ACCLAIM FOR
THE LIFE AND DEATH OF PETER SELLERS

'Lewis is consistently adept at making use of Sellers as a reference point in his scattergun but obsessively thorough exploration of British post-war theatrical, cinematic and comic culture . . . impossible not to admire the manic energy which he has brought to his material . . . rich and fascinating.'

London Review of Books

'An appreciator of performance who can stand comparison with Tynan or Pauline Kael, Lewis is also adept and subtle in relating work to life . . . each generates a myriad of insights into the other. Every part, every anecdote, every personal or professional relationship, is glossed with passages of refulgent intelligence . . . Lewis invokes Proust's and Joyce's handling of their heroes . . . [he] breaks the rules with a jazz-like insouciance, licensed to be playful by his years of dogged research.'

Literary Review

'Its publication proclaims the obsolescence of most of the many books written about Sellers: all but a very few, I fear, may now be safely consigned to the waste-paper basket. This new light Lewis sheds is a searching one, clarifying much which has been for too long obscure . . . [it] makes for absorbing reading.'

Roy Boulting, *The Oldie*

'The definitive biography. A wide-ranging and superbly crafted book, Lewis leaves no stone unturned in his quest to find the real Peter Sellers.'

Film Review

'Lewis's biography is a work of art in itself.'

Midweek

'Incredible energy . . . I believe that in fifty or a hundred years' time, when nearly every Booker-prizewinning novel has been forgotten and people will scratch their heads trying to remember the name of half a dozen English plays (or films) later than *The Caretaker*, books such as Lewis's will be crucial texts for anybody who wants to understand what British post-war culture was all about.'

Sunday Times

'Fascinating . . . no attempt at the objective. Lewis's method – humorous, jokey, self-querying – is itself the medium in which both the man studied and the man who writes about him appear to swim.'

Evening Standard

'Torrential psychological biography . . . A savage but satiating account.'

Daily Mail

'A fascinating, tragic and instructive story . . . vividly told.'

Sunday Telegraph

'Remarkable in scope and compelling as a study of Sellers the actor, of an era in film comedy, of the artist as paranoid egomaniac, and the biographer as obsessive sleuth and disillusioned hero-worshipper . . . a quirky and provocative book . . . vivid and rhapsodical.'

Spectator

'A probing, unconventional, intensely agile and alert biography . . . definitive . . . a vivid portrait.'

Entertainment Weekly

'It is by far the best, most literate celebrity biography of the year . . . Lewis writes in the tradition of Richard Ellmann, the noted biographer of James Joyce. His research here has staggering breadth and depth, as does his relentless power of insight tempered with humanity . . . Call this a blue-moon biography. They don't come often.'

Hollywood Reporter

The Life and Death of Peter Sellers

by

Roger Lewis

arrow books

Published in the United Kingdom in 2004 by
Arrow Books

9 10 8

First published in the United Kingdom in 1994 by Century

Arrow Books
The Random House Group Limited
20 Vauxhall Bridge Road, London SW1V 2SA

Random House Australia (Pty) Limited
20 Alfred Street, Milsons Point, Sydney
New South Wales 2061, Australia

Random House New Zealand Limited
18 Poland Road, Glenfield
Auckland 10, New Zealand

Random House (Pty) Limited
Endulini, 5a Jubilee Road, Parktown 2193, South Africa

The Random House Group Limited Reg. No. 954009

www.randomhouse.co.uk

A CIP catalogue record for this book
is available from the British Library

Papers used by Random House are natural, recyclable products
made from wood grown in sustainable forests. The manufacturing
processes conform to the environmental regulations
of the country of origin

ISBN 0 09 974700 6

Printed and bound in Great Britain by
Cox & Wyman Ltd, Reading, Berkshire

Credits

Permission to reprint copyrighted material from the following sources is gratefully acknowledged: BBC Written Archives Centre; the Mary Emett Collection (for the drawing reproduced on page 226); Faber and Faber Ltd. (for extracts from *The ABC of Reading* by Ezra Pound and *The Dyer's Hand* and *Collected Poems* by W.H. Auden); Victor Gollancz Ltd. (for extracts from *That Uncertain Feeling* by Kingsley Amis); Lord Grade of Elstree (for surviving material from the Lew & Leslie Grade talent agency); *Playboy* Magazine (for quotations from 'Playboy Interview: Julie Andrews and Blake Edwards', from *Playboy* Magazine December 1982, and also for extracts from the Peter Sellers interview by Robert Miller of October 1962); Elwood Rickless (Executor of the Peter Sellers Estate); Straight Arrow Publishers, Inc. (for 'The Strange World of Peter Sellers' by Mitchell Glazer, from *Rolling Stone*, April 17th 1980. © Straight Arrow Publishers, Inc. 1980. All Rights Reserved. Reprinted by Permission); Times Newspapers Ltd. (for quotations from 'Peter Sellers: A Monologue' by Dilys Powell, first published in the *Sunday Times Magazine* on January 14th and 21st 1962 © Times Newspapers Ltd. 1962); *TV Times* and IPC Magazines Ltd. (for the reproduction of 'Star Turn-Table' by Peter Sellers, from the *TV Times* of July 20th 1956).

The author and publishers have made all reasonable efforts to contact copyright holders for permission, and any omissions or errors in the form of credit given will be corrected in future printings.

To Barry Humphries
il miglior fabbro

Contents

... being is the reverse of subtle. It is simple, though the principle of analogy shows it to be paradoxically complicated as well. A locomotive is both simple in essence and complicated in detail; one would scarcely call a locomotive subtle. And one should beware of trying to describe a locomotive to the uninitiated by rationalistically describing its workings, beginning with the vapourization of heated water, lest its puffing power come to seem very subtle indeed. One does better to call it an iron horse.

Hugh Kenner, *Paradox in Chesterton.*

Introduction

"'tis in ourselves, that we are thus, or thus.' *Othello*.

My first movie love was Norman Wisdom. His films were telecast
in the early evening, and the off-register, horizontally streaky flicker
from the screen – we had a peeling teak-veneer Coronation era
Baird with a wonky CONTRAST control which plunged everything into a zig-zag of green shadow – is of a piece in my mind with
the rain-lashed industrial South Wales beyond the window panes
and my mother snarling in the kitchen, out of sight, creating a meat
tea from pastry speckled with soot and heated-up potato water.
Norman's hysteria and gormlessness, in the face of impossible
odds, were my own.

I enjoyed his films as a child because, always being told to
behave, pull himself together and quieten down, Norman *was* a
child – a child stuck in a man's body, obstreperous and defiantly retarded.* He seemed to be an innocent always placed in dangerous
or unpleasant circumstances – that is, he was pitched into adult
scrapes and he dealt with them by donning multiple disguises, by
pratfalls, and by pumping up the volume on being a fool or a funny
foreigner. In *The Square Peg* he for some reason finds himself the
identical twin of a Nazi General. In *On the Beat* he doubles the
parts of a constable and a gang-leader. Norman was all over the

---

* I refer of course to his rôles. Off-screen Mr Wisdom may very well be a Nobel
  Laureate in science, medicine, literature and the promotion of peace.

place. A milkroundsman, a window cleaner, a newspaper reporter, a jockey. Somewhere along the line I recall his ghastly croon dubbing an opera singer. But despite the costumes and showing off, his weeping and wailing, he was always Norman, a happy-go-lucky brat; if the innocence was mock innocence, or if there was any malice in his violent revenge on grown-up nonchalance (exemplified by Jerry Desmonde in impeccable evening dress with a boutonnière), it didn't register with me or spoil my fun. Norman had energy – unlike that other man-child, Jimmy Clitheroe, or Wee Georgie Wood, whose mummified features scared me then and terrify me now, as I remember them. Jimmy and Georgie, genuine dwarves, were freaks. Mother Nature had played a trick on them, and their having to wear blazers and carry satchels well into old age – when there was still a strong chance that they'd be spanked and forced to sing a comic ballad with an unbroken voice – was a sign of this. They aged without growing. Norman's nature, by contrast, seemed natural and, to me, the very spirit of *my* age. He was an escapee from all that school uniforms, organised team games and parental persecutions try and curb. He was displaced from my heart one Saturday afternoon by Peter Sellers.

I was making the most of having a cold and had been left at home alone, everybody else in Wales being intent on running about in the damp playing rugby. Wrapped in my mother's Glenurquart tartan travelling rug, eating Custard Creams and drinking Ribena through a straw, I settled, in a bored sort of way, to watch a double bill on the only channel not killing time with sports commentaries. The films were *Two Way Stretch* and *Wrong Arm of the Law*. As cops-and-robbers capers, with police cars having bells instead of sirens, they looked set fair to amuse me in the Norman Wisdom manner – the villains were folk heroes, with whom we at once sided in their battles against manic authority, personified by Lionel Jeffries, whose Nosey Parker and Sidney Crout are, I now see, comic variations on his hissing and spitting Marquess of Queensberry, the maddened upholder of all things Victorian in *The Trials of Oscar Wilde*. And there, amidst the slapstick, the explosions, the melodrama of characters getting themselves smuggled in and out of prison; there, at the centre of each film, was a self-absorbed, diffident, yet powerful presence, around whom the action and the rest of the cast whirred and whirled – Sellers.

In *Two Way Stretch*, when they are in the cramped gaol cell at the start, David Lodge and Bernard Cribbins do all the talking and complicated bits of business with a breakfast fry-up. A big fat warder further fills the room and carries off a cat. Sellers' Dodger Lane, however, is the focus of the scene. Sitting in bed, doing nothing except peer over the top of *The Investors' Chronicle*, he could be the greatest straight man who ever lived. His reactions to the pseudo-domesticity about him, his exasperation and world-weariness, are full of irony and resignation. Such texture, such reserve. I'd personally never noticed before that stopping still could be funny – where were Norman's cock-a-doodle-doo line readings and the dashing about I thought synonymous with humour? Even Sellers' weight was funny. Thickset and ponderous (from all that prison stodge), he was miles away from Norman's springy physicality. Here was a comedy of reactions – of the way everybody was knocking themselves out to amuse and attract the star. Sellers was solemn and hilarious, simultaneously. (In fact, Sellers often played these extremes off against each other. His art had little to do with the suddenness of jokes, except in the live-cartoon conventions of the *Pink Panther* series; his genius was for creating an atmosphere, vibrating and fluttering between gaiety and sorrow. Even Inspector Clouseau, as Sellers said, 'is a sad and serious man'.)

In *Wrong Arm of the Law*, Sellers played not, like Norman, a criminal mastermind and a copper, but an underworld chieftain, Pearly Gates, and his double, or public persona, Monsieur Jules, the couturier. Pearly is all Cockney wit and bottle; M. Jules, foppish, charming and camp. I'll never forget the moment when I first saw Sellers as the one go through a bead curtain and emerge as the other. It was a total transformation – voice, demeanour, temper. It was more than just dextrous; it involved no change of make-up or clothes. It went beyond acting. It was a reconstitution. This book originates in my desire to know more about the magician who could accomplish feats like that. Sellers, in that split second on the screen when I was on my own in Wales, and when my great curiosity was born, enacted one of my deepest desires – the ability to disappear and return as someone else.

☆ ★ ☆

Soon after I'd watched that double bill and had my rapturous encounter, there was a general uprush of interest in Sellers. I'd not known about the Goons before, yet here they were reuniting for *The Last Goon Show of All*, broadcast on Boxing Day, 1972. (What on earth was Harry Secombe doing in the trio? He was known to me then only as a pop-eyed concert tenor whose brother, the Rev. Fred Secombe, had married my parents in Machen church.) Though a performance for radio, it was shown on television and the variety of accents and impersonations coming out of Sellers – a tall, thin, grey man now, having once been squatter and brown – was definitely eerie. He stood there at the lectern and voices and ideas bubbled up from inside him, whisked and eddied over the airwaves, to richly amuse the Royal Family. Princess Anne clopped the coconuts for a horse noise, Prince Philip grinned, Prince Charles sent apologies for absence ('my knees dropped off with envy at the thought of my father and sister attending the show'), and Princess Margaret left the Camden Theatre on Sellers' arm. 'Excuse me, sir, how do you think the evening went?' asked a young reporter, who'd nipped to the stage door to meet the couple. Sellers pushed past regally without a word. As he was climbing into the limousine, the hack tried again: 'Excuse me, sir, just one last thing – how are you spelling your name?' – 'It's Sellers Schmellers, now fuck off,' boomed the star.

His was evidently a free-floating fizzy intelligence. In action, it was like witnessing a man being possessed by demons. Bloodnok's gastro-enteric groans, Grytpype-Thynne's caddish murmur, Henry Crun's senile mutterings, Bluebottle's epiglottal squawk etc., poured out with a restless, propulsive force. He was a Niagara. I remember going on from listening to Goon records to being interested in the masks and special effects of *Alice's Adventures in*

Wonderland – and there was Sellers, nutty and natty, as the March Hare. (Spike Milligan was the Gryphon and my old enemy, Sir Robert Helpmann, the Child Catcher in *Chitty Chitty Bang Bang*, was the Mad Hatter.) I recall not having the courage to join an expedition of cronies trying to bluff their way into the AA-rated *There's a Girl in My Soup*, in which Sellers, if the stills outside the nickelodeon were any clue, was impersonating the Earl of Lichfield. I started to familiarise myself with the Boultings' output and colourful trash like *Casino Royale* – then, as now, often on the box as midweek matinées.

From Fred Kite, in his one ill-fitting demob suit, to Evelyn Tremble, in a vast wardrobe tailored by Dougie Hayward, what became clear to me very quickly was that in Sellers I was watching an artist who could take a rôle to a lot of highs. I could see him, as Clare Quilty, in *Lolita*, compulsively enlarging his character, improvising through his scenes with James Mason, spreading across the movie like a damp stain coming through a ceiling; he sent himself further and further into his character's narcissism. I could see Sellers taking over – becoming an egocentric before my eyes; and acting was clearly an ideal home for his excesses, as it was for mine. Sellers, having aroused hidden feelings in me, became the hero of my adolescence, as Norman Wisdom had represented and idealised my childhood. I used to want to *be* Peter Sellers. I went about in tinted spectacles (rare then), a French fireman's helmet and a leatherette-effect lady's mackintosh from Peacock's, Caerphilly, which was the nearest I could find to an ankle-length Nazi greatcoat – the intention being to ape the Sellers who'd appeared on Michael Parkinson's chat-show, when he'd astounded me with his floor-show of stories, anecdotes, and exhibitionism. Sellers, of course, was reproducing Kenneth Mars from *The Producers*. (Mars reproduced Sellers' Dr Strangelove in *Young Frankenstein*.) I copied Sellers imitating everybody else. I used to goose-step up and down my bedroom, ranting that 'Churchill voss a rotten painter, *rotten*. Hitler, now zere voss a painter for you. Could paint an entire apartment, two coats, one afternoon!' My friend Harries used to record the stuff on a portable Sony.

It didn't end there. After seeing *What's New, Pussycat?* I decided I wanted to be a psychiatrist. Not because I was in the least bit interested in rehabilitating people who'd gone bonkers, but because (a) it was a licence to snoop and pry around people's fantasy levels and (b) I fancied myself in a Richard III wig and a red velvet smoking jacket living in a Parisian folly. (Psychiatry was out when I realised you'd need medical qualifications and I, surprising nobody, was in the Arts stream from the word go.) What I think I was doing, beyond all the teenage tomfoolery, was conducting experiments with personality. Adolescence, so threatening and fateful, is a time for assembling and assuming what will become the adult identity – a repertoire of mannerisms and inklings, a gathering of experiences, desires, anxieties and feelings, which are one way and another brought to order: our sense of self, which we will labour at keeping constant. We grow an armoury of attitudes, develop a style; what John le Carré's spies would refer to as our handwriting. What drew me to Sellers once, and once again as I approached thirty, was that he plainly had no such organising principle. His virtuosity implied that new and different selves, odd voices and elaborations, distracted him from moment to moment. And if he renewed himself for each film, why not for each day? Or for each person he was with who'd give him what he wanted?

☆　★　☆

It was this, the motor of his genius as an actor, his insistence on being discontinuous, which, I was to learn, constituted his madness. In his films he was concealing his neurosis, making a virtue out of the insomnia of his impersonations, parrotings, oddness. But in reality, to adopt a conclusion Sir Kingsley Amis came to about women, Sellers was off his head in more than a manner of speaking. When, at precisely double the age I was when running around the Rhymney Valley in a blue plasticine nose, I began my research into his life, it was primarily to explain why, having once loved the funny voices and carryings-on, I was now seeing in Sellers' transfigurations something sad and lost. The solution involves the fact that, as a schoolboy, I was responding to the delinquency in Sellers' masquerades and acts of flight. Now, studying a man who was fully alive only when acting, who could unknot himself only through mimicry, I am alert to the psychotic manoeuvrings, the emotional incontinencies, in a grown-up's always wanting to be a juvenile – in wanting 'always to be a little boy and to have fun'. Peter Sellers was the man in Peter Pan.

In interview after interview, Sellers explained his strangeness by claiming: 'I have no personality of my own, you see. I could never be a star because of this. I'm a character actor. I couldn't play Peter Sellers the way Cary Grant plays Cary Grant, say – because I have no concrete image of myself. I look in the mirror and what I see is someone who has never grown up – a crashing sentimentalist who alternates between great heights and black depths. You know, it's a funny thing, but when I'm doing a rôle I feel it's the *rôle* doing the rôle, if you know what I mean. When someone tells me, "You were great as so-and-so", I feel they should be telling this to so-and-so, and when I finish a picture I feel a horrible sudden loss of identity.'

The suggestion that when he was not employed as an actor he was an empty space, disembodied like a ghost (he told Kermit the Frog on *The Muppet Show* that 'There used to be a me, but I had it surgically removed'), was a convenient and complicated fiction. Convenient because he could detach himself from the consequences of his bad behaviour. (He was a moral amnesiac.) Cruelty to wives and family, tantrums in front of directors and colleagues, could be wiped from his mind, consigned to a trackless wilderness which is actually where the secrets of this deeply enigmatic man are to be found. When the camera wasn't turning he was often recessive and withdrawn, and it satisfied a need to pretend he didn't exist. As a first and obvious point, when he stated, again and again, that he had no personality or self, by fending us off with a blankness, the actor as zero, he was meaning to be inscrutable, magically invisible – like Shakespeare, say, a king of shadows. And secondly, whilst ostensibly searching for a personality of his own, he could give himself thousands of faces – and, though this was dismaying (he was befuddled by all the available possibilities), it came with a glorious freedom. 'I try to hop into a new personality as often as I can,' he admitted, not denying that his reformations went beyond the confines of the studio. (Theo Cowan said to me, 'He was happier making up and slipping into characters. If he was sitting here now he'd be doing somebody.')

Indeed, Sellers felt confined by anything which looked like stability or repetition. Thus the written-off marriages, the frequent changes of address, the fecklessness of his relationships. Domestic duties, for example, were incompatible with his wandering nature. As fame and money denatured him, and he became emotionally dead, he could go so far as abandoning his children, cutting them from his will. He wanted to be unconstrained, with no living connections. Milligan thinks it indicative that he never saw Sellers enjoy a hearth or home. He never put a kettle on and made a cup of tea; he'd never 'sit round a fireplace – all those primitive tribal things that give each of us a sense of ordinariness and order. They seemed to be denied to him. He *had* no fireplace.'

He hated rehearsal; he hated the live theatre ('because it means doing the same thing over and over again'). He thrived on whims and spontaneity. To this extent, at least, for all the mimicry, his characters are not artificial creations. Sellers was drawing on himself in some way. As his daughter, Sarah, concedes, 'I don't think Dad modelled himself on other people; it all came from inside. He was very psychic – in tune with what people were feeling. He didn't study people – it was more a feeling he got about people – intuitive. That's what he was like in his films and his life. That's the way he was. More than impersonation – because his own personality would change a lot. One day you saw him he'd be one way, another time he'd have picked up other moods. Very sensitive to things going on around people – quite often negative states . . .'

How did his twisted greatness come to the surface of his art? How did the surface, the faces and funny noises, connect with the subterranean talent – which eventually became a lunatic's mind, a harbour for insult and rejection, certain only that compliments and admiration were hypocrisy and conspiracy? What were the pressures shaping him? If the source of his originality and power as an actor lay in the problems he had with personal identity, was the price too high? Sellers, who in his demented wizard's way could work up a tiff into a declaration of war and a slight into a bloody feud, was capable of giving shadows substance, of subdividing into multiple selves – and a peculiar facet of researching this book was that in interviewing over three hundred of his relicts and dependants, colleagues and collaborators, enemies and advocates, I met about three hundred different versions and facets of Peter Sellers. ('See them all', orders the editor after the newsreel sequence in *Citizen Kane*. 'Get in touch with everybody that ever worked for him – whoever loved him – whoever . . . hated his guts.')

Like Charlie Kane, Sellers won't lie still in anybody's mind. On the whole he is remembered, a decade plus after his death, with a mixture of incredulity and horror – whilst at the same time there is a consensus that, regarding his films, he gave the public a huge amount of pleasure. In several pictures, of course, he played half the cast and showed how he could *be* three hundred people, if he'd wanted. The President, the Group Captain, the Nazi boffin in *Doctor Strangelove*; the citizenry of the Duchy of Grand Fenwick in *The Mouse that Roared*; the brothel-creepers in *Soft Beds, Hard Battles*; the yellow peril and his nemesis, Nayland Smith, in *The Fiendish Plot of Dr Fu Manchu*, which was released after Sellers' death and seemed to have been made by his ghostly remains. (Sellers also does assorted voices on the soundtrack which adds to the disembodied, spectral effect.) 'We are kindred spirits,' says Nayland affectionately of Fu, 'He is evil to my good, ying to my yang . . .' Sellers could dart across contraries on the screen – conciliatory Muffley, maniacal Strangelove, for instance, holding a conversation – and in real life he could veer, in the space of a minute, between heartless egotism and a suffocating generosity, the charm of the devil and invisibility. People remember him variously as stout or slim, frail or fleshy and with hair sprouting out of his shirt, werewolf fashion. The man of the people, the chum known to wartime colleagues and the stunt coordinator element, somehow coexisted with the toffee-nosed invitee to Kensington Palace, the treacherous business partner, the defaulter, saboteur, shit and genius. The various women in his life were unable to agree for me on whether or not, as a Jew, he was circumcised. Sellers, membrum virile and all, evidently shrank and grew, as if he existed in a hall of distorting mirrors.

No single person ever knew him. (He recoiled from genuine intimacy: husband, father, patron, client etc., were so many rôles and moods.) Nor was he open or certain about what might have been his own normal voice. For all their make-up and many-sidedness, there's never any mistaking Alec Guinness' purr or Orson Welles' rumble, which was like thunder across the bay. Sellers was not regionally bound by accent – and in Britain, especially, the grain of your voice is a signal of class and provenance, region and attitudes. The whole of your history and background is in the noise you make. (Where would Michael Caine be without the Old Kent Road, Sean Connery without Scotland?) Sellers' facility with dialect meant he could escape these constraints (another aspect of his curious freedom), with the delimiting factor that he was thereby rootless, placeless, with no point of origin. Sir Guy Grand, in *The Magic Christian*, has unassailably Mayfair tones, but when Sellers spoke to journalists on the set, such was the effect of Ringo, who played Sir Guy's adopted son, Youngman, that Sellers became a native of Liverpool. On other occasions he'd lapse into Cockney or a Yorkshire lilt. Then again he'd try to be flat, featureless – a drug-like stupor. (Oscar Moore, in *A Matter of Life and Sex*, says that Sellers' character in *Being There*, Chance the gardener, a Mr Nobody, speaks 'like a man with a needle hanging out of his arm.') Challenged, towards the end of his life, about how he *really* spoke, so ventilated was his conversation with take-offs and goonery, he said: 'I think it's something like what you're hearing now . . . Well, maybe I'm trying to sound a bit more posh. This voice is not made up, because I cannot relax and talk openly in someone else's voice. I've heard myself on recordings in background conversation, and I think I talk like this . . . I hear myself at other times, though, and I'm talking like this . . .' – and he modulated into South London. 'It depends on whom I'm with. Sometimes I start out in my own voice and no matter who I'm with, I take on their thing.'

It is an unnerving facet of Sellers that, as his own face faded, he created his own world by feeding off his companions. When he started copying people, he didn't recreate you – he took you over. He was like a real-life Leonard Zelig, the human chameleon in Woody Allen's film, who takes on the colour of his surroundings. (The young Allen worked with Sellers in *What's New, Pussycat?* and *Casino Royale*, and a Columbia executive, Leo Jaffe, once mistook Sellers for Allen at the Dorchester Hotel, precipitating a major Sellers tantrum.) But where Zelig's imitation game is benign and ingratiating, Sellers' was sinister and satirical. He'd throw you back at yourself, making self-expression an extreme of self-mockery. As Milligan said, 'Peter feasts off people – he finds himself so totally boring that he's got to escape from himself and find refuge and security in another personality – that's the only form of communication left open to him.'

☆　☆　☆

If ever there was an actor hollowed out and dissolved by the mysterious processes of his art, it was Sellers. There have been plenty of casualties of course: the humiliations and bruisings endured by Marilyn Monroe; the pill popping of Montgomery Clift; Rachel Roberts' and Richard Burton's celtic boozing; Charles Laughton's wheedling masochism . . . And the melancholy clown is nothing new, from Pagliacci's smeary pierrot's face to Tony Hancock's exasperation and suicide. What picks Sellers out is the comprehensiveness of his conflicts. He lived in reverse. Insubstantial off camera, coming alive through the lens; goading people into leaving him, or disagreeing with him, so that he could then feel forsaken; profoundly homesick, yet he never had a home; a solitary, he relied on being a public figure – nothing enraged him more than passport officials asking to see his documents. He once stormed past the customs and excise man at Heathrow and slapped a sticker on the fellow's forehead. He wanted the flattery of being waved through – to waft in and out of countries not bound by visas and the ordinary rules of wayfaring. Also, a passport is a proof of identity. For all his obsessions with the puzzle of who he was ('Having no genuine personality of my own gives me such a complex, you know . . .'), this actually was the last thing he wanted. Sellers wished to cross frontiers at will, not by queueing up with the mob, even if what he was waiting to board was Concorde and the next seat occupied by Dustin Hoffman. During the last few years of his life he travelled by private jet or chartered luxury yacht. He was constantly in and out of hospitals and hotels. New York, London, Copenhagen, Rome, Geneva, Majorca . . . 'This constant journeying of his', said Milligan: 'He's like a panther in a cage, pacing backwards and forwards for eternity . . . He daren't stand still because he'd sink and drown in his own tears, so he has to keep going though he knows he has nowhere to go.'

Translated into practical terms, Sellers' restlessness, his running, jumping and standing still, meant a compulsion to keep on making films and recordings, one after the other, regardless of whether they were any good or not. In 1960 alone, to give but one example, he released *The Running, Jumping, Standing Still Film*, *Two Way Stretch*, *Battle of the Sexes*, *Never Let Go* and *The Millionairess*. He travelled out of himself to become an old lag, an Edinburgh weaver's clerk, a hoodlum flashing a gold tooth, a medicine man from the Sub-Continent. . . . From 1948, when he was first employed by the BBC, to his death in 1980, when *The Romance of the Pink Panther* was in pre-production, Sellers was never out of work. (Indeed, from his early twenties onwards, Sellers, his complaining and feeling very sorry for himself notwithstanding, was able to live exactly as he pleased, if financial wherewithal is any indicator.)

He claimed to be searching for perfection. 'I just cannot take mediocrity. I just cannot take it on any level.' It is thus paradoxical that in a lifetime of films he made so few masterpieces (if the significance of Sellers was limited to his non-flops, you could count up the number of important pictures on the fingers of a two-toed sloth). And if he was such a perfectionist – 'I'm just a guy who tries to do things right. I'm a guy in search of the perfect "Something".

I've got a real psycho thing about it' – why did he more often than not behave so destructively and sulkily? He early on learned the despot's trick of surrounding himself with weaklings in a bid to enhance the look of his own power, and the collapse of *Casino Royale, Ghost in the Noonday Sun* and *The Prisoner of Zenda* was all due to Sellers' caprice. He tried to have John Cleese sacked from *The Magic Christian* because Cleese's performance was funnier than his own. (He had to be satisfied with the reshooting of Cleese's scenes where Cleese wasn't so favoured by the camera angles.) He had Piers Haggard sacked from *The Fiendish Plot of Dr Fu Manchu* because, shooting in Paris, he was jealous of the director for being able to speak French with the French crew. He decided to direct the picture from the top himself. Sellers' method of inspiring confidence and telling the company what to do was remarkably unfussy: he'd act out a scene, doing all the parts and voices, and he'd then expect everybody to copy him, exactly. (He didn't want actors, he wanted automata.) Clive Dunn went over to Paris to play a Beefeater: 'Peter would perform it; then I would do my version of Peter Sellers playing my part.' One of the few people to receive a note, as the theatrical profession calls a bit of formal instruction, was David Lodge. He played a police sergeant in charge of an identification parade. 'What I want you to do after you've delivered your lines', said Sellers, 'is to be like Gene Hackman.' – 'And what does Gene Hackman do?' inquired Lodge. 'Fuck all,' said Sellers.

Most of Dunn's scene and all of Lodge's were cut. Sellers then insisted that his own name be removed from the mess he'd proceeded to make from the extraneous footage,* thus crediting Haggard with a movie Haggard had long left – and which to this day he cannot bear going to see.

---

* Sellers sent this telex to Elwood Rickless on May 12th 1980: 'I hereby authorise you as my lawyer to inform Orion [the production company] immediately that my name must be deleted from every screen credit other than that of actor, i.e. no writing and/or directing credits whatsoever. This applies to both screen and all paid advertising. This, my decision, is irrevocable and leaves no room for any further discussion. Please deal with this as quickly as possible.'

Sellers courted people and exploited them. Hypersensitive to his own needs and treatment, claiming that a stray criticism or nuance could undo him ('A person can destroy me with two words. It can just be the way they say them, the inflection'), he was brutal to others, totally inconsiderate. Charles Feldman, producer of *Casino Royale*, had his health so undermined by Sellers' antics, he died soon after the film's première. Richard Quine's suicide went back to *The Prisoner of Zenda*. 'Was I really awful today?' Sellers asked Lionel Jeffries, 'Well . . . ' he started to reply, expecting Sellers to apologise for his misbehaviour. Instead, Sellers gave a satisfied laugh and hung up. Blake Edwards faced a nervous breakdown after dealing with Sellers on *Revenge of the Pink Panther*. 'I had so much pent-up rage and frustration within me,' he claimed. Peter Medak couldn't work for five years after the calamities of *Ghost in the Noonday Sun*. 'Nobody could control him,' he disclosed to me about his star: 'He'd create situations where he'd stop the production, which fell behind schedule on Day One. Little by little, systematically, he'd turn up later and later on the set. He should be in make up at seven, he'd be there at nine. Stuff like that. Every day there would be something else. He wouldn't film, supposedly sick – and then he'd be seen water-skiing in the harbour. Or he wanted to come back from the Cyprus location for a ball given by Princesss Margaret. He simply got on a plane and left for London. He sent back a certificate from a crooked doctor friend of his. So the film lost another two or three days. . . . After it was all finished, I got all the blame – for going over budget, for turning in a picture which wasn't box office. Yet the producers left me high and dry to cope with Peter Sellers. Nobody from Columbia would put their foot down with him. I was the only person trying to say no, no, no. Everybody else was willing to give him his head. By the end of the movie I wasn't talking to him. I couldn't talk to him. I hated him so much.'

So it went on. Sellers would discuss yoga and mysticism and relaxation methods, and then he'd slap his women around, smash up the furniture, pulverise jewellery and Cartier watches and toss the debris into the lavatory pan. People and possessions went, pell-mell, on to the Peter Sellers Scrap Heap. Which is why, I think, he was happy only when keeping company with his gadgets. His Leicaflex and Summicron-R f/2 50mm, Elmarit-R f/2.8 35mm and 90mm cameras, for example, which shielded him from the world: he could take pictures of it instead of participating in it. His succession of expensive motor cars betook him from whim to whim. He collected toy railways, hi-fi hardware, anything clockwork or robotic. Covetous and acquisitive, he could always then give his playthings away or abandon them the moment they started to bore him. Bit players often tended to inherit his bits. Vacuum cleaners, obsolete tape recorders, lenses, a mechanical elephant, archery targets, a trampoline. During the filming of *Doctor Strangelove* he decided to have a Rolls Royce engine transplanted into a Mini Minor. George C. Scott looked at the freakish conveyance outside Shepperton Studios and asked, 'Who on earth will buy the thing when you get tired of it?' – 'I'm already looking for a rich midget,' Sellers replied.

What was no joke at all was the way Sellers regarded his family as discardable, his wives as trinkets, through whom he could arouse the envy of others. Part of his intolerance over his children was linked to the fact that, in a real biochemical sense, he had made them – and this undermined his comforting fantasy that he was a nothing, a nobody, a trick of the light. Children, much more than wives (who could without too much difficulty be traded in when they'd lost their freshness)[*] represented a responsibility he wanted to shirk – and yet, though neglectful, he'd instantly become the rod-brandishing patriarch if he suspected them of independence or if they broke a rule he'd just silently made up. Children belonged

---

[*] 'I married Sellers at twenty-one,' writes Britt Ekland in her book *Sensual Beauty and How to Achieve It* (London, 1984), '[and] I will never forget the horror of finding myself for the first time in close proximity to a man on a twenty-four hour basis. How on earth could I deal with going to the bathroom? It wasn't enough to close the door: there was the odd odour to contend with, not to mention [. . .]' (pages 18–19.)

with a world of sun and solid things, as Chesterton would put it; Sellers was more for shades and chimeras. When he cut the children from his will, he was literally and conclusively dispossessing them – like the disposal of an unwanted fleet of vehicles; or perhaps it was more that wives and children were as films of his that could be disowned, and he himself removed from the credits.

☆ ★ ☆

Sellers was heartless. Hence the fittingness of all those heart attacks. He virtually died in 1964 and spent his remaining sixteen years in the shadow of a cardiac arrest. Perhaps the main aspect of his topsy-turviness was the interchangeability of life and death. He went in for spiritualism and table-rapping in a big way. (He was the biggest sucker for soothsayers since the Roman emperors.) If you died, your relationship with Sellers wasn't necessarily impeded. Larry Stephens, a co-writer on *The Goon Show*, continued to watch over his career. When his beloved mother died, at last he could have her to himself. He conducted transworld telephone calls with her by filtering the conversation through his medium, Maurice Woodruff. According to another of his psychic surgeons, Doris Collins, there was a fair old gathering of ghosts at his Memorial Service; and Lynne Frederick, his last widow, got Sellers' sanction, through Doris, to marry David Frost. A seance was held at Michael Bentine's house. 'It was a very moving experience, but I didn't cry,' Lynne said. 'In fact, Peter was a very happy man and he certainly hasn't lost his sense of humour.'

Sellers' morbidity helped him to explain his style of acting. If the characters he played were to have emerged from the dumb-show of his subconscious, how was the material placed there in the first instance? He decided he was a reincarnationist: 'When I am searching for a character', he said in 1974, 'I leave myself open, as does a medium. And I think that sometimes you can be inhabited by the spirit of someone who lived at sometime, or who was a bit like the person you are doing. And maybe they come in and use you as a chance to relive again.'

For *The Optimists of Nine Elms*, he reckoned he was invaded by

Dan Leno – perhaps not knowing that Leno, 1860–1904, whose real name was George Galvin, and who started out as 'Little George, the Infant Wonder, Contortionist and Posturer,' ended his days with General Paralysis of the Insane in a Balham bedlam.

That death was playing an active part in his life was further confirmed by a conversation he had on the set of *Being There* with Shirley MacLaine, herself a former Priestess of Isis, dairymaid at the court of Catherine the Great, or some such. He was feeling uneasy because the limo mock-up they were sitting in was situated on the same sound stage in the Goldwyn Studios as the one where *Kiss Me, Stupid* was attempted, before being scrapped (and started again with Ray Walston) owing to his heart attack; Sellers began gasping and clutching at his chest. 'This is the sound stage where I died,' he explained, before going on to tell MacLaine of his coma and the sense he had had of being pulled back from the next world by the doctors at the Cedars of Lebanon Hospital. When Dr Kennamer massaged his heart to get it beating again, 'I felt myself floating back into my body . . . I know I have lived many times before, and that experience confirmed it to me, because in *this* lifetime I felt what it was for my soul to actually be *out* of my body. But ever since I came back, I don't know why, I don't know what it is I'm supposed to do, or what I came back for.'

This is a variation on his multiple-entry visa and passport conundrums. MacLaine encouraged him to have confidence in his past-life incarnations. 'That's probably why you are so good at acting. You just have better past-life recall on a creative level than most people . . . You feel you are drawing on those experiences and feelings that you actually remember living in other lifetimes. . .'

'I don't go into this with many people, you know,' said Sellers, having warmed to his audience, 'Or they'll think I'm bonkers.'

That he thought he was a man who could cheat death and recur, because he was without end, throughout human history, is another example of his solipsism (shall we call it?) to be sure. Sellers was angry at being mortal. Though he might have considered himself invulnerable on one plane, he worried constantly about the future because he didn't want to see his death there. The prospect of oblivion always before him, he spent much of his time looking back. He'd revisit the boarding houses of his childhood; he'd reminisce. One of his last utterances (to Auberon Waugh, who tells me 'I had a premonition that he would die within the week, although he was up and about and apparently quite healthy') was 'I am proud to have been a Goon. I would like to be remembered for that' – despite the fact that, when *The Goon Show* was in full swing, during the Fifties, he was always threatening to walk out and demanding more money. (It was against his nature to be satisfied with being one of three, with Milligan and Secombe.) He hated growing old and time passing, so he coloured his hair and had his eyelids nicked and his neck tucked. Paradoxically, it was always little old men that he played when he was young (Percy Quill in *The Smallest Show on Earth*, Mr Martin in *Battle of the Sexes*, Morganhall in *The Dock Brief*, his many generals and geezers) – and he never did live to be elderly himself, dead at fifty-four, having long looked wheezy and frail, like his image of the hundred and sixty year old Fu Manchu, his final rôle.

Sellers' problems of self-representation and the mystery of his moods, explained by the spirits of the dead taking possession of him, is so much gobbledegook – except that deathliness is apparent in his work and knowing this adds to our understanding of it: the explosions and dismemberments in *The Goon Show*; the revenants in *The Smallest Show on Earth* watching silent movies; the murder spree of *The Ladykillers* and *The Naked Truth* and the annihilation of the world in *Doctor Strangelove*; the vampiral theme of *Hoffman*, in which Sellers plays a woebegone widower who imprisons a beautiful virgin; the death of the music hall in *The Optimists of Nine Elms*; the living death of the entombment in *The Blockhouse*. We might even add to the list Inspector Clouseau's misreported deaths and resurrections, premature funerals and orations. The death-register peaks with *Trail of the Pink Panther*, which Sellers seemed to have managed to make *after* his own extinction – and was explained by Blake Edwards' ingenious use of doubles and out-takes from previous pictures. But still. . . . And, of course, the sepulchral *Being There*, which takes place in a winter garden and is full of the feeling that death was closing in on its star, who putters off across the surface of a misty lake at the end. 'He lived for his work', Anne Levy, his first wife, said to me. 'He couldn't relax; he couldn't go on holiday, couldn't really just be himself. He was only happy when he was playing a part. And I don't think he ever got anything out of life eventually. I find it difficult to watch *Being There*, because it is too near the truth . . .'

☆　★　☆

Like Chance the gardener, Sellers was an erasure. On leaving La Haute Grange, his chalet in Gstaad, for the last time, he organised a bonfire of photographs and memorabilia – an immolation of his past. And he had no future. He felt he kept seeing omens (birds behaving oddly etc.), and when he flew to London, he insisted on paying a visit to Golders Green Crematorium, wanting to see the ovens – where five days later he himself would be torched, enkindled to the tune of Glenn Miller's 'In the Mood'. It adds up to a macabre story. Sellers' life, a fever chart, is a combination of cautionary tale and case history. To put it bluntly, he was more seriously fucked up than a chameleon crossing a kilt. As the flappers sing in *Zelig*:

> If you hold your breath till you turn blue
> You'll be changing colors like they do,
> And you're doin' the Chameleon!
> Vo – do – do – de – o. . . .

A friend recently reckoned that I must have had a scream, a ball, a lark, researching Sellers, the artful dodger. After all, there are the vocal marvels of the Goons, the Panovision pratfalls of Clouseau; there is the loony zieg-heiling of Dr Strangelove's arm and the innocent ingenuity of Chance, silencing muggers with his television's remote control. . . . There is much there, and in fifty odd other pictures, to generate laughter. But laughter, I soon discovered, was less than the half of it with Sellers – even when you left his emotional self-questioning and private life scandals to one side. Hunched before my video, watching those old Boulting efforts yet again, or locked in a bunker at the British Film Institute, discovering lost classics, like *Mister Topaze*, I was struck by the pervasive melancholia in Sellers' work. Has nobody ever *looked* at it before? Fred Kite, far from being the Napoleonic shop steward critics always describe, is a tremendously touching portrait of a clumsy idealist; Mr Martin, far from being the meek Scottish accountant, whom we are told Sellers plays in *Battle of the Sexes*, has eyes which glint with awakening anarchy and love; John Lewis, the librarian of *Only Two Can Play*, and General Fitzjohn, from *Waltz of the Toreadors*, aren't, as the reference books have it, lechers at all. Lewis is a thirtyish family man with a college degree whose quite normal demands are dampened by a low income; he lives in a squalid flat where his wife is exhausted by two energetic toddlers and the milk goes off because they don't have access to a fridge. Sellers expresses the man's ironic self-awareness of his plight – as he does Dodger Lane's in the prison cell. And as for General Fitzjohn, he is a sort of sombre Bloodnok, angry at growing old and impotent, and fantasising about the escapades of his youth, which probably never happened. The films were made together early in 1962, and in each Sellers is exploring the problems of ageing and loneliness – problems confronting him personally as his first marriage was drawing to a messy close. 'I never want to marry again,' he said, 'I feel it would be better to remain a bachelor and die a bachelor. I wasted twelve years of life with the wrong woman.' The General's resentment of his wife (Margaret Leighton) might be seen as Sellers' for Anne; Lewis' desire for Elizabeth Gruffydd-Williams (Mai Zetterling) is Sellers' for the white goddess who became Britt.

Even Clouseau, 'a fool who was shrewd around fools,' and who never smiles, was hilarious in a low-key way. Blake Edwards may immerse the character in explosions, firework factories, collapsing walls, and the rest of it, but Sellers decides to be imperturbable – Clouseau walks away as dazed and withdrawn as Keaton beneath a falling house. The actor took this almost supernatural immunity to an extreme in *Being There*, and to a further extreme as the immobilised, god-like Fu in *The Fiendish Plot*. The opposite of the tranquillised part is the manic Fritz Fassbender in *What's New, Pussycat?*, which really is a portrayal of lechery (Sellers was satirising the voyeuristic whimperings of sex-obsessed psychoanalysts); and Fritz grew out of Dr Strangelove himself, looking forward to the post-apocalypse breeding boom – looking forward to his rôle in personally re-populating the world.

If his famous portrayals have been misrepresented, Sellers' best performances have often been plain ignored – badly distributed, or unreleased, or accepted as fiscal losses by the Inland Revenue (which means they can never be shown for gain), or else the companies which made the films are long defunct and the prints lost. I'm thinking particularly of the depressive barrister in *The Dock Brief*, a work I had to hire on 16mm and project in my kitchen; the essay in corruption, *Mister Topaze*, which took me two years to locate – all prints, save one, were melted down and the celluloid sent to Nigeria to be re-cycled into combs. ('You mean,' said Milligan, aghast, 'that there are women in Africa combing their hair with Peter Sellers?') Why isn't the busker in *The Optimists of Nine Elms*, a part written for Buster Keaton, better known? Or the saturnine gaoler in *Hoffman*, the suicide in *The Blockhouse*, the psychopath in *Never Let Go* (where we understand why Bernard Miles wanted Sellers to play Richard III)? On anybody's reckoning, this is all the work of a great actor.

The sadness of Sellers is manifold. First, there is the unexpected grace and gravitas of the performances themselves (the rat-a-tat-tat Chief Petty Officer in *Up the Creek*; the laconic lawyer in *I Love You, Alice B. Toklas . . .*), which he was never encouraged to build upon; secondly, there is the regret that so much of his work was stupidly received when it came out, by producers, reviewers, and audiences, who seemed to want only goonery and superficial slapstick. It was tantamount to a cover-up. What chance had his career when *Never Let Go* was advertised thus:

You roared at – 'The Ladykillers'

You laughed at – 'The Mouse that Roared'
You howled at – 'The Naked Truth'
Now thrill and chill with Peter Sellers in his first completely straight role
– as a cold, heartless gang leader – showing at this theatre soon. . . .

The publicists went on to suggest that cinema managers invite the local police, probation officers, JPs, and crime prevention officers to a charity premiere. Marginally worse than this klunky wholesomeness was the bogus titillation heralding *Mister Topaze*: LEARN THE FACTS OF LIFE IN TEN EASY LESSONS, prompted no doubt by somebody noticing that Marcel Pagnol's hero was a schoolmaster.

Sellers was marketed as a laughter machine and he gradually allowed himself less depth. The biggest joke in *Being There* is that the protagonist, his responsiveness clouded and denied, is an ambling allegory of what had happened to the actor playing him. 'He *was* Chauncey Gardiner,' Shirley MacLaine said to me. In *The Bobo* his disconsolate singing matador is simply dopey, his Evelyn Tremble in *Casino Royale* is off-hand, dissociated, and the Clouseau of the late period *Pink Panthers* is flattened into a cartoon – he's far less animate than Richard Williams' credit sequence animations.

Sellers was gradually ruined by success; he was disabled by the very talents and susceptibilities which had made his name. Which is to say his gnawing professional insecurities grew into, and grew out of, deep personal insecurity – the way he found his sense of self dissolving and disintegrating, his mind a phantasmagoria of changing impressions, imaginings and affinities. He was constant only in his pathetic rage at being Peter Sellers. Everything he started to do was born out of this torment. People who met him, in the Seventies, found him either maudlin or hysterical. People who knew him found him either generous or vindictive. ('One day he gives us diamonds, next day stones,' as one of Timon of Athens' sycophants complained.) He was difficult to live with because he found it difficult to live with himself. He was terrified of falling short of other people's estimation; he flew immediately into a temper if he encountered what he took to be incompetence in anybody else. He was afraid that what was funny today won't work on the set tomorrow. His personal and professional insecurity was at such a pitch, success was as much a terror for him as failure.

The more he was paid (he was given Rolls Royces as inducements to read a script), the more he loathed himself, and the cars, the women, the alpine chalets and mediterranean yachts etc., only served to remind him that he wasn't happy. 'I'd like to be happy very much,' he said, so often it was his mantra, 'I'd very much like to be happy.' The patina of a high-living star covered up his real inner-life of suspicion and disease and he managed to make elaborate spending an expression of the despair: he'd organise parties he'd refuse to attend, refurbish houses he wouldn't live in, return from holidays because he'd taken against the people he'd chosen to invite. Timon again:

> He's but a mad lord, and nought but humours sways him.
> He gave me a jewel th' other day, and now he has
> > beat it out o' my hat.

Sellers hid behind his money – what he called his FUCK YOU money, the large amounts of money which bought him the power to hire and fire and to walk out if he felt like it. To those members of his private circus (his train in the Shakespearean sense of the word) his partiality became oppressive – phoning them all through the night, demanding their presence (and then absenting himself). But he had no real chums. 'I don't have any friends. I suspect everybody. I have the feeling that because of my success and fame they want to use me. . . .'

An edict unto himself, he played up on the set, abused the powers with which he was contractually invested; he was a chaos of uncertainty and bad judgement. He took rôles he should not have done (in endless cops and robbers junkets); he rejected rôles he should have embraced, rôles with which his inward, gloomy and secretive nature would have found sympathy. Great men great losses should endure, but even so it is hard to forgive Sellers for depriving himself of *When I Grow Rich*: he was to have been an impoverished professor of philology, visiting Istanbul to study medieval Islamic documents, who earns a little extra cash by reading American newspapers out loud for an old lady, a former burlesque queen who'd been a concubine in the Sultan's harem. She now lives in one of the decrepit royal villas on the banks of the Bosphorus and despatches drugs around the world in boxes of Turkish Delight. Sellers' co-star, in this exotic variation on *Sunset Boulevard*, would have been Marlene Dietrich.

A similar-sounding plot unfolds in Michael Frayn's *The Russian Interpreter*. Proctor Gould is an exchange student at the University of Moscow. He imports secondhand text books from England – and some of the volumes are receptacles for, yes, contraband and foreign currency. His smuggling is being spied upon by the authorities; and one of the ardent Communists, Raisa, becomes the hero's girl... The film rights to the literary property were acquired by Michael Powell; and in February 1967 he and Frayn went to visit Sellers, by appointment, at Elstead.* Though he had declared an interest in the project ('I like it very much ... I want to do it ... It should be done') Sellers, however, showing full command of his petulance and pretensions, saw Powell off in fine style. He'd recognized at once that, like him, here was a man very horribly full of himself.

Powell had arrived at Sellers' Surrey mansion in an open-top Rolls Bentley, poop-pooping loudly; he wore motoring goggles and scarves; and he had had the cheek to drive straight over the flagstones and into the master's personal garage. 'Is this Sellers'?' he'd then demanded of a blonde ten-year-old child, who turned out to be Britt Ekland.

There's only space for one Toad at Toad Hall. Sellers, loathing Powell as soon as he saw the vintage car enthusiast get-up, decided to be the very opposite of his ebullient guest. He shrivelled and became grey, cold, affectless – playing the wraith. His taciturnity was

---

* Powell's account of the episode in the second (posthumous) volume of his memoirs, *Million-Dollar Movie* (London, 1992), pages 525–32; Frayn has had his say in 'Remembering Michael Powell,' *Sight and Sound*, Vol. 2, number 6 (October 1992), page 24.

compensated for by the gang of wild-eyed agents and lawyers he'd invited to be present – fellows eager for their percentage of the seven hundred and fifty thousand dollars, which was Sellers' going rate at that time. (He liked seeing them try to contain their avidity.) Members of the household, dressed in their livery, came in and out with tea and, after a very long while, a cut-glass decanter of whisky. 'Glenfiddich,' said Powell. 'Michael is a connoisseur of the best,' said David Begelman (a talent agent, later a convicted embezzler, later still the president of MGM). 'Of course,' quipped Powell, 'that's why I'm here.' Sellers inclined forwards and bowed gently, working it all over in his mind.

The more everyone grew excited, heaping praise on Frayn's book, the less likely it looked that the material subject of contracts would be broached. Finally, Powell tried to come out with it. 'Peter . . . are you in?' – 'Oh, I see . . . yes,' murmured Sellers, as if he didn't quite know for certain what a contract was. 'You want a piece of paper?' – 'I want a piece of paper, yes,' said Powell brightly, it slowly dawning in a corner of his brain just what degree of deliberate objectionableness he might be up against.

On March 4th they all met again in a suite at the Dorchester, where Sellers had installed his own piped music system, which he refused to switch off. Ministering to the master was an augmented turn-out of lawyers and agents. Britt, bolstered by members of her family babbling in Swedish, reclined on a couch. Monja Danischewsky, who had written the screenplay for *Battle of the Sexes*, and now Sellers' choice for the Frayn screenplay, was another added voice. Was a food-taster there, too, to check Sellers' grub for poison? Nubians waving ostrich plume fans? Dwarves in motley? People practising Elizabethan dance steps to a viol da gamba?

Powell announced that *The Russian Interpreter* should be approached as 'out of Chekhov by Billy Wilder'. After giving ear to a bit of this, Sellers said: 'How about John Schlesinger to direct? Clive Donner?' People fell silent. Powell was startled. Wasn't the famous director of *The Red Shoes* and *A Matter of Life and Death* there before his eyes? 'Rather than bringing in a new voice at this stage,' said Powell, trying to pretend Sellers was making light, 'I propose to direct the film myself.'

'No, no, Michael, I wouldn't agree to that . . . I wouldn't approve that. It's not your subject.'

Powell went home and recorded the word 'Peterloo' in his diary – he had been massacred, in full public view. At what point did Sellers start to scheme and decide to take his malice to such lengths? When he was indoors and heard the poop-poop? When Powell barked 'Is this Sellers'?' at Britt (Sellers wouldn't have been wrong in detecting a sneer at stockbroker mock-Tudor ostentation in Powell's tone.) When people began to chatter as if his involvement was a foregone conclusion? When Powell's own expectations and assumptions about being in charge had seemed such an easy target? He may have scuppered the project there and then, on the spur of the moment – he couldn't resist the mischief of it. Surely Sellers' motive for revenge didn't go back to 1957, when he'd auditioned for the role of a Greek partisan in Powell's *Ill Met by Moonlight*? (in which Dirk Bogarde helps to kidnap a German general on the island of Crete.)* Powell had rejected the young actor and radio Goon, calling him 'an india rubber owl'.

So Sellers had a bit of luck ten years later, looking out of his window on that February afternoon to see a rival Mr Toad down in the forecourt. To his mind, his encounter with Powell wasn't about film-making; it was a struggle for domination. Perhaps, at some level, he did believe in the possibility of the film. He'd held prolonged discussions with his managers; he'd talked about the script. But, under the surface, in the violent surges of his semi-conscious, he was setting a trap.

The story doesn't quite end there. I wrote to Michael Frayn, asking him what else he could recall of the episode, and he said: 'Powell's option on *The Russian Interpreter* eventually lapsed, and it was then picked up by Sellers himself. My only contact with him, however, was a letter from Los Angeles in which he said he had

---

* The film was the subject of surrealist revision on *The Goon Show*. 'Ill Met by Goonlight' was the title of the programme broadcast on March 14th 1957.

"two of the finest minds in Hollywood working on the project."
That was the last I heard.'

Which is further evidence that it was Powell-as-Powell whom
Sellers was wanting to punish; and that he did recognize Proctor
Gould's surreptitiousness as being up his street.

☆ ★ ☆

Sellers was to have been Rex Harrison's Caesar in *Cleopatra*, Ron
Moody's Fagin in the musical *Oliver!* He was to have done a film
about the interior visions of a cross-eyed man, another about an
interplanetary alien for Satyajit Ray. He was to have been Captain
Hook capturing Hayley Mills' Wendy and duelling with Audrey
Hepburn's Peter Pan; he was offered the tramp in Pinter's *The
Caretaker*, Vladimir or Estragon in *Waiting for Godot*, Henry VIII in
Anne of a Thousand Days. Billy Wilder wanted him as Watson
alongside Peter O'Toole's Baker Street 'tec in *The Private Life of
Sherlock Holmes* (parts which went to Colin Blakely and Robert
Stephens). He was to have been Leopold Bloom, with O'Toole as
Dedalus and Diane Cilento as Molly, in a Wolf Mankowitz adapta-
tion of *Ulysses*. He was to have starred in a biopic of Chaplin. . .
And not only did Lord Miles want Sellers to play in Shakespeare at
The Mermaid, but 'Olivier wanted me to do "Lear" down at this
Chichester Festival place of his. . . Larry said, "Do it, you'd be
good." He said the best Lears were nearly always those new to
Shakespearean tragedy.'

The catalogue goes on and on and adds up to a resplendent
career which Sellers, because of his cocktail of cussedness and his
pathological lack of confidence, never had. That he always had a
hankering to play Hitler, and did so fleetingly in *Casino Royale* and
Soft Beds, Hard Battles, speaks volumes: 'I had no personality of my
own, at least I felt I hadn't, and I remember at one stage wanting to
be Hitler – so that in a great patriotic gesture I could commit
suicide and save the world. . .*

---

* The origin of the idea that Hitler was a baggy-pants comic goes back to Chaplin,
who recalls his first view of the Führer in a series of picture postcards: 'The face
was obscenely comic – a bad imitation of me, with its absurd moustache . . . and

The Life and Death of Peter Sellers.

☆ ★ ☆

In writing about Sellers – and in this book I want to see him as he really was, 'for I profess to write not his panegyrick, which must be all praise, but his Life' (James Boswell on Samuel Johnson) – I have had to become accustomed to inversions and irreconcilabilities. The great actor who was seldom in anything good; the materialist who liked to dematerialise; the star who created the problems he suffered from and whose bizarre behaviour grew in proportion to his fame, which unleashed his dormant lawlessness. . . . Though the subject of profiles galore when he was alive, and of a highly professional and polished authorised (by whom?[*]) biography (by Alexander Walker) the moment he was dead, Sellers' private life and public career have completely eluded his commentators. And, a dozen years and more since his death, this fantastically interesting and complex figure, who continues to be known and loved by millions all over the world, still gets to us in a special way. I feel that, like T.E. Lawrence and Andy Warhol, other of our century's Peter Pans, Sellers is one of those who stands in a symbolic relation to their age. As Milligan said of his fitful colleague: 'Peter's nightmares are our nightmares, too; his ghosts, our ghosts. He's Mr I Don't Know of the twentieth-century, he *is* Mr Twentieth-Century.'

---

disgusting, thin, little mouth. I could not take Hitler seriously. Each postcard showed a different posture of him: one with his hands claw-like haranguing the crowds, another with one arm up and another down, like a cricketer about to bowl, and another with hands clenched in front of him as though lifting an imaginary dumb-bell. The salute with the hand thrown back over the shoulder, the palm upwards, made me want to put a tray of dirty dishes on it. "This is a nut," I thought . . .'

My Autobiography, by Charles Chaplin, (London, 1964), page 316.

[*] I ask the question because Sellers' family did not co-operate with him – they collaborated on their own book, *P.S. I Love You*; and in an article in the *Standard*, on August 14th 1981, Walker made the comment 'Lynne Frederick does not mince words. I learned this when I approached her a year ago, on starting to write the authorised life of Peter Sellers . . .' The construction of that sentence does not seem to suggest to me that the widow instigated the project – so who was authorising whom?

If, on the one hand, I wish to explore the agony and the ecstasy of Sellers' creativity, I am also aware of the more pragmatic need to remind people that there was rather more to him than Inspector Clouseau. My purpose, when accounting for Sellers' career and explaining the considerable mythology which has accrued around his name, has been to find out what struck him day by day. I attempt to interweave the artist and the man. This has involved tracking down dozens of those lost or forgotten films I talked about earlier, hunting for recordings, screenplays, unreleased material and even unreleased whole features. I have examined written archives at the BBC and in the basements of Sellers' various agents and lawyers' offices. Directors, producers, and authors have given me files of correspondence, notes, draft scripts and unpublished photographs. (I particularly treasure Satyajit Ray's reports – the brownish ink on the thick mauve paper resembles dried blood.) I have collected copies of Sellers' eccentric telegrams and telexes and bootleg cassette tapes of his private conversation – all the memorabilia, the spots and dots, that remain of a life. And after all the inquiries, the legwork, the letters, telephone calls, tapes, the exhumations I have made, I find it impossible not to see something tragic in Sellers, sick at heart and alone, in those sunless hotel rooms right at the end.

☆ ★ ☆

PART ONE
The Man Who Never Was

It doesn't, in our contemporary world, so much matter where you begin the examination of a subject, so long as you keep on till you get round again to your starting point. As it were, you start on a sphere, or a cube: you must keep on till you have seen it from all sides.

Ezra Pound, *The ABC of Reading*.

Chapter One
Variety Lights

Peter Sellers' origins were in open-air concert parties, tatterdemalion music hall, and worse. In February 1911, his maternal grandmother, Welcome Mendoza, a relic of the Sephardic Jewish Community which had been given permission by Oliver Cromwell to settle in London and to establish a burial ground, used the money left to her by her husband, Solomon Marks, about whom nothing is known, to form a touring variety company. Having seen Seymour Hicks' *Under the Clock* at the Court Theatre, back in 1893, she'd become particularly interested in revue – which differed from traditional vaudeville in that emphasis was given to parades, costume display and dancing, rather than to individual novelty acts. Albert de Courville had introduced the form to England, having been impressed by Florenz Ziegfeld's *Follies* in New York; and revues, when they weren't being flesh-shows, belonged more with circus and spectacle than the theatre; they harked back to a world of misfits and wandering pierrots. Also, the tableaux and disguises, the black-outs and special effects, prophesy the cinema – the very development which would put an end to the revue's cheap magic.

Welcome, who adopted the stage name of Miss Belle Ray (Sellers was to have WELCOME WITHIN engraved on a brass plate outside his offices in Panton Street in punning homage), along with Andre Charlot and Austen Hurgon, devised an entertainment for the provinces, using a seaside theme as an excuse to get the audience to take leave of its senses. The chorines would fondle their ankles and comb their long green hair in the glow of the footlights;

they would then pretend to appear startled and they'd dive and plunge into a large tank, which had been constructed to look like a rock pool. Once submerged, the mermaids would peel and fellate bananas, and frolic with any other bits of fruit or greengroceries lying about. 'Very daring . . .' as Sellers once said. 'Of course the tank used to overflow; every time the girls dived in there was a great splash, and the musicians were always getting soaked.* And naturally thé management were always getting complaints from Watch Committees and so on about the girls appearing in nothing but bathing dresses.'

Miss Ray moved from Hackney, her ancestral beat, to Highbury Grove, N5, with her daughter Agnes, who as Peg was to become Sellers' mother. For professional purposes, however, Miss Ray was to be contacted c/o 35 Wellington Street, WC2, the 'Letter Box' of *The Era*, a trade paper. Sometimes she billed herself as Madame Belle Ray, the suggestion of being a continental artiste adding a touch of the exotic; but in the manner of George Formby's song about Mary who became a flapper with the cute little name of May, soon she was known as Ma, and had many an aquatic extravaganza on the road. By the Twenties, *Lido Follies* was in Dover; *Splashes* in Bradford; *Fun Showers* in Southport; *Mermaids* in Bath; *Ripples* in Newport. *Ripples*, for example, was written by a Mr Charles H. Allen. Its seventeen scenes included comedy sketches interspersed with plenty of warbling and hoofing. Gus Chevalier headed the cast, with Ernie Allen as his support. There was a Family Row episode; a Boxing Match; a Seaside Flirtation; a Bedroom Scene; a Rose Garden number; a Hawaiian Interlude. Rita Emmerson and Renalt de Winton danced a cat-and-canary sequence, the Challen Sisters rendered 'Digga Doo', Irene O'Dare sang 'That's the Good Old Sunny South', and Fred Tooze came on as the illusionist.

---

* He improved on this remembrance when he was on the *Parkinson Show* (BBC TV, November 9th 1974): The 'enormous water tank which filled the stage . . . eventually drowned the band because it broke,' claimed Sellers, miming the trombonists struggling for air, using their instruments as snorkels. 'At Huddersfield I think it was. Several were drowned. Seriously drowned.'

George Orwell, in his essay 'The Art of Donald McGill', has encouraged us to look down on revues and end-of-the-pier shows. The fat women and nigger minstrels, the jokes about silencing wailing babies, mothers-in-law, drunkenness, priapic grooms on honeymoon night, lavatories and bottoms – it is all vulgar and depressing, 'an utter lowness of mental atmosphere', which he claims views life as quarrelsome and dirty and marriage as a prison of drudgery. Orwell could almost be complaining about the *Carry On* films which, like revues and saucy postcards, laugh at sex and its consequences. The point should be, surely, that audiences actually enjoy seeing their desires and fears speeded up and caricatured. They are not being fooled by stereotypes – they collude with the actors; they, whose lives are perhaps never much of anything, appreciate the exaggerations and fantasy. It is cathartic – an outlet for emotion.

Orwell's pity would have been better directed not out at the orchestra stalls, but backstage, upon the blind concertina-ists, the stumbling card manipulators, the knife throwers with a strabismus. In my attempts to recover these rich and strange performances, leafing through disintegrating call sheets day after day, and sending myself home whimpering with migraine, I was beaten hollow with a sense of sadness – all this long-lost fun and tat, the come and gone laughter and applause; the gags, the little shows meant to delight, the suitcases of tricks and pantaloons being toted down gaslit lanes to railway stations on windy nights. The artistes and the audiences are now no longer there, yet Sellers' childhood, and the grief he carried within him, are to be found in this vanished world of terminus hotels, professional apartments (as digs were called) and morbidity.

☆ ★ ☆

Peg met her future husband, Will Sellars [*sic*] in 1921. She was appearing in *More Splashes* at the King's Theatre, Portsmouth. She played a charlady and an unfaithful housewife who flirts with the milkman. She sang 'Roses of Picardy' and introduced the band's scene-change music, 'There's a Long, Long Trail Awinding'. Between performances she went with her mother to the Corner House

5

Café where, because she was twenty-four* and getting on, she was encouraged to flirt with the resident pianist, who said he'd been the organist at Bradford Cathedral. Will amused everybody by tinkling 'I'm Forever Blowing Bubbles' in the style of a hymn; he then did hymns in the style of a cakewalk. He joined the Ray Company at the end of the week and he played in a Cossack sketch with a violinist, a Negro drummer, and a refugee from Moscow who owned an authentic balalaika. Sellers, incidentally, reproduced a remnant of the act in *The Optimists of Nine Elms*: lots of hey-hey, hey-hey shouts and gurgles, which begin slow and get faster and faster (the song begins as a dirge and ends as preposterous).

That he and Peg were only eventually married in 1923, at the Bloomsbury Registrar's Office, i.e. over two years later, suggests neither a need to hasten nor love at first sight. What might be their wedding photograph, the men in best collars and ties, shows Ma Ray, huge and draped in fox stoles, dominating her group of good companions. With her languid, droopy eyelids, hatpins and clutching a crocodile portmanteau, she's the Grand Duchess Gloriana from *The Mouse that Roared* combined with Crystal Jollibottom from *Ray's a Laugh* – a stately slagheap of a woman. Peg is on her left, neat, dimpled and prim – a governess, except for the slight actressy curve of her wide-brimmed hat. She is as alert as a bird, sharp featured and ready to flutter and peck. She could be a bird which would perch on the hippopotamus flanks of Ma, nipping at ticks. Behind her, hands defiantly in pockets, is Bill (as the Rays called him). His eyes are dark and the mouth sullen and pouting, the lower lip in an accentuated droop because of the cigarette lodged there. This is no put-upon chap – unless the marriage itself was something he'd rather not be going through, in which case he is acting. His stance, the sharpness of the waistcoat and the cut of the jacket, is that of a blade. He outstares the camera, whereas the others are on edge, guarded or (Peg) demurely flirtatious or coy. The brim of his homburg is angrily horizontal.

---

* Yet if she was seventy-two when she died in 1967, as Walker states categorically, then she'd have been twenty-six in 1921 – i.e. born in 1895, not 1897.

Besides him, his hat brim askew so his eyes can swivel up and hide in it, is Herbert Ray, whose features are a caricature of Peg's. Her beakiness is almost pretty in this photograph (she knows how to set herself off), but Herbert, or Bert, looks like a weasel – one of the anthropomorphised rodents in camel hair coats, a spiv, from *The Wind in the Willows*. He is gesturing with his right hand, as if offering something to the photographer for sale. Look, he seems to be saying, be reasonable. Of the other two fellows on the back row, the Negro drummer leans on his neighbour's shoulder, turning away slightly, as if to demonstrate that, of course he is the misfit in what you might think of as a family group. But instead of looking embarrassed (it is the neighbour, in the bowler, who looks tense and Bill who is the misfit), he succeeds in coming across as relaxed, at ease, his left hand, holding a cigarette, curled upwards to balance the composition (and to avoid igniting Ma's bonnet). He is photogenic – the eye drawn to him at once, not because he is black, but because he is jaunty.

In front, on Ma's right, are a young couple. The pale girl looking after the dog, Baby Bill (in a ruff for the occasion), is unidentified – perhaps she is Peg's sister Cissie, or Ve or Do, her sisters-in-law? Whoever she is, she doesn't have deportment, like Peg does, and her hat is clamped on her head like a burnous. She looks ill. Is that why the cherubic George Maloney leans close to her, in case she faints? Or is he afraid the dog will disgrace itself? Maloney's hat, which Ma obviously sat on earlier, gives him an idiotic aura. The photograph could have been posed for by the cast of a Peter Sellers film.

The newly-weds had no honeymoon. Though ostensibly residing at Aylmer Court, Aylmer Road, on the borders of Highgate and East Finchley, they went straight back to the theatre, to perform in *The Vanity Box*, which was across town in Willesden. By now, Miss Belle Ray had dispensed with being Madame Belle Ray and had settled for the maturity of plain Mrs Ray. She'd relinquished control of her company to her sons, and Harry Ray applied to the London County Council for accreditation, as Ray Bros. Productions

Ltd., under the Theatrical Employers' Registration Act, in December 1925. More than this, the tours were to be brought under the aegis of The London Syndicate Companies, managed by Walter Payne at Cranbourn Mansions, Cranbourn Street, WC2 (telegrams 'Twigsome,' Westrand; telephone: Gerard 5654). This was also the head office of Moss' Empires Ltd., which owned the chain of theatres where the revues were actually housed, week by week, across the country. It might have looked prosperous and efficient had not a personal disaster struck. A baby born to Peg and Bill had died when they were on tour with *The Vanity Box* in Dublin. The cast featured Mona Vivian and Will Hay, supported by the Mostyn Quartette, James Plant and Kitty Franklyn.

The baby's name was Peter.

☆　★　☆

John Updike, in his purple-passagey memoir, *Self-Consciousness*, says that it was seeing Sellers in *Being There* which made him want to look over his own life and search for lost time; the film (like an autobiography) is an analysis of origins and ancestry. Who is Chance? Where has he come from? Updike, likewise, wants to know what has determined his own character and shaped his destiny; he wishes to identify 'the essential self within its jungle of physiology and its mouldering tangle of inheritance and circumstance'. He re-visits scenes from his Pennsylvania childhood, makes a study of genealogy (Updikes have derived from Goonish names like Gysbert op den Dyck, Op dyck, and Updik – like Chance the gardener evolving into Chauncey Gardiner); and he goes about his inquiries with many a circling step and reiteration, 'like the inspired addendum of outtakes, under the credit roll, wherein Peter Sellers tries again and again to relay in his impeccably put-on American accent, the obscene message from the menacing black boy, and breaks up laughing again and again: Sellers, so incredibly clever, so lively in his impersonations, so quick, and now dead.'

The reason Chance will make a good President of the United States is that he has no family background; there is no hidden past to be revealed which might ruin him. (He is like a virgin birth – and he walks on water in the last scene.) Updike, however, says of ancestors that they 'lived that we may live. We reverence them because they participate in the mystery of our being.' Sellers himself didn't go in for much reverencing, but even he could see that ancestors – 'relations which grow on family trees,' as Old Sam puts it in *The Optimists of Nine Elms* – need to come and go if you are going to get born. His own illustrious forebear was Daniel Mendoza, the eighteenth-century prize fighter – Welcome/Belle/Ma's grandfather.

An engraving by J. Grozer from a painting by C.R. Ryley, produced to commemorate Mendoza's match against Humphreys at Doncaster on September 29th 1790, shows a rather pretty young man, stripped to the waist, his fists up in pugilistic pose. The picture was to have been the logotype for the company Sellers was forming with Wolf Mankowitz; and if you are sharp-eyed and look at what is hanging on the walls of Nayland Smith's cottage in *The Fiendish Plot of Dr Fu Manchu*, there is the framed print once again.

Mendoza was much more than a boxer. He was a ruin. His life, accounted for in periodicals like *Egan's Boxiana*, *The Fancy*, and *Bell's Life in London*, consisted of little but pummellings and exhausting pitched battles, sessions in debtors' prisons and grab-anything jobs to make ends meet. According to a modern editor of his *Memoirs*,[*] Mendoza worked as a glazier, a grocer's assistant, a waiter in a tea shop, a process server, a baker (specialising in cakes for the Passover), a recruiting sergeant, a tobacconist, and a publican. Mendoza, it was said, 'never was truly himself unless he carried on more than one activity'.

What he really was, his chronic unemployability aside, was a fledgeling actor. If the newspapers of the day described him as an exotic – 'the youthful Jew', 'the star of the East', and so on – he himself, in his many letters to the press, said he had appeared 'before the public in the character of a fighter on the stage'. His matches, against Richard Humphreys (1789), John Jackson (1795) or Harry

---

[*] *Memoirs of the Life of Daniel Mendoza*, edited by Paul Magriel (London, 1951.)

Lee (1806), which went to fifty-three rounds, were in the nature of brutal theatrical performances, with the combatants, gloves off, disfiguring each others' faces. Having been victorious against Humphreys in a re-match, Mendoza toured the music halls, a showman, giving exhibition bouts – and it was Mendoza's idea to put the bouts on a roped and raised dais, and that nobody be allowed on the stage during a fight except the principals and their seconds.

☆ ★ ☆

In *Memoirs of the Life of Daniel Mendoza*, the boxer presents himself as a Regency buck, an innocent hero always being dragged against his will into scrapes and duels of honour. He could be an invention of Henry Fielding. Fisticuffs were never his fault. It is comical, his high-minded detection of insolence. When some butchers' boys shouted and frightened his horse, 'I immediately dismounted and having singled out the instigator of the disturbance and insisting on his fighting me on the spot, I convinced him in half an hour that he had much better have let me alone.'

Mendoza's virtue is rewarded, and he hospitalised people wherever he went. For example, to Northampton ('the fellow was afterwards confined to his room for upwards of three weeks'); to Islington ('after the battle I was warmly congratulated by several gentlemen who professed their pleasure at seeing me so well recovered, and in such excellent health and spirits'); to Epping Forest ('I immediately seized the fellow who had committed the outrage, and having pulled him into the middle of the room gave him a severe thrashing in the presence of the whole company, none of whom offered to interfere'). And so it goes on. In Glasgow 'I threw a table out of the window upon them', and in Dublin he is challenged to a duel – but scorns the pistols and grabs his opponent and 'in the public room of the hotel, and in the presence of the whole company, gave him a severe caning'.

Mendoza thinks of himself as reserved ('I forbore to take many advantages which were in my power'), but the reader quickly has him marked as a particularly nasty delinquent who ages into somebody violent and mad. He goes about spoiling for a fight; all the better if an admiring and yelling audience gathers. His pranks, such as riding on his horse into a ballroom, 'to the surprise and entertainment of the company, chiefly consisting of sailors and their lasses', are rather over-boisterous; and when he disguised himself as a sailor (one of the 'gallant sons of Neptune') to go on a spree (and was arrested as a deserter) his chief recollection was of beating up a sergeant outside Chatham barracks. A hoodlum, he never learned manners or civility (invited to a foxhunt he scattered the hounds with his cart horse) and after his career had peaked when he'd met George III at Windsor ('No Jew had ever spoken with the King before'), he declined and fell, entering the Debtors' Prison in Carlisle, an archetypal rake's progression. Freed on that occasion by the Masons, he was hounded by creditors wherever his posters went up. He toured Lancashire and the North of England, gradually slipping down the bill. From having been a character who had held his own exhibitions, a name that relegated news of the French Revolution to the inside pages of journals and magazines, he was now part of a troupe, going on to crouch, dodge imaginary blows and demonstrate holds, and to display his scars, between the jugglers and the comic songs. His pride, as he recounted his heroic past, could almost be considered soulful: 'It was my custom at this time to exhibit the attitudes and manner of setting-to of Big Ben Johnson, Broughton, Perrins and Humphreys and to conclude with my own original attitude. Variety was thus afforded, and the company had by these means an opportunity of comparing, in some degree, the different merits of these celebrated pugilists, as their mode of fighting was successively displayed.'

Would the public really sit through such a lecture? Mendoza toured Wales, Hereford, Chester, Lancaster, Manchester, Halifax, Stafford, Nottingham, Newcastle, chased always by his debts. He finally met his match as a stooge sparring partner for Lord Camelford – who was more of a psychopath than he was: 'I found his Lordship a better proficient than myself; he struck with great force as well as skill, and I received a violent blow over the ear, which caused great pain at the time.'

His Lordship then took a rapier to Mendoza, which luckily broke, and when he went to look for a dagger, Mendoza saw his chance to run out of the house and 'as may readily be imagined, never felt the least inclination to re-enter it'.

☆ ★ ☆

Mendoza died in Horseshoe Alley, Petticoat Lane, on September 3rd 1836, leaving no money and eleven children, of which only ten are in the synagogue register at the Bevis Marks Hall (the Spanish and Portuguese Jews' Congregation, founded in 1657). These are Sarah (1788), Abraham (1790), Sophia (1792), Isabella (1796), Daniel (1797), Jesse (1801), Louisa (1803), Aron (1807), Isaac (1808) and Matilda (1810). The last but one of these grew up to be Welcome's father and after marrying a lady surnamed Lesser, helped to transfuse whatever we are to make of Daniel Mendoza into Sellers' bloodstream, where the circus and street-fighting lived and waited.

On one level, Mendoza's life was farce – the way, even when he goes with his wife to Vauxhall Gardens, he is 'assailed by sticks in all directions' and makes 'desperate resistance'. This is Clouseau and Cato, two hundred years ago, flying through the air aiming kicks and punches. Or the scene with Lord Camelford and the hecklers at the music hall – that is Sellers' and Milligan's view of the penurious, stupefied and eternally optimistic William McGonagall, forever flattened under weights, slapped full in the face by cabbages, and humiliated generally. In *The Great McGonagall*, the itinerant versifier, with his cardboard suitcase of poetic gems, like the wandering boxer, visits his Sovereign: not eccentric George III, but Sellers as Queen Victoria: 'This day I have given audience to a man who was a Scottish artistic genius. He read me some of the most exquisite poetry I have ever heard in my life with the rich and powerful tones of his voice which rose and fell like the sea. Both Prince Albert and I were deeply moved by him. But then he left and in came William McGonagall.'

On another level, however, what placed Mendoza out of the ordinary, the mock heroic idiom of his own *Memoirs* aside, and reverting to contemporary sources, was the way he attempted to capitalise on his violent streak ('the reward of money was high in his mind all his long life') by converting brawls into a recognised sport. Mendoza insisted on chalk lines to separate the competitors before the off; he suggested that umpires be picked 'from among the gentlemen present'; and he thought it a good idea if 'no person is to hit his adversary when he is down, or seize him by the ham, the breeches, or any part below the waist. . . .' His efforts to circumscribe his unruliness with rules – to use Richard Ellmann's phrase for boxing's other brute, the Marquess of Queensberry – was received in a variety of ways. To the readers of *Pugilistica* it was Mendoza's muscle-bound skill and dexterity which drew analysis. He was called a 'scientific professor in the art of self-defence' – a man whose style of jabs, grips and throws could be learned from and copied. *Boxiana*, however, viewed him more metaphysically than physically. Mendoza's career, it was argued, was evidence of that noble savage which lurks inside each of us; that spirit of courage and gusto which we tend to deny, with compromises, failure of nerve, old age. The pugilist exemplified a purified masculinity: 'he might be termed a complete artist'. He could have been dreamed up by the classics – and indeed the engravings and colour plates idealising Mendoza make him look as if he has stepped off a Greek vase. He is a pale dancer in profile. (Where is the smoke and blood?)

That Mendoza's juice and handing out of buffetings might be the refinement of something innate and beautiful would have been news to those who'd otherwise have steered clear of him as a one-man street-gang. But, his apologists responded, if Mendoza was a thug, what of the infant 'who is seen to lift up its little arm indignantly against the object that attempts to deprive him of his playthings'? By misconstruing an independent spirit as the divine right to be selfish and repulsive – this is the Mendoza of use to Sellers: the Sellers who justified his pitched battles with directors, producers, or any authority figure, by referring to his artistic integrity and his private and proprietary rights. The adult Sellers was still the boy who 'to protect his top or marbles . . . puts himself in a

posture of defence and dares his oppressor to the hostile combat' –
in the words of *Boxiana*, when its correspondent tried to get to the
bottom of Mendoza's youth.

Sellers, who took to an extreme Mendoza's asseveration that 'a
man ought not to be harassed with unnecessary and vexatious restrictions', may be given the boxing ring as a symbol of his modus
operandi. The hard flashes of Mendoza's eighteenth-century life
and times almost preincarnate the modern star's behaviour and
rant. He used to re-tell with approval a conversation he'd overheard
in Wales, when he was making *Only Two Can Play*: 'I remember
Richard Burton was down there and one of Kenneth Griffith's
Welsh cronies went up to him and said, "Do you know this Marly
Brandon then?" When Burton said, "Yes – he's a fine actor," the
man said: "that's as may be, boyo – but can you *beat* him?" And he
put up his fists. What he meant of course, was "can you beat him
up?" That's what counted in his world.'

If there was an extra dimension to Sellers' destructiveness, something that went well beyond the immediate provocation or catalyst,
it might go back all the way to the primal test of manhood. For the
Mendoza who defined boxing as a means 'to enable men to stand in
their own defence against the assaults they are daily exposed to' is
the knockout idolised by the Jewish community. As was said at the
time, 'Royalty besought him. Even the King! Who else among the
schoolfellows of his boyhood could have risen to such an experience! It was almost in the realm of fantasy!' The very same
realm Sellers would be in when he was romancing Princess Margaret and Roman goddesses like Sophia Loren . . . Mendoza, because
of his celebrity, helped to raise the profile and status of the London
Jews. His official fights and victories, owing nothing to teams or to
any equipment save his own muscles and daring, proved 'to a not
too friendly world that Judaism and courage often go together'.*

---

* This phrase comes from a paper by Lewis Edwards, 'Daniel Mendoza,' read
  before the Jewish Historical Society of England, in March 1938 – very much an
  anti-Semitic period.

☆ ★ ☆

Mendoza, the primitive, the poet, the ruffian, the conqueror and man of destiny – the 'intelligent and communicative man' in the opinion of *Boxiana* – was evidently as multiform as his great-great grandson. Sellers played him once. When he was regaining consciousness after his first big heart attack, the first programme he saw and enjoyed on the television was *Not Only . . . But Also*: 'He'd seen Peter Cook and Dudley Moore,' says Joe McGrath, 'and asked if he could do a guest spot on the show. We wrote a sketch about a boxer, called Danny, who had become an abstract painter, and who'd gone back to boxing again.'

Sellers held a palette covered with oils in one hand and had a boxing glove on the other – hitting the reds and greens and blues and then the canvas on the easel. 'It looks "taché-iste" to me,' says Cook. 'Nobody can accuse me of not loving my coloured brothers,' says Sellers. 'My day begins with a bit of road work, where I pick up my "objets trouvés". . . .' Meantime, Dudley is fanning him with a towel and using a paint rag to wipe his face down. Cook continues the interview: 'I don't understand why you have to paint in a boxing ring.' – 'Well, it's where I started. . . .' The bell rings and he runs out and continues painting. 'I believe Tintoretto was astigmatic,' says Cook. 'Well, I heard that,' says Sellers, 'some people are like that, some people ain't. Myself, I prefer birds.'

As a punch drunk old pug with finer feelings, Sellers' Danny is a nice little caricature – and very distant homage – and what further linked the historical Mendoza to the modern actor's temperament was their shared attitude to money. Mendoza earned large fees and spent it 'like a drunken sailor' ('All he knew of economics was that his money had been easy to come by'). Sellers, equally heedless and improvident, frittered away fortunes on cars and electronic toys. Yet where Sellers died a multimillionaire, the door-money from Inspector Clouseau rolling in, Mendoza's last years were 'piteous, lamentable, and ruinous' – words apt for Sellers in every sense *except* the financial.

Mendoza's widow lived until 1855, running a pub called the

Royal Oak in Whitechapel Road. Other addresses associated with Mendoza are 3 Paradise Row, Bethnal Green; 9 White Street, Houndsditch; and the White Hart Tavern, Abchurch Lane. According to the 1861 census, Mendoza's children were at 4 Wigmore Street; ten years later they were at 69 Nichols Square, Hackney Road. Amongst these thoroughfares Welcome (and then Peg) grew up – a landscape of prize fights and music rooms and girls singing in four-ale bars. Whatever effect her marriage to Solomon Marks may have had (sources differ as to whether she was wedded or widowed at the age of forty-four), that the touring revue company was established at all implies a need, late on in life, to revert to her grandfather's round of nomadic entertaining. There was a wanderer in her soul (as there was to be a restlessness in her grandson's).

Provincial music hall and revue, however, were not a healthy existence, especially at their lower levels, where Peg and Bill operated. People were over-worked by the non-stop shows, and there was a good deal of boozing. Suppers were served in the orchestra stalls and audiences and cast alike could swig on fizz at seven shillings a bottle or take concoctions such as sherry and egg or rum and honey for sixpence a glass. Peg became a soak in her final phase – gin concealed in Optrex bottles, all that. And there was almost a tradition of dying either young (like Sam 'The Ratcatcher's Daughter' Cowell, at forty-four, or George 'Champagne Charlie' Leybourne, at forty-two); or else you lingered on, degraded by poverty and disability – a common fate amongst the trampolinists and trapezists, the people who'd come up from the circus. (Mendoza himself was a wreck by the age of fifty-two; he lived to be seventy-three.)

It was no place for raising babies. The one-night cheap hotels, the damp, the unaired rooming-houses smelling of drains and mouse. The diphtheria, whooping cough, bow-legs, leg-braces, and meningitis. No wonder its adherents took to the bottle and broke their health. They never saw the sun. They lived by the artificial lights flickering off the dressing room mirrors or the float-guards. Peter Sellars (note the spelling) was a casualty. So was the child's mother. So was his younger brother, raised in his place.

Peg, highly strung anyway, and dependent on Ma for stability, was demented with grief; she'd take the layette kit out of its drawer and, as if it were a boy's collection of blown birds' eggs, weep on the tissue paper. To paraphrase Constance on the death of her son Arthur in Shakespeare's *King John*: grief filled up the room of Peg's absent child, lay in his bed, walked up and down with her, put on his pretty looks, repeated his words, reminded her of all his gracious parts, stuffed out his vacant garments with his form. . . . When you keep faith with the dead like this, your dead child is idealised; he never needs to fall short or be humbled by life's confusion and contingency. He'd be an angel. He'd be a boy forever.

Sellers' very existence, therefore, owed itself to anguish. Come to replace a lost boy, conceived as a double, he was literally born to be a great impersonator. He it was who'd stuff out another's garments with his form, put on his pretty looks; it was he who'd wear the little blue bunny shaped slippers and get silently measured against somebody who was no longer there. And it was he, *Richard Henry Sellars*, born a year after Peter, on Tuesday September 8th 1925, who had to fulfil Peg's super-normal expectations. He'd never be allowed to grow up; he'd never fail or be less than perfect – an attitude which doomed him instantly. ('I knew, you see, that his destiny was exceptional.') It was never going to be feasible for Sellers to be at home in this world. He'd always be afraid he was not quite real.

☆ ★ ☆

Flash forward half a century, to Sellers' last outflinging, when he was making *The Prisoner of Zenda*, *Being There*, and *The Fiendish Plot of Dr Fu Manchu*. What attracted him to the old-fashioned, Victorian atmosphere of these tales? (*Being There*, ostensibly modern, is set in a Nineties folly, Biltmore, in North Carolina, an ice palace where the clocks stopped long ago; and Chance wears dapper turn-of-the-century suits and hats.) It is not that they are simply romances about disguise, sundered twins, counterfeiting, and the illusion of order. They are also, each of them, stories about the problems of identity and who people really are – we are back with Updike's gaze down to 'the glittering bottom, alive with frogs and phosphorescence' of the pit of personality etc.. *The Prisoner of Zenda*, for example, is a campy cousin of Stevenson's *Dr Jekyll and Mr Hyde*: doubles who are opposites, and yet interlinked. In the Sellers film, the division is between a regal buffoon and decadent, Prince Rudi, and the honourable commoner, Sidney Frewin of Bethnal Green. (Their mother was a music hall actress, Tessy Frewin, and the two boys join in a chorus of her famous song: 'She was a sweet little dickie bird, tweet-tweet-tweet she went' – i.e. Sellers sings a duet with himself on screen.)

The two sides of Sellers' own nature are there: the night-clubbing and womanising versus the reclusiveness. And Sellers, indeed, could be both at once. When, to many witnesses, he was moping in his hotel in Paris, during the winter before he died, full of sorrow because his last marriage seemed to have failed, he was also, on the evidence of his chauffeur's log book, 'out on the town eating and drinking very late many nights . . . and the jet trips every weekend are very debilitating'. I quote from a memo sent to Sellers' lawyer on December 12th 1979 – the legal representatives had to decide how much of their client's exhaustion at work was the result of exertions at play, something which could have had alarming insurance ramifications if Sellers dropped dead during the making of a picture.

Sellers plays Rudi as a caricature of twittishness; he is perfectly brainless and nobody has ever talked with a lisp like that. But Frewin, the hackney-carriage driver, has a solidity, a decency; and he talks like Michael Caine. (Sellers coined Caine's 'not many people know that' catchphrase.) A forlornness comes over Sellers whenever he does an East-Ender or a Northerner, as though he is suddenly in touch with the sort of fellow he could have been, had stardom not made him run riot. *The Optimists of Nine Elms, The Dock Brief, Mister Topaze* – in such films as these Sellers played the unfamous, men who have not managed to come adrift from their origins; yet it is Frewin's fate, as Rudi's double, to be accelerated to celebrity and the public gaze, going from the stables to a new life in a

Mittel-Europa operetta. His prize is Lynne Frederick's girlish Princess Flavia. She has a knowing innocence to match his quiet depths. She is quite aware that he is an impostor and when, during the Coronation scene, she declares her fealty to the new King – 'I, Flavia, do become thy vassal, swearing to serve thee in truth, with love, life and limb' – it is impossible not to detect a private joke going on between the husband and wife team. The young or non-notorious Sellers, scruffy, a little greasy, puffy, bespectacled, fat, would not have been looked at twice by any Princess Flavias.

The fun of *The Prisoner of Zenda*, when Ronald Colman was doing it and not only Sellers, is in seeing the one actor appear on screen with himself – serving himself drinks, talking to himself. He overcomes his singularity. It is an obvious bit of cinematic illusion (and theatrical illusion, if you think of the Antipholus twins in *The Comedy of Errors*). When the camera allows Sellers to proliferate, however, what we see, and become conscious of, is his multiple personality. Which is the natural man? Which the spirit? Who deciphers them? Such questions loomed large in my mind as I travelled to Harborne, in the Midlands, to meet John Taylor, Sellers' stand-in and double from *The Fiendish Plot of Dr Fu Manchu*. When I rang the bell and the frosted glass door was immediately opened, I received the shock of my life: there stood Peter Sellers. Or, should I say, Sellers as he would be now, had he hidden himself away and survived into his mid-sixties.

☆ ★ ☆

Taylor, his voice actorishly velvet, though marred now and then by the Birmingham diphthongs which chimed in when he dropped his guard, told me that he had been a salesman, with a hankering for amateur dramatics. In his time he had appeared in concerts with Kenneth Tynan (who grew up in Edgbaston) and Hugh Manning ('the vicar in *Emmerdale Farm*'). He currently writes poems, or verses anyway, and *Love, Cricket, Peter Sellers* had recently been published, privately, by The Bowline Press, at £3.95. In my first edition copy (for which the author himself gave me change from a fiver) I was interested to read 'Lonely Man (Peter Sellers 1980)',

'Drifting Into Stardom (For Peter Sellers: A Sort of Obituary)', 'The Last Wrap 1980 (Peter Sellers' Last Film)' and 'On Being Cast in a Major Rôle in a Film'. The gist of these is best conveyed by a brief quotation:

> Months of playing make-believe,
> Months of traipsing round the set,
> Tracked by cameras to weave
> Scenes that all will soon forget.

Yes: the solitude of the famous; the transience of human achievement; the fleetingness of friendships, etc. It's all there, as it was in Wordsworth. Taylor struck me as a rather woebegone man, his face thin and pinched. Though he did his best to appear genial and courteous, I sensed he was apprehensive; he'd quite recently been through the adversity of a divorce and he didn't mind admitting that, in contrast to the experience of the last year, his adventure with Sellers stood out all the more as the big unexpected highlight in his life.

'My children's friends always thought I looked like Sellers, but I never made anything of the comparison, not until I went to meet a theatrical agent in London in May 1979. The girl in the agency suddenly said: "My God, I've never seen anything like it. Stand up again. There's Peter Sellers standing there." That was the first time anybody had remarked on any serious similarity. In June, the agency offered me three months' work, working with Peter Sellers – which I jumped at, even though I was only an actor part-time. That same week I went back to London and met Piers Haggard and the casting director at the YMCA on Tottenham Court Road. They made me walk around – I didn't know what I was supposed to be doing. My agent, Joyce, phoned me on the Saturday to say they were interested, and would I like to go for a proper audition, preferably on Monday, and "Can you bring five different comic pieces," which I had to learn over the weekend. . . . I duly did the audition on Monday. On the Wednesday I had another call – would I meet Sellers on the Friday. He was staying at the Inn on the Park.

I went in with Tom Smith, the make-up man. Sellers was with Michael Jeffery. We had tea and biscuits. Sellers suddenly said, "See you over there in Paris. We'll have some bloody fun." He gave me a list of addresses. His car took me to the wig makers, his tailors, his shirt makers, his shoe shop, and then back to Euston. Michael Jeffery had designed the Fu gear, and Sellers had said, "Whatever I'm having, duplicate it for John." We were identical in weight, height, our shoe size – except for the neck. He was a sixteen. I'm a fifteen and a half. I had to have a couple of sports jackets, trousers and ties for Nayland Smith. These all cost hundreds over ten years ago. The jackets were beautifully made in Savile Row, shaped and waisted. I kept some of the ties as souvenirs. I don't know what happened to all the rest, or to Fu's robes.

'Things started to get quite eerie during the test shots. I started on a Monday. Sellers arrived the following Friday afternoon. We went to a viewing theatre to see all the test film. It sent shivers up and down my spine, the likeness was so remarkable. You wouldn't know which one of us you were looking at. At the end of it, Sellers stood up, picked up his bag, walked to the doors at the top of the stairs and said, "Right, I'm off home. That bugger can do it." It really was remarkable. And it fooled Roman Polanski. He was at the Studios de Boulogne finishing *Tess*. He took hold of my hand, when I was Fu, and we did a waltz – he thought it was Peter.

'Ever afterwards, Sellers kept squinting and staring at me. "You give me the creeps, mate," he'd say. He told me he found it almost upsetting. "I've never seen anything like it," he said. "Where have we been at relative times in our lives? What did you look like when you were younger?"

'Well, I used to be quite chubby, you see, in my twenties and thirties; and I looked out a number of old photographs and the likeness was *there*. Most mornings I had to go and see him for a briefing and to collect the costumes. He'd always say, "You give me the creeps, mate, you really do." He'd phone me up at all hours of the night – at three a.m. for instance – and he'd say he wasn't ever happy unless he was involved in a film. "When I'm not in front of a fucking camera it's not worth being here." He had no other interest – he was bored even by his still photography. I never saw him with one of his cameras in his hand, not even in the Alps. He didn't read. He didn't listen to music. He phoned me once in quite a state. "I've got to get out of this fucking place." He wanted somebody to talk to. We had dinner near the Opéra. We resembled semi-elderly identical twins. "John," he said, "I'm wondering if I'll ever make another film."

'Well, he booked me to be in his next one, *The Romance of the Pink Panther*. I was going to be his double again. It turned out to be a hectic day or two. I arrived in London, went to my hotel, and called Sue Evans, his secretary, who said he'd been taken to hospital. Michael Jeffery phoned me late in the evening, from the Dorchester, having come back briefly from the hospital, and he said he'd be in touch the next day. The next morning I read in the Stop Press that he'd died. Ever since, I have been accosted so many times by strangers – long after his death, people would stop me in the street. I was in Leeds four years ago, and I was returning to the station, when three lads surrounded me. I was getting scared, anticipating a mugging, when they said, "Eh mate, you're Peter Sellers aren't you?" I mean he'd been dead years by then. . .'

In the folklore of the *doppelgänger* (German for 'double-goer'; defined by the *OED* as 'wraith of living person') to meet your duplicate is a premonition of death. Sellers, who had visited Roger Moore on the set of *The Man Who Haunted Himself*, must have felt as if he'd toppled headlong into a similarly horrific plot.* As *The Fiendish Plot of Dr Fu Manchu*, on Sellers' orders, was being re-re-re-written through the night, every night, by teams of hacks, belletrists, ex-playwrights, and just about anybody who could stay awake and hold a pen, this is exactly an element which was worked

---

* *The Man Who Haunted Himself* (1970), in which Moore is trailed by his double in the aftermath of a car accident, was directed by Basil Dearden who, back in 1957, had directed Sellers in *The Smallest Show on Earth*. Spookily, Dearden was to die in 1971 – in a car crash.

in at the last moment (though it was lost again when the film was edited after Sellers' passing). As Sellers intended it (and he threw the leaves of the script other people had concocted to the ground, in order to improvise it), the rejuvenated Fu, and Taylor as Nayland, were to walk off into the sunset together, the opposites reconciled, the doubles united. 'You are the only worthy adversary I ever had, Nayland. They were the good old days. We can recapture them and start all over again.'

Do the emotions, under the surface, reach back to the lost boy of Peg's? *The Fiendish Plot of Dr Fu Manchu* is crammed with old Goon gags and music hall allusions. Sellers was re-living things he'd already done (the Canary Diamond which Fu needs for his magic youth-restoring potion is a jewel chipped off the Pink Panther lode); and by going backwards Sellers' nostalgic cycle turned full circle: we came into the world like brother and brother: And now let's go hand in hand, not one before another.

☆ ★ ☆

'From the very beginning – why I don't know – I was called Peter,' he said in 1976. Alterations of nomenclature were not uncommon in his family. As we have seen, Welcome Mendoza became Mrs Solomon Marks, Belle Ray and Ma; Agnes Marks became Peg; Will Sellars turned into Bill Sellers – Sellars into Sellers having taken no more thought than everybody deciding to acquiesce in a printer's error on a flysheet. Richard Henry's instant alteration into Peter, however, was a signal that here was the little changeling boy to be Peg's henchman, and her control over him was both total and scant. The obnoxious everyday presence was the one she could goad, organise and bully. 'My son doesn't need to think,' she'd say proudly, 'I do all his thinking for him.' Sellers was pale, pampered, and protected. He had a beehive of hair which was smeared with vaseline to give it a healthy and glossy appearance. This repellent tangle on the top of his head almost symbolises the sticky, blobby inchoate mass, with no personality of its own, which Sellers liked to project in interviews: 'Now I'm probably one of *the* most unfunny people there is in private life. I'm dull. . .'

Where Peg could not follow, however, was into that part of his brain where he carried out his transformations. He got away from her through the conjurings and aliases of the theatre. 'I find', he was to say, 'that I operate much better if I'm behind a voice or a moustache where my own personality is disguised. I get a freedom that I don't normally have.' If Peg had lunch with him at the studio, and was asked afterwards how her son was, she used to say, 'I don't know. I didn't see him.' Sellers set himself loose by being other people, imitating and experimenting all the live long day. 'He used to go off on these flights of fancy,' says Joe McGrath. 'Sellers liked working in that semi-improvised way, when art and life mingle. He liked to feel he wasn't being constricted. A lot of the Quilty and Dr Strangelove stuff – he got into the character and was allowed to *go*. This is what Sellers was best at doing.'

☆　★　☆

'A man of genius', said Ezra Pound (Hailey, Idaho) 'cannot help where he is born.' Pound never stopped being a cracker-barrel Middle-West sage, sitting in a rocking chair on the front porch, nursing his prejudices; and it is a fact that the birthplace can form an artist – Dublin for James Joyce, Manchester for Anthony Burgess, Melbourne for Barry Humphries. Sellers was born less into a place than a condition. If it wasn't bad enough being ungrounded by his mother's interdependence of love and death, the vagrancy of the vaudevillians ensured a placeless childhood. 'I didn't always mean to be an actor,' he complained, 'I was carried on to the stage when I was two days old, but I never acted as a child. My parents were stage people. I was an only child and I was taken round with them on tour, living in theatrical digs. It was Mum and Dad's life and it had to be like that.'

Sellers, whom many might assume had been beamed down from the Never-Never Land, was officially born in Southsea, near Portsmouth, at 20 Southsea Terrace. His family had taken a flat above a shop selling sweets and postcards of the naval dockyards; and Sellers, like Holly Golightly's admirer, was always drawn back to the places where he had lived, the houses and their neighbourhoods. Revisiting the premises forty years on, he claimed that 'I knew where my cot was, the shape of the ceilings. It was uncanny, really uncanny . . . it all looked much smaller and older and sadder.'

He was delivered from his mother's womb by Dr Robert J. Lytle, MD, BCh, BAO, of 20 St Helens Parade, who was a lay canon of Portsmouth's (Anglican) cathedral; he was unhappy about Peg's desire to continue working – but she was insistent that she revert as soon as possible to the make-believe of the revue. *The Vanity Box* left the King's Theatre, in Albert Road, Southsea, on Saturday September 11th 1925. Peg and Bill remained above Postcard Corner to join up with *The Side Show* company, which had visited South Shields, Salford, Crewe, York and Darlington, and was at present in Southampton. The local attraction, meantime, was Dickie Henderson Snr, the father of the more recent Dickie Henderson, that little drunkard with a small amount of charm who is now dead. Henderson, it is alleged, is the one who carried Sellers in his swaddling bands on to the King's Theatre stage and led the audience in a chorus of 'For He's a Jolly Good Fellow'. ('I didn't know anything about it,' Sellers later claimed with some justification.)

The audience could well have been singing for Henderson himself. He had recently returned to Britain after an American tour. On August 17th he had begun a circuit of the provincial music halls that would last for three solid years. In a performance he'd given the week before Sellers' birth, a critic compared him to Dan Leno; and as 'Yorkshire's Own Comedian: The Man With a Genial Smile' he told stories about wives, mothers-in-laws, babies, neighbours, and other such themes which 'knock at the heart, stir the inmost fibres of being' and which were 'at once the Treasure of the Humble and the symbols of Wisdom and Destiny'. He sang 'Pal O' My Cradle Days' (reprised over the infant Sellers?) and was supported by Dave Davis' Swanee Minstrels, novelty juggling, and dancing by Dolly and Inez St. Vincent. Ted Marcel, 'the garrulous skating fellow,' skated and a soprano sang 'Nobody Loves a Fat Girl/But, Oh, How a Fat Girl Can Love.'

Henderson was something of a luminary, looked at from the vantage point of Peg and Bill; and Ray Brothers Productions Ltd. were glad to have an association with him, now that he was 'at liberty' in the theatre world's euphemistic phrase. Because he weighed sixteen stone, he had been tested by Hal Roach as the potential fat man in a duo with Stan Laurel; and though he did make a few films, his growling presence, as he chewed on a cigar, didn't adapt well to either silent movies or to the early talkies. He did not possess that loony aura which W.C. Fields and Oliver Hardy had – and which Sellers had – which makes you want to keep on watching them on the screen.

Born in 1891 (nine years Bill's senior, four or six years Peg's), by 1925 Henderson was already at the start of his decline. He dipped and splashed in and out of a lot of the Ray water shows, going away to make a new career for himself, returning when he'd failed; and his fate is of significance because it hints at the increasing fragility of the business Sellers' parents were in. Let alone the twice-breathed air and stink of digs and dressing rooms to make you droop, the idea of the wandering revue company itself, as Ma Ray defined it, was set to be extinguished within a few years. This only added to the twilit mood of Sellers' childhood. From every direction he met with things dying.

The singing and dancing in *The Side Show*, nevertheless, was 'exceptionally good and laughter abounds' – according to a critic who attended its opening at the Hippodrome, Aldershot, back in April. It was an hour or so of artifice and escapism, its songs and sketches being about recovery and hope. 'The prettiest item of the show is a duet, "My Lady of Quality," by Deci St. Clair and Harry Arthurs, and an Old English Dance.' After Southsea, Peg, Bill and their baby were on the road with this lot, and Sellers' first year, a pattern followed until he was five, went like this:

Week commencing		
October 23rd	:	Warrington
November 4th	:	Bradford
November 16th	:	Huddersfield
November 29th	:	Burnley
December 21st	:	Keighley

December 28th	:	Ashton-under-Lyne
January 18th	:	Manchester
February 22nd	:	Barrow-in-Furness
March 8th	:	Liverpool
March 29th	:	Newcastle
April 5th	:	Carlisle
April 19th	:	Hulme
May 24th	:	Aldershot
May 31st	:	Devonport
June 7th	:	Swindon
June 14th	:	Camberwell
July 19th	:	Sheffield
July 26th	:	Ilford
August 16th	:	Eastbourne
August 23rd	:	Edmonton
August 30th	:	Edinburgh
September 6th	:	West Hartlepool

. . . and so on and on, a treadmill out of Dante. During the Keighley engagement, the baby fell ill with bronchial pneumonia. 'A coloured doctor saved his life,' said Peg later – for whom the experience, the coughing baby in a Moses basket at the back of the stage amongst the props, and the black man emerging out of the fog, had the quality of an hallucination.

'I really didn't like that period of my life, as a kid,' recalled Sellers. 'I didn't like the touring. I didn't like the smell of greasepaint which hit you when you went into any stage door. The smell of size – that's the stuff they paint on scenery – and baritones with beer on their breath and make-up on the collar – all big voices, like "Hello, little sonny, how are you? All right? Little boy, dear little boy. Who is he? Who is he?" And I used to spend my time sitting in dressing rooms . . . so I didn't like that.' Yet he was to grow fond of at least impersonating these grandiose actor types, over-enunciating Wolfits, tumbledown Hendersons, normally called Warrington Minge, who can do little with their bouncing cheques except have them pressed flat at the Chinese laundry. Sitting in his hotel, during location work for *The Return of the Pink Panther*, Sellers spent his time leafing through the London *A-Z Street Atlas*, gathering names for a whole platoon of thesps: Theydon Bois, Turnham Green, Montagu Mews West (his favourite). Aside from being a gift to the caricaturist, these Victorian tragedians, Banstead Way, Hardwicke Court, etc., were, from the start, Sellers' way of demonstrating just how subtle his own humour could be. Anybody can ape an old ham making a fool of himself with quasi-Shakespearean diction, playing King Lear on stage and off. What Sellers could touch on was the desperation – the crumpled, ordinary and vainglorious flop lurking underneath the mannerisms.

His masterpiece in this regard is Dr Pratt in *The Wrong Box*. Though an unkempt, shuffling dotard, whose consulting room is awash with mangy cats and (we surmise) the unspeakable detritus of botched abortions, Pratt, in his frock coat and wing collar, is like a Henry Irving who has fallen from grace – the pathos he gets into his line 'I was not always as you see me now' is so gentle and expressive, we picture him in a private coach, paying professional calls on the aristocracy, or hobnobbing with Lord Lister at the Royal College of Surgeons. Or rather we don't. When these sorts of characters dream about their better days – Morganhall in *The Dock Brief*, General Fitzjohn in *Waltz of the Toreadors* – what Sellers suggests more than anything is their gullibility. His ripe and ancient magicians can respond only to things that never were; they are incurable romantics – and what makes the comedy deep-toned is the suggestion that hovering not very far away at all is the more tragic observation that here we have people who have had wasted lives.

There is perhaps not too much of this gloom in a sketch performed on television at the end of the Fifties. In *The Arthur Ploughshare Show*, written by Eric Sykes, Sellers was Pules Nogbart, who is visited backstage by a camera crew and an interviewer – whom he addresses as 'Oh noble messenger of pictures that delight the eye'. The joke is that this wonderfully declamatory old warrior keeps getting his Shakespeare plays mixed up, is interrupted and humbled by his dresser (who is sent out for four pennyworth of light ale and a bag of chips), and he resides, not in a nearby castle or grand hotel – but 'I always stay with Mrs Mackay, 11 Daisy Avenue'. He is preparing to play Bottom, and gets into the ass-head costume, though the stage is set for *Richard III*; he warms up with lines from *Hamlet*, though the posters advertise *Macbeth* – and Pules does a snatch of Macbeth-as-McGonagall, with spitting and hawking and throat-clearing Scots. Then, the final humiliation, it turns out he is in a variety theatre by mistake – and instead of bothering to race to his proper venue, he decides to stay put and do a ten minute spot after the juggler.

☆　★　☆

The brief notices on *The Side Show* which appeared in provincial newspapers, mentions now yellowed and crumbling in forgotten archives, the leaves about to disintegrate and cease to exist, seem to be the only references to Sellers' parents' career in existence. For example, when they were at the Palace, Bradford: 'Ray Brothers are staging "The Side Show" the principals being Fred Morgan and Harry Arthurs'; or at Ashton-under-Lyne: 'The Empire Theatre has relinquished panto for the production of the revue "The Side Show," toured by Ray Bros. Artistes are Spencer Cash, Will Sellars, Arthur Lewis, Monty Golding and a full chorus'; or at the Pavilion, Liverpool: 'The Ray Brothers Productions are presenting "The Side Show," an entertaining revue, in which appear Willie Cave, Arthur Lewis, Harry Ray's Syncopators, Will Sellers [*sic*] and Monty Golding'; or at Hulme: 'Ray Bros. Productions present here an attractive revue under the title "The Side Show". It has great vivacity and variety of interest, all kept well up to pitch by a well-selected cast. Chief among the players are Willie Cave, Monty Golding, Arthur Lewis, Will Sellers and Decima St. Clair[e], while specialities are provided by the Side Show Syncopators and the Six Cabaret Girls'; or at the Royal, Edinburgh, where it was now 'The New Side Show' presented by 'Mr Herbert Ray's Company': 'In the hands of Willie Cave and Monty Golding the humorous side of the piece is safe, and excellent support is given by Decima St Clair,

Arthur Lewis, Will Sellers, Betty Daley-La-Burl, Rex Parsons, Eric Gatty, Vera Elmore, and Eight Cabaret Girls. Mr Herbert Ray's Band contributes several selections.'

Peg's own act was called 'Fire and the Woman'. It was devised around the character of Sir Henry Rider Haggard's *She*, the jungle priestess who'd bathed in the Flame of Eternal Youth five centuries ago; and the idea was that Peg, portraying a princess who was immortal, had recurred throughout time as all its queens and heroines. 'My mother wore white tights,' said Sellers, 'and stood in front of a plain white screen. Behind the audience a magic lantern cast slides of different costumes on to the screen. The result was that my mother would appear as all kinds of women in history or mythology, from Britannia to Joan of Arc, and yet never really change.'

The concept of being a consistent blank whilst exotic other lives flickered across your face appealed to Sellers: 'My mother's act moved me in a way I still can't explain. She looked beautiful standing there like a white statue. . .' But it is not impossible to explain the impact the routine had on him. As she was an empty space, ready to be stained and tinted by fantasy, her performance was a version of Sellers' own procedure as an actor. A click, a fast fade, another slide. 'The colour and warmth and the applause and the feeling of being part of something that could give so much happiness to other people, made me want to be up there with her taking a more positive part than just watching from the wings.'

Watching and waiting, however, whilst his mother came and went phantasmagorically, were all there was to do. He was anonymous amongst the entourage – and they were always on the move: to Wolverhampton, Salford, Crewe, Southampton and Boscombe, after his first birthday had been celebrated in West Hartlepool. Sellers' youth lacked youthfulness and everywhere looked the same: 'The bedrooms were all alike, with marble wash stands and brass beds. I'd look up at the ceiling and say to myself "Oh God, I do wish we had a home."'

Whether he did voice that sentiment then, it was not one he did much about later, when he had ample chance. He had a definite liking for hotels and hospitals, places designed for transients, who'd leave no trace. Just as he could be lots of people – each new lantern slide taking its place – so he never seemed to mean to live in a single place. The Manor House at Chipperfield was exchanged for a suite at the Carlton Tower Hotel, which became a penthouse flat in Frognal Lane, then a room at the Dorchester. All this upheaval went on with a total disregard for wife and children. Physically, as well as mentally, Sellers would be scatttered and dissipated. Rimbaud, in *The Season in Hell*, says that 'I was forced to travel to ward off the apparitions assembled in my brain' – and there's something of this anxiety to Sellers. 'He thinks "Wherever I am, it's boring,"' says Milligan. 'Can you imagine the agony of that? If he hadn't made it financially I think he would have killed himself.'

Part of his problem was that, as a nomadic child, he never encountered other children, who might have knocked the edges off him and given him some perspective. He was surrounded only by busy adults and spent forces. He called his mother and father by their first names – and he was like a miniature grown up, but with a child's inner rage and loneliness. Children, indeed, in the music hall world, were represented by dwarves, like those banshees I personally recall, Jimmy Clitheroe and Wee Georgie Wood. Sellers never forgot being nightmarishly engulfed by a pack of munchkins called Fred Roper's Midgets, who jumped through hoops like dogs: 'I could never figure out why I couldn't make contact with them. They were the same height as me, but all had deep voices and smoked cigars and pipes.' Old men in infants' bodies – the reverse of Sellers.

With no people of his own age available, and with those of his own size being freaks, Sellers had no opportunity to make a pal; he had no contemporaries and, he never would, in all of his life, be capable of forming a secure friendship, with the give-and-take that such a relationship demands. He was close. He never developed the emotions that go with being able to share; he never overcame a maximum reluctance not to be selfish. The best he'd feel he could hope for from other people was loyalty – which he tried to buy by giving away cameras and presents of shockproof wrist watches and hi-fi equipment (symbols of his own detachment: listening and looking devices etc.). He very early on gave up hoping to attract affection.

'I'd make friends in one town for one week and then we'd move on. You'd hope, if you played that town again, maybe a year later, that the friend you'd made would still be around; perhaps, if he was the landlady's son, you'd be lucky. Then you'd hope that he'd remember you.' It was a mournful existence, Sellers' progress around Britain, enough to drive anybody in on themselves. The most affecting scene he ever played is in *The Optimists of Nine Elms*: Old Sam, who is wearing a dress-suit with a huge paper bloom in the button hole, so that he looks like Lear and the Fool in one, is sitting on a gilded prop throne, amusing the children by reciting his tired little Dan Leno rhymes. Gradually a melancholy creeps in to what he is saying – especially when he tells what is no longer a bit of patter about coming home from school one day and finding that his folks had moved, without leaving any new address. Why hadn't he taken the hint? For the past week they'd been wrapping his sandwiches in a road map. . . .

As a parable of abandonment it hangs in the air. Sellers sits there, like a deposed king, and under his calm many memories are stirring. It is one of those moments, on the screen, which seem beautifully finished.

☆ ★ ☆

It was easier, as he shed his yesterdays, to be thought of as somebody new. There is nothing more humiliating than spending time with somebody and then, when you see them again, and you are a blank to them, you realise you have been erased; you registered *that* much. You haven't imprinted at all. It is as if you were dressed in white and positioned before a white screen, but there is nobody to work the magic lantern's coloured filters. Was it for this reason that one of Sellers' choices of music, when he went on *Desert Island Discs*, was Victor Young's 'White' from *Tone Poems of Colour* (conducted by Frank Sinatra)? At receptions, as a successful man, unless he was holding the floor and working the room with his voices, people would always take a couple of seconds to realise who he was. (Harry Secombe said that Sellers, in hornrims and dour suits, had the charisma of a tax inspector.) Even in company he was isolated, loathing the way 'people expect you to be funny. . . . I go to parties and people hang around with their mouths open, saying, sort of, any second it is going to come now – and nothing happens, and they go away thinking, gee, I'm not going to ask him here again. . . Or somebody will lurch over and say "Do us one of those funny things you do on the films" – "What funny things?" – "Oh, I don't know. I saw you doing a funny thing in a film once. . ." Eventually you go to a party, in the hope it will quench all the thirst of all the people that want to see you* – because that's what your agent says. You arrive there – all the photographers in the world, all the press agents in the world: "This is your town, baby, you can buy it." An odd thing happens: they shake hands with you, look at you closely in the eyes for a few seconds – and then their eyes wander over your shoulder, to see who else is coming into the room.'

Nobody likes not to be memorable and one of Sellers' methods of defying his loneliness was to behave badly. His first action, as a toddler, was to push a woman, who was bending over the grate, into the fire, where she burnt her hands. He spat on people's heads and in their hats. He squashed a cat in a sofa-bed. He'd show his parents up in cafes, eat the last cake without asking permission, and he'd dismember toys he had been bought. If ever he saw a march band he wanted to conduct it; and when he was taken to see *Peter Pan* at the Shaftesbury Theatre he tried to jump off the balcony and join the Darling children on their flight to the Never-Never Land.

---

* In the 1970s, Sellers would expect to be paid – many thousands of pounds – to turn up at receptions: 'I was in his penthouse flat in Victoria,' said Peter Eton in 1976. 'He wasn't there, but I was talking to his secretary and a call came through asking him to appear for half an hour at a party – for an enormous sum of money. I said to Sue Evans, "Is he going to do this?" and she said, "He might." All that money just so the host could say, "I've got Peter Sellers coming along . . ."!'

Nothing here is out of the ordinary to anybody with frequent exposure to the under-fives. Most parents could cap that catalogue. What was abnormal was Peg's absolute refusal to reprimand her son. Whatever Sellers did was fine by her. It was like Papal Infallibility. Between Ma Ray, Aunt Cissie, and all the chorines, he was spoiled rotten. Being cheeky, being flip, was how he conversed. 'You didn't wash today,' his mother would say. 'I did, Peg, but I had my knees crossed, so one's still dirty,' he'd respond, to general glee. It doesn't take a nano-second for children to learn how much they can get away with, and Sellers was no exception. 'There were too many adoring, worshipping women round that baby,' remembered Herbert Ray, 'a good smacking would have done him the world of good. Those women would never let any of us [himself, Bill] come near the child. That baby's scream was their law. And how he screamed! If Peg went out of the room for a moment he just lay down on the floor and kicked and screamed. He was a horror, a monster; we would have gladly cut his throat.'

I can believe it. The tantrum was to continue as his way of expressing himself. Having been taught to wail at authority figures, starting with his own father, Sellers had no compunction about throwing a fit in front of a director, producer, writer, fellow actor. Or anybody. If a shop didn't have what he wanted – instantly he'd be in a rage. Jimmy Grafton, who helped him first to get work on the radio and who scripted that earliest of films, *Penny Points to Paradise*, was once witness to a revealing scene. They were in Victoria Street, when Sellers saw a complete outfit in cavalry twill he decided he wanted. Sellers started to get annoyed when the tailors didn't have one in exactly his size; or perhaps it was one in solid gold which he was insisting on. 'How dare you put something in the window you can't supply,' he raged. The manager offered to track down the requisite fitting from another branch. 'When?' snapped Sellers. By tomorrow, he was informed. 'I don't want it tomorrow. *I want it now.*' The manager offered personally to find the right suit by later on that very afternoon. 'No thank you. You've already wasted enough of my time.' And he stormed out, not pacified, noted Grafton (who doesn't say whether or not he should have hit his companion very hard), until he'd purchased a hat in Dunn's – for only then was 'the acquisitive urge satisfied'.

As he had been instilled with a contempt for the forces of law and order, his conduct never curbed, Sellers became accustomed to a star's mischievousness when he was still a child. His behaviour later on was an enlargement of the liberty hall he had lived in with Peg. In a curious sort of way, because his outrages were applauded, they became part of his desire to please – his way of keeping in with Peg, Ma etc.. This is the satirical moral distortion Sellers brought out in the 'Auntie Rotter' sketch in the Fifties. As a send-up of the patronising Enid Blyton way of talking to tiny tots – Sellers gurgles gleefully as the old lady encourages the moppets to chop up their families with a hatchet – the sketch also colludes with, and respects, the demon inside every child ('Here is your stabbing music. . . . Come along! No lazing!')

☆ ★ ☆

Sellers further thrilled his personal pack of Auntie Rotters by giving what Bill called 'a perfect rendering' of Albert Chevalier's 'My Old Dutch' and 'It Gits Me Talked Abaht': 'Even as a child of two,' Bill said resignedly, 'he had talent. We had a little evening dress specially made for him with top hat and silver-headed walking stick.' The performing monkey also appeared, c. 1930, in an advertisement for Mazda, the electric lightbulb manufacturers. Omega Lighting, the parent company, then called The British Thomson-Houston Co. Ltd., was in the process of trying to persuade people to convert from gas mantles. The point was made that electric illumination was healthier on the eyes, as well as being generally more efficient and beneficial:

MAZDA LAMPS
THEY STAY BRIGHTER LONGER
'Sight is priceless – good lighting is cheap'
Better Light: Better Sight
Mazda Coiled-coil lamps give up to 20% more light
than ordinary gas filled lamps.

A lot of children were used for the advertisements, which continued to appear until November 1936. There was a bi-monthly competition for models, and Sellers' portrait must have been ideal: the boy, unsmiling and stubborn, stares hard at the camera. These eyes aren't dim! Sellers resembles, in fact, Freddie Bartholomew or Dean Stockwell, one of those hateful Hollywood lambkins. His rich hair manages to be tousled and combed, and it receives a bit of a nimbus from the light source, off to the left. The monochrome gives his face a creamy, dreamy texture, which adds to the alien hardness of those eyes, those lips. (It is a portrait of Peter Pan.)

How the picture contrasts with a snap of Sellers taken when he was twelve. There, in cricketing whites outside St Aloysius', his school, he looks like Billy Bunter. His fulsome hair is unsuccessfully greased down – it looks like a lap dog has taken up position on his scalp and dropped dead. The outdoor light, instead of softening the face, as the lamp does in the studio photograph, fattens it. We see the shadow-accentuated crevices and the contours formed by pudgy cheeks and chins. Those plates of eclairs have taken a toll. Sellers blinks at the light (his eyes disappear into two dark holes) and he slightly tilts himself back, his mouth, a sharp black line, set in a sneer. But by leaning back he also pushes out his belly, and his trouser belt, into which his thumbs are thrust, is pulled up high over the blubber. The last thing he looks is sporty. Over one arm he has the red-with-green-trim regulation school blazer, which perhaps he has just collected before he betakes himself and his spotless kit home? The wall he is against, splotched with shadow, is ornate. Medieval? Victorian? Sellers, anyway, looks like a gargoyle which has recently dropped off it.

☆ ★ ☆

Sellers' first non-family environment was Miss Whitney's School of Dancing, King's Road, Southsea; he later went to Madame Vacani's Dancing Classes, when the family moved up to London. 'I longed for him to carry on where I left off,' said Peg. Underlying all the spoiling and the fussing and the petting, which to some degree over-compensated for the times when he was left on his own whilst the rest of them were on stage, there was, with regard to Peg's attitude towards her son, a conviction that he was other-worldly and miraculous. Her clinging form of love trained him not to be ordinary. She expected him to have the successful career she and her ancestors had been denied: Sellers would appease the penurious legacy of Daniel Mendoza. Here they all were, a hundred years later, still at but one remove from trestle table stages in pubs, gin palaces and the circus. Peg's boy, her Peter, her fair son, her food, her all-the-world, would change all that. He'd be a brilliant reduplication of herself. He'd *be* her; she'd *be* him.

Just about every single one of his problems were to stem from this. Roy Boulting believes that the smothering caused Sellers to resent his mother: 'I am absolutely certain that this woman he should have loved, professed to love, his mother, he genuinely hated.' She was certainly the only person for whom he had strong feelings of any complexion, and she drove out his capacity for affection towards anybody else. His wives, for example, were versions of his mother he could hit back at. But the fact that it was Roy Boulting who spoke those words is a clue. Roy is half of a famous twinhood in British films, the other component being his (late) brother John. They produced and directed pictures interchangeably and nobody could tell them or their artistic styles apart. Peg and Sellers were as twins. They could look alike. When Sellers climbed into drag for a scene in *The Magic Christian* (he is a nun in a disco), he called Joe McGrath over to him: 'Look, Joe. My God, I'm my mother!' With his own hair concealed under the wimple and his lean face powdered, he was indeed a Peg simulacrum. (He also once said, of Mendoza, 'Both Peg and I bear a most remarkable resemblance to him – it is almost uncanny.')

Mother and son were so interwoven, parapsychologists might like to investigate whether it is possible to be a reincarnation of a living person. Though Peg's passion created (i) Sellers' feinting and dodging and (ii) his bloody-mindedness, the effect in the short-term was the exclusion of Bill. 'Peg was overwhelming. She overwhelmed Peter,' Milligan said to me. 'When they kissed, mother and son, it wasn't pleasant. It was more like they were lovers – not that anything of *that* kind happened, I'm sure. He didn't become Oedipus Rex. But it was an unhealthy relationship, though a very deep and loving one. Though I don't know what stamp you put on that quality of love or on that kind of life. Bill was relegated to second place in the male heirarchy. Peg lived for, and top place was for, Peter and Peter alone. She doted on him and he doted on her.'

☆ ★ ☆

By 1929 Bill had started to have enough. The last time the family worked together, in one of Ma's divertissements, was when Herbert Ray opened his new revue, *Ha! Ha!! Ha!!!*, at the Bedford Music Hall, Camden Town, on February 13th. The show then toured under the London Syndicate Companies' banner. The book was by Harry Curwen, Bert Murray was the comic, Bert Roberts, Dorothy Brett and Graham Kendall were the singers and dancers; and also involved were Monty Golding (now spelt Goulding), Maisie Morris, Dulcie Max and Hilda Ellis. Peg had one last dip into her 'Fire and the Woman' routine; this was replaced on the road by Percy Boggis' 'Fun Spectacle,' the nature of which we can only but guess at. The numbers sung during the evening were:

'Shout Hallelujah 'Cause I'm Home'
'Girl of My Dreams'
'I Can't Give You Anything But Love'
'There's a Blue Ridge Round My Heart Virginia'
'Happy Days and Lonely Nights'
'You're in My Heart but Never in My Arms'
'My Rock-A-Bye Baby'

Sentimentalised homecomings and departures – these were the subjects of the songs. And when Bill left with the troupe, to tinkle daydreams for his audiences, Peg stayed behind in the quarters they were renting upstairs at the Bedford. She now had her son in her heart and in her arms. At root rootless, the pair began several years of flitting across London, as Peg became absorbed into the Mendoza house-agency side of the family. They occupied a succession of little flats on end-leases. Sellers, on whom nothing was lost (the low-grade music hall entertainers would come together as Old Sam; 'Fire and the Woman' would be adapted for Chance the blank, who is given a personality by the television screen), never forgot the litany of addresses. He thought he'd come to rest in London, but it was like traipsing the outback all over again. When he wrote an article in *Vogue*, in the last year of his life, he was specific about having lived 'in a flat at 43b Park Street (now Parkway), Camden Town, opposite the pet shop and above Heals the builders.'

The excuse Peg had for remaining behind whilst the others went off on tour was that Sellers needed to start his compulsory education. She dreaded this separation and did her best to cushion him against the depredations of the masses, who could not be relied upon to be as dainty as the pupils at Miss Whitney's or Madame Vacani's, by patrolling the school gates and telling the teachers what to do.

Sellers, knowing his mother didn't really approve of schools (she herself had left before the age of ten), saw immediately that this could work to his advantage. He would get her to bribe him to get up and go out each morning. Along the street was a toy shop and confectionery store, where he would feast on liquorice and sherbet fountains. In the window was a scale model of Sir Malcolm Campbell's Bluebird. 'I gazed longingly at this vision for days and eventually persuaded my mother that there was no hope in the world for me unless I could become the owner of this splendid, shining blue car. . . . Finally she gave in.' Sellers took the object to school – St Mark's Private Kindergarten on the Gloucester Road ('now Gloucester Avenue') – and he excited the admiration and envy of the class. It wasn't Christmas or his birthday or anything. One of the children in Miss Helen Penn's charge came too near for Sellers' comfort and 'I resolved to hit him if he came any closer.' The boy's ingenious reaction to the threat of violence was to nominate himself as the chap who'd thump everybody else out of range: 'Can I be the man', he asked Sellers, 'who sees that no one touches it for you?'* Sellers tells this story as the beginnings of his warped worship for cars ('a forerunner of things to come'). What it mostly prefigures, I think, is his tolerance of the boot boys and bodyguards, the men friends, from the outright effeminate homosexual to the burly stunt double element, whom he would get to protect and mother him.

His way of coping with Miss Penn, who had the cheek to try and impart crappy knowledge and rudiments like reading and writing, was to go into a trance – to teletransport himself elsewhere. Often, after one of Peg's heavy kosher lunches, the snooze was authentic. This retreat into a dream kingdom of his own Peg called 'The Imagines'. For reasons best known to himself, Sellers started to show signs of compulsive ritualistic behaviour. He'd switch lights on and off six times; he'd lift the lavatory seat up and down six times; he'd flush the cistern six times before quitting the jakes. If there was a superstitious motive behind the drill, akin to not stepping on the pavement cracks or spilling salt (Michael Sellers remembers a ban on open umbrellas inside the house and nor were bunches of keys to be left on the hall table because 'that was apparently a very unlucky thing to do') then a Catholic convent, dedicated to the dogmas of death and judgement, and heaven and hell, was going to be perfect for such a one of Sellers' susceptibilities.

☆ ★ ☆

[Oxford]
November 20th 1990

Dear Headteacher,

I am writing a biography of Peter Sellers, whom as you probably know attended St Aloysius' College in the late 1930s. Whilst I understand that Sellers' teacher, Brother Cornelius Reed, is now

---

* Sellers remembered and 'improvised' the line in *What's New, Pussycat?*: O'Toole is having girlfriend trouble, and Sellers' psychiatrist suggests that 'I could be the man that sees no-one touches her for you.'

dead, I am wondering if by any chance there are school records still extant? Old school magazines and the like? I'd like to write a little bit about the school, its make-up and rationale, in the 1930s – are there any 'histories' that you know of?

I know that Sellers was not actually a pupil for very long, but he returned quite often to visit his old teachers, especially during the years of his fame, and he apparently gave the school a radio, hi-fi equipment and (I think) a television.

I hope I can look forward to hearing from you.

> Yours faithfully,
> *Roger Lewis*

☆ ★ ☆

> St Aloysius' College,
> Hornsey Lane,
> Highgate,
> London N6 5LY
> November 21st 1990

Dear Mr Lewis,

Thank you for your letter concerning Peter Sellers. By a strange coincidence I came across the enclosed cutting the other day [below]. You may be able to trace Gerald Meteau – although I have no records of his address.

Before the war the school was an independent establishment but subsequently became a Grammar School under the old LCC. In 1971 it was extensively rebuilt and was reorganised as a Comprehensive School. Many of the archives dating from pre-War days have been lost.

[. . .] I also enclose for your general information a copy of the School's Centenary Booklet which may give you a little bit of atmosphere.

> Yours sincerely,
> *J.A. Mackersie*
> *Headmaster*

The Life and Death of Peter Sellers

☆ ★ ☆

The Schoolboy Sellers[*]

[...] Readers may be interested to learn the probable origins of Peter's inner rage.

In 1936 I was at St Aloysius' College, Highgate. Some weeks after a term had started, a new entrant arrived – Sellers. He was being placed with us much younger children because his previous schooling had been repeatedly disrupted due to his parents being in a touring theatre business.

Peter was very quiet, and must have deeply resented his being made to appear a dunce. In his later life he was brilliant in portraying characters who were outwardly fools but inwardly really very clever. This, I believe, was the driving force of his career – to demonstrate that he was NOT a dunce and that he brilliantly outshone the rest.

[...]

> *Gerald Meteau*
> *Worthing*
> *Sussex*

☆ ★ ☆

I don't think anybody thought Sellers was stupid. He was simply lazy and lacked application, as he well knew: 'I was never a good scholar. Perhaps I never really settled down to it,' he confessed in 1962. 'Perhaps that's what was wrong with my education. But I didn't dislike it at St Aloysius'. I've sometimes been back to see the people there . . .'

I never did manage to locate Mr Meteau, but with the help of Mr Mackersie's Centenary Booklet and some long conversations I had with Bryan Connon, another of Sellers' classmates, a picture of some of the best (note that qualifying double negative: 'I didn't dislike it . . .') years of my man's life emerges.

---

[*] This letter was printed in the *Guardian*, July 15th 1990.

The Founding Religious Order of St Aloysius' College, in 1879, was the Brothers of Our Lady of Mercy, from Malines in Belgium. (In 1961 the De La Salle Order took over the running of the school, under the stewardship of Brother Hilary Cluderay, and the Brothers of Our Lady of Mercy continued to run an independent preparatory school in the vicinity, but now that has also closed.) The Belgians had been invited to the Archdiocese of Westminster by Cardinals Wiseman and Manning, and the intention was to create an establishment for 'respectable boys of the middle class' – i.e. grocers' sons, in Connon's father's view. The school would be less exclusive than Ampleforth or Stonyhurst and science and commercial subjects would be taught, not just the classics. Peg chose it as her local equivalent of Dick and Winifred Henderson sending their brood to St Joseph's College, Beulah Hill.

By Sellers' time, St Aloysius' Boarding and Day School for Boys had two hundred 'day dogs' and one hundred and sixty 'boarder bugs'. They were accommodated in a building, completed in 1911, which looks from the photographs like Castle Dracula or an insane asylum – a charcoal pink edifice, an example of municipal Edwardian gothick. There was an ornate chapel, where Mass was said every morning and where hymns were sung every night – and Sellers enjoyed the high-camp of the incense-impregnated ceremonies, the lace-trimmed scarlet vestments, and the theatrics. Brother Cornelius, Sellers and Connon's master, 'was a convert to Catholicism and as such was more avid about it all than those born in the faith. He took his class to the chapel a lot.'

The services, their colour, light and precision, the singing and the recitatives, were like sophisticated revues. (The object, uplift, was the same.) Here was the world of the stage without the underlying pennilessness and misery. There was no need to strike the set and trudge to the midnight tram. Religion was a secure theatre. The antiquity of the words and routines, the decorum: it implied a branch of fakery you could come to believe in. The dead walked, had lives *after* death. Water became wine. Virgins gave birth. How was it all done? By magic?

☆ ★ ☆

Catholicism intrigued Sellers because he had just discovered he was a Jew – he was someone on the outside of the mysteries of faith. He was referred to as 'The Jew' in front of the other boys, and as he said in later life: 'My father was solid Church of England but my mother was Jewish – Portuguese Jewish – and Jews take the faith of their mother.'

What did being a Jew mean to him? The photograph of the sombre-looking fellow in a yarmulka (those little skull caps), which accompanied his obituary in the *Jewish Chronicle,* is not actually of Sellers, as such. It is a still of Harold Fine, the Jewish lawyer in *I Love You, Alice B. Toklas.* He was not barmitzvah'd, did not belong to a synagogue, and his four marriages were to non-Jewish ladies. Sir Evelyn de Rothschild, however, who knew him for over twenty years, sees Sellers as quite archetypically Jewish: 'He was a wanderer. He could never have roots, if you look at the way he lived and how he lived. He was restless – rushing from one side of the world to the other, an endless stream of people behind him. . . Wherever you went, you got the impression he was on the move somewhere else. He was never at ease with a lot of those film people, I never felt. He was always expected to perform – could never relax – and he was afraid people only befriended him for favours. I think he felt comfortable with me. He could say anything he liked and I wasn't going to take advantage of him. He would sit and talk to me about his problems most of the time – he always had problems of one sort or another, personal to him: worries about what he should do, where he had to live, his relationships with people. We used to go over that. Maybe because I represented something he couldn't be – here was I, outside the acting world and his professional career, and yet we were both Jewish. He was Jewish – people often forget that. Very cognisant of his Jewishness. It was part of his background, and maybe because of my name and posi- tion I represented another side of life which he hadn't thought about, and he had the opportunity now to express himself.'

---

* Sellers shared the page with the Shah of Iran, who had died the same week.

Sellers' Jewish heritage came up regularly when he talked to Wolf Mankowitz, too. But where the descendant of Meyer Amschel Rothschild, the legendary Austro-Hungarian money-lender, was sympathetic to the botherations besetting the scion of Daniel Mendoza, the son of a tradesman from East Ham remains much more sceptical: 'He didn't understand anything – at an intellectual level. He became at one time fascinated with Jewish things – because of his mother and Mendoza. That famous engraving of Mendoza looks awfully like him. He got interested in Jewish things and I spent a lot of time answering questions on Jewish subjects. He became a heavy would-be student of the Torah. He never got very far. He did this with Indian religions as well, and dropped those. The thing is, he was tremendously superstitious. . . .'

Sellers had spent his childhood observing and absorbing the little backstage rituals, the signs and magic symbols a nervous actor makes to give himself confidence and courage before he steps into the spotlight. He took it all to extremes, of course. The aversions to various colours; the obsession with omens and oracles; the way he treated astrologers as learned men: Sellers was out of *I, Claudius*. And yet what was to happen with him and the occult is implied, also, by his attitude to Jewishness. It was a way to try and justify feeling different, feeling a refugee from normal life. If the spirit medium-witchcraft side of the question made him superior (he'd been told early on he'd be a household name and live to be seventy-four – a prediction which became half right), Jewishness, like a stammer for Philip Larkin, was 'a built-in handicap to put him one down' – or, more accurately, if he wanted to pretend to be one down. It was a pretext for grudges.

Sometimes his touchiness came and went in a flash. On a breakfast television chat-show in America, in 1964, he was asked by the host if he'd care for some juice. 'I am Jewish myself,' snapped Sellers. 'No, juice *de l'orange*,' the host explained, gesturing to a jug. 'I'd love a little of that, too,' conceded the star. On other occasions, rooting for trouble, he'd allow his sensitiveness to take hold for weeks. *The Prisoner of Zenda* was made in Vienna, and Sellers attributed the cause of his anxieties to the fact that Austria was an anti-Semitic country. He banished six people from the film whom he believed had looked at him disparagingly, i.e. less than worshipfully. He took each individual aside and said, 'We don't have the right chemistry together.' One of his victims, the veteran unit publicist Al Hix, told me that he'd so looked forward to working for Sellers, being an admirer of his talent – 'but then I met the man, and it was such a shock. He was really dangerous. It wasn't as if you could call him childish; he was bitter and paranoid.' When Hix was sacked, the manager of the Wien Hilton, where the bulk of the company was billeted, no doubt fearing that his hotel would soon be emptied, offered to let the flack stay on at discount rates. When Sellers heard about this ('and he knew of everything that went on') he was furious. He made the production manager, Peter McGregor Scott, order Hix to move out. 'I reminded him that I had just been fired and that neither Sellers nor Universal nor the Mirisch Corp. could tell me where to live any more.'

As Sellers himself was residing at the Hotel Bristol, his attempted persecution of people he was unlikely to meet in the elevator or dining room is pathetic and spiteful. But he enjoyed the idea of riding people out of town. It had once nearly happened to him. Early in his career, when he'd bought his first Rolls, he thought he'd take it for a spin on the Continent. 'I was going to Calais,' he explained to Terry-Thomas' sister, Mary Hoar Stevens, 'but my new car wouldn't fit on the ferry, so I've decided to spend my holiday in Brighton.' (A typical Sellers reaction – a deckhand had probably asked him to reverse or manoevure into a tight space, and he could never cope with requests like that.) Mary said gaily, 'What a good idea! You'll like this hotel, Peter. It's very quiet – and there are no Jews here.' – 'Well, Mary,' said Sellers, equally gaily, 'There are now!'

Milligan told me that 'Peg had disregarded her religion – a lost Jewess – when she married Bill; and Peter was haunted by the uncertainty of his religion, and who he was, and he never did find out.'

The Jews whom Sellers played on *The Goon Show* were oy-vay caricatures, with names like Geraldo or Izzy; and concurrent with his death he was to be seen on television as a Jewish con-man, Monty Casino, urging viewers to invest their money in Barclays Bank. (His fee for the ad, shot in Dublin, was £80,000.) A bit further up the scale, he turned down the Alan Bates part in Bernard Malamud's *The Fixer* and Fagin in the Dickens musical *Oliver!* because 'I couldn't finally see any way of playing either rôle outside the usual interpretation.' Yet his reticent Los Angeles legal eagle in *I Love You, Alice B. Toklas* (which he made in 1968 instead of appearing in *Oliver!*) shows that there was a way to avoid the Yiddish weeping, wailing, smiting and the rending of garments. Harold Fine is filial, obedient, ambitious, successful – and full of tension. He has asthma; his jaw and shoulder tendons are firm-set. As a specialist in settling insurance claims, he is as cramped and confined as his clients, who sit in his office exhibiting their neck braces. 'I'm going crazy,' he admits.

As Sellers saw the film: 'It is a very interesting part. Probably the most interesting part I've played in my career to date. The part of a Jewish lawyer who eventually decides that the pressures in his life are so great he can't bear them; he can't face up to what he's doing any more. He earns forty thousand dollars a year and has a nice big shiny car; he has an apartment and a forthcoming marriage. But he eventually drops out, as they say. He decides to become a hippy – he decides to try a new way of life and samples their philosophy. And likes it.'

Harold wants to find a way of being taken out of himself; he wants to disappear, and so did Sellers. As can be readily seen, his understanding of the character amounted to self-identification, and he gave a nuance-filled performance which is several million cuts above the surrounding film. The plot merely requires any old staid mother-dominated executive sort to eat a chocolate brownie containing hashish. Then, drugged and giggling, he grows his hair and wears a kaftan etc. (In his granny glasses and wig, Sellers manages again to resemble Peg.) Sellers, however, didn't need Harold to smoke pot and pop pills to remain high and liberated; nor is he, as the low-key gloomy businessman freaking out in a flower-power smock, the object of derision which the script wants to make him. Sellers, without having to spell it out, conveys the melancholy of a man intuitive enough to know that, like his black suits and yarmulka, the blue and pink hippy shawls are another form of disguise. He has exchanged one kind of convention for another; a worse one, perhaps, because though marijuana makes the depression of ordinary life lift, its effects are illusionary. In the context of the film, it is no more than a gag when Harold keeps jilting his Jewish princess bride at the altar. Sellers, however, was attuned to deeper fears: 'At the end he runs off, because he doesn't know *where* he's going. He's a desperate man. Any man who would run out of a marriage ceremony in full swing has got to be a pretty desperate man. It's funny; it's tragic; it's all about today. . .'

Sellers (as Mankowitz said) may not have been able to argue and conceptualise up to the standards set by Oxford or Cambridge Universities, but he could act and convey abstractions like nobody else. Harold knows he cannot renew himself; he also knows it is ludicrous to be despondent about this fact. (Such knowledge didn't prevent Sellers' own despair – his personal temper was opposed to resignation.) Harold has tried to run away from home, and there is his mother, meddling and waiting. She wades in amongst the hippies in the commune, handing out admonishments ('Shame on you. Go on a diet'). When he tries to tell her about the hashish in the brownies being a recipe of Toklas' and that Toklas was a friend of Gertrude Stein's, Harold's defections are cut off short. 'Gertrude Stein. I used to know her. Lived in Oakwood.' Thus is the most famous American in Paris, muse to Picasso, Matisse and Braque, smartly slapped down.

Sellers conveys the man's humiliations well enough; but there is also a paradox at the heart of the character. For Harold to be able to claim 'for the first time in my life I feel free' he also needs to be 'just being, that's all'. Not thinking, doing, choosing, judging: nothing. He is in a state of suspended animation, ghostly and blurred. He is thrilled to shout out 'Harold Fine no longer exists!' This makes me uneasy because it seems all too similar to the anaesthesia of Chance, in *Being There*, who is of course a nullity; and I wonder how much can be read into the very last words Sellers spoke on the screen? In the final scene of *The Fiendish Plot of Dr Fu Manchu*, in the Himalayan palace, the Oriental mastermind promises that everybody is to be 'wiped out' – by an Elvis impersonation, as it happens, but that's not what people expected him to have in mind.

These descriptions, or depictions, of bliss are vaporous – like death. Is this how Sellers thought life should be? Happiness as a state of oblivion? 'He was incapable of radiant happiness,' says Milligan. 'Even with his children he could only get a sad happiness from them – no warm glow, as towards something positive that's happened in your life. For Peter, life is just a terrible journey.'

☆ ★ ☆

I Love You, Alice B. Toklas not only has the farcical weddings, it also has its knock-about funeral sequence, with the hippy contingent attired as Hopi Indians. The deceased is Mr Foley, the kosher butcher, and because of an L.A. hearse strike, he is taken to the cemetery in a multi-coloured van. Sellers himself, when he was about to be laid under, was transported to Golders Green, and the rites of the Church of England, by a more conventional conveyance. But on July 26th 1980 – a Saturday – there was darkness at noon. Black clouds and a downpour, lightning and thunderclaps, raged and foamed out of a novel by Mrs Radcliffe or a biblical epic by Dino de Laurentiis. (It was necessary for the hearse and funeral limos to turn on their headlamps.) It was as if someone in the world, a modern Caesar, too saucy with the gods, had incensed them to send destruction. The only wonder is that fire didn't fall from the sky. And before these strange-disposed stage effects started to happen, the phone had been ringing non-stop at the Dorchester. It was a terrified Cockney Jewish taxi driver, well known to Sellers. The switchboard eventually put him through to Michael Jeffery. 'I've taken Mr Sellers in my cab many a time,' the voice said, 'He spoke of his mum. He's Jewish and you *cannot* bury him on the Sabbath. You *must not*. . . .' Saturday is named for Saturn, the deity which the Romans depicted as an old man wielding a scythe. As gentiles often don't realise, the seventh day of the week is observed by the Jews as a day of abstention from all work and is regarded as sacred to the Lord, in commemoration of his rest from the work of Creation. (In the Christian church observance of the Sabbath has been transferred to the first day of the week, in commemoration of Christ's resurrection.) So what was all this about? A blasphemous note to end on? Some final rebellion? (Mendoza, it was regretted in contemporary reports, had no compunctions about fighting on a Saturday.)

☆　★　☆

St Aloysius' was unusual in taking non-Catholics on to its roll. Bryan Connon (son of an Episcopalian and a Presbyterian) recalls a strange mix of 'creeds and nationalities' at the school. Negroes, Indians, Americans, French, Dutch. The German teacher was a real German, Herr Knaudascher, who wore a top hat. It was this cosmopolitan aspect which appealed to Peg, who was suddenly nervous of how people would treat Sellers' semi-gypsy background and history. To look down contemporary registers is to see names like Carratu, Giacopazzi, Kurowski, Minella, Zenone. There were plenty of foreign accents for Sellers to absorb, in what was virtually (his short stay at St Mark's aside) his first foray into a world beyond the variety house. 'My ears were a sound radar that picked up every noise blip,' he later said of these years. The United Nations make-up of the classes had a more fearful dimension, of course. Victor Schlienger, another Sellers contemporary, tells me that, with many boys' families abroad, the coming war cast an especially sombre shadow over the school: 'the seemingly never-ending struggle of the Japanese with their neighbours, the horrors of the civil conflict in Spain, the ruthless behaviour of the Nazi regime in Europe, to name but a few'. There were plenty of pupils who could take current affairs personally, coweringly.

It was a school for refugees. Sellers later tried to laugh off being labelled as the class Jew – and one word-perfect in the Catholic liturgy at that – but the fact was, he *was* different. From the class photograph of the academic year 1936–7, Sellers stares across the years, gormless and huge. He has been made to stand directly behind Brother Cornelius, whilst all the other boys either sit or are given extra height by a bench – though even with this expedient he is out of scale. This is Gulliver in Lilliput,* the highly-embarrassed-relegated-Sellers of Gerald Meteau's letter in the *Guardian*. There is something quite sinister about his gigantism. It is as if all the boudoir fingers, treacle tarts, onion flans, brioche sausages and waffles, which Peg, Ma and Cissie stuffed down him, have inflated him cartoonishly. He looks like Daniel Mendoza.

Regardless of who he became later on, Sellers would have been memorable to his classmates because of his sheer size alone. 'He was extraordinarily large for his age – well over five and a half feet, and broad and chubby with it. A massive figure,' says Connon. His method of coping with the massiveness was to contrive to vanish into air. He wanted to be as anonymous as possible – and achieved this aim: 'It is difficult to remember Sellers making any impression whatsoever. He merged into the woodwork. He had little in common with any of us, and his educational standard was very low. He sat at the back of the class and kept to himself in the playground.'

It is as a nondescript that Sellers was recalled by Brother Cornelius in 1960:† 'He was just . . . average, not a memorable scholar, not a memorable athlete, no, nothing very outstanding at all' – except that Sellers was such a big boy: 'Although only ten years old when at the college he looked more like fourteen.' Because of his

---

* In later life, if there was a lull in the conversation at a dinner party, Sellers would mystify those present by reciting a passage he had memorised from *Gulliver's Travels*: 'The Most Mighty Emperor, Delight and Terror of the Universe, Monarch of all Monarchs, Taller than the Sons of Men, at whose nod the Princes of the Earth shake their knees, pleasant as the Spring, comfortable as Summer, fruitful as Autumn, dreadful as Winter.' Sellers would then helpfully add: 'You know, that Emperor was no more than six inches tall.'

† And again in 1980. Brother Cornelius, aged seventy-eight, attended Sellers' funeral and described his old pupil for the press as 'a quiet boy'.

lack of educational attainments he was given special treatment – no, not extra tuition or specially designed course work which might catch his interest. Nothing so enlightened. It was simply that, on Peg's instructions, he was not allowed to be caned – and the Brothers, out of the Lord He Knoweth what repressed sexual need, were enthusiastic beaters. ('Today those masters would be had up for assault,' says Connon. 'They were physically violent.') Masters slapped boys' faces and punishments started with a 'two-and-over' (two canings, as you bent over a chair); if you were walloped three times, the Brother Director would intone 'One for the school – SLAP – one for me – SLAP – and one for your parents – SLAP.' Sellers, instead, was given the meaninglessness of lines. Page upon page of copperplate. 'The next trouble', said Peg, 'was that he got so many lines that he couldn't have done them all if he stayed at school forever.' Some of the gobbledegook which he'd been made to copy out over and over again (like the passage from Swift) re-surfaced when he was filming *The Blockhouse*, forty years later. As a teacher imprisoned underground, Sellers' character, Rouquet, kills time chalking quotations over the walls:

> Now I am ten and growing tall
> My mother said to me
> Soon you will be strong enough
> To dive into the sea.

The little poem? Where did that come from? inquired a journalist who visited the set, a genuine dark and damp blockhouse deep under Guernsey. 'Oh, something I remembered from school,' shrugged Sellers, not willing to be drawn.

☆ ★ ☆

The deep sea Sellers was diving into was that of his own im-agination. He was stocking it with material which would be a bit more useful than his toilet flushing spells and household super-stitions. At the same time as he was forestalling humiliation by hiding at the back of the class and praying for invisibility – the classroom, incidentally, was situated at the Holloway Road end of the school, on the first floor, above the assembly hall and gymnasium and below the dormitories – he was also, as when in the wings, eavesdropping: 'I didn't talk much, I listened, and people thought I was shy.' The Rev. John Smallwood, in *Heavens Above*, is the obvious outcome of Sellers' attention to the details of this period. Sellers' priest, with his serene (and maddening) assurance and convictions, was inspired by the blessedly pure hearted Brothers at St Aloysius'. Radiating a grin, which is often a smirk, Smallwood is too bloody smug for this world, and so he is shot skywards in a space rocket at the end. He orbits the planet as a star – a heavenly body.

Smallwood is not only a bachelor, he is sexless. It must be the only Sellers performance that is totally free from any bodily appetite – lust, greed, thirst, hunger, and so on. (Even Chance has to totter out of his garden and into the streets because his meals, which he is accustomed to receiving on the dot from Louise the maid, have stopped arriving.) With his thick-lensed oblong spectacles and his severely brushed gleaming hair, Smallwood was an impersonation of Brother Cornelius. But Sellers' need for his teacher went beyond an actor's raw research. He kept up with the priest for the rest of his life, wanting, in some way, to acquire the man's certainties and composure. He treated Brother Cornelius as a guru, and Brother Hilary Cluderay, of the De La Salle Order, who was the Headmaster from 1960 to 1970, confirms that Sellers was 'often a private visitor', usually bringing a gift or a cheque for the school funds.

It became his habit to revisit in times of personal anxiety and chaos. A St Aloysius' secretary from round about the time the marriage to Anne was disintegrating, recalls: 'He was here in a state. Very tearful. I think he saw Brother Cornelius as a sort of sanctuary. He had come back to seek comfort. He invested a spiritual value in the school.' He turned up again after his mother had died, when 'I'll See You Again' had been played at her cremation. This time he discussed receiving religious instruction and just stopped short of committing himself to becoming a Catholic. He was looking (in the absence of his first wife and his mother) for a way of life that did without women.

Sellers also made the acquaintance of an Anglican priest, Canon John Hester, now of Chichester Cathedral. He officiated at Sellers' funeral and had flown out to anoint the actor in California after the heart attack in 1964 ('we had a day of National Prayer for his recovery' says Wolf Mankowitz). Sellers was into yoga. He was into the occult. He told the *Jewish Chronicle*, 'I am fully Jewish . . . a sentimental Jew. . .' His son Michael puts it best: 'Dad could be Jewish, Moslem, Hindu or any other religious faith on a given day. If someone offered a cut-price, special-offer-gift-wrapped religion that guaranteed miracles and a personal audience with the Maker, then Dad would apply for instant enrolment.'

Sellers wanted a direct line of communication with God – like the telephone wire between President Muffley, in the war room, and the (unseen) Russian premier, Dmitri Kissoff. (The end of the world is nigh and all they can do is bicker: 'I'm sorry too, Dmitri. I'm very sorry. All right, you're sorrier than I am, but I am sorry as well . . .' etc.) Though Sellers' doctrinal loyalties were fickle, his search for infallibilities and order; his need to explain why, despite being successful in his career, he felt uncomfortable and morose; and why, since he was a comedian, his life yet felt stark and tragic – all these were constant concerns. More than anything, he wanted to know if there was any purpose, or calling, beneath his artistic skills. A penetrable pattern? If he was meant to be a genius, how was he to understand what that talent meant? How could he put it to best use – and might it vanish? It was an unasked for greatness and not one which seemed to need intellectualising. As his first wife said to me: 'When he started making those ghastly little films with the Goons, he'd ring me up and say, "I don't know what to do with my hands." Later on he'd still be panicking: "I can't do this – I can't feel the man at all." Looking for the voice, and then it would fall into place. He'd hear a voice, which suggested a picture to him and his imagination would do the rest. Totally intuitive. No plan, structure, formula. It would either happen or it wouldn't.'

☆   ★   ☆

Sellers wanted what he did to be, not corny, like revue, but full of texture and richness, like the presentation of the Latin Mass. He was thrilled when a real priest, the Rev. Ironmonger, watched him shoot the church service scene in *Heavens Above* at Shepperton: '"Very convincing, very moving," he told me afterwards. It made me feel like taking the cloth.' Sellers always needed faith that his creativity was not a charade – that his performances had weight and strength. (This is what his search for perfection originally entailed.) The break-up of his marriages; the death of his mother; the dust and ashes of material success: traumas like these could trigger his insecurity and make him feel again the weakness of being the defenceless boy at the back of the Hornsey Lane classroom – who, knowing nothing, when asked to name one of the Seven Seas said 'the BBC'.

Emotionally a boy, he'd retraverse his boyhood sites ('to see and discover and taste the places that kicked me off'); and the places represented moods which refused to drop away. This is why, when he talked about his neuroticism or this or that crisis ('I don't think there is such a thing, you see, as idyllic happiness' etc.) his tone always had a whining edge. He was petulant, and the very melodrama of his spiritual searchings, so to call them, suggests something trivial and shallow. No matter how patient his inquiries, with Brother Cornelius or Canon Hester or Wolf Mankowitz, his desire, really, was for *gratification* – of a kind not procurable in the normal way. Spiritual well-being was the one thing he could not send his handyman, Bert Mortimer, over to Harrods to buy; the one thing nobody could give him in part exchange for a red Lamborghini Miura. There is farce, here, in the notion of this wildly impatient creature trying with all his might to discover what makes holy men tick. Sometimes he'd be hysterical at the lack of an answer (he led Canon Hester a dance); at other times he'd be plaintive. 'I'm just a real right twit,' he told an audience at the National Film Theatre. 'I am only a little thing,' he'd wheedle to Lynne Frederick, in the aftermath of some outrage, 'I am really Bluebottle and nothing else. All this acting is brown paper and string.' He'd disarm people, keep himself at a distance, by pretending to be a tattered Boy Scout, concerned with nothing much more than dolly mixtures and train spotting. He would become at will a manipulative child.

Hence the coyness of the telegram he sent to his school from America, when he was filming *Being There*, his essay on infantilism. He had promised to contribute a whole article to the Centenary Brochure, but in the end cabled:

> TO THE BOYS OF ST ALOYSIUS' COLLEGE. PETER SELLERS WAS EDUCATED HERE, BUT TO NO AVAIL STOP HE TURNED OUT A RIGHT TWIT STOP SEE THAT YOU DON'T DO THE SAME STOP EXCELSIOR! PETER SELLERS.

☆ ★ ☆

Of course it was by no means all unavailing. He didn't get topped up with solemn things and academic knowledge, but school was no less character forming for that. The combination of crafty naivety, genuine ignorance and saving shafts of quick-wittedness – all features of the Sellers known to Bryan Connon and Gerald Meteau – underprop many of Sellers' figurines, starting with Inspector Clouseau. And if the St Aloysius' era gave him a taste of mockery and a fear of being thought worthless, neither did it alter his loneliness. His chief company, apart from his mother, was to be found on the screen and out of the radio. 'Early on in life,' he once said, 'I found that *sounds* fascinated me. I became a listener.' Connon was a witness to this. When walking home from school, past the gabled and impressive Highgate houses (grace and favour residences for old ladies from the court of Princess Mary of Teck) and all the Catholic churches (built to accommodate the Irish over to build the railways), Sellers would imitate the goings-on of the school day: 'We were two boys,' says Connon, 'playing the fool. Him inventing the plots, me doing some of the dialogue. We'd use characters from *Monday Night at Seven* and other radio shows. We walked up the Archway Road towards North Hill and Highcroft, and what's interesting is not the wealth of his impersonations – boys of that age are always doing characters and noises. This is normal behaviour, not particularly unusual, so I wouldn't build on it. The point is more that he suddenly came so *alive*, on that twenty-five minute walk. He changed completely, when talking about the radio or films. He was mad about the radio – he could do all the voices. Then we'd arrive at Peg's, on Muswell Hill Road, and Sellers would change again. An extrovert away from the school gates, and then he'd go back into his shell just as we reached his front door. I didn't live far away at all and it is a curious facet of my having known Sellers that there was absolutely none of the interplay between the two homes that you might normally expect. I think I'd been keen to go into his house one day, but his mother was *not* encouraging about the idea. There was no encouragement for any people of his own age to become part of his life. No contact.'

☆ ★ ☆

If Peg wanted to keep Sellers to herself, she could not prevent the conversations he might conduct in his head, or behind closed doors, with Robb Wilton or Tommy Handley, when he felt the need to challenge his sequestration. Nor could she stop him from peopling his imagination with the cinema. Asked once who he would like to have been, who was his main movie love, he said, 'Just about everybody really.' The throng on the sound stage and screen made up for the solitariness of his life at home. The first film he saw, *Gold Diggers of 1933*, had impressed him for just that reason: 'There were a lot of people moving on the screen. Big dance routines going on. . .' Busby Berkeley's geometric choreography, the girls forming and re-forming as shapes and grand pianos, or tip-tapping on aeroplane propellors, and such, was a Ray Bros. revue with knobs on. Noisy, blowsy, absurd. As regards individuals, Sellers first fell for Loretta Young, and his first impersonation, around the house, was of Don Ameche, amongst the whoo-whoo of an angelic choir, making his folksy farewells in the Western *Romona* ('Well burn ma breeches – looka yonder there honey. The way I look at it is, he has just rode on a little way ahead – and when you get to the bend in that great road, he'll be there, awaiting for you'). The trouble was, there was nobody at St Aloysius' who looked like Loretta Young – 'so I went around wearing this Apache band around my hair, with a terrible headache, and when it slipped I nearly garrotted myself. However, such is life.'

Sellers also said he lost his heart to Hedy Lamarr, whom he saw in a Czech film called *Extase*: 'Her husband tried later to buy up all the copies – he considered it a naughty film [*Bluebottle voice*] not suitable for young men to see because they could come to harm see. [*Normal voice*] I don't care if I do come to harm. I went with a friend of mine to see it at the Electric Palace on Highgate Hill. He said, "During a certain place in this film what is on there, she runs across the screen, and you can see *it* as she goes past." That was enough for me. We rushed in there. I was wearing a heavy leather overcoat and was muffled up to the eyebrows, trying to do an impersonation of an eighty year old man, and actually we sat next to an eighty year old man, heavily perspiring, who said, "Do you come here often?" – "Only during the Lamarr season, you know." Anyway, we waited for this moment – and she ran across the screen so quickly that I couldn't see anything at all. I said, "When is it going to happen?" And the old man said, "It went there – it's gone now."

'Later, when I was at the Windmill, when things didn't go by *quite* so quickly, one was reminded of that. By that time I'd got over the aches and pains of the Electric Palace, Highgate Hill.'

☆   ★   ☆

Sellers' first erections coincided with his grandmother's death and his father's decision to walk out. Through Ma's family connections with the Mendoza Estate Agency, of Sidmouth Parade, Willesden, they had all had hutches to inhabit; through Ma, again, and Ray Bros. Productions Ltd., there had been employment. And they knew they were expected to be grateful. Homage had to be accorded Crystal Jollibottom-cum-Grand Duchess Gloriana. 'I remember her quite well,' said Sellers in 1962, 'I remember whenever one of my uncles gave me a toy or anything, she always used to say to me: "Your grandma gave you that. . . ."'

If Peg overbore Sellers, Ma manipulated Peg. Part of Peg's grief over the death of the first Peter lay in her failure to produce a grandchild – and she was approaching thirty when the lost boy was replaced. The Mendozas had always had huge families (today there are over seven hundred names on the ten generation pedigree which goes back to the eighteenth-century prize fighter), but Peg settled for Sellers. He was the focus for her attention, gave Ma somebody else to think about, and he easily eclipsed her already feeble feelings for Bill. Bill, indeed, was not simply the pit pianist. When he was approached in that Portsmouth café, his offer of a new job depended on whether he could drive a motor car. There was thus, from the start, an element of the underling in his rôle. He was primarily Ma's chauffeur, steering her scarlet Ford whilst she sat in the back, amidships, waving at people out shopping on the Edgware Road – a scene even more out of *The Mouse That Roared*.

When Peg and Ma stayed at the Bedford after the premiere of *Ha! Ha!! Ha!!!*, the mahout duties lapsed and Bill was gone; and when Ma died, sometime before 1933, Bill was even less needed or welcome around the premises. When the revue organisation went out of business, having finally been obliterated by the cinema, he went off on his own, with his friend Arthur Lewis, to play the piano at dances and bars. It was now that Peg moved to 10 Muswell Hill Road* (a 'tiny cottage' in Connon's eyes) and took over the lease of a junk shop. The shop dealt in broken furniture, chipped china

---

* On Sunday September 15th 1991, a group calling itself 'The Dead Comics Society,' founded by David Graham, unveiled a plaque above the door of this address: 'PETER SELLERS/1925–1980/Goon and comic actor/LIVED HERE/1936–1940 [sic]'. Present at the ceremony were Anne Levy, Michael Sellers (and his children, William and Hannah), Graham Stark, Bernard Cribbins, Alfred Marks, Herbert Lom, Burt Kwouk, Kenneth Griffith, Bert Mortimer, and Alexander Walker. Stark read out messages from Sir Harry Secombe, Michael Bentine, Lord Snowdon, and David Lodge. Donations raised the sum of £800, which was presented to St. Aloysius' College to create a memoral prize.

As we go to press – summer 1993 – I have just been informed that the half-metre diameter blue plaque has been stolen!

and glass, and utensils made out of copper. Peg was an outlet for the rubbish left behind in the Mendoza property by departing tenants. She augmented the stock by knocking on people's doors and asking them for their rags and bones. She collected old clothes, spoutless tea pots, non-legal-tender coins. These trips she called 'totting' or 'golding' and Peg would hope to charm her customers out of giving away at least some decent trinkets with their dross. Sellers was impressed by his mother's patter as, like Albert Steptoe, she exhorted and connived. As a set routine it was as impressive as the Brothers of Our Lady of Mercy chanting psalms: 'Good-morning-madam-I'm-from-the-London-Gold-Refining-Company-and-we-are-very-interested-in-purchasing. . .'

Some excursions were made with an 'Uncle Joe Barnet', who had a car. A spurious relative, hailing from the district of Friern Barnet in north London, not far from Muswell Hill at all, Uncle Joe kept Peg amused and ferried her about. 'Oi, oi, fat arse,' he'd shout at lady cyclists. But, said Sellers, 'he did have a smashing car. . . I vowed then that one day I would own a car of my own, a great car, the best there was.' (A machine, as it were, with which, like Uncle Joe, he could whisk his mother away.)

☆　★　☆

'Ever since I was a kid I knew one thing. That if I ever had enough money I would buy cars, cars, cars. . .' And he did: a Renault 750, two Mercedes Benzs, a Ford Zephyr, an Anglia, a Consul, a Prefect, a Zodiac, two Jaguar Mk 7s, a Jaguar E type, a Jowett Javelin, two Sunbeam Talbots, an Austin 7, two Austin A30s, two Austin A35s, an Austin 12 Tourer, an Austin 16, an Austin A70, a Nash Austin, an Austin Healey, a Sprite, an Austin Princess, a Van den Plas, an Alvis, a Lanchester 14, a MG TF, two MG Magnettes, a Volkswagen, a Hillman Minx, an AC Saloon, a BMW Setta, a Jaguar XK140, a Daimler Conquest, a Rover 1055, a Sunbeam Rapier, two Land Rovers, two Riley 1.5s, two Cadillacs, a Lancia Flaminia, four Rolls Royces, three Bentleys, two Aston Martins, two Lincoln Continentals, a Morris 1100, a Bristol 407, a Volvo, a Lambretta Scooter, a Mini Cooper, a Buik Riviera, a Bristol Viotti, a Lotus

Elan, a Corvette Stingray, a Fiat van, and three Ferraris, to name a few. There was also, at one time, an ambulance, kitted out with a stretcher, which would whizz the busy and momentarily prostrate actor between appointments.

The shortest time he ever owned a car was two hours: 'An AC. Took it out in the morning. Didn't like it. Took it back in the afternoon. Traded it in for an early one-and-a-half-litre Jag, which had a very tiny motor and very heavy coachwork – it was all you could do to keep the car going. Silver with red upholstery. That was the main thing – you could use it as a home, really. "Come and visit me in my car."'

Milligan regarded Sellers' private motor show with not quite amusement, as he explained to me: 'Always changing his cars, Peter. I used to call it Metal Underwear because he used to change them so regularly. But he played an appalling trick on me. In the early days of our relationship he bought an Austin 12 Soft-Top Tourer, 1929. My wife bought it off him. This car went backwards and forwards between us about four times. Finally, not long before his death, I was about to go to Australia, and he turned up at the door with the car, all restored, and with a bottle of Dom Perignon: "I want to give you this car as a present. It belongs to you. You've spent more time in it with your family than me." When I was in Australia, he decided to have it taken away and sold. That's one of the things he did – I don't know whether because of his illness, or what. Whenever he gave people things, there was always lurking in the back of his mind the thought that he wanted the gifts back. He gave Alan Clare a piano – that was taken away. . .'

I told Milligan that during my delvings I'd found a yellowing closely typed list, pages and pages long, of all the licence plate numbers of all the cars that Sellers had once possessed. 'It's like his testament . . .' Milligan didn't speak for a while. He sat stock-still and pale-eyed.

'Very sad,' he said at last, in a cracked and feathery monotone. 'A sad ending. That's sad. He left great pools of sadness. . .'

☆　★　☆

The absence of Bill ensured that, between mother and son, there were no serious rivals for affection. And if Bill was an absent presence in Sellers' life, he has been a lacuna in my research. Other writers have turned him into a cliché: 'a quietly graceful grey-haired man with sadly amused eyes' (Evans); 'the shy, quietly spoken Yorkshireman who came from dour but solid farming folk' (Draper); 'Bill Sellers came of the sort of country stock that always lent a hand to the neighbours in season. He had the look of a farmer's son, he was good natured and he also did as he was bid' (Walker); 'Bill originated from Yorkshire . . . He came from a working-class home in which family discipline was strong . . . Unlike the more dominant and animated Peg, he was modest, quiet and shy, prepared to play a supporting role which he uncomplainingly fulfilled throughout his lifetime' (Michael Sellers); 'He seemed to exist in a private world of peace at any price, particularly where Peg was concerned, and it's some indication of their relationship that you never thought of them as husband and wife, only as Bill and Peg' (Stark).

Bill has been turned into Chance the gardener from *Being There*, vapid, tossing hay, doing his best to deflect the stings and irritabilities of his wife, who could be a part for Agnes Moorehead at her most vampish. The fact is, far from being the weak man Peg wanted (like her father, Solomon Marks, another faceless male in this story: 'Nobody ever said whether he was successful or not, so I expect he wasn't,' said Sellers), Bill had had considerable resource: (a) to leave tenant farming for showbusiness; (b) to endure Peg for as long as he did; and (c) to have generated the following curriculum vitae: Sellers claimed that his father was in the Royal Navy in the First World War and the Merchant Navy in the Second. He was a ship's cook on the SS. *Rievaulx Abbey* and sang 'There'll Be Plenty of Boys in Khaki by the Sea' in the mess. He had been an organist and choirmaster at Bradford Cathedral and had become estranged from his family after appearing – so sinfully – at the Alhambra Theatre. He was Talbot O'Farrell's accompanist and Tallulah Bankhead's when she was in cabaret. He was a cricketer for Yorkshire. And (lastly) 'legend has it that he taught George Formby the ukelele – I don't know whether he ever did actually, but he used to boast about it. Anyway he probably did, because he was quite good on guitar.'

Bill is the Apocryphal Man. Did he spin all these yarns himself, or did Sellers invent a background for his parent, augmenting and elaborating upon the fantasies he'd been handed? Mrs Barbara L. Craven, Administrator of Bradford Cathedral, responded to my query by saying, 'I have made several enquiries about Mr Bill Sellers, but regret to say I have not been successful.' He nowhere appeared in the muniments as organist or chorist. The department of the Head of Navy Pay, Pensions and Conditions of Service, based in the Old Admiralty Buildings, London, could not help; neither could the Departmental Record Offices of the Ministry of Defence (Navy Search Division). The Registrar General of the General Register and Record Office of Shipping and Seamen also made a thorough search of the files but failed to find any trace of Sellers' father. And so it went on, culminating in this exchange:

> [Oxford]
> February 18th 1991

Dear Mr Stapleton [*Records Dept., The Middlesex Hospital*]

I am working on a book about the actor Peter Sellers, who died at the Middlesex Hospital in July 1980. I am trying now to find out about his parents' background – and as his father, William Sellers/Sellars died at the Middlesex in October 1962, at the age of 62, I am wondering if you have any records from that far back? Even if only a date of birth. Anything will be of help.

> Yours sincerely,
> *Roger Lewis*

> The Middlesex Hospital
> Mortimer Street
> London W1N 8AA
> February 19th 1991

Dear Mr Lewis

Re: Mr William Sellars [*sic*]

I regret, after extensive searching amongst our records we are
unable to trace the above named as being a patient here.
Therefore I am unable to help you further.

> Yours faithfully,
> *Jim Stapleton*
> *Medical Records Manager*

It is one thing not to have been a war hero; not to have played
county class cricket. It is quite another to have left such little evidence of your passing that you may as well have been disembodied,
a revenant, all along. Hence the poignancy of *The Side Show* write-
ups – proofs that Bill did put in an appearance. But though Bill has
faded into insignificance (archivally) and stereotype (biographi-
cally), what may reasonably be hypothesised about the father of
Peter Sellers?

That he had the determination (or fecklessness) to leave the farm
outside Bingley and to descend into the theatrical world (perhaps
indeed first learning some musical skills in the manse) suggests that
a creative need took him there. He was worlds away from the entertainment tradition of the Mendozas, and he enjoyed being affiliated
with it – it was like a boy's dream of running away to join a circus.
'Our Willie' had become Bill and, unlike Peg, who tagged along
with Ma, he had chosen his career – and, again unlike her, the pro-
tectiveness of family feeling was not something he took for granted.
If the Jews felt generically ostracised, Bill knew cold shouldering
from personal experience. By going into the music hall he had put
himself, as far as his kin were concerned, outside the clan. Despite
the attempt to appease the Sellars' side by calling a son Richard
Henry, when Bill took the boy to meet the grandparents in Yorkshire he was met off the three o'clock express with the words
'There's a good train goes back at five.'

If all that Tallulah Bankhead/playing cricket stuff is invention, as
it has to be, then Bill, like his son (when playing Dr Pratt et and no
doubt al), was a dreamer and romantic. And it is Bill, I think, not
Peg, who is Sellers' precursor as an actor. Peg's function was to provide the fire of ambition – but it was Bill's career, as a musician,

which Sellers was first to follow. He was an ironist, too. When Sellers was swankily taking his parents over the Harlequin Suite at the Dorchester, Bill said, with a view to defusing the playboy pretensions, 'Yes, Peter, nice, but nothing that a good joanna wouldn't improve.'

It has obviously been all too easy to mistake the nature of Bill's meekness and quiet, which I think points away from compliance. The busker's voice in *The Optimists of Nine Elms*, and that film's Formby and Formby-esque songs, acknowledge the timbre and repertoire of Sellers' father. Old Sam's loneliness, too, is Bill's – and his peppery temper. Bill is less Chance, in *Being There*, than Sellers' many rebels and reactionaries – characters like Mr Martin in *The Battle of the Sexes*, who would like nothing more than to kill the chirpy, interfering Mrs Barrows; or the lawyer in *I Love You, Alice B. Toklas*, who exchanges his suit for a hippy's motley; or the embattled Fred Kite . . . Sellers' muted, deeper characters (as opposed to his outright caricatures). From Bill, Sellers learned the art of stillness and observation; and where Peg tried to interfuse herself with him, Sellers saw his father as someone separate and individual. Bill was independent, and as such, in his interplay with other people, he could be subtle and variegated – and this was misread as anonymousness. Bill silently putting up with Peg is Sellers at St Aloysius', seeing the virtues of being inconspicuous – but let no man say that inwardly you cannot seethe.[*]

☆ ★ ☆

At the end of the summer term, in 1939, it was announced that St Aloysius' would close and that its pupils must prepare to evacuate to Stainsby Hall, Smalley, near Derby, for the following October. Sellers, who would not be fourteen (when mandatory education ceased) until the September, by rights should have been schooled for a further term. But Peg, her nerves abraded by the German bomb which had totalled her junk shop, wasn't having that – and Sellers never in his life caught up. She decided to gather her family – i.e. find Bill – and retreat to the country, taking with her an

---

[*] When this book is made into a film the actor to play Bill is Sir Anthony Hopkins.

antique copper kettle belonging to a Mrs Clarke. Bill was needed, quite simply, because without him Peg would never get a job – the quasi-divorced Jewess with an overweight son to support. Bill could find work piano-playing or something and Peg herself could tear tickets and take people's coats.

They went to Ilfracombe – where the Rays, or Wreys as it was spelled in Devon, were meant to have a connection with the Victoria Pavilion Theatre, though I have found no evidence that one of Peg's brothers owned the place, as Sellers maintained. ('The Pavilion Theatre was burned down afterwards. I think that killed my uncle – the loss of his theatre,' said Sellers airily in 1962, of a building still standing today.) The manager was a Mr A. Humphrey; and when in 1921 the theatre was enlarged, to accommodate an extra eight hundred people, the improvements were planned and paid for by the District Council.

The rendezvous with Bill took place in St Martin's Lane, near Long Acre. Seeing his father again was an important enough event for Sellers to want to stop and stare at the spot over forty years later. 'It's just over there,' he said to his male companion, Michael Jeffery, the two of them standing and looking. 'Me and me mum came to meet Bill.'

They had got together again. It was still going through his mind.

☆ ★ ☆

Chapter Two
Wartime

'You see . . . I was evacuated to Ilfracombe during the war,' Sellers told Freddy Clayton, a trumpeter in *The Goon Show* orchestra, 'and it was there that I got my first professional job. . . I joined one of the leading bands of the day. . .' – 'Which one?' asked Clayton eagerly, thinking of Geraldo or Victor Silvester. 'Waldini,' said Sellers. 'Who?' asked Clayton, mystified. 'Waldini,' said Sellers again, rather flatly and his expression getting pained, 'Surely you remember him?'

Waldini was really Wally Bishop (b.1895) who'd graduated from accompanying silent movies at the Olympia, Queen Street, Cardiff, to playing a cello in Roath Park and Sophia Gardens. Along with Bill Morgan, Benny Lodwick, George Cromer and Cliff Thomas, clarinettists and guitarists, he dressed up in colourful bandannas, made a gimmick out of Romany accoutrements, demoted himself from a Bishop to a Dean, took the Y off Wally, and Waldini and his Gypsy Band were born.

'Peter Sellers started with us,' confirmed Elaine Parsons, the accordionist in Waldini's Gypsy Band, when I spoke to her in Wales. 'He started with us in Ilfracombe. His father used to play the piano and his mother worked in the box office at the Victoria Pavilion Theatre. Peter, who was a jolly boy, dabbled in the drums, and I used to play along with him, to help his rhythm – in the empty hall. He used to enjoy keeping time. There used to be tea-dances in the town, another band on the pier, another on the band-stand itself, by Capstone Parade – Waldini had three bands going and Peter was generally in one of them. . . This was just before the war. The beaches were coiled with barbed wire and a lot of the amusements were shuttered up. Peter's father? A nice little man. Quiet. His mother? Peg? I sort of remember her as a little old woman, very short, and she always wore darkish clothes. When Peter got on a bit, he'd send Peg to Ilfracombe – and his chauffeur used to fetch Wally and I and take us to her hotel for tea and toast. She loved Ilfracombe and often stayed there, especially after Bill died. "Be ready at such-and-such a time," she'd say, and the chauffeur would come. Peter was married to Britt by then, who she didn't like. . .'

By chance, a recording of one of Waldini's Ilfracombe performances, in which Sellers participates, has survived. The seaside show is full of communal singing, operetta, clapping along and full-throated emotional stuff. Ruby, the soprano, sings a high descant over everybody else, and there is no end of Hungarian fiddling, lots of woozy scales and arpeggios. When the accordion dominates, it's like a circus band; when the violin takes over, with the piano in support, it's sinuous music to urge Dr Frankenstein about his business – colourful and jaunty, but with an undertone of melancholy. ('There are tears on the string of a gypsy's violin,' sang Sellers in a Waldini-inspired sketch on *The Muppet Show*.) The ballads, ostensibly about maids of the mountain yonder, go from climax to climax, and all deal with sending someone on his way, or holding someone in your arms, or not, as the case may be – i.e. they are songs about loss, and it is spooky, hearing these voices and artistes coming through the crackle, holding nothing back, promising that we'll gather lilacs in the Spring again and walk together down an English lane. Now aged and retired (and dead) there is a forlorn atmosphere about these stout coryphées and limelit tenors – an atmosphere that is to do with the whole rough magic of show business. Deepening it, too, is the knowledge that, under the cover of music such as this, Sellers' parents were reuniting after up to a decade of being apart. They were returning to the sort of low-level theatrics where they'd met, courted and begun married life; and they were getting together as a couple – for the very first time without Ma and the extended family. But now there was Peter, and the trouble was, as Peg used to crow: 'Peg never left Peter and Peter never left Peg. Did we Bill?' – 'You never did,' he had to concede.

Ilfracombe, where Sellers was to spend the only three years of his life that was in a single place, with its average yearly rainfall of 32.5 inches, its average summer temperature of 57 degrees fahrenheit (dropping to 44.9 degrees in the winter) and with its death rate of 14 per 1,000, was the last word in seaside genteelisms. From the boulder-strewn mixed bathing beaches to the enclosed pools (the charge was 6d for a machine, 'including all essentials'), from the croquet games at Bicclescombe Pleasure Grounds to the horse-drawn excursions and motor-coach trips to Watermouth Caves, Woolacombe and Clovelly ('thirty-three miles each way'), the scene was Victorian. It is Henry Crun's backdrop in *The Goon Show*, Mrs Wilberforce's in *The Ladykillers*. In the cafés and hotels, guests drank Chelspa Natural Aperient Water (for functional disorders of the digestive tract), and if they ventured up Capstone Hill or Lantern Hill, to view Lundy Island or the South Wales coast across the waves and foam, there were plenty of benches and cast-iron shelters, 'so that visitors can remain in the open air even on rough days without inconvenience, a matter of no slight importance to invalids'.

Entertainment amenities included the Scala Cinema, built in 1921; the Alexandra Hall, a concert room; the Gaiety Concert Hall; the Runnacleave Theatre; the Empire Cinema, in Northfield Road; the Palace Cinema, in the High Street; and the Victoria Pavilion, situated in Ropery Meadow, a series of lawns and ornamental flower beds (now given over to crazy golf and the War Memorial). Built to commemorate the Queen's Jubilee in 1887, at a cost of £6,000, the glass conservatory section was two hundred feet long, forty-five feet wide and forty feet high; it was filled with shrubs and climbing plants – 'and on a wet day' (my period guide continues) 'visitors repair there with their books, or to listen to the frequent concerts'.

It was Waldini's practice to open the second half by welcoming the 'many visitors from all parts of our great island'. Honeymoon couples were singled out for applause ('sit down – or you won't have much strength left') and parties from the Cecil Hotel (Separate Tables, F.A. Knill, Proprietor) and the Grosvenor (Replete with Every Comfort, Mrs Pickett, Proprietress) were told, 'We are very glad to greet you – we want your money.' As the old shags from the Fairfield Social Club, the Brighton char-a-banc tour, the Montebellow Hotel (Miss Creek, Manageress), and the Balmaha Boarding Establishment (Electric Light Throughout, Mrs. W. Simpson, Proprietress), dragged themselves to their feet for increasingly desultory ovations and the odd ironic cheer, Waldini apologised for the inclement weather and introduced the minstrel show. Gypsy bangles and bodices had been exchanged, during the interval, for curly wigs and black faces. The band now formed itself into a series of tableaux: cotton fields in the Old South, below-decks on a Mississippi paddle steamer etc., and we are told that, 'to have a song in the heart – that's why darkies were born'.

We have approximations of dirges and the blues, Al Jolson and G.H. Elliott ('The Chocolate-Coloured Coon') impersonations, 'Mamie', 'Carolina Moon', 'Lily of Laguna', and the banjos they are a 'strummin' and Show Boat is a 'comin' before we are returned to Ivor Novello and 'Over the Mountain Yonder' for the encores. The ladies in the audience sing along after a fashion and the piccaninnies on stage revert to Mittel-Europa whoops and sentimental caterwauling. As the local newspaper reported in a prose style which seems like one of Lord Jim's parodies of provincial journalism in *Ulysses* – or perhaps the sort of notice John Lewis supplies to the Aberdarcy Chronicle in *Only Two Can Play*:

> Music lovers are assured of a real treat at the Victoria Pavilion, for, commencing on Sunday Evening, they will have the opportunity of seeing and hearing for a week that famous combination, Waldini and His Gipsy Band. They have recently made appearances at several West Country towns, and Ilfracombe is indeed fortunate to receive a visit from this fine orchestra.

Waldini is a musician with definite ideas, and his various interpretations bear the distinct impression of his personality. It is fascinating to note the effective basic influence of the piano accordions in his musical structures.

Waldini and his musicians wear picturesque costumes, but the excellence of their interpretations renders them independent of appeals to the eye. The approach to the ear is emphatically all-sufficing.

Bill had joined the troupe and went on their incursions into Bideford and Barnstaple on Sundays and Thursday nights, for hunt balls – with Blodwen, Singer Superb (Welsh Eisteddfod Winner), Elaine and her Accordion, and Jeanne Humphries, posthorn. Peg tried to make herself useful looking after the tinker costumes, but Sellers had much more mundane tasks than even being a launderer and darner. 'My mother used to say that you should never ask anybody in the theatre to do another job you couldn't do yourself. So I was an apprentice, sweeping out after the performance. That was the first job – I got ten bob a week. And then after that I used to take tickets on the door; then I did front of house which, as most people know, is box office, and then from box office I went to assistant stage manager' – and he operated the limes and, when companies arrived with a play, trying it out before going up to the West End, he was co-opted as a dresser.

His mother was alongside him continually: *she* it was who executed the humble duties wielding the brooms and snapping the lid shut on the cash box while Sellers looked on. Peg drew a line, however, at climbing into the loft above the box office to work the spotlights. 'I remember one Sunday concert', said Sellers, nearly twenty years later. 'We had a chap on the bill called Herschel Henlere, a piano act. . . . He pulls his gloves off, and they bounce all over the place. Anyway, in the middle of this act, he says, "Strike me pink!" – and the idea was that he should be struck pink by the limes. Well, we had spinners on the limes, and one side was pink and the other was green, and I put the green on. . . . Mr Henlere was very annoyed about this, and I didn't get a tip at the end of the week.'

Sellers saw Paul Scofield and Mary Clare, pupils from the London Mask Theatre School, now evacuated to nearby Bideford, who brought Emlyn Williams' *Night Must Fall* to the town ('Not long ago I met Scofield,' said Sellers in 1962, 'I said, "I bet you don't remember where we met first time" – and of course he didn't'); he saw Ralph Lynn in *Rookery Nook*, with Guy Fane, Marie Ault, Vernon Kelso, Edgar K. Bruce and Joan Shannon (for one week, commencing Monday August 11th 1941, nightly at 8.30. Matinées on Tuesday and Thursday at 3. Sellers and Peg manned the box office from 10am. until 7pm.); and, when Joe Mitchenson arrived, to play in *The Two Mrs Carrolls* and *This Man is Mine* by Keith Helder, a split week with Diana Beaumont, who was Gerald du Maurier's niece, Ernest Barrow and Toni Edgar Bruce, Sellers was asked to go out and get cream fancies from J.H. Hasking, the baker and confectioner, 105 High Street.

'He got us all to sign his autograph book,' recalled Mitchenson for me. 'He was the cleaner – and very proud of the theatre, *very* proud of it. He was very kind, and we all treated him well. . . . I often wonder about the boy at Ilfracombe, who was always being around. Peter Sellers! And he went out and bought us cakes. . .'

☆　★　☆

The opportunity to rise from general factotum to performer had come on Friday October 11th 1940:

PARTY NIGHT

Waldini requests the pleasure

A Really Jolly Night.

Can you Sing, Dance or Act?

Prices of Admission 2/-, 1/- and 6d.

Members of H.M. Forces (in uniform) Half Price

Coaxed by Peg and coached by Elaine, Sellers decided to have a crack. He teamed himself with a local barber's boy called Derek Altman, with whom, as Selman Investigations Inc., he'd hunted for people's lost cats (when he should have been at large distributing posters). They strummed a ukelele and told a goonish story about a mad Greek oboist who was threatening the lives of the band. Their opening chorus went thus:

> We're Altman and Sellers,
> The younger generation,
> We always sing in the best syncopation,
> And we hope we make a big sensation
> With you-ooh-ooh!

'I suppose people knew us from seeing us give out tickets and so on,' said Sellers later, 'and probably they were well disposed towards us. Anyhow, we won.' The prize was a fiver.

Bill was sufficiently impressed to arrange music lessons for his son. Sellers was hopeless on the piano, having no patience, and he refused even to go and meet a replacement teacher when the first one had been sent packing (the first known instance of the future actor's high-handedness). What Elaine knew he wanted to concentrate on, however, was the drums: If ever she asked him 'How are you today, Peter?' or 'Where are you off to!' or 'What's for dinner?' he'd answer, regardless, 'I want to be a drummer!' When a band called Joe Daniels and his Hotshots had come to Ilfracombe on an engagement, and Sellers was allowed to have a bash on the drum kit once he'd removed the fruit rinds and dirty beer glasses off the stage, Sellers told his mother: 'Now I know what I want. I want to be a drummer.' Bill made arrangements with Harold Leeding, Waldini's percussionist, to have Sellers tutored properly, at half a guinea a go. 'In the empty theatre, lit only by a working light, I would take over his drums. . .'

☆ ★ ☆

' . . . it was the drums that I was really keen on in the early days,' Sellers said a quarter of a century later. 'I suddenly went mad about the drums. I spent months learning from a professional drummer; and I was pretty good.'

Good enough to appear in Waldini's *Symphony in Colour*, at the Victoria Pavilion on Sunday August 10th 1941, with Joan Port (Charm Singer), Nita (Solo Pianiste), Mona Rose (The Welsh

Deanna Durbin), Laurie Solari and, of course, Elaine (Super Accordioniste); in his *Night of Gladness*, on August 17th; and in the *In Town To-Night* concert of August 24th, when the musicians played 'interesting personalities from all parts of the globe,' one such being a soprano called Melissia doing Our Gracie's Sally Up the Alley screech.

Waldini was eased out of Ilfracombe by *Lilac Time*, with Yva Gordon and Sinclair Cotter (The Musical Comedy Comedian) and, of all things, Lydia Kyasht and the Imperial Ballet from St. Petersburg (Book Early to Avoid Disappointment); so Sellers and his father had to traipse the West Country, playing in pubs for two or three pounds a night. If the discipline of reading music and the precision of most instruments was beyond the boy, the ability to absorb himself in the beat and thump, the rolls and riffs of snares and timps, was evidence of a perhaps deeper and more instinctive talent. Within his limits of a given number, Sellers enjoyed improvising, making a melody out of the primitive thuds and cymbal crashes – it was jungle music, really, which harked back to the very heartbeat of those real nigger minstrels in the real American Deep-South, as they pined for their dark continent across the sea. Jazz drumming, as Sellers knew it, was both forceful, brutal – physical – and nostalgic. The music of slavery and migration, there was drama in it – and Sellers abandoned playing professionally when, after the war, he was unable to play expressively. Having to do what he was told at sedate ballroom dance evenings was not for him; the point about being a drummer was the freedom – being able to 'let loose and enjoy myself'.

There is a link to be made between Sellers' style of solo drumming and his eventual method of acting. Both must appear to be spontaneous, and both have a buoyancy, a weightlessness, which for all its skill and charm must, at its best, remain subversive – even belligerent. I'm thinking of Clare Quilty in *Lolita*, pinioning Humbert Humbert with gags and a rapidity of disguises; or Fred Kite, wearily treading across his carpet, wistful and defeated, his silent thoughts about his wife and erring daughter set to music by the sad, echoey trumpet and drum tattoo on the soundtrack. When he was making *The Magic Christian* with Ringo, 'I don't think we spoke about anything else other than drums and drummers.' Learning to play the drums, Sellers learned all about tempo.

Discovering the drums, he also discovered sex. The uprush of excitement he felt when making music coincided with the hormonal thrum. This was different to Hedy Lamarr's puzzling gallop across the screen in *Extase*. His sensibilities were newly stirred, like the 'boom-tiddy-boom' pulse Dr Kabir arouses in Sophia Loren in *The Millionairess*, or the tom-toms knocking and gyrating in Richard Rodney Bennett's score when the librarian is turned on in *Only Two Can Play*. Feeling very masculine because he was an employed, professional musician, in demand at fifteen because anybody any older would be in the services, Sellers put his coat across his shoulders and took girls along the cliff paths to Bull Point Lighthouse, there to see the white beam giving three flashes in quick succession every thirty seconds, and to watch the secret signals giving warning to mariners, now that Ilfracombe had its naval defences against German submarines lurking off the Bristol Channel. Or he took the ladies to the pier, claiming that he was related to its benefactors, the Wreys. But what he didn't do was take any girls out as Peter Sellers. Knowing himself to be plain and stout, he did his best to effect a transformation into Robert Donat – a winsome, bittersweet sort of an actor who had impressed Sellers in *Knight Without Armour*, which he'd seen at the Odeon, Swiss Cottage, when he was twelve.

'I was crazy about Robert Donat,' he said, 'and the girls I was with, they were pretty mad about him too, and I thought to myself – well, here is a chance to do an impersonation of him. You see, I could be, in a way, a bit like Robert Donat, but a girl's other crush, Errol Flynn – I hadn't a chance, you see. But at least I could *sound* slightly like Robert Donat – which I did. I remember I could say the word "because" like Robert Donat – the only word I could say, so I fiddled the others so that "because" came right in the middle. I relied on the "because" very strongly. She was very impressed, and she said, "*More!*" and I said, "*Because!*" again! I remember I was kissing her goodnight. I said, "Well, I have to go now, dear, *because* . . ." [*breaking into Bluebottle*], "Because my mother says I have to go home."'

Prepubertal Bluebottle's balls eventually fell into place in Taunton. Sellers was with his father, who was beginning to associate himself with ENSA (Entertainments National Service Association) units and to drift apart again from Peg. They stayed the night at a hostel – rooms above an undertakers, Sellers claimed – and Sellers was invited to take advantage of the black-out by coming in to comfort one of the women instrumentalists, who found the dwelling a bit macabre. Sellers developed this into quite an anecdotal set-piece in later life, where his devirginification involved falling over a coffin and virtually having the corpse on the floor into the bargain.

If sex and death were entwined from the first, more to the point might have been Peg's unique absence from Sellers' side. She was stuck back in Ilfracombe, helping the ballerinas get their tutus on. She normally slept with her Peter (Bill took a separate room or the couch), so it was a wrench when Sellers announced he was going to Lytham St Annes with his father, who was taking a job as concert party pianist for the 1942 summer season. Didn't this mean, at the very least, that he was leaving the Victoria Pavilion's set of drums behind? He'd take up the ukelele instead – hadn't he won the talent contest with a banjo when he was more or less just messing about? What about Waldini? He was going to Drury Lane, the ENSA Headquarters, to receive instructions for taking the Gypsy Band around RAF camps and hospitals. . .

As a bid for independence it was short-lived. Peg hadn't thought to follow her husband north, but she'd follow her son.

☆ ★ ☆

Waldini and his vagabonds were eventually pressed into service overseas, and Elaine wore out fourteen accordions under enemy fire. They toured through Italy, North Africa, India, Ceylon and Burma – where they met Sellers again. And such was Waldini's enjoyment of these adventures (his son, Ron Bishop, told me it was the only era of guaranteed employment, income and gratitude) that the postwar end-of-the-pier shows continued to have an ENSA structure and theme. Whether you were at Llandudno or Ilfracombe, it made no difference: 'You are not at the seaside,' Waldini told the holidaymakers, 'You are under the blazing sun of North Africa' – and his gypsies would pretend to make their entrance on camels. Waldini would then give an illustrated lecture on 'the little people of the stage, the unknowns' (such as himself) who'd rig up a rostrum in an engine shed and have car lamps for footlights and upturned petrol cans for seats. During the war, Waldini was at long last like a gypsy baron, his caravan rocking and rolling across the desert.

This nostalgia was still afoot as late as 1963, when Waldini attempted to excuse the grey hairs by saying, 'Kids, I'm with it – and getting more with it every day.' (He was not. The Llandudno Council cancelled his contract, and after a few miserable years playing at flower shows, dependent now not only on the weather but the limits of a bus ride out of Cardiff, he died in January 1966, aged seventy-one.) The band would play 'Maple Leaf Forever', Waldini explained about the hardships of a touring ENSA troupe, and then, suddenly, his coup de theatre, he'd hand over to 'my very good friend Peter Sellers.' Sellers, by 1963 an international star, had been prevailed upon to reminisce. He came over the loudspeakers with a Prince Philip voice that gradually grew, as the jumble of qualifying clauses proliferates, more and more Welsh:

I would like to pay tribute to the many artists who entertained the Forces overseas. When I was out in India during the War, in the Airforce, which was not being in the Army, you understand, or the Navy, it's different from that, many of the fellows in the Fourteenth Army, which, again, is different from the Thirteenth Army or the Twelfth Army, they used to team up in their own shows, to entertain themselves, and which is, when you think about it, quite a good idea, to team up in a show to entertain yourself. I've never entertained *myself*, because I've never teamed up with myself really, but I have thought about it. Anyway, sometimes a show from England

77

would arrive out there – which used to give the fellows a great feeling of home, because for so long, you see, we'd not seen any English girls on a stage. We'd not seen any English girls *off* a stage, or even *near* a stage. In fact, we'd not seen any English girls at all. Mainly because, I suppose, because of the shortage. You can't get English girls, you know, or you couldn't in those days. I think you can get them now. Get them! Get English girls Today! They Are Good For You! ENGLISH GIRLS. GET THEM. NOW! TODAY!

I have been affected by this commercial TV, you know. Excuse me. As Wally has probably told you, these English girls were the 'little people' of the stage. I don't literally mean little tiny people. I mean they were visible from ten yards away. They were the little people – oh, well, they *were* 'the little people of the stage'. They had no thought of stardom, their name in lights or anything like that. They were just put there to do a job of work. Well, for the job of work they did I would like to say [*Maurice Chevalier*]: 'Thank you *Little Girls* of the stage. English girls. . . .' And I'd like to give a big hand to all those – fancy giving a big hand to anybody. I must get a big hand and present it to somebody. I'll post it to somebody – a big hand to all those who relieved the monotony of things. And to Welshman Waldini, I'd just simply like to say [*stage Welsh voice*]: 'It's been lovely talking to you again, Wal, boy, lovely, smashing, see. My regards from Stanley Baker, Harry Secombe and everyone – and a long time since we played in Ilfracombe together, you know, isn't it? Lovely. Well, yes. . .'

☆ ★ ☆

The little people of the stage, the strangers to fame, included Sellers himself until he became indispensable to radio producers, clamoured after, just prior to *The Goon Show*. The unknowns certainly numbered Bill or any of the survivors of Ray Bros. Productions Ltd. The reason I have belaboured the music hall background and heaped up the detail, from the itinerary for *The Side Show* to Waldini's Ilfracombe concerts, is that Sellers, who emotionally lived in the past, lived in *this* past. Milligan described Sellers to me as 'Little Boy Lost – Forever'; and where he was adrift from were these experiences of his childhood and early youth, when he'd been implanted with a sensation of acting's magical properties, and had perceived, too, its sorrow and dejections. The grief which he carried within him has its origins at the end-of-the-pier and in third-rate variety houses, where he saw, yes, the shoddiness of glamour ('I don't like the smell of grease paint. . . . It used to waft out from the stage. I hated it . . .') but, more importantly, he became aware of people's need for fantasy and delusion; he saw that a demand for romance was not the audience's, or even his own (though it was), so much as a matter of life and death for the misfit actors and performers themselves. Sellers could see the deficiencies between aspirations and the achievements, and no artist has ever been so expert as he in expressing the tragedy of that gap between people's feelings and their skill.

This is most easily instanced by referring to Sellers' comic songs. Time and again he becomes the wheezy, rheumy old Cockney, proudly giving a concert in what turns out to be the bathroom. Or he puts his grandiloquent Shakespeareans through the humiliation of an audition ('Oh, will somebody *please* get him out of here . . .' murmurs the shit of a director). A salty rendition of 'Thank Heavens, you know, for little girls,' the voice Chevalier's mingled with the March Hare's from *Alice's Adventures in Wonderland*, is accompanied by a lusty military brass band – but then it fades away to be replaced with traffic noises. The glorious number was the daydream of a French cop on point duty. (It's nightmare equivalent is 'Singin' in the Rain' scored for the drums and fifes of the Coldstream Guards, all very loud, which climaxes as a huge orchestrated motorway crash and pile-up.)

Sellers' characters never let go of their dignity. Even when they are drunks, he gets their mock-gravity across. 'In a Free State' has a violent Irishman (Brendan Behan) smashing glasses and fighting his way to the gents, throwing a punch at the interviewer along the way. The joke is that the rascal thinks he's in the right – whereas really he's simply in a world of his own (like the bath-tub crooners, whose imaginations supply the orchestral strings). 'Suddenly It's a Folk Song' wonderfully sends up a bucolic idyll. The singers in the Somerset pub are drunk, the Irish jig is a drunken brawl, and the

Scottish tenor weaves in and out of the Sauchiehall Street rush hour, staggering on and off the pavement, waving a bottle.

When they sing, Sellers' creations are either inebriates, buskers, or flops. His Palm Court artiste, attempting to trill 'Only a Rose' against an out-of-tune piano and a jeering audience, which make him start to forget the lyrics and fail to keep time, is funny, because it is superbly executed, but also sad. Very often, his troubadours are out in the road, a drum and cymbal strapped to their backs, giving their all for throw money. 'Unchained Melody', for example, a number by Bluebottle and Eccles, is packed with the shrieks, crashes and thumps of a one-man-band. (Sellers' Nixon, when he is transmogrified into Hitler, at the finale of *He's Innocent of Watergate*, clumps off through the crowds as a one-man-band.) 'Any Old Iron', croaked with superb pace and phrasing, is an energetic alfresco skiffle, for washboard and spoons; and Minnie Bannister and Henry Crun's 'Dance with Me, Henry,' begins as a genteel tango and ends with explosions and crashing buildings, rock-and-roll riffs and gunshots, throughout which the cadaverous duo continue to warble on, unabashed. (They'd warble on after the end of the world itself.)

There are dozens of such numbers, thirty years' worth. Many end with destruction and noise – with some form of outright physical violence or personal decrepitude. This was the fate, week upon week, of the characters in *The Goon Show*. Major Denis Bloodnok is always ambushed and caught thieving, his impeccable Zulu War era credentials exposed as cowardice and disloyalty – but by some miracle Sellers makes him lovable. Bluebottle, the epitome of acne-daubed adolescence ('dressed in brown paper, cardboard and string'), is consistently mangled, but sustains himself with his heroic dreams – he thinks he is reincarnating Errol Flynn in *Dawn Patrol*. Henry Crun, misplaced in the 1950s, keeps himself alive by thinking it is still only the 1850s (so he is therefore not as ancient as he sounds); and Grytpype Thynne, an unsuccessful confidence trickster, who had to think up a new scam for Neddie Seagoon every week for over ten years, overlooks the farce his life has become by studious rôle-play: he's George Sanders or Basil Rathbone really, his ragged familiar, Moriarty, an aristocrat from France – Comte Toulouse-Moriarty of the House of Roland. ('Under Grytpype's careful management he is now bald, daft, deaf and worthless.')

In Sellers' menagerie, nothing is what it seems. Fools triumph; the self-confident collapse under the pressure of their pretensions. And, if you look for recurrences of theme and fetish in his work, across the whole span of his life, it is (a) the threat of failure versus the melancholia of what-might-have-been which gives his characters heart and (b) his best characters, like Clouseau, are the ones who don't know they are funny. Beyond the hopeless serenaders and the classical actors muffing their lines on the record sketches and tapes, the dark theme of the blundering and fatigued music hall entertainer is at the core of Sellers' ability to be (say) Percy Quill, in *The Smallest Show on Earth*, gazing in rapture at the unreachable idyll on the silent movie screen; General Fitzjohn in *Waltz of the Toreadors*, realising he married the wrong woman and that life has lost its savour; the useless matador in *The Bobo* ('Don't you cry for the bulls that die/Save your tears for the men'); the useless pianist in *The World of Henry Orient*, pursued by two girls who have overvalued his talent; the useless doctor in *The Wrong Box*, thinking his stethoscope tube is part of his own entrails. . . A large part of Sellers' personality and imagination remained stranded in his early years, and we can account for his anxieties, his inability to settle at a single address, his obsession with identity, by realising that, when he looked back to the embankments and castellated hotels of Ilfracombe, touring revue etc. with disgust, it was because it was as frightening as a fairy story.

☆ ★ ☆

What was crucial were his surroundings, the forces at work before his own birth (which laid traps for him), what he absorbed and saw. It all lay in his mind, like shadows and fog that wouldn't lift. The dilapidations of the barrister in *The Dock Brief* (who semi-minces like a failed matinée idol); Fred Kite's defeats; the loneliness of Mr

Topaze when he makes his corrupt million; the disappointments of
John Lewis in *Only Two Can Play* ('Don't stand there giving me
that little-boy face, you're getting too old for it'); the imbecility of
the pirates in *Ghost in the Noonday Sun*, who get lost in the Aegean
and stumble upon Ireland. . . . The innermost purpose of Sellers'
acting was to reproduce people making fools of themselves – when
they fall in love (*Only Two Can Play, Hoffman*), or want to blow up
the world (*Doctor Strangelove*), or have lots of sex (*Lolita, Soft Beds,
Hard Battles*), or when they think they are irresistible (*There's a Girl
In My Soup*) etc. – and to build on them extravagantly, robustly.
Sellers catches his characters coping with fresh or strong emotions
(jealousy, temptation, libido, fear). The return of a girlfriend from
the past, the suggestiveness of something better, the chance to
change – coping with feelings like these, or coping with the surrealism of a red alert against Russia, or, as in *Casino Royale*, being
a small-time croupier who is suddenly thrust into Ursula Andress'
bosom and boudoir – all this dislodgement makes his tribe of
major-generals and flâneurs suddenly stand out against their
backgrounds. They become people, like those on a stage, who know
we are looking at them. And if the source of Sellers' art was in recalling the sufferings and gaudy exposures of music hall, which
were also never far below the surface of his own personal craving to
escape from drabness (and thus linked all too closely with his follies
and instincts), he also feared he'd return to the end of the pier one
day – and be like the character in *The Optimists of Nine Elms*, living
off alms, or McGonagall (whom Sellers played on television long
before appearing as Queen Victoria in Milligan's film), writing
those poems nobody wants. As his career self-destructed in the
Seventies, with unfinished and unreleased whole movies, it was
almost as if he was willing, engineering, a decline and fall back to
basics.

   In one respect, at least, he *did* go back to the open-air concert
party. In July 1976, John Wells invited him to make a guest appearance in a programme called *The End of the Pier Show*, which John
Bird describes as 'a non-budget thing shot in the BBC's smallest

studio – smaller than the one they do the weather from.' Wells himself says: 'I was so amazed to be working with my childhood hero, I still find it hard to be objective. He was really surprisingly kind. I once rang him on a Friday night to ask him if he'd be in a Saturday recording as Adolf Hitler with Percy Edwards, the bird impersonator, as Hercule Poirot . . . and he turned up and did it for virtually nothing.'

That Sellers, who was a versatile mimic amongst many other things, had to share the billing with a comedian who came across as a noisy simpleton and who made his living by squawking, whistling and screeching, is a joke in itself. Wells' entertainment began with a seaside cinema organ and silent movie piano tinkles, and Sellers provided eager BBC announcer voices, Churchill's slack-jawed growl, and then came on as Hitler, giving a rendering of Noël Coward's 'Past Forgetting'. It all takes place in a railway carriage – *Murder on the 9.36 from Didcot* – and when Percy Edwards isn't doing dinosaur grunts, badgers mating, magpie cackles and 'the shy water vole', Sellers tries to impale commuters on an ivory tusk hatrack, prompting John Fortune to say, 'I'll find the swine who started this grim dance of death, I'll find the swine who kidnapped Crispin.' Hitler, whom Sellers plays as Fritz Fassbender from *What's New, Pussycat?*, eventually strips off his disguise – and he's Grytpype Thynne, an Old Etonian fresh from an afternoon of passion with the engine driver.

No doubt everybody involved thought of it as 'goonish'. Sellers, whom John Bird says, 'didn't seem to be doing anything, but was incredibly funny', acts everybody else off the screen. Where they mug and prance, giving performances which are in inverted commas (a hallmark of ex-University revue artistes, who signal frantically that they *know* it's all a load of old rubbish, this acting lark), Sellers goes beyond parody. When other people are simply silly and exhibitionistic, because they are above the stuff they are laughing at, Sellers is concentrated and his performances tingle. Wells and company send up tatty vaudeville, but have nothing to give, except their edge of condescension; Sellers' vocal quick-changes, the dexterity with which he moves, his lightness, are in the vaudeville tradition to begin with. For *The Goon Show* itself, which so influenced the humour of Wells' generation ('scenes containing omelette fetishism and enamel buckets of Bulgarian Yoghurt' is a pure Milligan-derived idea), was structured as music hall: the melodramatic playlets, the double acts (Hen and Min, Bluebottle and Eccles, Grytpype and Moriarty etc.), the musical interludes by Max Geldray and Ray Ellington.

We may go further. Dr Strangelove is a pantomime devil, and his tiffs with his false arm are numbers, routines. Quilty's sequence of disguises, in *Lolita*, is a series of skits. Clouseau and Cato are slapstick tumblers. Chance, in *Being There*, has a voice derived from Stan Laurel – who stepped westwards from the British music hall with Fred Karno. The multiple-rôle movies, like *The Naked Truth* or *The Mouse That Roared*, have about them an actor's joy in transformation scenes. Except in *The Prisoner of Zenda*, Sellers doesn't have to duplicate himself – make everybody the member of the same family, like Alec Guinness in *Kind Hearts and Coronets* – he can, instead, create the illusion of being a colourful crowd. He's a conjuror. The scenes he himself devised and shot for *The Fiendish Plot of Dr Fu Manchu*, after he'd sacked the original director, are perhaps the most revealing – for, when Fu takes time off from his villainy to play 'Daddy Wouldn't Buy Me a Bow-Wow' on the piano with Helen Mirren, and to talk about his nostalgia for the music hall, his tastes are Sellers'. Fu's embroidered satin robes are out of *Aladdin*, and his palace bedroom is littered with props and costumes, the bric-à-brac of theatre.

☆ ★ ☆

The attitudes inherent in Sellers' style were from the music hall, and his aristocracy of eccentrics was born backstage. He was fond of grotesques, the heightened effect, and he liked, also, the plaintiveness of tramps – who sing sad little numbers such as 'Sometimes', a track from *The Optimists of Nine Elms*, written by Lionel Bart:

Sometimes, it wasn't half as bad as all that, sometimes;
Don't know exactly what we had, but there were fun times.

Sellers was strangely happy when, for a sketch called 'Old Comrades on Hard Times', he got into a hobo disguise and busked in
Oxford Street with Secombe, carrying the hat, and Spike, tooting
on a trumpet. He himself banged a drum, and they collected the
grand total of £4.75. The result was broadcast on *Sing a Song of
Secombe*, at Christmas 1974. It was a comfort to know that, if this
were for real, there'd be no lower he could sink than the open air.

He was banging a drum for money, too, three decades earlier, up
in Lancashire. His father settled at Lytham St Annes, Sellers found
a job at a dance hall in Blackpool for £8 a week. He also learned the
ukelele properly. 'He was a wizard with it,' said Bill. Perhaps this
was the time when, one way or another, the Sellers family had a
brush with the Formbys? Bill joined an ENSA unit which included,
amongst its other three members, George Formby's sister, Ethel,
and Sellers himself played Formby ditties at factory concerts. 'Each
time he did this he stopped the show,' said Peg.

George Formby was to remain a Sellers favourite. On the *Parkinson Show* in November 1974, after singing the Bart 'Sometimes', and
remembering with affection that 'Dad taught me to play the banjo,'
he accompanied himself on the ukelele for 'When I'm Cleaning
Windows' and 'I Haven't Told Her, She Hasn't Told Me'. The
Harry Stoneham Trio have a tricky time matching the pace, and the
bass rather unnecessarily clumps in the background – ready to
come in and drown Sellers out, perhaps, if his fingerwork faltered.
But Sellers is nifty. He captures Formby's glee, but alters it slightly,
ages it and makes it wistful. 'He was one of my idols,' Sellers told
Judith Simons in 1980, 'I saw all his films. Two years ago I watched
a competition on BBC 2 with ten people imitating him, all in
blazers and boaters and singing "Leaning on a Lamp Post". I
thought there and then that one day I'd do a take-off of this event' –
so on *Sellers' Market*, his final LP, there is a sketch where the Wembley stadium is filled with the serried ranks of German, Russian,

Jewish and Chinese Formby impersonators – including John Travolta, dancing throbbingly to 'My Aunty Mabel's Knickers Have Got Holes in the Back'.

Now I am not a Formby fan, nowhere near, but there is an element in his idiot cheerfulness, and his getting in and out of scrapes, which needs explaining – because the harum-scarum little boy lost persona of George's is one Sellers could recognise and use; and all those shoddy films of the Thirties and Forties prefigure the *Panthers*. George, the fool who could play the ukelele with assurance, is like scatterbrained Harpo or Chico when they take up their instruments for the serious interludes, careful not to let us take all the gormlessness too literally. There's a quick manipulator under the goofiness; the awkward innocent is also shrewd. This was the mainspring of hundreds of plots – *Come On George, Let George Do It, South American George, George in Civvy Street* etc. – where George's imbecility is what protects him from harm (he's always encountering master criminals). Inspector Clouseau isn't far away from any of these descriptions: he, like George, is an inncoent abroad; George, like Clouseau, tangles with bikes, horses, gym equipment, naturist clubs, and ladders; and, like Clouseau, George, who was by no means any oil painting to look at, co-starred with desirable women. Sellers' character had his pulses set racing by Capucine, Claudia Cardinale, Elke Sommer, Catherine Schell, Lesley-Anne Down and Dyan Cannon. (Had Sellers lived to make *The Romance of the Pink Panther*, Clouseau would have gone gooey and turned to crime for the love of Pamela Stephenson.) In fact, the stories of the *Panther* films are of less consequence than the opportunity offered for Clouseau to embarrass himself, over and over, as a gallant. So, too, in the Formby films. George is always tangling with pretty women who have faith in him – who see beyond the twerpishness – Phyllis Calvert, Googie Withers, Florence Desmond, Kay Walsh, Coral Browne. Yet, where Clouseau is full of tension because he can't consummate a relationship (if he ever had it off, he'd relax and wouldn't be clumsy any more), George's great fear is that he will be successfully seduced. All women are spider women, imperilling his chastity – hence his primal cry of 'MOTHER!' He can't cope with sex (that's why *he* is wound up like a top), and has kept himself a man-child out of fear. His arms and legs fly in all directions at once as he yells and blushes.

Of course, like his skill with the uke, he's not such a dope. His songs are all saucy – the voyeuristic 'When I'm Cleaning Windows', the virtually priapic 'My Little Ukelele in My Hand' – and there's a knowingness in his chuckle, which is perhaps what audiences enjoyed. (It's certainly what Sellers responded to across his entire life.) George's immaturity and adventures are Peter Pan's, and in the formidable former clog-dancer Beryl Ingham he had his Wendy.

We have now crossed the line from George the actor to George the man. Though he complained that 'some folks seem to take me for a mug off t'stage as well as on,' there was in his general personality a remoteness and simpleness (not the same as simplemindedness) which he drew on in performance. (The plumper, silver haired and beautifully besuited Formby of the late Fifties – he died in 1961 – had a gracefulness which could have been a model for Chance.) Beryl, of course, masterminded the public's perception of his awkwardness – she could see that audiences would love him if he didn't come across as a fake. The appeal was in the simplicity – but the appeal was not universal. Michael Balcon thought Formby mentally retarded, and wanted the songs cut from the films. One of the directors felt that Formby could 'switch his simplicity on and off according to need' and Pat Kirkwood, from *Come On, George*, thought him 'in many ways . . . cretinous'.

In a broad sense this is also the paradox of Sellers, whom Milligan has called 'the most complex simpleton in the entire world . . . He had a level of immaturity that didn't fit in with his age at all.' And where Formby had Beryl, Sellers had Peg. Beryl forbade her husband the same leading lady, organised and protected his image, drove him to the top and negotiated his £100,000 contracts. She invested his money and got him accorded star status (all this during the years the Sellers family were living in diminished affluence in Ilfracombe). The result was that she kept him cut-off and childless and disabled him emotionally. The perfect show business marriage was a complete illusion. They'd given up sexual intimacy fifteen years before Beryl died, and Formby diverted his energy and interest to machines. He liked disassembling watches and clocks and he was always changing his motor car – he'd had over two hundred by 1949. He bought and sold houses and could never settle. He tried an Irish mansion (like Sellers) and had a manor house (like Sellers' Chipperfield).

The trouble with Beryl's keeping Formby a little-boy-who-always-wants-to-have-fun was that he became a lonely man, who needed the affection of an anonymous public. (Amongst whom, slightly less than anonymous, was Princess Margaret.) He was safe, but repressed. And the entrepreneurial aspects aside, Peg's treatment of Sellers resembles, and had similar effects as, Beryl's treatment of her husband. 'He knew what he wanted,' it was said, 'but he let Beryl get it for him.' As much as Sellers would say he resented Peg's fuss and control, she was his motor and in his marriages he was looking for a dominatrix – he was looking for an agent of his heart, a Beryl.

☆ ★ ☆

The first thing Peg did in Lancashire was to insist on Sellers having a better ukelele and his own drumkit – the better for him to be acceptable to ENSA. 'You see, he was so fussy about things,' said Peg of his instruments. 'A thing had to be perfect, or not at all. Peter had a *thing* about it.' In the autumn of 1942 they all moved southwards again, Sellers side by side with his father's unit on tour. They met up with Jack Salt, Waldini's saxophonist, and stayed with him at 22 Magdala Road, Cosham, Portsmouth. (Sellers sold Jack one of the first small valve radios, which was operated by a hearing-aid battery.) Then they were off on the road again – but something happened, because Bill and his unit, which included Mona Rose, 'The Welsh Deanna Durbin', as she'd been billed in Ilfracombe, went off alone, and Peg and Sellers turned up, early in 1943, outside 73 Middle Street, Brighton, looking for accommodation.

'Peter and his mother came to the door of the digs and the landlady was about to turn them away,' recalls Salt, who was now in

Brighton working for Alan Green's dance band at the Dome. 'I said I knew them and so she took them in. They stayed together for a few weeks, and Peter was then playing the drums at the Regent Dance Hall. Peggy said it would be better if we looked for a flat – so we went to Ross' Mansions, 10 Middle Street – the flat was on the first floor.'

Salt went with Sellers and Peg, and for a few months he experienced their ménage. Peg reactivated her old sideline. She went around the big houses of Hove, knocking on the doors, trying to buy antiques and rocks, which she'd re-sell in Hatton Garden, the jewellery quarter. Sellers, who only worked between seven and eleven at night, spent the day idling and listening to the radio. 'He was very skilled in his mimicry,' says Salt. 'He knew the whole of the ITMA* show. He would be in one room, and you'd be in the next, and you'd think the radio was on. He didn't make anything of this, though. Drumming was his interest. I'd reckon he was as good as any other dance band drummer of that period.'

Sellers boasted to Salt that he'd 'slept with every girl in his band'. (He'd later boast to his son Michael that he'd slept with every one of his leading ladies. Irene Handl? Margaret Rutherford?) Other liaisons were apparently with a coalman's daughter and the cashier in a cake shop. Peg, says Salt, was very strict and much of Sellers' romancing was invented and designed to shock her. 'His mother was very much his companion. She ran the home. She did all the cooking – huge, excellent meals concocted from our rations.'

---

* *It's That Man Again*: an influential radio comedy series, a welter of catch-phrases and puns, which starred Tommy Handley and Dorothy Summers. In 1942 the cast had been invited to Windsor Castle for Princess Elizabeth's birthday party, and 'the late King and his family fell about with laughter'. It commenced on July 12th 1939 and lasted (for three hundred and twelve episodes) until Handley's death ten years later. Characters included Mrs Mopp, Colonel Chinstrap, Ali Oop, and Claude and Cecil. They said things like 'splash my spats!', 'Butter my Bath bun!' and 'Can I do you now, Sir?' It projected an England where everybody, from the lower orders up, was a smart-aleck and far too quick-witted ever to get morose. Hence its morale-boosting popularity. *The Goon Show* would take off from it.

Though Cissie came to stay for a week, there was no mention of Bill – until Peg suddenly said, at the end of June: 'I'd like to get Bill together with us again. ENSA is wanting their units to go overseas. I've some experience as a wardrobe mistress. If we could form a unit for ourselves, ENSA will accept us for the Home Circuit.'

Salt went with them up to London on July 1st 1943 (they'd been living together since the New Year). They went to Drury Lane. Peg went ahead to talk business, Salt and Sellers waited in a café. 'I've got good news and bad news,' she said, returning. 'Peter has been turned down – he's too near to being called up. So we can't do what we set out to do. If you wish, you can still go though,' Salt was told. 'Waldini's new saxophone player has failed his medical, so you can go along.' Which he arranged to do, there and then. He returned with Peg and Sellers to Brighton, worked out his month's notice at the Dome, received his innoculations, and went off to be part of the front-line theatre.

Sellers, the authorities apprised of his whereabouts, was conscripted into the Royal Air Force the moment he passed his eighteenth birthday, in September. He was now ACH(GD) 22230333, a faceless service number assigned to aircraft-hand ground duties.

☆ ★ ☆

It took Hitler and the Third Reich to sunder Sellers and Peg; the Nazis also liberated Milligan from his mother. After the call to arms ('the sense of emancipation!' remembers Milligan, 'the feeling of freedom!'), no longer did these young men need to fear the spectre of a parent at the top of the stairs, calling them a dirty stop-out. Almost in gratitude, therefore, Sellers and Milligan made Hitler into a comic figure; and because, in the years to come, they dressed themselves up as Hitler at every possible opportunity, it is clear that their part in his downfall is counterbalanced by his rôle in their growing-up. In *The Great McGonagall*, for example, Prince Albert is Hitler in a kilt; in *Casino Royale* Tremble is disguised as Hitler when he goes to visit Ursula Andress ('Baccarat, a personal game with a bit of cunning involved. I could be', he says, with a

90

slightly Hitlerish rise in voice, 'the finest player in the world today'); and in *Soft Beds, Hard Battles*, Sellers' Hitler visits a whorehouse for what is virtually a silent-movie scene. The Führer inspects the line-up of girls, giving us time to admire the actor's make-up and the eerie exactitude of his physical mimicry, when suddenly he spies a Negress: 'Eine Swatzer!' he bawls, and storms out.

Better, curiouser, perhaps, were the off-screen pranks. Sellers liked to don an SS officer's uniform, and Milligan would be Hitler, to drive his black Mercedes around London. He'd look for a young constable fresh from Hendon to tease: 'Zer, excuse me please, officer, but vere iss zer Cherman Embassy?' ('I'm sorry, sir, I'm a stranger round here.') When he was making *The Revenge of the Pink Panther* in Hong Kong, Sellers, knowing that his hotel was expecting a coach load of Jewish tourists, strutted up and down the waterfront as Hitler.

'He'd got this *thing* about Hitler,' says Michael Jeffery, who was Sellers' companion in his last years. 'Peter really hated the concierge at the Plaza-Athenée in Paris, really hated him, and so he would go in and sing "Deutschland, Deutschland über alles" at the top of his voice in the lobby. . .'

Jeffery also witnessed another of these vendettas. 'When Peter was in hospital in Geneva, in Christmas 1979, there was one nurse he didn't like because she switched the lights on early in the morning. So he put a chair on a table, climbed up, and dismantled the fluorescent strip, and locked it in a cupboard. He then made me draw a swastika on his forehead, a Hitler moustache, and he just lay there, all night, waiting.'

To Milligan, I think, Hitler was an ogre whom you could try and defuse, or cope with, through humour. Sellers' Hitler(s), though caricatured, had an edge of cruelty – as Milligan himself detected: 'There has to be a reality to his impersonations – if he played Hitler, he'd end up in the bunker and commit suicide. He'd have no other choice. That's what makes him mad, you know.'

☆ ★ ☆

Peg, as can readily be anticipated, didn't want her son leaving home to fight Adolf or anybody else. Taking the cue from the saxophonist who'd failed his medical examination, Peg did her best to convince the Royal Air Force that Sellers was a wreck. 'She tried everything,' said Milligan. 'She must have gone through the entire medical dictionary to find a disease that would get Peter back into civvy street, back to her loving care and protection: "He's got flat feet, he's got a flat head, flat ears, he's even got flat teeth . . ."'

When she ran out of ear-drum perforations and heart murmurs, she took lodgings near by to Sellers' camps and watched over him, and guarded him, as she had when he'd gone through the school gates in north London. Peg was on patrol.

I have come across no evidence that suggests, however, that Sellers himself objected to conscription – as his Hitler nostalgia helps to indicate. He was well used to the itinerant life and its discomforts, and 'the only grim memory', he said on the British Forces Broadcasting Service (in 1980), 'was the usual grim memory for everyone, the training period . . . once you are out of that, you know, it's one big black market.'

Sellers treated the wartime as playtime – it would literally be for him a few years of laughter and song. Encouraged by Peg, and seeing for himself the pointlessness of being an armer-assistant in Cardington, Bedfordshire, he applied to join the RAF Entertainments Division: 'the trouble was that the men I was working with were technicians, fitters and so on, by profession; the work interested them. I wasn't in the least interested in pushing bullets into the wings of planes. It seemed more sensible for me to be doing something I was good at. Anyhow, I managed to get myself re-mustered and attached to the Ralph Reader Gang Show. In fact, I became an official RAF concert entertainer.'

Peg did her best to petition Pilot Officer John Cracknell, Squadron Leader Ralph Reader's Administration Officer, to prevent Sellers from being drafted overseas – all much to everybody's embarrassment. She went to the extent of planting a weeping willow in Cracknell's garden, at Sarratt, Hertfordshire (which was known ever afterwards as 'Peggy's Tree'), in the hopes of propitiating him. The tree would be the object of a strange veneration years later: 'Peter, as we all know, was very close to his mother,' explained Cracknell, a week after Sellers had died, 'and he believed he was in spiritual touch with her. To be close to her he would come here and pay homage to her by hugging the tree. It was a very moving scene. He was very sentimental and used to say, "I feel my mother here." He was quite sincere and not a bit theatrical. Last October [1979] he said he would love some cuttings from the willow to plant in the garden of his house in Switzerland. I gave him three beautiful cuttings and I hear they have grown beautifully. He told me the day he planted them was a Friday, which meant a double celebration, because every Friday he would light a candle to his mother. His last visit to me was strange. I thought he looked ill. As I walked out with him to his car on leaving, Peter suddenly came up and kissed me on the cheek. It felt strange. I had never been kissed before by a man. But it was a very warm gesture. I did wonder about him. I think he did have a premonition about the end.'

His premonitions, indeed, were connected with that tree – which did not quite flourish in Switzerland, despite what Cracknell believed. Sellers had to receive permission from the customs and excise department before he could export the saplings. It was quite a bureaucratic palaver. On the day he was to make his last flight to England, he called Jeffery into the kitchen at the Gstaad chalet. Two big crows were pecking at the cuttings, and one of the birds flew at the window and flapped against it. Sellers took this as an omen of death. He had the willow pulled up and burnt.

☆ ★ ☆

Though it obviously wasn't going to be as straightforward as telling Brother Cornelius to lay off with the stick, Peg needn't have fretted. Sellers was able to cope with military discipline by rising above it. In fact, rules and regulations brought out his rebelliousness and stubbornness, and the adult Sellers now starts to emerge. The grown-up society of his childhood had made him very direct, as far as dealing with other people went. Peg had given him no doubts about his superiority. As Jack Salt says: 'He would tell you to your face what he thought of you. He'd criticise your music, for example, whereas most people wouldn't do that.' And so, though molly-coddled, and demeaned, by Peg's presence, he was by no means a cat's paw. Actually, he felt inviolate, and he knew that the war would never be any more dangerous than being in the wolfcubs – a view shared by Ralph Reader.

Reader never forgot their first encounter. He was on an RAF station where the notices had been posted inviting anyone interested in joining the Gang Shows to make contact; and Sellers did. Reader was only allowed to recruit from the ACH (GD) rank; and of this group he was not permitted to approach engineers, tradespersons, or people with a useful skill of any description. 'What do you do?' he asked Sellers, who was classed amongst these lowest of the low. 'Play the drums a bit,' he replied. 'Anything else?' – 'Well I can do some bits of *ITMA*.' Reader said to come to the NAAFI (the Navy, Army and Airforce Institutes canteen) the next morning for an audition.

'The next day, as I walked in, I heard myself singing "Riding Along on the Crest of a Wave", even worse than I do sing it. I walked up the steps on to the stage and there was Peter Sellers entertaining six airmen, who were meant to be cleaning out the hall, by giving an impression of me! As soon as I stepped on the stage, the airmen, naturally, stood to attention. Sellers hadn't seen me and carried on until he realised something was up. He stopped and turned round: "Well," he said, "do you want a drink or do I get jankers?"'*

They had a cup of tea and Sellers was hired.

☆ ★ ☆

Reader was Sellers' second impresario, after Waldini. The difference between them was that where Waldini had given employment and security at Ilfracombe, Reader was the one responsible for helping Sellers to run away from home. He was put into the RAF Gang

---

* *Jankers: n.obs.* British services term for punishment of defaulters. Origin uncert. possibly echoic for jangles or janglers, the sound made by a provost sergeant's keys. See *Ross*, Rattigan's play about T.E. Lawrence: 'None of your lip, Parsons now – unless you want a dose of jankers.'

Show Unit Number 10, and he toured the Hebrides and the Ork-
neys before leaving for the East – and he was always to be more like
Ralph Reader than Ralph Reader. When Sellers went on a television show in the Fifties, called *Alfred Marks Time*, it was to appear
in a sketch as the great Gang Show showman: 'an uncanny impersonation,' says Dick Vosburgh, who wrote the script. 'The
orchestra and the audience were hysterical. Later we had the real
Ralph Reader himself on the series – we were told, "He was funnier
last time." People thought Sellers had been the real one.'

RAF Gang Shows had grown out of Reader's devotion to the
self-sufficiencies of scouting. He had been raised by aunts in Crew-
kerne (his parents having died of tuberculosis when he was a baby)
and as soon as he dared he scarpered to Ireland and New York. His
account of his childhood seems like the tale of a cheerful boy from a
Dickens musical. He would perhaps have been a reprobate, had he
not, first, decided to structure his life according to the precepts in
Baden-Powell's manly handbooks and, second, found a purpose in
life through show business. He'd appeared in village concerts when
he was in Ireland; in America he met Al Jolson and Jack Oakie,
with whom he toured. He even understudied Jolson (in a musical
called *Big Boy*), who was to remain his idea of the perfectionist
entertainer. Reader appeared in and choreographed Flo Ziegfeld
revues for Broadway and though he returned to England to work
for Sir Charles Cochran and devise shows with titles you'd never get
away with today – *Gay Deceivers, Yes, Madam,* and *Please, Teacher*
– he became much more American than British in his accent, dress,
and disdain for the London sloth and cold. He produced Ivor
Novello spectaculars at Drury Lane and directed the dance
sequences in various plays by Noël Coward.

Meantime, bolstering all this moonlight and filigree, there was
the wholesomeness of the scouts. Reader was a Patrol Leader and
made the observation that 'the healthiest smell of a Scout uniform
should be smoke from a camp fire' – though he had the lads on
stage, not running about the woods and glades. He organised concerts with increasing hundreds of participants – and in October

1932, when people realised the performances were getting to be annual events (an enthusiastic helping-hand backstage was Tom Driberg), the Gang Shows were officially born. They were a mixture of sketches and songs – 'Steer for the Open Sea', 'Birds of a Feather', 'These Are the Times', and, of course, the ritualistic 'We're Riding Along on the Crest of a Wave'. By order, this was sung at the start and end of every RAF Gang Show performance.

During the war, Reader produced patriotic masques and mystery plays at the Albert Hall, with Olivier, Henry V himself, in his Naval uniform, declaiming from Shakespeare; Churchill, the image of Sir John Falstaff, also put in a personal appearance. At the suggestion of Air Commodore Archie Boyle, District Commissioner for Lambeth North scout troup, as well as being the Deputy Director of Intelligence in the RAF, Reader went to France, with ten ex-Gang Show artistes, to give concerts under the ENSA banner. The rehearsals at Drury Lane and the previews at RAF stations outside London, and the set-ups in barns, tents and on the backs of lorries, went well – so the first RAF Gang Show Unit soon became officially established, with routings arranged by the Air Ministry (i.e. Cracknell). Reader avoided paperwork if he could and appeared as a guest star in all his Units. There were twenty five ultimately. Above Reader was a Wing Commander, who reported to a Group Captain, who was answerable to an Air Commodore. All these figures in the chain of command, none of them with a theatrical background, wanted to impose their stamp on the Gang Show. (The whole caboodle came under the jurisdiction of the Directorate of Air Force Welfare.) But Reader, who had total faith in his formula of apple-cheeked optimism and sentiment, by-passed the mandarins of Houghton House and met Tedder, Air Chief Marshal and top cheese. Reader, who by now had units in Normandy, wanted further men to tour India and Burma. Hence his subsequent search for such as Sellers – chaps on the lowest pay scale in the Air Force, who would not be permitted (unlike official bandsmen) to augment their income with extracurricular concerts.

Accounts of Ralph Reader's achievements tend to rub in what a hard worker he was – he never took leave, the audiences always cheered him to the very echo, etc.. Whilst not deprecating his enthusiasm, or mocking the corniness of the Gang Shows themselves (they became a national institution between 1932 and 1974, and I just about recall recoiling from them when they were televised); whilst I will not pause to frown over the fact that his modest monicker, at his own suggestion, was 'Chief', or to snigger at the latent pederasty in anybody who spends a lifetime turning the boy scouts into a chorus line (yes, I am sure, they were more innocent times) – I *do* want to see how the Broadway-cum-Baden Powell vision affected Sellers. The huge and benumbing Scala Theatre and Albert Hall rallies were not to Sellers' taste. Men, in the manner of chorines in the Busby Berkeley films he'd seen as a child, were merged into a mass. It was crowd art – which did, however, appeal to Ribbentrop, who'd met Reader at the Holborn Restaurant and had offered him work in the Hitler Youth Movement. (Reader later conducted six Wagnerian gods around London, and they dined at his home. He was still 'closely in touch by mail with various members of the Hitler Youth Movement' in 1939. The information was divulged regularly to Archie Boyle.) What Sellers enjoyed, once he'd finished the briefings in London, were the Gang Show splinter groups, the ring of a dozen or so on the road. It was a continuation of his ordinary life (without his parents). And it released a recklessness in him, quiescent perhaps since Ma died and he'd lacked a round-the-clock admiring audience if he'd felt like pushing people into the fireplace. Now, in a bunch of boys he could charm and amuse with his mimicry, bound for Bombay, he could freak out.

His unit included Gene Patton, Wally Sparks, Harry Kane, Les Osborne, Bill Wilkie, G.F.X. Taylor, Ben Novak, Maurice Arnold, and Dudley Jones, who was in charge. Sellers played the drums in the five-piece band and took part in comedy sketches. He also developed a ten minute solo spot, imitating *ITMA*:

Mrs Mopp: Would you do something for me, sir?
Handley: Certainly, Mrs Mopp – what is it?
Mrs Mopp: Would you take the elephant out of my room, sir? I never know which end he's speaking from.

Handley: Well, listen, Mrs Mopp – you throw a bun at him, and if it bounces back, it's the other end.
Mrs Mopp: Oh, thank you, sir. T.T.F.N. [Ta Ta for now]

Sellers also began, as he travelled the sub-continent by lorry and train, to pay attention to alien sounds and sights. The bearded holy musketeers and people who pissed in the street; the cripples, cows, monkeys and rats; the colour, dust and mobs clinging to the wagon-lits. With Ben Novak, Sellers developed a way of keeping back the natives, with their live chickens and tea things, when they threatened to swarm over the airmen's space – they'd start to quarrel in what sounded like Hindi, but which was, Jones explains, 'absolute codswallop. Neither of them spoke a word of it. But the four million Indians stood and gazed in wonder and no one ever tried to get into our carriage.'

As Sellers told Peter McDonagh in his British Forces Broadcasting Service interview: 'We became the remnants of the last of the British Raj. India was rampant with majors and colonels – types we have used since. Spike Milligan was born in Quetta, up on the North-West Frontier – his father was in the Indian Army – and he picked up the so-called Bombay-Welsh accent, and I picked it up, just through being there.

'We subsequently used it in some of the [Goon] shows, before the Asians started coming over here . . . I must be attracted in some way to them, whether it's to a certain tic or idiosyncrasy, or the warmth of their personality or their character. At the time, I didn't realise I was picking up their sounds, their styles and their thinking. I was too young to realise the general sort of feeling of Indian philosophy; but, in later life, of course I have.

'I like them. I like the fact that they were partly British, and the little in-jokes . . . When the British left, we did a good thing because, there's no doubt about it, the Indians were fed up with us. . . .'

By the end of 1944, they were in Calcutta: 'Laughs! Laughs!! and more Laughs!!!' the audience was promised by the poster. Performances were daily at ten-thirty, from Friday December the 1st to

Thursday the 7th, at the New Empire (though they stayed over until the New Year). The advance publicity, for 'A Ralph Reader Prodn.,' claimed that 'There are only ten of them, every one of them with a reputation on the Music Hall stage at home, and some who, I feel sure, will fill a big place in the entertainment world of the post war years.' They were indeed a hit. 'Two hours of laughter,' continued the local reviewer. 'The best of its kind in the last twenty years. Not a minute of boredom, not a second when we were not filled with admiration for the all-round talent of this happy group.'

The New Empire was in fact a cinema, built originally to house the touring theatre companies out from Edwardian England, but electrified with the arrival of the talkies. The General Manager of the Humayan Associated Theatres, in Calcutta, was Frank Wildish, who was thirty-five in 1945, and he wrote to me after I'd appealed for information on Sellers in one of the veterans' newsletters: 'My company gave the use of The New Empire (the cinema in question) to ENSA for free morning shows for the troops. Early 1945 I was back after nearly five years in the Indian Army, and one of the highlights of the ENSA invasion was Ralph Readers' *The Gang Show No. 10*, and Peter Sellers was in the show and gave an outstanding performance as the drummer in the all cast musical finale at the end of the first half. The show played to a packed house every morning . . . and in fact I went into the theatre each morning just to see and hear that fantastic finale to the end . . . and to watch this talented young man really give a resounding performance. After they played our one theatre in Calcutta, they went on tour under the control of Jack Hawkins and ENSA. However, Bill Sutton and Norrie Paramor [RAF officers] came to check that the "Boys" were keeping Ralph Reader's flag flying. Ted Shoesmith, a friend of mine also with Reader, told me that the Gang Shows did tour England after the war, playing all the known Empires. . . .'

Mr Wildish's letter confirms the critic's comment in the Bombay *Sunday Standard*: 'The "baby" of the show is Peter Sellers, aged 19, the boy-drummer and impressionist. A big future lies before him.'

☆ ★ ☆

A big future nearly lay behind him, for Sellers, if he is to be believed, was not content to confine his performances to the stage. As he said in 1962: 'I think it must have been while I was in India in the war that I found out I could do impersonations. I used to get up to all sorts of larks . . . We had skips full of costumes and uniforms for the performances – I used to dress up as an officer and stroll into the officers' mess [*high, slurred, upper-class note*]: "Hallo, mind if I join you? What unit . . . ? I'm from the Air Ministry. . ." Or I'd be a Flight Sergeant if I felt like it. Once I was a Sikh Officer. Once, when I was abroad, I dressed up as an Air Commodore. I must have been the youngest Air Commodore in the service – I was only about twenty-three. I put a bit of grey on the sides of my hair, it must have been too obvious for words – but, it was Christmas Eve, everybody was blind drunk, otherwise I should never have got away with it. I actually got talking to an Air Vice-Marshal, sitting at the bar, arm round my shoulders [*matey gesture, confidential tone*]: "I shaid to Tedder. . . ."'

Some sources put it about that it was Lord Tedder himself, Knight Grand Cross of the Order of the Bath, Commander-in-Chief (Middle East) and Commander-in-Chief of the (Mediterranean) Allied Air Forces and, later, Chief of the Air Staff and Deputy Supreme Commander next to Dwight D. Eisenhower and, incidentally, from 1950 a governor and Vice Chairman of the BBC, whom Sellers dared to mimic. Quizzical of demeanour, twinkling of eye, Tedder was 'the most unstuffy of great commanders' (according to *The Times'* obituary, June 5th 1967), 'who could be found sitting cross-legged, jacketless, pipe smouldering, answering questions on a desert air strip'. Sellers did indeed use him – Tedder is Nayland Smith in *The Fiendish Plot of Dr Fu Manchu*. But back in 1944? Except as part of a sketch? And on other occasions, when asked what he did in the war, Sellers pre-dated his Air Commodore stunt by four years: 'Even to me this seemed to be pushing my luck a bit far, for I was barely nineteen.'

Tall stories? It is all reminiscent of Dan Mendoza in a holiday humour, riding a Clydesdale into the Pump Room at Bath (or whatever) in his rollicking *Memoirs*. The wonder is that Sellers leaves off telling us he drove a herd of cattle through Monty's boudoir kitted out as a Regimental Sergeant Major in the WRVS . . . I have found no witnesses for the Far East pranks. When his tours took him back to Europe, however, and the Gang Show visited France and Germany, ('the Riviera, Cannes, and Bandol, marvellous luck . . .') people did start to notice a proliferation of anonymous flying officers and wing commanders – Sellers. The character actor David Lodge says Sellers once went into the Sergeants' mess as a Flight Lieutenant and led a rousing toast: 'Gentlemen, it has been delightful being with you this evening, but I am afraid I must drag myself away. My lad here [the towering and stocky Lodge] informs me that we have a long journey ahead of us. . .' And off they'd depart, the theatre troupe. 'I found it more agreeable', Sellers later reasoned, 'spending my time in the Officers' Mess than in the crowded other-ranks canteen. In good time I would withdraw from the bar and duly make my appearance with the Gang Show. In the early morning we would be off again to the next stop. No one knew or cared who the young officer in the bar was or where he had gone.'

The Sikh Flying Officer, organising rations of fresh food; the South African Group Captain, at large in Burma; the Indian fighter pilot, with medal ribbons and a white turban with the RAF badge, getting people to salute him in Dieppe; a Maharajah received with full honours . . . Even if Sellers was only some of these (a famous man's past engenders apocrypha), there was more passing through his mind than a simple desire to dress up and get away with it. At one level, of course, it was indeed straightforward roistering – a love of the danger of exposure and discovery, japes to get a lot of people admiring him. (That's how the behaviour has always been passed off by those who knew him: 'Peter was within an ace of being court-martialled dozens of times,' Lodge said delightedly in 1964.) But I rather think there was something unbalanced about the escapades. They were vanishing tricks. Sellers would leave behind, for a while, the muddle of touring and the pressure to be cheerful – Bluebottle's imbecile cub-scouting etc.. Now he could forage, amuse himself with the ease of his masquerades. It would be another ten years before he'd start to worry about disguise having closed him off from his real self ('What is me? I just don't know,' he'd sigh in *Picturegoer*). As for now, and whether he did become all those officers he confessed to, or whether many were mystifications, or obvious frolics he enjoyed with Lodge at Camp Gutersloh, the fact is he had a compulsion to flout the conventions of military life by treating uniforms as costumes and rank as a part you've been assigned in a play. He removed himself from the world by treating it as theatre (or music hall).

☆   ☆   ☆

As Sellers' confidence in his ability to be taken for other people grew, his acting genius germinated at the expense of a capacity (or desire) to differentiate fantasy from reality – and in the long term his divorce from reality would be complete. (When he was demobilised he strutted around England believing he was an earl.) This was no sudden derangement. The chopping and changing of childhood addresses, a mercurial mother, an affectless father, and the nature of the flickering and giddy profession they were in: all this was recipe enough to create a flighty, floating temperament, which wouldn't be disorientated by war, which could *use* the disruptions to advantage. 'Good night to you all, and God bless you,' he liked to believe he'd once said, with feeling, when quitting a sergeants' mess – where he'd graciously accepted a vote of thanks: 'I would like to thank you very much, sir, and say 'ow much we appreciate your coming into our mess. All the compliments of the season to you, sir.'

Sellers wished to be taken for a Lord of Misrule. 'Deceptions like these gave Dad a great kick,' said his son, Michael. *Deceptions*, note, not histrionics. When he was in France and Germany, travelling around the airfields, entertaining the victorious RAF and staying in what were until recently Luftwaffe messes (with their marble pissoirs and cubicles specially reserved for the Führer), Sellers became a dealer in fancy chocs, cigarettes and engine oils – liberating the military's quota and passing it on to the starved locals: 'you know ... flogging petrol on the black market in the South of France; a franc millionaire I was!' He was a con-man, a spieler, and he enjoyed being one step ahead of the Military Police. On his way from the Place Vendôme, through Lyon, Avignon, the villages and towns of the Languedoc and thence to the Pyrénées, he racketeered in shoes, soap, and blankets – which could be run up into jackets. 'A glorious orgy of free enterprise!' in the words of David Lodge. Sellers, good at sewing (had he helped Peg in her sempstressing?), made a suit out of a Canadian battledress, picking off the insignia and improvising shoulder pads from First Aid bandages. In Cannes, he arranged to sell a large tin of petrol for two thousand francs to the owner of the Toupée Nightclub – and this was an offence punishable by a long jail sentence there, Cannes being in an American zone. Sellers used his profits to buy champagne. (The exchange rate was 450FF to the £ sterling.) Back in Paris, he took a private box at the Opéra Comique and watched *La Bohème*, sipping endlessly at fizz.

Lodge found Sellers' behaviour ulcer-inducing at the time. He'd first met the harum-scarum drummer at a camp in Gloucester. He was another of Ralph Reader's recruits and Sellers had the next bed along in the hut. Sellers was arguing heatedly with a singer called Freddie Brent – and Lodge, getting fed up, handed Sellers a poker: 'Listen, son, if he keeps on, wrap this across his bloody head!' Amazingly, Sellers took him at his word. Lodge intervened, Brent went off in disgust, and Sellers could see Lodge would be valuable from that moment. Not only Sellers. Lodge met Peg and Bill before the RAF Gang Show set forth for France, and was told: 'David, I want you to promise you will keep an eye on Peter while you are over there on the Continent.' So Lodge became another figure to disobey and run rings round. When they took the boat train to Paris and reported to the Dufayel Barracks, a transit camp, Sellers, outraged that the Americans had taken the best billets – and then, as later, not liking to be told where he'd be dossing down – made his group pool their cash and find a hotel, which they did. A brothel in the Pigalle district. Lodge had to rescue Sellers from the arms of two whores and push a wardrobe in front of the bedroom door to stop his charge from getting out and back at them.

☆ ★ ☆

Sellers was in his early twenties. Why the chaperonage?

It was because carelessness and indifference to others had already encompassed his becoming a cold and absent father. As he said in 1980, reality slipping away: 'I've got an illegitimate daughter running around somewhere . . . She doesn't know I'm her Dad. Her mother decided to put her into a home, one of those places where they take away your name and people adopt you, and they never tell you who your real parents are. And yet sometimes, I really somehow feel her presence. And the awful thing is, I think she might feel mine too. I just don't know where to begin to find her and I've made several attempts. . . .' Explaining how he met her mother in India, Sellers added: 'I was a young twit and didn't realise what was going on around me. I was there because of the Second World War and we were the last remnants of the British Raj.' (A phrase he took to mean we were the conquerors and could do as we liked.)

How much of *this* is fantasy? Peter Evans, who wrote a book on Sellers in 1968, and interrogated him intensively on his past, recording hours of conversation and reminiscence, thinks we have to tread warily: 'Peter Sellers', Evans said to me, 'was created by Peter Sellers. He was liable to invent any new history and background for himself – for example, the lost love-child and the early romance, which he decided had haunted him for years . . . Now, he never gave any hint of this to me, and we'd been all over his early life.'

Just as dressing up as Air Commodores and Lord Tedder were improvements on what really happened, whoppers sanctioned by the time etc., with the point nevertheless being made that the impulse to manipulate and dissemble was genuine, so too may the adopted-away daughter have a number of ramifications. First, when the news was broken by Sellers, he was near death and the tackle of his heart, like Lear's, was cracked and burned. He felt he could only survive through the destruction of others, and was re-drafting his will, leaving people out and just as vindictively putting alternative names in. The principal non-beneficiaries were his three children. How it would have appealed to him, therefore, the vision of a lost child – who could take on, in his imagination, all the ideal qualities of absolute devotion and success, loving him more than words can wield the matter. He was duplicating Peg's feelings over his still-born elder brother: a lost child is a perfected child, immune from the depredations and lacks of those who live out their lives in the real world; real children might not feel like heaving their hearts into their mouths every five minutes.

Sellers' announcement of a hidden daughter, his preference for dream over flesh and blood, could be convincingly explained away, therefore, as a symptom of his solitariness and infirmity. He could cope best with those who didn't have a working pulse. If he *did* father an illegitimate child, then the futility of his quest wasn't missed by Lynne Frederick, his fourth and as it happened last wife: 'I can't say whether it's something that haunts Peter or not,' she told Roderick Gilchrist, briskly. 'How does one person know what is in another's heart? I know that Peter did try very hard several years ago to find her, but the adoption societies are very strict and would not open their books. ... You see, she doesn't know that she is Peter's daughter, because no one will have told her. . . . So it's not a case of her reading in the paper who her father is and getting in touch with him.'

It is possible that this 'several years ago' may have been connected with an Act of Parliament passed in 1975 allowing adopted people over the age of eighteen years of age the right to apply for information on their natural parents – a change in the law, incidentally, which inspired P.D. James' thriller about proofs of identity and forgotten crimes, *Innocent Blood*. ('I am the same person as I was yesterday,' one of the characters says, 'But who was I yesterday?' And of another character it is observed: 'None of us can bear too much reality. No one. We all create for ourselves a world in which it's tolerable for us to live. You've probably created yours with more imagination than most. . .') But that law is for the child, not the mother and father – though the publicity it received may have tipped Sellers off, encouraging him to unlock a secret. I'm guessing.

So, by the looks of Sellers' pose in the photograph accompanying Gilchrist's article, was Sellers. He leans moodily on the wrought-iron balcony of a Dorchester suite, his hand, no doubt to prop up his weary head, resting on his cheek. Though his eyes are hidden behind photochromatic spectacles (Sellers was one of the first people to wear these semi-sunglasses), there is no ambiguity about his vantage point: Sellers is looking down on the world – at the leafless trees, the speeding taxi cabs and buses in Park Lane; at the people dotted here and there whose lives have no connection with his own. Aware as I am that he has assumed the posture for a newspaper snapshot, I still sense an intense hopelessness about Sellers here. From where he is standing, no voice can reach him. The picture, entitled 'Sellers in London . . . "I've tried to find her"', imparts a bleakness – the more so, paradoxically, if he is having to play-act. A better caption, however, might be Sellers' remark made to John Taylor a few weeks earlier in Paris: 'You'd think a million pounds would buy you anything, but it won't you know.' (Taylor commented, 'He didn't tell me what it would not buy.')

☆ ★ ☆

Whether or not there was an actual child, rather than an apparition which filled a psychological need, it is possible to specify Sellers' candidate for the mother: Nora Barnacle, whom he fell for way back at St Mark's Kindergarten, Regent's Park. His first love. (Was she re-discovered in India?)* When he met Anne Howe, whom he

---

* Alexander Walker's 'Authorised Biography' mentions the episode only in the vaguest terms. The woman's identity is concealed behind the nickname 'Sky Blue' and she worked 'for a Government department in Whitehall'. The baby happened because Sellers 'got her drunk and deliberately made her pregnant.' Though I often think my subject was a very shabby human being indeed, statutory date-rape is not something I'd want to direct against him on this occasion.

was to marry, Sellers insisted on taking her around the streets and favourite places he'd come to know with Nora. 'He was already living in the past,' Anne said to me. 'And the strange thing about this was, we'd been married a while and I was in hospital having a miscarriage and Peg, whom I didn't get on with at all at this stage – she was always interfering – Peg decided to get hold of Nora Barnacle, and invited her up to the flat and invited Peter – knowing of his sentimentality over old times. She wanted to get them together again. Of course he told me about it. He did see her, and maybe they went out. I don't know.' Anne also added, 'You see, when I first met him and I had to traipse round the places he'd been to with his first girlfriend, it's because he'd had a child by her when he was quite young, when he went into the RAF.'

Michael Sellers continues the story: 'This other woman, the one Peg wanted him to marry – they had a daughter. My father claimed it was with her anyway. He brought her round to meet me once – years and years ago. I was sick in bed, aged about twenty, with glandular fever, and he brought this woman to see me. And they'd had a daughter, apparently. Someone I know knows where she is – the child. She must be forty now at least, and married. She doesn't know who she is as far as being the daughter of Peter Sellers is concerned . . . My father's old sweetheart was an ordinary, house-wifey type, far removed from his usual brigade of dolly birds. She made the comment about me that, "Yes, Peter, he's got a lot of your features. . ."'

A final sliver of evidence comes from Milligan, who said to me, 'You know he had an illegitimate child? Once, when we were in his car, he stopped outside a house in Highgate and told me to "go over to that house and ask them how my daughter is". Of course, I wouldn't go. His secret baby. *That* night he knew where she was.' The most likely explanation is that this was Nora's or her family's home. By sending Spike over with such a message, Sellers, with malice in his swelling heart, was calculating on causing maximum hurt.

There are connections to be made here with Sellers' own condition, of course, as Peg's changeling boy; and we might add in, too, his endless inquisitions about who he really was. 'I long ago gave up the search for my own personality,' he said in 1959, wishfully thinking himself a ghost. 'I sometimes feel I'm not really here as a person – only as a rôle in a play or a film or radio series.' But it would take a fabulist in the Edgar Allan Poe class to depict all the subterranean cross-currents which are at work. Richard Henry's becoming Peter; John Taylor eating his solitary meals; Anne's miscarriage; the dispossession of Sellers' known issue; the inquiries he said he made to the Registrar General for access to the original records of his lost child's birth – a lost daughter who was also an invisible step-sister . . . Also relevant to the psychodrama is his fondness for younger women as he got older – women who were his children's contemporaries. He said once to Dorothy Squires, 'Dot, love, I can't help it,' and she said, 'You are your own worst enemy, going round with all these starlets.' – 'But I just can't help it.' Sellers was a man divided against himself. Doubles, deaths; births, bereavements; disappearances, wronged suitors, and people discovering who they are. It is all one.

☆　★　☆

Sellers looked back at the wartime as his Robin Hood days. When Lodge, who grew up to become a man much dedicated to charitable work, a grandee in the Water Rats and the Variety Club, asked him to read the manuscript of his memoirs, *Up The Ladder of Obscurity*, Sellers commented: 'It was a very nostalgic and enjoyable trip down memory lane and it brought back many thoughts of the wild times we had together. It is a barrel-load of laughs for us, but they don't make 'em like us any more. You can't get the wood, you know.'

What comes through in Lodge's book, however, is that there was a fair amount of rage within the sapling Sellers' recklessness. He strutted about at night pretending his banjo case was a machine gun, and Lodge had his work cut out preventing Sellers from slinking off to find a woman. He did escape in Toulon – Lodge was nervous later lest his ward had copped a dose of clap (which presumably, in the absence of any hints about Sellers-being-a-father, Lodge must have assumed was the peril worrying Peg). 'Oh, he was a real ladies' man,' Lodge was quoted as saying in the *TV Times*, three years after Sellers' death, 'The trouble he got me into. . .'

But there was another side to the hot-headedness, a sullenness – a maudlin streak which was the obverse of the impishness. Two years after having known Jack Salt in Brighton, Sellers phoned him in Poona from Ceylon. He was feeling lonely. (This was 1945.) He was delighted to rendezvous with Waldini, the gypsy band now plying their Hungarian airs in Rangoon. He was ready to reminisce. One girl he met amongst the paddy fields and coconuts, and who was exposed to his serious side, was Marjorie Smith, a member of the WRAF stationed in Colombo. She herself was involved with a concert party, in between less colourful duties, and was initially disappointed that her show and rehearsals were to be scrapped to make way for Ralph Reader's merry men. They commandeered the dressing rooms and stage facilities. 'I can remember how disappointed I was that the dress I had laboriously made out of mosquito netting for one of my numbers wouldn't be seen. . . .' Despite her reservations, however, Marjorie Smith was enchanted by *The No. 10 Gang Show*. 'It was a very slick revue, with female impersonations, sketches, and a band that brought the place alive . . . The drummer was a gawky young man with dark wavy hair called Peter Sellers, and to this day I've never heard anyone play the drums with the same skill . . . This particular young man obviously had a bit extra. His female impersonations were hilarious and his self-assurance and style . . . were nothing short of pure professionalism.'

There is a danger, when people look back at an early brush with somebody who went on to be a star (in any field), that their recollections are honed, somehow, to fit. The past organises itself to prophesy the future that came about. Look at those books on Lord Wilson of Rievaulx which include a photograph of the child Harold on the steps of Number 10 Downing Street. The implication is that a force of destiny hovered over the lad, whereas, I'm sure, millions of tourists must have posed thus, in the days before the Prime Minister's residence was gated off. So with Sellers in the RAF Gang Show. Competent, lively, full of himself – but if he hadn't become

Peter Sellers, he'd have faded along with other members of the travelling units, each group consisting of a dozen men under the leadership of a Flight Sergeant. Twenty five Gang Show units at a complement of twelve is three hundred souls under Ralph Reader alone.

Where Marjorie Smith's account has value, however, when we are assessing and rejecting evidence (the biographer is a circuit judge, a forensic scientist, a historian of a one-person city state), is in the glimpse we suddenly get of Sellers in repose. He was encountered on the beach, where my eye-witness shared a fresh pineapple with him, and he moaned about the fact he couldn't sing. 'I really do wish I could sing, Marjorie. It would be marvellous to have a voice like Sinatra.' She asked him why he simply couldn't go ahead and get himself trained. 'Because I'm no good at it,' he replied categorically. 'There is one thing though that I'd like to be able to do even more – act. I don't just mean run of the mill stuff. I mean proper acting, something that will gain respect.'

We may make of that last emphatic assertion what we will, but the fragment about Sellers lamenting he'd not develop into a straight romantic player, that for all his own energy and twinkle he'd never be like the lead in *Anchors Aweigh* – that his exuberance was going to have to be differently expressed from Sinatra's or Gene Kelly's: that is worth attention. Never has a performer been more indignant about having to be a character actor than Sellers. (Charles Laughton's story is the sado-masochistic love-affair he had with his physical repulsiveness.) He was envious of handsome men, and did his best to convert himself into one.* The wafer-thin Sellers of *Casino Royale* and the long-faced cockerel, Robert Danvers, in *There's a Girl in My Soup*, are nearly five stones lighter than the burly figure photographed at radio microphones, doing the Goons. Paradoxically, the slimmer he became, the less funny his films – the lustre of stardom waned as he did. This is because – Evelyn Tremble in *Casino Royale* is the prime example – he'd decided he wanted

---

* And he tried to destroy at least one. His otherwise unfounded hatred of Anthony Franciosa, the co-star of *Ghost in the Noonday Sun*, is an example.

to stroll across the lens and be taken for himself, elegant and sophisticated. But the vanity would kill him. Losing weight very fast in 1964, the better to consort with Britt Ekland, he disrupted his metabolism and triggered the heart disease which haunted him always. (Taking off the pounds he'd gained for *Being There*, he arrived on the set of *The Fiendish Plot of Dr Fu Manchu* haggard, virus-prone, and inlaid with bedsores.) Sellers never forgave the world for not having made him automatically irresistible to women – so he'd always seduce them with a combination of his fame and the little boy lost act. Michael Sellers said to me: 'He knew he could have charisma. He explained to me one night, at a *Pink Panther* reception in San Diego, and I was using one of the maids for more than cleaning the room, and he said: "*You* have to be careful. In *my* position, I can have any woman I want." – "I know that. I can see that – but all these women are not available to *me*!"' Michael went on to add: 'He liked to identify with a lot of his womanising characters, especially Robert Danvers: "My God, but you're lovely!"' – though the joke *there*, is that Sellers was giving, vocally, a sly impersonation of Roy Boulting, who'd recently married Hayley Mills.

It was as if he regretted having to be a comic actor. That way, it was harder to be adored. Asked once about his early heroes, he said it was mostly good-looking people he admired: 'Mostly the handsome, the very handsome types – I used to envy them very much. Bob Wagner I did a film with once [*The Pink Panther*, 1963]. I remember sitting talking to him, and he said: "You know – I must say I've got great admiration for your acting ability. My problem is, I'm only good-looking." I thought, God Almighty – staving off all those birds! Which he was – they were coming at him – *aahh*! There's another one! Then another would go by . . . *Eeekk* . . . That one's mine, you have that one . . . ! If you really are particularly handsome – you've really got it made. You don't have to do anything else. You can come on and say [*William Mate Cobbler's croak*] "If you look like that, that's it!"'

Sellers seems not only to have confused womanizing with pheasant shooting, but to have also confused modelling with acting.

(Robert Wagner is bearable in *The Pink Panther*, and elsewhere, not because of his grin and dimples, but *despite* these attributes: he mocks the stereotype of the college jock.) Sellers was always to complain that his own was the only brand of performance demanding work – as if instinct and intelligence weren't necessary if you are a fellow girls look at twice. (Tell that to Sinatra, Dirk Bogarde, Paul Newman.) And note how he talks of women! Birds literally as waterfowl to be gunned down. (Such misogyny is rampant in *Casino Royale*, where bombs and mortars, in the shape of pigeons, home in on and destroy a platoon of Bond's beauties.) Sellers longed to be able to make an impression simply by being there – without having to exert himself. (His off-camera rages were efforts to do just that: to leave the impression of keen whips on crew and colleagues.) If he didn't play up, he'd vanish, like hailstones. Thus the rascality of the disguises and messing about – and thus, too, underneath, the wish that he didn't have to do any of it. (How he'd like to have lain back, a Sultan, dipping his fingers into bowls of hot cherry sauce. It would be like infancy all over again – in your bassinet, gazed upon with adoration by the houris waiting to take the stage.) Such were the lessons of his wartime experiences; and by 1964, in the wake of the blitzkrieging *Doctor Strangelove* success, he'd be saying: 'I mean I realise that certain actors project their own image on to the screen – those who are the same on as they are off. But I've never had the necessary statistics to be able to do that sort of thing, and so, anyway, I always wanted to be a character actor.' (As his father Bill would say, you never did.)

In November 1978 Sellers was to co-star with Lynne Frederick, who was nearly thirty years his junior, in *The Prisoner of Zenda*. (His remuneration: $32,142 per week; hers: $4,166.67, plus $2,500 joint living expenses.) Before flying to Vienna to begin the film, the ageing rakehell underwent plastic surgery. Yards of flapping, sagging skin were trimmed from his jawline and chins. (That's why, in *The Prisoner of Zenda*, he wears high collars – to hide the needlepoint in his neck.) He also had the bags under his eyes picked up and carried off. 'I went in the morning and was out in the afternoon,' he said of his trip to the clinic. 'I was recommended a plastic surgeon in Los Angeles who turned out to be an incredibly handsome young man. I went to see him and he said to me, "What is it you want done, Mr Sellers?" I looked up at him and said, "Why, I'd like to look like you."'

☆　★　☆

As a store of feelings to draw on and transmute, Sellers' war was, as they say, formative. It was by now clear that he had no moral sense, no judgement, and that he was never sure quite how to behave or gauge appropriate courses of action – or else he knew all too well and, as David Lodge told Peter Evans, 'All the time it was as if he was seeing how far he could go, what he could get away with next.' The anarchic glee found its way (artistically) into Sellers' taste for cops and robber pictures, *Two Way Stretch, Never Let Go, The Wrong Arm of the Law* amongst them – films in which Lodge, amusingly enough, is often cast in a supporting role which parodies his original real-life job as guardian and chum in the RAF Gang Show. Lodge's Jelly Knight, Dodger Lane's cell-mate in *Two Way Stretch*, for example, is a genial giant, crop-headed and unflurried by prison routine, who works away at his embroidery hoop – and the beauty of the scenes is that he is never less than Little John. The sewing is done casually, and seems a perfectly normal occupation. (The prison governor, Maurice Denham's Cmdr. Horatio Bennet, is an advocate of basket weaving etc.). Watching the film today, see-ing the easy relationship between Jelly and Dodger – Dodger full of wild plans which Jelly either talks him out of or, if he senses their genius, backs him up over – and knowing of the two actors' back-ground in the services: this enriches the flow of the performances they give. Jelly can never stop being amused by Dodger, even when Dodger is infuriating. And the pair of them play off against the third man in the cell, Bernard Cribbins' Lennie Price – the stooge who goes down the sewers or on to the roof of the moving train. (Lennie is a nervy equivalent of the rôle Sellers had in *The Ladykillers*.)

Sellers' craving for disguise, and its crisscross with crookedness,

is the chassis of his vehicle with Britt Ekland, *After the Fox*, shot on
the island of Ischia. Sellers is a gaol-breaking quick-change artiste
who is, by turns, a doctor, an Italian policeman (in full-feathered
head-dress, like a Colonial Governor) and a gesticulatory movie-
maker. Here we have the revue style of costumes and funny voices.
Sellers has no need to sustain each impersonation for very long.
The plot is convoluted, like the director, Vittorio Di Sica's orotund,
drawn-out delivery of an English word, and the film is worthy of
note at this point because of Sellers' evident relish at being, as in
Two Way Stretch and *Wrong Arm of the Law*, at the centre of a gang
– where he has a built-in audience, and none of its constituents can
be certain of what the boss will do next. Dodger Lane, Pearly
Gates, and Aldo Vanucci, are not just criminals: they are touched
with majesty (and with the intemperance and caprice that can traditionally go with being a king).

Interestingly, when Sellers himself was rich, he bought a court of
his own – first Chipperfield Manor, near Kings Langley, Herts, and
later Brookfield, Elstead, near Guildford. He fitted the seats out
with actors, film folk, critics, would-be bit-players, astrologers,
sycophants and real royals – and he could imagine himself monarchical. He'd spend his time, at his garden parties, recording the
gambols of his train with a cine camera – turning life into a newsreel, like the flickering, famous faces at Kane's Xanadu in the 'Time
on the March' sequence. David Lodge, before he married, was a
frequent guest at Chipperfield: 'Peter kept a razor, toothbrush and
pyjamas for me in one of the many spare rooms and I just used it as
my own.' It is impossible not to think of Lear's loyal Earl of Kent,
talking the King out of his tempers – for Lodge was the one Anne
knew who could calm Sellers down, when he started to get violent
and threaten her and the children with, as it might be, milk bottles.
'He'd keep the peace,' she said to me, '"Peter has poured a bottle of
milk on the floor" – and he'd come over and sort it out. Solid and
dependable.' As Lodge said in the *TV Times* piece, 'I don't condone
everything he did; he was apt to act like a child, a spoilt boy.'

Though he does not deny Sellers' ugly side, he would prefer

people not to refer to it and vex Sellers' ghost. (It is as if everybody is still answerable to Peg.) After Michael Sellers' portrait of a demon daddy dearest, *P.S. I Love You,** was serialised in the *Daily Mail*, he wrote in to the editor to complain:

AN INJUSTICE

I was immensely saddened by the excerpts from Michael Sellers' book 'PS: I Love You' which you have been publishing.

I was a close friend of the late Peter Sellers, from our young days as 'erks' in RAF touring concert parties to the day of his death. To see him painted as a total monster incapable of loving or caring or considering others, is to witness a monumental injustice to his memory. That it stems from the pen of his own children makes it unbearable.

Peter, of course, made mistakes and was sometimes hurtful, especially to those he loved dearly. His biggest failing was finding it almost impossible to say he was sorry when full of remorse. To paint the life of any man, warts and all, is one thing. To ignore totally the fair skin, beneath and between the blemishes is to commit a sin of hurtful insensitivity much more heinous than that levelled against the silenced victim.

David Lodge

The scaly, dermatological metaphor is apt. Time and again Lodge had to come between the dragon and his wrath. But if ever there was anybody hurtfully insensitive in the life of others, it wasn't Michael (and all the family collaborated on *P.S. I Love You,*

---

* I'll discuss this book more fully later on. For now it is enough to know that Sellers, though lapping his children in material luxuries, did his best to pass on to them all his own emotional insecurities – it is as though, as a father, he wanted to recreate the disruptions he himself had gone through. He didn't bargain on the sense and sensibility of his wife, Anne, nor on the fact that, after a dozen years of hell, she'd walk out. Nobody had rejected him so decisively before. In many ways, he never recovered from the shock, and revenged himself on his children by leaving them out of his will – an item I have already referred to.

the title of which isn't totally ironical) – as Roy and John Boulting
were quick to point out, replying to Lodge's letter c/o the editor of
the *Daily Mail* on October 1st 1981:

> [. . .] David Lodge's letter, if misguided, does him great credit
> [. . .] However, for David to claim that Michael Sellers' book
> paints him as a total monster is, in our view, ridiculous.
> Throughout, 'P.S. I Love You' is a cry of pain which David
> Lodge, apparently, has not recognised. For those of us who also
> knew Peter Sellers, Michael Sellers' story is only, and too sadly,
> too true.
>
> David Lodge, in the intimacy that he claims, must know this.
> Indeed, there are parts of his letter that support the very ideas he
> seeks to destroy.
>
> [. . .] It would be a pity if [. . .] he preferred the myth to the
> fact.
>
> > Yours, etc.
> > *Roy and John Boulting*

Anne put the problem succinctly: 'Suddenly, after he died, Peter
was canonized.'

☆ ★ ☆

Lodge is correct to try and argue for a sense of proportion where
Sellers' devilish practices are concerned – for Sellers himself tried to
suppress his greed and bumptiousness, by dispersing into impersonations of docile Indians. Dr Ahmed el Kabir in *The Millionairess* is
his most famous example. Sellers, his face stained the colour of
Mocha coffee, has to resist the blandishments of Sophia Loren's
Epifania Parerga – she's a temptress in Pierre Balmain pantyhose.
He, however, is too committed a GP, in his slum-district practice,
to bother about lust, love, and other human distractions. Kabir is
selfless, saintly. He lives to relieve the sufferings of others – sufferings brought about by tycoonery and sweated labour, the very

forces behind the Loren character's wealth. How paradoxical, and Shavian, then, that here she is, offering to fund the construction and running of a huge hyper-modern hospital.

Spoilt, rude, and insufferable, Epifania is much more like the off-screen Sellers himself, temperamentally, than Sellers was in resembling the Doctor; and during the making of *The Millionairess*, it was he who capered nimbly around Loren, trying to be the seducer. Their roles were reversed. He was avid for Loren *and* for Kabir's spirituality. As with the holy men of St Aloysius', Sellers envied his character's calm – which he describes in the film as a state he attains through yoga exercises: 'I try to forget who I am,' says Kabir, 'I sink down deep into my soul – an intermediary stage between being and non-being.'

Sellers was indeed trying to forget who he was – but through acting, not religion. And when he came across equanimity and poise, as in India, and found that other people's placidity nagged him, his way of buying into it was to mimic it. Acting *was* his religion because, to him, his performances were a sort of trance: 'You must keep the flow,' he said in 1962. 'When I'm working in the studio I always eat in my room. I don't eat with other people. That way I keep the flow. When I was playing the Indian in *The Millionairess* I found myself living the part in the strangest way; I almost *became* the Indian. I grew so much like an Indian that off the set real Indians would take me for one of themselves.'

He certainly impressed the great film director Satyajit Ray, who wrote a screenplay for Sellers, called *The Alien* – all about a leafy, lush rural community which has its life transformed by an encounter with an extra-terrestrial. (After infinite permutations and re-writes, the property, quasi-commissioned by Columbia, emerged years later as Spielberg's *E.T.*) Something extraordinary could have come of that project; it would have been hallucinatory, lyric. When Ray went to see Sellers, on the set of *The Party*, however, a coarsening was in evidence: the detail and imponderability of Kabir had gone, to be replaced with a brittle slapstick charm. The Indian sensibility was now an opportunity for gags; and before India fades from my narrative, I am going to hand over to Ray himself, who wrote me the following letter:

Calcutta, India
16.8.90

Dear Roger Lewis,

My abject apologies for the unconscionable delay in answering your letter of May 17th. These last three months were taken up with the completion of my new film.* Since I'm personally involved in all stages of post-production, and since I don't employ a secretary, my correspondence gets sadly neglected. However, I'm free now and have just picked up your card from the enormous pile that awaits my attention.

The Sellers episode is twenty five years old and is already a bit hazy in my mind (I don't keep a diary), perhaps because it ended in such an unsavoury fashion. However, I shall jot down for you whatever I can recall.

I think the first Sellers film I saw was *Tom Thumb*. I thought both he and the film were delightful. This was followed by a number of films in which his talent was not much in evidence. Then came *Doctor Strangelove*, and I was bowled over by his virtuosity in a triple role. Later I saw *The Millionairess* where I found his Indian English very amusing, though not authentic. Anyway, I decided to offer him the part of my Indian businessman in *The Alien*. Mike Wilson, who later negotiated on my behalf, had come down to Calcutta from Colombo with credentials from Arthur C. Clarke, who was a friend of mine and [to] whom I had told the story of *The Alien* in a nutshell. There was no screenplay as yet. Mike made me write it in two months virtually at the point of a gun. I told him there was an important part for Sellers in it, and Mike set about locating Sellers. It turned out that Sellers was in Paris (I can't recall why). Anyway, Mike and I found ourselves in Paris a fortnight or so later and

---

* Ray brought out two films during the period of our correspondence: *Ganashatru (An Enemy of the People)* and *Shakha Proshakha (Branches of the Tree)*.

met Sellers in his hotel. I told him what we had in mind. I made it clear that he wouldn't be playing the lead – but one of the four key rôles – an Indian journalist, an American engineer, an extra-terrestrial creature (ET anticipated by fifteen years!), and an Indian businessman. Sellers said this didn't bother him at all, and that he'd be delighted to work with me. Although he hadn't seen any of my films – 'Jonathan Miller thinks you're one of the best, and that's good enough for me.' The same evening we had dinner with Sellers in his hotel. He didn't know French but knew Franglais. He had us – and a sizeable group of waiters who had gathered around – in stitches with his mimicry.

Miller's credential notwithstanding, I was anxious for Sellers to see one of my films. Mike managed to obtain a copy of *Charulata** – which I rated as one of my best at that time – from London. We screened it for Sellers. He was visibly moved, and the first thing he said was, 'Why d'you need me when you have such wonderful actors in India?' I gave him three reasons: one, there was no actor in India who could play the part quite the way he could; two, I wanted to have the pleasure of working with him; and three, since *The Alien* was to be an international production, it called for the presence of at least one internationally known actor in the cast. Sellers appeared to be satisfied.

The impression I got in Paris was that Sellers was keen to work with me, and liked the idea of the film and his rôle in it. He suggested we meet again after we'd gone a little further with pre-production, and had a finished screenplay to show him.

The next meeting took place in Hollywood. We arrived there later in the year (1967) with the first draft of the screenplay. Most of my films had been based on my own first drafts, and this time too I felt there was no need for a second draft. Columbia had shown interest in putting up the money. So the reason of our Hollywood visit was not just to see Sellers, but also

* *The Lonely Wife* (1964).

to negotiate with Columbia and to find an American actor to play the part of the engineer.

Sellers was shooting (*The Party*), and asked us over to watch him at work and hand him the screenplay. We turned up at the studio where Sellers introduced us to Britt Ekland. We then proceeded to watch the shooting. Sellers was again playing an Indian with the unlikely first name of Hrundi, using brown make up and the same accent he had used in *The Millionairess*. Sellers had already put in a good word for the director, Blake Edwards – 'a genius at improvising sight gags'. I could see Sellers was really enjoying himself.

The scene that was being shot was the high point of the film – the scene of the party. Sellers was one of a dozen or so seated around a dining table. For some reason, Sellers was sitting on a low stool with his chin touching the table surface. Next to him sat an extremely well endowed blonde to whom he ad libbed – 'I once had a friend in Bombay called Bannerji*' – etc. Apparently it was the blonde's cleavage which made him butter his left thumb instead of the toast he was holding. After each take, Sellers and Britt would watch it on video. 'I think I can do better than that, Blake.' – 'Why, I thought that was great, Peter.' – 'No. Let's have another take . . .'

During lunch break, Sellers glanced through the script, stopping to read aloud some of the lines given to the businessman, smiling and nodding in approval.

Living in India, I wasn't familiar with the Goon Shows. On one of the three or four occasions that we met in Hollywood, Sellers introduced me to McGonagall. He had managed to procure a copy of McG's 'Poetic Gems' which he gave me. The inscription

---

* Singhiz Lalkaka Thingz and Babu Banajee (or Bannerji) were characters from *The Goon Show*, played by Sellers and Milligan. 'In all Peter's movies he would put in some private joke, just for the rest of us, that no one else would understand,' said Harry Secombe. ('Quick, nurse, the screens!' for example, was a line of Bloodnok's which Sellers was often prone to come out with.)

read: 'To Satyajit – Without dismay or delay/On this beautiful summer day.'

There was a scene in *The Party* where Hrundi was shown playing the sitar. Ravi Shankar, a good friend of mine, was then living in Los Angeles. Sellers wondered if there would be an opportunity to observe Ravi playing the sitar. On being told, Ravi Shankar promptly invited us and Sellers to dinner. After a gorgeous north Indian meal, RS gave a splendid recital with Sellers sitting cross legged on the floor, his eyes glued on RS's fingers for well over an hour.

The next and last meeting with Sellers was in the restaurant in the Beverly Hills Hotel. In the meantime Sellers had read the script and liked it except for the climactic scene. He went on to describe how he felt it could be made the more effective and affecting. I smiled and said I'd think about it. Sellers then came out with a surprising piece of information. He said he'd lately had his fortune told by an Indian astrologer. 'D'you know what he said? He said I'd soon be working with an Indian director.'

Also, on this occasion, I persuaded Sellers to try and see the first part of the Apu Trilogy when he was back in London.

Within a month or so of returning to Calcutta, I had a letter from Sellers. He had seen *Pather Panchali*,[*] and though he described his reaction in pure McGonagallese, it was obvious that he had been very impressed:

> In the year of 1967 and in the month of December
> An auspicious month coming as it does at the end of the year
> And not the slightest alike to November
> Is a month I will long remember.
> I received one day
> From Satyajit Ray
> Information I required without delay
> So that I could say to my friends the evening of that day:
> The film you are about to see

---

[*] *The Song of the Little Road* (1955).

Is the film of a Trilogy
And is called *Pather Panchali*
In which there is a scene of two children in a field of barley
Watching a train go by
Under an azure sky
So beautiful you want to die

— A few months later I saw *The Party*. I recall regretting that
even a first rate comedian could get enthused over a shoddy
script.* But there was one thing in the film which tickled me.
Towards the end, the following exchange takes place between
Hrundi and the American girl who has befriended him in spite
of his gaucherie:

H: I must go home to my pet monkey.
Girl (surprised): Your pet monkey?
H: Yes. Apu.

Even while in Hollywood, in a series of events too sordid to
describe, I could see *The Alien* project disintegrating. There was
an improvement in the situation after my return to Calcutta, but
only a temporary one, as it turned out. Being of a philosophical
turn of mind, I had prepared myself to accept the inevitable. At
this point came a letter from Sellers. To this day I haven't been
able to fathom why Sellers wrote what he did and the way he
did it. It was as cold and brief as an editor's rejection slip. It said
there was no question of Sellers' participation in *The Alien* project
unless his part was rewritten and expanded: 'I should tell you
straight away that though the part may appear more or less
complete to you, it does not seem so to me and I don't see how
I could contemplate playing it as it is.'

I toyed with the idea of answering in McGonagallese, but felt on

---

* Ray's biographer, Andrew Robinson, in *Satyajit Ray: The Inner Eye* (London,
1989) quotes from a letter Ray wrote to a friend in which he was much more
forthright in his disappointment: '[Sellers] plays an Indian in a Hollywood setting
– quite the most tasteless, heavy-handed caricature of an Indian ever put on the
screen. I was so disgusted that I would in any case have found it most difficult to
work with him.'

reflection that the occasion was too grim for such levity. But since I had to write back, and since I couldn't possibly match the frigid laconicism of his prose, I wrote in verse, an eight line dirge on the demise of our relationship –

> Dear Peter, if you had wanted a bigger part
> Why, you should have told me right at the start.
> By declaring it at this juncture
> You have simply punctured
> The Alien balloon
> Which I daresay will now be grounded soon
> Causing a great deal of dismay
> To Satyajit Ray

I never heard from him again.

> Best,
> Yours sincerely,
> *Satyajit Ray*

P.S. I took some photos on the set of *The Party*. I enclose one showing PS and BE watching a take on video. You're free to use it in your book in case you think it worthwhile.

☆ ★ ☆

Did Sellers think that Ray was a relative? Somebody to whom he could be pissy with impunity? Ray, a kind and generous, uncoercive man, six foot four inches tall and with a basso profundo voice, died on April 23rd 1992. When I look at his beautiful calligraphy, sheet after sheet of swooping lines and arcs – like a text out of the Arabian Nights or something that has flaked off a palace wall – I wish I'd been in a position, when he was still alive, to complete the story for him. I'd give a lot to have received another few leaves inscribed with his reaction. For, though Sellers betrayed Ray, he did not quite abandon *The Alien* – or the idea of Ray-the-absent-guru. At least three years after *The Party*, when *The Magic Christian* was released, and Sellers was appearing on chat shows to try and drum up publicity for it, he was coming out with this sort of comment: 'The *Pather Panchali* trilogy,' he said, 'none of those films made money, but they are great films. Kubrick, whom I consider one of the five great directors in the world, reckons that Satyajit Ray is number two or number one, and I think so too. . . He operates the camera himself incidentally. But for some reason he can't get distribution. Nobody's interested, so he has an art house showing, unfortunately.'

There we have a strong motive for Sellers' obduracy and insensitivity: Ray was not much better than a home-movie maker; his stuff, however artistic and well-regarded by connoisseurs, was not going to beguile a vain international star. (What did Sellers make instead of *The Alien*? The narcissistic *There's a Girl in My Soup*.) There is more to it than this, though. The coincidence of his mentioning Ray's work when *The Magic Christian* had recently been completed is of considerable interest.

The Magic Christian, according to Joe McGrath, was very much Sellers's project. (It was his home-movie.) 'He found the money. He really believed in the movie. That last sequence, with the businessmen going into the shit to grab the free pound notes – we went to America on the QEII, and had an agreement to shoot the scene at the foot of the Statue of Liberty. The shit vat had already been constructed. But Commonwealth United, our financiers, Bernie Confeldt, Henry Unger, people like that, suddenly took grave offence and cut off all our money – so Sellers said, "Fuck them." He raised the extra money himself, so that we could finish the film. We went back again to England and shot it outside the National Film Theatre. Dennis O'Dell, the producer, went into the NFT and said "We're a film crew – can we have lunch here?" – "No, we don't like film crews here. You're nothing but a load of trouble." Terry Southern, Dennis O'Dell, Ringo Starr, me and Sellers, we formed a company, Grand Films, to finish it. . .'

City gents doing the breast stroke and dodging turds; the equivocation of lucre and ordure:[*] this is a long way indeed from the

---

[*] Dickens draws the parallel in *Little Dorrit*, in the character of the tycoon Mr Merdle – and what French word can you pinpoint in that cognomen?

dream-times of Satyajit Ray. I don't think he'd have had much to say about shit vats, unless it was to point out the circular ironies inherent in Sellers, on the one hand wanting to satirise businessmen, and on the other, needing them, and becoming one himself, in order to make a film satirising money and its misuse. . . . But whatever else we might want to say about *The Magic Christian*, nobody is going to dispute its misanthropy. 'The whole thing shows you that every man has his price,' said Milligan, who claimed that Sellers loved it (especially the men-diving-in-tank scene) and 'I loved every inch of it, too. You've really got to hate people to love this film.'

Now whatever else we might say about Ray, he was *not* a misanthrope. His temperament, which imbues his films, is the exact opposite of the narrow and wretched vision found in *The Magic Christian* – it's almost possible to argue that *The Magic Christian* exists simply to deprecate Ray. His films are about possibility, not restriction; they are poetic. The humming telegraph wires, the sight of a steam train, flying insects alighting on a lily pad – simple glimpses like these are all he needs to create the feeling of fantasy in his work. (He is an Imagist – to alter a phrase of Ezra Pound's, Ray's shots and scenes are cinematic language charged with meaning to the utmost degree.) And it is flowers and blooms, the natural history of India, which fill the screen whether his themes are personal or political: the effects of the Second World War on remote villages, who don't even know who is fighting whom; the status of women and their liege lords; the feudal caste system; the country versus the town; modern education versus thousands of years of peasant ignorance (but is it ignorance, as such?). Ray's films are about confrontations and awakenings.

The Alien[*] was not only to have matched a spaceman, and his magical powers, with the hectic fever of rural India; it would also have set up Ray's big heartedness against Sellers' malignancy and

---

[*] The script is published in Ray's *The Chess Players and Other Screenplays* (London, 1989).

condescension. The role Ray wrote for him, Bajoria the business-man (the only rich man in a poor country – another collision) is an amazingly perceptive portrait of the actor. His avidity, his opportunism, his superstitiousness. The alien, having landed his ship in a pond, emerges from the water and begins a series of pranks and miracles. He interrupts the seasons, he gets the dead to walk out of their funeral pyres, he brings on the crops at night. (Here's how that scene is described: 'His eyes turn yellow, and he goes whirling about in the field while all the paddy about him ripens and stands aspiring in the moonlight.') He can listen to the conversation of whirring beetles and plants; he can see every detail of the moon's craters. (It is a replay of the creation of the world.) And Bajoria wants him – or rather, he thinks that the prongs of the spaceship, emerging through the petals and lotus blossom, are the minarets of a lost mosque. If he pumps away the pond water, reveals the temple, and restores it, he'll make himself into a hero. 'I'm giving religion a new lease of life,' he crows.

As we read the script we can see how Sellers' Bajoria was taking shape in Ray's mind. The character is super-subtle – obviously Indian, but full of Western habits and affectations. He drives a limousine; he continually snacks on boxes of candy; he smokes cigarettes. He sweats. There's something slightly sinister and corrupt about him; he taints whatever he touches – especially the space ship/temple, his involvement with which 'helps the country, helps his soul, helps his image'. It is Bajoria, perhaps, who is the alien. Whilst, obviously, not British or American, he is not totally integrated locally, either. (His motor car is an anachronism in the medieval-looking village – where even the space ship could be taken for a fragment of ancient statuary; the limo is *his* space ship.) Who else but Sellers could have portrayed somebody who wasn't quite one thing, wasn't quite another? Who was over-ambitious and always shifting and melting? With the jewelled rings on his fleshy fingers, talkative, nervous and wholly selfish, Bajoria reminds me of Quilty. The line 'Fish are clean! Ever caught a dirty fish?' is pure Quilty.

Though Ray was simply drawing on his knowledge of the kinds of Mephistophelean roles Sellers could best play, Sellers, who by the late Sixties wanted to be considered a playboy in the Cary Grant tradition, was far from flattered by the portrait of Bajoria. He didn't want texture or mystery any longer. He wanted to be kissable. He didn't want to acknowledge his unprepossessing aspects (moral, mental, physical) – hence, instead, the debonair Danvers of *There's a Girl in My Soup* or the pretty-ish women co-stars in every single one of his later films, from Sinead Cusack, in *Hoffman*, to Lesley-Anne Down, in *The Pink Panther Strikes Again*, to Helen Mirren, Fu's girlfriend: 'Oh, I could really go for you, Fu,' she simpers. Irene Handl and Margaret Rutherford were a *very* long time ago.

As when he physically attacked his daughter Victoria, who'd said of his performance in *Being There*, 'It's really good. You look like a fat old man,' Sellers could not dissociate himself from the person he'd become on the screen. His vanity was all-encompassing. Hence, I surmise, the huffy note ('as cold and as brief as an editor's rejection slip,' remember?) to Ray. But *The Alien* was also the film he most regretted never having made. I know this because he'd memorised, or expropriated, some of the script.

When Bajoria has a drink with Devlin, the engineer, and tells him about the pond and its temple, he starts to hum and sing:

Devlin: You sing?
Bajoria: Only when I'm very happy. Or very sad. This is a *bhajan* –
a devotional song.
(*Devlin gets out the beer and pours it out.*)
You keep time by clapping when you sing.
(*Bajoria demonstrates, singing and clapping.*)
Raghupati Raghava Raja Ram
Patiatapavana Sita Ram
. . . like this!*

---

* *Translation*: 'You are the purifier; You grant right understanding; Your name is Allah, Krishna, Rama, Rahim; You grant right understanding to all men.'

(Devlin claps in applause, then indicates the beer. They clink glasses and drink.)

Three months before he died, when Sellers was granting interviews to the world's press in Gstaad (to publicise *Being There*), he suddenly and with much reverence, came out with the above chant, attributing it to Gandhi. It was a lunatic, unexpected little exhibition, whoever he'd decided to pin it on. But it came from *The Alien*. As the dusk deepened across the mountains, did Sellers agonise over the lost chances? 'I was in India because of the Second World War,' he then said, adding (as always) 'we were the last remnants of the British Raj. It must have been a terrible set-up in the old days.' Well, marginally less terrible for the master race; and yet it is startling that Ray was running through his head, *thirteen years* after they had last communicated. Was Sellers trying to recall what it was like, his life (and art) before he decided to mistrust his own sense of wonder?

☆ ☆ ☆

The Party, to this day, is playing somewhere in the sub-continent. As Sellers himself said in the year of his death: 'In India it's still running, in Singapore, anywhere you go, like that, in the East, *The Party* is one of the favourite films.' (Hrundi V. Bakshi is a Hindu Inspector Clouseau.) The transition from giving a performance, in *The Millionairess*, to a series of skits, in *The Party*, is Sellers' guest appearance in *The Road to Hong Kong*, where he goodness-gracious-me's himself silly. In the scene, Bob Hope is being examined by the Indian doctor because he has lost his memory – and without being able to croon 'Thanks for the Memory', Bob is a blank. Sellers uses Dr Kabir's voice and Clouseau's stupidity – the gurgling noise in the stethoscope doesn't come from Bob, the quack is accidentally listening to his own innards: 'Too much curry in the cornflakes.' All Bing says, every other line, is 'Let's get out of here', and Bob, too, looks apprehensive. They are not very brilliant straight men for a Peter Sellers vaudeville sketch. He totally upstages them.

Sellers, once he'd broken on to the international market after *The Millionairess*, would always settle for caricature, cartoonery. What was the Chinaman outfit in *Murder by Death* other than a New Year's Eve party disguise? Sellers' Sidney Wang had simply stepped out of Charles Addams' credit sequence cartoon. And after the Oscar-worthy role in *Being There*, when he was again one of the cinema's hottest properties, what did he choose? To be bedevilled by the comic-book orientalism of Fu Manchu – an astonishing retrogression, explicable only by understanding how important nostalgia was to Sellers in his final months. As a child he'd listened to Harry Agar Lyons portray Fu on the radio, in a fifteen part serial; and he'd seen Boris Karloff in *The Mask of Fu Manchu*, with Myrna Loy. ('Next to Fu Manchu, Dr. No was a yes-man,' said Sellers.) Sellers, mixing goonery with music hall and corny old classical movies, was trying to re-live his past – and the advantage of the past over the future is that you know exactly what it contains.

Sellers' Fu is as wispy as cartoonist Al Hirschfeld's poster design; the original Clouseau of the very first *Pink Panther*, however, was not wholly the trench-coated blob in the DePatie-Freleng cartoons. Along with the clumsiness and solemnity, which are habitual to him, he tries to cope with the knowledge that he is a cuckold; his sexual frustrations add facets to the farce. Sellers plays it slow and he plays it straight. (Like Dodger Lane in the prison cell, it is for everybody else to rush through the connecting doors, hide behind the curtains and to dive into the wardrobe and under the bed, etc.. Robert Wagner and David Niven exhaust themselves, as David Lodge and Bernard Cribbins' characters do, in order for Sellers to steal the scenes.) By *A Shot in the Dark*, however, Clouseau had started to fall off buildings and into lakes; when the series was re-vived, in the Seventies, it was for Sellers to disguise himself as Toulouse Lautrec, Laughton's Quasimodo, and so on endlessly. Clouseau had become a third-rate variety artiste, muffing not his lines (though he cannot speak intelligibly) but his cases. He is a buffoon, in a way the Clouseau of the 1963 film was not. In *Revenge of the Pink Panther*, Clouseau, in a Long John Silver salty sea-dog get-up, even meets Alfie Bass down by the river – Bass reprising his old kipper smoker from *The Millionairess* . . . The bright sou'wester costume, plastic parrot, and the off-screen yell, as Clouseau falls into the water, are lodged as a cartoon comic-strip in my mind.

Sellers seemed to want to deny his gifts, which were for subtle and observant comedy. He flattened himself out – exasperated, perhaps, that he couldn't explain or get his private life to benefit from his perceptions and sensitivity, his depth. His error, I think, was to believe that intuition and stimulus should have been soft and sweet – should somehow have kept him alive. Instead of which, the mean-spiritedness he felt (instead of the spirituality he yearned for) shrivelled him.

'As you can see,' he once said to a visitor, gesturing to the throng of wig makers and costume fitters filling his house, 'life at the moment is fraught. If it weren't for my yoga I wouldn't be able to cope at all. I'd go berserk.' Yoga exercises, however, to Sellers, were not ways of coping but, far from it, another strategy for evading and avoiding his responsibilities. If he was needed, or if he just felt bored and/or mischievous, he'd stand on his head. He'd pretend he wasn't present – he was astrally meditating. Sir Evelyn de Rothschild's main memories of Sellers are 'his enjoyment of Indian foods. The last meal I ever had with him was in an Indian restaurant. And he used to run around my house and stand on his head. He was always standing on his head – for hours.'

His yoga was a clown's act. When Peter Medak went to see him, for example, he put on quite a show: 'One Saturday, a few months before we went off to Cyprus to shoot *Ghost in the Noonday Sun*, I said, "I must talk to you about this script. We've got to figure something out. It doesn't work." Talking to him, I realised, is it possible he's never actually *read* the bloody script? I was to see him at eleven in the morning. Bert Mortimer opened the door. "Where's Peter?" – "Peter is upstairs." I sat down in this mews house. I waited twenty minutes. "Look, where is he?" – "Well, go up and get him." I went upstairs and opened the door of the bedroom and a pair of feet greeted me. He was standing on his head doing a yoga pose. "Peter, it's half past eleven." He came downstairs. We started reading through the script, when the phone rang. It was Liza Minnelli phoning from New York. He babbled to her for ages and he put the phone down and burst into tears – started crying and crying. And that was the end of reading the script. We went for a walk. I realised we were in deep shit.'

☆　☆　☆

The nature of his intransigence would have surfaced in another part he never played – Orde Wingate, a surprising legacy from Sellers' Burmese days. In 1962 he described it as 'the film part I should like to play most of all.' He went to Israel to talk to many ex-Haganah people about him and 'I've done a good deal of research; and there's a script I'm trying to get hold of. The trouble is, if I were to play Wingate I should have to lose a stone. One couldn't play Wingate and not look lean. I'm not sure I could lose as much and stay healthy.'

A dietary motive is one thing – but what else appealed to Sellers? What did he *see*?

Orde Charles Wingate (b.1903) boxed for Charterhouse and rode to the Sudan on a bicycle. He spent, like T.E. Lawrence, much time in the desert, on foot and with camels. He mapped the Libyan interior and the Abyssinian frontier, and was sympathetic with the Jewish cause in Palestine (he was a friend of Chaim Weizmann's), where he organised night raids to combat Arab sabotage and terrorism. He had adventures with Emperor Haile Selassie, in Addis Ababa, routing the Italians, and Sellers would first have heard of him when Wavell, the Commander-in-Chief in India, instructed Wingate to conquer the Japanese in Burma. Wingate penetrated the enemy front, dropping soldiers behind the lines from the air, and was himself killed when his plane went down in a tropical storm, in March 1944. Wavell said of him: 'Wingate ... had a genius for novel and unorthodox methods of warfare and the opportunity and energy to put them into practice. Such men are seldom very tractable subordinates, nor are they always easy to serve...'

Wavell could be describing Sellers for me. The enigma of Wingate, and the anger and questing which inspired him, make explicit the two strands of Sellers I've been drawing out: the reflectiveness (which was moody and mystical) and the rashness – Wingate had an impetuosity which must have seemed almost crazy. Sellers responded to the drama of a heroic career (chasing around desert and jungle after dark – episodes for Dan Mendoza!), and felt an affinity, too, with Wingate's maverick nature. Both actor and soldier were loners who liked to spark off fear and wonder. When Wavell says that 'Wingate's dynamic personality won acceptance for his ideas,' we can imagine all kinds of persuasiveness and charisma being applied when he wanted to have things his way – again, like Sellers. Perhaps what both men shared was an ability to feign. To succeed at guerrilla warfare, to melt into the vegetation and the sand, you need, beyond the daredevilry, the actor's skill of invisibility. You have to deceive the enemy. Who knows, Sellers' Wingate might have been his version of O'Toole's Lawrence – if a director ever existed who could have brought out the complexity of Wingate's military mind, interwoven it with Sellers', so that the soldier became, like the actor, a masterful trickster. Wingate's effrontery and intelligence call for ironic treatment – not the conventional historic pageant generals and adventurers normally receive from the cinema. (George C. Scott's portrait of Patton is the only multi-faceted fighter I can think of – though the film he is in over-scales the power and the glory with action set-pieces, and Scott's Patton is perhaps really only Buck Turgidson on the loose from *Doctor Strangelove*.) Sellers, at his best when reserved or close, could have conveyed what his character was thinking – because Wingate's shrewdness and headstrong aloofness were qualities he himself shared; and which sent him mad.

☆ ★ ☆

Sellers was liberated from the RAF, with his Burma Star decoration, in 1946, after the Gang Show, under the ENSA Entertainments for Allied Forces banner, had presented *Jack and the Beanstalk* as '100 Minutes of High-Speed Variety' at the Théâtre Marigny, Paris. Sellers put his drums on the back of an open lorry and played 'When the Saints Come Marching in' all the way up the

Champs Élysées, at dawn. 'The above-named', said his Wing Commander on his release certificate, 'is strongly recommended for any work with entertainment.'

Back in Britain, life was not so amusing. 'After I came home I tried to get work as a drummer. I went to the agents. But it seemed that every drummer in London was out of a job. So I hung about in Archer Street with all the others. Sometimes I'd get an evening playing for some dance or other, but that was all.' Sellers got freelance assignments with Sid Seymour and His Mad Hatters and with Oscar Rabin's band. 'Yes, I played in London, Chiswick, round about, you know.' Playing for Don Costa, he got the sack: 'I fell off the stand during "El Relicario". Mind you, the stand was a bit narrow, and the tempo was a bit fast.' He then hung around with The Jive Bombers. 'They were a great little outfit. We used to meet in a café in Archer Street and sort out the weekly gigs.'

One person who saw the forlorn sight of Sellers hustling for work was Wally Stott, the conductor and composer who did all the orchestrations for *The Goon Show*: 'Archer Street used to be chock-a-block with musicians standing around hoping to get a gig for that night, or catching up with friends. Peter was in an RAF uniform, standing in a doorway – on the fringe of this activity, and with a side-drum under his arm, trying to get a job. . .'

Bill, returned from wherever, did his best to help his son: 'My father hired a hall in East Finchley and got an agent to come and hear me. I was sitting up there on the platform with my drums: the chairs were arranged round the walls, there was an empty space in the middle – it was all tiled, very cold and bleak; far away at the end of the hall I could see my father and the agent. Well, I did my piece. When I'd finished the agent offered me £7 to go to Burnley for a week. I shouldn't have got my expenses back. To put it bluntly, my father told him to stick it up. . .'

For a while he had recourse to a desk job at the WAAF (Women's Auxiliary Air Force) headquarters in Cadogan Square, helping to organise the itinerary for the all-girl Gang Shows which Ralph Reader had newly set up. Sellers also helped them to rehearse three times a week, and there he met Paddy Black (now Mrs Margaretta Neilly, of Belfast). One day he rang her and asked if she'd go to the flicks. She did so, and until her Gang Show left for a tour of Europe, they spent every available moment together. They danced at the Nuffield Centre and listened to music and the radio at the flat Sellers was sharing with his parents, 211B, High Road, Finchley, N2. 'He was generous and fun-loving', recalls Mrs Neilly, 'A mimic, who loved to perform.'

They went to see a film which was then showing in London and drawing vast crowds. Ignoring the long queue, Sellers said to his girlfriend, 'Watch this!' and guided her into the foyer. 'I wish to see the manager,' he announced. The manager arrived and Sellers, in a stage Irish accent, explained that Paddy, his sister, was due to go back to Dublin the next day, and wouldn't it be a pity if she should leave London without seeing this wonderful fillum, so could he please find them two seats you darlin' man? 'Isn't dat roight, Kathleen?' Paddy nodded, not trusting herself to speak. The manager nodded too, and showed them the street.

On another occasion, Sellers approached four young Scottish soldiers, whom he thought might jostle him, as they were the worse for drink, and demanded their names, rank, etc., declaring himself to be a Captain. One of the squaddies, swaying from side to side, told the fucking Captain what he could fucking do and where he could fucking go, the cunt. 'Peter was left looking foolish,' remembers his companion.

Sellers gave Paddy a fur-lined jacket when she left for the continent: '"You'll need it," he said, and I did.' He also gave her a brooch, or pin, in the shape of a large P, for Paddy. Paddy said that that was doubly apt because her real name, Margaretta, was often abbreviated to Peggy. Sellers was thrilled – 'because that's my mother's name!' Peg, meantime, took to her bed. Paddy seldom saw her, only heard an anguished and insistent 'Petar, Peeetarr!' summoning him away from behind a closed door.

Sellers, having been away for the best part of three years, was no longer comfortable with his mother; he didn't feel secure with her, and this showed itself in his over-anxiety to please. He'd continually telephone her during the evening if he was out in London. She made him feel guilty – as if he shouldn't have a life or any interests except for her. This tended to put a dampener on romance. As Mrs Neilly recounts: 'His mother would invariably call from the bedroom, and Peter would immediately go to her, after asking me to make myself at home. This went on until, in the end, I was obliged to ask, "Is your mother an invalid?" – "No," he assured me, "But she is poorly and will have to stay in bed for a while."' Peg would countermand any plans the couple might have made by sending Sellers off to visit his relatives, and she generally treated him like a child, telling him what to wear, 'ordering him to put his cap on as it was raining outside. I looked at Peter and he was decidedly embarrassed.'

Sellers was easily intimidated by Peg; the boundless love and devotion he was expected to demonstrate became a ritual, an act. Bill, however, was more stalwart. Mrs Neilly remembers thinking that 'here was a charming and gracious man, perhaps a little shy, but quick to start an intelligent conversation, especially when he learned that I came from Northern Ireland. He was genuinely interested and we had a discussion about the complexity of this troubled land.' As a Protestant who'd married into a Jewish dynasty, Bill knew about loyalists and outcasts at first hand. Whilst they were discussing the Ulster/Eire divisions, Sellers came in and started to reminisce about having been sent to a Catholic school – and being congratulated by Brother Cornelius for knowing the Articles of Faith. 'You see,' he said, imitating the master, 'he knows the answer and he's a Jew.'

As she had seen Sellers humiliated by an Odeon manager, soldiers in a state of beery exaltation, his mother, and (retrospectively) his teacher, it is little wonder that Mrs Neilly 'did not see a potential genius', only a fantasist. One afternoon he announced that they were going to see an earl, 'a relation who had a title of some kind'. He and Paddy took the bus to Cumberland House, Thakeham, Sussex, to meet Gerald Rufus Isaacs, the Marquess of

Reading. 'It was an enjoyable afternoon. Relics, regalia, and the family history were discussed and admired. When we left, Peter explained that the title was hereditary and he was next in line. . . .' This would mean, he went on, spelling it out, that if Paddy would consent to marry him, she would then become a Countess. What Sellers must have known was that the Rufus Isaacs', a family of distinguished lawyers and stockbrokers, were able to trace themselves back to Daniel Mendoza. So Sellers decided to interweave himself with his distant cousins.

Michael Isaacs (b.1800), of Mitre Street, London, had married c.1829, Sara, the daughter of Aaron-Enrique Mendoza – she was a niece of the boxer. Of their children, Joseph Michael Isaacs (b.1830) married Sara Davis, the eldest of thirteen (her mother, Francis Marks, was one of twenty four), and their second son became Sir Rufus Daniel Isaacs (b.1860) – a deliriously distinguished man. MP for Reading 1904–1913; Solicitor-General, March 1910; Attorney General, October 1910; in the Cabinet from June 1912; Lord Chief Justice, 1913–1921; Viceroy of India, 1921–1926; Secretary of State for Foreign Affairs, 1931; Lord Warden of the Cinque Ports, 1934. Created Baron Reading, of Erleigh, Berkshire, 1914; Viscount, 1916; Earl, November 1917; Marquess, 1926. Gerald Rufus Isaacs (b.1889), upon whom Sellers came to call, was his son and heir – a Bencher and Treasurer of the Middle Temple, Joint Parliamentary Under-Secretary of State for Foreign Affairs, 1951–1953, and an Honorary Colonel in the Inns of Court (TA) Regiment. He died in 1960, having published several volumes of biography about his father.

Sellers' base-born heart could not reasonably (or fantastically) have had any sort of a chance at the coronet. He was living in a dream world. ('Though he was definite the title was coming his way.') The second marquess already had a son, Michael Alfred Rufus Isaacs, a stockbroker and Major in the Queen's Bays, and he himself had a family well underway. The present (fourth) marquess, Simon Charles Henry, had been born in 1942. Knowing of Sellers' obsession with Alec Guinness, one can't help but wonder whether he intended to bump them all off – as Dennis Price does the D'Ascoynes? But there is a pay-off to all this genealogy. Simon Reading's brother, Lord Anthony Rufus Isaacs, was the producer of both *The Blockhouse* and the advertisement Sellers made for Benson & Hedges tobacco in 1973. 'He used to tell me that we were related,' says Lord Anthony. So even if Sellers' ruling class antics in 1946 were elaborate ways of impressing women (and to be unmasked as an aristocrat would fulfil any changeling fantasy – it is the plot of Sandy Wilson's *The Boy Friend*), his tenuous connection with the marquessate surfaced again nearly thirty years on. He liked to think himself different in blood from just about everybody. Lord Anthony, incidentally, and his sister Jacqui, were part of a circle which included Lord Snowdon, Princess Margaret, and Miranda Quarry, the daughter of Lord Mancroft, who became Sellers' third wife, in 1970 – until they divorced, four years later, Sellers' debonair period. (And his least relaxed. He came to despise being treated as the Kensington Palace clown. 'I say, Sellers, old chep, do something funny, there's a good chep!')

Paddy Black was more shocked at the back-handed proposal of

137

marriage than she was at the revelation that her swain was an incognito prince. 'As much as I liked Peter, the idea of getting engaged never entered my head; and if it ever had, this bizarre incident would have convinced me that it was something not to be considered.'

She had no need to worry about any long-term exposure to a crank. Her European trip beckoned and Sellers asked if he might sign her autograph album – to reveal another surprise. 'He wrote a message and signed it Peter Ray. When I questioned the signature, he told me that he intended to make show business his career, and would change his name.'

Sellers gave Paddy a photograph, signed 'From Smoke to Shamrock,' and the love letters he sent to her (now lost) began 'Darling Padarewski. . .' Mrs Neilly cannot recall much about the contents of the correspondence, except that when Sellers asked after a mutual friend, Florence Billington, from Oswestry, he spelt it 'Flah'.

She never saw him again. In the autumn of 1971, Sellers flew over to Belfast in a private plane with the yoga guru, Swami Vishna Devananor, and sprinkled ten thousand pro-peace leaflets upon the city. He later fell to earth and autographed many of them for fans and he gave a bouquet of flowers to Mrs Irene Gallagher, whose daughter, Angela, had been murdered by IRA gunfire. Mrs Neilly's children wanted her to find and meet her old suitor – but she wouldn't be persuaded. Even if Sellers didn't after all become Peter Ray, the superstar was no longer 'this wonderful lad with a mass of waving hair and just a little overweight'. Outwardly, and with nine years yet to live, he had indeed become a magnifico, more famous than any earl. The attempted rendezvous could have flopped, like Jack Salt's. The last time he saw Sellers was in 1951. Sellers had gone as a variety act to South Parade Pier. He was with Peg, and Salt was in Wally Fry's Band. 'He came to see me,' said Salt, 'when I was working in the ballroom, but he wouldn't wait until the interval. That was the last time I saw him – when he disappeared. Then, when he had his big heart attack in 1964, I went up to Elstead, where he was now living and recuperating, but the butler wouldn't let me in and I was turned away at the gate.'

✩ ✩ ✩

Chapter Three
Peace Work

To take his mother's maiden name like that, and become Peter Ray? It was a blatant attempt to appease Peg – a pseudo-marriage, a proclamation that no other woman could eclipse her in his eyes; and it was also a way of siding with her when it came to signalling displeasure at Bill's wartime disappearances with 'The Welsh Deanna Durbin'. 'Peg took him back,' recalls Anne Levy. 'Bill suffered for the rest of his life for going back. I think he always had to feel grateful he'd been taken into the fold again. A very close Jewish family and he was the outsider.' The flat at 211B, High Road, East Finchley (telephone TUDOR 7621) was a Mendoza property. Bill's job was to find and deliver furniture for what remained of the agency's other non-bombed sub-lets.

Sellers/Ray also kept up the falsehood that he was of lofty lineage – perhaps necessary to his esteem at a time of diminishing success. 'I couldn't get a job' he recalled of 1947, 'I was just living on Mum and Dad' (and *they* were being propped up by the network of cousins). It wasn't Rufus Isaacs he aligned himself with now, but another illustrious nineteenth-century Jew, Benjamin Disraeli, the first (and only – except for Sellers) Earl of Beaconsfield, who died in 1881. If Sellers didn't have a Regency pugilist to go on, he did have George Arliss' Oscar winning biopic – the cunning Prime Minister, with his lock of hair and stagey mannerisms, like Robert Newton's Long John Silver and Laughton's Quasimodo, a performance just begging to be imitated. The wonder is that Sellers didn't pick

Weissmuller, gibber and thump his chest and call himself Grey-stoke, the legendary Tarzan, lord of the apes.

It was as Lord Beaconsfield that Sellers upgraded himself in Norwich, whither he'd gone as a fairground barker, his ambitions as a drummer in abeyance. He'd grown bored with Syd Seymour and His Mad Hatters, 'because it was mostly a matter of hitting things every time Syd fell over', and he lost bookings for dance bands because he didn't have his own van to transport his timps and snares. So instead he strode around the carnival in a frock coat, twirling a cane, and inviting people to step inside the tents and see the Bearded Lady, the Death by a Thousand Cuts, the Siamese Twins. It was a circus side-show and Sellers, fooling himself into thinking he was a lost blue blood, was one of the freaks – a view which struck Milligan in 1969: 'Peter is a freak, not a genius, which makes him even more unique. His ability to reproduce another character is so startling, he himself must have some kind of mis-shapenness inside him. Once, when I was on stage with him, he came on every night as a different person. As I looked at him, he wasn't Peter at all. . .' It was as if, when performing, he was in the grip of a terrible enchantment.

The fol-de-rol ringmaster he played at the fair – all swank and beringed gloved fingers, and as grandiose and foxy as any con-man – merged into the attitudinising Disraeli when Sellers returned to his hotel. According to his own account, given to Alfred Draper, author of *The Story of the Goons*, porters and chambermaids bowed and curtsied and the manager allowed Sellers to make a ceremony out of signing the visitors' register. When Lord Beaconsfield returned from his evening stint with the Two Headed Baby and The Living Torso, however, the hotel staff had had leisure to decipher the curlicues of scratchy copperplate. Wasn't East Finchley an odd place for an earl to hail from? And wouldn't a patrician puff on gold-tipped Balkan Sobranies rather than Woodbines?

'Two gentlemen are waiting to see you, my Lord,' said the manager coldly.

Plain-clothes officers from the RAF Special Investigation

Branch, who had been apprised by the suspicious servantry, came forward out of the gloom of the lounge. They were looking for a deserter.

'Lord Beaconsfield?'

'What can I do for you?'

'Wouldn't it be more correct to say 2223033 Aircraftsman Sellers?'

'You have a point there, it would.'

Sellers produced his discharge papers (the one including the testament 'The above-named is strongly recommended . . .'), was laughed at and left alone.* He slunk back to London the following day, put his brass-buttoned costume back in the skip, and the survivors of Ray Bros. Productions Ltd. put their heads together to see if another job could be found. It was. Relief entertainments manager for the tail-end of the summer season at a holiday camp in Jersey.

'Was that fun?' asked Roy Plomley in 1957, when inviting Sellers to select his Desert Island Discs.

'Quite good. Going to bed very late and getting up very early. "Wakey, wakey, campers" . . . you know.'

He was still Lord Beaconsfield, though. Local newspapers took an interest in why a peer should be so egalitarian as to run the bingo competitions and adjudicate on knobbly knees. The job had actually come about because of Dick Ray Jr, who lived with his family in another part of the Mendoza parish, Rosslyn Hill, Hampstead. Dick's father, also called Dick Ray, was in the tab. business with his brother, Ray Ray, making curtains for theatres. With the demise of variety, after the war, there was little demand for the acres of levitating velvet – so Dick Jnr, when he came out of the RAF, instead of taking over his father's firm, went to Jersey to put on shows and operate as an agent. (He is there today, and owns the Jersey Opera

---

* Peter Evans, perhaps more realistically, says that Sellers pretended to be Lord Beaconsfield only on the telephone, when making his reservation, and that the military police met Sellers in the privacy of the manager's office.

House and Caesar's Palace.) Dick Jnr's mother and Sellers' Peg were sisters – so it was a close cousin for whom he went to work.

The Beaconsfield charade could no longer be anything except a hoot – and publicity, until he was sacked; and wasn't there perhaps, after all, a superfluity of bright people named Ray? Sellers was back to being Sellers when he went, next, to Peterborough, as the bottom of the bill comic in a show starring Dorothy Squires.

Dorothy, in sunglasses and white rabbit fur, was then starting out as a songbird with Billy Reid's Accordion Band. If Ethel Merman and Edith Piaf had mated, Dot might have been the result. She was never any stranger to controversy (she tended to biff policemen if they attempted to breathalyse her); and when her under-insured house caught fire, she quipped: 'Next time I'll live near water.' She moved to a riverside property outside Maidenhead, and was flooded.* Her ballads thus had to do with women who find fate an unpredictable jade; who are neglected and degraded – and her torchy numbers might easily be applied, too, to the trampish life of any performer: 'Sticks and stones is the name of the game/ For the clowns who choose to entertain.'

All apt for Sellers, whose George Formby impressions and uke playing were boring the audience in Peterborough to distraction. 'To stand on a stage and be the centre of such hostility is a frightening experience. I was literally shaking when I came off,' he remembered. 'During the interval between houses the manager came to the dressing room I was sharing with six others, and handed me a cheque for £12. "You're no good here, Sellers boy. Here's your money. There's no need for you to appear again." I sat there miserably, determined not to give up, but not knowing what to do.' Miss Squires, realising that her own vampish act was affecting the audience's mood, unpreparing people for Sellers' whimsicalities, interceded on the young man's behalf.

'I hear you've fired the comic,' she said to the manager, 'I'd like

---

* For this and more on an amazing woman, see *Loose Talk* by Tina Brown (London, 1979).

you to keep him on. You know Monday's always a bad house.'

'Well,' came back the grudging assent, 'I think he must be the worst comic in the business.'

Disconsolately, the non-comic went back to the drums, 'as I had quite an aptitude for that'; and he received £12.10s for a week at the Aldershot Hippodrome, commencing February 9th 1948. 'As a story of total and absolute disaster,' Graham Stark has said of Sellers' appearance there, 'it unfailingly reduced me to tears of laughter.'*

No doubt Sellers improved on the truth, making an anecdote of a low ebb into a misadventure to rival Clouseau – but at the time it was mortifying. The missed lighting cues and a pit band chewing sandwiches and lagging four bars behind . . . : 'I had a crushing defeat in Variety in Aldershot – a terrible thing it was,' was how he put it in more reflective moments. It was another experience to fill Sellers' heart with hate. And what this period was doing was to provide, not a fund of chuckles galore, but an excuse for Sellers to be an avenger for the rest of his life. When he misbehaved later on, reckons Milligan, and acted the role of deranged genius to perfection, 'every official that got ignored by Peter was not only paying for his own idiocy, he's paying for all the idiots in all Peter's past life; idiot producers who ruined wonderful material; idiot managers who told him he couldn't act; idiot BBC officials who treated him like a naughty boy. They were the enemy and had to be destroyed, or Peter couldn't survive.'

---

* Throughout his ribtickling book, *Remembering Peter Sellers*, Graham Stark is at pains to josh and remind Sellers of his beginnings – as if Sellers was nothing more than any other little old British character actor – his bit extra being access to a mother-lode of good luck: 'Time and again he defied faith by always falling on his feet and, if I was around to observe this phenomenon, I would give an unbelieving shake of the head and, to his great delight, mouth carefully these two words. . .' Which happen to be 'Golden Bollocks'.

Another example of Stark's rich humour appears in Michael Sellers' *P.S. I Love You*: Sellers has purchased Chipperfield Manor and all of his cronies are brought to the house to give it their approval; 'You've bought bleedin' Buckingham Palace. What the hell do you think you're doing?' is Stark's alleged reaction.

In 1948, however, Sellers was still trying to cling on. Remembering Ilfracombe, Jersey and the seaside, he went to the Kilburn Empire to audition before Hedley Claxton, an impresario who was casting his summer season revue for the Lido Theatre, Cliftonville, Margate. Reg Varney (later the work-shy driver in the appalling sitcom *On the Buses*) had been signed as the principal comedian. Claxton was now looking for a stooge for Reg. The following letter concludes the episode.

> Teddington, Middx.
> 28 Feb. 91.

Dear Mr Lewis,

It would be Spring '48. Two of us turned up for an audition at Mac's Rehearsal Rooms in Great Windmill Street. It was to play second comic in Hedley Claxton's Summer Show, *Gaytime* [. . .] Peter, who I'd not heard of, did George Formby, played the uke and told a few gags. I did some impressions and a shaggy dog story. I got the job – which paid £14 a week [. . .]

I worked on a couple of radio shows with Peter a few years later. We were there to do odd character voices. I think the shows were written by Frank Muir and Denis Norden. [*Listen, My Children* and *Third Division*.]

> Yours sincerely,
> *Benny Hill*

Sellers' patter, pretending to be that of a Red Indian journalist sending home his opinions of London to *The Pawnee Graphic*, was a bit saucy. Benny Hill, who sang a calypso, accompanying himself on a guitar ('We have two Bev'ns in our Cabinet/Aneurin's the one with the gift of the gab in it/The other Bev'n's the taciturnist/He knows the importance of being Ernest!'), stayed at the Lido Theatre for three years. After the audition, he bought Sellers coffee and cake at Velotti's Café, where they exchanged addresses and phone numbers and promised to pass on news of any jobs. In 1955, when Sellers was quite the radio star, but his face unknown, Hill told

Picturegoer: 'Watch Peter Sellers. He's going to be the biggest funnyman in Britain.'

☆　★　☆

Peg was also foretelling the future. She was trying to find an agent to represent her son and informing them, as Sellers sat there nervously fiddling with his gloves: 'My son is going to be worth a lot of money in this business. Listen to an old woman who knows.' Words which make her sound like a wild-eyed gypsy in a Verdi opera. Sellers said that his decision to audition for the Windmill, however, was his own. 'I had the idea of trying the Windmill Theatre. I got an act together – stories, impersonations . . . Those audiences waiting all day to see the nudes – it seemed lunatic for me to try. But I got the job: £25 a week for a month.'

Six weeks, actually, starting on Monday March 17th 1948. Sellers was in the 211th edition of *Revudeville*, 'entirely conceived and produced by Vivian Van Damm'. The Windmill shows involved lots of moon-faced girls (was there ever a less becoming era for hair-dos and cosmetics than the Forties?) baring their breasts and body stockings in tasteful tableaux. To get the performance past the Lord Chamberlain, the censor, the girls were not allowed to move. They had to be as pieces of classical statuary in a museum – alabaster casts of the Venus de Milo etc. – and they made the best of being permitted to waft themselves with large ostrich feather fans. To cover getting on and off the tiny stage (the floor made of glass, according to Harry Secombe, presumably to illuminate it from underneath), a curtain swished across – and a comedian stood before it on the apron to entertain the audiences while the girls bickered, adjusted their pompadours (did they set their curls with lard?), checked their nipple-tassels, and froze into more tasteful poses.

'Any additional artificial aid to vision is NOT permitted' admonished the souvenir programme – as if the auditorium was otherwise packed with gentlemen toting telescopes. 'As this theatre is open continuously from 12 Noon the Management respectfully informs its patrons that any seat vacated for more than 15 minutes will be considered free and therefore liable to be re-sold.' So, if you wanted to stay all day (the last performance started at nine p.m.) and grew hungry, do as Beefy in one of the J.P. Donleavy novels, and order a hamper from Fortnum's, across the street in Piccadilly.

Sellers' particular *Revudeville* opened with the girls burgeoning forth as 'Suddenly – It's Spring'. Then, after somebody called Robert Moreton had been on, the girls were back for 'Hearts and Flowers' and 'The Mermaid Song'. There was a trio, 'Once in a Million Lifetimes', with Jill Anstey, Raymond Waters and Josephine Hamlett, and this was followed by a sketch, 'Seconds Out', written and performed by the lugubrious Alfred Marks. Sellers eventually turned up in a sketch called 'Third Degree', alongside Johnny McGregor and Pat Raphael. Having endured that, the audience was rewarded with muffs a-plenty, when the tabs parted on 'Eskimo Blues'. On and on it went, 'Cocktail Time', 'News Girl', until Sellers had a solo spot. He did Flying Officer Kite and the *ITMA* characters, and a song written by Bill called 'I'll Never Worry'. Six times a day this cycle of tits, fans, gags and lullabies was repeated.

Van Damm's 'ideas man' was the composer and pianist, Ronnie Bridges: 'I played for Peter at his audition. He did a little story and a song, which he said he'd written himself with his father – this I doubted. I think it was a published song, called "We Know it Just the Same"; a George Formby type of song, which Peter did with a ukelele. We had a lot of talented youngsters, just out of the Forces. Harry, Mike Bentine. But Sellers was the most determined of the lot without any doubt. He had *business*. All the others wanted to get on, of course, but it wasn't the primordial thing in their lives. Harry was hoping to get on, so was Michael, so was Alfred Marks, but the *determination* of Peter . . . He was quite ruthless in everything he did.

'He used to lean on me quite a bit, getting me to play, without charge of course, for all his auditions with agents. We'd go to an agent's office, and I'd play for him. Every little agency in the Charing Cross Road. Yes, an opportunist. A very talented opportunist. These agents that I played for, he'd take them out for meals;

he'd give them presents. The first radio series he did, to get himself in with the BBC, he gave presents to each person in the cast – and this was unheard of; and nobody had heard of him, either. I remember a producer, Fred Yule, said to me, "This boy is giving us presents!" To get in, to make himself popular, to get more work. *Anything* he could do to get more work, was Peter – unfortunately.

'The snag was, with Sellers in the early days, he was only interested in people who could help him, and if he met somebody who could help his career more, you were forgotten. When Peter Sellers became big, he didn't want to know me – he tended to forget what I'd done for him. Harry and Mike were far more genial, and remain friends. Sellers was never genial.'

☆ ★ ☆

It succeeded though, didn't it – choking his virtue with foul ambition? Who else in his generation became an international star? Roger Moore (Dorothy Squires' husband) once said that you are not a star until they can spell your name in Vladivostok, and Clouseau's comedy travels equally as well as James Bond's suavity. (United Artists re-released *The Spy Who Loved Me* and *The Pink Panther Strikes Again* on a double bill.) As Michael Sellers said to me: 'The world danced to my father's tune. It's hard for ordinary people to understand if, when you are in any major city in the world, and you are hot at that time, just how people are only too willing to do anything to accommodate you. You don't have to queue; you don't have to do anything for yourself – like Royalty.'

Stardom, however, was won only at a terrible cost – to himself and to those whom he professed to love. When Sellers was breaking through from character actor to leading man, in *The Millionairess*, it was his family who had to suffer: 'By the time he was having his relationship, consummated or not, with Sophia Loren,' Michael continued, 'we had gone from being his home-life and inspiration to being a chain round his neck. He begrudged us for impeding his chasing after Loren. He had to pay our bills . . . He had to look after *this* . . . he had to do *that* . . . He resented us. He wanted freedom from family and obligation.' His family's opinion on the matter of his womanising didn't count because, as individuals, they no longer held any existence for him: they were simply hurdles keeping him away from his new pleasures. (That his new pleasures were to reach such a degree of dementia that he imagined Loren loved him back is a topic for the men in white coats – and this biographer – to classify.)

Peg gave up her freedom to facilitate her son's; he expected everybody else to be as accommodating. Uncle Bert made the observation that 'those first years after the war, when Peter was having such a lean time of it, aged Peg twenty years'. In addition to her over-assertiveness with agents – driving them away rather than the reverse – she pampered Sellers as never before, fattening him up, cocooning him. Milligan says that, because of this, 'he was in training for a heart attack from the age of twenty onwards. He ate everything that was fat and his mother told him always to rest and never overwork himself. He never did any exercise and I think he'd be alive today if he had. Isn't that a real Irish one? He'd be alive today if it wasn't for the fact he's dead.' He became, within the physical flab, purified egotism.

Ambitious past all thinking, Sellers may have dropped his vis-countcies and the desire to be Peter Ray – the former after the suicide of radio actor Peter Waring, arrested on a fraud charge (he made the bogus claim that he'd been a Lieutenant-Commander in the Royal Navy amongst other deceptions); the latter because of competition from Ted Ray who'd changed *his* name from Charles Olden* – but there was much mileage to be gained from being a Sellers. For a start, he was handing sub-editors their headlines on a plate: 'In A Sellers Market,' 'Best Sellers,' 'The Rest is Sellers' etc.. (Maurice Micklewhite became Michael Caine to give the press 'Caine Mutiny', 'Caine is Able', 'Candidly Caine'). Secondly, he was going through a period of being close to his father – practising the uke, learning his routines (which he was to replicate to such effect

---

* Thus making a nonsense of Michael Sellers' sentence: 'Ted Ray . . . was distantly related to us through the vivacious Ma Ray's kinsfolk.' (*P.S. I Love You*, page 33.)

in *The Optimists of Nine Elms*). And though Bill, his face as expressive as a standing pond, might look like the ghost of what he'd become if he didn't shift, Sellers knew his own greed and curiosity were of a different order – and besides there were other Sellers' to meet.

He decided, for example, he was a relative of the Rt. Hon. Sir Frederick A. Sellers, a judge on the Northern Circuit and a Lord Justice of Appeal (he died in 1979). He knocked on m'lud's door, at Highwood Lodge, Mill Hill, NW7, and asked 'my uncle Fred' for a loan of £100 to help him start his career. (He was seen off.) Nobody with a Sellers surname was safe, then or later. When he was making *Tom Thumb* at Elstree, he met a local divine, the Rev. Dr Robert Sellers, who lived in Cheshunt and was a professor of biblical and historical theology at London University. He cavorted in priest's clothes, and introduced himself to the congregation as the vicar's cousin, Sexy Recsy (recsy=rector). A few years later, at the Dorchester, he discovered that there was another Mr Sellers staying as a guest in the hotel. He pretended to be leglessly drunk and had himself carried to the namesake's room at three a.m., where, after rousing the occupant, the porters were to ask: 'Do you know this man?' They received an angry NO! The next morning, Sellers saw the second Sellers and yelled 'You bastard!' across the Grill Room.

☆ ★ ☆

Sellers, very proud, revengeful and ambitious, used the Windmill as a proving ground. 'And I'll tell you this,' he informed trumpeter Freddy Clayton, 'if you can get by there, you can get by anywhere. It really was wonderful experience.' When his stint ended, on April 24th, Van Damm decreed that the name *Sellers* be added to the plaque in the foyer: STARS OF TODAY WHO STARTED THEIR CAREERS IN THIS THEATRE. But, as Sellers said in 1962, 'Of course, that seemed like heaven. Then when it was over nothing else came of it. I simply couldn't get work with the BBC. I knew I could do impressions, but nobody would give me a chance.'

It was at this point he went outside his range, and won some eternal enemies. (My sources have requested anonymity.) Sellers became a Freemason. 'Sellers joined the Freemasons', I was informed, 'purely as a way of seeking advancement. He made a mockery of it. He bandied the phrases and signals about at the BBC, to impress producers and executives – but he only bought dishonour upon himself and humiliation to those masons who had sponsored him. A disgrace.'

That he'd automatically wanted to mock the brotherhood's theatricality and religiosity will come as no surprise. (He was unable to go through with the rituals for joining the Grand Order of the Water Rats because he kept laughing too much.) The craft was a Ray Bros revue and High Mass at St Aloysius' in one go. But the purposes of freemasonry, its mysterious boy-scout ceremonies aside, are charitable and social – the Grand Masters of the Order, especially in recent years, have worked hard to dispel the aura of an exclusive, secret sect. And when you are initiated, you swear an oath that you will not use the privileges of the society for personal gain. Sellers, by being the very worst kind of mason, the sort that brings the assembly into public hatred, ridicule, and contempt – well, it shows the emergence of the sort of man he was. For the record, scurrying about the Library and Museum of the United Grand Lodge of England, in Great Queen Street, I came across this entry in the registers:

Peter Sellers
Chelsea Lodge, No.3098, London

Initiated:	16th July 1948	Age:	22
Passed:	21st January 1949	Address:	East Finchley
Raised:	16th November 1951	Occupation:	Variety Artist

I had hoped to discover, in the relevant pages of the Masonic Yearbook, who Sellers' fellow brothers might have been at the Chelsea Lodge, between 1948 and 1951, to see what names can be cross-indexed and linked-up in his story – from Mozart to Jack the Ripper, a masonic sub-plot provides a not unengrossing underswell of grand guignol. However, it was explained to me that, as some of the members from those days may still be alive, it is against the craft's protocol to disclose such information to the 'profane'.

☆ ☆ ☆

It is true that, for all his running and jumping, he was standing still. Since coming back from Jersey he'd been trying, without success, to get employed by that fledgeling medium – television. He'd tried again and again to make himself heard. On January 28th 1948, for instance, he'd written to the booking manager at Alexandra Palace, Muswell Hill, 'in the hope that you can fix me an audition for television. I shall be in London for the next twelve days prior to variety at Aldershot . . .', and he added, 'my act . . . is that of a comedian.' He received the following form letter back:

Peter Sellers Esq.,
211b, High Road,
Finchley, East, N.2.

Dear Mr. Sellers,

TELEVISION

We have pleasure in inviting you to a preliminary audition at Star Sound Studios, Rodmarton Mews, Blandford St., Baker St., W.1, at:

12.00 pm on Monday, 2 February, 1948

This audition will not be held under full Television Studio conditions, but costume and make-up are obviously desirable though not essential. Dressing room accommodation will be available, and artists who intend to change and/or make-up should arrive not less than 30 minutes earlier than the time stated above.

Your performance should not exceed ten minutes in length.

An accompanist will be available, but you are at liberty to bring your own accompanist if you so desire.

In the event of your performance being considered of prospective interest for our Television programmes, you will be informed in due course of any engagement we are able to offer, or may be asked to attend a further audition, under normal Television Studio conditions, at Alexandra Palace.

We wish to make it clear that the BBC does not accept liability for travelling or other expenses which you may incur in connection with any audition(s).

Please state by return if you accept the above invitation: in the absence of a reply within reasonable time your place at the audition will be given to another applicant.

In the event of attendance, please bring this letter with you to facilitate admittance to the studio.

Yours faithfully,

for Television Booking Manager

He celebrated receipt of the above with Paddy Black – she remembers that he'd tried so hard to get the BBC to acknowledge his existence. The report card for Sellers' first audition describes him as a 'pleasant & vivacious young man in dinner jacket' and that his performance, which lasted eight and a half minutes, consisted of 'comedy impressions arranged as Black Market sketch, impersonating different types bartering for tin of sardines, followed by comic sketch "The Piccolo," with vocal finish'. 'The Gang Show' (and 'awaiting audition for Windmill Theatre') is mentioned as his only experience, and the conclusion is: 'A refreshing and talented performer. Parts of this act should prove ideal Tele. Variety.'
Sellers was informed of the next move four days later:

6th February, 1948

Dear Mr. Sellers,

TELEVISION

With reference to your preliminary audition on 2nd February, 1948, we shall hope to have the pleasure of inviting you to attend a further Test, under normal Television studio conditions, at Alexandra Palace, as soon as possible.

You will appreciate, however, that owing to prevailing conditions, we are unable at present to say exactly when this will be.

Yours faithfully,

for the Television Booking Manager

The 'prevailing conditions' were the winter snow storms – and Sellers was in a chilled limbo himself until the BBC contacted him again, which they did the following week.

13th February, 1948

Dear Peter Sellers,

TELEVISION

With reference to the preliminary audition you have already given, and our recent telephone conversation, we shall be glad if you will attend a Camera Test, under normal Television studio conditions, at Alexandra Palace, on Thursday, 19th February 1948, at 4.30pm.

You should arrive not less than 30 minutes earlier than this time, with a view to effecting any change of dress considered necessary to your performance. Dressing room accommodation will be provided.

An accompanist will be available, but you are at liberty to bring your own accompanist if you so desire.

We have arranged for a special coach to leave Broadcasting House (Portland Place) at 2.15pm on the 19th, in order to enable us to have a short rehearsal before the actual Test. If you would prefer to make your own way, however, please arrange to be at the Studio by 3pm, when the rehearsal is due to begin.

Please reply by return if you accept the above invitation, and bring this letter with you to the studio to facilitate admittance.

Yours faithfully,

for Television Booking Manager.

Sellers replied rather sniffily, on the 16th, that he had his own transport *and* accompanist, thank you very much – his father and Uncle Dick's Wolseley. Peg and Bill had collaborated on Sellers' script, calling it 'BBC Nightmare'. If a radio broadcast Sellers was to give later on in the year is any clue, the sketch involved a comic, killed on his way to the theatre, who goes to Heaven and is asked to give a performance, to cheer everybody up: 'A funny thing happened to me on the way to the cemetery . . .' And this is the excuse to impersonate voices, well-known then and forgotten today: Kenneth Horne, Richard Murdoch, Reg Dixon. . . .

The camera test went well enough for Sellers to be booked to appear on *New to You*, on March 18th and 23rd, at a fee of 7 guineas, and again on May 3rd, for 8 guineas. After that, television faded out, but this hardly mattered: he'd broken through to radio. Again, however, the start was sluggish. Sellers wrote to Michael Standing, the Head of Radio Variety, late in 1947 ('I am sorry I have not written before as I have just returned from Jersey'), only to have a note back from C. F. Meehan (Assistant Director of Variety), suggesting that he try Mr Dennis Wilson, at the Aeolian Hall, 'who will arrange for an audition as soon as possible.' On blue notepaper, engraved with the heading –

PETER SELLERS
'Bang On'

– and in the neatest, most elegant script ever seen outside of Miss Helen Penn's class at St Mark's Kindergarten, the following was set down on January 15th 1948:

Dear Sir,

[. . .] I received the enclosed letter from Mr. Meehan. I shall be

in town for the next three weeks prior to variety at the
Hippodrome, Aldershot. Shall be glad if you can arrange an
audition during my stay in town.

> Yours Very Truly
> *Peter Sellers*

As an example of Sellers the suppliant – a humble petitioner – it is
unique. But even in this batch of early letters, the schoolboy formality of the calligraphic layout does not quite manage to hide the
arrogance ('I would be pleased if you would give it your personal
consideration,' he says to Standing); nor does he downplay his
assurance: 'Bang On' indeed. (Is the allusion to his drumming, or to
being spot-on with his mimicry?) There is a raffishness, too, in the
references to 'my stay in town', and the briskness of 'shall be glad if
. . .' is almost off-hand. Sellers is only ostensibly polite. Wilson
replied on January 26th:

Dear Mr. Sellers,

Thank you for your letter received on the 15th January.

I am sorry it will not be possible for us to hear you at an
audition within the next two or three weeks, but this is to let you
know that we have added your name to our waiting list and we
hope to be able to send you an invitation in due course. Perhaps
you could let me have a choice of dates and times in March or
April when you are likely to be available. Auditions are normally
held between the hours of 4.0 and 10.0 p.m. every day
(Saturdays and Sundays excepted), but we shall not be holding
any auditions during the month of February.

In the meantime I should be glad if you would send me some
details of your act, together with any useful information about
your professional experience.

> Yours very truly,
> *Dennis Wilson*
> (Variety Auditions)

Peace Work

In response to Wilson's final paragraph, Sellers compiled this list:

PETER SELLERS, COMEDIAN
211B, High Road,
East Finchley.

Telephone. Tudor 7621/6628

Characters

Cockney – Spiv
Cockney – Honest-to-God
Cockney – Old Man
Refugee – Misconception English
Liverpool – [*somebody has written 'good'*]
Birmingham – [*ditto*]
Huddersfield – [*ditto*]
Scots – Cod [*ditto*]
Irish – a la Barry Fitzgerald style
Civil Service Types
All colonels
American – Brooklyn, New York, and South
Negroes
Welsh – South Wales
Horrific characters
Various straight characters

Impressions

All *ITMA* types
F/O Kite
Postman
Mr Burp
Peter Lorre
George Formby
Claude Dampier
Robb Wilton

157

Instruments

Drums (ex Pro)
Uke
Guitar
Bit of piano

Singing

Crooning
Cod Opera

This virtually covers Sellers' range from first to last – his final album, *Sellers' Market*, recorded in Paris during 1979, when *The Fiendish Plot of Dr Fu Manchu* was in pre-production, includes a track called 'The Compleat Guide to Accents of the British Isles', and on the record as a whole he mimics forty-eight different dialects. He was circling back – to a time when he had reasoned: 'I had an aptitude for dialects, and I'd studied them. I figured that the more dialects I could do and the more precise they were, the more chance there was of getting a job on the BBC. That's what I was after – to be a BBC voice man like Jon Pertwee, Maurice Denham and Kenneth Connor.' In 1979, he'd recently completed his dead-pan role in *Being There*; it was as if he needed to unloose his tongue, exercise his baroque facility for funny voices again. 'It was all Peter's inspiration,' the producer, Ken Barnes, told me. 'The "Guide to Accents" sketch was originally written by Miles Kington, but Sellers changed it, to make it more goonish. He was always inventing and deviating from the script.'

It is possible to see many of his future characters in the sounds he could make in 1948. The Rev. Smallwood from *Heavens Above* (Birmingham), Dick Scratcher from *Ghost in the Noonday Sun* (Irish), John Lewis from *Only Two Can Play* (South Wales) . . . Civil Service and colonel types would recur, overlain with Grytpype Thynne and Bloodnok; George Formby, of course, Sellers had absorbed and would re-deploy. Here is Sellers in embryo; and when it came to *Sellers' Market*, there was Sellers, about to die, full of nostalgia for his beginnings. Another track 'Don't Cry for Me, Argentina, There' was sung by a Cockney unsure of the words, accompanied by a drummer who'd lost the beat. 'The drummer on the record is me,' Sellers told Judith Simons proudly. 'I started in show business as a drummer and pianist and the beat is the music of the NAAFI.' He was also able, in a song called 'Eaton Square Blues', composed by Alan Clare, to be revenged upon the toffs at the Devonshire and Somerset hunt balls he'd long ago played at with his father. 'At every hunt ball I can recall there was some aristocrat wanting to pour his heart out like a man from Mississippi. They never addressed me as the pianist. When they wanted me to accompany their singing they would simply shout "Piano!"'

After these words appeared, Judith Simons was startled to receive this response from Sellers: 'I do not play the piano. I did not tell you I did and wish I had not seen Monday's *Daily Express*,' he curtly cabled. Why, she'd only printed an easy-going puff for his new record. Her editor must have stuck up for the reporter, because Sellers attacked again on October 15th 1979:

> Dear Show Business Editor Victor Davis: Your telex to hand. I do not send borish [*sic*] telegrams undeservedly. Only when it is disheartening to read badly written things I did not say. Peter Sellers. Show Business Person, Peter Sellers. P.S. Once again, Up Yours.

Even allowing for the fact that he was ill and mad, weekending on his own at Gstaad, this was an extraordinary over-reaction; yet it is possible to work out what was on his mind. He wouldn't have wanted to go into the motives behind 'Eaton Square Blues' with a newspaper interviewer, of course, but he'd been remembering Bill's belittlement, rather than his own, with that cry of *piano*! – and for the sake of anecdote he had simplified it all. He was sensitive, you see, to his father's having been held cheap, and seeing the mention of the piano player in print like that, the shame and contempt of the early days coursed back, memories flapping about him like uncaged birds.

As he modestly put it in 1948, he could manage only a 'bit of piano'. Bill was the one who'd lashed the NAAFI keyboard to the back of the van when they toured the West Country and Lancashire during the war. And Judith Simons, in her innocence, was not to know that Sellers' career, which had made him, as he told her, a tax exile,* was closely interwoven with Bill's discomfiture and frustration. Sellers had re-lived the crestfallen old man a dozen times – Henry Orient, the pianist, Juan Bautista, the ex-matador guitarist, Sam Hall and his uke, doing a wonderful balalaika, Clouseau scraping his violin, Hrundi Bakshi concentrating on the sitar; and let's add, too, Queen Victoria playing jazz piano and Fu Manchu's music hall organ . . . Sellers' characters have the urge to vamp, twang and fiddle, but they are barely better than gifted amateurs. They are too dippy to be hardened pros. And, flopping as musicians, they fail at their official occupations. The much-gored bullfighter; the film extra who knocks down the sets; Clouseau, unlucky in love and at solving crimes; Old Sam, reduced to busking; and by extension, there's Fred Kite, locked outside the factory gates. Such characters are not over-reachers, trying to get more out of life than it can reasonably give (that was Sellers' dilemma), nor under-achievers (which was Peg's problem, so she added her unfulfilled ambitions to her son's); but they are the people who don't jump out at you, whose eccentricity seems to come from their naivety rather than any demonic razzle-dazzle. Sellers got under their skin. Part of his riddle is that his success was based on playing bunglers and the outclassed. He understood the burden of their dreams; he knew what urged them on. And in describing this sympathy, in acknowledging Sellers' ability to unpack their hearts and let us sense their aspirations, we come close to what made him a great actor, able to produce great effects. Sellers' involuntary gift was the power of his imagination. If an artist is a person who makes something out of nothing (the blank canvas, the empty page, the silent

---

* 'Though I can't come to Britain I still know what is going on. I read all the newspapers and I have a friend who tapes the BBC programmes for me. . . And I listen continually to the BBC Overseas Service.'

orchestra), Sellers made somebodies out of his variations on Mr Nobody. His mice can roar.

☆   ★   ☆

Dennis Wilson, however, couldn't have been much impressed by Sellers' catholic list of voices and imitations – because he made no response. Did he think the welter simple showing off? It wasn't until the end of March, with Sellers at the Windmill, that another overture was made to the BBC, this time through a more professional channel. Sellers had finally found an agent: Russ Carr of Barney Jacobs Ltd., Piccadilly Circus, SW1. Miss Jean Raymond, for the agency, wrote to Wilson on March 30th, 1948:

> Dear Mr Wilson,
>
> We would like to draw your attention to PETER SELLERS, the 'Bang On' comedian, he is the modern type of entertainer with a fresh line of comedy.
>
> We would be pleased if you would take the opportunity of seeing him at the Windmill Theatre. Times 4.44, 6.29 and 8.14.
>
> Yours very truly
BARNEY JACOBS LIMITED

Across this official letter '? Waiting List' has been scrawled by an anonymous hand. Then, at the foot, another message has been added (and crossed out): 'Barney Jacobs' office will telephone later today to let us know when he can come either today or tomorrow or at 5.50 next Wed.' The note is dated '1/4/48'.

The reason for the sudden hurry was that Wilson had coincidentally just been to the Windmill – to see Robert Moreton. He'd watched Sellers' act by accident and had at last been impressed. Sellers betook himself to the Aeolian Hall with equal speed. It was his make-or-break audition – on April Fool's Day at that. 'I was shown into a room with a microphone. No one else was there and I did my piece.'

The concealed adjudicators scribbled these comments:

Peter Sellars [sic]

Jimmy Dyrenforth:	Singing not bad, though no great asset. Very good at dialects. Impressions good. Likeable personality. With better material he could be a real find.
Michael North:	Singing with ukelele – ordinary but not unpleasant. Impressions quite useful – especially Birmingham – Huddersfield – Col. Chin Strap – definitely worth seeding as he shows great promise. Needs new characters. Gd. personality.
A. Scott Johnson:	Good range of dialects and character studies. Half impression half dialect. Good professional personality. Wants much better material or he'll fail seeded. Audition showed characters but was not funny. Probably useful for production work.
Dennis Wilson:	Did shaggy dog story with many characters. Cockney – good. Brummagen – good. Huddersfield – good. Scots – rather overdone but good. F/O Kite – good. Merry-go-round – Postman – good. Very good voice for mike. Material old and weak at times. Ukelele unnecessary but not bad. Seed and note for production as well.

On the upper left and bottom right hand corner of the card, the word YES was typed. A handwritten scribble, 'Passed for Broadcasting' runs across the top edge. An acceptance letter was sent to Russ Carr the next morning:

2nd April 1948

Dear Mr. Carr

PETER SELLERS

Thank you for sending Peter Sellers along to the audition last night at short notice. I am glad to say that he did pass this preliminary test.

I invited him to come to my office this morning to talk over his audition and have arranged that he will be called forward for our final recorded audition before our senior producers as a solo comedy act, and later on I hope to place him in a production audition in order to give him an opportunity to show off his various dialects and characters in a scripted show. I have told him that for this solo comedy spot he will have to strengthen his material.

> Yours very truly,
> *Dennis Wilson*
> (Variety Auditions)

The hedging and the hurdles remind me of the studio talent scout's report on Fred Astaire's screen test: 'Can't act, can't sing, slightly bald, can dance a little.' Nothing happened for another two months. It must have been during this period that Sellers, believing himself to be getting nowhere fast, made his historic telephone call from a public booth in Soho. He recounted the caper many times, and did so with particular gusto on the *Parkinson* chat-show in 1974:

> . . . I noticed that Roy Speer was doing a radio show at that time called *Show Time*, and the compère was Dick Bentley, and there were lots of new acts, you see. And I'd written in I don't know how many times to try and get in on the show, with no reply. One of the big shows on the air was *Much Binding in the Marsh*, with Kenneth Horne and Dickie Murdoch. Well, you know, you do things at certain times. You feel you've *got to get ahead, you've got to get ahead!* So I phoned up and I thought, being a senior producer, Speer would probably know Horne and Murdoch, you see, who were very big then. And I thought, if I click with the secretary, I'll get put through, right? So I said, 'Oh, hello, I'm Ken Horne, is Roy there?' – 'Oh' she said, 'Yes he is' – and I *knew* I was all right. So Roy got on and said, 'Hello, Ken. How are you?' I said 'Listen, Roy, I'm phoning up because I know that new show you've got on – what is it? *Show Time*, or something? – Dickie and I were at a cabaret the other

night, saw an amazing young fellow called Peter, what was his name? Sellers. Peter Sellers. And he was very good. Probably have him on the show, you know. Just thought I'd give you a little tip – a little tip. . . .'

He said, 'Well that's very nice of you.' And then it came to the crunch, and I said, 'It's me.' He said, 'What?' I said, 'It's me, Peter Sellers talking, and it was the only way I could get to you, and will you give me a date on your show?' And he said, 'Oh, you cheeky young sod. What do you do?' I said, 'Well obviously, impersonations. . .'

Sellers went to see Speer at his office, who told him again he was a 'cheeky young bastard, this is highly irregular . . .', but he had a booking at last: *Show Time*, on July 1st 1948, rehearsals three o'clock until six, and the programme itself was broadcast from half-past seven until a quarter past eight that same evening. Sellers was paid ten guineas for his three and a half minutes. The programme was made at The People's Palace, Mile End Road, and a recording of Sellers' act has miraculously survived.

Dick Bentley informs us across decades that:

Now it's comedy time and the laughs are due to be handed around by twenty-two year old Peter Sellers, a new comedian who started his career in the RAF Gang Shows. Today, with his smart patter and impressions, Peter is a popular name on variety bills. So, if you're shopping for smiles, you can rely on a Sellers' market with – Peter Sellers!

The band plays a few bars of 'Happy Days' as an opening fanfare, and Sellers is suddenly explaining to us, rather formally, that he is going to do a sketch about a foreigner who has learned English from a short-wave radio set. And then he unleashes himself, doing all the hoots, rasps, whines and white noise, as well as an oriental voice trying to cut through the crackle, his sentences broken up by the interference. Sellers keeps a grip on the tale he's weaving – it isn't a mess. But he must have looked strange, standing on stage in his tuxedo, discharging such a commotion. There was no doubting the versatility, however, or his precision – or the rapidity of his vocal changes and delivery, which was like lightning. And, as he said in 1962, 'I began getting work. . .'* Indeed he did. He was back on *Show Time* on August 19th, and became a regular. He began to appear on Dennis Wilson's *It's Fine to be Young* (August 31st, September 7th, 14th and 21st) and A. Scott Johnson's *Tempo for Today*. He appeared on Speer's *Starlight Hour* eleven times in two months. He went on *Henry Hall's Guest Night*, recorded at the Jubilee Theatre, Blackpool . . . And Sellers' new agent, Montague Lyon, of Eagle House, Jermyn Street, had to write and admonish his client's employers for prolonging the taint of amateurism:

PRIVATE AND CONFIDENTIAL

August 24th, 1948

Jacques Brown, Esq.,
B.B.C.,
Aeolian Hall,
New Bond Street,
London, W.1

Dear Mr. Brown,

Further to our conversation yesterday re Peter Sellers' inclusion

---

* The performance was reviewed by Leslie Ayre, in the *Evening News*, on July 10th 1948, under the headline 'This Mimic Is Tops' ('I got a good write-up, the first write-up I ever had in me life,' Sellers told Michael Parkinson):

O. Henry once spoke of an actor who did 'impersonations of well-known impersonators'. Certainly many mimics give too little study to their originals. Peter Cavanagh ['The Voice of Them All' on radio] is an exception.

And now, in Peter Sellers, radio brings us another really conscientious and excellent artist and a genuine rival to Cav.

Tall, good-looking [*sic*], 22, Sellers was born in Portsmouth of a theatrical family. Entertaining in the war days, he was carefully studying famous radio voices. His first broadcast in 'Show Time' recently brought a scurry of agents and he's already fixed up a long series of Sunday concerts all over the country; and Roy Speer immediately booked him for the first available return date in 'Show Time.'

Peg had the notice framed. Peter Evans says 'It stayed on her wall until the day she in the 'IT'S FINE TO BE YOUNG' broadcast on Aug.31st, I trust you will appreciate the reason why Peter Sellers should not be announced during the broadcast either as being a very young man or having been at any time in [the] 'GANG SHOW' with Ralph Reader. We feel from the point of view of his future stage engagements it would be highly inadvisable to publicise the fact that he is extremely young or that he was associated with a service show during his R.A.F. career.

I therefore trust that when he is announced at the end of the programme as having appeared in it his name only is used without any build-up.

> Kind regards,
> Yours sincerely, *etc.*

The pattern would become a familiar one. Sellers didn't like to be beholden to his immediate past, or to the people left behind there (e.g. Ronnie Bridges) whom he'd climbed clear of. As Ralph Reader's boy scoutism was to be suppressed, so, later, he'd hate radio for holding him back from films – and he'd betray the people in any of those mediums who'd helped him to become who he was. Spike Milligan, Wolf Mankowitz, Blake Edwards, amongst others, were targets of Sellers' not being able to share a credit. (His wives and children received similar treatment.) But back in 1948, his professionalism and eagerness to please wasn't yet truculent; Sellers was starting to ascend and, hogging the air waves, he was like a one man chorus. A meeting between the variety booking manager and the head of variety was convened to discuss the matter of over-exposure. A memo dated November 19th states that:

On Saturday, 13th November 1948, Peter Sellers appeared in the series 'Tempo for Today', followed by an appearance on Sunday in 'Variety Band Box' and a featured spot in 'Starlight Hour' on the . Monday. Would it not be helpful if V.B.M. [Variety Booking

---

died' – after which it was destroyed, when Sellers demanded that everything of his mother's be incinerated.

Manager] were to inform producers if the artist they are booking
has already been engaged for the same or adjoining day?

It is signed by C.J. Mahoney. Underneath, somebody has apologet-
ically written: 'I know that this is normally done – but what
happened this time?'

What happened was that Sellers' ubiquity, and his skill at scatter-
ing himself as so many different voices, kept well ahead of the
paperwork – the score-sheets, contracts, and minutes generated lovingly by producers and Monty Lyon. Sellers, like Aldo Vanucci, the
fleeing fox in the 1966 film he made with Britt Ekland, was shimmering in all over the place: *Northern Lights, Everything Under
Control, Caribbean Carnival, Join in and Sing, Up and Coming, Calling All Forces, Bumblethorpe, Golden Slipper Club, All Star Bill,* in
which he recited the story of Dick Whittington in the voice of
Olivier's Richard III... His fee went from ten to twenty-five
guineas for approximately six minutes work, and he was doing
heaps of programmes every week.

Across the Atlantic, another wilful virtuoso was re-inventing
himself on radio – Orson Welles. Quite what Welles would have
made of *Workers' Playtime,* however, must remain an assignment
for the shade of S. J. Perelman. Sellers travelled everywhere for it.
He did *Workers' Playtime* at The Brush Electrical Engineering Co.,
Loughborough; Kay & Stewart Ltd., Huddersfield; the Central
Ordnance Depot, Donnington; Standard Telephone & Cables Ltd.,
Footscray; Huntley & Palmers Ltd., Reading; Courtaulds, Brain-
tree; a shoe factory in Tilbury... He infiltrated dozens and dozens
of mills and foundries, cheering up the proletariat as it re-built
England after the war. 'I've played for audiences of tractor drivers
with two-thousandths-of-an-inch foreheads,' he recalled. 'They
didn't understand a word you said, they might have been Russians.'
He also did *Variety Bandbox* countless times, and an edition from
January 15th 1950, which has survived, gives a flavour of how
people liked to be entertained in that long gone era.

☆ ★ ☆

To listen to old radio shows is, literally, to awake the dead. The phonograph hiss beneath the voices and music is like the air escaping from opened graves, and the particular programme I have discovered, which was done at the Camberwell Palace Theatre, London, resurrects it all: a Queen Mary and George VI atmosphere, with fogs and trolley buses, the Euston Arch and tin advertisements for Bourneville chocolate and Veno's Cough Cure; a time of soot and snow, with the colour leaked out during the war put back in by the gaudy of the Crazy Gang and Dame Laura Knight's backstage gouaches. Despite the rationing of foodstuffs, people are too plump for their coats – buttons are put under strain from canteen cookery and sandwich suppers. In this pre-deodorant era, when folk only took baths once a week, and everybody smoked, think of the stink, overlain, as it would have been, by menthol lozenges.

The show begins with a brisk rooty-toot from the orchestra, drum rolls and fanfares. The compère, Philip Slessor, speaks most precisely. Everything is formal and courteous. The audience, rapt, provides polite bursts of applause. Slessor, 'presenting the people of variety to a variety of people', introduces Kay Cavendish ('one of the first ladies of radio'), who sings: Alma & Ames, who play a rumba or a samba; and Reg Dixon, who sounds like Tom Courtenay, and does a recitation about ghosts. The performances are expert, contained, and we can *see* the ball gowns and dinner jackets. More than old-fashioned – this is a window on a vanished world. Nobody has a sardonic edge to their material. It sounds all so very innocent. So when somebody called Gerry Allen plays an electronic organ, it is horrible for a number of reasons. First, the tinny, cheap squawking doesn't go with the orchestra at all. Secondly, the effect is of a circus dog act. Thirdly, it may be a gimmick, but it is the way ahead. What makes *Variety Bandbox* an antiquarian experience is that it is popular music before pop; real musicians playing violins, instead of synthesisers and computerised simulacra. The programme is Edwardian – its technology and outlook belong with the hoots and puffs of steam trains.

We then revert swiftly to history, with Frankie Howerd giving a mock lecture on how to speak correct English ('Oooh, Shakespeare – turn away!'); and when Barbara Leigh ('petite, beautiful and Australia's own') comes on, her accent has been so carefully reconstructed, she doesn't so much sing a song as give an elocution lesson: 'The birds are mating/And while you're waiting/Time slips by' – an excruciating warble, the lyrics perpetrated by Jimmy Grafton. Bill Kerr appears as a morose Australian, to tell a tale about Wagga Wagga – he's a front-porch philosopher, wondering (boringly) what makes stamps and envelope flaps sticky – and then, at last:

> Here we have one of the really up and coming personalities that the past year or so's broadcasting has produced. With his amusing comedy impressions, I'm always very glad to reintroduce the rising star of *Ray's a Laugh* and *Petticoat Lane* and so forth – Peter Sellers!

After letting the acclaim die away, Sellers speaks with a dark voice:

'This is Peter Sellers taking you over to theatreland, to hear some excerpts from the new pantomime *Sellerinda*, with an all-star radio cast.' He then has his excuse to become Ted Ray, Crystal Jollibottom ('You startled me so, I've swallowed me upper set'), William Mate Cobblers (Buttons) and Soppy (the squeaky forerunner of Bluebottle). Most of the actual wireless mimicries he does I don't recognise and cannot judge (Robert Moreton, for example) – but it does sound like a crowd. Sellers does the ugly sisters, the broker's men, hecklers in the audience. He finishes with Max Miller and Crystal Jollibottom singing alternate verses of the testicular 'I've Got a Lovely Bunch of Coconuts,' and then he leads the community singing for 'Roll a Ball, a Penny a Pitch'. This merges into *Variety Bandbox*'s closing theme, everybody belting out, in a hurdy-gurdy rhythm, 'Give us another one, before you leave me' – the meaning of which I don't dare dwell upon.

☆ ★ ☆

He could have gone on indefinitely popping up in these sorts of spots, and the advertisement on page 169 was run in *The Performer*, on November 4th 1948. Inside a year, Sellers was at the Palladium, London's most prestigious music hall, sharing the night with Gracie Fields – his first flesh and blood appearance since becoming a busy radio feature. (He was on *Stump the Storyteller*, for example, with Osbert Lancaster and Gilbert Harding, improvising a story along a given theme, with given objects; and he was on *Woman's Hour*: 'let me have your script and any numbers you may want to sing', wrote Brian Johnston, the producer, before telling Sellers he'd be expected to 'take part in a quiz or game': seven minutes @ twenty guineas.)

His two-week season started on October 3rd 1949. Sellers was ninth in the line-up (Our Gracie the tenth). Others involved were Annell & Brask, trick cyclists, Two Berty Borrest, aerialists, The Stevil Sisters, acrobatic contortionists, and the Delta Rhythm Boys, gleemen. 'Of course,' he said, 'being on the BBC made it easier to get work in variety . . . the Palladium audiences were always nice to me. I liked the Palladium. You could be rude to them and they

didn't mind., I'd come on and say: "Heads up out of the trough!"
And they didn't mind.'

Sellers' act involved take-offs of Dick Barton and Reg Dixon (also
on the roster for real); he did impressions of the famous mingled
with his own characters, Jollibottom, Soppy etc.. He then
announced he was going to do an impersonation of Queen Victoria
'When she were a lad'. He went behind a screen and emerged in a
wig, an unlaced corset, army boots, and a large ginger beard. Some
people swear he carried a stuffed crocodile. He sashayed to the footlights and announced in grave tones: 'I'd like to be the first to admit
that I do not know what Queen Victoria looked like when she were
a lad.' Our Gracie had her work cut out topping that little exhibition. Wearing a black gown ('It's so tight I thought I'd have to
be wheeled on'), she sang 'You Made Me Love You', 'Alfonso, My
Hot Spanish Knight', and 'The Nun's Chorus'. But though the
audience sang along gaily and cheered her at the end, there was a
feeling that, with Gracie they'd met with things dying, with Sellers,
a comedy that was new born.

And Gracie didn't forget, either. When Sellers was making *After
the Fox*, seventeen years later, he went to see her, at her retirement
villa. Gracie took Sellers to tea, at a café she owned – and left him
to pay the bill. 'That's for you, love.'

Sellers was already feeling the need to develop and change. The
mimic is little better than a parasite feeding off the style and manners of the real achievers – and Sellers knew himself to be more
talented than the people he parroted: 'I hate everything I do so
much', he said, 'that I always think I'm going to go one better
before I die. I mean, I always think there's something left in me. I
know there is – there's something sort of in there somehow that I
want to get out.' That (apocryphal) stuffed crocodile is a clue to
what would hasten Sellers on to a new and more accomplished
career. He had a power inside himself, kicking and fighting to be let
loose – intimated in the long ago by the drums – an iconoclastic
streak; and he'd recently met the only man on the planet who could
help him to make any use of it – Spike Milligan.

☆ ★ ☆

PART TWO
Radio Days

He pressed a key in the semi-darkness, and with a rending crackle there leaped between two brass knobs a spark, streams of sparks, and sparks again.

'Grand, isn't it? *That's* the Power – our unknown Power – kicking and fighting to be let loose,' said young Mr Cashell. 'There she goes – kick-kick-kick into space. I never get over the strangeness of it, . . . waves going into space you know . . .'

Rudyard Kipling, 'Wireless,' in Traffics and Discoveries

Chapter Four
Old Comrades

There was always a great competitiveness between them – Sellers envious of Milligan's writing and inventiveness ('there's something about being left alone with that blank piece of paper . . .'), Milligan, in his turn, wishing he could break into films and make millions ('. . . he had the Midas Touch, chum. If ever that was passed on to somebody, it was Peter') – but the fact is, without the electrifying, jangly Irishman stinging him to the heart, Sellers would never have found his own unique style and method. I don't mean he'd have vanished. Sellers would have gone on to be like, say, Frankie Howerd, Dick Emery, or Benny Hill, a much-loved British comedian who'd died of a heart attack – but he'd never have been an innovator – veering away from mimicry to 'beautifully observed vocal cartoons' (in the opinion of the Prince of Wales). Milligan released something in Sellers.

'We hit it off from the word go,' Sellers remembered. 'We were brimming over with ideas and we had sessions where we sat around and built mad, lightning sketches. The only way I can describe the form of humour we enjoyed is that we took any given situation and carried it to an illogical conclusion. That's where I find my comedy. You take a situation and think what would happen if you didn't do what you would normally do but something else. It's the runaway idea. You take an idea and just let your mind wander. I became saturated with it.'

Milligan, through the dream-like trappings of the Goons, made Sellers into Sellers. He never had the same effect on Harry

175

Secombe, whose later career as a knighted doxologist denies his one-time feverishness. Am I alone in hoping that, when miming so seriously to a hymn, on top of a mountain in a gale, or just when walking through Sainsbury's on a Saturday morning, he'll burst into very necessary giggles – and demonstrate that Neddy Seagoon still exists? Nevertheless, Sir Harry, even if he has grown out of it all, is shrewd about Milligan's modus operandi: 'Spike had this crazy way of thinking, this illogically sane thing that goes beyond the gag. He's got a tremendous ability to evoke crazy mental pictures. He thinks visually, which is most unusual for a comic.'

The visions thus conjured gave Sellers a new reality – a home for his excesses. Goonery is a world without rules. Caddishness, cowardice and ignorance replace virtue and heroism, and become qualities to admire. The Rep. Company of characters, Eccles, Crun, Minnie Bannister and Bloodnok, amongst them, spend their time climbing Everest from the inside, searching for the piano Nappy played at Waterloo, or racing across the desert sands on a fifty-ton Wurlitzer organ. They encounter phantom batter pudding hurlers, head-shavers, and teeth-rustlers (who convert the gob crockery into castanets); and they travel gaily towards death and dismemberment by horse-drawn motor cars and atomic dustbins – transports which delightfully mutate: 'The ship was disguised as a train – to make the train sea-worthy it was done up to look like a boat and painted to appear like a tram. . . . ' Sound effects, advancing the action, included strangulations, boiling custard, exploding policemen, exploding fingers, exploding shirt tails. One instruction in the script, for a solo Chinese lady singing a high-pitched wailing dirge, was to be speeded up to get an agonising vibrato – to be followed by the line, 'Gad – how Our Gracie has changed.'

As Milligan says, 'We *had* to create *The Goon Show* – a fantasy world. You could make characters do what you wanted because you were writing the script. You always win. You can't get arrested in a fantasy world unless you want to. For anyone who found reality a bug, like Peter did, *The Goon Show* was sheer therapy. Characters, like Neddy Seagoon, could be struck, beaten, burnt, boiled, drowned, clubbed, nailed to a cross – and Peter would love it. For him the characters were real, and they came alive.'

One of the first things Sellers had in common with Milligan, therefore, was misanthropy.

There was much else to intertwine them. Milligan's parents, like Sellers', had appeared in music hall – though only as a diversion from his father's real job, which was as a Quarter Master Sergeant in the Royal Artillery, out in Burma and India. (As a boy he'd been a boxer, took dancing lessons, and had worked in the scenery dock at a vaudeville theatre in Poplar, East London.) Leo and Flo Milligan, as Leo Gann and Gwen Gorden, appeared at the Bombay Palace of Varieties in an act called 'Fun Round the Sentry Box', and they sang in the Governor-General's band – songs like 'Ramona, I'll Meet You by the Waterfall' – and Spike's bassinet (like Sellers') was placed in the wings. He was born into the last five minutes of the Raj, and his childhood was cushioned by servants and ceremony. (Regarding laundry, washing-up, etc., 'other people did that'.) The regimental dances and the starlight; the quiet of the sub-continent's nights; the order of the society (the Milligans were above the natives, but Spike wasn't allowed to play with officers' children): it all made for a sense of proportion and measurement, which Milligan has striven to rediscover in his life ever since. ('What happened to the boy I was?' he puzzled in 1959. 'Why did he run away?') For, in 1933, Leo was made redundant from the Indian Army. The family was ejected into a cold, unwelcoming England – which was to remain a foreign land, 'a damp, dead greyness that seemed to go on forever'. Milligan has lived the life of an exile.

His parents eventually emigrated to Australia. Towards the end of his days, Leo wrote his son a magnificent letter, which could be Bill talking to Sellers: 'I, too, had a creative mind, but was frustrated all the time . . . I suffered in silence, outwardly I was a happy and contented family man – I was a born actor.' Milligan himself is far from able to disguise his feelings. Periodically he suffers a nervous collapse. He retreats to his bedroom and communicates with his wife and children by telegram, or else he checks himself into mental hospitals, for injections of evipan and of pentothal sodium. He has had shock treatments and deep sleep narcosis – where he is generally anaesthetised for weeks on end. Such comas must be like dying and coming back – like Sellers' return visit to the underworld during his heart attacks. ('Of course, after his heart attacks Peter was never quite sure about which world he was living in. . . . It became as if he was always wanting to die again so as to enjoy the moment and talk about it. Then he died once too often, didn't he?')

His psychiatrist commented in 1958: 'He really wants to hide himself from the world,' and when he is not being ill, Milligan achieves this by eloping into his work – the goonish kingdom, which extends from the radio series to the post-apocalypse play, *The Bed Sitting Room*, the anything-goes atmosphere of the television Q programmes, and the farcical dust-heap he describes Europe and North Africa as in his war memoirs. (Hitler, Rommel, Mussolini, and Monty are guest stars in his hellzapoppin multi-volume picaresque.) Milligan likes to reduce behaviour to chaos and the ridiculous – for this is what he genuinely sees: 'We're a nasty bloody species . . . I'm very depressed about what's happening all over the world, when I see how ugliness has crept into our lives. . . You'd have to be a total idiot to be happy today.'

Thus, his archetypal hero is the tramp. In *The Bed Sitting Room*, he's Mate: 'Old cloth cap, ragged overcoat, zip-up boot slippers, large iron frame spectacles, old, about fifty-five, unshaven, long hair.' The joke is that, in a lawless environment, the tramp, a thick-witted outcast, is ridden with petty regulations – he's officious, a jobsworth. Pettifoggery keeps him alive: you can't park there, put that cigarette out, keep off the grass, etc..

Such rules ruin the peace and quiet of Milligan's other hobo-figure, William McGonagall – the artist as extreme down-and-out. In *The Truth at Last*, illustrated by Sellers in 1976, the poet is imprisoned, starved, operated on for piles, and infected with rabies; and when he returns home, 'his father split his head open with a loaded sock. Fourteen stitches later McGonagall repaired to his little room which his mother had carefully kept exactly how he had left it – filthy.' This would be a house fit for Eccles, the original stray:* 'Eccles was really the innocent creature that I was – the one that didn't want to cause any offence and loved simplicity, which I do. Yes, Eccles was the essential me.'

Milligan has played further variations on the shaggy tramp on stage in *Oblomov* and on screen as Racquel Welch's husband, in *The Three Musketeers*, as an inmate of the Bastille in Mel Brooks' *History of the World*, and as the traffic warden who eats his own wad of parking tickets in *The Magic Christian*. The wild-eyed hairy vagabond came together best as Ben Gunn, in the Mermaid Theatre's pantomime of *Treasure Island*. The castaway was an ideal Milligan self-image. As Sir Bernard Miles said, 'He is a man marooned, really. You could say he is Ben Gunn.' In public, the supertramp, a man without pretensions and thus pure and honest, is his preferred part. On chat shows he used to enjoy looking dishevelled. 'At times he likes to shock,' said Sellers, 'and walks into expensive restaurants dressed like nothing on earth. He imagines the public expects it. And it is true that people seem to expect us to be zany, crazy comics all the time. We aren't. . .' By looking a scruff, the lowest common denominator, there's a curious security – you know people can't drag you lower. (This is comparable with Sellers' mysterious fondness for buskers and music hall wreckages.) It's a defence – whereas, in reality, Milligan is obsessively punctual and spotless; he is highly organised, and much enjoys the Victorian graces. Until he retired to Henry James' Rye, he lived in a large Gothic villa at Monken Hadley, Barnet, where gentlemen were expected to dress for dinner and fine wines were served. The Prince of Wales was a

---

* Eccles, a relative of Disney's gormless Goofy, is also 'The Original Goon', according to *The Goon Show Scripts*: 'Educated at a Convent till age 7 – end of education. Has had 18,312 interviews for jobs. Has never been employed. Spends his days walking around saying "Hello dere" to anyone who will listen . . .'

That Eccles Street, Dublin, was Leo and Molly Bloom's address in 1904 is no doubt one of those coincidences which will keep professors profitably amused for generations.

guest. In his house in Sussex, I noticed, on the walls above the waxed and polished antiques, a drawing by John Singer Sargent and watercolours by Hercules Brabazon-Brabazon; shelves contain neatly labelled geological specimens and arrow-heads. You expect the master to appear wearing a quilted crimson jacket, a fez, and pince-nez spectacles.

If Milligan is Ben Gunn, therefore, he is isolated not in poverty and muddle but by a sense of nineteenth-century scrupulosity – perhaps his problems began when he realised he was born in the wrong era? (He should have been in Wyndham Lewis and Ezra Pound's gang, contributing to *Blast!*.) And the decorum he craves – the treasure island he's looking for – isn't cheap to maintain: 'I couldn't live in an ordinary community unless people were quiet and didn't smoke or have barking dogs. Most people are noisy, and it costs money to keep away from them.' He doesn't *mind* being a supertramp. He has no desire to rejoin the human race. He prizes his individuality, and even the attacks of manic depression can be used in his work: 'The moods come on very suddenly, and I try to exploit them to my advantage. . . It gives you a new spectrum of emotions that you didn't realise you had and you go to areas of emotional depth that are not accessible to other people. . .'

His illness gives him an intensity. (Breakdowns are for Milligan what the spirochete was for Flaubert, Keats, and Wilde – an affliction to aid art.) Whether his hypersensitivity was the product of his upbringing and experience, however, and whether his depressions are added extras or somehow traceable to his past: these are vexed questions. Unlike AIDS or syphillis, manic depression isn't contracted; it is not a viral infection. Nobody gives it to you. Nor is it, like many cancers, the result of the body deciding to turn in on itself, consume itself. It is not a cellular disorder, or a cerebral catastrophe, like a stroke. It hardly seems physical, though its effects (too much energy, or too little) have physical consequences. It is abstract – it affects thought and feeling, and personality. It is what makes you feel different, apart. It is all in the mind – out of reach.

And to the talented it gives an extra boost of superiority and/or inferiority. You suffer more – you are afflicted: 'A thousand grim winters grow in my head . . .' etc.

These generalisations, anyhow, can be made after examining Milligan's own descriptions of his disease, 'the black hopeless rose within me', found in his poems, letters, and interviews. A memo he sent to his secretary is indicative:

A. I'm not in.
B. I'm very very ill.
C. Don't let ANYBODY GO IN MY ROOM [. . .]
D. I've had enough – Jesus had it easy.
E. I'm at home.

That he could write the message at all suggests a degree of control; and if he is exhausted and prostrate, at least he can be grimly humorous (D) and he lets his staff know where he is (E) – which perhaps countermands (A). Is (B) self-pitying?

Milligan's mentality hasn't overthrown him; on the contrary, it made him as a writer. We are also expected to appreciate the sacrifice and cost. As he said just prior to *The Last Goon Show of All* in 1972, recalling its hey-day: 'The pressure and the tension of keeping up the standard drove me mad. I dedicated my whole life to it, seven days a week. Christ, it was terrifying. I used to get up, get to the BBC before nine, work right through the day and evening and get the last tube home. Sometimes I'd miss it and Peter would come and take me home in his car. It cost blood to put that show on for me. Sheer agony. It wrecked my first marriage and it wrecked my health. My nervous breakdown happened while I was on the show.' More recently he has said, 'I had to write a new show every week for six months. If Hitler had done that to someone it would be called torture. I was in such a state of hypertension, I was unapproachable by human beings . . .' He was taken, straitjacketed, to an asylum in Muswell Hill, whence he continued to write *The Goon Show* from, presumably, a padded cell. 'I have to write a script every week to make a lot of idiot people laugh,' he told the doctors. 'How can they fucking laugh when I'm in such fucking pain? I'm desperate.' When he was indisposed, Eric Sykes and Larry Stephens assisted with the scripts. Sellers effortlessly took over Milligan's voices (Minnie Bannister, Eccles, Little Jim, Moriarty). Harry Secombe paid Milligan's medical bills. When he returned to the fray, his psychiatrist, Dr Joe Robson, as a precaution, sat in the audience (with a large butterfly net?).

☆　★　☆

Like Sellers, Milligan had a highly-strung mother, who went one better than Peg and sent him to a girl's school, the Convent of Jesus and Mary, in Poona, 'to protect me from the realities of life', and his father, Leo, like Bill, was often absent on tours of duty. Milligan attended many schools (including one in Rangoon run by the Christian Brothers de la Salle, similar to the Order at Sellers' St Aloysius') – it was all disruptive, itinerant, and Flo, matriarchal like Peg, was at her most gratified when her son was ill in bed and needing to be nursed: 'She had total control then, you see.' When they came to England, for the penniless existence in Catford, Milligan never managed to mix with the British boys and formal education ended early. 'I sort of got lost and turned in on my self – into a world of fantasy.'

He had various dead-end factory or bum-type jobs in Deptford and Chislehurst, and his salvation was the trumpet. He sought escape, freedom, through jazz – as Sellers did with the drums; and, again like Sellers, he only began to find himself in the camaraderie of the Forces. The army game gave him security and brief happiness. Indeed, Milligan is the Siegfried Sassoon of World War II. After having experienced the fighting at first hand, he has re-lived it in slow-motion ever since – with those proliferating autobiographies, which commenced with *Adolf Hitler: My Part in His Downfall*. In compiling his books from journals, letters home, old comrades' diaries, contemporary newspaper clippings and Regimental archives, Milligan makes a comic brew out of the horrors of combat – he makes it bearable by making it goonish (more on this

later); and, in fact, his theories about comedy generally are militaristic. 'I try to go out into enemy territory,' he has said, 'where
nothing has happened before.'

Once conscripted into the 19 Battery 56th Heavy Rgt. RA, he
played in cabaret, *Boys in Battery D.*, and began to make up jokes
and exploit his gift for the spontaneous gag. 'We were the only
entertainment in Bexhill [the training camp] so we did some concerts there. We used to get dressed up in rags and tell jokes. People
used to laugh at me, but I didn't think of myself as being particularly funny.' After experiencing heavy shell burst at Lauro, Italy,
Milligan was sent to hospital at Afrigola and Portici, as a psycho-
neurotic. He was eventually moved to the Central Pool of Artists
and, through the director, Raymond Agoult, was cast in a variety
show called *Over the Page*, where the star, in this Combined
Services Entertainment, was Lance Bombadier Harry Secombe: 'a
little myopic blubber of fat from Wales who had been pronounced
a looney after a direct hit by an 88-mm gun in North Africa. He was
asleep at the time and didn't know about it till he woke up. General
Montgomery saw him and nearly surrendered. He spoke like a
speeded-up record, no one understood him, he didn't even understand himself; in fact, forty years later he was knighted for not
being understood.'

After demob., in the autumn of 1946, Milligan toured the continent with his band, the Bill Hall Trio, and tried to get
established.* Back in Britain, and following disagreements with his
mother, who was against the improvidence and temptations of
show business (' . . . a lot of snobbery in that, you know, because it
wasn't regarded as a proper job' – very *unlike* Peg), he shared a bedsitting room at 13, Linden Gardens, Notting Hill Gate, with
Secombe and Norman Vaughan. Secombe was already on his way.
He'd had spots on *Variety Bandbox* and, in October 1946, had done
a stint at the Windmill. (He sang a duet with himself, alternating

---

* His adventures are chronicled in *Where Have All The Bullets Gone?* (1985) and
Goodbye Soldier (1986). That description of Secombe comes from p. 183 of the
former.

the swollen larynxes of Nelson Eddy and Jeanette MacDonald, whilst messily shaving. He concluded by drinking the soapy water and the nudes complained that they kept slipping in his lather.) Despite Secombe's advocacy, however, he failed to have Milligan hired after his own season was through. 'NEXT PLEASE!' Van Damm had shouted from the stalls, when Milligan turned up for his audition loudly apologising for being fully dressed.

Milligan failed, also, to interest Val Parnell in the Bill Hall Trio, when they were appearing at the Hackney Empire. 'I didn't work at all,' he has said of this period, 'just sort of wandered around.' Despite the mendicancy (he was once reduced to being Alfred Marks' dresser), he kept himself trim (something Sellers never did), at Ladywell Athletics Track, Bellingham Baths, and the outdoor lido at Brockwell Park. Occasionally he'd earn 12/6 for playing (like Sellers in Archer Street) at a dance, with the Harlem Club Band or the Ritz Revels. One way and another he turned up behind the bar at Major Jimmy Grafton's pub in Strutton Ground, SW1, near the Houses of Parliament. Milligan pulled pints, made boffs and slept in the attic under a pile of coats. Grafton, in addition to being a Mine Host off the pages of Chaucer, wrote material for a radio comedian called Derek Roy, another *Variety Bandbox* stalwart (and his second cousin) – and 'Jimmy . . . asked me if I would like to write with him. He gave me a quid or two. I used to graft like bloody mad.'

☆ ★ ☆

It was at Grafton's, or points roundabout, that Sellers first encountered Milligan, Secombe and that other founder Goon, Michael Bentine. As regards precisely who first introduced who to whom, where and when, sources differ. Peter Evans states that Sellers met Milligan late in 1949 at the Bedford Music Hall, Camden Town (where Sellers, of course, had once lived): 'Secombe was self-consciously appearing in an all-male ex-service revue called *Soldiers in Skirts*. They met backstage together with another young comic called Michael Bentine.' Sellers' Authorised Biographer, Alexander Walker, repeats this information, except that now it is

Milligan and Bentine who are 'doing a show called *Soldiers in Skirts* at the Bedford Theatre, Camden Town.'

None of them was ever in such a production – Secombe's drag revue was called *Forces Showboat*; he wasn't required to doll up; it was in 1948, not 1949; and it was rehearsed in Clapham and performed in Harrow, not Camden, and then toured. (Amongst the chorines was the future Danny la Rue. When he broke his arm, Secombe suggested that he could hide the plaster cast inside a fur muff.)

The true sequence of events leading up to the convergence of such high-pitched talent seems to be:

(a) Secombe met Bentine at the Windmill. 'There's a Goon if ever I saw one,' he reported to Milligan, having found that they shared a fondness for animated cartoons by Max Fleischer. Bentine, with his partner, Tony Sherwood, had a piano and bongos act (called Sherwood & Forrest), where they dressed in undertakers' outfits and told, in wild Russian accents, some sort of fairy story. All very hectic, like Secombe's shaving – indeed, they took over from him at the end of his six week sentence. 'We quickly sized each other up,' remembers Bentine of the meeting in 1946 with a Camay-covered Welshman, 'and liked what we saw.' Bentine went on (inevitably) *Variety Bandbox*, and when his partner left to study music at the Guildhall, he reverted to his real name (after ruling out Mike Pike, Mick Park, Mack Tuck) and perfected a solo routine, a zany lecture, about a metamorphosing chairback: the bit of broken furniture became a comb, a plough, pair of handcuffs, a guillotine, prison bars, etc. (You can see him performing it in Sellers's early film, *Down Among the Z Men*.) Bentine was signed up by Monty Lyon, and Val Parnell hired him for *Starlight Roof* at the Hippodrome, Leicester Square, in 1947, with Vic Oliver and Julie Andrews. After that he toured in variety, appeared in cabaret at the Embassy night-club, Mayfair, and by August 1949 he was booked for the Palladium – as 'The Happy Imbecile', alongside Borrah Minevitch's Harmonica Rascals, and the Ink Spots.

(b) Bentine and Secombe met Sellers (and Benny Hill), through

Pat Dixon's *Third Division*, recorded at the end of 1948. 'This was the first time that Mike, Peter and I had worked together and was a forerunner of *The Goon Show*,' Sir Harry has remarked. No tape survives, though interestingly the show contained an early version of the mock travelogue Sellers was to make famous on one of his record albums, 'Balham – Gateway to the South', in which a crappy London borough is described as if it were Monte Carlo, say, or the Côte d'Azur. Frank Muir, its writer, said to me, 'Denis Norden and I employed Sellers first on radio in any meaningful way. Before he'd just been doing variety spots. *Third Division* was on the Third Programme, now Radio Three, the intellectuals' channel – though there wasn't a lot there, intellectually, with Sellers; nor was there much of a developed personality. He was a child. He was frightened, and the more successful he became, the more frightened he became. . . .'

(c) Bentine had begun to write some of Secombe's gags for *Variety Bandbox*. They received a letter from Jimmy Grafton, complaining that Secombe's comedy was 'too bloody funny' and hence making life hard for Derek Roy, the principal pantaloon. Secombe and Bentine went to the pub in Victoria and (says Sir Harry), 'I was able to introduce Mike Bentine to the man I had been raving about – Spike Milligan.' Bentine remembers seeing a wraith sitting up in bed wearing army boots and long-johns: 'This seemed to be totally in keeping with his persona.'

(d) *The Goon Show* came about, says Bentine, 'as a direct result of the evening Harry and I spent with Jimmy Grafton at the Grafton Arms. . . We later introduced Mine Host to the youthful Peter Sellers.' In his autobiography, *Arias and Raspberries*, Sir Harry concurs: 'It was a most propitious day for me, because this was the place where *The Goon Show* was born, and in due course Jimmy Grafton was to become my agent and manager. . . Naturally Mike and I took Peter along to Grafton's. He was so obviously one of us and his repertoire of impressions was formidable. Like the rest of us, he had been in the services and shared our lunatic sense of humour. Spike and Peter took to each other immediately and soon the four of us were meeting regularly.'

(e) Secombe, on introducing Milligan, warned Sellers, 'The only trouble is, he is quite mad!'; Sellers, asked what had intrigued him most originally about Milligan, replied 'His name!'; when Bentine was questioned on what drew him to Sellers, he said 'Because he had talent!'; Milligan's response to the same query was 'His haircut!'

(f) Milligan decamped from the Major's attic (accessible by ladder) to the spare room in 211B, High Road, East Finchley; and thence to a Mendoza property in Shepherd's Hill, Highgate. In these early days, he and Sellers still voyaged by public transport. 'Fares please,' said the conductor. 'Where are we going?' asked Sellers. Milligan produced a telephone from a cardboard box – 'Hello? is zat zer German Embassy? Vere are ve going?' He hung up and turned to Sellers, 'Düsseldorf.' When the conductor said he was only going as far as Wood Green, Sellers jumped to his feet: 'Quick – it's zer wrong bus. Hurry or we'll miss dinner. . . .'

(g) When I asked Milligan for his favourite memory, he said: 'One of the funniest moments of my life was being woken up in my flat – I lived opposite him – at three o'clock in the morning, and Peter was standing there naked in a bowler hat and asked, "Do you know the name of a good tailor?"'

☆　★　☆

The Grafton Arms was a playpen of competing egos. 'I used to tell jokes,' recalls Milligan, 'Harry Secombe was there and I'd play the piano a bit and Harry would sing and Peter would come in and do a few impressions of Kenneth Horne and others. Michael Bentine was there. We all used to laugh a lot. We had a strange sense of humour.' The atmosphere was clubby, private – freemasonic. When Sellers opened at the Palladium, he received a telegram which stated: 'I am instructed by the Goon Council to forward the following message of congratulation. Quote. Ooly-Dooly-Osh. Unquote. P.S. Ool. Signed KOGVOS.' *Osh* was a password; *ool* what grammarians call a roving noun, a word applicable in any connotation; KOGVOS, Keeper of Goons and Voice of Sanity, was Major Grafton.

Other people's secret codes can be very boring, but the success of

The Goon Show lay in the fact that millions learned to love its language – a language which went beyond words. Crun's Mnk-grnk-mnk-mnk-grmp; Bloodnok's Bleiough-aeioughhh-bleioughhh, or Bluebottle's Ye-he-he! Heuheuheuheuheuhe! 'Why talk? Why speak words?' Milligan told a journalist, sent round to the pub to witness the commotion in 1949. 'Everybody speaks words.' The actual word 'goon' itself came from America and was popularised, along with 'gawkery' (stupidity) and 'clerd' (a strong form of disparagement) by Fred Allen on his radio show – which Sellers, Milligan, Bentine and Secombe had stayed up all night listening to, upstairs at Grafton's, using a short-wave apparatus and antenna supplied by guess-who. It was a slang word, heard on the streets of Boston in the 1890s, spelt variously as gooney or gawney, and meant a brain-bereft simpleton. The first appearance in print was in E.C. Segar's 'Popeye' comic strip, in 1938; Alice the Goon was a subhuman creature, her speech-balloon filled with a cloud of scribbles. Subsidiary meanings include: a hatchet man or bully, hired by gangsters to eliminate opponents. (POWs called their German guards goons.) As a goon is the equivalent of a sap, a boob, a thug, the most unpardonable gawkery, fit only for a clerd, would be to say things that made too much sense. 'We didn't want to make sense,' said Milligan of his conversations with Sellers. 'The last thing we wanted to do was to make sense. So we worked on that.'

In addition to his powerful wireless, Sellers also introduced his Sound Mirror to the proceedings, a primitive semi-portable tape recording machine, weighing forty-five pounds and housed in a mahogany box. (He owned the first one, which conceivably ran on steam.) Into this device the quartet poured their gobbledeegook. *Picture Post* came to the tavern to do a spread on a lodge meeting and described goonery as comedy 'that doesn't despise your intelligence'. And, indeed, a paradox of the style is that, whilst eulogising idiots, you do need a certain mental agility to follow its flow. Your imagination is made to work. Eccles, so dopey he's in a state of grace; Bluebottle, 'a short thin shivering youth heavily wrapped up in rice paper and dental string'; Henry Crun and Minnie, clucking and twittering like startled chickens; Grytpype

Thynne, for all his attempts to be a master fraudster, always down on his luck – they are the dispossessed, scroungers, swindlers, and alms-hunters (worlds away from the middle-class domesticity of *Ray's a Laugh, ITMA, Men from the Ministry* etc.) – yet, as Sellers said, 'the public identified themselves with these characters and situations, because to many of them they were more than just funny voices. They were caricatures of real people.' This was certainly Sellers' own response. Strip down the surrealism and the characters represent characteristics: greed, hunger, jealousy, rage, innocence, ignorance; basic drives which we try and curb in ourselves, but which *The Goon Show* let out of school.

Though the quartet was in place by 1949, however, it would be another two years before their in-jokes and gibberish would be ready for the public. As the Major explained, 'these four young men are planning to form a new "crazy gang" when they have made even bigger names for themselves as single acts'. Milligan, by the autumn of 1949, had become the writer for a show called *Hip-Hip-Hoo-Roy* (starring Derek Roy, whom he now says was 'about as funny as a baby with cancer') and he was devising material for Alfred Marks, Bill Kerr, Dick Emery, and Secombe. Secombe was regularly on radio. Bentine had added a sink plunger to his chair-back and was beflummoxing the audience of *Folies-Bergère*, and Sellers – well, Sellers was on radio so often, even when he wasn't, people thought it was still he. He wasn't so much as speaking for the stars as instead of them. After the pre-recording of *Arthur Askey's Christmas Show*, on October 21st, for example, a nervous variety booking manager wrote to all Sellers' victims, explaining that they'll be hearing themselves on a programme for which they had no contract – they were warned that they'd literally be hearing things.

26th October, 1949

Dick Bentley Esq.,
c/o Ted Kavanagh Associated,
36 Bruton St.,
W1

Dear Dick Bentley,

'ARTHUR ASKEY CHRISTMAS SHOW' HOME SERVICE
24th December, 1949. 6.30-7.0.p.m
(Pre-recording: 21st October, 1949.)

As you probably know Arthur Askey has left for Australia but,
since he always does a programme at Christmas time, we are
anxious that this year shall not prove an exception. As such we
have prepared a programme in which he is presumed to be
calling on the parents of various Australian artists and one of the
people concerned will be presumed to be your father. The actual
voice of course will sound to be yours and the impression is
being done by Peter Sellers.

I hope I can take it that you will be agreeable to this. I should be
glad of confirmation that you have no objection.

> Yours sincerely,
> *Pat Newman*
> Variety Booking Manager

Bentley happily gave his consent for Sellers to duplicate him, as
did Miss Phyllis Rounce, of International Artistes Representation,
on behalf of Bill Kerr. Not all celebrities were amenable, however,
to Sellers co-opting them and turning the BBC into a one-man
operation. Gracie Fields, her shrieks in much need of satirical
deconstruction, had notified the Corporation that no unauthorised
impersonation may be broadcast. . .

☆ ★ ☆

Before the Goons became *The Goon Show*, therefore, they were
reaching for the highest ranks in entertainment as individuals – and
Sellers was there first. In 1950, Monty Lyon was negotiating with
Pat Newman for Sellers to be given a three-year contract. This was
to guarantee him a minimum of twenty-six broadcasts (as distinct
from repeats) in one or more series per annum, with the fees ranging from twenty-five to thirty-five guineas for each appearance.
The assurance that he'd not suffer from complete financial aridity,
however, didn't satisfy Sellers. As a man who did not wish to be

circumscribed, he found that the offer raised problems. Long term variety contracts were settled on Billy Cotton, Ted Ray, Henry Hall and Jack Train without ado, but Sellers felt, if he was beholden to the BBC, if they had first call on his services, wouldn't this jeopardise his availability for stage work? Yet, on the other hand, if he rose to eminence with the BBC, his popularity with the public at large would increase, and he could capitalise on this by making a snootful of booty, appearing at distant Hippodromes and Empire Theatres. Then again, if he was away travelling, how could he arrange to be standing at a microphone in London? Sellers was fond of independence, but the BBC (in the pre-ITV era) was a monopoly; he wanted to progress from penury, but he didn't want to be sold into bondage. The solution was to drag out negotiations for as long as possible. There was a lot of correspondence, to and fro, about how much notice Sellers would have to give, should a more lucrative offer than *Workers' Playtime* or *Henry Hall's Guest Night* arise. The position was summarised early in 1951, thus:

8th January, 1951

Montague Lyon Esq.,
Messr Lew & Leslie Grade Ltd.,
Regent House,
235-241, Regent Street,
London, W.1

Dear Mr Lyon,

Re: PETER SELLERS

Following on our preliminary discussions both on the 'phone and in my office we have, in line with various views expressed by both sides, revised to some extent the suggested offer we should like to make to the above Artist.

I now set out hereunder the principle points we should like to suggest:-

1. The Agreement will be for two years and will, as far as

possible, come into force on the expiry of any current contract.

2. During the period of the Agreement the Artist may not undertake work for any other broadcasting organisation without the permission of the Corporation.

3. The Corporation will have first call on the Artist's services from 1st September to 31st March in each year.

4. The Corporation will use its best endeavours to ensure that in each year of the Agreement the Artist is offered not less than twenty-six engagements in major productions and that they shall include one series of thirteen.

5. The Artist's fee for each major engagement shall be Twenty Five Guineas (£26.5.0.) in the first year of the Agreement and Thirty Guineas (£31.10.0.) in the second year, but the Corporation reserves the right to negotiate smaller fees for less important engagements such as gramophone record programmes.

6. The Artist will sign the appropriate form of standard contract for each engagement or series of engagements.

7. The Corporation guarantees that in each year of the Agreement the Artist's total revenue from the Corporation (including any mechanical reproduction or Television fees) shall be not less than One Thousand Pounds (£1,000.0.0.). If the Corporation fails to offer the Artist sufficient engagements to bring his earnings up to this sum, the Corporation shall pay the Artist the difference between the sum actually earned and One Thousand Pounds (£1,000.0.0.). If the Artist fails through any reason to accept any engagements offered by the B.B.C. in respect of the period 1st September to 31st March, the sum guaranteed under the Agreement shall be reduced by the amount of the fees which he would have received had he accepted the engagements. There will be no reduction in the sum

guaranteed in respect of engagements offered but not accepted in respect of any other period of the year.

8. Payment of the sum guaranteed shall be a complete discharge of the Corporation's obligations to the Artist under the Agreement and the Artist shall have no claim against the Corporation for loss of publicity by reason only of the Corporation failing to offer a minimum of twenty-six engagements in each year.

I should be glad to have your observations on this as soon as you can possibly manage; if you find the suggestions agreeable they will be incorporated in a formal contract which will be sent to you for signature in due course.

> Yours sincerely,
> *Patrick Newman*
> Variety Booking Manager

The chief developments following on from the above were (a) the contract would be re-negotiable after two years, not three; (b) the servitude was for seven months, not the full twelve, thus freeing Sellers for summer shows in coastal winter gardens; (c) these concessions were counter-balanced by piffling reductions in the suggested fees (point 5); and (d) what is that parenthetical reference in (7) to television? This particular draft fell through, in fact, because Sellers considered television a separate cake stand. Lyon informed Newman on February 13th that a fee of forty guineas would be expected 'per vision broadcast'. Silence then fell until March 6th, when Sellers' agent wrote, as if out of the blue, to say: 'I have had a few offers for this artiste to play in Variety out of town, and naturally do not want to commit him, until I first hear from you, as to when you will require him ... I am sorry to be rushing you on this matter, but you must appreciate that I do not want to lose work for my artiste.' The tone appears to be deferential, but the meaning is plain: Sellers is in demand. You need him as much as he needs you.

A contract was finally signed on April 26th, to come into force on July 27th – for a period of two years. It did indeed prove a bind. Dennis Selinger, who took over when Monty Lyon retired to breed pigs in Ireland (as he himself remarked, an unusual occupation for a Jewish man), was frequently writing to seek permission for Sellers to be released so he could play the Hippodrome, Dudley, for a week, or diversify in a late-night Delfont revue, and such. But what concerns us at this particular post-chaise stop in the narrative is Newman's point (4). By not tying Sellers down to any specific programme, by leaving the mention of a series very vague, the BBC, in their innocence, had left wide a gap through which a particular quartet of stumblebums would be thrusting.

☆ ★ ☆

Milligan freely admits that 'Peter Sellers was instrumental in getting *The Goon Show* on the air. He was doing very well on radio and went to Pat Dixon, a BBC producer, and said that we four would like to be together in a show.' Sellers had known Dixon (something of an eccentric who kept his office filled with memorabilia of the American Civil War) since working with him on *Third Division* in December 1948 and on seven episodes of *Petticoat Lane* a year later. He came to Grafton's, laughed at the antics, and promised that if a script could be concocted, he'd recommend a series to the planning department. Dixon had no real hope, however, of being taken up on this. The semi-drunken streams of consciousness in the saloon bar were little more than after-hours rags by delayed adolescents. He underestimated the Major and the Sound-Mirror.

Whilst the others were petting the pub's marmoset, Johnny, shooting lighted cigarettes out of each other's mouths with an air pistol, or demonstrating sumo wrestling holds, Sellers was fiddling with his tape machine, getting his pals to make battle-field noises, or to conduct long conversations in an incomprehensible Scottish brogue. The Major then suggested, instead of baffling people – say, why don't we fill up a spool for Dixon? With everybody contributing ideas, he wrote a script, shaped around Sellers, called *Sellers' Castle*. The characters and nonsense they'd tossed about, during the past eighteen months, were gathered into a decrepit stately home – to form a sort of Addams family – with Milligan's Eccles as the servant, Bentine a mad inventor locked in the dungeons, Secombe as a wandering minstrel and Sellers as Crun-cum-Bloodnok, the reigning Lord of Misrule. With the assistance of Barry Barron, who had a private recording studio in Bond Street fancifully called 'Gui-de-Buire' (the sprig of mistletoe), the Major made arrangements for the demo disc. To introduce the story, provide links, and to generally add an air of mock gravity, he got in touch with the newscaster Andrew Timothy – whom he had met in Iceland during the war: 'I was rung up one day by a chap called Jimmy Grafton,' Timothy says, 'and he recalled the Icelandic days; I said "Oh yes, my dear chap!" – "Well, come down and have a drink," he said. So, I went down to The Grafton, and he had had this idea of this zany humour – *The Goon Show* – and he was the inspirer of it, and a supporter of it, in the early days, because none of the Goons then had two brass farthings to rub together. He said, "We're doing a rather unusual show . . . and I wonder if you'd like to announce it and take part in it?" And I said, "Well all right, yes, fine." So we went to a sleazy recording studio in Bond Street, which was covered in dust, and we did this; I didn't think it was the least bit funny, very lame, and I thought it was ghastly.'

Grafton took the result and played it to Roy Speer sometime in 1950. Speer took the unusual step of inviting the cast round to read the script to him personally in his cubby-hole at Variety Headquarters – he wanted to be sure there *was* a script and that those concerned could repeat their performances. It had sounded so improvised. Jacques Brown was then given the task of making a pilot in the BBC's Piccadilly studio. Without an audience for the cast to giggle with, though, and repeating the material of *Sellers' Castle* for the third time, the atmosphere was cold and forced. The planners chucked it out. Dixon, however, could detect potential. One of the later producers of *The Goon Show*, John Browell, has said that 'there was one man at the BBC, Pat Dixon, who was firmly convinced that no matter how terrible the Goons were, he was going to persuade the BBC to keep them on and he did so.' Dixon had also heard some of the bootleg 'Sound Mirror' gibberish. He'd enjoyed it, and cunningly resurrected the idea of a series for Sellers just when his colleagues were trying to get that long-term contract signed in early 1951. The trial recording for *The Junior Crazy Gang,* on February 4th, was what induced Sellers to at last come to terms.

Dixon did not wish to produce the curiosa himself. He handed the programme to Dennis Main Wilson, as Dennis Wilson was now known – though not to Sellers, who preferred to call him Dennis Main Drain (revenge for those unanswered BANG ON letters of the late Forties) – and the pilot and early shows bear little comparison to what we'd recognise as authentic goonery. For a start, it was not called *The Goon Show*. The billing opted for clumsiness –

CRAZY PEOPLE
featuring
Radio's Own Crazy Gang
'The Goons'

The allusion to those madcap uncles, Bud Flanagan, Chesney Allen, Eddie Grey, Jimmy Nervo, Teddy Knox, Charlie Naughton and Jimmy Gold, was apt. At the Palladium during the war (and during actual air raids), and at the Victoria Palace in the late Forties and throughout the Fifties, they were Britain's premier practical jokers. In productions with titles like *March Hares, These Foolish Kings*, and *The Little Dog Laughed*, they threw buckets of wallpaper paste over each other (and the audience), ran off the stage and into the foyer, to give their performances there, darted into the stalls and emptied ladies' bags, and generally created the illusion of inflicting grievous bodily harm on one and all. They interrupted other acts (eg. by dropping cabbages from the flies or hiding essential props), drenched the scene-shifters with soda syphons, and dreamt up ways of making life difficult for George Black, the impresario – on one occasion by going to the trouble of filling his office with

---

* The total budget, to come out of the Experimental Fund, was £125, of which Sellers received 15 guineas, and Milligan £7.17/6 for the script.

thirty tapping and leaping children from the Italia Conti Dancing School, on the pretext that he was holding auditions. (George Black was their Sig Ruman).

They loved extending the nuttiness of theatre into real life. Eddie Grey bought a salmon and told the shopkeeper he'd call back later to collect it. He returned in disguise, snatched up the fish and fled to cries of 'Stop thief!' At other moments the gang advocated feeding charcoal to dogs and spread the rumour that dwarves lived in pillar boxes. Michael Bentine was once confronted in his dressing room by a dour-looking reporter, pencil poised: 'My name is Carstairs. I'm from the *Manchester Evening News*. Is it true that you have been taking drugs?' It took Bentine a terrified moment to recognise a member of the Crazy Gang; another few seconds again to see any humour in being set up. (Other disconcerting extramural rôles included playing at policemen investigating rapes, and doctors examining everybody for signs of cholera.)

They never had script writers and refused to go on the radio, finding it restrictive. Above all, they loved spontaneity, and in this as much as anything the Crazy Gang clearly pre-incarnated *The Goon Show* – the task of Sellers, Milligan, Secombe and Bentine being to find a sonic equivalent for their precursors' slapstick and inspired lunacy, which Churchill had said reminded him of the House of Commons. They had to get around fixed time schedules (the Crazy Gang were always getting audiences to miss the last train), engineers twiddling knobs and producers who had the power to edit what you'd achieved before it was broadcast. 'I've followed the Goons ever since they started on the air,' said Bud Flanagan, 'and I'm one of their biggest champions. They're brilliant – especially Sellers.'

☆ ★ ☆

'So we started,' said Andrew Timothy, 'and we used to do the recordings in the Aeolian Hall in Bond Street, and I thought I really was entering a mad house. We started recording – well, started rehearsing – on Sundays; the whole of Sunday went, and we'd start at 9.30, when the script, if there was a complete script, was delivered, and the Goons pored over it, criticised the jokes that the other Goons had put in, and thought of something much funnier themselves – and this went on steadily without a break until 7 o'clock in the evening, when there was a mass exodus, and the departure to a little Edwardian pub called The Grosvenor, just round the corner. . . .'

After that, they returned and made the actual recording. A witness in the studio audience during the very first of the *Crazy People* series* (which is what *The Junior Crazy Gang* had become after the pilot), would have mingled with a crowd of about fifty persons who were disappointed not to be getting free tickets for *The Bernard Braden Show*. They grumbled and clattered down many steps to find a small underground bunker, a low platform (no proper stage or tabs) and microphones with L plates. Bentine appeared to applause, adjusted the microphone stand to ten feet above his head, and exited, stage left, fiddling with his trousers. A piano was wheeled on, and wheeled off. Bentine reappeared, stage right, and went into a routine with an inflated inner-tube – he encouraged the audience to believe it was a canoe, Jane Russell's tits, and a Mexican hat. Secombe entered and blew raspberries, Milligan tried to break people's concentration with ad libs, and Sellers did his fanciful impersonations of Queen Victoria. The audience was rather more bemused than amused, and weren't totally overjoyed to be told, 'If this hasn't recorded properly we may have to go through it all again, folks, so fasten your seat belts or at least your raincoat.'

Despite the bonhomie, *Crazy People* divulged more caution than innovation. Sellers did little more than come out with his Dick Barton parodies; Secombe's character was called Jones, and he got up to horseplay at a health clinic, in Russia, and on holiday during the Yukon Gold Rush; Milligan's appearances were few; and Bentine's Professor Osric Pureheart, his inventor from *Sellers' Castle*, gave lectures on his jet engines or a solid lead violin for deaf musicians.

---

* The series (of seventeen) was recorded during the summer of 1951, the first instalment being on May 28th. Another series began on January 22nd 1952.

But nothing happens – there were no pay-offs. The scenes were monologues, or spots, and were interspersed with soggy musical interludes from Max Geldray, Ray Ellington, and The Stargazers. (There was no orchestra.)

They kept up the rhythm until July 1952. Sellers had introduced Major Bloodnok the previous August, and titles were growing Goonish ('The Bentine Lurgi Driven Tank', 'The Quest for Cloot Wilmington'), but the format continued to be, literally, sketchy. Secombe even contributed opera arias – straight, without farts. *Crazy People* was a concert evening. Except for a pastiche of Rider Haggard's *She*, on March 18th, entitled *Her*, in which the flame for everlasting life was cut off by the gas board, this was the variety circuit all over again. ('Handsome Harry Secombe' instead of Henry Hall). Sellers, Milligan etc. were introduced by their real names; characters and voices don't interact much; the sound effects were perfunctory. At the end of 1951, in between the first and second series, Main Wilson wrote a lengthy report on the programme – and the fact there had been so few novelties must have boded well for its future.

From a political angle, the comments about Bentine are intriguing and imply why he was prevailed upon to leave before the start of the third series in November 1952.* Main Wilson says that, first, Bentine's character's manic voice is too similar to Secombe's (as far as complaints from listeners were concerned), and secondly, the Osric Pureheart spot was getting cumbersome – ideally it should be 'more relaxed in pace ... with more movement and more *clever* plot and situation comedy'. Yet, achieving this would only be to give it the same style as the Bloodnok adventure,

---

* There were already jealousies between Bentine and Milligan as to who was the chief supplier of ideas. 'We would turn up for a session,' Sir Harry recalls, 'Spike and Mike would spark each other off, and at the end of the session both of them would go away thinking that most of the ideas were theirs. So there was a little bit of friction in that respect. Each one accusing the other of plagiarism, though not seriously. But that disappeared when Mike decided he wanted Sundays to the family. Which was fair enough, and he left.'

which was the show's climax: 'these two sketches keep coming dangerously close in style . . . resulting in lack of contrast throughout the half hour . . . I suggest that Michael should be built into Bloodnok's second-in-command as a subaltern, using his powerful and resonant "dwarling/Hyde Pork [*sic*]" voice – in other words a clot with a private income.'

Sellers interpreted all this as a duel, himself v Bentine. Not long before he died, at the age of seventy-eight, Andrew Timothy confessed that the atmosphere during the first read-throughs of the script could be distinctly unpleasant: 'When the Goons would settle down to see how big their own particular part was that week, there would be considerable annoyance if Peter seemed to have got a bigger part than Mike or vice versa . . . In fact,' Timothy went on, 'there was a permanent sparring match between Bentine and Sellers. Whenever we were sitting at the table reading through the script, any funny suggestion of Bentine's was immediately destroyed by Sellers – because he thought Bentine looked down on him. Bentine was Eton; he was more or less East End. Bentine eventually got fed up with this and left. Sellers was a difficult chap. The way he had of creeping into himself suggested impatience and anger. *He sort of crept into himself.* . . .' (It's where he went to meet his characters.)

Main Wilson's other suggestions, that they go all out to identify the Goon performers with the characters they play in the show, and that dialogue be kept down to an intelligible pace, – ensuring funny voices aren't gabbled, but shared with the audience – start to intimate *The Goon Show* proper, as (in a specific sense) does his concluding remark:

> We hope that Planners will agree to build the programme as 'The Goon Show' rather than 'Crazy People'. This is purely because everybody, both in and outside the business, refers to it as the Goon Show (or *that* Goon Show) but never as 'Crazy People' (which quite frankly could be applied to almost any comedy show).

Sellers used to enjoy melting into doddering Henry Crun to explain what happened next. 'In the early days we had a very small listening figure, but it soon got up to huge proportions. There used to be weekly meetings of the programme planners, and one week, one of the old boys looked at the agenda and asked an executive, "Tell me about this Go On Show."

"No sir, it's not 'go on', it's actually 'goon'.'"

"Coon? G.H. Elliott, d'ye mean?"

"No sir, that's chocolate coloured. It's 'goon' not 'coon'.'"

"Goon? What is a goon? White-faced coons?"

"I don't quite know sir, but they are having very big listening figures."

"Well then, they must go on."'

☆ ★ ☆

Up at Oxford there are dons working for maybe as much as forty-eight hours a year, establishing Shakespeare's texts. They sift through the leaves of the First Folio and the Bad Quarto, examining the principles governing the use of various spellings; they study Elizabethan Grammar and stagecraft; they footnote, gloss, ponder, fret. They hunt for symbols and lecture on imagery. Doctoral gowns are awarded and careers made if you can argue that (say) in *Timon of Athens*, Act III, sc.iv., 1. 58, Will meant to write 'If 'twill' rather than 'if 't twill'. But the academic industry buoying up the Swan of Avon is a dry sponge compared with the scholarship generated by *The Goon Show*. There are entire books (and countless articles) devoted to it – chief amongst them being Roger Wilmut's authoritative gazetteer, *The Goon Show Companion*, and Alfred Draper's biographical *The Story of the Goons*. Milligan, in collaboration with Sellers and Secombe, has published *The Goon Show Scripts*, *More Goon Show Scripts*, *The Book of the Goons* and *The Lost Goon Shows*. There are symposia (often held at Grafton's), conferences, monthly meetings of fans who communicate solely in old catchphrases ('What-what-what-what-what') and, most important of all, there is The Goon Show Preservation Society, which produces a learned journal once a quarter. *The Newsletter** is the place where you find out that 'The Tuscan Salami Scandal' is correctly 'The Great Tuscan Salami Scandal', and that ying-tong-iddle-i-po, another of the catchphrases and the lyric of a Goon song, is actually Mandarin Chinese for 'I must have sexual intercourse.'

By analysing draft scripts, phonograph rolls, variant recordings in the BBC archives, and badgering anyone left alive who toiled behind the scenes, researchers have plotted the show's development from a series of random light comedy sketches into classics like 'The Scarlet Capsule' and 'Tales of Old Dartmoor'. Rehearsal notes and jokes from one week would be worked into scripts designed for broadcast the next; stories were often recycled; characters gradually took on a life of their own, and spoke their own stage directions. ('Enter Bluebottle with a smile and a song. Stands waist deep in snow so that Neddy Seagoon will not laugh at my legs. Smiles grimly and jabs alpenstock in snow – ooooh my footy.')

For all this Goonology, however, and at the risk of coming across as a braggart rivalling A.L. Rowse, who makes mention at every possible juncture that he, and he alone, had the wit to unlock Shakespeare's heart and solve the cryptographs in the Sonnets, it does rather seem to me that the gist of *The Goon Show*, and the source of its power for its performers, has been overlooked until now. I mean of course that it was a surreal response to the violence and behaviour of the war. ('To think that nobody had ever noticed the obvious fact hitherto!' as Rowse would crow.) Explosions, machine gun fire, mortar blasts, bombs and shells: the noises of combat punctuate each episode. Poor old Major Bloodnok's stomach is a battle zone of mines and fizzing shrapnel; Moriarty makes the mistake of smoking 'a nice big long red cigar with a wick on the end';

---

* Study is in its infancy in America. *The U.S. Newsletter* for March 1978 has to inform subscribers that 'Bryan Secombe of the D'Oyly Carte Opera Company Ltd. is no relation to the well-known entertainer, Mr Harry Secombe.'

and Bluebottle and Eccles, as archetypal cannon fodder, have to be scraped off the walls after the frequent detonations and bangs. Right up until the final show in 1960, it was still the Germans the characters were up against. When Hen and Min take a clifftop stroll, in 'The Batter Pudding Hurler', they worry about the blackout and whether Hitler will invade Bexhill-on-Sea. A running gag is that whenever anybody strikes a match, a doodlebug is launched from across the Channel and scores a direct hit on Min and Hen's legs, which are blown off time and again. In 'Tales of Men's Shirts,' Britain's generals are busy typing their memoirs and aren't aware that their armies are clapped in a POW Camp – a German nick ('that swine – he and Belgian Tom'); and in 'The Jet Propelled NAAFI', a mighty aerial fleet is despatched to drink the surplus service tea. There are dozens of shows with army themes – in 'Dishonoured' it's the turn of the North West Frontier, and Eccles does the 'Dance of the Seven Army Surplus Blankets'; 'The Histories of Pliny the Elder,' has the Romans threatening the English much as the Nazis do, and everybody ends up inside an active volcano, which erupts apocalyptically ... Men marching, men grunting like pigs when at ease, army boots, (especially army boots: a PhD. could be written on the references to army boots in *The Goon Show*), bivouacs, tanks made of cardboard, pistol shots, spies, counterfeit uniforms, medals, court martials, top secret plans – all this forms the background of Goonery, a world of conscription and England in the Forties, re-lived in the Fifties.

☆　★　☆

The artistic style of the Great War was elegy – Rupert Brooke blowing his golden bugle over the rich dead; or the works left by those mutilated and annihilated Grail Knights, Wilfred Owen, Edward Thomas, and Henri Gaudier-Brzeska, writing about loss or sculpting angels. Death was spoken of as an aesthetic deed in itself – Peter Pan's awfully big adventure. Photographs falling out of albums from the period depict rather serious, beautiful young men, the sepia casting them in the shadows of a death-wish; these boys went off, full of nobility and stoicism, to be blasted to bits for the

King's shilling. It is hard to believe, at this distance, that it was allowed to happen – the combination of gallantry and waste was relentless and dehumanising. Photographs of No Man's Land are of a misty moonscape, craters and spindly trees; a world destroyed by dragon's breath. Hardly reality – more like jittery steel-engravings or raw material for Stanley Spencer or Paul Nash. Modern history quickly dwindles into pictures – or *the* pictures, for events are swiftly re-enacted by movie stars. (If I was sent back in a time machine to meet Mata Hari it would be a disappointment not to see Greta Garbo.)

The Second World War, however, was less of an Arthurian pageant. People had fewer illusions about barbed wire and bullets, and no patience with rhetoric. Is it only a coincidence that snapshots of officers and other ranks look less posed – less like a theatrical company stuck in the corner of a studio? Pictures, taken for *Time-Life*, for example, are of men boozing, smoking, muddy, exhausted, playing the piano or sleeping. Perhaps it was the first documentary war, as against the literary affairs of the past. Whatever, its artistic consequences were satire and humour – from Evelyn Waugh's ironically entitled *Sword of Honour* trilogy to Anthony Burgess' *Little Wilson and Big God*, to Milligan's adventure stories – as mentioned earlier, he has worked all his life with what he took out of the war. In this respect, it is interesting to compare *The Goon Show* with the art of Ronald Searle. Prison camps and torturers, which Searle met with when enslaved on the Siam–Burma Railway, were converted by the imagination of comic genius, into St Trinian's wicked and gleeful school girls. Searle's serpentine, brittle, scratchy lines, the way he uses the nib to jab and wound the paper, remind me of the Goons' jagged, broken-off narrative logic – it is as if form, for both the visual and acoustic cartoonists, was a trace on an encephalograph, and what we see or hear are the brain's hysterical, choppy waves.

I asked Searle about *The Goon Show*, for he was re-living his war in the pages of *Punch* at the same time as they were theirs over the airwaves. I wondered if, perhaps, he'd been to the Grafton Arms? This postcard flew from France:

I'm not a pub man. Not even Jimmy Grafton's, so far as I remember. I knew Sellers a little, though, and I used to go to the Goon rehearsal/recordings somewhere in a BBC cinema in Islington(?) [The Camden Theatre, Mornington Crescent]. It is too long ago really to be precise when it is needed. Can't say that I really liked Sellers. Too uneasy to be around with. I preferred Spike Milligan's sparkings off. And I remember having to leap to his defence when he was attacked for the send up of *River Kwai* on one of the Goon things, by a humourless public. . . .

The Goon Show often parodied contemporary war films, such as 'The Fear of Wages' (for Yves Montand's *The Wages of Fear*), 'Wings over Dagenham' (for any ace-aviator thriller starring John Mills) and 'Rommels's Treasure' (for James Mason's Field-Marshal in *The Desert Fox*), amongst many others. *I Was Monty's Double* became 'I Was Monty's Treble' and they had a go at Ronald Neame's *The Man Who Never Was* three times – perhaps because Sellers himself had dubbed lots of voices on to its soundtrack. There is also something about kitting out a corpse with false identity papers, to mislead the enemy over the invasion of Italy, which was goonish all on its own. David Lean's *The Bridge on the River Kwai* was thus an ideal subject: Japs, jungles, questions of honour. Though the episode was called 'African Incident', the plot mocked and followed the portentousness of Lean's epic closely – the source was further identified when Sellers gave an impersonation of Sir Alec Guinness' Col. Nicholson, falling on the dynamite plunger. This particular story was revived in 1962 by Parlophone. Sellers and Milligan, without Secombe, were joined by Jonathan Miller and Peter Cook. Amongst the gruesome sound effects the surviving Goons now wanted was that of a man's head being chopped off. A cleaver taken to a fresh cabbage bought in Alma Square did the trick and was (says George Martin, the producer) 'totally blood curdling'. After having made the album, however, EMI were confronted with a writ for copyright infringement. Not ony did people seem to think that Lean's film was sacrosanct and that Japanese atrocities against British prisoners of war, in the Changi Gaol, Singapore, where

Searle went, were no laughing matter; but Columbia were as proprietorial over the proper noun *Kwai* as Warner Bros had been when the Marx Bros lampooned *Casablanca*. The solution was ingenious. An editor went through the master-tape snipping out every 'K' – to create *The Bridge on the River Wye*.

☆   ★   ☆

Hilarity needn't only be a response to the war, a release mechanism. Farce co-exists within the service atmosphere already. The disorder people were subjected to, the immense confusions, had made a Goon show out of ordinary life. No railway station signs or road markings, for example; the shortages and queues – there's an entire episode devoted to 'The Lone Banana'; the blunders. Each of the Goons had this sort of material to draw on. Secombe's Seagoon relives comically many of the trials Sir Harry faced as a member of Operation Torch, the invasion of North Africa. Secombe saw heavy action and was in the thick of dive bombers and mortar fire for months on end. The mud, the lice-ridden clothing, sand-fly fever, malaria, took its toll – 'All the fighting had affected my nerves,' he has admitted. After the heat of Tunisia, he suffered exposure in the snows of Italy's mountains, and 'I found the bitter cold hard to bear.' He spent five weeks in hospital, lost two stones in weight, and when he met Milligan, who had experienced many horrors and had just been discharged from a psychiatric hospital near Sorrento, Sir Harry says rather cryptically, 'there but for the grace of God I too might have gone'.

The mangling of bodies and buildings, the gassings and the threat of atomic radiation – the objects of laughter on *The Goon Show* – these were lived through by Bentine, also. When he joined up he was nearly killed by the serum in a routine innoculation. He lost stones in weight and came out in abscesses. When he trained in the RAF Intelligence, he was issued with a Crimea era kit, attended lectures on field latrines, and dealt with the dropping of tin toilets over Berlin (the Germans accused the British of conducting bacteriological warfare). He tried to help officers escape from POW camps by secreting radio parts in jam and printing messages in invisible inks on grey blankets – 'personal evasion kits', they were called, and could *The Goon Show* improve on any bit of it? Like Secombe, he collapsed from the strain. 'My kindly C.O.', he says, 'had guessed how near I was to going over the edge.' He became emaciated, could not control his flow of tears, and reached, after years of training navigation crews, 'the limits of endurance'. He, too, was hospitalised for weeks.

Milligan has made no mystery of his invalid status. When he was caught in a bomb blast he 'started to cry and shake and shiver. . . . They gave me some tablets. . . , they gave me some tranquillisers, I think, which sent me to sleep, sent me out of the lines for seven days. Then they sent me up to the guns and as soon as I heard the guns go, I started to stammer.' It is a paradox that, hating noise as much as he does – a neighbour's lawnmower, for instance, or a surge of muzak, can to this day trigger manic depression attacks – *The Goon Show* should be so full of it. 'The Batter Pudding Hurler' has Crun fire an elephant gun, 'The Evils of Bushey Spon' a blunderbuss. The climax is always a huge explosion. After trying to rid Trafalgar Square of pests, in 'The Starlings', and rice puddings launched from catapults having failed to do the trick, exploding bird-lime is invented by Bloodnok – the starlings are despatched by the turning of central London into the Somme, with heavy artillery pounding away. When an instalment of *The Goon Show* ends, it sounds like the end of the world. ('The Starlings', in fact, excels itself for din. From the flocks of cawing birds to Crun and Churchill coughing and spluttering in parliament, to the rattle of dustbin lids and the whistles and rattles used before the military arrive, the show is a cacophony.)

Other key personnel were casualties of war. Max Geldray, the harmonica player, was also caught in a bomb blast and flung into a foxhole. He recovered consciousness in a field hospital, and was surprised to see so few bloodied bandages. Then he noticed that the men were shuffling, shivering, screaming, weeping. The commonest symptom of a mental scar was the inability to speak – 'this silence, and the way they stared out at the world,' he says, 'was the most frightening of all.' Geldray himself suffered nightmares, which left him feeling his body was being crushed and compressed. He was shipped back to England, put in a hospital for several months, and gradually his mind was restored. 'But still I could not look people in the eye, and I would continually stare at the ground as I walked about. Often, I would begin to cry.'

Dennis Main Wilson, the producer, as an officer in the Royal Armoured Corps, had been Head of Light Entertainment (*Unterhaltungschef*) for the Nord-West-Deutscher-Rundfunk, in Hamburg, part of the Propaganda Service of the Central Commission. He saw the results of Nazi atrocities in German occupied towns and, back in England, according to a profile on him in the *Observer* (June 1988), 'a sort of delayed shell-shock took hold of him for a while'. Throughout his career, the tension of those times recurred: 'He has, on occasion, overwound himself, which he does admit, and was once ordered to bed for a whole month to cool off.' Against which, Peter Eton, Wilson's successor on *The Goon Show*, who served in the Royal Navy and lost a leg; and Larry Stephens, one of Wingate's Raiders, who collaborated on the scripts with Milligan – well, their experience and intrepidity are no more than you'd expect in this roster of old comrades.

☆ ★ ☆

And Sellers? His war, as we have seen in an earlier chapter, was joyous. *The Goon Show*, quite simply, brought his lawlessness into focus – gave it expression. 'They really were my happiest days, those Sundays when we did *The Goon Show*,' he said in 1971 – and he'd repeat the sentiment over and over. 'I can really say that it was the happiest professional period of my life. I never had such fun, enjoyment or fulfilment either before or since,' he told Ray Connolly in 1972; and a few years earlier when making *There's a Girl in My Soup*, he insisted to Freddy Clayton that 'all my prayers were answered when along came *The Goon Show*. I think it all really started from there. Whatever the future holds for me, I'm sure of one thing, there will never be another era quite like that one.'

As he approached his end, his beginnings loomed large in his mind. In the last weeks of his life, he was saying, 'The Goon Shows were the happiest days I have spent in this industry – the entertainment industry, whatever it be. Those Sundays at the Paris Cinema or the Aeolian Hall – which is not there now, not looking like it did, anyway – were the happiest Sundays I have spent, the happiest times I have ever had. . . We were young men with very strong and ambitious ideas. There used to be a form of euphoria and we were swept along and we swept people along with us. We were in another world. Can't explain it. It was a happening . . . I have never had such good times. I never had such laughs.' Auberon Waugh, one of the last people outside of Sellers' train to see him alive, commented that, time and again, in a conversation which ranged over the wives, the wealth, the films, Sellers always returned to the nine years he spent doing *The Goon Show*; his reminiscences then seemed 'the truest and most deeply felt'.

The problem we face when trying to see the development of Sellers' ideas and technique, especially with regard to *The Goon Show*, is to make adequate allowance for his sentimentality and nostaliga. Only when suffering from vertigo at the pinnacles of international success did he start to idealise his radio days. And whenever there was a chance of reviving the series, he was the one who'd hesitate and spoil the deal. After the success of *The Last Goon Show of All*, a one-off, twelve years after the programme had officially finished, Peter Eton discussed the possibilities of further specials with the stars. 'They were all terribly keen on this,' he said in 1976, 'but recently Peter started backing out, having been frightfully keen. The other two, Secombe and Milligan, are still keen, available and willing – but now Peter is the problem.' Eton claimed that Sellers was employing a 'cultural adviser', an American, who was advising him: 'don't do any more "Goon Shows" – they're all passé!' Also, Sellers was about to re-encounter Inspector Clouseau, and had film after film lined up. 'So it's going to be very difficult,' said Eton. Totally impossible, as it turned out (and Eton has died now, too).

Sellers would always have a 'cultural adviser' or press agent, lawyer, manager or some such lackey to hide behind if he decided to change his mind, switch enthusiasms. To re-make *The Goon Show* would, of course, have been retrogressive. I think he was right not to take up Eton's overtures. So, as regards his pining for the good old days, what did he really mean? What he was looking back so fondly at was the way, with his voice alone, he could create a wonderland. This, the province of the radio actor, is not quite possible in cinema, where appearances, too, have to be deceptive. It is revealing that, when Sellers had the almightiness to get scripts rewritten, directors hired and fired, and sets torn down, reconstructed, and then never used, on, for instance, *Casino Royale* or *The Fiendish Plot of Dr Fu Manchu*, it was because he was trying to achieve, through the cumbersomeness of film studios, the fleeting quick-change of ideas he'd once accomplished at the microphone with no trouble at all ... But the years it took to shoot *Casino Royale* quite dissipated the zest the Goons could have brought to a James Bond parody, had they given a single Sunday afternoon's go at it; and quite clearly the welter of Goon catchphrases, jokes and even plot-lines in *The Fiendish Plot of Dr Fu Manchu* is demonstration enough that, to the last, Sellers wanted to transform radio into cinematic terms.* It was a conversion he never managed, one mutation he couldn't make. If some of his movies are failures it wasn't because he gave a poor performance (his Nayland Smith couldn't have been done better by Ralph Richardson) – it was more a problem of form (and of his off-screen rages and frustration). *Ghost in the Noonday Sun*, for instance, is full of more Goonery, and it co-stars Milligan, but a visual language and style are not found to match the imaginativeness of what went on in the Camden Theatre, the Aeolian Hall etc., two decades previously. The result is badly executed slapstick – where the essence of *The Goon Show* was

---

* *The Fiendish Plot of Dr Fu Manchu* (1980) borrows heavily from 'The Terrible Revenge of Fred Fumanchu', [*sic*] transmitted on December 6th 1955. Neddie Seagoon was the Chief Commissioner of Scotland Yard (played in the film by David Tomlinson), hunting for the bamboo saxophone thief. (Saxophones are blown into by Helen Mirren in the film).

speed. Columbia wanted to call the film *Goons at Sea* – which would have made even less sense than the one eventually used.

☆   ☆   ☆

Making *The Goon Show*, fair seed time had his soul. 'We'd get back together and think, God, how marvellous! That's why the show was, for *us*, such an enormous release; and we used to pack so much energy into the show; and all our ideas and thoughts went into the show; everything *we* had – we were just so keen to let people hear what was going on in our minds – this crazy, strange fantasy that used to take place in our minds [. . .] I remember when we first met up. We, all of us – Bentine, Harry, Spike and I, had this feeling that we *had* to do something; we had this thing inside us, this . . . We wanted to express ourselves in a sort of surrealistic form. We thought in cartoons. We thought in blackouts, we thought in sketches, we thought of mad characters, we thought of – take a situation, and instead of letting it end normally, twist it around. This grew and grew and grew and grew.'

Whether or not the vortex meant as much to the others in the long term, Sellers is certainly doing his best here (the 'we' and 'us' are royal) to describe his own creative processes and exfoliations. As an actor (and as a husband, father etc.) he relied on his instincts to an inordinate degree. This made him vulnerable and volatile, but taking him purely as a performer, for the moment, there was always going to be a sense of danger about somebody so versatile, and to this audiences responded. 'It was almost unholy,' remarks Milligan, 'this skill. It was as if he had no choice about the depth of his impersonations. That's what made it mad.' In *The Goon Show*, of course, Sellers' contribution went well beyond mimicry – except for Churchill or the Queen (as the Duchess of Boil de Spudswell), and saving the chance that Bluebottle was based on a scoutleader and Henry Crun on a lawyer in Lincoln's Inn Fields, his characters are inventions.* And it is the sheer quality of his gift of tongues which was now becoming apparent. The voices became characters

---

* Paradoxically, the more apparently real the characters, the more inventive was Sellers' performance. 'All the Goon characters are real, you know,' he said in

and he distributed himself amongst them. Bluebottle, the child; Bloodnok, the reprobate; Crun, the fool; Grytpype, the cad . . . Sellers cherished their oddities because they gave outer form to his own.

Whilst Secombe yodels and yells, and Milligan mugs, Sellers' acting, forty years on, has resonance and resolution. And if the Goons were caricaturing, in the main, what they'd endured for real during the war (idiots with power; the lying and cheating of propaganda; the fiction of military heroism – Main Wilson said that, 'For years we'd been sold the idea that the British Army never loses. Now, in the figure of Bloodnok, you had a Major who would take any bribe, tell any lie, to save his skin') – then Sellers wasn't reacting against trauma, like the rest, but expanding upon an intuitive spirit of rebellion and anarchy which was already within him. The war was a stimulus for Milligan. It was thrust upon Secombe and Bentine. For Sellers, however, the war intensified his delinquencies, and *The Goon Show* was a channel for his streak of cruelty and sense of the ridiculous, which were now heightened. He could *use* everybody else's excitable state (impersonate it?); their nervous illnesses struck, more figuratively, a nerve in him.

☆ ★ ☆

On his memorial plaque in Golders Green Crematorium there is the rubric 'Life is a state of mind'. This comes from *Being There*, and in the context of that film, and as a funerary ornament, it is vacuous, meaningless. If applied to the Sellers who was setting sail in the early Fifties, though, it is convenient. The state of mind which was being filled, in readiness for adulthood and independence, was one susceptible for exhibitionism, contempt, and anything anti-social. His fortunate friendship with Milligan confirmed his cynical vision and aloofness. 'Spike Milligan says, and God knows he's right, the world is full up with mediocrity, and you'll find it everywhere, and when you brush with it you brush up

_____

1958, 'William Mate [Cobblers], he's got a furniture shop near Spike's office. You go in and say, "What sort of wood is this?" And he says "Solid wood, that is."'

venom.' Sellers fed off Milligan's mental processes and leaps, identified with his knottedness and the intensity of his feelings. And when the once-assured Milligan broke down, over-worked by dreaming up *The Goon Show*, still he kept typing, even though he was in bed with boards strapped to its sides, because he was so violent: 'The scripts he wrote during that worrying time were better than before,' said Sellers delightedly. 'The fact is that everything Spike does is part of his war against the human race.' (Including becoming a patient in a mental hospital? When somebody asked him if he had any sympathy with the agonies Milligan went through to work out the show, Sellers simply snapped, 'I don't know why he did it for so long in that case.')

Sellers knew that the words his beloved characters spoke belonged to Milligan. Even if the characters had evolved at Grafton's and in rehearsal,* Milligan, concedes Secombe, 'had all the sweat of writing it'; but Sellers became proprietorial. He'd not been raised to share a single thing in his life, starting with his mother (Peg had nothing left for Bill); so towards Milligan, to whom he owed so much, he'd react with spite and envy. (His behaviour prefigures his bitterness with Blake Edwards over who should receive the plaudits for Inspector Clouseau – Sellers couldn't abide the thought of collaboration.) In America, for instance, where Milligan is not known, he'd use his friend's psychiatric problems to get an easy laugh. On March 20th 1964, he appeared on a syndicated talk show in Los Angeles, and told the host, Steve Allen, (who'd described *The Goon Show* to the audience as 'wilder than any comedy that's ever been done here') that:

> Well, it was a very interesting period of my life. I worked with a very brilliant colleague called Spike Milligan, who wrote the show. Who unfortunately is in a mental home at the moment [*laughter*].

---

* Zanies with names like Arnold and Mrs Fringe, Ernie Splutmuscle, Phillip String, Harold Vest, Sir Harold Porridge, seeker of the East Pole, and Yogurt Muleboot, 'a displaced Siberian haddock-stretcher', never made it further than the paper tape of the 'Sound Mirror'.

No. He gets a bit under the weather [*laughter*]. But anyway, you know, it was great fun.

The gods were tuning into Allen's programme; eighteen days later they made sure Sellers suffered a series of massive coronary attacks. (He was only able to survive because of the state-of-the-art cardiac unit at the Cedars of Lebanon Hospital.) Worse was to come. In April 1980, Sellers told the magazine *Rolling Stone* about the loneliness and cheerlessness of touring in variety – 'and Spike used to get suicidal because someone would shout at him. [Sadly] And you know, he eventually did commit suicide.'

Within three months of speaking those words Sellers was dead – but how can we explain a fabrication like that? (He'd even put himself on oath with the journalist, by saying: 'Everything I'm going to tell you during this interview is the truth; whatever question you ask, I won't evade it.') To be so anxious to appear the sole architect of your success, that you kill off a confrère: it's aberrant – but let's try and enter Sellers' sickness and explain the state of his mind. The first point is that by the Spring of 1980, *The Fiendish Plot of Dr Fu Manchu* was behind him and he knew he'd failed to pull off the most expensive *Goon Show* of all time; Milligan's tone and range didn't seem to have a look – Goonery remained all in the mind.*
Second, he was not living with his fourth wife and his romantic life was in ruins, again. Third, his heart problems were intensifying and coronary by-pass surgery was in prospect. . . . So there were professional and personal reasons a-plenty for being morose; he was

---

* The breakthrough, from fantasy to reality and back again, was made eventually by Terry Gilliam, who'd provided the absurdist animations for *Monty Python's Flying Circus*. As a film director, Gilliam has a great artist's eye – and in the pirate galleon-as-City office sequence in *The Meaning of Life*, in *Brazil* and *The Adventures of Baron Munchausen* (especially), he has made his own rococo style out of mixing Searle, Milligan, and that Czecheslovakian comedian, Franz Kafka. When I first saw John Neville's courtly Munchausen, in those magnificent plumed hats, flying on cannon balls and visiting the moon, I thought: I wish Peter Sellers was alive to be in this movie.

trying to find anybody to blame for his errors and wrecks except himself. But Milligan? Clearly, Sellers' identification with Milligan's emotional reserves ran very deep. He'd wanted to take possession of his friend's talents – Milligan fulfilled him – and the free, chaotic world of the Goons was paradise; but now, having heard the chimes at midnight, Sellers felt left out and afraid. Sellers, who had shot way above everybody else in his generation as a comic actor, was a born actor; and, it was a terrifying thought, perhaps he never had got inside Milligan's head – he'd only ever imitated him? Sellers, cornered by his own genius for mimicry, felt himself shrivelling. He was gasping and choking.

Milligan, an old man now, remains puzzled by Sellers' cruel remarks. When I met him, he was so pale, still and white-haired, he seemed translucent, a mandarin – a benign Fu Manchu: 'Peter would compete with people in peculiar ways. He hated it when I was doing something he couldn't do, such as restoring the Elfin Oak in Kensington Gardens. Despite his fame and his talent he was jealous of me. When I was with him he was very warm – then I'd hear that he'd asked somebody, "Why does Spike hate me?" I never had that hatred. I miss him very much, especially on a comedy level, because we used to discuss ideas which were way outside the scope of Hollywood. I'm a funny writer. I've proved I'm a funny writer – in books, on television, and on radio. But film making . . . In Hollywood, to get their ideas across they need fifty million dollars. Jesus Christ, that means somebody with sensitivity and delicacy is out. You've got to be hammered over the head by Arnold Schwarzenegger.

'I thought Peter was much funnier in *The Goon Show*, more laughs per minute there, than in the Clouseau films. More original, too. The Pink Panthers were based on classic silents – expensive Hal Roach. Peter kept a lot of things that were important to me – films in eight millimetre. Experiments in comedy. I asked Lynne Frederick after Peter had died – can you let me have access to them? She said, "Spike, one day Peter destroyed everything that

had anything to do with you – he didn't want to have any knowledge of you."* He destroyed it all.'

☆ ★ ☆

Whoever offered Milligan the Gryphon and Sellers the March Hare
in *Alice's Adventures in Wonderland*, made in 1972, missed a golden
opportunity to have had the pair cast as the warring and making-up
twins, Tweedledum and Tweedledee. For, if Sellers was consumed
with rival-hating envy and crooked malice before he died, Milligan,
in the long ago, had moments when he, too, was angered to the
heart – and on one occasion he was actually intent on committing
murder. He was up to his neck in scripts for *The Goon Show*; he was
having to cope with all the queries from BBC producers, sound
effects engineers etc.; his parents had just emigrated to Australia;
and he was living in a small flat with his wife June, who was ill, and
a new-born baby named Laura. Sellers, oblivious to these pressures,
and expecting to be enthusiastically greeted whatever the hour,
would swan in late at night to play a new gramophone record. . .
The frustrations were over-burdening and Milligan went for him
with a kitchen knife. 'I was so mad,' he has since said, 'I thought
that if I killed Peter it would all come right . . . What exactly happened I can't clearly remember, but I do remember shouting, "I'm
going to kill Peter Sellers . . ." I recall the ambulance taking me to St
Luke's Hospital in Highgate.' Sellers was saved by June, who
thoughtfully screamed and forewarned him (their flats were in the
same block): 'Peter!' Don't come out – Spike's going to kill you!' I
wonder if the cutlery was embedded in Sellers' doorway afterwards?

---

* The actual letter from Lynne Frederick, glazed and framed, met my gaze in the
downstairs cloaks, Chez Milligan: 'Dear Spike, I don't know how to tell you this,
but one day Peter destroyed everything that reminded him of you. I am very
sorry. What more can I say? Lynne.' The letter is typed, the signature bold. Milligan has appended this superscription: 'After writing six times to her, this is the
emotional reply I got from Lynne Unger – late Mrs David Frost, late Mrs Peter
Sellers, late human being.' Milligan has dealt with the tremendous hurt by treating it as an offensive joke – one which cuts both ways.

On Sundays, it was often up to Harry Secombe to keep the peace. Peter Eton used to take him aside and say, 'Look, there's been a bit of an argument. Get here early, so if there's any trouble you can be here to smooth things over.' There never was much trouble on the actual day of the programme, recalls Sir Harry, 'because if Peter had a touch of the sulks, and perhaps Spike would go to adopt the foetal position, really I'd think of some Army joke I'd heard and within a few minutes we'd all break out and all be laughing. And, of course, the brandy helped. By God, the brandy helped.'

The Goon Show, for Sellers, wasn't so much the finished twenty-eight minute product, as the whole afternoon and evening out, which was indeed lubricated by a cocktail of cognac and milk. John Browell, who laboured to produce the sound effects ('LONG SERIES OF SMASHING DOOR DOWN. GOES ON AND ON. GIVE IT VARIATION IN KIND. I.E. FIRST CONFIDENT CRASHES ON DOOR WITH AXE. THESE ALL VERY LONG. FAIL THEN RENEWED. THEN FURIOUS. THEN FRENZIED. THEN HEAVY FULL BLOODED BLOWS. FURIOUS SAWING. THEN HAMMERING ON DOOR WITH FISTS. MAD RATTLING OF THE DOOR KNOB. THEN FOUR OR FIVE HEAVY BLOWS. THEN A MAD FURIOUS HATCHET ATTACK ON THE DOOR.')* and later took over the programme from Peter Eton, has said that 'I noticed from time to time that the bottles of brandy were getting larger and larger, and I used to have to send my staff down there to drink copious quantities, to try and keep the cast sober. I had a sober cast and a drunk staff.'

Owing to the complexities on the technical side, the BBC were wanting the scripts delivered earlier and earlier – so that the boffins in the electronic department etc. could experiment with the new noises. This meant additional strain for Milligan, but ideally the

---

* After this destructive symphony, there's a short pause and Eccles says, 'I know when I'm beaten.' – 'Let me try,' says Seagoon. [*FX. Sound of hinge*] 'It was open all the time.' 'The Scarlet Capsule'.

time-table for *The Goon Show* was that the new script would arrive
on the Monday morning. By Tuesday the sound-effects people and
the producer would have knocked it into broadcastable shape. As
Browell says, of the scripts, 'although they were idiotic, they were
like great fantasies and there was a lot of serious talk and work that
went into them'. On Wednesday, the actual sound-effects were
tried out and, if possible, pre-recorded. Major Bloodnok's stomach,
for example, was achieved by overlaying burps, whoops from oscil-
lators, water splashes, cork-like pops, and light artillery blasts. As
for wolves howling, the Goons were told to do that one by themselves. On Thursday, the script was re-typed, duplicated and
distributed. On Sunday, at two o'clock, everybody would assemble
– Milligan worrying about the looming deadline for *next* week,
Sellers and Secombe having driven from wherever they were in the
British Isles, appearing in variety. Sellers would prepare for his
ingress by telephoning from his car, Secombe by singing 'Be My
Love' as he crashed down the stairs, There would be a first read-
through interspersed with cries of 'Cobblers!' and 'Ying Tong Iddle
I Po!' 'Anything that struck any of the artistes about the script
would be altered there and then,' says Browell. This was followed
by a stumble through on the stage, at the microphone, with the
sound-effects. 'Jim, the atomic bomb's not loud enough,' Milligan
might say. 'Louder, go on, until it gets to feedback point.' Wally
Stott next arrived with the musical arrangements, to rehearse with
the orchestra.

The Goons derived much mirth from hearing the 'Old Comrades March', a traditional military number with a distinct patriotic
underthump – an evocation of Chelsea pensioners, jingling with
medals, tottering in step along Whitehall on Armistice Day. 'We
will start with thirty-two bars of the "Old Comrades March" and
finish with a chord of C – played badly,' Stott would announce,
taking up his baton. The playing of this music, which became *The
Goon Show* signature tune, always had Sellers, Milligan and
Secombe 'in paroxysms of hysterical laughter', recalled Freddy
Clayton, 'while the badly played chord in C had them helpless on

the floor.' What was so funny? Simply the doddery dignity of the superannuated soldier, doing his best to look heroic, when really he's bewhiskered and well past it – the Goons could sentimentally see themselves getting to be like that, years hence, the spirit of adventure stirring in the veteran's heart. With the show over, and the play-out in full tump-tump-tump tiddle-tiddle tump-tump-tump, the Goons used to fall into line and march in procession around the stage. They'd continue frolicking until the producer, up in his booth, flashed the ALL CLEAR sign.

Stott, who has since had a sex-rectifying operation to become Miss Angela Morley, told me that 'I arranged all the music and composed the links for all ten years of the Goons, and for the last seven years I conducted the band. Outside the Camden Theatre on a Sunday evening there'd always be Peter's latest car – a different one every week. We were always expecting him to turn up in a steam roller. Peter played the drums on *The Goon Show*, during the afternoon and during the warm-up. When Harry sang 'Falling in Love with Love' in E-flat, Peter would run to the back of the band and take over the tymps. He used to play them like a caricature of a symphonic typanist – he was always changing the pitch and fiddling with the handles. Somebody also fired a gun. If Peter could get on Jock Cummings' kit of drums, he would; and he'd play it convincingly.'

They then had a final dress rehearsal, and eventually the audience, which had been queuing for up to four hours, was let in. Feeling antic by now, Sellers, Secombe and Milligan goofed and clowned. They'd clutch on to the tabs and be hoisted up and down; they'd pretend the wheeled music stands were scooters. 'Braces were a favourite,' says Browell. 'Peter would come along and do the old time music hall bit – "Ladies and gentlemen" etc. – and whip away Harry's braces, whereupon Peter's trousers would fall down. One terrible occasion when they did it, he wasn't wearing underpants.' Wallace Greenslade, the dirigible-sized announcer who succeeded the spare Andrew Timothy, was their main stooge. 'Sing us the news, Wal,' Secombe would say; Sellers, pretending to be sleeping under the piano, would simper 'Hello, Sailor,' to the assembling band; and Milligan, by now, would be standing on his head. Sellers once interrupted the actual recording – 'Stop the show – it's time to auction Greenslade's bum.' In no time at all, remembers Milligan, bids were coming in, 'even from the audience'.

It was Greenslade's job to introduce any VIPs who might be sitting in the front row – they'd stand to applause, and the sound-effects team would blast them with a round of machine-gun crackle. Every week, without fail, Greenslade pointed to the balcony and said 'Are you all right on the shelf up there? Good, because you can't get out, the doors are locked.' Milligan might then start to play the trumpet, Sellers to requisition Ray Ellington's bongoes, whilst Secombe sang hymns in a voice which started in range reserved for sopranos and finished up (recalled Freddy Clayton) 'in a land where only coloraturas dwell. Was he in pain? Appendicitis? Colic? But no, the man was laughing. It was all very strange.' He'd then have to race about the platform, picking up the leaves of his script which he'd scattered about. It was obviously tricky calling everybody to order to start the performance-proper – the messing about was so integral – and the audience was already chuckling when the green signal blinked on: 'Recording in ten seconds from now':

  Greenslade: This is the BBC.
  Sellers: Hold it up to the light – not a brain in sight.

☆ ★ ☆

We can derive a fair impression of what these live sessions were like from watching the videotape of *The Last Goon Show of All*, made in April 1972 as part of the Corporation's fiftieth anniversary celebrations. If you've only ever heard recordings (*The Best of the Goon Shows*, Vols. One and Two, was my first rummage) and have been used to filling the dark space of radio with your own mental picture of the characters and their deeds, it is a giddy, abstract experience finally to see the actors at it. Milligan, for example, looks embarrassed, ill at ease. He doesn't make eye-contact with anybody, or touch anybody – whereas Secombe, a pirouetting Toby Jug, is always nudging and jostling his way to the microphone. He's the one who generates the turbulence – and keeps the show together. (We can see what Peter Eton meant when he said that, if Sellers and Milligan 'were starting to wander off, you know, to backstage to talk, Harry would bring them back and stand them there. He was an absolutely sterling character' – and his total enthusiasm about the only element anybody could rely on.)

As for Sellers, he waves to his friends in the audience, talks to the band, leans over the footlights to chat to his children and wives, and only by the narrowest squeeze does he come back in on cue. He does a lot of pointing and ironic music hall ham bowing – he looks utterly happy, and he does whatever he wants. (Earlier on he'd demonstrated yoga positions, impersonated German officers, and shouted at the press through a megaphone – photographs of these feats appeared in next day's papers.) It is clearly suiting his sense of the spontaneous, and his sense of discipline, to be able to fool about and draw attention to himself. He simply lets his vocal skills get on with performing the script, it would seem, automatically. His timing and switches of character – Crun to Bloodnok to Grytpype to Bluebottle – are fast and spookily good.

It is as if he can be both concentrated and fixed on what he's doing and yet remain loose and indefatigable. Slim, at the microphone, he is snappy, hyper-responsive. His elbows, legs and fingers (which clutch the foolscap script) are all long and angular, like his chin and thin nose. Sellers is a human whiplash. He is at his most pure here, posing amidst the clutter of the orchestra, recording personnel, cables, booms and amplifiers. We almost don't notice that no actual Goon Show story takes shape. 'In my opinion' – and he's right – 'the script was very, very poor, very poor indeed,' said Andrew Timothy, brought out of retirement for the day because Greenslade had died (on the toilet in a pub called 'The George' in Langham Place, as it happens) back in 1961. What keeps *The Last Goon Show of All* going is the audience's goodwill.

In the past, the warm-up and the follow-up were technically

separate; but here, larkishness is prolonged for nearly an hour. It is one long preliminary. The Goons enter to much cheering; when they curtsy they pretend their aching bones have twinged. Sellers bangs the tymps, as of old, and Milligan upstages him by handing Secombe a bowl of milk and brandy during the inevitable reprise of 'Falling in Love with Love'. The style, throughout, is a parody of third-rate variety artistes; but if you were visiting from another planet or not aware of *The Goon Show*, you'd think that that's just what they were – a trio of loud buffoons telling one another a lot of bad jokes on purpose. What plot there is concerns Neddie Seagoon deputising for the Queen at state events; but this is soon forgotten about and all that happens is that the various characters are come across in peculiar hiding places. (If there is any subtext, it is that of concealment, or entombment.) Moriarty is inside the fuel tank of a vintage car, Bluebottle is in the gusset of Neddy's trousers, Henry and Minnie are inside a grand piano, Eccles is down a coal cellar, and Little Jim is inside Eccles' army boot. When Neddy gets nailed beneath the floorboards, inspiration aborts and, over Secombe's yells, Timothy comes forward to say 'That was *The Goon Show*, a recorded programme featuring . . . ' Apparently Milligan then butted in to say 'Goodbye *forever*', but this is not preserved on the video, though his snarl to the audience 'now, *get out!*' is. The last thing we see is the strange spectacle of Sellers dragging his children from the stalls on to the stage – why he wants this display of Happy Families we'll never know. (Except that it turns the affair into a home-movie.) Everybody lines up obligingly and self-consciously – Sellers dwarfed by his beefy son, Michael, who is dressed as Andy Pandy and has a haystack of hair.

☆ ★ ☆

That the script was a rattle-bag of catchphrases and hubbub, too slip-shod even to be mistaken for something the cast had improvised, is one thing. What was unorthodox was the smut. *The Goon Show*, apart from references to Hugh Jympton and Singhiz Thingz, was innocent of sex – this accounts for some of its charm. The 1972 swansong, however, contains laugh-lines about knee tremblers, knobs, Bloodnok's perversions, and 'Psst!' as 'pissed' i.e., drunk, which can best be labelled as childish – and the point about the original programmes is that they were childlike. For all the belligerence and insanity that went into it, the spirit of Goonery could often leap beyond pain and disaster. One way it achieved this was by going back in time, setting its plots in an indeterminate period of the imperial nineteenth century, an era of pioneering steam railways, Rorke's Drift, expeditions up the Limpopo, nutty professors journeying to the centre of the earth, or intent on other odd scientific missions, revolting tribesmen in the Punjab, discoveries in the pyramids, Sahara forts under siege, tiger hunts, and the search for diamond mines. In other words, *The Goon Show* recycled its Second World War violence through *Boys' Own* adventure annuals; its forebears and heroes were Sax Rohmer, Edgar Rice Burroughs, and Allan Quartermaine. 'Dishonoured', for example, concludes in India, and when everybody is blown up, Minnie comes to lay a wreath on a little stone – she's not to know it says 'Bombay 49 miles' in Hindustani. Bloodnok is normally in India or the Darkest Continent, selling the mess silver or hoarding concrete lamp-posts (as in 'The Evils of Bushey Spon'). Grytpype and Moriarty are often abroad in the Empire, racketeering, profiteering, swindling people out of gold ingots or King Solomon's treasure; and Neddy Seagoon (in the words of Main Wilson) 'expanded into a very strong character, embodying "Superman", "Dan Dare", "Flash Gordon" and "Dick Barton". Naturally he will turn out to be the most death-defying comedy coward of all time.'

London, too, is still Queen Victoria's capital, with its fogs, horses and carts, its clubmen in swirling capes. (It could be Anthony Hope's Ruritania.) And what's particularly Englishy English, in addition, are the loving references to Christmas. Plum puddings and turkey besplatter many an episode. 'Tales of Men's Shirts' has a sea battle in which the cannon are loaded with roast turkeys – the enemy retaliates with Christmas puddings and custard. The armoury in 'The Dreaded Batter Pudding Hurler' consists of mince pies, exploding sausages and, yes, Christmas puddings. The

Dickens parody, 'Christmas Carol,' has a pudding crammed with coins, which Grytpype and Moriarty want to steal; and in 'The International Christmas Pudding', the farinaceous ingredients come alive, are tracked to the Congo (or some such spot), and behave like a stag at bay, flashing the holly sprigs as if they were antlers.

Nostalgia for Christmas, for all the childhood excitements which it evokes, is perhaps what soldiers of fortune, when it comes down to it, fight for: times gone by spent in places they might well never live to see again. They romanticise, idealise, their home life and the past. It will all be over by Christmas – wasn't that the refrain, of men whose hearts were full of grief and uneasiness? War, adventure, wolf-cub braggadocio, and the oxymoron of military intelligence, all come together in 'Operation Christmas Duff', in which Bloodnok organises a gigantic pudding for Her Majesty's Forces Overseas. The mixture is prepared in the dry dock at Chatham. A flotilla of boats go back and forth, churning the steaming substance; depth charges are fired to bring up the raisins and 824 Squadron swoop down with candied peel. Flame-throwing tanks cook it, an atomic bomb heat-seals it, and the 74th Medium Regiment RA fire a round of threepenny bits at it. Bomber Command drops brandy torpedoes and 'they napalm it to set it alight'. We then cut to bar room noises – honky tonk piano, drunken singing etc.:

> Gentlemen, please, please. If the Chief of the Imperial General Staff will lay off the piano! Thank you. I have here orders containing four tickets for the Windmill, and this message: 'The pudding will be divided as follows: One slice to be cut and filled with anti-freeze for immediate transport to the Trans-Antarctic expedition. The remainder of the giant Christmas pudding will be fitted with wheels, a diesel engine, and driven to the Middle East depots for distribution. Signed, Field-Marshal Montgoonery.'

The Goon Show is encapsulated there – the army game, a lunatic scheme, everything undertaken fortissimo. Eccles and Bluebottle drive the pudding to the desert, misread the map, and end at the South Pole. Unknowingly, they've been going backwards – and one

of the Goon songs, for which Sellers provided the ropey piano obli-
gato, was called 'I'm Walking Backwards for Christmas'. To put the
clock back, to become again carefree kids, their minds brimming
with Keystone two-reelers and bright-hued comics from the news-
agent, Rider Haggard's exotica, Fu Manchu's threats, and music
hall conjurors – all this lay underneath the battle-scarred reality
which was the programme's stimulant. *The Goon Show* had a juvenile heart – which remained Sellers'. These are his tastes, right up
until the end, with his remake of *The Prisoner of Zenda* and what
have you.

☆　★　☆

The best thing about *The Last Goon Show of All* – an opus otherwise
adrift from the pulp melodramas which the surrealism bounced off
in the old days – was Rowland Emett's cartoon adorning the souvenir brochure. It is the only successful visualisation of the
programme's spirit I've come across. As such, the inside of Sellers'
head may have looked like this.[*]

Emett,[†] a visionary draughtsman and grandson of the Court En-
graver to Queen Victoria, once said of his cobwebby pictures, 'They
are doing a little job for England. You see, they spread the idea of
madness.' (His art was a reaction to the regimentation of the war).
In the drawing on p. 226, he wonderfully captures the daffy, pur-
poseless, ingenious side of *The Goon Show* – the bit between the
atomic explosions, bullets and people being hurled through closed
windows or blown to bits. His drawing is composed of wonky

---

[*] Reproduced by courtesy of Mary Emett.

[†] Emett designed Caractacus Potts' many inventions for the film version of *Chitty
Chitty Bang Bang*: the Hush-A-Bye Hot Air Rocking chair, the Little Dragon
Carpet Cleaner, and the Humbug-Major Sweet Machine. Best of all was an early
television set constructed from a parlour gramophone and a sewing machine,
with an egg beater for stirring up electrons and a valve made from a case of
butterflies. Ian Fleming's novel, in which the original descriptions of the models
are found, was the one book Sellers performed for his children: 'he read us
nightly passages,' wrote Michael, 'and dubbed in all the voices of the characters.
Yes, he did try . . .'.

perspectives, foreshortenings, and deformations of the traditional three dimensions. But, though wispy, it isn't weak or genial – notice all those spikes, peaks, arrows, beaks, twigs, icicles and piercings. (If you study it, it gets under your skin, like a splinter.)

We seem to be on a fragile isthmus at the end of the world. Bloodnok takes flight on a machine adapted from a bicycle, umbrellas and a fishing rod, and Eccles (is it?), squatting on the parched earth, his legs all intertangled, is about to fire a gun – or perhaps it is a telescope – which looks as if it is made out of the same tubes and pipes as his body and is wrapped around with his scarf. Scarves are what Minnie Bannister is knitting, up on the cliff. A scarf, or three-legged socks; or is she whittling at a bit of gnarled wood? It is hard to determine. She is being carried in a dustbin attached, like a satchel, to Henry Crun. Crun, a cadaver, whose tail coat looks like extra insectile legs, holds, in impossibly thin hands, a brown paper parcel containing Bluebottle. And what is *he* holding? A squid? More of Minnie's knitting? The picture is full of strange meta-morphoses. Eccles' spur has become a flower and his hat looks like the fold and whorls of a crustacean. Bloodnok's feet are turning into a bird's claws, his epaulettes into spiders – or even bristly wings. Grytpype, clad as Sherlock Holmes (because Sellers' voice in this connection may be more Rathbone's than, as everybody has always thought, George Sanders), has four legs – there's a centipede under that Inverness Cape. His suitcase contains his miniaturised double. You could also probably fit a tuba in there, too. And, why, there is a man with a tuba, arriving at the door! The hunchback in the tunnel's mouth, seeing off his master, must be Moriarty. He resembles a blackbeetle.

This is a restless picture full of creepy crawlies. If his penman-ship isn't bitter, slashy, like Searle's, Emett's curlicues are none the less disconcerting. He once said of his work – referring to his decre-pit steam engines and weird inventions, which appeared in *Punch* and were first exhibited, as 'Gothick-Kinetic Things!' at the Festival of Britain Pleasure Gardens in 1951 (but his comment has much aptness here): 'They had a lovely desperate look, as though every minute is going to be their last.' The portrait of *The Goon Show*, a picture which refuses to add up, is like the blueprint of a bad dream; it has dream logic. The focal point, disregarding Grytpype's magnifying glass and prisms, or the BBC microphone growing as a cactus, is the bursting alarm clock, buzzing with flies and descend-ing from Bloodnok's contraption, upon which Eccles has one eye cocked. It is either eleven fifteen or a quarter past six. Whatever, it is already later than you think.

☆　★　☆

Chapter Five
Her Man's a Scream

I had just written the confident sentence, 'The Goon Show was a world without women,' before remembering that I was forgetting:

> *Marian:*   Oh, sobs of despair – sobs! – locked in this dark dungeon with nothing but an old straw television set – this is the chamber of torture – oh, woe!, oh, misery! oh, fie! oh, whatever shall I do. . . .
>
> *Sellers:*   The part of Maid Marion is being played by Miss Charlotte Mitchell, and a ripe little ham she's proving.

– from 'Ye Bandit of Sherwood Forest' (1954). Charlotte Mitchell also appeared as a guest artiste in 'Tales of Montmartre', two years later. The proposition holds, nevertheless. (When 'Ye Bandit' was re-made in 1956 as 'Robin Hood and His Merry Men', Miss Mitchell's part was re-assigned to Bluebottle.) The brothers-in-arms involved in thinking up and performing the programme, over two hundred and thirty editions (and ten series) between May 1951 and January 1960, were too busy with their comic-strip heroics to be muddled by females. I suppose Henry and Minnie may have held themselves in a passionate clinch several hundred years ago, Bloodnok's consumption of curried eggs may be a sublimation of other, baser needs, and Bluebottle's acne implies a hormonal surge – but Goonery, incubated in a pub, inflamed by beer, full of sentiment about wars and derring-do, generally can do without any suggestion of wives, mothers, girl-friends (i.e. responsibilities.)* Though, as I said towards the end of the previous chapter, the sexlessness contributes a measure of innocence, the machismo does make matters, when you think about it, rather cruel and cold-hearted. 'There was no warmth in the writing,' said Peter Eton. 'It was all rather bitter – sardonic, perhaps. There is warmth in the characters – William Mate Cobblers, Bluebottle – but not in the writing. If you look at the scripts you will see this is true.'

Turning to drafts of the last shows, we find Eton was more than right. Goonery had become a slaughterhouse.

Sellers:	Any work?
Secombe:	No, there's a waiting list as long as my arm.
Sellers:	Quick – the chopper
	[F/X chopping through meat]
Secombe:	SCREAM!
Sellers:	Now what's the excuse?
Secombe:	There's a waiting list as long as my short arm.

The Goon Show was a fantasy of invincibility. Gunned down or minced up one week, the characters are back again the next. There is a love of speed (in the content – rockets, racing cars, jets etc.), and of gangs (in the performance atmosphere – from Gang Show to Goon Show in this respect was no distance at all). And not only were women not registering in the plots and dramatis personae, I don't think the programme appealed to them, either. They see through its cloak and dagger and extreme silliness – much as my own mother used to laugh herself half to death when she had to launder my father's masonic apron and polish his trowel. Perhaps this, too, is part of the comedy – a spoof on men's tough view of themselves?

'It was a masculine world,' Charlotte Mitchell agrees, 'and they

---

* Attention thesis-writers: compare and contrast the development of Goonery with C.S. Lewis, J.R.R. Tolkien and Charles Williams mysognystically meeting up, as The Inklings, to formulate Hobbitry.

laughed to keep themselves going. With me they'd decided they'd met a mad woman – I was very flattered. I'm not sure many women would have been. I was also eight months pregnant, though your shape is irrelevant on radio. It was hysteria really. Full of ad-libs and they put everything into the warm-up. I distinctly remember thinking, if I'm still alive by the end I'll be lucky. I was scared but I was able to cope with what they were doing because all I did was fall about laughing – and this is what they liked. During the week, when they were touring in variety, they'd get together and phone me up – at two o'clock in the morning. Once, I ran to get the phone – you expect it to be an emergency at that time of night – and I passed out. They continued being daft and jolly on the other end of the line. I lay on the floor with my head bashed in.'

Let's hope she wasn't still pregnant when she was concussed. Her testimony suggests that what the Goons enjoyed was an idolatrous audience, even if only of one. Charlotte Mitchell was put in the rôle of dizzy, dippy younger sister. She didn't reprove – she encouraged them to be more themselves than usual. (How would the chemistry have been altered if they'd found a Margaret Dumont character – a straight-man dowager type?) This, in general, was what Sellers personally wanted from any woman he encountered – total adoration. He'd woo them with his talent, which was passing strange, as his first wife confirms: 'At first I don't think he quite knew what his talent was. A drummer? Impressions? And I have to tell you he was wonderful. His act was just magic. I remember meeting him – Dennis Selinger introduced us. I thought "strange fellow" ... Then I saw him do his stand-up act at the Regal, Edmonton, one Sunday night, a popular variety venue, and I thought: "This is the most incredible talent that I've seen in years." I'm sure that's what attracted me to him, his talent. That's what the problem was eventually between us. I'm sure I was in love with his talent long after I wasn't in love with him.'

☆ ★ ☆

Sellers met Anne Howe in 1949, at the BBC studios in Great Portland Place. She was nineteen and a student at the Royal Academy of Dramatic Art. She was *not*, however, as other books have suggested, the former child actress Sally Ann Howes, who'd recently appeared in Korda's *Anna Karenina*. Her professional name was Anne Hayes, though Sellers soon saw to it that she'd not need to be going on with any career where she could deploy it. She had been raised in Melbourne, but all trace of an Australian accent had long since been eradicated by secondary schooling at Hendon, whither her mother had moved after the death of her father (or perhaps he'd simply gone off somewhere to plant tea?) What her background gave her, instead of Down Under Diphthongs, was common sense, patience, and a sense of the ridiculous – a combination, not as frequently found as you'd think, but useful when sharing a landscape with snakes and funnel-web spiders. The mix of unflappability and a delight in the bizarre was ideal for Sellers. What was additionally unique to Anne was that she could be strong and imaginative without needing to put it about that she was feisty – the madcap Mrs Sellers etc. Not prickly nor flamboyant – mannerisms adopted by many an intelligent woman in the world of the arts when they feel they need to register – she gave Sellers the strong domestic underpinnings for his fantasies and career. If Peg had nagged Sellers into becoming famous, Anne gave him the support to sustain and develop that fame during the crucial years of the Fifties. Of course, Sellers being Sellers, when he became an international success as an actor, out on the scrap-heap she and the children had to go. He felt it wasn't commensurate with being a sophisticated star and playboy to have an ordinary family home-life – so he destroyed it all. Quite literally.

'I can remember his breaking up every bit of furniture in our living room. Terrible tantrums. He'd lash out. He had this underlying violence. His mother never believed in attempting to teach him self-control. She always used to tell the story about how he'd pushed some aunt in the fire. She thought it was very funny and I'm sure she didn't tell him off. So he always got away with murder all the time. Peter was allowed to do anything Peter wanted. But she was more than a typical Jewish mother – she was crazy. More like a caricature of a Jewish mother, played by Peter Sellers. She ate him up. She ruled him. Everything he did – when he went into the RAF, she got him moved. Anything that Peter didn't like, Peter didn't have to do. Peg would sort it out. It is quite a thing to become an adult and have your own family and suddenly your mother isn't there. . .'

Talking about Sellers today, a dozen years since his death and over forty since they were married, Anne manages to be neither sentimentally forgiving nor, which is the more surprising, bitter. As she sifted over their life together, it is as if she was remembering the plot of a rather harrowing play she once saw, or a television bio-pic mini-series about other unfortunate people. Her detachment is the product of two supervening decades of happiness with the architect Ted Levy, who died of cancer in 1986. She now lives in a curious post-modern capsule, designed by her late second husband, built on the site of a coach-house off Akenside Road, in Hampstead. From the outside it is a plain garden wall, the door set at an angle. Within, an illusion of space is given by long narrow windows, a glass-sided patio, sloping ceilings and hexagonal sitting, eating and cooking areas. Here and there are drawings of harlequins and Rembrandt-era peasantry – that's what my memory has flashed up, anyway. I may well be wrong. I was too busy listening.

'He had sticky hair, over-stuffed suits, and was the kind of person who'd grab all the cream cakes for himself without offering them round. He wouldn't put his glasses on – and he was very near-sighted. He used to look at himself in the dressing room mirror, during variety, full of self-disgust, and say, "A big, fat, jolly boy, that's how I'm meant to see myself."'

By concealing his spectacles, he didn't have to see himself. Like Clouseau, he overlooked his fumbling and clumsiness – it didn't exist for him. Harry Secombe, too, pocketed his face furniture, but to make the audience disappear and to conquer stage fright, not to make himself vanish into the air.

'A lot of us used to go to the Edgwarebury Country Club, Earl Street, on a Saturday – Dennis Selinger, Spike, June [Marlowe, the first Mrs Milligan]. Peter asked me out. I was working in Rep., but this didn't deter him. He'd follow me around. I was doing an Alan Melville play. He'd always be there at the Stage Door. When I was away in Bedford, I did three months up there, he was at his worst. He'd arrive and say, "I've just taken a hundred aspirins," as I was about to go on. He hated the fact I was working. Very possessive. He wanted me to be with him every hour of the day. Also, it needled him that I was in the theatre – which is what he wanted to do. At that time all he was doing was variety and he wanted to be a straight actor and go on stage. So he resented me for that. Anyway, he said he'd taken an overdose. I didn't know what to do. "I'm going on," I said, "You'd better get on with it." He was always in Bedford during the week. He made sure I came home at weekends. He was afraid of losing me. He couldn't bear it, you see. He'd accuse me of having affairs. He would always accuse me of having affairs – nobody that he knew, with nobody specific . . . He was a very jealous and possessive person. When I was working at the Lyric, Hammersmith, he locked the door of my bedroom and wouldn't let me out. . .'

Was ever woman in this humour woo'd? Was ever woman in this humour won? Instead of running for her life from a lunatic, and perhaps fearing that he would do himself in and she'd be to blame, or as is more likely, seeing past the destructive antics to the lonely man beyond, Anne agreed to become engaged. Sellers proposal was novel. On April 9th 1950, he asked her: 'Will you be my first wife?' It had been necessary to pop the question quite loudly, too, because he'd locked Anne in a cupboard at the time. He'd let her out only on condition that she promised never to as much as look at another man again in her entire life. Nearly three weeks later, after some promptings by his publicity agent, or perhaps Sellers was simply busy hunting for a locksmith, the press broke the news: 'Her man's a scream,' said one paper. 'Twenty-year-old Melbourne actress Anne Hayes . . . has become engaged to radio comedian Peter Sellers . . . Here they are at Mr Sellers' Finchley home. . .'* Peg

---

* *The Star*, April 26th 1950.

and Bill's home, in that case, 211B. Anne soon discovered that she wasn't so much thought of as marrying Sellers – she was more the cause of his divorce from Peg. 'She was fine with me until we got engaged. She then telephoned my mother, saying, "Will you keep your daughter away from my son because she is going to ruin his life." Actually her language was more colourful than that. My mother was shocked. Peter had a terrible row with his mother, left home and found a flat in Montagu Square, off Baker Street. His first decisive adult action.'

Like Milligan, Anne found Sellers' and Peg's closeness repulsive. 'He'd go to say goodbye to her, and I'd think, "Hold on a minute. Who's engaged to him, me or her?" The way she kissed him – slobbery. Made me feel sick. She enveloped him in a mass of bangles and beads. I can't say that Peter was in love with his mother, but it was a classic love-hate relationship. He'd be cuddling her and caressing her, then he'd be pushing her away, telling her to go to hell, and then buying her something. Even though he was earning about £150 a week, which was a lot of money in 1951, equivalent to a few thousand a week now, he never had any money. He was always buying things. He'd buy you a gold watch and then see something else, for himself or for Peg, and he'd say, "Listen, can I borrow that?" and he'd hock it – to buy a toy train set . . . I didn't find he showered me with gifts, not until the time of our split-up – and once he felt insecure, out came the diamonds and the fur coats. Until then he never even knew when my birthday was – not from the moment I met him until after the end.'

☆   ☆   ☆

'We got married the year they started making *The Goon Show*' – on September 15th 1951 at Caxton Hall Registry Office, the groom's parents being conspicuously absent. They lived first at Flat 10, 29 Hyde Park Gardens, W2, where the rent was £13 a week. Sellers was also paying by instalments for a second-hand Rolls, which achieved eight miles to the gallon, and the couple's furniture was on H.P. from Heal's. All rather swanky, but their home lacked one essential: a telephone. (At 211B there had been a Hollywood-esque white instrument on the end of Tudor 7621). Michael Standing, the BBC Head of Variety, had to write to the viziers of the Centre Telephone Area, Shaftesbury Avenue, spelling it out that: 'Mr Sellers does a very substantial amount of broadcasting work for us amounting, I dare say, to the best part of a hundred appearances before the microphone each year' – and that it is quite a task, in any event, juggling all the jobs and bookings; logistically impossible without a. . . The response might conceivably have been satirical: 'I assure you we are very conscious of the important part which a telephone plays in the lives of people in the entertainment world.'

The residence must have been wired up pretty sharpish, because Graham Stark, who was often on the premises assisting his nibs with his photography, recalls the rooms being a whirl of barbers, tailors, scattered pages of script, and boxes of new cameras. On one occasion, Sellers was excitedly waiting for some glamour shots he'd taken to materialise in the developing tray, when the phone rang. Stark heard Sellers put on a laryngitic croak to speak to Peter Eton and excuse himself from a *Goon Show* rehearsal. 'The receiver went back on the rest. Pete [*sic*], voice now normal, gave me a look: " . . . You . . . have a go at the breasts, while I have a go at the bum. . . ."' – referring to the airbrushing of the monochrome bimbo.

If Sellers, so soon after his wedding, could shut himself away for hours on end ogling the nude pictures he'd personally taken of (amongst others) a friend of Anne's in a bikini – it doesn't seem to say much for his idea of a long-term commitment to a wife keeping herself to herself on the other side of the darkroom door. And in truth Sellers never, in all conscience, knew what the concepts of accountability and duty would have entailed. He seemed to be back to front on so many subjects; his own vision was that of a photographic negative – everything reversed. His attitude to colleagues and consorts simply depended on how long they remained convenient. He'd had his Lady Anne. The conquest was over. On to gratifying the next whim, be it acquiring another motor car, zoom lens, or what have you. Boredom was vanquished by spending sprees. 'Everything came easily to him,' says Anne today, 'he was never short of work. The only time we'd be short of money was when he grossly overspent. Once his accountant, Bill Wills, put him on a strict allowance of £10 a week pocket money, with a bit kept back to tip the stage hands. We'd started a trust fund for the children – so Peter broke into that.'

Retrenchment of a kind did come about on June 16th 1952, when the Sellers moved to 3 Highview, Shepherd's Hill, Highgate, N.6 (tel. Fitzroy 1136) – scene of Milligan's murder attempt a few months later. Here the rent (subsidised by the Mendozas) was only £6 a week. Milligan actually lodged in their spare room until his own wedding took place, when he decamped across the hall to another apartment. He and Sellers amused themselves by overlaying recordings of Chopin nocturnes with the grunts of a man straining at stool. This they'd play to guests during dinner, nonchalantly commenting after a while, 'the new Concerto by Le Roté – the pianist, he'd got the shits'.

'Spike was open, charming, in those days,' says Anne, 'before his breakdowns. We went out and bought Christmas presents together.' Milligan's intended, June, was in fact Anne's old Australian school friend. Because her dark looks could be thought of as Italianate, however, Sellers had affected all along to believe she was from Naples. When he'd made the original introductions, therefore, he'd presented a disguised Milligan to his future bride as a waiter called Jules, her tutti-frutti compatriot, to whom he said he was teaching English. Milligan appeared, like a blacked-up pantomime geni, wearing a velvet suit borrowed from the Combined Services Entertainment Depot. Master and willing pupil then launched into a recitation from the works of William McGonagall, the Goons' patron saint of artists who are so idiotic and self-enclosed, they are innocents. The tartan-tooled *Poetic Gems* was placed reverently on a satin pillow embossed with royal thistles –

Oooo-oooooo-beautiful midnight oil
Let nothing you despoil.
Ye are brighter than a candle
A' less messy to handle.

At one penny per quart
A considerable amount can be bought
And it casts a wonderful glow
Ying tong iddle i po

☆ ★ ☆

Ardent to the point of frenzy before his marriage, Sellers was 'inattentive, preoccupied and often thoughtless' immediately afterwards. 'He would go away and forget Anne existed. Then he would be remorseful, but only for a day.' These words expressed the opinion of Max Geldray, who provided the harmonica interludes on *The Goon Show*. He was in a good position to know what was going on because, during the week, when Sellers was touring the variety circuit, he was the one who accompanied him, going on stage as a musical interlude or playing the stooge in Sellers' actual act. 'At this point in his life someone said of him,' says Geldray, '"Peter Sellers will give you anything, except five minutes of himself..."' What you'd get instead would be minutes, maybe hours, of impersonation and dissembling. And why? Because Sellers, at that precise moment when you'd have thought everything was coming together right – i.e. with regard to home and career – that was just when he decided to be racked and tortured. 'You know, people hate a comic,' he said. 'They feel resentment against a comic. They sit there saying: Go on, make me laugh. Once you have a reputation, it's easier. Bob Hope, now, they say, now he's funny, we *know* he's funny. If you have a reputation they'll laugh before you've done anything. You can move your hand from one pocket to the other and they'll laugh. But if they don't know you...'

It hasn't really got much to do with familiarity or good report, though, has it, the pleasure we instantly take in seeing entertainers like, say, Eric Morecambe or Tommy Cooper? They simply love what they are doing so much, the audiences sense this and relax. Secombe can exude that level of generosity, too. He's ready, you feel, to give audiences everything. This was never Sellers' way. He was too self-centred: 'Once in Coventry – we were doing a three months' season, Spike Milligan and Harry Secombe and I. It was a revue. One of our acts was called Les Trois Charleys. We came on as acrobats, in white tights with red cloaks and leopard skins and gold head-bands, the band playing Da-Da-Dadadada-Da-Da, and we did all this sort of thing [*he stands up and demonstrates a deliberately quavering stance on one leg*] – very badly of course. I had a turn on my own – told stories, did impersonations. One afternoon I went on and played the gramophone. I simply took a gramophone on to the stage and I said: "Now I'm going to play a record for you." I put on a record and when it was over I applauded [*he claps gravely. The head is inclined as if in respect of a stage partner*]. And do you know, *they* applauded too! I went right through like that. I dispensed with the band altogether. . . . The record was one side of an LP – Wally Stott, I think it was, playing Christmas Melodies, "Jingle Bells," carols, all that sort of thing.'

As Sellers told this story (and he told it often), the point was the imbecility of members of the audience and his own Herculean efforts to get through to them. 'I was like Lenny Bruce to that vaudeville lot. We'd do "Goon Show" tours outside of London, and you're usually telling jokes to a . . . bunch of no-brow miners . . . They didn't know what you were talking about. I used to go over in *silence* . . . Those days were so bad. . .'

And referring to the horn gramophone stunt, he said 'You've got to do things like that or else you go absolutely crazy . . . So I said, "On behalf of Wally Stott, thank you so much." They went crazy about "Jingle Bells" and started singing it. I said, "Oh, I think we can stand to hear that again – and all sing it together!" – "Yes, that's right!" they roared. . . .'

Whether Sellers moodily outstared the audience or led the community in a chorus (accounts vary) there is no doubting the intensity of his contempt – and that's what the anecdote reveals to me. I don't think he really believed in the idea of an audience, except as a means of boosting his self-esteem. He cared about and was interested only in himself, not in the people paying to see him; he wanted not to have to do anything and still dazzle. 'I didn't wear any special costume for my own act. No funny make up, just an ordinary suit. Though once at Wolverhampton or somewhere I was desperate. I went on in a plastic mackintosh and a wide-brim hat, rather like a Sandeman's port advertisement hat. I wrapped myself up in my Pakamac, I tilted the hat forward so that the shadow came right over the microphone, and I did the whole turn like that: the audience never saw my face; they saw nothing but the top of the hat. One reviewer gave me a splendid crit. – he thought my way of performing was the latest thing. But I found out afterwards he was the local avant-garde boy. He used to lose his job every week. . .'

The ecstatic twerp-critic appears in *After the Fox*, when Aldo Vanucci's unintelligible black-and-white home-movie is unspooled in the courtroom – it's a series of jump cuts, camera jerks, and out of focus close-ups – and, clapping wildly at the screen, the fan is taken away in a butterfly net. Is that how Sellers saw himself? As a sacrificial victim surrounded by the uncomprehending? He wanted to be loved for who he was, and when only his petulance came across, he retreated into vituperation and self-pity. This is the source of his need, beginning to be expressed now in interviews and profiles, to convince people he had no actual personality to call his own – he tried to cover his lacks with mystique, make the absence of any nice attributes into a sort of supernaturally empty space.

'I am quite unaware of what I am,' he told *Playboy* at the beginning of the Sixties. 'A politician can see himself, can see what sort of an impact he's making. I can't . . . As for the face in the mirror – well, my appearance is fattish, sometimes happy, but always trying to achieve a peace of mind that doesn't seem possible in this business. This business breeds a tension that is difficult to live with . . . It's a tension of thinking that unless you are number one it's no good.'

☆　★　☆

When Milligan failed to get a response from the Coventry audience, he jumped up and down on his trumpet, made the mistake of asking the punters the rhetorical question, 'You hate me, don't you?', scurried back to his dressing room and, feeling degraded, tried to hang himself. Sellers and Secombe, dressed as morris men for a sketch called 'The East Acton Stick Dancers Festival', pushed through the door and disentangled their colleague from his noose before he came to harm. It is unlikely that Sellers would ever have crumpled like that. He was too proud-hearted to allow an audience to get to him and stamp him out, as if an actor was himself that flattened bugle. Hostility merely inflated his sense of superiority.

It was as a reaction to this grotesque and farcical incident – 'Let's be honest now,' said Sir Harry, 'we were all a bit scared' – that he decided to go on and do battle using the Christmas Carols. 'I couldn't repeat the act,' he said, 'but I had proved something to myself if no one else. I'd proved that you can mould an audience to like anything – if you try hard enough.' Sellers, taking Milligan's astonishment and fear personally, felt angry that he himself was only acceptable when he went about pretending to be somebody else: Tommy Handley, Jimmy Jewell, Ben Warriss, Jon Pertwee, Claude Dampier, or Robert Moreton. But though he may have coerced an audience into listening to an LP record, wasn't he himself billed as something of a human radiogram, all those voices tumbing out: 'Peter Sellers – Speaking for the Stars'? (Bentine said to me: 'He had a tape recorder between his ears. He'd start playing back my voice and gestures when I was with him – and I'd stop him and say, hang on, old love!')

The outright rejection of Milligan was what he'd dreamed would one day come his way, if he appeared without an armoury of other people's voices – which is what virtually happened at the Glasgow Empire, where he barely spoke half a dozen words. The Clydeside audiences were so notoriously ungracious, there was a net across the stage to protect the artists and orchestra from flying glass. Milligan had drawn the short straw and was booked to appear there on his own. A drunk yelled from the balcony. 'Are you Spike Milligan?' – 'Yes' – 'Well y're a fucking idiot.' 'Right,' said Milligan, 'Outside!' So they met at the stage door and Milligan gave the critic from *The Glasgow Herald* a black eye. Soon it was Sellers' turn in the life-disenhancing North. 'Is there anybody in from the *Herald*?' he asked. 'Yes!' came the answer from the balcony. 'Right!' said Sellers, marching into the wings and returning with his useful wind-up gramophone. He put on a record of 'God Save the Queen,' walked off the stage, hailed a taxi outside the theatre, and returned to London. 'The first time an Englishman had left a Scottish audience standing,' he claimed.

Sellers' performances were getting increasingly idiosyncratic, as he attempted to work Goonish flights of fancy into a traditional vaudeville spot – or was it, more basically, that he didn't give a damn? Max Geldray recalls seeing him crawling around the stage on his hands and knees like a giant baby, for no reason at all. He'd come on carrying a carpet or a picture frame, or wearing a shawl, and refuse to refer to these items – incongruous props, like Queen Victoria's stuffed crocodile in the Palladium act. At the Hippodrome, Wolverhampton, he interrupted Geldray's solo with the words: 'Sorry, sir, but I have to tell you something important. There's no danger mind you, but there is a fire drill next door.' – 'My God,' thought Geldray. 'He's going to clear the theatre with a fire drill.'

Because he was a radio star, few people knew what Sellers looked like – so he could trick the audiences into believing his little hoaxes. ('They didn't always know when we were gagging and when we were serious,' he said cheerfully.) Trailing a hose, he came back on clad as a Chief of the Fire Brigade, and pointed his nozzle at the stalls. 'I stood there on stage,' says Geldray, 'not knowing what to do.' Sellers, booted and belted, and wearing a huge silver helmet, proceeded to give a lecture on the pros and cons of his job and concluded by saying, 'I would like to thank you all for your attention. It is such a pleasure to deliver the message of fire prevention in such a luxurious temple of the Arts.'

Shouting 'Fire' in a crowded theatre is a traditional anarchist's action; so is shooting a gun in a public place. Sellers did that, too. When he was appearing at the Chiswick Empire, he gave an impersonation of Peter Lorre. On a darkened stage, with a gradually diminishing green spotlight, he wheedled as Joel Cairo, from *The*

Maltese Falcon, and he screamed out, as the persecuted child murderer in Fritz Lang's *M*: 'I cannot help myself! I cannot help myself!' Sellers shattered the inevitable silence which ensued by blazing off several rounds from a revolver. It must have been enough to have induced a mass loss of bladder control. 'I'd do anything,' he admitted. 'Jump up and down to change the number of the turn – if you jump you can sometimes make the numbers in lights at the side of the stage go round. When I was really pressed into the ground I'd do anything.'

Sellers continued with his Dada-esque experiments beyond the theatre – all the world was his stage, including the Hagley Road, Birmingham. Due to board with a Mrs Reeve, whilst he had a week's engagement in the vicinity, he arranged for her to take delivery of his prop basket. The doorbell rang, and there was the wicker hamper. Mrs Reeve couldn't budge it unaided, so she called her husband and son to come and help. The three of them, huffing and puffing, carried it upstairs. Sellers then unbuckled the lid from the inside, plucked himself from the linen, and stepped out: 'Thank you – it's my legs you know.'

One man who remained boot-faced at Sellers' cavortings was Val Parnell, the Booking Manager, and later Director, of the Variety Theatre Controlling Co., the General Theatre Corporation Ltd. and Moss Empires Ltd. 'Frankly, Sellers didn't make much impression on me . . . He always had a new twist for an act, something semi-zany. Off-stage he made the cast laugh . . .', he said off-handedly, though he nevertheless invited Sellers back to the Palladium for a show which ran for eight weeks, commencing on May 7th 1951. Topping the bill was Danny Kaye. Sellers was introduced as 'A man of many voices, a Teddy Bear-like refugee from the rest of the gang [of Goons]. . .' He did *Mrs Dale's Diary*, with Crun and Bluebottle, and interrupted himself with spoof ads, for such as 'Slushies', an oozing breakfast cereal, and 'Slim-Joy' bathfoam, which makes you so skinny, you go down the plughole. He ended with a duet shared between Grytpype-Thynne and the vulgar Yank, Josh Slocum: 'Don't chew tobaccy and spit it on the floor/expectorate in a cuspidor.'

Sellers definitely hawked and spat out the Palladium's *Mother Goose* from his system, 'Val Parnell's 7th Magnificent Pantomime,' in 1954. He was the Squire and played the part as Major Bloodnok. Eric Sykes wrote the script, Erté did the decor, and Shirley Eaton, who was Margery Daw, tells me: 'I don't think he enjoyed pantomime at all – it was as if it was something he thought he should do. He was stormy – temperamental – always ready with a tantrum if things went wrong – and yet then he could be very affectionate and extremely vulnerable. He was a very restless person, and he was never an attractive person, Peter – and he knew it. But he had charm. Women respond to that in men, and to their vulnerability. Peter used all this as part of his appeal. We all had our photos taken on stage with our mothers. Max Bygraves, Peter, myself. After his mother died – and he was absolutely distraught when his mother died – he tracked me down* and asked for a copy: "Shirley, darling, do you have a copy of it? I'll get another copy made for myself. . .". He never did return it.'

Max Bygraves remembers *Mother Goose* as a disaster for Sellers, who walked down the ramp at the finale day after day to no applause. The pains he took getting the make-up right – a false nose, almost luminous from sniffing at VSOP, the greying hair, etc., – were wasted; the conception 'did not travel across the footlights', because Bloodnok's eccentricity, as Bygraves astutely noted, was based on what could only be achieved on radio (the noises of battle, the stomach gurgles) and pantomime had simplified the character, broadening him into a slapstick Colonel Blimp. Worse, Sellers had no rapport with Richard Hearne, whose Mr Pastry creature had been cross-dressed as the dame. Mother Goose, as rich as you please, had sold her soul to become beautiful. She took a dip in

---

* Miss Eaton, well-known as the gold-painted cadaver in *Gold Finger*, had prematurely retired. She explains that 'I started acting on stage at the age of twelve, and continued until I was thirty-two, and gave my film career up to be a full-time mother. . . , and [for] family life in general, a decision I've never regretted.' She lives in St Jean Cap Ferrat, France. My conversation with her will continue when I get around to *The Naked Truth*.

a magic fountain and came out transformed with a diamanté wig and a silver play-suit. Sellers' Squire was meant to exclaim, 'What is this!' For one matinée he decided to do his part as Groucho Marx, complete with lope, painted moustache and eyes shifting wantonly behind his specs. Instead of his usual 'What is this!' line, he said 'I've heard of Lady *Dicker*, but this is *ridoculous*. . .'. The band appreciated the gag but Hearne, recalls Bygraves, 'would not utter the next line until Peter had given him the proper cue. Peter had picked the wrong one . . . as far as skylarking was concerned. Dickie Hearne was a rigidly trained legitimate actor who would stand there all afternoon . . . Even if you'd only twisted it up a bit, he would still stand there and almost demand the right line. It seemed like an eternity of silence on the stage – Peter couldn't understand – it was the first big laugh he'd had in the show.'

The following day, Bygraves found Sellers crying backstage. He'd received a letter, hand-delivered from the Moss Empires Head office:

Dear Mr Sellers,

I was in the theatre yesterday when you decided to change the text of 'Mother Goose'.

When I require you to make the members of my orchestra laugh I will ask you.

Until then, do the job you are being paid for, otherwise I will have you personally kicked out of the theatre.

> Yours etc.
> *Val Parnell*

☆ ★ ☆

Sellers was not somebody to whom you could say DON'T! or STOP! or NO! The only saving grace about variety, as far as he was concerned, was the chance he had to improvise. Isolated in the spotlight, he did what he pleased. 'If you went backstage,' says Anne, 'you'd hear every tannoy turned up, because he always departed from his scripts; there'd always be something new in his act, and I think it took tremendous courage for him never to want to be the same.' When inspiration failed, however, or he was thwarted, the after-effects were ugly. 'He became very aggressive – and I mean Peter had a lot of violence in him. Not so much verbal tongue-lashings – he was *physically* violent. I remember when he was doing variety, he got very frustrated one day sitting in his dressing room and he pulled all these large hooks out of the wall. The whole lot, in anger. And he'd lash out; he'd hit. Like a child, really. I don't think he ever grew up. I don't think he ever matured. He was emotionally retarded. His reactions to things were always childish – always hitting out, or hurting himself, or hurting some-body who was close to him. And then feeling terribly sorry afterwards. Living with him, I learned a tremendous capacity for blocking out things I didn't like. You only survived if you didn't think about it.'

Sellers treated his wife like he treated his audiences – in the final analysis, making due allowance for his posturing and detachment, there was little left in his attitude but disdain. The purpose of other people was to convince him he was marvellous. He used people up. Anne helped him to close the gap between music hall jesting and being a comic actor, Britt was a fashion accessory, Miranda his entry card into the ruling classes, and as for Lynne – he fed off her youth and ambition.

'He was destructive to anybody that was close to him, apart from Peg.' Anne found her mother-in-law an incubus. 'We had a row six months after our wedding. "My son doesn't have to think for him-self, I think for him," she was always saying – her refrain. One day she got on the phone about something and I said, "Look, will you leave us alone please." She started having a go at me, and I eventu-ally said, "Oh, fuck off" and put the phone down. In those days I did not use words like that, I have to tell you. We rarely spoke to each other after that – not until after the divorce, and I was well and truly out of his life, when she was almost a friend.'

After that debacle, and after Anne had had her miscarriage,

when Peg, laying plots and inductions dangerous, had invited Nora Barnacle, Sellers' old flame*, to tea, it was plain that, pregnant now a second time, Anne was going to need protecting. What this meant in practical terms was getting out of the peppercorn Mendoza flatlet and into a home of their own. With this scheme in view, Sellers, in January 1954, attempted to raise a mortgage with the General Accident Fire & Life Assurance Corporation Ltd., of Perth. When the building society started to deal with the proposal, however, and wrote to the BBC for confirmation of the applicant's gross wages and details of other emoluments arising out of his employment, the response was snotty:

> 22nd January 1954
> *Private and Confidential*

Dear Sir,

Mr Peter R.H. Sellers

[. . .]

According to our records, Mr Sellers has been broadcasting for us since 1948. He is, however, a free lance artist who is booked as required for our programmes and has never been a member of our Staff. It is regretted that in view of the clerical work involved we are unable to provide you with the information for which you ask [. . .]

> Yours faithfully,
> *G.M. Turnell*
> Assistant Head of Programme Contracts

Michael Peter Anthony was born on April 2nd 1954 and Sellers would not own his own property until February 21st the following year when, flush with the *Mother Goose* earnings, he and his young family moved to 72, Tetherdown, Muswell Hill, N20 (tel. Tudor 6607 and 0686). Why was Turnell so truculent? Perhaps because,

---

* Believe it or not, this is a pseudonym. Though the lady's real name is known to me, my publishers' legal advisors prudently suggest that as all confirmation of Sellers' illegitimate daughter and the identity of the child's mother had come

1. Gulliver in Lilliput: Sellers (standing behind Bro. Cornelius) at
St. Aloysius' College, Highgate (c. 1937)

2. First Photoplay: "Blimey, potato-worshipper 'ere!" Sellers and Milligan in *Let's Go Crazy* (1950)

7. *(Right)* All the Marx Bros. in one: Amphibolous in *Carlton-Browne of the F.O.* (1958)

8. *(Foot)* Ma Ray, Crystal Jollibottom, the Grand Duchess Gloriana – *The Mouse That Roared* (1959)

10. Mr and Mrs Fred Kite (1959)

11. "He became whoever he was playing" (Anne Levy): Lionel Meadows in *Never Let Go* (1960)

13. *(Right)* Topaze and Monsieur Muche
(Leo McKern)

14. *(Right)* "Now don't stand there giving me that little-boy face, you're getting too old for it": John Lewis in *Only Two Can Play* (1961)

15. *(Below) General:* "My God, woman, I hate you." *Emily:* "What difference does that make? I'm your wife." *Waltz of the Toreadors* (1961)

only two weeks previously, Sellers and his agents had refused to sign one of the precious long term agreements:

LEW & LESLIE
GRADE LTD
Regent House,
235-241 Regent Street,
London, W.1
Confidential
4th January 1954

W.L. Streeton Esq.,
B.B.C.
Broadcasting House, LONDON W.1

Dear Mr Streeton:

PETER SELLERS

[. . .] I have now gone into this matter thoroughly with Mr. Sellers, but cannot see that it would be beneficial to this artist to sign a long term contract, which I am returning herewith.

We feel that by signing this agreement Mr. Sellers would have to be on first call to the B.B.C. for the next three years, and as he has varied commitments in the entertainment field, especially with films, we obviously could not tie ourselves down as per the terms mentioned in your contract.

Mr Sellers has worked in very happy co-operation with the B.B.C. for the past few years, and I sincerely hope that he will continue to do so for many years to come. I can assure you that, even if he should not sign a long term agreement with you, he is only too happy to carry on working for you as he is at present.

Kind regards.
Yours sincerely,
for and on behalf of
LEW & LESLIE GRADE LTD
Dennis J. Selinger

(originally) from his nibs himself, there may be an element of doubt as to the credibility of that saga – and thus it could be dangerous to denote any genuine

Here we have the first reference to Sellers' forthcoming career in the cinema. With only quasi-home movies, like *Penny Points to Paradise* and *Down Among the Z Men* to his credit, he was already looking confidently ahead. The transformation of a radio voice into a screen presence will be the subject of the next chapter (within a twelvemonth of the above letter Sellers would be cast in *The Lady-killers*); and what needs explaining here is the nature of the training he was receiving, c/o the BBC, in addition to *The Goon Show*. For, if Milligan was giving Sellers the key to his buried thoughts, helping him to devise characters and noises which got to him in a unique way, there was another mentor on hand, demonstrating the more fundamental arts and crafts – Ted Ray, his spurious relative. Timing for example, 'is something you have to learn', Sellers said in 1980, three months before he died, 'but someone can't teach it to you. I learned timing from watching a great comedian who is now dead, God rest his soul, named Ted Ray. I worked on his radio show for about eight years. I was a straight man, and I also worked in vaudeville with him. I could *hear* when he knew the ultimate moment. I mean, he'd sling a gag at the audience and they'd laugh. And then he'd know the precise *second* to speak again to keep them on that level.'

In fact, Sellers appeared in *Ray's a Laugh*, concurrently with *The Goon Show*, for twelve years and far from being the straight man, he's the only funny element in it. Admittedly I have only sampled half a dozen episodes out of the thousands (I dare say) they made, but the gist was plain. This is the archaeology of comedy. A boneyard of gags and situations so feeble, they crumbled and I forgot them even as I was jotting them down. The first thing to set the teeth on edge is the close-harmony signature tune ('Come on and meet Ted Ray/He'll chase your troubles a-way'), and when the star greets us by saying, 'Hello boys and girls,' the smiles freeze on our

---

candidate(s). My sincere apologies and gratitude to the shade of Mrs James Joyce, who died in 1951 without knowing the first thing about Peter Sellers, for her guest appearance on my pages.

faces. Sellers joined the show at its outset, in 1949, when it had a variety format. Ted told a few disconnected jokes – 'I went to a big film premiere last week . . . which reminds me . . . isn't it strange the way things happen . . . seriously though . . .' – which were consistently mirthless. Then the very horrible blurred voices of the close-harmony lot came back again for a song – calling themselves 'The Beaux and the Belles', they are on a par with Bob and Alf Pearson, crooners of a kind, who chirruped gaily about lips or rain drops: 'We bring you melodies from out of the sky/My brother and I.' And you can fuck off back into the ether again as soon as you like, pal.

The musical interludes were quickly dropped in favour of an enlargement of the show's central section, the domestic scene between Ted and his wife, played by Kitty Bluett. Sellers was the various persons with whom their days were sprinkled. His most celebrated creation was Crystal Jollibottom, the crone from across the street – her exuberant gurgles are those of a contralto Bluebottle, she mutters and harrumphs like Bloodnok in drag, but otherwise she is a querulous, flirty, lush creation. We can *see* a fat old baggage hoisting up her petticoats. The audience come alive, too, when she arrives: 'I'll thank you to stop fiddling with me feather duster. . .'; 'Me unmentionables are caught round me scrubbing brush. . .'. When she takes a ballet class, Ray is warned, 'I'll thank you to keep your big nose out of me dying swan.' Her catchphrase was 'you old saucebox!' The mixture of innuendo and outright desire in this 'last of the GI brides' is rich indeed – Crystal is a pantomime dame, impudent and vampish, all whoops and sags.

Sellers was also Soppy, the boy who smuggled a telescope into the Folies Bergère and tells everybody to 'shut up, big gob'; and he played millions of yokels, cockneys, yids and wops. Luigi was a happy Italian, singing about 'my splaghetti, she is so be-autiful,' and Giuseppi was his taciturn twin: 'What you a-want supposing we a-got it?' he'd growl. Between them the brothers invented a garlic layer cake ('She is so nice, eh?') and macaroni sticks stuffed with bicarbonate of soda ('The indigestion she is a-cured while you eat of my beautiful straws'). Sellers played Wilberforce, an over-ingenious and dumb detective who prefigures Clouseau – 'Hist, never fear, Hugo's here,' he'd say, coming out of a disguise. (One week he was a tent pole and a mole on his neck was a knot in the wood.) And he was Cedric the scout-leader ('life gets hum'drum if you don't dabble') who met his match in Wilf the Tough ('We are going to get the gentleman's money *aren't* we, Sydney. . . ?'), a sort of menacing Grytpype-Thynne. . . .

The success of Sellers' one-man non-Goon Rep. Company in *Ray's a Laugh*, and in his other variety spot impersonations, was conveyed in a potted life history, written in the style of his characters and published in *Sound and Vision* as early as October 1950:

> *RAY'S A LAUGH is back and with it is Peter Sellers. Here are seven of his characters, real and imaginary, to give you a unique biography.*
>
> 'It's me, Crystal Jollibottom, you old saucebox, fancy wanting a story on how Peter Sellers started to do his impressions, oo-ah-ha-ha, it makes me go all goose-pimples to think about it.'
>
> 'I think you're thoppy . . . you are . . . I tell you he tharted it at hith thcool.'
>
> 'Quiet you two, this is Dick Barton, Special Agent. Here, Jock, Snowy, quick! Get me my dossier on that fugitive from the Windmill Theatre. Make it snappy now, there's no time to lose.'
>
> 'There it is! The clue we want – he's an old Aloysian.'
>
> 'Isn't that St Aloysius' College, Highgate, Captain Barton?' – 'Yes, Snowy.'
>
> 'Ach! the wee nipper went to school then.'
>
> 'Quiet, Jock, this is no time for comedy. It says here, our fugitive, instead of solving the riddle of the broken fraction, devoted his time to sinister business, that of entertaining his schoolboy gang . . . AND . . . with a stolen version of 'Itma'.
>
> 'He made one mistake.'
>
> 'What was that, Captain Barton?' – 'When he stole the Headmaster's voice and his idiosyncracies, and disguised them as one of his characters.'
>
> 'Ay, but the wee laddie didn'a get awa' we' it, though.'
>
> 'How do you know, Jock?'
>
> 'Ach! Snowy, the head wasna' so slow, his presence caught up wi' his

voice and retribution overtook the no' over-cautious impressionist in
the right quarter.'

'What happened then? . . .'

'Listen to the next recording of Dick Barton, Special Agent.'

'Are you ready, girls? . . . yes! . . . let's go. This is Syd Seymour
bringing you our latest find . . . Drummer Sellers, straight from his
debut with Joe Daniels and his Hot Shots. You want to know something?

'This drummer of ours started by sweeping up the stage at his
uncle's theatre, then learned the whole business by doing all the odd
jobs, Lime Boy, Props, Stage Manager, and if the energy he puts
into those drum sticks is anything like the amount he used to sweep
the stage – the dust clouds were thick over Ilfracombe.'

'The day war broke out! Peter tried to get into the R.A.F., and the
wife said to me, now there's a likely young man if ever there was
one! I said to her, I beg your pardon! and before I could get a word
in edgeways three years had passed and Peter was in the R.A.F. in
India, had met Ralph Reader and joined his Gang Show.

'Then I said to her, he's been in Burma, as well, then she said to me
. . . and before I could say I beg your pardon, Peter had been
demobbed, played at the Windmill theatre and was in 'Ray's a
Laugh'. It shows you how women will talk.

'By the time you've read this my old woman will have beaten the
longest unbroken run of any radio show, for talking. Just a minute,
while I see what the time is . . . Oh, dear! They've been open two
minutes. I must go and tell Fred, he doesn't like to be late . . . Ta
Ta.'

Sellers' vocal eccentricities seem all the more extraterrestrial
when set besides Ray's monotonous nasal delivery, which lay somewhere between a snarl, a drawl, and a bark. In the scenes with Kitty
Bluett – an Australian, apparently, who lost her original accent and
never quite succeeded in perfecting another one – Ted comes across
either as a bad-tempered old shag, a tight-fisted grouch, or a tyran-
nical bore. Kitty is always put down. 'Go on, scram!' he tells her. Or
'Kitty, you snatched my newspaper!' he informs us. 'Why do you
mess about with things you know nothing about?' he asks
rhetorically, if ever her conversation wanders off kitchens, curtains

or ordering the milk. 'Now run along, dear, please,' he says irritably, or 'Hurry up with my lunch, dear,' he demands, 'I've got something very important to do. . .'. These playlets, popular in their day, are vomiters now, the reason being that the battle of the sexes is unequal. Ted browbeats Kitty like Punch hitting Judy. It doesn't help that Kitty's range of whines and simpers, during the bickering, is such a rasp. They call each other 'darling' so frequently, the endearment flies back and forth like a dirty word.

Ray's a Laugh really is crap. George Inns, the producer, may have begun his career as a sound effects engineer, but primitive noises like doors opening, doors shutting, and door knobs rattling are about all he can manage here. (In one episode a Yorkshire Terrier's yap is closer to a chicken's cluck.) In fact, a lot of mileage is got out of this lone sound effect. 'See who that is, dear' or 'Answer the door dear, will you?' says Ted to Kitty, his twittering drudge. The stage is then set for Sellers' ingress, and when he speaks it is as if Mardi Gras has been let into the room. 'Let's get down to the hop-hall and lend me your frantic frame for the struggle, baby,' he says, as Al K. Traz, a gigolo from the Bronx; or, as Serge Suit, the Russian: 'I lerewike to hear Tchaikerowovsky's Serewugar Plerewum Ferewairy.' Sellers is exotic, but it doesn't seem as though he's just a versatile fellow doing the audible equivalent of pulling funny faces (which was the fate of Kenneth Williams). There is a curious reality to his caricatures – something which cannot be said of Patricia Hayes' malapropistic Mrs Easy, who is simply an actress pretending to be common. Patricia Hayes' East-Enders are trill and flat and make us realise what a talent Irene Handl had, when she partnered Sellers as any number of chars or busy-bodies or (magnificently) as Mrs Fred Kite. This is quite a conundrum: why certain actors can go over the top and still be believable and funny, where others, straining in the same style, leave an audience cold. It has to do with our being put off if we detect effort.

As much as Ted Ray leaves me cold, I can acknowledge that he does deliver his lines with conviction. When Kitty muffs her material (in one episode she says 'run a wace' for 'won a race' and remains on the edge of tears for the rest of the show), it comes as a surprise to remember that there *is* a script. Ray's crossness has seemed so off-hand and the jokes so pathetic, who would dare admit to having written any of it down in advance? Until Sellers irrupts, you'd think a tape recorder had been left running by accident in a suburban home. (I suppose the chauvinistic slant of husband and wife's sparring is authentically in period.) This was precisely why the populace tuned in. As Ray himself said, 'There is no doubt that Everyman and his wife identify themselves with my radio better-half and me. This hearth-and-home type of fun is really a fascinating subject . . . You just can't beat the real thing . . . I like to feel when Kitty and I are doing one of our sketches that all over the country married couples are looking at each other and saying: "But, darling, that's exactly what happened to us the other day!"' As a radio programme with a rationale of tediousness at its core, 'it was breaking new ground and, although I was hopeful, I had absolutely no idea . . . that people were going to rise so magnificently to the domestic humour of my adventures with Kitty'.

☆ ★ ☆

If Ray taught Sellers how to pace a line – he gave him his rhythms – he also, more tellingly, demonstrated that comic acting could be naturalistic. The two elements are connected, of course, and their impact on Sellers should not be underestimated. His artistry depended, no matter how nutbrain his given role, on the casualness of his inflexions. Even when elaborately made up – bulbous nose, lank wig, a seedy nineteenth-century tragic actor's costume as, for instance, Dr Pratt, in *The Wrong Box* – the words spill out guilelessly. We are not aware of Sellers, the other side of the character, manufacturing the entertainment. ('Look at that, sir. Scarcely human,' he sighs, blotting the ink on a fake death certificate with a live kitten.) In this film, especially, we can see that great acting is a product not of *obvious* artistry, but is a success precisely because of its apparent artlessness. Wilfrid Lawson, so drunk he can barely walk or speak – he communicates in a strange, wheezy hooting – is totally affecting. And Ralph Richardson, as the boring old uncle, is

253

blissfully trapped in a world of his own, foraging around the alleys and crannies of his mind for useless facts and figures, just as he rummages in the dozens of pockets and flaps in his raffish suits and coats. Sellers is in this class – he relaxes into his gifts, as Cocteau would say. He, Lawson, and Richardson stand out in the film that is full, ostensibly, of funny and talented people. Peter Cook and Dudley Moore repeat their supercilious master and sex-mad servant routine, Cicily Courtneidge and Tony Hancock mug embarrassingly, and the more John Mills (putting on a silly old sod's squeaky voice) throws himself around in his bed-shirt, the less interesting he becomes. You can see many members of the cast straining for laughs, clenching their jaws, the veins bulging in their necks.

The film, crammed with cameos, with a vague Victorian chase-theme rompishness similar to *Monte Carlo or Bust* or *Those Magnificent Men in their Flying Machines*, is an object lesson in who possesses a comic spirit and who doesn't. Admittedly, Bryan Forbes' direction, which is so slow the film seems to be enacted under water, doesn't help – and there actually are slow-motion sequences, when Michael Caine and Nanette Newman, decades too old for their roles, play stilted period lovers. Doubtless they are meant to be sending up the formality of courtship back in those days, but acting badly on purpose can go too far. Caine has said that one of his motives, as an actor, when playing 'little Cockney parts in English movies, [was] to play them correctly, with the correct accent, with some dignity . . . I always saw people of my own class portrayed on screen by upper-class people as a sort of caricature, as a sort of insult. We always wound up as forelock tugging, grovelling, monosyllabic oafs. And this always made me angry.' So, when reversing the process, in *The Wrong Box*, and it is he who plays the gentleman for a change, why did he have to make his character such a stereotyped chump? Or was he miscast on purpose – the unworldly Victorian medical student, batting his dewy eyes, a joke at the expense of Caine's rebarbative Alfie?

☆ ★ ☆

Whilst I am not saying that Sellers' sorrowful Dr Pratt (who appeared in 1966) is all thanks to Ted Ray – where would my man have been without Alec Guinness? – I am putting forward the argument that Ray was an indispensable element in Sellers' conversion from music hall artiste to multi-textured actor, whose fol-de-rols have weight. Ray, a generation Sellers' senior, was born in Wigan, George Formby's sacred site, and his father, like Sellers', was a pub pianist. Ray toured the music halls, as Nedlo the gypsy violinist, and had his own tales to tell* of dreary digs, clapped-out revues, and the coldness of England's northern towns. He started on radio in 1948, as the compère for *Henry Hall's Guest Night* (his bossiness was ideal for an emcee and it is no wonder his main film rôle was as the Headmaster, Mr Wakefield, in *Carry on Teacher*), which is where he encountered Sellers, who 'had just been demobbed from the RAF, and what a long way he has gone since those days'. (That sounds like a remark on a school report.)

Ray's a Laugh began in April 1949 and the first series ran for sixty-five episodes without pause. Sellers received nine guineas a time; this was soon increased to twenty-five guineas, then twenty-six pounds five shillings (the same as Kitty Bluett). Ted Ray himself received a hundred and five pounds each week. The cast rehearsed at the Paris Cinema and the show went out at half past eight on a Thursday night. Sellers eventually decided he wanted a vacation, and in March 1953 put his case to Pat Newman:

> As I have not had a holiday for the past three years, I feel badly in need of one and would like to go to the South of France for fourteen days, commencing the 4th of May. This would entail my being released from *Ray's a Laugh* for that period. As I have to start rehearsing for the summer show [*Show Time* at the South Parade Pier, Southsea] immediately afterwards there is no prospect of my

---

* Ray published two autobiographies, *Raising the Laughs*, in 1952, and *My Turn Next*, in 1963. You can hardly call them ill-written – like a lot of ghosted books they were recited and then transcribed by A.N. Other, a technique resulting in appalling infelicities, e.g.: 'Our Scoutmaster, Mr Grace, certainly had his hands full.'

getting a holiday at another time this year – even my Sundays have not been free because *The Goon Show* is always recorded on a Sunday. Right now my nerves are tuned up like an XK. 120 and I feel that if I do not get a holiday soon I shall have a nervous breakdown. I should be much obliged if you could arrange this for me. I assure you I would not have bothered you had I not felt it was really necessary.

Sellers' agent wrote a formal letter making the same request and only to this did the BBC respond:

11 March, 1953

Dear Dennis Selinger,

Re: PETER SELLERS

Thank you for your letter of the 10th inst. about the above artist [. . .]

Whilst I strongly support the essential need of artists having a proper holiday (since many of them are inclined to overwork) I must say this particular case seems to me to be a little tricky from our point of view.

Apart from the long term contract that Peter Sellers has had with us for the last two years I think we, anyhow, feel that, to a certain extent, we 'come first' and perhaps he should take into account the question of the possibility of overworking before he gets embroiled in late night cabaret amongst his other activities.

I believe he particuarly wants to go away at this time with the idea of joining Alfred Marks (I am afraid I suggested it would be no holiday as they would discuss 'the business' all the time!) and I appreciate that if he cannot snatch this particular time he will have to wait till his Summer Season finishes mid September. However, you will remember that he has already sought release from the last three editions of the current series of 'Ray's a Laugh' when he wanted to do the musical for Delfont which, had it come about, would have replaced the Summer Season. You will remember that, after due consideration, we refused this but it is interesting to note that, had we agreed, he would then certainly have been unable to take this holiday in May.

My own view – at the risk of seeming rather harsh – is that we will not feel able to release him; after all most of us have these clashes to cope with at times and, generally speaking, holidays have got to fit in to one's work schedule and I don't think Peter can really have it both ways.

Anyhow, this is a joint decision between my own section and those on the production side and I will take the earliest opportunity of discussing it with the latter. Should they be agreeable then the contract side of it would raise no objections.

You shall have our considered reply in a day or two.

> Yours sincerely,
> *Patrick Newman*
> Variety Booking Manager

In fact, it was to be a fortnight before Newman wrote again, for reasons which are contained in his letter of March 25th:

Dear Dennis Selinger,

Re: PETER SELLERS

This letter follows on my last one of 11th March and is merely to tidy things up [. . .]

I understand that since the request to us to release him so that he could have a holiday in May, he withdrew that request because he had anyhow cancelled his holiday for a Palladium commitment. Indeed, I believe the suggestion was that we should now pre-record four of the 'Ray's a Laugh' programmes – instead of three as we had agreed to do anyhow (to release him for his summer season). Unfortunately it is already sufficiently complicated for us to cope with the agreed three, and, with regret, we are unable to add on another one and make it four.

So the outcome of all this is that the position is what it was [at the beginning of March]. Incidentally, one cannot help but note that his urgent need of a holiday – so urgent that he seeks release from his BBC contract – seems to become less pronounced when there is a question of appearing at the Palladium.

By the way, I went to the Pigalle last week, but though the programme told me to expect Peter Sellers, I found myself listening to the Nesbitts instead. Really, one can hardly keep track of where he is and is not appearing, and I only hope he knows himself!

[...]

At the foot of Newman's carbon there is a handwritten note, saying that Selinger had telephoned on March 27th and 'everything OK'. Not so with Sellers himself, however, for there are further anxious scribbles: 'Sellers now asking for more money *now* – in the middle of the series! Selinger said 'NO' [to his client] but thinks Peter S. may attack me – so be it!!' It is initialled 'P.N.'

Newman was no doubt quite correct in thinking that Sellers was capable of coming to his office and making his case with a cosh. (Daniel Mendoza's descendant might make his entrance on a white stallion as well.) The artiste's reaction wasn't, as it turned out, violent. If the BBC wouldn't let him go, he decided he'd take up residence in the studio as a permanent fixture. A vexed memo was sent by Antony Derville to the chiefs of staff saying that, when Sellers was Guest of the Week on *Woman's Hour* he insisted on rehearsing his six minute interview for over two hours. Everybody was aghast. Nobody ever hung around longer than needs be, especially Sellers.

Didn't they notice the date of the transmission? April 1st 1953.

☆　★　☆

Newman, an impressive diplomat who could give his firmness a light touch, did well to stand his ground. Sellers' mind was always made up, his resolve fixed, until something better came along. And as for holidays – his family learned to dread them. 'I don't think I ever went on holiday without him saying "I want a divorce,"' remembers Anne. 'That was normal, saying things such as that. He was impossible on holidays – he'd get there and want to come back immediately. We went to the Cote d'Azur with John and Jackie Boulting. The moment we got there he suddenly felt he couldn't cope with John's intelligent conversation – so he left the hotel, on his own, and went to stay in Nice – "I'm going." – "But you can't!" – "Well, I am." – "You mustn't." – "I want a divorce." On holidays he'd have to be Peter Sellers relaxing, you see; and left to his own devices, there'd be nothing there. He had no cover. All his insecurities came out. He was aware he couldn't talk to anybody with any intellect, and he came across a lot of people who were bright – and he was lost. Ken Tynan, Sandy Mackendrick – completely and utterly lost. He blamed his lack of education, but that really shouldn't have made any difference in the end. To blame it all on to bad schooling . . . *Life* should teach you. . . He left school very early – I can't imagine him sitting in a classroom, can you? If darling didn't want to go to school, darling didn't go. . .'

Sellers did spend at least one holiday with the edifying Ted Ray and his teenage children. Andrew Ray was already a veteran juvenile actor (*The Mudlark* etc.) and Robin Ray would partially grow-up to be the know-all alongside Joyce Grenfell on *Face the Music*, a programme famous for its quiz master, Joseph Cooper, playing a piano through its locked lid. Michael Sellers informed me that they all frolicked at Pevensey Bay, on the English South coast, his father filming everybody with a cine camera. Was he hoping to remind himself later that they were happy? Peg and Bill were there, too, renting a little chalet.

The summer leaves are all faded now. 'Only vague memories of Peter at that time,' writes Robin Ray, 'Nice man, bought too many cars, child at heart – *great* fun. Sorry I can't be specific. . .' Fortunately, Michael is able to be less diffuse: 'When you were with him, a wrong word could put him in a temper for the day. "What do you mean by *that*?" he'd snap. You learned to be very peaceable and diplomatic. Going on holiday with him was a nightmare – keeping him happy for a whole fortnight or a month. Impossible. He'd invariably storm off home early.'

An off-putting facet of *Ray's a Laugh* is the way Kitty has to cope with Ted's ill-humour and pettishness. He is always threatening to sulk. For example, Kitty would like to buy a television set, but Ted is against the idea. She mentions a small table they possess, 'it's just about high enough. . . If we put two seats over there we could view . . .'; and Ted explodes. 'I'm sorry, dear . . .' mollifies his wife, 'especially as you were in such a good mood.' Such is his petulance, he is always being put into a bad mood by Kitty, or else he's grumpy anyway and Kitty is having to talk him back into sorts. (If she succeeds in cheering up her liege lord, she's told how grateful she should feel.) Was it all considered funny because a grown man, after his day at the office, came home and reverted to being a brat? Was that the joke? Infantile, in any event, is what Sellers was around the clock. If he had difficulty in being a husband, he hadn't a clue how to be a father.

'He was like a child with another child,' says Anne, 'quite unreasonable. He was very inconsistent. I wouldn't say that he was a good father at all. He didn't know how to cope with our children, and, later on, he often didn't want to see them – though, when he did want to see them, they'd more than willingly go.'

Sarah Jane Sellers, born on October 16th 1957, remembers being summoned: 'When we were with Dad, it wouldn't be unusual for us to be looked after by a secretary; all through the years, often when I'd see him I'd spend more time chatting to Bert Mortimer [Sellers' chauffeur]. It was very strange when I was a teenager, because he really didn't know anything about me. He didn't know who my friends were, whether I had a boyfriend or not, how I was doing at school. Nothing. He just knew I'd come and see him and that I'd behave in a certain way. I was quite shy and withdrawn. One or the other. I saw him a few times a year. In the early Seventies, we'd spend school holidays with him, especially in Ireland. I recall regular rows with Miranda there. After that, I didn't see him much. We were constantly on the receiving end of his moods – big blow ups. You'd be talking about something, he'd be full of beans, at the end of the conversation you'd realise that, somewhere along the line, you'd said something wrong, but you weren't too sure what it was – you'd get this sarcasm back.'

Her testimony chimes with Michael's: 'You could be happily, merrily going along – and one word would be enough. You'd have ruined his whole day. He would just *go!* And once his temper was gone, he'd take delight in upsetting as many people as possible. He was like a playground bully – he enjoyed making you cry, and once his victim had started to break down, he'd press his advantage. Cruelty took over. He lost control. After a while I'm sure he was no longer in control – because he used to be sorry afterwards, perhaps if only owing to acute embarrassment. But then he never genuinely apologised for anything. He did once – I think – when he whipped me for painting his Bentley. In later years he did actually say he was sorry about that.'

What happened was that Sellers had been showing off his new maroon car to his mates, when he noticed some minuscule flecks in the coachwork, caused by gravel from the driveway. Ranting and raving, he was coaxed back inside the house and presumably sedated. Michael, aged six or seven, having overheard the commotion, thought he'd set about fixing matters. He found a pot of Dulux red paint in the garage and daubed at the chips. Sellers, discovering the DIY re-spray, went wild. 'A major low point in my childhood,' says Michael, 'accompanied by the withdrawal of all toys, all permissions and privileges. I was in my room and all the toys were gone – except for his trains, which were still stacked on top of my wardrobe.'

'He suddenly had this wrath,' says Anne, 'Mike had said, looking at the patched up scratches, "But I thought I was going to make it beautiful again." Peter went berserk. Nearly murdered him.'*

---

* Stark, in *Remembering Peter Sellers*, wishing to show his hero in a non-violent light, recounts the episode very differently: 'Anne came down first, saw what Michael had done, climbed in her Mini, still wearing her nightdress and dressing gown, pulled Michael in after her and, with a basic intuition of a mother protect-

Milligan has claimed that he was on hand and intervened when the assault started to get out of all proportion. ('Peter got hold of the boy and shook him so violently . . . I thought he was going to kill him.')

I don't think Sellers much cared for the fate of the Bentley Continental in itself (so as to get rid of it quickly, he sold it on at a huge financial loss); the fact is, his was the over-scaled rage of the spoilt child who, unused to sharing, can't abide having his space invaded or playthings touched. Note Michael's reference to his father's out-of-reach train set. His mother remembers how they were acquired.

'When I was pregnant he went out and bought three hundred pound's worth of trains – for a child which hadn't been born yet. That sort of money would be a lot now on toy trains. I can't imagine what it would be equivalent to. . .'

Sellers was enraptured, watching the Hornby locomotives whizz purposelessly around the miniature tracks. 'He'd go out and buy a railway, and he'd set it up, and he'd play with it – and I wasn't allowed to touch it,' recalls Michael, 'until he'd finished. Once he'd finished and was bored, then I could play. He came home with this toy house building set. Oblong metal plates full of holes; you'd stick these poles in and slide in these panels – and he stayed up all night making this house, playing with it. Then he threw it back in the box and gave it to me. I was six years old – I couldn't make head nor tail of it. Didn't know what the hell it was about. He never ever made allowance for our age. . .'

---

ing her young, drove into the countryside where she stayed with Michael for the rest of the day. On being told the news, the coach builders came at dawn, wrapped the car in a tarpaulin, put it on a trailer, and took it away so no one could see what damage had been done. . .'

I don't know what's the most improbable here, Anne loitering in her lingerie, hiding in a field, or workmen arriving 'at dawn' – on the same day? The next? Who is meant to have tipped them off? And from whom are they meant to be concealing the defilement, if not Sellers? And wouldn't he notice the car's absence? What about his wife and son's absence? Where was baby Sarah meantime?

This went beyond inappropriate gifts. The rules were adult rules which we had to obey – although at that age, how could we understand his reasonings? Of course, this gave him the excuse for losing his temper. After a while, we'd learn the things he'd lay first claim on – what he reckoned he possessed. Including the homes. We never really had rooms of our own. "Mike's Room" was only mine for as long as it suited him. In my room at Elstead I had two chests of drawers. He'd taken on a new cook, who was to live upstairs in the barn; so he came into my room, threw my stuff on the floor, and said to this cook, "Right, you can use these chests of drawers." I had no say in the matter. . .'

☆ ★ ☆

Sellers begrudged his children their childhoods. He did his best, by behaving badly, to be more puerile than they ever were; and it puzzled him that he should continue to be accountable for them. As he believed himself to be a one-man species, their biological connections with him were a nuisance – a reminder of his own mortality. When Sarah was late sending a birthday card, or if Michael telephoned instead of writing a formal letter to acknowledge a gift, Sellers would be swift to tell him 'I no longer wish to be thought of as your father', or 'my final suggestion is that you have your name changed by deed poll. . . .'

Remember that Olivier had wanted him to play Lear? Sellers would go through that character's madness without the compensations of Act V's serenity and self-knowledge: 'They told me I was everything,' says the humbled King, ''tis a lie – I am not ague-proof.' Sellers, alas, was never cured of his flatterers, and his financial success allowed him to prolong his adolescence until his dying day. (His cardiac pacemaker was a macabre toy ticker.) The sole advantage of fatherhood, as he saw it, the only aspect he enjoyed, as Sarah says, 'was going out and buying toys that he'd then play with. He was therefore much more interested in having a son than bothering with a daughter. He wasn't mystified by me as a small girl – it was simpler than that: I hardly existed.'

Was that one of Lear's problems? All those bloody women and

nobody to get down and play choo-choos with? 'Goodnight, Daddy,' Michael was overheard by a journalist as saying, aged six in 1960, 'now you'll be able to have my electric train all to yourself.' Actually, I find Sellers' immersion in chuff-chuffs and toys the reverse of endearing. His little-boy-in-a-man's-body act was bound up with a lot of aggression and sourness. Bentine once revealingly said that he'd 'thought of the perfect Christmas gift for someone with Peter's attention span: a set of two thousand lead soldiers depicting the Battle of Waterloo, which Peter could play with for ten minutes, and then melt.' It wasn't so much Sellers' low threshold of boredom which was frightening, however, as his destructiveness and need for expressions of power. To lay waste both Napoleon and Wellington's battalions! He did once glue a miniature army together, out of a bag of coloured plastic pieces. He also went in for balsa wood aeroplanes and a mechanical helicopter. Anything, as Max Geldray says, 'that moved and crawled and flew and sparked and fired and banged'. He had a life-sized baby elephant, propelled by a Ford engine; remote control telephones and tape recorders, and there was a radio transmitter in the dashboard of his car. (He liked to leave disembodied messages in his office at night for the secretary to re-play in the morning.) He hid himself within the impedimenta. Others – Rowland Emett was one – could surround themselves with knick-knacks and it would suggest a whimsical, silly nature. Sellers, no. He over-did the high spirits. His behaviour was frantic and mean.

'Though you learned to weather him, as you got older, as a child he was bewildering,' says Sarah. 'Always, with Dad, you never *knew*. . . All of a sudden he'd be very annoyed and wouldn't want you around any more, and you wouldn't have a clue as to why.' I suggested to her that what was constant about her father's personality was that it wasn't constant. 'I came to terms with that after I'd grown up. And I also accept that he was mad. I accept that that's what he was. He couldn't have been a normal person to have achieved what only he did as an actor – so I don't feel angry at him. I feel differently now when I watch a film of his – I feel almost more sadness now than back then, when he'd just died. His films remind me of him. Before, it was like, well, he's still here. He might get in touch. Now, his films are more of a reminder. . . .'

Sellers induces melancholy in me, too – a complete outsider. By following his hunger for eminence and fame, as I am in these chapters, I can't help but see his death in the distance, the paranoia which preceded it, the corruption of his genius. There would come a time when the sight of other people's happiness filled him with irritation and pain – and the terrible thing is, this streak in his nature was becoming evident in the Fifties, in his attitude to family life. ' My mother tells me she heard me on the telephone, aged seven or so, humouring him to keep the peace, basically saying what he wanted to hear so he wouldn't go potty,' discloses Michael. 'And from then on it was a constant problem: how to deal with him? It was hard to explain. If he rang up and said, "Hi, Mike" – it was fine. If he said "Hello Michael," there was trouble in the wind, definitely. The same with my Mum. "Hello Annie" – fine. "Hello Anne" – something was afoot. It went like that. It could be the stupidest of things – the way you were sitting, if it was that sort of day.'

We can see from all this the further appeal of *The Goon Show*, the dream-world in which Sellers acted out his impulses – all those characters, liquidated week in, week out, like lead battalions. If a variation on Goonish make-believe rules seeped into his home life, Sellers also used the recording session itself as an opportunity to misbehave. In marked contrast to later on, in these early days he was not allowed to get away with it. (Though his early days were running out.) During the making of 'Shangri-La Again,' in November 1955, Peter Eton actually sent him packing: 'We were recording at the Camden,' the producer said, 'he did something which put Harry off. In the Max Geldray number I went behind and told him to stick to the script. We went back for the middle spot and he started fooling about again, and I said, "If you do that again, I'll fire you." He thought I wouldn't dare, so he did it again, so I had to fire him. Later he came back and apologised.'

Whatever misdemeanour he'd committed, news of his dismissal went right to the top – for on November 14th, Dennis Selinger, his agent, had been contacted, and his advice was for Sellers to lay the matter before Patrick Hillyard, the Head of Variety. So:

> with regard to a little bother I had at *The Goon Show* last night, for my part, the main cause of the upset was the result of extreme mental stress throughout the previous week, which is purely personal and has nothing to do with the show. I do admit that I was wrong in taking the attitude I did, but what one says and does in times of stress is obviously not calculated. If Peter Eton interprets this action on my part as an attempt to undermine his authority, all I can say is that he has completely misjudged my character, and forgotten the hard work and personal interest I have shown in the show during the past four years. As you know, we have had troubles before, and I have been the first to make that little extra effort to smooth things out; but apparently, the very first time I do anything wrong, I get the sack. I am surprised and shocked at Peter Eton's attitude, but however I have admitted I was wrong, and will leave the judgement of the whole affair to you.

Hillyard's response to this vainglorious bleat was a headmasterly salvo:

> 18th November, 1955
>
> Dear Peter,
>
> [...]
>
> With regard to 'The Goon Show' incident last Sunday, Peter Eton has fully reported to me what took place and, whilst you have explained that the attitude you took when Peter commented on your opening scene was due to matters not in any way relating to the show, I take the gravest view of your refusal to re-record the opening spot. I think it harmful enough to the show for an artist to give a performance below standard, but to absolutely refuse to remedy this is unbelievable behaviour for a professional of your standing. I have already had adverse comments on this particular programme from the Home Service,

who were quite unaware of the incident, and this distresses me very much.

Please do not think that I fail to appreciate the great contribution you have made to the success of the 'Goons' and that there can be many differences where so many personalities are involved – this is perhaps why I am all the more surprised to have had this report – but I must ask you to give me an assurance that this sort of thing will not happen again.

> Sincerely yours,
> *Pat Hillyard*
> Head of Variety.

Two days later, Sellers responded:

I repeat I am very sorry that I refused to obey Peter Eton last Sunday, and I do assure you it won't happen again. However, I am very distressed to learn that you think a short speech of ten or twelve lines can affect a thirty minute show to such an extent that the Home Service comment upon it. Are you suggesting that I was trying to undermine the broadcast? If so, I strongly resent this, as apart from the opening speech I as usual did my best. I heard the broadcast last week in Coventry, and in my opinion it went over extremely well. In passing, I would also like to add, we had in the audience last Sunday a very well known Actor Producer who is an ardent Goon fan, and he happened to mention that he thought it was the best show in the present series.

So fuck you, chum. Sellers, in typical spoilt gosling style, has turned upon those who dared try to chasten him. He's put *them* in the wrong. The trick is to overreact, play the innocent, give an exaggerated howl, and expect an apology to follow for the misjustice you make out has been caused. The horror whom Uncle Bert could never control, screaming the house down if threatened with a smack, still comes in handy – Sellers, man and boy, calculated his tantrums shrewdly:

21st November, 1955

Dear Peter,

[. . .] I certainly did not suggest that you were trying to sabotage the entire programme so please dismiss the thought from your mind.

So far as I am concerned the incident is forgotten, and I hope that you too will forget it.

> With kindest regards,
> Sincerely yours,
> *Pat Hillyard*
> Head of Variety

☆　★　☆

In truth, Sellers could afford to be cocky; he knew they'd pacify him eventually. Larry Stephens, Eric Sykes, or Maurice Wiltshire could manufacture the script if Milligan was wired up for electro-convulsive therapy; Kenneth Connor played Seagoon's Old Uncle Oscar if Secombe was indisposed. But Sellers, if ever he was absent, couldn't be replaced, not by a multitude. (Connor, Valentine Dyall, Jack Train and Graham Stark were drafted in when he missed 'The Spy or Who is Pink Oboe?' in January 1959.) The BBC grandees were more than aware of this. A year before the contretemps with Hillyard, the Head of the Light Programme, H. Rooney Pelletier, had had an idea for Sellers to introduce and discuss new gramophone releases. Sellers would pretend to be the proprietor of a record shop as well as all the customers popping in and out: 'Can HV [Head of Variety] see any objection to my giving the go-ahead?' HV certainly could:

From: Head of Variety.

Subject: PETER SELLERS   2nd July, 1954

To: Mr. H. Rooney Pelletier.
Copy to: [just about everybody]

Thank you for your memo of the 30th June. I must confess my

considerable surprise at your suggestion that Peter Sellers should participate in the type of programme you have described.

Sellers is a considerable strength to Variety programmes. He takes part in 'The Goons' (which is being revived in the Autumn) and the current 'Paradise Street' [with Max Bygraves], and he will also be featured in the new 'Happy Holiday' series beginning next week. If anything we are inclined to over-use him, but as he is the best in his particular field this is inevitable. To further dissipate his talents in a Gramophone programme would, in my opinion, be extremely foolish, and such a move would be bound to dilute his popularity in other series.

In other words I am completely against the whole suggestion, and can only express astonishment that discussions should have taken place without previous reference to this department.

Pat Hillyard.

The idea did not go away, however. On December 28th 1955, Sellers made a broadcast for the Light Programme called *The Listening Room*, produced by Michael Bell, a member of Pelletier's staff. Instead of a hi-fi shop, the characters were now forming a critics' forum: Grytpype Thynne, Bloodnok, Crun, and Bluebottle (for some reason re-named John Britanearly) passed judgement on, amongst other items, 'I'm Walking Backwards for Christmas' and 'Dance with Me, Henry' – a Hen and Min boogie-woogie. And in July the following year, Sellers (I have found no evidence of a ghostly collaborator) wrote this piece for the *TV Times*.

STAR TURN-TABLE

No hanky-panky introductions, that's me. Straight to business is the Sellers way. First of my disc favourites is a topical record 'Poor Old Joe' – variations on a Stephen Foster theme by Nikita Kruschev, backed by 'Slivovitz And The Same To You.'

This introduces a new close harmony team, B & K, with percussion somersaults by Tito and his Accordion Band. A performance full of unexpected nuances. On the new Russian speed, 5,000 revolutions per minute. (KREMLIN Da-Da.)

For classic-lovers there is the long-awaited 'Beethoven Violin Concerto No. 2,' with Egbert Huckmesser as soloist and the Hampstead Garden Sabra Orchestra conducted by Fred Spinks ('Route 102').

This has been transcribed and arranged from a hitherto unwritten manuscript discovered by Herr Doktor Baldi-Bontz in the Pumpfernickel Conservatoire, Munich. This will paralyse the pundits who imagined Ludwig van Beethoven wrote only one violin concerto.

How vastly superior this is to the immature first concerto will readily be understood when it is divulged that this is in eleven movements and takes fifteen and a half hours to perform in its entirety. Huckmesser plays the M.F. (mit feeling) passages with genuine chiaroscuro and the coda though a little short back and sides, is as crisp as Smith's.

Another point of interest is the handsome album in which the 39 Long-Playing discs are housed. There is also a built-in receptable to accommodate hot lunches.

This is a combined effort on the Pye-HMV-Decca-Philips-Oriole-DGG label. (Owing to the size of the label, this has had to be accommodated on a separate blank record.)

Hot from the presses is Justin Fidelhoffer and The Forces of Evil Trio in 'Let Me Hear That Melody Divine.' This is one of the 'live' tracks recorded last Hallowe'en at the Café Lucifer, and what sounds like hissing on the disc is actually the customers letting off steam by douching themselves with iced water (imported).

Among the interpolated instrumental 'breaks' are some hot licks from Père Nicole (better known to 'boppers' as Old Nick) and A Dixieland-flavoured chorus by the Stonehenge Skiffle Group, who have brought to a fine art the rhythmic manipulation of skulls and crossbones.

The trio, of course, are the identical little enchantresses who were such a hit in the 'blasted heath' scene from 'Macbeth on Ice' and their dulcet crooning behind Justin is reminiscent of their rollicking 'Double, double, toil and trouble' best-seller from the show.

Flipside, Eidelburger demonstrates why he is known far and wide among disc lovers as 'that old black magic man.' Starting off as a squelchy baritone, he goes into bass, counter-tenor and colouratura mezzo-soprano without once pausing for a gargle.

At the same time he recites 'Mary Had a Little Lamb' in the purest Mandarin Chinese, and juggles with a complete bedroom suite on his heels – the heel!

Travellers to the Orient will recall with pleasure many moments spent in peaceful contemplation of the beauties of nature when listening to Myron Blun's 'Casbah Delights'. This is a Staniswire recording (M&D 103).

For Cecil Sharpe fans there are also some delightful folklore discs available in the current lists. I can commend Madame D'Borscht's 'D'Ye Ken Fred Nurke', with the One In Harmony and the John Peelers, a charming troupe of strip-artistes trained personally by D'Borscht, who uses only a knout. ('Tartan-Bolshoi Ras-Dva-Tree.')

A rather unusual vocal combination brings together Ida Pules, soprano, with Mervyn Slegge, baritone, and the celebrated Hebridean tenor Frank Nong, singing 'The Foggy, Foggy Yok.'

The instrumental accompaniment on this disc is also noteworthy in that it sucessfully blends a harpsichord and two zithers with five specially-tuned dustbin lids.

Certainly 'Merrie England' in those days must have been a wonderful place to be deaf in. (New Era, 1984.)

Also well worth hearing is a full-length concert version on LP of 'Two Lovely Black Eyes', with the words and music by Edith Summerskill and the orchestra directed by her partner, Jack Solmons.

There is a short recitative by Ken Johnstone and Stewart MacPherson, and the arias are given tremendous punch by E. Summerskill herself and Victor Gollancz.

A gong ends each stanza, and linking the different sections of this massive work there is a moving chorus of punch-drunk promoters praying for remission of entertainments tax. (R.I.P. 9-10-OUT)

☆ ★ ☆

The scheme of rifling through items for purchase or sale goes back to March 1950, when Sellers made half a dozen shows called *Sellers' Market* with Miriam Karlin, using material which had been originally incorporated in *Third Division*. They played a couple of East End stall-holders and Sellers, of course, was also the various patrons and hagglers. Ronnie Bridges remembers them, late in 1949, coming to the Nuffield Centre,* where he played the piano each Tuesday and Friday, to rehearse. Sellers also brought the Sound Mirror. 'They worked on my song "Oh, You Sweet One," which Southern Music eventually published, with a photograph of Peter and Miriam on the title page. They experimented with *Sellers' Market* and recorded the material on paper tape. We all went back to Peter's parents' flat in Finchley to continue the rehearsals. I went there once and there was a family row. Someone had done something to upset Peg. Peter was furious. He wanted to go and bash them at the time and his mother had to restrain him. I remember that very well. And his mother looked after him and monitored every single thing he did in those early days. Then he met Anne

---

* The Nuffield Centre, a sort of returned servicemen's league, opened on the premises of the former Café de Paris, Piccadilly, in 1943, was destroyed a year later, and re-established itself in Adelaide St, WC2. Acts worked for free in the hope of being spotted by agents and BBC talent scouts. All four founder Goons made appearances there. Secombe, according to Milligan, 'rushed on, chattering, screaming . . . sweat pouring off him like a monsoon, and officers moved their chairs back . . . The audience thought he was an imported Polish comic and many wished he was back in Warsaw being bombed.' Milligan's own performance consisted simply of 'me and my guitar, without even . . . a script to hide behind,' and he told tales about the war (as he has continued to do ever since). Bentine did a zany Russian professor, lecturing on anatomy, with props that included a rubber chicken and a rubber glove, which got milked (and was no doubt not alone in receiving that treatment).

and got married – it was not acknowledged by his family, that first marriage. . .'

Miriam Karlin, owing to her own vocal mannerisms, was originally thought of, by Brian Seers, the producer of *Variety Bandbox*, as 'a female Peter Sellers'. She, too, recalls rehearsing at 211B, and her chief memory is of Bill, simply because 'anyone less like Peter you couldn't hope to meet'. She also remembers working with Sellers on *Variety Bandbox* itself: 'We alternated with Frankie Howerd, doing a comic scene called "Bless 'Em Hall" – all about a seedy stately home-cum-hotel, written by Jimmy Grafton. We played the guests and the proprietors. Peter would get into a terrible sulk if he didn't have enough of the funny lines, or if my lines were better than his. I mean, he'd be a real spoilt little boy – and I'd think, fuck, let him have my lines, if it'll keep him quiet. What do I care? He was always talking about his diet and slimming. He had enormous vanity. He always wanted approval and to be loved. And ambitious! He was eaten up with ambition. You didn't mind, though, because he was also obviously one of the most talented creatures who ever lived. We'd go out for drinks and things. Anne was around a lot, but Peg was vile to all women who came near Peter – but, of the two of us, Peg might have preferred me because I was Jewish at least. . .'

I wonder what would have happened if, instead of marrying a gentile actress, Sellers *had* courted another Jewish entertainer? Or would that have created worse ructions than the ones Anne already faced? Miss Karlin's stage and screen persona, it must be said, suggest what Peg the indomitable, the Peg who fed her son on witch's milk, might have been like. Slim, wary, and sinuous, her body inclining to an S shape, she even looks like the Peg of various snapshots. Miriam Karlin plays bird women. Her Mistress Quickly, for the Royal Shakespeare Company, in the early Eighties, was a sharp-tongued, red-headed madam, diligently keeping the books and running the Boar's Head, Falstaff's billet, as a business concern – she was not the wobbling waitress, over-weight and bawdy, which is how the part normally gets done (Quickly as a female version of

Sir John). She played the hostess Jewishly. Such was the hilarious way she came out with the line 'I cannot abide swaggerers,' I remember looking up the text when I returned home. She'd made an infectious game of the last word, half mumbling and mispronouncing it ('I do not love swaggering; by my troth, I am the worse when one says swagger; feel masters, how I shake . . .'), and I was ready to be convinced she'd made it up, interpolating a Goonish routine into *Henry IV*. What she'd done, being a watchful comic actress, was to deliver the orthodox text in such a way that it came across as spontaneous. Everybody else in the cast was spouting and quoting, she was possessed by the spirit of the part and was polished and sharp – qualities Sellers, too, had, and in abundance.

She appeared in two of his films, and dubbed Yul Brynner singing 'Mad About the Boy' in *The Magic Christian*. In *The Millionairess*, she's a Mrs Joe, toiling in the basement bakery alongside Vittorio Di Sica and Sophia Loren. Her Jewishness easily adapted itself to Italian flappability, and the Loren character's efficient re-organisation of the pastry cooks, incidentally, prefigures Karlin's Mistress Quickly in her nose for commerce. In *Heavens Above*, she's Winnie Smith, Eric Sykes' sister-in-law at the gypsy camp. With her turbaned head interrogatively and defensively tilted, a fag permanently in her tight lips, like a protruding, flickering tongue, and with her arms akimbo, she really does resemble the Peg photographed at Sellers' wedding to Britt Ekland – and it is not impossible to picture Peg, in another incarnation, squatting on a stool to milk a goat, bartering for partially plucked poultry, or finding an outlet for the surplus lead peeled off a church roof. Winnie Smith has acumen. Though a semi-hag, she's nevertheless glamorous compared with Irene Handl's Rene Smith, a toothless matron with a face like a cat's litter tray, and easily the most slummocky in Miss Handl's gallery of low-class belles.

Perhaps Miss Karlin's voice, prowling around vowels and making ordinary sentences sound like an opera libretto, was just too eccentric to succeed in concert for long with Sellers, because when the *Sellers' Market* and 'Bless 'Em Hall' format was revived, much altered, as a half hour show called *Finkel's Café*, in the summer of 1956, the writing team (Muir and Norden) was the same, but Sellers' foil was now Sid James. Though the setting was neither a boarding house, microgroove stall nor an open-air bazaar, the principle of putting Sellers at the centre of the public place remained and *Finkel's Café*, produced by Pat Dixon, was in fact derived from an American programme called *Duffys' Tavern*. The formula was to elicit boffs both from the people running the bar and the famous folk who visit it. Sellers, inter alia, became Eddie, manager of the caff. 'I shall play him Irish,' he vouchsafed. 'Something quite different from my normal style. No comic voices this time.'

That he was still considered nothing more than a versatile mimic was starting to rankle. 'To begin with,' he told a put-in-his-place reporter from the *Radio Times*, sent round to preview *Finkel's Café*, 'I am not essentially a funny man – in the sense that Ted Ray is a funny man. My normal approach to comedy is the actor's approach. I started as an actor, I'm still one. By the time I'm forty I should like to be established in the theatre and in films – as a straight actor.' Sellers was due to be forty in 1965. By then he would have demonstrated, with the exception of isolated masterpieces like the *The Optimists of Nine Elms* (1974) or *Being There* (1979), and odd performances like Mr Hoffman or Rouquet in *The Blockhouse*, just about his entire range. After that, when he should have been in his prime, he made over two dozen execrable pictures. Why? Why did he make a chaos of his talent? One reason is put forward by Anne: 'He didn't have any taste. He didn't know what was good or bad. He was very undisciplined – again, that's why a lot of his films turned out badly. What he needed was someone to guide him in his career.' (Someone other than the spectre of Dan Leno and others in the far-beyond, I suggested.) 'Now, whether he would have been guided, I don't know. He needed dictatorial treatment – like from Kubrick. He respected Kubrick, and there were very few people in his life whom he did respect. He respected the Boultings, mainly John. They saw something *there* and cast him as an actor. . .'

The BBC was not willing to treat Sellers as anything other than a variety artiste until it was too late. 'He gets a million pounds for a film now,' commented Milligan in 1979. 'He's not going to come along to the BBC for £75 and "Could you please speak up, Mr Sellers".' Back in the Fifties, during the protracted negotiations for the long term exclusive contracts, we can see that Sellers' very success, as a provider of funny voices, was keeping him from moving on. 'Sellers is quite brilliant in all he undertakes,' wrote Pat Hillyard in an internal memorandum, 'and is always a tower of strength.' But when Sellers 'made the point that so long as he is a supporting artist or a member of a team as in "The Goons", he can never receive a star fee, as might be the case if he had his own programme. . ., I pointed out to him . . . that his particular talents were being exploited in the way most suited to our needs, and that he could continue to make a much more valuable contribution to our programmes in the way he is now doing than if we were to star him in his own programme. . .*

If the derivative, re-hashed from the Yanks *Finkel's Café*, totally forgotten today, even by its authors, was the best the mandarins could devise by way of furnishing Sellers with his own personal equivalent of a *Ray's a Laugh*, no wonder he couldn't allow the corporation to continue having first call on his services. Also, 'Mr Sellers is doing a considerable amount of film work, also variety,

---

* Hillyard may have been putting the majority view, wanting Sellers to remain a team player, but back in September 1953, J.H. Davidson, the Assistant Head of Variety, had placed this (unresponded to) note on file:

Subject: PETER SELLERS
This artist really excelled himself in 'Top of the Town' – in fact Terry-Thomas had great difficulty in rising above him (Sellers) on several occasions during the course of the script.
Do you think we might consider starring him in a new show? I believe a personal talk with you [Head of Variety] would 'pay off'.

As an example of the disparity in fees, Terry-Thomas received eighty-five guineas for his own series and sixty-five if he went on anybody else's; Sellers received, at this time, thirty-five guineas, regardless of the spot.

both of which are not booked too far ahead' Dennis Selinger wrote. 'To ask him to sign a contract which only guarantees him £3,000 a year,* and which could quite possibly preclude him either filming or playing in variety where he could make this amount in a very few weeks, is quite out of the question. . . .'

As in his previous letter, of January 1954 (page 247), Selinger continues to lay stress on his client's career in films when, in truth, all Sellers had achieved in recent times was a bit part in *John and Julie*. (Regarding *The Ladykillers*, Michael Balcon was rather favouring Richard Attenborough for the role of the nervous Harry.) But there was no over-estimating Sellers' ambition, or mistaking where his eye was presuming to reach.

☆ ★ ☆

---

* On April 26th 1955, Peter Brough, Ted Ray, Terry-Thomas, Jimmy Edwards and Kenneth Horne were also offered, and accepted, the BBC's £3,000. As in 1951, Sellers was the only (to use a phrase common then) nigger in the woodpile.

Chapter Six
Sound and Vision

Sellers' creative frustrations culminated in his getting the Grades officially to inform the BBC, in early January 1956, that 'this artist now doesn't wish to be associated with *The Goon Show* ever again'. Towards the end of the month, when the contracts for a new series were being drawn up, he was 'still dickering . . . and though', wrote Patrick Newman, 'Spike Milligan tells me he's sure Sellers wants to go on, Harry Secombe's agent assures me that only last week Peter Sellers said he'd never do any more. . .'

Well, as we all know the Goons did go on, and as a result of his huff Sellers managed to get his fee up to fifty guineas a show (and soon to eighty), whilst Milligan, pacific before the money men, stayed on half-measures at twenty-five. To signify his boredom and general shirtiness, Sellers, in fact, put a lot into niggardly queries about loot. From the Winter Gardens, Eastbourne, he wrote complaining about a five quid underpayment. From the Star & Garter Hotel, Wolverhampton, he wrote to say that he no longer held 'any charitable feelings' towards the BBC, and therefore expected to be paid in full, all over again, for any repeats – to which Newman, countered, 'the basic fee is what counts and anything extra ought to be looked on as a manna from heaven . . . you begin to look on it rather as a right!' From the Castle Hotel, Norwich, he wrote, in the Irish dialect of *Finkel's Café*:

> Dear St Pat – You darlin' man, all my animosity is forgotten in view
> of the darlin' raise you've give t'me. What's Milligan going to do? Is
> he coming back as well? I'll be round for the beer quicker than you

278

think and I'll do as many 'Workers' Playtimes' as you want now that I'm in 'the monied' class.

He signs himself 'Voices O'Toole, One of the White Coons.' Did he seriously expect *The Goon Show* to be feasible without Milligan? That he could slip the question in suggests his waning loyalty and enthusiasm for the programme, and before long his insouciance got him into an embarrassing predicament:

4th March 1957

Dear Dennis,

PETER SELLERS

You may be interested to know that the above has quoted the fee he gets for 'The Goon Show' to an agent other than yourself. I must say it seems to me somewhat ill advised on the part of an artist to act this way but of course I am hardly in a position to forbid such an action and if Peter Sellers, or any other artist for that matter, wants to stand up in Piccadilly Circus and announce what we pay him I suppose it's his own affair. However, if he wants to take such action he must be jolly sure he quotes the right fee because if he doesn't that is certainly the moment when we will step in. In point of fact Peter Sellers quoted something slightly in excess of his present fee and although, after due enquiries, I am perfectly satisfied that it was a very genuine mistake on his part, (perhaps his arithmetic is a little weak), you will hardly need me to tell you how misleading and indeed, in my opinion, serious, an error of this sort can be. However, since we can all make mistakes, might not a very good solution be to suggest that he keeps his own business affairs to himself – then there can't be any complications, can there?

> Yours sincerely
> *Patrick Newman*
> Variety Booking Manager

Which was followed compunctiously by:

Dear Pat,

PETER SELLERS

Many thanks for your letter to hand dated 4th March and I quite agree with what you say about Artistes quoting salaries received to other agents, or, for that matter, so far as I am concerned, to other artistes as this can cause a tremendous amount of trouble.

I had heard about this before I received your letter and had already told Peter this was a silly thing to do as I am sure he quite appreciates. As you know, so far as the three boys are concerned they are so particularly friendly that they don't consider each other as business associates and, unfortunately, discuss lots of things with each other that they shouldn't!

On behalf of my Client I would like to say that I am sorry about this and will try to make sure that it does not happen again.

Kindest regards

> Yours sincerely,
> for and on behalf of,
> LEW & LESLIE GRADE LTD.,
> *Dennis Selinger*

Again, by manoeuvring himself into a position where he'd be connived at as a kid, a pup, a dreamer, Sellers was excused his mischief. He was, of course, in reality, sharper than a serpent's tooth. Before the start of each series, he enjoyed being the one who lingered until last, being the one whose signature was sought before the work could proceed – a small and satisfying power game. And not only in relation to *The Goon Show*. In 1953 he'd kept the *Ray's a Laugh* team hanging about: 'Further to my telephone call to your secretary this morning,' Selinger wrote to George Inns, the producer, 'this is to confirm that I have had a long talk with PETER SELLERS regarding "RAY'S A LAUGH," and it is understood that he will carry on with the show as per his contract, and that the billing shall remain the same, with the exception that the word "and" between Kitty Bluett and his name will be omitted.' *Peace reigns – for the moment anyhow* someone has jotted at the foot of the letter. *Thank goodness* someone else has added, in crayon.

That thinking about *The Goon Show* ultimately fatigued him to the point of apathy is revealed in this letter, which deals with the final series, a mere six broadcasts, recorded at the end of 1959:

29th May, 1959

Dear Dennis,

PETER SELLERS

I write to you not the least bit confident that I shall get any sort of satisfactory answer – after all, 'phoning you is quite pointless. I had thought for one moment of writing direct to Peter Sellers, but that I imagine would be equally useless. Or could it be that behind the facade of Peter Sellers Productions Ltd. some co-operative fellow exists, someone who really would be simple and ordinary and normal to deal with?

Perhaps I should remind you that we had hoped to do six programmes entitled 'The Goon Show' towards the end of this year. Messrs. Secombe and Milligan have expressed their willingness to partake and we have their signatures to respective contracts. When the offer was put forward it was made clear that the engagement of each of the three leading artists was dependent upon the signature of the other two, and if, therefore, Peter Sellers is not going to take part in the programmes there will obviously come a time by which it would be courteous, let alone business like, for us to withdraw the offer from Secombe and Milligan. The thing to do is to decide when that time ought to be.

We first sent you a contract at the beginning of March, but this was cancelled at your request, and another one issued drawn up slightly differently. This contract was despatched at the beginning of April. It is now the end of May. Naturally enough we would not expect you to conform to what is printed on the front of the contract to the effect that the offer is contingent upon a signed acceptance being 'returned to us without delay', if only because the word 'delay' is capable of various interpretations. For my part I would say that things are already delayed, but I would be glad to have your views. Do you suggest that we should wait until perhaps the end of June – is that rushing you too much? – the middle of August maybe? – late September?

I see the first recording is on the 20th December and I really think the other artists ought to have perhaps half a day's notice if it's not going to come off, don't you? Should we then wait for you to give us your answer the day before? (though, of course, this might be a little late in terms of script and the studio arrangements etc.)

Anyhow, just think about this and let me know what you think is reasonable . . . something *reasonable* . . . that's all we want.

> Yours sincerely,
> *Patrick Newman*
> Variety Booking Manager

☆ ★ ☆

When I listen to *The Goon Show* today, it is obvious that there was more to him than a facility for different voices. Sellers, going against the grain of the quick-change music hall gag format, gave his characters lopsided depths, moony aspirations. The great actor in him was stirring – and yet so far all he was was a noise, a sound, a package of sweet airs. Except for those who'd seen him in his bewildering variety sketches, or in the salutary failure of *Mother Goose* – when Sellers learned how hard it could be to imprint himself physically on a rôle – he was invisible. Not that this was true for studio audiences, of course. According to the reporter for *Sound and Vision*, in October 1950: 'Uncontrollable laughter you hear sometimes . . . during a not intrinsically funny moment in 'Ray's a Laugh' is almost certainly due to their witnessing a plaintive girlish voice emanating from the broad and weighty Peter.'

Broad and weighty is about right. In a quasi-documentary called *London Entertains*, made in 1951, Eamonn Andrews, conducting a tour party of Swiss school girls* about the capital's pleasure spots, visits Grafton's to see 'those crazy people'. From the two still photographs which exist, it looks as though everybody crowded into the Major's upstairs parlour – and Milligan, Sellers, Bentine, and

---

* The Swiss misses were played by members of the Eastbourne Girls' Choir.

Major's upstairs parlour – and Milligan, Sellers, Bentine, and Secombe, crammed into a brightly lit alcove, are obviously performing from a script. (Only Sellers and Secombe have copies, the other two peer over their companions' shoulders.) The smallness of the space and the intentness of the audience, the make-shiftness of the stage and the darkness of the rest of the room (where we can make out sticks of furniture, heavy black-out curtains, and picture frames hanging from the cornice) – all this makes for an atmosphere of clandestiny. It looks like a secret meeting. Is it a banned play they are reading from? Is this really Grafton's, or an attic in Eastern Europe during the Cold War? Sellers, beefy and blazered, is to the fore. (If there is a police raid, he can come and speak in his authoritative Air Commodore tones.) In one photo he holds his hand to his temple, in a dramatic pose; in the other, his hand is behind his back, he looks solemn, and it is Secombe and Bentine who are laughing. Those two seem to be having a good time.

Milligan looks a bit wary: in one picture he could almost be about to interrupt Sellers; in the other, his gaze goes beyond the sheets of foolscap Sellers is holding to rest on the girls in the front row. But Sellers is the focus of the comedy. Not because of his enormity, or the wave upon wave of his woolly hair, but because of his earnestness – which is almost a glumness. Sellers, right from the start, knew that 'there is one rule which, in the lighter side of my work, I always try to observe. Never try to be funny in a situation which is itself absolutely and essentially funny. The more normal you are the funnier that situation becomes.' All Sellers' great characters would be obedient to this principle – the doleful countenances of Fred Kite, Mr Martin, Inspector Clouseau, Chance – and he's doing it here. Secombe, his hair greased into idiotic fronds, plays the fool; Milligan, his rats-nest of hair carefully dishevelled, grins inanely – he's freezing a fake smile for the camera; and Bentine, cross-eyed and ringleted, looks as if he has just been hit over the head with a spade. You can virtually see the cartoon stars and tweeting birds floating across his vision. Sellers, robust and lugubrious, and ever so slightly parodying his despondency, is the only one who comes across as natural – *unnaturally* natural, thus the pleasing complexity of our response, and our apprehensiveness over whatever it is he might decide to do next.

He has wit, the others only their zaniness, which can seem rigged. He is apart, but what they do all have in common are their fringes and fuzz. As Geldray explained, the Goons had 'hair on an epic scale . . . Peter's was cut short at the back and over his ears, and left ultra-thick at the sides. It looked cut by a designer who was trying to create hair wings.' The absurdity of his appearance was what was going against him when he tried to break into films. 'All this time,' he said of the early Fifties, 'I couldn't get into films. I felt I had more to give than I'd been giving, but I simply couldn't get into films . . . I couldn't get a part. People would just look at me and that would be that. . .' What he therefore decided to do was apply his radio skills to moving pictures. 'I could find work doing voices – actors who'd had to go back to America before the film was finished and so on. I did lots of voices. Dubbing, looping . . . I did an awful lot of dubbing.'

One assignment was *The Black Rose* with Tyrone Power as Walter of Gurnie and Jack Hawkins as Tristram the Bowman. Sellers dubbed a Mexican actor called Alfonso Bedoya, whom you may remember as the primitive bandit in *The Treasure of the Sierre Madre*. This time he'd been asked to play a primitive *Chinese* bandit, 'but with his own accent on top of it,' explained Sellers, 'you couldn't make out a thing the poor fellow said – so I did an impersonation of him. . .' He did much more than that. Henry Hathaway's ponderous pageant, all about a Saxon prince having adventures in the thirteenth century Orient, jumps to brief quirky life when Sellers' characterisation comes off the sound track. He has given Bedoya an eccentric Mexican lisp overlain with a Deep South lilt, and with bits of Arabic throat-clearing thrown in. Whatever he sounded like before, now he's out of *The Goon Show* – and the dialogue is a tongue-twister anyway:

> *Sellers:* I have a message for you, from the Black Rose.
> She is the sister of my kindly master. She wishes

> to escape – she say she is going to England and
> that all Englishmen are gallant. Some report that
> her father was English, a Crusader taken
> prisoner.
>
> *Power:* Why is she called the Black Rose?
>
> *Sellers:* That is the name they give to the clove – the
> most precious of the spices. The bird who
> feathers his nest never leaves things to chance. I
> have a very well laid plan in which I will do all
> that's dangerous, if you are afraid.
>
> *Hawkins:* *[growling]* – Afraid! We'd do more for English
> blood any day than you'd do for an overgrown
> sapphire!
>
> *Sellers:* Oh! That's good! I will tell that to the Black
> Rose.

The above no doubt crucial exposition scene has horses and animals bleating and neighing in the background, as well as warriors shouting etc., all helping to counterpoint Sellers' rococo recitative. It could be argued that, slight though his association was, in *The Black Rose*, released in 1950, he worked for the first time with Herbert Lom and Orson Welles – if he was not quite alongside them, then he was at least underneath them, on the tape. (He had to say, 'Two days from here with his army' when Welles rode up and asked Bedoya a question.) Welles had appeared in the film to put himself in funds for the completion of *Othello*, which he was simultaneously trying to shoot near Hathaway's location in Morocco. Cecile Aubry, Maryam (the Black Rose), was one of his many candidates for Desdemona, and the surplus medieval costumes came in handy, too, for his under-budgeted Shakespearean project. Welles used *The Black Rose* to his advantage, borrowing, appropriating, pinching what he could. Sellers also went about his business subversively. Though nobody could have complained that he'd travestied the film, his delivery of Bedoya's part contains satirical resonance – just as Welles' performances of Tartar chieftains and Borgia princes always do. Welles, in historical costumes, is a wizard out of grand opera – you feel he really is capable of black magic. And Sellers was a magus, too. The actors instinctively add an ironic top-spin to what they have been hired to do – to show that they are larger talents, more exuberant, than anybody else alive. They are hungry to perform.

Mike Frankovich, who two decades hence would produce *There's a Girl in My Soup*, noticed this virtuosity when, as European head of Columbia, he was being driven to Heathrow to catch a plane to Rome. On the car radio was a play, at the end of which the announcer said, 'All the characters were played by Peter Sellers.' As Frankovitch recalls, 'We were doing *Fire Over Africa* with Maureen O'Hara at the time, and we required seven actors to dub the dialogue. I needed English and American voices of all classes. When I returned to London, I called Peter and asked him to do the seven voices and paid him £250 for the lot.' Sellers also worked on Frankovitch's *Malaga*, which 'Mike had just made . . . in Spain with his wife, Binnie Barnes, and Macdonald Carey . . . There were a lot of extras, and most of them were Cockneys who had never seen Spain, except perhaps the Costa Brava. The others were Spaniards who couldn't speak English at all, so I ended up dubbing the whole seventeen characters. So if you have ever seen *Malaga* they were all me! . . . In one scene there are eleven of these, all characters talking at the same time, all of them me . . . I also did four voices [including Bogart's]* in *Beat the Devil* and I did Churchill's voice in *The Man Who Never Was. . . .'*

☆　★　☆

There is an eerie appropriateness about Sellers, about whom Stanley Kubrick said categorically 'there is no such person', getting himself involved in the film version of Nigel Balchin's true wartime story. Operation Mincemeat was a top secret wheeze. A dead body,

---

* Sellers was needed for *Beat the Devil*, in 1954, because Bogart, involved in an automobile accident on his way to the location near Naples, had knocked his teeth out and bitten through his tongue. Naturally he couldn't speak coherently after that. Sellers also dubbed the Italian actors, who'd known no English and hadn't understood a word of John Huston's direction or Truman Capote's script.

kitted out with an unopened parachute and falsified secret documents, had been deposited off the coast of Spain – the documents would fool the Germans into expecting an Allied assault on Greece, not Sicily. As I mentioned in an earlier chapter, *The Goon Show* was on to the macabre comedy of this imaginative scheme instantly, and there was barely need to exaggerate when sending it up. Like the time Harry Secombe was put in a hospital bed for a week when all he'd gone to collect from the MO was a new pair of spectacles, the war *was* laughable, off and on. In *The Man Who Never Was*, a Goonish tone is set immediately when, over stock shots of Westminster, Sellers' Churchill is heard addressing the House of Commons. Far from giving the film a documentary realism, such a scene simply alerts us to the plummy play being made out of words like 'impedimenta' (to describe an army's equipment). Sellers can't help but over-colour the famous slack-jawed mannerisms. Later, when Laurence Naismith goes to confer with Sir Winston, Sellers' voice is again heard – this time booming through an open door: 'Let the plan be implemented!' In another scene, Churchill is meant to be occupying the other side of a very tall wing chair, and, as puffs of cigar smoke start appearing, I began laughing – for is Sellers himself concealed from view, manufacturing those blue clouds?

Churchill, whose actorish streak was vast (recordings of his hammy speeches belong with Charles Laughton's public readings from the Gettysburg Address rather than to archives of modern history), must have warmed to the bizarre elements in the tale. It wasn't any old body that was needed – they had to snatch a corpse that would fool the German pathologists. The whole business had to be thought through. The body, which actually expired of bronchial pneumonia, is packed in a canister of dry ice and given the name of Willy Martin. An entire identity is faked for him. His rank, his background, his interests. What would Martin have in his briefcase? Personal items like photos, love letters, theatre ticket stubs, and a Gieves & Hawkes bill are counterfeited. Eventually, the uniquely cast cadaver is dumped in the Mediterranean by a submarine – Martin's directors and stage-hands having studied ocean currents and off-shore winds – and the remainder of the film concerns the enemy's attempts to double check all the apparent credentials. Are a dead man's messages to be believed?

Sellers, in fact, is not only the ghost of Churchill. He provides the film with its babble. When some of the characters go to a cinema, his is the urgent voice of the newsreel announcer. When they are investigating parachutes and visit an air show, Sellers caws over the planes and reels off aviation statistics through a loud speaker. He's a drunk singing in the street, old hags in the music hall audience (sitting near to Clifton Webb and Gloria Grahame who have gone out for the evening to collect the ticket stubs), and he's also heard carousing to a hurdy-gurdy through the swing doors of a saloon bar. When Webb goes to Savile Row, to see Richard Wallis as the haberdasher, Sellers is the taxi driver's grunt of thanks on taking his tip; and lastly, when Cyril Cusack, the fifth columnist, has quite failed to invalidate the ingenious trails, Sellers is a variety of German generals shouting, 'Martin genuine! Martin genuine!'

Like Martin himself, who exists yet never existed, whose biography came out of nowhere, Sellers too, in this film, is peculiarly absent yet present. His vocal changes and ubiquity are a mocking commentary on the concept of single, ascertainable identity. His being everywhere like that, talking through walls and throwing his voice, like Michael Redgrave, the schizophrenic ventriloquist in *Dead of Night*, could be nightmarish – the effect is supernatural. And though of course it is only a special-effect, and films are only mechanically reproduced con tricks, knowing Sellers is there, within the fabric of *The Man Who Never Was*, still seems occult; or at least it does to me. But where Redgrave's split-up personality was scary, Sellers' disembodied dubbing was a chance for comic fantasy – and nowhere more successfully than in the Joan Collins vehicle, *Our Girl Friday* (aka *The Adventures of Sadie*). He plays the part of a splendid white cockatoo.

The idea is that Joan has been marooned on a tropical isle (actually Majorca) with George Cole, a pompous old fart called

Robertson Hare (who once appeared in farces put on at the Garrick Theatre by the Ray Bros. Ltd.), and Kenneth More, who plays a chirpy Oirish 'character'. It must be one of the worst performances the last ever gave. More, who never spoke his lines anyway, but shouted them, shouts in an approximation of a Dublin accent that is well up to the standard of Dick Van Dyke's Cockney in *Mary Poppins*. And Joan, as the spoilt swan daughter of rich and vulgar parents (her mother is Hattie Jacques), has evidently modelled her speech on Julie Andrews. 'Oh! I do wish this rotten old ship was on the bottom of the rotten old ocean,' she says, stamping her little foot. Later, that particular wish having been granted, and finding herself useful in the domestic department, cooking for the aged Lost Boys, she is a scold: 'Pat Plunkett sit down at once and have your breakfast!'

Throughout the film, she acts in the obligatory, stilted style of the Rank starlet – it's as if she's permanently posing for a stills camera. (When she moves, she could be sleepwalking and when she runs, she has that halting, sideways-on scampering of a ballet dancer in the grip of strong emotion.)

They wouldn't dare make the film today – 'We are alone on a desert island. Three men and one woman' – except as pornography. That's where Sellers comes in. His parrot screetch is the voice of lubricious thoughts. When Joan takes off her stockings, we cut to the bird, perched high in a palm tree, which lets out a long, filthy peal of laughter. Sellers has invented a multi-layered squawk, that's part whoop, part guffaw, part hysterical cackle. It is difficult to believe that a human larynx could produce it, let alone a parrot's. It's an other-worldly noise, full of grossness and insult. And, a parrot being a parrot, as the film drags on, Sellers' gurgles start to mimic Joan's own way of enunciating – when the men fight over her, and she gasps on the sidelines, for example, the cockatoo imitates her whimpers and concern.

Our Girl Friday, with its caves and huts, sunshine and seaside, ought to be about lust and desire, but instead it's all knotted up with arguments about celibacy and restraint. Robertson Hare, who keeps his tattered dinner jacket on, no matter what, puts Joan right off when he says: 'You are like some glorious being from another sphere.' For what does she mean by wearing her homemade bikini, to show off her bottom and boobs, if not to tempt the men with her own new-found earthiness? The last thing she wants to be is an inaccessible goddess. The only (negligible) humour in the film is in the gentlemen trying to remain gentlemen, making their pact not to touch Joan – when Joan probably wouldn't mind somebody copping a feel. Sellers' almost sinister cock-a-doodle-doo derides everybody's libido and pretensions.

☆ ★ ☆

As ingenious as he was, leaving his vocal fingerprints over other people's scenes, 'at that time I could never get into films as an actor. I always used to remind people, "Don't forget me if there is anything going in the acting line". . .' But they did, so he reverted to television. His first series was called *And So to Bentley,* and thirteen episodes were broadcast live from Alexandra Palace, beginning in October 1954. Sellers, along with Rosemary Miller, Peter Jones, Bill Fraser, and Jill Day, was in a comic team supporting Dick Bentley. Also in the cast was Charlotte Mitchell: 'Peter *cared* about these programmes. I remember seeing him bend all this cutlery in half in the canteen, because he was angry that things weren't being done swiftly enough. "*There's* one person who is going to be a big star," I remember saying, but the others disagreed, "He'll never be a star on his own, he has to be part of a group." But Peter had an instinct for what was funny and what wasn't – which wasn't true of the director, Brian Tesler. He could only tell if a scene was funny if he saw Peter and me laughing. "Keep that in, Charlotte laughed at it" became an in-joke. When I met Brian twenty years later, the first thing he said was "Still corpsing, Charlotte?" But as for Peter – it was as if something was always worrying him. He was easily upset. . .'

And So to Bentley, written by Frank Muir and Denis Norden, contained the cocktail party sketch, the army sketch, the law court sketch (in which a case of murder got mixed up with that of a man riding a cycle without a light), and it derived from a radio show

called *Take It From Here*. The beauty of putting Dick Bentley on
the box, after he'd been on the wireless since 1939, was that people
could finally see his long face with its range of quizzical expressions.
Born in Melbourne in 1907, he was a light-limbed violinist, saxophonist, and clarinettist. He could sing, dance and, immaculately
besuited, do comedy routines in music hall. He looks (in contemporary photographs) saucy and charming. In Sydney they
thought he was Noël Coward, and even today (I met him in 1990)
he has about him an air of Edwardian dapperness. Like his compatriot and protegé, Barry Humphries, Bentley has re-made himself
as an English gentleman, as far as his clothes are concerned. The
two of them enjoy the anachronistic rôle-play, with props like spats
and fedoras. And, just in case you might start to think the foppishness a bit over-elegant, they can come out with hair-raising filthy
stories when there are ladies present.

☆　★　☆

Old Ghosts
a play for mostly one voice

*Prologue: Dick Bentley is heard on the telephone giving directions to
somebody on how to find his flat. He double-checks all the arrangements
off-stage with his wife, a virago called Peta. All dialogue is repeated and
overlapped, with many mutters and courteous contradictions, exactly
like Hen and Min in 'The Goon Show'.*

DICK:　Ten thirty? That's the middle of the night to her.
What do you say to next Wednesday? How do
we describe Westmoreland Street? Near to the
heart hospital . . . On the fifth floor – press the
little button . . . At the end of Beaumont Street,
near New Cavendish Street . . . Two o'clock –
you mean after what some people call 'having
had their lunch?' We are not near any blinking
tube. . . Mmmm grnnkk. . . .

We cross-fade to the following week. A nervous, bumbling scholar, in

town for the day from Oxford (and whose weight and height, coinciden-
tally, are exactly the same as the present author's), is scuttling along the
street, examining the name plates of surgeries and infirmaries. He finds
the correct mansion block and puzzles out the brass and mahogany ele-
vator mechanism which appears to be based on the period appurtenances
in Captain Nemo's 'Nautilus'. Clanked skyward and met on a mezza-
nine, he is led into a genteel wee capsule, full of fine-looking porcelain
and oils, antique wicker chairs and, in the bathroom, antique brassières
and cami-knickers which, intended for substantial loins and a pigeon
chest, have been festooned near the window to air. Having set up his
recording equipment, Mr Lewis (for it was after all he) encourages the
two old parties, in whose company he finds himself, to reminisce. Dick
Bentley, attired for a country house weekend with John Galsworthy or
Ford Madox Ford, is chipper, corky, vague. His spouse Peta, assertive
and ostentatious, was probably once something of a beauty in the Theda
Bara manner. She smokes throughout and her speeches are interrupted
by a lot of hawking and coughing – and within a few months she'll be
dead of lung cancer.

PETA: Dick was compèring shows called *New to You*
and so on, at the People's Palace, Mile End
Road, and he introduced Peter Sellers and Leo
McKern, whom we didn't see again until backstage at *Brouhaha*. Sellers did a lot of voice-overs
and commercials. He did a commercial for a
wine company and got eighty quid's worth of
booze a month. We had dinner with him in
Whetstone and Anne cooked a roast chicken –
and all the way through the meal he served
Chateau d'Yquem, a dessert wine. You see, he
didn't *know*. He was all largesse and all these new
toys and stereophonic equipment, and his new
this and his new that . . . We used to see a lot of
him, especially when *And So to Bentley* was on
the television – a flop, unfortunately. Muir and
Norden had spent months on the first script.
Michael Bentine said it was the most . . .

DICK   (*helpfully*): You've heard of Michael Bentine,
have you . . . ?

PETA: We met him in Australia[*] ... But what happened was that the shows fell off after that. Muir and Norden simply tried to re-write *Take It From Here* – it folded. I phoned Ronnie Waldman[†] and said 'How can I get out of the contract? It's no good. It's not what we asked for.' I don't think Peter was that interested in it – because he was always on the phone negotiating for that part with Alec Guinness.

MYSELF: He had his eye on the movies.

PETA: My God he did. Dick said, 'He's never off the bloody phone' – talking to Dennis Selinger, his agent. Then he did *The Ladykillers* and from then on he became rather grand, you know. And he came round one morning with Logan Willick in a custom-built Bentley – because he'd always admired Dick's Bentley – and it had PS, like a coat of arms, on each door. A dreadful thing happened! Peter's son got up in the middle of the night and painted Daddy's car! And, you know, he kept giving masses to Logan Willick – and Willick always had to be in. . . .

DICK: Oh yes! Always had to be in. . . .

PETA: He was practically up his arse, you know. We used to call him Boots. . . .

DICK: Because that's all you could see.

PETA: This monogrammed Bentley was outside a pub,

---

[*] Bentine left for Australia on the S.S. *Oronsay* to tour the Tivoli circuit of music halls immediately after Sellers had nudged him out of *The Goon Show* in 1952. It must have been somebody like Peta Bentley whom he and his wife met at an upper-class party in Perth. 'Do come again, dear,' said the hostess. 'You've been no bloody trouble at all.'

[†] Ronald Waldman was Head of Light Entertainment on BBC television.

near Albert Bridge Road, for Willick's wedding reception. We went for a drink with Peter, and Galton and Simpson looked at the car and said 'Did you put that all on as a post script?' and Peter was very angry.

DICK (*to myself*): You were going to say something there? Mmm-mnk-grnk-mnk. . . .

MYSELF: The PS on the door – a vulgar touch.

DICK: Oh *yes*. No, no.

PETA: We didn't see much of him after he became grand – until he had his heart attack in Hollywood, and Dick sent him a book about Rolls Royces.

DICK: He'd had a heart attack, you see.

MYSELF: He nearly died.

DICK: He nearly died, yes.

PETA: We used to cut out pictures of Sir Alec Douglas-Home and glue them on photos of women with sagging old tits and send them to him.

DICK (*trying to get in*): I too had had heart trouble.

PETA: You said to him, 'I only got a little mention in the South Mimms local paper' – with Sellers, there was a day of national prayer. He and Britt bought a mansion in Elstead and invited us to dinner. Cottage pie and fish fingers served by a fucking butler. At one stage he thought he'd swallowed a bone – and there was all bloody hell to pay. I said, 'Look Peter, swallow a piece of dry bread.' – 'Oh no, I'm having another heart attack.' Britt spent the whole evening gazing at herself in the polished marble columns of the fireplace.

DICK: It's got nothing to do with what we are talking about, but I did a lot of work for a dear departed beloved gentleman who put in show after show after show after show. Jack Hylton. There must have been twelve people in the chorus, all men, and they were as queer as coots. I thought it funny – it was all to protect the single girl in the cast, Rosalind, who had these huge –

PETA: And Dick was too much of a gentleman to throw a pass.

DICK: Typical *Jack* – goes to great *lengths*.

PETA: Peter Sellers fell in love with Charlotte [Mitchell]. He told me. He was afraid to tell *her*. He told me. She's larger than Anne – but very attractive, like Anne. When he married Britt, he bought her everything. Clothes, jewels. Peter was taken in by the *glamour*.

DICK: He wouldn't be the first one in the theatre, you know.

PETA: She couldn't put up with him any more, Anne. He said, 'Of all the wives I've had, she's the one I should have stayed with.' It was Anne. We once took an Australian journalist to see him at Chipperfield – one Sunday morning. We practically had to make a formal appointment to go and see him. He had this fucking manservant. There he was in silk pyjamas.

MYSELF: Like a pasha!

PETA: But he didn't get along with the snobs in that village. Sellers! A bloody comic! When he was little he told us his mother had a cart and they'd go round the houses asking for old silver and gold. Next to being like gypsies. What a background ... And Peg tried to break up Anne's marriage – and when Peg was dead, Sellers kept in touch with crystal balls.

DICK: She's got complete recall, you know. I don't know the ABC – that's the end of me.

PETA: Spike used to keep going round the bend, and Peter said, 'We used to arrive to do a show and there wasn't a bloody script. We had to sit down and write one.' That *Running, Jumping, Standing Still* film of theirs – Dick was in that. Done in a bloody field.

DICK: I didn't know, you know, what they were trying to do.

PETA: He was away all day. He was meant to be a magician.

DICK: Oh yes? This is a surprise to me.

PETA: And you didn't get any money for it.

DICK: Oh, *that's* why I felt I could drift back home. . . .

PETA: Old pals wandering around a field making it up as they went along.

DICK: This thing you had repaired has been whistling for the last about –
(He points in the direction of a clock or electrified egg timer, but I myself never see exactly what's being referred to.)

PETA *(briskly)*: No it's not – it's something outside in the street.

DICK: Oh, is it? Well, we've had great trouble with this dear old . . . It's an old fashioned affair, frayed at the edges.

PETA: Wasn't Anne in the box office at the Palladium? Peter didn't tell stories very well –

DICK: *(cutting in)* 'Benny, life is like a cup of tea.' –

'Why?' – 'Don't ask me why. I'm not a fucking philosopher.'

PETA: He was a Jew. We lived in Springfield Road, in St John's Wood, and there was a fellow who loved telling Jewish stories, the ones Jews tell Jews, and we used to tell them to Peter.

DICK: Benny, he'd got his wife and little son, Benny, who disappeared for a while. So he said, 'Benny, where are you? *Benny?*' He said, 'Up here father.' – 'What are you doing?' – 'Fucking, father.' – 'Ah, that's nice – don't fight.'

PETA: These would crease Peter Sellers.

DICK: Jews have a way of escaping, of coping . . . Like the Jew who'd got into an exclusive club only by changing his name by deed poll. He jumps into the swimming pool and it's a bit cold, 'Oy vay!' he shrieks, 'whatever that might mean.'

PETA: When we saw his Manor House at Chipperfield, I said, 'My God, you've got good taste, Peter.' He said, 'I didn't do it. You ring up people, interior decorators, and they come and do it. *I* didn't do it.'
(*She exits to make coffee*)

DICK: Quick, before she comes back. There was this pub called 'The Two Queers' –

PETA: (*having sailed immediately back into the room*) . . . in the Lake District. He doesn't want to hear this.

DICK: It amuses me.

PETA: Oh, tell it if you want to. . .

DICK: There was this pub. . . .

(We fade to black as Dick Bentley gets into his stride with more jokes about Jews and homosexuals.)

☆ ★ ☆

As a postlude, I asked Charlotte Mitchell about whether Sellers had been in love with her: 'It was all a long time ago, and I find it impossible to take much of a compliment out of what Peta Bentley said. Peter was vulnerable. You can't be that funny as an actor without, in some ways, being difficult. He seemed to have a skin missing, he was so hypersensitive. Drawing on himself, all the time, to be funny, it made him frail. Anne used to come to the studio with the children [*sic*] in their woolly hats. He talked about his children with great love and affection – he was very proud of them. I knew him when he was happy. I wonder when he was ever happy again? What *happened*? He was sad, by the end. I wrote to him in 1964, when I thought he was dying. I saw him once, in later years, at Pinewood – but he walked past. He *did* see me, but he didn't want to recognise me. . . .'

It was as a result of *And So to Bentley* ('I laughed all the way through it') that she was invited to participate in *The Goon Show*, the Robin Hood panto which was broadcast on December 18th 1954. Sellers also took her photograph. Charlotte, in profile, sits amidst the muddle of a TV studio. Metal chairs, camera cranes, and discarded costumes abound. The lady looks young, eager, healthy, like an alert drama student. She is bright and apple-cheeked – you can quite imagine an infectious laugh, energy, bags of personality. If Sellers was in love with her when he took this picture, it's her confident high spirits he'd have wanted to possess. (He'd snapped, as she said to me, a 'jolly' picture of her.) At the time, his son Michael would have been not much above six months old. Anne, newly a mother, was perhaps not giving Sellers every moment of her attention – and he'd have resented her for this. Charlotte Mitchell, in Sellers' view, would have been unencumbered. He would never have seen a tired, preoccupied side of her. And all that guff about being a proud parent? That sounds like Sellers playing the rôle of new paterfamilias. I have seen photographs of him taken at this period and he's gesticulating with a pipe. Did he, weak and vindictive, go home to Anne and wear a tasselled smoking cap?

☆ ☆ ☆

To Sellers, except that he'd be seen across the whole country in one go, live television was no better than doing his act in music halls. He was still getting no experience in extending, or deepening, a role. On *The Glen Campbell Show*, for example, he was skittishy Scottish, making his appearance in a red beard and a long kilt ('to hide the curse I was born with – bad legs'), and he uprooted every Highland myth ever known: sheep stealing, porridge, meanness, heather ('the heather is as high/as an elephant's eye') etc.. All this Scotch mist is paraded, along with McGonagall doggerel, and Sellers seemed to act as a stimulant on the poor material, making its unfunniness part of why it's funny. He gets us to collude with him – his extravagance draws us in. He puts us on the side of the gifted entertainer trapped with trash. We help him make the best of it – as when he's a Southern preacher, yelping out 'cigarettes and whiskey and wild, wild women/They'll drive you crazy, they'll drive you insane . . .' – a sketch he reproduced on *The Muppet Show* a quarter of a century later. The very form of the Kermit and Miss Piggy programme was a send-up of musty music hall. Here Sellers, and Sellers alone, is fast and frolicsome.

That he's far too good for this sort of thing is demonstrated in a sketch where he's Inspector Tom Lengths of the Yard, a part he also got the chance to play again, in *The Case of the Mukkinese Battle Horn*. 'Every criminal leaves an obvious clue,' he says sombrely, 'like a pair of pantyhose in a trombone case or a flea collar in a church collection plate.' Sellers conveys the copper's weariness in the face of yet further law-breaking absurdities – and we'd enjoy more of this, but instead we cut to his portrayal of the underworld gang, his impersonation of George Raft menaces. 'If Pickles wants to play rough I'll have to call Knuckles. One peep out of Knuckles and Big Charley will take care o' him.' Sellers' gangsters, moon-faced and slow-witted, have the peculiar quality of being stereotypes acted out so well, that, like his Highlander, they go *beyond* cliché. In this instance, Sellers plays off everybody's memory of Warner Bros hoods and heavies, and turns them back into cartoons.

It's precisely because they are skits and sketches that Sellers is being cramped – he is forced to be, figuratively, sketchy. (The only comic actor I can think of who conquered and enriched the sketch format is Ronnie Barker, in *The Two Ronnies*, during the Seventies.) Michael Sellers once let me examine a photograph he'd found of his father posing in Hollywood with Mel Blanc, who gave voice to Warner Bros' Bugs Bunny and Tweetie Pie. Sellers must have wondered whether that would be his fate, a life-time in the service of slapstick animation. He was the voice of the Brooke Bond Tea chimpanzees and the Kennomeat bloodhound, whom he did as Alec Guinness ('My man always gets my food, don't you Sydney?'). It was still mainly as a mimic that television wanted him. All that remains of his appearance on Eric Sykes' *The Arthur Ploughshare Show*, for example, are his vocalisations. Having been introduced by wonky piano music, he bounds on stage as a homosexual: 'Goodness,' he says to Sykes, 'I don't like your tailoring very much . . . Oh, I say, *look*, just *look*! Aren't they a lovely audience? Look at the colours of grey and a dash of pink . . . I'd love to paint them . . . I want to get the aura of pale mauve laughter coming through.'

Sellers, I admit, is awfully adroit at camp squeals and over-articulation (he's back in his parrot range), but the target of the joke – the poovery of artists – is disagreeable, and the army song he proceeds to sing ('Oh a man on the march may be lonely/Though there are ten thousand men by his side') is a dubious link with Major Bloodnok. The ensuing army sketch is pathetic, it goes on too long, and Bloodnok is lost when out of the Goon context. (We can see why he flopped in *Mother Goose*.) Sellers relies on the character's explosive innards and harrumphs to get laughs, so much so that he gets to sound like Jimmy Saville, the bleach-haired disc jockey and hospital visitor. The slipping-in of the huge hampton joke ('You, Jampton, *you* Jampton'), which elicits a laugh from the band or stage-hands, suggests the actor knew all was lost.

He kept with it for the money, which, compared with his radio fees, was vast. He was paid five hundred pounds for appearing on *The Billy Cotton Band Show*, two hundred pounds for going on the *Six Five Special.** He was on *Don't Spare the Horses*, a variety show broadcast from the Princess Theatre; similar Saturday night entertainments beamed from the Palladium; Harry Secombe's eisteddfods, called *Secombe Here!*, broadcast live from Earl's Court, and which included Les Trois Charleys doing the stick dances; and you'd have also glimpsed him on *The Dickie Valentine Show* and as the co-host, along with Valentine and Margaret Lockwood, of the *Salute to Show Business*, convened on board a Thames steamer, the *MV Royal Sovereign*, and broadcast on September 20th 1957, to celebrate the second anniversary of Independent Television.† Also involved were Felix Aylmer, the venerable actor who played pilgrims and magi so convincingly, you feel he really did stroll into such as *The Black Rose* direct from the Middle Ages; Dame Edith Evans, Sir John Gielgud, Sir Ralph Richardson, Sir Michael Redgrave and Dame Celia Johnson represented the world of the classics (they performed excerpts from the plays mounted down the ages at the Haymarket Theatre); and William Holden, from *Sunset Boulevard* and *Bridge on the River Kwai*, represented the world of international films.

Sellers pretended to be the *MV Royal Sovereign*'s skipper-cum-barman. He kept his hair in the thick black cowlick of Amphibulous, the prime minister in *Carlton Browne of the FO*, and added the Hitlerian moustache of Fred Kite. He was dishevelled and slobby, deflating the mood of self-congratulation and glitter which carried the rest of the programme. He was remunerated with six hundred pounds, which was about what he'd come to expect: ITV

---

* December 14th 1957 and January 11th 1958, respectively.

† ITV started broadcasting in London, in opposition to the BBC, on September 22nd 1955, and within the following two years spread to the Midlands, the North of England, and Scotland, reaching about four million homes by 1957 – a fact disputed by Milligan, who reckons 'there were only 350 TV sets in England at the time'.

pay Spike and I fabulous money for "Fred" – more than we dreamed. They gave us co-directing status, too. If they hadn't, we wouldn't have done it. The money wasn't all that important. . .'

By 'Fred' Sellers meant *The Idiot Weekly, Price 2d* (half a dozen programmes, made between February and April 1956), *A Show Called Fred* (five programmes throughout May), *Son of Fred* (eight programmes in the autumn) and *Yes, It's the Cathode Ray Tube Show* (six programmes early the following year, when Milligan was replaced as script-writer by Michael Bentine). Why Fred? 'We all used this name Fred,' he once explained. 'We absolutely revered it . . . You can ruin anything with Fred. Suppose somebody shows you a painting. Oh, you say, that's beautiful, really beautiful. Yes, he says, isn't it beautiful: it's a Rembrandt. Beautiful, you say. Then you look a bit closer and you see it's signed Fred Rembrandt. It's no good, you can't take it seriously if it's by Fred Rembrandt from East Acton. Fred – it's the epitome of working-class names: Fred and Bert. Frank, now that's higher up the social scale . . . All right, Frank and Peter . . . That's why we had all the "Fred" shows.'*

Unlike the other TV spots and dots, the 'Freds' were concerted efforts to visualise *The Goon Show*. Sellers and his colleagues had tried since the very beginning to effect the transformation, but the BBC was not interested: 'I have some very good ideas for short sketches which Spike Milligan and Larry Stephens have written for me, which I think would do well on television,' Sellers had informed Ronnie Waldman, on October 4th 1951, just after the end of the first series of *Crazy People*. 'If these "clicked" I would like to try for a series. As you may know, Larry and Spike wrote *The Goon Show* and I think this material, presented visually, is a cert. Can you help me in this line? I should be very grateful for any suggestions or

---

* Fred isn't that hilarious today. (Frederick Delius, Frederick Ashton, Lynne Frederick.) There have always been plenty of famous Freds. But try dwelling on Kevin, Darren, Jason, Wayne etc., and you catch Sellers' drift. The Monty Python team chose *Brian* for the focus of their affectionate (?) scorn.

comments. I went to see R. Afton,* but was kept waiting forty-five minutes, so I packed it up.'

Waldman, like Afton, did not respond. The prevailing philosophy was that Sellers, a prodigy with sound, would be an embarrassment when brought into vision. 'Isn't it wonderful that there is such a thing as radio,' Roy Speer once said to Frederic Raphael, 'because otherwise people like Peter wouldn't have anywhere to work? He could never make a living as an actor with a face like that!' The BBC's loss was Associated-Rediffusion's gain. Yet though the 'Freds' were to become Sellers' chief contribution to television, very little of the material survives today. When Associated-Rediffusion merged with, or was supplanted by, Thames Television, in the Sixties, all the old tapes, film stock, and concomitant paperwork, was sent to a rubbish dump in Wembley. As the veteran technicians and producers always say, when I try and probe them about the past, 'We had no idea that what we were doing would be of any historical interest or value.' The atmosphere must have been like that of the pioneering, improvisatory motion picture industry in Hollywood – halcyon days, before trades unions etc. made life complicated and serious and reminded everybody that their games had to be conceived of and carried through as work. But, briefly, ITV had an amateurish, free-for-all zest, and Sellers' 'Freds' embodied this. As Bryn Siddall, who worked on the shows, remembers: 'It was hard for commercial television to attract technicians – nobody wanted to leave the security of the BBC; nobody wanted to leave the lucrative world of films – so Associated-Rediffusion had to hire staff from a bankrupted ballet company. That's why the carpenters, designers, and props-buyers went in for elaborate, ornate sets and costumes, which Sellers loved. Our art director was Timothy O'Brien [who now works for the Royal Shakespeare Company and the Royal National Theatre], a perfectionist. When Sellers wanted to play Napoleon in a sketch, O'Brien was able to send people to Paris to copy details from museums and galleries. Money was no object. No thought was given by anybody

---

* Richard Afton was a TV comedy producer – see *Trial Gallop*.

to a budget. We even had pure silk tents on one occasion – yet everything went out live and filming was very slap-happy. Extras would wander about at will, to be joined by members of the public. People would go in and out of shot. The programmes all over-ran. Material not used one week would be used at the start of the next. If they asked the props department for "sculls", and it was a spelling mistake, they got oars, and the *Hamlet* sketch would be, "Alas, poor Yorick, I rowed him well." Most weeks, no two people had the same script – and Milligan would re-write material on air. Once, a conducted tour entered the studio by mistake during a live transmission – Sellers incorporated it, by ad-libbing about these poor people. The following week, they were written in – they had to come back. We had all kinds of eccentrics wandering about . . . An uncle of Gilbert Harding's was found, Cuthbert Harding. He was wheeled about in a bath chair, dressed as a German general and playing a souzaphone. Tony and Douglas Robinson were used. They were a nightclub act called The Alberts. In real life they dressed as Cossacks and walked greyhounds in Hyde Park. We had Professor Bruce Lacey, an inventor, who provided exploding boots and a dinosaur that ate Peter Sellers during a newscaster sketch. They had a catchphrase, too, amongst themselves, which was "You can't get the wood, you know." Sellers was always saying that. . . .'

The 'Freds', by making use of whatever fell into the developing tray by accident – or at least by giving that impression – could make ill-discipline and dare devilry the basis of the humour. The programmes had the freedoms of a home movie, and indeed culminated in the team's making the eleven minute black and white silent, *The Running, Jumping, Standing Still Film* – which, as the co-director Dick Lester said, 'was an outgrowth of the filmed inserts we had been doing for the live TV shows. I'd enjoyed those inserts, because they were so flexible to work with. So the film was two Sundays shooting in a field with friends and chauffeurs and wives . . . We shot only one take for any gag . . . using Peter's 16mm Bolex with a zoom lens. The total budget for this shooting was seventy pounds . . . The editing, which was really just topping and tailing, took two hours. Every gag we shot, every piece of film that we shot, is in the finished film. We showed it to our wives by projecting it on to a wall in the living room. . . . '

Sellers loved the simplicity and informality of all this. He'd cause trouble, later on, in *Casino Royale* especially, when he'd try and force these nonconformist and liberal techniques on a top-heavy full-dress Hollywood-financed production. (Indeed, that he chose Joe McGrath, who'd worked on the 'Freds', to direct *Casino Royale*, suggests how he'd hoped, with his own inventiveness and Columbia studio's money, to re-create the happy anarchy of his early days on TV. It was not to be.)

☆ ★ ☆

' . . . the show is being written week to week,' Sellers confided in Herbert Kretzmer, the columnist of the *Daily Sketch*, 'so you probably realise the difficulties.' They were difficulties, however, which he (at first) enjoyed trying to surmount. If the actual script wasn't funny, he'd suggest they speak their lines against a back projection screen of riots in Belgium or a bed-stead travelling through the sea in the wake of a motorboat. Though Lester says that 'there was no tape. There was a primitive form of telerecording, but that was too expensive for the likes of us to use,' and though Bryn Siddall was certain that 'nothing survives of the programmes now', I have managed to find a fragment in the National Film Archive – which went something like this:

FADE IN on the big brass Rank gong which, when struck, shatters to reveal a chap in tin bath, which he then picks up – it has no bottom – and runs off with. We cut to Sellers, reading the news. He is sitting in front of a screen showing a motorist's point-of-view as a vehicle whizzes along country lanes. Milligan and Kenneth Connor run behind Sellers' desk, fight with each other, and go away again. Next comes a filmed sketch shot at Battersea power station, which is meant to be a building on the Scottish island of Scron. Sellers, as Admiral MacIdiot, arrives in a car covered with life-buoys. Milligan, seated on the bonnet, heaves-to at the front door with a boat hook and grappling iron. Sellers gets out the car by rope ladder and we then cut to Milligan, in beard and bearskin, shaving himself with a razor plugged into a tree – and later he's seen reading by the light of a bedside lamp which descends from the branches of a bush.

Next, a bearded lady tells us how to eliminate woodworm from your house – we get a clip of a battleship firing all guns. The lady then waltzes away with Valentine Dyall. Dyall, tall and gaunt, and with a resounding, sepulchral voice, had appeared in Olivier's *Henry V*. His diction was so impeccable, the Goons found him over the top, and therefore funny – as if he was a parody of an effete classical actor. This, anyway, was what they made him into. He appeared in many episodes of *The Goon Show*, playing pantomime villains. In 'The Canal' he was Seagoon's murderous father, and in 'The House of Teeth' he was a mad dentist; best of all, he was the Sheriff of Nottingham in 'Robin Hood and His Merry Men'. Milligan used him as the frayed Lord Fortnum of Alamein in *The Bedsitting Room* at the Mermaid (Ralph Richardson played it in the film), and he took many parts in *The Great McGonagall*. In the last, especially, he demonstrated his range, playing fops and Victorian gents with conviction, whilst also getting quite in the mood of the surreal format. Elsewhere, I'm not so sure. I always feel that Sellers and Milligan made fun of him rather cruelly, using him as a target for much of their anti-establishment, anti-straight acting, anti-cultural resentments. He was once made to dress up as a buzzard, for instance, and put in the vulture cage at Regent's Park Zoo. Sellers was seen to 'cry with laughter' when he watched the playback.

'I'm the Goon equivalent of the Marx Brothers' Margaret Dumont,' Dyall said good-naturedly. 'She's Mrs Dukesbury, that superb matronly figure in tiaras, big bust and black lace, nearly always insulted by Groucho.' But behind Margaret Dumont, a dowager in full sail, and virtually a drag act, you don't feel there is a different sort of gifted actress being forced into a decline. Her hauteur and her suffering are totally comic.

Anyway, Dyall exits and Sellers and Milligan come back on,

carrying dustbins. 'Jump into a dustbin and dance,' they sing. Sellers then spies Max Geldray through a periscope – Max starts to blow and suck on his instrument when (if only this had happened on radio), he's torpedoed.* We move, next, to an employment agency sketch. Sellers plays William Mate Cobblers playing Constable Pringe: 'I was a-wondering if you've got any unemployed criminules on your books.' Enter Dyall as a con-man aristocrat and forger, who is hired to go out and commit murders – to give the police force something to do. 'I now pronounce you criminule and constabule,' says a registrar. Mendelssohn and wedding bells start up, as the pair drive off in a patrol car, which has a JUST ARRESTED sign on the back fender.

Finally, Sellers gets to play Dr Jekyll. After all the usual business with foaming potions and test tube mixtures ('The Power! The Power!' says Milligan, off-screen, in a Moriarty voice), hairy cheeked Mr Hyde speaks – as Bluebottle. 'I *like* this game,' he says. 'Mr Hyde commits innumerable acts of atrocity with women,' pants the urgent newsreel voice, 'leading to hundreds of proposals from them. . .' Mr Hyde is pursued by Sherlock Holmes (Kenneth Connor) and Constable Pringe (now played by Dyall). They step in and out of false doorways, Connor swigs the potion and is changed into Patti Lewis (she waltzes away with Dyall again), and Sellers slaps a rubber suction steering wheel on his forehead and is driven off. . .

Transferred to TV, the Goonish imagination has less to do. The sketches aren't exactly inspired, and Sellers simply impersonates his own radio characters or mimics Richard Dimbleby or Laurence Olivier's Richard III – as Columbus: 'I've endured their sly mockery,' he says, whilst the wind whistles and the sea crashes, 'as they

---

* Actually, the BBC did try to drop him from *The Goon Show*, in 1958: 'Peter Sellers has just heard about our decision not to engage Max Geldray for the coming series,' the Variety Booking Manager wrote to John Browell, on September 25th, 'and Sellers says that he is not prepared to do the programme unless Geldray is in it . . . What now?' Geldray, of course, was re-engaged. Sellers could always afford to be magnanimous if his own talent wasn't under threat.

hint at that which they've not the courage to speak plainly to my face.' The staccato delivery and the mangled grammar are a faultless lampoon of Shakespearean gibberish, as well as encapsulating Olivier's own convoluted real-life speech rhythms ('illusion' is pronounced with four pecks, 'ill-ooze-y-on'). But though the material slips fast from the memory, Sellers' Olivier-as-Richard is chilling – as mimicry it is *too* good. He appears to embody both the King's amorality *and* Olivier's own ambitions and serpentine charm. In this sense, it is a dual impersonation, and becoming a fussy elvish'd-marked son of hell, seductive and repulsive, intersected with something deep in his own nature, where he had a heart like flint. We can see all this operating in a superb photograph, taken by Graham Stark, of Sellers in the full costume and make-up. (I have seen it written that Sellers wore Olivier's actual Richard III wig, having found it in storage at the Aldwych Theatre.) He sits back, in profile and in darkness, and what light there is picks out, like the glints off a silver hatchet, the severe nose, evil eyes, and lascivious mouth. (It is hard to credit it *isn't* Olivier.) Sellers climbed into the full fig again, a few years later, when he decided to perform the Beatles' number 'A Hard Day's Night' as a Shakespearean soliloquy ('It has been a hard day's night and I have/Been working like a dog . . .', he barked, very nearly imposing the requisite iambic pentameter. 'It has been a hard day's night, and I have/Been sleeping like a log'). I remember seeing him perform this number on television, in a Roger Furse castle set and with William Walton lute music, and I fully believed it *was* from *Richard III*, and that it was the Beatles who had gone and jazzed up the Bard. I hunted through *The Complete Works* to find the quotation, only to be disappointed – as I was when 'Goodness Gracious Me' wasn't in *The Millionairess*.

Sellers, like Richard, could add colours to the chameleon, change shapes with Proteus for advantages. Roy Speer's jibe about his featureless potato head aside, it is Sellers, and only Sellers, who claims our attention in the 'Freds' and associated stills. Whether he's dressed as a doctor about to amputate his own nose, or a rally driver sitting in a car made out of chairs and coats, or if he's doing things with a Viking helmet, or is a boxer, the Muswell Hill Mauler, in a leotard embroidered with shamrocks, he is in character and funny – but he is also something more. As with all the face-pulling photographs posed for during recordings of *The Goon Show*, where he, Milligan and Secombe would be requested to look zany and whacky, Sellers' expression always manages to be silly and sombre at the same time. He is strangely detached from what everybody else is about, and therefore (you feel) cannot be blamed for their imbecilities; and yet then he'll come out with ideas and disguises screwier than the lot. Puffing out his cheeks, to impersonate a gilded caryatid, holding up a box in a theatre, or simply staring into space, he's unpredictable, absurd, and sympathetic.

In the 'Freds', telling us about the efficacy of jumping out of air balloons, using hand-operated wings, you'd swear that, in place of a brain, he has one of Emett's engines behind his eyes. But, being on TV, the fairy tale potential of the moment is flattened – and we realise just how far Sellers has come on radio. Goonery seems rather retrogade here – and it does not fulfil him. There is far too much of Milligan's squeaky voice, in the fractions of the 'Freds' I saw; and far too much of Valentine Dyall altogether. Senile gabblings and upper-class drawls are thrown in for their own sake, as if they are automatically funny and that nothing more need be done. Military bands, explosions, and honky-tonk piano music are imported from *The Goon Show* (the sheer noise is from *The Goon Show*), along with rolling drums, amplified birdsong, and lots of over-hearty laughter from the orchestra and studio hangers-on.

The 'Freds' went from a refreshing misrule to a boring unruliness very quickly. 'It wasn't too bad at the start,' said Sellers. 'I think *Idiot's Weekly* and *A Show Called Fred* were the best of the series. But it was a strain for Spike, writing a new show every week. And later on – you know, we got together a group of young script-writers to contribute – well, they had some good ideas – but sometimes there would be a good beginning but no end. In script-writing that isn't enough; the jokes have to be organised. That was when the show began to go downhill' – aided and abetted, he should have emphasised, by his own irresponsibility. Once, out filming at a quarry near Harefield with Dick Lester, in the summer of 1956, he had to be taken home and work abandoned for the day because he'd literally pissed himself laughing. They were doing a dervish attack on a ridge. Sellers was leading his arabs against a line of red-coats, played by Sam Costa, Johnny Vyvyan, and the Alberts. Because of the dryness of the sand, Sellers couldn't get a foothold on the slope, and kept sliding back. He just couldn't reach the top. On the third attempt at storming the dune, he began to corpse, scrabbled frantically, gave up, and a trickle of urine streamed from between his legs, on to the sand, as he giggled and giggled. The rivulet raced him back to ground level. Professional incontinence indeed.

☆   ☆   ☆

'Goonery can't be done properly on TV because of the expense,' complained Sellers, forgetting that *The Running, Jumping and Standing Still Film* had cost next to nothing. 'We want a lot of films and cartoons, with humans appearing among the cartoon characters. . .' He might be prophesying the nonsense approach of *Monty Python's Flying Circus*, which would be so effectively made for television about fifteen years later; except that what actually concerned Sellers, who'd often recourse to diversionary ranting about 'expense,' e.g. on *Casino Royale* or *The Fiendish Plot of Dr Fu Manchu*, if he felt personally insecure, was not method or technical innovation, but how best to develop and sustain his quirky gifts, with all their overtones and undertones. 'I'm not a comedian,' he'd decided, 'just an actor-cum-what-have-you . . . I haven't the strong comedy personality of Arthur Askey or Harry Secombe. But even without that you can be successful if the material is funny. As I see it, I'd have to change my style [from clown and mimic to comic actor] inside five years – I'll be 35 then – so why not start the process now?'

His first reaction to the disarray of the 'Freds' was to decide he was disillusioned with Milligan – though, in actuality, an upheaval between himself and his creative godfather was 'something which I believe happens at fairly regular intervals,' Pat Newman had commented in a BBC memo (adding darkly: 'No doubt . . . the producer [of *The Goon Show*] or someone might like to examine this aspect in a little more detail' – and one thinks of a schoolteacher wading into a play-yard donnybrook to part a pair of battling infants, or of a marriage guidance counsellor. . .).

His second operation was a surprise (and a forewarning). He reverted to the beginnings of his career – by sending for Bentine. 'Lovely to have you back, Mike,' said Sellers, as the man he'd helped to transport to Australia returned from his exiles. 'Can you write some television shows for me? I've still got six more to do to finish my contract with Rediffusion. Could you please start right away?'

Sellers' bright and cheery request is an early example of his unnerving forgetfulness, which was to reach an amnesiacal abyss on *Ghost in the Noonday Sun*. He'd quite put out of his mind the fact that, but a few years previously, he'd schemed to have Bentine removed from *The Goon Show* – a campaign which was so successful, Bentine's forty-one programmes and *Crazy People* episodes had been melted down and wiped out of existence. Even his photograph (he says) 'had been neatly excised from the earlier Goon pictures,' and only since Sellers' death has he been able to have himself 're-placed in the group pictures of the original Goons displayed in many BBC buildings'. Bentine had become an un-person. 'I thought you were dead,' was the waggish sort of remark producers made now he was back.

Sellers' power, his ability to consign people to the wilderness and then recall them or be nice to them – in this early stage of his career because he was choked with ambition, later on because he was destructive and schizophrenic – is reminiscent of nothing so much as the Roman emperors. 'He used to forget things from one day to another,' said Peter Medak of his star-crossed Mediterranean movie-making. 'I saw him years later when I was doing another film at Shepperton and he'd forgotten anything had gone wrong between himself and me.

'"What's the matter, darling? I sent you a message. Why didn't you come over?" he said.

'"Because I didn't want to."

'"What do you mean? I haven't seen you for such a long time," he kept on.

'"Don't you remember what happened in Cyprus?" I was incredulous.

'"What do you mean, what happened? It was us and them."

'"It wasn't us and them – there was no *them* left. You expelled everybody. It was you and me."

'"I don't know what you are talking about . . ."

'He did not remember a single thing about it any more. . .'

By regularly emptying out his conscience, Sellers could rid himself of such human weaknesses and moral guides as, say, guilt. If he looked back, it was only to sentimentalise, never to apologise. Bentine came back into his orbit because Bentine was useful to him. That chair frame routine was *visual*, and the idea of objects like sink plungers etc. taking on a life of their own would inspire Sellers, one day, to vivify Dr Strangelove's false arm. Also, Australia and family life having knocked the Etonian edges off him, Bentine interested Sellers as an individual case-study. His Peruvian father invented things like flying boats and his mother bred parakeets; he was raised in stucco villas near Folkestone, paid for with revenue from the family's South American estates; and he claimed to experience psychic visions and hallucinations. The sombre side of the colourfulness was the way the exotic Bentins (as the name was spelled) were roughly, and offensively, treated by the xenophobic British. During the war, his parents were forced to sell their coastal home at a huge loss, and they were not allowed to own a wireless or, dottily, a bicycle. Bentine himself was not allowed to attend university, was suspected of being an enemy agent because of his interest in physics and technology, and when he worked as a press photographer, he was arrested and his camera confiscated. 'Oh God,' he said understandably, 'why must the British always treat my family like shit?'

Bentine had a real knowledge of rejection and of being on the outside. 'We can't have non-Europeans in the RAF,' he was told, but he persevered and, as we know, he became an officer and later expiated his wartime experiences with Goonery. In the broadest sense, his background may be compared with Sellers'. The wayfaring Jewish music hall artistes, belonging nowhere in particular; the South American immigrants, anxious to become English, adopting the local habits (bridge parties with the Edwardian gentlefolk), and yet then being scorned as outlaws and virtually interned. Sellers' total lack of education; Bentine's enthusiastic autodidacticisms. Sellers' vocal facility; Bentine's speech impediments – as a child, his voice box was damaged by a botched tonsilectomy. His subsequent delight in din, clamour and squawks began as mandatory, recuperative speech therapy. . . Their mutual obsession with spiritualism. . . .

The two men may be compared and contrasted – it was Bentine who officially led and represented the royal family at Sellers' memorial service on September 8th 1980 at St Martin-in-the-Fields – and in *Yes, It's the Cathode Ray Tube Show* their styles came together[*]. They would in fact have mixed and matched much earlier on the box, had not the death of George VI, on February 13th 1952, resulted in the cancellation of:

TRIAL GALLOP
– An experiment in organised chaos –
Michael Bentine, Peter Sellers
Leslie Mitchell, Leslie Randall
Peter Butterworth, Graham Stark
with
Jack Hayes, John Vivienne [*sic*]
Clementina Stuart, Anne Hayes

Devised and written by
Michael Bentine and Jimmy Grafton
Orchestra conducted by Eric Robinson
Produced by Richard Afton.

---

[*] Some of the scripts are reproduced in *The Best of Bentine* (St Albans, 1983), a volume which is dedicated 'To my good friend Peter Sellers who gave the joy of laughter to millions by his great comedy talent.'

Apart from (I believe) playing his stooge in cabaret, Anne didn't work with her husband on any other occasion – and this programme, which would have gone out live, obviously never existed in any form. (Clementina Stuart, by the way, is Mrs Michael Bentine.) Bentine's ambitions for it, however, are pertinent. 'I've tried to see the programme', he said beforehand, 'entirely in pictures.' Viewers would have seen a witch doctor taking a tour party around an atomic plant, and this was going to be the excuse no doubt to wheel on various mutants and nutty professors.

I'm afraid that, like the line in Keats about the sound of an owl being a 'night-bird's hated screech', I personally find Bentine's comedy too high-pitched – manic – for my taste. His sketches are exercises in noise non-abatement, and he provided Sellers with the opportunity to be Russians and Pakistanis at international conferences, a Scottish air controller talking down a nervous Indian pilot, a drunken toastmaster, Arabs bartering, and garrulous, pompous TV commentators ('Loyal, loyal Big Ben booms out the hour of noon') – and amidst the babble and prattle, the explosions in a firework factory, the contests between military brass bands, and the insects driving people mad with their incessant tck-tck, the wonder was that Sellers still managed to give depth to his characterisations. (At least he had characters to play now: the 'Freds', by contrast, were just so much running amok.) His favourite part was Mr Charles Crumpet, winner of the Film Extra of the Century Award. Suddenly, Sellers' sympathetic understanding of proud old failures, such as he'd known in Ilfracombe and points round about, came pouring out. Extras, or crowd artistes, are, says Bentine 'dreamers, hiring out their fantasies with tolerance and enthusiasm'. It is this sad whimsicality which Sellers could convey. 'Then I struck a bad patch,' the grand old man confesses to his interviewer, 'I was out of work for fifteen years.'

☆　★　☆

It was during this period, when he himself was very busy, that Sellers was contacted by Cardew Robinson, with whom he'd worked on *Variety Bandbox* and *Workers' Playtime*. Robinson had remembered that, after appearing on the latter, 'my wife came backstage and I asked her how my act had gone down. She said, quite truthfully, "You were a bit slow." Which after a bit led me to the realisation that professionals don't want any real criticism just after they've done a show – and this gave me the idea for a sketch. Two ex-school friends, one now an actor, and the other comes backstage after the performance, is asked his opinion, and gradually the piqued actor-laddie reverts to being a brawling Cockney spiv. I phoned up Peter and said would he do it – and also, would he be interested in a Gang Show reunion (where, again, I'd once worked alongside him). He said to write the sketch and to round up our Air Force colleagues, he'd do both. Within a fortnight it was all accomplished. The sketch was a great success – Sellers was superb at going from being the lordly actor to the East Ender; we did it on television in 1958, on *The World's Our Stage* – and we'd also started the Gang Show reunions. Sellers came to several, over the years, on one occasion even bringing Britt. I once went to a party at his house up in Hampstead. He had a new radio telephone – and he wandered off on his own all over the Heath ringing us up. . .'

☆ ★ ☆

Actors, earnest and dispirited, elderly and decrepit, lie within Sellers' Dr Pratt, General Fitzjohn, Morganhall, and Old Sam. His characters are men who believe themselves to be masters of illusion – or who are suffering from self-deceptions, if you prefer. Sonny MacGregor, Clare Quilty, C.P.O. Dockerty, Henry Orient, and his many confidence tricksters and crooks, are also play-actors, too, in the sense that they pretend to be what they are not. Would it be to get ahead of my story to try and see something ominous in Sellers' early and heartfelt appreciation of the actor's art – actors being, by their very natures, watchful, dissembling and mercurial? Applied to himself, acting was to entail an increasing lack of contact with real life. It was the tragic aspect of his comic genius that Sellers had nothing to replace acting with; and that beyond the jollity of his public appearances there was only solitude and disintegration. (As I once said in another book, 'Sellers filled his life with toys, instead of filling it with life.') And yet, portentously perhaps, he can imply even *this* in his fops and hams. At the end of the Fifties, Kenneth Tynan invited him to appear on an arts magazine programme called *Tempo*, produced live from Teddington on Sundays. It was one week ballet, the next week opera. 'One Sunday we were all surprised to see Sellers turn up,' a technician informed me. 'He stood at a lectern and recited McGonagall, and he did not laugh or even grin. In fact, all the crew without exception were in hysterics all day, and not once did Sellers crack up. Off camera, Bruce Lacey, in a brass helmet, was doing daft things, and still Sellers didn't corpse or even *look* at him. . . .'

Sellers introduced McGonagall as:

> A better poet was never seen in the City of Dundee at any time,
> And never again shall be as far as I can see in the meantime;
> His poem on the Tay Bridge is most beautiful to be read,
> As I found by reading it one cold night before I went to bed.
> Among the poets of the present day, there's none on earth who
> Can possibly be able for to gainsay,
> But that William McGonagall, poet and tragedian,
> Is truly the greatest poet that was ever found above or below the
> meridian.

The sequence was directed by Joe McGrath, who'd go on later, as mentioned earlier, to handle the megaphone on several Sellers pictures; and a still from the *Tempo* episode may be found in *The Book of the Goons*, where Sellers' McGonagall, swathed in tartan robes, looks like a Highland Oscar Wilde.* Milligan's McGonagall, in the 1974 film, was a tramp; Sellers' is an aesthete, in knee-breeches and spats with pearl buttons. You can tell, by his dramatic stance, that the botched balladry was being delivered as if it were a lecture on the way life imitates art, or on the hidden truths revealed by masks.

---

* In the book, the photograph is inscribed in Sellers' hand: 'Terence Milligan is a writer and actor and poet of high degree/Which is surely plain for all to see,/ Gainsay it I dare anyone who can,/Because T.S. Milligan is a good zany man.'

☆　★　☆

'I wonder if it is now possible for you to reconsider the Peter Sellers situation?' asked Ronald Waldman, in a confidential memo to the BBC TV Head of Light Entertainment, on April 25th, 1957. Having once so peremptorily turned him down, it had been galling for the BBC to watch Sellers succeed on the screen; and now that they wanted to entice him back from ITV, to sign an exclusive contract which would give him a dozen comedy shows and six drama programmes a year, he'd become expensive. 'He would want at least £500 per appearance. However, it is difficult to decline . . . such an excellent television artist and I am most keen to try and achieve this contract.'

The Grades pressed their advantage: 'Peter is definitely under the impression that you would pay him £500 per show which is what he has been getting on commercial television and, in actual fact, he got £600 for one particular show. Whilst he would like to work for the BBC he does feel that on principal [*sic*] he could not accept less than he has been receiving on the opposition channel. . .' The finances were never resolved; neither could Sellers quite decide on what material suited him. He'd go through cycles of enthusiasm and hesitation; he'd put people through hoops, and then he'd withdraw.

Michael Barry, the Head of Drama, attempted to interest him in 'a very special project over which considerable trouble is being taken. This is no less than a serial dramatisation of Pepys' Diary made by screen writer and historian Colonel Rawlinson. It is turning out extremely well as an amusing and human story and . . . would you like to play Pepys?' (It would have been for a fourteen week series, so Sellers declined.) Roy Speer, eating his words about Sellers' geekiness, asked him: 'Have you ever thought of doing a thirty minutes series *entirely on your tod*?' and went on to outline a duff scheme, whereby Sellers would play William Mate Cobblers or 'maybe a BBC fireman at Broadcasting House, . . . explaining what sort of things people did when radio was a popular form of entertainment. This could be your excuse for doing a sketch, a monologue, a song or what have you. We could do a macabre piece of Edgar Allan Poe. . .' (Dennis Selinger replied to the effect that Sellers was already 'very much overworked' and that therefore his client could not guarantee to give of his best and 'I am quite certain that you agree it would be unwise to go ahead on this idea unless we were all certain that you were going to get an absolutely first class result.')

He refused to appear in some S.J. Perelman playlets 'unless it is financially outstanding for him' – likewise: 'He feels that he is not the right person to read 'Brugglesmith' [from Kiplings' *Many Inventions*] on Chrismas Day.' The last thing they tried to tempt him with – ominously, in view of his future removal of Anne Howe, his serial polygamy and misogyny – was Maxwell Anderson's *Anne of a Thousand Days*, which had recently been a hit on Broadway with Rex Harrison and Joyce Redman – and thus yet another chance for the conceited Rex to be Professor Higgins pitting himself against a guttersnipe. 'Jean Simmons is pencilled in for Anne Boleyn and we would like to know if Peter Sellers would care to play the part of Henry VIII?' (Sellers said no because the production would have entailed three weeks of rehearsal beforehand.)

It is only fair to add that radio, too, was failing to hook Sellers:

[London]
March 13th 1991

Dear Mr Lewis,

[. . .]
Shortly after I took over the post as assistant head of radio
drama at Broadcasting House the actor Kenneth Griffith (who
has since become a well-known, if controversial, documentary
film and television director), with whom I worked on a number
of radio drama productions, mentioned that his friend Peter
Sellers was interested in trying his hand at some serious drama,
in particular Beckett's *Waiting for Godot*.

I, of course, was very keen to land such a prestigious star
performer in one of my favourite plays (I had only just published

my book on The Theatre of the Absurd) and so Kenneth Griffith arranged a lunch with Peter Sellers at the Carlton Tower Hotel in Sloane Street.

This went extremely well. Peter Sellers, armed with an array of cameras, photographed us during the lunch and seemed most keen to tackle the part of Estragon in the play. He spoke of his diffidence about acting, as it came to him in a mysterious way he could not fathom, and thus caused him great anxiety as he might one day wake up without this mysterious knack-beyond-his-control. Hence his eagerness to have an alternative activity he did know about, such as photography. He tried, on the spot, how he might do Estragon, what voice to adopt etc..

It was all agreed, the production was set up, but at the last moment, Sellers withdrew, ostensibly because of some film engagement; but my impression was that he simply felt too much stage-fright about stepping into high literary drama.

[. . .] The production was recorded (Nigel Stock took over) and broadcast [. . .] Kenneth Griffith played Vladimir . . .

> With best regards,
> Yours sincerely,
> *Martin Esslin*

Sellers' promise to play in Beckett's intellectual re-working of Laurel and Hardy (think of Didi and Gogo's bowler hats etc.) was taken seriously enough for the *Radio Times* to have carried his photograph announcing his forthcoming appearance – and the embarrassment of the cancellation 'seemed to me to necessitate a little chat with Dennis Selinger', said Pat Newman. The outcome of the pow-wow was that Sellers had gone into a sulk because he had expected the same fees for straight plays as he'd received for the traditionally more lucrative light entertainment. Esslin's department did not give up, however. On February 16th 1962, they wrote to Sellers c/o The Carlton Tower Hotel (whither Sellers had moved, the better to incommode his wife and young children) to suggest the following for the Third Programme:

THE KILLER – Ionesco. This is a wonderful play about a little man who cannot accept the fact that people have to die and is determined to find the killer who makes them die. He does in the end after many adventures face the killer who is a giggling half-wit and nothing he can say can persuade him to stop his killing.

OBLOMOFF – Gontcharoff.* This is an adaptation of the famous Russian novel about a man who is so idle that he even misses his own wedding. This is also a magnificent part.

The plays by Gogol which have not been done in this country – THE GAMBLERS and THE MARRIAGE, both of which have excellent parts for you.

There is something inadvertently funny (and piteous) about all these indomitable BBC eggheads sending Sellers classical plot synopses and trying to make him beetle-browed and serious. 'We are so eager to have you do something for us,' they'd write, 'that we should very much like to know soon whether you are interested in any of these and in which of them and when you would be able to do them.' We can see the nervy finger-twining, the bowing and the twirling and the fawning, in such an appeal. In time, Sellers would grow accustomed to everybody wanting to treat him like the most distinguished guest in an opulent restaurant. Sycophancy would become the norm (he'd have a psychological urge to be on the receiving end of it); and he would be, in every department, literally catered to. It was an increase on the glutinous veneration he'd fed

---

* Interestingly, it was in this play, re-titled *Son of Oblomov*, that Milligan had a West End success in 1964. Oblomov, as yet another unshaven hobo, became Milligan's daily opportunity to depart from any official script; people came to the theatre just to see the actor make up his lines as he went along – the pretext being that Oblomov, sitting in bed all day, was so lazy, he hadn't even bothered to rehearse his own story. Once, knowing that Sellers was in the audience with the royal family (out for the evening incognito), he simply stopped the show and started to chat over the footlights to his chum in the stalls. 'Why is Prince Philip wearing red, white and blue braces?' asked Milligan, amongst other sallies. 'I don't know,' said Sellers, '*why* is Prince Philip etc. etc.' – 'To keep his trousers up.'

off under Peg – and if, somewhere in his twisted nerves, he resented her extravagant doting, his flatterers, by casting themselves in the same baby-sitting role, only awoke his petulance and egotism.

There remained one person, though, who was cautious and non-spellbound – Pat Newman: various departmental chiefs 'might feel we ought not to pay Sellers less than Hancock, though as I see it,' he counselled, 'Sellers is rather a law unto himself these days. . . .'

☆　★　☆

The mention of Tony Hancock is suggestive – Sellers named him as 'my favourite comedian' in 1960 – for he and Sellers had a great deal in common,* starting with both of their sets of parents being in the part-time entertainment business. They'd worked together in the RAF Gang Shows (Hancock helped Sellers with the wardrobe) and they'd appeared together in *Orders are Orders* and *The Wrong Box* – Sellers' delivery of the line 'I wasn't always as you see me now. In the old days the sick and the groggy would come to me from miles around' made Hancock helpless with laughter. ' "Oh dear, the sick and the groggy," it became one of his favourite expressions', according to John Le Mesurier's widow, Joan.

Hancock had done his stint at the Windmill and had been auditioned for the BBC (as Anthony Hancock, the Confidential Comic) by Dennis Main Wilson. When Sellers was on *Ray's a Laugh*, Hancock was on *Educating Archie*; and *Hancock's Half Hour* was as popular as *The Goon Show*. Radio proved that they were comic actors, not stand up comedians . . . The two men had a fondness for fancy cars and place names that evoked old actors (Bovey Tracey, Throwley Forstall); they feared the prospect of long theatrical runs and were superstitious about the colour green; and, not the least of it, they had a sort of beguiling, canny helplessness which could be switched on and off depending on whether there were pretty

---

* John Mortimer has said that 'The two saddest men I ever met were Peter Sellers and Tony Hancock, and I give daily thanks to God, or destiny, that I never took up life as a comic.' Instead, he became a barrister and QC.

demoiselles present. Above all, they were neurotics, and Hancock killed himself in 1968, an alcoholic wreck, and Sellers spent most of his final decade out on the arctic edge of paranoid schizophrenia. (Milligan said to me: 'Hancock kept looking for something to do when he thought his star was waning; like Peter, he got rid of people systematically. They both destroyed themselves over and over.')

What interests me here is that, as with Sellers, Hancock the man overlapped in complex ways with the version of himself he played on the screen. Hancock's depressive, hectoring persona – that of the shabby genteel inhabitant of 23, Railway Cuttings, East Cheam, desperate to rise above himself and become famous, rich, knowledgeable, or distinguished – shares much with Sellers' gloomy fantasising. Both actors made being personally lost, bewildered and unhappy into a comic style. But where Hancock, consciously and ruthlessly, wanted to close the gap between acting and reality – arguing that 'you have to get rid of everything inessential. I want to stand there as I am. No props. No pretence. No defence. And say "There it is – here I am"' – Sellers, by contrast, had a horror of his individual hollowness, as he deemed it, being exposed.

Hancock's moroseness was the very content of his humour – a humour based on the boredom and exasperation of a man who hated being ordinary. Sellers' characters, instead of slumping and moaning, yawning and grunting, to get laughs, are in hyper-manic flight from the mundane. His people tend to be surreal, whereas Hancock was simply Hancock, sighing, shrugging his flabby shoulders, 'the bullying loser, the little big man, the idiot dupe inside all of us,' said Bill Kerr, who'd met Hancock originally, in Sellers' and Milligan's company, at Grafton's. Hancock's was a comedy of disillusion. At the end of his *Half Hour*, his schemes, to become a ladies' man, to open his house as a stately home ('Lord Byron Lived Here'), to be the keenest radio ham in England ('Look, don't bother,' says the skipper of a sinking ship whose May day! message the lad himself has intercepted, 'I'll just throw a bottle over the side with a note in it'), or to be public spirited as a juror or a blood donor – his schemes, they always end in ruin and the hero's come-uppance. Sellers, on the other hand (no matter how anxiety-prone he may have been in private), convinces us that his characters have exotic centres, weird dreams, which nobody will assail.

Sellers' characters have a well-defined sense of the ridiculous – and I'd go so far as to say that Hancock's success lay in his TV self having absolutely no sense of humour to speak of. He blusters too much. His homburg-hatted grouch was funny to the viewer because he was so literal – he has no idea how to be creative, though he thinks he has. (He thinks he's Bertrand Russell and Rembrandt in one.) His is the rage of the thwarted artist, and this was the very plot, incidentally, of Hancock's two main films, *The Punch and Judy Man* and *The Rebel*. And, if Hancock's characters yearn to be out-laws and outsiders, Sellers' cling to that little bit in their natures which makes them different already – it's to do with their self-confidence, the willingness to be laughed at, of the music hall turn. If Hancock had played Sam the busker in *The Optimists of Nine Elms*, for example, wearing that amazing technicolour dreamcoat in Leicester Square and when playing the uke for the football crowds, he'd have been an object of ridicule. That would have been the point of the story: Hancock, silly old sod, dressing up and making a fool of himself for throw money . . . He'd have been belittled. Sellers' Sam has tremendous intractability. When he's bedecked with flags and a variety of hats, he's a wizard in the West End streets. He's Merlin.

I am always made to feel, with Hancock, that the circumstances of life (it's as vague as that) deny him victory. With Sellers, his characters are too detached and solitary to be importuned – thus that touch of surrealism I mentioned. They have the ability to be taken out of themselves: Mr Quill, transported by silent movies, in *The Smallest Show on Earth*; Mr Kite's vision of the Soviet Union; Mr Martin's paradise of office quiet; General Fitzjohn's and John Lewis' eroticising; Clouseau, Chance, the Rev. Smallwood, and Nayland Smith's serenity . . . So it goes on. The characters are not fools; neither are they fall guys or impolite, as Hancock was. Sellers most Hancock-like performance was as Harry, in *The Ladykillers*, the tubby Teddy Boy, yearning for money. He is farcically undone, as Hancock would have been, had he found himself in Professor Marcus' gang. It's Sellers' only rôle, too, where he used his plumpness as part of the rôle. Elsewhere, being fat was not why he was funny. With Hancock, however, his puddingy features – bulging eyes, sagging jowls, thick hooter and clownish eyebrows, a face over-scaled and mouldering – did all the work. (A slim, cute Hancock is inconceivable.)

The 'biggest battle I ever won', Hancock said, 'was to do comedy in close-up.' But, where the television camera could linger on his Eeyore-looks for thirty minutes and it could all still be tolerable, Hancock's dyspepsia and dismay, prolonged to feature-film length, were a torment. What made him a star on the box denied him popularity in the movies – just as the moodiness and ennui which was comic in his work was tragic when it seeped into his private life. (One of the last things he said, before returning to his flat in Sydney, Australia, to top himself, was, 'What's ahead of me, but work, work, work?') He was therefore made for TV in a way Sellers, infinitely more varied as a performer, was not. The black and white gloom and blurry tuning were apt, too, for the mood – Hancock's old programmes appear made in the midst of foul weather, which emanated (like the fireballs and storms in Romantic literature) from somewhere toxic inside him.

☆ ★ ☆

Sellers, if he wished it, could be as invisible as the razor's edge (he could be Godot); and though the BBC wanted him to play a more manifest Beckett character, it was Hancock who, dismantling himself so thoroughly, *was* a Beckett character. 'There's an old man with a pipe,' he once said, bored out of his brain and gazing at the wallpaper. 'Screw your eyes up. Stare hard. Concentrate on that bit by the serving hatch.' He's kith and kin with Murphy and Watt, killing time. Tedium is their element, and Hancock, stripping himself of supporting cast and writers who wrote too many gags, wanted to achieve a purity of plotlessness and inaction – which he found in death, or in a wet Sunday afternoon alone in a bedsitter.

Sellers, who originally wanted to play James Bond in *Casino Royale* as a slack-faced, slouching sloth, as 'somebody like Tony Hancock, but of course Fleming would never let anybody do it,' admired his fellow actor at least enough to want to try and use his original scribes, Ray Galton and Alan Simpson, for his own ends.* 'We formed a company called Associated London Scripts,' Simpson told me. 'Spike Milligan, Eric Sykes, Ray Galton, and myself. Sellers was going to come in originally, but his financial adviser said Peter would only come in if we all contributed the same amount of money – whereas we'd planned to work on a ten percentage basis and take our chance. No, said the financial adviser, that means Peter will be parting with more actual money than anybody else because he's already making more . . . Hancock wouldn't come in, either. He thought it would all only benefit writers. Frankie Howerd did join us. Ray and I knew Peter well in the early days, when we had this agency with offices in Kensington High Street. Around about 1955, Peter came into the office and announced, "I need £400 or I'll be thrown out of my flat." He was married to Anne, had children, and hadn't paid the rent. Ray, Spike, Eric and I, we all gave him £100 in cash. Off he went. Spike said, "You won't see that again – he'll spend it." Three weeks later, Peter Sellers comes into the office again in a new suit, with £400 which he dealt out note by note, like playing cards. He'd just got the job in *The Ladykillers*, was flush, and came to pay us out. The point of the story is that there was once a Peter Sellers who was broke, before he became a star in America.'

But he was always running down his exchequer. 'He did worry about money,' Milligan explained. 'He'd put the names of his creditors in a hat – if they gave him trouble, he'd tell them their name wouldn't even go in the hat. He was for ever writing letters stalling banks. His credit went on and on and on. He never owned any of those cars; he didn't own a car for over ten years – all "on approval" or HP. . .'

---

* They wrote the screenplay for *Wrong Arm of the Law*.

Sarah Sellers concurs that 'he never curbed his spending. Birthdays or Christmas presents – it depended on how he felt. He'd either bother about you or he wouldn't. He never really went through a rough patch. He might have stopped buying boats for a while, but. . .'

☆ ★ ☆

Sellers, who couldn't settle on a television vehicle – Johnny Speight invented Alf Garnett for him, but he turned it down – and who believed they'd never pay him enough money in any event, grew to hate the medium. He went on variety shows and was paraded as a freak. People were always expecting him to be different, and he was plagued by his apparent plurality – in this was meant to be his excitement. He didn't like it that viewers didn't have to make the effort to go out and see him – TV stars were part of a traffic that included news bulletins, documentaries, weather reports, ads (the 'Freds' were full of spoof commercials) – and his reaction to the undiscriminating blitz was characteristic. He staged a tantrum during a live broadcast.

The programme was called *The April 8th Show* and went out a week earlier, on All Fool's Day (a fact nobody seemed to notice). Sellers had planned to give an impersonation of Harold Macmillan, and he was standing outside a set of 10 Downing Street, in readiness to be accurately pompous and insufferable. He was suddenly told, whilst on the air, that some high-up in the Corporation objected to the Prime Minister's being mocked. Sellers therefore marched up to the camera and, as the credits started to roll, angrily tore up the paper spool which had all the names of cast and crew carefully printed on it and began to create:

> Lies, I tell you, all lies, cheap, lousy, lies. They didn't tell you he was in the show did they – it's all Tom Sloan's fault I tell you – him and his lousy liniment. He's the cause of it – he's another foreigner – going to Ronnie Waldman's party tonight – they are all at it, him, Pat Hillyard, all of them – and him, he's in it. You didn't know about him. They are all gone. They are mad this lot.

It remains to this day the nearest thing to a nervous breakdown anybody has had on air. (It is reminiscent of Peter Finch going bonkers in *Network*.) What can be made out of his rant? Sellers clearly felt there was a conspiracy going on, a secret sect of heads of department and producers, who were thwarting his Supermac mimicry. But as to the specific identity (which keeps switching?) of each and every 'he' and 'him' in his speech – it is the incoherence of paranoia. It was Tom Sloan, however, the Acting Head of Light Entertainment, on BBC Television, who dealt with the matter – and his gravity quite quickly turned the affair into farce, which it was teetering on the edge of anyway, 'Sloan's Liniment' being a popular embrocation for sprains, groin injuries etc..

The first thing Sloan did was to send absolutely everybody he could think of the following memo:

> Acting Head of Light
> Entertainment,
> Television,
> 2nd April 1958

PETER SELLERS

I attach a script of the [*April 8th Show*] transmitted yesterday together with a transcript of what he said at the end of the show as he ripped the roller caption to pieces.

I propose to write to his agents, Lew and Leslie Grade, and express our extreme disapproval of his behaviour and draw their attention to the fact that he committed a breach of contract. I suggest that this is the most we can do on this occasion, but I will certainly see that Mr Sellers is only booked with my consent in the future.

> *Tom Sloan*

The letter of admonishment to the Grades, of the same date, went thus:

Dear Mr Selinger,

At the end of his show last night Peter Sellers made [various] remarks as he tore the roller caption to pieces.

[...]

I would like to draw your attention to Clause 7 of the contract in which it is clearly stated that no remark or interjection can be incorporated in the performance which has not been passed by the producer. Mr Sellers was quite clearly told by the producer that such remarks as he eventually made would not be permitted. He chose to disregard the producer and thus committed, in our view, a breach of contract. In addition to this you will realise that he uttered what could be considered defamatory remarks against a well-known product and since this was done against our clear instructions I would not consider the Corporation responsible in any action that may arise out of such statements.

Finally, I would like to make it quite clear that the fact that my own name was mentioned has nothing whatsoever to do with my attitude. I think it is a clear case of an artist disobeying a producer's instructions and I consider such conduct inexcusable and unprofessional.

> Yours sincerely
> *Tom Sloan*

Sellers, on receipt of the reprimand, pulled his usual stunt, turning himself into a yowling infant, wrongfully accused. He blabbed his case to as many newspaper columnists as would listen. 'I will never appear on BBC television again,' he said. 'I can only work where I am happy. I cannot work where there is such a childish outlook.' To Sloan himself he frothed:

This simply will not do. The allegations which you have seen fit to make are founded on the fallibility of the Corporation's own instructions, and there does not seem to be one scintilla of evidence to justify them, as the following statement of verifiable facts clearly exposes. Because the show on transmission was running early after a six minute cut during the last rehearsal, I was instructed to fill in the last two minutes on an ad-lib basis. This I did in rehearsal and used in substance the same words as were employed during the actual show, except that on the instructions of the producer, a reference to the BBC was omitted from the final performance. These remarks were designed to be in keeping with the general tenor of the last sketch and as the producer concurred in them it seems clear that there can have been no breach of contract (clause 7). At the same time it seems to me somewhat irrelevant to object to my remarks 'about a well-known product' after the show was over, when the producer did not object to the same reference during rehearsals. During the actual show I was asked to ad-lib for a little longer as it was running even earlier than anticipated and the remarks reported to you were spoken and contained the same substance as those spoken during rehearsals, apart form the omissions already referred to. [*Have you followed all that?*] From what I have said you can see that there appears to be a direct conflict between the evidence you have received at a distance and the events which occurred on the spot. This being the case [*Sellers begins to turn the tables*] I am inclined to take a conciliatory view of the whole matter provided that you are prepared to withdraw all statements in your letter derogatory to me, and in particular the references to disobedience and inexcusable and unprofessional conduct contained in the last sentence. It seems to me only right that this should be done [*Sellers has convinced himself of his own innocence*]. If however you are not disposed to do it, then I shall be forced [*by what impetus?*] to press for an impartial inquiry into the whole matter. In addition, allegations of this type should be made to me personally and not to third parties [*i.e., the Grades*]. This increases the gravity of what has happened [*i.e. the fact of the reproof, not anything he, Sellers, had done*] and I must of course reserve all my rights in this connection [*Those of the Mendozas who weren't Estate Agents were lawyers*]. Finally, I have had the closest and friendliest association with the BBC for about ten years now, and I cannot see why this should be upset by the fact that you chose to write an apparently precipitate and ill-judged letter. It is a very small pebble in a very large pool you know [*Who is? What is?*] and if it had not been for your references to unprofessional conduct etc., I daresay it would have come under the heading of debatable trivia. Such references however cannot stand. [*The great-grandson of Daniel Mendoza is out for a bloody restitution of his honour.*]

Sloan replied at length and immediately:

Dear Mr. Sellars [*sic*]

As you say, there appears to be a direct conflict of evidence between the facts as understood by me and by you and as a result I have made further detailed enquiries into the case.

Firstly, let me say at once that from further statements made by the two producers it is clear that you were not instructed not to make the remarks you did. It therefore follows that you were not guilty of disobeying a producer's instructions and therefore of unprofessional conduct in the sense that I meant it. I withdraw this assertion unreservedly and apologise to you for the fact that it was made.

However, both producers who were present in the studio on transmission day are quite adamant that they did not hear you make even the substance of such remarks in rehearsal as you made on transmission and therefore it follows that even if you made them and neither producer heard them, it would hardly be possible for them to instruct you not to say such things. They were also quite adamant that you were not asked to ad-lib for two minutes. On balance, I must adhere to the view that the ad-libbing in which you indulged was not formally agreed by the producer and that it was at least ill-advised if not irresponsible. I cannot believe that you were not aware of the damaging nature of some of these remarks and that to transmit them could not possibly have been within the policy of the Corporation. It is not enough to say that they were in keeping with the general tenor of the last sketch – there is not the slightest reason for using real names in such a context.

As far as the question of my letter being sent to a third party is concerned, I can only say that it has always been BBC practice to send such statements to the person through whom the artist is contracted rather than to the artist himself. In all formal matters concerning artists the Corporation always deals with agents and I saw no reason to depart from this view. As a result, I am sending Dennis Selinger a copy of this letter.

Finally, may I say that at no time did the BBC publicise this affair in any way. A reporter on the 'Daily Express' quoted to me passages from my letter to you and said that he had received them from you. To all enquiries we have said that the matter is closed and that you would be appearing on May 3rd.[*] I would suggest that things should remain that way because I can see no value in pursuing the matter any further.

> . *Tom Sloan*

It must have dawned on Sloan, when he was drafting the above, that he was dealing with either a liar or a lunatic – and that therefore, of course, truth, reason, and remorse were not likely to be forthcoming. His only course of action was to give up, concede defeat, as is acknowledged in the weary tone of his letter to Bill Wills (Sellers' 'financial adviser' in Galton and Simpson's account) of April 14th.

Dear Mr. Wills,

I have made further enquiries in view of the conflict of evidence and, at our end at least, the following seems clear. At no time did either producer give Mr. Sellers permission to make the remarks which were finally transmitted and which were the subject of my complaint. Secondly, the two producers assert that at no time did they ask him to ad-lib for two minutes. I think you must agree that no producer in his senses would have approved such remarks, and that the whole incident was unnecessary.

I do not think that there is anything I can usefully add at this stage. Our attitude is that the subject is closed as far as the Press is concerned, and I do not see how any further statements could serve any useful purpose.

> Yours sincerely
> *Tom Sloan*
> Assistant Head of Light Entertainment,
> Television

---

[*] In *The World's Our Stage*, where he performed the Dressing Room sketch with Cardew Robinson.

Sellers even outmanoeuvred poor old Sloan when that 'impartial enquiry' (which he'd said bluffingly that he wanted) was set up – he simply absented himself and hid out of town, whence he spoke to the press:

> Mr Sloan has now written to say he understands I wasn't given permission to ad-lib. This is nonsense. They don't know what the word means. The BBC said my behaviour was unforgivable and inexcusable. So is theirs. I'm getting half a dozen witnesses to sign a testimony saying I was asked to fill in at the end of the show. There's Graham Stark, Patricia Hayes, Mario Fabrizi . . . I did think of taking legal action – my lawyer friends say I've got a good case. . . .

Stark, in his risibility-tickling memoir, *Remembering Peter Sellers*, mentions the episode (with approval) as an example of the star's anti-authority stance. 'To use a lovely English phrase he never gave a bugger.' But Stark does not try to give the impression that he was there at the time of the outburst; as he tells the story, Sellers' battle with Sloan was something he'd overheard a producer outlining ('with malicious relish') sometime later, during rehearsals of a play he was doing with Warren Mitchell. If Stark had been an actual witness (as Sellers says), then surely, in his very own book, he 'd have testified first-hand, and at more length, about *The April 8th Show*, and would not have distanced himself with hearsay? Secondly, if he'd have been there, he'd have known the ugliness of the scene, and that it involved more than Sellers' 'not caring for power and social position' (i.e. other people's). So why did Sellers fabricate?

What the episode actually demonstrates is not a folkloristic Sellers – Sellers the champion of ordinary actors against the moguls, Sellers making a stand against the grim-visaged BBC generalissimos etc. – but Sellers the inheritor of Dan Mendoza's skill and savagery; a Sellers quite capable of converting fantasy into the only reality he'll abide by. Warren Mitchell said ironically to Stark that all those brainstorms 'did Peter's career a lot of harm!' And yet they *did*. If Mitchell (who made Alf Garnett his own after

Sellers declined the part) had thought about it, his words needed no exclamation mark – Sellers' behaviour, especially during the aftermath, when he became so certain of his version of the matter, ought to have been a worrying sign. It was a prophecy of his treatment of Peter Medak or Blake Edwards, or ultimately of just about everybody, when, overtaken by his genius as an actor, he started to dupe even himself. He'd dream something, and it was so. In this manner he became unanswerable. 'Everyone, who has had the misfortune to talk with people in the heart or on the edge of mental disorder,' wrote G.K. Chesterton, 'knows that their most sinister quality is a horrible clarity of detail, a connecting of one thing with another in a map more elaborate than a maze. If you argue with a madman, it is extremely probable that you will get the worst of it; for in many ways his mind moves all the quicker for not being delayed by the things that go with good judgement . . . He is more logical for losing certain sane affections. Indeed . . . the madman is not the man who has lost his reason. The madman is the man who has lost everything except his reason.'

☆　★　☆

PART THREE
Hope and Glory

Was what attracted him the nature of the job itself, the idea of having a secret self, inaccessible even to his friends, his wives and their former husbands and, as the agent of one intelligence agency inside another, a doubly secret self?

Was it not so much the cause, the vision of a twenty-one-year-old, never re-examined during a busy spy's life, but the love of deceit and by extension, of spying itself that kept him at his dead-letter drops and secret inks all those lonely years?

Murray Sayle, quoted in *Philby: The Life and Views of the KGB Masterspy*, by Phillip Knightley

Chapter Seven
First Photoplays

'I'm very happy away from BBC TV,' he said, and I think it is true to say that, apart from the odd chat show or variety spot, Sellers never did work on the box again.* Perhaps we need to remember what a cumbersome medium it was in those days – the heavy valve-driven out-of-focus cameras which couldn't pan or dolly; the sets constructed from cardboard and string (as if by Bluebottle); the un-editable magnetic strip or piano rolls (or whatever it was they used). Television's monochrome smudge was no place for actors – though it was an ideal home for a new strain of would-be actor: the anchor-man, the game show host, the TV personality. Sellers was in first with a portrait of the type – Wee Sonny MacGregor, in *The Naked Truth*. Sonny is repulsive, in the main, because he thinks himself so attractive. He flirts with the viewers, laughs at the contestants' feeble jokes, but we hardly need his snide, off-camera remarks to Porter (Kenneth Griffith), his dresser and catamite, to know he is insincere and slightly menacing. Sonny doesn't care that he's not quite human. Sellers, by demonstrating how TV presenters exaggerate their good cheer and rehearse their spontaneity, reveals that the likes of Sonny are really cold-hearted bullies, feeding off the adulation and power. TV, like nothing else, satisfies their need for

---

* Though he played the King of Hearts in Jonathan Miller's adaptation of *Alice's Adventures in Wonderland* (which was set in a Victorian madhouse), the form and approach of that production (photographed by Dick Bush and designed by Julia Trevelyan Oman) was cinematic, even if the result was only ever broadcast on television.

337

victims – and an extreme example of *that* type is Chance, in *Being There*, the moron whose very existence has gone by like a self-erasing video tape.

Like Wee Sonny MacGregor, Chance, too, isn't quite real; it is all down to Sellers' magic that illusions of depth and sensitivity are created. (Who else could have pulled it off? Chaplin? Alec Guinness?) All he knows is how to watch. Chance is woken each morning by the screen flickering into life, and he breakfasts and performs his ablutions to Mormon Choirs, Bugs Bunny, yoga classes, or splinters of old movies. There's a TV in the greenhouse when he sprays insecticide over the new leaves, another one in the dining room when the maid fetches him his bowls of baby food; and when he goes to sleep at night, the screen sympathetically decomposes itself into soporific white sound and snow.

TV is Chance's constant companion, interposing itself between his own station-hopping eyes and the real world. When he becomes inadvertently famous, what happens? He goes on TV. Back home, at the mansion he shares with Eve and Benjamin Rand (Shirley MacLaine and Melvyn Douglas), there are TV sets to distract him whilst Eve gets on with her self-administered orgasms; and when Ben falls ill, he is wired up to consoles and monitors – to TV screens. He dies and his spirit disappears, you feel, into the blips and splutter of the Frankensteinian sickroom apparatus. After death, the soul is as bodiless as a TV image.

It is a paradox that Sellers, who didn't much respect television, should not only make one of his best rôles a TV addict, but that he should also decide to personally identify with the character. 'I *knew* Chauncey Gardiner,' he said. Perhaps he meant that he could transform himself and that he had a tendency to copy things he saw and heard. He, like Chance, was malleable. But where Chance simply mimics handshakes and gestures, Sellers' impersonations, of course, could be comprehensive. (Chance is a doped Sellers.) What they actually had in common was a blankness, the emptiness inside. 'I'd often thought of him over the years,' said Sellers, 'but when I had to play Chance, I realised I didn't know what he looked like, or how he spoke' – because what had absorbed him up until then was the more instinctive reaction of knowing how the character felt:

'One thing had escaped me. The computer had said Chance had no identifiable accent or dialect [when a thorough check is ordered on his background by the President of the United States]. So I messed around for a long time with sounds. I have a whole sound set-up, and I spoke into a tape recorder, and then listened. I compared one sound with another sound with another until I found the one I was happy with – very clear enunciation, slightly American, with perhaps a little Stan Laurel mixed in. There's an almost total absence of colour – of inflection or emotion – in the voice. That was the most difficult part to play. The audience knows more about him than anyone because they see him first. They know he's never been out of the house, never been with a woman, a little soft in the head. . . .'

The concept of Chance the idealised man-baby, ignorant of the ways of the world, is what Sellers found appealing. He has no past, therefore no responsibilities. All he needs is food and shelter. Sellers plays a Chance who, when rapidly scanning the TV, hasn't taken in a jot of violent news or bruising docudrama. He's deaf and blind – blind Chance, ha! – to unpleasantness. He may as well have been watching the shifting configurations of clouds, as they turn from camels, to weasels, to very like a whale. 'I had to create a Chance,' said Sellers, 'that would be believable to the intelligentsia, and acceptable to the audience.' Is that how he came up with a benign version of Andy Warhol?

Like Sellers, the real and malignant Warhol, as a professional interviewee, was always stressing his personal nullility. The idea of nothingness and monotony were the basics of his aesthetic. By publicising his blanched face and bleached wig (he was an albino pierrot), deadpan and wedded, like Chance, to junk TV (and a student, besides, of the ways in which the medium alters our perceptions of the world), he claimed to be registering everything and that it was all the same, i.e. nothing. Warhol's pictures are as exciting as wallpaper – an analogy which I'm sure would have pleased him. He enjoyed tape-recording chit-chat (other people transcribed the cassettes and published them as instant books) and popping polaroids (which were blown up, screen printed and marketed as original works of art). Always fiddling with a microphone or a camera, he stage-managed the banal and tried to preserve the tumult of his life as it went hurtling by. All very similar to Sellers, who also threw people away like so many empty soup cans.

☆ ★ ☆

Television is disposable: 'Television didn't really exist then. Radio I'd had enough of. Vaudeville I just hated because I died everywhere I went.' So it had to be films. But films were 'a sort of closed shop. I never really wanted to do much in the theatre, legit. theatre as it's known among some circles. You see, I'd been a great film fan all my life. Whenever I go to America, I carry an autograph book around with me, and I never say, "It's not for me, it's for my sister," you know. I always say, "It's for me – would you sign there?" Like when I first met Walter Pidgeon, or William Powell, and I thought, "Oh God Almighty – William Powell!" I'd sat there and watched him for years, you know, and I mean, it's ridiculous to ask for an autograph, except that you feel you're compelled to. You want to. I'm an old movie buff. I can talk about all the old movies and even the new ones as well. And I wanted to be a movie actor, mainly because I knew that in the future I couldn't survive very well on repetition. Because if you're lucky, you get into a long run on stage and then you're dead. At least I would be. . .'

Sellers had an idea of the theatre as a treadmill, or as the equivalent of a loop of film in which he'd be trapped, constrained forever to repeat his actions and words. Cinema suited his quick temper. Scenes could be broken down into shots, which he'd do once or twice and then forget about. (He could subdivide his work into sketches.) It would be for others to edit, splice, weld and wrench a coherent story out of his fragments. One of the reasons he fell out with Billy Wilder, on the set of *Kiss Me Stupid*, was that the director liked a lot of takes; Sellers felt that this drained his performance of its natural rhythms, or its inspiration. In a strange sort of way, he was not enough of an actor to keep reduplicating a performance – the life went out of what he did if he rehearsed, over-prepared, went over things. I began this book believing that he was the perfect actor – his adaptability, his sensitivity, his observation. Now, deeper into the project, bearing witness to him, I think that perhaps he wasn't an actor at all, in the usual sense – because there was no technique or method. He simply had to become the people he played, and to accomplish this he needed to be emotionally and physically fluid; unhinged, you might say; mad. (The very plausibility of his performances ought to give us pause.) He never troubled to acquire the pro's knack of disguising his boredom. If you asked him to do a scene again, he'd throw a tantrum and push off home. Perhaps he was afraid that, through repetition, he'd collapse and deteriorate like a crumbling, melting sci-fi-monster? He'd lose the trick of it.

'George C. Scott,' said Kubrick, 'could do his scenes equally well take after take, whereas Peter Sellers was always incredibly good on one take, which was never equalled.' That's why, in *Doctor Strangelove*, if you look beyond and behind Sellers, the Russian ambassador or one of the war room throng are often smirking inappropriately – ruining the take, in fact, but because Sellers himself was so good, it had to be printed. (Peter Bull is quite a culprit – if he's in a shot but not speaking he's often out of character).

It was the same in the endless 'Pink Panther' series. One of the ways the films have all the polish of home movies is that, when Clouseau is being sombre, the rest of the cast are often on the edge of corpsing. Not infrequently, the editor has to cut away too soon, to save us the sight of one of Sellers' chums getting the giggles. At other times, we have reverse shots from stand-ins or sequences made by stunt men – Sellers was absent altogether, and Blake Edwards had to go about the day's shoot as best he could. If he was applauded afterwards, for the hilarity of scenes in which he himself did not personally appear (e.g. the Kung Fu fights with Cato), Sellers was again like Warhol, being paid for pictures ingeniously manufactured by doubles.

One of Sellers' early heroes was Jacques Tati (Clouseau wears M. Hulot's hat and mackintosh in homage), but he started to go off the master when he made the pilgrimage to France and found, instead of a loose-limbed real-life comedian, with whom he could have a few laughs, a dedicated and serious artist. 'All he did,' Sellers complained to Max Geldray, 'was talk to me about how great he is.' Evidently, Tati had an ego to mirror Sellers' own; in fact, what Tati had lectured Sellers on, in a typically analytic gallic way, was 'his comic theories. Ploog [Sellers' name for Geldray], the man has no sense of humour!' Worse, he was an actor-director who insisted on being 'free to take and re-take if it wasn't right, absolutely right. . .'*

☆   ★   ☆

Perhaps if live television, which consumes itself as it goes along, had been more technologically sophisticated and less lame-brained, Sellers would have given himself up to it – but then films meant glamour and lush romance, and Sellers wanted to mix his blood with its ghosts: 'I once got a fan letter supposedly from Jeanette McDonald, who as you know is now dead,' he said, looking back in 1967, 'and she asked for some photographs – giving as her address the name of MGM Studios, Culver City, and the number of her dressing room. I knew the fellow there so I wrote off to him and said, "Did she still keep, by any chance, this dressing room?" He said, "No, no". But I looked up, in an early *Picturegoer* annual, a photograph of Jeanette McDonald – and this fan letter had the identical signature.

---

* Sellers' disenchantment with Tati is in fact one of his more sensible criticisms. After the provincial French idylls of *Jour de Fête* and *Les Vacances de Monsieur Hulot*, films like *Traffic* and *Playtime*, made in 70mm, are pretentious and grimly unfunny, consistent with a man who claimed that 'the first rule of burlesque is that illogicality is logical, its strangeness rational and familiar to the people of its world. Its absurdity obeys a meaning to which its followers are the only ones who seem to hold the key' – which is well and good, and could apply to both Clouseau and *The Goon Show* (or anything) – but it is a bit cold. Tati worried away at his rules and lessons, and the mysteriousness of comedy seeped away.

'Much later in New York I met Myrna Loy. I always had a big crush on Myrna Loy, especially in her early films – *The Thin Man* series. This friend of mine, a public relations man, said he knew her and that she was a fan of mine. I thought, how marvellous, I'll take her out to dinner – which I did. But I was terribly stuck for words, I remember. I just couldn't think of anything to say – I was tongue-tied, looking at her – she was much older, but still a very beautiful woman – and I'm sure she was waiting for some sign of intelligent conversation. She said to me, "I've enjoyed you in . . . this that and the other. . ." And the fact that she'd ever seen me in anything I found quite amazing – because in my mind, she was always on the screen – and I had a great problem not asking for her autograph. All I was able to trot out was this, I said: "I hope you don't mind my asking, but did you use the same dog in every film – the one that used to go yacketty-yack around your feet? Asta I think he was called?"'

And before Myrna could take another spoonful of scallops, Sellers had launched himself into an impersonation of Nick and Nora Charles, bantering on the Twentieth Century ('All animals must go in the baggage car' – 'That's not an animal. It's my fur coat' – 'If it can wag its tail it goes in the baggage car') after which to-do, the actress informed him: 'No, we used a different dog in almost every film. They'd get trodden on, you know.'

The sophisticates from *The Thin Man*, Dry Martinis always within arm's reach, were parodied (an unnecessary development) by Maggie Smith and David Niven in *Murder by Death*, the revelry where Sellers played Sidney Wang, aka Charlie Chan, in a tangerine robe. Like the gathering of famous sleuths at Truman Capote's mansion (address: 22 Twain) in that picture, Sellers found America itself awash with celebrity, and he was unable, or unwilling, to discriminate between the rôles people had played and the actors as real people in their own right. When he met a star, he expected to be treated to a continuation of their performances. Sometimes the heat was indeed still being given off: 'I remember talking to Gary Cooper about his Deusenberg [motor car]. I met him once. We were doing some rough shooting out in the country. He'd been a fantastic idol for me, ever since I saw him in *The Plainsman*, with Jean Arthur, and he was killed by Porter Hall at the end . . . He got these two birds with each barrel. Bang! Bang! No effort at all. Didn't have the gun ready – just strolling along – Bang! Bang! – they were down. It really wouldn't have mattered to me if he'd got a catapult out, but the fact that he was as good with a gun as he was on the screen meant an awful lot . . . Effortlessly marvellous man. I really did imagine he was doing it with six-shooters at the time. . .'

At the other extreme, Sellers was crestfallen to find Stan Laurel living modestly in a little flat in a modest LA suburb; he was so unregarded, the address (849 Ocean Avenue, Santa Monica) and telephone number were still listed in the city directory. Sellers didn't want to know him after that. (Did he expect to be asked to help lug a piano across an Alpine ravine, or what?) He needed stars to retain their auras. When Tati wrote to him after their encounter ('I was ready to lie down and die for Tati! But when I met Tati! I've never been so disappointed. He's not at all like Hulot'), he didn't even have the common courtesy to reply. Stars, after all, are heavenly bodies, and Sellers, wished to zoom to such a supernatural height – to become a darling of the Gods, an *enfant du paradis*, in Marcel Carné and Jacques Prévert's phrase, his life encompassed by harlequinades, the acting and miracles never stopping. (How I'd love to have seen him play the comic Christ in Milligan's scheme for a Biblical epic called *God Ha! Ha!* The Sermon on the Mount and loaves and fishes bit was going to have been done as a Tommy Cooperish clumsy-clever sleight of hand magic trick, and a lot of mileage may be derived from the concept of the Almighty as a sadistic stage illusionist.)

But knocking on Laurel's door in Hollywood ('Laurel and Hardy – my two great favourites – very under-rated – the two funniest men who ever lived, probably') or escorting Myrna Loy to Peter Duchin's opening at the Maisonette ('where he was rather shy and as full of wonder about my career as any fan. He even asked for an autographed photograph,' Miss Loy confirms), or scouting across the underbush with Gary Cooper, pointing Purdeys at partridges at high noon – all that (and *that* included getting a better table at Sardis than Ray Bolger, because the erstwhile scarecrow, 'he ain't got no picture playing anywhere'), *all that* was a few years hence. For now he was in a makeshift studio situated somewhere in the Maida Vale/Marylebone region of London, making his very first photoplay, a short called *Let's Go Crazy*.

☆　☆　☆

If the documentary style of *London Entertains* made it look like bootleg film smuggled out of a secret meeting, the atrocious quality of *Let's Go Crazy*, also shot and given extreme unction in 1951, makes it reminiscent of a lost German Expressionist classic. The nitrate stock bubbles and burns as you watch. The photography is not simply blurred, it is fogged. You expect the grandsires of Dr Strangelove, Dr Caligari and Rotwang, the mad scientist in *Metropolis*, to materialise out of the smoke. The soundtrack music is atonal, and when we get a glimpse of the orchestra, the strings wearing legal wigs and the brass wearing cavemen wigs, and when we notice that, in the middle of the band, somebody is cooking over a campfire stove, we are ready to be told that imps like Tristan Tzara and Louis Aragon have collaborated on the script. There are piano keys sticking to people's faces, a Margaret Dumont type clashing the cymbals, and a little white-faced clown on the triangle.

Is the night-club set purposely stylised, with its eerie lighting effects and the jutting cut-off angles, or simply ineptly painted? For we are to be treated to a sort of abstract cabaret, with some of the performers and most of the guests being played by Sellers and Milligan. 'Do you serve crabs here?' Sellers, dressed up as Groucho, inquires. 'Well, serve my friend,' he says, getting a crustacean out of his pocket. 'He hasn't eaten for three weeks.' Such boffs are interrupted by some appealing jazz interludes, dreadful Irish ballads and an execrable French crooner – identified by the credit-roll as perpetrated by real artistes called Wallas Eaton, Manley & Austin, and Freddie Mirfield's Garbage Men. What seems to have wandered straight out of continental revue is a pair of acrobats who try to kill each other to a Rossini overture. It is quite impressive, especially when the man thrashes the woman with a violin and the lady retaliates by jumping up and down on his lungs with a pair of high heels. How accurately choreographed is it, though? Do they stop dancing mid-way and start scrapping for real? Meantime, Milligan, as a waiter, is in the background shaving a diner, and Sellers, presumably as himself (owlish, meek), glances at a menu. He then reappears as a bosom-heaving old lady, swathed in more sail-cloth than the Cutty Sark – Crystal Jollibottom, Municipal Dustcart Queen of 1951. Asked if she has a reservation, she is indignant. 'Reservation? What do you think I am? A Red Indian?' After some business with her fox furs catching fire, we then squeeze to the film's main scene – Sellers as an East End spiv (his vocal delivery Max Miller's) twitting Milligan, who is now a posh Etonian. Milligan, in fact, is pretty terrible and stilted, but Sellers, a slob in a kipper tie and a porkpie hat, times his off-hand insults to perfection. 'You've got a complaint? There's nothing wrong with this chicken that medical science won't cure, I'm telling you.'

Groucho-Sellers then lopes across the café: 'What I'm about to do has been censored,' he tells us. He exits, a girl screams, and he pops back to say, 'It's a shame you missed that scene.' Sellers is then the East Ender again, inquiring if 'You like potatoes?' – 'Worship them,' says Milligan. 'Blimey,' says Sellers, 'potato worshipper 'ere.' (I don't know why I find that so funny, but I do.) He then picks up the Etonian's food, looks at the camera, and nonchalantly eats. The affair flickers to a finish with Groucho tossing a fizzing bomb into the orchestra: 'This is one picture that isn't going to have a happy ending.'

Let's Go Crazy is so amateurishly done – it lasts thirty-two minutes and probably took less time than that to create – Sellers clean forgot about its existence. But as an experiment in visual and verbal non-sequiturs, it is something of a curious success, and you have to squint very hard to tell it is Sellers behind the various disguises, he is so deliberative. (Sometimes he is in the orchestra, at other moments he's in a false nose and moustache as the maitre d'.)

It is close in spirit to the well-known *Running, Jumping and Standing Still Film* – i.e. an attempt to put on celluloid what they'd enjoyed doing in radio. The director, Alan Cullimore, went on to produce, later the same year, the film which Sellers considered his debut, his 'very first appearance in front of a camera, if you like to call it an appearance, [*Penny Points to Paradise*]. Spike, Harry, myself, Alfred Marks, Bill Kerr and Paddy O'Neill once made a film for £100 each in Brighton Studios, . . . which was about the football pools. It really was a terrifyingly bad film! I played an old colonel of about sixty, but the make-up man was unable to make me look any older than I was. All he could do was to make my hair white. I looked like a very young man with white hair.'

He's rather better than that – his fatness (as with Hancock) already put years on him. Centre of attention, however, is the South Welsh flywheel, Secombe, who, as Harry Flakers, goes to stay at a Brighton guest house with his pal Spike Donnely (Milligan). The duo are fleeced out of the winnings by forgers and fortune hunters, and the frantic result has all the wit of a sub-George Formby or Norman Wisdom quota quickie. 'Harry, Spike and I were billed for it as the White Faced Coons – the word Goons hadn't registered yet: "Chocolate Coons or White Coons: Peter Sellers acts, Harry Secombe sings, and Spike Milligan plays the fool in *Penny Points to Paradise*." It was a pretty shocking movie and yet we thought – Hollywood here we come! We thought that, but we didn't come – neither did the film. . .'

The comic impotence is exemplified by such exchanges as:

SELLERS	*[lots of screams]*: Madam! This is a bathroom and not a nursery!
SECOMBE:	Another night like last night and I'll be a nervous wreck. Morning, Sheila – oh, I've got a terrible head.
PADDY O'NEILL:	It's an odd shape, but it will pass in a crowd. I'm just off to town, is there anything you want?
SECOMBE:	Morning papers.

PADDY O'NEILL: Mourning – somebody dead?
                       [*Milligan swings into shot as Tarzan.*]

You'd have to put your own head together with Susan Sontag and George Steiner to come up with a clever exegesis. There's simply too much plot, and Sellers said, of the retired military con-man he played, Major Arnold P. Fringe, 'it was a sort of character part – running around saying, "Ah, there you are, Harry m'boy!"; I didn't know what to do with my hands. If you see the film, you'll find me waving and pointing. "Ah, there you are, Harry m'boy!" Every time he came in the room, whenever anything was happening – "Ah, there you are, Harry m'boy!" Jimmy Grafton, who collaborated on the script,* he used to write that at the beginning of every piece of dialogue of mine. I'd come out of the loo saying, "AAAhh! There you are, Harry m'boy!"'

MILLIGAN: Harry, Harry – my name's Spike. You know, Major, this is wearing a bit thin.

SELLERS: Is it my boy? So it is. Ah well, we can soon rectify that. Two large gins please. [*Harry and Spike leave, fleeing the pub bore.*]

SELLERS   [*to himself*]: Ah, you'd never think it, would you? They all seem to have contracted the dreadful affliction, the Spondooliks. A most pernicious disease. The natives used to get it in their bazaars. They used to go mad and bite dogs. We had to shoot them. Sometimes we had to shoot the dogs as well. They weren't very pleased about it, you know. . .

---

* With John Ormond, whose Welsh accent Sellers used in *Only Two Can Play*.

Bloodnok, of course; but also the nutty nostalgia of General Fitz-john, in *Waltz of the Toreadors*, whose persona is here and intact. 'I'm always playing old Colonels, actually,' Sellers commented, and he's at it again in *Down among the Z Men*, made, as were all these little shorts and featurettes, for an impresario called E.J. Fancey. Sellers had scant respect for the minor mogul: '. . . we were working with crap. We thought, it didn't matter what you did, it's Hollywood! This is it! But this film fellow said, "They don't understand that Goon stuff . . . You've got to give it to them on the nail. And don't do none of them funny voices, because they don't understand 'em, either. . . ."'

Hence, after the glancing Dada of *Let's Go Crazy*, the obviousness of the sequels. Perhaps the biggest surprise of *Down among the Z Men* is the straight heroic role assigned to Harry Secombe – here portraying a grocer's assistant called Harry Jones. The point about Seagoon is that he was a screechy take-off of the romantic lead. Here, however, when one of the WRACs [Women's Royal Army Corps], played by a member of The Television Toppers, starts to mime at the piano, Jones-the-tenor mucks in, and doesn't muck about. We frost over as we do during the musical breaks in a Marx Bros. film.

This would seem an example of what Sellers meant, when he said that Goonery was suppressed – except that Secombe's cinema career, such as it is, has been full of attempts to render him lovable and gallant: *Davy*, for example, made at Ealing, in which he was a variety crooner offered an uplifting new start at Covent Garden; or *Sunstruck*, where he introduced Welsh Male Voice Choirs to a school in the Australian outback. In *Down among the Z Men*, his rôle suggests that within the roly-poly singer and good sport of *The Goon Show*, somebody very like Albert Herring has always been trying to escape – somebody earnest and sympathetic is behind the imbecile's mask. We feel for him when he's ordered to 'get back behind the cheese where you belong', because we've heard of Jones' private detective agency sideline, and it's amidst stirring adventures in that area where he wants to be at home. (It is as if Bluebottle's aspirations have been added to Seagoon's – and to Sellers' of the 'Selsman' Ilfracombe days.)

The early scenes, with Jones being fleeced of his savings by B-movie villains (one of whom is played by Andrew Timothy), and with Bentine's Osric Pureheart getting his grocery list mistaken for a secret formula, were shot on location in what might have been Britten's Aldeburgh. The streets are leafy and dappled, there is little motor traffic, and the shop fronts are quaint and Edwardian. I remember all this from when I first saw the film – it was slipped on to the TV schedules one Saturday morning, and I was staring hard, not sure that I wanted the Goons to have faces. They don't. They have grimaces. That's why the spreading chestnut trees, and so on, have remained with me all these years – compared with Secombe's idiot boy and Bentine's squint and explosion of black curls, the naturalness of nature stood out. And so does Sellers. Everybody does their utmost to be clottish, but his old colonel is on parade with remarkably little fuss. 'Sugar, daddy?' his orchidaceous step-daughter asks. 'By Jove, yes,' he says, by no means over-doing the double-entendre.

Sellers, as he would in his mainstream films, keeps still and leaves being frantic to the others. (He sits down for his scenes and, on the one occasion he stands, gets a laugh for his extraordinary jodhpurs.) Bentine, playing a character who is too brainy to walk straight, and who keeps a stuffed badger in his tent, talks nineteen to the dozen and is wretched; Milligan, as Private Eccles, enjoys the conscript comedy elements (the jazz riff reveille; supervising the WRACs' PT drill), and is already re-living the war. But it is only Sellers, as the military head of Warwell Atomic Research Station ('Fearfully Secret. Spies Please Knock') who is truly interested in giving a performance. He is suddenly acting properly. Reserved, slowly examining his food, or just posing at his desk, clutching at his heart in surprise, there are no eye-catching mannerisms – but it is exactly his large, sad eyes which we are forced to meet. Then, suddenly, we are yanked back into the toshery about espionage and undercover weapons, which soon goes to pieces and the remainder of the spool is given up to Bentine's chair-back routine, which I'll not mind never seeing again; and Sellers, casting off his old colonel, does a routine about American soldiers discussing a plan to escape a Panzer division. Decades drop off him as, switching helmets, he impersonates a lieutenant and a private. He alters instantly – the uninterrupted mid close-up shot allows us to marvel at and grasp the detail and economy of his changes of expression. It is as fascinating as those stop-motion sequences in old horror movies, when Lon Chaney Jr gets transformed into the wolf man. Except that here there are no special effects, as such. It is possible to see just how Sellers could have accomplished his war-time officer duplicities.

☆   ★   ☆

Sellers was morose. 'The essence of Goonery must be captured,' he argued, 'or we're liable to lose a lot of adherents. Which is just why the two attempts to date to make Goon films have, in the long run, done us a disservice, although they made a large amount of money. *Penny Points to Paradise*, which cost £9,000, has made, up to the present time [1955], £75,000. *Down among the Z Men* has also amassed profits running into thousands. In neither film was the story ours, nor had we any say in the direction. Until a brilliant director with an acute sense of contemporary humour, who would be prepared to let us co-direct, comes along, *The Goon Show* must remain purely radio entertainment; by allowing ourselves to be presented into unsuitable films, we end by pleasing no one. . .'

Television, as we know, offered only a limited solution ('Television is a muddle at the moment,' he said. 'It's where one goes to earn a quick pound'), and he had high hopes for their next outing, *The Case of the Mukkinese Battle Horn*, a twenty-nine minute hors d'oeuvre, made in November 1955. It was the better for not dragging its material out beyond the length of an episode of *The Goon Show* – and, it must be said, the lack of Secombe and Bentine, and their one-note performances, is for the better. (Secombe was busy on his TV show and was in demand for concerts.) In their stead is Dick Emery, who fits in well with the absurdist style. Indeed, unlike

Secombe and Bentine, he seems to know that *not* being too flamboyant is the key to comedy. He takes a number of roles – Nodule,
a museum curator, Mr Crimp, the janitor, etc. – and his jolly countenance, the obvious pleasure he's taking in dressing up, is, like
Secombe's giggle, infectious. We don't mind him.

Emery went on to have a successful TV career. He devised a gallery of popular characters, including pooves, bovver boys, toothy
vicars, and a vamp called Mandy, ('OOh, you are awful – but I like
you!' was the catchphrase, as she smacked a man with her handbag), and yet Sellers was still so much superior to this sort of artiste.
Why? Because Emery never went further than caricature. You
never needed to believe – it never crosses your mind – that his
funny folk had lives and thoughts beyond the sketch in which they
appear. Emery's acting was bright and colourful, like a saucy seaside postcard. He prospered, I think, because he knew his
limitations. He had no intense depths. He didn't need to excavate
anything except his enjoyment of drag and daffy costumes. His old
codger, Lampwick, for example, looked the twin of Sellers' William
Mate Cobblers; but where Sellers' infuriating senior citizen had recesses of frayed pride and melancholia, Lampwick was nothing
more than an elderly lecher with a filthy cough.

Off stage, as it were, he was rather more like Sellers, at least in
his appetites. He married five showgirls and said, 'I need a woman
who is prepared to put up with my miseries and my worries. I'm a
pig to live with, completely selfish. It's been murder sometimes and
I've paid in pain and money. I was looking for someone near perfection and I never found her, of course. I was looking for a mother
replacement, with a sexual life as well.' Such words could have been
taken right out of Sellers' mouth; yet the crucial difference between
the two actors is that Sellers' personality and flaws seep into his
work, whereas Emery's lies and guilt never did. Sellers' pent-up
feelings gave the art of comic acting new dimensions; Emery acted
to get away from the obligations and ramifications of a messy
private life. When he grew bored of Mandy, Lampwick, etc., and
refused another BBC series, in ridding himself of his characters he

was ridding himself of his illusions. He immediately proceeded to drop dead from a heart attack – as Sellers did, when he, too, could no longer fool himself that he was ague-proof.

Emery, said Milligan, 'was the last of a line. He was one of the very few people we would ever use in *The Goon Show* if one of us ever had to duck out.' In *The Case of the Mukkinese Battle Horn*, he has a matchless moment as Maurice Plonk, and has to do nothing more than wear a blobby plasticine nose and stare into the camera, with all the self-consciousness of a patient wheeled on as a demonstration model during a feature for medical students. He has nothing to do with the story – it's simply that 'We thought you'd like to see what a real idiot looked like.' The rest of the bunch, it therefore follows, must be contrived idiots, idiots under cover, fake idiots. Perhaps that's one of the Goon beliefs? There are too many people in positions of power who refuse to acknowledge their idiocy. Milligan said that the starting point for their humour was 'one man shouting gibberish in the face of authority, and proving by fabricated insanity that nothing could be as mad as what passes for ordinary living'. In this particular short, the target for satire is the police.

'Let us take a look at the world famous CID at work through the medium of a true real-life case,' says Sellers, in his newsreel voice-over voice. 'A factual documentary record . . .', about the theft of a tuba inlaid with emeralds, golden slave bangles, and priceless Grecian vases from Woolworths . . . Sellers' main character is Detective Superintendent Quilt (Milligan is his assistant constable), who moves purposefully, is heavily moustached and homburg-hatted, who is serious, and seriously dense. He is a Scotland Yard trial gallop for Inspector Clouseau. 'There's been a robbery,' he is told. 'Really? Anything stolen,' he inquires briskly. Arriving at the scene of the crime, his driver leaves him short of the door and he has to trot up to the museum entrance, pretending that he fully intended to be deposited half way down the street. The police photographers arrive, snap Quilt and Milligan in a wedding day pose, and hurry away again.

Milligan also appears as Catchpole Burkington, an actor in silent movies, who has placards for speech, and who causes the film to start to jerk and flicker – a technique re-used in *Ghost of the Noonday Sun*, where a long prologue sequence is shot in grainy black and white and scored for a pit piano. I don't think Catchpole advances the plot, which is no doubt why he has been invited to make a Goonish guest-appearance. Sellers and Milligan were exerting themselves to incorporate accident and irrelevance, even ropiness. The opus was made at Merton Park Studios, and whenever anybody visited the set, John Penington, the producer, would tell them that the actors were 'exhilarating to work with – but terribly trying. They're changing the gags all the time.' Later he and the director, Joe Sterling, put it more succinctly: 'They're mad.'

He was not totally jesting; half way through the shooting period, Milligan had one of his mental breakdowns. Sellers never quite forgave him and lost faith in the film – going on record to call *The Case of the Mukkinese Battle Horn* 'a very unfortunate affair which I would like to explain. This was going to be a short film made exactly as we wanted it. We had a group of filmmakers who were interested in doing this with us; but at the time it went to the floor, my colleague Spike Milligan was taken ill and we were left with an uncompleted script. These people couldn't put off the shooting date as they had already booked the studios, so we had to go ahead and literally write from day to day on the floor, which spoilt it. We had about three ideas in the beginning of the film which were good, but the rest was made up as we went along. This is no way to make a picture. . .' (But at one time he'd think it was.)

To put the blame on Milligan for what was, on the set, his own frivolity, is another example of his essential need to displace blame. It was Sellers who, if asked a question, would peer through a large magnifying glass and say, 'Follow that floor!'; Sellers who caused Pam Thomas, playing an ingénue rôle, to weep because 'Nobody tells you anything. I think that I'm in this scene now – but I don't know'; Sellers who goaded Barbara Cole, the continuity girl, into a shouting match: 'You've changed a line in that scene, haven't you?' she asked, despairing. ('You're privileged they've told you,' a props

man said, trying to comfort her when Sellers snarled an acknowledgement.) Milligan, and no wonder, retreated behind his Eccles
facade. 'Fine, fine, fine,' was all they could get out of him.

Sellers kept coming up with wild ideas, and then sulked when
nobody felt like using them. He wanted to have an animated front
door ambling its own way down a busy street. It comes to a halt –
and a man puts two milk bottles outside it. ('Is this funny?' asked
Joe Sterling, genuinely puzzled.) Then he said he wanted a window
frame standing alone in a field. A man draws up the sash, pokes his
head through, and takes gulps of fresh air. ('Are you laughing? Are
you holding your sides? Does this kind of thing make your jaw
ache?' Sterling continued.) Inconsequential gags like these make up
the eleven minutes of *The Running, Jumping and Standing Still Film*,
but for now, their absence from *The Case of the Mukkinese Battle
Horn*, like the non-appearance of Secombe or Bentine, is nothing to
mourn. For, despite Sellers' complaints, the film isn't a total dud.
Sir Jervis Fruit, the Assistant Chief Commissioner, is an amusing
portrait of Hercules Grytpype Thynne, from *The Goon Show*. As he
reclines on a chaise longue and speaks to Quilt on a white telephone, he is a send-up of other people's send-ups of homosexuals
and Liberace. He rolls his eyes and wears a smoking jacket with
braided cuffs. Fruit tells Quilt (Sellers talking to Sellers) to try looking for the battle horn in a pawn shop – an excuse for Sellers to
convert himself into Henry Crun. The hunchbacked elder statesman, in tasselled night cap, pince-nez, and Santa Claus wig, creeps
about his junk-strewn room (reminiscent of Peg and Bill's flat) and
tells Quilt that 'you can't get the wood, you know,' for battle horns.*
Sellers' Crun evidently came into being after a raid on the

---

* A Mukkinese battle-horn makes a reappearance in *Young Frankenstein*, when
Marty Feldman blows into one on the castle roof. This is one of a number of
Sellers homages in Mel Brooks' films – gratitude, perhaps, for Sellers' champion-
ing of *The Producers*. 'Last night,' he'd told *Variety*, 'I saw the ultimate film . . . it
is the essence of all great comedy, combined in a single motion picture!' What
was the appeal? The musical-comedy Nazis could be out of *The Goon Show*; the
Swedish secretary reminded him of Britt Ekland; and Gene Wilder's neuras-
thenic rages and crying jags reminded him of himself.

make up box. There must be pounds of the stuff on his face – and is it *his* face? To get Quilt and Crun into the same frame, was a double used?

The ending, a duel using a rapier and a revolver ('Touché', 'Three-ché'), is as random and frantic as the chase-in-a-wax-museum of *Penny Points* or the laughing-gas-making-everybody-collapse playout of *Z Men*. We are meant to be in Max's Club. Eccles does a Salome dance ('O fairest of the fair, O sublime siren', says Quilt) and, when the fight starts, musketeers and cavaliers come in from nowhere and join the fray, like they do during the pandemonium which concludes *Casino Royale*.

☆   ★   ☆

The end credits inform us that we have not seen either Freda Clench, an underwater soprano, nor Jim Pills, a saxophonist, let alone Lurgi the Wonder Dog, whose tricks we can hardly guess at. We might also add that we've seen little of what would make Sellers a revelation – his scope; his renewals; his audacity – but in fact there *is* something extra and significant about his appearances in these bits of piffle. Already he is attuned to the audience. This was not lost on a man called John Redway, the casting director at Associated British Pictures, a powerful conglomerate based at Elstree, which was partly owned by Warner Bros. and Pathé.[*] He it was

---

[*]   *John Redway & Associates Ltd.,*
    16 Berners St., London

    3rd November 1989

    Dear Roger Lewis,

    Thank you for your letter of the 26th of October.

    I am sorry to tell you that John Redway died in August. He was indeed a Casting Director at ABPC and was the person who persuaded the Boulting Brothers (with whom he had worked closely) to cast Peter Sellers.

    I'm sure John would have been happy to talk to you and in any case we would wish you every success with [your book].

    Yours sincerely,
    David Booth

Redway's was the first death amongst my expert witnesses. There have been who could perceive, before anybody else, that Sellers was being limited by *The Goon Show* and its spin-offs, and he suggested the actor for parts in, amongst other projects, two pictures planned by Group Three, a production company set up in 1951, funded by the National Film Finance Corporation (i.e. government grants), to knock off low budget features stocked with new (i.e. cheap) talent. Sellers didn't need much encouraging to hie himself hither to Beaconsfield Studios. 'As an actor,' he panted, 'I have always wanted to plan a career, distinct from Goonery, in films' – and he made a start in *Orders are Orders*, as a batman, and 'going a little further along the same lines . . . *John and Julie* provides me with another character part into which I felt I could get my teeth. . .'

What other performer would have used such tiny rôles as an opportunity to stretch himself? Hancock certainly didn't bother. He's in *Orders are Orders*, fat, slouched, and liverish, as Lieutenant Cartload, the despairing conductor of the military brass band. His scenes are not the least bit funny, though they are designed to be. A little of his round-shouldered grimacing, when the musicians hit duff notes, goes a long way. (Eric Sykes, credited for 'additional dialogue', is on cymbals.) Sellers, however, in a background rôle as Private Goffin, bored to death behind the bar in the officers' mess, is full to bursting with inventiveness and assurance. Hugely bloated, Goffin is not immediately recognisable as Sellers – he looks like Lou Costello. (We see why Peg kept force feeding him – to make him unattractive to women.) He is always snacking on pistachio nuts, crisps, or biscuits. Sellers has no vanity here. He has a terrible haircut, with various shaven patches, and speaks in a North London whine. When there's nobody special about he is slow and sullen; if an officer appears he jumps to and is ingratiating – his voice, suppressing a giggle, is virtually Bluebottle's.

'I know things about our Adj. a bloke never even heard of,' he

---

dozens since – though fortunately I took their statements before they dropped off the twig. The wear and tear on Sellers' contemporaries, who at the time of writing (1993) have an average age of about seventy, shows how swiftly a biographer becomes a historian – or a necrologist.

says, and Sellers is able to convey how Goffin feels when he's abashed. Another actor might have made the batman sly or sneaky; Sellers's Goffin is a mock-innocent. What he enjoys best about the film crew which has invaded the 1st Battalion, the Royal Loyal's barracks, is the chance it offers him to, first, get one over on the likes of Captain Harper and Colonel Bellamy – the latter played by Raymond Huntley with his impeccable, customary sneer – and, secondly, dragooned as an extra (one of a hundred and fifty men at a 'bob a knob'), he can dress up, play-act, and have adventures, which is precisely what Goffin is in the army for. Attired as a Martian and toting a cardboard gun, Bluebottle's games are complete.

The film director, Waggermeyer, is played by Sid James. He barks and rasps and is thoroughly unpleasant; he has a long way to go before he can loosen up and become the louche hero of the *Carry On* series. But the idea of a movie mogul muscling in on people's lives, causing maximum disruption, is one Sellers himself would return to in *After the Fox*, when Aldo Vanucci infiltrates an Italian town with his floodlights and cameras. Here, the scene where Raymond Huntley objects to the noise and muddle, reeling off military jargon about the necessity of acquiring various permissions and dockets, is one exactly mirrored in the later picture, when Sellers' Vanucci encounters the red tape of a local policeman. Vanucci loses his temper and throws mounds of official papers into the air. In *Orders are Orders*, Huntley is the one to explode. 'You can go to the devil, sir!' he huffs and puffs at James, the ploy to beflummox the director with bureaucratic regulations having failed. We do not, however, when watching the exchange, attend much to either Waggermeyer or Col. Bellamy. They are upstaged by Sellers. He does nothing more than float by, bearing a teapot, but his silent chortle – his enjoyment of both other men's discomfiture – steals the scene. As I said above, Goffin is a background character – and yet it's only his reactions which give the farce any perspective or depth. That's to say, only Sellers gives an original performance. The love-interest between the officers and the starlets is totally devoid of interest, for example. Brian Reece as Captain Harper,

Margot Grahame as Wanda Sinclair, and Maureen Swanson as Joanne Delamare, would barely pass muster as actors in a maladroit dubbed-from-the-German soap on live TV. Their stillborn court-ship is, again, thrown off-key by Sellers, who confides in Harper's girl that 'He don't give much trouble once you got his spurs off' – a line he delivers with a mischievous glint, and which Wanda can't meet or acknowledge at all.

Sellers takes over his sections in this film, spreads across them, just as the movie makers insinuate themselves into the army camp. During a reception in the mess, when all the officers are jabbering together, Goffin unpacks a picnic hamper of refreshments and serves out glasses of wine on a silver salver. It is his unhurried pace ('Sherry, sir?' – 'Not just now, Goffin') which gives the scene its tempo and measure. And when Waggermeyer brings his starlets on to the premises, to introduce them to the mess, Goffin clomps his way along a passage at the rear, Sellers timing his movements per-fectly, so that he arrives in close-up for his line. 'Who is this gentleman?' asks a moll with pointy bosoms. 'This is Mr Goffin, my assistant,' says Private Slee (Bill Fraser). 'He means colleague,' cor-rects Sellers, the scene now his.

What makes his performance noteworthy is that the liberties he takes, as an actor, perfectly match the calm and quiet insurrections of the character. (Later, famous, he'd not serve his rôles so self-lessly; it would be his own egotism which inflated, say, Fritz Fassbender, in *What's New, Pussycat?*, Evelyn Tremble, in *Casino Royale*, or Sir Guy Grand, in *The Magic Christian*.) It is thus unfair when the Colonel finds Slee and Goffin in their spaceman gear and lets them have it: 'You are just a couple of ordinary slow-moving Englishmen, thoroughly stupid and entirely lacking in any kind of sense. . . .' The rebuke has no particular resonance – it is snobbish and nasty – because Sellers, hidden within the silver suit, is lost from us. Goffin has no opportunity to roll his eyes (or whatever) and mutely throw Huntley's scorn back at him. After all we've seen, the reprimand is out of order – but in this film orders are bound by social class – and the underlying scheme of *Orders are Orders* is everybody in the audience's experience of the war and National Service. What could have been a satire on the imbecilities of obedience, however, is not undertaken. (There is even a speech about the importance of military discipline, in every rank, at the end, as people yell 'orders are orders' down the chain of command.) When the sci-fi props and junk, the ray guns and rockets, clog the barracks, and the soldiers are amazed at having to manhandle the stuff about ('Orders is orders' snaps a Sergeant-Major to a pop-eyed private who turns out to be Donald Pleasence), the joke is on the flummery and excess of film-makers, *American* film-makers, no less, and not on the army as an institution. (I refuse to believe that *Orders are Orders*, which was of course itself a feature film, was busy playing an ingenious little joke on itself – such a paradox is miles beyond its sphere.)

☆ ★ ☆

If *Orders are Orders* relied on everybody's brush with the call-up and being in uniform, *John and Julie*, the other Group Three effort, leans on the recent quasi-mystical ritual of the Coronation. The story, about a young brother and sister running away from home to see Elizabeth II crowned, ought to be (as Constance Cummings says) 'unbearable goo from beginning to end'. Actually, it is not. I surprised myself by much enjoying it – it is a hallucination of the early Fifties, and it is full of golden, harvesty colours. Perhaps the film succeeds because it has the inner-strength of a fairy story? The two blonde children (played by Colin Gibson and Lesley Dudley), journeying alone across the English countryside, borrowing bikes and sneaking on to charabancs, are resourceful and good, like Hansel and Gretel; they are babes in the wood, drinking from streams and hiding amongst the trees. Sid James' obnoxiousness ('Mabel, I want my dinner!') comes in handy for the rôle of Mr Pritchett, their step-father; and Constance Cummings, as an American tourist, travelling from the Southampton Ocean Terminal up to London, does office as a sort of good fairy, helping the youngsters on their way, her voice creamy and clipped.

Intermixed with the tale is documentary footage of the Queen processing to the Abbey – she is the goddess Gloriana in her coach. We see people like Churchill who, in his Garter robes, resembles Sellers' Crystal Jollibottom or the Duchess of Grand Fenwick; and we notice that the yellows and scarlet of the carriages and soldiers, in the stock sequences, are co-ordinated with Julie's glowing ringlets, John's palomino pony, Julie's mustard coat and John's primrose flags. There are posters of the Queen, in a buttercup ball gown sparkling with canary jewels, in shop windows; the rural buses have a saffron livery; and Molly Weir's guest house is decorated with bright yellow shields. All this creates a landscape that gleams and glows – and Sellers, as the young Dorset bobby on the children's trail, is named P.C. Diamond.

Sellers is way down the cast roster, between obscurities like Joseph Tomelty and Patric Doonan, about whom I can recall nothing at all. Again, it is a background rôle which he turned into a commentary on the foreground action. Cheerful and chubby, with brown, steamed hair, he ambles so slowly, he might be in a trance – Sellers has Diamond caught up in the film's fairy-story mood; he is bewitched, as the entire sceptre'd isle is on Coronation Day, and as such not once does he voice a fear for the children's safety. When Sid James comes into the station and yells at him, frowning and dreaming up punishments, Sellers leans across the counter and goes on reading his newspaper, unperturbed. He hardly looks up. He takes his time. 'The police have their methods, you know,' he eventually sighs, unflappable, like Shakespeare's Dogberry. A little later, he stands at the back of a group gathered in the bicycle shop, waiting for the children to phone. He sips his tea, looks at the Tri-Ang toy signs, and smiles to himself at Sid James' further outbursts – a silent criticism of the angry parent. Diamond is full to bursting with composure and confidence; he quietly enjoys the adventure. Sellers makes him seem almost blessed. Round and snug, to use a phrase of W.H. Auden's, in the den of himself, he is an early version of the Rev. Smallwood or Chance the gardener: characters with an inner, spiritual radiance, which Sellers could project in his performances, but could never attain in real life.

In *Orders are Orders*, Sellers' grins are ironic; Goffin is pleased to be doing something which will hurl one past the officers. In *John and Julie*, P.C. Diamond grins with happiness and jollity (linking him with Constance Cummings' portly husband, the American judge, who wears a red smoking jacket and functions as Santa Claus); and where Goffin unobtrusively mocks his masters, Diamond is amused by unfounded fear and concern – he seems to be in a wistful world of his own, listening, perhaps, to Eddie Calvert's trumpet wailing away on the sound track, a waltzy, lyrical theme, which merges into William Walton's uplifting Coronation marches and pomp. (It is the music of the spheres.)

It is an indication of Sellers' achievement that we never think, with Mr Pritchett, that the policeman is an incompetent. Somehow, Sellers holds the spell together; and there is much about *John and Julie*, especially its tone, which could never be recaptured now and must have been a gamble then. The very idea of young children at large makes me (at least) uneasy. Wilfrid Hyde-White, for example, playing the local magistrate, has that dark chortle in his voice which, to my nervous ears, gets to have a pederastic ring. Sir James, instead of packing John and Julie back off home, double quick, takes them in for the night. (He's like an old sage in the wild wood, and he later reappears, clad in plumes and brocade, as a Field-Marshal in the Household Cavalry.) But the children are enchanted, and even London, which blazes with ruby reds (buses, hats, lipsticks, flags), is free of danger for them. As they move through the crowds and brawls (led by Richard Wattis and Peter Jones, of all sedate people, in Oxbridge scarves) they pass Marne Maitland, who'll play the crooked Indian Maharajah in *I'm All Right, Jack*, and Katie Johnson, the old woman in *The Ladykillers*, who is gazing with adoration at a statue of Queen Victoria.

☆ ★ ☆

The dated decency and virtue of *John and Julie* only add to its charms. These days, moreover, child actors don't need to pipe up with such pert, posh voices; Colin Gibson and Lesley Dudley seem to have spent their entire waking lives in elocution lessons. They talk at top register, and the adults are as odd. They say 'poe-leece,' instead of, as now, 'pleece,' for police. Only Sellers sounds un-mannered (Sid James is loud and Joe Soapish; Hyde-White overdoes his low wa-ha-ha-ho-ho-ho), and he was anxious to learn how people thought he'd fared. 'It's early yet to assess the reaction to these films,' he wrote in *Picturegoer*, in February 1955, 'but would you let me know how you feel, about this "new" career in films. Will [the public] accept Sellers the "straight" character com-edian? . . . I hope the verdict will be fair to a funny man.'

Work did not flow in as he'd hoped – and it was during this period, when he was desperate for a film career,* that he fell out with Milligan more often than usual and began misbehaving during radio and television broadcasts. 'Doing *The Goon Show* series,' he explained in March 1960, 'had some draw-backs. As far as film-making is concerned and as far as one's part in films as a character is concerned, many film-makers tend to think of you as a funny-voice man, instead of being a serious actor. Consequently, if any-thing comes along, unless it is grotesque, they don't offer it to you. I, of course, don't consider myself to be an actor of grotesque parts. I can play these parts, but nevertheless I don't like to do any one particular thing. I know my own limits, but I don't want to special-ise in any one particular thing. . .'

Sellers' solution to the problem of how to break out from the cla-mour of radio to the acclaim of films was ingenious – he decided to experiment with some silent movie shorts. If, before, all he'd been was a voice, now he'd try and convey life in all its facets by not say-ing a word. Back he went to the Marylebone Studios, to make *Dearth [sic] of a Salesman*, *Cold Comfort*, and *Insomnia is Good For You*. The first was directed by Leslie Arliss, who had worked in some capacity on *Orders are Orders*; the others were directed by James Hill, who'd direct Sellers in *The Dock Brief*, and they

---

* Q: Was it obvious to you that you were going to be the one out of that Goon group to really excel?

A: It was to me, because I was *determined* to have a film career.

Rolling Stone, April 17th, 1980.

were written by Lewis Greifer and Maurice Wiltshire, who'd adapt *The Goon Show* scripts for *The Telegoons*. (Wiltshire lived in Sussex, near Winchelsea: 'I am mad about Winchelsea and would adore to live there,' Sellers told him in March 1961, when [i] his marriage was on the rocks and he was desirous of living anywhere except where he was and [ii] he was being sentimentally drawn back to the coastal resorts of his childhood. Coincidentally, it is Milligan who has retired nearby, to Udimore, a few miles inland from Rye.)

Also dating from this era is a twenty-six minute romp called *The Super Secret Service*, written by Milligan and co-starring Dick Emery and the Ray Ellington Quartet. Sellers was a bowler-hatted City gent involved in (another) secret formula plot. Apparently, the celluloid was junked at some point. Graham Stark recalls seeing shreds and tatters of it being utilised at Pinewood as grist to test Movieola editing machines: 'Made in a basement studio in Dean Street. . . , it's black and white, with sound, and it's absolutely terrible. . . . Peter [was] running about the West End, willing to work for fourpence providing it was a film.' So I have not seen it; nor have *Salesman* or *Insomnia* surfaced. But I did discover *Cold Comfort*, and it is both low-grade and brilliant.

Sellers' bowler-hatted City etc., who appears in all the little films, was called Hector Dimwitty; the idea was to parody government information newsreels, and Dimwitty is a sort of put-upon Pooter. The sight gags and nicely timed farce are overlain with a bright-voiced documentary scientist type, who tells us that (for instance) many of us will catch a cold today and fail to go to work – so instead of being spick and span on his commuter train, with the other Mr Nobodies, Sellers is seen as a dishevelled, heavy wreck in his storm-tossed single bed, who is addressed by an off-screen William Mate Cobblers:

> If you was to ask me you looks horrible . . . A cold? Sounds to me as though you've got something a bit more lasting . . . Like Albert Thomson – you wouldn't have called him a sickly man. Came home with the sniffs, and two days later he's got a funny-sounding cough.

> Cheeks sunk in, face all flushed, arms ate away . . . Went to see him
> on the Sunday – I missed him by half an hour.

Dimwitty makes his way myopically and wearily to the bathroom to
examine his furry tongue and stinging eyes. He is the image of 'flu-
racked forlornness. He opens the window – his pyjama trousers fall
down. He nips out to get the milk – door slams shut behind him.
He's locked out and at once it starts to rain. He manages to tip the
milk over his head. The simple pratfalls seem to be succeeding
because Sellers doesn't race through them; he doesn't let his arms
and legs spring everywhere, like many comics do when basically
having to mime. He knows, as Ted Ray did on radio, how long to
prolong a pause (it's for Dimwitty to have time to ponder) – how to
react to absurdity, rather than to think you have to be the cause of
it. (Sellers isn't a Norman Wisdom-style cretin.) The master of
what we might call becalmed exasperation is, without question,
Oliver Hardy. He was far funnier sitting in a puddle, or surrounded
by wreckage of some kind, taking stock, than he was when actually
falling over or being victimised. Sellers' most blatant Hardy-ish
moment was in one of the 'Panthers' when, having been bombarded
with cream cakes, Clouseau turned and gazed into the camera in
mute appeal. Sellers has learned that trick of sufference here –
though he cuts Dimwitty's recoil back to the bare essentials, giving
weight to the details: Dimwitty's slight, but constant, nervous fumbling with the edge of the bedsheets; or, short sightedness having
been established earlier, it is doubly funny when he squints at the
label on the nose drops and ends up by squirting a jet clear into his
eye.

So it goes on – for a pure seventeen minutes. He loses the ther-
mometer in the gunge of a mustard bath. He slaps Sloan's Liniment
[*qv*] liberally on his chest. Pause. We hear a few choked back Bluebottle whimpers of agony – and he grabs a carafe off the bedside
table and pours the water all over himself and the candlewick bed-
spread . . . He has difficulty swallowing a pill. It sticks to his tongue.
It sticks to the glass. He doesn't notice for ages – when he does, he
somehow swallows a mothball in error . . . The home-help prepares

a poultice, which is poured into a sock. Sellers, glum, amazed, and implacable, lies there in bed whilst this salami-sized collar is fixed around his neck with a safety pin. A mustardy gook squeezes out through an undarned hole – Sellers, with this absurd folk-remedy oozing down his fat, unshaven chins, with his down-turned inwardly-rolled lips, has the saddest of clown faces.

It is credible comedy. Yes, you feel, it could happen this way, if you were ill. The only off-putting note, oddly enough, is Sellers' urgent narration. 'Any fool can catch a cold,' we are informed, 'but it takes a real expert to hang on to it.' That dud aphorism squats miserably over Dimwitty's going to answer the phone in a draughty hall – and suddenly he has knocked over a vase of flowers and it is dripping on to his bare feet; so he hops on to the prickly stems and scattered blooms, to protect himself from 'a germ-laden floor,' and continues with his (unheard) conversation. Clouseau himself was never more deftly clumsy, nor so nonchalant.

☆ ☆ ☆

Cold Comfort, which in itself is nothing really, happens to encapsulate something of Sellers' genius in a way superior material, or a better quality production, often does not. I mean his ability to slow a film down. He's at it as Dr Pratt in *The Wrong Box*; in the scene where Fred Kite has been abandoned by his family in *I'm All Right, Jack*, and plods in and out of his lounge-room and kitchenette, knocking his fists against his thighs; and in *Lolita*, when Clare Quilty is first introduced to us at the school prom, and he is intent on a hypnotic, lazy, dance routine – a heavy, sluggish sort of salamander's twist. It is the actor's confidence in setting, through the character, his own rhythms, which comes across. Sellers, of course, had been a drummer. In fact, he'd been 'Peter Sellers, the Ultra-Modern Young Swing Drummer and Ukelele Entertainer', on the variety posters. Ted Ray, like Jack Benny, was a violinist. Sid Caesar was a funny saxophone player, Les Dawson played an out-of-key piano, W.C. Fields had his juggling, and Dudley Moore (a Magdalen organ scholar) has his nimble jazz. Milligan began as a trumpeter and Secombe has ended up as a hymn singer. No doubt the catalogue could be extended – to prove that the gift of comedy is related to a physical sense of beat, pulse, and measure. What makes such people artists, what empowers the best of them to deliver a gag (vocal or visual) such that it hangs in the air, and sets off resonances, is that they involve their nervous systems – their work (in Wordsworth's fine phrase) is felt along the heart, impudently, or emotionally, or with an edge. They whip up a rapport with us and leave us elated. The beauty of Sellers' next rôle, in *The Ladykillers*, is that Harry, the Teddy Boy,* seems to be listening to rock n' roll melodies playing inside his head. He moves about Mrs Wilberforce's villa with the lumbering tread of a spiv trying to cut a dash in a dance hall. It adds to the characterisation that Sellers is at least a decade too old for an authentic Ted – yet they do exist, these elderly Elvis fans and the hipsters that time forgot, and Sellers anticipates their creaking, shoulder-wiggling self-conscious mannerisms.

Richard Attenborough, agelessly baby-faced in those days, like Mickey Rooney, and Sir Michael Balcon's first choice for the part, would not have brought out this slight air of inappropriateness – which is so necessary for the film. For all the characters are anachronistic, out of their element, era, or minds. Alec Guinness' Professor Marcus is a German Expressionist comedian; Danny Green's hulking One Round seems off either the pages of Dickens or a Thirties boxing picture distributed by Warner's; Herbert Lom's Louis twitches and glowers like a Chicago hood – in King's Cross; and Cecil Parker's Major Courtenay, in a camel-hair coat and a luxuriant moustache, is the embodiment of every gentleman conman that ever tried to outwit the Inland Revenue or sell properties in the South of France to which he does not hold title. Hiding in the little old lady's house, where the clocks stopped when 'someone came in and said the old Queen had passed away', the gang

---

* *Colloq.* for Fifties youth affecting vaguely Edwardian style of dress – square cut blue velveteen frock coats and bootlace neckties, for example. One of Tony Hancock's abysmal impersonations was of Johnny Ray, thus attired.

a string quintet and Boccherini's tiddle-iddle-pom-pom-pom minuet underscores the film. The robbery is quite consciously set to music – Prof. Marcus is both enraptured and maddened by the violins on his horn gramophone; and when Sellers' Harry is killed off, the genteel tune modulates for a moment into a burst of the blues. *The Ladykillers* is a comic chamber opera – and as such was adapted by the Czech composer, Ilja Hurnick, in 1967, as a piece called *Dama a Lupici*: 'The Lady and the Robbers'.

☆ ★ ☆

'The first *real* film I made,' he said, 'was *The Ladykillers*. I can remember all of that very well. I used to watch Alec Guinness, who is an absolute idol of mine, do everything, his rehearsals, his scenes, everything. It was fascinating... Not that I could hope to be as good as Guinness. But he is my ideal ... and my idol.'

After Milligan, Guinness was indeed Sellers' great life-long inspiration and irritation. He wanted to have a film career like Guinness', and did; he wanted to do the equivalent of *Kind Hearts and Coronets*, and use the technology of cinema to play lots of rôles and encounter himself on screen, and did – in *The Mouse That Roared, Doctor Strangelove, Soft Beds, Hard Battles* etc. (Through the agency of special effects the world could see how full of himself he was.) *Kind Hearts and Coronets* amused him, in addition, because one actor re-appearing in a variety of minor roles, which in the cinema won you praise for your panache, had long been a tradition in tatty music hall, circuses and Rep.: Duncan coming back in a big false beard as one of the Thanes; the Red Indian fire-eater doing the dog act; and his wife, who'd earlier on had knives flung at her, climbing to the top of the tent to be an aerialist. When Sellers met Guinness he felt he'd lunched with a demure one-man Rep. Company. 'You cannot believe how quiet this man is. He's shy! He's got a switch inside. He turns it on, and another person pops up!'

Alexander Walker, who is a film reviewer for an evening paper, has said that Sellers, when abroad, would often call him up in the small hours, just as a new film of Sir Alec's was about to open, to ask, 'How is Guinness? How is he really?' He was praying for flops.

Wolf Mankowitz told me that 'towards Guinness' talent, Sellers was absolutely cravenly attentive and admiring. I remember we went, with our wives, to the first night of Rattigan's *Ross*. Probably the worst performance ever given by Alec Guinness. After being buggered by the Turks, he walked across the stage with a waddle that came straight out of the world of the Goons. Sellers and I both thought this was an absurd play and an absurd performance – and Sellers was happier than I'd seen him for a long time. This capacity for doing a *Kind Hearts and Coronets* – he was always coming back to that, always jealous of that film. He was never really able to do it because he was such an inventive mimic; and he assumed that that meant he didn't need scripts – his improvising would always compensate. Well, all that Sellers' invention does is destroy the structure. So you either have to be a writer, or get one. . .'

Sellers' party-turns were of Sir Alec – the impersonations of the Rev. d'Ascoyne, telling Dennis Price about his West Window; and Prince Feisal, in *Lawrence of Arabia*, coping with a corpsing O'Toole and blowing his lines about the Koran. One of his records contained a parody of a Guinness profile – under the non-disguise of Sir Eric Goodness – 'and you know, when I cut the Sir Eric Goodness [disc] I took it down to the theatre to play it over to Alec. It was while he was in "Ross".* He was very nice about it. He laughed. Then he said, "The impersonation is very good, but, you know, I don't think the *material* is very funny!" . . . Of course the whole idea of the record was that it was an actor giving one of those completely pointless interviews, saying absolutely nothing.'

And, to give one more example of a Sellers/Guinness conjunction, in the re-shoot of *The Fiendish Plot of Dr Fu Manchu*, Sellers' oriental sage, in the new, inserted scenes, suddenly speaks with Guinness' soap-and-honey voice – he's reminiscing with Helen Mirren's Alice Rage about the music hall, when he slaps his thighs eagerly and laughs in Sir Alec's rich, full throated guffaw. Coming out of the reed-thin Fu's devil doll mouth, like that, it is a spooky, devilish act of ventriloquism.

---

* 1960, at the Haymarket Theatre, London.

☆ ★ ☆

These are all facile Guinness gags; they show Sellers delighting in derision, and do not hint at how he was gripped. When Sellers expressed his envy, what he had in mind were not the classical stage appearances (Hamlet, Lear's Fool, Aguecheek, Richard II), but things like Fagin, Herbert Pocket, Disraeli, the d'Ascoynes (of course), and the heroes in *The Lavender Hill Mob* and *The Man in the White Suit*; Guinness was a star character actor, who found, through the different parts he played, a means of using up his anger and energy – converting these qualities, indeed, into vitality and flexibility. The Guinness whose magic operated on Sellers was the one whose imagination (like Shakespeare's) could encompass saints and sinners, the restrained and the grotesque. (Sellers, however, thrilled by the amorality of the artistic impulse, made the mistake of applying it to his private life, and this is what undid him.)

Sellers, 'poor, rich, exceptionally brilliant Peter Sellers,' makes an appearance in the very first paragraph of Sir Alec's autobiography, *Blessings in Disguise*, which is clue enough to the shared feelings and experience of the two men. 'Poor, rich, exceptionally brilliant Peter Sellers never seemed to get himself sorted out in spite of the fact that, apart from upset marriages, there didn't appear to be much confusion in his life.' Whereas Guinness was born out of wedlock and hidden in creepy hotels on the Cromwell Road, had a violent step-father, and his mother betook his few possessions to the pawn shop and left him a legacy of unredeemed tickets and unpaid bills. Indeed, Sellers' frequent bleating about his identity crisis ('As far as I'm aware,' he told the *New York Times Magazine* in 1960, 'I have no personality of my own whatsoever') comes to seem a bit pathetic when compared against the hard facts of Guinness' bastardy. He was known, in childhood, as Alec de Cuffe and Alec Stiven, and his father's name, on his birth certificate, remains a blank. Was he sired by a banker called Andrew Geddes? Or by one of Lord Iveagh's family on his yacht at Cowes? Never certain who his father was, no wonder he is drawn to Dickens. Over the years, he has been approached by weird women who claim to be his half-sisters, or by other spectral types who say they have news of his origins, and 'I began to feel I was playing some minor character part in *Bleak House* or *Dombey and Son*.'* His mother refused to enlighten him – and his domestic upbringing was the opposite of Sellers' – Sellers, who was loved not wisely *and* too well.

All the frenzy and disorder that spilled out of Sellers, Guinness keeps inside. It is what can break loose in the Ealing classics, for example, when his bank clerks or scientists, forced by circumstances to be humdrum, suddenly rebel and give in to the irrational. No matter how outwardly docile his characters, you sense great impatience and temper lurking beneath, which are being actively controlled. (As a child he directed his hurt and frustrations into crayon drawings of exploding battleships and war scenes.) Smiley, for example, the spy catcher, exemplifies this. That's as minimalist an outing as Sellers' Chance. Smiley's brain, behind that dusty face and those polished spectacles, flickers and fizzes, solving puzzles, making links, trusting nobody. Chance has no brain to speak of. He has the attention span of a bird. Both parts needed geniuses to play them, to lift Smiley clear of being a boring, over-shrewd civil servant and to stop Chance from being embarrassingly mentally handicapped.

Sellers, as we know, drew on Stan Laurel for *Being There*. Guinness, before he ran to fat, was Laurel's physical double, and his rôles, like Laurel's screen persona, have always managed to be both brisk and forlorn – giving them an undercurrent of irony, if not comedy, and always of ambiguousness. Like Guinness himself, his characters have 'something tucked away inside' (his words), which won't yield easily to classification; and it is similarly strong or

---

* When Sellers went on *Desert Island Discs* (February 4th 1957) his castaway book was *The Pickwick Papers*. Did he have in mind Dickens' actual novel, with its tales of a wife-beating clown, dead babies, imprisonment, madness and revenge, or Harry Secombe's 'If I Ruled the World' musical bowlderisation? I can see how The Pickwick Club would have held an appeal – chaps having a good time together, like the Goons at Grafton's.

unusual individuals, eccentrics, who claim his attention in real life – because they are larger than life. Martita Hunt, for one, downing huge whiskies, treating herself to pedicures, advocating compulsory colonic irrigation. Guinness is charmed by her silk-lined surroundings – painted toenails and the Sickert paintings – and her whole existence seems artsy and theatrical. He keeps going back to her grotto for elocution lessons, even though he's aware she's pretty ignorant of phonology, voice production etc. Her gaiety is an antidote to the drabness of Guinness' student existence; and he is amused by both the traffic of cab drivers, dropping in for sexual favours, and by Martita's hampers of smoked salmon and quarter bottles of champagne, which, during the war, were never in short supply.

Guinness is like a Dickens hero transfixed by a Dickens screwball, and Martita Hunt, a grande dame who played grande dames from the age of about thirty, is best remembered for her Miss Havisham in *Great Expectations*. Who can forget, along with Magwich grabbing Pip in the graveyard, the sight of the jilted old lady in her rotting wedding dress, enthroned amongst the cobwebs, and with the mice making a palace out of the petrified cake? Sellers used her in *Mr Topaze* as an indignant baroness; she descends on the provincial French school, covered in the pelts of endangered species and a hat of skewered coloured birds, and demands that her dotard grandson be given top marks and a glowing end-of-term report. It is a test of Topaze's integrity. Her scene is brief, histrionic, and we can tell why the actress became an alcoholic when she had to admit to herself that she was no Edith Evans. Martita Hunt is imperious and strident, without any recesses of wit or zing. (She's like a drag queen.) During the making of the film, so slack was her sphincter, owing to those daily enemas, and so gone was her care or control, owing to the drink, she kept farting and ruining her takes. Sellers, who was directing, became, as can readily be imagined, helpless with mirth. During one particular reverse angle shot, with the cameras focused on her aviary of a hat, she let riff a bottom-speak which Sellers described later as being 'like Louis Armstrong sustaining a top C'. He had to leave the studio, he laughed so much.

He phoned Bryan Forbes and said, 'I can't ever go back, because Martita refuses to acknowledge she's done anything – and this makes it funnier.' He used to imitate her tooting (Forbes tells me) to the end of his days.

Guinness stayed loyal to the wind-breaking waxwork, continuing to visit her as she declined from apartments to flats to a bedsitting room. She fell into the habit of smoking cigarettes in bed and more than once set fire to herself – again, eerily like Miss Havisham when she goes up in flames, 'shrieking, with a whirl of fire blazing all about her,' (writes Dickens) 'and soaring at least as many feet above her head as she was high.' Guinness himself remarks on the squalor of the boudoir, the singed holes in the blankets, and Martita Hunt's burnt wiry hair.

He came across another example of loony majesty in Edith Sitwell, holding court at the Sesame and Imperial Pioneer Ladies Club in Grosvenor Street. She carried on like the exiled princess of some distant fairy tale country, banishing folk from her circle if they said they didn't mind Beethoven, and expecting them to worship her own peculiar verse and books. Guinness obviously found favour, for he was invited to the Sitwell castle, Renishaw. Informed that Sir Osbert, a homosexual and dandy, hated babies ('babies made him feel ill'), his young son, Matthew, had to be hidden in a distant tower – and Guinness fretted all evening about (a) the deception of smuggling an infant in under the sacred roof and (b) whether his only child would be consumed by the Sitwells' pet baboon.

Dame Edith was quite capable of getting lost in her own garden ('Oh, do go and look for Edith,' Sacheverell says, 'She's inclined to wander off so'), and the exuberance Guinness admires in people is often coupled with an unworldliness – affected or cultivated to greater or lesser degrees. Tyrone Guthrie, for instance, whom he finds living in a decrepit red brick mansion in Co. Monaghan, had an incisive mind, directed Guinness as Hamlet, and allowed the housework to go to hell for decades. Guinness found a congealed sausage in the bookcase and the kitchen floor was so impacted with trodden-on peelings, it looked from a distance like marble. Again, the total effect, of the chipped crockery and the oil lamps, the out-size playing cards for Guthrie's blind mother, and the adjacent factory for Irish Mist Plum Jam, had 'an affinity with Dickens'. Or there was mollycoddled Sydney Cockerell, Curator of the Fitz-william Museum, who'd known Tolstoy, and who gave Guinness one of T.E. Lawrence's Bedouin robe cast-offs. Cockerell was big pals with Shaw – a character, says Guinness, who had no com-punction about laughing loudly at his own jokes.

Like Dickens, Guinness' mind is drawn to the grandiose and un-predictable; he can tell the difference between vanity (Noël Coward) and a 'very special glamorous presence' (Gielgud's) which is more resilient and true, but not necessarily better. He is absorbed by non-conformity, not fame; and former Russian acrobats, retired to dowdy hotels with 'unlit Turkey-carpeted passageways'; dishev-elled and crapulous old priests; sinister ex-missionaries, hitting out at schoolboys ('except handsome [ones] who were good cricketers') etc. all intrigue him just as much as celebrated DBEs and Knights. It is the spirit of the isolated rebel and misfit, which he himself pos-sesses, which he recognises; and he has transformed it into his actor's art. His portrayals of Lawrence of Arabia, in *Ross*, or Dylan Thomas, Jonathan Swift, or Gully Jimson, the grubby painter in *The Horse's Mouth*, are blatantly egotistical parts – and seem to be miles away from Guinness' own rather ghostly, reserved nature; but the furtiveness and forcefulness are there nevertheless, and he is at his greatest playing characters whose power is, one way and an-other, concealed: Smiley, watching and waiting; Hillary, the Kim Philby rôle in *The Old Country*, with his double lives; Obi-Wan Kenobi, the grail knight in *Star Wars*. Exactly what this inner energy is has long puzzled Guinness, and has led him to undertake many a 'casual search for a meaning to life', which culminated in his becoming a Catholic – the liturgy, punctiliousness, ceremony and poetry have given the actor, who is perhaps the actor Dickens him-self aspired to be, a sort of structure and stability; Catholicism has protected him from chaos.

☆ ★ ☆

Sellers, starting from his days at St Aloysius', never had the patience to adhere to a single religion; he wanted miracles to take place here and now and prayers to be answered instantly – if not, well then, God? Ha! Ha! During the speeded-up sword fight on the pirate ship in *Ghost in the Noonday Sun*, Dick Scratch withdraws to his cabin to pray for divine assistance. This is what it says in the battle-scarred copy of the script which Peter Medak gave me:

> SCRATCH is kneeling before a crucifix. For a moment we think he
> is a reformed man. In the various corners of the room we see the
> God of four different religions – a Hindu god with many arms – a
> Buddha with incense burning around it – a prayer mat with symbols
> of the Koran. As he turns from one God to the other he is seen in
> the appropriate costume of the priest of each religion.

Because of the fast-motion which prevails in the finished film – a gimmick of the editor's to give an illusion of slapstick zest – we don't get the opportunity to appreciate the gag – that Scratch is taking no chances. He simply scampers below decks, crosses himself and makes a few other wild gesticulations, and is then back running around amongst the duelling Maltese Corsairs. The scene makes no sense. In any case, the cabin set was far too cluttered for us to make out the various altars; and Sellers, doing his best to be awkward, refused to don the different clerical vestments. So it goes for nothing; and Sellers, too lazy to bother with the holy quick-changes, threw away a little homage to *Duck Soup*, where Groucho keeps appearing in different military uniforms (including that of a Roman centurion and a Confederate general) from shot to shot.

The scene, as glued in the script, was typed on tissue paper and dated November 3rd 1973. It is thus one of Milligan's contributions – Milligan having been brought into the production well after shooting had commenced on Cyprus, his brief being to inject some Goonishness that would entice Sellers out of his depressions. He clearly wrote in for Scratch one of Sellers' traits – the tendency to worship all manner of strange gods. Did Sellers pick up on the personal allusion, resent it, and was this behind his non-cooperation?

'I've no idea which emotional compass point he was on in his life,' Spike said to me. 'No idea. He went sideways. I once bought him a menorah as a Christmas present. You know, one of those seven-branched candelabra things used in Jewish worship. When he opened it he burst into tears. He was haunted by yesterday, yesteryear. Always telling Anne he wanted to come back to her; or that he wanted to see his mother again – all that lark.'

If Sellers lacked the discipline to think through individual religions, preferring instead to borrow the colourful highlights of several and inaugurate his own sentimental cults, he was at least aware of his divine urgings. 'Yes, I was religious,' he said. 'What I have to do is to find out how to worship God in the right way. I have to find my own way to pray to the God I believe in. I was very much interested at Haifa in the Bahia sect. I should say there's a strain of Buddhism in their beliefs. They take one commandment, you know, from various religions. They have a great feeling for beauty. Their temples and shrines are all very beautiful . . . My first problem is – well, Jesus said, didn't He: Pray behind your doors. I feel one shouldn't make a public show of praying, of being religious. Not that I mind in the least being seen praying. But there are the people who go to church hoping to be recognised: Look who's here! That's all right if it's just for a salutation, but . . . Pray behind your doors. One ought to want to do something *for God*.

'I don't really believe in organised religion. If you fast for a day, that may be good for self-discipline, but I can't believe – Look, God, I haven't eaten anything all day! – I can't believe God takes much notice. It's the same with confession. A man goes and confesses: I've done this and that, I'm sorry . . . All right, I absolve you . . . I can't see how anybody has the right to say that. It simply means that the man feels he can go out and do it again. . .'

Sellers himself, under such circumstances, would no doubt have felt that he personally was free to sin and be shitty as soon as he was out through the door; and as for praying behind closed doors, he either found that, in talking to God he was talking to himself, or that when he was on his own there was nobody there. There's a scene in *The Adventure of Sherlock Holmes' Smarter Brother*, when Leo McKern, as Moriarty, prays at a statue of the BVM; he wants to be pardoned for all his recent dastardly deeds. When he has finished meditating, he presses a keyboard, and the BVM starts flashing with festive lights, a bell tings, and the word ABSOLVED appears in a little window – the altar is really a department-store till. This is the instant forgiveness Sellers wanted; it was a celestial version of his mother's letting him get away with murder. I mention it because Gene Wilder, when he was writing, directing and starring in that film in 1975, spent each evening with Sellers, at Sellers' flat in Stag Place, Victoria, attempting to pick the master's brains. Whether Bialystock and Bloom thrashed out McKern's cash-register concept, I haven't the foggiest; but Sellers did say, of these tutorials, that 'What was running through Wilder's mind was, how do you separate yourself? You can see what other people are doing in front of the camera, but when you step out there yourself, you have only an approximation. You can't actually *see* it.' It was the problem Sellers had encountered with making *Mister Topaze* – you have to have, as an actor/director, an all-seeing eye, integrating your own performance into other people's; you are absent yet present. 'I would never take that combination on again, because it's just beyond my scope.' He did, of course, when he commandeered *The Fiendish Plot of Dr Fu Manchu* and requisitioned *The Bobo*; the concept of the film-director as a God of Creation, a master of the universe whose word is law, had a distinct appeal.

The first perilous divulgence of his madness came during the period of *The Millionairess*. 'I remember once after the film had come out an Indian came up to me in the street and said quite seriously that I was the new Messiah, that I should lead India into new paths.' Instead of shaking off the fellow as a crank, Sellers was receptive to the message. (Sellers was the crankier.) 'Oh, I suppose it's quite common for an actor to identify himself with the part he's playing. But I really do find myself living the parts I act.' Ergo, he quite likely was the Second Coming. It meant a lot to him, Chance's walking on water at the end of *Being There*. 'People are always saying,' he said, '"what is this guy all about, anyway?" Why don't they leave you alone and just accept what you do? That's one of the things I like about Chance. Who the hell is he? Is he God? Is he sent by God? Is he a moron, or what?' Sellers' final rôle, Fu Man-chu, was played as a living God; the plot, if you can bear to sit still and wait for it to emerge from the shellac, concerns the search for an elixir of everlasting life.

☆ ★ ☆

Guinness, before he took the veil in 1956, incurred his fair share of nuts and charlatans. He dropped in on a Buddhist meeting and found a Canadian in a white robe boasting of his sexual prowess; he took cover in a vicarage during the bombing of Bristol and saw the Rev. Cyril Tomkinson ranting about all the lady parishioners being lesbians. On going into retreat at a Trappist monastery, in Leicestershire, he noticed that the monks deputised to look after him, when out of sight of their brothers, couldn't stop talking. One, bringing his morning tea, 'eyed the biscuit enviously, but no doubt offered it up to God'. He doesn't mock or reproach. Guinness is as arrested by weaknesses and foibles as he is by the exotic; he is curious about people's psychological side-alleys and self-importance – in the follies that make them unique and of interest. The detached and humble attitude he personally takes – or which comes across in the theologically entitled *Blessings in Disguise* – is that of a parish priest. An actor, he actually says, is 'a kind of unfrocked priest', who celebrates mysteries, concocts rituals, and convinces audiences that they can see things which aren't there. He has happy memories of playing Chesterton's Father Brown, because, on loca-tion in France, 'my hand was seized by a boy of seven or eight . . . Although I was a total stranger he obviously took me for a priest and so to be trusted.'

It must be said that this kind of stuff can make for coyness and the solemnity-cum-spirituality in Guinness' performances can be tiresome, rather like the metaphysical passages in Iris Murdoch's novels which we all skip past when they start shimmering in. Guin-ness has made recordings of T.S. Eliot's poetry and such are his canonical tones, the maundering banalities ('All shall be well and all manner of things shall be well' – plagiarised from Julian of Norwich) are uplifted and virtually make sense. When Guinness plays Reilly, the psychiatrist/father confessor/God figure, in *The Cocktail Party*, it seems a deep and moving play. See it with another actor in position and Reilly is vacuous and fraudulent, tailor-made for Rex Harrison's comic touches.* Guinness brings a gravity and decorum to his work – and this can take over. Back in the days of *Kind Hearts and Coronets*, the weightiness could be used for fun. The surviving d'Ascoynes, in church for the funerals, already strike marble attitudes in their pew – they don't flinch and so merge with the figures on the ancestral tombs. But Guinness' Charles I, in the otherwise clunky *Cromwell*, is so much the image of a royal portrait, the actor seems to be posing for Van Dyck. (The long Stuart hair and goatee, let alone the suffering expression and martyrdom, are Christ's.) And in *Brother Sun, Sister Moon*, Guinness's Pope Innocent II, enthroned amongst Byzantine icons and gold, is so paralysed by holiness, he's an effigy.

Guinness' saintly stillness, which in *Little Dorrit* was used to suggest William Dorrit's bloated idleness, already seemed to be parodying itself by *Tinker, Tailor, Soldier, Spy*. When George Smiley was held in all those close-ups, we had world enough and time to notice how the make-up artist's face powder had settled on cheeks and crevices – like a patina of flakes and flour blown on to a statue during renovation work in a Cathedral. The light, glinting off his glasses, made the character additionally ceramic. Yet, somehow, the brilliant inner-life is conveyed: 'Invest him . . . with all the resources of science, past and present, with all the resources, if you will, of a wealthy government – which, however, already has denied all knowledge of his existence . . . This man . . . is, unquestionably, the most . . . formidable personality existing in the world today. He is a linguist, who speaks with almost equal facility in any of the

---

* Not even Sir Alec could take everybody in. One evening, after Reilly had asked Celia about her errant boyfriend, 'And what does he seem like now to you?', a brave patron in the stalls shouted out: 'A cunt.'

civilised languages, and in most of the barbaric. He is an adept in all
the arts and sciences which a great university could teach him. He is
also an adept in certain obscure arts and sciences which *no* university of today can teach. He has the brains of any three men of
genius. . .' – Which is not le Carré over-egging the pudding but Sax
Rohmer doing his best to give us a mental picture of the deathless
Dr Fu Manchu ('The yellow peril incarnate in one man'), Sellers'
last graven image.

Immobility was one of the secrets of comedy, Sellers believed.
John Bird once asked him straight out, what's the trick? 'He gave
me some advice which I never followed. He said: *Keep your head
still*. If you look at him, he does that. Everybody else is acting themselves silly – he is the centre of balance, like a dancer.' Then Bird
added (without being prompted by me), 'Guinness' technique is not
dissimilar. . .'

Which is true, because in *Murder by Death*, as the blind butler,
Bensonmum, answering the door and taking the guests to their
rooms, and staring at the world-famous detectives with eyes which
look but don't see, Guinness has made himself so stately and still,
he's hieratic – with his close-cropped white hair, his head is huge,
like an Emperor's bust. Maggie Smith, Peter Falk, Elsa Lanchester,
and the rest of the cast, scamper around him, like acolytes in olden
days, skipping and strewing the place with petals and garlands. Except for Sellers. Sidney Wang, in ceremonial robes and monster
teeth, is another totem – a stick-puppet. Bird summed up: 'You
look at Sellers' work, you think: What is going on? Why is he so
good? Despite the keeping still, and so on, there's nothing obvious
that you can copy and make use of yourself. As with Guinness, it is
great acting, and the greatness defies analysis.'

☆ ★ ☆

With serenity, motionlessness and basilisk stares to go on, we
have at least made a start. Clouseau might be Smiley's accident-
prone cousin, for they both bring evil-doers to justice and have
withdrawn, sombre personalities. They interrogate; they are underestimated; they are conscious of their dignity. They are stilled

points in the turning, duplicitious world. In attempting to solve crimes and expose lies, they are agents of order – or disorder, in Clouseau's case, for he cannot leave a house without first dismantling it, or Herbert Lom's office without igniting it. But there is no doubting his authority, which seems supernaturally abetted. (The fact that it's stuntmen who really do the work has its aptness: Clouseau splits up into doubles and doppelgangers like a subdividing angel or demon.)

Sellers and the spirit world is a large subject. Guinness, too, was prone to occult experiences at one time. The airless boarding houses of his childhood seemed haunted (by, amongst others, 'an impoverished Miss Havisham') and 'To this day I can still be apprehensive, on a grey day, when passing the shut door of a room I know to be empty'. His imagination furnishes it with goblins and cadavers, nameless secrets. He once owned a picture by Bernard Meninsky. In the manner of M.R. James' tale 'The Mezzotint', the canvas began to alter, and trees and bushes, in the landscape, started to writhe. All was (apparently) explained by the oddities having occured on the anniversary of the artist's suicide. Other 'phases of near-psychic experience' included Guinness' premonition about James Dean, whom he met in Hollywood. 'It is now ten o'clock, Friday the 23rd September 1955,' he warned, in the manner of Obi-Wan Kenobi counselling Luke Skywalker. 'If you get in that car you will be found dead in it by this time next week.' Dean was pranged. Guinness was right – the Force was with him.

He also took to consulting the Tarot cards – and must have become a serious student, because his fear, when aroused, was sudden and total. He threw the deck, wand, books of spells, and other unspecified impedimenta (a pointy wizard's hat? A cloak embroidered with pentangles?) on to a fire. This rough magic he abjured, it would seem, just before his conversion to Catholicism. The Tarot's symbols, he quite rightly saw, the chalice, spear, tree, and spiky crown, blasphemously alluded to the Crucifixion.

Sellers never ceased from his explorations of necromancy. There was always some table-rapping, tea-leaf examining, ouija board session, or voodoo rite afoot in his residences. 'I do indeed believe in extra-sensory perception. It happens to me all the time. When I'm driving I can tell if a man is going to cross the road in front of me, even if he's nowhere in sight. When I was a kid in Ilfracombe I got to know Terry Roberts quite well – he's the son of Estelle Roberts, the medium. So after the war I went to see her. She was extra-ordinary. While she was talking she'd suddenly turn away and ask: "What did you say?" – to the empty air, just as if someone were standing there beside her. She began talking about one of my uncles. She wanted to know if I had a picture of him. As a matter of fact I had: I had a snapshot in my wallet, he was in a group of people [see page 6]. I showed it to her. She picked him out at once; that's the one, she said. How could she have known? I'd never talked to anyone about my uncle. She really was extraordinary. She'd say: "*Nobody's dead.* There are no dead people, just people living another parallel life with us." One thing I found hard to believe. She said: "They have everything we have; they have gardens, and flowers, and food; they have whisky." But I don't know – after all, what are the words? "In my house are many mansions. . ."'

Sellers' predilection for the signs and symbols directed at him from beyond the grave, his reliance on spirit mediums and the voices of the dead, all imply his basic contempt for human life and reason. His insistence on taking the advice of fortune-tellers was one more way of being unmanageable; and by deciding he had an aversion to certain colours (green and purple mainly), here was a way of getting sets repainted, costumes remade, and bystanders in clothes of offending hues forcibly removed. As he said, the flap-doodle began in Ilfracombe, when he was evacuated with his parents and their pierrot shows. But it was in his bloodstream long before then. The backstage world, in which the Rays lived, and beyond that the inheritance of the boxing and circus rings, are full of superstitions. Show business was the meeting point of dreams and harsh realities; the masquerades were tawdry – but that was their strength. Audiences looked through them, like a congregation overlooks the props in a church mass, because you want to forget who you are; you want to be transported. (Hence, for Guinness, the way acting was a route to religion; and hence, for Sellers, theatre and theology's interchangeability.)

Though things like not whistling in dressing rooms can be ascribed to the prohibition on noises which would confuse the stage-hands and scene-shifters – for, originally, ex-sailors worked the ropes up in the flies and, as on a ship, whistles were used to signal to the men up in the rigging – many of the creeds and pieties seem nonsensical. When a cheeseboard fell on Sellers' head, he couldn't rest until he'd found out the reason why – an open umbrella drying in the boiler room. When one of his children fell off a horse, or if he had a bump with his car, it was because a bunch of keys had been left on the hall table. Michael remembers seeing his father look up at a flock of fan-tail doves cooing contentedly on the gables. 'Dad's face darkened. "It's those bloody birds. We've got to get rid of them – they're bringing us bad luck."' Sellers went to fetch his shotgun and blasted them to bits. 'I turned on my heel,' says Michael, 'and ran back to the forecourt to see the poor birds pitching off the tiles like broken shuttlecocks.'

It wasn't only the fowls of the air which Sellers found ominous.[*] He took against the children's first nanny, Frieda Heinlein, because she had once been a Lutheran nun and had asked if she could take her charges to Sunday School. He started calling her a 'German swine' and set about her constructive dismissal. 'You needn't say goodbye to Frieda this morning,' he told Sarah, in front of the good woman, 'because she won't be here when you get back.'

Nanny Heinlein's replacement fared little better. (He seemed to resent seeing his children being cared for competently.) In fact, rather worse, because Sellers tried to murder her, believing her to be a witch. He refused to remain under the same roof as Nanny Clarke and installed himself in an annexe of the Royal Automobile Club. Michael says that he then phoned up and said: 'What am I

---

[*] When I told Michael that one of my sons was born on Friday the thirteenth, he joked, 'My father would have had it strangled.'

doing here? I'm coming home. It's my house. If anybody is going to leave, it's that bloody nanny.'

What happened next is that he drove back to the house, collected a carving knife from the kitchen, and yelling 'I'll kill you, you cow,' stormed towards his employee's private quarters. He embedded the knife in the locked door (much as Milligan had done during another homicidal attack) and Nanny Clarke leapt out of the window, her fall broken by a rose bush. According to Michael's account, she hobbled to a neighbour's, was taken to hospital, and informed the police. Sellers told the constabulary that the woman was deranged, and they believed him. The violent scene, in retrospect, resembled nothing so much as a farcical set-piece invented for one of his films. (What was tragic in life was imitated for comic effect in his art, e.g. Mr Martin trying to stab Constance Cummings with an egg whisk in *Battle of the Sexes*.)

Since he was convinced that people were flashing him the evil-eye, or somehow in conspiracy against him, Sellers' paranoia was fed by the paranormal. But it had long been convenient to blame his cock-ups and terrible tempers on crossed knives and spilt salt. Anything external or other-worldly that could take the blame for his own mood swings or sense of disaster was conscripted – it was quite impossible for him, Peg's invincible golden boy, to find or admit to a murky source within himself. (Milligan said that Sellers 'thinks he's the only clean man in the leper colony'.) The crystal-gazers and horoscopes, he maintained, put him above suspicion and absolved him from having to take any responsibility for his actions. Even his big 1964 heart attack, he reckoned, was pre-ordained and a privileged preview of Heaven: 'I do remember one thing clearly,' he said of his death and resurrection, 'a feeling; a feeling that I would expire, but I wouldn't actually die. I remember there being a sort of large, strong, outstretched arm, pulling me – I knew as long as I clung on I wouldn't die. . .'

He'd been saved from his heart being drowned, and he believed, 'I shall live till I'm seventy-five and will die in my sleep shortly after that. I know that. I suppose I knew all the time I would never die during that Hollywood business. But you have to watch things. Even so, I think I shall most probably die about then, seventy-five, that age.'

'He thought he'd cheated death,' says Anne Lévy. 'He told me, "I've been there and I've come back." He was convinced he'd live until he was seventy-five. He always used to say, "I'm not meant to die." He thought he was immortal.'

Sellers' premonitions were out by twenty-one years.

☆ ★ ☆

If the occult was expedient, something you blamed bad luck and being a shit on, it was also a means of stretching credulity to the breaking point. Sellers must be one of the few people in history, at least since Nero's time, to have spoken to his dead dog. He was trying to contact his mother but he got his dog. 'Every time he went to see Doris Stokes he tried to get in touch with his mother,' says Milligan, 'but instead he got in touch with his dog, Chussy, a little white-haired Maltese terrier, who said it was very happy.'

The Land of Far Beyond was that of the Goons. When he was living in Ireland with his third wife, Miranda Quarry, he kept chickens. One day a hen went missing. 'I thought the fox had got it, but as Miranda was distressed,' he said, 'we had a seance. When Peg came through, I asked her, "Do you know where the hen has gone?" – "Of course I do," she said. "It's up in the rafters of the stable." – "Hang on, I'll take a look," I said. Well, I couldn't find the damn thing and told her so. "It's not there," I said. "Of course it's there," she said. "Go and have another look. But don't be long. I'm not sodding about all night looking for a perishing hen."' The next day he found his stray hen. Up in the rafters.

The crotchety banter is like that of Tony Perkins and his mummified ma in Bates' Motel. When she was dead, what with spectral pooches and disappearing chooks, Peg couldn't have had much peace. Sellers' seances interrupted her repose as his telephone calls at all hours of the day and night did back when she was alive. Indeed, his seances often *were* telephone calls. ('I still speak to my darling every day,' he said chirpily, a dozen years after her exit.)

He'd ring up Maurice Woodruff, Doris Collins, or another of his witch-doctors, and they, with one hand on the ouija board, would relay his mother's messages and advice. Sometimes the psychic bulletins were further filtered through Bert Mortimer, Sellers' valet. Bert would ring up Maurice, who'd issue instructions, which were then relayed to Sellers, who'd be across the room doing things with a Tarot pack. These telephone calls, from anywhere in the world, would go on for hours – would go on until Sellers received the predictions he wanted.

The despatches wouldn't have much mattered if Peg had confined herself to domestic pets or postcard banalities like 'Everything's all right, Peter darling. Don't worry, Dad's fine.' But unfortunately, her chatter started to interfere with Sellers' work. On *Casino Royale*, the film company built a set at enormous expense, but Sellers had a nightmare about it in which his mother came on to the studio floor and said she didn't like it, so he insisted it was torn down without being used. If you ever dare to over-stimulate yourself by watching a video of *Ghost in the Noonday Sun*, you will notice a discrepancy in Sellers' character's name – Scratch in one scene, Scratcher in another. This is because Sellers had Maurice with him during the filming and the soothsayer took him aside and explained that Scratch was an ancient name for the Devil.

'I now know why all this bad luck is being visited on the production!' the actor announced. 'Maurice says it is my character's name. The Devil is blighting the film – so I want every scene in which I'm called "Scratch" scrapped. Every copy of the script which refers to "Scratch" must be destroyed. From now on he's Dick *Scratcher*.' Medak's ring-binder file, with its sellotaped insertions and febrile ballpoint alterations, bears witness to this decree. Maurice also kept saying to Sellers that 'Today isn't a good day for being near water,' which given that it was a pirate romp they were making, on a reconstituted galleon out in the Aegean, only aggravated matters, to pitch it no higher.

Robert Parrish, a director who, like Medak, was abandoned in a foreign field to cope with a lunatic, estimated that Sellers' inner voices cost Warner Brothers, backers of *The Bobo*, approximately $71,428.57 for each day that the star declined to appear for work at Cinecetta. It was the same story on *After the Fox, I Love You, Alice B. Toklas, The Fiendish Plot of Dr Fu Manchu,* amongst many others. It all became too much for one executive. After stomaching delay after delay and the flimsy excuses of adverse ghostly prognostications, the producer took Sellers aside and said: 'Listen, Peter. It's very strange. But I've been hearing voices too. And you know what they told me? They told me that if you're not in tomorrow and ready to go, both your legs will get broken.'

Whether he was galvanised by the threat I've no idea; and the story may be apocryphal because most of the time Sellers got away with it. 'He got away with it time and again,' Milligan told me, his eyes glowing with amazement. 'He had a magic touch. He had a very bad name in the film world for being awkward, but he always got by. They kept using him. He never stopped working.' The reason he was indulged isn't so very difficult to address. *The Return of the Pink Panther* cost three million dollars to make and grossed a profit of thirty million dollars in the first year alone. Sellers' misbehaviour cost money, but it was written off as an investment. The upsets during *The Pink Panther Strikes Again* extended the twelve week shooting schedule to five months and put an extra four million dollars on the budget. It grossed forty five million dollars. . .

Charles K. Feldman shrugged off the insanities of *Casino Royale* because he wanted Sellers to beget another world-wide smasheroo like *What's New, Pussycat?* And so it went on, money being hurled at him in the hopes that he'd get his creative juices flowing. It made him the more disordered. He was the superstitious actor who crosses himself, kisses a goblet, chants a mantram a few times – in case. Pull it all in – something might succeed. But it was also a kind of hysteria. Partly genuine, partly a posture, Sellers' caperings were something he developed to fill the gap where opinions or a considered personality should have been. If he was anxious, uncertain, bored, or feeling malicious, he'd allow something ugly to occur.

To give *The Prisoner of Zenda* its lavish Ruritanian look, Walter Mirisch had arranged for a beautiful steam locomotive to be restored to its full period splendour and brought from the Austrian Railway Museum to the location, outside Vienna. With its rake of carriages and crystal and marquetry compartments, it made the Venice-Simplon Orient Express look like the 9.36 from Didcot. When Sellers, who had the say-so on everything, saw it, he said: 'What are you doing?' – 'What do you mean?' – 'The train!' – 'It's authentic.' – 'Are you trying to destroy me?' – 'What?' It was green, of course. Universal, the film company, obliged and re-painted the thing brown. They then had to re-re-paint it the original emerald before it could be sent back again up the line to the engine sheds.

By 1978, and *Zenda*, he was mad; but he could use his madness, too. He was calculating about these outbursts. They were worked up like a child showing off – and here is the link, once again, to Peg. He always wanted his astrologists to discover what his mother would have said, what her opinion was, and in a twisted sort of way, his caprices continued to be a way of trying to impress her. His bad behaviour, as I suggested when I catalogued his outrages as an infant, was a reflex action of his desire to please. Pushing an aunt on the fire or kicking over tables in restaurants, or breaking a mistress' nose with a jar of cold cream, or leaving one and a half thousand extras hanging about because he'd decided to fly somewhere a long way off and buy health food, are of a piece. 'When I complained to him,' said Blake Edwards, 'he'd sulk, not know his words, and carry on in an unprofessional way as if *we* were at fault and had to be punished. Then he'd disappear again and we'd find him in London having a massage.'

Peg never let him go.

☆ ★ ☆

Spiritual matters, which gave Guinness his core of faith and security, made Sellers spring apart. He chopped and changed from Judaism to Zoroastrianism to Vedantism; he travelled from Israel (where he found people 'almost anti-Semite') to India ('I went to see a lady . . . the other day who deals in numerology and she told me of my various incarnations and what Karma* I had to work off in this life') to the Philippines (to meet a sect which cured all known ills by poking around in chicken livers: 'These people are performing miracles. One day the medical profession will recognise their work'). And the quests had the frantic ardour of his constant exchange of motor cars or his trading in of wives.

Guinness made his submission to Rome ('I felt I had come home') at St Lawrence's Church, Petersfield, Hampshire, with sober-sidedness and dignity. Sellers' flirtation with Catholicism (after his St Aloysius' interests) took place in a suite at the Palace Hotel, Gstaad; and this episode, more than any other, demonstrates the differences between the two men – and points to their divergence as actors. Sellers, on his wanderings, had met a priest in Mexico who claimed to have cured himself of cancer by constant prayer. One day, out of the blue, Sellers decided he wanted him at his side. Many hours of transcontinental telephone calls later, involving embassies and consulates throughout Central America, the holy man was located and persuaded to fly Swiss Air first-class to Geneva. He must have been as bewildered as Frankie Pentangeli's brother is in *The Godfather Part II*, when he is uprooted from Sicily and brought to Washington for the morning to intimidate the committee of senators investigating the Mafia. The grim-visaged country bumpkin, wearing that funny hat with the red pom-pom, is as at sea amongst the sharks and dark-suited lawyers as the Catholic priest would have been amongst the Gucci-clad skiers and sybarites in the lair of the unregenerate rich.

Thirty six hours after Sellers had concocted the plan, the priest was installed in a suite at the grand hotel. Another suite, at Sellers' command, was converted into and consecrated as a temple. 'Only days before,' says Michael, 'Dad had been placing orders with room

---

* *Karma*: Hindu term, meaning 'Sum of person's actions in one of his successive states of existence, viewed as deciding his fate for the next' (OED). Sellers is therefore no doubt at large in the world again, reincarnated as a jackdaw or Osbert Sitwell's baboon.

service for champagne, caviare, club sandwiches and cartons of cigarettes. Now he was galvanising porters into preparing the rooms for Communion,' Life-size plaster statues, a wrought-iron crucifix, pews and a pulpit were installed. Sellers fixed up his hi-fi so that it would seep out woozy organ chords. The effect must have been of a chapel of rest.

The priest was 'quietly impressed by my father's spiritual feeling', and planned Mass for seven o'clock the next morning. Sellers' face fell at the news of this early hour, so he telephoned Michael at six-thirty and insisted on his presence as well. 'I'm asleep,' said Michael. 'This has nothing to do with me.' – 'Of course it's got something to do with you. What in name's sake do you think I flew the priest over here for? I'm not going to celebrate Communion on my own.'

The next afternoon, the priest was winging his way back to his peons.

☆   ★   ☆

Sellers' deep frivolousness and impatience, his need to receive instant pleasure, are worlds away from Guinness' modesty and quiet. (Can you imagine Guinness taking a priest to a press screening, as Sellers did, to bless the film and ensure glowing reviews?) But in making an obvious enough moral judgement we must take care not to throw in any counterbalancing aesthetic measures. Guinness is the nicer man; he is not necessarily the superior actor. It is simply the case that, after encountering Sellers and seeing the advent of Sellers' career, he became a different one. His vigorous characters climax with Professor Marcus, in *The Ladykillers*. After that, the insidiousness, the baroque flourishes, disappear. In the mid-Fifties, Guinness turned his back on the exaggerations which were once part of his appeal. It is impossible to conceive now that he's the same artist as the one who had played Fagin with such relish. The animated Cruikshank engraving ambling out of the darkness and confusion, his hooked nose protruding through the thick hair, and his eyes glistening over the emptied pockets of gold rings and coins, 'a dangling heap of clothes', in Dickens' phrase, was created by a bravura personality. Guinness – the Guinness admired by Sellers – was capable of sinister transformations. By the time of Christine Edzard's *Little Dorrit*, however, in 1988, the hallucinatory characters are left to Max Wall, Bill Fraser, and Cyril Cusack; Guinness' William Dorrit, played without recourse to one stick of make-up, is the very soul of impassivity. You can't believe that this particular Dorrit was ever a frisky youth; nor could you have predicted, looking at the young Guinness' work, that he'd be drawn to such muffled, soggy roles. Similarly, Mr Todd, in *A Handful of Dust*, was all nightmare malice, and Monsignor Quixote, in the adaptation of Graham Greene's novel, was all unworldly benevolence. The early Guinness was undifferentiated. His Herbert Pocket and his Ealing heroes and villains are people brimful of japes and strategems; they keep us wide awake with their flashes and spurts. They seem spontaneous. After *The Ladykillers*, though, as none other than Sellers observed, 'Alec likes to work out just what he will do before he starts. I have to "get inside the part" – feel it from inside.'

What I am building towards here is the idea that Sellers destroyed Guinness as a comic actor. Perhaps Sir Alec was already finding his own brand of exuberance a dead end? (He worried that Professor Marcus was too much of an Alastair Sim part.) Or perhaps in Catholicism, which he embraced a few months after the premiere of *The Ladykillers*, he found a form and channel for his tremendous drive; henceforward he didn't *need* acting in quite the same way? He makes the revealing observation in *Blessings in Disguise* that he has been known to break into a run to reach a church, arriving to pray 'in a state of almost sexual excitement'. It can be safely said that Guinness' later roles are invariably sexless – Obi-Wan Kenobi, Smiley, Reilly, and Monsignor Quixote, for instance, go one better and are actually celibates. This doesn't mean they are hollow and dry. On the contrary, sex has been superceded by piety and intellectual resource. (Guinness couldn't be more different than his confrère, Laurence Olivier, in this respect, who turned into Zeus as he aged, and gave erotic undercurrents to the versatility of his rôles.)

Whatever happened, whether it was religion's becoming more important to him than theatricality, or whether Sellers was the catalyst in his change of direction, Guinness got rid of his gaiety. When he was sent a script containing a part 'tailor-made' for his talents, he'd send it back by return, pettishly making the observation that 'nobody has been to take my measurements'. He was David Lean's third or fourth choice for Col. Nicholson, in *Bridge on the River Kwai*, but this was the kind of rôle – hard, undemonstrative, distant – which he now sought. 'False noses', he said disparingly, 'are too easy.' The putty protuberances, and all that went with them, were appropriated by Sellers. * He it was, sniffing and sneezing with ambition, whose restlessness and energy now found form in darting from one character part to the next; and whilst he was about it, as we'll see in the next chapter, he revitalised British cinema, virtually on his own. Sellers may have been a trifling, arbitrary man in real life, but before he lost his sense of control, his irresponsibilty, as far as acting went (and no further), was a virtue; it made him the actor he was. It's his own mercurialism which he puts on exhibition; his mystical thoughts and haphazard nature which filled out unremarkable characters in remarkable ways; his prodigality which revels and recoils around the remote mental crannies of Fred Kite, Mr Martin, Clare Quilty, Dr Strangelove, and the Lord He Knoweth Who else all.

☆ ★ ☆

Sellers was a *commedia dell 'arte* Alec Guinness. The sheer glee he brings to (say) Mr Topaze's discovery of crime, or the Rev. Smallwood's astral hymn singing, or to General Fitzjohn, high on his white charger, his eye-glass trained on the promenading schoolgirls giggling and romping in the dead bracken, contains the top-spin of an extra, sly joke. He seems to be sending a signal to the audience which says, in effect: Here is the Sellers version of Sir Alec! I'm out-Guinnessing Guinness! This message would have come across strongly when Sellers' films were first released, for every reviewer

---

* 'The man with the longest nose sees furthest.' *Russian proverb.*

made the comparison and rubbed in who they thought he was emu-
lating.* In fact, the homage might more accurately work the other
way about. If you look at Prince Feisal in *Lawrence of Arabia*,
Lieut.-Col. Jock Sinclair in *Tunes of Glory*, Hitler, in *Hitler – The
Last Ten Days*, or the Earl of Darincourt, in *Little Lord Fauntleroy*,
the accents and appearance Guinness adopts are Sellers'; and there
must be people across the world willing to swear on oath that, in
David Lean's *A Passage to India*, the part of Professor Godbole is
played not by Sir Alec Guinness but by Peter Sellers. We'll never
know if the elaborate dance sequence which Guinness extemporised
for Godbole, and which Peggy Ashcroft said she 'watched breath-
lessly', was cut from the final print because the actor was being even
more like Sellers than Sellers, or whether Lean was punishing Guinness for being inventive and original. (When he became renowned
for his tasteful epics, Lean's instincts for a performance left him
and he focused his attention, instead, on photographing cloud-
scapes, sand storms, snowflakes and motes of dust, daring them to
move.)†

But before the symptoms of rigor mortis set in with Lean, there
was Alexander Mackendrick, the Scot with an American passport,
who'd directed *Whisky Galore* and Guinness in *The Man in the
White Suit*. This 'sophisticated grown-up Peter Pan', in Guinness'
description, was a combination of scepticism and eagerness, of
'caustic wit and chuckling irony'; and all this, plus Guinness himself
in his rococo mode, plus a thirty-year old Sellers ready to show willing and as yet free from too many overt emotional blights, comes
together in *The Ladykillers*, a masterpiece of fairy-tale telling.

---

* The Authorised Biographer comments in strange surrealist and taxidermist
mood: 'In creating his film rôles, [Sellers] always worked from the outside in –
the opposite of Guinness, who created an interior life before, as it were, drawing
his skin round it.'

† Have any of you sat through *Dr Zhivago* recently? Such are the false whiskers,
opera chorus crowd scenes, and generally stilted acting, I was put in mind of one
of those interminable and slumbrous silent movie melodramas – especially as
Guinness, miming his way through the role of a humourless commissar, does
most of his speaking in voice-overs.

Mackendrick had begun his career by drawing strip cartoons for Horlicks ads.; he made out that the milky soporific repaired the battered body at the end of the day – Horlicks was an *elixir vitae*. He moved on from this to devising and designing commercials for the cinema, where he collaborated with George Pal, the stop-action puppet animator and the director (in 1958) of *Tom Thumb*. It's *Tom Thumb*, with its garish woodland colours and pantomime hyperbole which, in the Sellers' canon, *The Ladykillers* most resembles. The villains, as played by Sellers and Terry-Thomas, could fit with ease into Professor Marcus' gang. The theme – dreams coming true and going sour – is also the same.

'It's horrible to admit,' Mackendrick says, 'but one of the most interesting and exciting, and even rewarding, times of my life was during the war.' He'd worked for the PWB (Psychological Warfare Branch) Film Production Section, shooting documentary footage of Nazi atrocities and Italian lynchings, and all these deaths and murders somehow seeped into his imagination – they are the source of the off-stage bleakness and horror in his comedies, and of the direct and brutal betrayals in his tragedies, such as the under-valued and fucked-up-by-the-studio *A High Wind in Jamaica*. When he was required to record the exhumation of corpses hidden in a cave by the Germans, Mackendrick was appalled when the heads started to fall off and roll away ('bodies tend to rot at the neck'). He then found himself laughing uncontrollably at 'the terrible slapstick humour of it'. This is the temperament of a man who could set five grown men on to a defenceless little old lady and twist it around, so that she survives, in a world of her own, and it's the bewildered quintet which is wiped out: 'We'll never be able to kill her, Louis,' Guinness' character says to Herbert Lom's. 'She'll always be with us, for ever and ever and ever, and there's nothing we can do about it.'

Many and various have been the commentaries evoked by *The Ladykillers*. Charles Barr, for example, in his history of the Ealing Studios, regards the film as political allegory: 'The gang are the post-war Labour Government. Taking over "the House", they gratify the Conservative incumbent by their civilised behaviour (that nice music) and decide to use at least the façade of respectability for their radical programme of redistributing wealth. . .' Gavin Stamp, in an essay printed in *The Times* on November 3rd 1990, thinks the film inadvertently records the vanished charm of Fifties London. He has made blow-ups from stills and uses them to illustrate his lectures on the urban history of King's Cross: the film is 'set against a background which is shabby and ravaged, full of bomb sites and dereliction, and yet which is somehow authentic, vital and tough. No high buildings yet spoil the Westminster and City skyline; cars are always black; there are no plastic signs and Georgian terraces are properly grimy with dark-painted joinery. . .'

If Barr's paragraph is gibberish and Stamp's architectural nostalgia, if not irrelevant to explaining the film, is at best incidental (though I share his enthusiasm for red telephone kiosks and 'the surreal desolation of a Victorian railway landscape'), Stamp has at least put in some legwork. Lots of it. He informs us that the robbery was filmed outside Stanley Buildings, in Cheney Road ('a still cobbled backstreet between St Pancras and King's Cross termini'); that the crooks loiter near the Jesmond Dene Hotel, on the corner of St Chad's Street, when they are waiting for the arrival of the loot; and that Mrs Wilberforce's lopsided house was constructed 'about a mile further north', on Frederick Street, off the Caledonian Road: 'Frederick Street has been realigned, rebuilt and renamed (it is now Frederica Street) and diesels have replaced steam, but it is still possible to stand above the railway tunnel and see the strange, smoke-filled panorama.'

It says much for the enchantment of *The Ladykillers* that it can induce such pilgrimages and detective work; and it is true that, here and there, beyond the actors, Betjeman's London is going about its business. ('It is a London which I scarcely knew as a child,' says Stamp, 'but which I find hauntingly beautiful.') But to seek 'the real-life setting' for the film, to try and recapture the spirit of place, makes about as much sense as those tourist trails for Sherlock Holmes' sleuthings or those Princeton professors you see unfolding maps in Dublin, following in the footsteps of Leopold Bloom. It is not that Mrs Wilberforce, One-Round, etc., never lived, because Katie Johnson, Danny Green, Guinness, Sellers, and so on, did indeed walk upon those pavements pleasant in ancient time; it is simply that we are dealing here with make-believe and illusion, and if Mackendrick used a street directory it was only to transfigure it. *The Ladykillers* has all the solidity of a pop-up book – unlike *Passport to Pimlico*, say, which is actually about a London which is as lost as Atlantis, and where a Gavin Stamp-style analysis would be central to its meaning and not a gripping footnote. However, the urge is there and it is strong: to pay tribute to a time and place come and gone; to go and gaze at vistas which are not there now. It is not so very unlike my own obsession – to know everything about and explain a man I never met, who never knew I existed. Sellers, the stranger to my heart and me.*

☆ ☆ ☆

The story had appeared to William Rose in a dream: 'I woke up one morning, at about one or two o'clock, and wakened my wife, and said: "I've just dreamt a whole film. . ."' Mrs Wilberforce, Professor Marcus, the raid on the security van, taking strongboxes to King's Cross, the stringed instrument playing masquerade . . . Everything. It is thus Philip Kemp's account, in his critical biography *Lethal Innocence: The Cinema of Alexander Mackendrick*, which is the most enlightening. 'Perhaps Mrs Wilberforce,' he suggests, 'has fallen asleep within earshot of a radio and conjured up the gang from the depth of her psyche.' The violence and murder mood is thus 'an emanation from the dark underworld of Victorian morality'.

Well, yes it might be. But (as in Dickens), the characters don't need to have bizarre, hidden, or ugly thoughts and inklings; they

---

* The sacking of a city and the death of a famous man are bought into metaphorical conjunction by W.H. Auden in his poem 'In Memory of W.B. Yeats' (1939): 'O all the instruments agree/The day of his death was a dark cold day/ . . . / . . . it was his last afternoon as himself,/An afternoon of nurses and rumours;/The provinces of his body revolted,/The squares of his mind were empty,/Silence invaded the suburbs,/The current of his feeling failed: he became his admirers.'

don't need to possess inner lives at all. Eccentricity and goodness are there, stark, on the surface. We know Mrs Wilberforce is a one-woman protected species, a fairy, because she carries a wand – her parasol, which she keeps absent-mindedly losing. We know Professor Marcus is a troll by his outsize teeth and goblin's gait – he is as real as Rumpelstiltskin. And if, now and again, you are reminded of somebody else but you can't think whom, you'd be right. 'When I first saw myself in make-up I remember saying to Sandy [Mackendrick], "I look remarkably like an aged Ken Tynan; perhaps I'd better smoke cigarettes the way he does."' Thus the long, sneering face, the lank hair, the air of being a dandy with time to fill – revenge on Tynan for his little monograph on Guinness,* in which he argued that the actor was so nondescript, he'd make the perfect murderer. 'It was an absolute personal portrait of Ken, exaggerated for gothic effect,' Mackendrick himself confirms.

They are all exaggerated for gothic effect. Lom's Louis doesn't stop glowering; Cecil Parker's Major's moustache and canary-coloured waistcoat are out of a *Punch* cartoon; Danny Green's giant old lag, in his prison greys, seems carved out of rock; and Sellers' Teddy Boy, full of apprehension, pretends to be dipping and diving to Bill Haley and his Comets, or some such grandfatherly pop music. His Harry Robinson is totally jittery.

Sellers, as we know from his own mouth, watched Guinness like a kestrel. He was also, according to Tom Pevsner, the assistant director, 'very nervous and uncertain, and looking to Sandy for reassurance all the time'. His insecurity was noticed by Michael Balcon, too. 'He was desperately anxious. He kept asking: "Is it all right? Am I any good?"' It is just this lack of confidence which comes across in the character – and it is ideal. Sellers may well have been 'utterly sincere and genuine' (Balcon's words) when questioning

---

* Sellers bought a copy of *Alec Guinness* (London, Rockliff, 1953) and gave it to the Authorised Biographer, encouraging Walker to see that 'some of Tynan's . . . phrases and judgements might have been detached from Guinness and tied on to Sellers.' (Like balloons?)

his work, but underneath the prevarications, Harry was taking shape. He's always looking over his shoulder, or pretending to be walking away; he gazes at Professor Marcus, eager for instructions and desperate to be emboldened. Harry, wanting to learn from the master criminal, is Sellers himself, absorbing the craft of a master-mummer; he plays the role as a London Jew – as near as he dared to the son of Peg, his own hair slightly curled and a duelling scar added to his cheek. It is Harry who is the gang's driver – they have a vast black limousine, like a hearse – and it is Harry who tries to ingratiate himself with the old lady, helping out with her parrots (which Sellers voiced): 'You leave it to me, Ma. I'm very good with birds.'

It is not hard to imagine Harry as a mother-fixated East-Ender; and when Mrs Wilberforce creates the chaos with the barrow boy and the street marketeers, it is he who comments with amazement and awe: 'All of them out of business in ten minutes.' Katie Johnson's character is supernatural – her lightweight toddle is a hint that any moment she'll whirr aloft and take flight. Her face makes babies scream in their prams; her voice makes horses bolt. In the original script, she was to have been narrowly missed by a wrecker's ball on a building site, which swung past and crushed a car. Oblivious to it all, she's obviously Inspector Clouseau's fairy godmother.

Her house, a lopsided fairy-tale cottage, is a toy theatre. It is packed with fringes, drapes, antimacassars, velvet and lace; it has coloured glass screens and curtained partitions. It is a setting for shaping fantasies and fancy's images. There's no more marvellous sequence in British cinema than the one where Mrs Wilberforce's chums come to tea – dozens of Mrs Wilberforce doubles, it seems, a conclave of trim, elderly fairies – who have popped up through trap doors, chattering non-stop and bearing tidings of the robbery in King's Cross. Their costumes of feathered hats and pointy shoes – and parasols – are Victorian-era crossed with Walt Disney. The animated feature of *Cinderella*, with its bibbidi-bobbidi-boo atmosphere, had been released a few years previously, and some of its spare pixies are evidently at large.

The robbers are powerless before this massed band. Instead of stamping out the little old lady infestation, which size for size would be no contest, they are spellbound. The next thing we know, everybody is in the parlour, the Professor hunched over the pianola, Louis backed into a corner, and Harry, up against the door, has a cup and saucer in one hand, a scone on a plate in the other, and he has absolutely no idea how to get either of them up to and in his gob. It is then that they start to sing – the quavery women, the flat and defeated men:

Darling, I am growing old,
Silver threads among the gold,
Shine upon my brow today:
Life is fast fading away.

☆ ★ ☆

Inside the house, where the music we hear is that Boccherini minuet, often scored for a music box's tinkle, the light is mauve and lavender – a soft and cool glow. Outside, where objects are in harsh silhouette and the night skies are a dark blue, the soundtrack is full of trains screeching and trucks being shunted. *The Ladykillers* is one of the great railway movies, like *The Lady Vanishes* or *Murder on the Orient Express*. But chuff-chuffs are no more realistically used than the London street locations. Mrs Wilberforce's villa, lying in the shadow of Sir George Gilbert Scott's St Pancras, a forest of red sandstone, looks like a turret that has dropped off the station; similarly, Professor Marcus is a liberated gargoyle. In a scene which was cut from the final print, whilst he was making his first inspection of his rooms, he had to listen to Mrs Wilberforce whitter on about her previous lodger, a Mr Proudlock, who did nothing but stare out of the window and collect engine numbers. 'And, what', Guinness said, exasperation eventually getting the better of him, 'did Mr, eh, Proudlock *do* with the engine numbers he collected. . . ?' The pointlessness of the hobby is a glimpse of Hell.

The steam trains are the film's dragons. They send clouds of sulphurous vapour billowing about the house. When the Major is pushed off the roof, Harry is brained by One-Round, Louis is killed, or the Professor crowned (by the railway signal), smoke and gasses cover the violence – we never see anything nasty – and the bodies are taken, one by one in a wheelbarrow, across the vegetable patch to the viaduct; and they are then tipped over to the tracks, far below. It could be Quatermass' pit down there, a place where the souls of the dead breathe out of the tunnel and tombs. The trains whoosh in the mist and their lights shine and blink like dim yellow eyes.

If the house is a bit of broken gingerbread, the backyard a haunt of hydras, and the looming edifice of King's Cross a wild wood of twisted pinnacles and branches, the film's calamity – One Round's tugging at his double bass case and all the stolen money spilling out – has the beauty of falling leaves. The large white notes flutter from the cobalt sky in silence and slow motion. The men are mesmerised, as they were by the sudden appearance of the flibbertigibbets. There's nothing for it but to dash back inside the funhouse and plead for sanctuary. They wheedle; they cajole; they threaten blackmail. Mrs Wilberforce is adamant. The money must be handed to the police. They try sob stories:

The PROFESSOR calls in the MAJOR like an orchestral conductor.

MAJOR (*in emotion*)
No . . . no . . . I . . .

PROFESSOR (*gently insistent*)
Tell her.

MAJOR (*reluctantly*)
Oh, well – it's just that – well, at this very moment, Mrs. Wilberforce, there is waiting an invalid – a dear sweet, little old lady, not, may heaven bless her, unlike yourself. Waiting with patient serenity but with high hope, that she has nothing more to fear. (*pause*) My mother.

The PROFESSOR, behind MUM's back, nods to HARRY

HARRY (*on cue*)

With me, it's my little sister. She married a trapeze artist, Mum. Forced her into his act he did, a hundred feet up and no net. I told her I'd get some money to buy a little place for her and the kiddies. When I think of her up there, swinging to and fro . . . to and fro . . . (HARRY sees it in his mind's eye) . . . and her scared of heights, and all her little kiddies watching with their little eyes, holding their breaths . . . Just a little place on the ground, that's all she wants. . . .

PROFESSOR
Each of them can tell a similar story. I planned the robbery, Mrs Wilberforce. (*simply*) I wanted to help them.

A long pause.

MUM
No.

HARRY
Eh?

MUM
No. I don't think – even if what you say is true – I still don't think it can be said to be enough justification.

MAJOR
In the name of all that's *holy*, Madam! Have you no decent feelings whatever?

MUM walks back into the hall.

I have quoted from the scene at length because we don't get to see much of it in the actual film. * *The Ladykillers* was thought to be over-running, so chunks were lopped off by (as usually happens in such cases) the studio janitor. 'You know,' said Sellers, 'I might have got somewhere with *The Ladykillers*, but forty minutes were cut. A lot of *me* was cut with that forty minutes.' If you watch what is left of the above carefully on your Ealing Greats videocassette, you'll

---

* My source is the original shooting script, housed in the archives of the British Film Institute. My thanks to Philip Kemp for fishing it out.

notice a clumsy leap from the Major's 'My Mother' to the Professor's 'Each of them can tell a similar story.' Sellers was furious at having his big moment cut, and he lost confidence in the production.

'I myself was in *The Ladykillers* to get away from having to say the same lines every night for two years in *The King and I*,' Herbert Lom told me at the Reform Club. 'I'd taken over Yul Brynner's part and my head was shaven – that's why Louis wears a hat all the time indoors. Peter turned up in my dressing room after the show and *implored* me to get him a job on another film. He was convinced *The Ladykillers* was a disaster. He was sure of himself as a mimic, but not as an actor. As an actor he thought he'd be out of work.'

Mackendrick, too, was sad at having to sanction the retrenchment – though in recent years he told Philip Kemp: 'Bill Rose has one thing which delights me: when he gets hold of an idea he *milks* it – boy, does he milk it. In that scene in the kitchen where Cecil Parker is talking about "a little old lady not unlike yourself," there was a long speech from the Peter Sellers character which was very funny, and was indeed shot – but it just didn't play, it wouldn't go on that long.'

Since we now know what is missing, it is hard to be satisfied with the gap. It yawns. In fact, the rhythm, the absurd build-up, is wrecked; and Harry's 'Eh?' after Mum's 'No' loses its force – he's meant to be incredulous that his yarn hasn't won her over. I'd give a lot to have Sellers' little high-wire fantasy restored. His speech takes the mood off to a Goonish dimension, to a facetious realm which Mackendrick and Seth Holt, the associate producer, big fans of *The Goon Show* itself, had wanted him to supplement the film with when he was originally cast; it's why they lobbied Balcon for Sellers and not Attenborough, the young scarface of *Brighton Rock*. And of course it is *The Goon Show*, whimsical and fantastic, and with its psychopathic undercurrents, which lies behind *The Ladykillers*, linking them both together and to their Fifties era. Major Courtenay is Major Bloodnok; Mrs Wilberforce is Minerva Bannister; Professor Marcus, twisted and decrepit, is an Emett or Searle drawing of

Henry Crun, his madcap plan worthy of Grytpype and Moriarty. One Round is the brainless Eccles and Harry is Bluebottle – when he's alarmed, his voice *is* Bluebottle's. If the technology had existed, Sellers could have played them all – and in a way, he did. Michael Balcon, reminiscing in 1960, said: 'It would be easy for me to say now that I always knew he was brilliant. But that was not so. I admired him, thought he had possibilities. I didn't realise then what I now recognise, that he was a near genius, perhaps a whole one. Genius is a much-abused word, but I think Sellers and Guinness have it . . . One day we were all sitting in the studio canteen when over the loudspeaker came what sounded like the soundtrack from the film. But it wasn't the soundtrack. It was Peter impersonating all the actors himself on a tape recorder, including the camera director's remarks as well. People still talk about it in the studio – we were quite shaken.'

Sellers' spoof trailer for *The Ladykillers*, for this is what Balcon was hearing, was his acoustic version of *Kind Hearts and Coronets* – a chance to diversify, to be a multitude. Sellers had copies made of his handiwork, which I suspect Larry Stephens had helped him to write, and he gave them out as gifts at the wrap party. 'He gave us all farewell-presents of a piece of tape, on which he played an interviewer talking to Alec, Cecil, Danny Green, and me,' says Lom. 'We all listened to ourselves – and it was him. A great actor like Alec, or Cecil, Danny, me: no-one else could have done that. . .' Sellers was advertising his own cormorant-capacity for voices. His offering was less a souvenir of the shoot than a little token of his bid for prominence, and if the 'trailer' hadn't been so good, he could easily have been accused of effrontery. It was believed lost, long disposed of. But Tom Pevsner recently found an acetate disc in a recording booth (Sellers had had it professionally mixed) and he repaired it for Philip Kemp, who then passed it on to me. Here, coming out of the crackle, is my transcription:

Jolly, Fifties' Rank cinema music and fanfares, accompanied by the audience muttering and settling down.

COCKNEY LADY: 'Ere, I've forgotten me glasses, Bert.

OLD CODGER: Oh, gorblimey.

The woozy strings build and we swoop to a brisk newsreel announcer-type voice – to which Sellers gives an edge of bossiness, which gets gradually more openly contemptuous and idiotic.

ANNOUNCER: Once again Ealing Studios who have brought you such great successes as *The Cruel C* starring Mario Lanza, *The Night My Ship Died of Shame*, *Above Us the Joneses*, *Passport to Golders Green*, *The Man in the Right Boots*, now bring you their latest hilarious comedy, *The Lady-killers*, adapted from *Tomorrow's New Yesterday*, the Wurlitzer Prize-winning novel by Otto Heller; *The Ladykillers* tells of a ruthless gang of criminals headed by Alec Guinness, CBE, the man of a thousand faces – remember Fagin? He plays Professor Marcus, the cool, cunning, calculating leader. Herbert Lom, direct from his great success as Anna, in *The King of Siam*, plays Louis, the suave continental crook whose villainous past combines well with Major Courtenay – a masterpiece of underplaying by Cecil Parker of Vista-Vision fame. His partner in death is Peter Sellers of radio's White Coons. Next in this scintillating array of stars comes Danny Green as One Round, the punch-drunk actor-boxer. With him it's brawn, bulk, and a hideous sense of humour. And introducing Katie Johnson as Mrs Wilberforce, the lovely little old, little old landlady who in the end captivates the cold hearts of – *The Ladykillers*.

The insidious strings have continued over the above – they swell up again for a brief interlude, then:

ANNOUNCER: Here are but a few scenes from the Sir Ealing Balcon Michael Studios Production. . . .

Cut to the Boccherini String Quintet, which plays over

HARRY: How do we know we can trust her to do it right if she don't even know what she's doing?

LOUIS: I tell you I hate little old ladies. I want it settled here and now.

PROFESSOR: No one is indispensable, Louis. Only the plan, my plan. Do you agree. Major?

MAJOR: (*Bloodnokish*): Ha! Well, I .. . . I'm with you, Professor. After all, it is twelve thousand pounds all round. One-Round?

ONE-ROUND: (*Eccles*): I'm staying with Ma. I'm *staying* with Ma. *I'm* staying with Ma. What do you say, Louis?

LOUIS: I want it settled here and now.

ANNOUNCER: See them pleading with Mrs Wilberforce in a vain attempt to prevent her going to the bogies, the rozzers, the peelers, the flatfeet, the police.

The Boccherini is suddenly played at very high speed. Then –

PROFESSOR: Mrs Wilberforce, I really should tell you . . .

MRS WILBERFORCE: (*peculiarly like Crystal Jollibottom*): Don't you speak to me, Professor Marcus, I'm disgusted to say the least. Ah! I know what I must do. I must ask you to vacate my rooms immediately.

ONE-ROUND: Oh, now listen lady, we went to a whole load of . . .

MRS WILBERFORCE: (*suggestive*): You be quiet. *Your* dinner's in the oven.

ONE ROUND: OK, Ma. But I'm staying buttoned up.

Drum roll and fanfares

ANNOUNCER: All this, plus Frankie Howerd, bringing drama to the screen as the naughty barrow boy.

HOWERD: Eh, ooh, arrr, ooohh, arrr – ooohh!! [*etc*]

ANNOUNCER: No expense was spared to make this film the pick of the Ealing bunch this year. Here in a candid shot by our newsreel camera is a brief glimpse of the brilliant technique of Alexander Mackendrick, the director, hard at work on the floor.

Music disappears. Fade up of lots of chatter and hammer bangings from crew.

MACKENDRICK: (*diffident and Scots*): Tom, ah, Tom, ah, ah, can, um, we go? Tom?

PEVSNER: (*assertive, cutting in*): Yes, Sandy. Lock the doors and let's have it quiet. *I said QUIET!* OK Otto?

OTTO HELLER: (*cinematographer – Dr Strangelove voice*): No, no. Not OK. But who cares?

CAMP VOICE: We are waiting to shoot, Otto.

OTTO: Now he tells me.

CAMP VOICE: Right – Turn over.

TECHNICIAN: Mark it. Scene 5. Take 73.

Clapperboard snaps

MACKENDRICK: Action!

Speeded-up Goon voices – unintelligible

MACKENDRICK: Cut! Cut! Peter, Peter, that's, um, very good. We'll do another.

ANNOUNCER: Yes, folks, don't fail to miss *The Lady-killers*, coming to this cinema *soon*. *Coming* to this cinema soon. Coming to *this* cinema soon. Coming *to* this cinema. . . .

*Burst of Anton Karas' 'Harry Lime' zither theme as playout.**

☆ ★ ☆

---

* When Sellers was residing at the Hotel Bristol, Vienna, during the making of *The Prisoner of Zenda*, he hired Karas, then in his seventies, to come and play the zither privately for him over dinner. No doubt Sellers also raised his own flag and, like Grace Kelly, issued his personal stamps and coin.

Chapter Eight
No, Not Ealing

[Oxford]
July 10th 1989

Dear Sir Alec Guinness,

I am working on a book about Peter Sellers ... My intention is
to explore the ways in which his haunted personality and
experience shaped his art; and the book will give much weight to
the films. ...

To these ends, and given Sellers' high regard for your own work,
I am wondering [etc.].

☆ ★ ☆

[Petersfield, Hants]
March 5th 1990

Dear Mr Lewis,

[...]
I admired his talent – which had flashes of genius – enormously.
I worked with him only twice and always found him personally
agreeable and friendly, but I never got to know him.

During the making of 'Murder by Death' he had become pretty
odd – measuring his caravan with a tape measure to make sure it
was larger than everyone else's; deciding his mood by the colour
of a stone in his ring; not turning up for shooting – saying he
was ill – but seen lunching by David Niven in a Beverly Hills

restaurant; making extravagant demands on the management etc.
– all tiresome stuff which made me think he had become a little
unbalanced. I had the impression he greatly feared death but
can't remember him actually saying so [. . .]

> Yours sincerely
>
> *Alec Guinness*

☆ ★ ☆

Of the two British character actors who have managed to become
sound-era film stars of world renown, one went insane and the
other is cordial. Guinness exchanged his briskness (Herbert Pocket)
for a serenity (Smiley) and dispassionateness (William Dorrit). 'I
like to get away from myself as an actor,' he recently confessed,
before adding: 'Or I used to, but now that I'm seventy-five, I don't.'
Sellers, by complete contrast, was never able to curb his nervous-
ness and restlessness, and he used acting, along with his transient
enthusiasms for a variety of women, religions, and residences, as a
means of exploring, in a way that was almost detached – *entranced*
you might say – all the misshapenness that loomed inside himself.
Morbidly self-conscious, he was a man inordinately concerned with
his own lack of colour – so he put himself, and those within his
force field, through a series of tests and cues. He wanted to witness
reactions – and, missing nothing, prove to himself that he existed.

His arrival on Cyprus, for *Ghost in the Noonday Sun*, in 1973,
illustrates what I mean: 'We rented an incredible villa for him,' says
Peter Medak, 'an *incredible* villa. But trouble started immediately.
Peter turned up with his chauffeur and two hundred pieces of luggage. Before he did anything, he suddenly started unpacking one of
the suitcases and brought out the most sophisticated Sony stereo
system; he then unrolled a Gucci leather tool kit. "What are you
doing?" – "Wait a minute, baby, I've got to put my stereo together."
Then I tried to show him the bedroom and the rest of the house.
He took a compass from his pocket and started running through the
whole place. I took him to the master bedroom. "Oh that won't do,"
looking at the compass, "that won't do." He ended up in the maid's

bedroom. "That's where I'm going to sleep because this faces to the East." – "You are out of your mind. The mosquitoes are going to eat you up. This is terrible. . . ." Then we went downstairs and started talking, and he said, "Let's look up the credits of the producers in that copy of *Who's Who*." I said, "One is American – he won't be in there; the other is a gentleman called Tommy Clyde." He put the book down and said, "I'm going to get rid of them. I'm going to fire them." – "What are you talking about?" – "I've got to get rid of the producers." A week later he created a situation whereby the producers were fired by him; but I'm sure they would have quit or resigned anyway.'

He'd been similarly destructive and mistrustful (i.e. paranoid) on *Casino Royale*, about six years earlier. 'One of the problems that blew the film apart,' says Joe McGrath, 'was that Orson Welles and I got along really well. "I think we've got a chance here. We'll be quite funny," reckoned Welles. Sellers then got annoyed. "I didn't think you and Orson would take sides against me." – "I'm not taking sides against you, but Orson has the same feelings that you have – that there's a chance we can come up with some funny stuff." – "Well, I'll only attempt to come up with funny stuff so long as *he's not there*." So he and Orson came in on different days. He was frightened of the *scale* of Orson: his legend; literally his weight and immensity.'

'He was willing to sabotage the entire movie if it meant appearing in a scene with Orson and being outclassed?' I asked. 'Orson didn't have the same attitude about his career as Peter had,' McGrath replied. 'Peter *was* what he did. Orson thought: "I'll take the money and be here for four weeks. Let's enjoy ourselves." Peter's thing was: "My whole career, my *life*, is on the line here. I'm not going to let anybody mess around with my career." He was depressive, worried about money, and wanting to earn more and more of it; repressive with his children, pulling them about and sending them to expensive schools, and then not caring, or understanding, if they didn't fit into an academic routine. . . .'

Also to fall on *Casino Royale* was John Bluthal. 'When that started I was going to play five or six characters, spies in disguise, and so on, throughout the film. Then there was a row between Peter and Joe. After a while, Joe came to see me and said, "I'm sorry – I'm off the film." If he's off the film, my days are numbered, I thought. Sure enough, Sellers came and found me: "You and Joe – you are both the same, aren't you?" – "I don't know what you are talking about Peter." – "Yes – you both decided to make things tough for me. You're making it difficult." – "Peter, I don't know what the hell you're talking about. I don't know what your argument was. I'm playing some parts in this picture. You are starring in it. Joe's the director. . ." Anyway, I was sacked that night. He got rid of me. . .'

Immediately he arrived on a set, Sellers was foreseeing problems – in the early days, because he was conscious of his high artistry and didn't wish to compromise; later, because he wanted to preserve his fame and status; and finally, because only the deployment of crazy laws and the wielding of absolute power gave him any sort of sensation. (As Bluthal says, 'When Sellers was looking for trouble, four or five hundred years ago you'd be for the chopping block.') There'd come a point, which harked back to Nero, where he'd refuse to look at the colours green or purple. I have already mentioned the Ruritanian train story. His secretaries and personal assistants had to pre-inspect visitors and divest them of the offending hues; should you have turned up for a meeting in the wrong shade of pullover or frock, back out through the door you went. And why?

'Green has been a superstition of mine for a long time and purple was laid on me by the late Vittorio Di Sica. We were working one day and his script girl showed up wearing purple. Di Sica went into a foaming rage and sent her away all the time doing this – [and Sellers demonstrated the warding-off-the-evil-eye hand signal.] Just like that. Then he told me. "My dear Peter. Purple is the colour of death." That's where I picked that one up. Being a bit superstitious myself, I latched on to it myself. I figured de Sica must know something. And green. From my mother. She told me. It's certain shades of green. The hard, acidy green is bad. I pick up strange vibrations from it. It disturbs me.'

If he was taking the piss, pure and simple, he kept up the joke for about two decades, and there are hundreds of people who'll testify to his outlandishness. 'We were to do the restaurant scene in *Hoffman*,' says Alvin Rakoff, 'and Peter wouldn't walk on the set, because there were purple tablecloths. We compromised. "They are definitely not purple. Those cloths are lilac."' Sellers refused to meet Blake Edwards' mother-in-law because she owned a purple coat. 'My mother-in-law walked on the set one day in a purple coat, and I saw Sellers come through the door, and then he stopped, turned around, and walked off the set, and would not come back on again until I'd got rid of my mother-in-law.' On *The Prisoner of Zenda*, one Friday, Lionel Jeffries said, 'Well, Peter, I'm glad that's over.' They'd been shooting in an undergound casino, in stultifying heat. 'So am I,' said Sellers. 'But have you seen the roulette wheel? It's *green*. . . .' The scene had to be done again – which is why the green baize in the film is now blood red.

I must add that Sellers didn't only come out with these superstitious fears when he had an audience to impress. His private life was blighted by similar stipulations. In the summer of 1979, he was searching for a flat in Paris. He never found one to his liking – each apartment he was shown had a fleck of green or purple somewhere in its fixtures and fittings. In the end he moved to the Hotel Crillon, @ FF 1,564 per day. His suite consisted of a hall, a sitting room, a study and a bathroom. There was a double bedroom leading off the sitting room, beyond which was a second bathroom. However, the second bathroom was tiled in a light duck egg blue which Sellers decided was a shade of green. 'If you don't want it to make part of your suite,' he was therefore informed, 'you can use the yellow bathroom you first saw, and we can block this second bathroom off.'

Sellers got them to do better than that – the offending ablutions block was bricked up. These bouts of Roman Emperor-standard improprieties, I think, are all part of his search for a retreat – a place within himself, immured by fads and caprices, where he could feel

safe. Chance the gardener was his perfect refuge in this respect.
R.D. Laing, talking about schizophrenia being the ultimate refuge
of the super-sane, has argued that the mad go into that private
world to hide themselves – their fantasies are their protective
armour against the sensitivities and hurts of everyday. Chance represented the ideal – Chance is in total control of his own limited
little world. He can make things happen or make things not happen
in it by wielding his remote-control zapper. No wonder that Sellers
spent eight long years endeavouring to interest a studio in letting
him make the film and play the rôle. Chance's winter garden was
Sellers' great good place.

His enthusiasms were violent and short-lived, though all are connected to his search for inner spiritual harmony – i.e. his attempt to
be as all-powerful and perfect as a god. At one time he took up with
Tracy Reed, a tall dark girl, briefly famous, the daughter of Sir
Carol, the director of *Oliver.** (Tracy is Miss Foreign Affairs in *Doctor Strangelove*.) She was in his suite at the Dorchester and all
Sellers' guests had to do what Herbert Kretzmer (who was present)
called 'the Tracy thing' that night – which was to watch her suspend an amber necklace over a glass. 'Peter had decided she was a
natural diviner or dowser. Much of the evening was spent indulging
Peter's obsession – that all the answers would depend on the rotation of the amber stone.'

Kretzmer also witnessed another revealing scene: 'I went to
dinner with Spike Milligan one night, to Peter's flat in Stag Place. It
was dominated by a huge photograph of his swami. He was utterly
mad and impossible. Nothing had been prepared – no dinner. We
were sitting around and a lot of Indians arrived from the take-away;
a succession of Indians bearing tin foil trays, which Sellers dumped
on the smoked glass coffee table. There was no wine – he hadn't

---

* Sellers held up production for months because he was unable to decide whether
or not to accept the rôle of Fagin – and compete, as he saw it, with Alec Guinness' night gown and glass diamonds performance of 1948. (Harry Secombe was
Mr Bumble.)

done anything at all, except fuss around putting on rock records so loudly nobody could speak, whilst we were eating out of tin foil trays. He had no time for conversation. There was no period during that evening when there was any quiet or exchange; it was like we were humouring a drunk or a lunatic. After two or three tracks, off would come that record, and he'd spend a lot of time searching through his collection, wandering in and out of the room and disappearing. He had one of the biggest and most powerful telescopes money can buy. It was trained on Big Ben, upside down. Any distraction – to avoid being normal, attractive, and possibly revealing.

'I called Peter the next day to thank him for the evening. "Wonderful, your phoning," he said. "When one goes to a little bit of trouble to set up a dinner party, it's nice for people to appreciate it."

'I'd never known a man to take less trouble. "It was good to see Spike again," I said. "Yes – but he's turning out to be a bit of an oddball, isn't he?" And Spike had been perfectly coherent, sunny, wise, witty, when he got the opportunity amidst the clamour. Sellers was the oddball – but he'd reversed this in his mind. . .'

☆ ★ ☆

The Greenwich Royal Observatory-calibre telescope, topsy-turvily fixed on the inverted clockface of Big Ben, is symbolic, surely? Sellers always wanted to outwit time; to show himself indifferent to its destructiveness. He began, as a drummer, by literally beating time; and he believed that if he behaved heedlessly, irresponsibly, time would be knocked out of joint for him. He'd thump it into submission. He'd be Peter Pan, never growing up, never hastened out of childhood and away from Peg – his personal Wendy and Mrs Darling rolled into one. ('What are your exact feelings for me, Peter?' – 'Those of a devoted son, Wendy.') After he'd dumped Anne, Michael, and Sarah ('No one is going to catch me, lady, and make me a man') he decided to enjoy the mad streak. He dieted. He popped a lot of pills – to get this gaunt, Don Juan look (on view in *Casino Royale* and *There's a Girl in My Soup*). He drank. He did an

enormous amount of fucking, at which he was not all that good.*
Later, there was a hefty use of cocaine – because somebody, I
believe Keith Moon, had told him it would improve his potency,
enabling him to wave his willy and retain an erection all night. He
used to smoke pot, and during the years he was beyond the grasp of
the Inland Revenue in Ireland, he was really practically living in
outer space. He seemed disembodied and, when people went to see
him, he was so drugged and slurred, he was existing in slow
motion. He'd got time to stand still.

'I could hardly make any sense out of him,' says Leslie Linder, a
producer who flew to Dublin with a proposal for a film called *The
Phantom versus the Reich* – the idea was that Hitler, long a Sellers
comic hero, had not been killed in the bunker; he had escaped to
South America, where he was living with his idiot son and planning
to make one more bid for global power. A team of crack neo-Nazis
were to be sent to compete in the Royal Highland Games at Brae-
mar. Sellers had agreed to play Hitler père and fils. . . .

'I went over to see him with the writer Clive Exton. Peter was
stoned out of his mind. He and his girlfriend were so far gone, they
couldn't prepare lunch. They couldn't work out how a fridge door
opened, and Peter gazed with rapture at a tomato. I had to prepare
lunch for us all. And often, afterwards, if I saw him in London or
Los Angeles, he was in a drug-induced dream-world – on a different planet. It made communication with him impossible.
Everything was slow-paced. *Interminable*. . .'

It wasn't only marijuana and Bolivian Marching Powder making
him like that, in all fairness. He was never an addict – drugs were
simply a way, like going into a yogic trance, of taking a leave of
absence from reality. If it wasn't his schizophrenia giving him a
blank and glassy look then it might have been Lem-Sip – Sellers
being the only man in history to have overdosed on this all-purpose

---

* This is according to Wolf Mankowitz, who'd broached the subject with Britt
  Ekland – 'Ask her if you don't believe me,' Wolf dared. So far I've been too much
  of a cowardy-custard to follow this particular line of inquiry.

anodyne. And Sellers was also stuffing himself with prescribed medicaments for his angina – though that condition, a by-product of his first coronary, was, in effect, self-induced. After having lured Britt, the young Swedish starlet, into his bed at the Dorchester, in February 1964, he began, once they were engaged, to guzzle and snort ampoules of amyl nitrate. These opened his valves and ventricles, increased the gush of blood throughout his anatomy, and enriched his orgasms. By Tuesday April 7th, his heart had pumped itself inside out and it gave up the ghost.

Because he recovered, he believed more than ever that he had totally created and recreated himself: the fat boy who had slimmed, the radio mimic who was a film star, the written-off patient who came back from the dead. Look! I have come through! Henceforward, he thought, if he kept himself busy, manic, on the go, he wouldn't (as it were) have the leisure, the time, to die; or else, by attending to tinklings from mystical bells, and going in for supernatural manifestations and premonitions, he'd do his best to ensure he was not there when it happened. As much as he was obsessed by Sophia Loren, he once refused to fly to Rome for lunch with her because the newspaper horoscopes that morning had said 'this was not a good time to travel . . .' (Sellers was actually going up the Alitalia jet's steps at Heathrow before he decided to double-back.)

When time's arrow eventually did strike him plumb in the heartstrings, at 12.28 am on Thursday July 24th 1980, he was setting up *The Romance of the Pink Panther*. It was conceived for stunt-men, reverse angles and long shots, and Sellers himself would barely have featured in it. It would have thus proved his transfiguration – he'd have been starring in a film and yet only appearing fleetingly in it, like a wraith. (The man-who-never-was as the man-who-was-not-there.) The conceit was taken over by Blake Edwards, who cobbled together out-takes and a compilation of unattributed highlights from previous 'Panthers,' to create the illusion of a new feature film, *The Trail of the Pink Panther*, in 1982. Sellers' double, John Taylor, the man who had actually done many of the heavy make-up scenes in *The Fiendish Plot of Dr. Fu Manchu*, because Sellers was either absent or ill, was hired, on minimum Equity rates, to impersonate Clouseau for a morning of linking shots. The result is ingenious and a shambles, and of interest principally to copyright lawyers[*] – but it does convey the impression that Sellers had continued to materialise in films after he had cooled. . .

☆   ★   ☆

Of course, his dodges to use up time and to waste time, with his moods and fads, nymphs and narcotics, all imply a fear – the fear shrewdly scented by Alec Guinness – rather than an attitude for genuine disdain. It was bravado. This man in Peter Pan was as fretful as Captain Hook, forever hearing his nemesis, the crocodile, creeping towards him, the clock ticking louder and louder in its

---

[*] The one hundred and six page transcript of Mr Justice Hobhouse's Judgment of *Rickless v. United Artists Corporation*, delivered in the High Court of Justice, Queen's Bench Division, on May 24th 1985, makes interesting reading. As regards the debate over whether *Trail* damaged Sellers' reputation, or whether the law suit was for financial compensation for the use of clips and out-takes, the Judge said: 'Lynne Sellers suggested that her sole interests in this matter were aesthetic and did not involve any question of money. I do not accept this part of her evidence. I accept that she was genuinely concerned about the quality of some of the material proposed to be used . . . but I am also satisfied that she made it clear to Blake Edwards or others acting on his behalf that she did expect some substantial payments to be made for the right to re-use any relevant material.'

Figures vaguely bandied about were half a million dollars and ten per cent of the gross, plus two hundred thousand dollars 'to be paid to Lynne Sellers personally to serve as an executive producer of some kind'.

The Judge further disputed that *Trail* had done any damage to Sellers' posthumous reputation – there were no 'overriding ethical or aesthetic considerations which make it desirable that an injunction should be granted'. On the other hand, 'I . . . find that the damages which the plaintiffs have suffered as a result of the totality of the infringement by the defendants of their rights [to the use of clips and out-takes] is to be assessed at one million dollars.'

The plaintiffs, during the trial, had asked for *three* million dollars, which is what Sellers would have been 'able to ask while he was still alive'. (Which reminds me of a retort John Braine could have made: 'But you stupid bugger, he's not still alive.')

belly. (He had with him on Cyprus, when he kept being late for *Ghost in the Noonday Sun*, a computer digital clock that clickered out racing tenths of a second, and a facsimile of the wrist-watch Roger Moore wore in *Live and Let Die*.) Sellers knew his time was running out – we all do, so why did the concept particularly pain him?

Part of what made him mad was that he was insulted at not being made immortal. He had such a high opinion of himself, he couldn't accept that one day he'd cease to exist; that he'd wake up and not be there and that his eyes (in Emily Dickinson's phrase) would not see to see. He couldn't accept decay, age, feebleness. Thus his preference for keeping company with machines. The search for perfection through mechanical toys and contrivances, and the degree of his impatience when these gewgaws let him down, were not the activities or processes of a rational man; and what it all indicates, at least to me, was that when he was seeking to invest objects with the potential for infallibility, he was somehow transferring to them a little of his contempt and dismay over human frailties and lacks. He wanted things to be brand new and to retain their newness – but they never could, and their appeal quickly wore off. This went for cars; it went for women: 'Every man's dream,' he generalised, 'is still, I'm sure, finding a virgin. That's why marriage has gone on the rocks. The original idea was that the girl had never been with anyone else, and it was so pure. So I came to this conclusion that to be in love with the girl of one's dreams – who if possible was a virgin – was the ultimate happiness. I still want to keep the ideal situation where I can discover the ideal woman and undress her, reveal her, in this fantasy of mine. . .'

That is a repulsive fantasy for a variety of reasons, Sellers' sounding like Humbert Humbert being only the first of them. It wasn't exactly purity he was after, but power; and if he believed that young girls and virgins were spotless and innocent, like newly hatched eggs, he was either stupid and ignorant or a misogynist – and Sellers' vanity was one of his most overwhelming traits. Also, note, it is a woman's independent sexual life which is at fault, spoiling wedded bliss. Clearly, all he expected from a woman was that she should serve him. 'He had,' Michael told me, 'a number of older women friends, but they wouldn't stand for his crap and fickle nature; whereas young girls, he thought, would be totally besotted' – by his fame and will, if not by his physical frame. *There's a Girl in my Soup* and, especially, *Hoffman* (which was originally, unbelievably, entitled *Call Me Daddy*) pick up on the incestuous, predatory vibrations. In the former, Sellers, as a flamboyant TV gourmet, a frilly, proleptic Keith Floyd, seduces Goldie Hawn – who leaves him when she sees through him. (Women, to Danvers, are nothing but side dishes or fast food); in the latter, Sellers traps Sinead Cusack in his gloomy apartment for the weekend – *Hoffman* is beauty and the beast, where the beast is no handsome prince in disguise. He is morose, unleavened.

Sellers' final marriage, to a former child actress, was a fulfilment of several desires – which were detected immediately by Lynne's mother, Iris, who was naturally extremely alarmed at the idea of a prospective son-in-law being older than she herself was: 'I must admit that I thought Peter was a little odd. For example, there were the toys. He was fascinated by a radio which . . . picked up conversations between aircraft coming into Heathrow and the control tower. He went straight out and bought one and had Lynne call me in the middle of the night to play it over the phone . . . Sellers [then] telephoned Lynne from Germany to say he had a break in filming and was coming in [to England] specially to be with her. Imagine my surprise – and Lynne's shock – when he came through the Customs accompanied by another British actress. He said that there was to be a party at his flat [in Stag Place, Victoria]. I took Lynne there but we quickly left. But Lynne phoned me very distressed the following morning. I believe she had returned to the flat later, and I can only guess at what had happened to distress her so much . . . What mother can be expected to approve of the marriage of her daughter to such a man?' Outside of some dragon queen in the Court of the Emperor Tiberius, not one. Mrs Frederick and the last Mrs Sellers were not fully reconciled until after the actor's

death, when they clutched at one another for comfort at his funeral.
I quite like the eavesdropping on aeroplanes story – it connects with
Sellers' attempts to find any antennae which would receive message
of an astral and phantasmal import. (For anything up above the
world so high, light years off, he was all aquiver.)

But what about his fondness for these child-women? How is this
taste explained? That Sellers' girls got younger as he grew older is
another function of his attempts to live in a time warp; he wanted
to think of himself as a dashing young blade, and hide the fact that,
when he stared at a mirror, he saw one of the (his words) 'awfully
strange brigade of pudding faces who melt in the crowds. I hate
seeing myself. I'm not pleased with what I see in the mirror. I'm
just disgusted, watching a bit more of the ageing process.' He had a
horror of the flesh; so virgin's blood rejuvenated him? Even when
settled with Anne, he had his eye out for future victims, it would
seem. Once asked how he'd come to meet Miranda Quarry, his
third wife, he said it was when she was three years old: 'when I was
first married she used to play in the gardens near to where I lived'.
For some reason this detail gives me a case of the mild heaves.
Sellers didn't even pretend to want to educate the nymphets (as the
Woody Allen character does with Mariel Hemingway in *Manhattan*); it was enough that he expected them to look up to him, and
in gaining possession of them he was trying to demean them.

☆   ☆   ☆

Woody Allen, Chaplin (all those blind flower girls), Polanski: the
artists Sellers resembled or befriended (he attended Sharon
Tate's wedding and funeral and appeared in Polanski's peculiar *A
Day at the Beach*)* all collected maidenhair, and had no qualms
about putting their nympholeptic dreams into their films. Allen's
Husbands and Wives, returning to a strand of plot from *Manhattan*,
has a college professor leave Mia Farrow for a student in his own
creative writing class, named Rain: 'I feel myself becoming infatuated with a twenty-year-old . . . I'm sleepwalking into a mess.'

---

* See Appendix.

Allen's character, who claims, 'I don't want to hurt anybody or be hurt,' seems to find the company of young girls bracing – as Allen the director and author does in real life. As I write, the papers are full of his bust up with Miss Farrow and his *affaire de coeur* with her adopted daughter, Soon-Yi Previn. Sex aside, Allen seems to enjoy pixies (if his own films can be said to contain clues) because being accepted by them is therapeutic. They are not psychologically bruised, like everybody else in his rep. company. They are dew-fresh.

Nobody would make the mistake of thinking that all Polanski wants is to be accepted by youngsters – his drives are carnal and avid, and he is still a wanted man in America, having once jumped bail when he was accused of committing a lewd or lascivious act with a thirteen year old schoolgirl. After having had Miss Farrow fucked by the Devil in *Rosemary's Baby*, [*] he replayed the rape fantasy in *Tess*, when Nastassia Kinski, she of the crushed strawberry lips, was defiled by Alec D'Urbeville. And Sellers himself comes somewhere between these angels and demons.

He was not a rapist; he was not a nerdish neurotic pretending to be led. He was manipulative; he was an enervated vampire; and by the time he reached Lynne Frederick, there was not enough healthy blood left in his veins to sustain a hard-on. Between the *cardiac glycoside*, used to increase the heart's contractions, and the *glyceryl trinitrate*, a coronary vasodilator, used to lower his blood pressure and reduce the heart's work-load, his valves were popping open and shutting like the mouth of a goldfish, and the hydraulics in his loins clogged and wilted. 'We would try,' said Lynne, 'but it was difficult. He frequently felt he had failed in himself and would say, "I can't look at you". . . .'

The sexlessness, Sellers' genitalia a withered pear, dry and droopy, is horribly fitting. All his attempts to speed up his life, or to slow it down; his anxiety to buckle and pound the calendar, tackle

---

[*] Sellers, too, had an affair with Mia Farrow; but that, as Kipling would say, is another story. (See Chapter 15.)

tempo and silence the clock's tick; his hallucinogens, gadgets and strange gods, come together in a single object: a need to return to the past and, if possible, begin again. To rewind the tape; to go for another take. And why? Because as a child he'd had to act older than he was. Precocious as an infant, he was childish as an adult – and in his attitude to women, it was the safety of the pre-pubertal relationship which drew him deepest. He wanted to run along back to the childhood he'd never had.

☆ ★ ☆

Was a pre-occupation with the loss of innocence at the bottom of it?

'When his mother died,' Anne remembers, 'I had a children's shop in Hampstead called "Lollipop", and he suddenly arrived at the door – I was long remarried – in a terrible state. "Will you come for a drive with me?" We went on a long trip down Memory Lane. The flat where I'd first met him with Peg; his old infant school, where his first girlfriend was; the flat where I'd lived when he'd met me; where his uncle and aunt had lived . . . This sentimental journey. He was very sentimental about his past – he lived mainly in the past. After we'd split up, he looked back on our marriage and would think about that sentimentally – and then, suddenly, he cast me in the Peg rôle. He used to bring all his new women to meet me. He brought Britt. I must say, of all his wives afterwards, she was the best. She was great to the kids; she was very understanding – and I wouldn't have been her for anything in the world, because when he was married to her and I was married to Ted, I used to get letters saying, "I'm in Rome, but it isn't like it was when you were here. . . ." I'd have to get to the post every morning and tear these letters up – "Oh my God!", you know; it was very difficult for Britt, because he did a number on her about me, like he had on me about Nora Barnacle – except that this time it was an open threat. To have an ex-wife . . . She coped well.'

The Sellers who traipsed the geography of his childhood, and restructured his memories, was remarked upon, too, by Milligan: 'Peter will never be at peace, never be happy,' he commented in

1969. 'That's why he is devoted to the past. He needs the past to bolster up the present before he can even look at the future. Even bad memories are inverted as good ones – if they were in the past they were wrapped up and finished with: he came through that period and survived, and he gets an illusion of security. He cries for yesterday and this has made him very lonely.'

☆ ★ ☆

In the same way that Sellers did not acknowledge his divorce from Anne, if it so suited him; or ignored contractual commitments, if they got in the way of his whims, Sellers did not believe that death put you beyond his reach. He chewed the fat with both Joseph Grimaldi (1779–1837)* and Dan Leno (1860–1904) on various occasions. 'Do you hear his voice the way you hear my voice now?' inquired Peter Evans, about Leno. 'Yes, absolutely as clear as that,' replied Sellers, 'I mean a clear, clear voice, as if someone is speaking, but in *here*' – and he tapped his skull. 'Is the voice spontaneous, unpredictable, or must you call on it, summon its presence?' continued Evans. 'Sometimes I ask for help, sometimes it just happens. It can happen anytime, anytime at all.'

The inner voices made him next start to believe in the transmigration of souls – he had *been* Leno in an earlier existence; and this theory he put about during the making of *The Optimists of Nine Elms*, which is full of authentic Leno jokes and songs. (I increasingly think of old Sam as the greatest performance, mainly because, in the teeth of a plot about children and animals, Sellers totally avoids the sentimental, to which he was otherwise so prone.) When he starred in *The Bobo*, Sellers thought he'd been possessed by the spirits of gored bullfighters and, whilst on location in Italy, he decided he'd had something to do with the Colosseum and that he'd probably 'been a priest in Roman days. You know, it's the old *déjà-vu* thing, but every time I've been to Rome and wandered round I've felt it, especially one night in the Circus Maximus. It's now a car park, and about three in the morning I was sitting right in

---

* '. . . the genuine droll, the grimacing, filching, irresistible clown'. Dickens.

the centre thinking about all the Christians who had been sacrificed to the lions, and feeling that I must have been there' – in charge of the entertainment or up in the Royal Box, no doubt.

Sellers first set about earnestly communicating with the past when Larry Stephens, the Wingate Raider, Goon collaborator, and uncredited tinkerer with *The Ladykillers* screenplay, died at a young age. Sellers had been pleased with his material and wanted him to continue with their working relationship. He got Stephens, on his deathbed, to agree that 'when he died he would make every possible effort to get back. One day I just had a feeling that he wanted to contact me. So I went to see Estelle Roberts with that in mind. . .' As usual, her room was packed with ghosts. 'She suddenly turned her head and started to speak to someone. Then we went on talking. Again she turned her head. Apparently a group was with us in the room trying to attract Estelle's attention by tapping her on the shoulder. She got quite annoyed with them, and apologised to me for the constant interruptions. I found it very disconcerting. I couldn't see anybody! . . . "The young man you wanted to contact", she said, "has only been over this side a very short time and he's somewhat confused, so he's got nothing to say to you other than to give you an identification that you will recognise." I asked her what it was. She said, "Fred", which is the name we use as a Patron Saint. All things are built around Fred! I knew then that it *was* Larry. Estelle said that if I made further attempts later on he'll have many things to tell me. . .'

When it came down to it, Sellers had no confidence in the present tense – and refused to stay there. As I argued in Chapter Four, *The Goon Show*, a bow-window to exhibit his paranoia and render it comic, is full of killing, maiming, sadism and class-consciousness; it rantingly retraverses the war, Stephens' as much as Milligan's, Secombe's and Sellers', and it mocks nineteenth-century ideals of heroism. It is a look back in anger. Then, becoming a film star character actor, and being able to keep changing his own face, obviously satisfied a need; and I wonder if, in some obscure way, the versatility and the fear of death (i.e. Sellers' mourning in advance over his own disintegration) are connected? And did the mysticism and languor, which went on working underneath, and the commingling of his identities, which is what went on when he was acting, have a sensual significance? If his watching his mother in 'Fire and the Woman' was the formative experience I think it was, the answer to both questions is yes. 'My mother used to appear in sketches,' he said in 1962. 'There was an act in which a girl dressed in white tights stood against a screen, the coloured slides were projected on to the screen, so that she appeared to be wearing various costumes – she might be Britannia, for instance, or she might be a butterfly. I used to see my mother doing that; she looked very beautiful.'*

It was as if Peg had lived for millions of years, and had been every heroine and brilliant creature; and between the clicks of the magic lantern, she and the screen were suffused with eerie, pearly light – she was a white goddess, pure and chaste. Sellers tried all his life to join her in everlastingness. His wives were foster-mothers; his acclaimed character, Chance, a spotless child grown to a man's dimensions, was a dutiful and docile son (and he's blissfully impotent, as Shirley MacLaine's Mother Eve discovers); and Sellers himself, when he drove his sports cars very fast, seemed to want to achieve lift-off and journey into hyper-space and eternity. He liked to make films in Italy because of the highways: 'I got my Ferrari out here – you can belt down the Autostrada – great fun. Working in the studio all week you don't get a chance to do anything except a ten minute round trip. But at the weekends you can get out and do a bit of motoring. I love cars. . .'

'He was still a child,' says Milligan, 'running away from its mother, who keeps looking back, seeing how far he can go before she stops him. "How far can I get away?" he's saying, "and still be safe?"'

---

* 'Mum used to stand there in white tights, which was a daring thing then . . . and my Dad would be playing the old Joanna in the front there, something like that' – is how he put it on *The Parkinson Show*, in 1974.

☆ ★ ☆

But his favourite time-machine, the toy which really warmed his heart, was his camera. 'I love the workings of a camera,' he cooed. 'I always want to open it up while it's working and watch it. I've ruined more film that way!' – which was a pity, because a camera, with its dials, levers, cogs, springs and motors, is clockwork that retains the past, as Sellers knew.

'He had a habit', Simon Williams* told me, 'of holding up conversations or outings we were on to take pictures. "Quickly, quickly, take a photo! *Now*! We're all so enjoying ourselves!" He *loved* taking photographs. It was as though he didn't want to have anything to do with the moment *now*; he wanted to look back and see people and places with the benefit of hindsight. He was retrospective. "Sorry, it doesn't seem to be focusing," I said, when he'd thrust this solid gold Olympus at me. You see, in the view-finder he had his own prescription lens. In all my imaginings of the trappings I'd have as a rich person, I'd never have thought up that one.'

As Sellers had always felt lonely, at a distance, he naturally had an affinity with a camera, the voyeur's gadget. (When his aunt gave him his first Box Brownie, 'I felt a magical thrill running through my body.') On the obvious level, he enjoyed the technology and the jargon; the speed at which you could create; the images bubbling up like magic from the tanks and acid baths in the darkroom. Photography is the easiest art form, and the most detached; sophisticated cameras, with their automatic light gauges, electronic exposure-meters and depth of field sensors, do all the thinking for you. You don't need a brain of your own. Sellers was one of the first fans of the Instamatic. 'There's nothing to go wrong,' he said cheerfully. 'More often than not you can get the sort of results you might expect from a camera ten times the price.' (Photography is the art of the impatient – as the drums are the instruments for people who can't read music.)

---

* Simon Williams is Fritz, a young twerp, in *The Prisoner of Zenda*, and Robert Townsend, another upperclass twit, in *The Fiendish Plot of Dr Fu Manchu*.

As he squinted at the world through his ophthalmic viewfinders, Sellers put a frame around life. It was like making sure events occurred behind a proscenium arch. He got everybody to pose for him: 'On holiday I'm afraid I'm very restless. Wherever we go I'm always looking for subjects to photograph, and if the landscape doesn't compose itself or the people and the architecture aren't photogenic I get thoroughly cheesed off and want to start moving somewhere else, which is tiresome for my family.'

But on a deeper level, as Williams perceived, Sellers was responding to photography's mortuary aspects. Freezing the frame, arresting time, the cameraman makes little bits of the past, its images and occurrences, safe. You are able to attest, later on, that something happened; that you existed. Then, looking over an album (or screening your old movies), you can watch yourself ageing and dying. A flicker-book of Sellers portraits would show the overweight and pinguid youth slimming down to reveal a bony Jewish beak; the sticky pompadour becoming grey and bouffant; the stocky Mendoza frame getting to be frail and wispy – Harry Robinson, in *The Ladykillers*, ended up as Fu Manchu. An odd effect of the patchwork quilt that's *The Trail of the Pink Panther* is Clouseau's weight gain and crash diets from scene to scene, as the editor embroidered material gathered from across a twenty year span. And it wasn't only Sellers who underwent alterations. Burt Kwouk, who played Cato, Clouseau's oriental manservant, out of whom the shit is beaten in the slow-motion Kung-fu ballets, said that: 'What's interesting for me about that film is to watch myself progressively get older. It's full of clips from the early films. Gee, I thought. Who is that good looking young fella! As the years went by – two decades, almost – I could see that Cato was a sizeable chunk of my adult life. Herbie Lom doesn't seem to get a bit older. I don't understand that!'[*]

Photography, which gave Sellers what Roland Barthes, in his book *Camera Lucida*, calls a 'certificate of presence' – occular proof

---

[*] The answer has to do with wigs.

of being there – also served to remind him that he'd once been younger, happier, than he was now; less nearer the grave. So his archive, accumulated to confirm he'd had a past and to authenticate his fun, didn't make life any more acceptable to him. Indeed, as a man always foreseeing his own death – with soothsayers and all the rest of it – photography added to his agony. Before he left for London, the Dorchester Hotel, and his dying day, there were bonfires amongst the snow and ice of his Alpine retreat. He destroyed all his souvenirs. Having laboured to recreate and conserve the past, by recording the present, he suddenly had a new horror – that the albums etc. would outlast him. When he looked at his snaps, all he saw (Barthes again) was 'what is dead, what is about to die'.

Some items survived the inferno. Michael gave me a bushel of prints he'd found in an old trunk; Theo Cowan, Sellers' press agent, had some duplicates to hand from a Condé Nast assignment; and negatives of the schoolboy Sellers at St Aloysius' or that group photo of Peg and Bill's wedding were unearthed in The Mander Mitchenson Theatre Collection or handed on to me by Peter Evans (who'd received material direct from Sellers back in the Sixties). I recall that Sellers had a commission once, straight out of *Lolita*, to photograph famous people's teenage daughters. I have a magazine clipping of one in the series: Jennifer Selznick frolicking on a beach. A girl is wrapped in layers of shawl and chiffon, she waves a hat, and she is chasing a pelican. (A legend that the pelican fed its young with blood from its own breast made it in the Middle Ages a symbol of Christ.) Sellers has bled away the colour and the background. The girl is about to vanish into her capes, and the whole thing is sunless, flimsy, fading out. Other pictures I got people to describe – Elwood Rickless, for instance, Sellers' executor, remarks that 'Peter was only able to express himself through photography. At the chalet in Switzerland, there was a photo, taken in Sweden, of an old lady looking forlornly out of a double-paned window. Symbolic, I now see; for, like Sellers, she's totally cut-off.'

He let the lens tell of his loneliness. Steven Bach, the United Artists vizier allocated to *The Romance of the Pink Panther* – which, had it proceeded, would have given the company more grief than ten *Heaven's Gate*s – also detected something of Sellers' troubled spirit reflected in a blown-up still. Bach was taken on a tour of La Haute Grange and recalls that its master 'displayed quiet pride [in the] professional-quality photographs, one of which I especially admired, a nature photograph of a bird in flight, backlit by a starburst sun. . .' A little after Sellers had died, Bach received a cardboard tube in the mail, with a note from Sue Evans, Sellers' secretary: 'Mr Sellers wanted you to have this.' It was that silhouetted summer bird, cold and sharp.

I asked Bach about his bequest (a phoenix? an uncaged soul?), telling him that, of the few Sellers pictures I'd personally seen, all oddly mapped his isolation: he took snaps of lonely creatures and abandoned, ruined things. ('Yes,' I was told, 'perhaps Peter thought I would see in it exactly what I think I saw . . . *see*.') As I look at the half dozen prints beside me at this moment, as I write, their mournful message is unmistakable. If Sellers intended to speak from beyond the grave, he does so in the play of light and shadow on these crinkled leaves. The photographs are desolate, yet somehow pensive – Sellers has become the ghost in the machine. (He *was* a camera.) The two pictures of his private jet standing on the tarmac are really of the same subject as Bach's bird. The clouds and bushes in the background appear to merge with the fuselage, to become fantails and plumage. This is a futuristic bird, or perhaps a prehistoric one – a monstrous pterodactyl variant, with huge eyes and claws; a flying lizard. The human figures, dark and scuttling, do not signify. They are beetles. But there is a drama being unfolded down amongst the insect world, if we care to look. Who is that tiny girl, obediently posing? One of Sellers' daughters? The men in suits behind her are her bodyguards, and they overpower her. The way she is outnumbered is absurd – a joke. She still looks defenceless – and the snout of the aircraft might twist across and gobble her up.

The human story in the café scene is a sad one. All those empty tables and couples hurrying past. Sellers has no company except the ice bucket. Five people are glancing or staring his way – but the object of their curiosity is the whirring camera, not the man hidden behind it. Sellers is invading their privacy, after all. He has taken them by surprise. Only a tall girl in dark glasses looks in the other direction – haughtily so, perhaps. She flicks at her cigarette crossly. She is Sellers' focus of attention, and she bridles at the spying. The camera here is a Peeping Tom. But it is not the girl who captures my interest; it's the half empty bottle, the uninhabited wicker chairs, the used wine glass, the debris of a meal-for-one, the ship's masts puncturing the air like winter trees, and the melting ice – all the left-overs and ephemerality, which get in by accident – which I find rather telling.

For sheer bleakness, there's nothing to beat the portrait of a gnarled tree trunk, a giant piece of driftwood, striated and embedded with pebbles. The sea is out of sight. It has perhaps evaporated and this is an image of the dried-up ocean floor. It could be an arm, this tree trunk, ripped from its socket during the sort of primeval battle the Norse myths go on about. Or it is the eroded skull of a long extinct monster – a creature coeval with Sellers' jet planes. The bark, already turning to stone and crystal, is like bone. Sellers was evidently fascinated with the shape and texture of the broken roots and branches. The object is almost living. The effect is not of something worn and neglected, but of majesty and power (like Henry Moore's bronzes); and for a long time I thought that was that. Sellers had found and photographed a totem, a symbol of his aloneness and desire for preservation. (He had his name down for his corpse to be cryogenically suspended when he died. It is therefore on the cards, if Sellers went through with the scheme, that he will be up and about a century or so hence, being a nuisance all over again, like Bela Lugosi, thawed out of a glacier by Lon Chaney Jr, in *Frankenstein Meets the Wolf Man*.)

As I gaze at the photograph anew, however, I don't see Sellers identifying with the ancient storm-tossed megalith. I think that when he came across it, so concentrated and growing out of the shingle, his emotion was more like envy and resentment. He had no strength against it. The beauty of the object, twisted and blackened and crooked, is that it doesn't need to know what to do with itself; it is an image of soullessness. Greyness and cold are the subjects of the other pictures, too. Sellers seems to have gone out on his own very early one morning to take shots of lakes and ponds. Threadbare trees, in which no birds sing, criss-cross the photographs. (The woods are made of skeletons.) Wispy briars and branches and the ripples from the water further scratch and splinter the scene; there's a line of iron railings, like needles, and, in the distance, some sort of knoll, where a goblin, or changeling, seems to be dancing. It is the Peter Pan statue in Kensington Gardens, and it looms out of the fog as a tiny angel of death.

'Sellers' photographs,' I said to Milligan, 'these gnarled trees and deserted beaches, and the desolation he managed to convey in his pictures of the Peter Pan statue and the Serpentine looking like the River Styx in the Underworld – they are pictures of what was going on inside him. . . .'

'His inner world, yes. Photography – the art of loneliness in pursuit of the lonely. The only things that didn't let him down were his gadgets. Cars fitted with tape recorders, televisions, telephones. He had to surround himself with material gadgets to make him forget he was alone. The films; the salary; the fact he got a long way from Southsea, where he was born; a long way too from touring with his parents' vaudeville act; the RAF; India and Germany; six weeks at the Windmill; seven [*sic*] years with *The Goon Show*; three children; plays; pantomimes – yet it all came to nothing.'

☆ ★ ☆

The dust-and-ashes scenario has a romantic appeal, but it is not quite accurate. His look of being alone was part of his genius as a performer. So many of his characters are stranded – the librarian, the old general, the union boss; or consider Mr Topaze, in the forgotten feature film Sellers directed and put much of himself into, standing on the chilly château terrace. 'Has your money bought you happiness?' asked Tamise, chancing by with a party of school children. 'I'm buying it now,' says Topaze, cynically. 'Then I'll leave you to your shopping,' says Tamise – the last line of the film, and given a push and plagency by Michael Gough. Gough wanders away with his pupils; and it is Sellers (not just Topaze) who is left in a corner of that great cinemascope screen; a tiny figure, marooned and morose.

How else could Sellers have been? What else could he have done? We know from his disguises and protective camouflage during the war that he was never clammy, sticky, one of the lads. His relationship with Milligan, during *The Goon Show* years, was marked by envy and suspicion. ('I was not so much an out-and-out Goon as Harry and Spike,' he once commented, getting away. 'They were the real zanies. I merely contributed some mimicry.') He never had humility (like Guinness) and his attempts at self-abasement (yoga, gurus, etc.) come across as conceit. Auberon Waugh was surely correct when he remarked that, when Sellers was eulogising the Swami Venkesananda, who held his ashram in Mauritius, and telling him 'how they talked through the night, how the Swami understood everything, how he had learned self-know-ledge from this marvellous, saintly man . . . I could not avoid the suspicion that part of his fascination is that Mr Sellers could study his accents, his intonations and gestures, and practise them quietly to himself in the bathroom afterwards.' He was always acting, act-ing, and in the end he was as mad as the vexed sea.

Sellers' selfishness and sullenness may have been connected with his being a whopping case of arrested development; and he may have presented himself as the put-upon clown: 'People are all wrong about me. They see me on television. They hear me on the radio. They think I'm a pretty funny feller. So they ask me to bazaars and cocktail parties and dinner parties and expect me to be funny all the time.* Don't underestimate the effect of this, day after day, on the nerves and the patience. They come up to me with glasses in their hands and clipped accents in their mouths. They start talking about The Formula of Goon Humour, that sort of

---

* When a Captain and Mrs Brownrigg invited him to their At Home, Sellers re-plied by saying that he, too, would be staying At Home on the night in question.

thing. I dry up. I just dry up. I've got nothing to say.' He may have been quick to take offence and yield to a nervous frenzy – but (a) a lot of it was pseudo-immaturity; behind the blankness he could be cunning, and he was quite aware of the apologies and allowances people were making on his behalf; and (b) to say that his life and work all came to nothing, that nothing happened except loneliness, and that nothing can be made out of nothing, is contradicted by the facts. Nobody said to me, during the four years I spent on this book, 'Peter *who*?'

Sellers goes on. His children have had children and they all walk the earth (Michael's son is named William, for his great-grand-father); they have survived, and 'no one can deprive us of our memories . . . and we bear the name of Sellers with pride'. Secondly, over a dozen years since his death, every day I seem to meet somebody who had a brush with the sod and did not forget it: a doctor from Cardiff who'd seen Sellers turn into Hitler at a school prize-giving, ranting from the balcony; a graduate of Pembroke College, Oxford, who saw him looking grumpy on a plane to Copenhagen; a cab driver who'd ferried Sellers and his nymphets back to the Dorchester, and with whom he exchanged sly winks and a thumbs-up sign; a quantity-surveyor who'd once played in a band with Sarah Sellers' husband; a composer of incidental music for Shakespeare plays, who played the piano for a spiritualist meeting at which Sellers 'came through'; people who'd seen him in restaurants, behaving badly, or being inconspicuous . . . I have come to believe that everybody in the world had a chance encounter with my subject – Sellers, when he wasn't at the centre of your attention, getting himself over-wrought, was most likely the other side of the revolving door, or getting up to leave just as you came in, or alongside you at a hotel waiting for the lift. (Sellers, with an accomplice, would ride up and down in elevators pretending to pick pockets.)

At the edge of the frame, just out of reach, making his departure: Sellers seems as though he was both omnipresent and insubstantial. The despot, the prankster, the rakehell; the lunatic, the lover, and very likely the poet as well, playing hide-and-seek. 'All you could do', says Milligan, 'was watch him. Meeting him was like interviewing a ghost: "Will he turn up tonight, emotionally?"' If there was some doubt about what face he'd decide to put on or what personality he'd be trying out for size of an evening – when he was making *The Millionairess* and experimenting with being an Indian, Anne remarked that 'It's like being married to the United Nations' – there is at least, for posterity, his body of films and sound recordings; and cryogenics notwithstanding, Sellers is unlikely to succeed in repossessing or altering his work at this late stage. Though he was the first to suggest things be abandoned mid-way, he always found it difficult to accept that a film was finished. *I Love You, Alice B. Toklas* and *The Prisoner of Zenda* he tried to have re-edited; *Hoffman* he wanted to buy and destroy; *The Fiendish Plot of Dr Fu Manchu* he insisted on re-shooting.

☆　★　☆

Since he died forever in 1980, he has been an effigy, reliant on the TV transmission of his films, or availability on video etc., to be given the illusion of life. The ghostly traces and hidden presences revealed in photographs are one thing; but if you really want to summon up remembrance of things past, hear the chimes at midnight etc., look at old movies. The echoes, the faces, the cityscapes, and people differently dressed. In their diffusion of light and masses of shade they are little poems about life and death. Fred Kite's gaslit lounge room; Mr Martin's dreary counting-house, with its creaking floorboards and retinue of goblinesque clerks; the bunker in *Doctor Strangelove*, created out of deep and bold shadow; and in *The Blockhouse*, a candlelit crypt. Morganhall, in *The Dock Brief*, is as pale as a dead leaf, his skin the same grey wash as the prison wall behind him; and in the morning-after debris of Clare Quilty's gothic mansion, the melancholy mood seeps out of, or into, the black and white film stock. And Sellers could be frostbitten in colour, too: General Fitzjohn, for example, his scarlet tunic unbuttoned, framed against a marble grate (in which no fire flickers) tells his doctor that 'I make a noise, frightening the housemaids,

Lord of the Manor, . . . and the world says "what a man." But I'm empty my friend. There's nobody inside. I'm alone . . . I'm afraid.'

Behind the voice, a clock ticks slowly, immutably. Sellers' head is held in close-up, and in profile, and it is one of those moments in his films when his own intense personal conflicts are being confided. (Wolf Mankowitz wrote the screenplay for *Waltz of the Toreadors* and he knew exactly what to get Sellers to draw on.) If he did best, with toys and tantrums, to evade having to live a real life, he could at least, when these gambits failed, transform his life, work out his problems, by pretending to be somebody else. Sellers' films are particularly elegiac because, cast often as shuffling, wheezing grandads and crotchety fogies, he plays an age on the screen he never technically managed to reach as an individual. When he was young he enjoyed looking old, and he didn't get to be old.

The Air Commodore stunt was an example of how he tried to triple his age; but before that there'd been the disturbed childhood, with none of a child's habits. He was like a dwarf – little, but treated as if he was cocksure and big.[*] So when he was big he was (privately) childish and (professionally) a veteran; and when he talked about his childhood what mostly came back to him were the smells – especially the pomade and toilet water, the mildew and rot, the dirt and decay, of backstage at the music hall – a catacomb smell?

'Peg,' says Milligan, 'sacrificed her responsibility to her husband and made Peter the head of the household. Anytime of the day or night, he would call out, "Peg, Peg," and she'd drop everything and come running immediately.' He was stretched in all directions. (Like Shakespeare's Timon, 'The middle of humanity thou never knewest, but the extremity of both ends.') He'd never been a real child, as he was never allowed to play or develop; and precociously invested with a patriarch's power, he could then yet be intensely infantile, and get away with it – as a Roman emperor would. Perhaps only in acting *very* old indeed could he envisage a spot of calm?

---

[*] No doubt, like the deformed boy, Sloppy, in *Our Mutual Friend*, Sellers was 'a beautiful reader of a newspaper. He'd do the police in different voices.'

Henry Crun's senility is the obvious comic example. He's so dotty, he's in a world of his own, filled with Victorian bric-à-brac and weird inventions; or rheumy William Mate Cobblers, over-extending his official powers as commissionaire or car park attendant. Sellers plays old crocks, also, at the very beginning of *I'm All Right, Jack* (the clubman), *The Millionairess* (Epifania's father, speaking from an oil painting), and *The Prisoner of Zenda* (King Rudolf in his air-balloon). But, leaving these caricatures to one side, what concerns us now – as I zig-zag back to a chronological narrative after all these pages taking in a brief history of Sellers and time – is the twi-lit atmospherics in the films which followed *The Ladykillers*, and the way in which Sellers seemed to be trying to be on good terms with death – so that it would be like a continuation of life. He was a man who played old men when virtually a juvenile; he was a man who kept prophesying his own death, even in his early years.

☆ ★ ☆

Possibly he felt that, if he was elderly in his films, he'd stay young in real life – his films functioning like Dorian Gray's portrait? It comes as a shock, when watching *The Mouse that Roared*, to see the owlish milky-pudding that's Tully Bascombe. Sellers is suddenly playing a character of his own age (thirty-something), and it must be said he's rather unsatisfying. There's none of the delight in pro-posterousness which comes across to us when he is Fred Kite, say, or, to give an extreme example, Dr Strangelove, cackling with glee that the planet is about to explode. The romantic scenes with Jean Seberg make us want to look away, they are so gauche. But Sellers was thrilled to be doing them at the time. 'I hear you have a love scene,' said a journalist. 'Is it serious?' – 'Quite serious,' replied Sellers, 'Miss Seberg is charming, but I'm sure she would prefer the scene to be done by Gregory Peck. Though, of course, the Borg-nines have done it, so why shouldn't I?'

Ernest Borgnine, he of the piercing little piggy eyes, would be the first to admit he's no oil painting, but he does have a sort of brute force that is undeniably masculine, and which made him a success as vikings, cowboys, soldiers; he's a thick-skinned hero, and his range is to be found somewhere between Anthony Quinn's bluster and Rod Steiger's agonising. He took the Oscar in 1955 for playing a Bronx butcher who surprises himself by falling in love. *Marty* dramatises the eruption of tender feelings in a strong man's life – and it is done without too much sentimental billing and cooing. Love, as it were, completes the Borgnine character, it doesn't undermine him. Sellers had no pungency to carry off that sort of part; he could never be valiant, solid. Infirmity, indeed, is necessary to his style of acting – the ability to slip and slide and to adapt. (Sellers could no more have appeared in crude and melodramatic Westerns than Borgnine could have been cast as Clare Quilty.) What Sellers seemed to think all kissing and cuddling on the screen required was that the folk up there doing it be good-looking; he wasn't worried by context or emotion. When *The Mouse that Roared* was completed, therefore, and he inevitably disowned it, it was his vanity which was affronted. 'I enjoyed myself more as the Grand Duchess than I did playing myself in the love scenes,' he commented truthfully.

The Grand Duchess, as I've said elsewhere, is Crystal Jollibottom and his own grandmother; Count Mountjoy, the Prime Minister, is done as Alec Guinness. With this pair Sellers is rambunctious. He didn't make a sloppy Tully Bascombe mistake again – not until he was rich, famous and emaciated, when he did it all the time: with Britt in *The Bobo*, Ursula Andress in *Casino Royale*, Catherine Schell, Dyan Cannon, and Lesley-Anne Down in the later 'Panthers', Lynne Frederick in *The Prisoner of Zenda*, Helen Mirren in *The Fiendish Plot of Dr Fu Manchu* . . . I except from this catalogue of unsettling sequences, which are as tiresome as the intermittent love-bird episodes in the Marx Bros comedies, Goldie Hawn in *There's a Girl in My Soup*, and Sinead Cusack in *Hoffman*: there Sellers is made to confront his shallow attitude to women, and his slightly menacing manner isn't smudged. Roy Boulting and Alvin Rakoff, the respective directors, perhaps wouldn't let him do just what he wanted; they steered him towards exposing his creepiness and foolishness.

Sellers started to avoid his genius when he began to fancy his chances as Cary Grant or Gary Cooper. Observers like Milligan must have encouraged him in this ambition, for Milligan said to me that: 'With his degree of artifice he could take on, and take off, any-body – he could become Gary Cooper. He did impressions of people while he acted. That was the haunting part of him. He was uncanny. An uncanny actor.' Milligan is in the right of it about the spectral quality, the illusionism; but Sellers, even at his most trim and debonair, could never have the self-assurance and glow of a matinée idol. Some things cannot be imitated; when Sellers turns on his wan charm and opens his brown faraway eyes wide, we are in for mush and gracelessness. (He's trivialising his talent.) When it comes to the yearnings and reveries of duffers, nuts and clumsy chaps like John Lewis, however, and the actor in him is not erecting ornamental façades, Sellers is just about the most rhapsodic oper-ator of his generation – and of the previous generation, because that's where he insinuated himself.

☆ ★ ☆

The Ladykillers was his finishing school. He was the apprentice, Guinness (his nearest contemporary in the cast, being only a decade his senior) the sorcerer. Harry Robinson, as a crook too old for the modish togs he affects, is almost a satire on how Sellers might have dressed for Peg – suppressing his real age. (Sellers would like to have been the man that time forgot.) 'The first actor I found who was really wonderful to work with was Alec Guinness,' said Sellers. 'Although I didn't have much to do with him, the little I did was a great help . . . But I wasn't particularly good, and nothing else hap-pened for about a year . . .' Well, only *The Goon Show* and other radio appearances, all the Associated Rediffusion experience and the modest one-reelers, which I have dealt with; and there was *The Smallest Show on Earth*.

Conceived by William Rose (who'd dreamt up *The Ladykillers*) as a local riposte to Cecil B. De Mille's *The Greatest Show on Earth* (a ten ring circus with trapeze artists, lion tamers, and Charlton Heston all giving the big top the biblical treatment – in much the same way as the Old Testament had previously been given the carnival treatment), the film is muted, monochrome, and, where De Mille was overblown and festive, an object lesson in the art of film acting. Modesty and quiet are its virtues – decay and moribundity its moods – wet and cold its setting.

As the story of a crumbling pleasure palace, the Bijou Kinema, its fate and its inhabitants, *The Smallest Show on Earth* neatly encapsulates the themes of stopped clocks and revenants which I've been running off at the mouth about in this chapter. Sellers plays Percy Quill, the projectionist, and he's one of three alongside the veteran Bernard Miles, as Old Tom, the commissionaire, and Margaret Rutherford, as Mrs Fazackalee, the pit pianist during the silent movie days, and now the lady in the box office. The plot, in which Virginia McKenna and Bill Travers inherit the fleapit from an unseen shag called Great Uncle Simon, and do their best to flog it to developers who'll pull it down and build a car park, need not detain us long. Jean and Matt Spenser are an insipid couple and we resent them for being pushed at us as the stars. The bunglings of newly weds never makes promising material and with Virginia McKenna, the most governessy and watery actress, in my personal pantheon (after Julie Andrews), as the bride, their scenes are awkward and dull. Bill Travers, his young voice like Michael York's, goes through the film looking puzzled and tense – a grizzly bear. Does the fact that Virginia and Bill are married in real life somehow stop them from opening up when they are working together? They are the same in the *Born Free* things, or *The Ring of Bright Water*. Their instincts are in a grip. Put them in a scene with elephants, otters or cubs, however, and the Scottish no-nonsense brusqueness and detachment melts. They have a rapport with the animal kingdom which they do not have with each other, at least as performers.

Luckily, we can look behind and beyond the Spensers and their dignity to take in the true star of the film – the Bijou itself. Whether or not the original audiences, back in the Fifties, were meant to agree with Matt and Jean that it's a derelict and worthless place, that's not how it comes across now. It is a tiny, lost Edwardian paradise, tucked under a railway arch, wreathed in smoke and brimstone from the passing trains. The cinema, a domed and ornate Moorish temple, with barley sugar pillars and gloomy framed pictures of forgotten idols from the infancy of the flicks, seems cut out by scissors from the shadows and black air. 'It was a theatre way back; then a music hall; then an electric theatre,' Mr Quill and his cohorts explain; and they are the resident spooks.

The cinema is an architectural fantasia, like Mrs Wilberforce's villa in *The Ladykillers*. The mouldering rooms and out-of-kilter staircases, the horn gramophones and fancy gasoliers, the chipped tracery and plaster cherubs falling off the sloping ceilings, link up with the Titfield Thunderbolt and Genevieve, the motor car – they are all becomingly tumbledown and anthropomorphised. Kenneth More and John Gregson, at the wheel of their 1904-era Darracq and Spyker, are more at ease with their antique machines, chiding them and coaxing them, than they are with their official girlfriends, Kay Kendall and Dinah Sheridan. (The vintage cars are mechanical brides.) The puff-puffs, in *The Titfield Thunderbolt*, are also vehicles of nostalgia; the branch line, threatened with closure by British Rail, is an enclave of whimsy and vanishing Englishness. The ancient locomotives, rattling across the countryside, are large versions of a child's toy train set, or Rowland Emett's cartoons sprung to life. In *The Smallest Show on Earth*, Mr Quill's projection booth is the footplate of a choo-choo or the bridge of a ferry-boat. As he gets increasingly crotchety over the capricious levers and knobs, popping light bulbs and clanking magic lanterns, Sellers' character feels the need to take sustaining nips from a whisky bottle. The cracked lenses, mis-matched canisters of film and lost spools are the little cinema's equivalent of a senior citizen's decrepitude, hearing impairment and dimming eyes; Quill loves and adores his equipment as he would if nursing his own dotard of a relative. He is the only man in the world who can keep the junk going. He is married to it.

Miles, Rutherford, and Sellers make a magnificent trio. Old Tom, dressed in fraying brocade, slouched and growling, welcomes people into the Bijou as if they are crossing the threshold into Hell. He's less a ghost than a ghoul – Igor, for example, the hunchbacked helper of Dr Frankenstein. Mrs Fazackalee, stout and imperious (she could be a reincarnation of Maria Theresa, Empress of Austria herself), is one of Dame Margaret's best creations. Clad in black lace and jet jewels, flourishing a pince-nez tethered to her bosoms by black ribbon, she is Madame Arcati, from *Blithe Spirit*, a medium in mourning. The joy of a Rutherford performance is that, always booted, spurred, and costumed in layers of tweed capes and bonnets, she could yet convey spirituality and feyness. She was a shapeless, heavyset woman whose personality was nimble and light – hence her ability to be Miss Marple, Agatha Christie's female Sherlock Holmes; or, in Orson Welles' *Chimes at Midnight*, a peerless Mistress Quickly. Her favourite hobby was cycling ('the rush of wind in one's face, the sense of freedom') and it was no doubt her intention, despite her own resemblance to a massive, flightless bird, to get her bike airborne. Her huge wobbling chins and wrinkled nose seek and sniff out ectoplasm and misdeeds; and for all her old ladyish bits of business with handbags and foxstoles, with facial ripples and twitches, she's doughty and, it might be said, voluptuous. (She's an aged Salome.) You never deny the existence of the psychical matter for a moment when she's around, and it comes as no surprise to discover that she was a cousin of Professor Ernest Rutherford, the Nobel laureate, who had studied radioactivity and discovered the structure of the atom. The Rutherfords plainly had a genius for seeing what cannot be seen, and for being commonsensical about their imaginative leaps. ('Although I had never been a mermaid,' writes Dame Margaret in her autobiography,[*] 'I could

---

[*] Her life is worth investigating, for her acting genius was developed only at the cost of 'severe nervous illness . . . All through my acting career I have suffered from over-strain and breakdowns.' She checked herself frequently into funny farms 'in the hills behind Brighton'. She was also strangely beset by frauds and people who had had sex-rectifying operations. Her friend Gordon Langley Hall turned up one day as Dawn Pepita Simmons; and Prince Juan of Jordan, who claimed to be the estranged younger brother of King Hussein, and who wore blue silk-lined opera cloaks and carried an ivory baton, was actually a Portobello Road antique dealer, arrested and imprisoned in Manchester for passing forged cheques.

see no reason why mermaids should not exist' – the statement of a true scientist.)

If you wanted a single instance of Sellers' superior skills as an actor – some proof that he's in the first rank – you need look no further than his scenes with Margaret Rutherford in *The Smallest Show on Earth*. It's not that she doesn't swamp him – or that he successfully conceals the fact that he is three decades her junior. It has nothing to do with technique or tricks. What we notice is that Sellers and Margaret Rutherford can invest the material with more hush and resonance than perhaps its writers were aware of. There's a drollery about what they do; a fine, intuitive grasp – a clairvoyance, if you like. Dame Margaret once said that 'I am always surprised that audiences think me funny at all' – and it is similar, slightly whacky sincerity which Sellers brings to his work, and it turns his acting into a series of miraculous moments. As Frank Launder* says, 'an artist is one who has great moments, many great moments. These are the real artists and Margaret is one of them. I know a few who are in this class, but not many . . . Peter Sellers [is] the same type.'

They were at least alike enough for Dame Margaret to take over one of Sellers' own roles. When he decided he didn't want to be in the sequel to *The Mouse that Roared*, even though he'd arranged to have it directed by his 'Fred' collaborator, Dick Lester, it was Rutherford who filled out the crinolines and frills of the Grand Duchess Gloriana, in *The Mouse on the Moon*; and can you honestly spot the difference? Did Sellers have Margaret Rutherford in mind when he played the part originally? His Crystal Jollibottom is perhaps a little more common; Dame Margaret was properly aristocratic and vague. (Count Mountjoy was appropriated by Ron Moody, the future Fagin, and Tully Buscombe by Michael Crawford, the future Phantom of the Opera.)

In *The Smallest Show on Earth*, Quill, Fazackalee and Old Tom

---

* Executive producer, for British Lion, of *The Smallest Show on Earth*, and producer, with Sidney Gilliat, of *Only Two Can Play*.

don't walk in and out of their scenes and cubby holes; they seem to shimmer, disembodied, from the other side of mottled mirrors; they are at one with the dust and flecks of paint and shadowy alcoves. When Matt and Jean make their first, appalled, visit to the premises, their employees come from behind a curtain, nervous and frowning. The three of them quarrel and their talk continually overlaps. Sellers, with lank grey hair, is stooped and sad – physically he resembles Nayland Smith, one of his very last rôles. Mentally, too, perhaps, because both characters are totally self-absorbed – spectral. Sellers speaks with a Northern accent, lisped through his false choppers. (The film is set in a generic North of England city called 'Sloughborough,' but when the characters are met from the train, it is Hammersmith tube station they appear at, on the end of the Piccadilly Line.) Quill enjoys himself, in his eyrie, projecting *Killer Riders of Wyoming* and *Mystery of Hell Valley*; but there are never many people out front. Mrs Fazackalee, squat in the guichet as if it was a sedan chair, doesn't sell tickets, she accepts poultry or vegetables as barter. One evening, a crowd of derisive yobs turns up. Virginia McKenna, in bosomy Tyrolean gear, goes down the aisle to sell icecreams, and she's mobbed. Mrs Fazackalee then clomps into view, carrying the tray, and everybody cowers – she's a juggernaut.

When the Express whistles across the viaduct, Quill's apparatus has a seizure; he has to hang on to the flapping projector and humour life back into the dials and gauges. The celluloid snaps and what patrons there are left in the stalls go home in disgust. Quill puts on a record of the national anthem and stands to attention, quite alone. On his way back to his digs, he does a little skip in the street – a silly, perfect detail. Late at night, on another occasion, the three old eccentrics, having the place to themselves, watch a silent movie, Cecil Hepworth's *Comin' Through the Rye*, of 1916. Margaret Rutherford strums Chopin at the piano, Bernard Miles, on his own in the stalls, strokes the Bijou's cat and Sellers, transfixed, moves out of the darkness to explain what's afoot to the young couple, who realise they've blundered in on magic – 'classics, you might say', says Quill, with tears in his eyes. The caption on the screen in front of him says: *When you return this rye will be harvested, and this field as empty as your heart.*

Like the influx of fairies, singing and gossiping, in *The Lady-killers*, the scene's arrival is both a surprise and yet inevitable; and it is enchanting in more ways than one. The surprise is that there was room for it, amongst the gathering plotlines and workaday stuff with Leslie Phillips as a shifty lawyer and Francis De Wolff as Hardcastle, the manager of the town's gleaming Deco Odeon, whom the Spencers regard as their business rival. The inevitability lies in the fact that Sellers, Rutherford, and Miles are so well fitted for it; it extends and deepens the mood their characters would otherwise only give us in glimpses. The scene stands alone, and *The Smallest Show on Earth* would be nothing without it. Quill and his colleagues seem to have floated off the silver nitrate, tricks of the light. As they enjoy their session with sweet silent films, time is hanging in the air. Everything is evanescent, tenebrous.

We can only guess at the reverberations *The Smallest Show on Earth* set off in Sellers personally. The end-of-the roady building, with its chill and damp, and the feeling it emanates of come-and-gone entertainment and tat, is Ilfracombe and all the other reconstituted, decaying vaudeville venues of his youth, come back, as it were, to haunt him. But though Quill is tetchy, snappy, there is no bitterness – only nostalgia. As Milligan discovered, Sellers only really believed in yesterday (when all his troubles seemed so far away); 'Yesterday', Sellers once yelled at him. 'I get upset thinking about yesterday, because it's gone and it's so bloody buried, so irredeemable, and nobody seems to care. I can cry for yesterday.'

You can bet that he did give way to such jags of self-pity; and he'd have enjoyed monitoring himself being so moved, too. But though the general uncertainty over where his acting stopped and real life resumed was going to be a big problem, we can at least acknowledge that, when fully inhabiting a character, as he does Quill, Sellers, convincingly old before his time, can put his neurosis to beautiful use. I don't think he had to seek very far to find Quill's opacity. The North of England accent, the loyalty to the world of make-believe and show business which did nothing but keep you indigent; the suggestion that, deep down, you know you are beaten. Bill, of course, the absent or unnoticeable father. When asked, in March 1959, which was his favourite rôle to date, Sellers said 'Peter Quill' ('with an affectionately reminiscent smile'). That he misremembered the name (it's *Percy* Quill) and substituted his own is a slip I'll leave the followers of Dr Freud to elucidate.

☆　★　☆

The Smallest Show on Earth is quaint, as is *The Ladykillers* (for all that Professor Marcus' scarlet-rimmed eyes peer minatorily from the mauves, lavenders and violet tints). The films, along with *Battle of the Sexes* or *The Mouse that Roared*, are quintessential Ealing comedies – except that only *The Ladykillers* is officially in that category. Sir Michael Balcon had sold his studio to the BBC in December 1955 (the very month in which *The Ladykillers* was released), for £350,000, bringing to an end what Philip Kemp has called 'the faintly public school, all-together chaps flavour,' which had given the populace *Passport to Pimlico*, *Whisky Galore!*, *The Lavender Hill Mob*, and (famously) *Kind Hearts and Coronets*, as well as making heroes out of John Mills (*Scott of the Antarctic*) and Jack Hawkins (*The Cruel Sea*), among much else, mostly involving Alec Guinness. Artists and technicians had enjoyed the security of permanent contracts, and with the dispersal of the cottage industry to Pinewood (run by the Rank Organisation) or Elstree and Borehamwood (MGM), a certain confident and elegant tone left the British cinema forever. 'To comfort myself I used to say it was people that counted, not buildings,' remarked Balcon. 'This was not strictly honest, as over the years there had developed at Ealing a spirit which had seeped into the very fabric of the place.'*

---

* After the disassembly of Ealing, Balcon, Danishewsky etc., formed Bryanston Films, a gathering of independent producers; and they also became share-holders in British Lion, a distribution company which owned Shepperton Studios. John and Roy Boulting, and Sidney Gilliat and Frank Launder, were appointed to the British Lion board in 1958 – and, as 'Sir Michael Balcon & Associates,' they all

As for the people, Sandy Mackendrick went to America and, after a disastrous career watching his pictures get re-edited, or being simply sacked, he left the business to become Dean of the Film School at the new California Institute of the Arts (CalArts, funded by Walt Disney). One of his many unrealised projects was Ionesco's *Rhinoceros* with Sellers as Bérenger and Peter Ustinov as his friend, Jean. It was to have been set in a department store, with the armour-plated beasts hurrumphing around Harrods' basement – concepts Sellers retained, because *Casino Royale* has a Harrods scene, in which Evelyn Tremble is kitted out as a spy; and in *Hoffman*, Sinead Cusack, like a lamb-to-the-slaughter, is taken by her

---

took control of the firm, sometime in 1964. Bryanston Films Ltd. was eventually bought by Associated-Rediffusion. British Lion merged with Thorn-EMI, which became Cannon, which begat Weintraub Entertainment. Balcon resigned as Chairman, went off to run Border Television, and his position was taken by Arnold Goodman. . . .

Everybody seems to have had a slice of the pie. I make mention of all this for three reasons. First, boring as I personally find the politics of business, writing up the history of mergers, take-over bids, and backstabbings, is now a sub-genre all of its own. What with Jake Eberts' exhausting tale about the rise and fall of Goldcrest, *My Indecision is Final*, Steven Bach's story about the destruction of United Artists, *Final Cut*, and David McClintick's account of the David Begelman embezzlement scandal at Columbia, *Double Exposure*, there is material a-plenty to support the argument that the Borgias didn't fizzle out in Renaissance Italy. They migrated to the movies.

Hence my second point: the film industry is an off-shoot of banks. Balcon himself, for example, had the mentality of a cost accountant, and he found creative stimulus in financial deals. (His autobiography, *Michael Balcon Presents*, like Lord Grade's *Still Dancing*, is enthralling only if you enjoy balance sheets.)

And lastly: money-spinners, backers, investors, executive producers, footpads, highwaymen, and the people who sit in rented offices telling you that 'Yes, I can do lunch,' form the background to Sellers' career. You could write a book about a film star, his motivations and dispensations, from the point of view of finance, just as you may approach somebody else's Life & Times by way of his relicts, friends and enemies (Biography), his works and imagination (Literary Criticism), his mating rituals and handicrafts (Social Anthropology), his bodily uproar (Medicine) or his metaphysics and morals (Philosophy).

captor to look at the slabs of meat on the marble butcher's counter in the food hall. (Sellers' daughter, Sarah, is an extra, walking past.) For *Rhinoceros*, according to John Bird, who worked on a screen-play,* 'Sandy wanted a Laurel and Hardy version, but Sellers' agents said it wasn't a project for their client – too intellectual, of no mass audience appeal.' What David Begelman, Sellers' American repre-sentative, had actually said was: 'This is a fringe-theatre nutters' piece. You shouldn't be in this sort of thing, you're a big main-stream star actor.' (One doomed for a certain term to waste his genius being put in Sixties spy capers, cops and robbers spoofs, and regurgitations of Inspector Clouseau.)

Of other Ealing personnel, Monja Danishewsky, the producer of *Whisky Galore!*, wrote *Battle of the Sexes* and a part for Sellers in *Topkapi*. (Sellers turned down the scoundrely Turk rôle; it was taken by Ustinov instead, who promptly won an Oscar.) Charles Crichton, of the *Titfield Thunderbolt*, would direct *Battle of the Sexes*, and then virtually disappear until John Cleese re-discovered him for *A Fish Called Wanda*. (Cleese's barrister, Archie Leach – Cary Grant's real name – could have been played by the c. 1960 Sellers or the c. 1950 Guinness. The hue-and-cry, actually filmed in the cobbled backstreets of Oxford, is lifted from Ealing and only the sprinkling of dirty words and Americans puts a stop to our belief that Margaret Rutherford will swoop into shot on her push-bike.) Basil Dearden, who'd introduced Dixon of Dock Green, the avuncular cop, in *The Blue Lamp*, was the director of *The Smallest Show on Earth* and then died in a car crash. Bill Rose, having quar-relled with everybody because they said he was as loopy as Professor Marcus, devised, as I mentioned earlier, the Bijou as a mate for Mrs Wilberforce's cul-de-sac funhouse, and then went to America and wrote *It's a Mad, Mad, Mad, Mad World*.

---

* Sellers also saw a version Clive Exton had written for Mackendrick, in which the rhinoceroses appear in Hamburg – the bellicose animals as the Nazis, holding their equivalent of a Nuremberg Rally. How much of this idea worked its way into *The Phantom versus the Reich*? Was it yet another of Sellers' Hitler fantasies?

Sellers, therefore, got the benefit of the last five minutes of Ealing proper and made use of its graduates and faculty before they themselves spun off into outer space and variously fragmented. What did linger longer was what Balcon called the 'spirit'. Meaning what? At its worst a wartime patriotism that verged on xenophobia; at its best, a send-up of the British citizen's belief that the world begins and ends in London. As Constance Cummings (an American who now lives in Oxfordshire) said to me: 'Those films are so *English*. Their saving grace was their small-scale, and inner zaniness. There was a zany sense of humour, no matter how *straight* they were done.' Perhaps, to foreigners, there's something automatically hysterical about John Mills and Jack Hawkins' imperturbability? The way emotion is suppressed and valiant deeds are shrugged off as being of no consequence? The magnificent modesty?

The chivalry is medieval and is found in Shakespeare's *Richard II* ('This happy breed of men, this little world') and *Henry V* ('And you, good yeomen,/Whose limbs were made in England, show us here/The mettle of your pasture'), which Olivier had adapted as a contemporary war film in 1944 ('To the Commandos and Airborne Troops of Great Britain – the spirit of whose actions it has been humbly attempted to recapture in some ensuing scenes – this film is dedicated'). It took Guinness, a knight of doleful countenance, a reincarnation of Sir Andrew Aguecheek, to imply the anarchic streak that lay beneath the orderliness and punctuality, the uniformity and discipline; he brought out Ealing's, and therefore the gentlemen in England's, latent comic spirit. (He is even kitted out, in *The Man in the White Suit*, in quilted home-made armour, and he brandishes a round table as a shield – as if purposefully alluding to the chivalric theme.) Sellers, drilled in the violence and riot of *The Goon Show*, took the midsummer madness one stage further. If Guinness' characters were singular, dignified, then Sellers', once he started to receive star-billing, would be selfish and grasping – and I'm chiefly thinking, here, of Wee Sonny MacGregor in *The Naked Truth*, the film which followed *The Smallest Show on Earth*, and for which Sellers held high hopes: 'I want to be a star like mad,' he said. 'This is my first starring rôle in a film. I hope it clicks, because then I can get my teeth into other interesting rôles. That's what being a star means to me – being able to pick and choose.'

First, he had to seek permission from the BBC to be released from his radio commitments, so he could go to Walton-on-Thames Studios for the make-up tests. If this might seem a courteous enough request, it wasn't the way Sellers handled it. He wrote for the dispensation on May 21st 1958. The make-up test was the previous Friday.

☆　★　☆

Had you been leaning over the railings on the little footbridge that crosses the River Windrush, upstream from Ascott-under-Wychwood, sometime towards the end of the last decade, you would have seen an interesting sight. Along the edge of a ploughed field two characters approach, gesticulating and talking at the tops of their voices, and you'd be justified in thinking they are a pair of minor attendant lords lost from a Shakespeare play – Justice Shallow and Sir Hugh Evans, say – for, as they come into earshot, one of them, clad in a leather jerkin, is speaking in a dramatic, fiery way; the other, in an outsize Inverness Cape, is muttering and nodding agreement, and is also Welsh. What is it that so concerns them? The route back to the First Folio? No. Sellers. Kenneth Griffith is remembering his old colleague; his companion on this occasion – namely, the present author – is doing his best, whilst clambering through bush, through briar, to take mental notes on the speech, which went something like this:

'I remember him with great joy; and one of the most interesting aspects of it personally, these days, since he's *died*, is I quite often, when I observe something that is very funny, I long for him to be there – because his appreciation of it would be so extraordinary, and would add to my *own* appreciation. For instance I had this horrendous two years in India making a life of Jawaharlal Nehru for the Indian government, at Mrs Gandhi's request, who was a great admirer of my own films – and I was staying in Goa; and there arrived an Indian who'd lived ten years in America, and he was passing himself off as the *ultimate* American – and not succeeding at all. All the gear. Bermuda shorts; he'd walk around with flippers on – and would be so hilariously funny, and he'd bore everyone – plonk himself down at your table and chatter away. And there was one astounding coincidence when I was on a domestic flight in India – there was an empty seat – and who should clamber aboard but this Indian wearing a sola-topi, I'm telling you the truth. And Sellers would so have loved to have pulled him out of his creative hat at sometime; I longed for Sellers, only Sellers, to see him, because his perception of this piece of ridiculous human behaviour . . . And of course he could be ridiculous himself. Whether Peter ever saw himself as funny, I don't know. I think he probably did. We never discussed this.'

'There's a vulnerability and sadness somewhere in his life that comes across,' I said. 'We see it represented in *Being There*; and in *Only Two Can Play* there's a melancholy about that man's life and situation that Sellers gets at. Otherwise it would be an ordinary British comedy about adultery and it's not. . .'

'Kingsley Amis' original novel, *That Uncertain Feeling*, though pretty heavily done over by Bryan Forbes. But of course Peter was like that, too. He was most of the time melancholy and troubled, by his own fate. He had this melancholy and terrible doubts, neurotic doubts; so I don't think he ever tackled a job, so far as I know, without this compulsion that he couldn't do it, and he must get out of it. Which included of course *Only Two Can Play* – but every film, and I was in seven films with him, starting with *The Naked Truth*.

'The first time I ever saw him, I was walking up Shaftesbury Avenue, and I knew David Jacobs,[*] and he was with this chap,

---

[*] Dear Mr Lewis,

Thank you for your letter regarding Peter Sellers, with whom I had a wonderful relationship over the many years we worked together in radio; also, my late wife, Caroline, was his p.a. for quite a time so our paths crossed in various directions. I have a lot of memories, I'll just share a few of them with you.

When we were in a series called 'Curiouser and Curiouser', Peter, who as you who was Peter Sellers. I mean it was very early on in his career; he was just beginning to make a name – and Sellers was quite clearly delighted with me, and he showed that right to the very end, and I can recall two specific occasions. Once, on *I'm All Right, Jack*, when I had to report to Mr Kite that so-and-so had been working hard. Sellers says, "Very commendable, lad." – *Very commendable*, was it? Wonderful! – Well, at the end of my little bit of terrible sneakery, in front of the little group of actors, Sellers started to clap his hands. He did it again on *Only Two Can Play* – my first bit of filming on the terrace coming out of the house in Swansea; and I did something spontaneously eccentric, which was rather nerve-racking, because I wasn't a star like Sellers who could do what he wanted in front of Launder and Gilliat, and anyway he had money invested in it;* and certainly Launder and Gilliat didn't give *me* any encouragement – but Sellers was *there*, watching. And as my character left his house, swerving down the street, one arm swung and the other didn't, as he went off, and Sellers again applauded. "How *did* you *think* of that, boy?" Fascinated. Tremendous encouragement,

---

know was a very acquisitive character, bought the entire range of Twin Trix 00 gauge railway, and even before he had unpacked them he decided they were surplus to requirements and he offered me the lot for a minimal sum. However I turned it down as it would have spoilt my Saturday shopping spree with my young son when we used to go out and buy a carriage or a signal, one at a time. In fact I think Graham Stark bought them.

On another occasion we were recording a very funny piece about the Ancient Mariner, in fact he was the Ancient Mariner and I was the interviewer. It was so hysterically funny that both of us collapsed with laughter on several occasions. So impossible was it for us to continue together that Peter Sellers recorded his lines separately and, on another day, I recorded my lines. However, the very thought of him and the thought that I was alone in the studio made me laugh all the more. Fortunately the producer, Roy Speer, was a very kind and forgiving friend.

With all good wishes,
David Jacobs

* Sellers, convinced the film would flop, sold his ten per-cent share in the profits to British Lion for £20,000; within a few years that share alone had earned back the company £89,000. (The Authorised Biographer's figures are different – being £17,500 and £120,000, respectively.)

from one who insisted that I was his peer. In fact he treated me better than that. His acts of generosity . . . He made it clear, that day with David Jacobs, that he knew my work and was delighted to see me – of course, then I suppose in terms of films I was way ahead of him.* And on *The Naked Truth* I had an *astonishing* experience with him. I was his slightly gay dresser.'

'The relationship between the two of them is ambivalent,' I said. 'I think that's what gives Wee Sonny a certain strangeness.'

'Yes, yes, the characters do obviously care for each other in their own frigid manner. Sellers based the part on Wilfred Pickles,[†] whom hated – which was rather unfair. But he had a *loathing* for him, and that was the inspiration. But the experience was this: I went to view the rushes one day, and I was *appalled* at myself. Shocked. So all I could do was walk on to the empty sound stage in a state of *shock*; and I found Sellers there, in a terrible mood. He was in a bad temper; I'd never seen him in a bad temper before – and I said, "What do you think of the film?" And he said coldly: "What do you bloody well think? What do you think I think of the fucking rushes? *Terrible.*" I thought, well you're coming it on a bit, I know, but really . . . I said: "Well, I must say, I was very shocked at what I'd done . . . and I'm just walking here deciding I'll never make those mistakes again. . . ". He said: "What?" – "I'm thinking about it and I'm determined. . . ." He said "*What*? [hiss] *What*? [whisper] You were fucking marvellous – *that was the trouble*. ME. Did you see *ME*! It was *terrible*. What do you mean 'You'? You are what's made it worse for ME . . ."

'Very interesting. I still believe I'd done something I shouldn't have chosen to do in a scene; but it was his *deep distress* which amazes me to this day. But rushes! I learnt a long time ago in a film

---

* *Love on the Dole* (1941), with Deborah Kerr; *High Treason* (1952), with André Morell, directed by Roy Boulting; etc.

† 1904–1978. Yorkshire wireless personality and character actor – Billy Liar's dad in *Billy Liar*, Hayley Mills' in the Boultings' *The Family Way*. His radio show *Have a Go* was turned into Wee Sonny's television programme *Here's Tae Ye.*

it isn't necessarily what you have done as a performer – it can look bad because of the lighting; all sorts of other things can go wrong. This is a general thought on film acting: I've long thought of it as a boxing match. You win and lose rounds, and as long as you come out with a points decision, it all blends in, and those desperate sharp mistakes are lost.'

'Sellers was a Mendoza – he was out to bloody noses, black eyes.'

'Well, we became very close friends. On *The Naked Truth*, because he had a car and a chauffeur, I travelled with him a lot. He took me home and things; and he came to my little mews cottage in the only poor part of Belgravia, from work one day, and he would get very introspective; and he was in a very gloomy mood about his agent. So I told Sellers about John Redway, with whom I didn't hit it off very well. He was not a deep man, and if your face didn't immediately fit he could ignore you a bit, which was very serious for an actor/agent relationship. Anyway, I preached his virtues to Peter, who was in an introspective and gloomy mood, and he said "Do you think John Redway would look after me?" Now by this time, of course, what with *The Goon Show* and what-have-you, he was famous. I said, "Peter, I'm sure he would." – "Would you ask him?" I said: "Certainly." He said: "NOW." So I phoned up John Redway immediately with Sellers sitting there, and I remember it very clearly, because John said: "Yes, what is it, Kenneth?" A little impatiently; and I said: "I'm working on this *Naked Truth* with Peter Sellers." – "Yes, yes. What?" – "Well, Mr Sellers is here with me now and wants to know if you'd be interested in the handling of his affairs?" – "Are you serious?" – "Yes." And Sellers brought Dennis Selinger with him, who was his personal manager, I think, from the Grade Organisation. Dennis knew Sellers from the music hall days. They were both Jewish and I'm not sure they weren't in the Forces together. But again, Dennis suffered him and is a little bit unforgiving. You won't get the understanding of Sellers you'll get from me. . . .'

'In *The Naked Truth*,' I put in, 'we have a lot of English character actors. . .'

'Dennis Price, who very likely did end his days and his career in some bedsit, penniless. You know, he was a nice, gentle chap with a personal cross to bear. And society was against him. Terry-Thomas,* he's suffering so much from Parkinson's Disease. His money gone. I wanted Roy Boulting to come and visit Terry with me. Well, you know, Terry ... Very interesting, my relationship with such people – people who *raced* ahead of me, particularly the music hall people, stand-up comedians like Peter and Terry – they had a special regard for me; they put themselves out a lot. Terry would pick me up. He had a very exotic, handmade Scandinavian car. I asked him why there was no manufacturer's insignia on it. "I told them to take it off. Why should I advertise them? They don't pay me." I thought that was very impressive.'

'Did you know Sellers socially?'

'I knew him and his first wife very well as a couple. Anne. She was, as could be said, his best wife. Good, loving, caring. She talked to me quite often about how, once he'd got a lot of money, that everything became nothing; she said, "If I wanted a mink coat, he said 'get one'." So all treats disappeared. I talked to them *both* about keeping their feet on the ground, and I urged them both to travel on public transport, to which Sellers thought, immediately, that's a very good idea. A very good idea! He'd get like that. So of course he takes Anne on the Underground, and she's wearing a mink and he's Peter Sellers. He did it. And that would be it. He'd done it. He'd do it once. That would be it.'

☆ ★ ☆

Sellers acted the rôle of being a star long before he officially was one – though nobody seems to have objected. That limousine, for example, which collected Kenneth Griffith and took him to the studios for *The Naked Truth*, was actually a Hillman Minx piloted by Sellers' cousin, Ray Ray; and each evening, having dropped

---

* Who died on January 8th 1990, with an unanswered letter from me amongst his dribbled-on effects. (His last recorded utterance, mouthed in the direction of a retreating waiter, was 'fucking cheek'.)

Kenneth Griffith off at 'the only poor part of Belgravia' (Pimlico), Sellers returned not to a mansion with swimming pools and orgy rooms, but to 83, Oakleigh Avenue, Whetstone, N20, whither he had moved, on July 15th 1956, from Muswell Hill. The house, mock Tudor and suburbanly nondescript on the outside, was soon gutted, painted bright colours, and turned into a personal nursery. 'It was virtually a semi-detached place,' recalls Peter Evans. 'A little house full of expensive camera and hi-fi equipment, a drum kit, and toys for the children – all in the most appalling taste, and in such abundance you couldn't get in through the door.' When the local picture palace was demolished, Sellers bought the blue velvet seats, and other odds and ends, and built his own private Bijou Kinema in the attic – except that he called it the 'B. Jew,' and had this name stencilled on the beams. Here, pretending to be Louis B. Meyer, or some such magnifico, he arranged for screenings of the classics, in eight millimetre. (There were electrically operated curtains, organ music, the works.)

'It was a very modest house,' recalls Ian Carmichael, 'with a drum kit downstairs and a cinema up in the loft, up under the eaves. He used to hire films. "What would you like to see next weekend?" I said, "Audrey Hepburn and Fred Astaire in *Funny Face*," which he loved. *The Glenn Miller Story*, I went up there and saw that in his attic. . .'

Both films would have been not only unspooling there in his own house – they were also right up Sellers' street. *Funny Face*, directed by Stanley Donen in 1957, is a musical based on the antics of Richard Avedon, the photographer (played by Fred Astaire). Astaire goes off to Paris to shoot a fashion spread with Audrey Hepburn, a bookshop clerk duckling he's turned into a swan. What we (or Sellers) will have noticed, in watching it, is (a) the way the relationship between the cameraman and his model is made automatically romantic, and yet is also an unequal power-game; and (b) the discrepancy in ages: Astaire was thirty years older than Hepburn. When his desiccated nimbleness and her gaminesque charms come together, we think of a hypnotist and his victim, or of the old toymaker, Drosselmeier, making the virginal Clara a Snow Queen, in *The Nutcracker*; the young girl is brought out by the old man in disturbing, psychological ways. As Astaire's character literally has (Givenchy) designs on Hepburn's, the magical transformation of appearance and personality has a sinister, rapacious underside; the how's-your-father plot of *Lolita* is not far away at all. (There were plans, in the Sixties, for Sellers to play Captain Hook/Mr Darling to Audrey Hepburn's Mrs Darling – Audrey, all over again, would have been doing battle against a little spurt of unbottled machismo.)

As for *The Glenn Miller Story* (1954), that didn't signify sexual murk or defloration; instead it was autobiographical fantasy. James Stewart, as a bespectacled jazz trombonist, could be Sellers working his way up, married to the twinkling and dimpled Anne (played by the twinkling and dimpled June Allyson); and Glenn's sudden disappearance and death is a transfiguration – a guarantee of immortal status. (The film also contains Louis Armstrong and Gene Krupa, Sellers' drummer hero, playing 'Basin Street Blues'.)

With visions of Hollywood, flashbulbs popping, and spinning *Variety* front pages dancing under the pantiles, Sellers then thought he'd best start dressing like a star, and: 'You never saw such a bloody mess,' remembers Milligan. 'He was mad to look good and wore every accoutrement from the tailor except the ticket of sale. He wore gloves, a trilby hat – if there'd been a face-mask he'd have worn one of those as well. He'd leave his raincoat open to show that he had a single-breasted jacket underneath – thereby getting his inner self wet at the same time ...' The ambitious poseur was noted by Peggy Mount, too. (Peggy spent the interludes between takes on *The Naked Truth* knitting everybody knobbly blue sweaters with hood attachments.)

'We first met', she told me,[*] 'because we were both handled by

---

[*] I communicated with Miss Mount whilst she was appearing as the Fairy Godmother in *Cinderella* at the Birmingham Hippodrome. This season (1992–3), at that address, they are doing *Aladdin*. Who is it playing the Genie of the Lamp? Why, Britt Ekland!

the same man in the Lew and Leslie Grade Organisation, Monty Lyon. I recall us having coffee together at the time that Peter Sellers had a small part in the Palladium pantomime. He told me that his performance had overrun the night before, so he met with a certain amount of verbal criticism for doing so. Peter was put out. "I'll show Val Parnell when I'm a star," he said. "Go on!" I replied. "You'll never be a star any more than I shall." Fate decreed otherwise and, as you say, we met again making *The Naked Truth...*'

It was also to be Sellers' first film with Terry-Thomas. Thomas had been born and bred in Finchley and hated the place. He also hated his family for not being posh. 'I was ashamed of the lot of them,' he said, 'I just hated listening to their ill-formed vowels.' His double-breasted blazers, carnations, suede shoes, monocle and cigarette-holder were all attempts to appear a gentleman – though, of course, he failed miserably and simply came across as exaggeratively genteel; that was all right by Hollywood, of course, which eventually made him its (his words) 'favourite silly-ass Englishman'. He was a beautifully dressed bounder, who played scoundrels on the screen and was a shit in real life. (He eventually lived on Ibiza, in the sun with shady people like Elmyr de Hory and Clifford Irving.) He held it against Sellers that he resided in Oakleigh Avenue: Sellers 'seemed just a typical suburban father. Perhaps that was because he lived in Barnet, which to me was another Finchley – *dreadful!*' That wasn't all. He also disliked Sellers for being a Jew. (It is conceivable that the 'B.Jew' sign went up in order to rile him.) To Thomas, the adoption of 'very old-fashioned manners' (which presumably went with shiny waistcoats and top hats) meant you didn't really approve of Jews. He looked down on the journalist Bernard Levin as 'a sort of Kosher poor-man's Billy Graham'; he didn't like working with Debbie Reynolds, because 'I believe she was Jewish'; and he complained to Stanley Kramer, the director of *It's a Mad, Mad, Mad, Mad, World*, that as 'I am the only non-Jew in this huge cast, it's pretty tough going.'

Thomas' contempt expressed his fear of competition. He took rôle after rôle in Hollywood, as gentlemen's gentleman, cads or

Colonel Blimps, saying 'I'd hate myself forever if I turned them down – especially if, for instance, Peter Sellers took them.' Nevertheless, he believed Sellers' vocal dexterity 'a bit of a waste of time', and he at no time took the trouble to see that his rival had a skewed, intense manner on the screen, which made audiences keep wanting to watch him, to see what he'd do next. There's something uncharted about Sellers. Thomas himself, by contrast, was always totally predictable – leering, gap-toothed and calling all and sundry 'a complete shower'. He talked in catchphrases and looked like a trademark. (He called his gap teeth 'my most obvious giveaway trademark'.) Perhaps what we enjoy about his appearances (and there must be thousands of them) is that he never altered. We respond to his foppishness and shallowness as we do to the vulgar rituals of pantomime – we take comfort in the repetition. And, in *Tom Thumb*, say, or *Monte Carlo or Bust* etc., Thomas, cheating and conspiring, adapted easily to a cartoonish, pantomime format. He's at home there, with twirly moustache and long Victorian villain coats. But Terry-Thomas was Terry-Thomas. He had no mystique. He never gave a rôle any shading.

The difference between them as actors (and as temperaments) – Sellers' sombreness and giddiness, Thomas' sneers – is exploited in film after film, starting with *The Naked Truth* (and going on to include *Tom Thumb, Carlton Browne of the F.O.*, and *I'm All Right, Jack*). Thomas' Lord Mayley can't abide Sellers' Wee Sonny MacGregor, the arriviste. He says things like, 'My wife enjoys watching you on the television – I can't think why', or 'I never could stand you, MacGregor.' If Thomas ever did manage to rise above his habitual slick bullying, he did so when putting plenty of resentment into such lines as those. We might almost suspect him of being headlong and personal.

☆ ★ ☆

In that he was given the chance to don a number of disguises, *The Naked Truth* is Sellers' *Kind Hearts and Coronets*; he also inherited Dennis Price. This time around, however, it is Price who is to be the murderee, not the Guinness equivalents. Sellers had been apprised of the forthcoming film by his soothsayer, Maurice Wood-ruff. 'You will work for a producer with Z in his name,' decreed the clairvoyant. Who could that be? Darryl F. Zanuck, of Twentieth-Century-Fox? Franco Zeffirelli, the opera director? Adolph Zukor? Florenz Ziegfeld? No. Mario Zampi, the Italian responsible for Alastair Sim's *Laughter in Paradise*, in which a practical joker leaves money to four relatives in his will, and they can only claim their inheritance by making lavish fools of themselves.

Sellers didn't get along with Zampi, finding him indecisive. 'The way you are making this film is ridiculous,' he exploded one day, exasperated by the dozens of takes. 'I know much more about the camera than you do. I'll give you one more take and then I'm off.' For once in his life, Sellers may have been right. *The Naked Truth* is poky to look at; the simple plot (the bumping off of a blackmailer) is unnecessarily complicated; there are too many characters; the whole thing drags. It lacks style. The premise, however, was a good one. Dennis Price, pretending to be the editor of a scandal sheet, in which the ghastly secrets of prominent people will be revealed, bravely confronts his intended victims and explains that, for a few thousand pounds, he'll keep mum. 'Pay up in a fortnight,' he says, 'or I'll publish in a month.' What seems to me to be original about the film is that it has no hero (or heroine). They are all shits. Terry-Thomas is a racketeer and an adulterer; Peggy Mount's detective novelist, Flora Ransom, is a plagiarist and, in the long ago, was a prostitute in Shanghai (striding through her scenes in satin pyjamas, she's the only person in the film who seems wide awake); Shirley Eaton, as the model Melissa Right, is not the spotless innocent her Texan billionaire boyfriend believes her to be; and Sellers' Wee Sonny MacGregor, the much-loved television personality, is a slum landlord who charges his elderly tenants extortionate rents. In other words, the blackmailer's targets are themselves crooks – fully deserving the exposure and humiliation which ought to be coming their way. MacGregor especially.

If there's one thing Sellers never worried about as an actor it was winning the audience's sympathy. He doesn't make Sonny in the least bit nice. Off camera, the TV host's smarm instantly evaporates – it's not a commodity he wants to waste. The 'Jack of all Faces and the Ace of Good Hearts' is first seen in action, capering on the stage dressed in a kilt. The compère or warm-up man for *Here's Tae Ye* is played by a fresh-faced Peter Noble, who went on to edit the trade paper *Screen International*. When I ventured to ask him what Sellers was like in the old days, he said, 'So sorry, Roger. Peter was an odd, secretive, withdrawn chap and I hardly got to know him. On that film we didn't even exchange *greetings!*' This incommunicativeness of Sellers', however, was ideal cover for Sonny, who is taciturn. He comes to life when imitating the guests who appear on his show. If you are a Chelsea Pensioner, in one of their uniform scarlet bed-jackets, he'll whizz into the wings and reappear as your double. The crowds cheer, thinking Sonny a marvellous good sport. Actually, in duplicating the contestants, he's mocking them: see (he seems to say), you are not unique; you are easy to copy. There is nothing to you.

How much of Sonny, in fact, is Sellers? Shirley Eaton, who (as we know) had worked with him at the Palladium in *Mother Goose*, believes that the actor and the rôle were closely interlinked: 'Peter was like his *Naked Truth* character. High spirited, taking off like a small unguided missile; he was easily upset and he'd keep inter-rupting conversations to open and shut windows or to move to different telephones. Peter was a curious personality – I liked him, for his vulnerable nature, and of course for his genius as a com-edian; but like most people of genius he was at times very difficult. He was taken in by false admiration, and in the end he forgot the reality of himself. . .'

I don't think Sonny is a genius – his problem is his mediocrity, which prevents him from being a proper actor, hence the rubbish game shows etc. – but he is played by one; and as a portrait of a neurotic who behaves badly, and who knows exactly what he is doing, Sonny is a major creation. The problem, simply, is that Sellers' spookiness and powers are too much for the little post-Ealing comedy in which they are unleashed. Sellers is overqualified for what's demanded of him – or as he put it at the time (allowing us to read between the lines) 'I believe that directors shouldn't inter-fere with an interpretation of a performance. Mario and I have had differences of opinion. But then it makes life more interesting.'

If we can forget all the guff about Terry-Thomas being suspected by his wife (Georgina Cookson) of having an affair with Shirley Eaton, or the convoluted business with Peggy Mount and her shrieky daughter (Joan Sims) trying to drug Dennis Price (and poisoning Terry-Thomas by mistake); if we can sit through the many other such set-backs and wheezes and clear away the clutter of the film, to watch Sellers, we'll get a dose of his Shakespearean gifts. He even quotes from *Henry VI, Part Three*. Sonny, deciding that he'll pretend to be somebody else when carrying out the killing, ('Any one of a thousand characters I can create – and then destroy, just like *that!*') glides about his dressing room, crooning Glou-cester's terrifying speech (it could be Sellers' personal motto):

> Why, I can smile, and murder whiles I smile;
> And cry content to that which grieves my heart;
> And wet my cheeks with artificial tears,
> And frame my face to all occasions.

Paradoxically, when Sonny reframes his face as the bald bargee, inspecting Price's houseboat, the thick Irishman, speaking Welsh and trying to cadge gelignite off the IRA, and a large pointy-nosed police constable, paying a call on Miles Malleson (the hangman from *Kind Hearts and Coronets*); or when Kenneth Griffith is told to 'get out my Indian-Army-Colonel-with-overdraft clothes', all the impersonations are so fluid and shameless, it is Sellers who has become those different characters; Sonny is by-passed. (This hap-pens in the late period 'Panthers', when Clouseau is elaborately made up as Austrian dentists or Norwegian fishermen – it's Sellers having fun, and Clouseau disappears for a few minutes.) As proof of this, soon after *The Naked Truth* was released, a nine minute 8mm cine film was put on the market, called *5 Faces of Sellers*. You could possess your very own souvenir of the actor's (not the rôle's) self-transformations. We see him greet Wilfrid Lawson's Chelsea Pensioner, Sergeant Rumbold, tootling on a penny whistle. A subtitle then says 'In the Line of Duty', and there's a clip from the bobby scene; next is 'Rough Shooting', in which Sellers, as the Colonel, goes to purchase a thousand cartridges for his gun (actually Sonny wants the powder for a bomb); 'Barging In' is a bit from the houseboat sequence and finally 'A Drop of the Hard Stuff' sees Sellers' Irishman getting thumped on the plasticine nose.

There is some severe logic behind summarising Sellers' contribution to *The Naked Truth* as a series of quick music hall (or television) sketches. In terms of the storyline, that's all Zampi will have wanted from him. He'd then have fitted in nicely with Peggy Mount's falling out of windows and into a trunk, Terry-Thomas falling into the Thames and a lake, Shirley Eaton blowing up her flat, etc. But Sellers goes well beyond the clumsily executed farce. As we see when he dips into the wings to change his clothes, and he drops the Scottishness to puff on a cigarette (held ready for him by Kenneth Griffith), and reverts to a flat London accent, Sonny's malignancy is beautifully shaped. He's much more the cheat than poor Dennis Price who, as a performer, has lost all the cheek and cunning he had as Louis D'Ascoyne Mazzini, eight years previously. Now (and for the rest of his career – he died in 1973) all he can manage is haughtiness and/or superciliousness. His faintly Byronic good looks have disappeared, too. Where once he was curly-topped and well-fed, in *The Naked Truth* he is puffy and slightly flaccid – completely middle-aged. You can't imagine Joan Greenwood or Valerie Hobson going within a mile of him. Quite evidently, the string bag of brown ale bottles he clanked his way to the studios with each morning was having its effect.

The scene where he confronts Sonny about the Eastditch slums, however, is one of the most mesmerising Sellers ever played; we see how and why it was that *The Naked Truth* put people like Peter Hall (*Brouhaha*), Joe McGrath (*Casino Royale, The Magic Christian*) and Stanley Kubrick (*Lolita, Doctor Strangelove*) on to the phenomenon. Sellers has little to do except walk from the stage door to

Sonny's waiting taxi. On the way he is mobbed by fans and Price comes forward, wanting a quiet word. Sleepily, seamlessly, Sellers is ten different people within five yards. As the crowd engulfs him, a bird-like old lady (Edie Martin, who was Lettice, one of the fairies in *The Ladykillers*) shouts 'God bless you, Sonny!' and Sonny responds with a warm Scottish chuckle (he's every mother's favourite son), 'You tae, ma!' A pretty girl asks for his autograph, and he's suddenly smooth, telling her to call him; a plain one makes the same request, and he brusquely sees her off. Mario Fabrizi, a skinny would-be actor with a luxuriant moustache, whom Sellers actually employed as a handyman around the house and put in the background of a number of his films, says how marvellous he is – Sonny is all collusive smiles. He gives out kisses and rebuffs. Then Price appears – how much better the film would have been if his rôle, instead of being played as a shabby genteel con-man in a cravat, was more that of an Avenging Angel, his entrances wreathed with brimstone – and Sellers says with Grytpype Thynne silkiness: 'I'm so sorry I can't see you now.' Price mentions Eastditch, and Sonny's face falls.

It all happens in a few seconds, from leaving the theatre to getting in the car. It is a throwaway scene, for the blackmail threat itself is made in the ensuing footage over at Sonny's flat (with Kenneth Griffith flitting around as a witness, like a minor devil hunting for his trident). Our doubts about Price really start to pile up when he says, without irony, what a luxurious little pad his victim possesses – it is meant to be conclusive proof that Sonny has the means to meet the disbursements. Have you ever seen such a nasty flatlet, its frosted glass door opening directly on to the street? Lord Mayley's mansion is similarly cramped and badly designed. Zampi's camera backs everybody into a corner. And whose idea was it to shoot the night sequences on the houseboat, outside Flora Ransom's house, and in the woods? It's difficult to see what is supposed to be happening – Zampi, to keep down the budget, must have economised on his crew's use of electric light bulbs.

Sonny is upset about the blackmail. Not because of the money or because he is remorseful, but because he is caught out as a hypocrite. The idol of the poor old folk, who keeps the old folk poor in an insanitary block at Eastditch. His next guest, on *Here's Tae Ye*, is a fat old fellow with white hair, played by Wally Patch. 'So you come from Birmingham?' (as it might be) says Sonny, dressed identically and joining Wally in a chorus of 'The Old Kent Road' (they look like twin Santas in civvies). 'Oh no,' comes back the reply. 'I'm not from round here. I'm from Eastditch, and what a horrible place it is. . .' Sonny cuts him off. He goes berserk. 'Shut up about Eastditch. *Shut up about Eastditch*. SHUT UP ABOUT EASTDITCH.' It is very ugly – and goes on too long even to begin to be funny. Sonny's rage boils out of nowhere – it's Sellers'. There's no Scottish accent, or Londoner whine, or anything like that. The sound we hear is of a crack appearing in a frozen river, and we suddenly get a glimpse of the icy green waters rushing and seething up from deep below. It is out of proportion, and yet proves how inseparable Sonny and Sellers had become. The rôle is giving tongue to the actor's feelings.

The anger is frightening (it rocks the film), but it wasn't the only time Sellers let himself fly off, far from it. There are moments in *The Bobo*, scenes between Sellers' mild-mannered matador, Juan Bautista, and Britt Ekland's local beauty, Olimpia, which are too edgy to be funny; Sellers becomes Sellers, sour and cross, trying to bully reactions out of his wife, instead of being Bautista hoping to impress his inamorata. His own marital discord gets in the way. The impatience is off-key. In *Casino Royale* it was nearly lethal. As Joe McGrath told me: 'The first thing that happened is that he hit me, the director of this picture. We had a fist-fight in the caravan. He threw a punch and I hit him back. We got separated by Gerry Crampton, the stunt co-ordinator, who saw the caravan jiggling on its wheels. "I love you both, I don't know who to thump," said Gerry. Sellers and I started laughing and crying, but I said, "There's no point going on here, because somebody's going to hit somebody again." And he did. Sellers could be very nasty and surly. He hit one of the actors. He pretended it was a mistake, and people said he'd hit out presumably by mistake – but he meant it. He should have thrown a punch, as Evelyn Tremble, and missed this guy, in one of the scenes; but Sellers was so fed up, he hit out for real. He was particularly nasty to Jacqueline Bisset, in that scene where she holds up a bottle of champagne and he shoots the cork out. He threatened her with the gun before we did the take. He actually threatened her with the gun. I said, "Look this is being stupid, it's only a movie!" – "She can't get this right," he said, justifying himself. She really was afraid – when a gun is pointed at you it's very definitely not funny.'

It was almost as if, as he (Shirley Eaton's phrase) lost the reality of himself, he'd try and push people over the edge; only then could they join him. 'You always had to watch him', says McGrath, 'and figure out what mood he was in, which way he'd jump. He told me years later, "I don't have an awful lot of friends; but there are three people I can trust. Milligan, Harry, and you. Because we've been through hell together. You've actually faced me and thrown a punch at me. I know you won't put up with any shit. We know each other well enough."'

Thus spoke another Daniel Mendoza.

☆ ★ ☆

Though, to Sellers, it was always other people who were hell, what he could never acknowledge was that the hell they often had to endure was exclusively of his own devising. 'I'm the one who finally has to be in control,' he said of *Casino Royale*. 'When we were making that film, people were falling over everywhere. Charlie Feldman was in a corner ranting and raving. Joe was in another corner in tears – and I picked that picture up by the scruff of its neck and said: *This is what we are going to do* . . . Well, that was his version of it; the version of a man who only ever believed in his own desires and appetites. The fact that Feldman, the producer, was in the corner ranting and raving and Joe McGrath was in tears was because of Sellers, who wasn't turning up, or learning his lines, or doing what he was supposed to do for his million dollar fee. By any stretch of the imagination, there was only one person responsible for the destruction of that picture – and Sellers walked off the set for good, eventually, after refusing to share a scene with Orson Welles.

But he never admitted to any of this. The closest he came to accepting blame was to complain about the huge amount of money he was paid – a back-handed, round-about sort of admission that he'd yielded to temptation and shouldn't have done: 'I've certainly proved that I have my price. I proved that with *Casino Royale*. I was offered a million dollars to play James Bond. And I said, "You must be out of your bloody minds, because what about Sean Connery, Harry Saltzman and all that sort of thing?" The producer said, "Yes I know but I have this book and I'm going to make it." I said, "I certainly can't play James Bond. It is not my scene at all." We left it alone. And, much, much later, I was in Rome and they came along with a new idea that Wolf Mankowitz had thought up – but that wasn't for a million dollars. That was only for seven hundred and fifty thousand dollars, which wasn't enough. So every film actor has his price. . .'

The more he was paid, the worse he behaved. That's about the closest we'll get to adumbrating a general rule about Sellers. If you have ever whiled away a Sunday afternoon watching *Casino Royale*, and wondered why it doesn't make a bit of sense (scenes out of sequence; the disappearance of leading actors and the attenuation of plot strands etc.), it is because Sellers never completed his rôle and, having left hundreds of people in the lurch and with money pouring away, his disappearance meant that the holes where he should have been had to be filled in with out-takes, slow-motion dance routines, and David Niven talking on white telephones. As Ken Hughes, one of the many directors (including John Huston) called in to salvage a film out of the hours of meaningless footage which had somehow accumulated, summarises: '*Casino Royale* came to a ghastly halt. Sellers stated that he was no longer prepared to complete the movie. Feldman was left with a few scenes shot with Sellers but no movie. He now had to consider either closing the film down or continuing. Big money was involved, and he decided to go ahead. In a panic script meeting, it was decided that since they no longer had Sellers, they would have to improvise. Out of this chaos came all manner of Bond relatives, including the Bond who had played Bond in *O.H.M.S.*, George Lazenby, who was given a bit part. Meantime, the writers were writing like crazy, trying to save the day, and Feldman is hiring everyone in sight including Woody Allen, Niven, Huston, and Charles Boyer; and to save time on production he engages five directors: Huston, myself, Bob Parrish, Val Guest, and Richard Talmadge.

'The result was *total chaos*. Units were shooting in three separate studios. I was shooting at Shepperton, another unit was shooting at MGM; there were units all over the place. And none of us ever saw a completed script. I had to call the director at MGM to find out what *HE* was shooting so as I would know how it dovetailed into what *I* was shooting ... I shot my sequence, with Joanna Pettet, and no one came near me. I had an unlimited budget. I only saw the producer when I sent him a map of how to get to Shepperton Studios, and he dropped in for a day. But no single director knew what any of the others were doing, and not until we all sat down and saw it all cut together did we realise we had been conned into a total pile of garbage.

'The result speaks for itself. A mishmash that came into being because the star had walked out. Feldman said that Sellers had pulled out in breach of all manner of contracts; and I know for a fact that Feldman had a heart attack in the middle of all this and the general opinion was that Sellers was responsible. . .'

Hughes adds that they had to '"skate around" Sellers, and use doubles to cover him in unshot scenes, and stand on our heads to explain his absence from the screen. I myself never met him. Indeed, I shot a scene with Orson Welles in which I used a double for Sellers. Welles himself told me that Sellers wouldn't come anywhere near him. To shoot a scene with Welles, Welles went in one day, Sellers the next. The two never came face to face. This is evident in the cutting.'

☆ ★ ☆

Sellers' fingerprints are all over *Casino Royale* – he it was who got it to slip its sprockets. And he did destroy Feldman's health – something he maintained Feldman was getting him to do on purpose. 'Charlie Feldman is going to die,' he confidently predicted, 'and the reason he'll die is so that he can blame me – he'll say, *"There! Sellers killed me!"* He'll do it to spite me.' You have to be a special sort of raving lunatic to believe that people will actually drop off the twig to get one over on you. But, sure enough, a few months later, Feldman made the announcement that he was suffering from terminal stomach cancer; and, sure enough, he told anyone who'd listen that 'It's that bastard Sellers. *Sellers has done this to me.*'

Sellers at the very least was ulcer-inducing, and he'd aggravated Feldman's condition. He continued to show only scorn for the producer's plight ('You know,' he said, 'that film was fraught with incredible problems. The making of that film would make an interesting film in itself'); and if he couldn't quite blame other people all the time for the befuddlements he personally was causing his films there were always, of course, the portents, magic spells, omens and coincidences to wave a finger at. And, where *Casino Royale* is a few reels of obscurity owing to Sellers' absence (you could almost argue that his diffident Evelyn Tremble has been taken to extremes – he's now the invisible and creeping wind), *Ghost in the Noonday Sun* is chockful of ennui because he made sure he impaired the takes by sticking around to upset his co-star, Anthony Franciosa.

In the story, Dick Scratch and Pierre are rivals, each wanting to be the pirate king. Sellers took this to mean he had to drum up animosity towards the other actor – he had to hate Franciosa for real. 'I saw a rough cut,' says Dick Vosburgh, who wrote a hearty ballad to go over the titles, 'which included a take where Sellers insulted Franciosa – calling him a "two bit Hollywood wop bastard". He came quite out of character with a genuine and shocking snarl; and Franciosa looked back angrily at what was so plainly a personal taunt. I couldn't believe it: Sellers' naked hatred printed and put into a rough cut. But Gareth Wigan, Columbia's executive, seemed proud of having been able to trace enough usable film to assemble any sort of a version at all; and Medak said they'd get Peter back to re-dub the line at a later date.'

The chances of recapturing Sellers and forcing him to make good his errors and wrecks were remote. He was up and away playing Queen Victoria in *The Great McGonagall* and having speaks with Lew Grade and Blake Edwards over staging a reunion with Inspector Clouseau. (*Ghost in the Noonday Sun* was wrapped at the end of 1973; the opening blind-begger-with-minkey [*sic*]-scene of *The Return of the Pink Panther* was put in celluloid in the Rue de Paris, Nice, on Monday July 15th 1974.) Instead, Medak was compelled to use reverse angle shots, long shots, shots with stunt doubles etc. when attempting to camouflage the sections where Scratch's colourful rascally Irish cursing had overstepped the mark. It was *Casino Royale* all over again – except instead of being merely uncooperative, Sellers had now been actively seditious. 'His scheme was to do anything and everything to sabotage the film,' Medak told me, 'so that the film would not happen, and he'd get paid off. There was nothing he wanted more than to draw his salary and not do any work. He set this in motion – by getting the producers fired; he had the cameraman fired – Larry Pizer, who'd worked with him before on *The Optimists*. He was Peter's personal choice. Then he tried to get rid of me ... Three quarters of the way through the film, he came over to me on a beach in Cyprus – everybody had been there since six in the morning, and they'd had to get to this bay by boat as there wasn't a road; and he turned up at eleven, without his make-up, which took two hours usually to apply – and everybody was dying in this hundred and ten degree heat: "Oh baby, how are you?" He put his arm around my shoulder and walked me away from the crew; and he said: "What we've got to do – you should quit the film. Why don't you quit the film? That's what you've got to do. I have director approval, and I'm going to reject every director they are going to suggest. I will get paid off – and I'll give you half the money." I turned to him very gently and quietly and said: "You see that crew? They've been standing here since six this morning. You signed your name to a contract. So did I. The only way we are going to get out of here is to shoot our way out. You'd better go and put your make-up on."'

Sellers comes out of the episode even worse than this, if such a thing is possible. He was lying to Medak about not wanting to accept any replacement director. Night and day he was pestering people like Joe McGrath: 'I got these phone calls from him. At midnight he'd go through his little book, when he'd lost confidence in a production and its members. He lost confidence in me on *Casino Royale*. Totally lost confidence in me. Then he said: "Don't leave." I said, "If you've lost confidence in me what is the point of our even discussing this?" He asked me to take over *Ghost in the Noonday Sun*; and he'd ask Bryan Forbes to take over the films I did with him. Forbes and Dick Lester were both asked to do *Casino Royale*. I also got phoned about *After the Fox*. Peter wanted me to take over from Vittorio Di Sica. They were filming in Ischia. Sellers insisted that they flew British bangers in to the unit. A helicopter collected sausages from Harrods – a plane took them to Rome, Naples, Ischia. . . .'

☆ ★ ☆

Can Sellers' Roman emperor quality caprices be traced back to a source in (say) *The Naked Truth*? Did he learn something about himself back there? Zampi's desultoriness made everyone look ill and exhausted – save Peggy Mount who, as I said earlier, harrumphs through her scenes like Queen Celeste in Jean de Brunhoff's stories about Babar the green-suited elephant. Given Sellers' hatred of being bored, his general impatience and contempt for others, the sluggardly pace was agony. 'I remember one very difficult episode,' says Miss Mount. 'We were doing a very demanding shot. I had to enter the room followed by the camera and the shot had to embrace Miles Malleson, Shirley Eaton and Peter (disguised as a policeman). Nothing went right. There were some noisy bees on the set; an aeroplane went over; the camera squeaked; and so it went on. We had beer five days working on it, and just when we thought we had got it, a man in the gantry gave out a very audible snore. The comments were explicit, much to the annoyance of the union man on the spot who promptly called a strike in protest. The strike lasted another five days. We were eventually coming to the end of the sequence which required Sellers' false moustache to fall off, and it wasn't doing so. In desperation, and unseen by the camera, I blew hard in his face and, thankfully, the moustache fell off. . . .'

Sadly, for all their efforts, the scene is a shambles. Zampi had made his cast go over their movements and dialogue so many times, the final effect is inert and zestless. As farce, it seems under-rehearsed, it is so torpid; and as for Miss Mount's heavy breathing: Joan Sims, kneeling over Sonny, who has collapsed after taking a glass of drugged Amontillado, shrieks something like, 'Oh look, his moustache has dropped off!' Peggy then sighs heavily, and the moustache floats half an inch up Sellers' nose. It's hopeless; all to cock. How did Sellers himself refer to the experience? Off-handedly: 'One day Mario Zampi offered me a part. I was to play five different characters. I thought: Good! I shan't be typed. . . . But they were very dull. . .'

He did, however, retain a fondness for Sonny's Dubliner disguise: 'one of them was an Irishman – there's a still which I think is very funny; it's the epitome of all the Irishmen in their square-shouldered suits standing about in Mornington Crescent. . . .' In the photograph, Sellers' eyes are porcine and stupid and his nose so large and lumpy, it seems modelled on the snout of a bullock – Sellers has turned himself into Brendan Behan, whose drunken brawling and carousing he spoofed on several of his LPs: 'Suddenly It's Folk Song,' for instance, where a jovial crew go from music-making to fisticuffs, crowning one another with their harps; or that rancorous little sketch, 'In a Free State,' about 'Mr Bedham', the impossible playwright. As the interviewer does his best to squeak across his list of standard questions ('What childhood influences are there in your work?' etc.). Sellers, slurred, angry, panting and ready to commit murder to get at a drink, is hypercharged and he lifts the script up into a sadistic realm of his own: 'I'm not tellin' you nothin' you spud-faced bastard. I used to know a snivellin' bloody screw in the Dublin nick that looked the image of you. He got a piece of wet putty for a face just like yours – made me want to throw up each time I looked at him. I'm not writing nothin' – filthy stories for *Watch with Mother*, that's what I'm writing. What I dislike most of all is being asked stupid questions by a snotty nosed squit who ought to be strangled by his old school tie. *That's What I Hate...*' All this, plus undecipherable mutterings about how to get to the gents and the saloon bar – and of course we are meant to be in a recording studio at Broadcasting House, i.e. a cubicle of gentility.

The 'Mr Bedham' language, the colourful phrasing and distortions, is what Scratch's became when Sellers went for Franciosa and took the button off his foil. It wasn't as simple as Sellers coming quite out of character; it was more that he had melded into another, related, and more deadly one. Thoroughly disturbed, his aggression was released by acting – and yet not all of it was acting. Whilst he could pretend to himself that his outrages were acceptable if conducted on a movie set (where it could be argued that it was his inventiveness carrying him away), underneath there was real disintegration and formlessness. When they were making *The Naked Truth* he told Terry-Thomas, 'I've come to the part of the film which is scaring me to death. I'm supposed to use my own accent. And I haven't got one.' Hence the medley of Scottish, Irish, Cockney etc. which pours out of Sonny. His shifty personality is exhibited in his shifting voices; in the way he's charming or arrogant, as it pleases him. There's nothing about him you can trust. He *is* the thirty-something Sellers, slowly suffocating.

☆ ★ ☆

There are a few rather more transparent effects of *The Naked Truth* than mysterious, autobiographical hints. First, Zampi, the hands-in-the-air film director, voluble and short on talent, was impersonated by Sellers, as Adlo Vanucci, in *After the Fox*. Flamboyant, cocking a light meter as a monocle and having lenses slung around his neck like an alderman's chain, Aldo minces up and down and to and fro in the world as if it's still the eighteenth century. 'We film directors must give vent to our feelings,' he states, before throwing piles of a policeman's papers in the air, adding, 'And I have just vented!' (If the idiot foppishness is Zampi's, the fit and squeal are Goonish.) Secondly, the experience of the strike at the studio, during *The Naked Truth*, and the irrational power of the unions they all had a taste of, gave Sellers his material to draw on when putting Fred Kite together, in *I'm All Right, Jack*. He much admired the stubbornness of shop stewards – their self-satisfied sulks and tantrums, which had more to do with upsetting the master-race than spreading brotherly love amongst the workers. Thirdly, the vituperative relationship between Sonny and Lord Mayley – Mayley almost wanting to throw-up at the sight of Sonny in his house, but enduring him as a necessary confederate in liquidating the blackmailer – is repeated and exaggerated to out-of-scale pantomime proportions, in *Tom Thumb*.* Despite Mayley's snobbish class consciousness, he and Sonny are similar, under the skin. They are both grifters. So it made sense to team them, in vaguely Laurel and Hardy fashion, as a pair of comic baddies.

First, however, there was *Up the Creek*, a nautical revel sponsored by Mountbatten. Again, Sellers plays a double-dealer; but Chief Petty Officer Dockerty is all speed and adroitness (he's like Phil Silvers' Bilko, awash with scams), where Sonny left us with an impression of lassitude and sneakiness. Suddenly, Sellers is invigorated. His eyes sparkle. Maybe it is the strong Irish accent which he enjoys? Or the naval uniform – which makes him look a lot snappier than Sonny's dull and shapeless charcoal suits and narrow collars? He's still very fat, though, with chins galore, but this gives him authority, presence. We quite believe he's the brains behind *HMS Berkeley*'s sharp practices. He has charisma, and an answer for everything.

HMS Berkeley is a non-seaworthy sloop, anchored off Meadows' End (it could be the world's end, all gorse and heathland) in Suffolk.

---

* Some sources spell this as a twee lower-case *tom thumb*, but I'm having none of that.

The navy has forgotten about its existence – it is an accounting error, like the neglected colony of Gaillardia in *Carlton Browne of the F.O.* or the Ruritanian kingdom in *The Mouse that Roared*, or the sultanate by the sea, Huwayat, formerly a British Protectorate, in the play *Brouhaha*. (Sellers' habitats were cobwebby worlds set apart – islands of lost souls.) Dockerty and his crew of motleys keep pigs and chickens on deck; a public laundry operates in the boiler room; they make wedding cakes and other fancy pastries for the villagers ('This is for Mrs Green's barmitzvah') – the ship is an enterprise zone. They sell navy-issue rum and cigarettes to the local pub (Dockerty says that the HMS imprimature means Home Made Smokes), towels and soap to boarding houses, gun metal paint to the hardware stores. 'The navy never pays in this place!' a visitor is told proudly – for the navy is the supplier of bounty; their rate of exchange is barter or grateful gifts.

Sellers, his face transformed by a pair of oval tortoiseshell spectacles, delivers his speeches as patter. 'We might as well be flying the skull and crossbones,' he says, surveying his accounts ledger, totting up the profits. Indeed, Dockerty could be Dick Scratch's quick-thinking brother, for the *Berkeley* is being run on benign piratical lines. The people being robbed and swindled are the paymasters back in Whitehall – though the bosun has only a few old salts on board (Sam Kydd, Michael Ripper, David Lodge, Lionel Jeffries – little character actors familiar from a thousand British comedies), he's drawing the pay and privileges for a full complement. He personally does very nicely. His cabin contains flowers, a cocktail cabinet, a quilted eiderdown, and a budgerigar.

This, then, is the set-up: a rusting ship as a happy home, where Sellers' character is king; a microcosmic England, with the citizenry deriving pleasure from their harmless cheating and lying, talking their way into and out of anything, boxing clever. What goes wrong with the bamboozling idyll is what goes wrong with the film as a whole ('A good idea insufficiently developed' was Sellers' accurate verdict): the arrival of David Tomlinson's Lieutenant Humphrey Fairweather. Fairweather is one of those wet and chumpish upper class officer types usually played by Ian Carmichael. But where Carmichael conveys a sort of dreaminess – his characters are ineffectual and clottish because their heads are full of mist – Tomlinson's are a bit tetchy and exasperating. Noël Coward once described the actor as resembling 'a very old baby', and I think I can see what he meant. Tomlinson's full lips have a downward curl; he looks as though he'll stamp his foot in a rage. Even twenty-two years later, as the dapper Scotland Yard chieftain in *The Fiendish Plot of Dr Fu Manchu*, he rattles his teacup crossly, and the clear eyes and smooth cheeks are still in a beautiful state of preservation. He is a ditherer always on the edge of being huffy, but too well-bred to show it.

When Carmichael was pitted against Sellers in a class war (in *I'm All Right, Jack*), you felt that, in a remote and complex sense, the characters they played had similarly loopy ideas and quirks which would conjoin them. The relationship between Dockerty and Fairweather is more superficial and immediate – Fairweather never gets far beyond exclaiming incomprehension. (Commander Avery, similarly, has no idea what to make of Nayland Smith. All he can do, when Fu's nemesis starts to reminisce, is to look on in mild fascination.) Sent out to *HMS Berkeley* by the Admiralty, which has eventually discovered its oversight, he is easily fooled by the shyster he meets. 'Bosun,' he says, perplexed and wishing he was elsewhere, 'on the next pay parade I'll sit beside you – and watch.' His own extra-curricular interests, in ballistics, are too boring and contrived to concern us – except to say that it is one of his rockets which blows the ship up and gives us an ending.

When Sellers' Dockerty is in full panicky flow ('We couldn't very well *give* government property away, could we sir?'), his Londonderry accent is musical; his voice weaves in and out of the sighing which issues from Tomlinson and the grumbles of the crew members, who come up to him with their fears. He copes; he soars. The cook garbles something to the effect of 'What will happen when it is discovered we don't have a full crew?' Sellers, timing his pause to perfection, raps out: 'That's a very long sentence – which is probably what you'll get.' The cons continue under cover of darkness ('because there's no sleep for the wicked') and when Sellers scurries along the gantries and through the hatchways, the soundtrack cheekily toots Laurel and Hardy's 'Cuckoo' theme – cheeky because, though Sellers does have Olly's burliness, and the plot is another fine mess, Dockerty is no cosmic stooge, slipping and sliding and falling over. (He does, however, flash Fairweather a Hardyesque gaze when the depth of the new skipper's cluelessness over naval procedure is finally revealed.) *Up the Creek* isn't slapstick; it's a chance for Sellers to exercise his helter-skelter rhythms. Physically, as he glides about on his secret errands; and of course vocally.

To practise the voice, he bought one of the earliest reel-to-reel tape recorders. ('When I began,' he later confided of his technique, 'I used to go down to a studio with some kind of an idea and ad-lib for about an hour with a tape-recorder. Then I'd play it all back, choose what seemed to come off and work over that.') Doing the Irish brogue didn't present a problem; what Sellers wanted was to get the raciness right, so that when he poked the Able Seamen in the chest for emphasis, or looked mock-innocent when interrogated, his words and sounds would fit how he looked and moved. 'He was determined', remembers Tomlinson, 'to be taken seriously as an actor and not just as a clown who did funny voices.' Sellers asked his co-star, pointing to his gadget: 'Haven't you got one of these?' A few days later, he left a big parcel for Tomlinson backstage at the Aldwych Theatre. 'From a friend', said the enigmatic accompanying note. The recipient spent a year puzzling out who had sent it. Two decades on, in Paris, Tomlinson took delivery of another box: 'It's about time you had a new one,' wrote Sellers. It was another tape-recorder, the very latest and most expensive.

In the early days, Sellers confided his creativity to his tape machines; along with the camera equipment and motor cars, he could zoom about in, and try and control, time and space. Later, wives and children having been sent away, machines were his sole company. Yet even the tape spools, purring backwards, were no comfort. I asked Tomlinson what it was like to have known the Sellers who was first coming into his powers, in *Up the Creek*, and then encountering him again, on *The Fiendish Plot of Dr Fu Manchu*, after the end: 'If he liked you, he was wonderful, generous, funny. He never bothered me with talk of monumental depression – though I was aware that, in some mysterious way, he was *damaged*. He never read a book; he never went to the theatre or to the movies. He'd just sit on his own in the dark and brood. On *Fu*, he moved into the hotel with me, and he'd phone me at all hours. His Nayland Smith was very poignant. He was supposed to look through a magnifying glass, and he suddenly slapped a hand over one eye to help the focusing – a lovely detail and I laughed aloud. He hated applying the make-up for the aged Fu. Had there been a way of making films without make-up, without even having to turn up and be before a camera, he'd have been on to it. As for *Up the Creek*, that only cost about £150,000. Mountbatten intervened and allowed us to use a real battleship, as publicity for the Navy. The ship we were originally going to use was in a breaker's yard, and the owners wouldn't let us near it. Val Guest, the director, worked very hard, was very organised, and made himself a lot of money.'

The last point Sellers also made himself, in 1959: 'It was cheap to make and its takings have been fantastic.' (Translation: Though I'm not personally pocketing the door-money, millions of people are starting to go out to the flicks to see me.)

☆　★　☆

The varying of himself in criminal rôles was enlivening; at his best, in such parts, he was quick and controlled. He was born to play Clare Quilty, Nabokov's 'grease spot of mirth ... this semi-animated, sub-human trickster'. Something of his own wildness could be communicated when he also became Mr Topaze, going from schoolmastering to embezzlement; or Dodger Lane, nipping in and out of prison; or Pearly Gates, calling a meeting of the underworld fraternity and chairing it like an antic Pluto. Sellers would have made a definitive Father Brown (the detective priest played simperingly by Alec Guinness), because he, like no other actor, could have shown the way Chesterton's character subjectively imagines himself to be the murderer he's out to catch – he could have dramatised Father Brown's paradoxical process of 'feeling his remorse beforehand'.

Crooks and swindlers, with their front of normality, their alibis and insurrections, appealed to Sellers not only because of their slipperiness and dark secrets; he also identified with a hooligan's concept of social justice – he always put himself in embattled, aggrieved positions, so as to be able to fight, scheme, try and claw back what he believed was rightfully his: i.e. anything of yours he decided he wanted. This could range from your cufflinks to your car to your wife. When he was making *The Wrong Arm of the Law* he decided to add Nanette Newman to his collection. Michael Sellers says he remembers how it happened: 'My father offered to do a trade with Bryan Forbes. He rang him up and said, "I'll give you mine if you'll give me yours." Bryan said, "No Pete darling we can't do that," or something mollifying. Forbes didn't get angry.'

He'd have known there was no point. Sellers lived by makebelieve rules (he tried to swop Britt for Princess Margaret as well), and all you could really do was humour him. I think that what particularly obsessed him about Bryan and Nanette is that they were a happily married couple – he wanted to break into the relationship, or break it up, he was so jealous. 'He was always searching for a home,' Forbes told me, 'and he'd come to our house and look about him and plead, "How did you get this to look a *home*?" I'd answer: "Because all our things have accumulated over thirty years of marriage. We haven't had an interior designer in to choose everything, right down to the ashtrays" – which was Peter's way. He envied us our stable domestic life. He thought if he could marry Nanette, it would be his, too. He asked me if I'd mind if he married Nanette. I said, "It's not my decision – let's ask Nanette. . ."'

Sellers decided to lay siege to the Forbes' wedded bliss. 'He picked up Nanette from London Airport in an E-Type Jaguar, handed her the keys and said, "This is yours." The car was registered in her name. You had to stop him from giving you things. You'd admire something – he'd have Bert Mortimer deliver it the next day. Nanette has a Meissen figurine, which he said reminded him of her in *The Wrong Box*. I have a carriage clock. I admired his Hasselblad projector – Bert brought me one the next day; a Leica camera was also delivered . . . I'd try to pay for these, but he wouldn't hear of it. He invited us to dinner in Monte Carlo – he'd driven there from Italy. We were given a sumptuous dinner and there were exquisite presents on our plate, beautifully wrapped, from the most expensive shops.'

Once he had realised that this was one citadel he'd not prise open, Sellers vanished in some style. He invited the Forbes' to spend a holiday with him on his yacht: 'His yacht!' Forbes exclaimed. 'It had more power and gadgetry than the *Queen Mary*. It slept six. It had a full crew and a cellar stocked with vintage Dom Perignon. It cost Sellers about £90,000, and yet he still had the engines replaced with Mercedes diesel engines – incredible luxury. And he never turned up – there was a note saying: "Have gone with Bert to Vienna to learn the zither. P.S., regarding the map, the brown bits are the land and the blue bits are the sea." The Captain would say to us every morning, "Where'd you like to go?" We'd go off to Portofino for lunch. But Sellers was never there.'*

Apart from a deep desire to knock everybody out (all credit to the Forbes' for withstanding him), there was nothing else about him you could predict. Why was he so aggressive, exploitative, covetous? 'I find', he said, 'that I have been disappointed so many times in people, that I've become, not bitter, but I tend to approach people warily – in case they are going to clobber me. I find', he added, with no justification that I've been able to see, 'that I get clobbered a lot.' The snivelling tone is a performance. If anybody did any clobbering, literally or figuratively, it was Sellers. Other peoples' fear, especially, in mad-dog fashion, set him off. But, such

---

* This is the version of the story given to me by Mr Forbes himself. Another (evidently apocryphal) variation has Bryan and Nanette flying down to the yacht, in Sicily, discovering that Sellers had stood them up, and returning immediately – only for Sellers to claim he'd forgotten all about it: '*Did* I invite you? Sorry Bryan, love. It slipped my mind. *Did I* . . . ?' Either way, Sellers was an escapologist.

was his degree of mental topsy-turviness, and his sympathy as an actor, to achieve what he wanted, and to impose himself on the world through chaos, he seemed to almost completely become the people he was abusing – in the same way that he'd play back your own mannerisms or, as Wee Sonny MacGregor does, appear before you as your double. (He was a one-man *Rhinoceros*, denying you your individuality.)

His most frequent victims were his children. 'At eleven o'clock in the morning he'd love them,' says Forbes, 'and by mid-afternoon he'd be disinheriting them.' He hoped to extend his sufferings and moods by working on theirs. (It wasn't enough that he was ruining only his own life.) He expected them to feel how he felt. He wanted, as it were, to spread his sickness, like a vampire. This was his power; this was what he reckoned on as his right. 'I can remember times,' Sarah Sellers says, 'you'd be sitting there with somebody, and he'd get irritated with them, and all of a sudden he'd become them and talk back to them in exactly the same voice – awful, but amazing. Not just imitating the voice, but posture, looks, everything. It was hilarious and very embarrassing.'

Bloodcurdling is the word that comes into my mind. In James Hogg's novel *Confessions of a Justified Sinner*, a parable of egocentricity and demonic possession, first published in 1824, the religious maniac, Robert Wringhim Colwan, meets a master-mummer – who turns out to be Satan, who says: 'My countenance changes with my studies and sensations . . . If I contemplate a man's features seriously, mine own gradually assume the very same appearance and character . . . I not only attain the same likeness, but, with the likeness, I attain the very same ideas as well as the same mode of arranging them, so that, you see, by looking at a person attentively, I by degrees assume his likeness, and by assuming his likeness I attain to the possession of his most secret thoughts.'

This could be a description of Sellers' necromancy. Alexander Mackendrick once hoped to adapt a film from Hogg's book. Sellers would have been ideal for all the doubling and disappearing – and the novel, being about split personalities and paranoia, would have suited him in many troubling ways. Robert Colwan and the Devil: a gift of a part for a delirious actor who (in Hogg's words) 'by setting his features to the mould of other people's, entered at once into their conceptions and feelings'.

☆ ★ ☆

Had we been given the chance to wander around the sound-stages when they were making *Tom Thumb*, we might have felt plunged into a lunatic's landscape – everything so massively out of proportion, elephantine, that the human figure, small and undistinguishable, shrank away to nothing. One whole set was filled with Tom's cradle; another studio contained a wooden bench, sixty feet long, seventeen feet high, fourteen feet wide. A soldier's plumed hat, meant to be casually dropped on a table, was as big as a house and tethered by cables. The giant's bench and monster's cradle, in addition, were mounted on steel scaffolding, which could be rocked and tilted. There were teaspoons, yards long, paintbrushes, books and furniture legs, seemingly miles high . . . The purpose of the enormity was to diminish Russ Tamblyn, the twenty-four year old American tumbler cast as Tom; and playing the part in tight orange breeches and a slit white shirt, he's Peter Pan. (Is it my memory playing tricks, or does this Tom have a dagger slung across his hips?)

The myth which underlies fairy tales like *Tom Thumb, Pinocchio* and *The Gingerbread Man*, etc., stories about changelings and childless couples, is that of the infant Christ – immaculately conceived, raised by wise and simple peasant folk, the boys are led into temptation, or they fall amongst thieves and devils, and, their innate goodness shining through (aided and abetted by various angels or diaphanous fairies), they rout evil-doers and restore order, virtue, happiness, and such. This, certainly, is *Tom Thumb*, the most sentimental rendering of the lot. In the film, Tom's papa is Bernard Miles, a woodcutter (i.e. Joseph the Carpenter) and the Virgin equivalent is Jessie Matthews, a former soubrette and later the name-part in radio's *Mrs Dale's Diary*. June Thorburn plays the Queen of the Forest – she's a seraph, presiding over magic oak trees and celestial-looking bluebells and holly. (If the scenery is off a Christmas card, that's additionally apt.) But, luckily for us, Tamblyn's impish Tom goes against the grain of all this primary coloured purity. Not by being brattish or ungovernable, but by having a certain sex-appeal. This diminutive sort of Christ figure, with his golden head of hair and twinkling eyes, overflows with boisterousness and he has a dancer's awareness of his own body – Tamblyn is limbering up for the Mercutio rôle he played a few years later in *West Side Story*. As he darts through keyholes and penetrates locks (at the behest of Sellers and Terry-Thomas), you think: this Tom Thumb is a liberated flying phallus, a crowing cock.

What cannot succeed in the film in that case, Tamblyn's Tom being so knowing, are George Pal's celebrated puppet sequences. Tamblyn has to do a lot of acting alongside models and back projection screens. When the toys come alive in his nursery, ostensibly to amuse him, we wait patiently for all the hopping and leaping routines to be over, and for Pal the Hungarian stop-motion animator, to stop animating every blessed doll, pencil, button, jumping jack and kiddies' building block to come his way. There's worse than this, though. We wait very *impatiently* indeed when an utterly charm-free character called Woody (Alan Young) is on, trying to court the Queen of the Forest with alleged songs; or when Ian Wallace presents his dancing shoes at a fairground; or when the apple-cheeked old toymakers, hot toddy vendors, tattooed strongmen, balloon salesmen, and full company, their faces set in a rictus of jollity familiar to anyone who has ever watched an operetta at Sadlers Wells, take to the streets and mingle and jostle for the town carnival. (This chorus thinks acting is gesticulating.)

Why do we want this Franz Lehár stuff to be over? So that we can get back to Sellers and Terry-Thomas and their nefarious deeds. The characters, amalgams of The Brokers' Men in Christmas panto, the fol-de-rol actor-manager foxes in *Pinocchio*, Dick Dastardly and Muttley, and, as I said earlier on, Laurel and Hardy – i.e. any humorous down-on-their luck twosome – are luxuriously cast. They inhabit a region known as The Black Swamp – another postal district of Kenneth Grahame's Wild Wood or one of J.M. Barrie's Never-Never Lands. Ivan (Terry-Thomas) is the ultimate ne'er-do-well. As he puffs on a double cigar-holder, his black curls framed by a pointy Pied Piper hat, and his long flapping frock coat tailored, it would seem, for a foppish snake, he's every cheat and bogus gent Terry-Thomas played brought together in one place and cranked up for caricature – so that Ivan is a showman out of Restoration drama. (Though he doesn't have face powder or beauty spots, he does have a piratical earring. Perhaps we have hit on, here, the secret of this actor's success? No matter what film he was in – a St Trinian's with Joyce Grenfell, an American farce with Doris Day or Jack Lemmon – Thomas dressed and spoke as if ready to deliver the lines of Richard Brinsley Sheridan.)

If Terry-Thomas is a fox or a serpent, Sellers' Antonio, big and round, is a bear. Fat as Sellers was, he's still padded out – he's spherical, an effect accentuated by the large, curved, bashed Roman priest's hat that he wears. His leather coat, trimmed with clumps of mangy fur, is sewn together from unnumerable hides. Rotund, therefore, and carrying a caveman club, he's the hench-person, the stooge; and Sellers opts for Italianate, deep, ursine growls. 'Let's get reed of da kid now,' he suggests, 'so he don't open hees mouth.' He is couthless – where Thomas is all politeness. (Thomas, indeed, over-enunciates to such an extent, he seems to be singing.)

They capture Tom and, having taught him to tie bags of gold to their rope, sneak him into the Treasury. Whilst Tamblyn is about his business, in a set filled with wagon-wheeled sized coins, Sellers and Thomas are on top of the well-shaft and the film's best moments are the nods and winks which go on between them. Sellers, especially, his grizzly voice almost a whisper, does wonders with a brown-visaged scowl, a blank or a collusive look. Where another actor might use the garishness of the production as an excuse to burn too brightly and to hurtle around the cardboard painted castles, towers and woodland glades, trying to match the huge spoons, chairs and bassinets with an outsize performance, Sellers, remarkably, underplays. (If it is low-camp you want, fast-forward to Peter Bull, the burgomaster. When Bernard Miles and his missus have been erroneously arrested for the gold robbery, and sentenced to a whipping, Bull says: 'Tell the Town Lasher to prepare!')

It is in *Tom Thumb*, therefore, that the lessons of *The Goon Show* are seen to have been learned. On radio it was Sellers who'd had the star's presence; his voice which had had a swagger in it. Goonishness, Goonery, Goonism, what you will, with its mock deaths, mock heroism and nostalgia, gave him his central energy – and Sellers created characters and gave performances in which there was a big discrepancy between the calculated silliness of the story-lines and the genuine eccentricity of what he personally managed to accomplish. It's almost eerie, the way he touched in the foibles and curlicues, the psychology if you like, of cartoons. (He gave cartoons a third dimension.) As Antonio, a big blob of greed who doesn't know how many beans make five, he's similarly weird and stirring. For example, there's a terrific pantomime scene set in a ruined castle, presumably the very same Bavarian hideaway Dreyfus holds the deeds of in *The Pink Panther Strikes Again*. The robbers are attempting to count their swag and Tom nips in amongst the coins, knocking over the piles of gold and hiding and meddling with the doubloons – so that Antonio and his colleague start to suspect one another of cheating, and a fight starts: 'There's a crook in here, Ivan, and it's not me,' says Sellers. We can see and feel the dinosaurian reflexes and the primitive befogged brain cells which have had to crank into life to come up with that calibre of deduction.

During the battle, which Tom has inculcated, Sellers is oddly nimble. He uses his rotundity to become a rolling stone. He bashes Terry-Thomas with a chairleg, a broad sword, and a shield. He jumps over tables and makes a passage through the cobwebs with a firebrand. The violence seems to get things going inside his own head – for suddenly, banging Ivan's bonce rhythmically on the marble floor, he can count! And he does so with a vengeance, getting his own back on a fellow cut-purse who has no doubt sneered at his ignorance for years. All of Antonio's humiliations, defeats, resentments come out and are appeased. Clonk! Clonk! Clonk! (Our sympathy is not with Thomas for some reason – I was maliciously pleased to learn that he was on medication for his lumbago when this scene was shot.) Antonio still, however, cannot calculate what mathematicians call volume and capacity. When the villagery, baying and brutish now, having earlier been so wholesome, realise their error with Miles and Matthews and come after the real culprits, he is captured as he tries to squeeze himself through a tiny hole in the wall – a Tom Thumb sized chink. (It never takes much, in musicals or horror films, for fiesta crowds, traipsing about with wild flowers, to become mobs waving pitchforks, does it?)

☆   ☆   ☆

Up the Creek was released on November 11th 1958; *Tom Thumb*, six weeks later, on Christmas Eve. Would a tolerably aware contemporary picturegoer have noticed that Bosun Dockerty and Antonio the brigand were played by the same person? The one is all speed and unscrupulousness, the other all blockishness. What an early student* of Sellers' performances may have noticed is that, no matter how crude and simple the surrounding film, the actor himself is tenacious about giving his characters conviction, verve, interest. Already he had proved that, on the cinema screen as on radio, he could alter himself totally. (He was a shadow now, as well as an echo.) And, active creatively, in his private life he was restless and changeable. Soon it would be clear that he made the sort of films he did because of the kind of man he was – a man tortured by his search for a rounded identity, who needed to be free, and who, hardly of this world, disrupted the lives of those who tried to love him or work with him – because (says Michael) 'freedom to my father meant laying his hands on whatever he pleased and doing whatever he wanted all the hours there were'.

---

* I myself first saw *Tom Thumb* on a double bill with *The Wizard of Oz* at Bedwas Workmen's Hall, c.1974. I distinctly remember three things: (i) a surprise family programme in what was by then a bingo club interspersed with Christopher Lee and Peter Cushing revivals; (ii) Bert Lahr's ringleted lion; (iii) Sellers, in close-up, tapping the side of his nose knowingly – and doing it again . . . and again. He made a funny little moment out of nothing.

He was always on his way to somewhere else. What made him worth watching as an actor undid him as an individual; for, as an actor, Sellers could signify the things which were on his character's minds (Kite's dreams of Russian cornfields, Nayland Smith's duels with Fu's spiders, Dr Strangelove's bunker-room orgies) without ever standing still to know his own. At a certain moment, in the reproductive, mimic-prone world of acting, Sellers would make an imaginative leap – and it would be art. To achieve this, he was filled with a nervous tension; the nervous charge which we, his audiences, carry away. And the endless effort of it hollowed him out.

★ ★ ☆

Chapter Nine

A League of Gentlemen

... Broiling afternoon ... deck-chairs under the spreading ... the muted coo of pigeons in the immemorial ... delicate tracery etched against blue ... gently undulating emerald velvet sward ... cucumber sandwiches ... distant tinkle of ice in lemonade jug ... satisfying clunk of pad against willow ... distant insistent click of curate's false ... 'Oh well played, Ronald! ... Run, Doctor, run!' ... Doctor's reflexes not what they were ... short single ... hair's breadth ... flutter of applause ... soporific hum of bees in ... white figures moving in ancient ritual against time-honoured backcloth ... part and parcel of cherished national heritage ... warp and woof of very fabric ... Ronald caught in gully by bounder who looks as though he ought to be wearing braces, black trousers and snake-fastener belt ... 'Nice little knock, Ronald!' ... helped put us into double figures, anyway ... twenty-two for three ... not bad ... not bad at all ... clatter of crockery ... drowsy murmer ... shadows imperceptibly ... smell of freshly cropped ... democracy in action ... squire and labourer toiling side by side for the common ... glorious uncertainty ... all sorts and conditions of men ... regardless of race, colour or ... young thingummybob in next ... all pimples and Brylcreem ... hopeless ... notice out of corner of eye Mrs Bisset struggling with tea-urn ... ought to help her ... magnificent figure of a woman ... summer dress certainly shows off her ... wonder what she ever saw in old ... hypnotic drone ... stray dog ... harsh cawing of rooks high in ... six by young whatsisname ... sheer fluke ... plumb through old Granny Murchison's lavatory window again ... enthusiastic ripple and sporadic ... distant tinkle of broken glass ... hypnotic click of knitting ... satisfying clunk of bat meeting ... crimson orb setting in ... wonderful cloud effects

... just like galleons ... shadow of church spire imperceptibly ... white figures moving like ghosts in ancient ... where else but in England would you ...

The ethos of Ealing and its derivatives was of an England as a land fit for heroes; of the English as respectable and innocent; of Englishness as a relentless chirpiness (amongst the lower orders) or a muted and noble state of mind – and Sellers caught it beautifully in the piece he wrote (with Peter Munro Smith) called 'Village Cricket,' published in *The Boundary Book: A Lord's Taverners Miscellany of Cricket*, in 1962. Sellers, in fact, was not in the least bit interested in cricket, though he pretended to be. It was expedient, and good for a gag – as in the scene he improvised with Peter O'Toole in *What's New, Pussycat?* O'Toole, playing a wan-faced satyromaniac whose bodily fluids have been pumped away, attempts to convince Dr Fassbender (Sellers, at his most Germanic and nutty) that he is not a pervert, that he can exert restraint, and that he is a gentleman. How can he prove he is a gentleman? Because he knows the rules of cricket. Cricket is all the therapy the well-brought-up need. 'Is there any sex in it?' asks the doc incredulously. 'Cricket is a game played by gentlemen for gentlemen,' retorts O'Toole. 'Then it is sick, *sick* ...' says Sellers, vigorously shaking his head.

Cricket, so cunning and forceful a pursuit under its serene surface, was a game he felt he ought to affect enthusiasm for, being a Totteridge and Whetstone ratepayer; more to the point, a local charity side was captained by John Boulting. Sellers anticipated that, if he turned up and offered his celebrity services for a match, the conversation might swing around to an offer of work in a Boulting Brothers film. It went better than that. John and his brother Roy put Sellers under a five year contract, worth £100,000. At the press conference, convened to announce the deal, the actor smiled wanly as the twins went on about how they'd 'signed him up because he is handy with a bat and can talk cricket'. Sellers didn't demur. He gave every appearance of agreeing with them – 'not because I had to', he explained later, 'but because it seemed the right thing to do at the time'.

Sellers even allowed the Boultings to organise cricket matches during weekend house parties at Chipperfield Manor, where he moved early in 1960. On one occasion, the opposition side boasting a baseball player who hit the lobs high over the barns time and again, John and Roy whistled in their team (which included Graham Stark, David Lodge, and John Le Mesurier) and said: 'Gentlemen. We must get him out at all costs. It is a matter of honour. Even if we have to cheat.'

Eventually, however, Sellers' apparent capitulation to the arcane rules and rituals could not be taken straight. To the cricket chat, which he'd come out with when around the cricket-mad twins, he'd add a white jersey or he'd wear a cap. The satire culminated in his turning up, whatever the hour or venue, (the Jockey Club, Washington, for instance) attired in white flannels, pads, gloves, spiked shoes and visored helmet, and he'd be waving a bat.* It was the equivalent of throwing your voice back at you – Sellers would throw your habits and hobbies back at you. Or he might retain some of them. The Boultings gave him a personal model for a sophisticated, self-aware sort of Englishman; a slightly hazy, charming fellow – whom we get (partially) as Robert Danvers, in *There's a Girl in My Soup,* and as Major Robinson, in *Soft Beds, Hard Battles* (both of which were Boultings productions). It was a rôle he also adopted off-screen. To return to my plod across a wet ploughed field with Kenneth Griffith:

'The best hotel in Swansea was The Railway, opposite the station

---

* Sellers played a practical joke with a similarly slow-burning fuse on the Prince of Wales. Invited to lunch with Sellers and Britt at Elstead, in Surrey, the Prince noticed that he was being served with significantly less and less food at each course – until by the end he was receiving barely an eyeful. Sellers never acknowledged why he'd organised this – it was way before Charles started to go macrobiotic, and *nouvelle cuisine*'s anorexic designs were also well in the future. Milligan says it was simply 'sheer insanity'. (Another explanation is that Sellers didn't expect HRH to arrive with his bodyguards etc., and so told the cook to share Charles' grub amongst his whole train.)

– and we'd been put in there for *Only Two Can Play*. I moved in and I was settling down in this room, and suddenly Sellers came in and said, "Kenny, we can't stay here. It is bloody disgraceful. *We* are not staying here" – which alarmed me a bit, so he called for the manager, and it was a lady, and he said: "Mr Griffith and I can't stay here in these rooms" – and he marched out and we ended up along the coast in Porthcawl. Very happy we were in Porthcawl. We'd have long drives to the locations each day – and Peter would be depressed and withdrawn a lot and his vocabulary would be extremely limited. Now, in the car he'd suddenly become John Boulting; and he'd begin to comment on, say, the politics of the Middle East, with the vocabulary which was John or Roy Boulting's – a subject which he apparently knew nothing about as himself – but once he became the Boultings – John or Roy, and I had to become the other one (they both talked alike); so we'd have these long conversations about the Middle East, or something. He was always urging me to join in with this sort of fantasy – this fantasy world of becoming other people. Or suddenly he'd start off as, say, Alec Guinness; and I mean if you didn't know you'd swear it was Alec Guinness – and he'd talk then with Alec Guinness' vocabulary. It was a very strange phenomenon – and he was *released*, in a sort of way, to talk about anything that the Boultings or Guinness would discuss. You see, it's not just his voice which he could modify; he could rewire his brain to be these different people, and it was a very spooky talent.'

Being identical twins, John and Roy were accustomed to seeing double; with Sellers they were suddenly triplets – though Sellers did his best to modify his performance. Except for the cricketing masquerade, his efforts, in the Boulting's presence, to be phlegmatic, crisp, dithering if needs be, had an undercurrent of yearning. 'He was very aware,' Anne told me, 'of not having had any education. This was a terrible hang-up. When we went to the Boultings for dinner, and he met intellectual people, Peter was really out of his depth. Afterwards he'd say to me, "Was I all right tonight?" – like he was doing some play-acting. His life was theatre. He became even more insecure, meeting John and Roy and climbing up. He was neither well-read nor intellectual, nothing. He was nothing.'

☆   ☆   ☆

'My whole life', Sellers told Jerry Kosinski,* the author of *Being There*, 'has been devoted to imitating others. It has been devoted to the portrayal of those who appear to be different from what they are . . .' Thus, his dreamers and romantics, his mock heroes and monsters; and the believability of Fred Kite, say, grows out of the fact that the character's malapropisms and genteelisms reflect Sellers' own fears about his suavity being exposed as a sham, the mirror crack'd from side to side. Kite wants Ian Carmichael's Windrush to think of him as virtually an Oxford man, a compeer, as in the long ago he'd been up to Balliol College for a one day conference. 'Very good toast and preserves they make available at teatime, as you probably know.' It's like Fu Manchu, the Old Etonian – he used to run the laundry for the boys ('All those *collars*, don't you know'). There's a breach between what Sellers' characters actually achieve in their lives, and what they think they are achieving: all those old actors and music hall crooners with the stuffing knocked out of them, thinking themselves to be in the noble service of art and illusion; or John Lewis, the worn out librarian, overqualified for his pseudo-intellectual job, doing his best not to half-settle for what he's got and worried, in vague and indistinct ways, that something in his life is leaking away, that time is passing. And time's passage and youth's being the stuff that won't endure gets to be the subject of *Waltz of the Toreadors*, *Hoffman*, and *There's a Girl in My Soup*. In those, Sellers' characters appear to be successes; inside, they are desolate. As he was.

'Success hasn't enabled me to find out anything about myself,' he said with surprise and indignation. 'I just know I can do certain things. If you go too deep into yourself, if you analyse yourself too closely, it's no good for the job. You can either act or you can't. If

---

* Who killed himself on May 4th 1991, shortly after writing to me saying he would be happy to co-operate with my Sellers quest.

you analyse yourself and your own emotions all the time, and every doorknob handle, you know, you are up the spout.' Well, he could and he did and he was. He could act too well. He was always, as David Tomlinson said, brooding. He was up the spout – and yet he was also aware that, in terms of his high-powered career, his disaffections were necessary: 'I know that in this business success is so short-lived, so brief. It's not like being a part of [another sort of] big business that you're with for the rest of your life. That would lead to tranquillity. *But then I don't really want tranquillity.*[*] I almost want the whole thing to crumble around me. That keeps me at it – making me think I've got to be good . . . You do three bad pictures in a row and it's all over. [Another] part of the tension is the unreal life you lead. Being well-known is a problem to me. Whatever you do, somebody wants to say something about it or photograph it. But that's all part of it, part of what you want; you realise that's the life you've chosen. You're stuck with it . . . I can't achieve what I want to achieve. There's this constant gap between what one does and what one wants to have done. You go and see your rushes and you begin to wonder if you'll ever be able to judge your own work. And there's this other thing. The more success you have, the more people want to have a go at you in the press. And I just haven't got the confidence to shrug off what is said about me. . .'

Divisions are what unified Sellers: the man in Peter Pan (there's a line in *Hoffman* which bounces off the screen as autobiography: 'There are two people in all of us. The child in the snapshot and the monster the child grows into'); the success who feared the boredoms and meaninglessness of success and who was just about the best actor since Chaplin at portraying failures – not outright tramps, but the Kites, the John Lewises, the Old Sams, the Mr Martins – i.e. people with awkward and shapeless lives. He greatly feared death (as Alec Guinness testified) and yet courted it with spirit mediums and seances; and he died at least twice from heart attacks – on the first occasion emerging from hospital to say: 'I

---

[*] Italics added.

wasn't dozing off – I was dying. You'd feel okay . . . then you'd suddenly feel, "Ah – here we go again" – and that was death. . . .' He didn't like time to pass, he sentimentally looked back and reimagined events ('He once wrote me a letter,' says Anne, 'in which he said: "It has taken me fifteen years to get over you." He would ring me, when the children were with him, and say: "It's wonderful – I wish you were here." It was as though he'd wiped out the reality and the unpleasantness') and the very next thing he'd do would be to whizz about in fast cars, doing his best to use up time and speed ahead: 'Yes, I've got this car thing. It started when I was working in vaudeville. I'd always wanted a car. Then I bought one. Then I started to change them at an alarming rate. Since 1948 [he said in 1962] I've had sixty different cars. This chap, this car salesman in North London, opened up a showroom entirely for my benefit. I'd go to him with this mad lust for cars inside me, and see something I'd want and get it. And next day I'd be back, trading it in for another car. Now I've finally got what I want. The Bristol 407. It's perfect. I didn't know such a car existed. The Bentley Continental wasn't bad for room, for speed, for comfort and silence; but the 407 combines everything. I've had it over a month now, I'm happy with it, I'll only change it if they improve the model. I just love motoring. It's a search for perfection. Probably there is a link between this search and the other one, the one in my work. One is a search for perfection in a machine, the other stems from a great sense of depression at being unable to supply what I know I should be able to deliver.'

The man who switched cars also switched women and addresses – was always in panic and flight: 'My idea of permanence is about five years. I've always been restless. My grandparents were the same. Always on the move. I certainly have inherited this lack of a foundation, this lack of roots . . . I think being half-Jewish has a lot to do with it. That and the business. I have a feeling I'm not going to stay anywhere for very long. . .'

He was a collector who never kept anything. Once he'd bought and renovated a property, its appeal had evaporated. 'He begged me to have the flat in Hampstead,' volunteered Bryan Forbes, 'and he offered me Elstead. "It has too many bad memories for me." I said, "Peter, you've not spent more than a few weeks in the place" – which he'd had gutted and rebuilt at huge cost. Elizabethan bricks, seventy-four ornamental lakes, all that.' One of his last burrows was in Port Grimaud, adjacent to Herbert Lom's villa – who recalls: 'Sellers spent more than half his life in hotel rooms. All film actors do, of course, but Peter preferred this sort of existence. Elstead, in Surrey, was as close to a home as he ever had that I saw. But it was like a well-furnished film-set. I had a home in the South of France – several of the "Panthers" were going to be made there. Peter bought a house near-by and it took him six months to move in. Though it was a brand-new house, he had to have it remodelled, refurnished, refurbished. Finally, he moved in. I telephoned him from along the coast to wish him a happy home:

'"We're moving out," he said. "We don't really like it – and anyway, we don't like the French."

'"Why ever not?" I said. It typically didn't occur to him that I had a French wife.

'"We don't like the French because they don't speak English."

'The day he moved in, he moved out. Then he tried Gstaad – because Blake Edwards was there, Curt Jurgens was there. Peter had to prove that he too could afford to live in Switzerland – and then he hated that. . .'

Sellers' chalet, La Haute Grange, in the thin winter air of the megastar community of Gstaad, was a mausoleum – chilly and devoid of life, it belongs in the annals of gothick horror, right up there with Northanger Abbey and Bleak House. It was described for me in 1989 by Elwood Rickless, Sellers' lawyer and executor: 'Sellers was always deciding, "This is the house! This is tremendous!" But he was never able to settle. He heard people say Switzerland was the place, so he repeated the sentiment – and kept phoning me about a house he'd found: "I want it." He had very little money before *Return of the Pink Panther*. There'd been a string of flops and he already had a house in the South of France which he couldn't afford. Then, when he started to earn huge money, with the "Panthers", his then-manager, Denis O'Brien, said he should settle permanently outside of the United Kingdom, for tax purposes. Sellers decided on Gstaad – because Blake had a chalet there, and Sellers was always wanting to be like Blake, or be better than Blake. It was hugely expensive, the chalet he decided he wanted; and we, as his lawyers, were told we *had* to find the money. He was resolute. We tried to negotiate and reduce the price, but the vendor could see a sucker, and Sellers ordered us to pay . . . We found the money somehow – sticking together the cash with glue and string.'

Lynne then spent another fortune on interior decoration, and Rickless took Sellers over to see Leslie Waddington, where they picked out some paintings – a Lepine, an Ivon Hitchins and a Sam Francis – and carted them off to the chalet, which stood on a hill – most conspicuous, with ornate gables, and so on, all in contravention of strict planning regulations – but as far as playing king of his castle went, Sellers disappeared. Sellers didn't move in the same social set as Blake Edwards, and he had no idea how to play host in his own home. He never had people over. He had no friends. So he and Lynne were always taking off – which raised problems for his lawyers and accountants, because a residency permit is very hard to obtain and Sellers was not clocking up enough days. Well, it is over ten years since his death and the place is still part of his estate. Lynne is there a week a year, if that. The upkeep is vast. 'We let it once, to cover some costs, but Lynne instructed us not to do that again,' says Rickless. The house is cleaned three times a week. The lights come on automatically at seven and go off at one in the morning. . . There is nobody there. Except for Sellers' garments – which still hang in the wardrobe, awaiting his return, quite as if he is continuing to live. 'Going back without him to the chalet in Gstaad . . . was difficult,' Lynne told David Lewin. 'Logically and sensibly, I should have taken his clothes out of our closet. One half is his, the other half mine. But I couldn't take his clothes out. It sounds silly, I know, but I'll leave them there until I feel they should be there no longer.'*

It doesn't take much to imagine the light sinking in the hushed rooms, the curtains gliding open and shut on pre-timed electrified tracks, or to hear the sound of soft music tinkling automatically and forlornly from the hi-fi – like the breeze in the organ pipes in *Sunset Boulevard*. La Haute Grange is a haunted house; and it always was.

☆　★　☆

At the end of *Hoffman*, the enervated figure Sellers plays is having a dream house built in Hampstead – another vampire's lair. He takes Miss Smith (Sinead Cusack) off to view it. She's excited at his plans for the kitchen. 'I'd have lots of jars and check curtains,' she chirrups. David Lodge, as a hunchbacked Ygor, is down a hole under the floorboards, in the cellar (it's like a crypt), fitting a boiler. Benjamin Hoffman will have all he wants: a well-appointed pad *and* Sinead Cusack to be his Wendy Darling. Yet still he slumps in his chair, very alone, half gazing at the night sky, heavy, weary, depressed about the state of the 'soul behind this bloodhound face' – hangdog, more like.

But if that image is rather a subtle instance of Sellers' use of division and discontinuity – having all you want and it's still not enough; being disenchanted when dreams come true – then he was quite able, elsewhere, to make broad slapstick out of the appearance *vs.* reality conundrum. Inspector Clouseau is the world's greatest detective as well as being the world's greatest idiot. His skills at detection are inadvertent, and yet if people try to assassinate him, they bump off themselves; if they try to outwit him, they tie themselves in knots. He turns incompetence into a virtue. He is charmed – a Holy Fool. 'I originally got Inspector Clouseau', Sellers explained to Alan Whicker, 'from a conversation I heard between a concierge in a hotel in Paris and an American tourist. This concierge, believe me, was very sharp and used to tourists; a very

---

* As we go to press (Summer 1993), Mr Rickless informs me that Sellers' widow has finally agreed to sell the chalet ('thank heavens').

patient, nice sort of guy, but there was a twinkle in the eye. This tourist was asking: "We'd like to take in the Lido show and right after that we want to go and eat somewhere good and then we want to go on to the Crazy Horse and we'll need a limo for that 'cos there'll be around six of us," and the concierge said, "I'm going to tell you what I'm going to do. I'm going to book you into the Lido. Six places at the best table, right? I'm going to book you into the Tour d'Argent afterwards, a nice table overlooking the river, everything – the best view. After that I'm going to book you into the Crazy Horse – you see all the girls, and there'll be a limousine waiting for you." This guy says, "Hey – that's *really* good of you." Now he'd only repeated what this man had asked him to do, yet he got a bloody great five hundred franc tip. I thought to myself, that's old Clouseau really. He just listens to people and tells them what they think. That's why he has to be one-up on everybody. Somebody says, "There's a phone call for you, Inspector", and he says, "Ah, yes, that will be for me."'

Clouseau's Irish cousin, another ostensible failure who paradoxically succeeds, is Dick Scratch, the mangy ship's cook who becomes captain, wears a bejewelled turban, and thinks of himself as Douglas Fairbanks Jr. Had not Sellers, in his mad rages, unerringly deleted any vestigial good gag from *Ghost in the Noonday Sun*, we would have had a close-up of the ship's log – beautiful, neat copperplate calligraphy:

January 3rd 1648
Calm Sea. Clear Sky. Still Lost.
Signed,
Richard Scratch, Captain

Then, between the words 'signed' and 'Richard Scratch', a grimy hand would have appeared to uncertainly pen the letter X. Though Scratch stumbles upon buried treasure, loses it, reclaims it, loses it again, etc., he is lucky, (or unlucky) rather than perspicacious. In the world of slapstick, actions are mechanised, engineered; there's nothing much you can do if, as in the 'Panthers,' your folding bed

springs back, demolishes the wall and precipitates you into the
Seine, or if you charge at a locked door, hurl through it, fall out of a
window and splash into a fountain. And like Clouseau, Scratch is
never in total control – but things fall his way (figuratively) or fall
on top of him (literally). No wonder such characters are disjointed,
dazed.

☆ ★ ☆

It's Sellers' gallery of crooks which gave him the fullest opportunity
to demonstrate how people are often not what they seem. The
model prisoner who is simultaneously at liberty stealing a chest of
jewels in *Two Way Stretch*; the gangster who runs a dress shop, in
Wrong Arm of the Law, and a lock-up garage, in *Never Let Go*; the
escaped convict who pretends to be a film director, in *After the Fox*
– and who wishes, along with all Sellers' rebels, 'If only I could steal
enough to become an honest man.' Had *The Romance of the Pink
Panther* materialised, Clouseau himself would have become lawless
– stealing an albino gorilla from the Barcelona Zoo, amongst other
pranks. His objective? To pre-empt the hanky-panky of the film's
villainess, Pamela Stephenson, whom he loves – whom he adores so
much, he'll take all blame and responsibility for her scams. He
hopes this self-sacrifice will turn her back to virtuous paths. (If he
steals enough, she'll become an honest woman.)

Criminology is a series of false fronts. At its most crude the concept is exemplified in a dragged-out sketch which appeared on the
brother and sister sitcom *Sykes*, sometime in the early Seventies.
Sellers erupts into Eric and Hattie's life as an aged East End ruffian,
Little Tommy Grando, who purports to be an ex-school chum who
ran away to sea. He looks like a werewolf – a bad cropped-hair wig,
painted eyebrows, and jagged painted-out brown teeth. His rubber-
ised beak is the Irishman's from *The Naked Truth*. It must be one of
Sellers' worst performances – he doesn't hide his contempt for
being on TV. (It's a terrible guest-star spot.) He barely suppresses
his smirks; he is obviously enjoying himself – and he signals this in
a way that is amateur and boring. I suppose the voice is a variation
of Michael Caine's Cockney, especially as there is a ribald joke

somewhere about pumping a church organ and Tommy says, 'Not a lot of people know that. . .' We then learn that he's meant to be an old flame of Hattie's. Would I be alone in finding the sight of Sellers locked in a screen kiss with Hattie Jacques, a giantess from Picasso's rose period, slightly distasteful? He seems to be mocking her unattractiveness. (Remember that old song from the Ma Ray days: 'Nobody Loves a Fat Girl/But, Oh, How a Fat Girl can Love'?) Then, as the programme lumbers onwards (a single thirty minute take; no change of camera angle), and Tommy has various violent outbursts, such as beating up Eric because he assumes he's Hattie's husband, the temper and flick-knives get too much for the gentle suburban sitcom style. Sellers, brandishing weapons and being obnoxious, is back in the underworld of *Never Let Go* – he's verminous, and we can see what his Fagin could have been like. Sellers had such sinister reserves.

Well, of course, he's *not* an ex-school chum or an old flame of Hattie's, nowhere near. It was a ham-fisted con. Little Tommy Grando, who'd run away to sea, is an escaped convict. He's been using Eric and Hattie's place as a hideout and he has enjoyed invading their home, livening up their humdrum lives. With the cops laying siege, he disguises himself in one of Hattie's frocks and, a transvestite, makes a mincing exit. Sellers, who has breezed through his part without taking any notice of a director, can't help but be too convincing with his female deportment. He's another person again, in the dress and wig. The Dickensian brute disappears.

What was benumbing and foolish in *Sykes*, however, was revealing in *Lolita*. Quilty 'is not a starring role, but it attracted me in my urge to play parts that are always different from the others I've had. . .' In this, the first of the two films he made for Stanley Kubrick, an actor's frightening ability to slip from one identity to the next is the essence of the performance. Quilty is quicksilver; he's the mask behind the mask. Sellers is able to be different within the same movie without, technically, splitting himself up as the components of a crowd – i.e. Quilty is related to Sonny in *The*

Naked Truth and not to the inhabitants of Grand Fenwick in *The Mouse that Roared* or, indeed, to the macabre vaudeville of *Doctor Strangelove*; yet where Sonny is a profiteer, slum-landlord, would-be murderer, and much else, it is still Quilty who'll give us the creeps, and I don't think he does anything much worse than win and ditch the girl Lolita. Is it because we see him through James Mason's paranoid eyes? Or that his appearances and scenes, with their improvised speeches, are so unexpected and inconsequential – Goonish, but without Secombe's healthy laughter to draw their sting?

Watching Quilty, or watching out for Quilty, it is Sellers' own malleability and disquiets which we sense are being revealed. The very first scene, with Humbert Humbert arriving at the fogbound gothick castle, hunting for his enemy, seems to take place at Chipperfield or Elstead – the dustsheets, the shrouded statues and paintings, the bottles littering the floor, the overflowing ashtrays, the up-ended packing cases: the impression is of a permanent, hung-over party going on to celebrate moving-in day or moving-out day. We can almost choke on the stale cigarette smoke and the general airlessness and satiation. All the guests have gone. Quilty, like Sellers, is best imagined amongst the leavings of an orgy; the overturned sticky wine glass, the dirty plates, the refuse of a meal. As in the sight of shuttered music halls or out of season holiday resorts, there's melancholy symbolism (almost a *memento mori*) in the image of yesterday's decaying food and unwanted drink.

'Are you Quilty?' asks Mason. 'No I'm Spartacus,' comes back the reply. 'You come to free the slaves or something?' Leaving aside the little jest that it was Kubrick who'd directed old dimple-chin Kirk Douglas in the epic *Spartacus*, the reference inspires Sellers to arise from a covered theatrical prop throne and drape a blanket around himself like a toga – he becomes one of the Caesars. He takes a swig from a goblet and there is a dog-end floating in the dregs. 'Gee,' he says, 'that's so insanitary.'

It is a great scene – Sellers' whole disconnected, wandering and impossible nature is summarised in under ten minutes. Quilty is a patchwork-quilt of personality types, accents and attitudinising. At first you think he must be drunk, he's so dishevelled and all over the place. He rambles on about methods of returning ping-pong serves; about what it is like, the playwright's life; about how he could arrange for Humbert to attend an execution: 'Just you there and nobody else. Just watching. *Watch*. You like *watching*, Captain?' Sellers speaks now as an obscene Bluebottle – a flaccid, pulpy adult with an adolescent's cravings. But no sooner does Quilty remind you of one facet of Sellers, than he's gliding away to try on another face and inflexion; and, as brilliant as the broken-up, mad mimicry of Quilty is – his performance-within-a-performance – the point of the scene isn't the actor's virtuosity or flightiness. It's the way that what emerges from the litter and turbulence on show is a very strong and coherent sense of menace. Quilty and by inference Sellers are of diabolical origin, their courtesy a bogus thing.

He seems lazy and drained, and he assumes Humbert is a gate-crasher, or a guest who won't go. Then, noticing the pistol ('that's a darlin' little gun'), it dawns on him he's about to be killed – a Roman senator in the presence of his assassin. Humbert is so focused, intent on talking about Dolores Haze; Quilty shifts and shimmers, and the camera tracks his desultory progress around the room. He ignites a fag with a lighter made from an onyx boulder, strums chords at a piano of Liberace's. 'You are either Australian or a German refugee,' he says, pretending to play a guessing game and piling on the insults. 'This is a Gentile's house – you'd better run along.'

It isn't only a confrontation between men who loved and lost Lolita; it's a duel of acting styles. James Mason, classically trained, highly intelligent and cultivated, and with his lusts and yearnings kept under severe control; Sellers, loose, improvisatory, and with an ungovernable genius: it's Norman Maine springing apart because of Esther Blodgett all over again, in *A Star is Born* – Sellers being, like Judy Garland, full of flair and instinct rather than technique. Mason's contained fury, the same in Kubrick's film as it was in George Cukor's, also has the same motivation – which comes through in the character he plays. Mason's smile was always a grimace of pain and he flashed his teeth to inspire fear.* Garland's bluesy musical comedy actress, her fame increasing as her husband's wanes, and Sellers' glutted sybarite ('I got some pretty nice friends who could come and keep you company here') are immune to his usual tricks – to the ploys by which he normally takes command. They sully him. 'If you remember,' Mason said of *Lolita*, 'I wore a white suit in the film and Stanley Kubrick said to me, "Smile when you speak your lines and be charming, but all the time be thinking that if anyone dares to lay a finger on your suit and soil it you'll kill them. Keep thinking that and it'll come right. . ." He gave me an inner-dimension for the character. . .'

Mason is the man in the white suit, whom Garland and Sellers defile – and, deep down, Mason wants to be defiled and to let go: this provides the dramatic tension. Esther and Quilty are in a different order of being to Maine and Humbert, and to Mason himself – and the knowledge of this was a torture. Of *Lolita*, Mason said: 'I can think of only one minor criticism. [Kubrick] was so besotted with the genius of Peter Sellers that he seemed never to have enough of him. There was one scene in which Sellers, immersed in the character of Quilty . . . pretended to be an undercover detective for a full nine minutes while poor Humbert Humbert had nothing to do but look uncomfortable. I was Humbert Humbert.'

In *A Star is Born*, maddened by having to recognise the inferiority of his carefully crafted acting style, Maine gets in the grip of the grog. His ability to play immaculate gents shattered, there's nothing else he can give. In *Lolita*, Humbert is humbled by seeing his troubles and desires acted out for him by Quilty, and he is incited to murder. (He's like dry Salieri jealous of inspired Mozart in *Amadeus*.) As an over-fastidious man, he has written out, in a neat hand, a letter or list of all the crimes and humiliations Quilty is guilty of: it is a death warrant. 'Are these the deeds of the ranch?'

---

* e.g. see him in *The Seventh Veil*, rapping Ann Todd's knuckles as she plays the piano.

queries Sellers, taking the document and pretending to be a highly strung Southern Belle being served with a forceclosure notice. Mason starts to fire off the gun and he gets the victim in the leg. 'Gee, you hurt me, you really hurt me!' Quilty is incredulous, as he scurries amongst the shambles of toys and gadgets. He has discovered, against all expectation, a new sensation.

☆　☆　☆

Mason doesn't say it in so many words, but Sellers wasn't a gentleman. His own acting relied on exploiting the difference between a well-mannered, well-spoken surface of Englishness and a bosom filled with the poisonous fumes of contempt and guilt. He was always careful of how he'd look. Sellers, by contrast, never feared degradation. He wasn't aware that such a concept existed; and what this meant in practical terms was that his irresponsibility and shabbiness added up to an ebullience against which Mason, and people like him (i.e. people who were careful and indirect), would blunder.

You'd never get your bearings with him; there was nothing you could grasp. He may only ever have seen things from his point of view, but that perspective was always changing. 'You'd have marvellous times,' says Joe McGrath, 'with Milligan, Eric Sykes, Peter, and our wives. At other times, he'd just get up and leave. Or he wouldn't turn up. This is why he identified with Sir Guy Grand in *The Magic Christian*. Sellers had this feeling in his mind that he could do all those humiliating, mortifying things to people. He had a cruel streak and enjoyed setting people up, getting them to swim through shit. He was cruel with Cleese. Didn't give an inch with Cleese. In front of the crew and everybody, Sellers said, "Jesus Christ, *what* are you doing?"'

John Cleese was fired at the end of the first day of *The Magic Christian*. He went over to McGrath and said, 'I'm so sorry – I'm just so nervous when I'm actually up against *him* doing a take.' Sellers was merciless. 'Remove him. Get rid of him. Get somebody else for tomorrow.' McGrath said, 'Who?' – 'Anybody – we're never going to get anywhere with him.'

Meantime, Cleese was blubbing: 'It's the first real movie I've ever done. I didn't know it was going to be like this. He's a powerhouse.'

Cleese was reprieved, so long as he came in early the next morning to rehearse privately with the director, who explained that 'then we'll get Peter in and try out some business'.

Sellers still didn't know this and kept asking, throughout the night, 'Who are we getting tomorrow?' And he started to list old dependables like Brian Oulton or Colin Gordon. 'But Cleese is good and he's young,' argued McGrath. 'Well,' the star semi-conceded towards the dawn, 'on your head be it.'

McGrath and Cleese shot for two hours before Sellers displayed himself. The scene was cut together later in the editing room and Sellers said, 'All right, leave it' – but he was never happy with it. Why? Not because Cleese was especially incompetent, but because Cleese, as an obsequious salesman at Sotheby's, was more convincingly upper-class than the star – whose Guy Grand is meant to be a loopy aristocrat, and who comes across unfortunately as a bit of an arriviste. When Sir Guy says he wants only the nose from a Rembrandt, and takes a pair of scissors to the canvas, Cleese's whimpers of pain at the cultural devastation, mingling with his sobs of joy when pocketing the bribe, create a new noise: the strangulated cry of Basil Fawlty, swallowing his principles; or of Archie Leach, in *A Fish Called Wanda*, taking a microsecond to clear his throat before opting for Jamie Lee Curtis and crime rather than toffee-nosed Maria Aitken and the sedentary life of a High Court barrister. (Cleese performs an Englishman's neuroses comically as Mason did tragically.)

'Sellers wouldn't hide his annoyance with another actor,' says McGrath. 'He wouldn't put himself out to help anybody else's performance. His belief was you shouldn't be acting – and you had to be able to do it without rehearsal. Sellers would do that with actors – he'd lay them waste. He did have such energy and power, at one time. He wouldn't give people any benefits of the doubt. "I'm not here to help them," he'd say. If they couldn't do a scene his way – out. Now, he'd been the first to say, "Let's get Cleese", and the first to say, "Let's get rid of him." He had no allegiance.'

☆ ☆ ☆

When the bodies were falling during *Casino Royale*, Peter Evans asked him outright: 'What is this compulsion you have for sacking people?' Sellers said to him, quite hotly, 'I would get rid of my own brother, if he was not delivering the goods. If your sister had made you a typewriter, and it didn't work, *you* wouldn't use the bloody thing. If I find myself surrounded by incompetents and stupid people, I want to get rid of them.'

I find this remark a striking disclosure. It is more than an admission of ruthlessness – Sellers comes clean about wanting every resistance removed. By drawing an analogy between other actors and home-made Olivettis, and the like, he is saying that, to him, co-stars and colleagues were simply machines, objects without feelings, whom he could throw into a scrap yard the instant they displeased him. You prod and punch them; they do your bidding. He seems to have wilfully confused the tools of the trade with being creative; typing is not writing and acting is not mechanical – but he pretends that there is a connection. Secondly, why did he, an only child, bring brothers and sisters into it? Of course, he was *not* an only child. There was that still-born elder brother to haunt him – some innocent thing who had been dead all these years. And did he, as a scion of the Mendozas and the Rays, have an image of family loyalty as nepotistic – people moved into jobs, at which they were mediocre, as a favour, as charity? Thus had Peg and Bill got through life, having to be grateful. Sellers, however, wanted to rid himself of relatives (and rivals) on any pretext. (He rather fancied being a displaced person.) His isolation and the satisfaction he gained from violence was the result of self-possession – he wanted to be more than a novelty, the music hall child good at funny voices. He had to assert his strength and independence. He was miraculous; out of nowhere.

One way he exhibited this was to refuse to be with his mother when she was dying. (Peg joined the Choir Invisible on January 30th 1967.) He remained in Rome, stirring up hostilities on the set of *The Bobo*. He resented Peg for being frail, old, mortal; he decided he hated her for reminding him of where he'd come from – and this was a theme which had been gathering momentum for some years. Michael recalls that when his grandparents called, his father would often lock himself away in the darkroom and refuse to come out; or Peg would be taken for a drive in one of those limousines where a sound-proofing panel could be raised to cut off those in the back seat. Imprisoned in her glass and upholstery capsule, the poor dear would then notice all the window panes gliding down automatically, as her son revved up and accelerated through the North London suburbs. The blast of cold air and slipstream flung Peg about, cannoning her off the minibar and armrests like an untethered marionette. When the vehicle came to rest again a few miles farther on, she'd been lying inverted on the deck, her bloomers by now half way to High Barnet. Peter would have his little joke!

If the g-forces weren't matricidal, lady-killing, Sellers next tried neglect. Hattie Stevenson, his secretary for seven years, told me that 'Peg was only brought out to see him during his guilty moments. He wanted her in America, during the shooting of *The World of Henry Orient*, so I had to fly to London and accompany her back to New York on the *Queen Mary*. She was a very difficult person, an impossible person. She used to try and get around everybody by saying, "I'm Peter Sellers' mother, darling, and I want the best." A very embarrassing old bat; all the same, I was quite fond of her. If Peter came over to us, she'd say, "Now, darling, why don't you marry Het?" She used to call me *Het* as opposed to *Hat*, which used to irritate him intensely. Anyway, we did this voyage, which took five days. I was to be Peg's Travelling Companion – because *he* couldn't be bothered to take her out with him to America himself, or anything like that. I used to play bingo with her. When we arrived, she stayed all of two days, and he made me fly back to England with her because he couldn't stand her any longer.'

'What did she do to get on his nerves?'

'No idea. No reason for it. It was always, "Peter, darling. . ." Bert Mortimer used to be her driver. "Peter darling, I want a car and a chauffeur." He gave her all that. Bert and a car. Then he nicked

Bert from her, which upset her. A long series of chauffeurs after that. He made me fly back with her and then return to New York straight away. They were suspicious of me at the airport – smuggling old ladies in and out. He used to ring her up occasionally. She'd pushed him on in the early years, and that's why he was so stony-hearted with her in retrospect – she'd made him an actor, so if anything went wrong in the acting world, he saw it as her fault. She was an awful stage mother. She was exasperating. She dressed brassily; she used to have good things – but the way she put them on . . . The overall effect . . . We used to have to shop at Harrods. I used to have to go on these expeditions. Again, she was murder. "I'm Peter Sellers' mother." Showing off to everybody. She used to charge his account – and he accepted this.'

'What about when she was fatally ill?'

'He thought she was crying for attention – because she did use to do that, and he used to do that. You see, they were like twins.'

☆ ★ ☆

Sellers, when he confessed to Kosinski that he'd given his entire life to copying others; that he could have played any of us (rather better, no doubt, than our own efforts at being ourselves); and that his speciality was people who were not quite what they seemed: he may, I now see, have been referring exclusively to his own off-screen existence, dispersed and scattered, and full of fraudulence, as it was. When Peg died he was elaborately grief-stricken. He didn't care who saw him sobbing. As he wrote to Herbert Kretzmer, on February 3rd 1967, acknowledging a consolatory cable: 'It was, of course, a terrible shock to me as I was devoted to my darling Mother, but it's comforting to know that she died happily, and very proud of me.' Once she was safely dead, he could control his reactions to her, and start to misremember her. By the time Auberon Waugh located him, in July 1980, the song of lamentation was well perfected. 'Within minutes of meeting me, he told me that he was completely devastated when his mother died, rather as one might ask politely after a guest's journey. . . That was thirteen years ago, was it not? I said, putting on a sympathetic face. . .'

Sellers protested too much – even to the extent of privately canonising the parakeet Peg. 'Her influence! Oh God!' exclaimed Michael Jeffery with horror. 'Every Friday, Peter used to light a candle in front of her photograph. We went to the Cannes Film Festival, in May 1980, and hadn't packed the right sort of candles – he used night lights. He went berserk – it wasn't even Friday. He was worried we'd not be able to find any replacements. It was an obsession. He mentioned Peg all the time. . .'

Sellers was in his element with the cult of the dead. Sentimental and sadistic, there developed in him an idea that other people's distress and exits would enhance his own power and renew his strength – abandoning his mother, dumping wives, jettisoning children, firing colleagues, kicking dogs, it was his version of a pagan's human sacrifice. He even reached the point of trying to destroy people *before* they were to work for him – as is exemplified by Jonathan Miller's story: urgently summoned to Hollywood by Sellers. Kept waiting for a week in the Beverly Hills Hotel with no word from him. Reduced to rage and despair. Then limo'ed to the studios. There's Sellers on the set, shading his eyes to peer past the lights at this new arrival, and crying gladly: 'Jonathan! Long time no see! What are *you* doing here?'*

Admittedly, he hadn't always been as scheming as that, but the Boultings revealed great clairvoyance when they'd put him under contract, back in the Fifties. They could see how to make use of Sellers' sinking and whirling temperament. For, if Ealing films were all about decency, respectability, and conventions, temporarily flouted, the Boultings, who succeeded Balcon as purveyors of Englishness, turned England upside down. In a typical Ealing production, like *Passport to Pimlico*, people never defy authority for very long; to the Boultings, in *Brighton Rock* (adapted from Graham Greene's novel), or *Lucky Jim* (adapted from Kingsley Amis'), it is authority itself which is revealed as corrupt and substanceless. England's military (*Private's Progress*), judiciary (*Brothers in Law*),

---

* My thanks to Michael Frayn for this anecdote.

big business (*I'm All Right, Jack*) etc., are rotten to the core. Yet, though it is always said that the Boultings satirised institutions, like universities, the church, or Whitehall, I don't see it quite that simply. It's the individuals who make up the Establishment and fill the august professions which they had a go at; the sods and the worms out to impress, with their veneers and repressions. It is almost as if the twins took their lead from the final scene of *The Naked Truth*, when all Nigel Dennis' powerful blackmail victims, from throughout the kingdom, gang up to spring him from jail – the admirals, doctors, politicians, stipendiary magistrates and scoutmasters who don't want their ugly secrets being revealed in the witness box. 'Three hundred people worked on your escape,' says Sonny, awestruck. The message is clear: this land of such dear souls, this dear, dear land, dear for her reputation through the world, is populated almost exclusively with the covetous, the greedy, the hypocritical and the perverse.

Conduct unbecoming is what the Boultings took as their theme; and if they did deride one occupation more than most then, paradoxically, it was the actors they employed whom they lampooned – for Roy and John, in inheriting Ealing's sterling cast of characters – Cecil Parker, Terry-Thomas, Dennis Price, Raymond Huntley, John Le Mesurier, Irene Handl, Margaret Rutherford, Miles Malleson, Wilfrid Hyde-White, and so on endlessly – created a rep company of snobs and shits, cowards and swindlers, who had never aged. Dame Margaret's Mme Arcati for Noël Coward is identical to the old dowager in *The Countess from Hong Kong* for Charles Chaplin; Raymond Huntley was always an idle and supercilious old shag;* Wilfrid Hyde-White did small variations on his dodgy old

---

* Even, I venture to say, in real life – where he haunted the Garrick Club and whence he wrote to me; as Huntley must have encountered Sellers so frequently I'd asked if he had any memories of my man and his methods: 'I didn't know Peter at all ... Though we were, as you observe, often in the same films, we never really worked together.' I can think of at least the court martial scene in *Waltz of the Toreadors*, or Mai Zetterling's husband in *Only Two Can Play*, but who wants to argue? Huntley died on June 15th 1990, aged 86.

charmer routine; and Terry-Thomas was always the gap-toothed scoundrel. . . . Those who had been gallant and sound under Balcon and his kin were now encouraged to pick apart their impeccable drawing-room manners to show the bounder and blackguard beneath. And to anatomise the avarice and selfishness of the English sensibility, it was almost as if the Boultings played a game with the fact that actors, as part of the job, manufacturing emotions, speaking beautifully and pretending to be other than they really were, were confidence tricksters and counterfeiters by other means – and none more so than Sellers. Having attended to his work on *The Goon Show* and television, and having seen all his films, they knew that behind the veal-faced, tense and reserved chap on the cricket pitch, who had all the appeal of a civil servant shut in an office with sick-building syndrome, there lurked something hostile and ambivalent. He had a free-floating, absurdist capacity, which was exactly what the twins needed to galvanise their ensemble of genteel light comedy performers. By giving his drive and exhibitionism a chance, they made him a star, and in making him a star, they unleashed his meanness and spite.

☆　★　☆

Roy and John Boulting were born in Bray, Bucks, on November 21st 1913, worked in the RAF and Army film units during the war, and claimed (in *Films and Filming*, May 1961) to have begun their careers by sweeping dressing rooms, loading cameras, helping to paint sets, assisting in the cutting rooms and even 'on occasion and demand, though rarely and providentially,' they played in front of the camera as well as behind. 'Those, of course were the underpaid, under-organised, over-worked 'thirties, when conditions were disgraceful, and everyone seemed keen and happy.' The twins approached movie-making in the spirit of plucky amateurs – gentlemen-rankers out on a spree! In fact, they were cautious and prudent businessmen, perfectionists, who controlled all aspects of production, direction, and the writing of scripts. John died some years before I began my search for Sellers; Roy, to whom I wrote c/o Twickenham Studios, replied as follows:

Twickenham Film
Studios,
St. Margarets,
Twickenham,
MIDDLESEX
August 3rd 1989

Dear Roger Lewis,

So sorry. I have been leading a rather peripatetic existence and
your letter of July the 18th has only just come to hand.

Your request, I fear, presents me with something of a dilemma. I
am, myself, writing a book dealing with the B.B's fifty years in
the Film Wonderland. Our association with Peter, inter alia,
naturally provides a chapter and, of course, has a deal to say on
the subject of what you term 'his genius and peculiarities'.

The difficulty is obvious. Whoever comes out first is going to
make the other's observations on Sellers rather old hat. Or do
you see a way round it?

Please believe that I would like to help you if this is at all
feasible.

With kindest regards and every success with the book.

Yours sincerely,
Roy Boulting.

I responded to this by suggesting lunch at the Oxford college to
which I belonged, and we met within the week. If your image of a
film director is of a grizzled urchin in a baseball cap and sneakers,
or perhaps of a former Austro-Hungarian general wielding a riding
crop and a megaphone, then the man I met in the Lodge, sporting
neither a fizzing can of Cola nor Heidelberg duelling scars, didn't fit
the bill in the slightest. Puffing on gold-tipped cigarettes kept in a
small wooden box, Roy Boulting was more donnish than many of
the dons. My colleagues must have assumed I was entertaining or
auditioning a Rawlinson & Bosworth Professor of Anglo-Saxon, or

similar. Roy's erect and tweedy bearing, and his public school tone of voice, signified the old values – an Oxford of straw boaters and oars, bottles of sherry and port, leather-bound first editions, engraved invitations to commem. balls and beagling trips, Balkan sobranies, girls in Zuleika Dobson hats, the works. Perhaps it is because Roy himself was educated in Canada, at McGill University, Toronto, that he can hit off the English officer-and-gentleman comportment with such ease and confidence? Real academics, on the whole, are an unwashed, envious lot, over-weight from college puddings and bursting with smugness, or else they are scuttling, insect-like, along the shelves and walls of the Bodleián – totally unprepossessing. Dons, on the cinema screen, are always played by Sir Dirk Bogarde or Sir John Gielgud; they are given a quiet unmerited glamour and poise (Denholm Elliot at his most sodden and furrowed would be nearer the mark); but Sellers, no less, at least got the counter-tenor staccato voice right on his LP, *Sellers' Market*. His phonetics expert and folklorist, Don Schulman, travels to Oxford to record the natives, and after listening to a don's nervy squeaking, observes: 'His vocabulary stunned me . . . I was amazed he found it possible to form a sentence.'

Surrounded, therefore, by a fog of cuckoos and cadavers in drip-dry mauve shirts, Roy, in his regimentals, and the present author (wearing what? a negligee?), ranged over a dead man's life and times, as we drank whisky and wine.

'You had a crucial association with Sellers over many years?'

'Sellers made seven* films with us – which set him up for his career in Hollywood. He *started* with us. When faced with an extinction of his career, at the end of the Sixties, it was back to us that he came. We helped him to restore his name, with *There's a Girl in My Soup*. He was box office. And back to Hollywood he went

---

* *Carlton Browne of the F.O.* (March 1959); *I'm All Right, Jack* (August 1959); *Heavens Above* (1963); *There's a Girl in My Soup* (1971); *Soft Beds, Hard Battles* (1974). The Boultings, through Bryanston and British Lion, also helped to produce, i.e. had money invested in, *Battle of the Sexes* (1960) and *Only Two Can Play* (1962).

again . . . he was a vital part of our lives as film-makers; and it is fair to say that we played a very important part in the development of his career. . . .'

'Was he your Alec Guinness – assuming that you took over Ealing's market?'

'The first script we wrote for him, after *Carlton Browne of the F.O.*, he didn't want to do – *I'm All Right, Jack*. He didn't want to do the film – he couldn't find the jokes. We had to convince him that he was a fine actor. That he didn't need jokes and belly-laughs. For, at this time, he was heavily involved with *The Goon Show*, a different sort of thing altogether.'

'Wasn't it the streak of Goonishness, though, which made him unique – you could get him to jazz up your Raymond Huntleys, Irene Handls, and all that crowd?'

'Yes, but that side had to be implied, not set free any old how – which is what went wrong with his films later, when directors let him do as he pleased. We wanted a disciplined character actor. So for Fred Kite – and we laid seige to him to get him to be Kite – he obtained a shapeless double-breasted suit from Berman and Nathans. He saw newsreels of trades union delegates. He experimented with the voice on a tape recorder. He had his hair scalped and put on that Hitler moustache – an amazing transformation. When he looked in the dressing room mirror, it was no longer Sellers who gazed back. Even *he* couldn't recognise himself. . . .'

'What was he like, when Sellers was being Sellers?'

'He was really a Fat Boy. Big bloated face. He went through agony to get and stay slim. But for the films he originally made for us, he was fat. He was the archetypal spoiled, only Jewish child – stuffed with food and sweets by his adoring mother. . . .'

'Stuffed with ambition, too.'

'He was always citing Peg. Peg, this; Peg, that. He tried to convince himself she was marvellous – the ideal woman. But he was shrewd enough to have seen through her – to know that, underneath, she was rather pathetic and vulgar. But how can a son, any son, actually admit that to himself? She was always trying to push him on. . . .'

'She used to go with him to his earliest auditions – and his first steps were taken within his own family, they got him music hall spots.'

'When Sellers was a star, in every sense, she was *still* hustling on his behalf. She did it automatically, like he was some item of sale. Hustling, hustling. Everybody had to know how marvellous she knew he was. Peter would be *squirming*.'

'What about Bill?'

'I think what Peg wanted above all else was for Peter not to be another Bill – another music hall has-been. She'd get Bill to play these watery, sentimental songs at the piano. She said he'd composed them – sub-Ivor Novello tunes. Again, Peter would be embarrassed out of his skin.'

'It all rubbed off on him, didn't it? He'd have killed not to be another Bill. As he said once, "Talent will always find its own level". But by what means? At what cost?'

'He was methodically destructive of anything and everything that would stop him looking pre-eminent. When he lost weight, at the time of *The Millionairess*, and fell for Sophia Loren, Anne had to put up with him through all that. He was a monster to her; he neglected his children. He didn't give others a thought. . .'

'It would look good for the public image, squiring Loren.'

'Yes. He'd even wreck his own films, to be the centre of attention. Sellers could be very cruel. He'd destroy people with his impulsive acts and decisions. First day of shooting of *There's a Girl in My Soup*, he took a dislike to the continuity girl. He said she'd given him a look. "She's evil – she's directing evil thoughts at me. I want her replaced." – "Really, Peter? Is that so?" I took it calmly – wondering where *this* little bout of bad behaviour had sprung from. Next day he said, "*She's still here!*" I said, improvising my way through, "Peter, far from having evil thoughts about you, she's had several job offers lately, and she chose this film to work with you, because she admires you so much." So then they were friends. . .'

'You wouldn't tolerate his nonsense – but many did.'

'Hollywood allowed him to indulge himself with tantrums. He quickly saw that you could get away with murder if your films were successful; gradually, Sellers' weren't. I think he had five flops[*] in a row.'

'Which is when you made *There's a Girl in My Soup.*'

'Yes. It made money – so the nonsense started up again. People in Hollywood thought he'd be the next Danny Kaye; the next Chaplin! But film after film had failed. His agent started to get future films signed up, so that when one inevitably failed, Sellers would be on to the next and never be unemployed. Then he ruined himself in those incessant *Pink Panthers*. He was self-destructive – in his professional life, and in his private life. He could have achieved so much more, if he hadn't been so temperamental.'

'Can you give me some examples of his frantic impatience?'

'Well, one of the worst things he did, when he got going, was to surround himself with a coterie – little actors whom he had known since the war or who he'd worked with on radio. He tried to pull Kenneth Griffith into this group. He had another actor fired so that Kenneth Griffith could take his part in *The Bobo* – but Kenneth kept his distance and was circumspect.[†] Sellers liked people

---

[*] They comprise *Casino Royale* (April 1967); *The Bobo* (August 1967); *The Magic Christian* (February 1970); *Hoffman* (July 1970); *A Day at the Beach* (unreleased). I have excluded from this list *Woman Times Seven* (June 1967), because Sellers only took a cameo role; *The Party* (April 1968), because it continues to have a commercial and critical following; and *I Love You, Alice B. Toklas* (October 1968) because Sellers' performance, as a highly-strung Los Angeles lawyer, is wry and just about immaculate: he conveys exactly how Harold Fine feels, as he learns to relax. All this said, and though it is a fact that (a) few of Sellers' films in this period were rising out of the red ink; and (b) his own fee fell from the million quid mark (*Casino Royale*) to just £10,000 (*The Blockhouse* – unreleased), I personally always find Sellers watchable – even in trash, he reveals something about himself.

[†] He refused to sign a petition got up by Sellers to remove Robert Parrish as the director. Sellers, as a consequence, would not speak to Griffith for over a year. One thinks of *Richard III* and people with any independence of mind being gone whilst their fearful heads be on.

who'd laugh at the right moment; who'd tell him how brilliant he was. And this didn't do him any good – it spoilt his judgement. I don't think he was any judge of when he was doing good work; nor do I think he was any judge of material. But there are always flatterers, those who enjoy the company of the illustrious, who'll egg them on no matter what – as Sellers very well knew. His reputation for being a great giggler – it was not really high spirits, you know. It was insecurity. If he forgot his lines, or slipped up in any way, he'd fix the other actor with his eyes, to throw them – and *they'd* have to laugh first.'

'And yet if anybody tried to put him off, or to try out something . . .'

'Oh yes – he wouldn't have that. Totally egocentric – egomaniacal. He nearly bankrupted Columbia with *Casino Royale*. He chose Joe McGrath as director. Then, one Friday night, he walked out of the film and wouldn't come back – saying that the director was terrible; the director was ruining his performance and his career. Now Peter had chosen and insisted on the director, pushed for him over others with more established reputations . . . So then they had a great succession of directors, starting with John Huston. . . .'

'Who agreed to participate if Charlie Feldman paid his gambling debts. Huston was also given an Etruscan vase – which turned out to be a fake.'

'Well, I mention all this because we were meant to be shooting a film ourselves at Shepperton; but every single sound stage was filled with an expensive set for *Casino Royale* – though there wasn't even a finished script. We watched this with awe, total and complete awe. They had sets, but no script. Baronial halls, science-fiction laboratories, futuristic space stations. Another world. So these sets were torn down and burned unused. Such a waste – chaos – all caused by Sellers. Then, when somebody actually wrote a few scenes, all these sets had to be re-built – they had to be duplicated over at Pinewood.'

'Was Sellers mad, do you think?'

'In this period, the mid-Sixties, if it was madness, there was method in it. He loved the princely implementation of power and will that being a star entailed. He relished everyone being beholden to him. And, yes, towards the end there were times when he was out of his mind; and I'll also say this: not once were his crazy decisions artistically motivated. They were power games.'

'Didn't he mess you about, too, with *Soft Beds, Hard Battles*?'

'The whole film was a disaster from the moment of its inception. I couldn't shoot once Liza Minnelli arrived in his life. It was the unhappiest experience in my whole career as a film maker, and that's saying something. Sellers had said he'd be in it – playing six rôles: the clients of a Parisian brothel during the war – and we began the pre-production work. Casting; designing and building the sets. I was signing cheques by the dozen. Then Sellers announced he *didn't* want to be in it ... Well, we got him to sign a contract eventually. Fortunately, he had a new manager, Denis O'Brien, who suddenly got him to honour his pledges; but you could tell Sellers didn't feel he was obliged to be committed to the project. It's the only film I've made of which I'm ashamed. Sellers almost decided to be infatuated by Liza Minnelli on purpose.* He actually left the film, walked away – and he was in nearly every scene – to go and photograph her concerts. His absences were so bad and recurrent, I had to go to John, who was producing, and get him and the production manager to re-devise the entire shooting schedule. I said, "Give them time to go and screw one another to death, or whatever they are doing, and *then* we can continue our work." This was eventually done. Sellers cost us approximately £100,000 of our own money. It was that, or close the entire film down – and write-off more than a million.

---

* 'They were to be married within three days,' Anne Levy told me, 'so he brought her to meet me. I said, "I hope you'll be happy"; and he said, "I did so love her mother's films." It was as if he was marrying Judy Garland and wriggling his way into *The Wizard of Oz*.'

   In which a woman – Margaret Hamilton: not unlike Peg – turns into a witch. Or, of course, there was his fondness for *A Star is Born*. It was (jokingly) rumoured that Liza courted Sellers because he claimed to possess a sixteen mm. print of Cukor's original uncut version.

'I like to get to a set first, before any of the technicians. Seven a.m. at the latest. Sellers was called at six-thirty because he had elaborate make-up changes. One morning, he said: "Roy boy, you've got to meet her." I said, "Who?" He said, "Liza." I said, "I'd love to." He said "*Now*." She was in the dressing room with him. She said to me, "He's working such long hours. I want him to let me cook for him, let him relax. But no. He *insists* on going to night clubs, where the paparazzi will see him. He loves all that publicity. He said to me, 'I can't resist going out and being recognised.'"'

'What he enjoyed, I'm sure, was being seen to be courting Liza Minnelli – he was showing her off as his property.'

'There was a good deal of braggadocio about his relationships with women. I've known all his wives. Anne, lovely Anne, to whom he behaved apallingly. People who loved him, he deserted them. It was despicable what he did to his children – he was, as John and I once said in a newspaper article,* a man utterly unpredictable in

---

* John and Roy Boulting went into print about Sellers on two occasions: an 'Appreciation' (or signed obituary) in the *Guardian* on July 25th 1980; and an article called 'Catering for the new Sellers market,' in the *New Standard* (London) on September 29th 1981. The former piece elicited this public correspondence:

Sir, – The self-serving and grudge-laden tone of the Boulting brothers' 'Appreciation' of Peter Sellers is reminiscent of an aggrieved ex-wife still moaning 20 years after the divorce that it was she who 'made' her husband.

They pay themselves a generous tribute for persuading Sellers to play the rôle of Fred Kite, which they had 'created specifically to make manifest his talent ... as a character actor of unique quality.' They go on to say that his subsequent career as an international star 'did little to develop or extend his genius'.

Lolita, Doctor Strangelove, The Pink Panther series, *The Party* and many other films show Sellers' instincts to be far sounder than those of the talented twins. Certainly the Boultings' *Soft Beds, Hard Battles* did little to enhance Sellers' reputation in 1974.

'It is ironic', they add, 'that, at the very end, he should return to a simple character study of a genuine innocent in Hal Ashby's *Being There.*' Also ironic is the fact that it took eight years of persistence on Sellers' part to get this film made. John and Roy throw in their own idiotic theories about Sellers' relationship with women, but psychological insight is not their forte, as they his moods, physically violent when opposed, cruelly calculating in his deceptions and ruthless in his many betrayals and abandonments of so many who, over the years, served him with a loyalty and conscientiousness he rarely earned. I felt outright anger at, for example, his dismissal, after fourteen years devoted service, of Bert Mortimer. Bert waited hour after hour for Peter outside some night-club, where he'd be pulling some bird. One of the few people to stand up to him, in fact, was Miranda Quarry, his third wife. She was intelligent and wouldn't bend to his whims. Sellers had in-

---

demonstrated so hilariously in *Twisted Nerve*.

The twins accuse Peter Sellers of being 'mean and unworthy in spirit'. It is an apt description of their 'Appreciation'.
Peter Cook.
London W. [July 30th 1980]

Sir, – We read Peter Cook's reproachful letter with amusement as well as interest. Having known and worked with Peter Sellers over many years, our article sought to assist not only the artist, but the man. It seems that the other Peter would have had us, so to speak, 'cook' the books.

With a certain, sly skill – and by quoting us out of context – he attributes to us judgements we never made. What we *did* say quite specifically, was that, in our opinion, Sellers' work in Hollywood (Inspector Clouseau apart, to which we paid due tribute) did little to enhance his career or to extend his talents.

For Peter Cook's information both *Lolita* and *Doctor Strangelove* were made in this country by Stanley Kubrick.

In recounting how Peter Sellers arrived at the character of dim-witted shop stweard, Fred Kite, in *I'm All Right, Jack*, we were not seeking to serve ourselves (as Peter Cook chooses to believe) but to shed some light on the manner in which the artist achieved his goal.

As to Peter Cook's allusions to our own work, he need have no fear: we are quite as conscious of our own failures, as he very properly directs us. Perhaps, even more so. And we have no doubt that he, too, occasionally recalls [that] his own forays into [the] film world [. . .] have not always engendered universal enthusiasm.

Reverting to Peter Sellers: we *knew* him – did Peter Cook? –
Yours *John and Roy Boulting,*
London SW3. [August 5th 1980]

troduced her to me so proudly: "She was the publicity girl on such- and-such a film." – "Really!" I said, "I didn't think Miranda ever *worked!*" Her father was a Lord.'

'What about any other wives?'

'There was Britt; there was Lynne. Lynne Frederick was pertin- acious, ambitious. That marriage wouldn't have lasted. He left her in California; she followed after a month. Then she was back in Los Angeles and he was in Switzerland; and then he was dead. She once rushed up to me at the Dome Restaurant in Hollywood and greeted me as an old friend. I'd only ever met her briefly, at the party for Alex Walker's book.'

'She's very proud of having been Mrs Peter Sellers.'

'She survived him, in every sense. That is an achievement.'

'Sellers is quite the womaniser in *There's a Girl in My Soup.*'

'As much as we admired his talent, we had rather more than mixed feelings about the man. In fact, the talent apart, as a human being he was a disaster. Which made him ideal for Robert Danvers. The hero in *There's a Girl in My Soup* is a phoney; he's flash and false. There's a great deal of the *real* Sellers in Danvers. He was per- fect for the part – we didn't want any other actor (and we owned the screen rights). The film was co-produced by Columbia, who hadn't forgotten or forgiven him for *Casino Royale.* Mike Frankovitch, the producer, was aghast, cursing and swearing – but we held out for Sellers, and he was wonderful.'

'A paradox, that he was so wonderfully convincing – as a suave shit; as not quite a gentleman. You must have felt, with Sellers, that it was *Brighton Rock* all over again. Like Pinky, he saw a virtue in in- flicting pain, if a good film or rôle, or momentary pleasure, could come out of it. He was hellish, and one of the damned, and out of this came his art and transmutations.'

'He wasn't cricket, no.'

☆ ★ ☆

Being generous, I suppose you could say that there was nothing wrong with Sellers that divine intervention couldn't fix.[*] I mentioned as much in one of my subsequent letters to Roy Boulting; and I also said something about Sellers and the price he had to pay for being a creative genius, and 'When I think of Sellers, I keep wondering, was he Doctor Faustus?'[†] I was immediately upbraided, and rightly. I received a postcard depicting a detail from the illuminated manuscript of *Piers Plowman* (C-text, Passus VIII, lines 253–64; MSS Douce 104, fol. 39r): a peasant, dressed in a blue smock and a red cap, with an alarmed look on his face, digging in some shifting sands:

[August 29th 1989]

Dear Roger,

The card chosen as especially applicable to you; a writer dabbling in a Sellers Market. (The moral: only hard work can keep hunger away.)

Now a Boulting impertinence. Stop wondering about Sellers and 'is he Faustian?' When your research is done, you will probably know. Develop a theory now . . . and you are likely to find yourself trying to fit Sellers-the-man to that theory. And both 'artist' and 'man', by the way, constitute highly complex indivisibles.

Forgive me!

> With every good wish,
> Yours sincerely
> *Roy*

The interfusion, of on-and-off screen performances, is clearly manifest in *There's a Girl in My Soup* – as Sarah Sellers had immediately observed. When I asked her how does she think of her father now, a dozen years since his death, she said: 'I don't often sit down and watch his films, but I do collect all the videos. I like to have them. I like the older films – bits in all of them are hilarious,

---

[*] Alexander Woollcott on Oscar Levant, the original of Henry Orient.
[†] Thomas Mann's.

but other bits are flat, aren't they? I don't tend to watch the films as films – I watch *him*. The bits I notice – his temperament coming through. *There's a Girl in My Soup* – I can see a lot of him there. Expressions, gestures, mannerisms. Definitely.'

If Roy Boulting is correct, Robert Danvers was not a part requiring much out of the way research – and Sellers did aspire to being debonair. When he started to lose weight and traipse around night-clubs with dolly-birds, being debonair was an all-consuming performance. How did he prepare for such a rôle? No doubt the same way as ever: 'I start with the voice. I find out how the character *sounds*. It's through the way he speaks that I find out the rest about him. I suppose the approach comes from having worked in radio for so long. After the voice comes the look of the man. I do a lot of drawings of the character I play. Then I get together with the make-up man and we sort of transfer my drawings on to my face. An involved process. After that I establish how the character walks. Very important, the walk. And then suddenly something strange happens. *The person takes over*. The man you play begins to exist. I sink myself completely into every character I play, because he has begun to live in me. I suddenly seem to know what sort of life that man has had and how he would react to a given situation. . . .'

In knowing his characters inside out; in his being aware of what his characters were like and how they felt above, beyond and behind the lines of dialogue with which they were provided, Sellers, at his best, was thorough and scrupulous. So why do I find that little discussion of his methods bleak and shadowy? By bravely entering a new element, and transmogrifying, it is as if dark waves and blind surges have closed over his head, and have devoured him. Sellers has described his own annihilation. He speaks like somebody who is already dead.

☆ ☆ ☆

'As John Boulting always says, "Let's get down to the serious business of making a comedy." And he's absolutely right,' said Sellers. 'I've a great respect for the Boulting Brothers, and what they try to do; indeed, what they *do* do. I don't agree entirely with everything they do; I don't think that any one person who is interested in films can entirely agree with everything anybody else does. . . .' From Sellers, high praise – though hedged about with plenty of double negatives and abatements. The first cab of his off the Boulting rank was, as Roy mentioned, *Carlton Browne of the F.O.*: 'I had a great time . . . I play a Prime Minister of an ex-British colony, a bit of a rogue,' Sellers chuckled in the month of the film's release (March 1959). Later he was more dismissive, telling Terry-Thomas that he hated it.

The actor who might more justly have claimed to despair of it was Thomas himself. On the first day of shooting, at Shepperton Studios in September 1958, the shag who worked the barrier at the gate said to him: 'This will be easy for you, sir. A holiday. All you'll have to do is play yourself.' – 'Really old boy,' murmured Thomas, 'Play myself? I ask you!' Already Thomas was a prisoner of his own image. The rôle of upperclass nincompoop, this time called Cadogan de Vere Carlton Browne, is the one he'll reproduce time and again. The Foreign Office functionary, essentially idle, able to fake eagerness, and be consistently sly, allowed him to combine the scheming robber from *Tom Thumb* with the disdainfulness of Lord Mayley from *The Naked Truth*. His career, like a jelly plopped out from a copper mould, was now set. Sellers, by contrast, had liquefied and re-made himself. Gone was the pantomime of George Pal's puppetoons or the nail-bitten unattractiveness of Wee Sonny. As Senãr Amphibulous, top banana on the atoll of Gaillardia, a marmalade dependency which Britain has forgotten is part of its Empire, he is all three Marx Brothers at once. Sellers has Groucho's moustache and eyebrows, Chico's rococo Italianate accent, and Harpo's grin and swiftness. He dresses in the famous frock coat, bashed stove-pipe hat and baggy cummerbund; on less formal occasions he wears a crumpled white linen suit – Groucho's costume from *A Night in Casablanca*.

If only the film had much more of the Marxist medley. The idea of a tiny British colony lost in the fold of a map, still existing in some distant ocean with its Victorian rituals intact – the daily raising and lowering of the Union Jack at Government House; the Ambassador attired like a D'Oyly Carte baritone; Miles Malleson, as the viceroy, writing despatches with a quill and addressing them to Lord Palmerston or Mr Gladstone – has mouthwatering comic possibilities. *Carlton Browne of the F.O.* almost predicts the Falklands War: insignificant and distant outpost, a windswept sheep farm, which only comes into prominence when invaded. What is it that the Argentines knew that the British didn't? 'If there's anything there worth having,' says Raymond Huntley, the Foreign Secretary, referring to Gaillardia, *we're* having it.'

The Boultings' film certainly lies behind the superior television drama made about the first few hours of that real and weird conflict, *An Ungentlemanly Act.* Ian Richardson, in ostrich plumes, a brocaded frock coat and carrying a ceremonial sword, was Sir Rex Hunt – ostensibly the Governor General, but actually the very model of a modern Major General, from *Iolanthe.* The non-gentlemen were of course the Argentines, whose forced entry into Port Stanley displayed a distinct lack of manners. ('You came,' says Sir Rex, almost beside himself, to the dago Admiral, 'without an invitation!') Richardson and Bob Peck*, as the soldier in charge of the handful of British garrison troops, managed to convey not only English courtesy and English resolve – they also gave their performances an undernote of disbelief. They know they have been consigned to the ends of the earth, to a speck in the South Atlantic which has slipped everybody's mind – until. . . .

Without sending the material up for one moment, in fact by playing it so straight, all involved with *An Ungentlemanly Act* transported us back to an era of Ealing whimsicality. The sheep grazing on the lawn during a wreath-laying parade; the ambassadorial car being a maroon London taxi; the village pub serving an impressive array of Scotch, like the bar in *Local Hero* etc. Peck and Richardson were restrained, patriotic, sticklers for protocol; it wasn't the Falklands as topographical islands, the population, or the sheep and the

---

* Who tells me that all his life people have been saying, 'You know who you look like? Peter Sellers.'

penguins they were prepared to go to war for – it was Englishness itself. And as the young soldiers began to get killed, the concept started to look less quaint and anachronistic, and more and more mad. Principles are terrible things.

The theme of *Carlton Browne of the F.O.*, like the Falklands War, is exploitation and possession. The Russians and the Americans both have spies on the island and intend to get what they can out of the ignorant natives. The British, meantime, putting on a show of goodwill and munificence, demonstrate the biggest imperialistic joke of all: that when the Union Jack flew over a distant country, and it was added to the long list of British territories, and its wealth was plundered and its laws and customs were replaced by edicts from Westminster, the remote populations were the ones who became the foreigners – peoples to be looked down on as outsiders within their own boundaries. In the Boulting film, Ian Bannen's young King of Gaillardia is tolerated, earns respect and keeps his cool because he was educated at Oxford – he is virtually a gentleman. The unreconstructed exotic alien, the wog, is Sellers' rôle. With heavy lidded eyes and black oily hair, he has thick Latin blood pumping through his anatomy. Alone amongst the cast, Sellers is sultry – if he lopes, like Groucho, it is because he is bent nearly double from the heat. Sellers acts as if there's an equitorial sun in his sky, and it has made him dishevelled. Amphibulous is the only character who seems to be aware that Gaillardia is in the tropics, or anyway abroad. The rest of the rep. company (Kenneth Griffith as a geologist disguised as a British Council Morris dancer and John Le Mesurier in a bomber jacket as an Archduke, and so on and on) remain in Shepperton's damp and mildish Hertfordshire climate, unfooled by the odd cardboard palm tree stuck amidst the beeches and elms on the backlot.

Sellers, therefore, gnawing his cigars, dreaming up ways to make money for himself and his nation's exchequer, moving his shoulders and fingers in ways that are *foreign*, is out-of-key. He is a maverick – and there is thus an understanding between himself and Bannen as actors. Their few scenes together – a new, green king and an experienced politician – are the film's high spots. (Why not accept a few bribes, Amphibulous counsels, 'You get the Rolls, I get the Cadillac, and the people – they get the lavatories.')

In other hands, Bannen's role could be rather thankless. Ruritanian monarchs and student princes normally belong in operettas and are played stiltedly by crummy tenors (it's Gilbert & Sullivan again). Bannen, whom Roy Boulting worried was 'not good-looking in the generally accepted sense', is in fact a witty and virile artist, and he is convincingly royal. Perhaps because he was trained in Shakespeare, and was a protegé of Anthony Quayle at the Memorial Theatre, Stratford-on-Avon, he instinctively refused to stroll through his material – the king in *Carlton Browne of the F.O.* isn't fake; he has anxieties. He wants to behave correctly, and he comes across as rather chilly and authoritarian – he knows he has to be stern if he is to see off both the archduke, who wants him to abdicate and go and live in a hotel in Portugal, and the blandishments of the British, who want Gaillardia's deposits of cobalt for nuclear bombs. (There's enough 'to blow up the entire universe anytime we wish', says Raymond Huntley, as gleeful as I've ever seen him.) But this sovereign isn't a boring reformed playboy – which is how the part is basically written. Bannen, classically scrupulous, gives us instead a variation of Orlando, the spurned and spirited underdog hero in *As You Like It*, 'all gentlemanlike qualities' and gallantry who, as it were, comes of age in the Forest of Arden. It was the rôle he'd recently played at Stratford, opposite Vanessa Redgrave's Rosalind. In the film, it is Sellers who educates him and shows him how to relax – not overtly, but by example. Again, there is no dialogue for this – it is just that when the king sees his prime minister lounging on the beach having suntan creams massaged into his back by a sweet patootie, or when Amphibulous lolls on a big quilted bed chewing grapes and whispering down a white telephone, his expression isn't reproachful. He wants some of that frivolity.

Unfortunately, the film doesn't allow for these two actors to go very far with their bits of business or rapport (Sellers, as later with

James Mason, is brought out in new ways when teamed opposite an actor from a different, straighter tradition); we have to swerve off to slapstick military manoeuvres in the jungle with Thorley Walters, who is called something like Tiger, Buster, Thruster, or Slasher, and to the long sequence of the marchpast, when Terry-Thomas takes the salute: the Gaillardian Armed Forces comprise a biplane pulled by a donkey, a gun carriage pulled by mules, and fat smiling girls on bicycles. At the climax of the scene, the VIP dais collapses, resulting in a tangle of arms, legs, and medals. 'My brother-in-law promised the rotten wood would only be used for the public,' apologises you-know-who.

☆ ★ ☆

Carlton Browne of the F.O. is disappointing because it augurs so well. The nineteenth-century atmosphere of palaces and embassies; Miles Malleson, gout-ridden and in a bathchair, dreaming of St Petersburg; the corruption of the locals and the larger deceptions and casual cruelties of the imperialists; and Sellers, with extra hair sprouting from his nostrils, ready to invigorate the film with a music hall skittishness and gabbiness: it goes to waste and degenerates into a Superpowers *vs.* Underdogs plot, and I can't for the life of me remember how it is all sorted out. For some reason, however, Sellers chose to re-make the story time and again. In the course of the shooting of *Carlton Browne of the F.O.*, he was appearing at the Aldwych, soon to be the London headquarters of the Royal Shakespeare Company, in a play called *Brouhaha*, directed by Peter Hall, and which had opened on Wednesday, August 27th 1958. During the run of the play he also made *The Mouse that Roared*, which was released on July 17th 1959. All three dramas had to do with quaint wee lands of far beyond; their common theme was, if you like, the spirit of independence – or, as expressed by Sellers, with his overtones of shamelessness, the spirit of anarchy.

His weekly schedule was hard-fought. He set out for the studio at six thirty in the morning and arrived back at the theatre for curtain up at seven each evening. If he was shooting on location, he'd be driven off in his Rolls after the performance and he'd bed down for the night in his car. (The Duchy of Grand Fenwick was some woodland near Southampton.) On Sundays ('I used to live for Sundays, you see. Those Sundays, after a week of misery like that . . .') he'd rehearse and record *The Goon Show* or work on his songs and monologues for gramophone companies. His dressing rooms were thronged with hangers-on, discarded costumes and wigs, and there were always telephones ringing. When he spoke, Sellers assumed the voice and unruffled charm of Grytpype Thynne. He seemed to enjoy the turmoil – it meant he had no time to think.

If, during daylight, the Boultings were restricting or editing down his hyperactive talent, at night his gallivanting and his looseness went unchecked. That was the joy of live theatre. There was nobody to yell 'Cut!'; nobody to trim his performance afterwards with a pair of scissors; nobody to restrict him. Short of ordering the fire screen down or implanting him with a knock-out dart aimed from the rear of the stalls, his jazziness and impudence had an ideal showcase. 'Peter was outrageous,' says Anne. 'He took his camera on stage with him and snapped away at the other actors. He pretended to bang his head on the "fourth wall". He made up half of the script as he went along. He grabbed Leo McKern and started dancing with him – Peter just danced away from the play. Lionel Jeffries didn't like it at all. He must have thought Peter was bonkers.'

He'd have been in the right of it there. *Brouhaha*, by George Tabori, was about a sultan who, with the object of attracting superpower intervention and capital, goes about secretly creating disturbances, making trouble, and instigating rebellions in his very own country. He thinks that if he fakes a revolution, his kingdom will be put on the map. Sellers, as the potentate, had the Ian Bannen role; but, instead of being regal and commanding respect, he made his ruler into a man who was startling and reckless. The sultan was capable of anything and everything – and what the character did to his country, Sellers did to the play.

'All kinds of things used to happen,' he confessed, 'and in those days it was taboo to do any improvisation. But the middle act didn't work very well. The first act was very good, the last act wasn't too bad, but it really took a dive in the middle – and I was determined to try and beat this. And we'd worked out all kinds of things to do. Or at least I had with some of the actors who I knew I could sling lines at and who wouldn't suddenly freeze in the corner, like West End actors are often apt to do, if you make a move that isn't already pre-set.* So we had Lionel. You could do anything with Lionel Jeffries. You could do anything with Leo McKern. One day we were on and I said to Leo McKern "Why don't we do a balancing act in the middle of this scene, like they do in variety?" He said, "What a good idea," and I said, "Because I've just come off stage and it's like playing to *Hell* out there, you know. Teacups rattling, old people dying, you know." So I was given the sack I don't know how many times. I was bawled out I don't know how many times – and in fact I was told it was *not done* in the West End to do the sort of thing I was doing. But, this night I was talking about, I managed to get through it, until we came to the scene where I was dancing with Hermione Harvey. I took two or three steps too many towards the footlights – and I just went straight over, with her as well, and how we managed to miss a pile of old iron down there . . . We dropped literally eight feet from a standing position into the pit, with her on top of me. *Wham*! It was an enormous laugh. They must've thought there were mattresses down there and we did this every night. I don't know what they thought.'

☆　☆　☆

Sellers's retrospective version of events, in which he reckons he was heroically giving everybody a good time, differs markedly from the recollection of his co-star. I met Hermione Harvey, who now lives in Menorca, for toasted scones and almond tarts at Brown's Hotel, Dover Street, on one of her rare visits to London:

'I played Mrs Alma Exegis Diddle, the American ambassadress, who visited the sultan and his island. I had had one week to learn the part and I wasn't sure I could do it – it was all words, words,

---

* cf Richard Hearne and *Mother Goose*, in Chapter Five.

words, whilst Sellers, wearing his turban and hunting gear – jodhpurs and flicking a riding crop – was trying to seduce me. A few weeks into the run, he got so fed up with his costumes, he just didn't wear them. He came on stage in anything he felt like; he wore his own clothes. Or once he wore shorts, a snorkel, and a Dracula cloak. Which was not kind to the audience, because they didn't know *what* was going on. . . .'

'So he sabotaged the play?'

'He didn't appear at rehearsals until the last day. The director said, "He will try and distract you and make you laugh. You've got to know your words absolutely, so you won't be thrown." They tested my concentration with lots of surprise noises-off. Lions roaring. Trains going by. To put me off. I was very nervous about meeting Sellers, with this build up; but anyway, in I went. He was kind to me for about a week. He kept to the script and he didn't upset me. This scene of mine was in Act III and it lasted a quarter of an hour. It was a good part – but right at the end. It became nerve-racking, because you didn't know what he was going to do. It became his game, to make me corpse. Suddenly, one night, he started to recite the "Balham – Gateway to the South" sketch from *Songs for Swinging Sellers*. "Honey's off, dear," he kept squawking, meaninglessly. *What is this*? I thought – because the record hadn't been released. The audience was bewildered – nobody knew about this honey. The next night he came on pulling a dustbin and went and sat in it – which had nothing to do with the scene. Or he'd go on and invade other people's scenes and he'd start filming them with his cine camera. The other actors, Leo McKern and so on, didn't know *what* to do – except to realise that if Sellers wasn't on form, the play was dead.'

'If he was on form, then it came to life?'

'Whatever he fancied doing, he'd do. He once took my fingers, kissed them, and said, "You've got a moustache on your hand" – which sent me off into terrible giggles. This ordeal-by-corpsing went on for a little while, but then he got bored. He got bored with the matinées very quickly, so he rushed through them and then gave them to his understudy, Colin Ellis – which was hopeless, because everybody came to see Sellers.'

'To see him misbehave?'

'Sellers grew bored. He stopped caring. Came the famous night of the orchestra pit . . . Richard Waring, my husband, was in the Strand Theatre, just down the road from us, in a revue, and he'd heard word that "Peter was pissed." Sellers had been to Alec Guinness' knighthood party before the play, along with Anne Leon, who was in *Brouhaha* as the British resident's wife. She said, "Watch it tonight, Hermione. He's had too many. . ."

'Before the off, Sellers staggered on to the stage, in front of the tabs, and announced, "Ladies and Gentlemen, I am pissed. I have an understudy who is poised ready to take my place. But those of you who would prefer me to soldier on – say AYE!" There was, of course, a roar of AYE!

'Well, by Act III it was obvious that he was more peculiar than he was normally. In this scene we had to dance to a horn gramophone: "Shall we dance, Alma?" This time we danced the wrong way round – he reversed, tripped, and fell over the edge into the pit, dragging me on top of him. He was a heavy man in those days. The audience laughed, thinking it was meant to happen. There was no actual orchestra there, just a lot of ladders and equipment from the Old Vic Company, which used to rehearse at the Aldwych. And then he said in a very loud voice, "Where the fucking hell are we now?" – "We are in the pit," I said. He decided he'd hurt himself. I felt that the show must go on. He, however, had had enough. He climbed back on the stage and started to stumble off into the wings – ever the gallant, he'd forgotten about me and had left me down in the darkness. I called him back – and he did come and pull me out; and he momentarily returned to the play. The next line was "Let's throw caution to the winds, Alma!" which got a big laugh. We finished the scene and he went off to his dressing room, locked the door, wouldn't answer it to anybody, and wouldn't appear in the rest of the play. Poor Colin Ellis had to go on and finish for him.

The press were there immediately. I wasn't allowed to say Sellers was drunk. I had to say it was an accident.'*

'He was progressively irrational?'

'On the last night, Noël Coward, Milligan, Secombe, everybody was there; and Sellers insisted I had a moustache. "You must have a moustache. It's very funny." He painted this on my face himself. "Oh, Peter, please no" – I wanted to do my best in front of all these distinguished theatre people in the audience. He didn't ever think that he might have been spoiling somebody else's chances. To him, making me look a fool was just another laugh. Richard Waring was furious, "How dare you come on looking like that!" – "I couldn't do anything, *he* insisted." Sellers would override you. That night he came down from the flies on a rope. I just gave up. Afterwards, Graham Payne and Noël Coward held a party at Cheyne Walk. Sellers, the guest of honour, sat in a corner and sulked. He pretended to read a book – until somebody gave him orange juice mixed with champagne, when he perked up, jumped into his Goon characters, and was happy.'

'How would you sum up the *Brouhaha* experience?'

'Sellers was unbelievably unprofessional. He'd cut half the dialogue so he could jump to the end of a scene and go home. He didn't care about the other actors; he didn't care about the audience. He was more than eccentric. The way he went on, it was as if he was virtually insane. The whole cast would stand in the wings to see what he would do next.

'Which might only have encouraged him in his excesses, of course. . .'

☆　★　☆

Brouhaha was Sellers' playpen. Those who turned up to applaud his

---

* 'Goon's Tango Ends Up in the Pit,' said the *Daily Express*: 'Sellers had his left leg bandaged. An ambulance was called but he refused to go to hospital. His wife drove him home to Finchley. . . . Miss Harvey said in her dressing-room later "Peter would not give up. . ."' The *Daily Mail* quoted Anne Sellers as saying: 'When I went round to the dressing-room poor Peter was lying there saying some very unfunny things. After I drove him home the doctor gave him a sedative and he is now fast asleep.'

antics did duty for the cousins and the aunts of the Southsea childhood, who had urged him on when (said Uncle Bert, perspiring at
the memory) 'he was just a horror'. All eyes were on him. His wife
saw the production over thirty times – she chaperoned him like a
nanny. David Lodge had seen the play enough times to be able to
turn to her and ask, as Sellers capered down to the front of the stage
and clung there for a perilous instant before disappearing: 'Is this a
new scene they are working in to the show?' (As for Milligan, his
comment was metaphysical: 'You don't think that orchestra pit got
there by accident, do you?')

André François' set, from the photographs of the production
which survive, suggest that the Sultanate of Huwayat was purposefully made to look like a nursery: brightly painted overscaled
papier-mâché camels, minarets, well-shafts, domes and battlements. It was a child's pop-up book of Arabia brought thrillingly to
life. Sellers' sultan romped in this space, sneaking about with
buckets of paint to daub grafitti, bill-sticking, twitting the locals and
the visitors – an outsized infant. And, like an infant glutted with
toys and attention, he was soon bored. Sellers tried to justify his
boredom by saying (to Pierre Rouve) 'I don't like to remember
where to be on a stage. The stage is constricting. You can only face
one way.' He also fulminated (to Dilys Powell) against long runs: 'I
once saw an Agatha Christie play after it had been running for
years – the poor actors seemed to be dragging through their parts.
It put me against Agatha Christie. I should always be reading all
that into the books. Long runs! Eight weeks is enough . . . I got into
great trouble when I was playing in the theatre;[*] I was badly mis-
interpreted. I said an actor only gave two performances a week.

---

* His foolery and bungles elicited this reproachful letter from a Mr Jack Minster,
  published in the *Sunday Times*: 'Sir, – . . . Mr Sellers' remarks on the theatre were
  curious and could be very destructive . . . Particularly worrying is his statement
  that an actor can give only two good performances a week and that eight weeks is
  enough to devote to one part . . . But maybe Mr Sellers merely meant that an
  actor can give only two performances with which he himself can be satisfied,
  though (perhaps perversely) I would put this as rather high, especially within the
  limits of eight weeks. Does not professionalism come into this anywhere?

Well, it's a fact: an actor is really on top only about twice, perhaps only once in the week. You *try* your best every night. But it's only once or twice a week it works. And you know it the minute you walk on to the stage. . .'

If the Aldwych routine was draggy and stale ('I don't like the theatre,' he admitted finally), the character of the juvenile sultan, however, was a rôle with which Sellers, in his slithering and comprehensive way, could completely merge. He appeared on the television current affairs programme, *Tonight*, for example, in full Valentino fig. If Cynthia Judah and Ned Sherrin, the producers, had expected him simply to be subjected to a few minutes of interview-cum-plug for *Brouhaha*, they were in for a shock. Realising that *Tonight* was the sort of slightly pompous world-encompassing news review, with Ministers of State dropping by to discuss their own importance, Members of Parliament going before the camera to rubbish the government, and so on, Sellers arrived, in brownish make-up and billowing oriental robes, expecting to be treated and talked to as a Middle Eastern oil sheik. His assigned four minute slot extended to nearly a quarter of an hour, as he improvised opinions and pontificated about Egypt, the Suez Canal, pyramids, sand, Lawrence of Arabia etc.. The interview was conducted straight faced and for real – only when they'd got him finally off camera did somebody feel they ought to explain that 'That was Peter Sellers who is appearing in. . .'

Judah and Sherrin entered fully into the masquerade – Sellers' brand of irreverence would convert the sobriety of *Tonight* into the satire of *That Was The Week That Was*; and if the following gabbled letter is any clue, they must have appreciated that, in Sellers,

---

A professional surely is one who can do his job even when he does not feel like it. This being the outcome of discipline and practice. Unfortunately, in recent years there has been some much-published eccentric and wretched behaviour on the part of actors and actresses whose conduct has been exhibitionist and deplorable . . . Possibly Mr Sellers is not suited to the theatre and is ideally placed in films where his best performance can be trapped in a can for all time; or in television where only one performance (hit or miss) is seen by millions and soon perishes in the limbo of forgotten things.'

16. "A sad and tired look": Morganhall in *The Dock Brief* (1962)

17. Inspector Clouseau, Blake Edwards and Elke Sommer on the set of *A Shot in the Dark* (1964)

18. Goat's Cheese and a She-Wolf: Sellers and Sophia (1960)

CARLTON HAYMARKET WHI 3711

Weekday Progs.:
1.10, 3.30, 5.55, 8.20
Sundays 4.30 & 7.20.

HILARIOUS, AS A MAN WITH A MILLION TROUBLES
ALL OF THEM ROLLED INTO ONE WOMAN

TOGETHER, THEY MAKE SUPERB
ENTERTAINMENT!

SOPHIA **LOREN** PETER **SELLERS**

A DIMITRI DE GRUNWALD
PRODUCTION
THE MILLIONAIRESS 'U'

EASTMAN COLOUR

with
ALASTAIR SIM DENNIS PRICE GARY RAYMOND AND VITTORIO DE SICA
A **CINEMASCOPE** PICTURE RELEASED BY 20th CENTURY-FOX

Produced by   Directed by   Screenplay by   Based on the play by
PIERRE ROUVE   ANTHONY ASQUITH   WOLF MANKOWITZ   BERNARD SHAW

20. Dr. Strangelove
receives directions from
Stanley Kubrick

21. *(Right)* The White Goddess

22. *(Below)* A Very Public Wedding:
February 19th 1964

23. *(Foot)* Sellers with his new wife and new
father-in-law: note the microphones for the
nuptial home movie

24. *(Above)* Ready, Aim, Flee! Shooting Britt in Hollywood (1964)

25. *(Left)* A Pained Expression: Sellers in Disneyland, a few hours prior to his heart attack, April 6th 1964

26. A Jewish Double Act: Sellers (dressed as Henry Orient) and Mel Brooks in New York (1964)

CHARLES K. FELDMAN'S

CASINO ROYALE IS *TOO MUCH...* **FOR ONE JAMES BOND!**

JAMES BOND 007

CASINO ROYALE 007

28. Sellers (as Hrundi Bakshi) and Britt watch a playback of a take on the set of *The Party*. Photograph taken by Satyajit Ray (1967)

30. Aldo Vanucci in *After the Fox*: Sellers as a crooked film director (1966)

29. *(Left)* Sellers with a Britt lookalike (Leigh Taylor Young) in *I Love You Alice B. Toklas* (1968)

31. *(Below)* Robert Danvers and his latest dish (Goldie Hawn) in *There's a Girl In My Soup* (1971): Sellers as he would have liked to have been, i.e. debonair

32. *(Above)* The master and his state-of-the-art gadgetry (*c*. 1970)

33. *(Right)* A brilliant performance in a crappy film: The March Hare in *Alice's Adventures in Wonderland* (1972)

there existed now a creature whose capacity to dissemble was practically limitless:

30th December

Dear Peter,

I am so sorry I haven't written to you before to thank you for letting us interview you in *Tonight* on Friday 11th December, but I have been so busy that this is the first opportunity I have had.

It was lovely getting you on *Tonight* – at last! Sorry I had to rush away and couldn't thank you for it afterwards. Please come again soon: we love having you – especially me.

Happy New Year

Yours
Cynthia Judah
Tonight Programme

How could people have known, in 1958, that there was the virus of disaster lurking within the put-on artistry and success of Sellers' ten minute extemporisation? That *Tonight* spot was the limit of his attention span, and that's why films would suit him perfectly. 'He'd do two or three takes,' says Joe McGrath, 'and he'd get depressed if it wasn't working. He'd *never* want to try and figure out the faults. He'd want to stop, abandon ship. "Let's forget the whole thing." He never wanted to rehearse or to discover any depth or new approaches. Peter wanted, by living on his instincts alone, to do it and to be fully creative and funny; or else. . . .'

Cynthia Judah, however, was not alone in her pleasure. Consider this outburst of munificence. The BBC booking manager, contacted Dennis Selinger to say that 'We were so pleased with Mr Sellers last night, he was so funny, that we let him go on rather longer than we agreed. What we'd like to suggest, therefore, is an increase in his fee – from six guineas to seven.'

☆ ☆ ☆

After the low Gaillardian skies and Huwayat's sickle moons, his next (or overlapping) fantasy island was Grand Fenwick. It is meant to be situated in a valley off the French Alps; but, like the other sheikdoms and emirates, its precise location may best be said to have been right inside Sellers' head. He was lured by tales of remote kingdoms (they include Fu's Tibet and Prince Rudi's Zenda). He could identify with beleaguered and self-sufficient city states – they were places where his alienness had a home.

In Grand Fenwick, large and containing multitudes, he's not only Tully Bascombe, the Hereditary Grand Marshal, Count Mountjoy, the frock-coated and monocled Prime Minister, and Gloriana, the Margaret Rutherford clone; he is also the model for all the pigeon-flecked statues in the town square. The country is a single extended family – an ancestral Sellers has managed to spread himself everywhere. He is a body of people. (When, by means of cinema's special effects, Sellers has a conversation with Sellers, or Sellers encounters Sellers, it is like witnessing black magic at work.) Is the eugenic dispersal, or dilution, the reason why there has been no social or scientific progress since the Middle Ages? Grand Fenwick's army wears chain mail and the longbow is the national weapon; Gloriana and Mountjoy are costumed as Irene Dunne's Queen Victoria and Alec Guinness' Disraeli in *The Mudlark* – they exist, therefore, not in the real medieval period, but in a nineteenth-century reconstruction: Ruritania. Here, all is pageantry and purposelessness. Nattily attired brass bands march up and down, people wave banners embroidered with double-headed eagles, bunting is ever-present. It looks idyllic – but the populace is bored. How may they galvanise themselves? Why, declare a war.

If, originally, *The Mouse that Roared* was a satire on the post-bellum replenishment and wealth of Germany and Japan ('We declare war on Monday, we are defeated on Tuesday, and by Friday we will be rehabilitated beyond our wildest dreams'), the film now seems more to be about deviousness and greed; and its plot (the staging of a flop) prophesies, and further accounts for, Sellers' admiration of Mel Brooks' *The Producers* (where instead of phony war-games we have a phony Broadway musical, which unaccountably takes off, as Grand Fenwick's belligerence does). True, the cunningness at the story's core is well disguised. Tully, in particular, soft and fat and clad in a yellow shirt, looks carved out of cheese. He's a frightful nerd to have as a hero. And there is a lot of cosiness. Gloriana, chairing the council of war, gets on with her knitting; and the Declaration of War itself is penned beautifully in parchment and is decorated with wax seals and ribbons, like a college diploma. The quarrel having been picked with America (on the pretext they have spoiled the market for Pinot Grand Fenwick with an imitation plonk), the document is despatched through the post.

Tully and his chums, with their bows and arrows and suits of cardboard armour (they are amateur dramatic Robin Hoods), then set off across the Atlantic in a rusty tugboat to follow up the threat and to attack the enemy in person. They arrive in what is meant to be New York and there is nobody there – hardly any wonder because the New World, in this production, is glued together from model shots, primitive back projection and stock footage. (The result of this economising is that America looks less real than Grand Fenwick.) If Sellers, with his crossbow and hornrims, and resembling a retarded cousin of Woody Allen's, looks bemused, stupefied, it is not because he can't understand why there's no armed resistance; it's because he can't stop knowing he isn't anywhere near Manhattan. Even a total jerk, you feel, can recognise London's Lombard Street and City, deserted by its brokers and clerks on a Sunday afternoon.

However, we must suspend our disbelief and pretend that the shabbiness is anti-naturalistic and done with intent, like the cellophane seascapes in Fellini. What it would take mass hypnosis to get us to accept, though, is the romance between Tully and Jean Seberg's Helen. Seberg, a waif-like actress in the Mia Farrow mould, is utterly lacking in lightness and giddiness. This was tolerable in *Saint Joan*, when her dullness could seem like a martyr's earnest truth-telling; but the solemnity is hopeless in a comedy – and her sincere manner quite defeats Sellers. He is conscious, anyway, of his doughy body, and in his wobbling and wavering scenes with Seberg he keeps glancing away; he's awkward. Need the relationship between Tully and Helen have been so dismal? Could a genius in the audience have seen the spark of something? What they seem like to me is an early, crude version of the courtship rituals essayed with such agility by – Woody Allen. With the real, flexible, elvish Mia Farrow as his muse (or before that, the scatter-brained Diane Keaton), Allen overcame his unattractiveness and, in *Annie Hall, Manhattan,* or *A Midsummer Night's Sex Comedy*, he's quite the Priapus. (Indeed, he always gives himself beautiful co-stars, who adore him.) In film after libidinous film goblinesque boy gets elegant and neurotic girl, with wise-cracks.

☆ ★ ☆

Allen's cinema career began in Sellers' shadow. He wrote the original screenplay for *What's New, Pussycat?*, which Sellers broke up and waylaid with his precious improvising, and he played the part in it of Victor Shakapopolis, a backstage gopher at a strip club. ('How much is the salary?' – 'Twenty francs.' – 'Not much.' – 'It's all I can afford.') During the shooting, in London and Paris, he was frequently mistaken for Sellers. 'Britt said it was weird when I walked into the room where she was reading,' recalled Allen, 'because for a split second she thought I was her husband, and she even said "Peter?"' Worse was when it happened the other way around, and Sellers, then at a pinnacle of international fame, was mistaken for Allen, the neophyte who'd never been further East than Long Island. 'One day', Clive Donner recalls, 'an executive producer came into the foyer of the Dorchester, where we were all staying, and he saw Sellers there and he mistook him for Woody, and he said, "Don't worry about that guy Sellers. We'll take care of him..." And Peter immediately became and played along as Woody...'

To be avenged, Sellers' impersonation, or rather his expropria-tion, went further than the foyer. He took over the lines and situations in *What's New, Pussycat?* which Allen had carefully de-vised for himself. 'They would say, "That scene between you and Peter Sellers or you and Peter O'Toole. We're going to let the two Peters do it."' What should be Shakapopolis' sexual frustration, as he gathers up the discarded g-strings at the Crazy Horse Salon, turned into Fassbender's – who screeches to his valkyrie of a wife, 'I have hated you from the moment I first married you,' a classic Woody Allen quip. Allen was downgraded to a subplot; Sellers, who was only meant to be a guest star, having recently had a heart-attack, allowed his rôle to bloom and spread. 'There were fewer scenes in it for him when he accepted the part. That was one of the reasons he had decided to do it – it wouldn't overstrain him,' says Donner, 'but something curious happened . . . We did improvise a lot and Woody was petrified. . .'

In the scheme of things, what did it matter? Allen's rôle as the wide-eyed little maniac, the diminutive fellow with a fantasy of himself as dazzling (he's Chaplin's tramp brought up to date) is one he has perfected and had a good run for his money on to this very day. Whether the approach and form is farce, slapstick, pseudo-documentary, pastiche Chekhov, rip-off Ingmar Bergman, or what have you, Allen has sought (by getting increasingly high on serious-ness it has to be admitted) to analyse and demonstrate the politics of sexual appeal and male/female commitment. He has continued to play a smart and insecure Victor Shakapopolis.

Unless there was anything in the rumour that Allen was to have portrayed Sellers in a biopic produced by Robert Evans, he en-countered his sort-of double for the second and last time on that (his words) 'unredeemingly moronic exercise', *Casino Royale*. And, would you know it, *again* there was the case of mistaken identity, *again* in the foyer of a hotel – the George V in Paris, where Sellers was accosted by Leo Jaffe, the chairman of Columbia, and in-formed: 'That son-of-a-bitch Sellers is causing us nothing but grief on this picture. I wish to hell we never had signed him. You, Woody, are a gentleman.' Sellers transforming his voice once more into Allen's agreed with every word, disappeared into the night and was next heard from in Sweden – he'd gone into hiding with Britt Ekland's mother, and he refused to return to the film.

Allen called *Casino Royale* many names ('the film stinks as does my rôle' etc.) yet the jumbo-sized tastelessness and prodigal wastage aside, the opus did at least allow him, as Little-Jimmy

Bond ('the tallest dwarf in the world' according to a script conference memo), to develop his humour of the inferiority complex.
(Who was it that called him the first stand-up Freudian?) If Victor,
ogling at the Paris equivalent of The Windmill, is so near yet so far
from nookie (in the original conception, Allen would have been the
O'Toole character's buddy, feeding off his debonairness vicariously;
now it is Fassbender who has the agog companion rôle),* then in
Casino Royale, Jimmy, frustrated beyond endurance by his un-
appeased gonads, decides to become a Bondian master-villain. He
cannot abide his uncle, David Niven's, amorous successes – with
reason. They are off-putting for us, too. It is impossible to believe
that platoons of cherryripe teenage bimbos would find Niven's
wrinkled face and small charm arousing or even interesting. So,
anyway, Jimmy instigates various crimes and misdemeanours in
order to flush out 'the old fashioned gentleman in his retirement'
for a show down.

Little Jimmy, calling himself Dr Noah, resides in a space age
HQ, with black shiny floors, rotating rooms and long empty corridors decorated with gigantic Pop Art thumb prints that owes its
existence solely to the ingenuity of a movie-studio's well-funded design department.† Niven, as 007, and a group of yet more dumb
beauties, wander the labyrinth, are menaced by a deep voice – purportedly Dr Noah's (actually Valentine Dyall's) – and, as in *The
Wizard of Oz*, the mountebank behind the curtain and hidden in
the thick shadow of a winged arm-chair is revealed as a little squirt.
The little squirt, however, has concocted a bacillus which will destroy all men over four feet seven. Jimmy has a post-apocalyptic
vision of a world full of beautiful women, and where all the chaps

* But then, in the original conception, it wouldn't have been O'Toole but Warren
Beatty; and the sex mad psychiatrist wouldn't have been Sellers but Groucho
Marx. *What's New, Pussycat?* was to have resembled Byron's *Don Juan* crossed
with *Horse Feathers*.
† The art director was Michael Stringer, and he met Vincent Korda in the street:
'What are you working on at the moment?' – '*Casino Royale*' – 'You can't be! I'm
doing it.' – 'I'm doing it as well,' said Korda.

are shorter than himself. 'Let's run amok,' he says to Daliah Lavi, whom he has strapped to a pink dentist's chair, 'or if you are too tired, we'll walk amok.' Somehow she pops a time bomb pill in his Bollinger and the film, which has been in danger of never ending, falls off the sprockets when he explodes, taking the planet with him. (Sellers reappears in the credit roll, having dropped out of the film hours previously, as an angel strumming on a harp.)

☆ ★ ☆

Which transports us back to *The Mouse that Roared*. Sellers' sallow Tully meets Jean Seberg when he blunders into an Institute of Advanced Physics and captures her father and his new hydrogen bomb – a fizzing rugby ball capable of destroying two million square miles. (It is a Doomsday Machine, and Dr Alfred Kokintz – 'He's eccentric. He likes to work alone' – as portrayed by David Kossoff, is a benign Dr Strangelove.) That is why, by the way, the Fenwick army finds New York deserted. An air raid or fire drill is in progress and the half dozen extras portraying the American population are hiding in a cellar. They are very cheerful – they love the bomb, because 'whoever has the bomb has the world by its tail'. At school you will have been taught to underline those words in pencil and to write DRAMATIC IRONY in the margin.

On the boat back home, with the nutty professor and his daughter as hostage, plus their oval high explosive, which clucks and ticks like a mechanical egg, much hilarity is derived from the tossing seas. Tully reels in and out of his cabin and looks nauseous. The prof is worried about his bomb down in the hold. The army, still in their chain-mail, attempt gymnastic exercises on deck – they are as maladroit as the pirates in *Ghost in the Noonday Sun*. It is as if these scenes have been thrown into the film as an interlude, to kill a bit of time whilst somebody off screen came up with a way of continuing and developing the storyline. Grand Fenwick now 'controls the destiny of the world' – but what of it? When we get to dry land and meet Sellers' other characters again, they are not the sort of people to be much interested in a hectic plot. Gloriana, swathed in blue chiffon and ostrich plumes, gives a recital on her harpsichord and sings in a gurgly contralto. 'Do give my love to your president, and to Mrs Coolidge too,' she trills to an American ambassador, come to get his country's bomb back. Calvin Coolidge, of course, had retired from office, aged fifty seven, in 1929; but it's not because the duchess is senile and rambling (which is how Margaret Rutherford played the rôle in *The Mouse on the Moon*) that she makes these mistakes. Sellers' Gloriana, a hippopotamus dressed by Norman Hartnell, is simply and resolutely in a cuckoo-land of her own. Facts of history and chronology are not her concern – she's beyond them. Similarly, for Count Mountjoy to have to scamper around the castle, to a silent movie piano yet, is demeaning. He seems to want to find the bomb and give it back or let it off, or something tedious. As Sellers conceives him, his slightly exaggerated sleekness and purring voice gesture in the direction of Hercules Grytpype Thynne, no less; he ought to be besotted with a totally lunatic scheme out of *The Goon Show*, not stooping to a television sit-com chase, which climaxes with four-star generals from the world's big nations chucking the bomb, one to the other, in an American football game.

The director, Jack Arnold, was best known for his science-fiction films, like *The Incredible Shrinking Man*; and that's what he does to Sellers' flamboyance – he miniaturises it, puts it up against a broad and coarsening New World *vs.* Old World polemic, which leaves me, for one, perplexed. The film is full of inconsistencies, logical jump cuts. Not only is the love-affair between Tully and Helen implausible because the peformers lack the vital chemistry, it also makes no sense in terms of the drama – *why* should she like him? He's her captor and Tully's theft of the bomb and his refusal to render it harmless is foolish, to put it no higher. Mountjoy, who does want to defuse the bomb, and the international crisis, is condemned to grape-treading. Why? And why does the Kossoff character decide to stay when he's been so badly treated?

I don't think we are meant to question, or even to acknowledge, the hole-riddled cheesiness that's *The Mouse that Roared*. It is a film people always remember fondly, despite the fact that its execution is such a shambles; it's the fancy behind the way the story is told which grabs the imagination. Grand Fenwick taking on America – and accidentally winning, by default, or what-have-you, is an underdog fantasy. It goes back to *Henry V*: a small band of mud-stained men beating, against the odds, three-score thousand beautifully equipped French knights at Agincourt. Or, biblically, it's David and Goliath. I once met an Irish senator who told me it was the favourite all time film of the Dáil Eireann – and *of course* it would be. But if you dwell on it, and actually sit through it again, the pro-quaint wee country and anti-superpower stance isn't handled very sensitively. 'The little nations of the world,' the film concludes, 'should be in charge of the bomb.' Oh yes? Libya? Iraq? Uganda? Haiti? Little bits of what was Yugoslavia?

☆　★　☆

As prophecy and political satire, therefore, *The Mouse that Roared* is sentimentalising gibberish; its romantic scenes are limp; and simply in terms of cinematography it is uncraftsmanlike. Nobody was more surprised by its success than Sellers himself: 'Tom Thumb did well in America, although . . . the film that has really done incredibly well there is *The Mouse that Roared*, for what reason I don't know, because I didn't like it very much. But over there in the first four weeks it took over a million dollars, which is more money than any other British picture ever to play there has taken in that time. In New York they were queuing four deep, if you please, from the Guild Cinema right round the block. I think that it was quite a good picture, but it didn't appeal to me, I'm afraid. I don't want to comment on how it was made. I wasn't, shall we say, entirely pleased with the way it was made, and therefore I think that certain things were not taken advantage of, and other things went right over the top. Nevertheless, the idea was good, and of course it was angled for America. And I suppose that that is the eventual answer. You can't argue with the distributor and say, "But I didn't like it"; he will only reply, "I'm not interested in whether you like it, my boy. I've got the money to prove that the public likes it." There's absolutely nothing you can say.'

Well, there are one or two things. There's no mystery as to why the Americans lapped it up. As a continent of plainsmen and little old world villagers, uneasily federated, they quite identified themselves with Grand Fenwick, the small and spunky lonesome state. That America itself, in the film, is meant to be a nebulous and slightly menacing Big Brother, indistinguishable from Russia, could easily be overlooked – for what do the stereotyped big-chested CIA colonels and Washington bureaucrats (who believe 'We've always been nice to little countries all over the world') have to do with real, individual American citizens? Real Americans, seeing 'a bunch of fifteenth century Europeans' coming down the street, toting crossbows and halberds and using Thomas Cook's *Guide to New York* as the campaign plan, saw in Sellers one of the Pilgrim Fathers. (The double-headed eagle on the Fenwick flag might be less Austro-Hungarian than a derivation of America's emblem of power, nobility, and generosity, the bald-headed eagle.) He wasn't an invader – he was an ancestor.

It is muffled, but inside *The Mouse that Roared* is the spirit of adventure – or adventurism. 'My country,' said Sellers in March 1959, interviewed on the set and wearing robes, lace, and strings of pearls, 'the smallest in the world, declares war on the United States, hoping to be defeated so that American aid will pour in and balance our budget. Unfortunately, we win!' As he saw it, summarising succinctly, the film was about chicanery and topsy-turvy bravery – which was fine. But what of the deeper drives of wilfulness and deceit which Sellers, who was never straightforward, could convey? *The Mouse that Roared* is over before it ought to have begun; with Fenwick, a speck, in charge of the entire planet, we might have had some true Goonishness and hazardousness. But the actor isn't given the chance to try things out, and as he said himself, 'I can imagine seeing myself in that film in America and saying "Hmmm. . . ."' Nevertheless, the picture did occasionally insinuate itself during Sellers' future career. Gloriana, the harpsichordist, became her cousin, Queen Victoria, la-la-la-ing to a jazz piano in *The Great McGonagall*; Mountjoy's pseudonym, Bobo, gave rise to a whole film of that name – *The Bobo*, which is about a demure warbling matador; and Sellers called one of his yachts *The Bobo*. On his last LP there is a drunken blues number, 'Come back to me Bobo,' sung in a horribly flat and indistinct way by the Prince Rudi voice from *The Prisoner of Zenda*: 'Bobo', to Sellers, was an endearment that meant any over-dignified idiot, and he personally used it when talking to and of his wives.

The kidnapped, bearded professor, beautiful daughter, and Doomsday Device plot is duplicated in *The Pink Panther Strikes Again*, where, for the second time, it lies inert. The Kossoff rôle is taken by Richard Vernon, who is called, in puzzling homage to *What's New, Pussycat?*, Dr Fassbender. (His daughter, Margo Fassbender, played by Briony McRoberts, has nothing whatsoever to do and makes less impact even than Jean Seberg.) The comic cognomen is tossed in meaninglessly – especially as, in a film where normally reliable actors like Colin Blakely and Leonard Rossiter are over-doing it, trying to be amusing, Vernon pockets his scenes by keeping silent and looking fed up: i.e., he is the exact oposite of Sellers' arms, legs, voice and hair akimbo Fassbender from the Sixties roundelay. Yet, if the prof and the bomb routine wasn't enough to pilfer from *The Mouse that Roared*, how about putting Clouseau in chain-mail and getting Sellers to revert to being Tully, running around in an Alpine hunting lodge set?

Tully, as you'll by now have gathered, is perhaps Sellers' least entertaining performance; but it was a rôle (part Bluebottle, part mock-innocent) which he found useful to adopt in real life. (Women would be drawn to what seemed like his helplessness, his passivity – they'd want to mother him.) He even favoured archery as a hobby and filled his garage with painted straw bulls-eye targets and quivers of arrows. Word of this reached Michael Bentine, who decided they ought to visit Robin's Oak, in Sherwood Forest, and practise their skills in the shadow and atmosphere of the legendary bowman. 'I think that branch up there,' said Bentine, taking aim at the top of the tree. Years later, when the tree was pruned or felled, the Nottingham locals were delighted to find the arrowhead embedded in the bough – it was conclusive evidence at last. . . .

Once Tully had aged, however, and his mildness had thickened into an attitude or outlook, the character he becomes is Chance, in *Being There*, shuffling through the dead leaves. Both speak with Stan Laurel's flat, dopey lilt; both are failures who paradoxically succeed – Tully being appointed prime minister, Chance being considered presidential material. Compare and contrast the two performances and you'll see the differences between the early and late period Sellers. As a young man, playing a young man, he was featureless, blobby. We wait, in vain, for the inspired silliness (which was his gift on radio) or for his sadness (which emanated from his oldsters) to spurt out. Twenty years on, and again playing an opaque character, there is mystery, rather than weakness and numbness; Sellers, who allowed himself to revert to his youthful plumpness to look like Chance, is no dead weight. He is affecting – the last thing his performance is is slack. Moving with the slowness and tentativeness of an oriental sage (we can see why Fu Manchu had to come next), with each gesture and banality counting for something, we yet get the impression that Chance is peculiarly loose and free. Kosinski (his name is Polish for *nothing*, incidentally) was thrilled by the portrayal: 'Peter Sellers understood my character of Chauncey Gardiner better than I, for good reason . . . He has no interior life. No sense of himself. No notion of what he was or who he would like to become . . . He is, in fact, beyond definition by himself and entirely defined by society, which perceives him for what he is not.'

This string of epigram, describing a personality so adrift and distilled it must be mad, literally unhinged, is, as a description of Sellers, only partially accurate. For, despite his pains to commandeer *Being There* and everything pertaining to it ('I liked when they said in the film that the computer can't pin down where he comes from'), Chance was not Sellers as he really was, but as he'd liked to have been. It was the ideal of the empty space; degree zero; every moment, as reality erased itself, a fresh start. As with Tully's gormlessness, the wistful nullity of Chance was another fiction, a device with which to hide the truth of his paranoia, avarice and calculated nastiness. To give a small but representative example of how Sellers was Sellers, not Chance the bowler-hatted gent: on *Being There* there was a runner who prepared and brought his lunch. Steak and salad every day at one pm. sharp. After a month, Sellers suddenly turned on this chap and said 'What's this?' – 'Your steak and salad.' – 'You *know* I'm a vegetarian.'

'He said this really seriously and maliciously,' says Michael Jeffery, who witnessed the outburst. 'One minute he was up, the next down. Totally unpredictable. He found doing *Being There* traumatic. Until two days before they started he hadn't found the character, and he was in a state; and he used to get annoyed if I spent time talking to other people. I had to be *his* – his friend. He'd get shirty if I as much as nodded to Shirley MacLaine. . . .'

He was so suspicious and disenchanted, and so lonely and full of waste, having driven wives and children off, he had to pay somebody to keep him company. I asked Michael Jeffery what it was like, this rôle of salaried chum: 'It took me at least four years to get over his death. I'd have recurring dreams – because we used to go to Golders Green a lot to see the rose bush for Peg and Bill, and I dreamt he'd appear from behind the tombstones, in disguise, saying, "It's me. I just had to get away from people." I had this nightmare for at least a year. I'd been with him for over four years – and towards the end it was twenty four hours a day, seven days a week. And I'd never lost anybody close to me before. He fed off your energy. Everything I did was for him. . . .'

☆ ★ ☆

'What are your immediate film plans after *The Mouse that Roared*?' he was asked in the spring of 1959.

'I'm making *I'm All Right, Jack*, with the Boulting Brothers,' he replied.

In the character of Fred Kite, the Boultings, who could see Sellers for what he was, made full use of their actor's obduracy (which is not the same as strength) and infantilism (which is not the same as childlikeness) – i.e. the extreme points, or twin peaks, towards which Sellers would always veer, as an artist and as a man.

Wily and, when you tried to get the hang of him, far away from everything, Sellers was brought out by Kite – 'a very serious part,' he said, 'and the only way to tackle it was seriously'.

Sellers maintained that he'd been offered a new beginning; and when, in later years, he roved over his career, he wiped out what had gone before, as if it had been of no consequence. ('It wasn't until *I'm All Right, Jack* that I had a hit'; ' . . . this script came up, *I'm All Right, Jack*, and I really got away with that one'; *'I'm All Right, Jack* really got me into the film industry'; 'My first real chance was *I'm All Right, Jack*. Fred Kite was a good character to play. Those days were wonderful days.' etc.). In fact, the rôle grew out of his early work, where he'd learned that humour and comedy was not the same as plain funniness; and Kite was far from being a sudden new direction. He himself described the part as 'that hardheaded tryer Fred Kite – on the surface such an infuriating old blockhead and yet, somehow moving – who did his best according to his own lights'; and it was clear to the Boultings that there was no actor living *except* Sellers with the psychological quality, the furtiveness and strangeness, for the rôle.

'The Boultings wrote him an amazing part,' says Ian Carmichael. 'We were all reproducing our characters from *Private's Progress*, but Fred Kite was new and Sellers took it with both hands. The Hitler moustache was his idea. The mangling of the English language was his own – that wasn't on the printed page as I remember. Kite poured out of the Boultings; they loved writing that part and Sellers loved playing it, when he got into it – which he did, very much as a straight actor. John Boulting continued to keep him on a tight rein and Sellers was lucky to have such a director. Sellers got on quite well with Terry-Thomas, except that Terry had a problem with remembering his lines. Boulting was a perfectionist and he'd go on doing takes until Terry stopped fluffing. *Many* takes. Between twenty and thirty, here and there. Peter didn't like this. He believed the continual repetition was losing spontaneity. He was murcurial, instinctive. He didn't like a lot of takes and he didn't like rehearsal, and he was impetuous with money. He'd gone through thirty cars already, and he'd go out and buy a new Hasselblad camera with all the fitments, or a Bentley, or a new drum kit. . . .'

☆ ★ ☆

Carmichael is correct about the lower-middle-class Hitler moustache – 'a stroke of genius' in Milligan's opinion. ('He must have chosen that because he did all his own make-up'.) Sellers also allowed himself to be scalped. 'I really did live the part. I had my hair cut Gestapo short and rarely went out,' he said. He still had to sally forth to record *The Goon Show*, however, and on the sleeve photographs for Parlophone's *The Best of the Goon Show*, Volumes I and II, you can see what he looked like with his brutalist barbering. (He looks like a mad monk.)

And the malapropisms and mispronunciations were Sellers' – one source of inspiration being his own mother. 'Oh Spike,' she'd once been heard to say, 'I do like a bit of friction. I'm very fond of friction – reading friction.' Kite, in full sail, says 'jeropadising,' 're-valant,' 'sitawation,' 'indawidawal,' and so on; and Sellers copied this from a chief grip at the studio who said 'prosholium' for 'pros-cenium,' and who, when Sellers once tripped over a cable, didn't exclaim 'Oh Christ!' or 'Whoops!' or 'Fuck!,' but came up alongside and said, 'Can I assist you in your predicalament?'

Sellers enjoyed putting Kite together: 'Kite came from my watching television clips of various members of the TUC coming and going from Downing Street, and fellows holding up microphones: "The situation, as I see it, is that the negotiations have reached a point of stagnation and all that can happen now is that they will re-verberate to the detriment of the masses. All I am prepared to say at this juncture is that my colleagues and I are going to withdraw and consult." Kite was built up from a collage of that sort of people. Once I have got the voice, I work from the voice upwards, having worked in radio. Some actors work the other way round. They get the make-up first and fit the voice to it. But the voice tells me a lot about the character, so I can start to see it and fill it out, put things on and take them off, for two or three or four weeks. . .'

Kite's voice is low and clipped – formed by a lifetime of whispering secrets and strategies to a huddle of like-minded factory foremen. He is so enraged by the exploiters with carnations in their buttonholes, who own the workshops and foundries, his speech is strangulated; he is pop-eyed with indignation. He also does his best not to be gruff. The Dennis Price, Terry-Thomas etc. characters aren't only hatefully richer than Kite, and of a higher class, they are also more eloquent. Kite's ludicrous misuse of words occurs when he tries to rise and outmatch these paymasters, and there is something very unpleasant about the scenes where we see that his snarls and follies simply amuse them.

'I had a bit of luck with the character of the shop-steward in *Jack*,' Sellers said, continuing to identify his raw material. 'There was a trades-union official I used to know at one of the studios: "I've seen 'em all come and go, you know," he'd say. When I came off the set: "you was 'avin a bit of fun today, I seen you . . ."; then: "Why don't you come along 'ome some night and meet the wife?" He was the type who always had about six pencils in his breast pocket; or else he rushes about with a little notice board in his hands and a list of names on a sheet of paper fastened on with paper clips – I'm sure it's completely useless. I suppose I modelled the character from [all] these sources.'

Trades union congressmen, studio henchmen and bureaucrats (who had called that strike which Peggy Mount mentioned during *The Naked Truth*), and the television news, however, were simply stimulants and residues. Kite was more a product of Sellers' own numberless facets and urge to prevail, as he was the first to try and explain: 'Very often, as an actor, I find the character I'm playing takes over. When I'm going to play a rôle, I work out in broad lines what the man is like; then the character takes over. Of course, you have to know your lines. Knowing your lines perfectly is one hundred-per-cent important. After that, it isn't a matter of technique; it's a matter of – well, in some way I know how the character would behave.'

With Kite, the understanding went well beyond the staccato voice; it involved those beady, yearning eyes and the way Sellers knew that his character would wear his watch on the underside of his wrist. Kite's wrists, in fact, loose and flapping, are a significant mannerism. They thrust his hands at right-angles to his arms and body – like claws or stubby flightless wings. Kite, after all, has an office. He pushes paper. He is proud of being able to wear that lumpy double-breasted suit, weighted down with propelling pencils. He *doesn't* work with his hands or have to don proletarian dungarees. You could almost regard him, with his big, moony baby cheeks and perspiration, as a creature in mid-metamorphosis from the factory-floor underclass to the managerial level. And this, the sense we get that he wants to better himself, gives him a curious rootlessness and anguish.

One of the merits of *I'm All Right, Jack* is that it doesn't take sides in the class war. Indeed, under the coverings of their respective languages and costumes, the bosses and the labourers are much of a muchness – they are all shits, lying and toadying. Except, of course, for Carmichael's decent and dreamy Windrush (he's Lord Peter Wimsey as a young man); and, in a more inscrutable way, for Kite, who is suspended between the genuine menials and tycoons. Windrush, 'a university man . . . brought up as a gentleman,' wants to escape the hypocrisy of his tribe and live amongst what he imagines are the virtuous poor. He purposefully travels down in the world. Kite, similarly romantic, keeps himself going with reveries of Soviet Russia ('Russia, Russia, it's all we ever get in this house,' complains Irene Handl, as Mrs Kite). The astonished and faintly embarrassed meeting between the two men, who are each out of their natural element, gives the film its focus.

☆ ★ ☆

Whenever I see *I'm All Right, Jack*, I'm surprised anew at how *un*focused it is. I've never quite grasped the ins-and-outs of Richard Attenborough and Dennis Price's confidence trickery. (As Coxie and Uncle Bertie, they are directors of rival missile manufacturing firms.) I do not understand how Margaret Rutherford, as the dowager Aunt Dolly, all bosom and bustle and breathing fire, can witter about 'one of those horrid unions' and yet then, when there is a General Strike, and people are waving banners and cheering,

she's proud to announce 'what a nation we are once we are stirred!'
Nor am I able to relate to you, with reasonable promptness and
conciseness, how and why the strike starts and spreads, why Coxie
and Uncle Bertie *wanted* the strike, and for Windrush to trigger it,
and then why they change their minds; or why, come to that, Kite
and his colleagues down tools in support of Windrush and then
send him to Coventry (or is it the other way round?).

The film is as convoluted as Kite's diction and grammar; the plot
'reverberates back to our detriment'. And what a long time it takes
before all that plot is given a push. We start with a pre-title scene in
a London club, with Sellers, made up with a heavy fall of talcum
powder, playing an old codger of Victorian vintage who is 'on the
way out' – a Bloodnok or General Fitzjohn sort, an officer and a
gentleman, who is being usurped by the postwar ne'er-do-wells,
bounders and wasters. Barring its use as a practical illustration of
Sellers' ability to walk with the stiff-legged, tilting-over-arse-back-
wards gait of the elderly, the scene is redundant. For, once through
Michael ffolkes' wispy sub-Searle titles, and past a very horrible
dated rock-and-roll song, we come across Miles Malleson, authentically ancient, naked in a deckchair, shelling peas. He has dropped
out of modern life in disgust – the Nature Colony is a monastery
with sex ('Not a natural blonde, of course,' he says of a naked lady
playing tennis) – and he is interviewing his son or nephew, young
Windrush, on his career plans. The interrogation is half-hearted. It
is not something a gentleman is brought up for, work. Young
gentlemen are meant to go and run the army, head the church,
become judges in the High court, and to accomplish it all through a
combination of inherited and feigned intelligence, enthusiasm, and
an air of confidence – 'above all, an air of confidence.' *Work* is vulgar; it is unaristocratic – and if we don't much object to the
complacency and pride of this argument, it is because Malleson, as
always, has such taste and simplicity. He's an innocent, and very
knowing.

In that sense, Carmichael's Windrush is a chump off the old
block. You can see how his temperament will blossom and relax in

the years to come – and the film ends with him, too, naked in a deck chair, shelling peas. The only way to avoid contamination by a world full of shits (the working class trying to be middle class, the middle class trying to be upper-middle class) is to go into retreat. It was an option Sellers fancied: 'I think,' he said, 'that probably Windrush thought to himself in *I'm All Right, Jack,* "The only way I can get away from these characters, the big business men and the unions, is to go back to one of these nudist colonies and live my life there." I think that's a fair comment.'

The film's series of prologues continues with an extended, expendable sequence, where Windrush proves, as his aged parent/guardian has predicted, just how unfitted he is for industry and normal life. (His idea of normal life, we surmise, is a Bertie Woosterish one of country-house weekends and squirting soda-water.) He tries to get appointed as an executive trainee at a detergent factory, where he is bested by a bespectacled creep played by Ted Ray's son, Robin. He is taken on a tour of a confectionery factory, is force fed with the products (eclairs and nougat), and he pukes copiously into a big brass vat. (This episode is an aberration – the monstrous machines and mixers, ovens and boilers, have goblin faces and tubes like intestines, and are jokily stylised in a way that is out of key with the rest of the production's muddy realism.)

Eventually, perhaps forty minutes into the film, we reach the domain of Kite and his cohorts. When Sellers comes on it is exhilarating. After having been lulled by all the fatheaded stuff about Windrush's incompetence, suddenly, here is energy, here is assurance. Kite, his eyes as bright as glass, marches across the yard, in close formation with his comrades (including Kenneth Griffith and Cardew Robinson), to confront Major Hitchcock (Terry-Thomas); and we are held by him. What is the management up to, employing Windrush, an obvious twerp? It is 'bare-faced provocation of the workers'. Okay, says Thomas, in his card-sharp way, let's sack him. Kite continues to stare and blink into space. He's achieved what he demanded, but something isn't right. 'Incompetence,' he announces at last, 'doesn't justify dismissal.'

If the film was nothing more than sallies of this kind, it wouldn't be negligible; but what makes it a classic are the bits between the industrial relations jokes, the bits underneath the surface. Windrush, the Oxford graduate, reinstated, Kite is clumsily conciliatory. 'I enjoy a bit of serious company and intellectual conversation,' he says, going on to explain that Mrs Kite occasionally takes in a lodger. Windrush's face is a picture – Carmichael superimposes a panic-stricken east-west shift of his eyes with a polite and frozen smile – which merges and slides into a woozy, smitten grin of glee when he meets Cynthia, Kite's daughter, who polishes spindles. 'Capital, Stanley, capital!' Kite says, delighted, when Windrush agrees after all to come and inspect the rooms. He's rapt, and totally blind to the flirting going on under his nose.

Sellers was so smoked and kippered in the rôle of Kite, the home life scenes, with Irene Handl, stout and boisterous, and Liz Frazer, blonde and pneumatic, were to remain amongst the best he ever played. In the factory, amongst his troops, Kite's music, on the soundtrack, had the bounce and spring of a military band. Home again, however, in his parlour at the end of a busy day, he is fagged and faded – and the music, too, sags. The drums and trumpets slow right up and are vaguely bluesy. Kite takes his jacket off and puts it across the back of a lumpy Victorian chair. He massages his toes before the coal fire. He tucks into a bowl of stew and wipes his plate clean with a large slice of bread. When Windrush arrives, he perks up: 'Mother, where is that Australian burgundy we had?' He is thrilled to be able to talk books – and he is downcast when Windrush rushes away with Cynthia and leaves behind the little stack of volumes he had pulled down specially from his shelf. He gazes after the couple blankly.

Kite may succeed at work – by blowing his whistle and *stopping* people from working ('The natural rhythm of the British worker', says John Le Mesurier's time-and-motion inspector, 'is neither natural, rhythmic, or much to do with work'); but at home, or as a man rather than a rank, he is defeated. Sellers, without recoursing to any sentimental ploy, conveys the man's essential loneliness; and when the womenfolk walk out on him, Irene Handl accoutred in a cloche hat, he is crushed. To the noise of their offstage packing and door-slamming, he droops and slouches. (The drums and trumpets aren't bluesy, they are simply listless.) He decides to hold a press conference, is puffed up again by the sight of a throng of reporters, but once more he is disheartened – his thunder stolen by Windrush, to whom the hacks really want to speak. Kite prowls around the knot of journalists, with their flashbulbs and notebooks, being ignored, and he is flabbergasted.

Abandoned in his own house, the journalists, Windrush, his wife and daughter, and everybody, gone, he soon converts and reduces it to a masculine piggery. The sink is full of dishes, there is toast on the floor, gathering fluff, and partially full bottles of rancid milk abound. At this point, totally dejected and wearing a pinafore, he is interrupted in the washing-up by Terry-Thomas. At least it will be company, of a kind. ('Do you imbibe?')

If, in *I'm All Right, Jack* the welders, fitters, and fork-lift truck operatives are so bored, and have so few incentives, they are happy to become shirkers (strikes are workers' playtimes), the likes of Major Hitchcock and Dennis Price ('simple businessmen') never do anything at all, ever. They almost strive to be idle. They ensure that there is nothing to fill their days with except luncheon appointments and leaning back on a couch to read the newspaper – whilst occasionally barking to subordinates to: 'Well, get on with it!' Thomas calls the proletariat 'stinkers' and 'rotters'. He hires the John Le Mesurier character, Waters, to produce a report to justify wage cuts and bonus reductions. It is all exactly like a story Thomas himself told Kingsley Amis:

> There's a fellow called Telfer who makes more pork pies than anybody else in the bloody *world*, old boy. So the Americans went and asked him how he did it – incentive schemes, graduated bonuses, productivity scales, vacation benefits, you know the kind of thing. 'No,' he kept saying, 'no, I never do anything like that, no, I just let 'em turn the bloody things out the best they can. Oh, now I come to think of it, there is just one thing – every so often I goes down to the yard and I bawls, "Faster, you fuckers!"'

Hitchcock comes to Kite's place to see if the fucker can get the other fuckers back to work, else contracts will be lost and (as Coxie spells it out later), 'the strike goes on and we all lose a hundred thousand smackers'. If the scene does have a relevance to the furtherance of the plot, and I'm sure it does, this is not how I remember it. The two men, who are enemies, achieve a rapprochement (after a few drinks) and, by the end, the Major is darning Kite's socks. Kite keeps his apron on throughout, and the atmosphere of the scene is cosy and domestic; the incongrousness of it is perfectly understated. Suddenly, these men who are so mighty and full of themselves are playing house. And Kite, at his moment of greatest power, in command of a General Strike, is actually feeling very hollow, very bereft. 'Have I managed to live my own life?' he seems to be thinking. 'Have I been simply an egotist, peering only after destiny and fame and my name in the newspaper?' The rhythms of the scene, coming after Kite's other disillusionments, imply these ruminations. Kite also seems to sense, in the shadows stirring in his room, that he is quietly growing old. When he glances at his wedding photograph, the face reflected in the glass is weary and bloated, past its prime. It only lasts a fraction of a second on the screen, but we know that Kite is overcome by the bitter taste of failure and incomprehension.

It is impossible to believe that Sellers was only thirty-three.

☆ ★ ☆

I'm All Right, Jack concludes with a riot in a television studio; it is something of a cop-out, like the turmoil at the end of *Casino Royale*, where cowboys and Indians, circus animals, parachutists, and presumably anybody who wandered in off the street and fancied a fist fight, hurl themselves through the scenery and the lack of a plot is to be hidden behind the spectacle of destruction. In the Boulting film, in place of sea lions and tomahawks we have Windrush shouting slogans: 'The phoney patriotic claptrap of the employers' . . . 'The fiddles of the workers with their points-of-order' . . . 'Everybody wanting something for nothing' . . . 'When a deal is fine for Uncle Bertie it's a wet and windy one for everybody else . . .' . . .

'Waving the union jack and nobody can see what you are getting up to behind it. . . .'

It is assumed that Windrush, in blowing his top, has gone mad. Actually, in the midst of his struggles and difficulties, he has had to telegraph to us, and round up, the film's themes and targets. Crude as this method is, we can at least now be sure that the Boultings intended their satire to get at the violence and barbarism within the English sensibility – the inward aggression which is outwardly manifested in the forms and rituals of, say, cricket. When Windrush throws the bag of money in the air, the bribe given to him by Coxie, the studio audience, the film crew, the members on the panel of speakers, swarm towards the billowing banknotes. Punches are thrown (Kite goes down), lamps and cameras topple over, and so on. For some reason, the little local difficulty ends up in court. Raymond Huntley, as the magistrate, flickering his invisible serpent's tongue, automatically sides with Tracepurcell – who may be a swindler ('Business – high finance and that'), but at least he's an English swindler. Huntley's uncivil civil servant, in this corrupt context, poised at the bench, self-confident, polished, and essentially indolent, captures, in his forty-five second cameo, the intended drolleries and spirit of the film that have been somewhat dispersed in all its previous waves of incident and discussion. In the person and figure of Huntley we can see what generals and judges and gentlemen actually are: they are people who enjoy being rude and unaffectionate.

Sellers himself would return to the subject in *The Magic Christian*, a decade later. Sir Guy Grand, a megalomaniacal practical joker, uses his money and ingenuity to humiliate, disconcert, chasten. He lets a black panther loose at Cruft's Dog Show; he takes a pair of scissors to a Rembrandt, to horrify John Cleese (as previously mentioned); he encourages Richard Attenborough, as the Oxford rowing coach, to nobble the Boat Race – that kind of carry-on. The mercenary motive melts and warps the most honourable heart. Grand uses his aristocratic position, his sense of being superior, to wage a malicious war. He is a scourge – unscrupulous and cynical.

Sellers' favourite scene was the anti Satyajit Ray one where Grand constructs a large tank or vat, pumps it full of greenish yellow ordure, scatters cash across its surface and then invites the citizens of London to come and collect their FREE MONEY. Hordes of bowler hatted gents (they look like Fu's dacoits) have no compunction about diving into the mulligatawny soup . . . And if you think it sounds peurile and less than subtle, you'll be in good company. Irene Handl phoned up Sellers to say, 'Peter, you know I love you, but the other day I saw *The Magic Christian*, and you know when that scene with all the excrement comes on at the end? A lot of us OAPs went out. I don't honestly think people want to see excreta on the films.'

'But the point was, love,' said Sellers, 'I know it was a hardhitting scene, but it really meant that people will swim through shit for money. Which is absolutely true.'

'I don't know if the OAPs would do that.'

David Frost – who'd marry his widow, Lynne Frederick – once asked Sellers: 'Do you think money is the root of all evil?' He replied in a voice which had the trace of a lisp, a becoming impediment put on to indicate humility: 'I think you can do just about anything with it . . . You can buy anything with it, buy anyone with it. I started without a penny to scratch my backside with, like most of us. So I gathered around myself a lot of material, unnecessary things, to begin with. Until I found they were useless. They didn't bring me happiness. And it is a quest for that that I think we are really talking about, aren't we?'

☆ ★ ☆

With the success of *I'm All Right, Jack*, which won Sellers the British Film Academy's Award as the Best Actor of 1960 ('I would like to say on behalf of me mum and dad that I am very pleased to return to the villas with the prize,' he told the mystified Duke of Edinburgh, who was presenting the trophy), he decided to move from middle-class Whetstone to the gentrifications of the Home Counties. Before he left London, however, Sellers organised a firework party at his old house – he would send himself off with a bang. It was to be his farewell to (half-way) ordinariness. He'd never again live in a street.

As Angela Morley, the former Wally Stott, explains: 'Around 1960, when *The Goon Show* finished, I nearly bought Peter's house in Oakleigh Avenue, Finchley. I put a deposit down, and he was selling it to me for £10,500. Before I could complete the purchase I had second thoughts about how far out of town it was. I'd always lived in Kensington. I withdrew from the deal and Alfred Marks put in an offer – but Peter had already decided to have his fireworks. Mario Fabrizi and such people were in the garden with rockets, lining them up. Peter was inside the house,looking out, shooting all this stuff with his Arriflex 16mm cine camera. One of the rockets fell over after it had been ignited and headed straight for the plate-glass window – smashed through that and set fire to the living room and dining room, singeing Peter's drums and doing considerable damage. . .'

The inadvertent bombardment, the miscalculated pyrotechnics, are somehow apt; a warning signal. (Did the episode inspire the exploding firework factory sequence in *The Revenge of the Pink Panther*?) Sellers was migrating to a level of stardom, wealth and international recognition which would give him all the personal satisfaction and pleasure of Dante's first circle in Hell. But being handed something or achieving something, only to find it is not quite right, is the Sellers hallmark. He derived humour from the way his characters tried to overcome, by fast-talk or pure ignorance, life's various calamities, choices and limitations. I know Quilty is killed and Roquet, in *The Blockhouse*, commits suicide by slitting his wrists and plunging his arms into a sack of cooking flour, but the majority of his creations are charmed, being either zombie-idiots (e.g. Chance) or worldly-wise (e.g. Fu Manchu), who only wants to be told good news because he is in no state to receive bad news. Clouseau, for example, carefully examining a fizzing bomb, before it goes off, as he expects, right in his face, is left none the worse for wear than streaked with soot.

Sellers' characters absorb their hurts and pangs – perhaps they are repositories for the actor's, too? Kite, whose dreams of glory break over his head like rainclouds, would certainly fulfill this function. 'I don't think I've ever met anyone who is completely happy,' Sellers once confessed. 'I don't know whether it is possible to be completely happy, because either one is terribly happy, I mean as far as one's business life goes – that goes marvellously well, and it seems that one's domestic life doesn't. I've never met anyone yet who could honestly tell me that *both* were going absolutely marvellously well. . . .'

Follow his pro-and-contra, home and work, argument to its end and the world is doomed to cancelling itself out. Sellers himself, in being never acquiescent and in always demanding *more*, never struck the balance; he feared the boredom of it.

If Kite's private life, then, in the subtlest and most allusive of ways, mirrored Sellers', then it should be added here that *I'm All Right, Jack* was not the last of the character. In 1971 there were tentative plans for a sequel. 'I'm waiting for John Boulting to come up with the next stage. At the moment it's in a very early draft stage,' said Sellers. The labour force would now have been going on about their holidays on the Costa Brava, their wives would gossip over gin and tonics at coffee mornings, and Kite was destined to become a member of parliament; perhaps prime minister or king of England.

Nothing came of the film, but a version of this modernising was to have survived on the album *Sellers' Market*, recorded in the summer of 1979 for United Artists. As Ken Barnes, the producer, explains: 'It was Peter's idea to do a send-up of the then new Prime Minister, Margaret Thatcher, in conflict with trades-union leader, Sir Fred Kite. "What About the Workers" was conceived as a pop single and features June Whitfield as Maggie. The record company was more than happy about releasing this. And, initially, so was Peter. This was then followed by another sketch with Sir Fred doing battle at Number Ten Downing Street with Mrs T.'

Unfortunately, and amazingly, the reprise of Fred Kite does not come off. Sellers can't get the voice right. Twenty years on from the original film, he is too terse; the depth and play of mind has gone. The evocation of a missed and crestfallen life is not something he can renew. And though Mrs Kite was a battleaxe, Mrs Thatcher, whom from the first was portrayed by cartoonists and comedians as Boadicea reincarnated, is a very dull foil. (She cannot compete with Irene Handl.) This isn't June Whitfield's fault; her impersonation of those slow, measured, patronising tones is careful and attentive. But she cannot, and nor could any actress or drag queen in the ensuing dozen years, find any recesses of humour in the woman. Mrs Thatcher, like morning prayers in the workhouse, was beyond the reaches of comedy. So Sellers, in making up to her, is stalled; and though scored for full orchestra and choirs, the song is thin and dreary:

KITE: The strike is solid through the land.
THATCHER: But I'm the one who is in command.

As for the sketch, in which Kite is bribed with a peerage, perhaps the fault is in the weakness of the script – Kite, invited to luncheon, is offered ratatouille: 'I have never been a lover of rodents,' he says. Pâté de foie gras? 'Thank you, I will take a glass.' Or is it that Sellers' timing is off? He doesn't pause, he goes dead. Admittedly the tape I heard was in a rough edited stage, but this in itself is illuminating. I heard him as he was, before any post-cogencies or electronic polishings. When the album was being prepared, in California and Paris, from about the month of March 1979, Chance the gardener had come and gone and Sellers was melting into his Fu Manchu and Nayland Smith – but he lacked lustre. 'My ambition in the cinema, since I came across it,' he said at the time, 'was to play Chance the gardener in *Being There*. I have realised that ambition, and so I have no more.'

It was with this ghostish, leave-taking Sellers that Barnes contended. 'His instincts weren't so good. No sense of a comic's timing – he'd allow sketches to go on too long. Perhaps because he wasn't a comedian but a character actor? I discovered that the way to keep him happy was to keep him laughing. Irene Handl said, "He's an empty vessel – give him a character to fill himself up with, he's happy."'

On *Sellers' Market* he had the choice of about fifty personages, from Oxford dons to Welsh gossips ('Why don't you shut your mouth you *stupid old twat?*'), from George Formby singing authenticated new Formby songs ('With My Little Plinker-Plonker In My Hand') to end-of-the-pier baritones – but there is no Fred Kite on the finished disc. Had Sellers suddenly acknowledged that his work was faint and flat?

It has transpired that, when Mrs Thatcher was elected, Sellers had sent her a note of congratulation from the Inn on the Park, where he was staying with Michael Jeffery. He received a very friendly and courteous handwritten personal reply. He was so touched by the letter, and as he hoped one day to receive a knighthood* (when he moved back permanently to England from his Alpine cage, if the income tax was reduced), he decided to axe all material connected with the first lady from the record. 'The UA executives,' says Barnes, 'were most disappointed about this – because its topical value would have helped sales enormously.'

With due allowance for the prospective Sir Peter's self-interest, not wanting to hurt Mrs Thatcher's tender feelings marks his only known gentlemanly act.

☆ ★ ☆

---

* Sellers had been awarded the CBE in 1966; but as columnists had been hinting for years that he was 'as established and distinguished a star as Sir Alec' and that 'as a result of his fine work he will one day become Sir Peter', Sellers considered the honour an insult and he threw the insignia in the bin. He was envious of *Sir* John Mills and *Sir* Richard Attenborough, and once remarked: 'John and Dickie played it by the letter. Trust them to do the right thing. Do you think I live out of England by choice?'

PART FOUR
His Marvellous Years

Anne: I would I knew thy heart.
Gloucester: 'Tis figured in my tongue.
Anne: I fear me both are false.
Gloucester: Then never man was true.
Shakespeare, *The Life and Death of King Richard III*

Chapter Ten
Chipperfield Circus

If the last the cinema-going world saw of Fred Kite was his expression of wonder and worry during the tumult at the television studio, that was not quite his positive final – or most excessive – appearance; and I am not alluding to the stillborn encounter with the Conservative Member for Finchley. A group of people, perhaps numbering no more than a hundred, saw him take form, like an unbottled goblin, on the island of Cyprus in 1973:

'On the second day of shooting *Ghost in the Noonday Sun*, by lunchtime it was incredibly hot,' recalls Peter Medak. 'I was in my trailer asleep, and I suddenly awoke to all this laughing and shouting – and I start listening, and I thought it was Peter entertaining the troops and giving an imitation of Fred Kite. As I listened more and more – it was all "Brothers" and "The situation as I see it" and "I refuse to bear the conditions we are working under" – I started to wonder, what was going on? I went out. He had gathered all the actors around himself, he'd elected himself the shop-steward, and he made this insane speech about how everybody is incompetent. The producers are incompetent. The director is incompetent. The whole picture is organised in an incompetent way – and it is not fair to actors to work under these conditions – and never in his life had he heard of doing a comedy in hundred and ten degree heat on a boat. The catering is disgusting. The tents are not air-conditioned . . . He was doing *I'm All Right, Jack*. I'll never forget Peter Boyle's face – he was dumbfounded. He kept looking at me. Then the entire crew gathered around – and Sellers said there should be a vote taken: hands up those who believed that the director was incompetent? About a third of those present – make-up people, all his flunkeys (he'd had some of his mates cast in the smaller rôles, real sycophants of Peter, who formed a circus around him and who'd laugh at his jokes) – raised their arms. I was so furious, I jumped into a jeep, drove off at a hundred miles an hour down a dip, and shouted: "You are out of your fucking minds, the whole bunch of you!" There is one thing I can do, I thought: go back to Hungary; and so again I yelled, *"You can go and fuck yourselves! the whole bunch of you!"* I drove off in a jeep to the sand dunes and then wondered what to do next. My whole crew is back there! I had to continue. . .'

It should be noted that the film had been Sellers' project for years;* that he had been billeted in one of the grandest villas in the Aegean (certainly the only one on Cyprus with green grass in its garden); and that he had a luxury yacht moored alongside the pirate ship set for his personal use. He'd never wanted the picture to succeed – it was simply an exercise in power and paranoia. He manipulated people; put people up against each other. If you wouldn't side with him, if you disagreed with him in the slightest, he'd take against you; you were justifying his mistrust. Peter Boyle, to this day, has never seen manoeuvrings to compare with it: 'I was only there for a couple of weeks. I mainly took the job, playing a scimitar-waving brigand, Ras Mohammed, because I was such a fan of Peter Sellers. We got along fine, but there was a point where he went absolutely crazy. He staged a giant tirade. He'd called a meeting and he insisted on everybody's presence – *everybody* had to be there, including the rival Turkish and Cypriot drivers. When everybody was there he told us that everybody was incompetent – *everybody*! It was magnificent. I still remember this incredible scene – the wackiness of it! It was great acting. The epic and dramatic

---

* 'Sellers has already decided on his lapsed Catholic-Southern Irish voice and the humour from his incompetence,' wrote Thomas Clyde, of Cavalcade Films Ltd., the co-producers, to Wolf Mankowitz, who wrote the original (uncredited) screenplay, on June 11th 1971.

nature of it . . . The whole thing – amongst the dunes, the exotic setting; the caterers, drivers, producers, the director. . . "If you don't all shape up, I'm on the next plane out of here!" Sellers was both scary and ridiculous. I got the feeling that, though he was a genius, with his mimicry, voices, dialects, he didn't get any reassurance out of comedy. He didn't see much that was funny. His life was no laughing matter. But even his mad speech was inventive. He couldn't stop being inventive.'

☆　★　☆

Excessive, suspicious and delusion-crammed as Sellers was once he'd become an international star, the forces which destroyed him were the forces which had created him. He was constantly playing some new part, except that, like Barrie's sentimental Tommy, 'playing is hardly the word . . . for into each part he puts an earnestness that cheats even himself, until he takes to another. . .' Sellers was intoxicated by the novelty and freedoms of acting, the deep and ever-widening sea in which he was immersed; and to revert to 1959, when he was teetering on the brink of triumph, Sellers must have known that the scene in the house with Terry-Thomas darning the socks was important, and rich in meaning, because he insisted, some weeks later, that the Boultings return to it and re-attempt it. He had to taste Kite fully. Sellers 'made a thing' about this, according to Thomas; and it was a huge request. The Kites' interiors had already been dismantled and it was no joke re-assembling the set and carefully matching the muffled, carboniferous lighting tones with previous shots. 'This re-take was the one used in the film,' said Thomas, 'but in all fairness to Peter, I couldn't see any difference [in his] performance [which], to me, seemed identical to the first one [i.e. take].'

If it is on a par with his grasp of grammar, Thomas' degree of observation is not to be trusted. That has always been the fun of him as an artiste – he's all bottomless surface and self-consideration (those huckster's waistcoats, that ebony cigarette-holder); he'd simply not have noticed any of Sellers' shadings. Indeed, the growing difference between them as actors, their diverging styles, gives the scene extra pungency. 'The great thing about working together', said Sellers, 'is that we never try to outshine the other.' But there was no need for any rivalry or competition. Where Thomas was content to refine his pip-pip cabaret and radio persona,* and never to break new ground, Sellers was caught up in his new character, expressing himself through it and wanting only to give Kite conviction. ('In fact,' said Sellers sweetly, 'Terry and I feed each other with lines. This makes for the over-all good of the picture.')

The lesson we take away from *I'm All Right, Jack* is that Sellers, by making his rôle so his own, was finding a way to enlarge his imaginative experience. Next to him, the rest of the cast, whilst full of interest and intensity, have the unambiguousness of medieval puppets – like the morality figures on Roy Boulting's *Piers Plowman* postcard. We can tick them off: Arrogance, Snobbery, Sloth, Greed, Youth, Age, etc., each impersonated by an ex-Ealing and pro-Boulting stalwart, who fit their rôles only too perfectly. Sellers, however, has singularity, abandonment. He's not like the rest of them. (He can't conform, mingle and merge, even if he wants to, and be a rhinoceros.) Kite, and the roles which follow, Mr Martin, Inspector Clouseau, Dr Strangelove – all the way up to Chance, the burnt-out case – are rare and luminous. Sellers is the embodiment of magic realism. It is little wonder, then, that when trying to come to terms with the strength of his identification with a character, with his own plenty and consummations, that Sellers should invoke the paranormal. How else, and why else, should he be, like Bottom the weaver, so *translated*?

It is during this period, the late Fifties, that Sellers had started to rely on soothsayers, signs and tokens: 'He was a great believer in spiritualism,' Ian Carmichael reminded me. 'I lived in Hampstead in a house opposite Maurice Woodruff's, a man who devised horoscope columns for the London evening papers. Peter's car was there

---

* So vain was Thomas, and proud of his impeccable demeanour, when *Private Eye* published a cartoon depicting him as staggering unshaven out of a stage door (implying that, underneath the tailoring, he might be ordinary and dishevelled), he immediately issued a writ for libel.

regularly. He was there a *lot*. Peter wouldn't make a decision without consulting Woodruff. He felt strongly about the spirit world. He thought Larry Stephens was trying to get in touch with him – he felt *very* strongly about this. Certain things would happen – that's Larry Stephens. . .'

Sellers said of his Woodruff visitations, in 1959: 'It's like a drug. The man's fabulously accurate. I keep on going to find out . . . to find out.'* Whether or not he needed the guiding hand of a collaborator from the early *Goon Show* days, as he began to flourish as an actor, is dubious. Sellers didn't particularly want to see into the future; he wanted Stephens to help him keep a grip on the past – Sellers, the instant nostalgic. But much more to the point is the analogy he perceived between Woodruff's procedures and his own: 'As soon as I can get hold of something – a character, a voice, some make-up, I can then use that as a shield, get within it, and hope to make the character live – I act as a medium, if you like, and let the character come out through me . . . I think there is something psychic about my acting to a certain extent, yes. . . .'

The process was magical, or perhaps mystical: 'When I assume a character it takes over my personality completely. I find myself slipping into an almost trancelike state. The character takes me over. He exists in my body. I don't have to ask myself how he would react to this or that. I know the character acts for me. During the production of a movie, I lunch alone in my dressing room to keep the trance intact. I try not to talk to anyone, or become interested in anything that would not interest the character.'

Acting, for Sellers, had now gone well beyond mimicry or the expectations of caricature and satire. He wasn't copying whatever material came his way; he was transfiguring it. He could get a character's aspirations across – that's to say, he could convey what wasn't actually spoken or said or made explicit. Sellers, who had overflowed with accents, who possessed oceans and cataracts of

---

* Wolf Mankowitz described him less caressingly: 'He was a really unattractive little homosexual personality who had a strange hold on a lot of show business people; they went to him before any deal and he'd fix their astrological charts.'

trills and warbles, could be evocative with a look, a gesture, a sense of remoteness. Not just Kite, plodding to answer the door bell, but hundreds of examples: Clouseau, holding a bomb and waiting patiently for it to go off, or Clare Quilty, at the school prom, photographing Lolita, or Juan Bautista, observing that he was turned bright blue, or Old Sam, standing to a salute in the pet cemetery – a moment about which Anthony Simmons has said to me: 'Sellers had grown tired and bored with the film. He wanted to get away and begin *Soft Beds, Hard Battles* with the Boultings. His mind was on that. So they are meant to be in the graveyard, and Old Sam sees what the kids have done for him, and the girl looks at him – Danny Kaye said they should kiss. "It is a love story, about a father and a daughter," he claimed. Well, I couldn't accept any kiss, but there is a *look*; and Sellers could imply all the emotions you wanted in a simple glance. Anyway, we were shooting in Hyde Park, with the horse guards, and I received a message that Peter was ill. I carried on filming with the children – so that that rather moving glance of Old Sam's was shot on a different day, from a different angle. Sellers and the girl, Donna Mullane, never actually looked at each other. But it works on the screen.'

It's all done by necromancy, illusionism.

☆ ★ ☆

Sellers, in reconstituting himself, and unbosoming himself, made acting hallucinatory – 'an affair of ghosts,' if I may use V.S. Pritchett's phrase, coined to describe the novels of Henry James. James, incidentally, once remarked that 'To project yourself into the consciousness of a person essentially your opposite requires the audacity of great genius.' Sellers, beyond question, had the audacity, and the genius; he could body himself forth as other people, variously near or far from his own branch of solitude. What's at issue is the quality of his consciousness, its continuities, its brittleness, its incongruities and its lapses. And with regard to extra-sensory perception and the calling-up of spirits, let us continue for a moment with *The Optimists of Nine Elms*, which Sellers made fourteen years after *I'm All Right, Jack* (i.e. when he was, at forty-seven, nearer to Kite's probable age – though to play Old Sam he gave himself another two decades again).

It was for this production that he decided to be possessed by the soul of Dan Leno – Leno, the clog dancer, monologuist, and Drury Lane pantomime dame, who'd played at Sandringham in 1901 before Edward VII, and who later went insane. Simmons gives us an idea of how and why the haunting happened: 'He had decided on a flattened Yorkshire accent for the voice. For the face, Stuart Freeborn prepared the make-up of the slightly protruberant teeth, and a pair of false ears, and he built all this on a model, on a plaster cast of Peter's head. We showed him this. Then we took him to Berman and Nathan's for the costume. Special shoes, with a hump in the soles, to create that funny, rolling walk. Gave a similar effect to long clown shoes . . . So the character gradually built up. A nagging process. We found that big, flapping coat, which could be turned inside out, and the lining was of many colours. We spoke to his chauffeur, his various girl-friends, his wife, his soothsayer, getting them to give Peter plenty of encouragement. I found him some primitive microgroove records of Dan Leno, which nearly put him right off – because Leno's voice was so non-resonant, like a cracked bell. But he became obsessed with Dan Leno. He simply felt he was the spirit of Dan Leno reincarnated. A medium, who didn't know what we were doing at the time, put him in touch [*sic*] with Dan, to give him the right sign. Sellers had to go through with this rigmarole before he'd broach the issue of a contract.

'I, meantime, had started to re-write the script, changing and adapting a lot of the dialogue into Leno's own doggerel verse style. His odd, quaint little phrases. I found I could write "Leno". For example: "I can't go home, the old man said, there's a rat inside me house. The little girl laughed, said don't be daft – it's only a pink sugar mouse." Sounds like Leno, but was mine. Then I went through the script with Peter in tremendous detail. We were *prepared* – and he could have no cause for losing confidence in the material later on. When we started filming, I'd be told by the third assistant when he was in a fair state of mind, and I'd go and see him in his caravan, early in the morning. It had to be before the teeth went in – the moment the teeth went in, he was no longer Peter Sellers; he'd become Old Sam. I'd go over the day's work with him. I'd then rehearse with the children, leaving Peter quite alone. The camera would be rehearsed. Peter then came out and did the scene. This was our routine. He'd walk through it – no rehearsal.'

'An improvisator,' I said.

'He loved an audience – he loved getting a laugh. On the second or third day, he was to busk outside Fulham Football ground, with the real crowds. He was in amongst the crowds – with heavies on the sidelines to whisk him away if there was any danger. Peter sang and danced, ukelele numbers of his father's, he said; and the children did their stuff, passing round the hat. After the match, the children follow him through the park. The scene was shot the same morning. "Peter's feeling nervous," I was told. I went and sat in the car with him, and we chatted about the implications of the scene – pushing the pram of junk, turning around and giving a little nod to the urchins. We shot the scene and the extras applauded. From then on it was marvellous. He knew he had the part in the palm of his hand.'

'It is called *The Optimists*,' I said, 'but the atmosphere on the whole is wintery, doomy, melancholy. . . .'

'It is about death and a lonely man,' replied Simmons, 'and Sellers was a lonely man. I'd work with him in the evenings; and the producer's secretary would have to come in and hold his hand until the early hours for him to go to sleep. He was very odd.'

☆ ★ ☆

The false teeth were the source of his happiness. He was delighted in Battersea market, for example, when he was approached and asked, 'Where can I find Peter Sellers?' People not with the film unit had no idea of his identity. He was in the character fully; there was nobody else. Picture, then, the panic when the choppers went missing. 'Only one set was made, for some reason,' says Larry Pizer, the cinematographer, 'and there was a right old Red Alert. The teeth had vanished from the dressing-room trailer. They'd got thrown out somehow when the caravan was cleaned. It was a serious and yet strangely stupid moment. Sellers was totally disabled without those teeth.'

Sans teeth, sans everything. Lacking the dentures he lost the character; and in the absence of the character, who was he? Suspended between rôles, he had to struggle against anonymity: 'I get the same thing old Peter Finch gets. We call it the Blacks. They descend on me, the Blacks, usually after seeing the rough cut of my last picture in some private cinema. And it's the end, just the end. The whole thing looks terrible. Then I just want to pack it all in and look around quickly for a means of employment or suicide. Who can you talk to? Who'd understand your problem? Who can you unload your mind to? Then, after a few days, you get over it. I . . . drive; I try to lose myself in something, anything. . . .'

Whatever went on in Sellers' head, he was incapable or unwilling to share with those around him. He didn't like to respond, as a human being, to other human beings. He preferred his motor cars, his clockwork and robotic things; and then there were the distractions of his disguises. Hattie Stevenson says that 'I shall never forget – while he was making *Doctor Strangelove* – he asked me to pop down to the studios with some letters. I walked on to the set (the very lavish one they had when he was playing the bald-headed president) – they had just broken for lunch – and I walked straight past him. Having worked for him for two or three years, I didn't even recognise him.'

In describing for me what he was like on the set, Hattie, along with Simmons and Pizer, by saying that Sellers himself had vanished, simply echoed Roy Boulting's voodooistic discovery of all those years previously: 'He wasn't Sellers at all. He was a man called Kite.' And if you encountered him elsewhere, when he was ostensibly off-duty, still he'd be pouring himself, from hour to hour, in and out of dramatic poses. Simmons once saw him at a dinner party chatting up a young woman. The concentration and devotion Sellers brought to bear on the task were remarkable: 'He could turn his charm on and he could equally easily turn it off – because, you see, he'd not be involved with the lady. He'd be rooting for himself, for his own success. Just like *There's a Girl in My Soup*. He had to feel that everybody was concentrating on him. He was very alert to feelings in his "space". He came to our house for Christmas lunch, with his children, and he was telling story after story – hilarious company. But it was, like his womanising charm, switched on, done for the moment. We didn't exist for him as individuals – only as an audience. He was pitching to an audience.'

Did the floor-show ever abate? On the whole he didn't dare allow many curtain drops. Audiences, any non-particularised mass, fed his egotism. Whether you were in the cast of *Brouhaha*, the stalls during his early music hall days, the crowd thronging the recordings of *The Goon Show*, the suffering crew on his international film sets etc., or in his family recovering from an outrage and goggling at one another in amazement, you were meant to surrender to his private games. Otherwise he felt unsafe and exposed. He felt diminished – and he complained about this until his dying day. 'I tend to be rather disappointing, socially. If people are looking for a laugh, they've invited the wrong person,' he stated in an interview published a week *after* his death in 1980. 'They should invite someone like Peter Ustinov, a very fine raconteur, a very funny fellow, who doesn't mind being the life and soul of the party.'

Sellers never used the word 'raconteur' flatteringly. He once greeted Terry-Thomas in Hollywood by saying, 'Ah, T-T, the *raconteur*,' meaning, ah, here comes one (as Sir Kingsley Amis would say) in need of a medium-strength kick up the arse. There is a world of difference though between Ustinov, an entertainer who is like Father Christmas at his post-prandial ease, and Sellers, who was either manic, mesmeric, or sulky and wanting to walk out. Ustinov's film performances, too, have an air of the after-dinner speaker (urbane, apparently effortless, faintly bored); he is always, you feel, beneficent and responsive. He lacks hostility. And like Robert Morley, Sellers' co-star in *Battle of the Sexes*, who was admittedly more brisk and shrill, Ustinov is not an actor who'd benefit from any form of disguise; he doesn't need make-up, vocal variations or any other sort of metaphorical trapdoor to fall through and be taken out of himself. Whether he's Captain Vere, Charlie Chan or Hercule Poirot, the rôles he plays are thrown over his own temper and breadth of mind with the lightest pressure. It all adds up to an uncomplicatedness. Sellers, however, much more crabbed and sorry for himself, clung to his transformations.

☆　☆　☆

Not even the company of Milligan, the man who understood him best, could alleviate his self-involvement. Indeed, when they were together the garrulity, japes and palaverings were non-stop. It was almost as if, seeing in each other one of nature's solitaries, and mindful of the occasion when Milligan had wanted to kill the star (the abstracted celebrity that Sellers had become), the two men did their best to *avoid* a normal confrontation; they didn't dare meet as their real selves – they had to put on a double act. Leslie Linder remembers an occasion in their company which quickly turned into the semblance of a sketch from one of the 'Fred' shows. 'I spent a crazy evening with Peter and Milligan, but the funny person that night was not Peter, it was Spike. Peter was driving and we came up behind a Securicor van that had these watchdogs in it. Milligan hated the idea of animals being locked in a vehicle, so we stopped the car and he and Sellers crawled along the ground and opened the back of the truck and let the alsatians out . . . They had a strange relationship. Spike was a good conversationalist; but it was Peter who, by the end of the evening, would have everybody's attention – because he'd simply imitate everybody who'd been there. Quite remarkable; quite sinister.'

Sellers' talent was diabolical; he could be everybody, except himself – and thus did he assert himself. With Milligan, he'd pretend not to be competitive by communicating in the code of *The Goon Show*. (They had to have fictional creatures interposing): 'We really cared desperately about the characters,' said Sellers in 1971. 'They became real, so real for us, as they are now. I get letters every other week from Milligan, addressed to Bloodnok – because Bloodnok we keep alive regularly. Moriarty and Thynne are more or less dead now through hunger . . . I still get and send letters from and to Hen and Min. We had special notepaper printed. Whacklow, Futtle & Crun, solicitors at law. We send them occasionally to odd people when they don't pay us for odd moments.*

The Goons were their go-betweens, and they both kept an eye out for Goonish manifestations in real life. Sellers would send Milligan a press clipping about, say, an American mayor who'd conducted a search for his mislaid dentures (they were found up a telegraph pole); Milligan would telephone Sellers in France from Australia and they'd talk as Goon characters:

SELLERS [*Pakistani*]:   Hello, Hel-lo? What is happening?
MILLIGAN [*Australian*]:   Just a minute – I'll put yez through.
SELLERS: Through – but I am through. Is Mr Banerji in?
MILLIGAN: No, this is the Woy Woy Exchange.
SELLERS: Woy Woy? What is a Woy Woy?
MILLIGAN: It's a telephone exchange.
SELLERS: What is happening? Is Mr Banerji there?
MILLIGAN: What?
SELLERS: I was speaking to Mr Banerji and he was cut off.
LEO MILLIGAN [*Not in on joke*]:   This is Spike Milligan's father speaking.
SELLERS: I don't wish to speak to Spike Milligan's father – I want to speak to Mr Banerji. . . .
LEO MILLIGAN [*to Spike*]:   This isn't Peter Sellers. It's a wog asking for Mr Banerji.

And so on. If a chat show tried to pair them, they'd do their best to be daft – predictably daft. They'd switch chairs, mutter and screech as Hen and Min, Bluebottle and Eccles; Sellers would sing tunelessly ('I want to be unhappy, but I can't be unhappy, until I've made you unhappy too-oo-oo') whilst Milligan did trombone noises. Anything, to deflect a serious conversation. When an interviewer once asked Milligan, in Sellers' presence, whether 'You

---

* The 'Authentic Inter-Goonal Correspondence' is published in *The Book of the Goons* (Robson, London, 1974).

recognised and were seeing a reflection of yourself at all', in the sombre documentary he'd written for Tony Palmer, *Will The Real Peter Sellers (Stand Up)?*, he couldn't bear to be drawn. 'No,' said Milligan, 'I was pissed.' (In the documentary, which Sellers tried to ban, Milligan had said: 'The real Peter Sellers won't stand up until he's dead.') And if the talk started to concentrate a bit much on the international film scene, with which Milligan had no connection, he might interrupt Sellers (who'd be saying that 'Satyajit Ray, you know, he is a very sensitive and brilliant and wonderful man') and chip in with a few dud limericks, which he claimed he had just composed there and then – emphasising that he had been feeling left out.

The dynamic duo rose, or fell, to new levels of mischief when interviewed by David Frost, just prior to the release of *The Magic Christian*. Milligan, ignoring his cue, sloped from behind the scenery and, with Sellers' encouragement ('Come in, Min'), made gun-shot noises and jumped up to touch and grab the sound boom. Sellers then joined him in imitating monkeys and chickens, before launching into a song: 'Jews and shepherds come away, come away . . .' Milligan, going over to sit on Sellers' lap, next pretended to be a ventriloquist's dummy – and the twosome became Archie Andrews and Peter Brough, with many a 'Tarrarrrr!' to highlight their terrible jokes. After that, they came to rest as Eccles and Bluebottle. . .

Listening to their mugging, to the contrived chaos and the slobber of shouts and goonery, what I personally detect is that, first, both Milligan and Sellers believed it incumbent upon them to rebel against the manners and customs of a television talk show; they feel obliged to deconstruct it. ('What do you make of these people?' Frost wearily asks his other guest, Ringo Starr, as Sellers does a Jimmy Durante impression. 'I think they're wonderful,' he says, in such a deadpan way, his irony cuts the zanies right down to size.) Secondly, submerged in the mass and welter, concealed amidst the leaping and bounding, is their great and abiding rivalry. They try to out-do one another, top one another. 'I thought I had the same

comic ability as Peter Sellers,' Milligan said in 1987, 'because I used
to match him in the Goon shows, but the cards fell right for him
when he went into films and never came right for me.' But Milligan, surely, would be the first to admit that he is not anything of
an actor; what he is (like Ustinov) is a personality. In Richard
Lester's *The Three Musketeers*, Mel Brooks' *The History of the World
Part One*, and what-have-you, he's always scatty, hairy, jittery and
amiable. He almost parodies acting; he can't prevent himself from
letting you know that *he* knows that actors simply strut and fret
their hour upon the stage and then, a ten ton weight falling on their
heads from nowhere, they are heard no more. Hence the garish,
gaslit music hall artificiality of *The Great McGonagall*, a film I love.
(Nobody else does, however. 'There was a ghastly silence on the
first night. I've never heard a silence like it. You'd think we'd made
a film about a leper colony,' its star recalls.)

Milligan's gift is for comic conceptions, rather than performance;
he is crammed with ideas which, set free on radio, and which
worked in snatches on television, would, he has always believed, be
snuffed out by the heavy industry of cinema. 'Peter and I did phone
each other a lot to exchange comedy ideas,' he told me, 'and I miss
that. I don't know anybody his equal in comic ideas. We used to
say, oh let's film this! But we couldn't. Too exotic; too exquisite.'

Sellers, who had been given, as I argued in an earlier chapter,
structure and form by Milligan – he was, in many respects, minted
by Milligan – would never have returned the compliment. In fact,
his statements about Milligan (whom he did call 'a near-genius') are
the reverse of generous. They are anti-tributes. 'He and I . . . have
had a love-hate relationship over a long period. . . His compliments
. . . are always two-edged. I think he feels that all the things that
have happened to Harry and me in the way of success should possibly have gone to him. . .' Asked, in the mid-1970s, if there would
be any more Goon shows or similar collaborations, Sellers said:
'Spike has this enormous ego these days and it would be difficult to
work with it. He seems to be uniquely jealous of me as a person. . .'

☆ ★ ☆

What is the state of mind behind this remark, to which my immediate response is simple disgust tinged with disbelief? Sellers was speaking to Alfred Draper, author of *The Story of the Goons*. They'd met at the actor's penthouse flat in Roebuck House, Stag Place, SW1, which was decorated with photographs of the Queen Mother and Prince Charles, a yoga shrine, a pair of plimsolls mounted and glazed, and the famous Cape Canaveral telescope, through which the master watched the expanding universe and diners munching at the top of the Post Office Tower. Sellers, as so often when stalled between films, was bed-ridden with a virus – he had completed *Murder by Death* and he was soon to begin *The Pink Panther Strikes Again* (during which 'he got stranger and madder' according to Blake Edwards).

Also in the apartment, and what a significant souvenir it must have been, was the framed wedding day photograph from *I'm All Right, Jack* – the very same snap that Kite himself glances at during his darkish night of the soul. Kite, in his Sunday best, looks at the camera proudly; his Hitlerian moustache is neatly brushed and his boutonnière consists of a large fern and a frilly bloom. He is militarily correct and old-fashioned, with his rounded collar and shiny shoes. Irene Handl, as the blushing bride entwined with orange blossom, is either only three feet tall or she's kneeling down besides her lord and master. The formality of the pose, and our being uncertain as to whether she has fallen over or is a dwarf, gives the picture its comedy. It is authentic Thirties, and yet full of concealed ridiculousness – as well as being very human and poignant. (People do look awkward and over-done for their marriages.) It's the difference between Kite in this photograph, plump with promise, and Kite during the sock-darning evening, when he realises, in a flash, that the life he has led has failed him, that gives Sellers' performance its great interest and mystery. He would return to the drama of a pale and wasted life, and give it extended treatment, in *Hoffman* at the end of the Sixties – a film in which 'he did himself' (or so Milligan said to me).

579

Sellers was always swinging between doubt and elation. When Draper encountered him in his web, high above Victoria Station, with only the far-away cries of departing trains, his photograph collection and the astronomy equipment for company, he was bitter that he was only newly rich because of Clouseau's resurrection. He was aware that his experiments in serious rôles had (commercially) flopped – i.e. *The Blockhouse* or *The Optimists of Nine Elms*, about which its director said: 'The interest payments against the film are more than it could ever earn.' His hopes, if he was to break free from slapstick, cartoonery and the increasing broadness of 'a faggot cat', as he termed the panther that is pink,* were already pinned, as fixedly as Kite's fern, on adapting Kosinski's novella, *Being There*, which he had been given (by Victoria Lindsay Hogg) on its publication in 1971; and where he will have read that:

> with all its life, even at the peak of its bloom, the garden was its own graveyard. Under every tree and bush lay rotten trunks and disintegrated and decomposing roots. It was hard to know which was more important: the garden's surface or the graveyard from which it grew and into which it was constantly lapsing.

If it was indeed the case that Sellers, as he admitted, 'read the book every six months', then he will have been well aware of this passage; and he will also have perceived that, in terms of his own existence, in relation to his own brooding and backward-reaching temperament, it was an apt metaphor. He himself, despite his need for fresh starts, fresh wives, fresh homes, fresh characters, was more susceptible than anyone to the call of the dead – to the tangle of pugilists and music hall troupers, radio waves and assorted phantoms out of which the creature Draper met in 1976, had sprouted. The forthcoming *The Pink Panther Strikes Again* was not only a

---

* Quoted in an interview conducted for *Rona Barrett's Hollywood*, on December 18th 1975 at Burbank Studios, during the making of *Murder by Death*. Asked 'What about Alec Guinness?', his co-star, Sellers replied: 'Lovely chap, but I must say the snoring on the set does rattle the grips a bit.'

replay of *The Return of the Pink Panther*, of the previous year, but that money-spinner itself branched off from *A Shot in the Dark* and the original *Pink Panther*, both released in 1964. Sellers was imitating his own ancient imitations. And now here was Draper wanting to dig up *The Goon Show*, and asking if the likes of *The Last Goon Show of All* will be repeated . . . Sellers felt himself to be running, jumping, and standing still. His touchiness on the subject may be illustrated by this brief bout:

In 1972, the Goon Show Preservation Society was inaugurated. Sellers responded to an invitation from the Secretary to attend a get-together by sending this letter to the headquarters at 7 Frances Gardens, Ramsgate:

> 11 Eaton Mews North
> London SW1
> 1st January 1973

Dear Michael Coveney,

It was with delectation and delight that my old military hands, trembling tenderly, held your brief but nutritious note.

It would seem that you are all gathering in a small hut off the Edgware Road. Has it perchance sauna facilities? All meetings of people who are kept specially for meetings and feel no pain should derive extra benefit from the Scandinavian steams.

I will be unable to be present on this occasion as I distrust everybody, including you, Sir, and I will leave the safety of my quarters only under durex and/or the highest provocation. Therefore I am unable to give you a date or any other wog sweets.

No doubt Milligna, the well known typing error, will be with you, and you him, if that is correct. How dare you!

Meanwhile, Sir, I am yours furtively,

> *Denis Bloodnok*, Major Retired.
> Military Person in Waiting to Ralph Reader.

Though Sellers declines to appear before his fans, his repudiation of them is graciously and amusingly done.* What a witty old buffer, you'd have thought; and how nice of him to take the trouble to reply 'in character.' When, however, the society's newsletter ran a review of the revived Clouseau series, in which it was pointed out, unarguably, that *The Return of the Pink Panther* was simply a romp and that it lacked subtlety, Sellers salted away a grudge. In 1978 – five years later – when Coveney wrote to him again, asking if he would like to accept the post of Patron or President or somesuch, his rejection of the offer, so kindly meant, was swift and indignant. The following telegram arrived at Frances Gardens:

DON'T CONFUSE CLEVER CRITICISM WITH PSEUDO SURBITON INTELLECTUALISM. I DO NOT WISH TO BECOME AN HONORARY MEMBER OF THE GOON SHOW PRESERVATION SOCIETY.

('We are somewhat encouraged by the thought that he pays some attention to what we print in the newsletter,' commented Coveney. 'And I don't live in Surbiton.')

☆ ★ ☆

It is one thing to be sentimental about the past, and to put on demonstrations of weeping and wailing that would have silenced Donald Wolfit, ('Oh Christ,' he once gulped to Graham Stark, 'Whatever happened to Aircraftsman Sellers?'), it was quite another for the critics and the public to accept, or lament, that he was going

---

* 'Sometimes I wish I could be like anybody else, just walk down the street and nobody know me. All this autograph hunting, now . . . I used to think how wonderful it would be to be asked for my autograph . . . I used to dream of a day when someone would come up to me and say: "I was very deeply moved by your performance; it was the most beautiful thing I've ever seen." And then when people began to recognise me it was all quite different . . . I used to dream of it. But it's all quite different. Now you just take it for granted. It's just part of your life.'

backwards. And so he lashed out at Milligan, the instigator, the inspiring principle, the wonderful talker; and he also said to Draper: 'I disagree with Spike that tomorrow can never be as happy as yesterday. I live for today and tomorrow.'

With that comment,* what Sellers' is up to comes across with a horrible candour. He was projecting his own perniciousness and envy on to Milligan – imputing to Milligan his own shudders and chill. He was intent on this, spreading discord and trying to absorb Milligan's life into his own, back on *Ghost in the Noonday Sun.* As Medak explains, 'Spike is the most organised, level-headed, kind-hearted person I have ever come across – whether it's towards individual people, or trees, or animals.' This is true. He loves Victorian buildings and preserves their fixtures and fittings (e.g. porcelain doorknobs); he salvages things like the dressing-room mirrors from the about-to-be-demolished Bedford music hall; he has made people aware of the unnecessary vivisection carried out for cosmetics; he was thrown out of Harrods when he tried to stuff twenty-eight pounds of spaghetti down the throat of the food hall manager, in protest against the forcefeeding of geese for pâté de foie gras.

'He'll always go out of his way to do something good,' Medak affirms. 'He came to the film late on to jazz up the script and to put one-liners in it, which he's brilliant at. He wasn't there to accommodate Peter – so Peter turned on Spike, and there were days when they wouldn't speak to each other. Spike tried to get him to do things – everybody's complete effort went into keeping Peter alive, into keeping him functioning.'

I think I can understand, at last, why Sellers wouldn't go along with the *Goons at Sea* concept; why, divided and frustrated, he was determined the film should be a fiasco. He couldn't bear it for

---

* The exact opposite of the remark quoted on p. 444 ('The truth is that Sellers knew that yesterday he was happier than he could be tomorrow,' Milligan once told Peter Evans. An accurate forecast, as it turned out, because everything about Sellers, except his wealth, was to diminish.)

Milligan to triumph; for Milligan to hew laughs out of the heat and dust. Which Spike might well have done, because his ingenuities and suggestions (all, of course, ignored or botched in the execution) are light and frisky. *Ghost in the Noonday Sun*, with a budget of two million dollars, could have caught fire and been *The Goon Show's* cinematic breakthrough; crammed with a bit more corniness and loopiness, its plot, about lost treasure and idiotic desperadoes, is ripe for Ned of Wales – a thought which crossed Dick Vosburgh's mind: 'The producers couldn't decide what to call it; and they wanted me to write a little lyric that would be understood by Americans. *Ghost in the Noonday Sun* became *Goons at Sea* became *The Ballad of Dick Scratcher* became (and they were pleased with this one) *The Black and White Pirate Show in Colour*. I said, "if you would just hire a studio for a day, and get Secombe, and have a Goonish preamble – I could go through all the Columbia pirate pictures, and do a *Hellzapoppin*, with Sellers providing a voice-over."'

Sellers would not co-operate. Even he could appreciate that, having done his best to misshape and thwart the production on the spot, there was no benefit in imposing further chaos at this late stage – and anyway Vosburgh's scheme, you never know, could succeed (like the paradoxical, undesired smash that's Bloom and Bialystock's *Springtime for Hitler*). But the idea stayed with him. After the shooting of *Being There*, and he was hot and nominated for the Oscar, he attempted to personally buy back the negative from Columbia – and he said to Medak, 'I would love you and I to re-edit it, get Spike back to do a narration, and we could get it released.' He tried to purchase a work he had hated – because the origins of his hatred were so complicated; his motives receded, like tendrils, to the start of his career and the beginning of his fame. 'There is such brilliant stuff in the film, we can make magic out of it,' he kept saying. 'We really ought to put our heads together.'

Columbia wouldn't part with the material, even though they had never distributed it. The most likely explanation of this is fiscal – the costs of the film had been written-off against tax and it would be an accountant's nightmare re-opening the books and seeing if it could turn a profit. Economics aside, however, Sellers' change of heart is what's of interest. To Medak, it is final proof that 'he was definitely schizophrenic', and not simply cussed or conventionally *difficult*. 'His switches of mood were terrifying. One day we got off the boat at this lovely harbour in Kyrenia. He came and put his arm around me and said, full of calm menace, "Why don't you quit the film? Quit the film." – "What are you talking about?" – "I don't think you are enjoying this movie, why don't you just *quit* it?" And he stalked off. An hour later at dinner he'd treat me like his long lost brother and best friend. He really was quite insane.'

☆ ★ ☆

Milligan describes his experience on the picture as 'like being given a statue. Chip this away, a bit here and there, and make it look better. I did a rush job. I wasn't working – I had to make a living – so I went out there. . .' He needn't be so dismissive about his (un-utilised) contribution. I particularly like the harkings back to Eccles and Bluebottle logic ('Smoking stunts your growth. But for this [a hubble-bubble pipe] I'd be seventeen feet three'), and what about a flashback to Scratch's youth, as the pirate tells Jeremiah, the cabin boy, of his father's great estáte (we were to see a grotty field) and how he helped him to supervise the farming (we see Scratch in harness pulling the plough); and how he serenaded a princess (a toothless crone) from his white charger (a donkey); and how he duelled with a King (an old codger who belts him); and how he ran off and became a buccaneer (policemen chuck him off a pier)?

   This sequence, which exists solely as a yellow, crumbling leaf, dated and gummed into the script on November 3rd 1973, would not only have been a neat superimposition of sound and vision, it would also have been a jibe at the tendency, Sellers' in particular, to romanticise, change and puff-up one's past. It was a little scene de-signed for a fantasist; and this is only my personal impression, but as I examined Medak's own copy of the script, a binder of faded coloured paper, crosshatched with doodles and pencillings, it dawned on me that Milligan's re-writes ('I had to re-write every

morning. I'd be woken up – "Can you re-write this?'") seem to en-
cipher, through Goonish rant and subconscious touches, his
intricate and perplexing relationship with the star. I have already
mentioned, in connection with Sellers and religion, how Milligan
filled Scratch's quarters with altars and shrines of every denom-
ination. What else except a glimmer of something suppressed can
explain the impulse of this speech – spoken by Billy Bombay (Milligan's character) to Scratch, when they meet by chance in Algiers:

> I've sailed with you 'afore . . . You never ever kept a promise, and
> you never will. You're the dirtiest scum I ever sailed with. You're a
> crook and that's what you'll always be. In any case, I got a treasure
> of my own. . . .

Considering Milligan composed that, am I wrong to detect an
undercurrent of real feeling? Or here is another example, on sky-
blue tissue paper and dated November 14th:

> SCRATCH: Ohhh, no, no – I'm too young to die.
> BOMBAY: You're just the right age.
> SCRATCH: Let me go and I'll give you anything you want.
> BOMBAY: You 'aven't got nothing.
> SCRATCH: Then I'll work for you – I'm a great cook and lovely
> dancer.
> BOMBAY: Say your prayers, matey.
> SCRATCH: Which one would you like?

Medak has scribbled across this exchange: 'Done 2 takes – P.S.
[Sellers] refused to rehearse it, also [to] do final take to get dialogue
right. P.S. *walked off*, to lunch 1.40. [Unit] back from lunch 2.30.
Waiting for P.S.'

Was this one of the occasions when, not bothering to return,
he'd be seen later waterskiing or scuba diving in the harbour? Or
else he might be half way to London, off to another party at Kensington Palace?

✩ ★ ✩

'Peter and I are like Gilbert and Sullivan,' Milligan had said in 1960, when *The Goon Show* had ended and the 'Freds' fizzled. 'We love and hate each other at the same time. We're really like oil and water. We don't mix. It's just a matter of chemistry I suppose. We have a completely opposite approach to what we want to do, but by hammering it out we come to some agreement. But it's hellish going. When we get together we smoulder. When we talk to each other over the phone there's always at the back of our minds the thought: "You're wrong and you bloody well know you're wrong." You see, I'm deeper than he is. He takes things seriously – but in a quite different way. I think he's perfectly aware, too, of the state of "homo sapiens", but he thinks "What's the use?" He doesn't think deeper than that. I think humanity's a failure, but he doesn't care to think about that. I think he's an enigma; he is to me, and I don't think he understands how much talent he has got. We always clash about the quality of perfection we want to achieve. I think I'm a greater perfectionist than he is, where the production of ideas is concerned. Basically he is uncertain of himself and that makes him more sensitive as a performer.'

Sellers' wandering consciousness (he was as twisty and pixilated mentally as he was nomadic in his homes, fleeting in his whims, and fickle in his relationships) is what Milligan is describing here. He mutated from rôle to rôle, went from film to film, caring for and believing only in his own interests and amusements; and always, underneath the arrogance and the dashing about, he was afraid of his inability to understand what he was doing. Do you know that cartoon, attributed to Einstein, of the rock climber? The think-bubble, above the figure's head, as he clings to the precipice, is filled with a succession of incomprehensible formulae – which turn out to be advanced mechanics for the transferral of centres of grav-ity within the joints of the human body. Half an inch up or down? This way or that? Apply this to Sellers' performances: *he* is the one clambering nimbly, ascending, levitating, in defiance, it would seem, of nature's laws; *we* are the ones working out the formulae. Strange things happen in re-adjusting one's balance – and Sellers, with his intuitive torrents, had that to a degree which was a miracle.

At least he did in the late Fifties and early Sixties; after that came the boring international capers, bad behaviour, loads of money, parties which lasted for days in a row, and the chance to fuck beautiful young girls etc. Sellers didn't have enough personal resistance to such luxuries (would *you*?); and, never having appreciated his own capacity, for either dedicated serious work or indolence and hedonism, he'd say to a journalist: 'I feel that I want to be very, very, very discriminating . . . I think that I have a lot of things to do in my life . . . I want to do many, many things . . . I have great, great, great ambitions to do something as an actor which I will leave behind me, because I know I have it in me. I *know* I have it in me . . .' – and then he'd follow this up immediately with *Where Does It Hurt?*, a dismal hospital farce, notable only because it connects with Sellers' morbid interest in heart attacks and the blissful vegetative existence of a patient; *Alice's Adventures in Wonderland*, which, though full of marvels (Ralph Richardson, Robert Helpmann, Sellers' March Hare), totally lacks zest; and then came *A Day at the Beach* (unreleased), *The Blockhouse* (unreleased), *Ghost in the Noonday Sun* (unreleased).

Sellers' rise and fall, and then his rise again, in the marketplace with *The Return of the Pink Panther* and as an actor with *Being There*, is out of a fairy tale – the more so as the archetypal, mythological cycle was about to turn once more, with *The Fiendish Plot of Dr Fu Manchu* – Sellers' final and, in my view, megalomaniacal attempt to obliterate his feelings for Milligan with a super-dooper version of *The Goon Show*. As Piers Haggard explains, with regard to Sellers' last gasp: 'I got a call from Orion. My name had come up as a last resort on a project they were in deep shit with, *The Fiendish Plot* . . . I was summoned to see Peter Sellers, one of my heroes, at the Inn on the Park in May 1979; it was there I learned that there had been a script already, but that at some point he'd decided it was rubbish and he wouldn't do it; he had written a slim number himself which he pressed into my hands. [*] I later discovered that the

---

[*] Sellers wrote his screenplay aboard a yacht he'd hired in the Mediterranean called the *Berengaria*. As he maintained that he had put out to sea to deal

script he'd hated, Orion had been extremely pleased with, and very hopeful of. He'd taken against it. I read Peter's script – a series of Goon Show sketches, showing Goon Show preoccupations – the Royal Family, absurd policemen, etc. – some of which was funny. I detected a sort of innocence and charm about his story – which was interesting, because the Sax Rohmer original tale is inherently deeply racist; actually not very pleasant at all: casual murders, swinish chinks; then these dacoits, who are even more swinishly chinky. Sellers' was more of a fairy story slowly unfolding – a balloon drifting across, a flying English cottage, a wistful English detective. A germ of a comic fantasy narrative, set in the past. . .'

The reasons why it all went wrong are not difficult to discover. 'Orion, who had spent over a million dollars already, were trying to hold on to Peter Sellers. They wanted to do a Peter Sellers film. They were willing to do almost anything to please him. Every blessed thing was tempered with "How do you think Peter will take it?" He was cocooned and cosseted from the start. Everything was gift-wrapped to be sold to Peter, in the most elaborate way. Increasingly, I, as the director, became angry and despairing at not being able to have a normal relationship with my leading actor. He was worried what Fu would look and speak like, for example. He had no idea what he was going to do in this major part. I wanted to be able to help him, but he would not open himself to me; wouldn't trust me – even though he'd said to Orion, "I'll only do the film with Piers, so fuck you." And then, shortly before we began shooting in Paris, I finally had a meeting with him on his own – with the intention of discussing the myriad artistic details to do with making a film. Well, my first proper meeting with Peter was also my first experience of Peter in depression, which was puzzling and frightening. He was sitting in his dressing gown over near the window and the room was, or felt, very dark. He looked dreadful and sad. He sat like a graven image, very sombrely. He was on his own.

'substantially with the preparation of the Fu Manchu script,' and was thus not vacationing, he sent the bill, from Halsey Marine International Charters Ltd., for $51,000 fees plus $20,024 running expenses, to Orion – who paid up.

I later looked back and saw this moment as a premonition – of the insanity I had got myself into. Because from that point everything became *worse*.'

☆ ★ ☆

If only he'd died after *Being There*, for his own sake. He cannot have been pleased with himself for living life as it should not be lived; for behaving as one should not behave. The fear of life, the fear of death, the fear of human contact, the fear of loneliness. The sadness is in considering how gifted he was, and how much mental disturbance and unhappiness there was by the end. (His fate ought to put anybody off wanting to be a star.) And the story, as if it wasn't operatic enough already, doesn't even end with *The Fiendish Plot of Dr Fu Manchu*. Sellers was reaching new and spectacular peaks of fever and frustration on *The Romance of the Pink Panther* (which was to be his revenge on Blake Edwards). I will simply drop into my cauldron this letter from Steven Bach:

> Munich
> West Germany
> January 16, 1990

Dear Mr. Lewis,
Thank you for your letter regarding Peter Sellers.

He was in a very delicate state during the time I knew him, constantly vacillating between extreme fragility and monstrous abusiveness of others. I remember seeing him in Cannes [May 1980] slightly before meeting with him in Gstaad ... In Cannes he was in a state of shock – ambulatory but barely – that he had not won the best actor prize he had expected (and deserved, in my opinion) for *Being There*. This exacerbated an already impossible situation.

... Clive Donner[*] is a lovely man and a good filmmaker

---

[*] Donner had last worked with Sellers in *What's New, Pussycat?* He was to direct *The Romance of the Pink Panther* and was present in Gstaad both for discussions with Sellers and to meet any United Artists personnel. (Bach was at that time the company's senior vice president and head of worldwide production.)

who was ideal in one sense for Peter: he is a gentleman who
would not inflame Peter's never-very-latent paranoia. On the
other hand, Clive's very decency was a disturbing factor to Peter
who had worked it out in his head that if you weren't overtly
trying to fuck him you were doing so covertly, so there was
simply no way of winning with him. I think Clive knew all of
this, and he probably knew that deep down Peter had the bully's
mistrust and contempt for anyone who gives in to him, out of
whatever compassionate or human ground or need. Clive did that
– as Clive out of compassion would – and somewhere Peter saw
that as a) duplicitous and/or b) weak. These may sound mutually
exclusive, but nothing was so logical with Peter as to have been
governed by normal patterns of thought. He was, quite simply,
deeply unbalanced, if not committable: that was the source of his
genius and his truly quite terrifying aspects as manipulator and
hysteric.

My personal fondness for him and my admiration for him as an
actor do not override my feelings that he was on very important
levels a monster, and I try to say that with all the compassion I
may possess. No one suffered from it more than Peter Sellers, of
course, but he *had* to, and many people who did *not* have to
were put through it by him and I think he knew it and expected
it and somehow enjoyed it. It may be that his ability to create
havoc and nightmares and survive them was a proof to him of
his own reality, something he could only get in touch with
through the reactions of others. I don't know, and the world is
not in current need of other amateur psychologists.

I should warn you about this: many people were involved in that
last project and not all of them behaved much better than Peter.
Clive did, certainly. I tried to. So, I think did his co-writer [Jim
Moloney]. But not everybody did or could or would.

Good luck with your project.

> Sincerely
> *Steven Bach*

☆ ★ ☆

This is the tragicomic culmination of Sellers' proclamation, in 1960, that he intended 'to become so successful that I can name the *parts* I want and play them the *way* I want'. And who would have gainsaid him that ambition back then, with *I'm All Right, Jack* making his name and *The Mouse that Roared* making money? And who would have regarded the following, from 1957, as minatory: 'I've got an awful lot out of life – a beautiful wife, lovely children, a pleasant home. Being a star couldn't add much to that. It's the power that counts'?

The power, which to Sellers meant seeing how far he could go in abusing people's patience and demanding homage, certainly didn't reinforce or augment either his professional standing or his personal happiness. Power, i.e. the opportunity to be intemperate, wrecked film after film, marriage after marriage. He never saw it this way, of course. He saw himself as Prince Valiant. Around about 1970 he said: 'I'm going to defeat all these berks that are around me. And I'm going to *do it*. I'm going to do it one of these days and I think very soon, because I'm getting that way *now*; because I have a name for being very difficult. I'm not difficult at all. I'm not difficult. It's just when people just don't seem to *know* or have the basic knowledge of what makes A and B tick, that gets me. For example, I am written up as being *nasty* on the set. I'm not nasty on the set at all. It's just that when you try and argue a point with someone, not argue, discuss a point. . .' And so wheedlingly and endlessly on. Sellers' wantonness was often carried out under the guise of rectitude. He alone was trying to appear strictly professional; he alone was aiming for the heights: 'I am a very ambitious person . . . I have a burning fire inside me to do certain things which I know I'm going to do. . . And no sod is going to kill it in the future because I'm really. . . .'

Fade out Sellers, mix in Milligan for a concise summary and translation: 'He hated people, you see. He hated people because they used to stop him from doing what he wanted.' Not that he knew what he wanted particularly, beyond everybody capitulating and acknowledging that he must never be curbed. His loathing extended from the studio, to his behaviour off-screen, when as we know the self-recreations didn't cease, to his having it out, too, on inanimate objects. (Sellers was a barnstorming version of Clouseau: a man whom the universe seems to be *against*.) Herbert Kretzmer recalls an evening when Duke Ellington was in town, 'and I managed to get tickets. We went off in Peter's Rolls to the Royal Festival Hall. He couldn't find a place large enough to get the Rolls in easily – there were plenty of parking spaces, but they'd have called for some manoeuvring.* And an astonishing change came over Peter. He decided to forgo the concert. "To hell with it, there's no place here for my jam jar. Let's go back to my place and I'll run *The Producers*." This hadn't been released yet, but he had a sixteen millimetre print. He was clearly in no mood to be argued with over this. An evening with Sellers was an evening with Sellers. It was of absolutely no consequence to him that the rest of us were missing the concert. We went to Clarges Street, where he lived with Britt. He set up a projector and the screen – and he didn't have a take-up spool. He spent the next hour and a half, obsessive, on the telephone, looking for a take-up spool. He tried to track down Tony Armstrong Jones. We sat around with drinks and cigarettes. Finally, he got hold of a nightwatchman at the Technicolour Laboratories in Hounslow – "I'm only here with the key," said this William Mate Cobblers type on the other end. Peter then started to describe what a take-up spool was to this idiot. He wanted this fellow to go into the factory, find a take-up spool, phone him back, and he'd send a car for it. Needless to say, we never saw the film, we never saw the jazz concert. A totally wasted, pointless evening, beholding this madman. It put him in a terrible temper. . .'

☆ ★ ☆

---

* This is either reproduced or prefigured in a scene in *I Love You, Alice B. Toklas*. Harold Fine is very tense when he's in his car, a Lincoln Continental. He drums his fingers on the steering wheel and gets hot under the collar. When he tries to park, he is bewildered by the signposts in the multi-storey. The big car then gets stuck fast in the concrete layrinth. In despair, he has to abandon it and hitch a lift in a psychedelically-painted van. In the context of the film, and no doubt in America, too, the loss of your vehicle means the loss of your identity.

In the early days, when he could still slip through the streets unnoticed (because the public 'knew me just through weird noises on the radio') and before the investiture with power writhed him into many strange shapes; when he had hope and his imagination was a fertilising force rather than traceably desolate and productive only of anguish – then, in two weekends in 1959, between the end of *I'm All Right, Jack* and the start of *Battle of the Sexes*, Sellers put his random, startling and unpremeditated way of doing things to lasting use in *The Running, Jumping and Standing Still Film*. This eleven minute opus must be the most successful home-movie ever made. Leonard Mosley, from the *Daily Express*, heard about it and said he had a friend who was gathering material for the Edinburgh Festival – where the film won a prize. It went on to the San Francisco Film Festival, and won first prize, The Golden Gate Award. Then it was nominated for an Oscar. 'It won awards all over the place,' said Sellers. 'It got on to the festival round. Like going to a cocktail party. You pass your film from Cannes to Moscow. . .'

It is often slipped into television schedules to this day; and it was a particular favourite with the Beatles, who invited Dick Lester, who'd helped to edit it, to come and direct their own Goonish features, *A Hard Day's Night* (which in turn inspired Sellers' Shakespearean rendition of the soundtrack) and *Help!*

'There was never any attempt during the filming of it, or during the post-production of it,' says Lester, 'for it to be of any commercial use at all – it was really just a chance for Peter to play around with his camera.'

Whether he was mucking about or not at the time, Sellers would speak, after the fact, as if he'd fully intended and had personally masterminded a miniature epic. 'If I can get a footing with my films such as *The Running, Jumping and Standing Still Film*,' he pontificated in March 1960, 'which I only made as a demonstration to show what can be done without dialogue, I want to inject this type of thing into a British screen comedy. . .' And a decade later he was saying, marginally less proprietorially: 'It all started because Spike Milligan and I once said we wanted to experiment in visual humour. We got as many friends together as we could and went and found a field. That was all we had – friends, a field, a roll of film. We shot ideas – that was all – and linked them together. . .'

'We got away with it, with that little short,' Milligan said to me. 'It's the only example of Sellers' real sense of humour. His sense of humour wasn't Inspector Clouseau – it was much more abstract than that.'

Abstract? It was the very word Sellers himself had used. 'I find this abstract humour very pleasing. There's nothing to worry about, to think about. Things that happen in it either amuse you immensely or don't amuse you. It's a fantasia in a way, you might even say it's bizarre.'

What was a delightful stream of consciousness for Sellers was hard work for other people. Lester's testimony is revealing on this point: 'Peter relied a great deal on Spike in our period – Spike was the creative force, Peter was the performer. I think Peter envied, in the best sense, Spike's ability to create. Peter was a wonderful adaptor of other people's ideas. He honed them and made them into something infinitely better. . .; but in terms of raw creation, certainly Spike was the creator of almost all the ideas that came up.'

John Browell, producer of the tenth and final series of *The Goon Show*, in 1959, has said that *The Running, Jumping and Standing Still Film* 'was being made during recording periods. . . . Very often Sellers and Milligan were rehearsing ideas for it while we were trying to rehearse in the Camden Theatre, and sometimes I was not quite sure what performance I was rehearsing for. . .' Those cavortings are lost to us, of course. So besides the 'Freds', which apart from the mildewed fragment I described in Chapter Six, no longer exist (and if we leave to one side the Queen Victoria cameo in *The Great McGonagall*),[*] then *The Running, Jumping and Standing Still Film* is the only example we have of Sellers and Milligan functioning together frictionlessly outside of *The Goon Show*

---

[*] Sellers also provided some scribbles (you can't quite call them cartoons) for Milligan's book *William McGonagall: The Truth at Last* (1976).

proper (for all that *that* series was replete with tantrums and for all that I'd take grave issue with Lester's sub-clausal 'in the best sense', above). Or, to put it another way, their friction is concealed – and *The Running, Jumping and Standing Still Film*, however it came into being, and at whose instigation, is a transubstantiation of Goonish sound into Goonish image.

☆ ★ ☆

Indeed, its recurrent theme, or motif, is that of cameras and lenses; and as it is printed in a yellowy sepia wash, it is reminiscent of a Victorian photograph album. As with *The Goon Show*, the atmosphere is turn-of-the-century – people wear top hats and frock coats, deerstalkers and crinolines, and their bric-à-brac includes horn gramophones and brass bedsteads. The action, too, seems to be taking place in a billowing Baker Street fog c.1890 – everything is indistinct and murky, the result (as Sellers explained) of shooting it on 16mm film stock and blowing it up to 35mm – 'there are very few facilities on 16mm to do exactly what you want to do, it takes ages for a thing to be blown up, and then nobody's really geared for it. Everyone is geared for 35mm.'

The blurriness, however, suits the mood of reverie – the dream logic. We begin with a close-up of a moonscape, which turns into Leo McKern's mottled face, seen through a telescope. 'The broad framework,' said Sellers, 'was one person looking at another person looking at another person, and it carried on like that. Each person brought you into the next scene. It was very simple, but the ideas were funny. Like finishing up with Graham Stark being beckoned into close-up and socked on the jaw.'

Before we reach that pleasing climax, we iris-in and iris-out on a parlour maid, kneeling over and scrubbing a patch of grass; and we come across a photographer (Sellers) hiding behind a tree. He carries an old-fashioned solar flash and a tripod. He sees Milligan having trouble erecting a tent, takes a picture of him, and goes to develop his negatives in a running, babbling brook. (Henceforward, when the photographer wanders into view, we cannot be certain it is Sellers – for the character takes to wearing a snorkel and face mask, or else he is disguised under the Box Brownie's blanket.)*

McKern reappears, playing the violin – his music-stand is half a mile off and he scans his notes through his telescope. He also spies Graham Stark being trussed to a large kite, which fails to take off. (Sellers' house at Whetstone, incidentally, was decorated with mezzotints of air balloons, vintage steel engravings of da Vinci inspired autogiros, and he also owned books on the early history of manned flight.) David Lodge then comes on, dressed as a circus weight-lifter. He tosses a caber and hurls a discus – which is shot down by Sellers, who is back in a trilby and gaiters as a gent out a-hunting. He fights a duel with Lodge, a sword-fight using gun and a machete – a gag from *The Case of the Mukkinese Battle Horn*.

There are other bits, like a lady, sitting for her portrait, whose face has been covered with little numbers and demarcating figures; and a strange aesthete (Bruce Lacey) who plays a record on a tree-trunk turntable – and Sellers does a little jig in the distance. But, like a dream, the film is hard to remember once it is over. It has charm and it is scatterbrained. There is no need to prise much more from it – except to notice the seriousness, the intentness, of the characters. (The film could be going on inside the head of Percy Quill in *The Smallest Show on Earth*.) It's as if we have watched, or have been transported back, to a genuine summer afternoon in the late nineteenth-century, when Mr and Mrs Pooter were alive, and there were suddenly steam trains and flying machines, horseless carriages, phonographs, bioscopes – all manner of newly patented inventions and eccentric devices to enable the human frame to whizz, soar, listen, look. Science-fiction was becoming everyday fact; and what *The Running, Jumping and Standing Still Film* does (the title is the clue) is to celebrate movement, melt, fluidity, in time and space. The little film drifts past you.

☆ ★ ☆

'The Running, Jumping and Standing Still Film', said Milligan in

---

* A snorkel and face mask were Sellers' 'luxury' on *Desert Island Discs*.

November 1987, 'I made that with my ideas. That was me. And it was perfect.'

It wasn't, as he explained to me three years later. 'I had to go to Australia, and Peter handed it over to Lester, who clouded it by putting a jazz tune on to it. A fatuous soundtrack, which has nothing to do with the film.' He is right, the bird-whistles and snare drums are monotonous and tarnishing. What is instead required, to set the vanished past to music, is a plangent silent-movie piano theme composed by Erik Satie; something that would grace a Sunday in the park with Sellers', and the others characters', meaningless pursuits.

It was indeed when Milligan was in Woy Woy, Sydney, visiting his parents, that 'Dick and I edited it in my bedroom at Whetstone'; and it was then, on Sellers' instructions, that they must have added the credit titles – which would bring a blush to the chartreuse cheeks of Mr Toad: 'A Peter Sellers/British Lion Production,' – 'Devised by Peter Sellers,' 'starring Peter Sellers,' – 'produced by Peter Sellers' . . . Sellers, in fact, in his squirearchical tweeds, could be said to prance through the film as Kenneth Grahame's conceited amphibian from *The Wind in the Willows*. He hops into most shots, toting a gun or a camera; he lurks in the undergrowth and the background, scanning the other clowns suspiciously. He doesn't want to be left out. And Mr Toad, bounding from hobby to hobby, not willing to be censured by Badger or Rat, spending money freely on himself, having adventures with motor cars and donning disguises, is the creature whom Sellers now became. 'Do you tend to spend freely on yourself?' *Playboy* magazine asked Sellers in 1962. 'Yes, very freely,' he freely replied. 'I used to think, one day I can buy this and that, and now I can. Buying what I want is not really extravagance. If you bought what you don't need, that would be extravagance. But then I can always persuade myself that I need what I buy. I don't believe in being the richest man in the cemetery. . .'

Sellers' income had risen from £17,000 a year in the middle-Fifties to twice that by the end of the decade. He'd received £7,500 for *I'm All Right, Jack* and would be paid £9,000 for *Battle of the Sexes* and £15,000 for *Two Way Stretch* – which means that, by the early Sixties, when he had films opening every other month, the least he was looking at was £150,000 a season; and in fact this figure edged towards the quarter-of-a-million mark by 1963, when, for *Doctor Strangelove*, his fee was £1,600 a day for eleven weeks. The big money had started with *The Millionairess*, in May 1960. As Wolf Mankowitz explained to me, 'Sellers at that point was a totally different creature – tubby, very plain, frightfully myopic, anxious about his career, extremely unpretentious, devoted to his first wife, Anne, a charming lady who put up with quite a bit of trouble. Apart from doing the odd film part, he didn't appear to have any grand and lunatic ideas. He was getting relatively quite small money for his films; I believed that if we developed significant properties for him, we could push his money up – make a package deal and get part of the producer's percentage profit. All that shit. So I started to develop various ideas; and one brought to me for Sellers by Anatole de Grunwald, who had received a limited licence from the Shaw Estate, was for *The Millionairess*. I put the suggestion of Loren and Sellers starring together in *The Millionairess* to Sophia and Carlo Ponti. I talked to them about it, and they seemed pretty interested; and Sophia had seen some of Peter's things and thought he was the funniest man living; she was very keen to play the part. Naturally, I was too. On that basis de Grunwald drew up the contracts and I made the deal, with £50,000 for the two of us. Sellers had £37,500 and £12,500 was for me – and I wrote the screenplay. That was more than he'd ever received up until then. . .'

And he needed it. 'Peter has always overspent himself,' said Milligan at the time. 'He realised early on that he was never going to be happy unless he spent and spent and still had money left over, and this must always be part of his pattern.' His chief means of indulging his squandermania, in December 1959, was to leave the firework-charred Whetstone property for The Manor House, Chipperfield, near Kings Langley, Hertfordshire – and everything about him changed. His acting had always transcended the film studio because of whatever he did, was up to, was interested in. Now Mr Toad had acquired Toad Hall. He altered his walk, his laugh, his wardrobe, his demeanour. 'The graciousness with which he now entertained', recalls Peter Evans, 'had no connection with the informal, suburban dad in Oakleigh Avenue. He was Lord of the Manor and Anne was the chatelaine.'

Chipperfield was a Crazy House. Schizophrenic to begin with, being Queen Anne in front, Elizabethan at the back, the property was quickly re-shaped to suit its new master. 'I have only to hear about a new electric oven with a built-in fridge, and I've got to have it,' said Sellers. In addition to such appliances, he had the lawns mined for a swimming-pool and the outlying tithe barns restored, one to be filled with a large set of trap drums, the other to contain his five hundred metres of model railway track. What was the library he turned into a stereophonic workshop, called The Gramophone Room. Though he possessed thousands of jazz records, it's not accurate to say that Sellers actually managed to listen to any of them; he never relaxed to Ellington or Basie. He was the sort of infuriating knob-twiddler who, never satisfied, kept jumping up to adjust the speakers (concealed behind the Tudor panelling), tap the amplifiers, wipe the jack plugs and to check the treble and bass levels. Needless to say, the sound system was co-ordinated to flickering psychedelic lights.

Like expenditure, which rises to meet or exceed revenue, the more space Sellers had available to him, the sooner he filled it with his Mr Toad toys. 'I *cannot* walk past a toyshop,' he admitted. 'It has a fatal attraction to me. Hamley's in London's Regent Street is a Utopia.' One afternoon he came home with a model combine harvester, a collection of toothpicks and a blonde wig. ('I'll give the toothpicks to Terry-Thomas and the blonde wig I'll send to Yul Brynner as a Yule Tide gift.') And of course, poop! poop!, there were the cars. Chipperfield had ten bedrooms and two garages, and obviously this should have been the other way around. Sellers had owned fifty-two cars since the end of the war. His fifty-third, bought to adorn his new house, was a blue Cadillac convertible with a black hood. (It was parked alongside the giant mechanical elephant which Sellers had acquired in 1958.) 'I drive up to London,' he said. 'But if you are a family man it's difficult getting the right car. This one hasn't got enough room, that one is difficult to handle, the other doesn't hold the road. I think I've got the right one now [his fifty-fourth?], a Bentley drophead coupé. My wife drives a hotted up Mini. They're wonderful cars.'

Sellers also installed another of his smallest-shows-on-earth, a 16mm cinema complete to the last detail. After the success of *The Running, Jumping and Standing Still Film*, the most commonplace home movie (Michael, aged seven, taking a bath; holiday travelogues) had to be edited, dubbed, scored for an orchestra, and preemed, to use a *Variety* word, before 'anyone who's silly enough to accept an invitation to the house'. And accept they did. Sellers played the grinning host at weekend parties for Kubrick, Sophia Loren, the Boultings, Bryan and Nanette Forbes; and Wolf Mankowitz, Herbert Kretzmer, Graham Stark and David Lodge, and their wives, would often be present, playing cricket or sipping drinks. Alan Clare, who'd known the master since he was the occasional drummer for Oscar Rabin, used to get a band together. 'There was smoked salmon and footmen in white gloves serving it,' recalls Bloom, Alan's wife. 'I once made a cheesecake, which Peter loved, as a contribution for one of his receptions. "They're not having *that*," he said, and put it in the fridge for himself later.'

To maintain the larder, sweep the tennis court, and polish the Georgian silver (the canteen of cutlery is now on the shelf in Gstaad); to safeguard the armoury of shooting sticks in the varnished hall stand; to arrange the briar pipes, the fishing tackle, and to press his thornproof knickerbockers; and finally to serve the breakfast kedgeree and tawny port, Sellers employed a Spanish gardener ('we call him Dirk Bogarde'), a handyman named Dewberry (whom Sellers put on a record album as a Flat Earth Society member, raging against balls, bottoms, breasts and other sundry spheroids), a butler, Bruno, who clanged his head on the cast iron chandelier when serving dinner ('Any minute now . . .' Sellers would whisper expectantly), the German nanny, various kitchen maids and scullions; and he had also opened his London office at 37 Panton Street, Haymarket, SW1 (Telephone TRAFALGAR 1585/6). Here Hattie Stevenson, his secretary, and Bill Wills, his accountant and manager, were encamped.

'I'd never had a job before,' says Hattie, 'I was straight from secretarial school, and a friend who knew Anne Sellers said, "Why don't you have a go?" I didn't know he got through a secretary a week – if you *stayed* a week you were lucky. "Go on – as a laugh. You'll get to meet him and everything." So I went down to the studios where he was making *The Millionairess* and met Ray Marks, known as Ray Ray, his cousin, who was his valet before Bert took that rôle. "Bad luck," I was told. "He's in a filthy mood. He's got a headache. Filming hasn't been going right." But all Sellers said to me was "Hello Miss Smith,* when would you like to start?" No interview – and having said that, he was notoriously bad at making snap decisions. But this one worked very well because I stayed for seven years.'

☆ ★ ☆

The empire had formulated itself quickly. Owing to the success of *The Mouse that Roared*, which took over two million dollars during its eight month run in New York, offers of work were starting to arrive from America – Sellers was asked to consider a £25,000 fee to play Mephistopheles opposite Laurence Olivier's Faust in a networked television Masterpiece Theatre type programme, for example. It was one of the many tantalising projects which Sellers rejected. I mentioned a few of these in my Introduction. The Beckett, Pinter ('I should like to play in Pinter') and Brecht ('I was offered *The Good Soldier Schweik*') plays; Julius Caesar in Elizabeth Taylor's *Cleopatra*; the stuttering, shuffling emperor in a John Mortimer adaptation of Robert Graves' *I, Claudius* (the rôle abandoned by Charles Laughton and played on television by Derek Jacobi);

---

* 'Miss Smith' is what the Sinead Cusack character is called, every other few seconds, in *Hoffman* – and she's from the office typing pool.

Captain Hook in *Peter Pan* – I personally sat through Spielberg's *Hook*, in which a great subject was thrown away, despising every moment of Dustin Hoffman's mewling, runty performance. The rôle cried out for Sellers – a notion alluded to every minute Hoffman was on the screen, because he was made up to resemble, and his voice tried to imitate, Terry-Thomas.

Had he lived, Sellers would have been top of the list for the Penguin or the Joker (I can easily superimpose Sellers on Jack Nicholson, enthroned on his carnival float, releasing poison balloons); and when still with us he was John Huston's choice for Freud, in *The Secret Passion*: 'I am jolly interested in the Freud idea for John Huston,' Sellers told Roy Speer, in March 1961, 'but I don't know how I can fit it in this year. I have two interesting subjects to do – *That Uncertain Feeling* [which became *Only Two Can Play*] and *Waltz of the Toreadors*, so I can't very well do Freud until the end of the year, but maybe Huston can't wait that long.'

He couldn't – Montgomery Clift played the rôle, bringing to it all his introspection and agony. (Clift suffered from a hyperthyroid condition that caused muscle spasms and cataracts; he was additionally bullied by Huston, who took against him for being a homosexual. The film was re-cut by the studio and nobody was surprised when it flopped.) How would Sellers have fared? He did his best to get out of his other commitments to find out. As Leslie Linder, who worked for John Redway, recalls: 'Two weeks before shooting started on *Waltz of the Toreadors* Sellers said, "I've had an offer from America and it's a lot of money – it's a smashing part." I said, "How can you even consider it. You've signed a contract to do *Waltz of the Toreadors* which you desperately wanted to do. You can't walk out. The whole crew is ready; it's ready to go ..." He said, "Well, if I was with MCA" – the biggest and most powerful agency in the world. "Look Peter. You know where they are. When you leave this building, you turn right at the entrance and you go to MCA. There's nothing we can do about it." He stormed out, and though he came back a couple of days later, he'd been very angry and he even took legal advice.'

He would have liked to have played Freud if he could. It would have been his first encounter with a director of undeniable diamond-hard vision and first-rate artistry. Afterwards, Sellers' career might have followed a totally different path – for, in the days before psychoanalysts meant Dr Fritz Fassbender in *What's New, Pussycat?* and anybody vaguely Viennese or German meant Dr Strangelove; when Sellers was as subtle as a sphinx, and didn't feel, as he did towards the end, that he had to be dressed as a Nazi stormtrooper to get laughs (and to get by); *then* he would have been ideal for the stubborn Jewish revolutionary, full of possibilities, who (said Huston's posters) 'alone fought against his own dark passions, against the taboos of an outraged world . . . He alone dared to search beyond the flesh.' Freud was a sort of lost Messiah or biblical patriarch: 'This is a story', intoned Huston on the soundtrack, 'of Freud's descent into a region as black as hell, man's unconscious, and how he let in the light.' It's not so much that Sellers' Freud would have been a way of facing up to his feelings for Peg and Bill; it's more that, with Huston as his guide, Sellers would have created a character whose off-centre nature and essential loneliness (and arrogance) chimed with his own zig-zag mind.

The concept behind *The Secret Passion* was that the meanings of dreams would become clear after a detective-story style quest. Freud as a Victorian-era Clouseau? Freud as Fred Kite in a big black beard? What Sellers' miscarried or ploughed projects suggest is that producers and writers were thinking of him for extravagant, despotic, showy roles; it was recognised that he could bring, or touch in, with his instinct and innovation, a sense of torment, under the sovereignty, or he'd convey a softness, where another actor might be straightforwardly rigid. Sellers had a shifty pulpy genius (which Kubrick snaffled up), but he was not keen on being reminded of this. 'I've never played me, not at any time, so there's no such thing as Peter Sellers' rôle,' he once snapped – unable to perceive, as others could, that it was precisely for his superabundance, the multiplication of his aspects, and for his deceitfulness and guile, that he was wanted.

'I don't even bother reading scripts any more that are sent me with an accompanying note: "This is a typical Sellers,"' he continued, implicitly conceding that he'd deny himself the very characters best suited to his mentality. That's why Clare Quilty stands out amongst the wasteland of cops and robbers flapdoodle (which he entered into freely because 'it keeps you in touch with a certain section of public'). Sellers' vanity and hypocrisy are used in the Nabokov role and were not the forces ensuring he'd swerve away from it – as was the case with *Expresso Bongo*. Wolf Mankowitz, who always had a novelist's regard for Sellers, once calling him a cockatrice (a fabulous reptile hatched by a serpent which deposited its eggs in or on the larva of another lizard or insect as on the spot food for its own progeny), invented the rôle of a rather spivvish, openly opportunistic theatrical or musical agent, a Svengali-like hypnotist and hustler, who takes a huge percentage of his young client's earnings and whose speech patterns, ingratiatingly and automatically, adapt and meld with the accent of the people he's talking to. He is foxy; he uses others ruthlessly – and Sellers considered the offer of the part an impertinence: 'I turned down *Expresso Bongo*, the part that Laurence Harvey did, because I didn't like it. I thought that it was an incomplete part; I didn't like the script, although Wolf's a great friend of mine. I explained this to him, and he quite saw my point and quite appreciated why I didn't want to do it. He's a very intelligent fellow, not the sort who will be put off by petty annoyances. I haven't seen it yet . . . However, I still stick by what I say. It was a two-dimensional character and wasn't real. I know these characters very well, because I've lived a section of my life amongst them. I know the way they talk, the way they carry on, I've a lot of friends amongst them. I've been in the band business and know it all, and this fellow wasn't true, wasn't right. They don't act this way, they don't talk this way. And so therefore, without a major re-write, it would not have been possible for me to play it truthfully. I couldn't have sat down and said, "I've got faith in what I'm doing." I suppose if I didn't know these characters so well I could have done; I could not have shut myself up and thought, "Well, you know, it's a part." I can't do that. And so I turned it down [in favour of *Two Way Stretch*].'

☆ ★ ☆

Wasn't real . . . wasn't true . . . wasn't right: Sellers' phrases are to the point. He was quite aware, if the above speech is any clue, that the deficiencies in Mankowitz's fictional character were actually reflections of the faults and flaws to be found in his own real personality; but he did not want to confront this, or to know about it. Thus, as I said, Quilty aside, his feckless lack of moral quality was deflected and concealed behind gold bullion raids, jail breaks, scams, stings, harmless jewel thefts. The criminal fraternity, in Sellers' films from the middle-Sixties onwards, represent fun and freedom – life as a spree, a giggle. Dodger Lane, Pearly Gates, Aldo Vanucci, and their gangs, belong, like Scratch and his pirates, in the tradition of lovable rogue. Sellers gives these figures texture and he plays them as befits a virtuoso, but film after film was (his words) 'another romp like *Two Way Stretch*'. When he was successful and internationally known he avoided, like a sleepwalker keeping away from the top of the stairs, putting much of his improbity before the public.

His reaction to Mankowitz, who'd seen into him and through him, was more true to form: 'He took vengeance on me and at the time I thought his gesture totally selfish, malicious, disloyal, dishonest and stupid. What happened is that, as I had found him biggish money for *The Millionairess*, I received his go-ahead to build up Sellers-Mankowitz Productions Limited. He designed the stationery, incorporating his Daniel Mendoza portrait, and he briefed his bankers, lawyers and accountants. I personally, on the basis of Sellers' name, had made arrangements with half a dozen very important artists who'd be associated with us – like the early United Artists, when Mary Pickford, Douglas Fairbanks, Chaplin and D.W. Griffith made and distributed their own films. We'd have been artists in association who could make major deferments and therefore get some money for films which would be controlled internally. Dream stuff, because if you are successful a major takes you over, and if you are not successful you'll disappear anyway. But that was the idea. With projects in hand, such as *The Survivor*, a story about an Austrian undertaker, *Memoirs of a Cross-Eyed Man*, a satire on showbusiness, being written by Frederic Raphael, some adaptations of my own novels, and Joyce's *Ulysses*, with Sellers as Bloom, I had got finance – £250,000 in cash which was also being met by a bank; so we had half a million set with which to make relatively low-budget high-quality films. Of this company, Sir David Webster was going to be the Chairman; Jack Hylton was putting up some money; Howard Samuels, who was a socialist millionaire, was putting up money; and Lord Goodman convened the meeting. A morning meeting. Sellers and I were to attend and have all these arrangements finalised, at the Royal Opera House in Sir David's office. That morning I received by hand, half an hour before leaving my own office in Piccadilly, a letter from Sellers withdrawing from everything – on the grounds that he couldn't afford the £10,000 which he was meant to make by way of a deferment, which was nonsense; and he blamed me for doing too much, for doing too many things.'

☆ ★ ☆

Like Alun Weaver in Kingsley Amis' *The Old Devils*, Sellers was not a man you should rely on for anything more important than the way to the Gents. His treatment of Mankowitz replays, in essence, his behaviour towards Milligan, or anybody else with talent and individuality. He had to destroy them.

Looking over the vestigial paperwork of the abortive company, it is clear that (a) Mankowitz has not misremembered the episode and (b) Sellers, in wrecking this scheme, and in rejecting what it stood for, hastened his own decline as a serious actor and dissipated his greatness.

The first document of consequence is a memorandum, dated April 22nd 1960 – i.e. just under a month before shooting began on *The Millionairess*.

SELLERS MANKOWITZ PRODUCTIONS LTD

DIRECTORS –   PETER SELLERS (chairman)

Wolf Mankowitz

SHAREHOLDING	100 Ordinary £1 shares, divided as to 50 each between the two Directors.
OFFICIALS	R.D.A. Wills, General manager.
	Mrs A.M. Sagar, Secretary
Auditors	Messrs. Baker Todman
Solicitors	Messrs. Travers Smith, Braithwaite & Co.
Bankers	The Westminster Bank Ltd.
Agents	John Redway Ltd.
Managers	P.S. Management Ltd.
Office Staff facilities	To be supplied by Crispian Ltd., at a weekly fee of £15 for the time being. Exclusion Overseas Telegrams and Telephone calls to be charged separately.

A. OBJECTIVES

1. The main objects of the Company are to hold under contract script writers, actors, directors and producers for the production of motion pictures by the Company.
2. To acquire the rights to suitable properties as a basis for the production of motion pictures.
3. To produce motion pictures.

B. ASSETS

1. Wolf Mankowitz and Peter Sellers will be under contract for one year from July 1st, 1960 to the Company, to provide their services through their respective companies, as script writer and actor respectively. It is hoped to put Diane Cilento under a similar contract as an actress shortly.

2.

a. The motion picture and television rights in the book 'Memoirs of a Cross-Eyed Man' are being transferred to the Company.

b.   The motion picture rights in the book 'My Old Man's a Dustman' are being transferred to the Company.

c.   The Company has registered the original title 'The Man Who Corrupted America' with B.F.P.A.

d.   Titles under (a) and (b) will be registered with B.F.P.A. on assignment.

GENERAL

The Company's first production is likely to be 'Memoirs of a Cross-Eyed Man'. This will be scripted by Wolf Mankowitz and Peter Sellers and Diane Cilento may also star.

Finance for this picture has been offered by ABPC and Continental Distributors Inc. on not particularly favourable terms. Other possibilities are that initial finance or credits up to £50,000 may be supplied by the Directors, that the Laboratories may give credit for the same amount, that small investors may be persuaded to put up the sum of, say, £15,000 and that the bank may complete the requirement by the advance of the remaining £130,000. This is being investigated by the G.M. with Mr. Langton, the Westminster Bank, the Laboratories and sundry possible investors.

Other plans include a package deal which is now being investigated for the Company to provide the services of W.M. and P.S. to a foreign company for the making of a picture called 'The Reason Why'. This would be a Company production. [. . .] Executive producer, Herbert Wilcox.

FINANCE

In order to put the Company in funds initially, P.S. and W.M. have agreed to make loans to it, of £2,500 each, provided that a picture is made of 'The Millionairess' scripted by W.M. and starring P.S.

NOTE ON
SHAREHOLDING

The existing shareholders should agree that if at any time they wish to sell all or any of their shares to any third party, they will first offer such shares to the other shareholder at the same price as they would have been able to obtain from the third party.

Mankowitz began to solicit the interest of Walter Reade, whose firm had distributed Sellers' other films in America, for a partnership deal in New York. Reade, and Continental Distributing Inc., of 1776 Broadway, promised to co-produce and co-finance two pictures within a three year period. By June 10th, however, when routinely discussing Raphael's fee for the *Cross-Eyed Man* screenplay[*] with Bill Wills, Mankowitz started to sound a little

---

[*] Raphael, who received £1,500 for the task, says that he recalls going to see Wolf in his office above the Wedgwood shop in Piccadilly, where he was shown a big matchbox stuffed with fivers. 'I was eager to shine and to have access to his kind of matches and I agreed to write the script he wanted. He gave me a few examples of what, in his literary days, he might have called his "level of intent" (very low) and I went home to do my damnedest . . . By the time I had completed a draft, Wolf had indeed fallen out with PS and I don't think PS ever saw the script, which may account for his continuing high regard for me. We used to meet around London . . . and when we did so, Peter would say, "Amazing, isn't it, Freddie? Here we still are and they haven't rumbled us yet." I was flattered . . . to be associated with PS in the club of successful imposters.'

Raphael also told me that his view of these times is conveyed in a short story, 'Quixote/Shmixote', collected in *Think of England* (1986) – where Mankowitz is lightly disguised as Jake Nathanson:

He offered me a cigar, which I refused, and asked me to pass the oversized box of matches next to the third telephone. When he opened it, I could see that it was crammed with five-pound notes. 'Other box,' he said, helping himself *en passant* to enough fivers for six months' rent on the cottage I was living in. He still had difficulty shutting the lid. 'Think you can write comedy? Because I want somebody can write knockabout. Nothing subtle. I'll give you a for instance. Picture starts on the Rock of Gibraltar. Bloke feeding the apes, OK?

apprehensive: 'I can't understand, incidentally, why Peter's and my contracts with one another are taking so long to draw up. I really think that we ought to push them through and get them signed as soon as possible, especially as we are now entering into various commitments which are predicated by the existence of these contracts between us. If you would thump your solicitor I will keep on thumping mine, but do let's get it signed up.'

On August 26th, Irving Wormser, on behalf of Continental Distributing Inc, wrote to Mankowitz pointing out that contracts for the American co-production deal with Sellers-Mankowitz Ltd. had been sent 'several months ago but I have not heard from you. Please let me know whether you received them and what is happening.'

The solution to the mysterious silence was about to unfold. Here is the document Mankowitz received on the fateful morning:

> 37 Panton Street
> Haymarket, S.W.1
> 30th August, 1960

Dear Wolfie,[*]
Since I saw you, I have been thinking a great deal about your
new company and it doesn't seem to me, on very full
consideration, that it is going to be the right step for either of us
if I become a member of it.

First of all, I have got to concentrate on being an actor.

The Barbary apes. Throws one a banana. Bugger throws back the peel, and our bloke goes arse over tip, knocks down this Arabic princess. She slaps his face and the stupid *schnook* falls helplessly in love . . . OK, so he's this modern Don Quixote, he thinks she's an Arabic princess, whereas in reality she's a nice Jewish girl from Dalston modelling *schmuttahs* on some cruise liner anchored in the bay. This bloke, he's so ugly she won't give him the time of day, but there's more to him than meets the eye. Has to be, you're right there. I've got Peter for the part; I've got a commitment from him and that's why I can't afford to piss about with somebody can't give me the crap I want. University boys're the kind of trouble I don't need. I want a hundred and twenty pages, tops, and it's got to be a knicker-wetter . . .'

[*] When Sellers tried to soften you up with a coy endearment trouble was on its way.

Everything else is subsidiary and, knowing how worried and anxious I get about that, I simply don't want to have another responsibility which like it or not I should worry about.

Secondly, even if I became mèrely a director of your company in name only and have no other involvement, people seeing my name on the paper will think otherwise and I shall be presumed to be involved which in my mind would be just as bad.

The third point is that of money and it does seem clear to me at the moment that I can't afford the sum of £10,000 to invest without creating another responsibility which, in the interest of my main work, I want to avoid.

There would be advantages particularly in the feeding and development of ideas in the company in the way we both want, but it seems to me that if we can successfully co-operate as we have done in the past without a company, the same could apply with a company irrespective of whether I am a member of it or not. As you know, I definitely want to direct 'Polyandra' when you have finished it.* I mention this because I don't want you to think that anything I have said in this letter could interfere with that or similar projects. Generally speaking, my feelings are that my future for the next few years is [as] an actor, solely and simply, and that I must avoid any other activity which might even remotely be detrimental to my main aim.

I value my association with you in a way which we both realize and I want to keep that association loose and pliable so that it can be ready for everything called on it with no strings.

> Muzzel,†
> *Peter*

It wasn't only the timing of this letter which was implacable; its actual content doesn't add up. Why should Sellers, who never cared what people thought, care what other people might think if they

---

* Nothing further was ever heard of this project.

† Yiddish for something or other.

saw his name printed on the stationery? How does that diminish him in his own, in anybody's, eyes as an actor? And hadn't Mankowitz, with *The Millionairess*, actually demonstrated that the route to riches was to receive a percentage of the producers' take? As for £10,000: Sellers always had £10,000 for another motor car. . . ; but in case Mankowitz started to think about any of these contradictions, and had plans to march over to Panton Street and argue his corner (though in any event Sellers, he found, 'had been completely unavailable'), a second sheet of paper arrived – what in the legal world is called 'Counsel's Opinion':

The Association of
Peter Sellers and Wolf Mankowitz
and their respective companies

It seems that all parties are now agreed that the above association whatever else it does should not inhibit or prejudice the personal careers of either party. On the one hand Peter Sellers is an actor with his own particular problems and on the other hand Wolf Mankowitz is a writer who considers that he has reached saturation point in his writing and can only expand in the direction of production. It does not seem to be in keeping with Peter Sellers' career objective that he should yet engage in general production or commit himself to any major financial deal. Wolf Mankowitz, however, if he is going to have a chance of success as a producer may well have to accept some such deal.

Therefore, while the objectives of Sellers-Mankowitz will remain exactly as they were it does not appear that there is anything but danger in trying to tie either Peter or Wolf up to Sellers-Mankowitz as closely and as quickly as has been perhaps anticipated. Sellers-Mankowitz could well now become a holding company for properties for development which it will buy and develop according to its financial capacity. This capacity could be arrived at by loans of money possibly in equal proportion from Peter and Wolf's associated companies respectively for say the next two years until it has reached a point where it can finance itself in general production. To fill the next two to three years it is now suggested that Peter and Wolf and their respective companies should join together to make say four films in the next four years in which they will both be associated as actor on the one hand and producer-writer on the other. This sort of plan seems preferable to the very close-knit tie-up with all its concomitant inhibitions to the personal side and yet allows both Wolf and Peter to associate freely on a general, comfortable and smooth programme.

Having been dropped in the shit, Mankowitz was left with the humiliating task of breaking the news to the Walter Reade people:

22nd September 1960

Mr. Irving Wormser,
Continental Distributing Inc.,
1776 Broadway,
New York 19,
N.Y., U.S.A.

My dear Irving,
I'm sorry to have to report after all the trouble that you've gone to – but even more that I've gone to – that the Sellers-Mankowitz company is virtually kaput. Sellers is taking over the company and I don't know what his plans for it will be. They may involve me as a script-writer from time to time, but there's no longer a mutual commitment between us.

This dissolution has not been of my seeking and [is] probably as big a surprise to Sellers. The fact is that he really feels best able to serve himself by proceeding on his own, and I hope that he's right.

Nevertheless it does make the deal for two Sellers pictures with you quite meaningless unless you can conclude a direct agreement with Sellers himself. I have encouraged him and his manager, Bill Wills, to do this – to make a direct agreement with you leaving me entirely out. I don't know whether they will do so, but I understand that Bill Wills is getting in touch with you direct.

I fear that I lack some finally essential quality necessary to a producer. I don't know that I mind not having it. I'm only sorry that in this case my lack of it should have let you and Walter down.

Since all my production plans this year hinged on this partnership with Sellers, my situation is currently chaotic. In fact back to normal.

Yours ever,
Wolf

☆   ★   ☆

For all his avowed professionalism in his letter ('I have got to concentrate on being an actor' . . . 'I value my association with you . . .') and for all that the statement channelled through his lawyers seemed cool, sensible and empty, Sellers, in private, was pleased with his own revengefulness. Under the guise of a 'career objective', and seeming a saint when most he played the devil, he had been quite consciously spiteful; he had found a way, by leading Mankowitz on and then abandoning him, of appeasing his jealousy and arbitrariness.

'Wolf and I couldn't find suitable subjects to work on together,' he lied, adding, 'Wolf is doing so many things it's difficult to keep track of him. In my opinion, though I doubt whether Mr Mankowitz* will much value it – he has too much on his plate. He is a very strange person with so many things on his mind. In my view he should concentrate more on one thing, like screen writing, and leave the impresario business alone.'

As when he complained about Milligan, Sellers' words are impeccable, irreproachable – as a *self*-diagnosis. (He thinks himself the physician; actually he's the foul disease.) Mankowitz, neither at that time nor later, made any attempt to dissemble his own disappointment. He had been a classic gull† and didn't see any advantage in

---

* Sellers' use of your full courtesy title didn't guarantee your safety, either.

† *Gloucester*:   I do the wrong, and first begin to brawl. / The secret mischiefs that
I set abroach [i.e. that I set running] / I lay unto the grievous charge
of others. / Clarence – whom I, indeed, have cast in darkness, – / I
do beweep to many simple gulls. . .

Richard III, I,iii

pretending otherwise: 'He's not exactly on the dole, is he?' he said of Sellers in the autumn of 1960, when the press heard of the split in their indissoluble partnership. 'The truth is he has taken over Sellers-Mankowitz completely and I leave it to you to guess who got pushed . . . For six months I have devoted myself to forwarding the Sellers-Mankowitz operation and its collapse leaves me free. I am unbusy. I can tell Mr Sellers – actor, producer, director, script-writer, and recording star – that I shall be glad of the rest.'

Sellers' response to Mankowitz's comment was as straight as a hazel-twig: 'If you are sufficiently well-known and in demand you can have freedom anyway – you can set up a good subject very easily, with anyone.'

☆　★　☆

Here is the last surviving note from the saga – its epitaph:

> 37 Panton Street,
> Haymarket, S.W.1
> 29th November, 1960

Dear [Wolf]

I am quite happy to take over the payment of the Sellers-Mankowitz stationery. As you know, this will be added on to the items already listed* and, when I have them altogether, I will send you a debit note for half the amount.

> Yours sincerely,
> *R.D.A. Wills*

☆　★　☆

Whatever other relevance the foregoing little demonstration of power might contain, it is proof enough that Sellers, as a wheeler-dealer, and hence as a popular star, was not going to remain at the level of offbeat, whacky one-reelers like *The Running, Jumping and Standing Still Film*, despite what he said: 'We may do a series of

---

* The items included a bill from the White Elephant restaurant for £6-17s. 'This was for dinner for Miss Loren and Mr. Ponti.'

short abstract comedies,' he announced in March 1960, when news of the Golden Gate Award came through; before, in the next breath, completely changing his mind: 'Financially there's no money in them. From that point of view they are a waste of money and time . . . I would like to make a full-length one, not necessarily abstract comedy but a silent-film in that respect, with some music and sound effects . . . *The Running, Jumping and Standing Still Film* was done on 16mm, but we are going to do the next one on 35mm because it is so much easier.'

On standard-gauge celluloid, non-abstract and with a soundtrack (because 'these things build up atmosphere enormously'): Sellers was veering back towards the conventions with which *The Running, Jumping and Standing Still Film* had broken; and he was also getting away from any dependence on Milligan, who'd expected a break-through in his own career on the basis of that little short: 'I'd hoped people would take me up on it and use me in films for ideas,' he said to me. He recently amplified the remark in a television inter-view: 'I tried to say to people, "Look, you don't need ten million pounds to make a film, you can make one for as little as fifty pounds." I thought someone might take me up on that and say, "Hey, if you can do that, hey, he's our man." But that never hap-pened.'

When I visited Milligan for this book, in his spotless, waxed and polished house, where all the pictures are screwed to the walls with little shiny brass brackets, and where the Victorian horsehair and button-hooked chairs and couches float on two acres of snow-white carpet, like boys and girls changed and immobilised by a witch's spell, he made one remark which particularly stuck in my mind: 'Funny about Peter – Peter never ever came to me for a film script. He never said, "Spike, write me a film." I don't know why.'

When Milligan spoke these words, in his slightly tremulous thousand-year-old man way, his mood was not resentful or bitter; he was intent on conveying something much more like regret – even of concern. Not a regret for himself and his own loss, or chagrin because Sellers never made any effort to put him on a

Hollywood studio's payroll. Nothing so vulgar and imputable as that. His tone, I'm convinced, was sorrowful *for* Sellers; and there's a connection with what he went on to tell me next: 'He spoke to me on the phone from Paris. He said, "I'm a bloody fool. I've left my children nothing in the will at all." I said, "That's terrible, Peter. You work all those years and leave them high and dry." – "You're right, Spike. I'll have to leave them in it." I told Lynne Frederick this, but she wasn't interested.'

His own children; Milligan as mentor; Mankowitz as a partner: Sellers rejected them all out of the same underlying principle – mad, calculating and self-protective, he had to expel those who were not malleable or who might surpass him by, say, living longer or by being more greatly loved. He got rid of people one by one; and then, his heart being his own executioner, he got rid of himself.

* * *

Chapter Eleven
Bubble Bubble

It wasn't Milligan, therefore, who was able to capitalise on *The Running, Jumping and Standing Still Film* – but Blake Edwards, for the short was 'one of his favourite things' and it inspired the structure of *The Party*, nine long years later. 'The idea that Blake had', said Sellers, 'was that we should just have an outline, and work around it, and try and think things up. He's very good at thinking up ideas and bits and we used to work together quite well. We took for a theme an out-of-work Indian actor who's gone to America to appear in a television series, and because he was no good he got the bullet, you see; and he rolled up at this huge Hollywood party and nobody recognised him. There were some remarkably good things in that film. The end went wrong – mainly because Blake was at that time busy with getting *Darling Lili* together. There were masses of people, I remember, around the set whilst we were doing a scene with a lot of soap-suds – and people were flying in saying "Blake, we got to, hey Blake, Blake, BLAKE. . . !" And this somewhat put Blake off. He couldn't concentrate on what we were doing.'

One of the visitors to the studio, as we know, was Satyajit Ray, who to his dying day couldn't understand why Sellers had failed to grasp the feebleness of the material. *The Party* is indeed rather slow and (the chicken portion pinned to a tiara; the ever-unspooling toilet roll dispenser) dogged; and Hrundi V. Bakshi, Sellers stained a coffee colour, is a sub-continental Clouseau without a case to solve. After a prologue where he is chased off the North West

Frontier set for wearing a wristwatch, during a sequence meant to take place in 1878, and having blown up the *Gunga Din* fort by accident, the rest of the film unfolds in a Californian ranch house crammed with gadgets. The floors shift and split apart to reveal a pool; walls are made of glass; there is a stream running through the atrium – in which Hrundi loses his clompy white shoe. I'd say that the location for the party is the star of *The Party*. The building is a mixture of Ancient Rome, Sixties Americana, and Sellers' own gimmicky taste. When Hrundi fiddles with an electronic console, flames roar in a distant grate, the burbling brook becomes a torrent and the gentle fountains turn into geysers, the drinks table rotates and a public address system blasts people with muzak. It is a booby-trapped pad. Hrundi is the booby.

Like many of Sellers' characters, he is also an innocent. He slinks about the house, dignified, his hands behind his back. The very soul of courtesy. When he smiles his big toothy lop-sided grin, people are compelled to respond civilly. As when Clouseau traps his arm in a spinning globe, or Chance spouts his gardening homilies, or Nayland Smith reminisces about being chased up the Nile by a Yucatan tarantula ('the deadliest, most intelligent and highly sexed insect known to man'), the other people in the scene, by-standers and eye-witnesses, stare at this idiot, and suck on their cigars, as if transfixed. *Is* he an idiot, they seem to be thinking? Or a genius? Hrundi, as an Indian, is automatically the outsider at this Hollywood reception; but he's more than foreign. He's an alien – virtually from outer space, the way Sellers plays him. Everything from cutlery to flush lavatories seem to be objects he's encountering and fingering for the very first time. He does his best to fit into the world inhabited by the rest of us, but he misreads it (he's a Goon at sea).

'Pay no attention to me, sir,' he says, 'I'm merely spectating.' It is Hrundi's ambition to be invisible – like Chance, who says 'I like to watch.' But it is we who do the watching, Sellers who is the centre of attention. His gift, I think, is that he throws himself into these passive rôles so completely, it really does seem as if he is photographed by accident – he is not, you'd swear to it, aware of being

620

spied or eavesdropped upon. (This is how his violent characters operate, too, by being indifferent to others.) In the midst of the cinema screen, and within that, in the hurly-burly of a movie studio with all the heavy engineering of artifice, Sellers can look totally alone and forlorn. Not even Chaplin could manage that; he always had a winsome and dewy eye on the audience. He was ever ready to acknowledge applause. Sellers, by contrast, creates an impression of privacy (and of mystery). Might this have something to do with his radio apprenticeship – when he'd been all-powerful, absent-yet-present, and when nobody could see him at the end of the microphone? When I picture Chaplin, I imagine the tramp as a circus clown, peeping over his bunch of violets at the audience and suddenly showing his pearl white teeth.

☆ ★ ☆

The Party wholly lacks the nineteenth-century surrealism of *The Running, Jumping and Standing Still Film*: what it chiefly has in common with the short, in that case, is a looseness of form and a looseness of content, which all adds up to something inconsequential. That's not a totally pejorative remark. The drifting, desultory behaviour of people in their leisure moments, off-duty in the park or mingling and gossiping at a soirée, would seem to give the films whatever links to intelligibility and sense that they may possess. But the one hour and thirty six minutes of *The Party* on Warner Home Video lasts a very long time indeed. (It is a short stretched out to feature length until it snaps.) I found myself wanting to invent bits of business of my own, to fill up the time. Much more could have been done, for example, with the guests' false hairpieces, plastic teeth, costume jewellery. Hrundi, in flooding the house and washing away the Chagall watercolours down the sink, could also have undone people's nice manners and social coverings-up – he could have reduced people, indeed, to the naked barbarism and whimpering madness of Dreyfus in *The Return of the Pink Panther*. Instead of which, and God knows how, the film ends with a painted elephant being given a bubble bath – i.e. with whimsicality and nowhere near the grotesque.

It is also virtually a silent movie. Long stretches contain no dialogue or anything much beyond a soft hubbub. There aren't even the boioioinngggs! and ppflaapps! and tschinks! and tschunks! with which Tati underscores M. Hulot's mimes – and if, as Sellers said, 'Tati's an idol as far as I'm concerned, he's a great, great, great film-maker,' then why didn't he purloin a few more hints and signals from the master, not just the obvious swipe of a chãracter (Hrundi; Clouseau) who is clumsy and choreographed at one and the same time.

The best use of sound-effects in a Sellers film, as it happens, is to be heard in *Battle of the Sexes*. Mr Martin, the weavers' clerk, has an aversion to noise – so every squeaky nib in the accountant's office, every cup and saucer on Pat Hayes' rattling tea tray and, worst of all, every derisive note of Mrs Barrows' quacking American laughter, is accentuated, heightened. When a man's peace and quiet are wrecked by the ping of alarm clocks and the burr and clatter of intercoms, electric adding machines and typewriters, his thoughts, ineluctably, turn to murder.

☆ ★ ☆

With Fred Kite's heavy-set melancholia still upon him and *The Running, Jumping and Standing Still Film* (which 'as it happens . . . only took two days') in Lester's care, Sellers left for Scotland on June 6th 1959. He was to spend a week, with Constance Cummings and Robert Morley, shooting location sequences, under Charles Crichton's direction, for *The Catbird Seat,* as *Battle of the Sexes* was then called. The alleys near Edinburgh Castle were used for the situation of Mrs Barrow's flat; the hills and fields on the city's outskirts, at Arthur's Seat, became the remote island dwellings of the crofters and their spinning wheels. (The remainder of the film was made at Beaconsfield Studios, near London.)

'I remember once, we were waiting on the pavement for the light, as one did in those days,' says Crichton. 'Sellers was standing by a bus stop with his flat cap on and holding a stick, and another old man drew up, who was identical. They did a sort of slow dance, watching each other, neither of them able to believe the evidence of

622

their own eyes. They looked like twins. I wanted to turn the camera on and capture this piece of street theatre, except that we couldn't have used any of it . . .'

Sellers was now white-haired, stooped, neat, mild, and attentive. 'Just imagine a man who has spent a lifetime with a stodgy Victorian firm,' he said, 'and you will know what I am going to look like.' Mr Martin's veins seem to contain not blood but a mixture of milk and water – for Sellers almost glows, he is so snowy and pale. (Alec Guinness was the man in the white suit; Sellers is the man in the white skin.) 'I personally think it was about the best performance he ever gave,' continued Crichton. 'He hadn't had a big part like that before, only cameos and supporting roles. A leading part, and he took it very seriously. I didn't help him enough; I didn't reassure him enough. Did anybody, in fact? Because later on he always played flamboyant parts. But I think Mr Martin was *the* most considered performance he ever gave. It was poignant. He was far better at these sorts of rôles than the flamboyant parts, which I think coarse, but which did make him rich and famous. He was also very inventive. That scene where he's backing towards the kitchen door and he pulls out the knife – but it is an egg whisk. All Sellers.'

Battle of the Sexes was the first outing for Sir Michael Balcon's gathering of independent producers, Bryanston Films. Were they hoping for an international or transatlantic subject? 'Harold Hecht in Hollywood had rights to the story and he invited me to America to direct it,' says Crichton. 'I arrived in Los Angeles and there was nobody to meet me. Usually there is. I didn't have a single dollar in my pocket. I borrowed some money to call the studio, and got Hecht's office. "Sorry Charlie, didn't anybody tell you? We've given it to somebody else." They had a plan of combining it with another Thurber story. "It's all nonsense," I said, "You'll never make it." For once in my life I was right: so Danischewsky re-acquired the rights from Harold, and I'd arrived in Hollywood and went straight back home again.'

The story had begun a life as a four thousand word New York

fable by James Thurber; you'd not expect that it could have been successfully transplanted to Scotland – and when I asked Crichton 'Why Scotland?' he simply said, 'Works, doesn't it?' (Danischewsky knew Scotland very well because of *Whisky Galore,* and *Battle of the Sexes* uses some of the same actors.) And yes it does work. Mr Martin's self-effacement is a strength and virtue in Edinburgh; he has presbyterian restraint and reflectiveness. As Mr Erwin Martin, in the original, he is simply submissive – one of the millions of veal-faced losers and commuters trudging along Fifth Avenue, like one of the damned in a play by Elmer Rice. Perhaps, however, in slipping into his soft Edinburgh sing-song, Sellers missed being able to wrap his tonsils around the colourful American slang – because visitors to Beaconsfield Studios heard him muttering, 'I'm lifting the ox-cart out of the ditch all the time and I feel like tearing up the pea-pitch. But I suppose I'm in the catbird seat in more ways than one.' He'd then obligingly translate: 'Lifting the ox-cart out of the ditch means that I'm working hard; tearing up the path means going on the rampage; and being in the catbird seat means sitting pretty. . .'

The ballyhoo about Sellers' involvement in the post-Ealing company reached the front pages of not only the *Bristol Evening News* and the *Brentwood Gazette,* Essex ('A woman in business is acceptable – provided she sticks to jobs like making tea. But a woman who bursts into the quill pen calm of the accounts department and proposes introducing twentieth-century business efficiency methods – no Sir!'), but also of the *Johannesburg Star,* South Africa, and the *Malay Mail,* Kuala Lumpur ('Mr Sellers will be introduced as the head clerk in a firm of Edinburgh tweed weavers'). He was getting known. As an individual, however, getting to know him and trying to fathom him was proving increasingly uncertain.

'He was a little bit vacuous,' said Constance Cummings. 'When he was not playing a scene he sort of disappeared, like a mirage. He was not a man to hurl himself about. He took the greatest delight in Mr Martin and in these characters he played. He hurled himself into those, but he didn't throw himself about.'

'Mr Martin is sad and lonely,' I suggested.

'And Peter was a quiet man. I got the impression that he had this longing, this yearning. He felt himself to be inadequate and he was conscious of having been disadvantaged as a child. He spoke of his sad life as a child. But we never met outside of the film.'

Sellers also shrank from Crichton.

'I never knew him socially. He didn't keep up any contact with me. He was very keen, at one time, that Danischewsky, the writer and producer, he and I should continue together and make more films. I don't know what happened. He lost belief in all of us, and *Battle of the Sexes*, before it came out. Then, years afterwards, Princess Margaret said it was the best thing he'd ever done . . . and then perhaps he regained his belief?'

'The cycle of excitement and disenchantment,' I said, without surprise.

Constance Cummings was not aware of any of Sellers' doubts or denunciations. Indeed, it is quite clear that, around her, Sellers carefully kept himself secretive and in character – except once: 'Yes, he was charming, and so *quiet*, and also a great giggler. There was a scene we had where a blind man walks down the stairs. Peter and I were absolutely *finished* by this scene and poor Charlie Crichton – I don't know if he pretended to lose his temper, or whether he really did. . . Whichever, it didn't help very much. The blindman's dog was a retired police dog – so he was trained to cope with every dangerous eventuality. They'd built this rickety staircase without banisters – because the camera was meant to follow us up and down. And they got this dog, Astor, up on the platform, and he was meant to lead the blindman down. On *Action* he was to start guiding his master down the steps. Well, this retired police dog took one look down this staircase and just crouched – as if to say: "That is too bloody dangerous. I'm not going down *that!*" Still makes me laugh to think about it. Peter and I began to giggle. They had the dog at the top and finally they decided that they would shoot silently, with the trainer at the bottom hissing, "Seek, Astor, seek, seek!" trying to get this dog down the stairs. And Peter and I

The Life and Death of Peter Sellers

were standing there waiting for this man to pass us with the dog, and the dog wouldn't budge. Peter absolutely *went*. He lost all control and just dissolved. He had a sense of humour which simply couldn't resist something like that. Charlie got very cross with us, not with the dog. We were helpless. We'd be standing quite po-faced, but the minute the clapper went and Charlie said *Action* . . . both of us, *helpless*. "Seek, Astor, SEEK, SEEK!" The dog never did do the scene; but if Astor had, *we* wouldn't have anyway. . .'

'I had heard that Sellers, even then, could be difficult. A bit uppity,' says Crichton, 'but on the whole of that picture I had a ten minute argument with Constance Cummings, because she and Sellers kept corpsing, and that was all.'

☆ ★ ☆

'My role in *Battle of the Sexes* is a serious one,' offered Sellers. 'I spoke to a chappie the other day who said, "Oh yes, but it is funny isn't it?" So, perhaps I am wrong . . . It's a jolly well-made picture, lit by Freddie Francis, who did *Room at the Top* . . . Here again there are things in it that I'm not entirely happy with; but then I don't suppose I'll ever find anything that I'm entirely happy with, even in my own stuff . . .'

Disregarding Sellers' grumbles of dissatisfaction, it's not that Mr Martin is not funny because he is serious; it's more that he is undemonstrative and the humour derives from his calm looks and glances of reproach. Like Clouseau, when a doorknob comes off in his hand and he gazes at it, or a doorway leads not to the outside corridor but to a broom cupboard, Mr Martin, during the period of time covered by the film, is finding that his life has been booby-trapped – and he reacts with a cunning that he didn't know was in him. Mr Martin, says a patronising American voice-over (Sam Wanamaker) 'may not be cast in a historical mould, but, [he] is a hero just the same.' I don't think he's heroic, exactly; it's more that, confronted by circumstances which are horrible and boring (Robert Morley's pompousness, Constance Cummings' hollerings), he can apply himself to sorting it all out. And, realising that 'you can always rub out an error,' he is as agile and unruffled planning a murder as he is totting up columns of figures in his office. He doesn't, therefore, become a new or different person – he simply develops or enrichens what's already there in essence.

Like in *Two Way Stretch*, which followed immediately after *Battle of the Sexes*, Sellers, by some instinctive means, keeps very still and quiet, lets everybody else strut and fret, and steals the scenes. (He casts himself in a silent movie again – we watch, and register, his meditations becoming visible.) He is a particularly effective focal point of a steadiness and nonchalance when the supporting cast includes a high-spirited circus elephant like Morley. An elephant? I'm always put in mind of beribboned or otherwise dolled-up animals when I see Morley on the screen. In *Theatre of Blood*, for example, he plays a namby-pamby drama critic (done in by Vincent Price) who accompanies himself everywhere with at least three ringleted lap-dogs. The poodles look like macabre appendages of his own body – as if they had sprouted from his belly and are still connected to his entrails. In *Battle of the Sexes*, clad in a kilt which contains enough tartan to curtain and carpet Skibo Castle, he resembles, more than ever, one of Dr Moreau's mutants -- a turtle crossed with a Cavalier King Charles spaniel, blown up to monster size.

That Sellers' restraint, in the face of Morley's fuss, never looks like discomfiture (we don't feel he's in retreat); and that his expressionlessness is, paradoxically, expressive, is a great achievement. As soon as we see Mr Martin, a cloth-capped figure tapping his way along the street, grey-haired and never catching anybody's eye, we register his diffidence – and also his control. He is not shiftless. He is not nervous. He is careful – at the wake for old Mr Macpherson, when the others are deeply into the whisky, for example, he sips at a glass of ginger ale. He also flinches from any gossip about girls and family. (Indeed, there are no home life scenes for him – no Irene Handl, off-stage, preparing his meals.) Mr Martin belongs to nobody.

The film's first joke is that old Mr MacPherson, who entrusts the welfare of his weavery to his chief accountant, is played by Ernest Thesiger, the epicene actor from *The Bride of Frankenstein* (and a dead-ringer, incidentally, for Jean Cocteau). That this skeletal crow-like mannikin could be capable of fathering anything, let alone the hundred tonnes of Robert Morley, is a concept that belongs in the annals of exotic natural history. But Thesiger's deathbed scene at least alerts us to the exaggerations and antiquities that will be found in the rest of the building. (Is the House of MacPherson an off-shoot, after all, of the House of Frankenstein?) Mr Martin's office is piled high with ledgers, parchment scrolls and bushels of quill pens. 'It's like something out of Dickens,' Mrs Barrows says disparagingly; but the clerks, Mr Martin's underlings, are goblins out of a fairy tale forest and cousins of Henry Crun from *The Goon Show*. Mr Meekie and Mr Munson, talking in whispers and wearing wing-collars, scurry though the undergrowth of papers and sit in their little dens and cages; they have eyeshades and little cardboard sleeves on their forearms, to protect their cuffs from splatters of ink. (They are Santa's elves.)

Into this tottering edifice of speaking-tubes and controlled chaos ('I don't suppose you'd call it a system, but we do find what we want when it's needed') come Cummings and Morley. The lady is an advocate of efficiency and the application of 'psychology to business'; her rotund swain, not understanding a word of her jargon and gobbledegook, but besotted by her zest, turns her loose on his inheritance. She goes through the office building like an apocalyptic plague. From her lips, the word 'quaint' falls as a term of abuse. She is particularly contemptuous of Mr Martin's thirty-five years with the firm. 'Aren't you in the catbird seat,' she purrs. 'Baseball term – sitting pretty.' She can see that he'll have to go before she'll get anywhere.

Morley gives her a conducted tour of the premises; he's anxious about this because he hardly knows the layout of the place himself. 'You'd never think this was a chair,' he says. 'It's not,' says Mr Martin, 'it's a pair of steps' – one of those semi-circular platforms with a pole attachment found in eighteenth-century libraries. One way and another, Mrs Barrows and MacPherson manage to knock over the goblins' files, spill the glue pots and open a window, to create a whirlwind of paper. (Mr Meekie and Mr Munson move slowly to catch the falling leaves – they are enchanted by the scene.) Having, in thirty seconds, wrecked the cross-reference and card-indexed order which had taken centuries to form and grow, it doesn't take Mrs Barrows longer than a quick-fade and lap-dissolve before she has insisted that MacPherson 'break with tradition' and replace the Victorian furnishings with Fifties junk – pot plants and cactuses, ugly knobbly wire sculptures, anglepoise table lamps, abstract pictures (which resemble the commercial graphs) and graphs and financial charts (indistinguishable from the jagged Miros and Klees). In the counting house, Mr Martin and his men, still dressed for days of sail ships, gas jets and hansom cabs, crouch over answering machines and adding machines, stroking the instruments and murmuring to them, as if propitiating bad-tempered semi-domesticated pets.

Mr Martin could probably adapt to the technology; what gets to him is Mrs Barrows' personal manner. She treats the men like naughty boys. At the same time that she's jabbering on about productivity, complaining that 'we can't dwell in the past', and such, she's straightening people's ties, unmussing their hair, picking at invisible fluff, cutting them off when they try and get in with an opinion or a reply. MacPherson loves this bossiness – Morley's eyes gleam. Constance Cummings is a nanny fantasy. Mr Martin, however, you can see it, is starting to calculate inwardly. Crestfallen, because he's just been called a 'fossil', a 'Rip Van Winkle', he can see that a nasty modern ceramic, on the other side of the room, is about to drop off the mantelpiece accidentally. He makes no move to save it. It smashes – and he allows himself a tiny grin. It is an omen. He will rebel.

☆ ★ ☆

As the film chunters on, Morley's performance becomes increasingly wayward. As one of Mrs Barrows' plans is to put the Hebridean crofters in a big smoke-stacked factory, he delights in playing with the scale model of it made by the architects. It is a dolls' house and toy fort, with little twinkling lights, plastic trees and Matchbox motor cars. You suddenly think: The House of Mac-Pherson is endangered not by that meddlesome woman but by this basket case. Charles Crichton agrees: 'The picture was damaged by Robert Morley, who *overflows*. Constance hit the right level. Morley plays it like a great baby. He's not right. But at the time he was much more famous than Peter Sellers. . . .'

Morley once said: 'I don't work, I merely inflict myself on the public,' and I doubt if anybody will wish to argue with that. It was left to Vincent Price, enacting a parody of *Titus Andronicus*, to chasten him once and for all – in *Theatre of Blood* those lap-dogs are baked in a pie and forcefed down Morley's gullet through a funnel. In *Battle of the Sexes*, his poutings, sulks and whinnying voice, being pervasive, being insistent, turn him into a background noise. If we do manage to blot him out, it's only because Sellers, in making Mr Martin's face increasingly soft and sorrowful, has become the undisputed centre of attention. The buzzes of the new intercoms are finally what do it. Mr Martin creeps back into the building at night and jumbles up all the labels and codes on the switchboard. What in another's hands might have been a straightforward sabotage-under-the-cover-of-darkness operation is, in Sellers' performance, quite a set-piece – and this is what happens in the remainder of the film, now that the formalities, motives etc., are firmly in place. Sellers is given long scenes in which he can luxuriate in his character; he tries out variations on his character. As a result, drab little Mr Martin is gripping (in a way Morley's MacPherson, monotonously petulant, is not) and it is a pleasure to see him tuning the nightwatchmen's radio to a Strauss polka and throwing files in the air and snipping name tags with a pair of scissors, his midnight anarchy *choreographed*.

Unlike Kite, who is embarrassed and humbled if left in solitary confinement, Mr Martin doesn't mind his loneliness. When he allows himself a sword-fencing flourish of his umbrella at the marble busts of the MacPherson ancestors, we can see how happy he is, not being watched. (He can be himself when he's on his own.) His elation continues the following day. Morley is going bonkers, in his mission control, because the intercom's lines are all crossed (he wants Mr Meekie and he gets the tea lady), when, to add to the chaos, dozens of packing cases containing clocking-in machines for the crofters are delivered. Mr Martin smiles with pleasure at the confusion. 'You're a canny man you are, Mr Martin, you are that,' says the porter. 'Aye,' he responds, inaudibly. As the rest of the staff exit, and MacPherson and Mrs Barrows go off arguing, he does a little pirouette and tosses a handful of the sawdust packaging (again) into the air. It is an inspired, eloquent moment – and Sellers doesn't have to utter a sound.

Mrs Barrows, bested over the time-clocks scheme, escalates her side in the war: sack the oldsters, she commands, scrap the vintage car, forget tweed, send the crofters to the caves, and make synthetic fibre for the masses. Hearing this, Martin, too, is galvanised. She's put him down by calling him 'Samson' and 'my little boyscout' once too often. A Sherlock Holmes film gives him the germ for the perfect murder. If he bumps off Mrs Barrows and purposefully scatters false clues about – whisky, cigarettes – he'll be the last person the police will suspect (his transition to master criminal may be compared with John Cleese's development from barrister into jewel thief in *A Fish Called Wanda*); and his preparations for the deed result in dialogue which can only be called Goonish. He has no idea about whisky brands and blends, for instance. At the off-licence, what he wants is a flat-shaped bottle to fit his pocket. Sellers (I surmise) improvises an exchange with the shop assistant – or, at least, the muttering comes across freely, loosely. A bottle labelled 'Killwillie' seems the correct dimension:

SELLERS: Killwillie? Och, no, no. I don't like the name.
PROPRIETOR: It's a good fit and a very good blend.
SELLERS: No, no. I'd like a different name with another bottle.
(*Proprietor finds a bottle called 'Auld Aquaintance'*)
SELLERS: Try it in there; try it in there. . .

As in *A Fish called Wanda*, character is plot. In Crichton's later

film, we wait to see Cleese make his escape from the courtroom
with Jamie Lee Curtis; in *Battle of the Sexes*, we are anxious for Mr
Martin to show his mettle and do (as Bluebottle would say) what a
man has to do. The resultant sequence is excellent farce. It is as if
eggwhisks and furniture all conspire to thwart Mr Martin on purpose – like objects and animals in Disney's cartoons, which come
alive and turn human to help the heroes and heroines in their hours
of need. Mr Martin cannot really be allowed to draw blood – he
must be protected. Therefore, when he's standing on a chair and
preparing to club Mrs Barrows, she moves out of range with a milli-
second to spare (it looks as if he is merely uncorking a bottle); he
goes to stab her and the connecting door in the kitchen swings shut,
and the knife is embedded in its panels (it looks as if he'd been
using the knife to dislodge the icetray in the fridge). The scene, like
the sabotage scene and the clock scene, is a dance. Mrs Barrows is
brisk; Mr Martin is thwarted. He is about to push her out of a window when Morley arrives. Sellers speeds about the flat retrieving
his umbrella and cap, planting his evidence and covering his tracks.
We never know which door or hatchway he will be behind – it is
scrupulously done.

'My favourite scene – when he wants to murder me,' remembers
Constance Cummings. 'He thinks about pushing me out of a window; he gets the knife and sticks it in the door. That was great fun
to do. I always loved that complicated farce. You had to be very
meticulous to do it all absolutely dead in the right second – has to
be neat, neat, neat. Peter kept thinking up things to do. He did it
very seriously. Much of it Peter invented – he *took* to that. He was a
genius and he had a neatness, in the way he moved and in his
words. I'd say he was a miniaturist, with his love of precision.'

☆ ★ ☆

It was a love he would stop labouring for and lose. The later series
of Pink Panther films are hardly anything more than slapstick
sequences, for example; but the richer and more famous Sellers became, the more lethargic was his acting. Sometimes, in the martial
arts scraps with Cato, the houseboy, we see four people, if not

more, doubling for Sellers in various corners of the set. In his contract, at the behest of his insurance company, was the phrase 'The artist shall not be required to do scenes of a hazardous nature.' Define *hazardous*! To Sellers, by the middle Seventies, getting out of a parked car he considered hazardous. You never knew what he'd refuse to do or on what pretext. As Burt Kwouk, who endured the karate chops and explosions, recalls: 'Peter was a genius, and one of the reasons I say this is because he was capable of giving wonderful performances and he was also capable of giving the most god-awful things you ever saw in your life – this means that, to me, the line is very fine. If he wins, he really wins . . . This is one area where I admired him, the willingness to take chances. But it all had to come off the top of his head. In the stuff I did with him, anyway, you had to ride with him, with whatever the hell he was doing. Sometimes it wasn't easy. Because he was a major star, and the person with the most clout, and the person being paid the most, he was expected to have control, a say on this or that. But as an actor *he* needed to be controlled. He went in and he did it and everybody deferred to him – and everybody is saying, "Yeah, that's great! That's terrific. Yeah!" Which is wonderful if you are insecure, like Peter. Everybody flattering you. But he *knew* in the back of his mind that it wasn't quite true. Everything he did on the Panthers wasn't great and terrific. So he was suspicious of praise – and very suspicious, it must be added, of criticism. He couldn't *understand* why people disagreed with him; he was volatile. An up and down performer. He'd had an uneven life – and so he also had an uneven career. He had an uneven personality – all part of Peter Sellers. . .'

If the producers chucked money at Sellers, in the hopes of coaxing his talent and inventiveness into being, it ought to be mentioned that John Taylor, who was passed off as Sellers-and-Clouseau in the grave-robbing *The Trail of the Pink Panther,* was remunerated with zilch and treated without ceremony; and still he's no better or worse than the master (and his stunt doubles) when it came to falling over a lot. Which speaks volumes about the extra aura Sellers must have had. As soon as Sellers had died, and the decision was made to concoct the film from old out-takes and new linking material, 'they were pressuring me to get down to Pinewood that same afternoon', says Taylor. 'No formal proposition was put through my agent.'

The assistant director expected to use Taylor for three hours. Taylor worked for three days – the opening scene, where Clouseau is walking along the street looking at billboards; then he went into a restaurant and had a fight with a dustbin. 'Joe Dunne, who used to do Peter's stunts, was there, and gave me advice on how to fall over this bloody rubber dustbin, doing judo on it. Only after I was scraped and bruised did they think of applying towelling pads to my knees. And I was also Clouseau on the roof – looking out over the city, and getting splattered by bird droppings. There was nobody else appearing with me in any of these shots – just me, so it was quick.'

Taylor was considerate and professional – two qualities which Sellers, because he was a star, i.e. because he didn't need simply to be competent, had abandoned. As Blake Edwards puts it, when Sellers' career was at a low ebb 'he'd be co-operative and wonderful to work with'; but the moment he became famous, he was 'a monster . . . angry, sullen . . . He wouldn't show up for work and he began looking for anyone and everyone to blame, never for a moment stopping to see whether or not he should blame himself.' Hence, for *The Pink Panther*, his first adventure out of England,* he did his best; for *A Shot in the Dark*, which followed the acclaimed *Doctor Strangelove*, 'he just got bored with the part . . . and the shit hit the fan.' Sellers then made his less-than-magnificent continental films, *After the Fox, The Bobo*, and of course *Casino Royale*, so crept back to Edwards and made *The Party*, on which

---

* *The Pink Panther* was made in Rome and Sellers' fee was £80,000 for five weeks' work. As soon as he was offered the job (at short notice, because Peter Ustinov had withdrawn from the rôle of Clouseau), he telephoned Graham Stark to gloat: 'Well I didn't call him Golden Bollocks, or lucky bugger. I think I probably just said "Christ!" Such a sum was beyond our comprehension, and gave Peter the first inkling of just what it could be like out there in the international marketplace.'

'our . . . experience had been a good one'. *The Return of the Pink Panther,* five or six years later, rescued Sellers from his string of un-released features, and after that 'we got very rich' – and Sellers remained ungrounded for the rest of his life. 'I mean,' says Edwards 'Sellers was a pretty strange gentleman to begin with, but that awful heart he had apparently affected his memory. If you gave him any kind of intricate physical moves in scenes in which he also had lines, he became literally incapable of doing both. I remember a scene in *The Revenge of the Pink Panther* in which I started re-hearsing him on all kinds of funny moves that would have just been par for the course in the early Pink Panther movies; there was abso-lutely no way he was able to do it, so I stuck him up against a fireplace and kept his moves to a minimum. Under normal con-ditions, that scene would have taken no more than the morning and possibly part of the afternoon to shoot. It ended up taking about two and a half days. . . . We got more and more away from Clou-seau's character involvements and we put in more and more physical comedy so that we could use doubles for Peter.'

Sellers' dependence on, and his periodic rejection of, Edwards and Clouseau follows the pattern of his behaviour towards Milligan, Mankowitz or the Boultings: he was industrious and/or perfidious as it pleased him, his mood-swings being dependent on his sense of power. If he felt he didn't need you, he'd misbehave to make up for the times when he did have to be compliant – and the severity of his agitation and exhilaration was manic depressive. Psychoanalysts would say that Sellers had turned the director-actor relationship into a version of the mother-son bond, with all its love-hate ram-ifications. Cognitive psychologists would argue that, on the contrary, Sellers' problem was that he found his career and exist-ence unrewarding and he was therefore full of self-disgust. Other sorts of therapists might say that Sellers' early experiences, traips-ing England's music halls with his parents, had instilled a sense of helplessness.

Whatever the students of the mind might come up with, the fact remains that on *Battle of the Sexes* (to round off my discussion of that film) his ability to go from being the elderly shag with a walking stick at the start, to doing the nimble jigs in the middle of the film, and then to pull off the full-dress mazurka at the end; to make the adjustment from muffled clerkiness to sombre-countenanced would-be killer; to make his characterisation coherent, credible, and to get us incontrovertibly on his side; and beyond these basics, to imply that, hidden inside Mr Martin are other Mr Martins: this is the performance of an actor in his prime. And, like in the Keats poem about the ripe fruits, ready to decay, the plump, gambolling lambs, ready to be meat, the bee's store of honey 'o'er brimming their clammy cells', Sellers' moments of perfection were in a conspiracy also to be the commencement of his rot.

☆ ★ ☆

'Damn it! If I'm ever going to be happy surely the time is now?' Sellers said angrily to Herbert Kretzmer, at Chipperfield. 'I've got everything, everything. Two lovely kids. And Anne. God, I don't want another wife. I don't want other children except my own. Well, what's wrong? Why can't I be happy now? What am I looking for?' At first he thought his goal might be financial. 'I think the ideal thing,' he told the *New York Times Magazine*, on March 27th 1960 (when *Battle of the Sexes* was about to open in America, and when *I'm All Right, Jack* and *The Mouse that Roared* were still doing brisk business) 'would be to work like stink, get somewhere, have a nice house, give your kids a good education and have enough money – say £200,000 – to sit back and think, "I don't have to work any more."'

When Sellers allowed himself the leisure to meditate, however, he achieved no complacency, but other things. He was bent on making his aspirations and desires into anxieties; and even happiness was to be feared and could induce a depression, because (a) it wouldn't last and (b) if it did, he'd get jaded: 'I tried to think about what is happiness, and I suppose it is those brief moments that come to you – that you can say, "My God, I'm really happy today," or something's happened. . . And then it goes – and I suppose if you had happiness all the time, you'd probably get blasé with it; you'd never appreciate it when it came along.'*

Sellers talked of happiness as an object, a possession, not as a condition or a state. Death, similarly, if his talk about being snap-frozen and warmed up by scientists at a future date is to be believed, was another commodity – an optional one at that. Death, indeed, he took as a personal affront. It implied how little he counted. Hence, I think, during his marvellous years, 1959 to 1963, his decisive efforts to summon up remembrance of things past. He'd outwit time by going back in time. 'How do you fancy a week-end in Paris?' he asked David Lodge. 'I'll take Annie, you bring a girl, and we'll recreate some of those times we had at the end of the war.'

John Osborne had written *Look Back in Anger* four years pre-viously as an invective against the hypocrisies and illusions people take out of the past; Sellers looked back angrily too – but his rage was the rage of the sentimentalist who *wants* to impose false colours on yesteryear, who *needs* to deceive himself that he can grow young and fresh by retrospection. Sellers booked rooms at the Hotel Favart, by the Opéra Comique, where he and Lodge were quartered a decade and a half ago. His Rolls took his party to London airport, and on arrival at Orly, a Columbia limousine trans-ported them to their billet. They had lunch at La Fouquets, went to

---

* Sellers, in dwelling on loss, joy, glory, transience, etc., seems to be re-enacting the history of English Romantic poetry – like Barry Humphries, who writes in his memoirs: 'Twenty years ago [. . .] I walked one sunny morning down Lower Regent Street [. . .] Half way down the hill, I had to stop, and sit on the doorstep of a shop. I had the most extraordinary sensation that something was seriously wrong, and I was convinced that I was having some kind of heart-attack. For a while I sat there, panic-stricken, breathing deeply and wondering when I was going to pass out. In front of me the legs of pedestrians endlessly scissored past. Which leg I wondered, would I grab, and cry to its owner: "Quick, for God's sake, get a doctor! On this sunny day in London, I am dying." But I did not do that: I sat a while longer on my doorstep until I decided I was not dying at all. With a rush of joy I found at last the label to my strange and alarming condition. I realised I was happy.' (*More Please*, London, 1992; page 315ff.)

a cabaret at the Chantilly, and then moved on to hear some jazz at the Blue Nun. *Up the Creek* was unspooling in Montparnasse and Sellers was met and made a fuss of by Kenneth Hyman, the executive producer from Allied Artists and Seven Arts (for whom he would eventually make *Lolita* and *I Love You, Alice B. Toklas*).

Such a trip would make anybody walk tall – not Sellers. Despite the retraversing of his past, in order not to feel an erasure, all this new opulence and applause did was serve to remind him how tenuous was the hold on fashion and fame. He knew he could lose it as quickly as it had come to him. 'I accept myself,' he said uncertainly in December 1959, 'but sometimes I get worried. It's success that does it, I suppose. You worry about how long it's going to last. You have a marvellous living. You're suddenly able to afford a vast mansion in Chipperfield . . . And you wonder how long it's going on. And you wonder how long *you're* going to go on.'

When the band of brothers called the Goons broke up, and he moved out of London, and on to the international circuit, Sellers repined for his early days at the Ilfracombe Pavilion, in Ralph Reader's Gang Shows, and his gigs as a drummer: 'I'm not really afraid of being poor. When I was poor I was happier – I didn't worry. [Now] I get terribly depressed . . . I get *terribly* depressed; suicidal; black!' He took out his frustrations on the fabric of Chipperfield Manor itself. 'This is quite perfect,' he announced, showing a visitor the blossom in his garden in June 1960. He then insisted that all the beautiful apple trees lining the lawn had to be cut down. 'Why weren't they with the rest of the fruit trees in the orchard?' he complained, very testily, when people objected to his vandalism. ('Dad didn't think he had done anything wrong,' says Michael.*)

Chipperfield's sense of history, the spirit of it as a place which had persisted across the centuries, started to irk him. Sellers remembered that, when he visited the empty house to arrange for the re-wiring, somebody had said to him: 'It will be ten years probably

---

* 'O if we but knew what we do/When we delve or hew/Hack and rack the growing green/ . . . After-comers cannot guess the beauty been.' G.M. Hopkins.

before the villagers accept you.' He returned to this comment and took offence. He sloped off on his own to eat a Chinese meal at the Shangri-La, Brompton Road, and started to resent his wife and colleagues who had 'talked him into going on with' the purchase of a stately home. *Ten years!* He wasn't going to wait ten minutes: 'One tries to create roots,' he said 'it's vital for the children. I want to get them settled, so long that they have a feeling of belonging somewhere. But they've probably inherited my restlessness. They never seem to mind moving.' In other words, Sellers was going to unseat and disorientate his brood whenever he felt like it; they were assumed to have no opinions which might diverge from his own.

'He was monomaniacal,' Michael said to me. 'The world did revolve around him, especially as brought up by Peg. So it's not a case of saying: fame made him lose touch with reality. He'd never had much to *do* with reality. And suddenly he went on private jets; he walked into customs, and if they gave him any trouble, he'd stalk straight through and say "Fuck you, I'm off." He was nearly arrested once and had to be warned. "We know who he is, but technically he should be arrested for what he's just done." He then decided he had a fear of flying, so we went to Rome on the train – fabulous luxury. When he was doing *The World of Henry Orient* in New York, we went on the *Queen Mary* – and on that ship the second-class and the first-class couldn't swim together. They used to empty the pool and refill it for the first-class passengers . . . There was no way you could get a fix on him: on the one hand he ran down other people who thought the sun shone from all their orifices; but in the same way, *he* had that public figure disease. . .'

'He'd have wanted the pool emptied and filled yet *again* for his personal use,' I suggested.

Michael laughed and then said, 'My father wasn't actually with us on those trips. He'd have summoned us but we'd be on our own; or with his secretary or a nanny. We turned up on his boat the year before he married Miranda, 1969; I was fourteen or fifteen. I arrived in Venice for a cruise with him around Italy to Monaco. We got a water taxi which took us miles to his yacht. We drew up beside the boat, he was on the deck and he threw *his* bags into *our* taxi. "Where are you off to?" I said. "Back to England." – "But I've come to be with you – and to see you." – "Sorry, love. I've got to go." With that, he disappeared. I'd seen Miranda, actually, back at the airport crying, and getting on a plane and presumably he went back and made it up, because the next thing I heard was: "We're getting married. Isn't that great?" If I'd said *"No"* that would have been a real rocker. Like with Lynne: "Aren't you going to congratulate me?" I didn't say anything. I didn't ring him up. Nothing. Then one day he forced me to mutter, "Yeah – congratulations."'

☆ ★ ☆

Sellers behaved as a potentate. That was fine in the context of *Brouhaha*, or in any of his other Ruritanian or Arabian fantasies; it was a bit harder to take when he was autocratic in his home life – his imperialistic attitude extending towards, and encompassing, even his guests. 'In the early days he was wonderful company,' says Herbert Kretzmer, 'especially at Whetstone. But come Chipperfield – he wasn't a lot of fun to be around eventually. He became increasingly friendless. There were a lot of people he'd *known* for a long time, a Peter Sellers "crowd" or "gang" that was often at his country house, but he began to go out of his way to hurt people.'

Wolf Mankowitz, who remains unforgiving over the saga of the Daniel Mendoza colophoned production company, would agree with this assessment: 'Sellers very quickly started to live a very expensive and expansive life, and he was spending money on a large scale – so he suddenly started to look as if he was a much bigger star than he was. One of the shittiest effects of his sense of elevation was that he began to regard the rest of humanity, writers, producers, people who'd helped him get on, other actors not quite on the Sophia Loren – Cary Grant level, as his own personal court of performing dwarves.'

Mankowitz was *used*; Kretzmer had a taste of the fitfulness, too. 'Sellers would encourage and more or less commission projects. People would get put to work in a fever of enthusiasm – and then, Sellers' own enthusiasm not lasting the night, he'd get Bill Wills to be the bearer of bad news. I went through one of these experiences. We were going to record an album of children's comedy songs; and on the day he came to hear them at a flat in Queen's Gate that had a piano, almost the first thing he said was, "Right, let's get on with it. I've got a driver outside." People had been so excited to know that he was coming. It was impossible to get anything going with a man who has got a car waiting outside. We'd anticipated, and deserved, a couple of hours to play a dozen songs.'

These songs, incidentally, would have involved the same team as 'Goodness Gracious Me', the duet Sellers had sung with Loren, in their characters from *The Millionairess*, and which had earned him five thousand pounds in the first few weeks of its release on disc: 'I mean, what would bring in the same money?' he said. 'And let's face it it's bloody good money. Yes, there are the records, too. . . The cheque came in and I looked at it, and it was for five thousand quid. It was a record which got into the Top Ten. At the time I hardly knew what the Top Ten meant – I suppose I knew they were tunes. . .'

'He tried to get out of doing "Goodness Gracious Me",' recalls Kretzmer: 'He didn't want to do it finally, though the theme of the heartbeat and the doctor, and the idea of a song to push the film, was all his inspiration. He'd liked it originally, but he went off it. He'd even insisted on a B-side, "Bangers and Mash", because he'd taught Sophia Loren some Cockney slang. It was George Martin who said, "We've got Sophia Loren coming to EMI Studios at ten o'clock on Saturday morning, and I'm coming to fetch you at nine." He was dragged into the studio.'

☆ ★ ☆

Sellers' contempt was severe – abnormally severe. There was no healthy scepticism or wisdom about his judgements. He was simply easily piqued, disbelieving, resentful. He was 'basically not a nice man', says Blake Edwards with commendable understatement. 'I would defy anybody to tell me what was nice about him.' The best illustration of this, in the Chipperfield period, is the famous Graham Stark-in-boot-of-car story. The full dress version goes like this: Stark receives an urgent phone call from Sellers in the early hours of the morning; he puts a mackintosh over his pyjamas and whizzes over; Sellers is standing next to his new car, holding a piece of chalk and a torch: 'There's a rattle or squeak coming from the rear of the car, I can't place it, can you help me trace it?' (Those sorts of things always made Sellers crazy.) Stark has come all this way, is relieved that there was no genuine emergency, and says, 'OK, let's get on with it.' Sellers says, 'No, – you've got to climb in the boot.' One thing leads to another and Stark does indeed end up in the boot, with Sellers driving around North London, steering on and off the kerbs to accentuate the squeak – meantime Stark, using the implements he'd been handed ('Take these'), the torch and the chalk, is making little circles and crosses where the sound was coming from; and of course the experiment had to be at dead of night, to cut down on any competing traffic noise. 'They had gone four miles down the road,' Michael tells us in *P.S. I Love You*, 'when Dad was stopped for speeding by the police.' In Stark's own account of the episode,[*] he says he had been persuaded ('in a moment of weakness') to climb into the boot because Sellers had called him a 'fellow lover of fine machinery, a connoisseur of quality merchandise *and* his closest personal friend' (italics in original). It is impossible to imagine Sellers using such words without, at the very least, the hint of sarcastic edge, and so events must have proved: Stark –

> gingerly climbed into the capacious boot, carefully holding up the lid by a few inches. Ever so carefully and slowly did my friend drive, but neither he nor I reckoned on the sod's-law factor, namely the young moron in the sports car who cut Peter up very savagely. Reflex actions are hard to control and Peter put his foot down and off we went. The lid slammed shut, I bounced up and down in the darkness, while carbon monoxide filled the cramped space at an alarming rate. . .

Only when the racing vehicles came to rest at a red light did

---

[*] To be found in his book, *Remembering Peter Sellers*, pages 40–41.

Sellers remember that Stark was still concealed in the luggage compartment, conscientiously doing as he'd been bid, with torch and chalk. Now, whether it was night or day, whether people were actually wearing pyjamas, whether the constabulary was involved, whether or not there was indeed a sports car which Sellers felt compelled to chase, whether there was any bumping off and on to the pavement etc., it remains that (a conflict of material evidence aside):* (a) the story is not apocryphal in essence and (b) it is open to a wide variety of interpretation.

Milligan, incidentally (and this ought to be of interest to a psychiatrist), has at least twice claimed that *he* was the dupe. On *The Don Lane Show*, recorded at the Comedy Theatre, Melbourne, sometime early in 1980, he was playing the piano and entertaining the audience when Sellers and Irene Handl ('the famous composer') appeared via satellite from London. 'Spike, why don't you have a chat with Peter, out of character perhaps?' suggested Don. Milligan proceeded to tell the squeak-three-a.m.-call-out-car-boot story: 'This is true, for God's sake believe me . . .' – 'That's right, Spike' responded Sellers flatly. The second occasion he projected himself as the stooge was in a story called 'Peter Sellers' Rolls-Royce Christmas';† and this time around it is December 24th and snow is falling yet. The policeman opens the boot 'to find an unshaven tousle-haired man. . . in his pyjamas on his knees drawing little white crosses on the floor . . . "Oh, it's *you*. Merry Christmas" . . .'

To Milligan, the point of the story is Sellers' formidable single-minded nuttiness; it is a gag from *The Goon Show* come to life. (He refers to 'my lunatic friend Peter Sellers', 'my loony friend', 'what

---

* Yet another variation (Alfred Draper's) makes Sellers out to be lunatically absent-minded: '. . . during the drive Sellers spotted a business acquaintance, stopped the car and went for coffee, completely forgetting the actor in the closed boot. It was only much later on his way home that Sellers heard the desperate hammering in the boot and remembered Stark . . .'

† Collected in *Scunthorpe Revisited*, edited by Jack Hobbs, London, 1989, pages 11–13.

was he getting at?') Sellers is crackers, you feel, but also mesmerising; you, too, would have been tempted to become a party to his schemes, because you'd want to discover how the surrealism will be resolved. You are in the presence of a magician – one who (after reading Michael's account) can turn an accomplice into a gull. For when Michael tells the tale, there is no build up, or absurdity – just 'one day he put Graham Stark. . . in the boot to trace an annoying rattle'. Suddenly, Sellers is hurtling along, oblivious to Stark's discomfort; and what all this indicates, plainly and horribly, is that, to Michael's father, human beings were a stage further back in his concerns than machines. The car had a squeak; so what if Stark was bruised and asphyxiating? This is also the lesson the reader takes away from Stark's own paragraphs, too: Sellers considered himself a perfectionist. If he hadn't solved the problem of the rattle, he'd have changed the car. If anything went wrong with his possessions, he'd throw them away, his patience would snap.

Taking these variations and facets together, there is still one element missing: Sellers the prankster. I cannot but suspect that along with the goonishness and/or the pernicketiness, a large part of him thoroughly enjoyed the thought of a poor boob being locked in the trunk. Similarly, when shooting the scene, in *The Pink Panther Strikes Again*, where Stark is a Bavarian innkeeper puffing on a meerschaum, Sellers 'went into convulsions' because the pipe had been surreptitiously filled with marijuana. Stark, who didn't discover the reason why until months later, says his head 'felt as if it was stuffed from ear to ear with cotton wool, and as if the tympani player from the Royal Philharmonic was . . . thumping both my temples'.

People skilled at practical jokes are the reverse of good sports; they enjoy watching the suffering they inflict on the nice and the innocent – but is there anything else they gain by it? W.H. Auden, in his essay on Iago, 'The Joker in the Pack', has this to say:

> The practical joker despises his victims, but at the same time he envies them because their desires, however. . . mistaken, are real to them, whereas he has no desire which he can call his own. His goal,

to make game of others, makes his existence absolutely dependent upon theirs; when he is alone, he is a nullity. Iago's self-description *I am not what I am,* is correct. . . If the word motive is given its normal meaning of the positive purpose of the self, like sex, money, glory, etc., then the practical joker is without motive. Yet the professional practical joker is certainly driven, like a gambler, to his activity, but the drive is negative, a fear of lacking a concrete self, of being nobody. In any practical joker to whom playing such jokes is a passion, there is always an element of malice, a projection of his self-hatred on to others, and in the ultimate case of the absolute practical joker, this is projected on to all created things.

☆ ★ ☆

There we have Sellers. His complaint (or boast), in a thousand interviews, that 'I have no personality of my own. There is nothing I put forward as specifically me' – his credo of dullness and blankness – is actually the most dangerous thing about him. By insisting that he was the actor's version of the writer's empty sheet of paper or the painter's dun canvas, he wasn't telling us what an expert artist he was, getting all those different voices and expressions to peter across his face; he was telling us how alienated he was. Constance Cummings found him quiet, charming, unassuming – may not they be the same aspects as somebody who was remote and withdrawn, filled with a kind of fear?

'Though he was different in every film,' Miss Cummings said to me, 'you never asked, oh, who is that in that part? You knew it was Peter Sellers. This recognisability, when they are transformed, marks out the greatest actors – Larry Olivier, for all his false noses – you never said, who's *that*? If Peter kept himself to himself, when I worked with him, it's because, behind it all, he was afraid he'd be *found out*, in real life, as an unfunny man. I thought he was a bit like Willy Loman, and he'd have been terribly good in that play, wouldn't he?'

Olivier fondled the idea of being in *Death of a Salesman*, too. Willy Loman's contradictory mix of heroism and phoniness, sentimentality and flashes of nobleness; his crassness, his lying, his despair, his sheer *talkativeness*, has an instant appeal for any actor (the play is mid-afternoon soap opera blown-up to Shakespearean size) but it wasn't Arthur Miller whom Constance Cummings sent Sellers' way – it was Marcel Pagnol. *Mister Topaze* had been translated and adapted by her husband, Benn Levy, and made into a film with John Barrymore in 1933.*

'*Mister Topaze*,' she explained to me, handing over the crumbling folder containing Levy's original notes, 'is about a very mild schoolteacher; it's quite a funny play. I saw it in New York with Frank Morgan. He gets corrupted. Finds he has a hidden talent for shady deals. Becomes a dynamic man, through deviousness – not honesty. *Perfect for Sellers*. He must have recognised something deeply congenial in the material, for he directed it. One of us put Pagnol into his head. I wonder if Benn suggested it, or whether I did, because he'd be so *right* for it.'

☆ ★ ☆

Mr Martin gives thought to murder, Mr Topaze to fraud. The romp which Sellers rushed into making immediately after *Battle of the Sexes*, however, was *Two Way Stretch*, in which, as Dodger Lane, he's an habitual, not a new or would-be, criminal. You can't imagine Dodger's life without its lock-picking, safe-cracking pursuits; he exemplifies what John Huston would call 'a left-handed form of human endeavour'. 'I think it's a good idea to do that kind of thing now and then,' commented Sellers – did he mean break the law? Appear in a simple crowd pleaser? Or walk from one film to another without a break? It was now December 1959. He'd made

---

* 'It is difficult to convey this film's effervescent quality because in the wit there is sadness and in the sadness there is wit. John Barrymore is the bearded old professor whose innocence in a world of lovers and rogues is the fundamental joke. From this seems to spring a whole garden of satirical philosophy. In the end he shaves off his beard, blackmails his associates, makes whimsical advances to Myrna Loy, and distinguishes himself as the biggest rogue of them all.' *Sunday Referee*, April 30th 1933.

'John Barrymore gives manifestly one of the finest performances which the audible screen has produced.' *Cinema*, March 15th 1933.

The theme of the knowing innocent was irresistible.

pictures at such a lick, there was skirmishing amongst the people who fixed schedules and premières – and *Two Way Stretch* beat *Battle of the Sexes* to the screens by a fortnight. Sellers himself had his work cut out, inspecting his performances. He was in the middle of shooting *Battle of the Sexes* at Beaconsfield Studios when his previous film, *I'm All Right, Jack,* had its first non-rough cut preview in Soho. Anxious beyond measure to see how it had turned out, Sellers organised a fast car to take him to the Beaconsfield Cricket Club ground when his day's work as Mr Martin ended. From there he was whisked, by specially chartered helicopter, to the South Bank Heliport, where another fast car was waiting. . . The dash cost him £200. (Approximately a year's wages for a girl shop assistant.)

As for *Two-Way Stretch* itself – it was not stretching, but it is revealing. If you turn back to page xii, you'll see it's the film in which I first encountered Sellers, on a television double bill with *Wrong Arm of the Law,* all those years ago in Wales, when I was whiling away a Saturday afternoon, blocking out the roar of the rugby crowd, and semi-listening to my father, in the butcher's shop, chopping the Sunday joints (and hence it's where this book has its point of origin). Sellers is stripped of make-up and eccentricity; he does not add decades to his demeanour, and his voice is unreconstituted Cockney. Dodger needs a haircut and to go on a diet – and so might he therefore resemble the real, young, flabby Sellers? The one known to David Lodge during the war? (Lodge is perfect as Jelly Knight, Dodger's grinning chum in the choky.) Indeed, instead of ageing himself for once, Sellers is going in the other direction. Dodger's giggles, the pettiness of his crimes, his one-track mind in respect of his girlfriend, Ethel, all suggest a juvenile offender. If, at first sight, Sellers doesn't seem to be exerting himself much, on second glance we can appreciate that, to knock a decade and a half off his real estate (thirty four), and to remove, or suppress, his own airs and peevishness, all his skills as a dissembler are being employed. And he holds our attention, this sagging, plump Peter Pan, by keeping still; he makes lethargy dramatic: we sense the craftiness which has gone in to getting people to wait on him. (When he wakes up and is coming round, he laps his dry lips – exactly as Chance does, when he is getting up out of bed for the day; and Chance, too, is totally spoonfed.)

Sellers spread easily into the part. 'You *feel* with Peter as he reaches for a character,' said Robert Day, the director. 'He works his way towards the perfection of the rôle.' Which he must have reckoned he'd reached without ado, because the actor certainly enjoyed showing visitors the set ('come into my cell') and explaining the plot, not something he'd do when in a tizzy. 'I'm afraid I am rather an unrepentant law-breaker. I like my comforts, as you will observe.' The contraband in the gaol, the cooking outfit, the wine and spirits cupboard, the well-stocked larder and portable radio: it was like Peg the hoarder's flatlets during the war. 'I don't take kindly to eating in the prison dining room,' Sellers continued. 'I have two cell-mates, Lennie and Jelly. We consider we are doing a favour for the Governor when we get him some stones for the rockery. Soapy (Wilfrid Hyde-White), in the guise of a padre professing to look after the welfare of the prisoners, is one of our former confederates, and has plans for a million pound robbery. He has a scheme to smuggle us out of prison.'

Hyde-White, also, didn't mind giving away the story: 'Dodger Lane, Lennie Price and Jelly Knight have nursed a grudge against Soapy Stevens. They believe I shopped them on a mail van robbery. The Governor and Chief Prison Officer Jenkins are due for imminent retirement. Contented with their lot, the three prisoners await their pending release, until I arrive on the scene. I reveal my plan to seize a million pounds' worth of diamonds from a van passing near the jail on the night before the three are due for release. If they can get out of prison and back again without being spotted . . . they will have a cast iron alibi and a fortune. I also seek the help of Lennie's mum and Dodger's girlfriend . . . who is waiting to put up the banns after five years of somewhat chaotic courtship. It is an amusing and unusual part for me.'

Unusual? Hyde-White, like Cecil Parker, was at his best when

playing a caddish variation on his gentlemanly screen persona.[*]
(Like Major Bloodnok, he had the affability of a man who'd not
think twice about robbing the regimental cash box.) But what *is* distinctly unusual, in all this exegesis by Sellers and his co-star, is that
no mention is made of the character, and actor, who bursts through
the film like a shipwreck flare – Lionel Jeffries' Sidney Crout.
Crout, the martinet prison guard, not only has the best line ('Silence
when you are talking to me!' – appropriated by Sellers in *What's
New, Pussycat?*, when Fassbender hurls the logical conundrum at
his wife during a fight); he also has the best comic sequences. E.g.
the dynamiting of the quarry. 'What are you afraid of?' he sneers at
Dodger, Jelly and Lennie, as they dive for cover. 'A little bang?'
Crout emerges from the explosion and smoke, his clothes in ribbons, his face streaked with soot – exactly like Clouseau, in *The
Revenge of the Pink Panther*, who survives bomb blasts with his dignity intact, and whose still-smouldering uniform ignites Dreyfus'
office.

Sellers was jealous of Jeffries' crackpot performance, and no wonder. Crout's normal level of speech is a scream – he's a screaming
skull – and far from being 'over the top' (as Sellers sneered), the
point of the characterisation is that the man's anger has to be contained. As much as he'd like to, he can't run amok. The peak on his
cap is as sharp as his beaky nose; his shoes are polished to a mirror-
brightness; the crease in this trousers could sever a limb. Crout, you
feel, is under intense pressure not to sob and thunder (we can virtually see the steam whistling out of his ears); he knows it is an
achievement to get through half a dozen words without the suggestion of a shriek. It is a brilliantly strangulated performance; and
Sellers made use of it twice. The correctness, the observer of protocol, the man who remains exact and diligent in his job, no matter

---

* Life eventually conjoined with art: Hyde-White frittered his money away on the
race track and was declared bankrupt by the Inland Revenue. He died in debt
and neglect in America, on May 6th 1991, unable to afford the fare back to
England. Though (it goes without saying) I'd written to him for information on
Sellers, he was slightly senseless by the time I'd begun my research.

what disasters befall him, is clearly Clouseau, as those scorched pants signified; the high-pitched rage is Dr Strangelove. The Nazi inflections breaking through; the rogue arm flying off to give a salute: these mannerisms derive from Crout, sitting in Commander Horatio Bennet's office, and having to listen to a talk about the rehabilitation value in basket-weaving and fretwork classes. Crout, using all his powers of will to prevent himself from having a fit, says he'd rather go for rock breaking and the treadmill, if it's all the same by you. . .

Crout is a demon in a pantomime, yet also curiously credible, i.e. unique. As I said back in the Introduction to this book, his drive to hunt down deviants, and his serpentine walk, which intimates his inner twistedness, are the Marquess of Queensberry's, whom Jeffries had recently played in *The Trials of Oscar Wilde*. Queensberry, in addition to persecuting Wilde through the law courts, devised a set of rules for the art of boxing – in this, and in respect of his personal brutality, he was a temperamental descendant of Dan Mendoza. Jeffries, you'd be forgiven for thinking, was getting more like Sellers than Sellers in respect of the outlandishness of the parts he took – and this wasn't lost on at least one of the pair of them. They met again on *Wrong Arm of the Law*, another mirage of Ford Consuls, Jaguars, and Sunbeam Rapiers. After the first fortnight, when Sellers had been playing the gangland dressmaker, he realised that the best rôle was Jeffries' policeman, Nosey Parker – infuriatingly so, because Sellers had originally been given the choice of the two parts. He suspected Jeffries of again stealing the film. 'Lionel, I've made a mistake – it's *your* film. I've picked the wrong part.'

Sellers, as ever, was avenged. 'He was professionally and personally jealous of anybody he was making a film with,' says Hattie Stevenson. 'He'd organise a row, an argument. Lionel Jeffries – he was furious with him. *Two Way Stretch*, *Wrong Arm of the Law*; he was really angry, and tried to put him down. . .' After his heart attack in 1964, he asked Ray Galton and Alan Simpson if they had a quiet little story which would suit him. They had a draft screenplay handy called *The Spy with a Cold Nose*. 'We arranged to meet Peter

Sellers, now married to Britt, at Elstead, one Sunday,' recalls Simpson. 'We gave him the script and he started falling about at the first gag. He was giggling so much we thought he'll be having another heart attack. He loved it: "We'll produce it ourselves – do it all ourselves. We'll have Lionel Jeffries and myself as the vet and the doctor. . ." Then he couldn't decide which was the best part to play and he kept excitedly changing his mind. He got as far as hiring a studio and we were very excited because he was so keen. Then we had a call to see Bill Wills, and we thought, that's OK, we have to sort the money and contracts out. Peter was not there. "Peter said to tell you he can't do the film. He's already under contract to Charles Feldman." – "Surely he knew that when we saw him?" He'd already long signed to make *What's New, Pussycat?*; but Peter thought contracts didn't matter. He believed he could always rearrange things. Typical Peter Sellers: over the moon; the next day not interested. For three or four weeks he had us all running around. Then, again typically, he didn't tell us himself he was out. It was very frustrating and annoying. *The Spy with a Cold Nose* was eventually made with Laurence Harvey and Lionel Jeffries. Peter Sellers and Lionel Jeffries would have been better.'

☆　★　☆

Sellers avoided Jeffries until 1978, and *The Prisoner of Zenda*, when, suddenly, 'he claimed a paternal relationship with him', says Simon Williams. 'He would phone Lionel at all hours of the night, saying he wanted advice on this and that. He treated David Tomlinson in exactly the same way on *The Fiendish Plot of Dr Fu Manchu*'. The odd thing about this is that Jeffries was actually a year younger than Sellers (and Tomlinson was only eight years his senior); but nearly two decades on from *Two Way Stretch* and *Wrong Arm of the Law* etc., Jeffries had changed out of all recognition. The thin, angular, manic tenor of Crout and Parker was now a bewhiskered, baritonal old codger; and Jeffries had long since ditched nasty or wayward characters in favour of the crusty grandfather (*Chitty Chitty Bang Bang*) or the nutty knight in armour (*Camelot*). In *The Prisoner of Zenda*, as General Sapt, he doesn't have much to do except wear a thrilling succession of Austro-Hungarian uniforms, each plastered with medals, ribbons, frogging – he's the image of the Emperor Franz-Joseph. And as the films which Jeffries himself had directed (*The Railway Children, The Amazing Mr Blunden,* * *Wombling Free*) suggest, the actor's tastes were now for soggy nineteenth-century near-classics, with a Disney-ish gloss; he had (like Guinness) relinquished his fervour. And therefore (to Sellers) he was no longer competition.

It was not uncommon, however, for Sellers to be exceeded. George C. Scott's ape-like General Buck Turgidson, in *Doctor Strangelove*, is funnier than the President, the RAF officer, even the mad doc himself; and Sellers, who was meant to play the Texan pilot, too, 'was infuriated, really frightfully angry', says Hattie Stevenson, 'that Slim Pickens played the part so well in the end'. When I watch the later Pink Panthers, it is Herbert Lom's repertoire of nervous ailments which I look forward to most, by way of laughs; and for sheer, immediate mirth, it is often not Sellers who is the cause of the tomfoolery. In *Mister Topaze*, for example, he is upstaged by Leo McKern's bumptious M. Muche, the headmaster, who roves about the ramshackle school buildings, inspecting the torn charts, flicking the dust, and pocketing stray pencils. His eyes dart and jitter, his nose is always sniffing, his eyebrows are huge and bushy – he's like a jack-in-the-box. And he's not the only character who is pantomimically overblown. Ernestine, his daughter, played by Billie Whitelaw, moves with a cartoon trot and wiggle; in her red frock, and carrying a bottle of red ink ('I'll open it for you, if I may'), she is a caricature of pertness. Michael Gough, as Tamise, Topaze's fellow academical clerk, is so abstracted, he has his head in a Latin grammar when he's doing the cooking; he is so poor he wears his overcoat indoors ('gets a bit cold in here when the gas runs out'); and he is so tall, when he bends or turns, his body becomes a human question mark. Then there is Nadia Gray, as

---

* With the eighteen year old Lynne Frederick (playing a much younger Victorian schoolgirl called Lucy), making up to an elderly ghost, played by Laurence Naismith.

Suzy Courtois, the torch singer, who is clad in more leopard skins, furs and stoles than Norma Desmond in *Sunset Boulevard* (her cigarette-holder is two foot long – it's a wand); or Martita Hunt, as the (farting) Baroness,* who almost seems in drag: her hat is like a huge crescent moon, which casts her face into an eclipse. When she draws herself up to her full height, the camera pulls downwards – so the illusion is she's actually *growing*.

Given that Sellers directed the film, and therefore masterminded the stage effects, we can see how he pushes his cast into giving redoubled, vaudevillian performances: Muche paces up and down, ready to pop; he plucks at his beard; he puts on his pince-nez like a visor. Herbert Lom, as Castel-Benac, the crooked financier, also wears out the carpets with his agitation. To signify his wealth, it isn't any old château he lives in – this one is marble from the cellars to the attics, and there are indoor pools and cages, here and there, containing ibises and peacocks. And Sellers, who with Lionel Jeffries had encountered the Marquess of Queensberry, now met Lord Alfred Douglas in such a setting of gilded cherubs and music boxes – John Neville is the young cad, Roger, a blackmailer; he is elegant and has a touch of frivolity. He might have been cast through his tailor.

Indeed, what with the music-hall-sketch structure of the scenes, the exaggerated silent movie melodramatics of the acting, the preposterousness of the costumes and the painted decor: the film, all crazy appearance and surface texture, has been assembled from a wicker skip belonging to the Ray Bros. For if, during the early years of this century, a camera had been trained on a touring theatre company's production of a French musical, it might look like this. (*Mister Topaze* is a musical without any music: the cast falls easily into tenor-baritone-bass, soprano-mezzo-contralto registers.) Except, that is to say, for Sellers himself. Topaze, who says, 'I am completely alone in the world,' is also alone in avoiding the artificiality which otherwise, and elsewhere, prevails. Sellers has surrounded himself with flamboyance; he remains muted and

---

* See page 372.

small-scaled: the very thing he's *not* is frenzied. And he's the one we watch. When he is sacked from the school because he won't improve a dunce's exam results, his hurt somehow registers right to the depths of his woebegone beard; and he walks slowly off. He's kind and scholarly, and looks for the good in people, and the object of the film, is his refusal to be degraded. 'A lot of things are different,' he says at the end, when he is wealthy, 'but it doesn't matter so long as the man inside is the same.' Of course, without it's having to be said out loud we can sense that the inner man has altered – he's become disillusioned. All he has to do to get people to throw away their principles is to say 'How much?' *The Magic Christian* is thus the sequel to this film. *Mister Topaze*, in spite of its French carnival background, gets to be bitter and dark. Its message – that everybody is basically cheap – is summed up in the cabaret number (written by Herbert Kretzmer) sung by Suzy the vamp:

I like money and I'm not afraid to say so,
Although it sounds unfeminine and brash,
The pound, the franc, the yankee dollar,
The rupee and the peso,
The language doesn't matter if it is all hard cash.

(*I Like Money* was the film's American title, incidentally). Sellers, by being unremitting, has made acting itself a form of detachment. Topaze is at the centre of the story, and yet also, implicitly, commenting upon it, above it. And this is an extended example of what happens in other films. Sellers has the ability, paradoxically, to be the focus of attention at the same time as he's diffuse. Other actors are full of comic flourishes; he is the one who stays in the mind. Hence, George C. Scott's chimpanzee whoops and grimaces are not funny until juxtaposed with President Merkin Muffley's deadpan expression of reproach. Herbert Lom's mad giggles and twitches are the funnier because of Clouseau's contrasting calm and genuine concern. So it goes. In *Only Two Can Play*, Graham Stark's Mr Hyman is the definitive portrayal of a dirty old man haunting a public library; he paws the books on medieval Welsh pantyhose and virtually ejaculates across his gaberdine. This is quite funny (it is like a skit from the 'Freds'); for its full effect, however, it requires Sellers, as John Lewis, to lean across the desk and, half bored and half disgusted, to take the volume from Mr Hyman's grasp, and rubber stamp it. (You can see that what he'd rather do with the book is fumigate it.) The scene has purpose in the furtherance of nuance. We can tell from Sellers' expression that Mr Hyman represents a nightmare version of Lewis' own thwarted lusts; after another decade of unfulfilment, he might be the one, creeping about the stack, hunting out the rude bits, eyes a-gleam.

Stark, like Scott and Lom, is the comedian; Sellers is the straight-man. At his best he was always the straight-man.* In *The Million-airess* he's the straight-man to Sophia Loren; in *Woman Times Seven* and *Being There* he's the straight-man to Shirley MacLaine; in *There's a Girl in my Soup*, he's the straight-man to Goldie Hawn. There's nothing chivalric about this. Sellers doesn't peaceably step aside and allow these ladies their laughs. On the contrary, he is very much in evidence, implicitly mocking feminine silliness – especially that scene in *Being There*, when Shirley MacLaine's Eve is masturbating with a vengeance, rolling over the rug and rubbing herself obscenely against the bedpost, and Sellers' Chance looks away, to find the television more interesting. (The scene is *effortlessly* Sellers'.)

When he is forced into slapstick, however, in the later Pink Panthers, or in *Waltz of the Toreadors*, in the scenes where General Fitzjohn falls off a balcony into a waterbutt, something essential to Sellers' talent is getting demeaned. Where his skills lay was in apprehending some other person's quirks, turning them over in his

---

* America's funny straight-man was Jack Benny. In 1956, Sellers was contracted to appear on a Jack Benny television special being recorded in London. During the rehearsal, however, Benny spoke to his director, Ralph Levy, and insisted that Sellers had to be removed: 'Our deliveries are so similar and our tempos are identical. It will hurt the laugh reaction.' Sellers was replaced as guest star by Sean Connery.

mind, and reacting. He reacts at top speed in (say) *Lolita* or *What's New, Pussycat?*; he reacts with dinosaurian slowness to the world about him when he's Chance the gardener. What I seem to be leading up to saying, here, is that Sellers, the once upon a time radio voice and mimic, was able to convey, to perform, the shiftings and changings of thoughts and dreams, i.e. things that are outwardly neither noise nor movement. He stands there and his inner turbulence is registering.*

☆ ★ ☆

Sometimes it was Sellers' personal sensations which got in the way of his characters' consciousness – as he admitted. 'I'm thinking, when I'm working, only about that work,' he said, referring specifically to his glazed expression on and off the set during *Being There*. 'Shirley MacLaine couldn't figure me out at all; she just couldn't. But Jack Warden did; we were great buddies. And Melvyn Douglas, jeeze, I found myself in scenes with him where I was so carried away with the force of his acting that I forgot my lines. Almost by just looking at him. The whole experience of making *Being There* was so humbling, so powerful. And I'd often say, "Cut!" and people would come running, saying, "Is anything wrong? Don't

---

* A good example of this is in *I Love You, Alice B. Toklas*. It is Harold Fine's wedding day and he is standing at the altar. All the time that the cantors are spouting from the scriptures and the congregation is shuffling expectantly, we can see that Harold is coming to a momentous decision. He's building up to his decision to bolt. He turns to his bride: 'You don't really know me, Joyce, *I* don't know me.' He marches out up the aisle and throws away his wedding weeds. Suddenly he's in a suede jerkin, bare feet and beads. 'We have left the machine,' he intones, 'and by so doing have opted for survival.' A guru says to him: 'When you stop trying to know who you are, you've found who you are.' Harold says: 'I'm trying to stop trying' – a line which Sellers can't but deliver without irony.

  The Los Angeles Jewish lawyer-into-hippie is one thing; what interests me is the agitation that Sellers is able to convey beyond the surface calm and civility. Harold always looks as if he has a headache, he's sullen and he's permanently *embarrassed*: embarrassed by his Jewish momma, his clients, his intended, his car, his new hippie friends. Sellers, immensely detailed, conveys the man's unsupportable tensions.

you feel all right?" And I'd say – and I know this is a bit Chance-like to say a thing like this – but I'd say, "Oh no. I've just never seen anything quite like this film."'

In other words, Sellers' receptivity to another actor's versatility had very definite limits. If Douglas was excelling, Sellers would ruin the take, by coughing, drying or coming out with some gobbledegook excuse. It had for a long time been thus. The all-star bill of *Murder by Death* was a torment. ('Maggie Smith's a dear girl. She lets me shine her Oscar twice a day. Even tips me for polishing the bloody thing. What more can you ask of a co-star?') I have already mentioned, in earlier chapters, his bad behaviour over Orson Welles in *Casino Royale*, and John Cleese in *The Magic Christian*. It wasn't so much that he was competitive; the problem was that he was such a bad sport. 'He was very envious, Sellers, of other actors,' says Wolf Mankowitz. 'I'll never forget the occasion when Orson and I, two rather large fellows, were travelling down in the lift one day in Grosvenor House, which was where Charlie Feldman was operating. The door opens and Sellers was there. At that time Sellers was not talking to Orson, and he was none too keen on me, either – because I'd never done him anything but good and I'd helped raise him up to an international level. He wouldn't go down in the lift with us. He said it wasn't safe. Orson was very pissed off, "What the fuck is he talking about?" – "I think he means the combined weight, Orson," – "What the fuck does he weigh anyway? Skinny as a shrimp. *Looks* like a shrimp, come to think of it."'

Sellers ranked his dieting amongst his major achievements. Not that being slim and slender improved him as an actor; and maybe a lot of what was unpleasant about him can be traced to his vanity. 'I used to write his fan letters and sign them,' confesses Hattie Stevenson, 'but he used to sign all the photographs. He was very, *very* fussy about what picture to distribute. He used to find one he liked, then he'd get bored with it. Actually, he didn't like any of the ones that were taken of *him*, as opposed to him playing a rôle. He wanted to look dashing and debonair – the image he later created in *There's a Girl in My Soup*, which, I'm telling you, he didn't foist in real life *at all*. He hated himself as chubby and bespectacled. He was really unhappy with himself. Later he nearly had anorexia, in a male kind of way: "Look, Hat, I'm so *thin* now."'

Sellers was happiest when he felt superior. That the members of his audience who troubled to write to him were so insignificant, his private secretary was instructed to forge his responses, is a measure of his indifference; of how *disdainful* he could be. He claimed to hate it when strangers tried to speak to him: 'They'd shout to me, "'Ullo Pe'er, 'ullo Bluebottle . . . There's Pe'er Sellers; 'ow are yew Pe'er . . ." You couldn't really say it was a name; it came out as one word: Pe'rse'r. Taxi drivers would say to me: "I seen you. Harry Secombe: very funny it was" – even the name would be the wrong name.'

The way Sellers went on, you'd think he was the only famous man in history to be misidentified.[*] The journalist David Lewin was once alongside him walking down a London street. 'Are you Peter Sellers?' asked a woman timidly. 'Not today,' snapped Sellers, refusing to break his stride. This rather goes against the grain of his belief that he was 'so plain-looking, so average, I don't see how you can tell me apart from anyone else in a crowd'. He was, in fact, punctilious about how he was to be approached and addressed. 'In private I always called him Peter, but in the office and in company he insisted on "Mr Sellers",' says Hattie Stevenson. 'He was adamant about this. He used to get cross about the familiarity of the "darling", "love", "Pete" stuff of the film studios. Didn't like that at all. He absolutely *hated* to be called "Pete".'

Sellers wanted the respect and awe accorded to a god. He was absent yet present; invisible and anonymous, yet also needful of

---

[*] He could have taken heart from Peter Ustinov's story about being identified as John Huston's father ('you're Walter Hustonov'); or perhaps from this account: 'I sat for a while on a bench in Oxford Street. It was very nice until a chap on a bicycle stopped by me. "I know you," he said. "Oh, yes?" I said. "Yes," he said. "You're Sir John Gielgud," he said. "Fuck off!" I said. Then I walked home. It was a lovely night for walking. So many stars.' Sir Ralph Richardson, quoted in *Blessings in Disguise* by Alec Guinness (page 275).

ceremony. Simon Williams recalls the 'regal feeling' which swept the ballroom and coronation sets during *The Prisoner of Zenda*. 'The lights and the camera, the extras and the supporting players, would be prepared. The cast would be called in ascending order of importance, Lynne Frederick being beckoned penultimately. Then Mr Sellers himself would deign to grace us, surrounded by this train – Michael Jeffery, his dresser, Harry Frampton, his personal make-up man. It was the second-unit director's job to ensure that Lynne wasn't seen talking to me or to Stuart Wilson when Sellers appeared on the set. It was *insanity*. Because he'd recently had a lot of skin removed from his neck, by plastic surgery, he'd get very irritable about the costumes. He'd start losing his temper, twitching in annoyance, and a real Sellers accent would spurt out – he'd be sounding like the Jewish boy from Finchley, instead of upper-class like Jeremy Lloyd.

'Sometimes he simply didn't materialise, in any shape or form. Or he'd rip the Prince's or Frewin's moustache off, revert to being angry, and he'd just go – without explanation. Richard Quine would have to think up things to keep the crew looking busy for the rest of the day. Close-ups of sugar bowls, anything. Quine was an old man, broke, he hadn't worked for years. Sellers was nothing but nasty to him. We all felt acutely embarrassed, and Quine did commit suicide soon afterwards. All Sellers wanted was to be spontaneous. The comedy had to come to him when he did a scene the once – and then he'd fuck off. Sometimes he'd radiate displeasure and you'd wish you could say, "What is it you don't like about the way I'm doing this scene?" He wouldn't help. And if you were obviously good and funny he'd let you know he felt threatened by it. "Come on – you can't have it both ways," you'd feel. . .'

Both ways? Sellers wanted it every which way; and, by the end, there was no pleasing him. Piers Haggard, who'd watched helplessly as Sellers systematically destroyed the script, the shooting schedule, the performances of other actors, and just about anything and anybody not nailed down, during *The Fiendish Plot of Dr Fu Manchu*, says that the star had overshot any normal definition of madness; Sellers was in a fairy tale region all of his own – and the worst thing was, he was bolstered, and encouraged to stay there, by the spinelessness of the producers, who'd have let him get away with murder so long as he completed a film. 'Nobody would say to Sellers, at any time, "If you do not turn up you will be sued." Nobody, at any point, did anything stronger than threaten to phone Marty Baum, Sellers' agent in Los Angeles. How may that have worked? We were in Paris. It was like the Court of the Mad King – where , if the King says, "It's black"; it's black; if the King says, "It's white"; it's white. If the King says, "Everybody wears no socks today," everybody wears no socks today. Whatever it is the King wants, is enacted; whatever it is the King might want, is imagined; and whatever it is the King wanted yesterday – it is remembered, in case the King might want it today, or tomorrow. And everybody at the Court of the Mad King is reduced to a neurotic gavotte to no purpose – and that is what it was essentially like working with Peter Sellers.'

☆　★　☆

The Court of the Mad King was underway nineteen years earlier, at Chipperfield, where Sellers had installed (in miniature semblance of Charles Foster Kane's private menagerie) two dogs, a cat, a goose, and an aviary of songbirds. He also wanted to add people to his collection – a human zoo. Kenneth Griffith – on anybody's estimation a most brilliant creature – could see what was going on and didn't seem to object: 'There was an area where he admired one as a curious person; and he had great imagination, and he wanted to express affection and professional respect, because he'd take to you as a *character*. He was an inspiration; he made you laugh. He was audacious. He had a creative vision that soared above most. . . .'

Yes, indeed; but he'd also devour you, give him half a chance. Herbert Kretzmer had noticed that Sellers no longer invited his guests, he summoned them; or, worse still, he was starting simply to expect their presence: 'I remember one night in Harry Saltzman's flat in Adam's Row where he got insane. "I don't see enough of you," he said. "Why don't you come out?" – "Peter, all you have to do is phone and I'll gladly come out . . . I just don't want to hang around. . ." That angered him. He actually bunched his fist and hit the wall between us. I mean really *very hard.* "Life has been diffi-cult," he said by way of explanation. "Why don't you show more sympathy?"'

Sellers never appreciated that other people might have an exis-tence beyond the compass of his own. One of his persistent anti-social habits was to telephone people when he knew they'd be asleep. Once, in Los Angeles, he wanted Alan Clare, who was in London, to recite the lyrics of 'Eaton Square Blues': 'What time is it over there?' Sellers asked Ken Barnes, who was with him in Cali-fornia preparing the *Sellers' Market* album. 'Two a.m.' – 'Right, let's get the bugger up.' Ben Arbeid, the producer of *Hoffman,* told me that 'Sellers was forever phoning at two or three in the morning – no qualms about rousing people from their slumbers – like a dicta-tor.' The most extreme example of this ego-centrism would be funny if it wasn't proof that he was completely off his head. Sellers threw a tantrum because Piers Haggard was in the lavatory. 'Very late one night, I was in the bathroom and the phone rang and it was Peter. My wife answered and said something quite harmless and really normal, like, "Hold on a minute – I'll get him." I came to the phone – but telexes flew to his lawyer, agent, Orion about how my wife had been rude to him. We got calls all through the night about this, from anxious executives in Hollywood; and my wife had cer-tainly not been rude to him. That is a vivid example of how *insanely* touchy he was.'

On another occasion he kept Lord Snowdon on the phone for hours – Snowdon eventually terminated the conversation as gently as he could – it was nearly dawn – and a telegram promptly arrived: 'WHY DID YOU HANG UP?' Another time, because Lynne Fred-erick, who was living in Los Angeles, wouldn't answer her phone, Sellers sent Michael Jeffery, who was with him in Gstaad, all the way over to California by jumbo jet to knock on her door. ('She was still out,' says Jeffery, 'so I stuck a note on her car.')

The only person known to have told him to go to hell when he rang at a god-forsaken hour was a Mrs Wolfenden, landlady of a boarding house on the Isle of Wight. As he floated out of reality, it became increasingly impossible for him to have friends in any normal sense of the word. He was unknowable, like a phantom. You never knew what form he'd take – or how he'd sound. 'So many people ask me why it is my voice constantly changes depending on whom I'm talking to at the time,' he said. 'Like an American accent when I'm talking to Americans. It's because I don't have any actual voice of my own. I don't ever do it intentionally, but it happens. It's very difficult to sustain a voice for any length of time without letting it tail off after the first week. I try and completely absorb it so it goes right over me and into me. . .'

Constancy was obviously an intolerable effort. He set up any number of false appearances and employed Theo Cowan, a publicity agent, to help with the circumvention. Cowan, who told me that the press were always after Sellers, helped to nurture a popular and likeable image. He fended off newspapers in the midst of his client's marital mishaps and heart attacks ('I told the press that Peter was fit and that "he went cycling yesterday"'). He encouraged interviews and lunches with sycophantic journalists; he protected Sellers from the kind of profile-writers who'd have exposed the Arch Goon as a shit. Cowan saw his job not as generating gossip and news-breaks, but (as he said to me) 'in husbanding the garden, getting Peter to avoid storms'.

Behind the façade, or back in the potting shed, as it were, Cowan knew all too well what a monster he had germinating. 'You could never plan ahead. For twenty years I worked on an hour-to-hour basis. I got used to his reneging, in the morning, on a promise he'd made the night before. The secret, if you were to ride with him, was to listen first and gauge his mood. You'd say, "Let's think that over, Peter . . ." He was not a man who could deal with permanence. Everything was *now*, how he felt *now*. His mood could change in the middle of a sentence. You'd go to a restaurant with him – "Marvellous place, love." He'd ask for something, Château this or that. They haven't got it. He'd get up and storm out, and leave you there. . .'

By his very nature he was friendless – not because he was loutish and tactless particularly (qualities which, in any case, it is possible to put up with); or because he was implacable and distrustful. He was isolated because, as Milligan put it when Sellers was still alive: 'He wants to be accepted as normal when he knows he's not . . . The real Peter Sellers will have vanished long before anyone gets too close – perhaps the enigma is more real than the man himself?'

To give this will-o'-the-wisp at least the appearance of being functional Sellers had business colleagues; there were usually executives on hand to discuss a forthcoming film; he had lawyers clocking up their fees and agents extracting their percentages – but unless he felt you were a subordinate he was filled with apprehension. Thus the importance to him of his secretary and valet – the retainers, servants, people who were paid to keep him company. 'He never wanted you to have time off,' says Hattie Stevenson. 'He wanted you to have no life of your own. I was sacked so many times, you wouldn't believe it, and always over the most idiotic and footling things. He'd lose his temper, or if things weren't going right, then you were out. We were in New York once, and he was in the process of buying Elstead, and he was waiting for the plans to arrive. Every morning he'd say to me, "Have the plans arrived?", as if I was purposely withholding them. "No." In the end he got really furious and shouted, "Right – well you're fired." So I said, "OK, *fine!*" I'd been working about two years with him. "*Fine.*" I got on the phone and started to make the reservation for my flight home. About half-way through the day, he poked his head around the door again: "And what's more, you can fly back Tourist Class." Then he came back later on and said, "Next week, remind me to. . ." This was his way of saying you're not going; he'd forget about it. I could cope with that – it didn't bother me. I used to find it quite amusing. Another time, he fired me in front of the whole world. It was the *Waltz of the Toreadors*' première. The reviews were being dictated to me over the telephone from New York and I couldn't hear what they were saying very well; and I only got half of it down. I said, "Leave it with me. I'll type what I've got and call back." I arrived at the première and he bellowed down the stairs with all the stars there, including royalty, "Have you managed to read your own shorthand yet?" If he was in a foul mood, you just *ran . . .'*

Hattie's male counterpart, in Sellers' entourage, was Bert Mortimer, who approached his women. 'I . . . got the job of obtaining the phone number or address of a girl he had heard about. Yet while I was ringing around getting the information, he would look into the mirror and say, "Why do they want me? I'm not handsome."' Mortimer, a big strong bloke, also fetched and carried for him, drove for him, cleaned the cars, cleared up after him generally, bailed him out, and covered for him, every day between 1960 and 1977. He was Sellers' bodyguard, and if nobody tried to attack him, Sellers would try and create complications to justify the incumbency. One night, for example, they were out dining in Cyprus with Titi Wachmeister, the daughter of the Swedish ambassador to Washington. When a middle-aged man at an adjoining table, quite innocently and civilly, leant across to speak to Titi, Sellers flew into a jealous rage. He made Mortimer drive him back to the house. He shoved all Titi's belongings roughly into a suitcase, and they returned to the restaurant, Sellers, by now foaming at the mouth. Titi, embarrassed at having been abandoned, had joined the man and his girlfriend – and the three of them were now confronted by Sellers, who resembled a Hogarth portrait of a Bedlam inmate, brandishing the suitcase above his head. 'In a blind rage,' says Mortimer, 'he threw it on top of their food and wine and ordered Titi back to England on the next plane.'*

As he knew that Mortimer would always spirit him to safety, Sellers could luxuriate in violence, or threats of violence. Mortimer was a form of conspicuous expenditure, conspicuous consumption – Sellers consumed another man's life with his own puny desires.

---

* Some accounts have Sellers flinging the Vuitton suitcase on the *wrong* table, the clothes and dirty laundry springing out and covering a group of totally innocent diners. But this sounds too much like Clouseau.

(Mortimer used to joke: 'My wife said that if we ever divorced she would cite Sellers because I spent more time with him than with her!') Another formidable person he tried to exploit, though he was never on the payroll, was the stuntman Gerry Crampton – who scaled ropes for John Rhys Davies in *Raiders of the Lost Ark*, rode the horse that reared over Ben Kingsley's head in *Gandhi*, dived into the acid bath for Jack Nicholson in *Batman*, and has fallen through plate glass windows for Michael Caine time without number. When I met him he'd recently returned from a wrestling bout with a Siberian tiger.

'I'm not an actor, so I was no threat to him,' this courageous operator told me. 'And I didn't need him, because my speciality is big action films. I knew Peter from *The Millionairess* onwards. We had a great time on Ischia doing *After the Fox*. He used to like to see me dive-bombing into swimming-pools, when the Italians were lounging along the edge. That gave him the giggles, seeing them scurrying. But on that film I was virtually twiddling my fingers. One car chase, one fall – but he just liked me around, Peter. He asked me to be on all his films. I'd say, "Peter, I'm a stuntman, what can I do?" On *Ghost in the Noonday Sun*, I organised five stuntmen and we played pirates for five months. Sword sharpening, climbing up cliffs and castle walls. But other than that . . . I worked on *The Blockhouse*. I fell off a roof when the fighter plane comes over; I doubled for the man who was punched in *Casino Royale* – I escaped that film to do *The Dirty Dozen*. I did no end of fights in Chinese restaurants in the Pink Panthers . . . There was a gymnastics scene in *Soft Beds, Hard Battles;* and I went to see him when he was shooting off the Fulham Road on *The Optimists of Nine Elms*.

'But mainly I was always getting Peter out of scrapes; somebody would upset him on the set, or in a night-club, and he'd call, "Gerry". He used to ring me up at all odd hours. I was at the Britt wedding and the Miranda wedding. I was invited to the Lynne wedding, but I was in India. Lynne, when she found out about me, said, "He's just a stuntman!" The Britt wedding was all set up as a gigantic home-movie production. David Lodge was the joint best man with Graham Stark, doing a commentary. I took five heavies, from the stunt boys, down to Elstead with me to stop the press from invading the place – and once the press realised they weren't going to get any joy, we went indoors for champagne. The Miranda wedding was at Caxton Hall, with a reception at Tramp's. On that occasion, Bert Mortimer was the best man. Her two pekinese dogs were the bridesmaids. And then I was the usher at his memorial service. I showed Olivier in. "Who are you going to put me next to?" I sat him down next to Bernard Cribbins.'

☆ ★ ☆

Cinema may be a world of illusion ('magic time' in Jack Lemmon's irritating phrase), but as illusionists go, Gerry Crampton and his team-mates actually have to do all the brave and death-defying things which the actors get given the credit for on the screen. Sellers, when he wasn't treating them as his personal Praetorian Guard, was shrewd enough to know that the stuntmen made him look good; and he liked to believe he was in league with them, could knock about with them. Stuntmen appealed to Sellers because they were the cinema's link with circus and tumblers – i.e. with his own origins as a descendant of Daniel Mendoza, the showman boxer. The last film he saw, on television at the Dorchester, the day before he died, was John Wayne's brutal and shameless *Brannigan* – in which the Duke, as a Chicago cop, chases around modern London wishing it was the Wild West. 'Father identified many of the stuntmen appearing in it as those he had worked with at some stage in his career,' recalled Michael. 'His mood brightened . . .'

Crampton, when he was in charge of the dare-devilry, would often put Joe Dunne in a shot to double for Sellers. ('Joe could imitate his funny walks.') Dunne and his family now live in Hollywood, and they remember Sellers with amazement. 'I saw what he could be like,' Joe said, pointedly, in a letter to me. 'I never socialised with him outside of work, ever . . . In Cyprus he had this house to which we were all invited one weekend. Myself, Ann, my wife, Matthew, my son. When we arrived, we were met by Bert who told us Peter had decided to go back to England . . . He constantly had arguments with Tony Franciosa, on the set of *Ghost in the Noonday Sun* – so much so, that eventually Franciosa's close-ups were shot over my shoulder, with me doing Sellers' dialogue. The stars wouldn't work on the same set together . . . He had a memory you couldn't believe – he would mimic all the old radio shows. He would mimic anybody and he could keep us laughing for hours at a time. Then, the next day, he wouldn't say a word.

'After *Ghost in the Noonday Sun*, Sellers asked for me on *The Return of the Pink Panther*, and he insisted that I was on every one of his pictures; *The Pink Panther Strikes Again*, *The Revenge of the Pink Panther* . . . He said I was his "good luck charm" and that he had to have me. I worked on *Prisoner of Zenda*, with Richard Quine's American stunt co-ordinator, George Robotham, and when I visited Los Angeles, sometime in 1978, I left a message for Sellers to say I was in town. He called back a few days later, very early in the morning. He was just off to start *Being There* (a movie which obviously required no stunts) and he ended the short conversation with, "I'll talk to you when I get back." We never spoke again. I'd suddenly fallen out of favour and was no longer the "good luck charm". Once Lynne Frederick entered his life he dropped people who'd had a relationship with him that was longer than his new wife's . . .* When he was preparing *Fu Manchu*, he had the production manager call me and offer one day's work in the following

---

* Bert Mortimer, after sixteen years of service, was dismissed in a curt letter, handed to him by a hotel chambermaid when he was getting ready to join Sellers and Lynne on a yacht. 'I couldn't help but wonder that Lynne wanted to do herself all the tasks I'd been performing for Peter,' Mortimer told the *Sunday People*. 'When they returned I stormed into their room and demanded an explanation. Peter was highly embarrassed and asked if we could come to a compromise. The pair stayed on while I returned to England – still supposedly working for him. But the matter didn't rest. I soon received a similar letter to the first – and my life with Peter Sellers was definitely over.'

Others whose employment was terminated at this time include Denis O'Brien, Sellers' business manager; John Humphries, of Travers Smith & Braithwaite, Sellers' lawyer; and Theo Cowan, Sellers' publicity manager.

Of this personnel, Cowan died on September, 13th 1991; Humphries was left

December. I didn't even reply. I'd worked tremendously hard for not very much money and had made Sellers look great for seven years – so I had been offended when, for no good reason, he'd dropped me. But he continued to send Christmas cards, written in his own hand, as if nothing had happened. When he decided to make *Romance of the Pink Panther*, he suddenly decided he couldn't make it without me. I was his "good luck charm"! I didn't want to work with him again – so instead of turning him down flat, I tried to price myself out of the job. I asked for an enormous amount of money. The producer said he'd get back to me. He called the next day. Sellers MUST have me. They would pay me my fortune. I still didn't want to do the movie, and of course it was never made. . .'

Matthew Dunne, who today is Blake Edward's assistant director, has a signed photograph on his wall – a still from *The Pink Panther Strikes Again,* which bears the inscription: 'To Matthew, with sincere wishes, your dad's double, Peter Sellers.'

☆ ★ ☆

Picking people up and discarding them; behaving wretchedly and expecting others to cope with the mess; cancelling, or simply not turning up, for flights and cars which had been booked by Theo Cowan (a minor sin in the scheme of things, but crappy and symptomatic); the importance of a valet, a Jeeves figure, who as Wodehouse would say, 'in this matter of shimmering into rooms is rummy to a degree'; duplicates, doubles, decoys: Sellers, bolstered by his retinue, was monarchical. And his largesse was monarchical. Kenneth Griffith again:

'*The Bobo*. He insisted I should be in *The Bobo*, you see. So we are in Cinecitta, and I am with my lady, who became my last wife, and

---

£5,000 in Sellers' will; Mortimer now works for Max Bygraves; and O'Brien got into dispute with Sellers' estate. When, as a result of Rickless *vs.* United Artists, the estate was paid a million dollars' damages (plus interest and costs) for the posthumous out-take compilation *Trail of the Pink Panther,* O'Brien, as Sellers' former manager, claimed that, by virtue of a 1977 agreement which allowed him to participate in certain films where he also acted as Sellers' agent, he was entitled to a share of the money recovered from MGM-UA.

we lived in a little apartment up a narrow street in a colourful part of Rome. We lowered a basket on a long piece of rope for our groceries. And Sellers had a great grand villa outside Rome with Britt Ekland, who is in the film, that was a bit of a nightmare, too. However, so I said to Sellers, who had the Rolls and Bert – whom he later betrayed very badly, who was his close, good, loyal decent chap – Peter was capable of that sort of thing – and anyway, I said: 'Peter, you are living in the midst of this beautiful countryside, why don't I come out, and we'll go for a walk?"

'"Fantastic, Kenny! Tomorrow!"

'I went to this fantastic villa. We had some lunch. Then he says, "Bert, get the Rolls out." – "What's this? We are going for a walk?" He says, "Drive Kenny to the Spanish Steps." We got to the Spanish Steps.

'"Bert, pick us up in a hour's time."

'He immediately turns to the left, down Rome's equivalent of Bond Street. He's walking – and he's not accustomed to walking, you see. Then we come to this shop I've never heard of called Guccis.

'"This is a very good shop, Kenny, let's have a walk round in here." So he walks in. "Oh, Mr Sellers, were the shoes all right?" – "Yes, excellent." He'd bought a dozen pairs. "Fine, beautiful . . . Kenny, I've got a friend who has a birthday. You've got such good taste, what do you think I ought to buy?" So I said, "Male or female?" – "It's a man." – "An attaché case, something a chap has every day, which you've given to him and not only is it a nice thing, but he thinks of you every day . . ."

'"Thinks of you every day, ha? Marvellous."

'So there they are, all arrayed, and he says, "I do think you've got such good taste. Brown or black?" – "These things are so subjective, but being a Welshman I'd go for black, but that's the Welsh puritan in me."

'"Bring out all your black cases."

'Dozens of Gucci cases brought out. "Kenny, which in your opinion, is the best?" – "Well that one's beautiful."

'"Put Mr Griffith's name on it, will you?"'

'And he gave it to me. Tears touch my eyes at the memory of the man, for all his failings and the things you hear against him. . .'

Was it generosity? Or an inducement to make Griffith think well of him? Once Sellers started to be able to support his fantasies he splashed jewels and presents around – not because he was generous, but because he had no sense of the reality of money. As Blake Edwards says, Sellers was very *very* selfish: 'I mean he was generous – quite often he would give all kinds of gifts – but they were bribes. He was generous in material things, not really generous in his heart because he really didn't know how to do that. When I say "generous", he was generous because he had his chums, he would see to it that they were hired. That was to ingratiate himself and make himself liked, among other things.' As Griffith concedes, there was possibly an ulterior motive tucked away inside the Gucci briefcase – but when Sellers tried to collect the favour he now considered owing to him, he found he'd picked the wrong man:

'On *The Bobo*, whatever Peter said, was. We were in Spain and then Rome. One day I came to do a scene and Peter was directing, and Robert Parrish was sitting in the background. Nothing was said to me – no explanation. *Nothing.* And so I carried on – and he was really coping with Britt Ekland. I remember we went to about thirty-six takes, and I was bang on every time, and I knew if she got it right. . . It was a nerve-racking experience that went on and on and on. I think Peter had said, "Okay, I can do it for this scene." But he continued to be in charge until the end of the day. I was disturbed by this, but nobody said anything to me. I went to my dressing-room, and I was taking my make-up off,* and I thought I'd go and look for Parrish. I knocked on the door of his office.

---

* In *The Bobo*, Griffith is Pepé Gamazo, a journalist with the *Barcelona Express* who prints false stories about Olimpia (Ekland) in order to blackmail her lovers. (It is pretended that she is under sixteen.) Pepé, a gormless idiot, is himself desperately in love with Olimpia. In his black wig and horn-rimmed spectacles, Griffith is made up to look exactly like Sellers, c. 1960.

Everybody was going home, but a voice said "Come in!" "Bob I'm troubled. No one has explained – what's been happening today?"

'"Well, Ken, Peter decided to take over the direction of this film."

'"What! Did he discuss it with you?"

'"No. He just said he was taking over."

'"Robert, that's terrible. How do you feel?"

'"Well, I'm sitting here thinking about it, and I think the best I can do is to just make sure the film is finished."

'I was very sympathetic because I was very fond of Robert Parrish.

'"Just carry on, Kenny."

'Back in London, Theo Cowan came to see me. "Peter wants you to write a piece about what you think of him as a director on *The Bobo*."

'"I can't do that, Theo. It would imply that I had accepted what happened to Robert."

'"Kenneth, every other actor has done it."

'"Well, I'm sorry, Theo. I can't be a party to this – unless I can write about what really happened."

'For six months Peter wouldn't speak to me. Once, in Leicester Square, I was with my last wife. In the middle of the square, there's Peter and Britt Ekland. He cut me dead.'

☆ ☆ ☆

It is this sense of volatility, of a character who was both heedless and absorbed, which comes across in Dodger Lane. Sellers managed to rebut Jeffries' Crout's rococo rage, and salvage *Two Way Stretch* for himself, by reclining on his prison cot, or by leaning against a wall, becoming the very image of mock-regal indolence. Dodger is a man who has used his quick wits to get everybody else chasing their tails, doing everything for him – a master-delegator, waited upon hand and foot. David Lodge and Bernard Cribbins cook the breakfast and worry whether it's up to standard; Wilfrid Hyde-White works out the robbery plans, and is made to fret . . . Gaol is Dodger's court; the fellow prisoners are his flatterers, and the warders, until Crout's advent, his equerries and chamberlains.

And it is, like the armed forces, a closed society of men. Dodger doesn't much mind this – he's too desultory to think ahead about marriage or anything appertaining to it. 'We've been engaged for five years,' Ethel tells him, 'and I got nothing to show for it.' – 'Then you're dead lucky, aren't you,' comes the reply.

Liz Frazer, who plays Ethel, the girlfriend, was Sellers' daughter in *I'm All Right, Jack*; and Ethel's mother, Mrs Price, is another petite dynamo set in motion by Irene Handl, who'd been Fred Kite's wife. I mention this so as (a) retrospectively to marvel at how convincingly Sellers had aged himself in the earlier film, and (b) to remark that, whatever the type of person Sellers was playing, there was always an underlying intransigence. The intensity of that self-will, much muted in Mr Martin, hidden behind insouciance in Dodger Lane, was about to burst through the surface – of Sellers' life and his art. Early in 1960, he said: 'If I do a film that I am considering at the moment it will mean playing the part of a real horror, a really nasty bit of work, a rôle which is entirely different from anything that I have played so far.' The film was *Never Let Go*; the difference was that Lionel Meadows is not light and comic – he's Sellers' Richard III.

Never Let Go was made between *Two Way Stretch* and *The Millionairess*. Richard Todd tells me that Sellers had originally been cast as the meek little salesman, the Willy Loman-ish John Cummings; but he insisted, instead, on being the psychopath – and so he and Todd exchanged rôles. It was one of the most extraordinarily self-revealing things he ever did – equal and opposite in every way from Chance the gardener. Chance is empty, bereft, dead already; Meadows is zestful and an incarnation of the devil. Chance is Sellers at the end of his life; Meadows is Sellers at the beginning of his international fame. Perhaps Sellers wanted what he deemed to be a Lionel Jeffries/Sidney Crout rôle; a pantomime genie, after the inwardness of Mr Martin and Dodger Lane, and the preceding shuffling old figures? His need for variety in his work ('I don't particularly want to do any one thing for too long') matched, as we shall see, his mood off-screen. Sellers made *Never Let Go* in what he

called 'a black hell of depression,' i.e. he was beginning to go mad –
and this darkness is all too visible.

☆   ★   ☆

Todd (echoing contemporary reviews) also told me that Sellers, as
Meadows, began on an outrageous note, and that there was simply
nowhere to go after that; the audiences laughed in embarrassment.
In fact, Sellers starts over-the-top and just keeps on levitating and
magnifying. It is beyond question a performance to set beside
Olivier's Richard III – indeed, as a result of *Never Let Go*, 'I was
going to open the Mermaid Theatre with Bernard Miles in *Richard
III*, but we did not have the time to prepare it. . .' Like Richard,
Meadows is an exercise in horror-comedy, acted out with great
glee. The problem is simply that the surrounding plot has not
been devised or written by Shakespeare. *Never Let Go* is like an
episode of *Z-Cars* awkwardly graced with a villain of supernatural
proportions.

---

* Rank Film Distributors Ltd., instructed their cinema managers to send the following letters to local car dealers, H.P. people, commercial salesmen, the police,
magistrates, and probation officers:

Dear Sir

On the [date] the new British film 'Never Let Go' will be showing at my theatre.
I am certain that you and your many members would like me to draw this fact to
your attention, primarily because here is a film I feel they should not miss.
'Never Let Go' is a tense story that spotlights the stolen car racket – and a cold,
vicious gang of thieves. Heading the strong cast is Richard Todd, Peter Sellers,
Elizabeth Sellars, and the exciting new teenager Adam Faith – in a non-singing
dramatic role. This film is presented with a new and forthright determination
about a subject that must be exposed – before it is too late. 'Never Let Go' is a
picture to make you think . . . I know you will enjoy it.
Yours sincerely . . .

Dear Sir,

In the reasonably short time since Peter Sellers made his film debut, he has
rocketed to fame by recording success after success – and his many screen portrayals have been received with jubilation from both Press and public alike. Now
with 'Never Let Go' – his latest film – Peter Sellers chalks up yet another un-
forgettable performance. Yet, here is a Sellers that you have never before seen –

The plot, as the original posters and press advertisements left you in no doubt, concerned THE CAR RACKET EXPOSED. Cummings, a cosmetics salesman, has his under-insured Ford Anglia pinched, and so, as A MAN WITH TOO MUCH TO LOSE – AND A NEW LIFE TO GAIN, he sets about trying to find the damn thing. In a HIGH-TENSION THRILLER THAT PINS YOU TO THE EDGE OF YOUR SEAT FROM START TO FINISH, he descends into the criminal underworld and confronts YOUR FAVOURITE STAR, PETER SELLERS, [WHO] HAS A CHANGE OF FACE IN HIS LATEST FILM. SEE HIM IN A NEW TYPE OF RÔLE IN HIS LATEST FILM. SHOWING AT THE REX ALL NEXT WEEK.

As in *Death of a Salesman*, Willy Loman–Cummings is made to bear all the world's problems upon his weary shoulders. He's not doing too well toting his case of lipsticks and face creams around the department stores; he hopes that by splashing out on a little car he'll be able to whizz around more shops in more towns. The increase in his commissions will earn the money to pay off the debt incurred by the purchase of his wheels – so his careerist dreams are compromised instantly by a spiral of debt. Going with the financial insecurity, of course, is a personal uncertainty – Cummings' job requires him to project a breezy, joshing kind of confidence. He has to ingratiate himself with managers and floor-walkers. But he lacks the quickness and thick-skin that this requires; Todd, actually, almost overdoes the man's sense of despair and humiliation even *before* the Ford Anglia disappears. (The hero of *The Dam Busters* shrinks and snivels like Peter Lorre.) A salesman, first and foremost, has to sell himself – and this, we quickly deduce, in itself is an affront. It is emasculating.

Had Sellers played Cummings, as originally intended, when John

---

for, in this, his first completely straight role, he plays a tough and ruthless gang leader. This is something you will not want to miss and it is my pleasure to inform you that 'Never Let Go' will be showing at this cinema the week of [date]. Yours faithfully . . .

Guillermin and Peter de Sarigny's script was called *Moment of Truth*, I dare say there'd have been more to the rôle than cold sweats, fear, incredulity. Todd plays a worm that turns; he learns to use his fists and, after that, he's a real man. (He's proved himself worthy of being a hero in *The Dam Busters*.) Todd's conception of the rôle is emblematic. Cummings is weak; he is tested; he is strong (I doubt if he'll go back to selling cosmetics). What the man is really meant to be like, you feel, is the vigorous quasi-gunslinger who goes back to Elizabeth Sellars *after* the end. He simply needed a bloody nose to bring him out. (The militaristic tune on the soundtrack, 'When Johnny Comes Marching Home', has all along implied his credentials, without irony.) Sellers, by contrast, would not have implied a moral judgement on the salesmanship side of the question. He'd have been much more ambiguous about the little deceptive chuckles and backslapping with the department store people; we'd then see him burst apart when the car is stolen and gather himself, and his anxieties, for the showdown. Cummings would be a rôle-within-a-rôle. Sellers could have shown us the posturings and little subterfuges needed to get by in everyday life; and how slight adjustments to the kidding and disingenuousness make you a failure or make you a success, make you well-liked (Willy Loman's phrase) or despised. For to get by it is necessary to act – to hide your boredom with your boss, your contempt for your friends and colleagues; there is a difference between how you seem and what you are – and keeping the two going, keeping faith to both, is an effort. Hence Meadows' power, or advantage (as Sellers plays him – I can't think how Todd would have played him). He finds the effort easier because inner and outer man are totally fused. He has a tenacity (he never lets go); and it's tenaciousness, his grip on the rôle he has assigned himself, which Cummings develops and strengthens. (Ideally, Sellers should have taken both rôles.)

☆ ★ ☆

In the film as we have it there are no parallels, or psychological overlaps, between Meadows and Cummings; there is no subtlety. (The film is in every sense black and white.) If Todd represents mankind as the bare, forked, gibbering animal, who turns out noble, and a bit trite, Sellers is the vindictive deity, hurling thunderbolts and causing tempests and eruptions (the characters are unattracted opposites); and as befits a red-hot savage, and a tale about the underworld, the film begins with bonfires and welding-torch sparks. The smoky scrapyard is Meadows' kingdom, fronted by an Art Deco Michelin House sunburst portico. (The locations were shot in a area of Paddington since demolished. The interiors were done in three weeks at Beaconsfield Studios.) Meadows' henchmen, flitting about in the sooty rain like demons, are busy re-conditioning the stolen cars. Tyres are changed, engine numbers are altered, plates are swopped, and bodies are re-sprayed. Finally, a log book is forged containing the licence details of a genuinely crashed car – a mechanical corpse, reincarnated. In fitting old vehicles with new identities, there is more than a suggestion of the fake passport and false papers plot of *The Man Who Never Was*.

The car-breaking is 'a well-organised business', which the police are apparently helpless to combat. The documentary-type information about all this, however, rather detracts from Sellers' mannerist, disjunctive performance. When his crimes are specified, Meadows is demeaned. Who cares about the cars? What matters is not poor old Cummings, the travelling salesman who can't travel, who trudges about on buses and is late for appointments. (Todd semaphores the man's frustrations without ado.) What is transfixing about *Never Let Go* is not sympathy with the downtrodden, but Sellers as a force of evil. 'I know how to handle people, you see,' Meadows says to Tommy Towers, one of his minions, played by the nineteen year old Adam Faith. To demonstrate what he means he crushes the boy's hand under a record player lid.

As in *Richard III*, the anti-hero's own enjoyment of his excesses bespeaks more energy and liveliness than all the lamentations of the virtuous. Sellers even invents a special voice for his villainy. Words squeeze down his nostrils and out through his clenched teeth; it is the sound of a creature more used to breathing flame than having to talk. The accent is either Yorkshire crossed with South London, or

Leicestershire with a touch of the Irish thrown in. Probably it is a syncretion of all of these, plus others. You feel that when Meadows is off-screen he'll be lubricating his larynx by sucking boiling water from a copper kettle spout. It is a voice incapable of not sneering. 'Me, I'm in the garage business,' Meadows says at some point, *'legitimate* business.' Never has the word legitimate, spat out slowly, a syllable at the time, seemed so ominous and diabolical. His face, too, is framed to make no expression other than a snarl. Sellers, utilising his punch-drunk boxer's build, seems hewn from a misshapen and discoloured rock. (Mica schists? Carboniferous limestone?) Meadows' hair, above his steel-grey sideburns, is a black thorny bush and his moustache is a malignant blister. Like many spectacularly ugly people, of course, he is very vain. He is dapper in his bow tie and blazer. In every scene he is adjusting his collar in mirrors, shooting his cuffs, checking his pompadour. (Coincidentally, Jack Nicholson's Joker does the same: he gazes at his outfit and courts the amorous looking-glass. When Jerry Hall assures him he looks great, he glares at her and says matter-of-fact: 'I didn't ask.' The devil is a dandy.)

When Meadows clips over the cobblestones we know there is a cloven hoof inside those brogues. His spruceness ('I like to see everything nice and clean and tidy') and his avowed perfectionism and business philosophy ('I've learned that money makes money, Tommy') deflect attention from his corruption and inner squalor. He is particularly despotic towards his women, whom he calls his tarts. Nothing pleases him more than to devise punishments and tortures for them. (The tarts are the ones who press his suits and polish his furniture.) Jackie, always in a state of déshabillé and stupefaction, wearing black pantyhose and drinking gin, is slapped around and thrown across the bed. Meadows then despises her the more because she gave in to his sadomasochistic demands. She's imprisoned in the flat, and when the Adam Faith character (hell's own angel who does a good deed) comes to set her free, Meadows' stomping and raging is terrifying. Of course the audience would laugh during this destruction orgy – no other response is possible to

677

the sight of an overgrown man ripping apart frocks and an eiderdown, his mentality suddenly that of a three-year-old. Audiences laugh at Dennis Hopper, too, in *Blue Velvet*, when he shakes them up, and that's whom Sellers prefigures here. (He's also Bill Sykes going for Nancy.)

After giving Adam Faith the broken-bottle treatment, Meadows is round at Todd's digs. ('Nice place you've got here. What do you pay? Four pence a week?') He insults Cummings, and tells him he could be his sweeper-upper ('You're about the right size'); he takes a swipe at Mrs Cummings (Elizabeth Sellars – her character very tellingly called Anne); and, fully an ogre, he growls at the children. Sellers has metamorphosed into an animal now, a raging bull, and he next pays a visit on Alfie Barnes, an asthmatic newspaper vendor, who may or may not have been tipping Todd off about what he witnessed the night the car vanished. 'You're just a useless old man,' he says, putting his fist through the oldster's fish tank, and then – in a close-up as surreal as David Lynch's severed shell-like ear in *Blue Velvet* – he stamps on a terrapin with his heel. Alfie, cast into despair by his squashed crustacean, sticks his head in a gas oven, and at last the police start taking an interest, trying to find the connections between car thefts, harassments, suicides.

The cops, however, remain offstage (they are heard only as the clanging bells, getting closer, of their Black Marias) and *Z Cars* becomes *Gunsmoke*. We are made to follow Cummings, the vigilante, on his quest: 'I've got to hang on. I've got to see it through.' And instead of Meadows, with his grinning menace, representing the fears inside himself which Cummings is being made to confront, the film develops into a basic man in a white hat versus the man in black, who has to be vanquished. Meadows, meantime (and rightly) is contemptuous of his foe ('Do you think I'm going to let a lousy lipstick pedlar take me apart?'), but even he has been informed about the need for an orthodox shoot-'em-up finale. He's suddenly there, in the garage, in readiness for the duel. ('All right, little man, what are you waiting for?') He sacks his henchmen and bullyboys ('*I don't need you!*' he screams) and is suddenly very alone. Even Cliff (played by David Lodge as a thuggish variant on Dodger Lane's second-in-command) scarpers out of the door. Sadly, the script writers skip the scene, the equivalent in *Richard III* to the night before Bosworth, in which Meadows might have been seen to agonise over letting go; we don't know, psychologically, why or how he loses his grip and comes to sense that his reign is over. In Shakespeare's play, the king makes a great speech ('Methought the souls of all that I had murdered/Came to my tent; and every one did threat/Tomorrow's vengence on the head of Richard'); in *Never Let Go*, Meadows appears with his hair mussed. Sellers is denied poetry; he simply omits to change his shirt and neglects his personal hygiene.

The fight scene, Cummings' rite of passage, is realistic, dirty, messy; chains, spanners, hoists etc. are brought into play. Despite Cummings' victory, however, I can't recall his achievement. I don't remember feeling joyful for him. This is because Sellers' performance is so hypercharged, you feel Meadows could rise from the dead (you almost want him to); only an exorcist could get rid of him.

☆ ★ ☆

As when Alec Guinness, in the final, annoying shot of *The Lavender Hill Mob*, gets up from the café table, handcuffed, so the ending of *Never Let Go* is the one demanded by tradition. The bad (as they do not in real life) have to end unhappily – Dracula has a wooden stake hammered through his heart, the Joker plunges to his death from the Gotham City bell tower, the Wicked Witch of the West dissolves into an oily puddle. Sellers' exhibition of dementia, which is otherwise in this satanic class, begs to break with such rules and conventions. Meadows is the kind of jeering and lewd bogeyman who won't go away; he incarnates, or focuses, a spirit of arrogance and self-reliance that is abroad, pervasive – especially in Sellers' career. The power of the imagination which created the part, such that we can clean forget about the complacency and sentimentality of the film he was actually in, lies within the grandiosity of Strangelove, the causticity of Quilty, the vanity of Henry Orient etc.; but, more interesting, I think, are the bonds between Meadows' self-determination, and isolation, and Sellers' ostensibly mild characters. It is not that the likes of Sellers' Dr Kabir, Rev. Smallwood, Hrundi Bakshi, Benjamin Hoffman, Mr Martin, and so on, are deceivers and libertines; what I mean is that each of these reserved men have a measure of fundamental obstinacy. Kabir won't capitulate before Epifania; Bakshi remains at the party he's wrecking; Hoffman won't let go of Miss Smith; Mr Martin will do anything to preserve his peace. They will not give in. They are in worlds of their own, mentally and often actually, and they want to stay there. Clouseau's obliviousness is really only a farcical egotism. He's wrapped up in himself – as is Chance, who looks as if he'll become President of the United States, his benign self-centredness having been mistaken by everybody for spirituality and wisdom.

Chance's early try-out, Smallwood in *Heavens Above*, also never loses his radiant and seraphic grin, even when the howling mob attacks him and throws him on the municipal dust cart. He seems to enjoy the humiliation – it's a saint's pride – and as the Bishop of Outer Space, up in his rocket, he is gloriously alone. There's nobody in sight to try and contradict him. The film, indeed, is *about* Smallwood's stubbornness: Cecil Parker, as the Dean, Miles Malleson, as a psychiatrist, and others, do their utmost to make him compromise over something or other, but he won't. Likewise, Juan Bautista, in *The Bobo*, is peculiarly private. He quietly exults in the fact that his skin has been dyed an indelible bright blue. It is a stigmatum – visible evidence of his difference, his isolation. When he walks off out of Olimpia's house, children bait him and dogs bark at him; we zoom aloft for an overhead helicopter shot of his progress through the city's sunny boulevards. If it is meant to be a funny ha-ha conclusion to the film – it isn't. Bautista is turned into a freak – and he retains his dignity. He is thus doubly saddening.

How much does it take for gravity, dispassionateness, inscrutability, etc., to become botherations, aspects of selfishness? If Meadows, a character crammed with nastiness, is one extreme, and Chance, as one of the walking dead, is the other, then a mingling of chemical components from them both will produce the raw emotional material for Sellers' rôles. And he veered between the poles himself. If, as Bautista, he was all graciousness, as the star actor-cum-unofficial director of *The Bobo* itself, he was all tempestuousness. 'I'm not coming back after lunch if that bitch is on the set,' he stated. 'Tell me which one and I'll take care of it,' said Robert Parrish, who had already had to sack the script girl. 'The one over my left shoulder, in the white dress. . .' Sellers was referring to Britt Ekland, of course.

☆　★　☆

Vladimir Nabokov, in his careful study of Stevenson's *Dr Jekyll and Mr Hyde*, points out that Hyde isn't a separate entity who comes and takes over the good doctor; he's an amplification of the hypocrisy and spite that is already present. We see enough of Jekyll, before he starts experimenting with potions, to know that he is unforgiving and capable of skulduggery. Hyde is this side of him which 'chained down, began to growl for license'. Exactly the same thing happened to Sellers. The plucky young actor, who had to hate restrictions and proprieties if he was to survive, deliberately chose to play a deeply unsympathetic character. What this suggests to me is that Sellers needed to give shape, form and expression to his quarrelsomeness and yearnings for destruction. Something lurking in him wanted to make use of Lionel Meadows' malevolence. Where was he in his psychological development at this point?

A clue is given by a remark Anne made to Peter Evans. Evans, invited to Chipperfield, had been taken on a tour of the tennis courts and swimming pools. 'You're very quiet this evening,' he said to his hostess. 'With all this excitement [Sellers' established reputation; the forthcoming film with Loren; the money and the trappings of fame etc.] you should be bubbling with excitement.' Anne, staring at the blue floodlit sheet of water, said: 'Bubble, bubble. Isn't that the noise people make when they're drowning?'

Thirty years after hearing those words, Evans said to me: 'Such was Sellers' nature, he had the Star Syndrome very badly from about 1960. He was moving on, and upwards, and Anne was going to be jettisoned. The big time. He was getting a very firm view of himself which precluded old baggage – his nice wife, the kids, things like *The Goon Show*. Hollywood beckoned; Sophia Loren was coming to work with him. It is hard to remember now just how hot he was at that time. In terms of the Sixties, and as far as showbiz and money went, Sellers was as hot as you can get – hotter than Satan's bollocks. He was in the same class as the Beatles.'

Anne is philosophical about the transformation of her former husband from actor to icon: 'I was the only one who knew him from *before* – and I don't honestly think I'd have wanted to cope with him as a superstar, which is what he allowed himself to become. The fat impressionist from a variety family, who toured the music halls, who was ugly – suddenly to become a leading man: it's like a film, isn't it?'

☆ ★ ☆

Because Sellers was bored with Anne and the children, and was ready and waiting to fall in love with Epifania Parerga, it was convenient and easy for him to think of his family as enemies. Instead of *Never Let Go* being a catharsis however, an outlet, the violence in the film was continued and extended behind Chipperfield's iron gates. Acting all day with Richard Todd didn't deplete him, it fired him up. Anne used to have to get the children fed and out of the way before he returned from the studio. During this period, she recalled for me, 'he was totally impossible. The rôle and the man became indistinguishable – he acted the rôle of Lionel Meadows even under his own roof. He became very aggressive. Particularly towards the end of our marriage, and then ever afterwards, he'd *be* whoever he was playing; he'd come home as the person. Yes, for *Never Let Go* he was *very* aggressive.'

Having found it, he couldn't lose it – the rôle would never let him go. He'd always been touchy when he was preparing a film, walking around the house, trying to find the voice, movement, look. He spent a lot of time acting in front of mirrors – and now the evil reflection wouldn't fade. For once in his life he (backhandedly) admitted as much. Asked by an interviewer whether the complete identification with his performances affected his home life, he first said 'Not at all' (meaning that he himself was what he was); then he added: 'My wife is aware of it, though, especially when it's a nasty part, as in *Never Let Go*. I was sort of edgy with her while we made that film. Then, while I was making *The Millionairess* . . . I was very serene.'

Oh, well, that's all right, then. *Edgy?* When he saw Anne calmly leafing through a magazine he flung a vase at her; he ripped a chromium towel rail off the bathroom wall and bent it into shapes, like Dr Grimesby Roylott with Sherlock Holmes' poker in 'The Speckled Band'; he smashed the pictures in the bedroom; he did his emptying-milk-bottles-on-the-floor bit. Another evening, he tore up his wife's best frocks, because he didn't like it that people complimented her on her appearance. He plucked apart a mink hat and snapped a string of pearls. (He later decided that 'pearls were for tears' and wouldn't allow Britt to possess any.) Anne became a prisoner, as Michael records: 'As long as she was in the house and giving him her undivided attention, then Dad would be content. If he was working in the studios he would ring three or four times a day to check her movements. If she left the house even to go shopping she would be subjected to interrogation.'

Once, she tried to have an hour or two to herself – she came back to Chipperfield to discover the contents of the drawing room in fragments. Porcelain had been ground into the carpets, the tables and chairs were matchwood, unread leatherbound classic novels were ripped to confetti, and cushions were disembowelled. Then Sellers started on Anne herself. 'My headboard and my parents' bed were separated by a thinnish wall,' Michael told me. 'I remember my mother pleading with him to stop – to stop hitting her and to stop threatening more and more violence, I learned later. What I learned was that he wanted to kill her. He was in the middle of making *Never Let Go*. He made me sit down and watch that film. I was frightened by that fight scene between Meadows and Richard Todd – he assured me that there were plenty of crew members standing by to prevent the swinging chains and winches from actually hurting him.'

His father involved in mock-battles at work; his mother covered with real bruises at home (no stunt doubles deputising for her); Michael was six years old when he was subjected to all this.

☆ ★ ☆

Chapter Twelve
The Spirit of Romance

Sellers' attention was only held by what was in prospect – by what (for the moment) he did not possess. The rest was dross, and dulled his blood. His demands could be quite small (a weighing scales, a jar of royal jelly, a toaster), though they were often still very far from being reasonable. When he was making *The Pink Panther Strikes Again*, at Shepperton, he needed such an amount of waiting-on, he had his own personal props buyer – a chap on hand around the clock to whizz up to London and obtain whatever the master wanted, at whatever cost. To decorate his dressing-room trailer – a self-contained luxury flatlet on wheels, where the star had already installed a white-liveried chef – Sellers decided he needed a Paddington Bear. Not *any* Paddington Bear, you understand. This one had to have the exact colour combination of coat, hat and wellies which Sellers could clearly see in his mind's eye. Some poor sod was then made to trudge in and out of Hamleys, John Lewis', Selfridges', Harrods, and the other West End stores, where there were Paddington Bears aplenty – but no-one had quite the right costume mix to fit the bill. You'd get the hat and coat, and the wellies would be wrong; the wellies and the hat would be correct and the fucking duffle wouldn't come in the right shade. In despair, Sellers' minion tried to bribe Harrods' toy department: 'Look, why can't we swap the hat on this one for the boots on that . . .?' Harrods would have none of it. After *three days* of wandering and persistence, the props buyer tracked the ideal blend of outfit down to a little shop in Flask Walk, near Hampstead Heath. Sellers, of course, ungraciously shoved the thing in the corner of his caravan and never looked at it. Did he give it away? Throw it away?

A Paddington Bear model would have cost (what?) twenty or thirty pounds, maximum. Cars, dreams that money can buy, are a different order of expenditure, but in fact the same principle applied. Sellers didn't care how much money disappeared – getting his way was what counted. 'Peter always knew what he wanted and because he was so definite we all hated to ask him to compromise,' a former member of his staff told me. And, indeed, it would have been the equivalent of heads rolling in the sand (excoriation and the sack) if you'd returned from a shopping expedition on his behalf full of apologies and explanations. He just would not accept it – he'd scent a conspiracy. He was the Mad King in a fairy story, who sends people scurrying off in all directions on an impossible quest. While he was making *The Party* he decided he wanted a Pontiac. He made a list of the exact colour, type of brakes, level of air-conditioning and the pattern on the tyre treads which the car had to have – or else. When, after a hunt across America, a vehicle fitting his specifications was found, Sellers (still dressed as Hrundi Bakshi) delightedly ran out of the studio, hopped behind the wheel and drove straight back to the house he was renting on Bedford Drive, Beverly Hills. (Whatever vehicle had brought him to work that morning was now simply abandoned.) Sellers then spent the remains of the day taking hundreds of photographs of his new bauble. One week later, however, he was saying, 'I hate this terrible car. I've got to get a Corvette. It must be white, with hard and soft top, FM-AM and all the extras . . .' This time the car was airlifted from Detroit.

In a little short made in 1969, called *Simon, Simon*, Sellers is to be glimpsed driving a blue Lamborghini. We see it incur a minuscule scratch. Sellers gets out and looks at the car in disgust. He snaps his fingers. A red Lamborghini appears instantly. Sellers gets in the replacement and zooms out of shot, with never a backwards glance. 'It gave the impression of unlimited cars at his disposal', says Graham Stark, who directed the film. The scene does more than that, I think. It's not simply wealth and infinite resources which come across with Sellers. He didn't accumulate possessions, he dumped them. The cameo in *Simon, Simon* shows that after he'd detected the slightest blemish – real or imagined – all his acquisitions were fit for was the scrap-heap.

And as with cars, so with women. He sprang from model to model as the novelty wore off. 'When a marriage or love affair is over I just have to get rid of everything associated with it,' he said. 'The houses I bought I sell right away, often at a loss, because I can't wait to get rid of them. The cars I had are changed, which is why I have bought and sold so many in my life. About eighty I think at least.' As Bert Mortimer said soon after his ex-master's death: 'Many of his women he treated in the way a child plays with a new toy. After showering the lady with flowers, gifts and compliments he did not want to know when the conquest was made.' Once somebody had been appraised, anticipated and controlled, like a machine, there was nothing left for Sellers except dissatisfaction. The experience of Trudi Pacter, a journalist whom he met after the break-up of his marriage to Britt Ekland, would seem to be indicative.

'There will be a lot of pretty ladies in my life now,' he told her. 'I like pretty ladies.' Their first evening out together was a success – Pacter found Sellers completely charming. On the second evening, however, when the maître d' asked 'In what name is the table booked?' Sellers screamed: 'Who the bloody hell do you think the table's booked for? For Christ's sake, don't you know who I am?' From then on, nothing was to his liking. 'This just isn't good enough,' he said, hurling the dishware to the deck and stomping out. He later tried to make it up to his date by organising a private party in her honour at a Chinese restaurant in Kensington. Pacter spent a lot of money on a frock because Sellers had said, 'Put on something nice. It's important you look beautiful for my friends.' When she made her entrance, the rest of the company were scruffy and casual. 'Don't you think you are a little over-dressed,' said Sellers, in a way that should have made bystanders want to hit him.

'Why don't you pop home and change?' She did just that. Roman Polanski drove her there and back. She returned to find Sellers going on about his death and resurrection: 'I died once in my life, and it could happen again. I live in fear that every day could be the last one.' A doctor present, believing that Sellers was fishing for sympathy and expecting a contradiction, compliantly said, 'Peter . . . That heart of yours is as strong as anyone's in the room!' If this was what Sellers had wanted somebody to say, another part of him hated the rebuttal and coded it as hostile. So (Pacter reports) he stood up, walked over and slugged the man into unconsciousness. And was this demonstration of physical strength meant to prove, or disprove, the doctor's comment about his ticker?

Polanski, in his memoirs, *Roman* ('Frank, Shocking, Revealing'), records the episode slightly differently.* He names the doctor as Tony Greenburgh. The discussion was not about Sellers' heart and his day-return to the Underworld. They were arguing, instead, about a doctor's moral responsibilities. If (said Greenburgh) a patient was intent on destroying his health by smoking and drinking to excess, then a physician cannot be held accountable for any subsequent respiratory illness or liver and kidney failure. Sellers couldn't cope with the quite normal and common give and take of dinner table debate; he also didn't like the idea that anything that might go wrong with his life could be his own fault. He was so incapable of accepting criticism, or liability, even infirmity and ageing had to be blamed on the negligence of someone else. (He point blank refused to see that he was a participant in his own dissolution.) His voice rising in pitch and volume, he countered by yelling: 'You're wrong, doctor. You're wrong. *You're fucking wrong.*' Only when it became necessary to enlist help in prising Sellers' fingers from Greenburgh's throat did Polanski and the other guests see that this was not play-acting or an elaborate joke – but that, far

---

* Unless, of course, Sellers made a habit of inflicting GBH on members of the medical profession when he dined with the happy-go-lucky Polack, and this was another occasion.

from it, Sellers was truly demented. 'Tony was choking and turning purple as Peter genuinely tried to strangle him . . . .'

Later, in the car going home, Sellers reverted to his hideous little-boy-lost performance; he blubbed and pretended that being grown-up was all too much. 'They don't understand, none of them understand,' he wept to Pacter (it was always a comfort, his belief that he was misunderstood). 'How can they? They're all so much younger. [Polanski by eight years – that's nothing] I try to keep up with them. I wear these ridiculous clothes. I play their games. But never will they accept me. I'm just an outsider, a middle-aged man [he was forty-four] who pays the bill at the end of the evening.'

Pacter never saw him again, which must have been a relief. Sellers went on to spend Christmas with the rest of the evening's company in Cortina. He had another bout of boiling and bubbling, got depressed, and returned to England on Boxing Day.

☆ ☆ ☆

That women, like cars, were in the category of mechanical things is illustrated by another anecdote involving Stark. He once sent Sellers a letter purporting to advertise a plastic kit which, when assembled and rigged up to a small battery-operated engine, turned out to be a life-sized horizontal doll complete with all moving parts. 'Just think what we can do with it!' said Sellers, apparently taken in. 'Especially when we get the motor going!' Only when Stark started guffawing did he realise the hoax. ('He joined in the fun but his laugh didn't cover the disappointment.')[*]

Sellers should have played a megalomaniacal inventor like Dr

---

[*] Sellers did attempt to get his own back. According to Michael Sellers' *P.S. I Love You*, 'Dad and Blake Edwards . . . hoaxed Graham into sending for some newly discovered German virility pills – he did not realise that the advertising sheets he was shown were "dummies" specially printed to dupe him' (page 128). It was no doubt on another occasion entirely that Sellers talked excitedly to someone else altogether about The Mongolian Monk Penis Enlarging Ointment. Again he faked the testimonials. Again he maintained that people were scrabbling to send their postal orders off to the address in Copenhagen – whence a confederate mailed back tubs of rancid garlic butter.

Coppelius in *The Tales of Hoffmann* – an evil genius in an opera cloak who creates a robotic beauty. 'I'm continually searching for this woman . . .' he said in 1969. 'I keep reading of the great women behind great men: they mother you, they are great in bed, they are like a sister. They're not there when you don't want to see them; they are there when you do want to see them. I'll find one one of these days.' And once he had got it to sing its clockwork aria he'd have been free to smash it to pieces. Why was Sellers like this? Why did he want to despiritualise his relationships? The reasons are fundamental. As Milligan had said: 'He can never be happily married because the person on whom he most depended is dead. He was an only child, and his mother naturally wanted him to have the best in life. . . When she died he lost the perfect set-up – except that this boy never really got over it.'

I don't believe that Peg's death was the problem; it was the pressure she exerted when she was alive which did the damage. She'd made her son incapable of loving anybody. What he required, instead, was that women should be seen to love him – more, to adore him. (Similarly, with blokes he wanted not friendship but loyalty.) I am reminded of Jed Leland's analysis of Charles Foster Kane:

> He married for love. That's why he did everything . . . . All he really wanted out of life was love. That's Charlie's story. How he lost it. You see he just didn't have any to give. He loved Charlie Kane, of course, very dearly – and his mother, I guess he always loved her.

Sellers, similarly sick with self-love, couldn't see that it was his own twisted up narcissism which damned his liaisons before they had begun to bloom. As everybody attests, he was an expert at the gigolo part. The wooing; the courting. He enjoyed that. Bouquets; gifts. (When he was making *Hoffman*[*] he invited Sinead Cusack out to dinner. She asked where they were going. A helicopter was

---

[*] Could the title (the name of Sellers' character) conceivably be an allusion to the Offenbach opera or to E.T.A. Hoffmann, the German romantic poet of unrequited love?

heard flapping and descending near at hand. 'Paris,' said Sellers.)
But afterwards? What rôle did a husband play?

He addressed the puzzle whilst deciding what to do about Lynne
Frederick. 'I've learned that I'm obviously a difficult person to live
with, and I've chosen the wrong ladies to make that work – because
they were probably all very fine in their own way, but not with me.
I now know that I have to be terribly, terribly *terribly* careful,
because it does make all the difference in the world once you sign
that little piece of paper; every time that paper's been signed it has
changed everything. Strange. I don't know what the chemistry is,
but it always works. A romantic at heart. Yeah, I want to marry,
you see. My ideal has always been achieving the ideal marriage –
the great romance that lasts throughout a great romantic marriage.
I mean, why not? But I'm so scared of it now. I'm afraid I might go
and lose what we have simply by saying "I do" all over again. . .'

Wedlock was the devil. If Sellers couldn't see, more and more
clearly as the years went by, that his cycles of obsession-leading-to-
boredom were getting repetitious, he must have been blind on purpose; and you'd have thought even he might have perceived that
marriage, meaning a commitment (to someone else; to the future),
was not a state his grasshopper mind was cut out for. But he never
seemed to accumulate knowledge of this kind, and what was past
and what was to come (as Shakespeare says in his bitterest play
about the battle of the sexes, *Troilus and Cressida*) 'is strewn with
husks and formless ruin of oblivion'. Sellers, as a consequence, liked
to try and exist in a permanent, heedless present-tense – as Chance
does; and as he gained power in the cinema industry, always wanting to re-shoot or abandon ship, so did he try and wipe out mistakes
in his private life, by starting over. You re-wind the tape and have
another go.

Which is not to say that he blundered into one pair of arms after
another, totally open-faced and hopeful; and he never did a single
blessed thing against his will. I think that, cruel and manipulative,
he actually liked this pattern in his life. Since he treated women
with the flippancy that he gave to trading cars ('I buy things because

I want them, and I only buy the best. The one thing they have in common is excellence' etc.), it gave him pleasure to see an attractive woman, an ambling status symbol, submitting to him – just as, later, during the inevitable roundelay of squabbling and forgiving, he would wonder at how easy it was to stand outside of another person's pain and distress; which would lead to his next, inevitable thought: How lonely *he* was! And for a while he would be dejected, claiming (as he did in 1963 when the divorce from Anne was declared absolute): 'I no longer get any kicks thinking about falling in love or the great glamour of the great chase. All that jazz, all that kid stuff. Sometimes I figure that women are basically all the same and you can't tell what they are really like and how they are going to behave until you have lived with them for a damn long time. . . . There's nothing more I want in my life than to love somebody and be loved. But I haven't ever been able to get it excepting, of course, from my parents. But that's a different thing.'

☆ ★ ☆

Never Let Go, a horror-comedy about a man who hates himself, starring a man who loved himself, was, Anne can see in retrospect, 'the beginning of the end of our marriage – when his career was on the up; then he did *The Millionairess* and thought of himself as a romantic lead; and he had an affair with Loren. He was awful when he was supposed to be having an affair with Loren. I don't think it came to anything physical – though he swore to his dying day that they did . . . It was purely mental, in all senses. He was *mad* about her. He used to chase her around everywhere and ring her up at all hours. She had a great affection for him and humoured him. But he was obviously madly in love with her – and he insisted on coming home and telling *me* about *her*, like I wasn't his wife. He'd talk to me on a level that maybe I was his mother. Wolf Mankowitz said "What he wants is a mother"; I said "Well I'm not his *bloody mother* and he can *piss off* as far as I'm concerned" – I really use the English language beautifully – "I'm not getting into this. I'm not having this. I'm *not* having this being treated like his mother; and I won't be his mother. I'm not his mother . . ." And Peg was still alive, but if she was aware of Peter and Sophia she'd just think, "Oh well, that's just Peter! He's having a nice time." She'd go along with it. She'd not see that it wasn't easy to live with. It wasn't easy to live with.'

Mankowitz confirms that Sellers was going bonkers on purpose: 'He started to get disturbed in the course of *The Millionairess*. I have pinpointed the very moment when, in my opinion, he started to let go. I used to drive back from the studio with him in a Rolls he'd got at the time. He stopped the car, pulled over and said, "Look I've got to tell you something. I'm in love with Sophia." I said, "Everybody is in love with Sophia. Naturally, that's the idea. They should be in love with Sophia."

'"No, no – this is serious. We are in love. I'm going to get together with her . . ."

'"Really? Does she understand this? Does she want to leave Ponti? That's most unlikely. There are lots of reasons why she should stay with Ponti."

'"Well she doesn't know about it yet."

'"Okay, fine. If you can make it, make it. Somebody might one day – but don't talk about it. Tell me, but don't tell everybody."

'"I've got to tell Anne."

'"What have you got to tell her? That you want to fuck Sophia Loren? Eight hundred million men and women want to do that. It's not unusual. If you had already done it, maybe you'd have something to tell her – but perhaps then you should definitely *not* tell her. I don't understand. What are you going to tell her?"

'"That I'm in love with Sophia, and I'm going to do everything I can do to make certain we can be together."

'"A bit rash?" And hardly rational.

'"Well, I'm going to tell her."

'"What for? I beg you – don't. She adores you. You've two children. Nothing is happening. I want to tell you, Peter, with the utmost confidence and conviction: *all this is a fiction*. Sophia will never leave Ponti. She has all sorts of reasons – psychological as well as financial ones – for staying with him. Their money is so tied up together. He controls her. There is no way she is going to leave him. He leaves a Sicilian armed guard to sleep across her threshold. You don't know what you are getting into."

'"Yeah, but she adores me. She told me so – and she's very sweet to me. We have great fun together."

'"Yes, that's her. She loves having fun. But she's been with Ponti since she's sixteen, since she was a dancing girl in a travelling troupe . . ."

'That very night he told his wife about this, and the marriage relationship started to degenerate fast. He embraced a false sense of reality. A clear indication of this. We drove on to his house; his chauffeur took over the car and drove me back to my house. He told her. This is when it first became perfectly clear to me that he was losing the ability to differentiate between fantasy and reality. Everybody goes mad about a woman every so often; that in itself is not a certifiable form of insanity. This was more than that. There was more to it than that. This was dangerous. And he started to chase her around a lot and he became quite a nuisance.'

☆ ★ ☆

If the stars are what we have now to replace the gods – Olivier was Jove, Burton was Mars, Sellers was Mercury (patron of sleep, dreams, thieves, and conductor of dead souls to Hades) – then Loren is clearly Venus Aphrodite. Though she wasn't exactly created in the sea, as form from the foam brought forth on the cusp of an oyster shell, like the Botticelli painting, her origins are equally mythic. She was born in the bastards' ward in Rome, in 1934, and raised under a volcano, in the Naples slums. Her father (like Bill) was a feckless piano player, named Riccardo Scicolone; her mother (like Peg) was a thwarted actress, who had once won a Garbo look-alike competition judged by Luigi Pirandello, and her name was Romilda Villani. 'My mother,' said Loren, 'has the ferocity of a lioness,' and she encouraged her daughter to enter beauty contests and to seek work as an extra at Cinecitta. (Loren is in the crowd scenes in Mervyn Le Roy's *Quo Vadis*.) The movies were seen as a means of overcoming poverty – as a gateway to something magical; and in

Loren's case this is not a sentimental overstatement. From a child-hood filled with the problems of basic survival and sacrifice – her neighbourhood was bombarded by battleships during the war, and the Germans destroyed the water mains – suddenly she had man-sions all over Italy, France and Switzerland. The compound of Villa Ponti, for example, at Marino, outside Rome, is littered with mar-ble and gold fountains, Etruscan frescoes, Renaissance statuary, and pictures, by Matisse and Modigliani, of voluptuous women – earth goddesses.

She met Ponti when he was adjudicating one of the Miss Rome beauty contests in 1950. He was a producer, wheeler-dealer, agent and lawyer. Affable and tenacious, he became her sugar-daddy (he's over twenty years her senior) and gave her confidence and security. 'Without him I am nothing,' she said, 'I have no intention of giving myself to any other man.' They were married in Mexico in 1957, and it's at this point that her life-story started to get complicated. Ponti had been married in the long ago to one Giuliana Fiastri. Though he had been divorced from her, Vatican officials did not acknowledge the separation – and the wedding with Loren was con-demned as bigamous. The couple were threatened with excommunication and gaol. To establish the legitimacy of their re-lationship, and to be able to have children who'd not have outlaws for parents, therefore, they had to take French citizenship – which Ponti did in January 1965, and which Loren did in June of that same year. (Divorce remained illegal in Italy until 1970.) They were remarried – or legally married, in the eyes of the church – in April, 1966.

The above paragraph is a laughable simplification of legal-papal-bureaucratic shenanigans which dragged on for years, generating mountains of dossiers and a king's ransom in costs. It is sufficient to be able to grasp, however, the conscientiousness – doggedness – with which Loren and Ponti set about becoming orthodox and dig-nified. They had no intention of being bohemian or rebellious; Loren, in particular, had no wish to replicate the lackadaisical atmosphere which had existed between her own mother and father

– and as for becoming a mother herself, to duplicate her own fate and raise illegitimates was unthinkable, unholy. Her life's ambition was to become *la migliore che possa essere*: the best and most respectable person there could possibly be. This was the set-up which Sellers thought he could so easily overturn, the citadel which it would be a piece of piss to penetrate.

He met her on Wednesday May 18th 1960, two weeks prior to the release of *Never Let Go*. He was on the platform at Victoria Station to receive the Golden Arrow, and his first words to her were: 'Welcome to England. I've never had it so good.' The pair were transported, like royalty, to the Ritz; and at the party which then took place, to celebrate the commencement of *The Million-airess*, Loren was heard to comment: 'He's so shy, don't you think? So different to the ordinary man. So shy, so gentle . . . I'm sure we'll get on well together.' Sellers explained that, 'I don't normally act with romantic, glamorous women. You'd be scared to. I'm more an introvert than an extrovert. She's a lot different from Harry Secombe, you must admit.'

Sellers then moved across to Loren and kissed her on the cheek – fifteen times. ('But it was only for the photographers' sakes,' he emphasised.)

☆ ☆ ☆

The Millionairess, according to what its producer, Pierre Rouve, told Paul Sherrif, the production designer, 'should be set in a kind of no-period, where orchids in one's buttonhole were not viewed with envy, where tipping with gold sovereigns was commonplace, where people, rich beyond one's comprehension, loved the idea of being rich beyond one's comprehension, where "to be" or "not to be" were worlds apart. In the period, in fact, where millionaires were million-aires and loving every minute of it.' Or, as Rouve said to me, 'the film is a parody of Thirties opulence; everything is heightened and artificial'.

Perhaps the artificiality is not heightened enough? Or was it that

Asquith,* the director, was literal-minded and not the man to bring out any surrealism – any screwball zest and spontaneity? (That Katharine Hepburn had played the rôle on stage, and wanted to do so on film, suggests the material's potential for eccentricity.) Or is it Shaw who is the dud? He could never overcome his intelligence and the expected – and therefore never reached the hyper-intelligent realm of Wildean folly and paradox. In any event, instead of an erotic charm and sheen, *The Millionairess* is full of airs and ostentation, and I find it hard to sit through. The film is really a series of tableaux to show off Loren's looks; and when the forty-degree lens is not being used to narrow her face, her big-lipped pout is the spitting image of Lucille Ball's. She appears in one damned wide-brimmed hat with a lace veil after another (the Cinemascope screen functions as an art gallery frame) and these pink or blue or peachy vast puffy creations are teamed with elaborate furs and stoles. Thousands of arctic foxes and poodles must have laid down their life for this production. (It isn't drama, it's millinery.)

What it all anticipates, by a few years, is Cecil Beaton's hat-orgy in *My Fair Lady*; and the problem with *The Millionairess* (like the one solved for *Pygmalion* by Lerner and Loewe) is it is not a musical. It ought to have been; for what survived of the Loren–Sellers partnership is the song 'Goodness Gracious Me' (with its unlawful pregnancy allusions: 'Oh doctor I'm in trouble' etc.) – though it is not actually sung in the film proper. As Herbert Kretzmer, the lyricist recalls: 'Sellers called me one day – and it was all his idea; a very good idea. "There's a scene in the film I'm making with a very glamorous patient. I'm the doctor and I'm quite indifferent to her but I'm fascinated by her heartbeat – and I was thinking, if you

---

* Sellers imitated Anthony 'Puffin' Asquith as Newton Tweedale in his sketch 'The Critics' – a send-up of the ludicrous and pretentious Radio Three Programme, *Critics' Forum* (now defunct), in which a group of egg-heads used to exchange commonplaces about the latest books, films, and theatre openings. (Tweedale's nervous, nibbling voice doesn't inspire confidence.)

could come up with a song around that idea of the heartbeat and an Indian doctor – then Sophia and I, she's got a sweet voice, could do something."'

Sellers, who had lost his heart to Loren, was explicit about the cardiological chorus (and the boom-tiddy-boom on the soundtrack is a bit spooky in view of his recurrent heart attacks); but with his genius for how things were heard – for atmospherics – he could tell that the film would be flat and stillborn without some melody. He had already refused to play Kabir as Arabic. 'It is too much of a gurgle, a throat-clearing sound, which we'll all do in the hours of our death,' he told Rouve. 'I can't find any fun in Arabic.' Indian, which he remembered from the war, had a different combination of sonorities. It could curl; it was a bargaining sound – a bazaar sound. Rouve's job was to convince the Society of Authors, on behalf of the Shaw Estate, that the character could be altered. 'They said, yes; because it had been a disaster when Robert Helpmann had done it on the stage. He didn't have a musical delivery – the language wasn't able to sing.'

And yet does it this time around? Sellers seems to mumble his way through the film. He has darkened eyes, a copper complexion, jet black hair, and he thrusts his lower jaw out, to get his tongue and teeth around the Hindi. 'India resists organisation,' he says, when Epifania shows off the new glass and stainless steel hospital. What is this meant to imply? That the ill actually prefer an insanitary hutment full of chickens and goats? Why be ungrateful? Surely a patient would be glad of some efficient up-to-date treatment. Shaw's repartee – the soulful doc versus the cold and spoilt bitch – is a load of blah. Sellers is more himself, which is to say his character comes alive, not when he talks, but in the silent throwaway glimpses – at the big, echoing empty hospital he smiles quietly to himself as he experiments with the electronic automatic doors. He is amused by the nonsense of it, the magic of it. He's more absorbed by those doors than by Epifania, and who can blame him? 'I am the most interesting woman in the world,' she says, 'because I'm the richest.' Perhaps Hepburn could have given this line a snap, but when Loren comes out with it, sulkily, petulantly, we realise, with a thud, that what is advertised as rich and interesting in *The Millionairess* is, in fact, monotonous. Epifania is bored by her wealth, and Loren, a consummate artist, plays her boringly. Kabir is not interested in her capitalistic creeds (e.g. 'Money is power, security, freedom'), and Sellers, equally consummate, plays the part unengrossingly.

What went wrong? 'It was hoped', Rouve explained to me, 'that Asquith could balance Sellers and Loren without commanding them – because they were two difficult creatures. We got our players on the pitch. Appalling! They froze! Sophia was so frightened – yet she was supposed to play somebody who was so totally self-assured. All her possible complexes about her hard upbringing appeared. Peter was equally frightened. He was nervous of Alastair Sim, who plays the slightly corrupt lawyer, until Sim went over to him and said, "Look, I am an admirer of *The Goon Show*." The problem was to make the film without going into any discussions of what Shaw might have meant – because had we mentioned, Asquith or myself, anything slightly academic, it would have had Sophia and Sellers running, howling. Peter had played Fred Kite, but he never grasped the mockery of unionisation, and the tycoons versus the workers, that is in *The Millionairess*. Nor were either of them happy about the film's mockery of money. I remember very distinctly hearing Peter say one day, between takes, "All that money – you don't give money away. You feel superior when you've got money." And Sophia started to talk to him about the post-war poverty of Naples; and she said how she, too, had learned the importance of money – it got her away from her beginnings.'

☆ ☆ ☆

'Vitality in a woman is a blind fury of creation. She sacrifices herself to it.' *Man and Superman.*

'A coquette is a woman who rouses passions she has no intentions of gratifying.' *Attrib.*

'What really flatters a man is that you think him worth flattering.' *John Bull's Other Island.*

'The secret of being miserable is to have leisure to bother about whether you are happy or not.' *Misalliance.*

'Morality consists in suspecting other people of not being legally married.' *The Doctor's Dilemma.*

And so on. There was more of a George Bernard Shaw comedy going on between the stars off-camera than ever found its way on to the screen. 'After all those marvellous men you've acted with – people like William Holden and Charlton Heston – I must seem almost insignificant,' said Sellers. 'Peter – how little you know. It's what's behind the looks that counts,' Loren replied. It was during their confidence-building chats, whilst they lounged in the studio in their name-stencilled canvas chairs, reminiscing about how they had got going in show business, that Sellers began to get woozy. 'She really threw me,' he told Donald Zec, Loren's biographer, in 1975. 'I thought then, and still think, that she was the most beautiful creature I'd met in my life.' Because his co-star started to give him reassurance, by laughing at his funny voices, he wildly over-interpreted it. He decided he was suddenly aware of a different atmosphere with Loren – who was at her best, at her grandest, and using all her seduction. To his way of thinking, she was continuing to be the millionairess; she represented energy and vital forces.

'I adored her,' he continued to Zec, 'and I had the feeling all the time that it was mutual . . . I mean she adores my kind of humour. She loves my jokes and we got on famously. One day during the film I told her that I was in love with her. A day or two later she came on the set in a beautiful white dress, by Balmain I think it was. She was in a wistful mood. I said to her, "Anything wrong? Has anything upset you?" "No, no. I'm fine . . . I love you that's all."

'I believe if Carlo went tomorrow, God forbid, she'd come to me. I tell you straight. As it is, I'm happy that she is fulfilled. She has what she wants. Carlo and I are good friends. He's always pleased to welcome me in Rome. And in a way, he has accepted this special relationship the three of us have been through, taken me as one of their family. I think Sophia is a marvellous actress who still hasn't reached her true greatness. I love her and always will.'

The infatuation with Loren was due not only to her overwhelming sexual presence ('You see, I'd never played a part like this before. I always thought they faked this kind of stuff' – i.e. the scene where Kabir massages Epifania – 'but there she was with her bra down. I thought, 'strewth if I touch her she'll give me one') but there was also a parallel between their careers. She was the girl who had made it on a world-wide scale; and she, more than anybody, encouraged Sellers to embark on the search for international fame. 'All the hidden dreams of Peter Sellers seemed to coagulate around Sophia. All his confused aspirations,' says Rouve. Sellers also revealed that his favourite line in *The Millionairess* came during the big-new-hospital sequence. Epifania is boasting that there are beds for more than five hundred patients. 'Ah,' says Kabir, 'but would you know their names?'

That was the one thing he'd brought out of the film – the nameless boy, from nowhere.

☆ ★ ☆

But what about the love-affair? 'The woman the least interested in sex that I have met in my life is Sophia Loren,' Rouve vouchsafed. 'Sophia had had unspoken-about traumatic experiences as a young girl in post-war Naples; and just about the one thing she would *not* do is sex – because it connects with the one moment in her life which she was striving to forget. Her great obsession was children. Legitimate children. It is not difficult to see what her own illegitimacy had meant to her – the fact that she had not spoken to her father, ever, because he would not marry her mother. Too many elements which kept her away from sex. Sellers wrapped himself up in a complete fantasy. She had that sense of the solidarity of the slums with him; she was close to him – and she likes laughing. Peter would reduce her to hysterics with his complete repertoire. Chaplin did the same. I introduced her to him for *The Countess from Hong Kong*. Chaplin went through his repertoire for her benefit in his sitting room. She creates a mood of warmth and understanding – she brings people out . . . .'

Many of the immortals on Mount Olympus had been enchanted.

Chaplin taught her how to do 'a little quiet clowning. She wanted to be much more facetious but I said, give the audience a treat, let them do some of it for you.' Noël Coward reckoned 'she should have been sculpted out of chocolate truffles so that the world could have devoured her.' Clark Gable said: 'This girl makes you think all the wrong thoughts'; and Alan Ladd entered the *Dictionary of Quotations* with his comment: 'Working with her is like being bombed by watermelons.' But these sorts of courtesies are in the category of teasing and joshing ('I love that cow!' said O'Toole, after *Man of La Mancha*); and she has been able to shrug it all off, saying: 'maybe actors have been in love with me, but there was never any danger. . .'

Sellers, however, was disquieting and anguished. Though he claimed he had turned into the Indian, which was crackers enough in itself ('an Indian came up to me in the street and said quite seriously that I was the new Messiah, that I should lead India into new paths. I even began to feel I could heal people'), it wasn't Kabir's purity which was coursing through him but Epifania's fury and fatuousness. (He was Shaw's heroine and not the play's hero.) Her fondness for electrical gadgetry and orange bed sheets – Sellers' taste; her tendency to telephone people at half-past four in the morning – a Sellers' trick; her huge sulks when she can't get her way – Sellers' traits, as also her alternate giggling and glaring. Kabir says that Epifania is the kind of grown-up brat who 'demands toys – then tosses them aside without unwrapping them,' a description which matches Sellers to perfection; and Epifania's way of degrading people with her wealth is an anticipation of the sour everyone-has-his-price ethos of *The Magic Christian*: 'Is there nothing one can get with money, except more money?' asks the doctor sadly. To which the millionairess's shitty reply is: 'Well, one can get most men, yes.'

And, as Epifania over-dramatises her reaction to Kabir's rejection of her advances – she's suicidal – so did Sellers become increasingly frenzied and insufferable. Especially with Anne, who was getting cold-shouldered. 'It was total madness the way he kept blabbing to me about Sophia Loren. Total and utter madness. If he had behaved in a normal way towards me I'd have gone back to him; and I suppose I'd never have left him – if it had been just a fling or crush. But it was all mad. He'd lie in bed and say, "I can feel her spirit coming into the room". It was *mad*. "Oh, Christ, what is going *on* in my life," I wanted to yell, you know. And he'd spend our money on her – because she had some jewellery pinched,* he toddled off and bought her some very expensive pieces. He was totally, totally obsessed with her – in a way which was a madness. This was the start of the real break-up of our marriage. It had always been up and down, but Peter was Peter and it was something you accepted; and I can't say I was ever particularly happy or unhappy. We had wonderful times and miserable times. From way back I'd ring up Dave Lodge and say, "For God's sake get over here – he's absolutely impossible." He'd throw things around etcetera. I don't think I ever thought of divorce at any stage. I'd been brought up in an old-fashioned way that meant once you'd got married you stayed married, for better or for worse. Divorce was never in my mind. It was when we moved to Chipperfield and he started *The Millionairess* that it all got too much – the obsession went on long after he'd finished the film. He'd still be ringing her up. He'd do it in the next room. I'd hear all this patter and canoodling and think "This is awful." I decided I was going to leave – he was doing *Waltz of the Toreadors*. I said I was leaving. I couldn't stand it any longer, and he said, "Well, I'm not going to work." He refused to go. Bill Wills rang and said, "Would you stay on until he's finished the film?

---

* Valuations of the hoard vary from source to source: £82,000 (Evans); £85,000 (Walker); £185,000 (Zec); £750,000 (R.J. Minney, in *Puffin Asquith*, London 1973). Everybody agrees, however, that the sapphires, diamonds and emeralds were uninsured. The robbery took place on a Saturday night and Rouve was in charge of helping the police with their interviews and inquiries solidly until Monday morning – when 'Peter Sellers' nerves cracked. He fainted and had to be taken to hospital. We had, of course, to go on with the shooting. The shooting could not be stopped. We spent the rest of the day taking close-ups of the tired, greatly upset Sophia Loren – and the close-ups were really beautiful.'

Because he won't come in to work and we'll all be in terrible trouble." So I stayed. It was always some form of blackmail. When I did leave I had to do so in a very sudden way, finally – when he was away. Because he was a scary person. I was scared of him, you see. He was physically violent when he lost his temper. We had rows that went on for hours – for fifteen hours I think there was one. I'd go to sleep in the middle. It was a nightmare, because he was mad. You can't put it in any other way. He was quite mad.'

☆ ★ ☆

Because she was unobtainable, Loren stayed Sellers' ideal woman; even from beyond the grave he was faithful to her memory and inspiration. Interviewed through a ouija board by a psychic named Micki Dahne, he said, 'Sophia was my ultimate woman, perfect in my eyes. I dreamed of her constantly. One of my only regrets about my life is that we did not marry. I would have made any sacrifice to have had her as a wife.' When he was still with us on the ground, Sellers was equally as effusive – almost as if he was setting out specifically to disregard Mankowitz's advice about shutting his trap: 'I was never in love as deeply with any woman the way I was with Sophia,' Sellers told Zec. 'One day Basilio Franchina [a Ponti henchman] came to me and said "When the husband he finds out about this there will be trouble . . ." I told him, "Well if he has to find out about it, it's just too bad."'

Sellers cast himself in a bedroom farce – Loren's own *Marriage Italian Style*, perhaps. While he was making *Mister Topaze* in the Loire Valley, 'he used to cry a lot,' Michael Gough recalls, 'because he couldn't get through to Sophia Loren – she was closely guarded. Sellers said that they couldn't ever go to his place, nor to her home, and hotels were out because tongues would have more than wagged – so all their "courting" was done in the back of his car. . .' The delusional life was still being lived during *The Dock Brief*, in the Spring of 1962. One of his many anxieties (according to John Mortimer) 'was that he was being pursued by the Mafia because of his undoubted affection for Sophia Loren'.

He was still rambling a decade later: 'I enjoyed working with Sophia Loren because it was like you know the first time I was in a major film and it was like I was really shit scared and I didn't know what to do with myself. Every day it was, "Hello, Miss Loren," "Goodbye, Miss Loren," "How are the jewels, Miss Loren?" She'd just had another bad jewel robbery at that time, and she was fun, you could crack gags, you know . . .' When a journalist asked him, eleven years after *The Millionairess*, whether it had been a professional love or a spiritual love, Sellers said: 'Both. We had the same sense of humour, in fact we had a lot going in common, and we fell in love – just like that.' That must have done wonders for your ego, said the reporter. 'It certainly did,' confirmed Sellers. 'I was about two stone heavier than I am now, and most unattractive. We're still great friends. Yes, I would make another film with her if the right subject came along.'

It never seemed to do so. Sellers wanted her to be in *A Shot in the Dark* and *Casino Royale*. He had himself photographed as Napoleon, in order to get a part in *Madame Sans Gêne*, which was made near Bari in 1962. Loren played the wife of one of the admirals of France, who comes from the Paris slums; she gave it her Neapolitan vulgarity and did battle with Bonaparte, the head of the secret police, and so on, who became her stooges. The part went to Robert Hossein. When the casting was announced for *A Countess from Hong Kong*, Sellers longed to play the valet, Hudson, a rôle conceived for the unavailable Noël Coward. (Hudson is ordered to marry the Loren character, a Russian aristocrat, so that she can clear American immigration. The gag is that the Jeeves figure is the one person in the world who wrinkles his nose up at being handed Loren on a plate – and this could have been quite a joke at the expense of either Coward's homosexuality or Sellers' concupiscence.) Chaplin, however, thought that with Loren and Brando, and Margaret Rutherford as a dowager, his tale of a shipboard romance was already getting top-heavy with stars. The part went to Patrick Cargill.

On the other hand, Sellers turned down rôles. He refused to

appear in *Topkapi*, for example, because it would have meant co-starring with Maximilian Schell – of whom he was jealous for having co-starred with Loren in *The Condemned of Altona*. Here is how he explained himself on that occasion: 'I read the script and thought it was a great part. I went around to the Dorchester, and Jules Dassin [the director] was charming. I said, "I hope you won't think this sort of presumptuous of me, Mr. Dassin, but who's playing the German in it?" He said, "Maximilian Schell." And, wrongly, I'd been told by a *lady friend* that Schell was very unprofessional on sets. So I said, "Well, I've heard that he is a very fine actor but difficult to work with." Dassin said, "No, no, not at all, whoever told you that?" So anyway, my agent calls me up and says, "Well, you really talked your way out of that one. What is this about you won't work with Maximilian Schell?" I said, "Well, well . . . I . . ."' [Italics added.] Sellers' inability to see that when it came to unprofessionalism and irresponsibility, he, and he alone, led the field, is almost winning.

But if Sellers and Loren were not fated to be conjoined professionally, Sellers did his best to try and meet her on location in a private capacity. He haunted the set of *The Fall of the Roman Empire*, in Madrid (where he was cross to ricochet into Dick Bentley); and when Loren returned to Italy, he turned up at the Villa Ponti – Circe's bower – and begged to be able to install the hi-fi, hiding speakers and tape decks behind the walls. (Was he in disguise, like Clouseau in *The Return of the Pink Panther*, calling at Christopher Plummer and Catherine Schell's villa to repair the telephone?) Most embarrassing of all, he couldn't be shaken off during the shooting of *Two Women*, which was being made between Venice and Naples. Loren was renting a large house and Sellers arrived and moved in.

The actress wanted to concentrate on her rôle – of a careworn mother who is raped, along with her daughter, by Allied Moroccan soldiers at the end of the war – and she would waddle off to her bedroom at nine each evening, bolting the door. She barely spoke to Sellers, who'd sit eating spaghetti and shellfish with Rouve and Vittorio Di Sica; but he still hung about for three long weeks. 'In Italy, with Sophia next door, he'd emerge and sink an enormous Campari for breakfast. He would go and sit in the middle of nowhere, this village in the mountains; and then in the evening he'd endeavour to be noticed by making jokes and doing his Goon voices. He'd show off – but Di Sica, Sophia, and the young Belmondo *they* were all show offs. It was difficult for him to compete. I would occasionally translate for him' says Rouve, 'and after a while he'd sit there and drink.'

Sellers was finding the repudiations a new experience – like being shot is a new experience for Quilty. He saw much more of Loren's sister, Maria, who was engaged to Romano Mussolini, than he did of Loren. Maria, too, had wanted to be an actress. Paramount had even offered her a script, on condition that she had plastic surgery. Romano, the son of *the* Mussolini, was a competent jazz pianist. At the party to celebrate the successful completion of *Two Women*, Maria encouraged her fiancé to play something. After listening to the music, and deciding he was enthralled, Sellers felt he ought to express his appreciation. He sauntered over to Romano. 'Gee,' he said, 'I'm really sorry about what they did to your Dad.'

☆ ★ ☆

Sellers took his fantasticated indiscretions to elaborate lengths. He'd stage it so that visitors to Chipperfield would overhear the most intense telephone calls – calls which were evidently between lovers; calls between people who had been intimate. He'd say it had been Sophia the other end – and for an actor of Sellers' cunning it was easy to pitch woo down a dead line. To prove to Milligan that 'he and Sophia had a thing going between them' he took his chum all the way to Rome for an afternoon out. 'He wanted to see Sophia Loren in Rome, and he asked me to go with him. He did his best to canoodle with her – looks and everything. I had to go all the way there, wait in a hotel room, and then fly back to London. A bit much, isn't it? I had lunch with him during *The Millionairess*, but he didn't want to break out of the character – and very embarrassing it was, his talking as an Indian all the time. He was very excited about Sophia, I do know that. He grew a beard – for this' – and Milligan tapped the back of his hand under his jaw to indicate Sellers' double chins.

And indeed, on *Mister Topaze*, which was made next, Sellers is heavily bewhiskered. In the original Pagnol play, when he gets to be a businessman, Topaze is a celebrity; he is invited back to his old school to present the prizes on Speech Day. Tamise, his former indigent colleague, is asked if he'd like to come and be his secretary. In the Sellers version, however, Topaze is alone in his castle and Tamise walks away. The impression conveyed is one of loss, lucklessness, idleness; and of gathering gloom. 'Being rich', he says, surveying his new palace, which gives him no joy, 'is the only thing that gains one respect.'

The line (Rouve wrote the screenplay) could be from *The Millionairess*, and there are other, more private, allusions. When Loren first met Ponti, and was asked to make a screen test, the cameraman said: 'She is quite impossible to photograph. Too tall, too big-boned, too heavy all round. The face is too short, the mouth is too wide, the nose too long . . .' Ponti discussed this report with his future bride thus: 'Would you consider doing something to your nose and maybe losing twenty pounds or so off your weight?' At last here was a man who didn't go gooey with the hymns-to-a-goddess approach, who didn't mind telling her she was ugly. The temerity of it bound Loren to Ponti for life. She yammered that she came from Naples. She didn't know where the next loaf of bread or plate of pasta was coming from – so as for cosmetic surgery! Outrageous! That is why, in *The Millionairess*, there's a (non G.B.S.) scene where Epifania, having been rebuffed by Kabir, goes to see a psychiatrist, played by Dennis Price. 'How can I be more attractive to men? Should I get my nose fixed?' Ponti, incidentally, came to see that scene being shot, and Rouve had to whisper a running translation to him – 'and he shot bolt upright at that line'.

In *Mister Topaze*, Sellers is the one who gets his physiognomy scrutinised. At the expensively designed movie-set garret where he lives (fogged window panes, rusting boilers and pipes, a clutter of dusty books and old clothes), Tamise tries to galvanise his friend's

courtship of Ernestine, the headmaster's daughter, by saying: 'You
have a commanding nose . . . a learned brow.' Topaze takes up the
theme (Sellers appears to improvise – the words come out so
naturally): 'My nose is commanding from the front, not from the
side.' It is the sole reference to Topaze's appearance and vanity in a
film which is otherwise concerned with abstracts like corruption,
honesty, and the boredoms and isolations of success; and nothing
more comes of any Topaze-Ernestine romance, or indeed of
Topaze's inflamed masculinity. Sellers, who of course directed the
film, included the interpolated scene solely as a homage to Loren.*

But there is more to it than Sellers' appropriation and replication
of Loren's conk complex. As a director, Sellers impersonated Di
Sica, who is in *The Millionairess* as Joe, a baker and spaghetti manufacturer (Mrs Joe is Miriam Karlin – Jewishness and Italianness, like
Indian and Welsh accents, are similar); and as we know, Sellers had
watched Di Sica handle the megaphone during *Two Women*, for
which Loren won the Oscar. Sellers had noticed that Loren was
basically an imitative actress, which is why Di Sica, who couldn't
really direct so much as act it all out, was for her. She could copy
him. He was charming and endearing and would be trying to tell
you something that didn't make sense. In a conversation, he'd be
acting; he conveyed a state of mind or feeling. And this is how
Sellers tried to take charge of *Mister Topaze* – as if it was a Sophia
Loren film. The Di Sica style had percolated to him.† 'He never

---

* 'Sophia was convinced that the right side of her nose wasn't as attractive as the
left. She had a theory that her left profile was more suited to comedy, and the
right side to drama. So for this film she had to be photographed either full face or
with her left profile. In the completed film [*A Countess from Hong Kong*] there
was just one scene that showed her right profile for the briefest moment. Sophia
was so upset that she tried to make us re-shoot the sequence. Charlie [Chaplin]
considered it, but the scene involved back projection, which takes ages to set-up.
He finally couldn't be bothered – just for the sake of her nose. I think Sophia is
still upset.' *Remembering Charlie*, by Jerry Epstein (New York, 1989), page 183.
† As soon as they were both available, Di Sica and Sellers roped each other into
After the Fox. Sellers, says Rouve, 'wanted to be in the neighbourhood. Rome.

came to terms with what cuts in to what, the technical side,' recalls Rouve. 'With that he had to be helped – but only to the extent that a typist has influence on the work of a novelist.' The actors and the casting were all Sellers' ideas. McKern as the headmaster; Herbert Lom as the swindler – Lom, who had a semi-heavy attitude in *The Ladykillers*, here does a spoof on the Lom of his previous films (and prepares the way for the twitchy Dreyfus). Sellers knew what he could extract from such performers by acting things out for them. And what of his characterisation? On Topaze's desk, during his affluent phase (his secretary, Colette, is Joan Sims, still a bag of nerves from *The Naked Truth*), there is a bronze figurine of a Greek youth escaping from a nymph. The symbol can be decoded to mean that with money now at his disposal, and with material luxuries as palliatives, Topaze hopes that he will somehow be above, or absolved from, base and bodily cravings – he's monkish and withdrawn; he has leapt free.

It is not difficult to see that Topaze on his terrace, moping and believing that he is enlightened at last ('I'm just beginning to learn how the wheels go round') is Sellers himself, beyond the touch of ordinary humanity, and continuing to get crazily self-absorbed. As he said to Herbert Kretzmer at the time, with his marriage disintegrating and Loren distant: ' I had nobody to talk to. I felt I wasn't company for anybody. I've never been so low in my life. The days were all right. The days I worked. I worked non-stop. I set out to *lose* myself in work. I made film after film, almost anything to take my mind off Anne and the kids. . . At night it wasn't so easy. I got so dejected and introspective that I would sit at home alone for hours, going over my childhood days in my mind, trying to fathom things out.'

☆ ★ ☆

What was Loren's reaction to Sellers' crack-up and amorous seizures? Mostly, it would seem, she kept mum; and in any event,

---

Sophia. All that milieu. Peter wanted to stay there. I doubt very much if he saw her. She was by then doing *Lady L* in Vienna' – with Peter Ustinov.

as nothing had happened between herself and her quondam co-star (whom she privately referred to as 'Goat's Cheese'), there was nothing to document. Hence the omission of his name from her autobiography, *Sophia: Living and Loving*, ghosted by A.E. Hotchner in 1979; and thus there is nobody playing him in *Sophia Loren: Her Own Story*, the mini-series for television based on the memoirs, made the following year. (Loren, who plays herself when young, sees her life as the triumph of rags-to-riches over gynaecology – the birth of Carlo Jr and Eduardo are the high spots. Rip Torn is Ponti; Edmund Purdom is de Sica. And anyway, who, since the death of Kean, could possibly have incarnated Sellers?)[*]

He was furious at the inexplicable absence of at least one long chapter dedicated to his grand passion ('Sellers is outraged by this dismissal of an event that he believes changed his life,' said *Time*); and when his own biographer, Peter Evans, had a conversation with him in 1980, and asked 'Do you manage to stay friends with your lovers, wives and girlfriends after the event, Sellers said (pointedly): 'Certainly with Sophia, we are great mates now.' It was a remark (Evans tells me) 'which fell very naturally into our chat'; and Sellers wrought his fantasies into many an interview towards the end of his life – one significant development being that he now started to assign blame: he more or less called Loren an adulteress and Ponti a cuckold. He seemed to believe that, all along, he'd been the hunted not the hunter: 'After all, our relationship was one of the things that helped break up my first marriage. Miss Loren was *always* phoning me and I'd go rushing all over Italy to be with her. It's odd that

---

[*] 'Richard III should woo less as a lover than as an actor – to show his mental superiority, and *power of making others the playthings of his purposes*. Mr Kean's attitude in leaning against the side of the stage before he comes forward to address Lady Anne, is one of the most graceful and striking ever witnessed on the stage. It would do for Titian to paint. The frequent and rapid transition of his voice from the expression of the fiercest passion to the most familiar tones of conversation was that which gave a peculiar grace of novelty to his acting . . .' . Hazlitt on Edmund Kean as Richard III in *Characters of Shakespeare's Plays* (1817). [Italics added.]

someone who apparently meant so much in her life – or so she *said* – should not figure in her life story. The only reason I can think is that she was married at the time. But it's not as if her husband didn't know. Carlo knew *very* well . . .'

But Loren has not been totally mute. As long ago as 1962 she was telling Lillian Ross:* 'I hate to hear actors say things like "when I play a King, I *become* a King," because to me this is really phony talk. You feel what the character you play feels, but not completely. You never lose control. When you kiss on the screen, you don't really kiss.' That is an implicit and effective demolition of Sellers' style and pretensions don't you think? And when Zec's book was published, containing extensive interview material from potty Peter ('. . . this magnificent, fantastic woman, a really very, very beautiful woman', and so on endlessly), the actress took explicit exception at last. As Zec said to me: 'This is the one area that Sophia Loren was upset by. She questioned the assertions and comments that Sellers had made – especially his claims that there had been a love-affair. She didn't like the implications of what he was saying. She is a moral lady; she hates cheap gossip, and she thought that whole business lacked dignity – it implied she could be frivolous in her marital relationship, and she was hurt for the embarrassment it caused Ponti. She also feels that she has been falsely implicated in the break-up of Sellers' first marriage. . .'

Well, no one could accuse him of ever behaving rationally, and obviously his excitable claims about Sophia Scicolone coming close to being Sophia Sellers are so much moonshine. The piteousness of that is no surprise. He had dreamed it up – the wishes and long-ings were father to the thoughts. But what began as delight – the fat radio Goon co-starring with a world-famous broad – quickly became nightmarish and absurd, and deeply embedded psycho-logically. Sellers was 'a crazed manic figure' according to his son, Michael, in the aftermath of the Loren passion. As proof of

---

* In *The Player: Profile of an Art* by Lillian Ross and Helen Ross (New York) page 54.

this he sold Chipperfield Manor, without asking for Anne's opinion, and shoved the family in a hotel. This peremptoriness did not go unnoticed by the press, to whom Sellers explained: 'We left our house at Chipperfield because we simply couldn't get proper service there. It's the Couple. You ring up the registry for a Couple – the wife to cook, the husband to work in the garden and so on. Now we've got a very nice German Nanny: the children love her, she's really good.* One evening I get home, the cook comes to me and says: "I'm not going to stay and be pushed around by a domineering German." – "Well now, what happened?" "Well, she came into the kitchen and she flung the sponge down. I'm not going to be pushed around by a domineering German." – "Yes, but what did she *say*?" – "She didn't say anything, it was the way she flung the sponge down." – "So what do you want me to do?" – "I'm handing in my week's notice." – "All right, never mind the week's notice, you can go today." – "Oh. . . Oh. . . well, if *that's* how you feel . . ." . . . "Hello, is that the registry office? Have you got a Couple?" And off we go again. That's why we left Chipperfield; it's the Couple.'

Despite this little sketch, Sellers' problems of domesticity and daily living were not farcical but maniacal. And he was quite right about a warring couple – he was himself subjecting Anne to endless tyrannies. 'You never knew what he was going to do. I went to stay with my mother when we separated. My mother lived in Bovingdon. Peter was in Hampstead, and he asked if he could come and see me. We arranged to meet at the end of the long drive. "You'd better come in," I said when I met him, because he seemed to be in a terrible state. He was dazed and blank. Don't forget, I'd known him since I was about seventeen; I was now thirty one – and he suddenly looked at my mother and said, "Who is that old lady?"; "That is my mother," I said. He'd known her a very long time. He was so odd, I said: "I think I'd better take you back." I drove and whilst we were on our way, he kept asking, "Who am I? I don't know who I am." He went into this whole speech about dark green, which he

---

* However, see page 383.

called Levy green, because Ted [Anne's second husband] had used it to decorate his house; and he kept asking who I was, who he was – a whole performance like he'd lost his memory. I drove him from Bovingdon to Hampstead, took him to the flat. He went in, slammed the door, wheeled round on me and said: "Right, you're not getting out. You-are-not-leaving-this-flat. *I will not let you out.*" It was then four o'clock in the morning. I had to phone the doctor: "You've got to come over. He won't let me out – and I want to leave." He came and stayed with Peter and sedated him. It was *terrifying.*'

☆ ★ ☆

And the terror predicts the mood and plot of *Hoffman*, which was made in 1969 – by which time Sellers had repeated with Britt, and others, the sorts of horrors he had perpetrated on Anne.* In *Hoffman* Sellers is depressed and sluggish, and yet he also suggests a terrible repressed energy. His eyes seem hooded and his long face is dark bottle-green and blueish, like an El Greco. It is almost a ghost story – Sellers creeps about the shadowy flat and the shuttered rooms as Nosferatu, the original bloodsucker. 'How attractive you look in the fading light,' he says to Miss Smith; and when, later on, she complains of a sore neck and he applies it with liniment, ('your

---

* According to Bert Mortimer, Sellers faked a wasting illness with Miranda Quarry: 'I recall vividly a weekend party that he and Miranda . . . had been invited to in Wiltshire before they wed. He disliked such gatherings because they were always packed with "chinless wonders", as he laughingly put it. I was enjoying a quiet weekend in Surrey when Miranda rang, begging me to rush down. Peter was behaving most oddly. When I showed up I was told he was in bed, calling distraughtly for "Bert". I thought he could be seriously ill and was taken to his bedroom where he lay, near motionless in a king-sized bed, repeating my name. But as I looked anxiously at him he gave a large wink. Then I realised what he was up to. I asked that we should be left alone. And as soon as the others had gone he hissed: "For God's sake get me out of here. I've had enough of this" . . . I told everyone he was ill, helped him to my car to take him home, and off we drove, with Peter laughing up his sleeve.' (Quoted within an article by Shan Davies in the *Sunday People*, August 3rd 1980.) The other distinguished personage who feigns collapse to get his way is Mr Toad.

neck . . . so young and defenceless'), we fully expect him to sink his fangs into her throat. Instead he sings a song – a dolorous vampire's love lyric:

> Once I knew a pretty girl
> I loved her as my wife
> But I put my hands
> About her neck
> And robbed her of my life.

Sinead Cusack's meek little colleen, in her neat wee beret, is a lamb-to-the-slaughter. 'I want to eat you,' says Hoffman, 'I want to consume you – what do you think of a man who wants to do that?' You'd think she'd want to be going a long way somewhere far off to avoid such an epicurean nutcase; but it is too late. She is a prisoner. She flees to the stairs – but Hoffman sails serenely down in the elevator and reclaims her. 'I do have full use, Miss Smith. Any man suffering massive sexual frustration would be out of his mind if, on getting the girl of his dreams, he didn't put her to *full use.*'

Sellers' Prince of Darkness doesn't get to release his tensions in any normal (or violent) way; instead he toys with the girl and prolongs his own agony. (The film has a sado-masochistic undercurrent.) Donald Pleasence had played the role of Hoffman on television, so it is easy to imagine the grand guignol variation on beauty and the beast which lurks within the material. (If Peter Lorre had been alive, it might have been a vehicle for him, too.) But Sellers, however, is sinister not through any cackling, hooting, or exophthalmic virtuosity; he is formal and polite (he is the more scary for being solemn and correct). He is full of silent staring and noiseless snooping and slinking. It is as if his permanently twilit apartment has been purposefully designed as a voyeur's maze. We are never quite sure which door he will come through – some locks fail to click; some thresholds seem to materialise in solid walls. Hatches, glass partitions, unexpected corners – and there is Hoffman's leering face, to elicit a shudder. ('A charming schoolgirl smile you have there, Miss Smith,' he purrs, when she believes herself to be unobserved.) And though, with his unexpected entrances, he is in every single scene of a one hundred and eleven minute movie, the character can slip out of sight, too, just as abruptly as a revenant would.

Sellers' stillness – the immobility he shared with Guinness, and which is deployed as autistic for Chance and gnomic for Fu Manchu – is utilised, for this one occasion in his career, as a source of fear. You expect Hoffman to start bleating like the cornered child murderer in *M* ('I want to escape . . . to escape from myself! But it's impossible. I can't. I can't escape . . . Who knows what it feels like to be me? How I'm forced to act . . .' etc.). The level of intensity on offer is like Lionel Meadows' – the difference being that, in *Never Let Go*, Sellers did not hold anything back. Here all is muted, crepuscular. There's not another performance to compare with Benjamin Hoffman until the courtliness of Sir Anthony Hopkins in *The Silence of the Lambs*; and that psycho-thriller's juxtaposition of eating-sex-death-cannabalism is predicted here. 'Hurry,' says Hoffman, 'Life is awaiting us. Eat or be eaten.' Other Hannibal Lecterish apothegms include 'Women are always hungry for something'; 'Most girls escape being chopped up only because they can cook'; and 'If a man could eat a girl's soft young body like ice-cream, he would not have to struggle to live with her soft young mind. . .'

That, in addition to everything else, Hoffman (and *Hoffman*) is repellently misogynistic, is hardly an observation that needs making. He trots out dozens of put-downs (they are automatic, like Old Sam's Dan Leno patter): 'It is not only homosexuals who don't like women. Hardly anybody does,' for example, or, 'When a woman starts complaining it means she is feeling at home'; and what we hate about it all is that Miss Smith accepts these judgements. She succumbs to them and makes herself available to him, even though the script has required her to deliver home-truths like: 'Look at you! Who wants you? You are mad and you are ugly.' (If Jodi Foster's determined young Special Agent, jogging through the woodlands, is a modern version of Sinead Cusack's elf-maiden, evolutionary history has made many a leap and bound in the twenty-odd years between the two films.) But Hoffman's problem isn't a straightforward hatred of women. What he hates most is that part of himself which needs them (for sex and other domestic duties); and he hates women the more when they yield. It is the hatred of a man who is dependent on his victims, and yet who wishes to be celibate and aloof: 'Every girl is a flower garden with a compost heap at the bottom. And many a noble man has had to drown his dwarf wife in a zinc bath or strangle an idiot girl on a muddy common in order to draw attention to himself.' Slaying women, or at the very least subjecting them, is the male's rite of passage. When a woman is dead you possess her wholly – she has no independent life left.

Sellers' phrasing here is masterful. He pauses, potters about the flat, moves from thought to thought, adds to his idea. It is the key-speech in *Hoffman* (and, not incidentally, it expresses Sellers' own view of women); it's the moment when the central character realises that he is disgusted by what he craves. ('Lips that touch kippers shall never kiss mine,' he says riddlingly.) To try and cope with the temptation and lusts, he reduces women to their component parts – he verbally dismembers them: 'You are here to be two arms, two legs, and the bits that fit in the middle,' Miss Smith is informed. She stares with terror into his big sad eyes. (Later, there is a close-up of Hoffman asleep – suddenly his eyes snap open, to give us a jolt.) But is it terror? Miss Smith hasn't been provided with much of a mind. We never feel there's much going on inside her head. It is wholly Hoffman's – or Sellers' – show. Miss Smith is a virgin-defilement fantasy who might have stepped from the shiny, coated pages of a holiday brochure or soft-core magazine. 'To awaken one morning and find a strange and beautiful naked girl asleep by your side. My dream, every man's dream,' her possessor says. (She is like Sellers' dream of a mechanical kit model girl.) Hoffman can hardly believe she is real, and neither can we. He sniffs the air when she sails past; he buries his face in her coat. He's always wanting to help her to wash and he frequently invades the bathroom when she takes refuge there. He goes on about her skin and hair and warns her against fungal ailments and infections. Either Miss Smith can rise above being nauseated by these anti-endearments, or else she is too stupid to see beyond them and twig that language portrays its user. 'You don't seem to like women, do you?' she says eventually – and incontestably. 'Yes I am filthy, yes,' he responds (again riddlingly), before letting fly some self-pity as he stares in the mirror:

> My maniac face. Girls all over the world are afraid of men with my expression. Plain, sad-faced men. Mature, sexually starved men. In offices, busses and trains. Men who've missed the boat. Their day is coming. Their revolution is almost upon you . . .

☆   ★   ☆

If Oscar Wilde is correct when, in the preface to *The Picture of Dorian Gray,* he says that 'To reveal art and conceal the artist is art's aim,' then it is apparent that with *Hoffman* something has gone wrong. Contempt; fastidiousness; anger; humiliation; sullying and being sullied: the moods and nuances in the work make it less of a film than a confessional, as Sellers knew. 'It's the first time I've been called on to play what *they* – the producer, the director, the author* – call *myself.* It's a very difficult rôle to play. It comes out of a lot of anguish.' Just how much anguish Ben Arbeid, Alvin Rakoff and Ernie Gebler were shortly to discover: Sellers tried to buy the negative and destroy it. He was confronted by a self-portrait, which revealed his internal monstrousness, and, like Dorian Gray, he wanted to plunge a dagger through its heart. As Arbeid explained to me: 'Benjamin Hoffman is very lonely, very insecure, very self-deprecating; and these were all terms used by people to describe the real Sellers. So there was much of the character already in our actor. The part called for that vacuum factor of

---

* 'Ernie Gebler, who wrote the screenplay, said that he wanted me to play myself. I told him that was very difficult because I had no idea what I was really like,' Sellers told Philip Oakes in the *Sunday Times* on December 14th 1969.

his – his way of filling himself with everybody and yet being no-body.'

'His ability to be everybody else, except himself,' I put in.

'This was not the sort of rôle that would normally attract him – he usually went for bravura stuff. Hoffman was not that at all. He had to play the internal self which wasn't there to start with. He couldn't rely on mimicry, and he went through the torture of not knowing who Hoffman was because he didn't know who he was . . . I remember when I first acquired the rights. I had an office in Hay Hill, off Berkeley Square, and I bumped into Sellers, who was living a few yards away in Clarges Street. We had a short exchange – I thought, "Christ, he'd be great as Hoffman."* And he was. He was so good, so convincing, he tried to buy the prints and burn them. Not because he was ashamed of the film, but because he recognised aspects of the inner man he thought he'd hidden for ever. He wanted to suppress himself – Peter Sellers the man, not Peter Sellers the performer. But it was impossible for him actually to pur-chase the negative. The company – Anglo-EMI – had accepted the picture. He had had ample opportunity to discuss the film with me before it was delivered to them as a finished piece. Sellers just wanted to *eliminate* it.'

In the event, political manoeuvrings at the studio resulted in the burial of the film, which was barely advertised or distributed. (Few people today have heard of it, let alone seen it.)† As Arbeid explains the palace revolution: 'There was a conflict in the executive corri-dors of the film company, as to who was in charge; a personality clash between the man controlling the studio, and with whom I made the deal to make the picture, Bryan Forbes, and the man

---

* Ben Arbeid first saw Sellers, shrieking in a darkened room, in 1955. He was the production manager for *Our Girl Friday* (which was recently released on video cassette, incidentally, as *The Adventures of Sadie*) and he recalls 'that some idiot was spending hours in the recording theatre doing parrot voices, whose name I didn't know until much later – when it turned out to be P.S.'

† The great photograph by Roy Jones, which adorns the cover of this book, was taken in Sellers' dressing room at Elstree during the making of *Hoffman*.

who was then chairman of the parent company, Bernard Delfont. It was almost as if the projects Forbes had instigated were deliberately not being promoted.* The only film which took off was Lionel Jeffries' *The Railway Children*. They were not *sold*. They were opened, but they were not sold. Very easy to do with *Hoffman*, because it was an unusual piece; not what you'd expect of a Peter Sellers performance. . .'†

That it was not what Sellers had expected from a Peter Sellers performance, either, was evident very early on to Alvin Rakoff, who went to meet him in Clarges Street: 'He greeted me – wide-eyed, hypertense, slightly manic, with an Austrian accent. And his first words to me were the first words of the film. "Miss Smith, come in." As best as I could I quoted some of the lines back at him. He calmed down eventually, and I said, "I don't think it needs to be an Austrian accent." I knew that Peter had to find the accent – the gimmick into his man's character. "Why can't you just do it straight? You can, you know." This was the biggest sales pitch, director-to-actor, that I did. "Don't put on a funny wig, don't put on funny glasses, don't put on a moustache, don't put on funny clothes" – he had a wardrobe of Austrian lederhosen; in order to make this eccentric, sinister man work, he was going to play it full of laughs. "No, no. You don't need all that." So I had to calm him down – and the opposite happened. Peter, having always played comedy, wanted a tragic edge. He went the other way – his Hoffman is dark and slow. I kept trying to get Peter to do it faster, but he wouldn't. His pacing. He argued for this brooding quality. "I'm

---

* 'I wish Bernie Delfont had had the courage of my convictions more often,' is Forbes' comment on the period, quoted in *Halliwell's Filmgoer's Companion* (Ninth Edition, 1988).

† Producers and directors would often whisper to me of rumoured managerial feuds, accounting department shenanigans, mystery deals, and other business agreements etc., to which they were not a party, but which assisted, or determined, the commercial failure of their ventures. So did Sellers, through his many flops, create debts or, as is hinted, did the written-off expenses he ran up shelter the cinema industry from the burden of taxation?

waiting for this moment to arrive. The girl of my dreams. I'm opening the door. I would be in this terrible state." That's why he is so black and cringing.

'There were strange imbalances in the man. Manic depressives could have taken lessons from Peter. One day he had a scene in the bed when Miss Smith is leaving him. He couldn't get the lines right. He started screaming – then he couldn't stop laughing. He kept pinching himself, so as not to laugh, and to get this line out, which he did eventually. Then he got bad tempered and left the studio. We didn't know if he'd come back the next day or not. He did return, as a matter of fact. We were to be given a bonus if we finished on time and on budget. The completion-guarantors, through Arbeid, were to offer myself and the technicians five thousand pounds each if we came in on the dot. Because Peter was notorious for walking off a production and disappearing for two weeks – so if we could keep him happy, we'd get our bonuses. We did it, we brought it in – and the upper echelon had been so concerned about Peter's misbehaving. Everybody remembered *Casino Royale*.

'He became Hoffman; he was Hoffman. He could do subtleties and variations, thousands of gradations, in a characterisation. An extraordinary talent, and as a director almost you had to decide amongst the eight different ways he'd want to do a two minute sequence. "Which one do you want?" he'd say. "Why?" And he'd expect an answer. He knew that he was always in turmoil; he was changing as an actor, going through a metamorphosis of some kind, starting on the path that leads to *Being There*. Death obsessed him. He kept thinking about it, because he didn't want to accept it. He said he'd set aside the money to be frozen when he died. He told me all about this, and he wanted to know why I wasn't going to do it. He was *obsessed* by death. I said, "Peter, suppose you are thawed out in a hundred years time – maybe even longer; suppose it is *several hundred* years. The world will have changed. You'll not fit into it any more. You'd be in a zoo, a freak. Or like meat in our deep freezers, you'll deteriorate." None of this could dissuade him at all. . .'

721

Of course not. He knew all about being a freak, a misfit; and far from disintegrating further, the ice would arrest his decay.

☆ ★ ☆

The beauty of cryogenics, to its proselytisers, was that you could control your going hence as well as your coming hither – you could outwit 'the fellow in the bright night-gown', as W.C. Fields always referred to death. Suicide only deals with the first half of the promise, but the principle of management is the same. You regulate your own exit – nothing is left to chance. Seven or eight years prior to *Hoffman*, when Sellers was ridding himself of Anne, so that he could be born anew as a young romantic leading man, he tried to give the impression that he was happy: 'I was amazed by the reaction *The Millionairess* had on women,' he explained, 'I suddenly found myself receiving extremely pleasant fan mail. Believe me this was quite a new experience. I've never considered myself to be at all the romantic type. And I wouldn't argue with anyone who described my looks as homely. But I must say I do have a giggle whenever I read these rather flattering fan letters.'

But behind the scenes, suicide was his constant threat: 'And with Peter, you never *knew*,' says Anne. 'I remember he once asked me over to his flat with the children, and he said, "Right if you leave this flat, I am going to jump over the balcony. I'll meet you downstairs." I had to get him to come back with me to my mother's. It was mad, and calculating, because he knew I'd never take the risk that he wouldn't leap, especially with my two children in the flat. With Peter, you never knew if he'd jump over the balcony. But in the end he didn't do anything dramatic – he just killed himself slowly. He used drugs, too, when he married younger women. Sexually he couldn't make it like he wanted to. When I was with him, he never took drugs and he drank very little. After he had his first heart attack, he was on cocaine a lot.'

'The charmed life became a cursed life,' I said.

'When I was married to him, any studio or newspaper publicity was about "Sellers the family man"; until we split up there was never any *strange* publicity. Then we split up; Bill died; Peg died.

He had no family. He'd been called the Arch Goon – and once he started to get into films, he didn't want to be seen as the Arch Goon. He wanted to be regarded as an actor. And it took him a long time for him to be recognised as an actor. But he still didn't have any taste. All those "Pink Panthers" – he's worthy of better. There was always a fight in him – perhaps because of his over-possessive mother. It must be a hell of a fight for a man to be totally dominated, like he was for so long. Maybe he thought he could dominate me, to make up for it, which was to be true in the end, because I gave up the theatre in desperation. He won that battle. He gave me such trouble when I was working. And I had Peg to fight. It had to be one or the other, I couldn't cope with an attack on two fronts. And then I had Mike. The funny thing about Peg was, when Peter and I split up, she absolutely begged me not to go. She'd grown used to me. Once Michael was born we'd sort of made it up – it was too much for her, a grandchild, she had to come and see me. I can't say I ever liked her, but we did tick along, and I liked Bill tremendously. And I remember Peter telling me his parents did split up at some point. He remembered when he was small going in a car with his mother and an uncle, and they picked his father up on a street, where they'd arranged to meet him. . .'

That will be the same event which Michael Jeffery got to hear about, when he and Sellers were walking along St. Martin's Lane.[*] It evidently clutched at his heart. Why? I think it is because, when he was reaching back, searching for lost time, he could see that that was the moment in his life when he learned about disharmony and division – and it left a profound impression. Bill's absences hadn't been noticed; it was his new, crestfallen presence which had been so off-putting. Was Peg going to share her tenderness? Was Sellers expected to? 'When I first met Peter, he was twenty-two or twenty-three, and he was already focused on his childhood,' says Anne. Her future husband was already trying to see what it was he had lived through – and he never was able to resolve his sympathies and emotions about the past. His father's

---

[*] See page 66 above.

humiliating return, the falsity of the unity his parents subsequently presented to the world – and all this overlaying the instability of his here-there-everywhere boarding house infancy: Sellers was aware that ordinary domesticity was not something he had ever known; and maybe, as his mind was flooded with memories and comparisons, he realised that it was not something that was for him at any stage.

'My father liked one-off payments', says Michael. 'You settle a bill, an account, and that's that. The continuous expenditure a family involved upset him – a continuous drain on his resources.'

'On his emotional resources do you mean?' I asked.

'He'd forget about us for months on end, if he was away doing a film; and then, when he'd run out of other people to amuse him, and he was lonely – then would come a phone call. But never any apology or explanation for the long silence or neglect.'

When Anne left he grew bitter and retrospective. As he confessed to Herbert Kretzmer: 'Why, I wondered, does one marry the wrong person? I began keeping a kind of diary. I began putting it all down, all the things that had happened to me, as much as I could remember, all the way back. It kept coming back to the same questions. For instance, when I met Anne Hayes, why did I rush all over the country trying to persuade her to marry me? Maybe I was one of those actors nobody could live with. Anyway, I never found the answer.' Well, no. He'd never in a million years have admitted any blame – he could not see that Anne left him because he was psychotic and violent. But there is more to it than this. When he and Anne swung apart it was like when Peg and Bill swung apart – and this was one way of bringing the past up to date. It was also one way of getting close to a side of his mother that was a mystery to him – how she'd felt when she was walked out on. And had her sense of grievance (mingled with gladness) communicated itself to him? Because the ironic twist in this tale is that Sellers, though he had tormented and victimised Anne without stint, felt himself to be the victim, not the aggressor. It had never occurred to him, when he was inflicting his tortures, that Anne might move on to have a happier life elsewhere – or that she'd find her protector in the very man whom Sellers had hired to decorate his flat, Ted Levy.

☆ ★ ☆

The fact that Sellers had bought a seven year lease on a top-storey flat (for £31,000) and had disposed of the freehold security of Chipperfield (sold for £41,000) is evidence enough that he intended reverting to a bachelor existence, though he pretended otherwise: 'My wife and I recently sold our home in Chipperfield and for a while we lived at the Carlton Tower Hotel. That was a sort of clearing-house while we looked around,' he told *Playboy*. 'I liked living at the Carlton Tower. I liked the atmosphere. Now we've taken a flat in Hampstead. I want to find out if flat living is OK. . .'

West End hotels, and penthouse apartments, were luxurious versions of his childhood boarding houses. As the manager of the Dorchester said to me: 'Mr Sellers was such a regular guest; he was in and out quite a lot at all hours. Film companies would put him up in the Oliver Messel suite, when they wanted him to do some entertaining. He was always here holding receptions. All his wives used to come here and use the hotel. It was more or less his London home, and he knew all the staff – they were almost like his own personal staff. He knew all the floor-waiters; they knew what food he liked. He liked the twenty-four hour service. Being Mr. Sellers, he would want breakfast, say, at any hour of the day or night – and it would be brought to him without any problems. There were fewer security precautions in those days – but when he was here, everybody would know where Peter Sellers was, and we'd see that nobody else would get his key. . .'

Sellers could pretend he was a sultan – the sultan from *Brouhaha* perhaps – and a hotel's liveried servants did duty for the admiring aunties backstage in Southsea and Ilfracombe. Though he knew that this sort of limitless pampering was what he wanted, he still went through the motions, however, of hunting for a fixed family abode: 'Darling,' he was heard to say down the phone to Anne, 'I'm afraid that old thing of Sir T's is hopeless. No, it's a dreary place – quite impossible. But I think I've got something for you to look at on Monday.' He then turned back to his interviewer (Dilys Powell) and said: 'Houses! You wouldn't believe the places I've looked at lately. And the estate agents – I must do an estate agent one of these days. No, I say, we don't want to go to Baron's Court. "Don't want to go to Baron's Court. Now there's a semi-detached house at Rickmansworth, five bed, three recep ..." We think Rickmansworth is a bit far out. "... Bit far out. What would you say to a bungalow by the river, kitchen garden, boat-house." The river always seems rather damp. .. Yes, I really must do an estate agent one of these days.'

He didn't (in so far as I am aware); but he did find himself imitating the fellow who was putting the finishing touches to an eagle's nest in Northwood Lodge, Oak Hill Park, NW3. 'I am a person who has no real voice of his own,' said Sellers, as ever trying to imagine what it would be like not to exist. 'I'm like a microphone. I have no set sound of my own. I pick it up from my surroundings. At the moment I've got a South African architect working on my new flat in Hampstead, and so I tend to speak in a South African accent all the time.'

To discover that he was in the presence of a curious echo was disagreeable; to find that his vocal double was maltreating his wife and children was insupportable. Ted Levy had to intervene. 'In South Africa, all Ted's generation wanted to listen to was *The Goon Show* – so Peter Sellers was Ted's idol when he came over to Britain and designed our Hampstead flat,' says Anne. 'Ted didn't notice me – he was far too overwhelmed to meet the legendary Peter Sellers; but then he saw how he behaved – disgustingly. If Peter decided to be charming, there was nobody more charming in the world. He had the devil's charm. And then he could be the opposite. Ted thought that, in real life, Peter was *disgusting*. He was his greatest fan – and then, well. . .'

What happened is that, to make the best of living in a flat, and to try and keep the family together for a little longer, Anne threw herself into decorating the place – into trying to make it a home. She therefore accompanied Levy on expeditions to look at furniture and ceramic tile samples. When they returned, Sellers accused them of having an affair; and so relentless was his campaign, he achieved what he feared – he pushed them together. This (in circular fashion) justified his rage and dejection. 'The evil forces consuming Dad', wrote Michael in his book, 'were to make poor Ted pay a horrendous price for what Dad termed an "injustice".' The children almost became accustomed to their father raving that 'Ted Levy has destroyed my life. He has taken your mother away from me. I'll kill him, I'll kill him.'

Levy did indeed think his hour had come. At two o'clock in the morning, Sellers discovered where his enemy lived and set out to confront him. He hammered on the door until Levy was roused from sleep and let him in. Sellers was wearing a heavy overcoat and gave the impression he was armed. 'He wore an expression of hate, anger and frustration, the like of which I'd never seen on the face of any human being before. I was convinced now that he was going to murder me.'

Levy, as calmly as was possible under the circumstances, said that he was not the cause of any marital bust-up, and that surely the Sophia Loren episode hadn't helped. He also pointed out that Sellers had already started to sleep around, and that if Anne wanted to leave or stay with her husband, given those sorts of circumstances, it was none of his, Levy's, business. . . And so on. Sellers left around about then and returned to wherever Anne and his sleeping babes were abiding. Perhaps it was another occasion altogether when his viciousness became extreme. 'I used to wake up in the middle of the night with them rowing, and her screaming, "No, Peter, don't don't *don't*." Then it would stop and she'd scream some more,' Michael told me. 'And I remember he said, up at the penthouse, "You'd better not be here when I get back – or I'll kill you."' And off into the dark he disappeared again – but at least that request and threat made a change from the one where he wanted to keep Anne a captive.

Arguably, the psychological harassment of his children was worse than his physical maltreatment of his wife – who at least could wear long black Dior gloves and dark glasses to hide the contusions. He constantly dragged Michael and Sarah from their beds to tell them he hated their mother and was going to divorce her. Once, because it was about four o'clock in the morning and his solicitor didn't seem to be in the office answering the phone, Sellers pulled his infant son from his bed and told him he had to remember everything that was being said, that he was an official witness. One such statement that was flung about and which Michael obliged by not forgetting was (to Anne), 'You must get out of here and never come back.' A similar scene took place with Peg present. As Michael told it to me: 'The great ordeal with Peg was giving her an endless hug every time we saw her – it was like "Hello-o-o-o-o-my-daaarling-g-g-g!" and you'd be clamped on to her bosom and you'd say, "Yeah, I love you too Peg". She'd ask how much you loved her and exactly how great it was to see her; she'd feed the lines and we'd give the responses, and she'd feel happy after about half an hour of that. She was never nasty to us – she reserved her scorn for my father's women. She came to our aid a lot of the time, especially when there was an argument before he was to go off to America. My birthday is in April, and he said quite kindly: "Are you coming out for your birthday?" – "No, I want to stay here for my birthday." – "*How dare you*! I'm your father. I'm going to give you a ticket, and if I say you'll come, *you'll come*." – "All my friends are here. I want to have a party here with my mates." It went on and on, and eventually he threw me out – out of the Dorchester, in fact. His finale was to demand, "Who do you love the most? Me or your mother?" So Sarah goes, "I love you both the same." Nice and cool. But I said, "My *mother*." By then I'd had enough. I wasn't going to play his games. I didn't feel like placating him after what he'd just put me through. So – "Right. *Out*. All your stuff will be turning up at your mother's house soon."

'Peg made the peace for us. "Cool down. Calm down. Let's have a cup of tea," she'd say.'

But is wasn't peacefulness, as such, which reigned. Sellers was simply diverted into ranting about something else. He'd always say his children didn't love him; that they were all against him and using him, none of which was true. (It needs to go on record that it was Ted Levy who – voluntarily – paid for their education and who supported them: Sellers was meant to pay ten pounds a week maintenance, and only when the arrears totalled two thousand pounds, and he was threatened by court action, did he grudgingly cough up.)

As can readily be seen from the above deposition, both Peg *and* Sellers required people to quantify their affection; they were too wrapped-up in themselves to understand that 'there's beggary in the love that can be reckon'd' (as Antony warns Cleopatra). And Sellers' persistence in putting his children on trial ('Which of you shall we say doth love us most?') made him a mad and modern Lear. Far from showing a loving nature, his demands (like his mother's) expose a jealous and selfish brooding – and Michael, whose obstinacy was feeble compared with his father's positive derangement, did have to go to America, of course he did. ('Right. That's it. He's going to America'), where he was left in the care of Bert Mortimer and Hattie Stevenson.

☆   ★   ☆

Sellers played the rôle of aggrieved innocent and deceived nearly everybody, himself included.[*] He invited Herbert Kretzmer up to

---

[*] ' . . . he finally sued Anne for adultery with Levy . . .' wrote Evans, succinctly, in 1968 – which was true, Sellers did; but as the subject of *The Mask Behind the Mask* was still alive at the time (as was Levy) it was perhaps not possible to explore the background. In fact, Anne sued Sellers for divorce first, but he threatened to counter her petition, challenge her in the courts etc., and drag things out in an ugly and public fashion. (It was out of the question for *her* to be seen divorcing *him*.) Faced with this option, Anne and Levy decided to let Sellers go ahead with his marginally less gruesome ploy, which was to allow him to be the first to sue, naming Levy as co-respondent. In the event, Sellers still blabbed publicly: e.g. Kretzmer's interview, 'Sellers: Now I Will Tear My Palace to Bits,' in the *Daily Sketch*, on March 9th 1963, in which he said: 'Yes, I do feel bitter, it's no good denying it. They have behaved badly.' Only Graham Stark, in *Remembering Peter Sellers*, has got it right and seen it the other way around: 'Peter was the loser, and well he knew it.'

the penthouse, showed off the stained wood ceilings and matching fabrics, and then said: 'I can hardly wait to get all this Ted Levy stuff out. I'll change it all to French country style. I can't live in this place the way it is. It holds too many memories. I'm going to pull the whole lot out by the roots and start again. I want to see nothing around me to remind me of Anne, or that man, or the life we used to live here. In any case I never really liked this place . . . It's so heavily *Teutonic*. Like a hotel or a ship. Know what I mean? Over-masculine. It's just not me, love. It's not me. Anne, or course, loved this place. She was enamoured of this chap's designs and colour schemes. They kind of overruled me, always around, the two of them, buying wallpaper and wood and stuff. Gradually I caught on. I saw this thing growing. I'm not very articulate but I'm quite perceptive . . . I could see what was happening, but I didn't want us to break up. I bought Anne a house near here so we could separate. I thought it would be a solution if, maybe, we didn't actually live together for a while. I desperately wanted Anne back, well, because of the children and because I was still in love with her . . . I have children now, two of them. They are the big thing in my life. One has to think of these things. . .'

To find another monologue that so craftily interweaves lies, hypocrisy and all-over baseness, you'd have to go back to the dramas of Molière. The masculinely drab decor, like the idea of the flat itself, was his own inspiration. The hotel-cum-ocean liner effect, again, had enthralled him; and as for Anne's enthusiasm, she did well to try and make the place comfortable, within the limits of Sellers' instructions, especially as she'd rather have been still at Chipperfield or perhaps Whetstone. Sellers' threats that he will tear the place apart are simply spiteful (wouldn't it be simpler and cheaper to sell up and move on?); the comments about still loving Anne and how much he loves the children are sentimental and hollow; and is it possible, logically and practically, to 'separate' and yet also not to 'break-up'? But to dissect the speech in this manner is all too easy.* That, to Sellers, love was an issue of power and will – part of his compulsion to possess and dominate – is by now very clear, and this would never alter. So what interests me about the performance is whether or not he was aware that he was giving one? Did he not realise the situation? The bulk and gist of his words, which complain about his isolation and urge us to picture his injuries, as a new couple were off gallivanting, make sense only if they can be imagined as being voiced by Anne, had she wanted to describe what it was like when Sellers was doing his utmost to give the impression that he was gadding about with Loren.

In talking about Anne and Levy, therefore, Sellers is referring to himself and his goddess – and he did so in a deliberate parody of his wife's grief. For as Anne said to me: 'When he was having his affair with Loren, nobody mentioned it to me, and I thought in my stupid way, if nobody is talking to me about it, it isn't going to happen. I really cared about his career, and I cared about him as a person. I gave my *time* to him – but I should have seen what was going on. The first time Loren came out to Chipperfield, we had to have a huge party – Peter spent the afternoon filming it and taking photographs. She arrived in a yellow dress and a vast *My Fair Lady* hat covered with flowers. Michael said, "I don't want to meet her. She looks like a chicken!" – which I loved! Another time I had to go into town and meet them for dinner. Michael looked at me and said, "You look like a fairy princess, Mummy, you look beautiful" – which is an unlikely thing for a child to say, and I thought he's the only person who's going to say that tonight. Because I know my husband won't. He's with his girlfriend. Michael had intuitively picked up that something was going on. But with Peter, he was

---

* I must mention that, far from being able to eradicate the place from his mind, when Sellers was scouting around London in the late Sixties, deciding upon locations for *The Magic Christian*, he told Peter Evans that his favourite residence had been 'the penthouse up at Hampstead. Now that had a fantastic view. . . Do you know, on a good day you could almost see Jimmy Grafton's pub. Where it all started. Spike, old Harry, Mike Bentine . . .' Evans comments, understandably elegiac: 'He could almost see yesterday. The only thing he could ever be sure of.'

playing the part of a romantic actor, and playing it in real life; and I always felt there was much more to Peter than one ever saw.'

☆　★　☆

When Sellers' first marriage broke up, he was left broken up – and if he didn't know Wyndham Lewis' admonition that 'in order to live you must *remain* broken up' – which means, I presume, that if you are not to ossify and grow dull it is necessary to keep on the move and to search for constant stimulus – then he certainly showed a marked fidelity to such a concept. Yet – and this is the great paradox with Sellers – what was divisive in his life was put to creative use in his films. Out of the welter of projects now offered to him, in the wake of the release of *The Millionairess* around the world, he chose those in which his struggles and uncertainties could flourish (or at least be mimicked). Asked, at the time, did he feel a compulsion to work, Sellers said: 'Well, what else is there? I don't really want to do more than two pictures a year. That's the ideal. But then you get to a position where you really get mixed up. There's all this stuff to sift through and you don't know what to do. I think there is a certain pattern an actor falls into. A lot of actors try to break it. You meet them and they say they've found it, like Buddhism. Some Indian bloke who stands up against a wall all day. That's it. That's the secret. And they hold up walls for a while, and next time you meet them they are back in the old routine, doing the same old job. I suppose the thing is to take off to some little place and think – that would be good.* But I don't relax easily. And the moment you do stop work, they all descend on you – you get all the moguls with ideas; producers, they come round and they say, this is good, Peter, this is wonderful, they say, we must do it right now, and you say, all right, and most of the time there isn't even a script. . .'

There was a script for *Only Two Can Play*, however, and Sellers

---

* One of the reasons Sellers gave to the BBC for withdrawing from *Waiting for Godot*, in January 1962, was that he had 'promised to take his family to India for three months after *Waltz of the Toreadors*'. Nothing more was to be heard of that passage.

was fascinated by it, almightily so. John Lewis' relationship with Mai Zetterling's Elizabeth Gruffydd-Williams is a carnal version of Dr Kabir and Epifania's serenades; and beyond that, Lewis' restlessness and his sense that he is trapped and is being worn down chime with Sellers' own fear of boredom, stability and a settled marriage. Elizabeth Gruffydd-Williams, in floral headgear and clutching a topiaried poodle, stands in for the full-of-poise Sophia Loren.

'When I was first asked to make this film I was a little doubtful about it,' said Sellers. 'I'd read the original story, and I don't mind admitting that I wasn't too keen about it.* I was handed a film

---

* This dismissive remark, in translation, means that he hadn't read it, i.e. Kingsley Amis' novel, *That Uncertain Feeling*, first published in 1955. If he had, he'd have relished the brilliant and farcical scene in which Lewis, caught in Elizabeth's bedroom, makes his escape disguised in the costume of a medieval Welsh woman, which happens to be handy:

. . . I got on the bus. Holding my skirts aloft with what at another time I'd have considered impressive skill, I went upstairs. None of the double seats had both places vacant. I sat down at the back next to a man in rough clothes who seemed to be asleep, and put my bonnet on. It would help to hide the wig, which under a good light was unlikely to be very convincing, and would establish quite certainly what I was, or rather what I was supposed to be. An old woman with glasses in the seat in front turned round, smiled rather charmingly at me, and addressed me in the language of my forefathers.

Pretending to be deaf would probably have been my best bet at this point, but I didn't think of that. Aware that some slight paradox was inherent in my doing so, I told the woman, in the tongue of the Saxon invader and exploiter, that I couldn't speak any Welsh. The voice I adopted for getting this across, however, did me great credit: I had forethought to pitch my ordinary voice well up instead of relying on piping away in falsetto, where control's likely to be poor. I was so pleased at having thought of this that I started feeling more cheerful than at any time since jumping out of the window. A few stares had come my way since I'd boarded the bus, but these were dying down now. And in a quarter of an hour or so I'd be off, making like a whippet for a lovely field full of bushes that lay just fifty yards from my stop in Cwmhyfryd.

The old woman's smile had faded and she remained silent. She was probably a farmer's wife from Denbighshire and thus isolated from the great English-speaking community of the free world. In a moment, having determined that

The Life and Death of Peter Sellers

script and after I'd read it I couldn't resist playing in the film. It was such a wonderful and funny script' – by Bryan Forbes, who tried to improve on Amis' original by incorporating some gags of his own. The scene where Sellers is trying to seduce Mai Zetterling in the American convertible, for example, and the car is mobbed by a herd of Friesians, was based on a real experience of Bill Kerr's – whose coitus was made interruptus by cows when he was in the RAF near Peterborough. Another interpolation is the bit on the crowded early morning bus to work, when Sellers, to goose the bosomy typists, cops a feel and then pretends to have a withered

---

I'd indeed been speaking in English, she'd say 'Dim Saesneg' and that would be that. What she did say was 'You're an imposter.' (page 130ff).

As the first scene in the film has Elizabeth coming to the library for a book on Welsh national dress – so that she an replicate the designs for the Amateur Dramatic Society – the loss of the above, which would otherwise connect, is a pity. Another (more crucial) aspect which Sellers overlooked – or did not know about – was that Amis, in conversation with Clive James, called The Fuck:

. . . On the whole [the movie was] not bad, but I was very disappointed that there was no fuck. Because it's vitally important, that fuck. And not for sexual reasons alone. It terrifies you, what Lewis gets himself into as a result of it. He gets into a panic and basks fraudulently in a glow of moral principle about the job being fixed. What *I* didn't realise at the time of writing, so how could he, was that he was scared, and wanted out. The attack of principle gets him off the hook. In the film, where the screwing is cut out, all he has is an attack of principle, which makes him look priggish. I suspect Sidney Gilliatt [producer] didn't like the decision either, but the heroes of romantic screen comedies didn't fuck in those days.

(*The New Review Anthology*, edited by Ian Hamilton [London, 1985], page 55.)

Sellers also fibbed about having read and evaluated Nabokov's *Lolita*: 'I didn't like *Lolita* – the book, I mean – but I like the script.' As Wolf Mankowitz said to me: 'Sellers was incapable of even reading a script. You'd have to do an imitation – and he'd get hold of that, and he'd copy you, and he'd read his own lines eventually. He never had any intellect at all. He'd hardly ever read a book, not from beginning to end. He could simulate certain things. And he'd pick up the wrong ideas very quickly.'

I believe that the only book he read from cover-to-cover was Jerzy Kosinski's thirty-thousand word *Being There*.

arm, like Richard III's. 'He'd get stuck on a line or stage direction like that,' Forbes told me, 'and he'd be *helpless*.'

Only Two Can Play differs from *That Uncertain Feeling* in that the former is a simple seven-year-itch sex romp ('as you say, it was just a romp,' Sellers said to Dilys Powell a little peevishly), and in the latter libido is a sympton and not the cause of the hero's desire to have an adventure. In Amis' original, Lewis is a man who is in the process of discovering that he's no longer young. 'Now don't stand there giving me that little-boy face, you're getting too old for it,' his wife shouts, when she confronts him with his womanising, i.e. his disloyalty and selfishness. That line isn't in the film (though Jean's harassed anger is), and the miracle with Sellers – his genius – is that he can imply all the feelings and guilts which are in the book but which the film otherwise leaves out. The way he yawns, the way he slouches around his kitchen, the way he leans on the counter and against the shelves at the library: we can see that Lewis, suffused with tediousness and staleness – with a lassitude so extreme it is almost languorous and pleasurable – is on the brink of going to seed. In other words, though this is a film, and one designed as an adulterous farce at that, Sellers is incapable of being superficial. His performance has a *novelistic* spaciousness and reticence – almost as if Sellers' underlying processes were like Henry James', who'd only need the tiniest glimpse of an idea – half an anecdote overheard at a dinner party, say – to be able to worry it into a full-length drama. ('I amplify and improve a little,' James scribbled in his notebook, as a character for *The Ambassadors* came to him. 'It touches me – I can see him – I can hear him. Immediately, of course – as everything, thank God, does, it suggests a little situation. I seem to see something, of a tiny kind, springing out of it. . .'). There was no need for research, and with Sellers (at any rate) what he accomplished did not require an analytical brain. His understanding was instantaneous. Whatever outrages and mess he committed in reality, when it came to his art he could be sympathetic and unifying – his puerility and crudity were transformed.

☆ ★ ☆

'Perhaps,' I said to Kenneth Griffith, 'he was frightened to analyse his talent in case it went away.'

'Yes, he had these fears. If he knew how it worked, he couldn't do it. This was one of his terrible doubts and fears – didn't know quite *how* it happened. He, over *Only Two Can Play*, went through this terrible neuroticism. "I can't do it Kenny. I don't know how to be a Welshman. I've got to get out of it." Always he'd say, "I'm going to get out of it."

'"Look, Peter, why don't you and I go down to Wales a couple of weeks before we start, and I'll have a think about what you have to do, and I'll introduce you to one or two Welshmen who are rather like John Lewis. Educated lower middle-class." One was John Ormond, a BBC producer and poet, a great friend of Dylan Thomas, and who looked like a Welsh owl. Dylan called him "l'enfant horrible." I said, "I'll introduce you." So I arranged a supper party at a pub in Tiger Bay, to which I invited the two men I had had in mind, John Ormond, and the other was a newsreel cameraman called John Pike, a bit of a boy. Pike would dress immaculately – blazer, hands in pockets, dapper, so. . . A great ladies' man. Suddenly his eyes would focus on your own clothes, and the whole façade of his sophistication would crumble as he'd say, in a strong valleys accent, "Get that tie in *London*?!!"

'I wanted Sellers to have a look at these chaps;[*] and the moment he saw them all his problems were solved. He said, "That's it. I'm all right."'

---

[*] I have not managed to discover anything more about Pike, but Ormond, who died on May 4th 1990, was exactly as Griffith described: a third-rate sub-Dylan Thomas versifier, the author of *Requiem and Celebration* (1969), etc. According to an obituary in *The Times*: 'increasing ill-health kept him to well-beaten paths in Cardiff where he enlivened those favourite pubs in which regulars and barmaids would occasionally be startled to hear him rap out love poetry and satirical verse between rounds of drinks'. Which makes him seem more like Amis' Gareth Probert (played by Richard Attenborough), rather than Lewis – unless Ormond was an omen of what Lewis might nightmarishly become: Alun Weaver, in *The Old Devils*.

Like Henry James, he'd received ('all throbbingly and yearningly and passionately') a clue, or a key, and the way grew straight. Indeed, Sellers was so comfortable as a Welshman, there was no stopping him.

'He'd become someone else, and extend his vocabulary, and he'd develop an apparent interest in subjects he'd be reluctant to embark on on his own. One evening, he said, "Kenny, you know Swansea" – which isn't true – "I think we ought to go out for a meal. Where shall we go?" I recommended a little Chinese restaurant. "Fantastic." Bert found the place. We sat down, the three of us, and in came several hulking colliers and their demure girlfriends. They sat down rather noisily – particularly the men. Then after a while we could hear: "I'm not going to bloody ask 'um. Who the fucking 'ell do they think they are?" We realised they were referring to us. "Bloody stupid, you are. On the telly? Go on . . ." Unnerving. They were talking about us, and rather offensively. Uneasy, I was. Suddenly, one of them finally lumbered over to us:

'"Here," he said, "my girlfriend do say you are on the *telly*. 'Sat true?"

'This to Peter Sellers at the height of his fame. Sellers chipped in with a Welsh accent:

'"Oh, norr," he said, "I'm afraid your fee-on-cee by there is mistaken. Norr, norr. Mr Jenkins, by here, and me, we're on the administration side of the Llanwern Steelworks."

'"There warr you bloody fool," this lout called back, "They're not on the telly. They're in the office at the steelworks in Newport, for God's sake."

'And he backed off.

'"*Hold on!*" said Sellers, "Hold on! Now that isn't strictly true, what I've told you. Because you know when Her Majesty the Queen opened the second half of the steelworks? Well, of course, it was very carefully and *fully* covered by the BBC television. And I have been told, but I can't guarantee this, but it has been reported, and word has got about, that as the camera tracked down, following Her Majesty the Queen, both Mr Jenkins and I were distinctly *seen* . . ."

'He got away with it, and he dragged me into it as Iuan Jenkins, my character in the film.

'"Iuan, you have heard it said we were clearly *seen* . . . This is what we have been *told* . . ."

'Though he was conscious of how different he was – set apart by his talent if nothing else – in other ways Peter was very anonymous.'

☆ ★ ☆

There is a particular scene in *Only Two Can Play* which gets it all across – when Lewis attempts to perform his ablutions in the squalid bathroom, with its steamed-up mirror and rust-pocked sink. He is preparing to shave, and is squinting at the reflection of his dewlapped face, when an old man emerges from behind the partition which hides the jakes. Coughing and wheezing, the codger exits, leaving behind what must surely be a radioactive pong. The plumbing is primitive and the chain for the flush cistern is situated above the basin (we might have mistaken it for the light-pull switch), where Lewis is now stooping, gazing at the grey scummy lather he is about to apply to his skin. He glances at the gently swinging handle on the chain as if hypnotised by it. A few seconds later he grabs it and stills it; he also pulls up the tab on the Air Wick to maximum length. His failure and despair crystallise in that moment. He is overweight, zestless, underpaid, with a wife and children to support. Did he get to be a graduate (BA, Univ. Coll., Swansea) for this? Jean, in her turn, is fast losing her looks (Virginia Maskell's bony, wan prettiness exactly fits Amis' description: 'It was saddening to remember how lustrous, as well as abundant, her hair had been before she'd had the children; to know how necessary that careful make-up was, and how angular her hips and shoulders had become'). She is wearing herself out in the top-floor flatlet, surrounded by soiled nappies and no hot water. There is also no fridge, phone or television set.

The appearance of the Mai Zetterling character, therefore, is to Jean an affront (Elizabeth Gruffydd-Williams is rich, shiftless, childless) and to Lewis an avenue of escape. The white goddess brings out in him what he might have been like when he was younger. Sellers, as with Kite, doesn't allow caricature to warp his performance: when Lewis is aroused by a dream girl what we register is the extent of his self-delusion. He thinks he can rush about like a horny teenager, and then again he knows he can't. We sense Lewis' own ironic awareness of his plight – and this is where Sellers finds the comedy: in the division between a desire to be irresponsible and the knowledge that his character is too mature (i.e. basically decent and moral, i.e. cowardly) to set himself free.

Off the set, Sellers constantly carped about Virginia Maskell and wanted her removed from the film. (Her confidence duly undermined, the actress made one more film and she killed herself in 1968.) Was he treating her like that because he was treating Anne like that? Did Sellers, whose domestic problems were enciphered in the film, try to duplicate those problems when he was making the film? (Lewis himself, by contrast, is tender with his wife: 'Her face is one that I can never see without wanting to smile for one reason or another' – another sentence of Amis' which Sellers, sunk in the rôle, communicates on the screen without having to say a word.)

If he stored up (unjustified) rancour for one woman, he doled out (unwanted, unreciprocated) attention on the other, for he decided to have a shot at romancing Zetterling, as if she were an encore of his antic hey-hey over Loren. Luckily, Amis himself came to her rescue, though he may not have known this. When Sellers went off into this funny voice routine, which had worked so well during the leisure moments on *The Millionairess*, Amis interrupted him with impersonations and gags of his own. No doubt he did his Edith Sitwell Face, his Crazy Peasant Face, his Sex Life in Ancient Rome Face, and his Evelyn Waugh Face. ('Someone once took photographs of them all,' said Philip Larkin, 'I wish I had a set.' So do I.) Amis was also adept at Russians, Germans, gun shots, jeeps backfiring, gangster films, war films and a mime that involved Humphrey Bogart flashing a torch round a cellar.* The distin-

---

* For these and further recollections of Sir Kingley's histrionic talents, see *Required Writing: Miscellaneous Pieces 1955-1982*, by Philip Larkin (London 1983).

guished novelist in his younger days was evidently a one-man version of *The Goon Show*, and he much impressed another writer who has always fancied his chances as a comedian, Clive James, who has reported that 'Amis' mimicry is not quite in the same league with that of Peter Sellers as to accuracy, but the mind and invention behind it make it a feast for the Gods. He is a brilliantly entertaining man.'

That established, here is how Zetterling recalled the behind the scenes socialising in Swansea: Sellers and Amis 'tried to outwit each other with reminiscences and dirty jokes, Kingsley punctuating his with resounding farts, to everyone's embarrassment. . .'

Thus was Sellers' frantic ardour dispersed.

☆ ★ ☆

Bottom burps and imitation games to one side, another reason why Sellers would have hated Maskell is that she, like him, was giving a vivid, downbeat performance. Jean is flustered, cross and left on her own to cope with the kids all day. The half-bottle of sour milk on the food-cupboard, the sticky lino floorings, the coin-in-the-slot gas heating: the domestic surroundings in *Only Two Can Play* could have come from a Ken Loach or Lindsay Anderson docu-drama about life in a sooty city, and Jean and Lewis add up to a realistic portrait of an airless, wormy modern marriage. That's what is in the book; that is what comes across on the screen. Sellers, however, was simply envious of his co-star's skills, and as a manipulator he didn't like having to share being at the centre of things. No doubt he'd have preferred Lewis not to have had a visible wife at all. Is this what he was scheming for? An off-camera She Who Must Be Obeyed? A Her-Indoors? Could Lewis' home-life have been signalled simply by the little brown paper parcel of sandwiches he totes to work?

Incidentally, did Larkin, who was a librarian, inspire the character of John Aneurin Lewis? Larkin, says Sir Kingsley in his *Memoirs*, found the ideal solution to one's difficulties with girls: instead of taking them out and spending money on them, Larkin reasoned that 'I can toss off in five minutes, free, and have the rest of the evening to myself.'

The fact is, Lewis and Jean exist on a naturalistic plane; everybody else is flamboyant and cranky. Griffith, who is genuinely and habitually Welsh, is Welsh in a way which would be a ponderous and semi-offensive racial slur if Iuan Jenkins had been conceived and played this way by an Englishman. His voice is chapel born and bred; his rolling gait has been formed by chasing goats up and down the mountains. He has the pop-eyes and hunched shoulders of a never-very-far-away bardic convulsion. Mr Hyman (Graham Stark), the dirty old man who at last returns the much-stained *Concise History of Codpieces* to the branch library, is likewise funny in an over-the-top Pink Pantherish way – as is Richard Attenborough in a ghastly little beard as the poetaster; as is Mai Zetterling's vamp, who when she whispers into her ormolu telephone puts me in mind of Claudia Cardinale, one of Inspector Clouseau's temptresses. Such attitudinising works against Sellers' discreet, diffident Lewis – and perhaps another actor would have been demolished had he accepted the part and then been thrown in the ring with a lot of busybodies and comedians. Sellers, however, makes the fact that he does not properly belong to this crazy gang the key to his performance. His own dissociated sensibility is shaped to Lewis' quiet, suggestiveness, and cynicism. Lewis is indirect, infectiously humorous, and he thinks himself a misfit because he is interested in women's breasts and jazz. In a film where everybody else (save Jean) is cartoonish, and therefore less than human, Sellers, unafraid of appearing bland and weary, holds our attention because he makes lethargy seem droll. We are alert to what is going on behind those half-awake eyes. Lewis, imprisoned by home and job, gives grudging acceptance to the fact that there is not, after all, going to be much more to his life than respectability.

Lewis is related, in Sellers' canon, to Dodger Lane, who is literally in clink. (The titles, *Two Way Stretch* and *Only Two Can Play*, could be exchanged and still mean as much, or as little.) Dodger is one of Sellers' most domesticated characters, and he hopes against hope that the jewel robbery (which of course is bungled) will be his means of escape from a domineering Irene Handl and a shrewish

Liz Frazer. The little photoplay would have been a negligible prison caper without Sellers; and Lewis, too, without Sellers there to convey the self-mockery and the genuine frustration, would have been a bit of a bore in a boring film. As it is, a film about boredom is exceptional and interesting. We sense Lewis' fantasies – like Walter Mitty's – and Sellers holds it together. Sellers could take an ordinary man and convince us that, inside his head, some of the brain-waves are floating free. Now that I come to think of it, many of his characters are dreamers – men inspirited by romance. If it weren't for their fantasies, they'd be defeated, tragic. Morganhall, in *The Dock Brief*, for example, fools himself into believing he'll be a great advocate: 'Dimitri de Grunwald wanted to make it very quickly,' says Pierre Rouve, who again wrote the screenplay, 'whilst he had Peter's goodwill after *The Millionairess*. It was meant to be an anthology of what Sellers could do, using Attenborough in a more secure rôle, as a more continuous character. The old lawyer, his dreams – romantic: "What would I be, if. . ."'

We see him, in a flashback, at Oxford during a 'beautiful long summer' – but as the others dance in the quad and go off for picnics on the river, the young law student is left behind in his rooms, struggling with his Latin textbooks. As the years pass, he remains in his chambers all alone, doing the crossword. The title sequence unfolds over images of caged birds – and who is the more constrained? Henpecked Mr Fowle (Richard Attenborough), who kills his hooting and guffawing wife because she wouldn't leave him; or the barrister, who needs the criminal classes because they are his livelihood? The film is full of cages, locks, bolts; when the sunlight shines on a wall the striped shadows form bars. Sellers is wonderful at oscillating between Morganhall's hopefulness and hopelessness – and when he says, 'Oh, Fowle! The wonderful new life you've brought me!', we know that he'll screw up on his big day in court. And he duly does lose his papers, drop his legal tomes with a clatter and forget his speech – he dries, like an actor, and he is derided by judge and jury. 'I had only to open my mouth,' he says later, 'and pour out words.'

It was Morganhall, not the defendant, who was really on trial; and when it came down to it, and his dreams of glory were set to come true (Morganhall becoming a rival to Sir Edward Marshall Hall), he backed out – as Lewis backs out of having an affair with Elizabeth Gruffydd-Williams. Faced with the choice between romantic yearnings and their fulfilment, Sellers' characters often seem to need to recoil. 'Reality', as Hoffman says, as he shifts right across the bed to avoid touching Miss Smith, 'betrays us all.' Reality is contingent, it is crammed with unknown variables, like other people and their inner mysteries; it is intrusive and inadequate.

Though Sellers' characters often fear failure and rejection, therefore, they fear the actual and the responsibilities of commitment more. 'There are ways and ways of losing,' commiserates Fowle – who is set free, not because of his counsel's forensic brilliance, but because Morganhall was deemed incompetent. The old barrister can never be free, in that case; he is hampered by his humiliation. Sellers' face, of course, seeps with a sense of failure and sadness – but it is the same face Morganhall had when he was in his college study, cut off from the undergraduate larks. (It is an expression, a 'sad, tired look', which he shares with Fowle's budgerigars.) And we can sense that, though permanently crestfallen, there is something in his nature, which makes him accept solitude, that is rather fearless. Morganhall could be seen as a sombre version of Clouseau, who likewise learns to live with ridicule – to such an extent, indeed, that ridicule becomes a consolation. (Hence his imperturbability in the midst of chaotic firework factories and exploding houses – to a man who falls into lily ponds and walks into cupboards every day, that's nothing.)

☆ ★ ☆

Sellers instinctively feels his characters' slights – the obvious examples are Juan Bautista, when he is dyed blue, Henry Orient, after his calamitous piano recital, the Rev. Smallwood, when he is stoned and thrown on the dustcart. (That same dustcart, incidentally, is the getaway vehicle in *Two Way Stretch,* and the prison location is used again in *Heavens Above* when Smallwood has a brief

743

scene as the bound and gagged gaol chaplain.) But what interests me at the moment is not so much the proud outsiderishness – the embattled martyr element when they muff things – as the rather more compelling suggestion, lurking under the surface, that Sellers is trying to come to terms with his own experience of being a fool. He was mortified over Loren, and in the films that followed on from *The Millionairess*, foolishness is a sort of shelter: for Topaze, Lewis, Morganhall, Smallwood, Henry Orient, and so on, it doesn't much matter if people think them clowns. They themselves are indifferent to the sniggering – for they have mysterious imaginative lives, a private wildness inside, where the limitations of the world may be overcome. Such was Sellers' virtuosity, he could make the quality of this interiority seem virtuous, or arrogant, or vain, or deluded, by turns; and when Emily asks General Fitzjohn: 'Inside your head – what's going on in there?', he is thrilled to be able to respond 'My head, madam, is out of bounds. It is the only place left where I can get a bit of peace.'

To each of his characters, Sellers gives a little of his personal instability and erratic nature. The way he was becomes the way they are. But did his receptivity to derision – which made him all the more stubborn when it came to his saying that he and Loren loved each other – in fact reach further back? Much further back? I mean to his music hall childhood, with its twilit old actors? His parents, playing the piano and ukelele or dressing up and disguising themselves as a cossack (Bill) or national heroines (Peg), earned their living by appearing before audiences and asking to be loved. This is certainly the atmosphere of *The Dock Brief*. Sellers plays Morganhall as a silver-haired leading man down on his luck; his posh, dark voice has a note of apology in it – he's like the sort of leading man who'd have toured provincial theatres during the war, exempted from military service by a wooden leg or a buggery charge. Interestingly, John Mortimer reports that Sellers had been uncertain how to play the part until, having lunch at Shepperton Studios, he ordered a plate of cockles: 'the shellfish came to him with a whiff of the sea and the memory of Morecambe. They brought a faded north-country accent and the suggestion of a scrappy moustache.

He felt he had been thrown the life-line of a voice and work could begin.' The Lancashire coast was where Sellers went after Ilfracombe, for more end-of-the-pier shows, and the north-country accent was his father's.

Though, by the time shooting began, Morganhall's inflexions had been reconstituted as RP – Received Pronunciation or BBC English, as it was called in the days of Andrew Timothy and John Snagge – the suggestion of a distressed and melancholy artiste remains. When Morganhall is handed the brief, he is so delighted he is flirty, seductive, gay (in the original meaning of the word); he flourishes the bat-wings of his gown as if he is soliloquising on the cardboard mezzanine at Elsinore, and when he practises his speeches in the empty well of the court he is a classical actor rehearsing. Then, after curtain up and he gets stage fright, he more or less gets booed and pelted with rotten eggs and tomatoes – as the ropey, grave and dignified tenor does on *The Sellers' Market* album, when he warbles a few bars of 'Only a Rose', accompanied by an out-of-key honky-tonk piano.

Sellers saw himself in these permutations. In *Waltz of the Toreadors*, which was made after *Only Two Can Play* and before *The Dock Brief*, he plays a man who plays the part of the great seducer – and General Fitzjohn, when he goes a-courting, does the equivalent of falling off the stage and crashing into the pit. He gets drunk in the bar of Ghislaine's hotel, finds her bedroom, and falls off her veranda. Then again, counter-poising the farce is a sense of elegy. His lost love, when she reappears, makes the general think of the wasted years and the problems of ageing – and as Sellers himself said: 'The thing about Anouilh is he can be tragic, then in the middle of a scene he can turn to comedy – and back again.'

The film, directed by John Guillermin, who'd allowed Sellers to be so demonic in *Never Let Go*,[*] suffers from just this commutation.

---

[*] Guillermin went on to specialise in big game and monster movies: his curriculum vitae includes *Tarzan Goes to India* (1962), *King Kong* (1976), *Sheena Queen of the Jungle* (1984) and *King Kong Lives* (1986).

One minute the general is poetic and rather moving, as he tells us about his suffering and sense of mortality ('It's nice, isn't it?' he says to a virginal housemaid he is about to wearily deflower. 'It doesn't mean anything but it makes one feel less lonely'); the next minute he is Major Bloodnok, storming into Dr Grogan's house and fighting a duel with his furled umbrella. ('If you wanted to hook Sellers' interest,' Mankowitz told me, 'you picked out one of these Goon characters. Sellers would immediately want to do it.') Perhaps *La Valse des Toréadors* had a Gallic charm and lightness of touch, a way of intermingling farce and tenderness that was urbane and not coarse? Perhaps General Saint-Pé, as Fitzjohn is called in the original, was coherently tragicomic, his fate bittersweet? Translated into *Waltz of the Toreadors*, however, the film is broken-backed – the slapstick, the jokes, the romp *vs* the shadowiness of the old man and wife in their cobwebby mansion – and Fitzjohn, who wears the full scarlet dress uniform and medals of a Grenadier guardsman in every scene, seems to have come adrift from a D'Oyly Carte touring production of *The Pirates of Penzance* – he's another of Sellers' old troupers.

In fairness, it should be noted that the film suffered at the hands of a timorous producer, Julian Wintle,* who cropped Margaret Leighton's miserable-and-abandoned-wife speeches and interspersed them with back-projected sequences in which she is meant to be at large on her bicycle, her nightdress and waist-length grey hair streaming in a studio wind-machine hurricane. (Emily is a former opera singer, and her antics make her madder than Donizetti's Lucia di Lammermoor.) The attempt to make a serious character silly is artless, benighting; yet, after another burst of bleakness ('I'm dying for want of your love'), off she bolts on her bike again, this time to get involved with a fox hunt – and the fox takes refuge in her pannier. None of this is funny, and instead of

---

* Anne Francis, in her book *Julian Wintle: A Memoir*, tries to exculpate her husband by saying: 'The delicate feat of the balancing of art with the commercially viable had been Beaconsfield Independent Artists' [the production company] aim from the beginning, and one from which they felt they couldn't digress.'

ameliorating the film's gloominess – or figuratively shedding light on it – the indecisiveness of the film's style, tone and intentions is simply affirmed.

It was a mistake, from the beginning, to Anglicise the original material. Promiscuity and sexual consummations do not belong to the English comic idiom. In French farce, the running in and out of doors and windows mimics the antic penetrations of love-making – all those fissures and holes in the body begging to be filled. In Britain, by contrast, humour derives from sexual failure and frustration. Donald McGill's postcards; the Carry On films; Amis' *That Uncertain Feeling* and the wilted phallus that gives its name to *Jake's Thing*: husbands are prevented from cheating on their wives, boys don't get the right girls, etc. because there is too much guilt and embarrassment built in to the national character to allow for much pleasuring. The British are simply unsuited to sex, which is struggled with, rather than enjoyed. Hence, where General Fitzjohn, because he has an eye for bottoms and breasts, seems lecherous, General Saint-Pé, his continental counterpart, was curiously pure and enviable.* His tragedy – though that is too strong a word – was that he felt the life-force to be ebbing. He is having to cut down on his daily quota of orgasms. General Fitzjohn's fate, by contrast, is more melancholy. He is not only sexually impeded (his impotence being signalled to us by one of Emily's arias: 'I know what a woman feels when she's left unsatisfied'), he is also encumbered with regret about a missed opportunity – the way he had failed to 'live in the sunlight of a glorious love', with Ghislaine. We are presented with the big English romantic theme: loss.

☆ ★ ☆

To the English, happiness survives as fantasy – a dream of the Golden World past, a mingling of memory and desire. To the

---

* Sociologists might like to note that where Benny Hill, during the last years of his life, was shunned by the British and denied access to television, in France he is a national hero. (His death was the subject of headlines and newsflashes.) 'Binny 'eel,' as they call him, a little fat man pursuing bikini-clad maidens, is a figure with whom every male over the age of fourteen can readily identify.

French, happiness is appetite – an expression of vigour. *Waltz of the Toreadors,* which is often stilted when it tries to be pensive and dull when it opts for slapstick, is also uncertain – preposterous – in its tone. As a French (copulative) farce acted out with such Englishness (the general's castle, at Alfriston, on the Sussex Downs, was also the location for the D'Ascoyne seat in *Kind Hearts and Coronets;* other scenes were shot at Eton), what might have been ribald in Anouilh either now strikes us as out of key (e.g. the general having a quick one behind the counter in a High Street haberdashery: 'It was never so hot in India,' he says, Bloodnokly) or as plainly vulgar. If Grogan and the general were French, I'm sure I could accept their chit-chat ('Fascinating how these ancient machines still work so efficiently,' one or other of them says, referring to a veteran car, leaking steam and exploding, though of course the innuendo is obvious); between Englishmen, however, of the Edwardian period in which the film is set, but not only then, comments like these provoke a snigger and a blush. 'Well', says the General, giving the doctor permission to minister to his hypochondriacal wife, 'you'd better go up and lubricate my old heap. . .'

That would be a nice line if Sid James said it to Kenneth Williams, with reference to Joan Sims; in the context of a film that is trying to create a climate of sophistication and disenchantment, though, it is a bit fresh – it is a music hall gag. On the other hand, it is apt for Sellers, for whom cars and women were synonymous; and Sellers, like Ralph Richardson, who played General Fitzjohn on Broadway, had the talent to imply mystery and helplessness under the surface defiance and swagger. But he is on his own. Cardew Robinson, as a gangling undertaker suffering from lumbago, looms in the background of various scenes, looking perplexed. No wonder Sellers tried to give him a piece of business. 'Peter said, "Don't just go out – make a comedy exit," which I did by giving myself concussion on the door frame.' Robinson similarly stood about in Fred Kite's factory; and John Le Mesurier and Raymond Huntley, who were also on patrol in *I'm All Right, Jack,* again oblige by putting in an appearance under the mélange that is Anouilh's Anglicised sky. Le Mesurier is a vicar, instead of the time-and-motion inspector; Huntley, having changed into scarlet and gold, is still sitting as a stipendiary magistrate. Cyril Cusack as Dr Grogan, is both other-worldly and worldly-wise, a mixture that remains uniquely his own to this day – he's a leprechaun, and I'm always afraid he'll disappear in a cloud of fairy dust. When he putters into shot in *Waltz of the Toreadors*, aboard his Tony Huber 1900, it is only for us to marvel that Sellers, who was still only really in his thirties, is totally convincing as a sagging oldster – as Grogan's contemporary and chum (Cusack was already in his fifties when the film was made). The character really only exists for the General to have somebody to talk to; his sympathetic presence prevents Sellers from having to spout what are technically soliloquies.

Over balloons of VSOP the general complains about his wife and expresses regret about his mistress, and he is correct to be exasperated on both counts. The former, when she is not bicycling, is made to shriek and moan like a Greek chorus. (Anouilh was fond of grande-dames: he wrote whole plays about Eurydice, Médée, and Joan of Arc – Emily, as played by Margaret Leighton, however, could out-caterwaul any one of them.) Of the latter, and the romance at the Cavalry Ball, whilst the band played the schmaltzy 'Waltz of the Toreadors',[*] and he was a dashing dragoon, he says: 'It all seems to me, Grogan, like some fantastic flight to the moon.' (As I suspected, Fitzjohn is a visionary in the tradition of Baron Munchausen.) Ghislaine, who does not seem to have aged in the intervening seventeen years since the precipitate bunny hug, reappears wearing huge fancy hats and elaborate lace pantyhose – costumes perhaps discarded by Epifania Parerga; and she keeps pretending to commit suicide – again like Epifania Parerga (even to

---

[*] When the film was released, unaccountably with an X certificate, in April 1962, the 'Waltz of the Toreadors' sheet music, composed by Richard Addinsell, was made available by Filmusic [*sic*] Publishing Company Ltd., 110 New Bond Street, London W1.

the extent of jumping into a lake so that she can later parade in her scanties to get dry).

Here we have the appeal of the story for Sellers. Dany Robin, in her lime green and peach Zuleika Dobson outfits, was playing Loren (in Sellers' imagination) and Margaret Leighton (again to Sellers) was standing in for Anne. He had filtered his fantasy life through *Only Two Can Play*; here, in another man-wife-mistress triangle, he was doing it again – and much more rancorously.

☆　★　☆

The film everybody else is in was not the film Sellers is in. When General Fitzjohn decides to write his memoirs – an account of his soft beds and hard battles – and takes refuge in his private chambers, a Great Hall stuffed with hunting trophies, memorabilia from the East, armour, swords and toy soldiers, the completeness of Sellers' self-absorption is profound. Dr Grogan has no access to these scenes. Nobody has. In *Only Two Can Play*, the aspirations and despair of the librarian, and his dream of fair women, ironically cut across the actor's own domestic drama – and he took comfort in the rôle. In John Lewis, we had watched Sellers' vulnerability and absurdities, sure enough, but the mood was softer, more amiable, and we could respect the hero because he knew himself to be idiotic. When General Fitzjohn goes upstairs to his lumber room, however – to a castle-within-the castle, with its wide staircases, wax-encrusted chandeliers, and its draperies and damask – he is torpid and knotted-up. If the decor is meant to suggest grand opera, it equally implies the theatricality of horror movies, and if Sellers was to have fallen on to all fours and turned into a werewolf, I for one would have shown no surprise, as the make-up man has already made him so sallow and green.

Lewis learns a few adult lessons – that 'Ye trancéd visions, ye flights ideal' (Keats) must yield to real everyday pressures and responsibilities; that the search for personal happiness can depend on, or involve, the pain it causes to others, so you must learn restraint and self-sacrifice – and part of the film's success lies in our knowing full well that Sellers himself could never face up to an awareness of this kind. (*Being There* works in a similar fashion: manic Sellers camouflaging himself as moronic Chance; and *There's a Girl in My Soup* does, too: unsavoury Sellers coming on as Don Juan.) But the thing about *Waltz of the Toreadors*, when General Fitzjohn is walled off from the world in his gothick web, is that all the moping, the deep jealousy, the aridity, the hysteria, is authentic. Sellers, like his character, was dooming himself to disintegration. 'Under this fancy dress of a uniform', says the general, 'is the heart of a boy dying to give his all' – a boy who will not grow up on purpose, who is a demanding, perpetual adolescent. In *Waltz of the Toreadors*, Sellers' mind is on display up on the screen; we are on the other side of his craziness with him – and when the general and Emily (whom he meets on the landing, and she follows him into his out-of-bounds den) indulge in the following exchange, it is impossible not to feel very ill at ease:

> GENERAL: [*whispering and then rising in intensity*] I want a divorce . . . Damn you . . . Damn you. I'm leaving you.
> EMILY: [*the opera diva artificiality giving way to sincerity*] . . . A woman belongs to whoever takes her and keeps her . . .
> GENERAL: Then, let them take you, madam, with my compliments.
> EMILY: . . . I am your wife, before God and the law. I'm your wife. I will follow you to the ends of the earth.
> GENERAL: [*defeated, resigned*] And when I die, will you follow me then, too?
> EMILY: When you die I will cry out, 'I was his wife.' My name will be carved on your grave; and when I die, I'll come and lie by you for good.
> GENERAL: [*with extreme loathing*] My God, woman, I hate you.
> EMILY: What difference does that make? I'm your wife.

☆　☆　☆

There is always a chance that the above dialogue could be put across as a leg-pull – the badinage of a couple who trade insults as endearments, * just as there is always a possibility that the Queen

---

* There is a touch of Noël Coward's *Private Lives* in it, perhaps? 'What happens if one of us dies? Does the one that's left still laugh?' And do the warring Amanda

will one day invest me with the medal ribbons and chain of a Knight Commander of the Royal Victorian Order. How did Ralph Richardson do it? Or Trevor Howard – who played General Fitzjohn in London? ('Who gives flawless performances?' Sellers once asked himself. 'Trevor Howard.* Trev is a wonderful actor.') Sellers, however, is completely bitter and exhausted. It is one thing for the film to be muddled about its pan-European pedigree, and for it to have endured producer interference; it is quite another for its star to wrest certain scenes and to fill them with his personal malignancy. For, I am convinced, the power of the harangue is coming from deep inside. Elsewhere in the film Fitzjohn is variously genial and/or sorry for himself. Nothing prepares us for the spitefulness of this particular confrontation; nor do attempts to defuse it, later, succeed. (When Emily is off bicycling and looks as if she is going to pedal under a passing steam train, the General is distraught; when he finds incriminating love-letters she has forged to Grogan, he is possessive.)

It is one of those moments – like the temper trantrum I discussed in *The Naked Truth* – when Sellers goes beyond acting, to achieve a pitch that is unconnected with the rest of the film, or with his conception of the character, and which is insane. It happens in *The*

---

and Elyot go back to Beatrice and Benedick –

Benedick: What, my dear Lady Disdain! are you yet living?

Beatrice: Is it possible disdain should die while she hath such meet food to feed it as Signior Benedick? Courtesy itself must convert to disdain if you come in her presence.

Benedick: Then is courtesy a turn-coat. But it is certain I am loved of all ladies, only you excepted: and I would I could find in my heart that I had not a hard heart: for, truly, I love none.

Beatrice: A dear happiness to women: they would else have been troubled by a pernicious suitor . . .

Much Ado About Nothing, I,i.

* In 1980, Howard reprised a surreal General Fitzjohn, and embodied a great deal of Major Bloodnok, in the cult comedy *Sir Henry at Rawlinson's End.* (Family motto: *Omnes Blotto*.) Also in the cast was Denise Coffey, who in the 1962 film is one of 'Sellers'' daughters.

Bobo. He and Britt (who is playing 'the most desirable witch in Barcelona') have a scene in a furrier's shop. Olimpia wants a mink coat. She is accompanied on her expedition by the mild matador – except that, inexplicably, as Olimpia examines the pelts and talks to the manager, Juan Bautista starts to behave very meanly and petulantly. (He is *out* of character.) He grabs a plate of biscuits from an assistant and he looks bored and sullen. Did Sellers resent having the scene stolen from him? The joke is that the effeminate manager gets carried away by exhibiting his wears – and he minces across the shop floor modelling the hats and muffs. (Puffin Asquith was in the habit of wearing Loren's hats during *The Millionairess*, and giving little twirls.) There is a distinct cloud across the scene, as if Sellers couldn't stand being ignored a moment longer. Bautista's face, normally long and thin, with large liquid eyes and capped and straightened teeth, gets puffy. Sellers delivers his lines with an angry rap. And then we cut to the street, and an exterior location, shot on a different day, and Sellers and Britt revert to having a kindliness between them. Inside the shop, Sellers grabs Britt's wrist; outside, they are holding hands. There is a lightness in the air which, after the foregoing agitation, is equally ruffling. (There is a discontinuity of mood.)

There is a similarly overheated atmosphere in the early part of *After the Fox*. This time Britt is Sellers' sister, Gina. He, having escaped from prison, heads home and is disgusted to learn that she has designs on becoming an actress. He is the outraged Latin family man – 'Remember, I am de poppa and de brother ... When de poppa goes, the son becomes de poppa. Momma, I am de poppa now.' Aldo Vanucci's jealous rage, however, is a husband's. When he grabs Gina from the set and frog-marches her back to the Roman apartment, the argument which ensues is a marital row. The ostensible joke is that Aldo, the jailbird and habitual crook, is laying down the law about propriety and delinquency – thieves' honour. We do not register this much because Sellers' own contempt and cynicism get in the way. 'Harlot' and 'starlet' are flung about as interchangeable terms of abuse. Gina is told that 'You are never to mention acting again!' Then Aldo asks the momma (Lidia Brazzi) to turn away so that Gina can be thumped: *'You will do what I tell you,'* brother dins into sister. She disregards him, goes back to the film set, and he storms after her again, for some reason in the plumed helmet of a full fig officer in the carabinieri: 'This time I kill her!'

As we know from the testimony of Kenneth Griffith and Robert Parrish, this is the gallant way Sellers treated his wife in real life. Michael, too, recalls his father screaming at his step-mother: 'You're a lousy bloody actress. Can't you get one scene right? Why don't you listen to what I tell you?' Britt's additional problem was that Sellers wanted to turn her into Sophia Loren – a scheme which is about as mad as Caligula deciding he'd make his favourite horse a consul. It is not my intention or concern, in making such an allusion, to denigrate Britt's career and capabilities. (She is a gamine Ursula Andress, an erotic Elke Sommer.)[*] Sellers himself did enough of that, especially in his later years, e.g.: 'Every move she makes she ruins a life. It's her hard, driving, ruthless ambition. A professional girlfriend and an amateur actress,' he would say, in one of those gibbering comments of his which by now we can decode as making sense only if it is taken, in substance, as a revealing *self* diagnosis. (We can see him in the way he saw other people.) What amazes – and amuses – me, quite simply, is how he thought an incredibly beautiful blonde from the frozen North could be converted into a raven-haired she-wolf from the Mediterranean. In every department, from temperament to chastity, they are as different as fire and ice.[†] But still he advised his bride 'if you do the *right*

---

[*] She is by far the best thing in the otherwise wan *Scandal*, the 1988 film about the Profumo Affair. She plays Mariella, the hostess of an orgy – and, recumbent upon a sofa, with gold tassels on her nipples, she is like a reincarnation of Cleopatra. As Profumo, Stephen Ward and Ivanov arrive with Christine Keeler and Mandy Rice-Davies, and the rumpy-pumpy gets going in the out-of-focus background, guess what is on the soundtrack? Why, Sellers and Loren singing 'Goodness Gracious Me'.

[†] In a book called *Who's Had Who* (London, 1987), which bears the imprimatur of Faber & Faber, and which therefore must be taken as an authoritative work of

films at the *right* times then you could be bigger than Loren.' He made a start on this by getting Britt to dye her hair black – though he had to be satisfied with a wig – and then they made *After the Fox* and *The Bobo* in Rome (though the latter is ostensibly set in Spain), because 'I love acting there. Rome is one big open-air Actors' Studio. Ten yards away you see what looks like a punch-up. You get closer, and you see it's only someone getting street directions.' And Cinecitta was convenient for the Villa Ponti, where Sellers was always angling to get invited – and where Britt (who felt herself to be 'the little Swedish mouse' in the Great Presence) noticed that Loren could never relax: 'Every appearance she made, even within her own household, meant that she had to be properly dressed and made-up.'

Is this what Sellers wanted for Britt? That her naturalness be replaced by a stately mask and that her every appearance become a grand entrance? Is that how he thought goddesses behaved – like Maria Callas taking a curtain call? Whatever, the Italianising of Ekland proceeded apace. *After the Fox*, he said in November 1966, 'is a return [after his heart attacks] to the ambitions I have for Britt . . . Britt had to wear two wigs at once for one scene – a red one when playing a part in the film-within-a-film, with the brunette one under it . . . you couldn't get angry with Britt as a blonde. But you could slap her around when you see her as a Roman *ragazza*, all teenage cheek.'

Hence the authenticity, and offensiveness, of the surliness in the

---

reference, the entry on Britt Ekland describes her as 'the prime female rogerer . . . a sweet, rather trusting young Swede, dead keen on sex and not letting her search for true love stop her getting lots of it' (page 199). She has been romantically linked with Count Ascanio ('Bino') Cicogna, Patrick Lichfield, Warren Beatty, George Hamilton, Lou Adler, Ryan O'Neal, Rod Stewart, Les McKeown (former lead singer of the 'Bay City Rollers'), and her second marriage was to James McDonnell, alias Slim Jim Phantom, drummer of the 'Stray Cats'. Michael Sellers, interviewed by Lynda Lee-Potter in the *Daily Mail*, on September 29th 1981, went on the record to say: 'The thing I like about Britt is that she's honest. She doesn't deny the truth that she loves money, likes young men. I must be too old for her now, I guess.' (Her step-son was then twenty-seven.)

brother-sister encounter which I described. All Sellers' resentments came out: he hated Britt for not being Loren; he could shout at and hit Britt as if she was Loren. He made it quite impossible for her to succeed; no matter how good she might have been if left to her own devices, he had to undermine her. He knew best; he could not allow her any independence, whether in judgement, thought or deed. As Britt herself said as long ago as September 1966, before she was willing to admit what a mean-spirited warped egomaniac she was lumbered with: 'Peter saw daily what I had done in the film the day before and one day he saw a scene I had done when he was not on the set. He came home and told me it was the most terrifying thing he had ever seen, that it was really awful. It was like someone just put a big foot on me and crushed me to the ground because up till then I was convinced that I was just marvellous and everything was swinging – how easy it was! I got so unhappy . . . Peter . . . just said, "I don't want to be mean to you, but just go along and have a look at this thing you have done."'

To further build up his wife's confidence and self-esteem, Sellers resorted to what we might call the Lionel Meadows tactic. He intimidated Britt to such an extent (by throwing chairs at her, for example), she had to flee their villa in the middle of the night and seek refuge with Neil Simon and his wife, Joan, who had rented a house across on the Appian Way. When they all went to Ischia, for six weeks' location work, Sellers sulked in his room at the Hotel Regina Isabella, and expected Britt to remain caged with him. He wouldn't allow her to see much of her family, who had come from Stockholm to join her, because they tended to babble away in Swedish and he felt excluded; he was even suspicious if she went into the nanny's suite to check on baby Victoria. 'There were perpetual rows,' Britt has written, 'and sometimes our precious furniture got broken. In one row I chipped one of my front teeth. The flaw is still visible today.'

Apparently, Sellers had upended a bed, which very shortly before Britt had been asleep in, and one of the castors clonked her on the gob. He also dissassembled her Cartier watch, without telling her, and it was a bit of shock seeing the little cogs and springs eddying in the lavatory pan, like coral fragments at the bottom of a reef.

☆ ★ ☆

To adapt a line from *Carmen Jones*, once he'd loved you, that was the end of you. 'I loved them all', he confided in the spirit medium, Micki Dahne, after he'd died. 'I adored women and constantly need [*sic*] to be with them. They were the driving force of my life – my work was only a means to be with them.' There was, however, sadism in Sellers' attitude to sex and women. He wanted his partners to suffer because he despised them for yielding; if they had succumbed to his chit-chat then they were weaklings – and because they were weaklings, his degradation of them was vindicated. And so on, round and round. Better, by far, was to have remained aloof from him, absent and indifferent – like Loren: 'above them all stood Sophia – she was my Goddess. I dreamed of her constantly. I prayed that we would be together one day. . .' However, he reiterated before the astral signals faded at last, 'I really loved all the women in my life when I was with them. . .' Quite so. Once they'd quit his pad in the service elevator, they would already have started to cease existing.

With Sellers, after he'd had you and, as a possession, you were relegated to a lower order of being, he was, as General Fitzjohn says of his particular liaisons, 'bored to death'; and, like the unhappy hero of *Waltz of the Toreadors,* who believes himself to be encumbered by wife, family and the obligations of rank, so did Sellers consider himself inconvenienced. He looked at Anne and the children and blamed them for his own staleness. He identified with these saturnine aspects of the rôle to such a degree, he marred the film – the scenes with Margaret Leighton, as I argued earlier, are *too* powerful.

'He wanted to play General Fitzjohn desperately,' recalls Leslie Linder. 'But the producers were very worried about him, having heard that he was difficult. Eventually, after weeks and weeks, we talked them into it.*

Julian Wintle and Peter de Sarigny, the backers, were correct to have misgivings. As Anne Francis, Wintle's widow, remembers: 'From the outset of production, Julian was bedevilled by the problem of attempting to control ever-rising costs. Sellers, engaged in domestic arguments, moodily, and too often, kept the film unit waiting.'

I pointed out to Anne (Levy) that the domestic arguments *in* the film seemed to impinge on the domestic arguments *surrounding* the film, and she readily agreed with this: 'Things going on in his private life did tend to come out in his films – because in *Waltz of the Toreadors* you have an old soldier trying to disentangle himself from his wife to chase his girlfriend – abandoning his family security – and, by coincidence, all this was happening to Peter. We were at the Manor House, or had just left it, and I went to see him on location. Had a *terrible* row there.'

If the animus for art was being provided by real life, Sellers, when he granted an interview to Herbert Kretzmer (the 'Sellers: Now I Will Tear My Palace to Bits' piece), and had seemed to talk so openly and wrathfully, was actually requisitioning lines of dialogue from the film to describe his own feelings: 'I wasted eleven years of my life with the wrong woman. No. I mean that. Something has been wrong with us for a long time. Did you never notice it before?' That's what the general says to Dr Grogan. How aware was he of the source of what he was saying? Sellers had become the

---

* It was during this pre-production period that Sellers started to stray and became interested in John Huston's *Freud* – which suggests that, one way and another, the actor was determined to confront his dementedness and torments, and that he was keen to go on a journey of psychological detection. The interpretation of dreams is like the junkyard of the Goons – you try and make use of whatever bubbles up from the unconscious; and psychoanalysis also tries to recover the lost past. As a theory of the mind, it hunts for sources and certainty; and as philosophy, or quasi-religion, it would seem right up Sellers' street. However . . . Though. . .

Ronald Colman character in *A Double Life* – the famous matinée idol who finally flips when he is playing Othello, loses his identity, and whose jealousy and murderousness is inspired by Shakespeare's lines and plot.[*]

Anne told me about how upset she had been by the publicity surrounding the divorce – and at the miraculous way Sellers had posed as and convinced the public that he was the injured party: 'How dare you write this about me! I said to Herbert Kretzmer, when that article came out. "Herbie, you were in my house on many a weekend. You know Peter, you know me, so you know that half of what Peter is saying is lies." – "I know darling, but that's my job. That's the interview Peter gave." – "You can go to hell!" ... People only wanted to know about the star, and I felt it was a betrayal of friendship – but I did realise, when Peter and I split up, that there was no such thing as loyalty. It was all down to work and money. The only person I remained friendly with was Spike. He wanted to make sure I was all right. "Is there anything I can do?" And Theo Cowan I still saw. None of the others came near me after I'd remarried – one of his cronies told me: "I can't see you because Peter doesn't want me to." Peter told everybody: "Don't have anything to do with her." It all swung around later – and he resented it that I'd been snubbed. He then didn't like it that they'd done what he'd told them to do, which was to have nothing to do with me ...'

☆ ★ ☆

---

[*] 'You have to keep *watching*,' Milligan had warned, 'because there's often a complete difference between what Peter says and the emotion of him. He often just repeats statements he's read about himself so as to prevent you from getting any closer to him.'

PART FIVE
The Afterlife of Peter Sellers

Why is it that one runs to one's ruin? Why has destruction such a fascination? Why, when one stands on a pinnacle, must one throw oneself down? No one knows, but things are so.

Oscar Wilde

Chapter Thirteen
The Crack-Up

His attitude to women, therefore, is to be hit upon in *Waltz of the Toreadors* – as it was to be again in *There's a Girl in My Soup*, which exposed his shallowness and vanity, and in *Hoffman*, which dealt with his bloodlessness and predatoriness. His wandering loyalties and strange vulnerability; his changeableness and fight to be free; his miraculous way of putting innocents in the wrong; these are the irks which course through the General's rain-lashed house. Sellers' affinity with the character even extended to his eyeing up of the nymphets in the cast – one of whom grew up to be Prunella Scales: 'I am of course only admitting to being sixteen years old at the time of *Waltz of the Toreadors*,' she told me. 'I remember Peter Sellers being very serious and helpful; in the lunch breaks he would sit and improvise scenes from the General's life with me and Denise Coffey – and Peter did, one evening, ask me to go to the cinema with him. To my eternal regret I said no, because I had a date in London. Heigh-ho . . .'

Sellers was evidently intent on reviving himself with young company. He'd do this with increasing regularity – clear his life and fill it with new friends who'd not last long enough to become old friends. His psychic surgeon Doris Collins witnessed a revealing scene in this regard: Sellers giving a double performance on the telephone, speaking in one voice to a girlfriend, in another, with his hand over the mouthpiece, to Mrs Collins. 'Oh darling. I'm so sorry. Hurry up. You know how much I miss you – My God, I hope she never gets here – I can't wait darling. Catch the next plane over

– I hope she misses it, she's such a pain.' Both speeches, says the medium, were made with total conviction. 'I felt sorry for the young lady . . .'

If the future Mrs Timothy West/Sybil Fawlty gave him the cold-shoulder, he had better luck with the former child actress Janette Scott (a daughter of the magnificent and still-going character actress Thora Hird), who was thirteen years his junior. I met Miss Scott – now Mrs William Rademaekers – at a restaurant off Sloane Square which I shall call *Michael Cassio's*. The point is, for all that Sellers had his dream-figure in Loren and kept making films that expressed either his solitude or the pitfalls of romantic entanglements (real and fanciful), intermittently, in the holes and corners of his life, he gave vent to his lust and emotional sado-masochism. The clandestine relationship with Janette Scott underpins everything that I have been unfolding.

'Peter, not long after we'd started going out together, mentioned Sophia Loren, and said he'd thought himself so unattractive a person, he was totally bowled over when she came up to him on the set one day and said, "I want to roll in the hay with you! I want to roll in the grass with you!" The moment changed his life – and he led me to believe he'd taken full advantage of the invitation. But he was probably just trying to impress me and had made the entire saga up . . .'

'I'm sure he was – he gave Britt the same story. You realise that it was Epifania, in the film, who goes on about making hay whilst the sun shines? That wasn't actually Loren talking at all.'

'In those days I was a very big name in this country; I'd started starring in films when I was nine. By the time I met Peter, in the year he made *Doctor Strangelove* [1963], I had grown up in the public eye – as everybody's favourite girl next door; and this image was carefully guarded – and having down-to-earth parents, they'd have not wanted my name in the papers, romantically linked to

Peter Sellers. A year earlier there'd been front-page publicity because I was going to have my first screen-kiss.[*]

'We had known each other vaguely – we were aware of each other. I had gone to Vidal Sassoon's for one of his first short hair-cuts, and then I went on along to the first night of *The Bedsitting Room*, at the Mermaid. There was a party afterwards on the stage. Amongst the guests were Peter Sellers and Dennis Selinger – my agent, Peter's agent – and the next day Dennis Selinger called me up and said, "I've got a rather strange request. Peter Sellers wants to know if it would be all right for him to telephone you and ask you out." I was so amazed he'd gone through Dennis, I said "Would it?" almost as if I was asking him for permission. "What do you mean?" I continued. "Is there something weird about the man?" Dennis didn't sound absolutely certain it would be all right, but he didn't specify anything. . . .

'And so it was a secret romance. I wouldn't go out anywhere in public with him; he wasn't about to force the issue himself. I was living at home with my parents, because my house in Stewart's Grove, Chelsea, was being redecorated. Peter was very generous – he never arrived at my parents' house without bringing gifts, for my parents as well as for me. He was very keen on photography – he was always wanting to photograph me – but because I spent my professional life being photographed, although he often asked me to go on photographic expeditions, I never went. But he was *always* wanting to photograph me. . . .

He moved me into a flat at the top of the King's Road, which he said his company owned.[†] He installed a record player, Stan Getz

---

[*] From Bryan Forbes – in the film about young lovers fleeing to Gretna Green, called *Now and Forever*. Having endured a screen test, Forbes was told: 'after mature consideration, it had been decided that Janette Scott could not receive her first screen kiss from a divorced man.'

[†] Rumours abound about what manner of company Sellers had formed or became involved with. In another article by Herbert Kretzmer, called 'A Wizard Running the Peter Sellers Empire' (*Daily Sketch*, June 15th 1963), the public was

records and a (school of) Picasso painting. This was an excellent arrangement because we didn't need to go out for dinner. I did the

---

introduced to Richard Dawson Azerley Wills, known as Bill, whose job it was to 'simmer continuously with shrewd and complex plans aimed at improving Peter Sellers' financial status and finding new ways of conserving, spending, or spreading Peter Sellers' fortune. . .'

'I don't really mix with Peter's crowd,' Wills was quoted as saying. 'Nor he with mine. I keep to the shadows. If I became too intimate then my influence over him would be affected. Yet I am more fond of Peter than any man I can think of. I am a great believer in his talent, even genius. I love his success. He, on the other hand, has always had a fantastic respect for my private life. For instance, he never rings me on a Sunday.'

Wills was Sellers' whole-time manager and agent – negotiating the contracts (see the Wolf Mankowitz correspondence in Chapter Ten); organising Sellers' private investments and stock market portfolio; handling the insurance premiums etc. 'I am trying to build up a situation so that in ten years' time neither Peter nor I need regard money as anything but a bag of rice to last us for the rest of our years. Peter will then be able to let his talent and genius flourish completely unadulterated by any kind of financial compulsion . . . All I am really doing for Peter and myself is to build up a happy life.'

Ten years hence, Sellers was nearly broke – he was (according to Bert Mortimer) 'down to his last few thousands' – and his affairs were not repaired and improved until he became a client of, first, Denis O'Brien, of EuroAtlantic Ltd., Cadogan Square, and then of Elwood Rickless, of Whitman & Ransom, Waterloo Place. So what had happened?

It would seem that at some point in the mid-Sixties, when Sellers received huge money for *Casino Royale*, Bill Wills was sent to Switzerland to establish himself (and his family) in a canton, and to form a company called Sedata Ltd. As Hattie Stevenson recalls: 'There was some Swiss scheme – a Swiss person and Bill Wills persuaded Sellers to go into a brick making company. "It's a very warm winter we're having this summer," this heavy-going German-Swiss bloke would say. The whole thing unfortunately failed, and Sellers had invested money in it.'

Leslie Linder said to me: 'Peter had this blind faith in Bill Wills. You couldn't criticise Wills. He encouraged Peter to buy cars [what Wills called Sellers' 'phantasmagoria of equipment'] – Peter thought him a financial genius – and money *was* rolling in.' Wolf Mankowitz concurs that Wills, 'a little accountant', was 'one of the few people whom Sellers trusted'.

The most intriguing side-light comes from Bryan Forbes, who told me: 'The only time Peter Sellers didn't talk to me – for a year – was because I told him I cooking. About this time [March] he started *Doctor Strangelove*. Whilst it was being filmed, on several nights he'd arrive for dinner, but neither of us would eat anything, because he was so upset. He'd break down and cry, and say he didn't think he'd be able to go on with it – the strain of doing the film. We went out to dinner several times to Stanley Kubrick's Victorian flat in Kensington. Everything was very nice and friendly – but not too close. They were not buddies. They rarely spoke of the film.

'On other evenings, we'd be at his penthouse in Hampstead – at the top of an ugly modern tower block. Peter was inordinately proud of it. I found it as cold as cold could be. The huge windows looked out on to grey clouds – there wasn't a speck of colour. We might as well have been in a hotel lobby. Anyway, I acted as hostess for innumerable dinner parties there – Kubrick, Sterling Hayden, Robert Wagner, George C. Scott. Peter would swagger to meet them from the lift: "Well, man, how d'ya like the pad?" Bert, his driver, was always shadowing him. Peter was a good host, but he spoke incredibly quietly – and I got the impression that the meals were gone through out of policy and courtesy, and not out of any pressing need to get together with friends. Sterling Hayden, who

---

had seen his accountant at the gaming tables . . . putting two hundred pounds on each spin of the wheel. I said to Peter, "I wouldn't want my accountant to gamble like that." Peter said, "How dare you criticise Bill Wills."'

However, despite my best efforts over several years, I have failed to locate Bill Wills to hear his side of the story (a number of people told me that he was last seen as a taxi driver – though the Public Carriage Office, the licensing department for London's black cabs, had no record of the name); and I must therefore conclude that he has handed in his dinner pail. Yet all the hearsay aside, it is the case that the value of and income from shares may fall and you may not get back the amount you have invested – so Sedata's failure was not Wills' fault; if Wills enjoyed a flutter occasionally, it was his own money he flung about – there is no question of impropriety; and lastly, Sellers, quite on his own, got through fortunes. 'He spent it as though he had a hose attached to the Bank of England from which the money just poured out,' said Milligan. Neither Wills nor the entire membership of the Institute of Chartered Accountants could have prevented his improvidence.

was as dense as his character [General Jack D. Ripper], tried to date me, and didn't get the gist of the fact that I was with Peter. He insisted that I went out with him. Both Peter and I were rather insulted by that. But the vast majority of evenings, it was just the two of us in the flat off the King's Road; and he also moved himself into the Dorchester – so he could rely on the room service and the attention. He was feeling the emptiness of the Hampstead flat – full of gadgets, as it was, and buttons he'd press to make the curtains open and close.

'Like in a crematorium,' I exclaimed.

'Peter was far too proud of it for me to say I didn't like it.'

'So what did you do?'

'On weekends he had access to the children and he was as good a father as it was possible to be: (a) for him; (b) under the circumstances. Michael and Sarah would come along, and we'd put on pretend shows, or record pretend radio programmes. Peter had enough equipment to run a real radio station. He always showed off his gadgetry to visitors. I must say, I felt closer in spirit to the children than to Peter. He was thrilled to introduce me to the children as "I'd like you to meet Peter Pan." I'd played Peter Pan at the Scala Theatre, and he'd seen me flying around the stage. If the weather was nice, we drove out into the country. Peter would take us to some woods with walkie-talkies – the two children would pretend to get lost, and we'd try and track them down.'

'You were all of you babes in the wood.'

'I spent a lot of time with the children. Perhaps I might have become their step-mother? Sometimes there'd be pretend games of movies. Anyway, I felt I was able to cheer Peter up. During these crying spells it was obvious that he got depressed either very easily, or that there were deeper, psychological reasons. I understood any technical problems that would bother him about film-making – I could explain those away – and for the first couple of months he was generally happy and wonderful. He started talking of marriage. He wanted us to go to Japan the following Spring and to marry when the cherry blossom trees were out in full flower.

Things were indeed going very well, and it might have happened. But little by little, the ploys I was using to cheer him up weren't working so successfully. Bert called me up late one night. Peter had locked himself in the bathroom and refused to come out – and he was so worried about him, could I come over and help . . .? I drove over there and sat on the floor outside the bathroom door, until daylight. Talking through the bathroom door trying to cheer him up. This sort of depression repeated itself several times. I therefore had to start backing off – I couldn't cope with all this.

'He was threatening suicide. Our talks didn't make a great deal of sense – he went on about this overwhelming weight he felt; everything was too difficult. . . It was always the burden of his work he talked about. I tried to tell him that no film on earth could be that important; that if he tried, he couldn't be bad. These rambling conversations went on from eleven-thirty until the dawn. A lot is said, and yet nothing is said, because nothing really works. Twice this particular all-night suicidal session took place – once in the bathroom, once in the bedroom. Finally, he'd come out and put his arm around me – more big-brother-and-little-sister than lovers. "Sorry if I've put you through it . . ." And off I'd have to go and make a dreadful film called *Siege of the Saxons*, which I was making purely for the money. My ex-husband had got through my savings with his gambling debts. I wouldn't let Peter help me financially, but he kept giving me all this jewellery which I could very happily have sold – none of it was very well chosen, just expensive, Jewish, heavy, encrusted with gold and lots of diamonds. Tasteless, which I wore not to hurt his feelings. To this day it sits in boxes in my bank, because I can't sell it, nor can I wear it. . .

'Peter then started not turning up for dinners I had cooked. A duck sat in the oven drying out, I recall. A couple of times I called the Dorchester late in the evening, and they referred the call down to the restaurant. This hurt me dreadfully. As I was about to move back into my Chelsea house, a letter arrived: "Jannie – it just isn't working, is it? Dreadfully sorry. Love you a lot, Peter."

'A few months later I met David Frost.'

'Who many years later would marry and divorce Lynne Frederick.'

'Curious, the movement of the chess pieces. I lived with David for several years. I was in New York meeting my agent and David was setting up *That Was the Week That Was*. I got two phone calls in rapid succession from two of Peter's friends, both of them saying: "Jan, Peter met this Swedish girl a few days ago, and he's going to marry her. Please come back and talk some sense into him." One friend begged me to go back to him; the other just wanted me to speak to him. They both wanted me to stop the wedding. I decided to have nothing to do with it. You could have been entangled in the ups and downs of Peter's emotional life forever if you didn't draw the line.

'What I discovered is that greatly manic-depressive people need you to think of something *new* that will cheer them up – they *drain* you. I have rarely been so emotionally drained as I was by Peter. He left me an emotional husk. He was so self-centred, he couldn't see any hope outside of himself. He began to use me – and he became resistant to me, as to a drug.'

'So then he was away to feed off Britt's vibrancy in a similar way.'

'And he started to supplement women with real drugs. He tried to offer me marijuana. The friends who called me in New York were afraid of the drugs he was boasting about using with Britt. Poppers – amyl nitrate – which affected his heart, and he did have a heart attack soon afterwards. I think now that, in some strange way, he enjoyed all these crying jags – self-indulgence and self-pity, which he carried to extremes. He'd like to surround himself with people who'd make a fuss of him when he was down – which gave him a false sense of reality, because he'd worked hard at being unhappy. Could it be that, as a child on tour, he'd gained attention and affection from his mother only when he was unhappy? He mentioned his mother often. Mort Sahl said to me that what you've got to do, as a Jewish son, is to be angry. In your mind, you try your mother; you convict her; and then you forgive her.'

'Did you see Sellers again?'

'Years and years later, in a Chinese restaurant, when he was married to Miranda, and I was married to Mel Tormé. He telephoned me in Beverly Hills and we went out to dinner, along with my parents. Miranda wore a see-through blouse and my darling Dad could not take his eyes off her titties the entire evening. You couldn't even talk sensibly to him – and Peter was exchanging winks with me about him. None of us could understand how Peter could be at ease with the effervescent, amusing Miranda.'

'He was attracted to her High Life – but her presence only helped to remind him all the more that he was from Finchley. So he was doubly filled with indignation.'

'They just weren't a couple. I couldn't see it at all. A few months later I read they'd split. Peter's parents were not dissimilar to my own – my father was a drummer in the pit when Thora Hird was on stage in *The Desert Song* at the amateur dramatic society. Peter was really happy with my parents, and in a strange way I was only ever part of a package that included them. They represented his own background to a certain extent. I can see him now taking off his glasses to wipe the tears of laughter away after something my mother had said – something about her overhearing a woman on the bus say: "See that over there? That's the second largest power station in the north of England. And what's more, *I* know the manager."'

☆　☆　☆

Doctor Strangelove – or *Dr Folamour*, as they call it in France – lives up to its title. From the fornicating flying machines over the title sequence to the crazy Kraut yanking himself up and out of his wheelchair in the final scene (the flaccid graveyard worm is suddenly *homo erectus*), the film is filled with strange, dehumanising kinds of loving. The red alert is sounded because a general, suffering from impotence, finally flips. 'Women sense my power and they seek me out,' he says with quiet psychotic reasoning. 'I do not avoid women. But I deny them my Life Essence.' Believing that his sperm count has dropped owing to secret chemicals pumped into the water supply by the Russians, he pushes the end-of-the-world buttons. Up in the B-52, the pilot examines the emergency ration packs – an over-sexed adolescent's dream-kit; chewing-gum, condoms, lipsticks, nylon stockings. 'Gee,' he says, 'a fella could have a pretty good weekend in Vegas with all that stuff.' Over at the Pentagon, Buck Turgidson keeps getting calls from his floozie ('Look, honey, I can't talk now – my President needs me'), who won't be put-off by any silly war games ('*Of course* it isn't only physical,' he implores); and the Russian premier, when he is located, appears to be in a bordello. The theme of gonadic stir-craziness peaks when General Ripper's HQ is finally taken: Col. Guano is reluctant to let Mandrake use the phone – he thinks the British officer is in drag, a 'deviant prevert [*sic*]'. 'What do you mean suit?' retorts the pukka officer. 'This happens to be a RAF uniform.'

What with Strangelove's dream of fertilising women down the mineshaft (and gorging himself on the animals which ''vill be bred unt *slaughtarrh'd*'); the chaps flicking through *Playboy* in the bomber; General Ripper's obsession with his infertility; Turgidson's mistresses; the guns spurting out spent cartridges; the Coca-Cola machine spraying Col. Guano full in the face; the nervous chewing on phallic cigars: men at war and men and sex are one and the same. In *Doctor Strangelove*, the characters seem to fear it, or are useless at it – so they take out their frustrations in bringing about the apocalypse (the ultimate orgasm). The nuclear bombs go off, and the popping mushroom clouds are like those close-ups of delayed-action blooms and pollen puffs which used to be cut in to B-movies, along with waves breaking and trains entering tunnels, to mimic the agonising ecstasy of coming. (Kubrick's symbolism is on a level with the imagery in *The Blue Lagoon*.) The irony, of course, is that *Doctor Strangelove – or: How I Learned to Stop Worrying and Love the Bomb* is not about love, but death; not about insemination, but annihilation; and this is its only irony, in fact. I find it a suffo-cating, portentious film, and its fascination – which is therefore considerable – principally lies in what it reveals to us of Sellers' own extremely post-adolescent view of a world he was not terribly happy about inhabiting. For, as much as there was a screenplay and a structure laid down in advance, 'during the shooting many substantial changes were made in the script,' Kubrick has said. 'Some of the best dialogue was created by Peter Sellers himself.' And if many of the scenes in the film were improvised – and Sellers *is* the film – all that material has had to erupt from somewhere, surely? *Doctor Strangelove* (and *Lolita* too) give outward form to their star's anger and madness.

I ought to declare, before continuing, that I am very much in a minority – perhaps, who knows, a minority of one? Though he has long been the subject of adulatory books galore and learned articles beyond number, I am afraid that Stanley Kubrick's work leaves me cold and impatient. The mention of his name, like Nietzsche's or Zsa Zsa Gabor's, makes me the reverse of uplifted. Funnily enough, the film I can just about tolerate, *Spartacus*, is exactly the one which the director has sought to disown (Kubrick insists on total control, from posters to seating arrangements in cinemas, and on *Spartacus* he was subordinated to Kirk Douglas); and yet it must remain the case that, Sellers' bravura appearances in subsequent things aside, the Roman slave epic is the only one of his goodies with considered performances: Olivier, Laughton and Ustinov understand their characters as human beings, rather than grotesques.

For, elsewhere, all is grotesquerie. (In a Kubrick film, to be interesting and to register you must be barking.) Jack Nicholson staggers and whoops around *The Shining* like the monkey in *2001*; the ape in that film, waving its bone as a weapon, is a duplicate of George C. Scott in *Doctor Strangelove*, grimacing and pounding his chest in the War Room; and Malcolm McDowell's Alex, in *A Clockwork Orange*, is a trial run for his Caligula, a man who willingly becomes a beast. These aren't characters, they are primates – and as such they are caged and constricted. (Dr Strangelove himself is imprisoned in his wheelchair.)

Like when people start running on at the mouth about Michael

Powell, I find that I can't wait to leap in and say, no, Kubrick is a vastly overrated talent; and where Powell's films are vulgar and per-fervid – cramped – Kubrick, because his films are humourless and stifling, is unimaginative in a different way. Whilst I do not doubt that he toils hard, sequestering himself 'in a country house about twenty miles from London', or that he is absorbed and intense – the message put across smartly in Michel Ciment's *Kubrick* (translated from the French by Gilbert Adair) and *Stanley Kubrick Directs*, by Alexander Walker – there is such a thing as over-preparing and being over-deliberate, and *Full Metal Jacket*, for example, would seem very well named. The experience of watching it was like being forced to don a lead-lined suit; I was dragged down by it, I felt bludgeoned by it – and I am sure that this was the director's in-tention. The viewer had a small taste of the horror of Vietnam – but at what point does the degradation of the audience become too sneery and manipulative? *Full Metal Jacket* is relentless, and by the time of the final fade-out, senseless.

Similarly, I found that sitting through *Barry Lyndon* was soporific – I was bludgeoned in a more genteel manner. Though beautiful to look at, in a strolling-for-eternity-through-an-art-gallery sort of fashion, because all of Thackeray's brio had been removed, and Ryan O'Neal is so bland, the end product was headachey, inert. And isn't that true, too, of *Lolita*? Inertia would seem to be what it is about. Sellers' Quilty is hung-over (when shot at he hides behind a Gainsborough portrait, which could be of the Marisa Berenson character in *Barry Lyndon*); and James Mason (looking migraine-ridden) is doomed to drive from one identical motel to the next, never to get anywhere – except to end up in a strait-jacket, like McDowell's Alex. In *Paths of Glory* there is a poison gas to disable people; in *Doctor Strangelove* there is the radioactivity; in *2001: A Space Odyssey* men are imprisoned in space-ship pods, like frozen corpses; and in *The Shining* Jack Nicholson, after going mad in the traditional Jack Nicholson way (a way brought to baroque perfec-tion in *Batman*), dies from the cold in a remote snowbound hotel.

All of which suggests that a sensation of heaviness and soullessness is not getting into the films by accident – it is endemic – and
Sellers was smitten.

☆ ★ ☆

Asked, towards the end of his life, what he was most proud of
having done, Sellers said *I'm All Right, Jack* ('I loved doing that'),
Only Two Can Play ('I loved the Kingsley Amis book which Bryan
did the screenplay for . . . A fine movie. That really stands up'); but
his chief conjunction, he knew, was 'my meeting with Kubrick, who
is a god as far as I am concerned, and you can watch *Doctor Strangelove* now and it is even better than when it came out. It is a
remarkable film.'

Apart from Peg and Loren (his goddesses), Kubrick would seem
to be the only personage in the Sellers line-up who managed to
escape from censure and the after-effects of disillusion. Kubrick was
his ideal, and he testified to this in hundreds of interviews across a
seventeen year period: 'I take my hat off to Stanley . . .'; 'I think I've
enjoyed working with Stanley Kubrick more than any other director, apart from John Boulting . . .'; 'I think Kubrick is one of the
five great directors in the world and I look forward to working with
him again some time . . .'; 'I'd do anything he wanted to make –
film the phone book, anything'; 'I admire Stanley Kubrick so much
– he is a painstaking, brilliant and generally self-efficient director
. . .'; 'You see, Kubrick – I always keep bringing Kubrick up because
he's a great person in that way – I mean you can discuss anything
with him. You can chuck ideas at each other – and the outcome of
the thing will either be his or yours. The end product is all that
matters. The end product. So you don't have to carry the argument
away from the set – you can be good friends off the set, but you can
argue your bloody heads off on the set, it doesn't matter. That's all
that matters. What you are doing at the time . . .'; 'I think Stanley
Kubrick and John Boulting are two directors who've really got into
me and I feel I've produced near to my ultimate best as an actor
with them. I think *Doctor Strangelove* . . . is one of his greatest films.
I saw it again the other day and it has even more impact now than it

had then. A wonderful film . . .'; 'Kubrick is marvellous to work with. You see, on a film everyone has something to contribute if they are interested in what they're doing. It's the same with actors. If a director is open to their contribution of ideas then he can gather and bring much more to the picture. I'm a creative actor and all the things I did with Kubrick came out of long discussions . . .'; 'Stanley Kubrick . . . understands me. [He] seems to know what goes on in here . . . (said Sellers, tapping his skull.)[*]

And so on fulsomely. What Sellers had found, for the space of two films, was a serious-minded Milligan – though perhaps this mentor (who in photographs resembles Dame Flora Robson in a frizzy black beard) wasn't *that* serious-minded, if what Shelley Winters says is true. She recalls that, when they were shooting *Lolita*, Kubrick always arrived at and departed from the studio by bicycle, whatever the hour or weather. She kept trying to offer him lifts in her chauffeur-driven limo, to no avail. 'Shelley,' she was eventually told, 'Stanley Kubrick two years ago decided he would not fly in a plane. Last year, he decided he would not ride in a car. He will only trust his bicycle.' Soon afterwards, Winters heard that the director had taken to walking to work. 'I don't how they got him to Ireland to shoot *Barry Lyndon*,' she says. Neither do I,[†] but the phobia, or eccentricity, might explain the grey Hertfordshire skies and English foliage in *Full Metal Jacket* (it resembles the tropics at least as much as Gaillardia does in *Carlton Browne of the F.O.*); and of course *Lolita* and *Doctor Strangelove*, which have American settings, were made in Britain – because (says Kubrick) 'Peter Sellers

---

[*] Sellers' sole disparaging remark was also his most hilarious ever. He claimed not to have liked *A Clockwork Orange* because 'surely we've had enough violence for a while . . . I used to enjoy seeing the odd gangster film a few years ago. But I am a Yogi – and am against violence completely.'

[†] I am not sure that they did. *Barry Lyndon* was made at Wilton (Salisbury), Petworth (Sussex), Longleat (Wiltshire) and Castle Howard (Yorkshire). The scenes set in Germany were shot by a second-unit. 'Stanley never went there,' says Ken Adam, the designer. 'Stanley didn't want to go further than twenty miles from his home, claiming that we never know what we may find at our own front door.' Quoted in Michel Ciment, *Kubrick* (New York, 1980), page 205.

was in the process of getting a divorce and could not leave England for an extended period, so it was necessary to film here.'

Whether by accident or design, therefore, Kubrick (b. New York) is an English director – and his work shows an interest in the English sensibility, in peculiarly Englishy themes: class, chivalry, hypocrisy, repression, patriotism, xenophobia. Which was ideal for Sellers – the actor had returned to the climate of *The Goon Show*; and where Milligan's scripts had a dream logic, Kubrick's films have nightmare logic, which similarly liberated him. In one particular instance, *The Goon Show* – or, to be accurate, one of the 'Fred' shows – specifically overlapped with, or inspired, a great screen moment: 'In one of the Freds,' explained Sellers, 'we decided to see what we could do with the glove puppet idea. Harry Corbett and Sooty were very popular, so a shot was set up of someone who, to all intents and purposes, was Harry Corbett with Sooty. Sooty kept hitting him and "Corbett" was saying, "Stop that little Sooty! Stop it!" But little Sooty wouldn't stop, so suddenly he gets a slap and becomes stiff. He drops out of sight while the man says, "He is a naughty little Sooty doing that, isn't he? What a naughty Sooty! Sooty mustn't do that again." Then Sooty comes up with a gun in his hands and fires and the man slumps forward. Then the camera crabs round and you see that "Corbett" himself was being worked by someone else with his hand up the back of his jacket. He looks round, startled, and says "Oh!" It was a very weird moment. One day, Stanley suggested that I should wear a black glove which would look rather sinister on a man in a wheelchair. "Maybe he had some injury in a nuclear experiment of some kind," Kubrick said. So I put on the black glove and looked at the arm and I suddenly thought, "Hey, that's a storm-trooper's arm." So instead of leaving it there looking malignant I gave the arm a life of its own. That arm hated the rest of the body for having made a compromise; that arm was a Nazi. When it tried to choke Dr Strangelove, the other arm had to hit it. It was the same thing as the Sooty sketch – the arm or hand having a life of its own, hating the rest of the body.'

Despite Kubrick's grimmer air, the prevailing belief that man is not a deeply rational creature is the same as Milligan's philosophy; the rowdiness, mutilations and explosions are the same; the asperity is the same. Underneath the surreal antics and jokes of *The Goon Show*, Milligan never lost sight of the war; he created humour out of shell-shock, combat fatigue, dirt and danger. (Neddie Seagoon's mock heroics are a mockery of heroism: he, Eccles and Bluebottle are regularly dismembered in pursuit of impossible goals, like a strip cartoon adaptation of *Paths of Glory*, which Kubrick made in 1957.) And, if one of the purposes of war is the chance it offers chaps to assert their manhood – they can come of age by being violent – this, Goonery's great satirical theme, is the theme, also, of *The Killing* (with Sterling Hayden), *Paths of Glory* (obviously), *Spartacus, Doctor Strangelove, 2001: A Space Odyssey, A Clockwork Orange, Barry Lyndon* and *Full Metal Jacket* (again obviously). Armies, duels, weaponry, thuggishness, machismo, and power: this is Kubrick's world – a world (like that of *The Goon Show*) without women, on the whole. (Shelley Winters and Shelley Duvall turn up not as women but as banshees.)

☆ ★ ☆

The Shining is a war film, too, in this respect. The Jack Nicholson character reverts to being a slouching beast and he stalks his wife and son with an axe; he wants to assert his ultimate authority over them, and the patriarchal spirit (Kubrick seems to be saying) is basically destructive, predatory. (What the matriarchal spirit might be like we are never told.) Hence *Lolita*, which is about the perversion of the father–daughter bond. Humbert Humbert moves in on the Haze household, and goes through with marrying Charlotte (Shelley Winters at her blowsiest), the better to ambush the prepubescent Dolores: 'Lolita, light of my life, fire of my loins. My sin, my soul. Lo-lee-ta: the tip of the tongue taking a trip of three steps down the palate to tap, at three, on the teeth. Lo. Lee. Ta.' Nabokov's original novel intermingles several skirmishes: Humbert *vs*. his deviancy ('We are not sex fiends! We do not rape as good soldiers do. We are unhappy, mild, dog-eyed gentlemen . . . ready to give years and years of life for one chance to touch a nymphet');

Humbert *vs.* Charlotte ('You're a monster,' she tells him, when she finds out his secret and his calculation. 'You're a detestable, abominable, criminal fraud . . .'); Humbert *vs.* Lolita, who is incapable of returning the intensity of his possessive love ('It had become gradually clear to my conventional Lolita during our singular and bestial cohabitation that even the most miserable of family lives was better than the parody of incest, which, in the long run, was the best I could offer the waif'); and Humbert *vs.* Quilty, his sinister double ('To have him trapped, after those years of repentance and rage . . . To look at the black hairs on the back of his pudgy hands . . . To wander with a hundred eyes over his purple silks and hirsute chest foreglimpsing the punctures, and mess, and music of pain . . . To know that this semi-animated, sub-human trickster who had sodomized my darling – oh, my darling, this was intolerable bliss!').

The film,* however – not surprisingly for all those decades ago, and total paedophiliac candour would be more than a challenge today – doesn't do much with the forbidden fruit element, and Sue Lyon, in a large floppy sun hat, whilst pretty and teenagery, would not be mistaken by anybody for a child. ('She was my child, Quilty.' – 'I am very fond of children myself . . . and fathers are among my best friends' – dialogue *not* in the film.) What this means, in effect, is that an atmosphere of warped, dangerous eroticism is lost; the specific act of child molestation is lost; so Humbert's guilty passion is lost. *Lolita*, the film, has as much connection with *Lolita*, the novel, as a production of *Othello* in which the blackamoor is portrayed as being white; and the sexual relations between James Mason and Sue Lyon, in fact, far from making us retch at the idea of the beast with two backs, are less off-putting and more chaste than Leslie Caron and Fred Astaire in *Daddy Long Legs* or Audrey Hepburn and Fred Astaire in *Funny Face*. (*Q.* Why did Astaire keep getting these incestuous-type roles? *A.* Because he was courtly, nimble, and totally sexless [and not apparently queer]. His dancing wasn't the prelude to anything else; or representative of

---

* Made in the winter of 1961–2, between *Waltz of the Toreadors* and *The Dock Brief*.

anything else. His dancing was all there was. He's safe-sex set to music.)

Kubrick's *Lolita*, therefore, comes down quite fast to rather vaguely being about James Mason's ability to show what a man's face looks like after years of secret suffering – and Peter O'Toole reprises the screaming-skull look, incidentally, in *Goodbye Mr Chips*. Both Mr Chips and the film Humbert are narrow and crotchety academics; and romance in any form is feared by them and not welcomed by them because it upsets their scholarly calm and self-composure. The musical of *Goodbye Mr Chips*, it is interesting to note, was created for Rex Harrison, who turned it down – he correctly saw that it was Professor Higgins all over again; but isn't that what Kubrick's *Lolita* is? A shadowy version of *My Fair Lady*, in which the flower girl is revealed as under-age? (How old is Eliza Doolittle meant to be, anyway? For all his talk and preachifying, the inmost meaning of Shaw's drama concerns an old professor finding happiness with a young girl, who can unbend him.)

Mason's Humbert Humbert is a Higginsy creature of bad temper and moods, all right, but so would you and I be if wedded to Shelley Winters' Charlotte – a terrifying portrait of a suburban vulgarian in a leopard-skin belt ('culturally we're a very advanced group, intellectually'), which belongs right up there in Kubrick's gallery of grotesquerie with the waxy painted faces of the lords and ladies in *Barry Lyndon*. Their scenes are a straightforward – bitter, recriminatory – battle of the sexes. They more or less go for one another in slow-motion, like the monkeys in *2001: A Space Odyssey*; and once 'the noxious mama', 'the stupid Haze woman', 'the brainless ba-ba' has been killed off, the girl and her step-father drive away, and Mason's cause for concern, and reason for frowning, is his ward's consumption of chewing-gum, milk-shakes and trashy magazines. (Lolita is going to mature into a double of her mother.)

☆ ★ ☆

So, unless the viewer wants to decode Mason's grimace, and attribute reasons for the suppressed violence in it – is that why Quilty's murder is shifted to the start, so that we do not forget that this silky fellow can kill? – *Lolita* avoids what it is meant to be about. Except,

that then there is Sellers, so full of implication and outlandishness
that Winters was moved to say: 'Peter Sellers seemed to be acting
on a different planet.' This is a very perceptive remark, and the
extra-terrestrial origin, as we know already, was *The Goon Show*.
Quilty fools Humbert with false identities and funny voices; he
scampers across the film exactly like the young Sellers himself, free-
associating behind the microphone at the Camden Theatre, twitting Wallace Greenslade or the dyspeptic producers. (It is as if
somebody had already made the James Mason–Shelley Winters–
Sue Lyon film, and then elves and goblins got at the negative and
interspersed it with Sellers.)

After the evocative prologue, in which he plays ping-pong and is
gunned down ('the first five minutes are pretty stunning,' Sellers
always conceded),[*] Sellers' character not only keeps reappearing, in
disguise, to gleefully upstage Mason; there is also the sense that his
mutations, by being so fluid and imperious, are in themselves a
form of hostility. Quilty (at least in the novel, which is presented as
a madman's paranoid fantasy) is meant to function as Humbert's
liberated double and Id ('instinctive impulses of the individual as
part of the unconscious' *OED*); he is his tempter and tormentor. It
is perhaps easier to see Mason as the unwitting stooge in a music
hall act – like Grytpype's Moriarty.

We first see Sellers as the distinguished author at a High School
prom,[†] going through the motions of slow jazz steps, a shuffle

---

[*] I have discussed the scene already (page 501 above), in the context of Sellers'
non-gentlemanliness, and when introducing the argument that Sellers' rebel
characters and his own lawlessness led to an ability to convey menace – which he
now brought to completeness in Kubrick's films.

[†] In this scene Sellers is Nabokov's Clare Quilty to perfection: 'American drama-
tist. Born Ocean City, N.J., 1911. Educated at Columbia University. Started on a
commercial career but turned to playwriting. Author of *The Little Nymph, The
Lady Who Loved Lightning* (in collaboration with Vivian Darkbloom), *Dark Age,
The Strange Mushroom, Fatherly Love*, and others. His many plays for children
are notable. *Little Nymph* (1940) travelled 14,000 miles and played 280 performances on the road during the winter before ending in New York. Hobbies: fast
cars, photography, pets.'

really, and looking at his watch. He is bored and cynical and can't recall anything about Charlotte except that didn't she have a daughter with 'a lilting, lyrical name'? I don't think his nibs was ever as authoritative and frightening as he is in a long shot in this scene, lazily dancing, absorbing people's high regard for him; Quilty is nasty, supercilious, and as bloated by fame as a television personality. His 'toad of a face' (Nabokov) thus connects very well with Wee Sonny MacGregor in *The Naked Truth* and Robert Danvers in *There's a Girl in My Soup* – other men who succeed at appearing charming and normal, whilst underneath there is rottenness and revulsion. In case this doesn't sink in the first time, when Quilty is next glimpsed he is preening himself on a poster, or a leaf torn from a magazine, pinned up in Lolita's bedroom. It is an advertisement for cigarettes: 'Clare Quilty says "I am sometimes without a pen, but not without a Drome".' I cannot swear to it, but the face on the photograph is awfully like one of Sellers' own authentic publicity shots of the period.

Thus, the significance of *Lolita*. Quilty, a man who is always trying something on, and who is ungraspable, embodies a lot of the personality of the actor playing him. Sellers has said that he never met Kubrick until 'right before *Lolita*. He came straight to me and asked me to play Quilty . . . To me, that was an enormous honour' – and I must say it was a casting decision of genius. (I'm not so certain about his original choice for Humbert: Noël Coward.) Kubrick could evidently discern that, behind the levities of *The Goon Show* there existed a talent towards which we react with both admiration and animosity; Sellers is so quick and ticklish – one moment Bluebottle, the next Bloodnok, etc. – that he can never be totally trusted. He enchants us and baffles us, and his endless re-creations also implicitly criticise the rest of us for being rigid and conventional, for being stuck with who we are. And this is how Quilty mortifies Humbert: he mocks the complacency of his self-estimation and forces him to reflect upon his own vileness and falseness (as Iago does Othello; as Hyde does Jekyll.)[*]

It is apt, therefore, in a parodic way, that Quilty next appears as a policeman – as a guardian of law and order he cuts a devilish figure. Humbert has taken Lolita on the road. They stay each night at an identical motel (so that they cover the miles but never go anywhere), and Quilty is always one step ahead and intent on kidnapping the girl. In the darkness of the lobby, and later on the veranda, Humbert tries to sit quietly, nursing his abjectness, when he is broken in on and subjected to long, fierce monologues. 'What do you do with your excess energy?' he is asked rhetorically. The cop's apparently innocuous chatter, which drones on, like muzak in a lift, is full of innuendo and taunts: 'I enjoy judo. The pain. I lie there in pain, but I sort of love it. I lie there hovering between consciousness and unconsciousness. It's really the greatest.'

Humbert puts up with the smirching, and does his utmost to be civil, because he is wary of being arrested, his perversions exposed. He checks himself and Lolita in each evening as father and daughter, but he knows sooner or later he will be disbelieved – and Quilty knows he has this fear, and pumps him further for information. Humbert, not to appear rude, starts to vouchsafe one or two things about himself, such as Charlotte's recent death, to which Quilty responds: 'Gee, fancy, gee, a normal guy's wife having an accident, gee. . . Gee, I keep getting carried away, me being so normal and everything. . .' Quilty (or Sellers) then starts to riff about normality – '*I'm* a normal guy and I think *you're* really normal and everything' – and it goes on and on, a fuzz of insult, gibberish,

---

[*] Nabokov's interpretation of Stevenson's fable was brought to bear on *Never Let Go* (page 681 above); you may also like to look up, vis-à-vis Humbert and Quilty, *Othello*, Act III, Sc. iii:

> Utter my thoughts! Why, say they are vile and false;
> As where's that palace where into foul things
> Sometimes intrude not? Who has a breast so pure,
> But some uncleanly apprehensions/ . . . in session sit/
> With meditations lawful?

home truth, in which *normal*, crunching like *honest* in *Othello*, refers to its opposite.

When Sellers, fiddling with his spectacles, faces away from Mason, and leans over the balcony towards us, his whole boxer's body is made ogreish by the shadow. The contrast between the bulk and the benumbing feminine sing-song which pours from his lips adds to the grotesquerie – for Quilty's ungainly monologues more than comment on Humbert's thoughts; they *are* his thoughts. They are his hysteria breaking out. 'Are you with someone?' Humbert eventually struggles to say, desperate to be polite and to withdraw. 'I'm not with someone,' says Quilty, in a line to give us the shivers. 'I'm with you.'

☆ ★ ☆

Where did Quilty's monotonous voice – at once panicky and relentless, like a radio sports commentator who can't be cut off – come from? 'Stanley wanted Clare Quilty to have a particular American sound. The sort of voice he wanted me to imitate was Norman Grantz's, an impressario – he puts on jazz concerts. I'd seen him introducing Ella Fitzgerald, saying, "Here is America's first lady of song. . ." A very sibilant sound. So Stanley sent him a letter and a tape, and said, "Could you record some of the dialogue?" Well, he's not an actor, and when I played back the tape, he'd introduced it saying, "Gee, Stanley, thanks – I received your letter – and gee, I don't know how I'm going to do all this, but anyway – here goes. First man. Hello there, Captain. Second Man. What are you doing in here? Third Man. Gee I don't know. I'm nothing to do with that. . ." It was hysterical. You heard a voice, speaking too loud, saying ". . . Jesus Christ, this is a whole script for God's sake, I mean you really do ask for some strange things." Then you hear some rustling of paper . . . And that's where Quilty came from.'

Only in part – but Sellers liked to reassure people he was merely a mimic,[*] that the wickedness was not his. 'When you did the

---

[*] A view often still propounded by, for example, Michael Bentine – to me personally and in the press: 'Peter's secret was that between his ears was one huge, magnificently tuned tape-recorder with instant playback. . . .' (*Sunday Mirror* August 3rd 1980)

character of Dr Strangelove,' said a talk-show host in 1964, 'you did that, of course, in a German accent.' To which Sellers responded: 'Well, I was stuck, because I didn't want to do just a sort of normal English-broken-German accent. So on the set was a little photographer from New York – very cute little fellow called Weegee, you must have heard of him . . . And he had a little voice . . . and used to walk around the set and he'd say, "I'm looking for a girl with a beautiful body and a sick mind." I thought that if I put a German accent on top of that, you see . . . then suddenly I got into Dr Strangelove, who is really Weegee. I don't know if he knows it, but it's Weegee.*

'Well, he knows now. The secret's out,' said the host. 'Bit of an anti-climax,' said Sellers.

And also untrue. Back in *Lolita*, when Humbert comes to rest after this trans-American voyage, it is to teach at Beardsley (as in Aubrey) College. (The name is a joke, like Camp Climax for girls was a joke. Climax, incidentally, is the name of the town in the lubricious *Kiss Me, Stupid*.) He and his child-mistress rent an old dark property, and the more he complains about untidiness and cooking, the faster the romance withers: 'You just want to keep me locked up with you in this filthy house,' she shouts, with complete justification. Humbert won't let her mix with her classmates and speaking to boys is forbidden. Under the guise of an autocratic father he is getting to be the insanely jealous lover (i.e. Othello), the girl is getting shrewish (i.e. like Charlotte) and it is not long before the campus psychiatrist, Dr Zempf, pays a call. Lolita is starting to

---

* Sellers returned to this story in 1980, and filled it out with extra detail: 'On the set we had a special stills guy called Weegee, who is now dead. He was very famous and he took a lot of pictures for *Life* magazine in the old days. When all the hoods used to get riddled with bullets, he was always the first photographer there [hence the nickname: it was as if an ouija board had tipped him off, it was so uncanny that he knew where to be], and he'd get as good a shot as possible for the Mafia, and then get twenty-five dollars from *Life*. He used to talk in a strange little voice, like, "Hey, Peter, I really have an idea for a shot here." So I put a German accent on top of Weegee's.'

behave oddly, he says. Does she know the facts of life? The curves of her body are beginning to attract the interest of young chaps at her school, but she is not responding. Her boredom with sex is not right. 'She is suffering from acute repression of the natural instincts.'

The Freudian gobbledegook, like the speech about martial arts and normality/abnormality ('Gee, I wish I had a lovely tall pretty small daughter like that') glistens with sarcasm; again, however, Humbert does his best to hear his visitor out respectfully. The prying policeman seemed to know more than he let on; so does the psychiatrist. Humbert is so relieved not to be charged with statutory rape and unlawful sexual intercourse on the spot, and hoping to allay Zempf's threat 'to investigate thoroughly ze home situation', he agrees to allow Lolita to take part in the end of term play, which happens to be a production by Clare Quilty . . . The demon is closing in – and there he is again, in person, taking photographs of the satyrs and shepherdesses from the wings. . .

He is not seen thereafter. Paradoxically, his presence is the more spooky and intensely felt for this absence. Humbert decides to make a run for it from Beardsley, and a large, mysterious sedan follows him at a discreet distance. He receives anonymous phone messages. The disembodied voice of Dr Zempf is heard, asking for a report on his current sex life. A pair of dark glasses turns up in Lolita's room, testifying to some invisible caller. And then Lolita herself is spirited away, making Humbert's deepest fears come true: the graceful and baleful rival has won. We flash-forwards a few years. Lolita is tracked down, married and living in poverty as Mrs Richard F. Schiller. Bespectacled and drab, she is no longer the nymphet. Humbert can't decide whether to kill her or bestow money on her and try and forget her. ('I was weeping again,' Nabokov has him say, 'drunk on the impossible past.') What he does is to inquire: 'Who was Clare Quilty?' – 'Why,' says the girl, amazed he hadn't known, 'all of them, of course.' At that moment Humbert knows Quilty must be killed – executed.[*] 'He wasn't a normal person,' Lolita continues, not realising the effect her words are having, 'he was a genius. I guess he was the only guy I was ever really crazy about. . .' Quilty is her lost love; she is Humbert's. In *Lolita* the characters are dispirited by romance.

☆ ★ ☆

Like Quilty, Sellers was not normal; and his genius, too, lay in being able to produce any one of a thousand different convincing faces or voices from up his magician's sleeve. But was it really *genius*? 'Peter could be every living, breathing thing,' said Milligan, who once stated that Sellers was more than a genius – he was a circus freak, or sideshow or psychiatric specimen. Pressed as to what exactly he meant by this, Milligan continued: 'Peter had such a large area of unexplored emotionalism within him, in which he could drown. He's always on the edge of ferment, of tears, of hysteria. The actual business of living made him afraid. . . .'[†]

Hence the recourse to magnificent, limitless dissembling – Iago's 'I am not what I am' – and it is important to see that this is not the same as saying that Sellers was an impersonator, who parroted Norman Grantz and Weegee, and that was that; and nor was it simply the case that, having found Quilty and Strangelove, he himself then retreated behind them. 'Many people claimed he hid behind the characters he portrayed on the screen. That was absolute rubbish,' said Lynne Frederick soon after her husband's funeral. 'Peter regarded those kind of remarks as a big joke' –

---

[*] How come Nabokov missed alluding to this:

> I too would pelt the pelted one:
> At my shadow I cast a stone.
> (Melville, *Shelley's Vision*.)

[†] Milligan on Sellers often sounds like Milligan on Milligan. Lynne Frederick was unerring when she remarked, shortly after her husband's death, 'Spike Milligan had the key . . . Spike was able to unlock Peter's mind, to unravel his thoughts. They were very much alike, and there was a strong bond between them. . .' (*Sunday Mirror*, July 27th 1980). The big *difference* is that Milligan is a good angel and Sellers was a bad.

despite the fact he had laboured long to palm journalists off with them. The truth is that Sellers was not only a chameleon – he was 'an *emotional* chameleon', as Milligan explained to me; his rôles were coloured by his own rage and disingenuousness, and so it is no wonder that he affected to dissociate himself from them. How could he admit, whilst he was alive, that the will, energy and desires of his characters spilled over from, and revealed, his individual consciousness and lack of inhibition?

This is especially the case with the Kubrick films, because what might have begun with mimicry was let loose by improvisation – as Sellers once explained: 'While we were making [*Lolita*] with Stanley Kubrick . . . we did something interesting. If a scene didn't seem quite right, we'd read it from the script and pick out the parts which went best. Then we'd sit round a table with a tape-recorder and ad-lib on the lines of the passages we'd chosen; in that way we'd get perfectly natural dialogue which could then be scripted and used. It's the spontaneous to-and-fro, waiting to hear what the other person says; no matter how good an actor is, he can't get that effect if the dialogue isn't right.'

In terms of *Lolita*, though, it was not *dialogue* which was perfected but *monologue*; Kubrick purposefully encouraged Sellers to go too far, so that the actor's bamboozling of Mason, Winters, etc., represented Quilty, the character's, spellbindings. 'I could never connect with him,' Winters has said of Sellers, 'and whenever I complained to Kubrick . . . he would agree with me. But he didn't change [Sellers'] performance, and this very frustration that I had in real life was what was so sad and funny about Charlotte. I never felt anyone was listening to me when I talked . . . I didn't understand the lonely quality it gave me until I saw the film.'

Quilty is the great solipsist – or egotist, if you want to put it no higher. But where have we heard all this stuff about improvisation and tape-recorders before? Why, at Grafton's during the Sound Mirror days. ('When we used to meet we all got high,' said Milligan looking back in August 1980, 'but not on drink. It was the sheer adrenalin that did it – the fun of being together.') Kubrick had given Sellers back the psychological atmosphere of *The Goon Show*.

He steered him toward making full use of his imaginative faculty – and Sellers, with gusto and assurance, leapt into his own unconfined inner labyrinth, a place full of sunshiny and snowy memories; a silver-grey grotto of neuroses, crammed with dream-visions and ghosts: Bill playing a flaking upright rosewood piano by candlelight for 'Fire and the Woman.'; Peg, creeping with him like a snail as he went unwillingly to school; wartime licentiousness; radio days and responsibilities; dead babies and crumbling houses; the music hall; non-stop voyages around the wilderness of provincial cities; gypsy violins and pit trombones . . . and a billion other hints and sparkles. But Sellers' imagination was not fixed, like wax flowers under a belljar. It was an aggregating and modifying force – 'it dissolves, diffuses, dissipates, in order to re-create . . . yet still at all events it struggles to idealise and to unify' (Coleridge). In the workings of his mind, Sellers re-shaped, fused and blended the patterns of his life and temper; and the result of this free activity (as Kubrick himself has said) was that 'he could certainly play any conventional rôle, but his real genius lay in embodying over-the-top, larger-than-life characters and pulling moments of pure comedy out of them. It's true that he could start first from the voice, but he achieved far more than vocal authenticity and dexterity. He was also the only actor that I ever knew who could really improvise. Improvisation is sometimes useful in rehearsal, to explore a rôle, but most actors, when they improvise, stray into a repetitive sort of hotch-potch, which leads them down a dead-end. While Sellers, by contrast, even if he wasn't on form, after a time fell into the spirit of a character and just took off – it was miraculous. A good part of Dr Strangelove came from his inspiration. I filmed him with many cameras, never less than three, so that I lost nothing.'*

---

* This was Kubrick's response to a question put to him by Robert Benayoun in October 1980: 'Peter Sellers, whom you have used in two of your most famous films, is dead. Do you think that he was an all-round actor who could play any rôle or that he excelled above all in creating grotesque characters?' Published in *Positif* (Paris), February 1981. (Translated from the French for me by Anna Lewis.)

☆ ★ ☆

Sellers' tragedy is that, such was the pitch of his hypersensitivity, fact and fiction intermingled. What he dreamt up about people he proceeded to believe was real. We know that from his reactions to the Loren business. (Sellers was like Coleridge's description of Don Quixote: 'a man in whom the imagination and the pure reason are so powerful as to make him disregard the evidence of sense when it opposed their conclusions'.) On the other hand, there came a time – worse, in many ways, than when he was maniacal – when his imagination failed to be excited and he became sullen and lethargic; his hypersensitivity was replaced by – or exposed as – touchiness and vanity. Such was the case on *Casino Royale*. Peter Evans, who had watched the disaster unfold, told me: 'The genesis of the failure of *Casino Royale* is in *What's New, Pussycat?* In the latter, they gave Sellers his head, allowing him to ad-lib and mess about with O'Toole. There was a lot of spontaneous so-called creation on the set, and they got away with it (to Woody Allen's dismay). *Casino Royale* was not intended to be free-wheeling, but Sellers suddenly decided he wanted to be Sean Connery, and Charlie Feldman said, "I'm going to let Peter do what he wants – he got us out of trouble before on *Pussycat*. I think – give him some rope, it'll be OK." So what Peter wanted he got, and that's when it started to go badly wrong. It was a very big example of how dangerously crazy Peter could be. He completely and utterly destroyed that movie. People were sacked, scripts were abandoned . . . Columbia pretended that they meant it to be a multiple-director omnibus movie – but they were floundering, and yet because it would have been too expensive to close the picture down, they parted with more and more money. Peter was coming into the studio and having wonderful ideas, and they'd be building the sets in the afternoon; the next morning he'd come in, and they'd have dressed the set, and he'd have changed his mind – he didn't want to do that scene any more. And Charlie believed Peter's genius could pull it together.'

It didn't – and Sellers kept plummeting. Because he came increasingly to rely on his unique slant and intuitions, his conception of a rôle had to come together all at once or he'd panic. Permanently anxious about what was happening to him, his only reality – his only existence – was to be found in what automatically bubbled up from his lower depths. And there started not to be anything there – the quality of his creative imagination deteriorated. One of the saddest, maddest exemplifications of this happened during *The Revenge of the Pink Panther*. The idea was for Clouseau and Cato to enter a Negro night club, disguised in zoot suits and Afro dreadlocks. 'Peter', says Blake Edwards, 'was then supposed to come out with a lot of what Clouseau thought was very hip black street lingo and, of course, screw it all up. Peter absolutely couldn't *get* it. That made him very angry and resulted in a very unpleasant day on the set. About two o'clock in the morning, though, Peter telephoned me, as was his wont, to say, "Don't worry about tomorrow. I know how to do it." I told him that was terrific news and asked what he was going to do. Peter said, "I want to surprise you, but don't worry, I've talked to God, and he told me how to do it." . . . The next morning, he came in and wanted to do the scene immediately. We still had some work to do with the cameras, but Peter said, "Leave things as they are and just roll it." I said OK, and Peter made his entrance at the top of some stairs – and it was perfectly obvious that he didn't have *anything* planned. He just believed that by some miracle he'd do something brilliant, but what he did was awful. Afterwards, I said, "Do me a favour, Peter. In future, tell God to stay out of show-business." I did it as a joke, but it didn't work. Peter drifted off into such a depressed, morose state that you could hardly hear him when he performed, and his whole physical being seemed to wither. We had to cut the entire sequence and replace it with a new one . . . in which we used a double. It was very sad.'

It was bad enough, towards the end, when directors like Richard Quine and Piers Haggard tried to sort him out in advance by asking him to rehearse. Sellers, who got so that he couldn't step into the same performance twice, could not repeat material. Everything had to be accomplished in one take. He was completely desaturated. As

Jeremy Kemp (who played Duke Michael) told me: 'I'm afraid that by the time we came to make *The Prisoner of Zenda* he'd *gone*, really. He had a very poor view of the director, Richard Quine, a man who had not made a film for several years – but this was an excuse. Sellers was simply not functioning. You can't picture Peter Sellers doing a gag, getting it wrong, mistiming it, and saying, "Oh, that was all right," can you? It wasn't laziness – he was ill, physically and mentally. His mind wasn't operating properly – his mind was disintegrating. He was going insane. Not just turning in a poor performance, exactly; he would simply fumble something, and not know. Had he been on form, this is the kind of vehicle he'd have relished: doubles, rags to riches, fairytale castles ... His way of working had always depended very strongly on the elusive thing called *instinct*. He'd know how long to wait. He *knew*. But his instincts had deserted him, and when that happens, we tend to wonder whether he's been on the sherbets. But Sellers wasn't known as a drunk or a drug addict – though I must say, after four o'clock he'd be more astray than ever. His dresser was marching about with bottles of Chablis. There must have been something going terribly wrong in him to turn to I don't know whether it was coke or crack or pot or pop or what. *Miserable*. There were many delays. I was thoroughly aware that all was not well. Peter came over to a group of us by the caravans and said, "How terrible that Quine has kept you waiting. I'll talk to him about this, the bloody useless article." But the delays were all caused by none other than Sellers. Lionel Jeffries, in particular, was very upset and concerned that such a once great talent had lost all sense and control.'

Simon Williams, who reminded me that *Being There*, with its hollow man, had intervened between his first experience with Sellers on *The Prisoner of Zenda* and his second on *The Fiendish Plot of Dr Fu Manchu*, said that 'there were days when we had to pretend to corpse. One of Peter's great pleasures in life was giggling – so we'd not only have to act in a scene, but act breaking up, just to prove to him that the old magic was there, which it wasn't. A very unreal experience.'

The Prisoner of Zenda, with a script by Dick Clement and Ian la Frenais, lost momentum quickly. 'The Frewin character', says Williams, 'became lugubrious. Maybe Peter was playing about with how to portray Chance? Find a heavy pathos? I don't know, but something was going on in him. And the scenes as Prince Rudi in the casino – there were endless delays, because he wouldn't have green within a hundred miles. The set was re-dressed and re-dressed. Another of his protective obsessions was only to sleep with his head pointing nautical north, and one wondered if he really believed in this sort of nonsense? Or was he just trying to have everybody on? On another occasion he suddenly said, "This is not funny, it's boring. It has lost everything" – and he ordered everybody to have Vitamin B12 injections. He made people do this a few times. He said it would perk them up. Or he found a tape called *The Legend of Gunga Din*, which is where the idea for *The Party* came from. Galloping, with pauses and gunfire, then it carries on; cannons and machine-gun fire; more pauses, and then the galloping starts up again – and so on and on and on. Sellers had Quine play this tape in the studio. We all got bored with it, but Peter would do the full crying-with-laughter, wiping-tears-from-his-eyes routine. He had to have these ways of getting in the mood. He had to feel funny to act funny. . .'

But how could he, with his presumably baroque apparitions of standing before the mouth of an open sepulchre, and the hooded skeleton there pointing him down into the darkness? 'He'd often talk of his interest in being frozen when he died,' continued Williams, 'and he was frightened of death. He told me about the experience of soaring above himself, when he had a heart attack, and he'd be watching the doctors jumping on his chest, wondering what the fuck they were doing. When he was Fu Manchu, he gradually got to be quite godlike and immobile . . .' – as if all the conduits of his blood were iced up; and with his stringy white oriental beard, this grained face of his was hid in sap-consuming winter's drizzled snow.

It was with an intensified stillness – an effigy – that Haggard had to contend: 'It became clear that Peter didn't know what he wanted, except to disagree vehemently with the suggestions of people he'd decided to take against. Which was everybody. Problems in the script were never solved. I left new pages at his hotel, but he refused to collaborate with me over them; "What shall we do here?" I'd ask, referring to various scenes – but if the experience of preparing the film was misery, shooting it was worse. If I'd been remotely sensible I'd have left the project. I felt, foolishly, a sense of responsibility. Orion had hired me to salvage the project. That was the implicit moral bargain. But that's not the way to do anything in the film business. Anyway, one still *hoped* that Peter would sort himself out, that the magic would happen. We were casting in Paris and finding locations in the French Alps. There was more aggravation on Peter's costumes – can't be green; insane superstitious tremors. John Bloomfield, the costume designer, was summarily told that Mr Sellers' clothes will be designed by Michael Jeffery . . . Then Sellers wasn't actually available for work of any description – he'd gone to London, for advice on his impotence, and hadn't returned. We were all expected to swallow this. There was a struggle about Fu's eyes. In the script, Peter had written "yellow eyes" and he said, "I'll wear contact lenses." He pulled back from this idea. He arbitrarily cut down the make-up. We did some tests, and suddenly during shooting he said, "I don't want to do it like that any more."

'Like an idiot, I kept waiting for the thunder clouds to pass and tried to find ways of being positive. I remember the very first day we were on location, outside that cottage, with the lawnmowers and the sprinklers. He didn't think he had anything to offer; he didn't seem to want to try – and this seemed to me very unusual, not to say tragic, behaviour. It was as if he wouldn't allow any artfulness – from anybody. The problem I was getting, even with Nayland Smith, a rôle which was not encumbered by make-up, was that his sense of timing had gone. He was slow and whispery, and taking too long. Five seconds, lengthening pauses, between his words. Monstrously *slow*. No adroit editing in the world could pull this together. So I was not succeeding in directing him – there was no performance there to shape. "Don't speak so slowly, for Christ's sake, have some *energy!*" It was an illness – a depression – utter, utter listlessness.

'We carried on – but the work couldn't be any good under these conditions. I was reduced to going to his dressing room and trying to introduce the ideas of the coming scene – it was like talking to a backward child, full of dancing around, cushioning phrases – and sometimes, when he did the real thing, and *performed*, one was *extraordinarily* pleased. But it was never really any good, and I was clearly not in the process of making a good film. I'd want to try something out. He'd say, "I don't think so." There was a tendency that he'd not exert himself. There were leaden sections in the film. Dead sections. He slowed right up, and wasn't always available. Nobody censured him. The belief back in Hollywood was: "We have a Peter Sellers film shooting in Paris. We're bound to get something out of it."

'I never saw him socially. He never allowed me to have a relationship with him. I soldiered on and shot nearly everything, and actually there's some good stuff which Sellers had destroyed when he had me sacked: lots of sequences I was fond of – the dacoits running amok in a theatre during an opera, leaping from the dress circle and into the Royal Box; an elaborate sequence in the botanical gardens, with Fu's fellows camouflaged as colourful flowers and blooms. There was a lot more. Anyway, we had eight or nine days left, but decided to shut down over Christmas. Peter and Mike Medavoy wanted to look at all the rough cut film, and either before that, or after that session, Peter said he didn't think he could work with me any more. This was after four months, with only a little bit to go. He decided that either I should go or he should go. "You've made a pig's breakfast of it, Piers, and so have I." He realised he'd not been doing well – and I'd completely failed in instilling some life into him. I'd failed to get a performance out of him. Normally, you find ways of working with people – but he was unable and unwilling to do this. So I was fired from the picture. He had Lynne Frederick brought in as producer, and it was somehow edited and finished off and released after he'd died. I didn't supervise the cutting. The stuff he shot – for I did see a rough cut: Orion wanted my comments – was a bit silly. He had a lot of footage where he is swooning in Helen Mirren's bosom. He also re-shot the scene in the doctor's surgery, where Sir Nules Thudd is strapped down and examined for "elephants on the knees"; and I saw a memo – "Piers's version of this much funnier than Peter's". The sadness is in considering how gifted he was, and how much mental disturbance and unhappiness there now was, at the end.'

☆ ★ ☆

The Fiendish Plot of Dr Fu Manchu is no worse than *The Pink Panther Strikes Again* or *The Revenge of the Pink Panther* – it is rather superior, actually, what with Alex Trauner's magnificent sets: Chinatown, opium dens, dragons, abundant baskets of orchids, a Himalayan palace, underground laboratories. As Haggard suggested, however, no editor could salvage a coherent film from the spools as exposed at the Studios de Boulogne, Paris, the crack cinematography and the scenery notwithstanding. The Edwardian interiors, with their candelabra, mirrors, marble busts and carved ceilings, have a French fuss; Fu's headquarters has a vast polished red, blue and yellow mosaic floor – but what of it, when Fu's long black fingernails come and go from shot to shot; when references are made to George V's equerry, whose scene (with Eric Idle) has been excised; when the dacoits are all suddenly bandaged and bruised, and we have no idea why; when the Fu of the Tower of London scene is such an obvious double, we wonder if this is intended as part of the plot; when Sellers' own voice, barely disguised, issues forth from dubbed minor characters . . . ? And so on and on. Despite the background opulence, the overall effect gets to be rather shoddy.

The interest of the film, therefore – over and above its being Sellers' terminus – must lie in something other than its execution, and so it proves. *The Fiendish Plot of Dr Fu Manchu* is a summary – virtually an anthology – of Sellers' life and work. It was as if, by alluding to all his other films and experiences, he hoped he could agitate, stir up, his imagination and prove that his wasting lamps had yet some fading glimmer left. (It was like trying to give emergency treatment to stimulate a stopped heart.) Thus, David Tomlinson has been brought in from *Up the Creek* and John Le Mesurier from just about everything; Steve Franken was the waiter in *The Party*; Simon Williams reminded Sellers of Ian Carmichael; Clive Dunn is a beefeater, as he had been in Michael Bentine's *It's a Square World* on television, in which he had also played Fu Manchu, setting sail in a war-junk up the Thames to bombard the Houses of Parliament with cannon fire, 'and Peter must have remembered this'; and Burt Kwouk, renowned as Clouseau's houseboy, makes a brief appearance as Fu's servant ('Your face is familiar'). As Kwouk recounted it to me: 'He wanted me to be in *The Fiendish Plot of Dr Fu Manchu*. I said, send me the script. He said not to worry about a script, just come over to Paris. So I went over, and if you've seen the picture you'll see that they set fire to me. I turned up at the studio and discovered this – and I said, "Why didn't you fucking tell me on the phone you were going to set fire to me? You must've known." – "Well, you wouldn't have come!" And I said, "Too fucking true I wouldn't have come." But they paid me quite well; I was put up in an expensive hotel. . .'

David Lodge was summoned to play a policeman – the desk sergeant he had been in *After the Fox* and *The Naked Truth*. ('Who wouldn't have accepted the invitation for an all expenses trip to Paris?' he said to me jokingly.) He had to organise an identification parade, and Helen Mirren, disguised as Queen Mary, sailed in to examine the line-up. The entire sequence, lasting approximately seven or eight minutes, was later discarded, as were whatever contributions John Antrobus had made to the screenplay. Sellers, who was too proud and jealous to allow himself to go cap-in-hand to Milligan, tried to do the next best thing – and he hired the co-writer of *The Bed Sitting Room*. (Antrobus also contributed to the script of *Wrong Arm of the Law*.) He spent a long time at the studio, only to be informed, on June 25th 1980, that he was to be denied any credit. 'In my opinion,' Sellers told him, 'it is to your advantage not to have your name on the picture. Because of the dreadful cutting insisted on by Orion, I have now removed my name from the film – other than my acting credit, which I'd also have removed if it had been possible. I am deeply disappointed with their final version which bears very little relationship to what I had visualised and worked towards.'

It was typical of Sellers to blame others for chaos he'd created. For the record, I asked the editor, Russell Lloyd,* for his opinion of the film, and he said: 'In the cutting room we had a good relationship. Peter listened. But he was very intolerant with some people – he didn't like producers or directors, and he'd made life *very* difficult for Piers. However, as I cut the picture, it was clear that Piers had a great eye for the photographic. We used most of what Piers had shot – except for an elaborate theatre scene, which Peter decided was too farcical, too contrived. He wanted everything to look natural, and for the humour to come from that . . . He was very ill during shooting. The doctor would say, "He'll be well enough by Thursday" – when really he needed until Monday, but he kept on going. . .'

He kept going, even though he loathed what he was doing, because he knew when he stopped he'd die. 'We all knew about his heart attacks,' says Burt Kwouk. 'We were aware something could happen. He used to make jokes – "I'm trying to give them up!" – like coronaries were on a level with an addiction to cigarettes. He was always talking about the time he'd died for seven minutes. "I *died* for seven minutes. My heart *stopped!*"'

There are citations, even, to cardiology in the film. Indeed, Fu has to devise his fiendish plots because his elixir vitae – his supply

---

* Lloyd cut many of John Huston's pictures (e.g. *Moby Dick*, *Reflections in a Golden Eye*, *The Man Who Would Be King*) and he was hired to make sense out of *Casino Royale*: 'Huston's part was the most coherent,' he told me – i.e. the David Niven/ Deborah Kerr non-Sellers section. He also worked on *After the Fox*: 'It was cut originally by an Italian lady, but the producers wanted it re-done; Vittorio de Sica insisted on speaking in Italian – my Italian was a lot worse than his English.'

of heart drops – has run out. (Kwouk's character smashed the last
bottle of this specific when his sleeve was ignited by birthday cake
candles.) Periodically, and in the absence of medication, Fu experiences breathlessness and faintness, and he fends off
unconsciousness, and gets his blood circulating, by zapping himself
in an electric chair: 'It might keep me going a few days longer,' he
says. Sellers felt the same way about his pacemaker, which was implanted and replaced three times in 1977 alone. It was his least
frivolous gadget. The pulse generator, containing batteries and
electronic circuitry, was employed to treat the heart block which
lingered from his acute myocardial infarction – his heart attack of
1964. The exacerbation of his angina was a sign of a worsening condition and Sellers' death resulted from a clinical picture of
hypotension, shakes and shivers, mental torpor, and blood pressure
so low it dropped off the scale. When Fu receives intensive boost-
ers, therefore, by putting his fingers in light sockets and by standing
between a pair of fizzing, spitting Dr Frankenstein-sized AC-DC
transformers, it is not really a gag; it is a straightforward dramatisation of cardiopulmonary resuscitation.

Sellers showed more jocosity the following Spring – in April 1980
(just prior to his departure for Cannes) – when he was shooting a
television commercial in Ireland. He was pedalling an old bicycle
and was hit by severe chest pains. He spent six days in the coronary
unit at St Vincent's Hospital, Dublin, being looked after by nuns.
Joe McGrath, who was directing the million pound ad for Barclays
Bank, went to see him, thinking he could be of service. 'Can I do
anything for you, Peter? Make some telephone calls, or whatever?'
The waxen-faced Sellers, lying on his bed, near to death, said: 'Yes,
go over to my brief-case. Inside you will find a pair of gold Gucci
jump-leads. Put one end on your heart and one on mine, and give
me a start, will you?'

One is reminded of that line in *Love's Labour's Lost* – Berowne ('a
man replete with mocks'), to prove himself worthy of Rosaline's
hand in marriage, is packed off to try and cheer people up in hospitals; he's not sanguine about the commission:

> To move wild laughter in the throat of death!
> It cannot be; it is impossible:
> Mirth cannot move a soul in agony . . .

– as Sellers discovered. Though he filled *The Fiendish Plot of Dr Fu Manchu* with purloined gags which had amused him – the jet-propelled throne is Truman Capote's from *Murder by Death*; the canary diamond is the pink panther painted yellow (its museum display cabinet is the same as the one in *The Return of the Pink Panther*); the open audition for Queen Mary decoys is lifted from the Hitler lookalike contest in Mel Brooks' *The Producers* – or with personal references which meant something to him – the cross-legged, pipe-waving Tedder posture for Nayland Smith, the Daniel Mendoza etching on the wall, Alec Guinness' rich chortle ('As they used to say in the Navy, there's only one way to go . . .'), and all the music hall nostalgia ('the music hall has been one of my pursuits and delights since I was a young man,' says Fu, perking up): despite these spindly props and talismans, Sellers was aching for air, medically and metaphorically. And so of course his forlornest hope was that he'd be oxygenated by *The Goon Show* – 'Yes, it's like the early *Goon Show*,' he freely confessed of his ambition for the film. 'It has all the comedy of the ridiculous.'

A man married to his lawnmower; a Wiltshire cottage which turns into an air-ship (the interior, thanks to Trauner, is as well-appointed as the *Nautilus*); a complaint called 'elephants on the knees', which eases off at sundown when the creatures go to find water (in *The Goon Show* there was an ailment called 'monkeys on the knees'); a torrent of Goonish names (Alice Rage, Rex Finchley, Mavis Thing, Charles Rotten, Constable Groin, Warrington Minge, Arnold Wretch): Sellers clutches at ingredients from the radio series but, as Milligan said in the *Dictionary of National Biography* entry which he compiled on his friend, though he 'made a desperate attempt to recreate the "Goon Show" atmosphere by making the film *The Fiendish Plot of Dr Fu Manchu*, which he co-wrote, . . . alas he never ever was a writer, or ever would be. . .' Sellers throws in the funny names and the asides, but there is no punch, no structure – no point. As he must have admitted to himself, because he abandoned the idea of working Max Geldray in – 'I thought I could find a part for you,' Sellers told the mouth-organist on Christmas day, 1979, 'but alas you look too Jewish.'

The Goon Show, for all its tangents and flim-flam, used to succeed best when there was an underlying storyline – whether *Boy's Own* adventures, gaslit Victorian melos, or wartime tales of hair's breadth 'scapes. Episodes may have given an impression of being slapped together by a pack of kindergarteners, but the material had been carefully composed and run through beforehand; and Sellers, sulky even in those days, would always abide by producer's decisions. (Was he storing up resentments for later life?) In his dealings with Pat Newman or Peter Eton, there was a definite tension – Sellers' unruliness was never very far off – yet when he made *The Goon Show* (or films with the Boultings or Kubrick) he was still a professional and (grudgingly) one of a team, and that is why the recordings may still be listened to (and the early films watched) with pleasure. Sellers was not – as so often later – spoiling things for everybody (himself included) *on purpose*.

Two decades after *The Goon Show* had ended, his ambition had carried him far beyond crappy things like co-operation or conceding points. (There are plenty of flunkies, lawyers and tycoons to back up a film star if he wants to be a bully.) If ever challenged, the ghost of Daniel Mendoza would rise and walk, and Sellers would get sickeningly self-righteous: 'A lot of people believe or feel that if you get into an argument on the set with them, they are to go stark raving bloody mad for some reason. I don't know what it is. If, consequently, you take it, you sink absolutely, or you have the luck, and it is luck, to work with great directors only. I've had that maybe only just on two or three occasions. The rest of the time it has been a bit ropey. But it won't be in the future, because . . . whatever I have, and it may be nothing, but whatever I have I'm going to put it up there . . . and *do it*. That's the way I feel about it right now anyway . . . You know. . .'

Translation: nobody was going to stop him from doing exactly as he and he alone wanted; and, indeed, the first thing to go when he was a star was his fragile self-control (a faculty allied to judgement and conscience, which Sellers never had). And so, if Goonishness fizzles in *The Fiendish Plot of Dr Fu Manchu* because Sellers couldn't see that the all-important Fifties post-war context – in which it had flourished, and of which it had been so much a part – had disappeared, is there any other incongruity, or autobiography, which he imposes on the film and which, likewise, won't flutter into life?

Yes: Sellers abandons the entire concept of Fu's machinations, which may have been amusing – the chain of bizarre burglaries, of Balkan gold, Yeti bones, a mummy from Zagreb, the Leningrad and George V diamond, which, crunched up together, form the elixir vitae – and, throwing away what the film is meant to be about, fills the space with the spirit of romance – all those dread seduction scenes with Helen Mirren, which Haggard mentioned seeing. Decrepit as he (and Fu) was, Sellers still had to inflict his supposed irresistibility on his audiences. (Fu's long hair could be Robert Danvers' grey locks in need of a trim, and his boudoir has a big circular bed, like the one at the centre of the set in *There's a Girl in My Soup* – which, in its turn, with its automatic curtains and mirrors, was based on the Hampstead penthouse.)

☆ ★ ☆

It makes no sense, and serves no purpose, in the film itself, when Alice Rage, saxophone-playing policewoman and Queen Mary impersonator, goes over to the enemy side (Fu has her kidnapped, and when she is unbundled in his den she doesn't object). Mirren tried to explain her character's motivation by saying: 'There is a scene in which Fu is ageing fast, and I promise to do everything in my power to make Fu young – or at least *feel* young. The thought kept flashing through my mind, "Am I *really* saying these things?" But I *was*, and the feeling was rather good.' Gerontophilia like this replaces Sax Rohmer's fondness for poisonous orchids, scorpions and clockwork tarantulas. Sellers, having rid the project of Haggard, and of any residual controlling intelligence, decided that he wanted to be 'doing something outrageous in the name of Fu' – and what this meant, in effect, now that he commanded an entire film crew and could act out his mad impulses, was allowing himself to become a lover of little girls. Fu's voice grows dark and chocolatey, owing to his 'extraordinary sex-appeal. After all, if you've devoted 150 years to devilish cunning, you're bound to get good at it,' said the star.

The way Fu lopes around his apartment, inspecting the drugged chalice and the fragrant bath oils, recalls Danvers' half-crouch, half-run, as he checked appurtenances like fresh bed linen and the champagne bucket. The compulsive or would-be skirt-chaser, however, whether John Lewis, General Fitzjohn, Clare Quilty, Henry Orient, Fritz Fassbender, Evelyn Tremble, Juan Bautista, Harold Fine, Mr Hoffman, or the womanising late period Clouseau (whose fervour is checked by knotted belts and ties) is always an aspect of Sellers himself – who once said: 'I don't think it's possible to have women friends. I don't believe in platonic friendship with women. Sooner or later something springs out of it.' And who also said, when reference was made to his weight loss: 'That was in an attempt to become more attractive to women, I suppose, and to be able to wear more attractive clothing. But it is difficult – I adore chocolate and good food. Also vicars I like very much. I go to M'Gumbas, the only cannibal restaurant in London. They do "Vicar Provençal" there and it's really marvellous – vicars and chocolate. A vicar a day keeps the verger away. . .'

Fu doesn't list the eating of human flesh amongst his diabolisms, though it would not be out of place. *Hoffman*, in which digestion equals sex, is full of slurping, cooking, feeding imagery. ('Women are always hungry. Fallopian tubes with teeth . . .' is one of Ernest Gebler's witticisms. ' A man is excited by splendid breasts, Miss Smith. He gets an instinctive feeling of well-being, of food in the offing', is another.) On a rare foray beyond the fortress of the flat, the two characters visit the Harrods Food Hall, and Miss Smith, as Hoffman's sacrificial victim, is posed beneath mutton carcasses and serried ranks of feathery pheasants and grouse. (They were also meant to lick their ice-creams on Wimbledon Common, but on the day they came to shoot the scene Sellers was niggling and bad tempered. 'He had to react to the sound of the ice-cream van,' says Alvin Rakoff, 'and he said that the timing of it was wrong. Then he said, "Oh fuck the fucking ice-cream van . . ." so that was that.')

The gastronomy metaphor of *There's a Girl in My Soup* would seem more playful by comparison – light and airy like a soufflé, after *Hoffman*'s bloody inner organs, nutty gizzards, liver slices and fried hencod's roes. But, in fact, the underlying philosophy, that women are kitchen utensils, or platters to be scoffed and then spat out, is common to both films – they are misogynistic, and surely not only because, two decades later, we are more enlightened about feminism and justice for all? Hoffman lacks confidence; he is nervous of what will happen 'if the prisoner within me has escaped'. Danvers, by contrast, has nonchalance to burn – but the two men intend gorging on females, and the sweetmeats they capture don't really mind. (It's a crude masculine fantasy – that women really want to be dominated and torn apart, otherwise how can you handle them?) Sinead Cusack's Miss Smith could change places with Goldie Hawn's Marion, and *Hoffman* and *There's a Girl in My Soup* wouldn't alter – because they are, in fact, the same film. They are a variation on the fable of beauty and the beast.

In *Lolita*, when James Mason mounts Shelley Winters, he stares hard at a photograph of Sue Lyon on the bedside table; in *There's a Girl in My Soup*, when Danvers squirms on top of Gabrielle Drake, and slams in the lamb, his eyes stray to the television screen – where his own smarmy face is on, telling housewives the recipes for banana splits and skewered chicken. The real Danvers then turns back to the girl and he says 'You have a delicious flavour . . .' If he is Narcissus, the TV is his pool. When he is presenting his programme he wears velvet coats and curled, Roman consul hair – he affects effeminacy; in the privacy of his own bathroom, however, we have the chance to corroborate Britt Ekland's statement: 'Sellers' hairy cladded chest did much to perpetuate the argument of mankind's evolution from the gorilla.' (King Kong is also on view in a shower scene in *Casino Royale* – after his Billy Bunter boyhood

Sellers liked to adopt middle-aged muscle-man poses.) In the last shot of the film, he is slapping cologne on his chops when he catches sight of himself in a mirror and murmurs, 'My God but you're lovely!' – his catchphrase. Hoffman would seem to believe the opposite of this: 'A man's face doesn't matter all that much,' he says plaintively. (It is a line Charles Laughton would have relished up in his bell tower.) In fact, he is equally vain; it is simply that his shames and emotional problems are on show. Danvers is superficial, the public image; Hoffman is the man behind the mask.

Both facets are wrought into *The Fiendish Plot of Dr Fu Manchu* – Sellers tried to give the Oriental mastermind a comic neuroticism: 'The poor blighter is 168 years old,' he said. 'His henchmen have to plug him into a wall socket every morning to keep him ticking. The police of six continents are searching for him. And he still hasn't conquered the civilised world, defiled its women or pillaged its cities. The man deserves some sympathy.' Sax Rohmer meant him to be the supremely confident 'Lord of the Fires'; Sellers had the possibly excellent (and anyway undeveloped) idea of making him not unlike Clouseau – the wicked criminal who, for all his posturing, is a flop. Fu could have joined Old Sam, the Shakespearean music hall artiste who is now only a busker; or Fred Kite, Mr Martin, Morganhall etc., in Sellers' gallery of dolorous clowns. Instead of which, there are these Fu/Alice Rage scenes, which are lewd – a bit gross – and go right back to the old days of *The Millionairess*, when Sellers first got it into his head to be Cary Grant. 'He once said to me', says Joe McGrath, 'that he'd reached a stage in his career where he could have been Cary Grant for the rest of his life. After *There's a Girl in My Soup*, he said, "They are paying me a lot of money just to be Cary Grant. . ."'

As far as Sellers was concerned, Cary Grant never had to make any effort to do anything; he merely had to turn up – he had no ugliness to overcome. 'I'm not a star,' Sellers complained a thousand times, 'I'm a character actor. The character actor must tailor his talent to the parts that are offered. If I were a leading man, a tall good-looking sort of chap, you know, a chap who has a way with him, who gets parts tailored for his personality, like Cary Grant, then I could regard myself as a star. I'm not a star because [*altogether now*] I have no personality of my own.'

You have only to see the sogginess of Sellers the seducer – in his scenes with Ursula Andress in *Casino Royale*, Britt in *The Bobo*, Claudine Longet in *The Party*, Leigh Taylor-Young in *I Love You, Alice B. Toklas*, or Lynne Frederick in *The Prisoner of Zenda*; or to have wondered why you were bored and irritated when Danvers and Marion take off on their whirl around France, from the Loire Valley to Cannes ('Do you like it?' he says, on seeing the Côte D'Azur in the distance. 'Then let's get it') – to appreciate the ruinousness of his Cary Grant-style aspirations. As a great screen lover Sellers does not ring true. In *Casino Royale*, for example, he is slim, lit carefully, made up with lip gloss and a hint of mascara, but he is also pallid and very, very dull. (When everything stops for Sellers and a co-star to get romantic, it has all the joyfulness of those wretched Nelson Eddy–Jeanette MacDonald duets.) What Sellers enjoyed, I think, and thus had no compunction about pouring on to the screen, was his playboy affluence – a rôle he maintained in reality, with his penthouse pads, mews cottages, hotel suites and private jets. (He wanted to be glamorous – couldn't he see that this turned him not into Cary Grant but Clare Quilty?) In 1962, when at his peak as an actor, he said that if he ever played James Bond he'd satirise the machismo: 'Ian Fleming . . . he's hysterically funny. The idea of taking, say, a spent match, and imagining that somebody would go to the trouble of making a terrible death-dealing weapon out of it – out of something like this – it's hysterically funny. I should like to make a comic film from one of the Fleming books. What's the name of the man? Bond. James Bond, yes? Bond ought to be not one of those mammoth characters, like Mr Universe, but some great flabby type. . .' Five years later, when just such a project was meant to come about, Sellers, thinner, vainer, married to Britt, and determined to make us understand that he now thought very well of himself indeed, had quite forgotten his original scheme. He didn't want to parody urbanity, he wanted to be regarded as urbane

– and his ordering of *forty-five* changes of costume for himself for *Casino Royale* is a sign (or symptom) of his rampaging pompousness and swank. (The tailor, Douglas Hayward, invoiced the film company, which refused to pay, arguing that the clothes had not been authorised. When Hayward complained, Sellers said: 'That will teach you never to make anything without a contract.')

To be Cary Grant requires more than immaculate togs and an excellent set of manners; you need assurance and you need to be able to tantalise, and Sellers is at his worst when he tries this on, without irony, without self-mockery. As a romantic he has no warmth – and so he suddenly has no depth. One of the paradoxes of Sellers is that when he was hired to play a caricature (the shop steward, the commonwealth prime minister, the Teddy Boy and so on, figures which might have been sketched by Osbert Lancaster, Ronald Searle or Michael ffolkes), he was unpredictable, resilient, full of humanity and/or scoundrelism. Deciding, in the Sixties, to idealise himself and be expensive-looking – both in art and life – he robbed himself of his wit. As a cartoon, he'd found recesses, juice; as the man about town he was mediocre and flat. He'd got rid of his soul.

☆ ★ ☆

The only beneficial effect of Cary Grant on Sellers that I can see is that he encouraged him to quit, if not heart attacks, then smoking: 'C.G., Cary Grant, did that for me. He said: "I don't know why you smoke, my darling. You're all you've got." He always called me that. That's my real name. My Darling Peter Sellers. I was Christened My Darling – and Customs Officials always read this out over my dutiable goods. . .'

Grant did well to appeal to Sellers' ego – that, unique unto himself, he must preserve himself; on the other hand, that Sellers was only Sellers, and that he did not actually double, split up, scatter and divide off simultaneously into new and multiple selves – this, the fact of his mortality, was one of his great disappointments. He was all there was, all he had to go on. 'Honestly, I don't really know what I'd have done without films,' he confessed – without a medium to make him unreal. 'It's true,' his son Michael told me 'that his characters were much more full of life than he ever was. Far more interesting than he was as a person, as an individual.' And Sellers himself once said that, as an actor, he left a copy of himself at home – the version he saw in the mirror, who was ageing and ordinary: 'There are many men like me,' he wailed, 'some of us sit in Tubes, some are faceless . . .' Whereas the Sellers who flamed into being at the studios, by contrast, after a short journey in a chauffeur-driven limousine, was full of eagerness and unfading.

The concept is vaguely vampirical – Sellers in his coffin or frozen in his tomb all day whilst a supernatural emanation is off re-generating, and having a good time. It is also inaccurate. The point about Sellers, before his vain-gloriousness got in the way, was that he could give a character poignancy and a degree of nobility not by ignoring dishevelment and the effects of growing old, but by draw-ing on just these feelings and observations. (Ordinariness and mortality were hardly left at home; they were what determined shadows and gravity, and have a basis from which his performances got a lift.) Mr Kite in his kitchen, Mr Martin in his office, Mr Quill in his projection booth, and the rest – they are dandruffy, dauntless, and honestly acted. Sellers raised the profile of nondescripts. They had quirks, oddities. But by the time of *Hoffman*, say, a definite, contemptuous edge – a streak of bitterness – had come to the sur-face. (He'd become inhuman.) He used to play old when he was young, and he was happier in those rôles; and by wanting to look twenty-five when he was middle-aged he was simply continuing the trend of living his life back to front. (Who would have predicted, however, watching *The Dock Brief*, that one day its leading actor would sack a team of publicity consultants because they'd released to the press a photograph in which their client was seen to have a double chin – as happened on *The Prisoner of Zenda*? Actually, Hat-tie Stevenson might: 'He hated old photographs, of when he was fat. Everything had to be thrown away.')

Sellers' main characters are lonely – or loners. They are entirely themselves. It is impossible to imagine Dr Strangelove, for

example, having any family or progenitors. (He sprang from a
nuclear accident, similar to the airborne bacilli which created Lionel
Meadows.) Hrundi Bakshi, in *The Party*, is self-sufficient (that's
why the flirtatiousness with Michele seems so tacked on); Inspector
Clouseau is in a world of his own (the assistant he's saddled with,
Hercule, in *A Shot in the Dark*, was a mistake not repeated); and
who can forget Dr Pratt, in *The Wrong Box*, wreathed in cats and
fantasies? If the Sellers and Loren relationship worked in *The
Millionairess* – and it did succeed well enough for a record album to
be made of their duets* – then it might have had something to do
with the way Dr Kabir rejects Epifania. The film is not clouded or
sentimental (as *Hoffman* is: Miss Smith incredibly makes herself
available and will come and be a chambermaid – 'Can I choose the
things for the new kitchen?' she asks, like a child excited by a
Wendy House; as *Only Two Can Play* is: Lewis and his wife im-
probably operate a mobile library van together). Kabir is left to his
solitude, as Topaze is (the threatened romances with Nadia Gray
and Billie Whitelaw do not take place), or as Old Sam is, in *The
Optimists of Nine Elms*.

In the last film, dressed in a turban and a coloured coat with
crested moons and frilly sleeves, Sellers is a dream-figure out of
Dickens. The London locations (as photographed by Larry Pizer)
are Dickens'† – the poisonous skies, grey mud flats and rubbish tips,
the pipes and sparks of the steelworks and the gasworks, the teetering bridges and catwalks, the bonfires along the river's edge, the
dust carts and garbage-laden barges, the fences, walls, wire-mesh
cages, chimneys, weed-clogged railway tracks and the fog; and the
music, by Lionel Bart, is hurdy-gurdy music hall, like from *Oliver*!
'Peter first saw the final cut one Saturday morning when he was still
freshly in love with Liza Minnelli. They both loved it,' says

---

* By EMI (Parlophone), entitled simply *Peter and Sophia*, as if they were already a
  legendary partnering, like Dick and Liz, or Bing and Bob.
† Sellers', too: 'Makes a very good Grand Marnier Soufflé does the chef 'ere,' says
  Old Sam, as he and the children trundle past the Dorchester.

Anthony Simmons. 'Liza cried her way through it and there was mascara all down her cheek . . . At that stage the film only had a rough piano score built out of a few Lionel Bart songs, played at home by one of his minions on Li's piano. . . Later, when scored, orchestrated and dubbed, the film changed. We never got back to the raw emotion of a single old piano. . .' But most of all Sellers is Dickensian because nothing is concealed. The huge nose, the teeth, the little jig of a walk, the outlandish costumes (Sam is a dilapidated dandy for whom all-the-world's-a-stage) are fantastic, and exaggerated – but what is being exaggerated (or enhanced) is the truth of the character's nature.

His hovel (which he might have inherited from Fagin, along with the flapping coat) is like a theatrical warehouse, with scrapbooks of press clippings, yellowing and disintegrating posters (advertising THE HALL FAMILY & LITTLE SAMMY), and a lot of Sellers' own past seems to be stored here: the Dan Leno-ish little rhymes and sayings; the Russian dirges and balalaika, from Ma Ray's shows; the banjo playing and Formby songs which Sellers had learned from Bill; the wardrobes of pierrot suits, ruffs and parasols, which Peg was once mistress of. But beyond the bric-à-brac, there's Sam's fear and mistrust, and his protective brusqueness. The loneliness which comes across in the film (and which, free of self-pitying and sorrowing, is allied to independence) is at the root of Sellers' discontent, and is what made him an actor. As a child (like Little Sammy who grew up into Old Sam) Sellers had been isolated, and his entire career was a means of expressing that isolation. Left in the care of households of aunts and landladies, whilst his parents were away pursuing a different life before audiences and in pubs, he had known abandonment; and when his mother returned, and over-did her affection, he knew the opposite extreme, a possessiveness which was pathetic and horrible. One way and another, the buffetings and experiences boxed him in and made it impossible for him to return love – and what he expected from others was a total, uncritical adoration. As Milligan mused: 'His second wife, Britt Ekland, he married eleven days after he met her – no wonder it didn't last, people said.* But he wanted the security his mother had given him, and so naturally he thought it must come through marriage. He was always trying to replace the security of his mother – and that security was a dream. It bore no relation to the real world, where people are hard. The real world, full of obligations and liabilities, was like a violent attack on his warm, glowing mother-son relationship. It hacked him to pieces.'

☆ ☆ ☆

The deep appeal of *Being There*, with its Little Boy Lost hero, can immediately be understood. Chance isn't shy or mute, or a zombie, he is a child – the child trapped in the big body ('You's always goin' to be a little boy, ain't you?' says Louise the maid). To acquire the novella's film rights, Sellers set about bewitching and bewildering Kosinski. 'It started in 1971 when I was in London,' said the author. 'He left me a message saying C. Gardiner had called. It turned out to be Peter Sellers. For seven and a half years he sent cables [such as "Available my garden or outside it"], letters on special headed paper, and left baffling messages on my answering machine. Gradually we became friends and whenever we met he would do a Chauncey Gardiner act. I gave in finally.'

---

* There was still time enough to have some 'Thank You' notices printed. This one was sent to Herbert Kretzmer:

> We want to thank you for your telegram/letter/card on our wedding day. It was sweet of you to think of us. We're sorry for the delay in writing to you but due to circumstances beyond our control we were hijacked on to Sam Spiegel's yacht and suffered severely from exposure to French cuisine. Any gifts in the form of money, old cars, used but laundered underwear, gold false teeth, trinkets, baubles, Danny La Rue, bangles and beads will be gratefully received and should be sent to:

The Mr and Mrs Peter Sellers Recovery Fund,
Lichtenstein Buildings,
Bahamas Trust Investments Ltd., London, S.W. 19
(For the attention of Mr Squirn.)
That's all for now folks!
25 Eaton Place, London, S.W.1 [tel.] 235 4494

Sellers, to get what he wanted, serenaded Kosinski as he would a woman (he once sent Britt three consecutive telegrams: I, LOVE, and YOU); and it is no surprise to note that, after *Being There* had been wrapped, Sellers saw no need to continue cordiality, and he pissed on the author without stint: 'Jerzy Kosinski wanted the part himself. That's why he wrote it for a young man of Olympian, god-like beauty. I saw Chauncey Gardiner as a plump figure, pallid, un-exercised from sitting around watching television. Too old? A lot of people said that. I just told them, "You're wrong, I'm right." Hal Ashby managed to bring it off. Jerzy? He has always wanted to be in films. He is now appearing with Warren Beatty. Huh!' [As Lenin's chum Grigory Yevseyevich Zinovyev in *Reds*.] Sellers sensed Kosinski's vanity – and it was similar to his own vanity. It was Kosinski whom Sellers blamed for breaking the sensitive news of his surgical tucking and patching: 'I don't know where those things come from or why people like Kosinski say them,' he ranted. 'I suppose it makes interesting reading for some people, but it in-furiates me. It isn't true.' (It was, as we know.) Sellers' revenge was idiomatic. He added to his repertoire of party tricks the very Polish Kosinski trying to get his tongue around the very Anglo Saxon sound of 'Fuck off!'*

During the run up to the film, however, he was careful only to be serene. 'I remember after years of telling me he could play Chance . . . once, in Malibu, he proved it,' said Kosinski. We were walking

---

* Some months after originally writing this page, I came across a description of Kosinski, by Paul Theroux, which is so apt and illuminating I have to quote it: 'He seemed a bit paranoid and insecure, and vain in an unexplainable way. One night in Berlin he had gone back to the hotel and put on a type of male make-up, giving his pale Polish complexion an instant tan. What was that all about?

'He told me that he was afraid of assassination attempts, of being the object of sinister plots. But it was the opposite that he feared – not notoriety. He was afraid of being ignored, not taken seriously; he could not stand being regarded as insignificant, or of his gifts being belittled. . . He liked power. He wanted to be respectable. When he ceased to be respected – in the end he had actually been mocked for being a lightweight . . . he killed himself.'
The Happy Isles of Oceania (London, 1992), pages 615ff.

in a garden at a friend's house and he saw a small tree that was drying out. Dying. He bent stiffly, picked up the hose, and began watering the little tree. Very quietly. Complete contentment on his face. He *was* Chance. Nobody thought Chance was even a *character*, but Peter *knew* that man.'

The rôle was Sellers' melt-down – he put all the nothingness he had into it – and his sense of exclusion, of being impossible to reach, went back a very long way. In 1962, when Anne left, he felt somnambulistic; it was as if he was staring at a void, and that death was at the centre of his life: 'I'm nothing,' he'd say, 'I wasn't baptised. I wasn't Bar Mitzvah'd. I suppose my basic religion is doing unto others as they would do unto me. But I find it all very difficult. . .' He had no faith ('I'm not comfortable about organised religion'); he had no interest in current affairs ('I have a Victorian outlook') he had no connection with other people ('I don't like taking part. Becoming part of some large group never does any good'). All he had was his mother. When she cooled, whilst he was making *The Bobo*, in 1967, he went into mourning and never came out: 'I remember when my mother died . . . , even though I have children alive, she was my last close relative. I felt a great feeling of loneliness. I couldn't just pick up the phone and speak to her any more. I felt that a lot.'

Well, there were the seances, which blighted his marriage to Miranda Quarry ('He spoke to his dead mother. . . . He became very interested in psychic powers and often talked of the "voices" he heard,' she told a journalist); and there was a film to take to his bosom, and which he championed as he had *The Producers* – Hal Ashby's *Harold and Maude*. 'I thought, "Why is *Harold and Maude* playing to such a tiny theatre?" So I got a friend in L.A. to get hold of the distributors, and they didn't want to know, man. I offered to pay Bud Cort and Ruth Gordon's fare to London so we could launch the film properly. . .'*

You don't need a framed psychoanalyst's diploma on the office

---

* When I asked Michael Jeffery what lingering effect Sellers had had on him, he said, 'It was Peter who introduced me to *Harold and Maude*.'

wall to be able to see that *Harold and Maude*, a black comedy in which a twenty-year old demented urchin and an eighty-year old hag make whoopee, was *Peter and Peg*. (Was Ashby's original allusion to *Pat and Mike*, which Ruth Gordon and Garson Kanin had written for Hepburn and Tracy – cinema's great odd couple – in 1952?) The actors even resemble Sellers and his mother. Bud Cort, who was a pudgy-faced Peter Pan in the Icarus fantasy, *Brewster McCloud*, is now, having fallen to earth, merely goblinlike. Ruth Gordon, who had won the Oscar as a witch next door in *Rosemary's Baby*, is a thin painted bird – her flowery clothes and ponchos are her plumage. (But she's still a bad fairy.)

A charitable reading of the film might point out that it leaps across, or joins up, the generation gaps. Nobody need grow old in spirit – Gordon is fey and fresh, etc. etc., and she brings out the moody, introverted boy. She continually sings,in her moist-lipped warble, a Cat Stevens lyric: 'If you want to be free, be free/If you want to be free, be free'; and perhaps, by being so old, she's ageless – and in the long ago she might have been known not as Maude but Moth or Mustardseed; she is otherworldly, like the inhabitants of a Shakespearean forest. As an enchantment, however, is just not how we take it all in. When Gene Wilder eloped to a motel with a sheep, in *Everything You Wanted to Know about Sex*, or when Zero Mostel seduced Estelle Winward ('Hold me! Touch Me!'), in *The Producers*, the scenes were foul and bizarre – and funny. Comedy is quite cancelled out in *Harold and Maude*, for there can be few more squeamish moments in screen history than Cort and Gordon's sharing of a post-coital cigarette. Maude's wrinkled dugs may be hidden by the bed sheets, but because, with her degree of experience, she'll know every trick in the book, the film is nothing less than a flirtation with necrophilia – and death is the film's big joke.

Harold has a fondness for morbid practical jokes. He enjoys the consternation he causes when he pretends to disembowel himself, set fire to himself, or dangle from the rafters. His car is upholstered in purple and black – i.e. it is a hearse – and his way of using up an empty afternoon is to attend funerals, anybody's. Maude, too, is a funeral freak. This is how they get chatting, noticing each other at gravesides – and so love and death commingle. The old lady invites the young man back to her home, a reconditioned railway carriage (she has a dozen front doors); and after that they whizz about the city having adventures. They are symbolically married when Harold eventually gives her a ring and she promptly throws it in the river, 'So I'll always know where it is . . .' (It compares with 'Love means never having to say you're sorry' for mawkishness. Is the film intended as a satire of *Love Story*, with senility instead of leukaemia, and Bud Cort's sinister flabby-cheeked baby features replacing Ryan O'Neal's boyish rude health?)

Sentimental and silly, freakish and charming – *Harold and Maude*, in which the hero finds a mother and a lover, was destined to appeal to Sellers' incestuous fantasies, and it duly and 'absolutely blew me out . . . So a few weeks or months later, when I read *Being There*, I thought, "Well, the guy to do this is Hal Ashby." I sent him the book with a note saying, "Need to see you, read this." He saw everything it had to say. We then started our quest [for backing and Kosinski's consent] . . . It was particularly difficult, yet I was going back to the old days, away from these Clouseau things I was doing – which are fine for what they are, but I found I was getting in a bit of a rut. I just wanted to break there, desperately, and do some other things. And do you know, I've been after this for six years. Hal Ashby had done *Harold and Maude* and I was going through a very bad patch. Nobody wanted to know me. They were crossing the road in order to avoid bumping into me at that stage. And Hal fell in love with it. And we made a promise to each other that if ever we got a break with it, he would come to me, or I would come to him. And suddenly Hal phoned me one day in Vienna, and said, "I hesitate to say this, but I think we've got it off the ground. It's really going to go." And I'm glad in a way it didn't happen before. Because those days would have been wrong. The progress that's been made, politically, economically, satirically since then has been enormous. So I'm glad it's been done now.'

☆   ★   ☆

A development in world events aside (*Being There* became topical because Chance predicted Governor Reagan – an imbecile camouflaged in the White House), the chief advances, affecting the film's tonalities, were ones made by Sellers himself – i.e., he had travelled nearer to his death. As his executor, Elwood Rickless, said to me: 'From the time of *The Pink Panther Strikes Again*, in 1976, he knew he was dying. He knew he had little time left . . .' and this is apparent in every shot in the film; it is as if the picture is saying (with Philip Larkin), *beneath it all, desire of oblivion runs.*

Being There ends with a funeral (Melvyn Douglas') and commences with a corpse – that of Chance's (unnamed) employer, whose demise means that all the servants will have to be let go. ('It's like what he did to us,' says Michael, on behalf of himself, Sarah and Victoria. 'A lawyer coming along and explaining, "I'm sorry, there's no provision for you in the will. You have nothing."') Chance potters about a bit in the walled garden; he rakes the gravel and prunes a leafless bush; and then, when Louise, the maid, fails to arrive with his lunch, he packs his bags and, eerily calm, makes his solitary way into an overcast and windy Washington. This, we are meant to believe, is his first excursion beyond the old dark house, and Sellers is like a man who has just alighted on a new planet: motor cars, shops, muggers, the entire streetscape: O wonder! How many goodly creatures are there here! How beauteous mankind is! O brave new world. . . (The montage reminded me of *Tarzan's New York Adventure*.)

Chance's discoveries, however, are quickly cut short. Entranced by a bank of TV sets twinkling and winking behind a plate glass window, casting a lavender glow across the pavement, he steps back to get a better view – to a TV addict the display has the splendour of the Sistine Chapel (it is an electronic altar) – and he topples off the kerb. He is straightening up and recovering his balance – his focus, all the time, on those wonderful screens – when he is nudged in the knee by a huge black limousine, and out pops Shirley MacLaine. Assuming, from his bowler hat and dark grey double-breasted striped twill suit, that he must be a gentleman (doubtless she'd have instructed her chauffeur to step on the gas if the car had hit a poor Negro), she insists that Chance's contusion gets examined by her personal physician; so he is inside that funereal limo and being ferried off to be looked after, all within a few minutes of leaving his old home.

The meeting between MacLaine and Sellers, in the film, is as contrived an accident as Kane's first encounter with Susan Alexander out on the road when she has the toothache. Neither of them are scenes the probability of which we are intended to think about too hard. The point is, characters from different circles have collided. Susan, the whining soubrette, is elevated to a world of opera houses and castles, where she is unhappy and out of place (she resents being made to acclimatise); Chance, by contrast, *is* content. The Rand mansion (which resembles Kane's swamp-enclosed Xanadu) is a shadowy labyrinth, not unlike the mahogany and marble place where he was raised, i.e. it is another mausoleum – and cadaverous Melvyn Douglas, propped up in a glass oxygenated room, is a replacement for that sheeted, anonymous employer, whose nineteenth-century togs Chance has appropriated. Chance, who does not have much of a long-term memory, probably fails to notice that he is living anywhere different; and his *indifference* is interpreted by his new-found (childless) friends and benefactors as well-mannered restraint. It is classy not to be impressed or gush over the palatial surroundings – it is alluring. Soon Chance's gardening homilies are being quoted as snippets of wisdom (like the sayings of Confucius or Fu Manchu), and his subdued merriment appears civilised and poised. Here we have, then, a mental defective who is considered innocent and true – a superior being.

At that point (if this indeed were *Tarzan's New York Adventure*, or an equivalent) a satire on modern America, the cult of the celebrity, the prevalence of television and the conversion of news into entertainment, and God knows what else, could have taken flight; but, rather like *The Mouse that Roared*, a dramatic situation is constructed only to be ignored. This sort of avoidance wrecked the earlier film – it makes *Being There*. Off-stage, as it were, the President is despatching his minions to discover Chance's background

('What do you mean he has no background? I quoted him on TV didn't I?'); and so with plot consigned to brief flashes and glimpses, we can see that the purpose of the film is not action and incident (still less satire) but reverie. Is this more obvious now, all these years after its release? That the film is an allegory of Sellers' own disconnectedness?

Sellers had no roots, no fixed addresses, as a child, and so he had no roots of personality – no sense of *being there* – as an adult. As late as 1978, he was still saying: 'I don't have a home, don't have any roots. Which is nothing unusual. I've been a gypsy all my life.' Whatever characterisation he fancied, whatever mood struck him, he was; he became it utterly. If he played a blank, then he was a blank. He'd not shake it off until the next assignment came along – so from the little fat man in the snowy château he proceeded to be the gnomic Fu. It interests me that, for all the horticultural talk in the film, we see no blooms, no life. *Being There* is a winter garden; roots are snapped off.

Melvyn Douglas' Benjamin Rand is a dying plant; his personal hospital is like a greenhouse and, with his big bony hands and square, dislocated jaw, he resembles a pot lily. The dried flower arrangements, which adorn the mansion, are wreaths; and Johnny Mandel's theme music, picked out on a piano, sounds like the tinkle of icicles. We hear it a lot when Sellers and MacLaine tour the rose beds. MacLaine's character is named Eve, and this is a barren garden of Eden. We see acres and acres of brown nothingness and thorns. If it wasn't for Eve, however, the deathliness and decay would be stultifying; she's the only person with energy (it is on the cards that MacLaine will age into a human woodpecker like Ruth Gordon) and it becomes pretty clear early on in Chance's stay, when she floats into his bedroom wearing a negligée, that she is yearning for some sex. Benjamin, who is way past any stirrings in the trouser-snake department, tacitly gives Chance his consent to go ahead and give the lady what she craves, but he can't. He has no sex-drive.

Chance cannot read or write, either; we almost feel he is above the need for such attainments. Similarly with sex. His impotence makes him holy (Catholic priests vow celibacy, but Chance is already an evolutionary step beyond them), and he induces impotence in others. The President is unable to make love to his wife, after he has met Chance. We have a number of shots of Jack Warden's pale and puffy face as he tosses and turns in his bed, and I was reminded of those Hollywood biblical epics in which a burly cowboy, such as John Wayne, dressed as a Roman centurion, eventually vouchsafed the opinion that 'Truly, He was the Son of God,'; for what upsets the President is that he has met somebody who is not corrupt. Eve, meantime, starts to glow. Proving that having to make us see Harold and Maude actually in bed together was not an unique lapse in taste, Ashby gets Eve to start masturbating in Chance's presence. He gives up watching after a few seconds – he is far more intrigued by Bugs Bunny on the television. The scene goes on and on, though. MacLaine having convulsions on the carpet; Sellers watching the box. I first saw *Being There* with a student audience, and we were a pretty liberal lot, always ready to scream with derision when the need arose. Eve's finger pie made everybody embarrassed and silent. The scene isn't funny; it is not unintentionally funny (a student audience's favourite target).

Its function, in terms of the story, is that Eve believes she has made love to Chance without touching him – she is therefore not technically an adulteress; she may even still be chaste. (How could she touch anybody with those four inch Fu Manchu fingernails? It's a wonder she didn't scissor herself to pieces.) What is actually at issue is Chance's vegetativeness. He's not interested in learning about things; and in appearance, too, he is sleepy and amphorous. 'I had to put on a lot of weight to play Chance, and I cut my hair terribly short, because the kindly, efficient maid Louise used to cut it for him. I knew it was right for Chance. And I've had the most terrible battle ever since to get this fucking weight off. When you get to be my age it's so hard.' In the event, his wasting heart made him meagre. He suffered from chest pains, feelings of faintness and anxiety – and, as he explained to Max Geldray, in *Being There*, 'I look quite plump . . . which was *deliberate*, I wanted the character to look stocky. However, now I have lost almost thirty pounds! and have made myself rather weak in the process, but it was necessary for Fu Manchu, or me maybe.'

Sellers' instinct was right to make Chance thick-set – he's mono-lithic. The actor has reverted to Daniel Mendoza dimensions, and I also think there is an echo, in the impassivity, of that uprooted tree trunk photograph, which I discussed in Chapter Eight as a symbol of the primitive and everlasting. Chance is white-haired and quiet, and there's nothing to him except the externals. He has no thoughts, no raging elements, which is why Milligan said 'almost miraculously . . . Peter Sellers himself seemed to be totally ex-cluded.' For, indeed, who is this sweet-smiling agreeable creature, with Stan's voice and Ollie's build? Fuller of face, heavy of tread, Sellers harks back to Fred Kite, especially to the scene where the union boss, rigid and on his best behaviour, is quizzed by Malcolm Muggeridge on an ersatz-television programme called *Argument*. But most of all, in portraying a character whose life is eroded of all except the essentials – Chance eats, sleeps, seeks shelter, parrots whatever he's told – Sellers had reverted to the safety of the nur-sery. Eve will protect him, mother him (she is, of course, Mother Eve), and their frictionless relationship is an idealised symbiosis of the bond between mother and child, a timeless Peter and Peg.

In *Being There*, Sellers achieves a state of perfect nostalgia. Exact-ly what this meant to him personally is something he tried to get across in an impromptu speech at the Cannes Film Festival in May 1980: 'Various people, including the well-known Mr Walter Mirisch,* said "Why do you want to make this film? You need a hook to hang it on." . . . This *Being There* film is the most unique film that has ever been made, and I mean *has* ever been made in the history of film making . . .' Hyperbole, yes, but to Sellers *Being There* propounded his view of Heaven, and to most sane and nor-mal people it looks like Hell. Chance's every need is catered for.

---

* The producer of *The Prisoner of Zenda* and, to Sellers, an enemy.

The Rands, who function as parents, have limitless wealth and power. They do not try and unmask their guest – who is literally a foundling. The dark side of the idyll is that Chance had died but he's not dead; Sellers seems like a ghost returned to haunt himself and the huge house is a house of death, its grounds forever chilly. No birds sing; no leaves will sprout on those skeleton trees. It gives me the creeps, actually, the atmosphere of the Rand mansion, Chance's paradise garden – as it did an earlier guest. Henry James stayed at Biltmore, the Vanderbilt pile in North Carolina used for the location, and dubbed it 'impractically spacious', 'a castle of enchantment', 'a phenomenon of brute achievement':

> ... Roll three or four Rothschild houses into one, surround them with a principality of mountain, lake and forest, two hundred thousand acres, surround *that* with vast states of niggery desolation and make it impossible, through distance and time, to get anyone to stay with you, and you have the bloated Biltmore ... utterly unaddressed to any possible arrangement of life, or state of society.[*]

☆ ★ ☆

The childhood Sellers regressed to, as Chance, is benign, but it is still autistic; the character has avoided (or been deprived of) social interaction, so he retreats to what psychiatrists would recognise as 'uninterrupted self-isolation ... a life not too remote from a nirvana-like existence'.[†] Thinking about his own childhood, and what we know of it, I wonder whether Sellers' early years were blighted by unacknowledged mental illness? The term 'childhood schizophrenia' is generally applied, by the diagnostic system of the American Psychiatric Association, to any manifestations of 'autistic, atypical and withdrawn behaviour; failure to develop identity separate from the mother's; gross immaturity and general unevenness and inadequacy of development . . .'– and Sellers felt isolated from

---

[*] Quoted in *Henry James: The Master 1901–1916*, by Leon Edel (New York, 1972), pages 270–1.

[†] My source for this scientific material is *Abnormal Psychology*, by G. Davidson and J. Neale, (New York), 1978. Chapter 15, 'Child Psychoses'.

society long before fame, money etc., allowed him to reserve secluded hotel suites, book private jets, and travel in darkened limos. It is not very surprising that sufferers from childhood psychosis go on to become adult schizophrenics, and Sellers could have ticked off not a few from that sinister list, above. He absolved himself from responsibilities – he gave up – and this rather feckless moral attitude, optimistically acted out as wistful idiocy when he played the Mr Nobody of *Being There*, meant something quite different in practice. It meant being appalling to his wives and children, alternately showering them with gifts or threatening to kill them; it meant divorces and disinheritance; it meant abandoning friends for years and then telephoning them persistently in the small hours; and it meant making life grim for people trying to help him, because he didn't appreciate presumption ('I never *tell* people to do anything, because I never do anything myself when I'm told to do it, only when I'm *asked*').

Heartless and sentimental (he died literally of a broken heart); generous and stingy; violent and crying easily; rancorous, hyperactive or unresponsive: Sellers would have worn out teams of mind-doctors. By the time of *The Pink Panther Strikes Again*, says Blake Edwards, 'if you went to an insane asylum and you described the first inmate you saw, that's what Peter had become. . . He was certifiable, and anybody who says he wasn't just doesn't know. . . It manifested itself in the way he treated women. I don't think Peter liked women at all, and I think that had a lot to do with his mother . . . Peter had a classic love-hate relationship with her . . . ' – and, thinks Edwards, one of the reasons Sellers hated him was because they were dependent on each other for Clouseau's success. 'He must have loved me kind of like I loved him, and hated me to such a degree that it was kind of like [I was] his mom, that terrible tearing feeling. I know he had a big emotional investment in me . . . but he hated the fact that I was so responsible' – for scripts, direction, conception.

Edward's words are corroborated by my conversation with Herbert Lom at the Reform Club: 'Peter was a great imitator – to the

34. *(Above)* Nosferatu the Vampire: Sellers as
he really was – *Hoffman* (with Sinead Cusack as
the recumbent virgin) – 1970

35. *(Right)* A Living Death in *The Blockhouse*
(1972)

36. *(Right)* Homage to the Music Hall: Old Sam in *The Optimists of Nine Elms* (1973)

37. *(Below)* Insanity on Cyprus (a): Sellers snoozes alongside Peter Boyle. Peter Medak shakes a stick (1973)

38. *(Below)* Insanity on Cyprus (b): Milligan and Peter Medak attend to the script whilst Sellers sulk

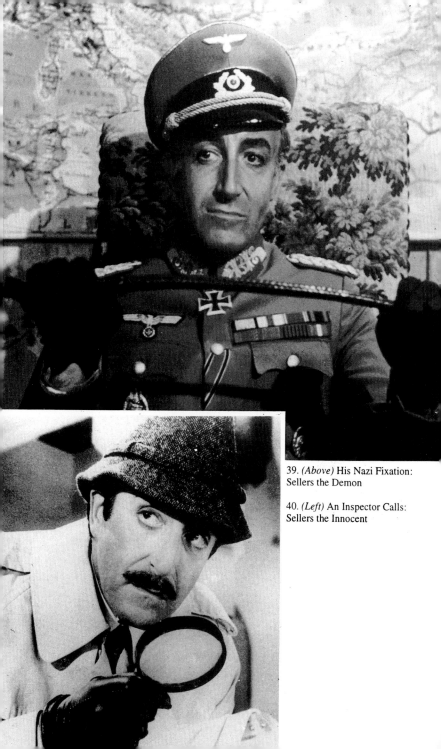

39. *(Above)* His Nazi Fixation: Sellers the Demon

40. *(Left)* An Inspector Calls: Sellers the Innocent

41. Off his head in more than a manner of speaking: in Vienna for *The Prisoner of Zenda* (1978)

42. His last young bride: Sellers in the French Alps with Lynne Frederick
(thirty years his junior) in 1979

43. Mr Nobody: Chance in *Being There* (1979)

44. "Sellers: Where Is His Love Child?" – Looking into the past from a balcony of the Dorchester Hotel (1980)

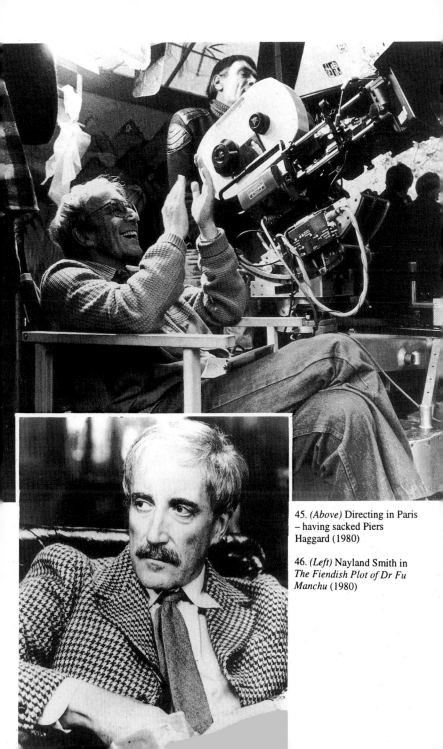

45. *(Above)* Directing in Paris – having sacked Piers Haggard (1980)

46. *(Left)* Nayland Smith in *The Fiendish Plot of Dr Fu Manchu* (1980)

47. The fellow in the bright night-gown: Sellers awaits the inevitable (1980)

extent that, when he'd thought out a character, he'd imitate himself in the part. Clouseau was always "him" or "he", never "I". "I thought up a great idea for him yesterday . . ." He was a typical mixed-up guy. He couldn't cope with fame, women, money – everything confused him. And that was his nice side. Little Boy Lost. A superficial judgement would be to say: You have fame, women, money! You have arrived! But he was always insecure. When he went to a party, he always thought everyone disliked him. So he surrounded himself with cronies. He referred to women only as "birds". On the day after he married I had lunch with him in Hollywood. He said he was off to Germany to see a bird. He was always on the lookout for a new distraction. Vegetarianism, for example. He travelled everywhere with a vegetarian cook. Then he was back on red meat. "Vegetarianism didn't do anything for me." He didn't possess any culture, any background. Nothing to fall back on – to the extent that he never knew whether to accept or reject a rôle. He came to me once in a state, "because I don't know what to do!" King Lear had been offered to him. "Why play King Lear?" I said. "It's a trap." I advised him to turn it down. But he'd been thinking for quite some days, "Perhaps I'm Lear?" He was lost. He had so little knowledge of himself, he didn't see how inappropriate he'd have been in a classical tragedy. He thought he should accept, but had he done so, it would have been a disaster.'

'Yet he became like Lear,' I suggested, 'dispossessing his children, banishing people, mad and foolish fond.'

'There is a difference between *being* Lear and *playing* Lear.'

'Was his emptiness almost innocence?'

'He had no culture – it was astonishing. He was like the President of Czechoslovakia, years ago, when it was asked if he'd accept a book as a gift: "No," he said, "I've already got one."'

'He had a difficulty with abstractions,' I said, 'and a greater difficulty with people. He hovered between the two, certain only of his gadgets and the successfulness of his temper tantrums.'

'Peter was extremely talented. More talented than people gave him credit for, but Blake, for instance, had to give up directing him.

He gave him the screen and had to let him get on with it. They were never friends. Blake was a maturer man, compared to Peter. More experienced. And for some reason they fell out – so they didn't speak any more. This happened in the middle of a film. Messages had to be conveyed by assistants. "Tell him to come through that door and sit on that chair." – "Tell him I don't want to. . ." We had to stand around. Embarrassed. Now I was sad about this, because I knew this would have to be the last *Panther*, and I wanted the series to run forever; so I tried to reconcile them. And they did meet. Blake Edwards had a yacht, so Peter had a yacht hired. They came together like King Alexander of Russia and Napoleon, who met on some raft. And they did make it up and we made more films. But it was a shaky alliance. Blake showed me telegrams he had received: "YOU ARE A ROTTEN HUMAN BEING. YOU ARE A SHIT, AND I CAN AFFORD TO WORK WITHOUT YOU. I DON'T NEED YOU TO GET WORK. LOVE PETER." That sort of thing. Emotional, uneven, unbusiness-like.'

☆ ★ ☆

Chapter Fourteen
Love and Death

In the midst of the craziness and ugliness, Sellers met Lynne Frederick.

'Lynne is different to all the ladies I've been attracted to. She's a good one, that girl; and a terrific bloody actress. I met Lynne at one of Dennis Selinger's parties. He introduced me to my first wife [and to Janette Scott]. I think she's a smasher. We were mutually attracted to each other. She's the one girl who's been cheering up my life for, I don't know how long. . . It's certainly working very well, and please God, if it goes on like this, it will be a real treat. I've known it very different in my time, as you know. On the other hand I think, why should we get married? I'll be in a better position to answer that in the New Year when I've got myself sorted out a bit, find out what I'm doing. When her film comes out, which is soon. I want to see what impact a big success will make on her. How will success affect her? Because she will come into her own when this film comes out – *The Voyage of the Damned*. I think she will become a very good actress in the full sense of the word actress. Although she doesn't want to be – she wants either to be a housewife or continue studying physics. Everyone I've met, including Malcolm McDowell, was knocked out by her performance in this film. I suggest she continues with her career and becomes very selective . . . She says now that all she wants to do is good work; and occasionally, or "If you want, I'll give it up." I just want to see how she takes to the applause. She has to go through that. I hope it works out. It would be nice if it did. It's all very happy there. All very happy. . .'

The above monologue was recorded by Peter Evans in December 1976. He tells me that 'I'd had lunch with Sellers – all very pleasant. He was on good form, telling his stories, outlining his plans. Lynne was present, and he'd be bringing her into the conversation; she didn't need a great deal of encouragement for that, which I thought slightly dangerous, knowing Peter. She'd step on his lines. But he was very tolerant, very loving, and very well-behaved. I came home, and that evening I got a call from him. He'd completely changed. The calmness and the tolerance and the amusement of lunchtime was gone. Completely gone. He was in a terrible state. He was in a fearful, worked-up condition. I had to promise him I'd not mention Lynne Frederick in any interview or piece I might be writing; that, if he were already married he was going to divorce her; and that all this was between ourselves – but "It has been a ghastly mistake and *she's out of here* . . ." That was within a period of three or four hours. . .'

Woody Allen, when he had to linger in London for months on end because of *Casino Royale*, said that the great thing about England was that it had all four seasons in a single day. Sellers, similarly, blew hot and cold. His relationship with Lynne, whom he married on February 18th 1977, oscillated from ardour to hatred, reconciliation and remorse – and, of all his wives, she had the most consistently terrible time. (How could it have been otherwise, given Sellers' deteriorating condition?) When groom was in Europe and bride was in America, she'd receive telegrams signed 'Your nearly ex-husband'; then a dozen roses would arrive. Sellers would state categorically 'It's over', then he'd wax lyrically about how 'We met in a previous incarnation'; the next day, his moods having whirled again, he would fire off a telex: 'Dear Lynne, You have no sense of humour. At least not mine at any rate. Yours, Peter.' This would be followed by more bouquets, accompanied by a note: 'I didn't mean it!' Understandably beflummoxed, Lynne gave an interview to Roderick Mann, in May 1979, in which she said: '. . . we have both consulted lawyers, though nothing's happened yet. I mean neither of us have filed for divorce. We talk every day [by long distance telephone] and I know he feels just as badly as I do about the break-up. Peter says he thought it would be forever. But so did I . . . I've told Peter that I'll fly to Switzerland next month to help him move into the house we bought in Gstaad. It's a lovely place: a real dream house right on top of a hill. I've promised Peter I'll decorate it for him, and I'm the only one who knows where everything goes. I'll go to London first to help him close up the flat there and arrange for the furniture to be moved. I know Peter is talking of a reconciliation, but I cannot predict what will happen when I see him. I'm sad about the house in Switzerland, just as I'm sad about what's happened between us. I knew I was his fourth wife . . . and my mother warned me against marrying him. But I was sure we could make it work. The age difference [she was now twenty-four; he was fifty-three] has had absolutely nothing to do with it. I've always preferred older men. Even if this marriage to Peter fails, it won't turn me off going with older men. I prefer them because I like to be with people who've done more than I have in life . . . It's hard to say how I feel now. Peter and I shared such a lot together: we went through so many highs and lows. And I still love him, of course. You don't suddenly switch it off . . . It hasn't made me bitter or angry, though. Just sad. . .'

Sellers' reaction to his wife's philosophic resignation was to accuse her of conducting an affair with Mann, the journalist who had done nothing more than take down her words. He also had her tailed by a private detective and told Michael: 'I can't take any more. She's messing me about. She's got the hottest pants in Hollywood. No wonder she doesn't want to come back here . . .' Michael told his father he was imagining things – which was to put it mildly. Sellers had always liked to accuse his other wives of infidelity. He was as operatic as Othello when it came to the strength of his jealousy; he would have kept his women locked up in a tower if he could. Now, however, he was exhibiting the histrionics and exaggerations, and holding the irrational beliefs, of a patient in the grip of dementia. 'He became very cruel, hurtful and destructive,' says Blake Edwards. 'He was an emotional and physical bully, especially to ladies.'

☆ ★ ☆

She was his child-bride, upon whom he showered furs and pearls beyond price ('I can deny thee nothing'); she, in her turn, was coquettish and lively – thrilled by the bloodsports he took her to see, by the erotic pavannes at court, by the sudden attention of the powerful. When we see them in the bedchamber together, his impotence and ravaged bulk, and her Pre-Raphaelite slenderness, are an obscene conjunction – it is horrific to think of them having sex (cf. Harold and Maude); and soon the old king, disgusted with himself, humiliated by his sense of failure, is raging and howling in the palace corridors, mad with visions of plots and disloyalty. If that little outburst wasn't bad enough, even when he's calmer there was always his melancholy disposition, his sense of being lonely within his rank, which would wreck what remained of any relationship. Quick to anger, ready to give ear to slanders and surmises, he interprets his new wife's natural flirtiness as inherent impurity; he allows her to be imprisoned on false reports and driven crazy by meddling lordships. . .

Lynne Frederick's rôle as Catherine Howard, in *Henry VIII and His Six Wives* (directed by Waris Hussein in 1973), was a frightening premonition of her life with Sellers: his paranoia, boredom, greed, impotence, fury, envy, and his reliance on the musterings of whispers, gossip, conjectures. Like Henry, Sellers was deplorable and improvident; and, like Bluebeard, he was capable not of love, only violation. His version of love was a clinging, a leeching – the unnatural demands of a creature totally obsessed with itself. Lynne, full of tenderness and pity, however, decided that what he was crying out for was protection – and as his daughter Sarah said to me: 'She did do a lot for him and I could see how he'd think it was good. She took care of him in every way. She took over the jobs and rôles of all those countless people he'd had around him – secretaries, chauffeurs, valets, cooks . . . She was totally dedicated to him. . .'

Sellers' helplessness became Lynne's inspiration – and she was right in one respect. Sellers, who was searching for Peg in all of his wives, wanted to be mothered. Finally, he'd got what he deserved, and more: 'I was his mother, his sister, his daughter, his lover, his wife,' said his widow towards the end of 1980, 'and he became for me my father, my lover, my friend.' What the pair of them mostly were in fact was patient and nurse. 'He was now sick enough, things had gone far enough, that he no longer wanted the hassle of running his own life,' says Michael. 'This is how it started. Bert Mortimer left, or was induced to leave; Denis O'Brien was dropped . . . Bert had been great. He was like an uncle . . . I always used to help him to wash the cars. For years I helped him to do the cars . . . When Dad would go gallivanting off, he'd be left in charge of me and Sarah. He was with Dad for sixteen years, which was in itself a feat. He was the right-hand man. Drove for him, picked stuff up, liaison officer, an organiser . . . But Lynne took control, basically. My father thought she knew what was best for him – so he let her get on with it.'

Lynne had the good intention of managing Sellers' existence – of becoming necessary to him. 'Peter was insecure, uncertain and anxious when I met him,' she told David Lewin a week or so after Sellers' funeral. 'He was insecure about himself and his relationships with others, particularly women. He believed he did not appeal to women because he wasn't attractive. "See my nose, it is crooked," he'd say . . . Gradually I helped ease his anxieties . . . I told him I found him very attractive, that I had from the beginning. I told him I liked his hair grey and he shouldn't tint it.'

First there had been Sophia Loren, re-awakening in him the adolescent idea that 'I am a child of the cinema. When I grew up, we all went two or three times a week and we saw romantic men like Errol Flynn carrying beautiful women off into the sunset.' Next came Janette Scott, listening to his midnight cries through a locked bathroom door; and now, the would-be suicide having gone completely off his rocker, it was Lynne's turn to minister to the lunatic in Intensive Care: 'The change I made was to help him even out the graph of his emotions: the highs got lower and the lows got higher. It didn't become a straight line of course – with his talent it couldn't.' Indeed not. The straight line would have been that of the electrocardiogram informing you that the patient is dead. Lynne did calm him down for a while – for the duration of the *Being There* shoot, for example, which was, however, ungraciously followed by 'one of his depressions . . . he had an enormous sense of anti-climax at the end of what he knew was his finest work'; and so the pair separated. 'We had been together solidly without a break for three-and-a-half years. And no matter how close, no couple can live in each other's pockets like that. We decided that it would be sensible to have some time apart.' Piers Haggard told me that 'one of the troubles with *The Fiendish Plot of Dr Fu Manchu*, was that Peter and Lynne were having problems. She was always somewhere else, and didn't appear until after shooting had started – and it always did him *good* when she was around. Got him going a bit.'

As that evidence suggests, Sellers put an incredible strain on his bride. It is no wonder they were to diverge. Sellers denied Lynne any separate emotional existence. 'He constantly needed my support to help him get through the day,' she said in August 1980. 'I felt it was my duty to boost his confidence.' Two years earlier, just before the start of *The Prisoner of Zenda* in Vienna, she'd voiced a similar opinion: 'Peter is a very dear person and he desperately needs somebody to look after him . . . He continually needs his confidence replenished.' This around the clock ego-massaging and shielding from reality took the form of never appearing to hold an opinion that was contrary to his, throwing away negative newspaper reviews, and seeing off people whose presence might have ruffled the star: 'He's not good at taking criticism,' Lynne told *Time* magazine four months prior to Sellers' death. 'He magnifies everything at least ten times. We dismiss things that he will take to his heart and then take to his bed over. It may be that he remembers he has a pacemaker or heart disease or that he is on his fourth marriage and has been unlucky in relationships. Or that someone he thought of as a friend may do something which convinces him he never should have trusted him.'

Sellers was clearly a hopeless case. He scented betrayals everywhere. Nothing was trustworthy. He held other people in such contempt, I wonder whether hating others was what gave him peace of mind? Lynne, meantime, whilst having enough misgivings about Sellers-the-man to have signed a separation agreement on June 15th 1979 (which gave her a fifty grand annuity and a million dollar house in Los Angeles) continued to be faithful to Sellers-the-legend – to the *idea* of a wayward, wonderful stage-front genius. 'I feel it rather sad,' she said twelve months before they split up, 'that Peter reached his age while not being really happy. I am very young, and I am happy . . . He is young in mind, and I am old in mind, so there is a meeting someplace . . .'

Does any of this gush sound familiar? The Lynne/Sellers relationship, suitably idealised, is the one foisted upon us in *The Fiendish Plot of Dr Fu Manchu*. 'I don't think age matters,' Alice Rage coos to Fu and he, ecstatic, promises her the earth. 'You shall have everything your heart ever desired,' he purrs. When she strips down to her camiknickers, the better to blow into her saxophone, he murmurs, 'Don't mind me. I'm just a feeble old man.'

Feeble and sterile Sellers might have been – he now corresponded not to Chance from *Being There*, but Melvyn Douglas' Benjamin Rand – he still had his wealth to deploy. In a Last Will & Testament dated July 27th 1979, drawn up by Alfred von Grunigen in Gstaad, Sellers stated that 'As adequate provision has been made for my wife *Lynne Frederick Sellers* in a separation agreement . . . it is my express wish that no provision be made for her in my Will.' After a few pecuniary legacies, including fifty thousand Swiss Francs to the community of Gstaad and Saanen 'for cultural events in the interest of the local inhabitants to be decided by the community council' (yodelling competitions? Après-ski piss-ups? Julie Andrews Lookalike Contests?), the balance of Sellers's loot – his residuary estate – was to go to the British Heart Foundation. When Lynne returned to him, briefly, later on in the year, Sellers scratched all this latter bit out. In a codicil dated October 29th 1979, in Paris, the residuary estate was now to go to 'my wife, provided that she shall survive me by a period of thirty days' – so fuck the British Heart Foundation.

Quite who was to receive this-and-that and how much is not of significance to the present argument; what does matter is that we can see Sellers quite blatantly, and pathetically, trying to buy devotion. Lynne would not be a party to his wiles, though; and even when he made Orion (after Haggard had left) pay her seventy-five thousand pounds to be a 'production executive' for a mere three weeks ('She'll be helping generally where she can,' said the film company vaguely), 'the general feeling as regards Lynne,' says Simon Williams, 'was that she was not "with him".' The separation agreement was not cancelled and when *The Fiendish Plot of Dr Fu Manchu* wrapped, Lynne spent most of her time back in America.

☆ ★ ☆

She was far from being the only woman who thought she could save him – and, when he was still alive, she was pragmatic about what the future might bring: 'I believe Peter and I were meant to meet, have a relationship, get married,' she said in 1978. 'But what will happen I don't know. It might last only a couple of years or it might go on. There's nothing I can do about it. Our marriage has a time it will run.' Sellers underscored the suggestion that this was a transitory match – i.e. that his unhappy marriages would resemble each other: 'There's no telling how long a marriage will last,' he said, 'and this is certainly a dicey business for it. I don't know too many people who make a go of it. The reasons are obvious – separations, temptations . . . Some survive just a few months . . . But I am very happily married. . .' And then, as we know, he'd be changing sides and informing Michael: 'I'm going to have to tell Lynne that I can't go on with it. It's just not worked out. She doesn't understand my way of life. I shouldn't have married her. . . .'

Mr and Mrs did manage to appear together at the Cannes Film Festival, between the 9th and 23rd May 1980. It was Sellers' final public appearance. He looked so emaciated – his 'flesh refin'd by death's cold hand' (Donne) – that as he and Lynne strolled along the Promenade de la Croisette he resembled a reliquary being trundled out by a favourite nun. For the hacks and flacks who flapped about him, he said: 'If ever I catch a cold – it's a heart attack, seizure, head fell off, knee gone.' That he was indeed brittle was the impression he gave when the American television presenter, David Sheehan, shoved a microphone into his face and asked for his views on the festival. 'People come to sell their wares,' he snapped. 'It's not a festival, it's a bazaar. *A bazaar.*' If an actor had thought Cannes *wasn't* a trade fair, Sheehan may have had his scoop. As it was, Sellers looked ripe to walk amok, throwing the money-changers out of the temple.

He was equally fissile in private, quarrelling with Lynne and (says his lawyer) 'just generally flailing. He was desperate. He knew he was going to die – this terrified him, and this was why he grabbed at projects: to keep himself going, to keep himself alive. United Artists were committed to *The Romance of the Pink Panther*, which Blake didn't want to direct; and though the script was terrible, U.A. were giving in to Peter on every point. Which was not the way to deal with Peter Sellers. When he had complete control over everything, the result was *The Fiendish Plot of Dr Fu Manchu*. A disaster. One time, he walked off a film, hid in a London hotel room, and I had to find him and take him back ... During his last few months his marriage was in great difficulties; I went to see him in Cannes, where he'd decided to hire a ship. He was all over the place – ordering me to serve divorce papers, ordering me not to do so ... Eventually he shut himself below decks, and then he went off on his own...'

By now he'd made sure he had no friends – only show-biz acquaintances and sycophants. There was nobody with whom to share his problems. Lynne, too, was treated like a retainer – doing everything for him, doing his bidding. ('He consumed every minute of my life,' she said the day after he died.) He would overpower women. He was wilful – which is not the same as being strong, as having strength of character. And as a starlet in her early twenties trying to cope with and run a homuncle practically foaming at the mouth, Lynne's experience was a reduplication of Britt's – a fact she was not keen to acknowledge. 'Britt Ekland!' she snorted on July 27th 1980. 'How could she understand him? They were married fifteen years ago, and Peter had changed a hell of a lot since those days.' Quite so. He'd got worse.

In 1966, Britt told *Photoplay*: 'When you are single you think as a person alone . . . You seldom think of anyone else. But now I think in two of everything. Instead of making one cup of coffee, I make two. And I have to remember if Peter takes sugar! You become more concerned for the other person than for yourself. You can no longer just go ahead and do what you like. You mature because you have an enormous responsibility to the one you love. . .' If asked about the age gap (sixteen years), she'd say, 'In Sweden we have a saying, "The younger the branch, the better it bends"'; and she'd add (in interviews conducted, like all of Lynne's, at the Dorchester), 'I am very careful about my appearance, especially for Peter's sake. When he comes in at night I have changed, combed my hair . . . I'd never let him see me wandering round in curlers or a dressing-gown. I know he's been a whole day at the studio so I make myself look nice for him when he comes home. I think everyone should do that for their husband.'

Britt had offered herself as a vassal only to have her self-sacrifices and compliance derided. It is rather a shame that the cosy scene she tried to create was spoiled when Sellers decided he liked stamping on her wedding ring until it was flatter than a squashed piece of bubble gum (this happened so often, Garrard's grew accustomed to re-shaping it); or that he liked to threaten her with a double-barrelled shot-gun; or that, when they were staying at the Excelsior Hotel in Rome, he decided to rip up her clothes, smash her cassette-radio and rant and rave until three-thirty in the morning. 'I want you to come to the hotel immediately,' he ordered Franco Reggiani, his Italian agent, 'and collect my wife. She is leaving Rome this instant. Our marriage is finished.' Then, turning back from the phone to Britt, who was cowering in a corner – the position to which he'd reduced Anne – he said: 'Just get out of here and don't ever come back. I never want to see you again, you bitch.' Britt (and Reggiani) walked the pre-dawn streets in terror and sanctuary was eventually sought at the Hotel Flora. Sellers ordered the captain of his yacht to throw his wife's luggage overboard (the suit-cases were found in a heap at Brindisi) and Bert Mortimer packaged up her effects in England.

Looking back over their years together, Britt said, in the week of the funeral: 'Being married to Peter was like riding on a roller-coaster. One minute you were flying high, the next you were running low – and I'm sure that his other wives found that ... I know Miranda Quarry couldn't cope with Peter's black moods, either. God knows, their marriage lasted little more than a year. Peter always felt insecure, about his physical appearance especially. He feared the macho-type man posed a threat to him, so he was jealous if another man even glanced in my direction ... I am sure Lynne was a loving and devoted wife. We all were, but none of us could reach him. He was an unhappy, troubled human being. We wanted to help him, but he could not even help himself ... I could not help but look at Lynne [at the funeral] and wonder how she was feeling. I thought back to sixteen years ago. I could have been standing there as a young widow. It almost happened that way. He had eight successive heart attacks [in 1964] that nearly killed him. For days he was on the brink of death. ...'

☆ ☆ ☆

Was he a homosexual?

A thread may be traced through the films. In *The Naked Truth*, Wee Sonny and his dresser bicker like a pair of old-fashioned queens (this low campery was reproduced in *A Day at the Beach*); and then there's *The Magic Christian*. In Terry Southern's original novel, Guy Grand is a cynical Santa, a preposterous Puck. He goes into cosmetics and markets a shampoo based on a recipe used by the Egyptians in the preservation of their dead. He buys a news-paper and introduces a policy of misspelling proper nouns and over-doing the use of foreign phrases 'to antogonise the reader and to obscure the facts'. He incites racial riots by skywriting abuse: JEWS ARE FULL OF CRAP and FUCK YOU in mile-long smoke-letters. He inserts mischievous new scenes into revered films: Walter Pidgeon leering at Greer Garson and brandishing a dagger in *Mrs Miniver*; an amputee with metal hooks for hands groping a woman in a hammock in *The Best Years of Our Lives*. And so on. There was scope here for a Jack Nicholson-type Joker. Southern's Guy maddens people. His pranks account for 'the faces, and especially the eyes, of people in the cities . . . .' What Quilty does to Humbert, Guy does to people wholesale – he makes them paranoid. Sellers, however, loses this aggressiveness. His Guy has no glee. He is bored, listless – like himself. (Guy's house is full of discarded gadgets, games, a giant TV screen, etc.) In appearance, with his hair a tall, tapering quiff, he is an apathetic version of Robert Danvers; and if the film, lacking the panache of the novel, is inert and dumb, there is at least one new whimsy. Where *There's a Girl in My Soup* was about misogyny and automated humping, into *The Magic Christian* Sellers introduced a homosexual curiosity and undercurrent.

The film begins with Sir Guy picking up a boy in a park and adopting him – Youngman Grand (who does not feature in the book) is his catamite – and their pranks and bribes are queerish: enticing Laurence Harvey to play Hamlet as a male stripper; getting boxers to stop punching and start kissing; that sort of thing. Interviewed on the set, at the Theatre Royal, Stratford East, during the shooting, Sellers pretended to be an arts journalist ('This is Nudbolt Thules') telling us, in hushed tones as the lights go down, about the significance of what we are watching – i.e. sex in Shakespeare. In the opening soliloquy of *Richard III*, for example, 'Shakespeare does mean that Richard's sexual member is rather small and therefore misshapen; and he needs to have an erection to *strut* before the wanton ambling nymph. And in "To be or not to be that is the question," he means "To be homosexual. . ." Or does he not? Only the viewers can decide . . .' So it goes on. Polanski is seen playing a hare-eyed loner propping up the bar in a gay night club. Yul Brynner, en travesti, sings Noël Coward's torch song 'Mad About the Boy' – or, to be accurate, he mimes to a track made by Miriam Karlin ('Peter came up to me in a restaurant in Curzon Street. "Mim,

I've got just the thing for you . . ." You see, I have a low voice'); and because *The Magic Christian* is rambling, episodic, and anything can be tossed into the stew, we are given glimpses, now and again, of near-naked Negro musclemen and, down in the ship's engine room, cracking a whip, the Queen of the Amazons, played by Raquel Welch, presides over a platoon of butch lesbians pulling at oars.

Sellers is all over the film – voice-overs, grumbles and lines for the extras (he *is* the crowd); and, most intriguing, he wanted to appear, in a subliminal shot, dressed as a nun and for the nun to resemble his mother. 'There's a very quick disco sequence when they are on the train going north; and there are nuns in it,' Joe McGrath explains. 'Quick stroboscopic flashes of nuns – and he's one of the nuns. He wanted to dress up as a nun. On the morning we were doing it, he called me into the dressing-room. "Who is it? Who am I?" I said, "Your mother". He said "I never realised until I started getting dressed up that I looked exactly like my mother." She looked exactly like him.'

☆ ★ ☆

I don't think I want to let my mind linger too long on the significance of that. (It makes Sellers seem comparable with Norman Bates in *Psycho*.) Suffice it to say that to a psychoanalyst the problem would be as clear as day and homosexuality not an option but an inevitability: the seductive mother (Peg) and the distant father (Bill), and Sellers replacing Bill in Peg's affections – to the extent that she discouraged any friendships or interest in other women (that's why 'birds' or 'tarts' were all right: they are a lesser order of being); and when he did go with them, and compelled himself to marry them, he was filled with guilt and felt degraded, and he had to get violent to assert his masculinity . . . Or something pseudo-scientific like that. Sellers, with Fritz Fassbender in *What's New, Pussycat?*, gave the world one of the funniest portrayals of a shrink who is more bloody barmy than any of his patients ('Why don't we all take off our clothes? It's so modern, you know'); and, in that film, the O'Toole character's compulsive promiscuity ('A little pleasure, a little pain, and then always back to the ladies') is a complaint

Sellers affected to suffer from after the discarding of Britt, when he preened to the press: 'If one more doll just so much as makes a pass at me, I think I'll run out into the street and leap into the nearest river.'

Which brings us to Clouseau – who is often drenched, doused, dipped, ducked and dripping after an encounter with a woman.* In *The Pink Panther*, the first in the interminable line, he is married to Capucine, who with her long neck, Nefertiti profile and Yves St-Laurent threads, is classical beauty incarnate; and her elegance extends to the slapstick routines with Sellers. The pair of them are foiled Gallic lovers. Clouseau's own pratfalls occur because of all his suppressed frustration and tension; he can't manage to get into bed with his own wife without hours of calamitous foreplay, as he trips and stumbles. He's going out of his mind trying to remain nonchalant. He jabs his finger in dramatic emphasis – it catches up somebody else's nostril. He makes a dignified exit – into a cupboard. Ask him to switch a light off – he'll pull the ceiling down. If he goes anywhere near a bathroom, a sink, taps or a water source of any kind – there'll be a biblical flood.

The character was conceived as a mockery of virility. 'I arrived in Rome to work for Blake Edwards.† Wow! Suddenly people at the airport to meet me. Wow! What am I walking into? Wow! Here we are. New life. Rome. Smells. Beautiful, wonderful things. Anything could happen. Anyway, driving back into Rome – "How do you see Clouseau?" I'd read it once. "Well, he's a sort of below-par French detective." We later invented all his accident-proneness. It came out during the early discussions. Blake said, "How do you visualise him?" I said, "Well, Frenchmen, to show their virility, believe in growing a nice, thick bushy moustache. . ." I thought, Clouseau

---

* Blake Edwards would seem to have a thing about water where Sellers was concerned. The Clutterbuck mansion, in *The Party*, is full of pools and streams – giving Hrundi a lot of bother with soapsuds, sprinkler systems, hose-pipes, overflowing lavatories, and fountains in the bidet. The film ends with that elephant being given a bubble bath.

† In the winter of 1963; and for a *per diem* of £2,666. (Graham Stark's calculation.)

must have a thick moustache to prove to somebody or other that he's virile – and in command, you see. That would be the first thing. And the hair fairly short, you know. And he'd use this French/English accent.'

So what happens? He stands too close to electric fans and we hear a sudden *ping*!; billiard cues go for his groin; prongs and levers attack his crotch. He's always being threatened with castration. Then again, the joke of *The Pink Panther* is that it is a sex comedy in which the characters don't get to have any: Claudia Cardinale's whorish princess gets drunk on champagne and passes out on Niven's Sir Charles; Capucine fends off Robert Wagner; Niven is always called away or otherwise distracted if Capucine comes close. Nobody succeeds in getting their rocks off – nobody manages to keep possession of the rock, the Pink Panther jewel itself. And it is Sellers' film (not Niven's – he 'just sat back and watched Sellers take it from him because he knew there was nothing he could do,' says Wagner) for one big reason. Clouseau, by the look in his eyes, appears to be registering, and reflecting upon, the strings of misadventure; and, no matter what, he believes he is fully rational and controlled. It's the rest of the world which behaves oddly – which is out of joint. Clouseau, scratching his violin (his homage to Sherlock Holmes), is magnificently pensive. Niven, Wagner, and the rest, are shallow and basic; they are not required to do much more than pose before expensive backdrops (Riviera nightclubs, Cortina ski slopes) and hold wide-brimmed champagne glasses. (They are cartoons.) Clouseau, by contrast, has a mind, a sensibility. 'There are people like Clouseau all over the world,' said Sellers. 'He's a man with great in-built dignity, you see, great, great dignity. He's an idiot, and he knows that, but he won't let anyone else know that. . . .'

What he doesn't have, after the first film, is a wife. Instead there is Cato, his houseboy, with whom he enjoys a comic sado-masochistic relationship. If, in *The Pink Panther*, Clouseau was an unsuccessful heterosexual – his bottled-up feelings making accidents occur almost telekinetically – later on his world is distinctly queerish. I don't simply mean that Cato hides in his master's bed and bath tub (in the unmade *The Romance of the Pink Panther*, he'd have been preached on the cistern whilst the Chief Inspector was at stool), or that Clouseau (like Holmes) is generally bachelorly in his habits and pernicketiness. (Women, in the later films, are just there to stand on the sidelines and giggle.) I mean, rather, that there gets to be a preponderance of transvestite killers and fag jokes. Cato cross-dresses as a geisha; Clouseau is attacked by a transvestite in the Bois de Boulogne, and ends up in skirts and wig himself. In *The Pink Panther Strikes Again*, for example, the one in which Dreyfus escapes from the lunatic asylum, becomes a James Bond villain, and tries to kill Clouseau, there is a long, unpleasant scene in a gay bar. Michael Robbins is a transvestite butler who dances cheek-to-cheek with Clouseau, gets shot, and plants a big kiss on the Chief Inspector's lips before dying. And the film begins with an extraordinarily tasteless gag. Dreyfus, having fallen four or five times into the lake, is gasping for air. Clouseau pulls him on to the bank and sits astride his back, rhythmically pumping the water from his lungs. Cut to two old ladies regarding this with horror. Cut to their point of view (Clouseau and Dreyfus in the middle distance): they obviously assume some alfresco sodomy is in progress. Cut back to old ladies hurrying away.

☆ ★ ☆

Though Sellers came to hate Edwards because he was jealous of him, there were odd moments when he was lucid and good-natured enough to admit that 'as far as fun goes, I think I had the most fun working with Blake . . . I'm pleased to say that wherever I go in the world I get the impression that [the Inspector Clouseau] films are probably the most popular things I've done. I'm always being asked to make another one.'

If it hadn't been for Sellers' truculence, it would have been the ideal working relationship: Edwards' knack for slapstick, Sellers' goonishness. But Sellers (as with Milligan and Mankowitz) would not be beholden; he had an aversion to the sharing and involvement connected with the word *rapport* – and as Lom said, it didn't take long before director and star were only communicating through intermediaries. Danny Shelmerdine, who worked as a clapperloader on *The Return of the Pink Panther*, recalls that the actor 'was very unreasonable – and quite oblivious to the ways in which his unreasonableness affected the life of the crew. He wouldn't turn up, when we'd spent all day preparing for a shot. We'd be told, "Peter is not feeling well." His general mood was apathetic. He had no enthusiasm for the film. And this is how he always was. He was either enthusiastic about a future project, and wanted *this* film out of the way; or the current film bored him, so he just wanted it out of the way, pure and simple. Whatever he was obliged to be doing now, today, irritated him. It was difficult to get him going in the mornings – though he found that being Clouseau came easily and naturally to him. Then he'd start laughing at the potential of a scene – which Blake would have prepared – and he'd eventually *go*.'

Edwards (like Kubrick) would spend ages setting up multiple cameras for comedy sequences and Sellers would materialise and improvise his way through – and disappear again. By arriving on stage to execute a routine and make a quick exit, Sellers had imposed on the cinema industry the self-containment of a music hall act. (He'd returned to his origins.) The director would plan the next scene on the bill, and meantime use doubles and stuntmen and stand-ins. But it was not only the agreeableness of these conditions which suited Sellers (up to a point); Edwards' sly, sophisticated, cynical creative temperament was congenial. He is fond of filling his films with spies, gangsters, murderers and madness. Themes of insecurity and collapse have been explored (tragically) in *Days of Wine and Roses*, as Jack Lemmon and Lee Remick get in the grip of the grog, and (comically) in *The Great Race*, when Lemmon* tries to get a grip around the throat of the smug Tony Curtis – who plays the whiter-than-white Great Leslie. And he's very fond, too, of transvestism – the games people play with sexual rôles. The

---

* *Author's note*: In my younger years, in Monmouthshire, I would attend Fancy Dress Parties as Lemmon's black-garbed Professor Fate.

murderer in *Gunn* is a drag queen. The killer in *Experiment in Terror* disguises himself as an old lady. Aberrant social behaviour (being a criminal) is connected with deviant sex – and this, again, Edwards has dealt with amusingly and bitterly. Regarding the former, there's *Operation Petticoat*, about the disruptive presence of women nurses on Cary Grant's submarine: 'Maybe Congress made you an officer,' raps the Cap'n, 'but God made you a woman and a woman shouldn't mess around with a man's machinery.' At the opposite extreme is *Victor/Victoria*, a film which is a homage to female impersonation and gender confusion. (It includes a great performance by Robert Preston as an over-the-top, ageing cabaret star – one of those rôles I wish Sellers had been alive and sane enough to play.)

Edwards has made many cops-and-robbers films and television shows (*Gunn, The Carey Treatment, The Tamarind Seed*). He sees the figure of the detective as a man who restores order to a chaotic world, who deciphers its puzzles and plots. (He is an unmasker.) Hence the spoof of Clouseau. The divisions and ambiguities developed and approached by Edwards in dozens of other hit-and-miss films – good and evil; niceness and squalor; sourness and sentimentality – now receive crude cartoon exploitation. Clouseau survives endless assassination attempts, on top of all the scorn and derision; yet he's never less than heroic. Dreyfus, driven crazy watching a fool succeed, stabs himself, guillotines his thumb, shoots off his own nose – a gradual dismemberment which turns him into a cloaked phantom-of-the-opera, cackling at his pipe organ in a remote mountaintop castle. (Sellers stole that image for Fu; and he also re-made *The Prisoner of Zenda*, directed by a former Edwards associate, Quine,* because of the Zenda send-up in *The Great Race*.) Dreyfus is France's most august policeman, the Commissioner; and he is also a strait-jacketed bedlamite, scrawling KILL CLOUSEAU on the walls of his padded cell. Clouseau, in his

---

* Richard Quine co-wrote, with Edwards, *All Ashore* (1953) and *My Sister Eileen* (1955) etc.

turn, *is* as triumphant as Holmes, despite the setbacks. And, like Holmes, he loves disguises.

In *Gunn*, a detective, living and working undercover, becomes paranoid and full of self-doubt. 'Hey man . . . Who are you?' Peter Gunn is asked. 'Even if I told you,' he replies, 'you wouldn't believe me. I don't even believe it myself.' The Clouseau films do not address any remotely serious or deep issues connected with identity – on the contrary, Clouseau's carnival costumes debunk the very concept of a cop (or an actor) taking on the colour of his surroundings, melting into the night, and all that stuff. 'I glide through the underworld like a shadow,' Clouseau vouchsafes in *The Revenge of the Pink Panther*; and then we see him as Toulouse-Lautrec, a Hong Kong coolie, a Mafia Godfather, a Swedish herring-merchant, and as a Catholic priest officiating at his 'own' funeral. (Dreyfus gives the oration. His happy choked-back chortles are interpreted as grief-stricken sobs.) Yet perhaps that is what it is all about? We are right back with red bulbous noses and boutonnières squirting water at the end of the pier. (Again, Sellers' origins.) Like an exhausted, resentful music hall artiste, condemned to trot out his cheap skits day after day, night after night – Clouseau vaulting down a stairway; Clouseau getting jammed in a revolving door . . . – Sellers could no longer be bothered to stay in character consistently. Often, the clenched-jaw Gallic suavity just falls away; he stops being Clouseau and is bored, and himself: heavy, puffy, flashing his own chest hair and Shanti-Om medallion.

The later Pink Panthers are shoddy, plotless, hectic – they are revues. (What plot there is, in fact, is taken from *The Godfather*, *To Catch a Thief*, *Topkapi*, *The Maltese Falcon*, *Goldfinger*, and *Doctor Strangelove*: in *The Pink Panther Strikes Again*, Dreyfus constructs a 'Doomsday Machine'; however, 'compared to Clouseau, the Doomsday Machine is a water pistol'.) The best bits are those we know from Denis Norden's out-take compilations, *It'll Be All Right on the Night*, when Sellers got the giggles trying to talk to Dyan Cannon and when mispronouncing his lines, or the scene with the mobsters breaking wind in the elevator. I personally do not find the cutting-room floor material especially amusing, for the cock-ups weren't happy accidents. Sellers made his mistakes on purpose. 'I search through the scripts to find some words I can play with – "officer of the *law* [leu]" sets them off,' he boasted. In the finished film we see the results of the corpsing – scenes have to be trimmed back to virtual jump-cuts.

Clouseau, a conscientious cuckold in the original film, degenerated eleven years later into a clown; and the editing and continuity are home-movie standard. But the idea of these expensive productions looking so cheaply made; the notion of a brilliant comic actor being so bad *he* (not Clouseau) is the one who has to be hidden inside suits of armour and thick make-up disguises, and his appearances generally faked by lots of reverse angles and medium long-shots of decoys in trenchcoats: all this ingenuity and incompetence makes for clod-hopping camp. Allied with the cross-dressing and dozens of night-club locations, the fuddled, forced, sleepy atmosphere is almost decadent. Though as unsubtle as a circus, tacky and superficial, under the surface of this burnt-out group of films, therefore, is Sellers' fatuousness and stagnation.

☆　☆　☆

Yes, but was he homosexual? (It would have suited Peg if he had been.)

He couldn't cope with women at all; he couldn't cope with his daughters, he couldn't cope with his wives. If he suspected they were trying to outwit him, compete with him, or have thoughts of their own, he could always rely on his superior physical strength to regain the advantage and settle arguments. (Once, infuriated to hear Miranda Quarry justifying, on aesthetic grounds, Sam Peckinpah's use of screen violence, Sellers, the advocate of yogic calm, countered her claim, and put the case for non-aggression, by punching a hole in a restaurant wall.) Most married men, with families to support, knuckle down and accept a measure of responsibility; but to Sellers, responsibility equalled docility. The welfare of other people was not for him. He didn't want anyone near him who was an equal. He was as cold and lonely (i.e. as independent) as a homosexual – and as for his tomcatting? Didn't he work too hard at that? Didn't he dramatise his rakishness to disguise his aridity?

Wednesday June 23rd 1976 was the hottest day in London for nineteen years. Hugo Vickers, the biographer of Cecil Beaton and Vivien Leigh, was dining at Les Ambassadeurs, in Park Lane, and confided in his diary* that:

> at the next table sat Robert Danvers. When I say Robert Danvers, Peter Sellers was so much playing that part that it seemed it was he. Next to him sat a very attractive little brunette about my age [twenty-four] or younger, and beside her at the top of the table someone . . . extremely well known, but I didn't know who it was. Robert Danvers was wearing a dark velvet suit, and dark glasses – square ones in a gold frame. One arm was about the girl's shoulder – and the conversation was on the subject of suing Lord Grade. . .†

---

* Warning, celebrities! Mr Vickers is going to be the Harold Nicolson of the century's end. He also noticed Sellers attending 'a concert given by the citar player Ravi Shanker [oh, that Ravi Shanker] at St George's Chapel in 1970 (part of the Windsor Festival), accompanied by Miranda Quarry. I was disappointed by his lack of stamina. He left at the interval.'

† Why should Sellers possibly want to sue Lord [Lew] Grade of Elstree? Aside from the fact that Sellers was once a client of Grade's booking agency decades previously, the only connection that I can see between the two men was that *The Return of the Pink Panther* was originally to have been a television series for ATV. Edwards preferred reviving Clouseau in a film, however, and Grade, knowing that United Artists, who held the rights, anticipated a disaster, only agreed to finance the production after Edwards had said, 'Lew, I won't take a nickel, and I've talked to Peter and he won't take a nickel. All we want is expenses and ten per cent of the gross from the first dollar on . . . Lew made a wonderful deal with . . . UA . . . all it wanted to distribute it was five per cent of the profits. After it released the movie, it just took off, and from then on, UA decided that the Pink Panther was important. The studio allowed Grade back into the next one, but after that, the Pink Panther became entirely a UA project.'

My surmise is that Sellers, greedy and grudging, would have been behind the decision to push Grade out – for that only meant more gross receipts and moolah coming his own way.

Grade is rightly proud of his reputation as a businessman of loyalty and integrity (he couldn't be more different from the shifty Sellers); and, as a merchant

The girl was bored by the long business chat, and decided to start making love to Robert Danvers. First her hand massaged his leg – then it massaged – well, luckily we didn't see! Then a finger crept through his hair, and inserted itself in his ear. He did not flinch despite the provocation. . . . He went on talking to his friend . . . I was jealous, and called her common to my table. We left at about one o'clock. The Sellers party left earlier.

I am reminded by this vignette of that master of plurality, Clare Quilty, bored and disdainful, waiting for the people to fascinate him; and Sellers, similarly cold and depleted, was on the alert only for new sensations. And he found one. His final years were spent living not so much with Lynne, as with a man. It was not a physical relationship – which, since Sellers had lost the power of erection, was impossible. Rather, it was a curiously emotional association. Michael Jeffery was like his mother and a son-surrogate rolled into one. At last here was a marriage without the inherent ordeals of marriage. ('I think a relationship goes wrong as soon as you get married,' Sellers had always said. 'Immediately, there's a psychological hang-up. Getting married is the quickest way to break it up.') Jeffery was womanish without the disadvantage of actually being female; he could fuss and cajole, henpeck and defuse tension – and as Michael Sellers, who witnessed the menage at La Haute Grange, said: 'Jeffery got on well with Lynne, as well as with Dad, so he was taken on. At times my Dad would say, "Oh, I wish I had a man like Bert around!" Michael Jeffery could *mother* him, which Bert couldn't; campish people can mother you. That was what my father wanted. They sent one another up something rotten. But this

---

adventurer, he had organised spectacular launch parties for *The Return of the Pink Panther* and *The Pink Panther Strikes Again*. The first extravaganza was in Gstaad – the town was painted pink. A pink aeroplane flew journalists from London. Pink champagne flowed at the Palace Hotel. The Henry Mancini Orchestra gave a concert with Julie Andrews. The second squash was in Hawaii. Guests were able to avail themselves of soft toy Pink Panthers, sports outfits with the Pink Panther logo, Pink Panther writing sets, travelling shaving sets, toiletries etc.

new chap could tend him in ways Bert couldn't – it was a light, easy, dressing-room atmosphere.'

The master-servant distance suited Sellers. I went to meet his former cup-bearer at a flat in Chalk Farm, North London. I thought he looked like a buddah – and then I noticed, on a side-table, a number of squatting onyx and ormolu buddah figurines, so Jeffery was evidently living up to his bric-à-brac. There were also framed autographed photographs of Sellers, fragments of Fu Manchu's kimonos, lemon and red, and a book about garden gnomes on display. (The latter bore the flyleaf inscription: 'These will be better at the BOTTOM of your garden than those other things, Peter, July 1979.')

'I met Peter on *The Revenge of the Pink Panther*. I was employed to look after him, his costume-dresser; and before then I went to meet him at Stag House, Victoria, with the wardrobe supervisor, Tony Nichols. There were a lot of people around. We had a shirt-fitting. We all left, and Tony got a phone call from Peter: "Who was that young man you brought with you?" – "That's Michael, who came to talk to you to see if you got on, because he's going to look after you on the 'Panther'". – "Oh, is he? I'd better see him again, then." So I went back and met him again. I did the "Panther". I came back to England, and I was living in Richmond, and I kept getting phone calls in the middle of the night – and would I be on the next film, *The Prisoner of Zenda*, in Vienna? He was at the Bristol and I was at the Hilton and he used to invite me out to dinner – every night when Lynne left. He insisted I appeared in the film – I was Oscar Wilde at the Café Royal, who made some remark to Prince Rudi. But this scene was later cut out. Then we went to Los Angeles to do the Special Effects – the doubling and superimpositioning. He said, "I'm staying here. Would you stay?" By that time I'd become a bit more than a dresser – a bit more like a Personal Assistant.'

Sellers was offended by the scissoring of Jeffery from the film. On March 27th 1979, he complained to Walter Mirisch about 'many of the worst imaginable [editing] errors . . .' that had been made: 'Why on earth,' he asked, 'other than your dislike of the reference to Oscar Wilde at the Café Royal was it omitted??? It MUST be put back.' It was not, nor were references to the Prince of Wales and Lillie Langtry reinstated; and Sid Frewin's cockney ('The old bottle gone, eh?') was curbed – all in deference to the ignoramuses in 'Arizona or Orange County,' Sellers alleged.

I asked what being a P.A. involved doing. 'Not a lot. Really just keeping him company when there was nobody around. More of a companion – that's basically what it ended up as, in a way. In between films I travelled with him as a companion. I used to cook, or take it in turns with Lynne, if she was there. I was never his driver or involved in pulling birds for him, which I understand were amongst Bert Mortimer's duties. Instead he used to send me off to his soothsayers' – I'd have to deputise for him at palm-readings and things, to find out his future.'

'So you were in California together. . .'

'He and Lynne had Candice Bergen's house. I was with him – he'd phone up (I had the guest cottage in the garden) and take me to dinner or the cinema. Then came *Being There*, and he let his hair-dye grow out. Quite nice, this salt-and-pepper look he had. He allowed himself to get chubby – then you see his Nayland Smith: so gaunt. For months he spoke like Stan Laurel. It was like living with Stan Laurel – and he had a picture of Stan Laurel, signed by him, up on the wall. After the film we went on holiday together, without Lynne. We flew from Los Angeles to Miami to Barbados. He'd decided he and I would go on holiday together, on our own, to Oliver Messel's house in Barbados – which Lord Snowdon had told him about. We flew on a regular flight to Miami; then a private Lear jet to the island. In the Bermuda Triangle the engines cut out. We were playing backgammon and were out of our seat-belts. The pilot, co-pilot, hostess (the pilot's wife) – suddenly it was weird. No noise. We were bounding off the ceiling and hitting things. Peter started chanting *Shanti-Om-Om-Shanti* – a mantra – and there was an awful cracking sound. I gather that the engine heaters weren't working, and this was the sound of ice breaking, but I thought the fuselage was splitting. I really thought we were going to die. The pilot's face was crimson and covered in sweat. Eventually, the engine spluttered on again. We had to land in Puerto Rico, because we'd jettisoned the fuel on the way down – the idea being that had we crash landed we might not have become a fireball. We refuelled. Peter and I went to the bar and had a drink. Straight back on the jet – so by the time we arrived in Barbados it was late at night, and the customs men decided to be officious. Peter hated customs men, and refused to go through Heathrow, only Stansted. There was a lot of fuss over bringing his Long Wave radio to the island. That upset him. The driver didn't think we were going to arrive, so he'd gone home. We had to get a taxi for the half-hour drive to the house – and the staff had gone home. Nothing to eat. It was night and we were expected in the early afternoon. Peter was livid – hopping mad. "I know what we'll do," he said. "We'll go to London." The pilot, who was in a hotel in Bridgetown, was got hold of. "Can you take us back?" Peter refused to go to bed. I went into the sea at four o'clock in the morning and was attacked by jelly fish.

'We flew to Miami, and on to New York, and just missed the Concorde. We had to stay overnight in the Kennedy Hilton, an awful place surrounded by barbed wire and guards. Again, Peter wouldn't sleep. Next day, we got on to Concorde with Dustin Hoffman and his mother and Justin Henry from *Kramer vs. Kramer*.[*] Hoffman and Peter were discussing doing a film together. In London, we discovered that all the rooms at the Dorchester were booked, so we had to go to the Inn on the Park, where Peter was given Howard Hughes' old suite. We still hadn't slept – because he wouldn't sleep in New York. We hadn't slept for two days. It was the day of the General Election [May 3rd 1979], so he insisted we stayed up all night watching the results coming in. When Thatcher won he sent an immediate telex to Number Ten Downing Street

---

[*] Hoffman was to beat Sellers, and Chance, to the Best Actor Oscar for that grinding *feuilleton*.

asking her to reduce the income tax so he could move back into the country.* There was a reply from her saying that the next few years will be very hard . . . Next, the journalist David Lewin came round and Peter said he was going to divorce Lynne. The press immediately besieged the hotel. I had to fend off the phone calls by pretending to be "Ted Blake", which Peter loved, because that's Blake Edwards backwards. They put it all in the paper . . .'†

I asked whether it was around about now that Sellers began writing his own script of *The Fiendish Plot of Dr Fu Manchu*? For it was in the May, at the Inn on the Park, that Haggard first met the actor; and Sellers' brooding – the failure of another marriage ('the killer with marriage is this business of "till death us do part"'); his enviousness over Milligan and Edwards; the general re-traversing of his life – set off a film which was to be, in effect, a dying man's rash act; a final act of paranoia.

'We went off on the *Berengaria*, which was moored off Cannes and Antibes, in June; and we'd sail to a small island with a monastery on it, St Honorat, one of the Iles de Lérins, and he'd pour his troubles out. I was totally inadequate to solving his troubles.'

'Which were what?'

'Mainly his impotence, the loss of his virility. He went and had acupuncture treatment in Geneva.'

'Needles in his nuts? Bodkins in his balls? Tin tacks in his testicles . . . ?'

'He wanted me to have it done first – to see if it hurt! We then flew from Switzerland to Paris for the day to meet Yannoulla Wakefield, the production manager, and John Bloomfield, the costume designer. We went to the Mediterranée for lunch. Half-way through the meal, he stood up and shouted, "I can't say it's been a

---

* See page 562 above.

† The *Daily Mirror* smelt a rat: '[Sellers] seemed determined to play a cat-and-mouse game with [enquirers]. A man calling himself Ted Blake . . . answered the telephone . . . He sounded suspiciously like the actor in his Inspector Clouseau rôle.'

great pleasure meeting you" – and he stormed out of the restaurant. He was getting in the car to drive off without me. He was in a foul, foul mood; he wouldn't say what had happened. He sat there, on the private plane, in absolute gloom. We were nearly home when he said, "*You* can do my costumes." Even John Bloomfield, who is a really nice guy – quiet, and so on, and I thought Peter would like him – said: "Do you think he did that scene over lunch for *you?*" Well, I'd rather he hadn't.

'Once we started shooting, Peter wouldn't go to view the rushes – and then he decided he would, after weeks and weeks, and he stormed out again, this time off the entire film. He went to Switzerland. Mike Medavoy, Eric Pleskow, Zev Braun – all the Hollywood big-wigs came over. Peter was in Intensive Care, in Geneva. I was in Paris and his driver took me all the way to the hospital. He was all alone. To get in, I told the nurse I was Mr Sellers' son; *he* told them his younger brother was coming. I had to sneak back out and get him a hamburger at eleven o'clock at night.'

Another visitor at the Geneva hospital was David Tomlinson, who sensed that Sellers was channelling his energies into, and keeping himself going by 'a pathological hatred of producers. When he had a heart attack, over Christmas, Zev Braun, who really did care about Peter's health – who was genuinely appalled at the thought of Peter Sellers dying – tried to see him in Gstaad. Peter said "The only person I want to see is David." I flew to Switzerland and met his consultant, Monsieur Bloc. But I could not persuade Peter to be kind and rational towards Zev. I said, "He's a decent, honourable man." Peter said, "I think he's a sack of shit."'

The film resumed; Lynne arrived 'with a revised dissolution agreement, signed by her, with instructions as to how Peter is to sign so that she can hand-carry to Geneva' (legal memo); sets were rebuilt for Sellers' re-shoots; people were inconvenienced (Simon Williams, for example, who had a commitment in the London West End, in January 1980, had to commute back and forth to Paris every single day for three weeks); Jeffery was given the task of moving Sellers' effects from the Crillon to the Lancaster; and the lawyers declared 'a pure *force majeure* [unforeseeable course of events discharging people from a fulfilment of their contracts] situation.'

☆ ★ ☆

When Sellers became the director, he found a (literally) touching scene for Jeffery. Elsewhere, the doubling had been done by John Taylor; but in the last sequence, when Nayland finally gives Fu the magic rejuvenating medicine, 'I played Fu's hand, with the long pointed fingernails. Peter thought Taylor's hands were too fat for a close-up. Then, after that, it was back to Gstaad. It was too quiet there. Peter wasn't a skier. He didn't like being there in season. He was waiting for the spring to come. Once you'd walked past the cows and the flowers, there was nothing to do. A beautiful house, La Haute Grange, but very boring. Nothing to do. We'd go out for walks; we'd go to the Palace Hotel for dinner. He'd be on the phone a lot in the late afternoon, early evening, at night, to America. He'd be on the phone to Lynne for two or three hours at a go. She was away a lot towards the end. If he was down, he'd be on the phone to Spike or Tony Snowdon. Peter and Michael, his son, were getting very close; he came to stay and we'd go to the English pub and play darts. The funny thing about Mike – he never cried when his father died. A long while after, we went out to dinner – he was never jealous of me, for getting more attention from his father than he got; for we've got the same name and are about the same age. Anyway, he asked me if I thought his father had loved him. I said, "Of course he did, deep down and in his own strange way." Mike said he had to go off to the loo, he wouldn't be a moment. He was gone ages. When he came back I could tell he'd been crying his bloody eyes out. This happened to all of us. We went through a lot mentally with Peter – we all did. When he died I stayed at Helen Mirren's for a while, and then I went to Africa for *Flame Trees of Thika*. I was lucky I was out of the country. There was a lot of shock and bitterness. Peter sapped you of energy – I myself was on the verge of a nervous breakdown, especially after those weeks and weeks in the snow, when there'd been just the two of us: Finally, he pushed this note under my door.'

Jeffery handed me a sheet of paper, dated, across the top corner, Wednesday 23rd March 1980:

> We have spent a great deal of time together over the past weeks [wrote Sellers], and I think it would be a really good idea and beneficial to us both if, after the Cannes Festival, you found a film to work on until we are ready to shoot [*The Romance of the Pink Panther*]. I will naturally keep you on your retainer so please don't feel in any way [that this is] some kind of termination of employment – quite the contrary, as I feel, in Margaret Rutherford's words 'you will return like a giant refreshed'. As we both know, inactivity doesn't suit you, and there won't be anything for you to do during the period I mention. Please give my suggestion some thought – if you decide not to work on a film then perhaps you can take a holiday or spend some time with your parents and friends. Whatever you decide I shall look forward to your returning in time for 'Panther'. In the meantime we have Ireland and Cannes to look forward to and enjoy. . .

Jeffery said that he took the letter as a test, which it was. He moved out immediately into a single room at the Palace Hotel, but he was soon recalled to service, as he fully expected to be. ('We had our ups and downs, like any friends.') I think, though, that between the lines a lot more is being implied about Sellers' pain and unease than his wish to make a spot check on allegiance. By driving somebody away and not quite wanting them to go; by displaying grandeur and helplessness; and by intermingling benevolence and poisonousness: Sellers was a man who wanted to be alone so that he could feel forsaken, or anyway distinct. Wives and children, whose ties to him were more natural than Jeffery's, and who might love him only according to their (biological; emotional) bond – he feared that these sorts of people might revolt against him (as he would, if he was in their position). It was Jeffery's function, by contrast, to be limitlessly patient and to appear over-adoring. He was paid to be subservient, which Sellers was free to code as abasement; and as Jeffery mothered his master, Sellers could assert his filial superiority.

His sickliness enveloped everybody and the atmosphere, during those last months, compounded by his entanglement of guilts, was awkward at best. Michael Sellers says, apropos of his visit to Gstaad: 'the drugs for his angina would knock him for six. He'd take the tablets to calm his heart down and he'd be gaga for a number of days. But in other respects he was unaltered – i.e., he was unpredictable. It was the February of the year he died. On the second night, I was knackered, idly staring at my plate. I just wanted to go to sleep. He took Michael Jeffery off to one side and demanded, "What's the *matter* with him?" In a way, he didn't allow for other people, if they didn't fit into his plans; unless they did what he wanted them to do . . . Not that he was always clear about what his plans might be from moment to moment . . . He'd create rules for us, as children, and then admonish us for breaking them – but he'd not have made us privy to what his rules were in the first place. We did whatever he wanted to do, or he just left us; very rarely, if ever, would he bend to our needs; we fitted in with his needs.'*

☆　★　☆

Jeffery designed the costumes for the Barclays bank commercial in

---

* The fourth person to enter the chalet, making the characters quorate – in readiness to enact a *psychodrame* by Jean-Paul Sartre, you might suppose – was Auberon Waugh, who told the readers of the *Sunday Telegraph*, on July 27th 1980: 'In his wife's absence, [Sellers] was being looked after by his assistant, a young costume-designer in tight corduroy trousers who wore a gold stud in one ear and walked with the unmistakable skip of a former ballet dancer. He was called Mike Jeffery. It was Mike who cooked him his meals, made sure he kept his appointments and scolded him if he forgot to put his boots on when going out of doors. . .' Waugh thought that 'there seemed a certain amount of aggravation in the air between them. . .'

In a letter to me he was more explicit: 'I remember the interview with Sellers – I think it was the last he ever gave . . . I received a strong impression that . . . his "minder", a heavily camp figure . . . seemed to hate him; and that he spoke bitterly of his children, although I cannot remember the details. His son, as I remember, turned up in the evening and we had a rather tense dinner party in his house.'

Ireland; he was with Sellers during that hospitalisation, too, and he said that 'Peter sat there telling the doctors and nurses what was the matter with him.' For Cannes, however, he was relegated to baggage handling. 'We had two private planes. One for Lynne, Peter and me; another for the luggage. For once in his life, Peter had done his own packing. He had these corduroy jeans, and when he realised he'd forgotten them, I had to fly back to find them. A two day journey, from Cannes to Gstaad, where it was snowing.'

Sellers was reunited with his trousers, and momentarily with his wife. There were others flitting in and out of his life, too, as it drew wretchedly to its close: United Artists personnel, somewhat grotesquely trying to force another Clouseau out of a dying man (Steven Bach described him as 'a spectral presence, a man made of eggshells'), and Jim Moloney, who came to collaborate on *The Romance of the Pink Panther* screenplay. In this script (for which Sellers received a million dollars; he'd have received two million more had the film been made), potty Peter built in a few references to lost time – the Russian hey-hey-heys that he was so fond of; Waldini-style violinists and accordionists – but, on the whole, if *The Fiendish Plot of Dr Fu Manchu* was about music halls and shadowlands, then *The Romance of the Pink Panther* would allude to Sellers' years of fame and emptiness. The locations would have been luxurious: châteaux, Venetian palazzos, private railway carriages, Rolls Royce rides in the South of France, swimming pools, villas, yacht clubs, Left Bank night-clubs and expensive restaurants. (There are rather a lot of gags involving waiters spilling champagne and skidding on caviar.) Of all things to cannibalise from the past, Sellers seemed to want a lot of rigged roulette-wheel jokes, rich people gambling jokes – that is, he returned to the idle-class ambience of *Casino Royale*; and his baccarat-keen heroine, Clouseau's adversary, the 'International Arch Criminal, The Froeg', could have been Ursula Andress' Vesper Lynd, right down to her Bond-ish walkie-talkie, secreted in her lipstick.

The film would have had no actual story; nor even scenes – just blocks of (supposed) action, where the stuntmen could exhibit their talents (there aren't any jokes, either): the Chinese Laundry scene, with steaming, hissing pressing machines; the Toy Factory scene, with robots and rockets; the Three Ring Circus scene, with the villains escaping up on to the trapezes; the Pogo Stick Chase sequence . . . There's little, here, which they hadn't already put on to the silver nitrate in the silent-movie era; and Sellers' own international-transatlantic super-rich Monte Carlo or bust tone is very dated, very Sixties. That is why he wanted Clive Donner, of *What's New, Pussycat?* (and other swinging Sixties iconographs, like *Here We Go Round the Mulberry Bush*), to direct. Sellers, yet again, was trying to outwit his ageing body and pretend, by glancing and gazing across all the come-and-gone seasons, that it was really twenty years ago, and that he had twenty years yet to live.

But what of Clouseau, wouldn't he be cadaverous? Not necessarily, for we'd hardly see him for his disguises. He'd be inside the springs and stuffings of an antique chair, in an albino gorilla costume, or made up as 'the famous English clown, Grock', or as a moustachio'd W.C. Fields. (It would have been John Taylor's film.) What was quintessential Sellers, however, was the flirting and courting of Clouseau and The Froeg, which would have stopped the film dead – scene upon scene of champagne toasts and sweet nothings; and, underneath the romance, the inevitable self-pity: 'I'm going to shock you, Cato. I know you have always thought of me as being the irresistible, debonair, ladies' man. That is only a clever appearance. In truth, beautiful women have never been attracted to me.' Cato, who was never the inspector's confidant, is unlikely to have had any thoughts on the matter, one way or the other (he was to wreck Clouseau's wedding by pretending to be a choirboy and starting a Kung Fu duel in the church); that is solely Sellers speaking. And how was Anastasia Puissance, The Froeg bride, envisioned? She was to be 'breathtakingly beautiful, her long, jet-black hair set off by alabaster skin and topaz eyes. She radiates a deep and mysterious sensuality, tantalisingly amplified by the outline of her perfect and long-legged body as accentuated by the tightly wrapped towel . . .'

Beyond the eye-popping intensity of the adolescent prose – all radiation, amplification, accentuation – we can immediately picture Sophia Loren, Sellers' one big excitement. (Anastasia receives advice and hears ancestral voices from a family portrait, as Epifania does in *The Millionairess*.) The script, completed a week before his death and mailed off to United Artists on July 16th with a cover note from 'Peter Shakespeare' ('No joking, I think it's bloody terrific, and I hope you will' the proud author stated), was to be his final attempt at connecting himself with a woman whose presence had inspired and disturbed him. 'It shows a facet of Clouseau's character which hasn't been seen before,' he explained to Auberon Waugh. 'He has a real-life romance with a French countess who tempts him away from the Surêté.' Loren's foreign air had quickened his impatience; he was ready, after meeting her and being cast off by her, never to take, or to demand, less from the world than he wanted. His irresponsibility, his hostility – his adherence to the pleasure-principle – went uncontrolled. He was careless and indignant – and, in a cartoonish lightweight way, Clouseau is glad to fall from grace and experiment with crime. Like Sellers himself, he gets to be conscious of his alienation.

Funnily enough, Loren had seen Sellers in his last year. Or rather she hadn't. 'I went out to lunch one Sunday to an Italian restaurant in Paris,' says John Taylor, 'and Loren and Carlo Ponti sat next to me. She squinted at me and said, "It *is* Peter?" This went on all through the meal. She and Sellers had spoken earlier that very day, and she said: "It was a very great surprise when I saw you sitting opposite me there. He's not meant to be here!" Even if she knew I wasn't Sellers, I think she thought I still was – and that I was Peter, out in the city on his own, playing a part.' Taylor said that Sellers would go on at great length, confiding in him about his solitariness. 'When I said my children were coming over to Paris, he said, "Nobody ever comes to see *me*". Yet Joseph Losey, Ursula Andress, John Derek, Polanski, they all came to see him; and I think Sophia Loren would have been happy to see him.'

In between uprooting the saplings of 'Peg's Tree', because the ominous crows had pecked at them, and lighting bonfires, during the last weekend in Gstaad – 'He decided to get rid of all the photographs of Lynne,' says Jeffery, 'and anything to do with Britt was put on' – Sellers was having consultations with Clive Donner, who recalls that: 'There had been a final and irrevocable break with Blake. A curious relationship, extraordinary. Sellers was noted for developing a scene, seeing the rushes next day, and demanding it be done again. His personal doubts and insecurities cast aspersions on Blake's comic judgement – and this caused many a conflict. After *A Shot in the Dark*, Peter said to me: "I saw the rough cut – that's it. A total disaster. I don't want anything to do with it. I never want to see it again." He was astonished at the success of the film – and yet he'd broken with Blake. Because of success, the money, etc., ten or eleven years later he went back. At last, however, the *final* break. And Peter very much wanted to make *The Romance of the Pink Panther*. He said, "It will be the last one, the best one" – and he personally asked me to direct it. At Christmas 1979 I went to Gstaad; we met again in the summer, by which time Peter had written the script, with Jim Maloney, with whom he felt comfortable. But it was getting to be a complicated set-up – there were other emotional and political problems involving his wife, Lynne, and various executives. Lynne was to be executive producer. She was good, and good for him. A bright lady – but she did not take part in these discussions. She was in America. I worked with Peter in Switzerland, trying to get a comic flow to the scenes in his script; United Artists were very keen for us to proceed. We spoke to a production manager, who flew from Paris. I had to get back to Los Angeles by the end of the week. Peter said, "I'll see you on Saturday. I could do with a few days in England first. I'm going to meet up with Spike and Harry on Tuesday." I remember flying with him in a private jet, early on the Monday [July 21st], sitting opposite him, and he was wearing a tracksuit with a zip. I said to him, "Peter, where is your pacemaker?" – "It's here!" he said, brandishing his scars. "And there's a new one coming out and I'm going to have that fitted." An extension of his gadget fixation. We met up again

on the Monday night in London. On the Tuesday morning I spoke
to him on the phone before leaving for Los Angeles. When I
arrived in Los Angeles he was dead.'

☆   ★   ☆

The narrative is picked up by Michael Jeffery: 'We spent our last
afternoon on an outing to Gruyère. I took some snaps of Peter on
the ramparts of the castle. The day after that we flew to Stansted
with Clive and Jocelyn [Rickards, the art director]. On the way to
the Dorchester, we stopped at the crematorium. The times we'd
been to the crematorium and got to the gate and he wouldn't go in!
When we actually went in I was very surprised. We smuggled in
our flowers, a rose for Peg and a rose for Bill; we lay them just
under the bush and then we went to see the new plaque. "Do you
want to see the ovens?" he asked. "No I *don't*," I said. We went on
to the hotel. He saw Elwood Rickless that afternoon and we went
for a walk around St James' Park, and over the bridge where they
did a scene for *The Magic Christian*. He'd always say, "This is
where we shot *The Magic Christian*,"* even if we crossed it three
times a week; and we'd do a traipse around the pond.'

Rickless remembers his visits to the hotel suite: 'He wanted to
finalise a trust fund for Victoria, who was then aged fifteen. The
figure of twenty thousand pounds froze in his mind. He didn't seem
to see that, because of inflation, the twenty thousand which Michael
and Sarah had received when they reached the age of twenty-one,
would now be worth a lot less. His attitude was: "I started with
nothing. I came up from nothing. They have had twenty thousand
pounds, which is twenty thousand pounds more than I had." And
he was looking back happily to the days when he earned twenty-five
quid as a stand-up comic. Even when he was capable of commanding millions, at the back of his mind he'd rather have been a
stand-up comic. This was the impression he gave me, anyway –
that he never came to terms with the demands of stardom.

---

* The pre-credit-title sequence, in which Sir Guy wanders amongst the tramps and
  bag ladies, and meets Youngman (Ringo Starr), whom he decides to pick up.

'He was flying to America partially on *The Romance of the Pink Panther* business, but chiefly for an angiogram and tests – all preliminaries to major open-heart surgery, which was his only hope of prolonging his life. (He should have had this sort of operation fifteen years earlier, but he had a dread of going under the knife.) He stopped off in London to see Spike and me. I saw him on the morning of the day he collapsed. He looked very unhealthy – ghastly, ghostly. At the same time he had a ruddy complexion and was wearing a tracksuit. He'd been standing on his head to give himself colour. He looked pale and sickly and flushed at the same time.

'I must say, few people die as well-prepared. His Will and legal affairs were in perfect order. . .'

An angiogram – correctly, angiocardiography – involves the selective injection, through a catheter, of a contrast medium (a dye that shows up on X-rays), into the major artery of an arm or leg, in order to demonstrate the anatomy of the chambers of the heart and to observe the bloodflow patterns. Though it is an uncomfortable and hazardous procedure, anaesthetics are avoided, if possible, because sleep-inducing gasses would suppress the true state and picture of any narrowing or obstruction. There is a risk, in severely ill patients, that the radio-opaque contrast medium itself will produce, or provoke, a blockage or a heart attack. (Other side-effects can include thrombosis of the catheterised artery or vein, embolisms and haemorrhages.) Such was the advanced state of Sellers' disease, he would not have survived the techniques employed to evaluate its precise nature and extent.* He was never going to make *The Romance of the Pink Panther*, or any of the other projects queuing up in the distance: Richard Condon's *Arigato*, directed by

---

* In the thirteen years since Sellers' death, angiograms have been superseded by echocardiography – the use of ultrasonic beams, similar to the scans women receive in pregnancy, when the foetus can be seen squiggling about on a black and white television screen. In November 1980, Lynne Frederick presented a £12,400 pioneering echocardiograph machine to the Middlesex 'to reciprocate in some way the enormous love and care which the staff here showed my husband'.

Stan Dragoti, with whom Sellers made a series of commercials for Trans World Airlines, in 1975; or Preston Sturges' *Unfaithfully Yours*, in which Sellers would have been a cuckolded concert conductor, who fantasises about ingenious ways of murdering his straying child-wife. (The film went ahead in 1984 with Dudley Moore and Nastassja Kinski.)

Rickless, who had the task of arranging payment of his client's hospital bills, was told by a consultant at the Middlesex that had Sellers had the angiogram, he wouldn't have pulled through it; and Michael Sellers concurs with the gloomy prognosis: 'He was too ill to be saved, according to the doctors who examined him. They couldn't even get their probes and needles up into the arteries and valves near his heart. It was all too clogged. They said he would have died during the routine preparation for surgery. He'd never have made it. Too late. Only four years earlier, however, he'd met Dr Christiaan Barnard, was invited to South Africa, and agreed on a by-pass operation. My father was allowed to photograph heart surgery in detail – and it suddenly dawned on him that *that's* what they'd be doing to him in the next few days. He went back to his hotel room, booked a flight, locked the door, wouldn't come out, wouldn't speak to anyone, and left. Subsequently he got ill again, needed treatment, and he and Lynne went off to meet those charlatans in the Philippines, who extracted pigs' entrails from the ends of their fingers whilst they were massaging his heart. They advised him to stop taking medication, which he did. They said, "You're fine now. You're cured." He believed them, and he promptly keeled over. He was put in a proper hospital and fitted with a pacemaker.'

At the time of his death, his heart was as big as his chest – a huge swelling of tissues and tentacles, fluttering to little effect; with its pipes, fronds, frills and fringes – its pinkish passementerie – Sellers' heart was like a great, sad sea-creature, out of its element, a fish in air. 'He was having constant heart attacks – we were forever getting urgent calls,' says Rickless. What Sellers was growing accustomed to were Adams-Stokes attacks, mini heart attacks, during which he blacked out for a few seconds owing to ventricular tachycardia (excessive heart beats) or fibrillation (quivering and irregular beats). The pacemaker was meant to prevent these, but evidently complete cardiac arrest, and death's terror, was imminent.

'We had lunch,' says Jeffery. 'Dover sole and salad. He had a second helping. Sue Evans, his secretary arrived. I went to get his clothes ready for the evening, and Sue suddenly yelled, *"Michael!"* He was sitting at the table, his face bright blue, and he fell sideways off the chair. He was blue and purple and lying on the floor. The Dorchester's nurse was there within seconds; they called a doctor and Peter was given mouth-to-mouth resuscitation. It was pretty horrible. We followed the ambulance in the car to the Middlesex Hospital, a six minute ride away. Michael Sellers arrived . . . Yes, it was on Peter's mind that he would die.'

Sellers was on the Dorchester's sixth floor, in suites 611 and 612. Those rooms do not exist any more. They were lost when the hotel was gutted and refurbished a few years ago. I would find it hard to explain quite why I find that so symbolic and right, but I do.

☆ ☆ ☆

A little before The Goons were due to arrive at the Trattoo restaurant, on Tuesday July 22nd, Alan Clare, the pianist, received a phone call.

'Well, Peter won't be coming tonight,' said Milligan, at the other end of the line.

'Oh why? That's a shame,' replied Clare.

'Because he's dead.'

'Come off it Spike. Don't play games like that.'

'Well, he hasn't been breathing for about twelve minutes – doesn't that mean he's dead?'

'So he's died?'

'But Harry and I are still coming over, with Britt.'

'But she and Peter were bosom enemies?'

'Well, I'm bringing her over just the same.'

'*Tonight*? If Peter's just *died*? What *for*?'

'Well, I'd like to hear her side of the story.'

Love and Death

So Milligan listened to this long harangue about what a bastard Sellers had been to her.[*] Secombe remained at home; and, Clare says, 'I was surprised when I met Britt. I thought she was just another toy which Peter had gone around the corner and bought; but I quite liked her – she was intelligent and nice.'

She had flown from Stockholm, with Victoria, the moment she'd grasped the gravity of the news ('I knew that my first duty was to bring Victoria to London. I felt it was right she should be at her father's bedside, like his other children.') Also jetting into town was Lynne Frederick, who had only said in an interview four months previously: 'I love the life in California and Peter hates it. I bought a house there, and he bought a house in Gstaad. When I can, I'm in California with a reluctant Peter . . . I think the pace of life there is too fast for him. . . It's a fifty-fifty chance whether we get a divorce. . .' Michael Sellers would put the odds much higher. During his last conversation with his father, Sellers had said to him: 'She annoys me. I just wish the divorce was over and done with.' He was worried about the forthcoming surgery and worried that Lynne would try and take charge of him: 'What if she shows up at the hospital? I don't want her there . . . She's bound to catch up with me. . . .'

All Sellers needed to have done, of course, if he genuinely felt so oppressed, was to re-summon Elwood Rickless, add a new codicil to his will, and sign the papers. He did not – or shall I say, if such was his intention, he did not have time to act upon it.[†] In the

---

[*] By coincidence, *True Britt*, in which she had revealed the trauma of her marriage, had only recently been published. In the light of her former husband's death, she said (commendably) 'to attempt to retract anything I have written now would be hypocritical'. In any event, facts are facts, and Sellers' murderous rages are facts. There is something structurally cultural, incidentally, in the way that the (chauvinistic) press automatically sided with Sellers and condemned Britt for her revelations. Evidently, in the Britain of thirteen years ago, it was deemed a far worse crime for a woman to tell of her maltreatment than for a man to be violent (i.e. masculine and assertive) in the first place.

[†] If Mr and Mrs Sellers were at such sixes and sevens, however, who booked the cosy table for two at Scully's Restaurant in Beverly Hills, for Friday July 25th –

event, Lynne did catch up with him at the hospital, though hardly the hospital he had in mind. Despite what Milligan thought, when he dined with Britt and Alan Clare on the Tuesday, Sellers was not totally deceased. He was in a deep coma – and his brain, starved of oxygen during those bright blue moments on the Dorchester carpet, when his heart stopped beating and his breathing ceased, was now irreversibly vegetative. Lynne, landing in London on Wednesday July 23rd, after an eleven hour flight (arrival formalities were waived at Heathrow to get her to the Middlesex as quickly as possible), was confronted by a death-bed scene. Sellers had had emergency treatment in the ambulance, to combat the unconsciousness and loss of pulse; he needed further, or continued, resuscitation in the casualty department, and only then was he transferred to the intensive care unit. 'He is critically ill,' said Mr David Johnson on behalf of the hospital. 'He has received a lot of drug therapy in intensive care.' Later on Wednesday, a further bulletin was posted: 'There has been a deterioration in Mr Sellers' condition, which is now very grave.' He was hooked up to a life-support machine; an endotracheal tube was introduced to ventilate him; electrodes were glued to his arms and chest to relay plips and plops to computer screens – and his entire body was wrapped in foil, to preserve its heat. The effect was of a flimsy armour for the frailest White Knight.

'He is in a coma and unconscious,' Lynne told the press. 'But he had hung on for me to come. Of that I am sure . . . there is no clinical or medical explanation how he could have stayed alive with all his senses gone . . . He had worked so hard to stay alive until I could get to him, but finally it was too much.'

Perhaps, in one final crazy decisive deed, he intended gathering himself enough to spit in her eye?

☆   ★   ☆

Lynne's birthday, and the day Sellers was due to arrive in Los Angeles? The table remained set but empty all evening in his honour.

'After Sue and I were having lunch and he went blue and collapsed,'* says Michael Jeffery, 'I lay on the floor of the hospital in
the nurses' office for two days. The Sister said, "He's stable. Go and
get some rest." And just as we returned to the Dorchester the
phone was ringing. "He's deteriorated. Can you come back . . ." by
the time we'd got back, he'd gone. It was terrible seeing him on that
machine. We used to hold his hand and talk to him – Michael,
Sarah, Victoria and I, and then Lynne – there was a chance he could
hear us. As it was coming up to the Friday, I suggested to Michael
that we bring the shrine-photograph of Peg. But he died on the
Thursday [just: at 12.28 am., July 24th]† and the funeral was on the
Saturday.'

The committal was to take place on the Jewish Sabbath, but that
didn't seem to matter. 'Mr Sellers' death was entirely due to natural
causes,' said a hospital spokesman. 'His heart just faded away . . .
Every effort was made to keep his heart going, but it just did not respond. It was just not possible to restart the heart. It ceased to
respond. He had really had all the drugs and all the machines it is
possible to have. There is a limit to what can be done.' In Malibu,
the former Serpent of the Nile and Helen of Troy – she, who like
the Mona Lisa, has been dead many times – sat up with a bolt.
'Something has happened to Peter Sellers!' said Shirley MacLaine.
Later on, when a reporter telephoned to confirm her premonition,
she thought: 'Yes, you probably think he's dead, but he's really only
left his latest body.' Nearer to home, at Willen, a village near Milton Keynes, the spirit medium Doris Collins experienced heart
murmurs: 'I heard a voice saying: "Doris, God help me." I would
say it was Peter reaching out to me. . .' In London, Graham Stark

---

* When Sellers went blue – prior to going alabaster white and comatose – he
turned back into Juan Bautista. As he once joked: 'Not smoking gives you that
wild-eyed look and turns you blue. You can see the effects in *The Bobo*. I play an
out of work matador, who is blue, through no fault of his own.'

† The death was announced to the throng of reporters and photographers outside
in Mortimer Street at 2 a.m., giving the newspapers time to make up their front
pages for the morning editions.

left the celebrity party for Alan Parker's *Fame* because, though not a believer 'in extra-sensory perception, some hunch . . . told me that this wasn't the night to go dancing.' He toasted his pal silently with a cup of tea: 'Here's to the memory of Leading Aircraftsman P. Sellers. . .' And on a beach in Mallorca, Bloom Clare, Alan's wife, found herself crying and crying.

No doubt there were eagles and comets, lionesses whelping in the streets, and any number of portentous things as the great necromancer was flying beyond the sheltering sky. 'I'm well-prepared for when I enter the after-life. My mother has talked to me about it frequently since she died in 1967,' he'd said whilst at the Cannes Film Festival, so very recently. 'I feel her through vibrations in my head. When I had my first heart attack in 1964 and was actually dead for almost three minutes, I saw my mother. It was just too early for me to die. She pulled me back from the grave. She is always here looking after me, helping me in a crisis. We're as close as any mother and son could be.' Peg must have been an amazing woman if she could march into the underworld and behave like a gliding ghost three years *before* she was actually grassed over. Indubitably deceased by 1980, however, she was able to warn Sellers that 'the day will come soon when she will tell me it's time to pack it in. It will happen simply and I have no fears'[*]

The grave was not the end – Sellers had always believed that. He'd gained inspiration from the dead (e.g. Dan Leno, for *The Optimists of Nine Elms*); he'd heard voices and he'd frequented seances. He'd been born into the crepuscular music hall, a world which was vanishing, and as a young man he'd made himself grey and dusty, to play melancholy oldsters – and the paradox is, though he   could

---

[*] First and last, he was Peter Pan – who 'went in a hurry in the end, because he had dreamt that his mother was crying, and he knew what was the great thing she cried for, and that a hug from her splendid Peter would quickly make her to smile. Oh! he felt sure of it, and so he flew straight to the window, which was always to be open for him . . . But the window was closed, and there were iron bars on it. . .'
The Little White Bird, by J. M. Barrie.

act old, he didn't want to be old. He had a dread of being an invalid, and getting old and sick. He wanted to be forever young – but instead of remaining youthful in his enthusiasms, he grew spiteful, disruptive. He didn't actually care for (real) children, yet he'd aim to please, like a child, and mainly he'd aim to hurt. (Lynne, wise to the Peter Pan performance, would respond by being Wendy: 'I would just say, "You know, it's naughty to do things like that [*what?*] and I don't like you for it." But I never stopped loving him.')

☆ ★ ☆

Sellers told Herbert Lom that he was proud only of two films: '*Doctor Strangelove*, in which he always believed, and *Being There*, where he walks on water at the end. Otherwise he was disappointed and mixed up.' I think it is possible to understand how these works are connected. They are about immaturity and morbidity. Sellers' films, from the early black and white efforts to Fu undergoing funny Adams-Stokes attacks, are often funerary and (fleetingly) poetic; and Chance in his winter garden and the politicians and soldiers wilfully covering the planet with mushroom clouds symbolise a satirical extreme of sterility and dereliction. The atmosphere of *Being There* is passive, doped, and that of *Doctor Strangelove*, by contrast, is anxious and busy – but in both, men behave like children; and is it a coincidence, or what, that the one was made at the peak of Sellers' early fame, and the other right at the end, when his lacks and losses were, miraculously, converted into an acting style? (Between 1963 and 1979, cult oddities like *The Optimists of Nine Elms, Hoffman* or *The Blockhouse* aside, when the magician clapped his hands, no dove appeared.)

Being There was a lullaby and a swansong, Sellers being the pale faint swan who chanted a doleful hymn to his own death; *Doctor Strangelove*, still in the nursery, is brattish. (The war room is a playroom where grown men can express themselves by smashing up the world.) The only tender – maternal – moment is the credit sequence, with the planes suckling – re-fuelling – in mid-flight. (The nuclear bombs, couched in the fuselage, are a pair of eggs.) After that, it's a boy's own story. George C. Scott sulks, pouts and interjects; he is thrilled by his visions of bombs and mega-deaths – by record-breaking statistics. Peter Bull, as the Russian ambassador, is sullen and sneaky (he is covered with hidden cameras and espionage equipment); he is given to going off in huffs and having spoilt-boy tantrums, like his petulant boss, President Kissoff. Major Kong, aboard the errant B-52, takes a childish glee in the gadgetry at his disposal. The jaunty pilot sits astride the nuclear bomb, wearing his stetson, as if it is a buckeroo – a hobby horse. Doctor Strangelove himself is the class swot, fiddling with his pocket calculator and slide rule, and goosing people with his over-boisterous hand; and Merkin Muffley, the president, is like the weedy teacher's pet, left in charge whilst the adults are off elsewhere. (Group Captain Lionel Mandrake, over at Burpelson Air Base, is public school prefect isolated with the school bully, Sterling Hayden's General Jack D. Ripper.)

The performances are frenzied (and funny) because these grown men, with their uniforms, guns and dens, take themselves so seriously – they don't realise that they are only six years old, mentally. No wonder the original idea was for Sellers to have taken on the whole kindergarten. 'In fact,' he admitted, 'I was going to do them *all*. Stanley Kubrick was convinced I could. I could do no wrong, you see. Some days, Stanley used to be sitting outside my front door saying, "What about Buck Schmuck Turgidson?, [the rôle played by George C. Scott] you've got to play Buck Schmuck." And I'd say, "I physically can't do it! I don't like the rôle anyway, Stan. And I'll try and do the Slim Pickens thing, but I mean I think that's *enough*."'

As it turned out, Slim Pickens himself was hired to play the Slim Pickens rôle, Major Kong. Sellers decided he wasn't happy with his attempts at a Texan accent – though the official reason he gave for abandoning the sequence was a broken ankle. However, says Hattie Stevenson, 'it was *not* a broken ankle, but he still insisted on getting put in a plaster cast so he could get out of the part. He then became terribly sarcastic and nasty because Slim Pickens was so good.'

With infantilism prevalent on screen and off, Kubrick's decision to lop off the last reel is to be deplored. 'After a screening of *Doctor*

Strangelove I cut out a final scene in which the Russians and Americans in the War Room engaged in a free-for-all fight with custard pies. I decided it was farce and not consistent with the satiric tone of the rest of the film . . .' Has ever a director so mis-understood and failed to perceive the drift and nature of his own work? The film builds to that pie fight – it should culminate in the children's delight in destruction. It was an error of judgement to deny us that;[*] now the film ends abruptly, with Peter Bull going off to photograph the big board computers and Strangelove tottering out of his chair. Also, we have seen the cakes and jellies – a chil-dren's party tea – all through the film, in the background of the underground bunker; and a pie fight would have given all those sober-looking men around the table (sixty of them) something to do.

Ken Adam, the designer of the looming James Bond-ish sets, doesn't help my feeling of frustration when he says that it was 'un-doubtedly one of the most extraordinary custard pie battles ever filmed. The characters were hanging from chandeliers and throw-ing pies which ended up by covering the maps of the General Staff. Shooting lasted a week and the sequence ended with the president of the United States and the Soviet ambassador sitting on what was left of the pies and building pie castles like children on a beach.' Peter Bull[†] claims that the sequence took a fortnight; that two thou-sand pies (made out of shaving foam) were provided every day; and that when he and Sellers were waist-deep in the goo, they sang 'For he's a Jolly Good Fellow' – which led into Dame Vera's 'We'll Meet Again' over the end-titles. The actors were banned from the studio canteens because they trod gunk and stale cake everywhere; and (says Bull) 'the corridors, lavatories and dressing rooms looked quite extraordinary, as if some creature from Outer Space, con-structed rather loosely from a lot of vegetables, had been cruising round'.

---

[*] Kubrick's address is 'Boreham Wood', Hertfordshire, England. Please write to him or telephone and petition for the reinstatement of the pie fight.

[†] In his memoirs, *I Say, Look Here!* (London, 1965), pages 111–17.

The person who recalled the pâtisserie tournament best was Sellers, who looked back in April 1980 with much merriment to 'the famous alternative ending . . . Stanley has a copy of it. The pie fight started with the Russian ambassador photographing the big board again, and George C. Scott rushes over and chases the scared ambassador behind the buffet table. The Russian says, "You vill pay for diss!" And he picks up a large pie and goes to hurl it at George C. Scott. He ducks and it hits me, the president, full in the face. Scott says, "Gentlemen, our beloved president has been struck down in the prime of life by *pie*! We demand merciful retaliation!" And of course, the whole army, air-force and navy hate each other anyway and they start on the ambassador and then they start on each other. Strangelove eventually turns out like – you know when you see a bug and you spray it and spray it until it's slimy and can't move? Well, just everybody pelted him until he couldn't get up. And he's trying to get back on his chair and the more he grabbed it the further it went away from him. In this sea of muck, cake and what-have-you, [Peter Bull,] George C. Scott and the president are seen in a corner like little kids making mud pies. Their minds are gone. Suddenly, you see a heaving mess drag himself out and it's Strangelove. He gets a gun and fires it in the air and says: "Gentlemen, gentlemen, don't you realise what will happen to us all in a moment? This pie is non-protective! We must go down to the shelter as quickly as possible. Don't worry about showers, we have plenty down there. Through the mine shaft!" And as they all go out of the room you hear the song "We'll Meet Again."'

☆　☆　☆

Sellers had clearly enjoyed himself; he'd been back where he wanted to be – in early childhood, engrossed and rampaging. As he did not take other people seriously, it never worried him that the rest of us were being denied the scene ('Well, Stan felt it was a bit long there . . .'). But if a missing ten minutes is a tantalisation, what about a missing whole feature?* *The Blockhouse*, which hardly anyone has ever seen, functions, in effect, as a sequel to *Doctor Strangelove* – it is about the candlelit years seventy-foot underground, with collapsed walls of a thirty-foot reinforced concrete thickness separating the survivors from any way of escaping back to the surface. One by one the men – yes, as so often in a commendable Sellers film, there are no ladies present – lose their reason and die off in grisly fashion.

It is a film of portraits; of icons, in a way. Down in the underworld, ravaged faces peer from the gloom: Charles Aznavour as a sharp-faced, beady-eyed chancer from Marseilles; Per Oscarsson as a weird blonde giant, who thinks he can hammer and chisel his way to freedom; Jeremy Kemp, as a Polish officer who tries to keep his dignity, and who goes to pieces; and Sellers. It is simply a scandal that his performance, as Rouquet, the schoolmaster, has been allowed to slip into oblivion – but that's by the way. The fact is, in terms of the pained, cheerless Sellers whom I have tunnelled out in this book, *The Blockhouse* is the crucial opus. It is about a living death. The men get iller, older, paler; they don't know how long they have been trapped. Time no longer has any meaning. They put on blankets and come to resemble strange, hunched medieval

---

* The difference is that the director is not the cause of the interdiction. As Clive Rees explained to me: 'We ran out of money making it and Hemdale International Films came in to pick it up – and they came in to pick up a Peter Sellers War Film. They saw the first reel cut together, spitfires and explosions. It's all quite exciting – great, they thought, the funny stuff is to come – and, of course, it didn't get funny at all. It is quite remorsely in one direction – harrowing. Not a sign of hope. They found it very difficult to accept that. Perhaps at that time it was not the kind of film many audiences would have wanted – though people who do see it remember it vividly . . . It was not the sort of film which could be distributed, and Hemdale treated it as a tax loss . . . At the time I was resentful about their behaviour or lack of understanding about the film – it wasn't the kind of film they were expecting at all. Beyond their comprehension – I don't mean intellectually, I mean commercially. They were all probably right.'

Of the many kindnesses I was shown as I wrote this book, one which stood out was the special screening of the single extant print of *The Blockhouse* which Clive Rees arranged for me.

figures; and with all the candles, the bunker is like a cathedral under the earth. There is little action. The film succeeds in its mood – fear, claustrophobia, the endlessness of the webs of darkness encircling them – because of the feelings which emanate from the actors.

Clive Rees explains how this texture was achieved: 'We had a special technique for shooting. Seventy feet underground. Very quiet. And so I'd say *standby* – and there'd be silence. I'd wait, sometimes a minute. Then we'd turn the camera on; then wait a bit more; then I'd say *Action*. There was a terrific feeling that got to the actors, and it made it easier for them to be emotional. When Sellers begins to weep, because he's moved by Aznavour giving him a drink, during the party sequence – he just *did* that; he didn't need any help with make-up or chemicals in his eyes. He just could do it. A wonderful actor. Peter did get so involved in the part, and he went through periods of depression and worry, as he always did – but that was used, and was embodied, in the character he played. He was smoking a lot of dope; he was on macrobiotic diets and he stood on his head a lot. He'd get up at five in the morning to do his exercises and he'd come to rehearsals by eleven. He'd look completely wrecked by then, which suited the picture. We'd start shooting at one o'clock and work through to seven or eight without a break. It meant for the whole morning we were outside. There was a relaxed atmosphere – until the moment they put on their costumes, and walked into the blockhouse, and it was as if something psychological or spiritual had occurred. The effect of being seventy feet underground? Bodies buried in the walls? I don't think we'd have achieved the same thing in a studio. It was a six week shoot. By the fourth week everybody was totally into their parts, knew what they were doing, and we began to shift through it.'

☆ ★ ☆

It is D-Day 1944. The Allied planes are bombing and strafing the Normandy coast. A few men, in a Nazi slave-labour camp, seek refuge in a vault. The passageways start to collapse, so they climb deeper – like Alice tumbling down the rabbit hole. Suddenly: bang, crash, blackness. Pinpricks of matches come and go. Then, a man carrying candles slowly comes into view – he has discovered a supply of wine, cheese, bread, tinned stuffs, jam, salami, barrels, enough to last for years. Two narrow ventilation shafts bring fresh air. 'We got food, we got drink, we got clothes – we're safe.' Except that 'We are trapped . . . .'

If Hell was photographed, it would be similar to these catacombs. Sellers' Rouquet is the least demonstrative of its denizens. He's always quietly examining things: the ladder, the wine, the firebrands. He jots in a diary. He makes calculations. He's methodical, pedantic – ever the schoolmaster. By timing how long a candle lasts, he works out the passage of time – soon they have been buried alive for seven weeks, and excitement – all that booze! all that grub! – has turned to fear. Peter Vaughan, as Aufret the Nazi collaborator, retreats, like a frightened animal, to a remote corner and, with plenty of harrowing shrieks and gurgles, cuts his own throat with a serrated can. Because there is nothing to drink or wash with except alcohol, many of the men intensify their hopelessness with stupefaction – Kemp's Grabinski dies in a drunken brawl. Other characters fade and pine away.

Rouquet, however, tries to stay alert. He recites the poetry he has memorised and chalks lines and rhymes on the walls ('deliberately a lot of Dante's *Inferno*, though it would have been pretentious to keep that up', says Rees.[*] In Chapter One I mentioned that Sellers also drew on his own stock of schoolday verses). He plays chess with candle stubs ('There is no point playing with you – you always win,' he is told) and he organises a game of dominoes – in a speech Sellers improvised. 'The origin of the game dominoes – it sounds Greek, "dominos"; maybe it was discovered by an Englishman in Greece, and he brought it back.' Rouquet explains the rules – it is the longest speech in the film. 'It was the character's one lapse, which I think important, into being more typically Sellers.

---

[*] I also noted bits of Donne, Keats and Pope. Fact: Rees was taught by Dr Leavis at Cambridge.

We based it on an idea: an African sees his brother taken by a cro-codile, and he laughs at the shock of it. I wanted to get people over the shock of Aufret's death – get the film going again. It was im-portant to get some comedy. Peter and Jeremy were very interesting – because Jeremy loathed ad-libbing. He's classically trained – likes to know what's happening. Peter can ad-lib any old thing, and the two of them together were quite a blend.'

'"It comes from the Greek *dominos*" – all that. . . Completely im-provised!' concurs Kemp. 'He made it up there and then. It went on for a longish time. Several minutes – until I could bear it no longer. The wit and ingenuity of this attribution of a game of dominoes to the Greeks . . . It worked. Peter was able to give free range to his ex-temporising powers, but there was no sense of it being other than this man Rouquet, a schoolmaster from Northern France, doing the talking. He never budged out of character. Poignant, and rather beautiful – and the muted, detailed, miniaturist performance contrasts very sorrily with how he'd grown by *The Prisoner of Zenda*.'

As a prisoner in the sunless cellar, where they have forgotten what the progression of the seasons was like, Sellers is to be glimpsed in the background of most shots, punctiliously dipping his food in a pinch of salt (he's not a slob like the others) or trim-ming his beard (the very beard which he sported on *Michael Parkinson Meets the Goons*, on October 28th 1972). His big brown liquid eyes slowly take everything in; and he has a way of slightly opening his mouth and moving his jaw anti-clockwise – as if he is about to speak but decides against it – which is one of Chance's mannerisms. (The accent is French – non-idiotic Clouseau.) After a while we notice that he is having trouble with his little spectacles, or is it his eyes? Down in the dimness, he is failing to focus on his dis-integrating books. He huddles in corners. With a short tilting back of his head, he lets out a sigh. Suddenly, he has the screen to him-self. He is looking at a sepia postcard. The creased picture is of the school where he'd taught. He puts the treasure back in his spectacle case, snaps it shut, and goes off, out of frame. We see him clipping open a bag of cooking flour. He cuts his wrists and plunges them into the powdery sacks, letting his life drain away. It is as if he is falling asleep. His life extinguishes with the last of his candles. (A title caption informs us that the Aznavour and Oscarsson characters spent their last four years in total darkness. They were rescued in 1951, one of them dying instantly from the shock of the light, the other three days later. Villagers had heard bangings and cries, but thought the site was haunted.)

Sellers' character articulates the fact that, in extreme circumstances, it is perhaps better to end your life than to live on into further mental and physical disintegration. That is why he kills himself – which he does in the same neat, practical way he'd brought to everything else. Rouquet is a sensitive man – we pick up his emotions and what he is going through without there needing to be dialogue or interplay. As an experiment in what the art of acting can achieve, I'd rate it higher than *Being There* – perhaps because Sellers makes no attempt to dominate any scene, and *The Blockhouse* is not sentimental.

More true to form was Sellers' obliviousness to other people's feelings. He'd snap away with his stills camera or make his funny voices. As Rees says: 'He could be incredibly sensitive, and yet also be totally blind to things – like Jeremy Kemp can go through a very difficult period when making a film. He can become quite disturbed. For that last scene – singing the Christmas carol – he wanted a doctor present. He found it very hard to do. He needed a doctor there all the time, and he was crying all the time. He was on the verge of a nervous breakdown. Everybody knew how delicate this was. When Peter heard afterwards, he hadn't realised at all – and yet he'd be completely sensitive to other things. Everybody could see that Jeremy was in a real state. When the camera turned over, though, he was in total control. He was classical in this way. Sharp and professional. But it was as if it had all swept out of him, the living death in the blockhouse, and it frightened him, and he felt alone. . .*

---

* Kemp agrees that 'I got too close to it – and it wasn't a nice place to work; it really was built by slave labour. One knew bloody well that there were some of

Though Sellers conveyed the impression that he could keep the mood jokey, by coming out with goonish rubbish between takes, entertaining the crew; and though he seemed to combat a place where people were cutting their throats with tin cans by living in sybaritic digs – an elaborate set-up with a butler, antique furniture, champagne flowing – he was equally distressed. On occasion he'd weep, owing to problems he was having with his marriage (to Miranda), people supposed. He'd fall into deep sleeps on the set – yogic trances, it was alleged. Bert Mortimer, who ran the household on Guernsey, where the film was made, had long been used to his master's threats of suicide – an old gambit 'to get what he wanted. It was a form of emotional blackmail.' Anne had seen him promise to leap over penthouse balconies; Lynne would see him brandish fistfuls of pills – he'd insist on being told exactly why he shouldn't take an over-dose. Bryan Forbes and Nanette Newman had had to stay the night at Elstead when Peg died, because the grief-stricken mother's son was like to fall upon his sword . . . Such antics are worthy of *Harold and Maude*; but during *The Blockhouse*, suicide was no longer a game. Because he was on an island, remote from the world, and working in a deep cavern, where his character was severed from the world, Sellers' strange, strong fears and sense of dissociation were intensified. 'He was playing the part of a French school teacher . . . and had to slit his wrists, plunge them into a bag of flour and die,' said Mortimer. 'He was so wrapped up in the part, I believed he might actually do it. And Peter was nervous himself that it might actually come about. I was out of my mind with worry about it, because for many years I had lived with his suicide threats.'

Sellers didn't attempt anything dramatic – perhaps there weren't the right sort of people in the vicinity to try and impress? In default of suicide, it was as if he resolved to flinch, in the future, from the serious and confounding business of drawing on himself when acting; henceforward he would be shallow, vulgar, careless (and

---

them in the walls. Certainly with me, I got very jumpy, towards the end. Always good to get out into the light of the sky . . . I was the one who showed signs of succumbing to being down that foul, dark hole.'

intermittently brilliant): *Alice's Adventures in Wonderland* (the March Hare); *Where Does It Hurt* (an embezzler); *Soft Beds, Hard Battles* (multi-rôles); *Ghost in the Noonday Sun*; *The Great McGonagall*; then all the resurgent Inspector Clouseaus; then *The Prisoner of Zenda*; then, after *Being There*, *The Fiendish Plot of Dr Fu Manchu* . . . If films of the mid and late Sixties were bad, those of the Seventies were worse. Down in the blockhouse, when Sellers felt perdition catch his soul, instead of killing himself, he buried his career – though, in saying that, I am aware that I am talking about a man who gave more pleasure to the public than almost any other actor since the grafting of sound to moving pictures. What he achieved was more than most people manage – hence the huge scale of his failure, too. It was a failure, I think, of energy. Look at his eyes, in those films I've just listed: they are vacant, strained. Sellers lost his glint. The climate darkened. His paranoia, sense of futility, aggression, explosiveness, vanity, hysteria, procrastination, and intentional bad behaviour all got worse.

It is interesting to compare how good he was on the island of Guernsey with how bad he was on the island of Cyprus, a year later: 'He enjoyed screwing people up,' says Dennis Frazer, the chief grip on *Ghost in the Noonday Sun*. 'We'd spend ages preparing a shot, and he'd suddenly say, "I'm not doing that tonight. I'm going home." He was soul-destroying. You'd struggle getting the equipment ready and he'd disappear. When Richard Burton let people down it was because he was drunk and incapable of acting. With Sellers it was malice or madness.' Along with the psychological disorder went the physical crumbling – his heart, like the clock inside the crocodile, gradually running down as time ran out; and on top of all that, there was his humiliating last match with Lynne – proof, should any be required, that 'I am a romantic and being a romantic has been the cause of making so many mistakes . . . I am really looking for a mother figure and a great bird all in one. You must remember that beautiful women are not always the easiest to live with. But, then, God knows, I'm not particularly easy either.'

☆ ★ ☆

Rouquet, entombed and watching the lights go out, one by one, is a symbol of what happened to Sellers, whose life showed not development but reduction – the frenzy of *The Goon Show*, the bustle and gaiety of the early films, his sheer virtuosity *versus* the deadness, the blackness (and blankness), his fires extinguished. He began by aspiring, he ended by raging. (He attained what Samuel Beckett called a 'nullity of being'.) When Lynne met him he was already half a ghost, hovering in a Roebuck House apartment which she considered 'faceless – like a large Hilton hotel suite. Even the few paintings looked as though they had been moved in by a firm. The bedroom was functional, the walls were white and bare . . .' Thus the habitat, thus the man, who was as chilled as stone. The bathroom cabinet contained such an array of pharmaceuticals, Sellers called it Boots the Cash Chemists.

Conversation, too, between the young girl and the wasting man was of death or (a related topic) sterility. Michael Sellers once heard a harrowing tape his father had secretly recorded of a private phone call to Lynne, in which he told her about his horror of impotence and of a consultation with a Dr Brock: 'I told him that the problem resulted in a rift between my wife and me and was causing an awful lot of pain and depression . . .' The journalist David Lewin was in the right of it when he said the marriage was not about beginnings – new starts, new hope – but endings – for Lynne had told him: 'Peter would talk to me often about what to do when he died and . . . death was not a taboo subject in our home. He had been ill with his heart . . . before, and . . . we discussed it openly. He would go over and over the plans – almost like a dress rehearsal – for getting him back home, so he could be cremated in Golders Green, where the ashes of his mother and father are.'

When the day dawned to carry out the last wishes, on Saturday July 26th 1980, it was as if Sellers, like Prospero, had bedimmed the noontide sun. London was plunged into a perilous night. The sky was full of flying shapes – witches? – the winds ripped at the trees and chimneys, and cross-blue lightning flashed upon the funeral procession as it headed, twenty-five minutes late, along the Finchley Road to the furnaces.

Love and Death

'We left the Dorchester in two limousines,' says Michael Jeffery. 'Lynne and the children in the first; me, Ve and Do, Peter's aunties, Iris Frederick, Lynne's mother, and Lynne's grandmother, in the second. Jet black. Like midnight.'

The fifteen minute (Anglican) ceremony was conducted by Canon John Hester, who remarked: 'In its own way it was the right weather for the occasion, with a thunderstorm to give Peter a suitably theatrical send-off. It would have appealed to his sense of humour.' Fewer than thirty mourners were allowed to attend,[*] though approximately two hundred people gathered outside the chapel to pay their respects. Lynne, by making it an invitation-only do, had hoped to debar any ex-wives from the service. 'I even had to turn away . . . Peter's first wife, Anne Howe, because I thought if I invited one ex-wife I would have to invite them all . . . and I wasn't going to do that.' Britt, however, demonstrating the independent streak which Sellers had hated her for (and which any sane person can see is nothing but admirable), decided to break the embargo; she wanted to look after Victoria, who was sobbing non-stop – and also 'I went to the funeral to pay homage to a man whose life I once shared. It was my duty to show him that respect. After all, Peter was my husband, and in the early days of our marriage we were very close.'

Lynne didn't see it that way. As she made her way down the aisle, towards the oak coffin – was Sellers inside? I have failed to trace the undertakers. Had he been spirited away to a secret crypt and freeze-dried?[†] – she suddenly bridled. Later, in a reception at the Dorchester (which Britt steered clear of), she flew at Victoria:

---

[*] They comprised: the widow and her immediate family (to whom she had very recently started speaking again after a four year estrangement. 'The bitterness is still there,' she was to say later); the three children; Jeffery; Milligan; Secombe; Bentine; Ve and Do (Mrs Vera Elmore and Mrs Vera Marks, the last survivors of Mr Herbert Ray's Company); David Lodge; Graham Stark; Alexander Walker; Evelyn de Rothschild; the Earl of Snowdon; Theo Cowan; Jim Maloney; Brother Cornelius; Dennis Selinger; and Britt Ekland. Plus assorted spouses.

[†] We may call into question the truth of this exchange: *Parkinson*: 'You were at the funeral, weren't you?' *Milligan*: 'Yes – so was Peter.'

'What was your mother doing there?' Michael Jeffery had to intercede: 'Please don't cry, Victoria. We all knew your father once loved your mother, so please don't pay too much attention to what Lynne is saying. She's too upset to know what she means . . .' Nevertheless, her anger – it was almost as if the prima donna resented being upstaged – was all over the front pages the next day. 'I certainly didn't think she was going – and I didn't invite her,' Lynne was quoted as saying, from the Dorchester's Harlequin Suite. 'Britt never visited Peter in hospital. I decided who would be able to visit and I did not think it would have helped things if I'd let Britt visit him . . . I was amazed when she turned up in the chapel.'

The funeral service had included a reading from the gospel of St John, Chapter XIV – verses normally designated for the Monday before Easter:

> *Let not your heart be troubled, neither let it be afraid. Ye have heard how I said unto you, I go away, and come again unto you. If ye loved me, ye would rejoice, because I said, I go unto the Father: for my Father is greater than I. And now I have told you before it come to pass, that, when it is come to pass, ye might believe . . . Arise, let us go hence . . .*

Before the congregation did so, Canon Hester explained that, in place of the normal hymns and arias, Sellers would trundle on to the pyre to one of his requested tunes – 'In the Mood'. Michael Sellers had gone out and bought the LP the previous day. His father had always said that the big band sound was wonderfully inappropriate – hence, wonderfully appropriate – for solemn occasions. Milligan also recalled Sellers' desire to play a last prank as he took leave of the world. He'd once asked him, 'Is there any special hymn you would like to be played?' – 'Yes, "In the Mood".' – 'Is that Hymns Ancient and Modern?' – 'No, it's Glenn Miller.' Bentine said it was Sellers' *least* favourite number – that, when he'd been a dance hall drummer, he had to beat time to it for hour upon hour. He came to hate it so much, he was, in retrospect, fond of it. Stark, too, could hear in the rooty-toot-toot rhythms an echo of the younger Sellers. He has said that only when 'In the Mood' started to

pipe through the chapel speakers did a full sense of loss finally over-
whelm him: 'There, in my mind, ... was Leading Aircraftsman
Peter Sellers, smart as paint in his best Air Force uniform, confidently gliding across the dance floor at the Nuffield Centre,
holding a pretty WAAF in his arms.' He felt that, had he but
glanced upwards, a spotlit rotating sphere would have been dangling from the chapel ceiling. *

The crowds, press photographers and the policemen in their rain
capes, pressed against the celebrity mourners as they quit the building and found their limousines. The following day, Michael Sellers,
Michael Jeffery, Ve and Do, Sarah and Victoria returned to Golders
Green to examine the wreaths. They were surprised to see a long
queue of people intent on the same errand. Jeffery went to the front
and whispered to the attendant that 'Mr Sellers' family would like
to come and see the flowers' – so they were ushered along, very
conscious of being stared at. Messages scribbled on the cards
were Goonish and Pink Pantherish: 'Farewell, Pink Panther'; 'Ying
Tong Iddle I Po Forever'; Burt Kwouk's floral tribute was signed
'Cato', Harry Secombe's ('Bluebottle is deaded now') 'Neddy Seagoon'.

'I took Ve and Do to see the rose bush, which had had two fully
blown roses on,' Jeffery told me. '"One for Peg and one for Bill,"
Peter'd said. When I went up with Ve and Do, there were the two
blooms still, and one bud. Peter would have loved that.'

☆　★　☆

That's so fucking corny, I thought to myself, as I left Michael Jeffery's flat and walked to Chalk Farm Underground station,
intending to return to Paddington and Oxford. Instead I rode the
Northern Line three stops to Golders Green, crossed over to Hoop
Lane and entered the crematorium gardens, where the recently

---

* Sellers set a trend – according to *The Times* (December 8th 1993) he 'changed the
British way of death forever. Gone are the days when a tearful rendition of
"Abide with Me" sufficed ... Whitney Houston's "I Will Always Love You" is
top of the funereal pops [followed by] Pavarotti singing "Nessun Dorma", and
that personal anthem of many, "My Way".'

dead are sprinkled like slug repellent across the soil. Sellers' is rose bush number 39802. There is a small plaque nearby, placed by Lynne: 'My darling husband I will always love you'; and on the wall behind is the *Being There* gibberish:

'Life is a state of mind'
WITH EVERLOVING MEMORIES
PETER SELLERS
C.B.E.
1925 – 1980

I was aware of the corny impulse behind my own pilgrimage: Hamlet in the graveyard, handling the clown's skull and asking it: 'Where be your gibes now? Your gambols? Your songs? Your flashes of merriment?' But when he was alive, Sellers wasn't Yorick, he was the prince – a mother-fixated man 'Constantly occupied with the world within, and abstracted from the world without, giving substance to shadows, and throwing a mist over all commonplace actualities . . . His senses are in a state of trance, and he looks upon external things as hieroglyphics' (Coleridge); 'he who has felt his mind sink within him, and sadness cling to his heart like a malady, who has his hopes blighted and his youth staggered by the apparitions of strange things; who cannot be well at ease, while he sees evil hovering near him like a spectre; whose powers of action have been eaten up by thought; he to whom the universe seems infinite, and himself nothing; whose bitterness of soul makes him careless of consequences, and who goes to a play as his best resource to shove off, to a second remove, the evils of life by a mock representation of them – this is the true Hamlet' (Hazlitt); 'the whole drama is the tragedy of the convulsed reaction of the mind from the flesh, of the spirit from the self' (D. H. Lawrence).

I knew that my adventure was almost over, and that one of the meanings of Sellers had come to me. Looking at the flowers and leaves, the ashes and atoms, the memorial stone benches with cobwebs at their corners, and at the flakes and silt swelling into gusts of wind, I could see that Sellers, in the dissolutions of his personality when he was alive, and in the transmutations he continued to make after he was dead – into dust, blooms, obituaries, thousands of different, jostling recollections – had demonstrated the essential alterations – of one thing becoming another, and another – that (against the odds, given how I have belaboured Sellers the King of Shadows) are on the side of life. He was like a running stream. You only have to ask yourself 'Did Sellers have a death wish?' to grasp this. And of course he didn't want to die. He lived a pretty wild, unhealthy sort of existence, and it was his body and brain which let him down. But it was not a death wish – more like the opposite. He had a biological and constitutional tendency towards melancholia, and he fought against this and tried to be vivacious – indeed, his intractability (if you were not on the receiving end of it) could be deemed heroic. There was great comment in his work, especially in the forlorn characters. Everything he saw and heard he turned to mimicry, impressionism, immediately, like a reflex. His joy of observation, and his joy in expressing what he felt, may be traced right from *The Goon Show* to *Being There*: when he looked at the world he saw its ludicrousness.

What my other conclusion was you may discover in the last chapter.

☆ ★ ☆

Chapter Fifteen
The Evil That Men Do

The astute reader – and the root-faced reviewer – will have noticed that, what with all the digressions, diversions, curvilineations and white-water pages, day-to-day detail – addresses, telephone numbers, the calendrical grid – was, with certain exceptions, let go in 1963. Here is why. On Sunday August 12th 1990, the following begging letter was published in the *Los Angeles Times*:

> ### SELLERS MARKET
> I am working on a major biography of the late Peter Sellers, the greatest British comic actor since Charles Chaplin, but also something of a haunted, hunted personality in real life. He died exactly a decade ago in London, but his homes were in California and Switzerland.
>
> I have received the fullest co-operation from Sellers' family, friends and enemies in Britain; I would now much appreciate hearing from any American colleagues and acquaintances. So would anyone with any information, letters, telexes, recollections, etc., no matter how trivial, please contact me? With a legend such as Sellers nothing ought not to be known.

Amongst my many respondents was Michael Selsman, who had been Sellers' account executive at Rogers & Cowan, a public relations firm. He said that Sellers 'was an unusual client, even for an actor. Troubled doesn't begin to describe him.' For my interest, he

enclosed a carbon of a letter he'd written, twenty-seven years previously:

> Mr. Peter Sellers
> 1 Northwood Lodge
> Oak Hill Park
> London N.W.3, England
> February 1st 1963

Dear Peter,

As promised, I hope to outline here a plan for us to follow in
representing you.

To answer your question, we do not intend to carry on as before.
We intend to carry on a good deal better than before. Between
us, and I mean Henry Rogers, Warren Cowan, John Springer
and myself, we have several concrete ideas which we feel can
contribute to your activities. The firm will remain the same, with
myself and John Springer reporting to you and solely responsible
for the job to be done for you. Arthur [Jacobs] will have nothing
physically to do with the operation, but will contribute his
thinking regularly, as he is retained by Rogers & Cowan as a
consultant. I've just learned that Warren Cowan will be coming
to London for a few days and will be calling you immediately
upon his arrival.

I think, Peter, that it is strange indeed that our national
magazines have not covered your career as thoroughly and
importantly as should have been the case long before this. I think
our immediate job is to re-evaulate the magazine situation and to
initiate extensive text and photo pieces on your behalf.

The national trade press is another important area and as far as
its columns and news pages are concerned, I feel you have been
fairly and consistently covered as to your legitimate business
activities. However, I think one facet of the trade press has been
ignored and that is the editorial column which should point out
your continuing and growing importance to the world film

industry regarding the amount of business you stimulate at the box office and the image as an actor you project.

Another important function we should try very hard to arrange (so that the excellent friendships you made with important press here and in New York not be allowed to lapse) is a monthly trans-atlantic telephone call to people like Hedda Hopper, Louella Parsons, Abe Weiler, the Wire Service people, etc., on a subject previously decided upon and on which the writer will have been thoroughly briefed. We feel that you should not have to bear the expenses in this matter, and so we'll suggest to the motion picture company you are currently working for, or to those companies soon to release previously made films, that they set up a budget for this.

Another matter we shall attend to is to continue what I feel has been such a successful series of trade ads. We shall try to arrange for these ads to be placed by the companies you are working for and those you will be working for, expressing their pride in your having agreed to do a film for them.

We have not taken full advantage in the past of the very good relationship we had with Theo Cowan. I will endeavour to correct that and to remain in constant contact with him so that his efforts and ours can be doubly important in both our countries. Of course, we are always in touch with Freddie Fields and his group, so we are at least as apprised as they are.

Additionally, there are articles to be written by us of both a humorous and straight-forward business nature which will be sent to you for your approval in advance. We can place these importantly with the wire services and newspapers in major cities including Los Angeles and New York, where they are most important. We would embark upon this immediately.

In sum, there have been whole areas of neglect which you can rest assured will be corrected. Co-ordination with your current activities will be constant and as I once worked for Nat Wise, Stanley Kubrick's new advertising-publicity man, an excellent relationship exists. And you know, I think, my relationship with the Mirisches, et al.

I am not forgetting by any means to include the fact that we will be placing, on a daily basis, trade stories and column items which we will obtain from Theo and the various companies you are working for. So with the foregoing and other things we are still discussing, I feel we will go a long way in overcoming your wariness.

You mentioned in your letter you would probably see us for the Billy Wilder film. There is a chance, due to the fact Carol's current picture for Otto Preminger 'The Cardinal' will be shot in Europe, that I may come over in late March. In which case, you'd be the third person I would contact upon arrival . . . the first two, of course, being wife and child.

If you have any thoughts, Peter, about what I have said here, one way or another, or if there is something I have not said, please let me know and it shall be done. Naturally, if you have the time I would appreciate an occasional note containing the kind of information that would make good publication news.

I will be in touch with you weekly, sending you your clippings and whatever important information I think you would like to know or what could be of value to you, and I will keep you especially posted on the activities for 'Lolita'.

> Best regards,
> *Mike Selsman*

We can see from this (propitiatory) letter – clearly sent in response to some rocket – that Sellers was a madman who thought he was Sellers. He had become, by 1963, the star he wanted to be, and he did not wish to resist his own legend. He was sucked into a machine that manufactured façades, false fronts; and the truth, the reality, of his nature and temperament was to be hidden. He would address long letters to newspaper reviewers, for example, not because he had any personal respect for them, but because he considered them an important component in his fame; their good opinion was worth fostering. (One, dated September 23rd 1963, sent to Alexander Walker from New York, plugs *Shot in the Dark* – 'we should be all set for a very good time, and a cracking film in the process' – says how well *The Pink Panther* is going down – 'I think it should be one of the comedy hits of next year without any doubt' – and ends with the helpful information that 'We shall be making *Shot in the Dark* at MGM Boreham Wood, which is where we made *The Millionairess* . . .') Sellers didn't write letters to friends – he issued publicity statements. (Hospitalised with a heart attack, he responded to Peter Evans' get-well-soon message by saying: 'I don't intend to work until February or March next year [1965] so I shall just laze around and take pictures of celebrities. If you want any, let me know' – Evans was the show business editor of the *Daily Express*.)

Peter Evans told me that Sellers had a brilliant nose for news, for getting himself coverage. 'It was Sellers who helped me to get that job on the *Express*. He kept giving me very good stories about himself and other people. I was selling these stories as a freelance. I could depend on a front page Sellers story about once a month.' Sellers trusted Evans, and later entrusted him with his life, or Life. 'As a showbiz columnist I consequently got to know Sellers extremely well . . . In about 1965 we started talking about doing his biography – his idea entirely. Would I like to do it? The more I listened to him talking about himself, the more I realised that he had secrets in him, depths, and a history, and I hadn't realised this. . .'

More on *The Mask Behind the Mask* later; my present point is simply that Sellers, under his apparent gregariousness and ingratiation, was quite consciously and cunningly furthering his own career. Rampant ambition is all very well, but Sellers was avid and devious. (As a character in *Sweet Smell of Success* says, 'I'm nice to people where it pays me to be nice.') He turned himself into a commodity. He stopped being real. How this contrasts with his first dealings with fame, when he'd visited America a few years previously, in

April 1960.* Then he had taken umbrage at being referred to as 'the property'. As he told Dilys Powell: 'It's strange the way people look on an actor. I went to America for the première of *I'm All Right, Jack*. I didn't think the Americans would understand about British trade unions, but the film was a great success, they loved it. I was interviewed by everybody in America, so it seemed to me; if my friend Graham Stark hadn't been with me I think it would have killed me. When I arrived in New York, straight by taxi from the airport, I went up to my hotel room and I found it was crammed with people. There was one character on the telephone; just as I came into the room I could hear him say, "I must get off the line, the property's arrived." That's what it is: one is just a property.'

At the time he appeared to accept – or ignore – this estimate, and set about having a wonderful all-expenses-paid time in a wonderful town. (Later on in his career, he'd have turned on his heel and stalked off at the slightest hint of disparagement.) Outward bound First Class by Air France. Penthouse suite at the Hamshere House Hotel (other guests included Lucille Ball and Vivien Leigh). Sardi's. Trader Vic's. Russian Tea Rooms. Four Seasons. Receptions and meals thrown in his honour by British Lion and the Walter Reade Company. 'Yeah, like dere eye yam, walkin' up Fit Avenue and who dis eye meet? Dis swingin' guy eye meet is John Boulting. It's my director! It's the director of dis movie eye yam in – 'I'm All Rightie Jack' – which is the smash I tell you of the season. . . ' The reviews of *The Mouse that Roared* were circulating as

---

* This was not Sellers' first excursion to the North American continent for work purposes. On Wednesday November 28th 1956, he had flown to Toronto to appear on the Canadian Broadcasting Corporation's *The Chrysler Show*, performing one of his Olivier/Richard III sketches. Others on the bill were Tito Gobbi and Larry Adler. The compère was Hume Cronyn. A Mr Ernie Bushnell, the Assistant General Manager of CBC, was to welcome Sellers and explain the popularity of Goonery to the television audience.

Memoranda in the BBC archive express disquiet over Sellers' tight schedule – he had wanted to return via New York. What (fretted a producer) 'if he lingers too long on the far side of the Atlantic, or if his plane gets lost in the fog. Where does that leave this week's *Workers' Playtime?*'

the Boulting production opened. *Battle of the Sexes* was to arrive shortly; casting for *The Millionairess* had been announced. 'Jolly nice,' said Sellers. 'I just love your English understatement. Jolly nice? Man, your notices were goddam marvellous,' he was informed.

Sellers bought a Cadillac ('I'm a mad fool') and Stark took some amusing snaps of him which were printed in the *Daily Express*: Sellers conferring knighthoods on waiters and cab drivers; Sellers, in winter wonderland gear, skiing down the steps of Grand Central Station; Sellers pretending to be a gorilla on the top of the Empire State building. 'I was amazed . . . Mate, it looks like what you'd call a success,' he summed up, when the British press met him off the *Queen Elizabeth*, twelve days after the beginning of his round trip. (The hailing of the conquering hero effect was slightly marred when a member of the public mistook Sellers for a ship's steward and asked him the way to the promenade deck.)

It was the twelve days which shook his world. As Stark observed, all Sellers' high spirits and pranks for the camera aside, the New York adventure was 'a turning point. Up to then Pete was Pete. A carefree, comical lad. Now he was a valuable, must-be-carefully-nurtured asset that could make a lot of people a lot of money.' And Sellers slowly seethed over the evaluation for the rest of his life, and beyond: he stipulated that no American was to be present at his funeral. He decided that all Americans were commercially-minded vulgarians, who measured success in terms of money – they were 'immersed in the theology of making a fast buck' (*Sweet Smell of Success*, again); they were brash and insincere. When he was in the Hamshere House penthouse, someone said (one would imagine self-mockingly): 'Look down on the town, Peter. All this is yours now.' Sellers refused to collude. Remembering his overnight visit to America after the brief appearance on Toronto television, he said (with unmistakable coldness): 'I'm exactly the same as I was the last time I was here, and you ignored me then.'

He wasn't. First, between 1956 and 1960 he had accumulated a formidable list of achievements. He had made a dozen films, ranging back to *The Ladykillers*. ('Most of my part finished on the cutting room floor and it was three years before I had another picture,' he cock-and bull'd to Cecil Wilson of the *Daily Mail,*[*] who'd come to have an audience with 'this suave, solid young man . . . just returned home . . . after a New York triumph that has set Hollywood fawning at his feet'). Second, he was no longer the same because the man who had once said disingenuously, 'Some people say I ought to aim at being a big international star. I don't think that works with a character actor. I think to do that you have to be another kind of actor: a hero-player, not a character player,' had become the man who was now going to look ahead and 'see it this way. I'm thirty-seven and the next eight years are the most important for me. In that time I've got to internationalise myself. That doesn't mean I shan't make films in Britain. It simply means that I'll make only big films which get an international audience.'

As we have seen, in his drive to internationalise himself he destabilised himself. Out went Anne and family life; in came Britt – and then out *she* went. Out went intelligent, original, cagey black and white performances, full of rewards and mystery; in came the soulless rubbish of the Age of Aquarius. (Out went, you could say, Irene Handl and Margaret Rutherford; in came Capucine and Claudia Cardinale.) He wanted to empty his life and start again – to such an extent, he did not appreciate being reminded of who he was: 'Someone comes up and says, "Eh, ain't you that Peter Sellers?" And if you don't pass the time of day with them they say, "That Pete Sellers is a bleedin' big 'ed." So what do you do? You have to chat to them.' No you don't – as he shortly discovered. You hire a chap like Bert Mortimer to ferry you hither and thither in a limousine. You stay in expensive hotels. You fly in the First Class cabin. Money frees you from the need to mix with mortals, and as Paul Theroux says 'it is the easiest thing in the world to become corrupted by the good life . . . after you have tasted luxury, you are changed, and there is no cure for it . . . It could be a crueller punishment than torture – giving a person a taste of heaven, creating a habit, and then whisking the victim away to suffer without it.'

---

[*] 'Mr Sellers Buys Car No. 53 – Of Course It's A Cadillac', Friday May 6th 1960.

This is not totally true. Stark, who shared the New York pampering, showed no signs of corruption afterwards. He went on as before, a happily married man working as a nice little comedy bit-player. He did not become habituated. Sellers, however, who had betrayed symptoms of being seriously unhinged just prior to departure, when he completed *Never Let Go* and let his aggressiveness spread across his home-life like a bruise, refused to treat the adulation and attention as a holiday from reality. He took it as his due – and in due course he would act the part of a superstar, with all his dolly birds, fast cars ('Cars are freedom,' he once said), and travelling everywhere unnecessarily. He'd even get *others* to travel unnecessarily. In 1968 he flew a repair man from Nice to Venice to fix the hi-fi on his yacht: 'I could have fixed that thing myself, of course. But I found that man in Nice and flew him in because I like to watch experts at work. They're pretty rare these days. I found one in London once, a Mr Berry in the Tottenham Court Road, but he suddenly upped and emigrated to Canada.' (Can't you just see the Praetorian Guard being despatched to cut the contrary Mr Berry's throat?) Sellers would take up residence in an invented world; and what was begun with Lionel Meadows – the unbottling of his ugliness and brutality – was transformed in America, when he was encouraged to believe in his own invincibility;[*] and the process was completed on his return to England, when he met Sophia Loren – 'and the biggest giggle is that since I made *The Millionairess* with Sophia Loren I've become a heart-throb. For the first time in my life I've been getting erotic fan letters. Marvellous. I guess women think that if I was good enough for Sophia I'm good enough for them. . .'

Sellers was a dedicated pleasure-seeker – and he was (like Theroux's hypothetical torture-victim) afraid that it wouldn't last: 'the public's very fickle. Only too often when I go to see my folks, they

---

[*] *New York Times Magazine* ('Arrival of Sellers,' by Walter H. Waggoner), on March 27th 1960, eulogised the 'medium-sized young actor with the Face of Anonymity and the Voice of Everyman [who] is Britain's newest film sensation. . .'

say to me, "Of course you remember So-and-So?" And of course I say I do; but I really don't. It's somebody who's dropped right out. If everything came to a stop, what could I do? After all, I've got a wife and family now . . .' The hypocrisy of that last phrase fairly shimmers on the page. Though (as Leslie Linder puts it) 'all of us who knew him felt that his biggest mistake ever was leaving Anne, whom he then proceeded to treat as his mother, by taking his new wives and girlfriends to see her, looking for approval,' it is the case that Sellers was very intent on severing ties, fragmenting, and reconstructing himself; and it is also the case that he feared for the precariousness of his new life and felt the strain of upholding a playboy persona. (He removed his face to reveal his masks.)

When Peg and Bill reminisced about the old ghosts of music hall, therefore, Sellers envisaged himself amongst them. His, after all, was a music hall talent; *The Goon Show* was music hall; and as an actor he adapted, or adopted, a music hall method. (Alvin Rakoff said to me, of *Hoffman*: 'He would come in and do each scene as a separate sketch. I kept reminding him of where we were going, and I tried to keep a continuity to the performance, otherwise, when the picture was joined together, he'd have been so many different characters.') Is that why, in the Sixties, he began to behave so badly, to try and (perversely) make this bad dream of obliteration come true? Was he guilty because he knew his acclaim wasn't deserved? He recreated the wanderings and rejections of his youth; he worked it so that people would loathe him, thus justifying his paranoia (I lost count of the people who confessed to me 'I ended up hating him'); he appeared to be self-destructive and heedless. Robert Graves was shrewd when he said 'Peter Sellers – I grieve for him! He must be a very unhappy man with so many terrific talents which he probably despises.'* There was indeed a tension between Sellers' hedonism and hysteria, between his desire for liberty and terror of dissolution.

---

* Graves wrote those words on June 18th 1968, in reply to a letter from Milligan of the previous March, in which it had been stated: 'I'm having a sticky time with my marriage, and no light of hope on the horizon, it's making me permanently

On the other hand, what if instead of desiring banishment from the acting profession, he was perhaps testing its limits, like the mad Emperor who dares the populace to assassinate him? What he despised was the actor as dancing bear, doing what he was told; so he rejected artistry and the discipline that goes with it. What he enjoyed was exerting his own power – defiling, degrading – and once Anne and the children were gone, he gave up the pretence of having to care for others. He became uncontrollable. He liked to insist upon hiring weak directors, because he could bully them (it is interesting that he never sought out Kubrick again – Patrick Magee's Mr Alexander, in *A Clockwork Orange*, and Hardy Kruger's Captain Potzdorf, in *Barry Lyndon* are Sellers-esque grotesques; and what about Jack Nicholson's devilish Jack Torrance, in *The Shining*?); and yet, because he didn't know how to manage his gifts, and had no judgement, the bigger and brighter he shone as a star, the worse his films – and the more he thought people were trying to get him, were lying in wait for him, which they weren't. He shifted blame, went in for bombast, and came and went as he pleased. Robert Parrish, for example, who took over the helm of *Casino Royale* for a few days, found himself, Orson Welles, all the extras and the crew, made up and ready to work at eight forty-five in the morning, as per their contracts. Sellers did not arrive for another two and a quarter hours – he'd stayed in his car, circling Shepperton Studios, wasting time and abrading people's nerves on purpose. (He had a telephone in his limousine and he kept calling a lackey on the set, for up-to-date reports on the general restlessness.) Welles spent the morning telling anecdotes about his favourite restaurants and practising magic tricks. When Sellers eventually arrived, ostentatiously dishevelled and un-Bondlike, Welles boomed, 'Welcome, Mr Sellers! How good of you to join us!' He had

---

depressed. I went to dinner with Peter Sellers night before last, and . . . his second marriage is over, only he's happy about it.'

From *Dear Robert, Dear Spike: The Graves and Milligan Correspondence*, ed. Pauline Scudamore (Stroud, Gloucestershire, 1991), pages 80–83.

arranged for a spotlight to pick out the wretched star. 'Let's have a big hand for Mr Sellers!' Sellers, momentarily startled and magnificently befooled, made himself into air, into which he vanished. Nobody heard from him for two solid days – though people continued to go through the motions of assembling on the set at nine, going for tea at ten, breaking for lunch at twelve, returning to their dressing rooms at two and leaving for home at five;[*] and then he said he'd come back only on condition that he never had to see or speak to Welles, on screen or off, ever again. He claimed that Welles was trying to put a voodoo mind-grip on him.

☆ ★ ☆

I think we can see why Sellers hated Americans – 'and he hated Americans with such a venom, you'd have thought he was Red Indian on his parents' side', says Milligan. They were competition. They were an entire continent of people magnified to be like him: unrestrained, driven, ready to put up a fight. After Ealing, the Boultings, Englishness, and leagues of gentlemen, Sellers, on a visit

---

[*] Amongst the obedient souls, killing time, the following respondent:

[Malaga, Spain]
March 14th 1990

Dear Mr Lewis,

Thank you for your letter of February 28th with reference to . . . Peter Sellers and *Casino Royale* . . . I played the small but amusing part [of Lady Fiona/Agent Mimi] entirely at the request of John Huston, with whom I had worked in *Heaven Knows Mr Allison* and *The Night of the Iguana*, and for whom I had great affection . . . Charlie Feldman offered me a sizable sum with enormous daily costs if production went over the ten days I was to work. Suffice it to say I worked for eight weeks – most of the time spent in my dressing-room. You can imagine the amount of money I took home! This money was put to build a swimming-pool at our house in Switzerland. It was christened 'The Charles K. Feldman Memorial Swimming Pool'. I did not know that very soon after *Casino Royale* he passed away. He was a very sweet and kind man for all his idiosyncrasies . . .

With kindest regards,
Deborah Kerr.

895

to New York, was suddenly confronted by what must have seemed like his own venality running wild. It was an ideal environment and society for him – so, peevishly, he affected to recoil from it in distaste. E.M. Forster once said that America is so accommodating, you make your passage there and 'you can usually find in it what you look for' – and in the looking-glass new world, Sellers saw charm openly being deployed as no more than a cover for aggression and push; he saw mercilessness and aplomb; superabundance and psychoses. Hattie Stevenson, who was with him in 1963 for *The World of Henry Orient* confirms the way Sellers was projecting *his* distemper and bad manners on to others: 'He didn't like New Yorkers – he thought they were rude. He'd go into a shop, and he thought they didn't treat him with enough respect. There was a different law applying to himself, but he didn't like rudeness in other people. He used to think things rude which I didn't. He'd detect slights and hostilities where there were absolutely none. . .' His paranoia was ever-increasing; and in addition to his philistinism, he imported, or imposed, his private collection of poltergeists and demons on America, too: 'He decided New York was too hot, so everybody had to move out to Long Island. We stayed in a clapboard traditional American house and Sellers was convinced it was haunted. Everything that happened in there he'd attribute to the spirits. Even Bert was carried away. He was sleeping in the library and his bed moved. Pictures would fall off the walls. Sellers would hear footsteps coming up the stairs in the middle of the night. He emerged from the shower and discovered that the socks he had left on his bed were now on his chair. . . . It got to a pitch one night when it was a full moon. At two a.m. Sellers demanded that we all got up. He was between girlfriends, so it was just him, Bert, me, the nanny, and the two children – he roused us from our beds, made us pack everything up, and we moved back into New York, to the Regency. Theo Cowan was amusing about the sudden flit and rang me every five minutes to find out if we were still there or if we had moved recently.'

Out of the twenty-three projects which Sellers was considering for his American debut (what were the ones he rejected, I wonder?) *The World of Henry Orient* is an odd and revealing choice to have made. The film was based on Nora Johnson's novel about Oscar Levant, a morose pianist and actor (*Rhapsody in Blue, An American in Paris*), who said of himself, 'In some situations I was difficult, in odd moments impossible, in rare moments loathsome, but at my best unapproachably great', and who also claimed, 'I'm a controversial figure. My friends either dislike me or hate me. . .' In place of the whiffs of sulphur that such a choleric character suggests – Orient/Levant could have been a mad-genius type, like Anton Walbrook in *The Red Shoes* – Sellers decided to subvert the megalomania. Henry isn't quite a pit pianist, but he is decidedly on the slide. (His pianism is Liberace's in aspiration.) He is vain and pompous, pathetically puffed up. As Sellers himself said – under no illusions about what he was trying to accomplish: 'I play a phoney, an awful second-rater full of affectations and poses. He's a concert pianist by profession and a woman-chaser by preference. He's a rogue and a liar, with his wavy chestnut hair, his incredible monogrammed wardrobe and his charming, charming words and ways, including a hint of a foreign accent, which he believes tantalises the ladies. . .'

Though this be Manhattan, Sellers is drawing on the strolling players and gypsy accordionists of the Ilfracombe substratum. (Orient's Italian accent is a put-on, like Waldini's Romany spielings.) Henry is not what he seems. The Latin lover antics are thwarted – by the two young girls who follow him and plague him; his Carnegie Hall debut is a botch. He is at his best, alone in his apartment, a creature of fantasy, preserving his looks with a hairnet and red satin eye shades. (With his thin waxed moustache, Sellers astoundingly resembles Salvador Dali.) Despite the clinches with Angela Lansbury and Paula Prentiss, this is another of Sellers' lonely-are-the-brave performances – perhaps a compendium of them: Valerie and Marian, the fourteen year old girleens, are a brace of Lolitas; the failed romancing of married women is John Lewis; the continental accent-switching is Pearly Gates/Monsieur

Jules from *Wrong Arm of the Law*; the slapstick karate agitation and the frantic pushing of a statue against a door to block the path of pursuers is Clouseau; and so on. But where, in the past – in *Waltz of the Toreadors* or *Dock Brief* or *Mister Topaze* – there was a note of elegy, a pang of gloom, a sense of mooniness, in *The World of Henry Orient* Sellers seems closed-off. He is billed as the star – we have great expectations of the film ('SELLERS *the* KING *of* COMEDY *in his* ZANIEST ROMP EVER!' promised the posters) – but his scenes are cameos, virtually skits. He is brilliant in them – he just lacks resonance all of a sudden.

His genius was to play failures in such a responsive way they became paradoxical successes; there was a division, which we could accept and enjoy, between their shallowness and Sellers' deep waters. He had the intuitions of a true artist – and these, once he had sought and been through the entrance to the VIP lounge, he denied. He no longer seemed quite all there – he was mad. When, prior to *The World of Henry Orient*, he chose to play Lionel Meadows, Kabir, the passive Indian doctor, Topaze, Lewis, General Fitzjohn, Quilty, Morganhall, the Rev. Smallwood, and the original Clouseau, Sellers was able to re-work, dwell upon, dodge, exorcise or fictionalise the circumstances of his life. His ambition, hypocrisy, meanness, his mood swings from black violence to off-white innocence, as a marriage was running down, made him transform his being into his art – he was his own central subject. When he said, 'I must tailor my talent to a rôle', that is precisely what he did. He elided with it, colluded with it. For, as Edvard Grieg once said to Percy Grainger: 'I have always found that they are mistaken who would divide the artist from the man; on the contrary, the two are indissolubly wedded one to the other. In the man can be found the parallels of all the artist's traits – yes, even the most minute.'

Even after 1963, after *Doctor Strangelove*, in which Sellers took a childish rage to an extreme and symbolically annihilated the planet, this remained the case. The difference was that, now he had become an official celebrity – up for an Oscar indeed – instead of being an actor, and getting on with the job, he started to have a *conception* of himself as an actor; and instead of having experiences spontaneously, he adjusted and stage-managed his life, and made his life theatre. Henry Orient was the first sign of this falsity, and the extent of Sellers' dissociation – to use the psychiatric term* – can be seen by the way in which he believed himself to be Henry Orient away from the set.

'He decided he had to make conquests,' says Hattie Stevenson. 'He'd tell me who he was after and ask for advice. A girl sent him her photograph – beautiful face. He said, "I must meet this girl." He made me or Bert ring her, and arrange for a meeting at Grand Central Station. Bert and I were made to go along in case he didn't like her, and he hid behind a pillar. The girl appeared and she was totally huge. We had to go and say, "So sorry he couldn't make it." She was very persistent, however, and in the end he agreed to meet her if she slimmed down. He then proposed to her and gave her an engagement ring. That lasted all of a day. Then he got rid of her. He proposed to countless women. . .'

☆ ★ ☆

Sellers returned to England on October 3rd 1963 ('because I have had New York in a big way, mate. They are all too rude here for me . . . it's the man-in-the-street – or the woman-in-the-street – because it's the women who run it here . . .' he jabbered to Walker).

---

* Here is a most suggestive notion; this is Sellers, isn't it, the mother-fixated actor-sorcerer:

> According to the psychoanalytic view . . . of dissociative reaction, one part of the mind or consciousness splits off or becomes dissociated from another part. The individual engages in activities of which he or she later claims to be unaware. The types of dissociative reaction are tied together etiologically [are assigned the same cause] in psychoanalytic theory, being viewed as instances of a massive repression, usually relating back to the unacceptable infantile sexual wishes of the oedipal stage. In adulthood these oedipal yearnings increase in strength until they are finally expressed, usually as an impulsive sexual act. The ordinary form of repression is obviously no longer sufficient; the whole event must be obliterated from consciousness. The person succeeds in this by splitting off an entire part of the personality from awareness and by acquiring a new identity for the dissociated portion of the self.

> *Abnormal Psychology* (op.cit.), page 155.

He took up residence in the Dorchester and began work on *Shot in the Dark* – which in itself was an ominous sign: Sellers was starting to repeat himself. He expressed his anxiety and irritability by making everybody uneasy. 'He complained about actors, actresses – just generally starting trouble,' says Blake Edwards, who tried to put a stop to the nonsense by pushing a note under Sellers' dressing-room door: 'Come on, Peter, act like a professional.' It was not an appeal likely to have much chance of success: 'It was like punishing a bad little boy,' the director realised later, 'and taking a parental attitude about this whole thing. He pouted and went up and down with his attitudes . . .'

In fact, now I come to think about it, having followed Sellers on his way up to 1963 – his marvellous years – and having seen him roll all the way down, towards death and disaster (his making and unmaking) I would go so far as to state that it was only repetition which awaited him in the future. As Wolf Mankowitz said to me, 'Sellers had that Clouseau thing going years before. He used to do that funny French number – all his comedy goes back to his early radio days.' Quite so. You can line up the characters he subsequently developed – like Marcel Duchamp's *valise* – a miniature collection of all his works, gathered up and put in a box. All there.*

---

* A small but representative example of this is the album *Fool Britannia*, recorded at midnight on Tuesday August 6th 1963 at the RCA Victor Studios in New York. Sellers was joined by Joan Collins, Anthony Newley, Leslie Bricusse, Daniel Massey and Michael Lipton in order to send up the Profumo calumnies.

It is a bit flat now, I fear. That entire Profumo–Christine Keeler–Stephen Ward–Mandy Rice-Davies scandal, so-called, seems as remote as the Corn Laws. The tracks, called 'Countess Interruptus', 'Twelve Randy Men', 'Two Old Ladies Locked in Conversation', and so on, allowed Sellers to reproduce his repertoire of Cockney chancers, Italians, Jews (film producers and theatrical agents), snoring admirals (Bloodnok), New Delhi radio announcers, chortling Russians, a muck and brass Fleet Street editor (who has a Lionel Meadows abruptness), Hooray Henrys (Grytpype Thynne), the Queen (smiling and waving in her own home) and the prime minister ('When I said, "Never had it so good", I didn't mean *that* good'). Hugo Vickers informs me that Vivien Leigh was in the

☆ ★ ☆

Before he himself was gathered up and put in a box, and died forever, he had died a lot. (Death was an experience he kept living through; and his fear of death helped ruin his life.) It was always his heart. 'He used to think he was having heart attacks,' says Anne. 'I was driving home with him one day, from *Brouhaha*. "I think I'm having a heart attack." You'd never know if it was for real, or if he was having you on. "Don't you think I should drive the car in that case?" I said. "No. I'll be all right, just leave me alone, I'll be all right." He's driving this car, he's insistent that he's having a heart attack, and he gets home and went straight to bed. "You'd better call the doctor," he said. I summoned Dr Studley: "It's the usual. He's having a heart attack at the moment." – "Right," he sighed. "I'll be there." It wasn't.'

'I don't know whether I ever consciously worried about having a heart attack, as my ex-wife Anne says I did. I can't be sure,' said Sellers in 1965. 'True, my father had three coronary attacks, but it was actually prostate trouble that killed him.'

Bill had died in October 1962. He ended his adult life, as he had begun it, in a spirit of amiable sponging. The patronage of the Mendozas, however, was parsimonious compared with his son's handouts. Sellers bought his parents a flat, 7a The Grove, Highgate Village, N.6.; he gave them a twenty-four inch sized screen television set; and (said Bill), 'Peter gives us an allowance and it's a pretty big one. He paid £1,500 for my operation in the London Clinic. He buys us a new car every year, and now he's sending us away for a very expensive holiday.'

As the dutiful son, Sellers was irreproachable. Peg and Bill, after all, were his most devoted fans. 'I know my parents are proud of me now. My Dad always reads out my write-ups, but I'm sure he's pleased. My mother – I believe I've done all she hoped for me.' He didn't actually see them very often, but that didn't matter. He'd left what could be taken as a duplicate of himself in their care – what in

audience the night it was recorded, and she went over the jokes with Jack Merivale many times later.

spiritualistic parlance is known as a familiar: a parrot. 'I'm all right, Henry,' it squawked. 'Sometimes,' said Bill, 'the parrot says, "I'm all right, Henry Sellers," and uses the most filthy language. We have to cover him up.' *Bollocks* was his favourite word. His owners delighted in his devastations. (They soon gave up confining him to a cage.) He ripped the curtains and pecked at the chairs; he disembowelled cushions and dive-bombed Peg when she was in the bath. He was rewarded with packets of seeds shipped from the tropics.

As an imitator and a conscience-free destroyer, it was like bringing up their poltergeist Peter all over again – and Sellers' real name, you may remember, was Richard *Henry*. In addition to his birds of the air and other gifts, however, Sellers also made at least one attempt to find his father a foot-hold in radio. Now that he was an established star, he'd hoped he could get Bill's songs broadcast – but it was not to be. The George Formby–Ivor Novello ditties, sentimental and winsome, were deemed derivative.[*] Sellers received the politest of rejection slips from the BBC. Nepotism was allowed to fade away amongst the rigmaroles of bureaucracy:

[Broadcasting House]
3rd January, 1954

Dear Peter,

I understand that your father has written a number which Don Peters wants to sing on the programme [*Variety Bandbox*]. I am afraid that if we do broadcast this it will have to be passed by the Dance Music Policy Committee. This means that Peters can't sing it this coming Sunday. Can I have a copy of the number with your father's written consent for Peters to broadcast it attached?

I am sure you will think this is another of those silly BBC things but unfortunately it is the policy and we must abide by it.

Hope you're feeling better. See you Sunday.

---

[*] By one of those coincidences which make you want to believe in the moving hand of Fate, the Sellers family rose bush in Golders Green is right next to Novello's lilac tree. His plaque gives his dates (1893–1951) and bears the legend 'Till You Are Home Once More'.

The Evil That Men Do

All the best,
[*no signature on carbon copy*]

☆ ★ ☆

The plight of the failed entertainer is at the heart of Sellers' work (Henry Orient is part of the pattern); his second film in America – his first in Hollywood – continued the trend. *Kiss Me, Stupid*, his next project after *A Shot in the Dark*, is about a songsmith and piano teacher – a small-town dreamer – who gets the chance to play his tunes to Dean Martin. (One of the mediocre ditties is called 'Sophia';* the joke is that Orville J. Spooner's compositions are actually hitherto unpublished works by George Gershwin.) Martin's car has broken down in Climax, Nevada; he has time on his hands whilst the garage fixes it and he can be on his way; what else is there to do? He grudgingly agrees to go across the street to Orville's little house, which is flanked by two huge lolling phallic cacti, for an audition – and then he scents Orville's wife, Zelda, played by the beauteous Felicia Farr (her profile is Garbo's). Billy Wilder's film gets to be genuinely cynical and lecherous quite quickly after that. Martin, who is playing an intensification of his real cabaret performer self, is a bourbon-stoked ageing heavy-lidded Don Giovanni. He doesn't simply chain smoke – he chews and swallows the fumes and snorts them like a dragon. Orville's dilemma: does he allow this creature to flirt with his wife? Will that make him better disposed towards purchasing his songs?

Wilder's films, as I once argued†, are all studies in scarlet.

---

* The lyrics – apt for Sellers – are by George's brother, Ira (1896–1983):

Listen to me, oh Sophia,
Have you any idea,
How much you mean to me – ah!
Every day more and more.

Say the word, sweet Sophia,
Let our hearts intertwine,
Oh, from the earth I resign,
Oh Sophia, be mine.

† See the section on *The Private Life of Sherlock Holmes* in the Robert Stephens chapter of my harlequinade, *Stage People* (1989).

From *Double Indemnity* to *Sunset Boulevard*, from *The Apartment* to *Irma la Douce* – line 'em up – he is fascinated with pimps and prostitutes, gigolos and men and women who are for hire. (Does that include film directors and actors of all sexes?) *Kiss Me, Stupid*, in which a frustrated artist contemplates cuckoldry if it means he will get to be famous, glories in the obsession. It is a slutty film, and yet it is also adult about adultery. (*What's New, Pussycat?* is puerile by comparison.) Zelda doesn't object to Martin's attentions – she is aroused by the idea of breaking free for a little while, of being unrestrained and dominated. (Wilder seems to imply that within every prim provincial housewife there is a minx who wants to be slapped around.) Orville, in his turn, is aware that he is turning his wife into a tart, that he is putting his wife up for sale; and if that isn't moral problem enough, he also happens to be habitually sexually jealous and nearly mad that he will be jilted. He suspects Zelda of carrying on with the dentist, the milkman, and he even screams with rage at his nerdy piano pupil, whilst the boy hopelessly plonks out the 'Moonlight Sonata'. 'I married the prettiest girl in town', he yells, 'and she is going to leave me one of these days, I just know it.' Orville is a runty fellow incongruously married to a sweetmeat he can't handle and fears he'll lose. Martin's appearance, therefore, triggers his greatest fear (desertion) and dream (celebrity).

What are we doing in Nevada? These people should be wearing curly wigs and fluttering fans in Restoration England. To complicate matters there is Kim Novak's authentic hooker, Polly the Pistol. She is constructed out of curves, undulates across the carpet, and looks like a human version of Betty Boop. If Zelda thinks 'it was fun being a hooker for one night,' Polly, who lives in a trailer park, yearns for a different kind of life. 'I'll swap you for the wedding ring,' she responds sadly. Under the cover of darkness, the women carry out what in Shakespeare's day was called The Bed Trick: they impersonate each other under the sheets, change places, and the men on top never know (lesson: all cats look grey in the dark).

It is a knavish, carnal story. There is no nonsense about Martin

('What's with the broads round here?') being gallant – he leaves a five hundred dollar tip in the caravan for Mrs Spooner, thus debasing her as a strumpet; and Orville is not only a pimp, something in him is attracted to, and revels in, the humiliation. His fury is like Ford's in *The Merry Wives of Windsor*, desiring what he dreads:

> who says this is improvident jealousy? My wife hath sent to him, the hour is fixed, the match is made. Would any man have thought this? See the hell of having a false woman! My bed shall be abused, my coffers ransacked, my reputation gnawn at . . . This 'tis to be married! This 'tis to have linen and buck-baskets! Well, I will proclaim myself what I am: I will now take the lecher; he is at my house: he cannot 'scape me; 'tis impossible he should; he cannot creep into a halfpenny purse nor into a pepper-box; but, lest the devil that guides him should aid him, I will search impossible places. Though what I am I cannot avoid, yet to be what I would not shall not make me tame. . . .

☆ ☆ ☆

Wilder called Sellers' Orville 'superb', and Sellers too, at least initially, was content. 'I might say that it's long been my ambition to work with Billy Wilder. The two directors I've always wanted to work with are Vittorio Di Sica and Billy Wilder. I think Wilder is one of the greatest, if not *the* greatest, comedy directors, I think, in the world . . . My two favourite pictures that he made were *Some Like It Hot* and *The Apartment*. They were beautiful pictures. . .' The interviewer, Steve Allen, then asked what *Kiss Me, Stupid* was about and Sellers had to ruminate: 'Well, *Kiss Me, Stupid* used to be called – ah, now, wait a minute. What did it used to be called? It used to be called. . . Anyway, it doesn't matter. It's now called *Kiss Me, Stupid*. It's a film that Billy Wilder is making . . . We have Dino as well, and Kim Novak, and it's proving to be very enjoyable indeed. A wonderful opportunity.'

If indeed he ever had thought the opportunity wondrous, Sellers didn't seem to consider that to be the case for very much longer. These words were spoken on March 20th 1964. On April 7th he was wired up in the Intensive Care Unit of Los Angeles' Cedars of Lebanon Hospital. 'He will do anything to get out of being in this fucking movie!' one of the producers exclaimed. Wilder, apprised of his leading actor's collapse, said, 'What do you mean, heart attack? You've got to have a heart before you can have an attack.' The fact is, having got away with murder on *A Shot in the Dark*, and considering himself beyond curbs and controls – courtesy and co-operativeness were for mere mortals – Sellers had arrived in California ready to be temperamental. The first problem was that Wilder held a screenplay to be sacrosanct. He did not welcome improvisations on the set. His scripts – written in collaboration with I.A.L. Diamond – were scripture, and how this differed from the spur-of-the-moment ideas and brainstorms encouraged on the studio floor by Kubrick and Edwards. Sellers, after having tasted a pell-mell approach, did not appreciate reverting to a more disciplined style – though it was, for example, the Boulting's style, and once-upon-a-time Sellers' inventiveness would have overcome restrictions, made a virtue out of them. But now, uncompliant, certain he had no more to learn, 'I ended up in the middle of the film becoming very ill, so it was never completed with me in it anyway. Perhaps you are just not meant to do certain things.'

Sellers' second complaint seems paradoxical in the light of the alleged constraints he felt he was under: Wilder, for all his dictatorial attitudes towards his actors – i.e. his expectation that they will be professionals who adhere to their lines – liked work to proceed in an atmosphere of high wassail. Sellers, who didn't have any friends in Hollywood, felt left out. 'I used to go down on the set of *Kiss Me, Stupid* with Billy Wilder,' he said, 'and find a Cook's Tour of hangers-on and sightseers standing just off the set, right in my line of vision. Friends and relatives of people in the front office came to kibitz on Peter Sellers, actor . . . I should have ridden to the set on horseback . . . and bawled out: "Who are all these damn civilians? Get them out of the range of my cannons!"'

As we know from *Brouhaha*, his antics during his vaudeville days, and the mystifications on stage during the recording of *The*

Goon Show, Sellers didn't care for audiences, unless they were drooling with adulation, and even then he was aware of them only to have power over them. We may go further. He didn't much care for fellow performers, directors, or his films as wholes (except for *Being There*: he believed, correctly, that the out-takes over the credit roll broke the spell); he didn't even like looking back at his own performances, once they had been captured by the camera ('I wish I had the calm and the ability to appraise what I see there on the screen,' he said during the making of *The World of Henry Orient*.) All that mattered to him – at home or at work, in public or private – was doing what pleased him. From moment to moment he wished to be absolute, supreme.

What dismayed him during *Kiss Me, Stupid* was that he was uncertain about overcoming resistance. Looking back in 1976, he claimed: 'I had a very sad and depressing experience working with a director whom I admired tremendously – Billy Wilder . . . When I got on the floor, I realised that there was no way for me to work within Wilder's system . . . Placing oneself entirely in someone's hands, even Wilder's, brilliant as he was, just wasn't right. He and Izzy Diamond's words were golden, but they were very set in their ways. . .' The real quandary, therefore, wasn't so much the disallowing of deviations from the script; and still less was there an impasse with the gawpers. These were symptomatic of a more general indignation – namely, Sellers' refusal to be beholden. He decided to be stubborn to punish Wilder for giving orders; and the more people cried shame on him, the more determined and cruel Sellers grew – until, in an astonishing outburst, he reckoned that it wasn't only Wilder and the cast and crew of *Kiss Me, Stupid* who were ranged against him and to blame for his unease: it was the whole of Hollywood. 'I have had Hollywood, love,' he told the *Evening Standard*. 'At the studios they give you every creature comfort, except the satisfaction of being able to get the best work out of yourself. America I would go back to gladly tomorrow, but as far as film-land is concerned I've taken the round trip for good. The noise and, to coin a phrase, the people.'

This is highly reminiscent of the grudges he had aired about New York in his letter to Walker of the previous Autumn. He hated the East Coast; he hated the West Coast (adding to the symmetrical effect is the fact that Walker was the chap who wrote up the *Evening Standard* interview). Between his experiences on America's extremities had come *A Shot in the Dark*, which he had hated, too. What we are seeing here is a man whose vehemencies were ingrained, whose independence had become exaggerated until he was inaccessible and belonged nowhere, and whose dissatisfactions were destructive and no longer part of any drive to attain perfection: 'The trouble is,' he said in January 1963, 'you find yourself trying all the time for satisfaction and then never really being satisfied with yourself. I suppose that's good for an actor – but sometimes it is awful. Like a battle you can never win.' Where possible, the battle against himself was re-deployed as a battle against other people, to whose feelings he was always indifferent. It was with something like surprise, therefore, that he opened a telegram a few days after his anti-Hollywood babble had been printed, and read: 'TALK ABOUT UNPROFESSIONAL RAT FINKS'. It was signed by Wilder, Dean Martin, Kim Novak, Cliff Osmond and others – good for them – of the *Kiss Me, Stupid* company.

As Sellers would have been aware, a rat fink is one of the terms of opprobrium used in the film by Polly the Pistol. She is a former manicurist, and she believes that men with small cuticle moons are finks. Two finks she has met are Martin, who gets a headache if he can't copulate, and a hoola-hoop salesman, who once ditched her. Sellers was being placed in this category of slime. As when the St Aloysius' masters had threatened the rod, BBC producers or booking managers had upbraided him, Tom Sloan had castigated him over the liniment tantrum, Blake Edwards had asked him not to be boorish, and Anne had left him, he couldn't see it, of course. He felt suffocated, persecuted, cold against them. In an attempt to broadcast his conviction that he was not the one in the wrong, the following notice appeared in *Variety* on July 1st 1964: 'I am [not] an ungrateful Limey or rat fink who has been abusing everything in

Hollywood behind its back. I did not go to Hollywood to be ill. I went there to work and found, regrettably, that the creative side in me couldn't accept the sort of conditions under which work had to be carried out. This is a personal matter. I have no criticism of Hollywood as a place, only as a place to work in. The atmosphere is wrong for me. At the same time anyone is at liberty to say that I am wrong. . .' And so, wheedlingly, on and on.

☆ ★ ☆

The advertising space for Sellers' self-justifications cost him either £250 (Evans) or £750 (Walker); leaving aside the classifieds, do not his words and tone suggest he should have been certified? For, if his transgressions over *Kiss Me, Stupid* connect with his life-long dismissal of authority, his behaviour also – more specifically and interestingly – fits with the crack-up which overtook him in the early Sixties, when he became unsettled in every sense: geographic, careeristic, spiritualistic.

Whilst it was possible – nasty, foolhardy, humiliating and priggish, but still possible – to publicise his disagreements over Wilder's *modus operandi* ('I suppose I just automatically accepted that he would be great for me. Well, he wasn't'), there were deeper, murkier forces at work inside Sellers which he didn't dare voice. The first of these has to do with Bill. In 1976, Sellers added another, new, reason for his unhappiness with the film: 'I couldn't make anything of the character,' he claimed, 'because I didn't know people like that.' The failed songwriter, the hen-pecked husband, the overlooked man, withdrawn and fidgeting: Orville, piano-playing and organ-playing in the local church, seething and miserable, was somebody Sellers knew, all right. But if *Kiss Me, Stupid* alluded, no doubt coincidentally but still unmistakably, to his father's prostration – to the life of a man who was not important – then, much more unnerving was Orville's overlap with Sellers himself.

Two days prior to his departure from England to begin the film, Sellers had married Britt. Less than a month prior to that he had met her for the first time. As he described the romance himself in 1965: 'The best thing that ever happened to me was walking down that Dorchester Hotel corridor the moment I did. I was staying there, you'll remember, while I made *A Shot in the Dark*. I'd moved out of my apartment [in Hampstead] . . . and I hadn't yet moved into this house [in Elstead]. So there I was lording it in the giant Oliver Messel suite. Alone. One day I walked down the hotel corridor and there was this unbelievable chick coming the other way. "Who is that?" I said to Bert Mortimer, my chauffeur-valet. He knows everyone. "Britt Ekland," he said. "She's here for talks with Twentieth-Century Fox – I read it in the paper." "Wow," I said, or words to that effect. So the same night I sent Bert round with a note and asked her to come in for a drink. Which she did. I was knocked over, absolutely stunned. I couldn't believe it. She was so great. She wore a simple dress and her hair was like sunlight. Unbelievable! Well, you know what a camera fan I am. I asked her if I could take some pictures of her. She thought it was a fun idea – and from that moment we were never apart. Three weeks later [on February 19th 1964] we were married. It wasn't until much later that I came across a slip of paper with the initials B.E. My friend Maurice Woodruff, the clairvoyant, had forecast six months earlier that I'd meet a girl with those initials and marry her – but I'd completely forgotten.'

Actually, Woodruff hadn't been quite that precise. What he had said was that a person with the initials B.E. would figure in Sellers' life in a general way. Woodruff, who was in the pay of film companies to steer Sellers in the direction of their projects, was meant to be laying the ground for the acceptability of Blake Edwards and *A Shot in the Dark*: if Sellers had thought it was God's will that he made the movie, maybe he would have been less truculent about returning to Clouseau? The actor, however, failed to make that connection. He married Britt instead. Academics may like to address the issue of how history's course would have been altered if, on that fateful evening in the Dorchester, Sellers had run across Buddy Ebsen, Barbara Eden, Barry Evans, Barbara Everest, or Bernard Evein, the art director of *Woman Times Seven*.

Notice too, in that self-pitying image of his solitude and abandonment in the luxurious hotel suite, how easily Janette Scott had slipped from Sellers' mind. He talks of himself as if he was haunting rather than living – and then along came Britt, for him to feed off. 'For two years, until I met Britt, I had been terribly despondent. I was working to forget how unhappy I was.* I never took any exercise – and if I did it was one of those frenzied ten-minute bouts which are quite useless. Then there was the smoking. With me it was causing insomnia. I would sleep maybe for six hours, but out of those six hours I wouldn't get any more than half an hour's real rest. So I was taking tranquillisers – I was getting into the pill area in a big way.'

Was it marijuana which made Henry Orient and Clouseau, in his second outing, look so glassy? The picture Sellers tried to project, of the lonely man-beast saved by a goddess of the Spring, is far from accurate (though he tried to repeat the fable again with Lynne Frederick). Sellers may have found Britt arousing, and he did want to enjoy her, but she was less of a real person, in his eyes, than the object of his brutish attention. He wanted to overpower her, and he infected her with his malaise. She didn't save him – he nearly destroyed her. 'Our moments of real happiness', she was to confess, 'were rare and far apart.' Eventually she would try and take an overdose.

Britt, who was twenty-one and had barely serviceable English, had been offered a contract by Darryl F. Zanuck, and she was staying at the Dorchester pending instructions to fly to New York for screen tests. She remembers Bert Mortimer knocking on her door with his message, and she found him rather persistent. Sellers was

---

* As I suspected (see p.893 above), Sellers wasn't working to acquire a long-term secure future for his children. As the Penguin says in *Batman Returns*, he was Number One, everybody else was treated as Number Two. This came across even in his vague, off-hand statements: 'I don't like lazing around. The money isn't really important. It's nice – but when you've got a nice home and a good start in life for the kids what else is there?' Then, turning the caring-family-man image on its head to reveal the reality of his selfishness, he added: 'After all, who wants to be the richest man in the cemetery? I'd rather have a ball.' (*Today*, January 19th 1963.)

disclosed in his suite eating Chinese food. He kept shooting her glances and began talking about photography – the camera being his concupiscent device, or dare I say tool.* He taught her how to smoke a joint, grabbed her and started snogging. The next morning, the contents of the Dorchester's florist stall – proprietrix: Miranda Quarry – were carried up to Britt's room, along with the card, 'Hope you slept well – Clouseau.' Over the next few days, the young Swede was seduced with Asprey's trinkets, Garrard's jewels, crocodile-skin accessories and a Lotus sports car; Sellers took her disco-dancing and to expensive Mayfair eateries. Five days later, Britt was obliged to travel to New York, where she stayed at the Drake Hotel. Sellers telephoned her incessantly and informed the newspaper columnist Roderick Mann: 'I really believe this may be more than just a casual relationship. Funny, isn't it? I keep saying to you I'll never get hooked again; that I'm tired of having my heart bleed; but here I am, waiting to be hooked. My trouble, I suppose, is that I can only be attracted to pretty girls. And that's courting disaster from the start. Especially if you tend to be jealous, like me.'

Sellers' jealousy was Shakespearean – it was an emotion connected to his pride in the rights of property-ownership and his fears of a slave's revolt. As quickly as he could, he locked Britt up. He was at Heathrow on February 12th to meet her off her plane and give her an engagement ring. (They were officially betrothed in the cleaning ladies' lavatory at the airport, to avoid the press photographers.) The marriage was held in Guildford Registry Office on the following Wednesday. Norman Hartnell made the bride's frock, and the building was filled with white flowers and (a Swedish tradition) candles. Hundreds of people jostled outside, and the crowds followed the newly-weds to the gates of Elstead. (The next time Sellers drew the fans like that it was his funeral.) There was a smorgasbord luncheon and a supper later at the Tiberio restaurant in

---

* 'Time stops. We share a brief, intense intimacy. But it's unearned. It has no past, no future. And when the sitting is over – when the picture is done – there's nothing left except the photograph . . . the photograph and a kind of embarrassment.' Richard Avedon.

London. Sellers had the whole day filmed by sixteen millimetre cameras and he later added a commentary and a musical soundtrack. Don't you find that an odd thing to do in itself? Sellers, by designing his day for posterity, and living his marriage through a lens, was already empty. By busying himself making a movie he was confirming the artificiality which was now gripping his life. He felt far-off. He didn't believe he existed, except on the screen. For, though shot in his home, this was no home-movie. You could have run Pinewood with the equipment at Sellers' command. That Graham Stark and David Lodge, part of the furniture in many of his official films, introduced the guests, and were cast as Sellers' best men, added to the fantasy world. Microphones were secreted in vases and button-holes. Interviews were conducted with the principal players – and there, on what Milligan would call Minnie Mouse legs, was Peg, with her pterodactyl face. She'd seen Anne off – and now this, a girl-bride. Peg survived another three years, feeding herself on gin and cigarettes. To compete with Britt, she took to wearing hot pants and boob tubes. She painted her face with lashings of Mary Quant mascara and rouge. The effect of the sexagenarian bobby-soxer must have been like one of those pox-ridden screaming skulls in the Bedlam sub-plot of a play by Middleton & Rowley.

☆　★　☆

Sellers was then bound for California and *Kiss Me, Stupid*; Britt, thrilled to be in possession of her Fox contract and a United Kingdom work permit (not easy to obtain), was due to appear in *Guns at Batasi*, which was being made in Britain by John Guillermin, the director of *Never Let Go* and *Waltz of the Toreadors*. Instead of a honeymoon, however, and the excitement of entering a new, strange life, Britt was chilled to discover that she'd been carried over the threshold into a nightmare. 'The true character of Sellers began to emerge. His incredible affection soured rapidly into an habitual jealousy which filled the first few weeks of our marriage with despair.' In the widening circle of Sellers' madness, affection didn't change places with jealousy, as such; the strength of his emotion intertwined them. In his diseased opinion, the only constants

913

were deceit and slipperiness (he assumed other people were just like him in that respect). His underlying bitterness and grievances came out, and instead of playing Orville J. Spooner, he *was* Orville J. Spooner – who worships Zelda, but can't trust her. Sellers had spies on the set of *Guns at Batasi* and he himself telephoned Britt persistently, cross-indexing and double-corroborating the reports. 'I would have to describe my day almost minute by minute,' his wife said.

Sellers was convinced his pond was going to be fished. Like Orville, he snooped on his pretty bride, cross-examined her, and tried to have the mileage checked on her car. Ford, in *The Merry Wives of Windsor*, justified this sort of prurience by saying, 'if I find her honest, I lose not my labour; if she be otherwise, 'tis labour well-bestowed'. That was Sellers – or Orville, the character having rubbed and exposed his nerves. He accused Britt of casting-couch capers with Zanuck – he resented the producer for having discovered her first – and when he asked about her relations with John Leyton, the star of *Guns at Batasi*, his inquiries grew increasingly lewd: 'Has he asked you out? He must have chatted you up by now? Tell me the truth Britt . . . Are you sure you don't fancy him? . . . What kind of scene? You didn't have to kiss him . . . ?'

Like Ford and Orville, Sellers' obsessive questioning suggests that, in spite of himself, he was thrilled by the concept of cuckoldry. Was he uncertain of his manhood? Was it his latent homosexuality coming out? (Get busy, psychoanalysts.) He'd been the same with Anne, accusing her of falsehood, and he'd be the same with Lynne – when, beyond all shame, and much to his son's disgust ('Mike, I've got to know the truth'), he set private detectives to follow her. He did not wish her to be seen talking to Simon Williams and Stuart Wilson on the set of *The Prisoner of Zenda*. He felt threatened by any male less antiquated than Melvyn Douglas – the exception to the rule being Michael Jeffery: 'Lynne and I had a dance routine and Peter used to get us to do it,' he told me. 'He used to love sitting back and watching us.'

Given all this psychopathology, it is little wonder that Sellers' work in *Kiss Me, Stupid*, despite his diversionary tactics and meannesses, was brilliant. So brilliant, he burned himself out, his heart a phosphorescence. When I watch the film today, I feel I'm being horribly unfair to Ray Walston – who took over the rôle of Orville; I keep wondering what Sellers would be doing, and how he'd be doing it better.* ('I came to the picture a week after Sellers had gone to hospital,' he told me. 'Some of the crew said he was somewhat frustrated with Wilder's methods of direction, although I think that might just be true of any actor who worked for Wilder. He was very adamant that the actor do it his [Wilder's] way.') Walston's Orville is old-ladyish, fey. He is nervous, jerky; he gnaws his nails and patrols his little house with a clockwork soldier strut – or is it his metronome which guides his movements? (The house was designed by Alexandre Trauner: it is as cluttered as the apartment in *The Apartment* or as Nayland Smith's cosy cottage in Sellers' final film.) Walston is shrill and pop-eyed – his Orville is nasty, charmless and shallow. Sellers would have been all these things, too, no doubt; but he'd have transfigured the rôle. The rage would have been real and unfathomable (instead of simply tetchy); the sinister sadomasochistic streak in the material would have been more strongly implied; and beyond all this, I think, there would have been some sympathy, as there is for General Fitzjohn, Fred Kite, or John Lewis – other Sellers characters having trouble with the missus. There would have been slyness, awkwardness – a creepiness that was almost beautiful.

By 1964, however, it was too late. What made Sellers an artist on the grand scale was what made him mad: the intensity and excitement of his imagination. He passed between dreams and reality 'as through tissue-paper' (Barrie) and he could not sustain a performance of Orville's calibre; and in any event it was too close to him. *Kiss Me, Stupid* penetrated to Sellers' own fears, which he was not willing to explore; it resonated through to his subconscious. He was being prevented from breaking up the script into a series of

---

* If anybody knows of the whereabouts of any Sellers *Kiss Me, Stupid* footage – he shot for six weeks on the film, after all, so there'd have been a great deal – do please let me know, c/o the publisher.

semi-extempore sketches; and as each scene approached, his malignancy grew, his sexual frenzy grew, and he sent for Britt in person. He enticed her to Hollywood for an Easter weekend break and he wouldn't allow her to return to her film – he made out she was suffering from nervous exhaustion. 'Britt you are a sick girl,' he said. 'You don't want to crack up totally, do you?' He had already taken the precaution of filling the wardrobe, at his rented house, 924 Hillcrest, in Los Angeles' Trousdale Estates area, with clothes and shoes of her exact fitting. (She never wore a single outfit he'd bought. 'The conservative American dresses didn't match the flamboyant Ekland image,' I was told.) He was going to keep her prisoner and wreck her work on *Guns at Batasi* – or, as he conveyed the drama to the papers, adroitly putting the responsibility for the flit on to Britt: 'Swedish Bride Flees Country to Be with Bridegroom'; 'Britt Flies to Her Man'.

Britt arrived on a Friday and she was meant to be back in Pinewood within seventy-two hours. She was not, and a writ for breach of contract was immediately issued. Sellers ignored it.* He decided to take his family – Michael and Sarah were present – to Disneyland. As Hattie Stevenson recalls: 'Just prior to his heart attack there was a strained family atmosphere. We went to Disneyland. A family. Anne relied on me to look after the children to a certain extent. One day in Disneyland, one day in the shops in Beverly Hills – Sellers thought he'd done his bit. It was odd being in Disneyland – his acting the part of a family man, and with him not being a good father. He'd brought the children over to America – and then he'd ignored them.

'The night he'd had his heart attack, we'd been all day in Disneyland, and had had a reasonably nice day; the children had got on well with him – so Bert and I decided to go out for the evening. We decided to drive to Mexico – we'd do it through the night. And we got back, at seven o'clock in the morning, on the Monday, to find

---

* He eventually compensated Fox with $60,200 – this being the cost of re-shooting Britt's scenes with Mia Farrow.

we'd been left a note by Britt: "Peter has had a heart attack. Am in Cedars Lebanon." I started laughing. "Good God, the lengths he'll go to so he doesn't have to make this film. . .' He'd been complaining and grumbling and finding any excuse because he didn't want to go into the studio.

'We were all staying in Spyros Skouras' villa.* The phone rang all night – it was daytime in Britain. I was at my tiredest. I never had any sleep for three days. Anne rang me and said, "Bring my children back immediately." Sellers had said to Bert: "Don't let the children go home." A very difficult dilemma. We convinced him in the end it was the best thing for me to fly back with them. So I brought the children back. Britt was bothered about her furs – would I take her minks back to England? This was all she seemed anxious about. So I arrived at Heathrow wearing her mink. All the reporters and television cameras were there, waiting. My mother [spouse of His Honour Judge Melford Stevenson] rang me: "*Where* did you get that coat from?"'

☆   ☆   ☆

They had stayed the night of Saturday April 4th at a Disneyland hotel, and on the Sunday morning they visited a cowboy ghost town in the Californian desert. (Bert took a photograph of Sellers dressed as a saturnine gunslinger.) The staff then went on their way across the Mexican border; Sellers, Britt and the children returned to Skouras' Greek temple. Whilst his wife frolicked with Sarah and Michael in the pool, Sellers leafed through the script of *Kiss Me, Stupid* – he had a six a.m. start for the studio on Monday – and, once the babes were settled in their nursery (Michael was eight, Sarah four), he brought Britt to bed for rumpy-pumpy.

He had forced pot upon his bride; now he liked her to inhale poppers whilst he squirmed across her belly. Britt wasn't impressed

---

* 'The only Greek tragedy I know is Spyros Skouras' (Billy Wilder). President of Twentieth-Century-Fox. The chief executive, coincidentally, of the company Sellers was messing-about, by refusing to allow Britt to complete her rôle in *Guns at Batasi*.

with the aphrodisiacs. The chemical vapour reminded her of an operation she'd once undergone in Stockholm for her adenoids. Sellers, however, was transported. The drug (supplied by his diet doctor incidentally) caused a dilation in the coronary arteries, leading directly to an increase in coronary blood flow, which in its turn, after Sellers had had his orgasm, led to a sudden overload in the amount of blood leaving his heart and a corresponding reduction in the stream of blood on its way in. The heart, its rhythmic pumping action sabotaged, galloped, fluttered, and shut-down. Sellers, still reeling from his ultimate come, was on his way to the bathroom when the fires in his chest started and pains flashed down his arms. He told Britt to phone the heart specialist, Rex Kennamer, who had been recommended to him by Elizabeth Taylor (one of our century's great sufferers). Kennamer arrived at the villa, took a cardiogram and gave Sellers a sedative.

The doctor then left. He returned within a few hours. The results of the electrocardiogram (ECG) had been processed – electrodes had been attached to Sellers' limbs and chest wall and readings taken – and he said: 'You have had a mild heart attack.' He wanted Sellers to enter hospital for tests. The oracle had spoken. Sellers was curiously pleased. He had a good excuse for shirking Monday's *Kiss Me, Stupid* stint, Britt had a good reason for not flying back to *Guns at Batasi*; and so they departed for the infirmary immediately. The children were given to the maid – it is at this point that Bert and Hattie returned to the empty house and disbelieved the news.

For the first time, since he had begun working and living in America, Sellers was happy. The New York flatteries and fawnings were nothing; the Hollywood party circuit was nothing; Billy Wilder was nothing ('I still have a few idols but now I consider them no more infallible than the man next door. "Okay," I say to them, "now prove you're as great as I think you are." Now the responsibility is all theirs'); when it came to dying and not dying, though, America was really something: 'You've got to have top billing to get into a five-star joint like this,' beamed Sellers, as he checked in to the exclusive (i.e. expensive) institution. (This was thirty years ago: Sellers' room was sixty-five dollars a day, exclusive of medical fees.)

Britt backtracked to Hillcrest Road for a nap. The day was filled with the battle about the children. 'A real test of nerves,' recalls Hattie Stevenson. 'Sellers wanted them in California because he had just re-married; he wanted Britt to take over as their mother. Anne, meantime, wanted them away from the publicity.'

If Sellers' hospitalisation for observation made the London evening papers on the Monday, what happened next filled the front pages all over the world. ('It was like when Kennedy was assassinated,' remembers Wolf Mankowitz.) In the early hours of Tuesday morning, a nurse making a routine check discovered that Sellers was (according to a bulletin) 'unconscious with no blood pressure and no pulse'. Emergency cardiopulmonary resuscitation was applied. He was given a direct current blast of two hundred joules, a chest massage, and shots of anti-arhythmic drugs. He was taken to the Intensive Care Unit – wittily known as the Eleventh Hour Ward – and re-connected to cardiograph machines, heart stimulators and a ventilator. 'He has had a serious setback,' said a hospital spokesman. 'This looks like a close one. A blood clot from yesterday's coronary thrombosis has blocked the vital conduction system of the heart. Doctors are using a pacemaker which electrically stimulates the heart ... he has been given stimulants ... anti-coagulants ... oxygen ...' At four-thirty a.m., there was a second massive coronary attack and the word went out that Sellers was 'deteriorating'.

Britt was brought to the hospital and informed of her incipient widowhood. Dr Kennamer was joined by Dr Eliot Corday, America's foremost heart surgeon. 'Everything humanly possible is being done,' said Britt. 'But a few prayers would be very useful now.' In London, Peter Evans recalls the doom-laden ticker-tape messages which were chattering into the *Daily Express*: 'Sellers obit see embargo ... important see embargo ... not to be published until death announced ... not to be released until death official ... see embargo.' Ian Carmichael, up in Hampstead, was urgently beckoned by Associated-Rediffusion – as he told it to me: 'When he was at Cedars of Lebanon Hospital he was not expected to survive. I was confronted by the television people. They were preparing a memorial programme for that evening because Peter Sellers would be dead. Would I be the anchor-man and provide the linking commentary between the clips? Spike and Harry were also to appear. "Will you come to the studios now and rehearse?" I was given a script. I had to read, "Today, on Tuesday April 7th 1964, at [blank for time], in the Cedars of Lebanon Hospital, Los Angeles, Peter Sellers died." And it was macabre, because he was still alive. The producers, and so on, were so wrapped up in it, I got the impression they'd be bloody annoyed if he lived – which he did. I met him later on. I never told him about it.'

☆ ★ ☆

Sellers, meantime, like Orpheus, was in the underworld: 'It's weird when I think of it. That I was dead, I mean. I had eight heart arrests. After six, they didn't think I could take any more. Nobody ever had. They told Britt there was no hope. But it wasn't my turn for the wooden overcoat, apparently. The first time, my heart stopped for one and a half minutes. If they had been a second later getting me down to the pacemaker machine, I wouldn't have been worth saving. My brain would have been damaged. Fortunately, I never knew what was going on. They kept me heavily sedated. When I did come round, I saw these five guys in white coats holding me down [*a very understandable hallucination*], for the jolt from the pacemaker machine is so great it can throw you off the bed. The staggering thing, of course, is that when I thought I was just falling asleep, I was really dying . . . [I lay] like a collapsed puppet, with wires and strings all over me.'

Sellers' first comment, when he regained consciousness, was 'Who are all these cats?' He was diagnosed as having endured an acute myocardial infarction with a complete heart block. 'After a period of rest he could be a new man again,' said Dr. Kennamer. 'His heart by that time will be back to normal. . . . There is no reason, with proper convalescence and treatment, why he should not be just as active again in the future as he has been in the past. His millions of fans will not be disappointed, provided he follows medical advice given to him.' Milligan and Secombe sent a telegram: 'YOU SWINE BLOODNOK. WE HAD YOU HEAVILY INSURED. HOW DARE YOU.' Sellers, or Bluebottle, responded: 'I AM DOWN HERE IN THIS HOSPITAL WHICH IS IN THE LAND OF AMERICA, AND I DON'T LIKE THIS GAME, NO I DON'T. I AM NOT DEADED, I TELL YOU, I'M ALIVE. THINKS "I HOPE SO".' Sellers also designated McGonagall to commemorate his resurrection:

> O, beautiful Hollywood,
> You are a sumptuous place,
> Lived in mainly by Film Stars,
> And also several members of the human race.
> Blue would describe the colour of the sky,
> Which makes the inhabitants really want to live,
> But alas, some of them die.*

Confined to his bed, Sellers delighted in Goonery.† By April

---

* This verse was quoted by Alexander Walker in his obituary of Sellers, entitled 'Alas, Some of Them Die,' printed in the *Evening Standard* on Thursday July 24th 1980. The article, couched as a personal tribute, is a superior piece of work to the rather anodyne 'Authorised Biography' which he proceeded to pen immediately afterwards. The article includes at least one admirable flourish: '[Sellers] fired directors, turned whole scripts inside out to fit his own way of experiment, made many bad choices out of the idiosyncrasies of the moment and sent many a producer – as well as many journalists including this one – long tartly worded telegrams vowing he would never work, speak, or would have anything to do with them again except as a hit-and-run relationship in a fast car.'

† Full of himself for having pulled through, Sellers was dictating letters and scribbling notes to Milligan nearly every day: 'You'll never get me . . . you swine, because I too have you heavily insured!! So we shall see who's the first to collect' (April 15th); ' . . . I don't like this game but I shall be back in East Finchley soon. I say to you, love and electric twits and things' (April 17th); 'The pills what Majer Bloodnok sent to me made me go all funny in my littul hed and I was put in the hospittle. They said I had eten poisen but I no that deear Majer Bloodnok would not want to killéd me. Anyway I'me orlright now and I'me staying at Hanks Snake Howse and he is kind to me' (n.d.); 'No doubt you have heard of me. I

9th he was (in the hospital's phrase) 'holding his own' and he pulled funny faces for the nurses. He ate meatballs and rice and said, 'I feel great.' Thousands of letters and messages were arriving from fans. 'A whole new world opened up for me,' he claimed, 'I didn't realise it meant so much to people whether I lived or died.' He was on top of the world: 'I feel like the Miracle Man who came back from the dead!'

The physiological and psychological impact of his heart attack on his remaining decade and a half is incalculable. He was worried about his health – what he should eat, what he shouldn't eat. He had many a fad. He was very attuned to the problems of his body – which would be hypochondria, except that he'd had that glance across what he called 'the valley of the shadow'. A heart attack would have a long-lasting effect on the way of life of any human being – and Sellers was no exception. But then the whole of his make-up had *always* been sensitive. Anne told a reporter at the time: 'he looked after himself so well, and took such care of his health that when I heard the news I just couldn't believe it. It seems

---

served in Her Majesty's Royal Deserters during the Sepoy Rising in India, and apart from mild attacks of dysentery which come upon me from time to time, I am in fine shape . . .' (May 22nd); 'Having served HER MAJESTY in various capacities all over the globe, I am distressed by the continual threatening letters I receive from various people who claim that I am this SCANDALOUS SCOUN-DREL AND BAWDY MAN Dennis Bloodnok' (June 23rd); 'I am, unfortunately, completely bald due to loss of hair, and have now been able to secure the services of a crepe hair wig, kindly loaned to me by the Old People's Crepe Hair Wig Association and Minge Fund. This, however, has given rise to several rumours that I am a female impersonator, and bear some other name . . . ' (August 10th); 'In case you have never heard of me, my name is Rex Finchley, Private Investigator, specialising in divorce procedures, re-arrange-ments and other situations that need constant surveyance and certain things . . . ' (August 31st).

See *The Book of the Goons* (op. cit.) for the complete and inventive texts. Notice how, at first, the jokes are to do with illness and bodily functions. As Sellers' health improved, the theme is that of mistaken or new identity. Rex [King] Fin-chley is a name used in *The Fiendish Plot of Dr Fu Manchu*, sixteen years later.

incredible that anyone so fanatical about health could be ill. He was obsessed with physical fitness. But Peter lived at quite a pace, and with all the worry it must have been bad for him. He was an obsessional worrier.'

She was not to know that the deciding factor – the trigger – was her former husband's new fondness for narcotics, or that he'd had one chemically-exalted fuck too many. But she did tell the press that: 'He was haunted with the idea that he would die from a heart attack, like his father and several uncles. It was on his mind constantly.' For Milligan, indeed, the heart attack was fated – almost psychosomatically induced: 'He had about forty heart attacks before the real thing turned up. Years before he had this heart attack he always worried about it, was always searching for the bloody thing as if it were a letter that he knew had been posted and hadn't arrived.' Do those who fear death, deep down, think that they deserve it? Sellers' permanent anxiety states, aggression and impatience were all likely to complicate organic heart disease. He was ill because of what he was. Today, doctors would call such a condition 'cardiac neurosis' or 'neurocirculatory asthenia' – palpitations, headaches, stress, dizziness, sudden fatigue. Then again, all these symptoms could have been quite justly explained away as basic over-work: 'I used to work with a kind of frenzy, just so that I could lose myself in it. I drove myself harder and harder, but I did manage to lose myself entirely in my films. No holidays, reading scripts, rehearsing, always on the go. . .'

Yet he wanted to be like this; he had been busy since 1948, when he made his first BBC broadcast. He could never stand being merely himself – contingent, relative, mortal – and vacations, the spots of time between projects when he was not obliged to rôle-play, always made him malignant. Hence the valium and tranquillisers he was guzzling already, before the departure from America. They assisted the process of getting out of himself; pills made it easier for him to go on being a disturbing influence, claiming complete freedom. The capsules he'd inhaled with Britt were part of this pattern. This heartless man's heart attack, therefore, vindicated him. First, it came in handy as a way of – retrospectively – blaming all those who'd ever dared to thwart him or interrupt his pleasures; it was a way of making his enemies feel guilty. Secondly, it was a sign that he was not inconsequential. Indeed, he claimed – like Lazarus laughing – that he was immortal: 'One of the cardiologists told me that what I'd been through wouldn't hit me till later, and it's true. The other day I started thinking, "Man, I died!"'

As for the after-effects, Sellers didn't change, as such; on the contrary, his long established traits were magnified: his torments and tensions, his deliriums. As he grew older and iller, his psychological problems may well have been linked to his pulmonary disease, and exacerbated by the medication he received; but the chief result of the Cedars of Lebanon adventure was the way it confirmed for him his earliest inkling – that he was marvellous, eternal, everything that Peg had promised. At the end of the last chapter, I said that Sellers, for all the moping melancholia, was on the side of life. He was unabateable, a wild thing. I understated the case. He wanted to live *forever*. As an actor, he was infinitely resourceful. When one character ran out, he'd assume another – and this is how he wanted to be in reality. When one life expired, he'd be back in a new shape and guise. 'It was virtually a case of having another time around,' he said in 1971, 'because I did in fact die. I was dead for up to two minutes. I learned that later, though I cannot possibly describe it to you. I suppose when you think about *that*, you think to yourself – well, having come back from wherever it was. . .' Sellers' voice trailed off. He was trying to convey what it was like being a phenomenon. He was eloquent elsewhere, however, in his films – when Clouseau survived death and destruction to bounce back time and again, when Chance walked across the waters, or Fu Manchu found that he could rustle up the secret recipe of ever-lastingness.

☆ ★ ☆

Sellers very quickly came to the conclusion that he had survived because he was infallible. The first sign of a rift with Britt appeared when he took offence at her practicality. 'Did you know I actually died?' he inquired. 'What do you mean?' Britt asked. 'My heart stopped,' he stated. 'Yes, but you weren't dead,' she said. 'Yes I was,' Sellers insisted. 'He was disappointed when I told him he had *not* died,' Britt explained later. 'He wanted to be able to tell people what it was like to be dead and then come alive again. But I convinced him he hadn't *really* been dead, even if his heart had stopped beating.'

She convinced him of no such thing. Sellers was far too enthralled by his own mythic, phoenix-like, version of events to want it sullied by crappy things like medical knowledge (the paroxysms are a condition called ventricular tachycardia); also, he believed that he had lived not so much because of the well-equipped hospital and professional expertise, but because the world downed tools and prayed. 'I mean, having thousands of people writing to you telling you they're praying you'll recover. God, it taught me a lot.' Not about humility, of course – Sellers, by contrast, felt messianic, justifiably not commonplace. 'I can't guess why I survived,' he fibbed. 'Thousands of ordinary people all over the world wrote saying they had prayed for me – so perhaps the power of prayer does do something when it is directed. I don't know. Perhaps if it isn't your turn to go, it doesn't matter what happens, you'll survive. But it's no good making guesses. I mean – was it fate that made it happen in Hollywood . . . ? There's something else. One of the things that really staggered me was discovering for the first time that I am not just another actor to some people; that they really care about me.'

They had as high opinion of him as he had himself – isn't that what he meant? After a fortnight in the intensive-care unit, Sellers was moved upstairs to a private suite (number 503) for a further month. 'The decor is much nicer and I'm feeling much better. As you know, I'm well off the critical list,' he wrote to Peter Evans on April 21st. (The letter ends with the solemn valediction, 'God bless you.') He was discharged at the end of May (with a ten thousand pound bill)* and on June 4th, two months after the start of his illness, he became the one-hundred-and-forty-sixth star to have his footprints set in cement outside Graumann's Chinese Theater. He signed his name inside a Cupid's heart. 'I have given up smoking, and I am absolutely through with all the frenzied film-making. I want to start living again. I have got this lovely girl and I am going to relax now and see all the places I have never seen. Perhaps it takes the hand of death upon your shoulder to make you realise how wonderful life really is.'

He sketched his precise plans for the near future in – aptly – *Life* magazine: 'What we shall do is this. I live in one of the most beautiful parts of England. I have bought myself a red-setter, to take long walks with. I also have a pair of matched palominos, for riding. I've ordered a nice, fast, new car – my eighty-fourth, a blue Ferrari. And I want to take Britt to a discotheque one evening and have a hippy-hippy-shake. . .' Britt expanded upon the idyllic designs. The couple planned to go to New York to see Richard Burton and Elizabeth Taylor (and swop medical anecdotes); then they would begin a belated honeymoon in Switzerland, Spain, and the French Riviera. . .

None of this came to pass. Back in England, Sellers made those nasty comments which elicited the rat-fink rebuke. From his happiness in the hospital he plummeted into a depression which would never lift, except intermittently, for the remainder of his days. He was a messiah without a mission. 'I don't know why I'm here!' he said to Shirley MacLaine (a receptive audience). 'I don't know what I came back for this time! . . . I can't figure out my purpose.' His problem was that, believing he'd had a glimpse of Heaven – 'I looked around myself and I saw an incredibly beautiful bright loving white light above me. I wanted to go to that white light more than anything. I never wanted anything more. I knew that was love,

---

* According to *Photoplay*, April 1965. Evans says it was £12,000; Walker, £26,100. The wide variations aside, 'It was worth every penny,' said Sellers. 'Compared with the alternative, it would have been worth it whatever it had cost.'

real love, on the other side of the light which was attracting me so much. It was kind and loving and I remember thinking, "That's God"' – there was going to be nothing *this* side of paradise which would gratify him. If Paul Theroux has argued that a man may be corrupted by the pamperings of a five star hotel, think what it must be like to reach the Elysian Fields only to be turned back. You'd be pretty resentful. So it was with Sellers, a man unconsoled by earthly powers.

☆ ★ ☆

His heart attack – that ecstatic moment when the attention of the whole wide-world was upon him – became part of his long search for perfection – a cosmic variation on his struggle to find the flaw-less motor car, the non-hissing hi-fi, the optimum lens, the most desirable dwelling and the immaculate woman. (The consequence of his manic dissatisfactions was that he was increasingly startlingly imperfect as a human being.) He was soon untempted by Britt – and *before* she was induced to absent herself from *Guns at Batasi*, when he was ostensibly lonesome in Hillcrest Road, frothing like Orville J. Spooner and every other cuckold and jealous husband in dramatic literature, even *then* Sellers was leading a double life. He was sighted in Acapulco with Stella Stevens. He'd hired a private plane and the trip was conducted in great secrecy, naturally enough. Unfortunately, the Mexican night-club had a house photographer. 'If we had come down here in broad daylight you people wouldn't give a damn', snarled Sellers. 'But try to keep our lives private, and there's always a Johnny-on-the-spot.'

Coronary problems recurred; bad marriages recurred – all problems, actually or figuratively, of a breaking heart. His muse-figures, who inflamed him with their unattainability recurred – the Sophia Loren erotomania was repeated with Nanette Newman. 'We were up at Hampstead,' says Anne. 'He rang up Bryan Forbes, and said, "I'll let Anne have a divorce if you'll let me have Nanette."' The only way to cope with this was to treat it as a joke – to pretend to indulge him. 'He was in love with Nanette,' Forbes said to me, 'and he did want to marry her. Nanette was the only person who could talk him out of his black moods. She loved him, and does still, but as a friend – she was never *in* love with him.'

As when he'd allowed the plot of *The Millionairess* to overtake his life, so did Sellers extrapolate a romance from *The Wrong Arm of the Law*. Nanette played Valerie, a sweet and innocent supergrass, first seen modelling a wedding dress, who reported Pearly Gates' pillow-talk to a rival gang of robbers – they, disguised as policemen, intercept the scenes of crimes and commandeer the swag. There are several bedroom sequences – 'Don't push your luck, gel. It doesn't take much with me. All of a sudden. Whoosh! The old war wound starts to throb and I go berserk!' – and Sellers was smitten. Nanette received the Janette Scott treatment – i.e. she was required to use up her energies explaining to Sellers why he needn't kill himself (he'd bought guns for the purpose on two occasions); and if he believed he'd found a Wendy for his Peter Pan, he was spot on. Nanette has a sympathetic understanding of a child's imagination. In 1983 she wrote the foreword to Catherine Haill's book, *Dear Peter Pan*, a collection of letters sent by children to the actors and actresses who had appeared in the early productions of Barrie's play; and her words on that occasion could be referring, very specifically, to Sellers: 'Peter makes his audiences believe that staying a child is more fun, that being grown up is not the blissful state that adults maintain it is, but is really a time of responsibility. Barrie gave to Peter the magical power that most children long for, whether it be going to the moon, or being Superman . . . Peter . . . is forever. He is the rebel, the exception to the mould, the enviable one who cocks a snoot at rules and regulations and gets away with it . . . Wendy [is] the "mother figure". Wendy is sane and sensible, knowing that one day she will be a proper mother. . .'

Peter Pan is actually a psychopath ('I forget people after I kill them,' Barrie has him say in *Peter and Wendy*); so was Sellers. Britt, after a bout of maltreatment, would seek refuge at the Forbes' house near Wentworth. She'd pour out her heart to them and Nanette said firmly: 'You have no alternative, Britt. You've got to leave him.' Sellers then arrived, acting the rôle of abashed, conciliatory husband, and collected his wife. Alone in the car with

Britt, returning home, he'd revert to taciturnity and abuse. Sellers, on anybody's estimation, was an arch-manipulator, Britt was an innocent victim of a monster (was she Tiger Lily?) and Miss Newman, according to her own daughter, Emma Forbes, can only have descended from the Darlings: '. . . She is the best Nurse Nightingale you could ever wish to have. She makes being ill a pleasure. She is the sort of person who makes your pillows nice and plump and mixes up delicious honey and lemon drinks. She is a very smiley person . . . an optimist and great fun to be with.' No wonder Sellers wanted her. He wooed her with furs, jewels, and the E-Type Jaguar. He tried to follow the Forbes' on holiday. ('We were a trio for a time,' Forbes says with resignation.) He tried to fight the flab. 'There was Peter Sellers, the fat Jewish boy, the Goon; then there was a transformation and it happened in my house,' Forbes said to me. 'He saw a headline in the *Express*: "Mastroianni: Peter Sellers with Sex Appeal."* He threw the newspaper down, went on a crash diet, and didn't want to be thought of as a comedian ever again. He was burly – never naturally thin – and all the drugs he took to lose weight must have shortened his life. LSD I know he took. He got up in the middle of the night – pitch darkness – and he ran around claiming to be photographing the beautiful sunsets.'

To bolster his petition, Sellers sent the Forbeses letters from Pratt, MD, *The Wrong Box* character, and he recorded tapes in his Bloodnok voice. The gifts, the gags, the slimming proving unavailing, in

---

* The article on Marcello Mastroianni, who had induced a lather of jealousy in Sellers for appearing with Sophia Loren in *Marriage Italian Style*, was written by Peter Evans. He soon found himself on the receiving end of a strange telegram: 'PETER EVANS DAILY EXPRESS FLEET STREET EC4 I AM AVAILABLE AS BARITONE FOR AQUA-SHOW STOP CAN TREAD WATER OWN SNORKEL WILLING TO SWIM LOVE ENGLAND['S] MASTROIANNI'. Sellers was pretending to be amused by Evans' headline, but he was evidently displeased. The allusion to Ma Ray's *Have a Dip!* and *Splash Me!* entertainments suggests that, the way Sellers tabulated things, if you weren't romantically adorable, a leading man, then you were worthy only of the bottom of the bill. The cable summarises his insecurity and self-pity.

the end he began to get bitter, surrealistically vengeful. Elsewhere in this book I mentioned the abandoned yacht story – when Sellers invited Nanette and Bryan to join him in the Mediterranean and he never showed. There were other crazy occurrences. Because Forbes had complimented Sellers on the food one evening at Elstead, Sellers got it into his head that Forbes was going to try and lure away his chef, and that he was doing this because of latent homosexual tendencies.* 'Sellers put forward this scurrilous and false rumour about Bryan,' says Hattie Stevenson, 'and it was crackpot, his indignation. "How dare he . . . etc., etc.". In his mind he convinced himself he had the moral right to acquire Nanette – and he really did pursue her. During this period, if ever Bryan phoned, I was under orders to "put him off the trail". Sellers did his best to create the atmosphere of an affair – and he made me, completely innocently, imply that they were gallivanting off on afternoons together. It was total fiction.'

Total madness, I think Miss Stevenson must mean; but Sellers out-did himself with his next School of Sophia compulsion: Princess Margaret. 'Sellers used to say to me "Ring P.M." as he'd call her; and I'd say, "It's not my place to do so." She had a direct line at Kensington Palace, a magic number, and Sellers knew what it was. She accepted all his funny phone calls and funny voices, but we had to bow and curtsey, keep to the proprieties. Sellers used to go out with the Snowdons and I'd babysit at the Dorchester, if he had weekend access to the children – and he'd come in late with the Queen's sister. I suddenly had to get up and curtsey. You are not meant to leave before she leaves, but I used to try and go home – and I'd be compelled to stay and have a drink. Even in an informal capacity she was very formal – in a Dorchester suite, with nobody there save herself, Sellers, and me.'

☆ ★ ☆

To Sellers, the Saxe-Coburg-Gotha-Mountbatten-Windsors, with their long history of tours and public spectacles, were a show-

---

* The chef, Ray Gurton, eventually did leave Sellers' employ, and went to work for Cecil Beaton.

business family, like the Mendoza-Marks-Rays. Britt has written that she would 'squirm with embarrassment at the demeaning lengths he would stoop to in order to ingratiate himself with the royal family. It was contemptible.' His behaviour may or may not have been contemptible, but it wasn't ingratiation. Sellers was being subversive. He was taking them on – proving himself superior to them. At one of those celebrity line-ups after a gala screening, when the princes and princesses shuffle along the foyer and have a brief word with each star, Sellers, asked, 'What are you doing now?', decided to take the Queen Mother literally and, grinning fit to bust, said, a bit incredulous: 'Why, standing here talking to you, you silly old bat'. (The last four words were spoken only in his head.) He was similarly obstreperous at the charity première for *The Pink Panther Strikes Again*. He wanted Lynne Frederick to be presented to the Prince of Wales. 'Make sure Lynne's invited and is in the line-up,' he told Charles Berman, who was organising the event. 'I've promised her that she will be.' Her name was duly submitted to Buckingham Palace, and an equerry asked, 'This, um, Miss Frederick. Is she Mr Sellers' wife?' She wasn't, at the time. 'Is she in the film?' Again, no. 'Well, she can't be involved.'

Sellers, as may be guessed, got the shakes but good: '*What*! What you mean is that they won't have her. That's what you mean, isn't it? Well, I'm not fucking coming either. And that's that,' he informed Berman. He sulked in his apartment at Roebuck House and the evening went ahead without him. 'I think it was very bad form,' said Prince Charles, who after all was the one being snubbed, not Lynne. 'Peter was bloody rude.' Despite the ruckus, H.R.H. agreed to come back eighteen months later and adorn *The Revenge of the Pink Panther.*[*] Lynne, as the official Mrs Sellers, was guaranteed

---

[*] H.R.H. The Prince of Wales was willing to indulge Sellers because he adored *The Goon Show* – and, indeed, he contributed a Foreword to *More Goon Show Scripts* (London, 1973), in which he said: 'I discovered the "Ying Tong Song" in record form and almost at once I knew it by heart – the only song I do know by heart. I plagued everybody with its dulcet tones and "Solo for Raspberry Blower" to such an extent that when my small brothers heard a recording for the first time they thought it was their elder brother ... No matter how much

a place in the line-up; but what angered Sellers this time was the presence of Blake Edwards and Julie Andrews, whom he feared might upstage him and get treated as the leading lights. So anxious was he to position himself, and Lynne, at the head of the queue, he arrived at the Odeon, Leicester Square, early – too early. 'Where do I go?' he inquired, hurrying into the cinema. 'Er, straight up the stairs,' Berman began. 'That's where the presentations will be. In about an hour' – but Sellers was off before hearing the last bit. A few minutes later, having discovered the mezzanines and auditorium deserted, Sellers and his bride, fuming and perhaps feeling that they'd made themselves look like pricks, marched out again. Sellers was yelling, 'I'll kill him! That fucking Blake Edwards! He got me over here [from Port Grimaud] and there's no one up there! Wait till I get hold of him!'

Why Edwards should have had anything remotely to do with Sellers' miscalculations and his botched E.T.A. is an issue for the psychiatrists. (Edwards had written and directed the film *ergo* anything irksome connected with it Sellers displaced as Edwards' fault.) A search party had to be sent out into the Charing Cross Road, Shaftesbury Avenue and the Strand to round up the dippy star. (Were they equipped with a large net and a tranquilliser dart?) He was found in a pub near Panton Street (where his office had once been situated) and persuaded to return. 'Oh no!' Berman was thinking. 'Not again! We've got a repeat performance of last year. One prince and no star . . . It was a damned close-run thing.'

As a star, Sellers put himself above a prince – above everybody. He was superhuman. The royal family evidently recognised (and were willing to countenance) his anarchic-genius qualities, for

---

"fashion" in humour changes, there will always be thousands of people whose minds are attuned to the kind of mental slapstick and imaginary cartoonery that typifies Goonery. For that reason I am always hoping that many more "Goon Shows" in record form will be made available to their dotty and devoted supporters. . .'

Was it the 'Ying Tong Song' and 'Solo for Raspberry Blower' which drove poor Princess Diana away?

despite his effronteries (Princess Margaret called him 'the most difficult man I know') he was a frequent visitor to Clarence House and Windsor Castle. Perhaps, they thought, if the monster in the secret room at Glamis had been unfettered, he'd have been like this? Sellers would get up from the dinner table and pretend to be Sweeney Todd: 'I wish the world was one big throat and I had the cutting of it!' he'd announce, curdling the blood and pretending to be an actor in an old-fashioned melodrama. Aware of the regal fetish for kilts and scottishness, he next danced the Highland Fling over a pair of crossed sabres. He whizzed along the passages on a tea-trolley. ('You'll find it's much safer to ride one of the horses out in the paddock, Mr Sellers', said the Queen.) The Duke of Edinburgh, not to be left out, set fire to the table-cloth.

The royal family need their playtime and private moments to be as organised for them as their regimented official duties. Time can't be allowed to drift by, as it does for the rest of us. They rely upon, like any inmate in a long-stay maximum security hospital, a vast staff of professionals and a rigid routine. Chamberlains, major-domos, cup-bearers, ladies-in-waiting, keepers of this and that. Sellers functioned as the court jester, venting his folly. He wasn't given a bladder on a stick, but he was expected to throw himself into Charades (Britt had to mime being a lobster), Blind Man's Bluff and other such games from the Edwardian nursery which form the royal family's mental atmosphere. When, on Boxing Day, Sellers went shooting, he played the part of the Indian Army Colonel – Purdey, tweed jodhpurs, black boots – who had appeared as one of Wee Sonny's disguises in *The Naked Truth*; when he went water-skiing in Windsor Great Park he created hilarity by getting himself thoroughly ducked – their highnesses were not to know his incompetence wasn't being faked. 'He's fallen in da wahtar!' they squealed – a Goonish catch phrase. (Lord Snowdon, taking pity, invented an extra-long twin cross bar, so that he could stand alongside Sellers and offer instruction – to no avail.)

☆ ★ ☆

More in Sellers' line than parlour games, rough shooting and sports, was the regal theatricality. He played the present Queen twice: on a special edition of *The Goon Show*, called 'The Starlings', where she was called the Duchess Boil de Spudswell, who opens London's anti-bird zone ('May all who stand on it perish' she quavers – Sellers being at his most mezzo); and secondly on a (feeble) *Fool Britannia* track – the Queen admonishes Princess Anne for horse riding in the house, and Sellers' voice is what he called his 'It's Chocolate Time' voice: a breathy, Kensington female voice, based on a Cadbury's cocoa advertisement. In 1974 he made *The Great McGonagall* at Wilton's Music Hall in the East End. This was a vision of imperial England as vaudeville – with Victoria herself, the original royal en-chantress, positioned on a dais in the centre of the stage, surrounded by cardboard hills and cardboard deer. (She speaks in a haughty contralto that combines the Duchess of Boil de Spudswell with 'It's Chocolate Time'.) It is possibly my personal favourite of Sellers' lost films; it is full of genuine cavortings and starts with Sellers mincing about in the dressing-room applying make-up to Milligan – layers of putty, grease paint, a snout, a wig. (Milligan's head is turned into a kiddie's junk model.) There is silent-movie ooompahhing music; we see the clapperboard snap and the cast assembling and changing their costumes. The film doesn't hide its artifices, yet has its own powerful logic. Apart from Sellers' Victoria (he named his second daughter Victoria because of the aura of dewy roses and nineteenth-century bric-à-brac) and Milligan's poet, the actors play lots of parts – this is a travelling rep. company from the nineteenth century, lit by gas flares and footlights, hamming it up amongst flaking plaster thrones and bright red curtains, scaffolding and dust sheets.

What I particularly like is the incorporation of out-takes – they preserve a ramshackle flow. John Brown, the Queen's emissary, arrives with an invitation to Balmoral. The actor (Victor Spinetti) is having trouble with his beard and fluffs his lines. 'It's OK, keep run-ning,' says Joe McGrath, off camera. 'I'd like to do it all again. I was way over the top,' comments Milligan. The director isn't keen on starting again – he wants to maintain the energy and pace. 'What am I supposed to do here?' persists Milligan. 'Am I supposed to re-peat what he [Spinetti] says?' In the next take, Milligan dries. 'He stopped because he [Spinetti] laughed this time,' interjects John Bluthal. Milligan looks into the camera, at a loss. The fourth take: nothing happens. 'You didn't say *action*!' says Bluthal. McGrath says, 'I'm trying to.' Finally, Milligan successfully repeats the line: 'Balmoral Castle. Next Thursday. Four o'clock.' McGrath says, 'OK, lunch', and the actors tear off their wigs and exeunt – and we see them eating at a trestle table outside by the catering lorry.

If *The Great McGonagall* (which is virtually unknown) had been made by Czechoslovakians with unspellable names and brought to the West in a badly dubbed scratched print, it would be regularly listed in the *Sight and Sound* poll of egg-heads' best films. Sellers was 'in his element', McGrath told me, with the Goonish music hall and magic lantern style, with Prince Albert being dressed as Hitler, with Queen Victoria humming along to a jazz piano. 'Peter loved having the dress on as Queen Victoria. He was on a high as an actor,' says John Bluthal. This enthusiasm may have been due to the fact that ten years previously, for the real Queen's thirty-ninth birthday, he had made a fifteen-minute home movie which had util-ised similar techniques. At a personal cost to himself of six thousand pounds – home-movie it may have been but, like the Britt wedding day photoplay, it was professionally edited and dubbed – Sellers had deftly interlinked his own nostalgia for ropey music hall sketches with the royal family's instinct for tableaux. (The lavatory at Kensington Palace, incidentally, is situated in the centre of a large bathroom – a throne.)

In the Queen's film, Britt played Queen Victoria and (or perhaps as) a silent-movie vamp; Lord Snowdon was a one-legged golfer and a queer gangster ('That's *entirely* my concern,' he lisped when asked, by a Brooklynese Sellers, how he was gonna wipe out a rival mobster); Princess Margaret was Herself; and Sellers was Fred Thrump, an illusionist. He was going back not only to his Palla-dium act, when he'd been the hapless quick-change artiste holding a stuffed crocodile and claiming to be 'Queen Victoria when she were a lad';[*] he was also, as so often, tempting fate and reverting to (and mocking) the earnest vaudevillians who filled his childhood. (In many respects, and as a man who alters all the time, he always *was* one of these quick-change artistes.)

Thrump did the standard sub-standard repertoire – Richard III, Hunchback of Notre Dame, Captain Bligh, Toulouse Lautrec – and then, after the 'Goodness Gracious Me' Pakistani doctor, he said 'I will now do, in what I can safely say is the world record time of six and one quarter seconds, my celebrated impression of Her Royal Highness the Princess Margaret'. Sellers ran behind a screen and threw coats, bloomers and baggy shirts into the air – and the *real* PM emerged. She waved to the audience, sashayed back behind the screen, and Sellers re-appeared: 'I broke the record! Six seconds!' The film ended – another homage to Sellers' past – with the entire cast singing 'We're Riding Along on the Crest of a Wave'. The film was less *Goon Show* than Gang Show.

☆　★　☆

As he had been capable of believing, with Sophia and Nanette, that a film-set relationship was a real relationship, it took no effort at all to believe that he was in love with Princess Margaret and that she would marry him. He sent her romantic letters (which at one point he wanted back, pending the day when they could be buried with him in his coffin); he tried to get his spirit medium, Maurice Woodruff, to predict the regal wedding day – he pointed the astrologer in the direction his predictions should take by passing him the cryptic message: 'With equal pace, impartial Fate knocks at the palace as at the cottage gate'; and he gave Snowdon hi-fi equipment, cameras, a CIA bugging device capable of picking up conversations within a hundred metre radius, and a Riva speedboat in what he hoped would be part-exchange. Princess Margaret, he said, wore the same size bra as Sophia Loren – what further possible sign and portent did the world need?

---

[*] He repeated the gag on *The Muppet Show* in 1978: the deadbeat matinée idol attired in Viking Helmet and a corset, trying to impersonate Queen Victoria at Bognor.

As crackpot behaviour it was well up to standard. At least Loren had had Ponti to return to and be normal with and Nanette Newman was safe within the security of her marvellous ménage. But Princess Margaret, as Sellers saw, was defenceless. Her life, like his, was histrionics. 'I've never known her especially enjoy protocol,' said Sellers, 'but she knows she has to live with it. Yet I have taken her out to lunch without a detective or chauffeured car and she simply doesn't enjoy that.' In other words, actually liking the bowing and scraping isn't part of the issue; she simply cannot operate without it. She'd be unable to cope – at one with those dazed women you see in streets and parks who transpire to be psychiatric out-patients. To give the impression that she'd be adequately looked after, Sellers adopted strange tactics. He invited the princess to his house in Clarges Street and (like the little boy in *Home Alone*) he had tapes of chatter and hubbub playing so that it seemed an off-stage party was in full swing.

Sellers turned his pad into a theatre; the other place – or factory of make-believe – he often met the princess at was the studio, where she would be his special guest. (When she visited *The Magic Christian* she got in the way of the action and was sat on by Graham Stark.) He was most put out, on *Casino Royale*, however, when she seemed intrigued by Welles. Sellers had boasted all morning that she was due to appear. 'Then, Princess Margaret *came*,' laughed Welles, 'and walked on the set and passed him by and said, "Hello, Orson, I haven't seen you for days!" *That* was the real end. *That's* when we couldn't speak lines across to each other. "Orson, I haven't seen you for days!" absolutely killed him. He went white as a sheet because *he* was going to get to present *me*.'

Sellers was already adopting a proprietorial attitude; Princess Margaret's presence meant that he could compliment himself on his choice of powerful friends. Snowdon was a companion, too, in his own right. Both men enjoyed practical jokes (Snowdon thinks it a hoot to pass people pens that emit electric shocks); both, obviously, were passionate about photography. One of the reasons Snowdon's portraits are successful, I think, is that his work has a comic edge. Do his subjects collude? Do they know how much they are revealing about themselves? John Mortimer's episcopal signet ring and chubby drooping hand; Iris Murdoch's bag lady coat; Barry Humphries thrusting his head through a urinal; or Robert Runcie, the Archbishop of Canterbury, looking like a melting wedding cake in the robes he'd had designed for the royal wedding of Charles and Diana in 1981: above and beyond the technical expertise of such shots, we can detect an impish intelligence and imagination being brought to bear. But Snowdon never captured Sellers as Sellers, only Sellers as, say, Old Sam, in *The Optimists of Nine Elms*, pottering about in the mud on the edge of the Thames, flapping open his coat to reveal the Union Jack lining. In any case, 'we tend to put off taking photographs and talk endlessly about the latest cameras, electronic gadgets and fast cars,' he has written. '[Sellers] will go down in history as one of the great performers of our time.'

Snowdon also appeared on the *Casino Royale* set, much to the surprise of Joe McGrath and Charles Feldman, who had barred journalists and photographers from the studio. It turned out to be Sellers' doing. Snowdon took some snaps of Britt just prior to her wedding (Sellers tried to encourage her to unbutton her blouse and appear dishevelled – he wanted the readers of the *Sunday Times* to see what the Arch Goon had acquired); and the Snowdons and the Sellers went on holiday together in Sardinia as guests of the Aga Khan, with a party that included Princess Alexandra, Angus Ogilvy and Kirk Douglas. Such a trip might well have symbolised Sellers' arrival in High Society, you'd have thought. But he was not satisfied. He wanted to be a renowned photographer – 'If I hadn't been an actor, I would like to have been a photographer' – with an earldom thrown in. Back at Elstead, at dinner, when the Snowdons were invited to see the home-movie for the millionth time, Sellers was pleased to observe the marital friction. 'PM used to be very nasty to her husband,' recalls Hattie Stevenson. 'They used to say the most awful things to each other. I can remember dinner parties and they'd argue right across the table.'

Sellers didn't help matters when he instigated the Affair of the Mighty Mellotron. (It rivals in absurdity 'The Mighty Wurlitzer' episode of *The Goon Show*, in which Neddie Seagoon breaks the land speed record in a cinema organ.) What happened is that he was staying at the Dorchester, having grown bored of Britt, and to keep him company in his suite he had a Mellotron. 'This was the first time we'd seen a Mellotron,' says Alan Clare's wife Bloom. 'Peter decided to buy one for us. A huge thing which filled our flat. We lived round it. Peter had been thinking Alan could do arrangements on it – but it couldn't change key. Eventually Peter decided he wanted to give it to Princess Margaret. "If you don't want it, Princess Margaret will have it." Some men came and took it away. Spike complained that Peter gave things, then took them away again – so then we got eight hundred pounds of Knights Piano, which arrived by post.'

The mechanical monster – all tubes, flues, flashing lights and gears ('It's capable of doing forty knots,' said Sellers) – was delivered to Kensington Palace. Princess Margaret couldn't be kept from it. She perched on the stool and attempted Phantom of the Opera arpeggios. She pretended she was coming up through the floor in an Odeon. The trouble was, the instrument finished off the doomed marriage. 'She adored it; he positively loathed it,' vouchsafed the courtier, Robin Douglas-Home. It was a big souvenir of Sellers, there in the royal front room; it became a symbol of the couple's dissent. Snowdon moved out. Sellers did his best to move in. 'Once you've got over the fact that you are sitting down eating bread and eggs with the royal family, you realise the whole family together is just a very normal family,' he who had no conception of family normality bragged. (Was this aspect of his character – the Sellers who sinks in our estimation as he starts to consort with the ruling class – inspiration for the obnoxious revue comic, played by Rowan Atkinson, in *The Tall Guy*?)

Unlike Sophia and Nanette, who did their best to put some distance between themselves and Sellers, with Princess Margaret, whom he was now calling 'Ma'am Darling', it was Sellers who retired. The official reason he gave was that he'd wanted to have an affair but 'couldn't because I knew I would never be able to look Tony straight in the eyes again without feeling guilty'. Sellers was not one to experience guilt or compunction, and the real reason for his withdrawal was that Princess Margaret refused to marry and ennoble him. 'It's amazing. Princess Margaret has made it quite clear she won't marry again. Having been through it once and, God knows, marriage breakdown happens all the time, she won't do it again. She is a very resolute woman. When she decides to do something she goes through with it.'

Sellers was particularly hurt by the Roddy Llewellyn gossip – he wished that such rumours were accruing to him. 'I've never discussed Roddy Llewellyn with her,' he said sniffily, before having to admit: 'He has been at Kensington Palace when I have, but I've never noticed her show any sign of outward affection for him.' Sellers felt resentful, overlooked. He went to stay at the Royal Lodge, Windsor, and phoned Michael Jeffery asking if he'd ring back 'and pretend to call me away for an urgent appointment. Get me away from here. I am so bored.' The ruse worked and when Sellers returned to Jeffery, at the Inn on the Park, he gave him a stack of Clarence House crested notepaper and a roll of toilet tissue – the royal family use that uncomfortable grease-proof stuff customised with the coat of arms. The next day, Ma'am Darling's detective was downstairs at the hotel. What was about to happen? Arrest for the pilferage? Execution for the lie about the frantic summons? The detective was returning Sellers' three-quarters empty bottle of shampoo which he had left in the bathroom. 'Princess Margaret had commanded her staff to bring this nearly finished bottle all the way from Windsor specially,' says Jeffery, agog.

Was this an example of regal waste-not want-not economising or, as I see it, an act of defiance? (The detective's petrol would cost more than a jeroboam of Silvikrin.) But then who precisely was defying whom? Sellers, in leaving indiscreet traces of himself in the private quarters? The Princess, in pettishly signalling to her would-be swain that if he wants to clear out early, he'd better take his rubbish with him? They were obviously very aware of each other and had formed a strange alliance. 'I have had some good times in her company. She is great fun to be with, very kind and, at times, of great help to me,' Sellers said. Whether the relationship was actively sexual is almost an irrelevance. (One of her staff, questioned on this point on my behalf, answered snootily: 'Well, if she did, she had her eyes closed and she forgot about it immediately afterwards.') The point is that they were both shut off from people and superior, the princess by her position, Sellers by his nature. He had thoroughly enjoyed himself up until her rejection of his marriage hints. They had been to Ronnie Scott's jazz club; they had held seances. Suddenly, it was as if he had never been important to her; he felt inadequate and contemptuous. He telephoned Kensington Palace and, pretending to be Snowdon, gave a lurid description of nights on the tiles with Lady Jackie Rufus-Isaacs, Snowdon's current inamorata. She did not find this amusing, but neither did she retaliate. She was too isolated to feel the force of his coldness. Sellers' final taunt came in 1979. Ma'am Darling wanted to see him and she scribbled the following memorandum on a scrap of paper:

From Princess Margaret, Countess of Snowdon

May 25th – R.L. [Royal Lodge, Windsor]

May 30th – P.O.W. [Prince of Wales]

May 31st – I'm in Newcastle

June 1st – Away for Weekend

June 5th – *King and I*

June 6th – Kinetic Art

Sellers opted to squire her to Yul Brynner's revival of the Rodgers and Hammerstein musical. He insisted on taking Michael Jeffery, too. Sellers bought the lad a full-dress Yves St Laurent evening suit in Geneva. As late as he dared leave it on the day of the show, Sellers announced that he couldn't be bothered to go. He told his secretary, Sue Evans, to phone up Constance Spry for some flowers. He stood her up. He'd done his best to be incredibly discourteous, and he succeeded. He'd been so sensitive that he was not himself the man born to be king, he was senseless.

Ma'am Darling never got in touch with him again – though his influence did linger, as it so often did. Sellers had awoken in Princess Margaret a talent for doing impressions. To this day she likes to have a go at making amusing Bloodnok, Eccles and Clouseau noises. When he was invited to a private reception at Kensington Palace, Michael Holroyd, informed in advance of his hostess' party trick, attempted to ingratiate himself by – it has been alleged* – screaming with laughter and banging the table. It was the best Bluebottle the distinguished biographer had ever heard.

Princess Margaret had been speaking in her normal voice.

☆   ☆   ☆

Sellers' blue-blood fantasies went back a long way – to the remote Mendoza link with the Rufus-Isaacs'; to his belief that he was the Earl of Beaconsfield. Lady Jackie Rufus-Isaacs' brother, Lord Anthony, produced *The Blockhouse*, and he told me that 'when he came to dinner, he'd be playing a character, and he'd remain as that character throughout the entire evening. This enabled him to tell the most outrageous lies about himself. He was brilliant like that.'

It was an effort, though, and one wonders why he bothered. Revenge? In 1958, he had asked Herbert Kretzmer: 'Do you care for the Mayfair clique?' – 'Can't stand them,' Kretzmer answered, somewhat surprised at the question. 'I hate that chi-chi set,' said Sellers. 'Hate 'em.' The resentments may be traced (like so much in his life) to the end-of-the-pier, when he had had to beat time in a dance band. He never forgave America for branding him with success; he never forgave England's hunt-ball types for treating him as a failure. Some shag in Somerset once called him 'that blasted kettle-drummer' and a Brighton swell, during the same period, had referred to him as a 'ruddy muckface'. Now, however, the class

---

* By William Donaldson in *Great Disasters of the Stage* (London, 1984), page 45. ('The Least Successful Impressionist'.)

which had noticed him only to look down on him were attempting to flatter him – but Sellers wasn't to be beguiled. Their flatteries didn't amount to much. According to him, what his rich hosts and hostesses were still expecting was entertainment. The difference was no money taken at the door. The Mayfair set were commanding performances from him for free – and doing him a service by receiving him. 'You find yourself sitting in a chair', he said, 'and people are crowding round saying, "He's bound to come up with something any second – he's jolly funny, I know he's funny, I've seen him being funny. It's only a matter of time. Turn away from him, and look back when he's funny. . ."'

He lampooned these sorts of condescending idiots as Prince Rudi in *The Prisoner of Zenda*, whose vowels are so plummy he has a speech impediment; or as the drunken toff in Alan Clare's song 'Eaton Square Blues', wailing 'Come back to me, Bobo.' It is fair to say, however, that Sellers' loathing for the nobility concealed a good deal of fascination. A famous man has access anywhere, and for all his mockery of 'Hooray Henrys', 'Chinless Wonders', 'the Nigels' and 'the Eaton Square Mob', he chose to run and mix with the clotted cream. When asked why – or perhaps *why for fuck's sake*? – his answer was that of the detached actor, gathering material: 'I feel a completely new world has opened up, [of] people that I probably would never have met, and as an observer of human nature, I find this [*le mot juste*] fascinating.' I think Sellers the anthropologist can be quickly discounted. If he had started to associate with royalty because their company augmented him, his acquaintanceship with the landed gentry – a spin-off of the Ma'am Darling cocktail circuit – was part of a similar drive to attain rank and station. First, these were people (like him) above the common mass; second (unlike him) they were established – they had history, pedigree. They knew who they were, where they'd come from. Sellers, with his personal background of vagabondage, found this alluring. There was a strong suggestion of a different, better world. He wanted to acquire it; he thought that then he might no longer feel so fluid, be in such painful flux.

And so he began to attend dinner parties, where he could dis-simulate; he went to Ascot, Henley and Covent Garden. (This is the period when he dressed, spoke and comported himself as Robert Danvers.) He wandered in silk-lined rooms and perched on golden furniture – and he married Miranda Quarry, the step-daughter of Lord Mancroft. It was one of the worst decisions of his life, and proof of how berserk he was. He'd assumed that he could judge lords and ladies by his own standards – that they would pride themselves on knowing him, as he'd felt himself enhanced by befriending the palace. It was not to be. He was seen through and denigrated as never before – or at least not since his early drum-ming days. (He'd managed to make history repeat itself.) Once, invited to Mrs Desmond Guinness' stately home, the hostess greeted another of the guests, Michael Fish, the dressmaker, effu-sively: 'Mr Fish, I know exactly who you are!' She then turned to Miranda and said, 'My dear, how absolutely marvellous to see you again.' She then glanced Sellers' way and commented, 'You must be Peter Sellers, Miranda's new husband. I'm afraid I've no idea who you are. You see, I never ever go to the pictures.'

There was going to be no prospect of his being appreciated as a source of reflected glory; and as a self-made man, concerned for his career, his money and flash were deemed infra dig. Instead of get-ting himself accepted by an élite, he'd further divided himself from people – he remained a stranger. 'I feel I'm a totally different person [with Miranda's crowd] to the person I am when I'm with my own friends. [Who are they? The other Goons?] You know, I think I tend to be very boring to those people. But then, you see, people who don't know you, or know anything about you, tend to think of you in terms of some film they remember you in and probably ex-pect you to be someone you're not. I'm very introverted in this way. Very guarded. I don't open up at all, and I think that must be very boring to them. I let them believe what they want to believe, and if they think I'm a bore then they must get on with it.'

☆ ★ ☆

The two obvious cinematic results of Sellers-and-the-idle-rich were

There's a Girl in My Soup and *The Magic Christian*. (In each he was superficial, glazed, languid.) The latter's première was held on December 11th 1969 at the Odeon, Kensington, and there was a gala party afterwards at Les Ambassadeurs, Hyde Park Corner. The guests included the Beatles, the film's cameos – Polanski, Yul Brynner, Laurence Harvey, etc. – and famous faces like David Frost, the Monty Python Team (Chapman and Cleese wrote the uncredited screenplay), and Britt, from whom Sellers had been divorced a twelvemonth previously, who was escorted by her step-son, Michael. Princess Margaret and Lord Snowdon watched the film together but arrived separately at the bash – and the earl went and sat at Lady Jackie and Lord Anthony Rufus-Isaacs' table. Miranda did not materialise: '[She] isn't speaking to me right now', Sellers explained. No matter; he played at being a king – Rex Finchley – with Ma'am Darling. It was all rather an extension of a film fantasia; Sellers had melted into the rôle of debonair man about town. He was Danvers and he was Sir Guy Grand – and Danvers and Sir Guy are so totally certain of themselves, they are remote and reckless; there is no interchange when they meet other people – they don't need other people, except as the equivalent of blow-up dolls for sex (Danvers) or as accomplices for practical jokes (Sir Guy). They are both half-dead.

If Chance the living saint is Sellers as he wanted to be, Danvers was Sellers as he liked to think he was. It was brave of him, I think, to play an ageing playboy, whose hairbrush is clogged, whose belly flops over his belt when he forgets to suck it in. He was parodying his own public image – the forty-something endlessly chasing the teeny-somethings – and he gave his capped-teeth grin a big workout. Danvers goes to society weddings like Harold, in *Harold and Maude*, goes to funerals: for the bodies. *There's a Girl in My Soup* begins with a swift seduction of the bride (Nicola Pagett) before she goes away on honeymoon; and barely have the credits finished rolling than our hero is in bed with a bridesmaid (Gabrielle Drake). Then comes the fling with Goldie Hawn – it isn't love; it is simply that Marion is always one up on Danvers' stratagems: she can see him for what he is, and this amuses him. The film concludes ninety minutes later with the approach of another bimbo – they seem to come off an assembly line – named Paola, played by Françoise Pascal, with whom Sellers proceeded to have an affair. The first time he met her was when they did the scene in the garden, swinging the child. Danvers can't take his eyes off the au pair's wobbling boobs – and neither could Sellers. He enjoyed staring at her bosom so much, he insisted on seventeen takes. 'I don't think I can do this scene!' said Sellers, who kept saying 'boom, boom, boom' as the knockers swayed back and forth.

Françoise was currently being squired by Terence Frisby, who had written the screenplay. At a party given by Victor Lownes in the Playboy Club to celebrate the wrap, she met Sellers again. 'Do you want to come back to my place?' he asked. 'Sure,' she said. He made her sit through hours of tape-recorded gurgles and yelps – not post-modern music by Karlheinz Stockhausen, but playbacks of his Indian voices and throat-clearing practice. He produced marijuana and when she was doped he took her to his web. 'Peter was a nice guy,' she says. 'I only slept with him twice. He was an awkward man, even in bed.'

There's a Girl in My Soup conveys Sellers' predatoriness – the fellow with tons of money, who doesn't know what it is like not to be pampered, who does what he likes all the live long day. Sir Guy, in *The Magic Christian*, is Danvers taken to a caricatured extreme: the upper-class accent is drawlier, the hair-do is more preposterously bouffant, the tedium at the centre of his life is more intense, and his pocket is deeper. Indeed money – what people will wade through to get it – is the film's motive. It is meant to be a satire on cupidity. 'I've always been aware of the power of money', Sellers once said. 'The way they wave it in front of you to get you to do things. In fact, you can buy anyone in the film industry, and I mean anybody – including myself.'

The film is a chain of bribery scenes – Cleese as the condescending Sotheby's auctioneer, allowing the Rembrandt to be ravaged; Graham Chapman as the captain of the Oxford eight, willing to spoil the University boat race; Milligan as an officious traffic warden, chewing and swallowing the No Parking ticket he has issued (the concluding exchange was ad-libbed; 'You needn't eat the plastic', said Sellers. 'I'm here every Thursday', said Milligan. 'Fridays are better for me,' said Sellers, whizzing away). Despite all this, however, it isn't Sir Guy's victims who are exposed as wormy and cheap – it's himself. If you ask yourself who is the most culpable, the giver or taker of bribes, it has to be the former – he's the instigator, taking advantage of human weakness. Sir Guy's – and Sellers' – cynical empty-heartedness is revealed in every so-called gag. Sleepy-eyed though he be, at the core of *The Magic Christian* is the turbulent tempter 'ere the accuser of mankind: Satan. (Sellers has a silver streak through his hair – a devil's quiff.)

Was Sellers ever aware that Sir Guy's actions, which he endorsed, rebounded upon him? That to be so rich, you believe yourself above the law, is not an admirable supposition? '*The Magic Christian* gave him the chance to express what he felt about the human race in a commercial film,' says Milligan. 'The whole thing could have been written *about* Peter instead of *for* him.' One of his pranks, which wasn't always appreciated – it illustrates his lordliness in all things – was to enter a cockpit after landing and to tip a pilot as one would any common taxi-driver in London or New York. Colonel Hamilton Lawrence, USMC (ret.), who was the chief pilot for a charter company called Executive Jet Aviation, based in Geneva, recalls a hundred Swiss franc banknote being stuffed into the shirt pocket of his uniform: 'Nice flight,' said Sellers. 'Have a drink on me.' – 'THIS WAS MY FIRST TIP, EVER!' gulped the pilot. 'Does one tip a retired colonel of American Marines as one would some Brooklyn cabbie? Should a passenger paying in the order of a thousand dollars per hour for private jet transportation feel any obligation to tip his crew at flight's end, especially with a piddling equivalent of twenty-five American dollars? PROBABLY NOT.' The colonel passed the money back to Sellers, who 'looked unbelieving but accepted it without comment'.

There seemed to be a confusion in his mind between his

personal love of money – and the goodies and freedoms it allowed – and his contempt for those whose services or products he felt he needed, commissioned and had to pay for. 'Now is the time to enjoy it,' he said of his loot in October 1962. 'If I see some gadget or car and want it – I buy it. I have the bloody thing. Everybody's provided for, and I'm in the black with the tax people, so what I've got is my own, and I enjoy it. I certainly haven't got a guilt complex about spending . . . I don't believe in doing charity work publicly [or privately come to that].* I don't believe in this Look-God-I've-been-good-today mentality. If I do it, I want to do it unseen, not to make my niche up in Heaven a little larger.'

The possession of large amounts of money, which started to come his way regularly in the early and middle Sixties, unwrapped new temptations – principally, the capability to get away from things, to become self-inclusive and unapproachable. The great evil of money, as applied to Sellers, is that he could dodge life; and when he said – as he did often – 'people will swim through shit if you put a few bob in it', it is not the swimmers who deserve our scorn, it is the moon-struck madman on the sidelines, flinging in the coins. This is the Roman emperor again, Caesar Sellers, unwittingly giving us an image of *his* avarice, *his* greed; this is how he soiled co-stars, directors and producers. He was thrilled and sickened in equal measure when folk obeyed him (weaknesses were confirmed). 'Deep down, Peter, too, has little regard for the morality of the human race,' Milligan has said, to no surprise.

☆　☆　☆

Twinkle, twinkle, little star,
Who the hell do you think you are?

The royal family didn't get uppish with him (it was *he* who was

---

* Here's the bare bones of a joke Sellers used to tell: billionaire wants to give money to an orphanage – 'Make out fifty grand to each child – hold on, look, before Christmas, take out eighty grand in cash – ten thousand for each child – cross that out – oh, fuck 'em.' This comment on Sellers' attitude to money and other people may be strung along – shaggy dogged – into a twenty minute spot.

uppish with *them*), but Sellers, according to the gentrified descen-
dants of 'a Dubliner born plain Arthur Guinness whose grandpa,
they say, got accidental eminence when he let the hops burn
brown,* was deemed to lack class and breeding. The Mendoza and
Rufus-Isaacs link was distant and tenuous, and anyway Jewish – as
was the (defunct) earldom of Beaconsfield, which had been created
for Benjamin Disraeli; and then there was the problem of his being
an actor, an unholy, threadbare trade (Miranda didn't know who
Henry Fonda was when she was introduced to him at a party).
Sellers tried to compensate for these lacks with his money – astro-
nomical amounts.

His credo was put succinctly and honestly in December 1976, in
the midst of a discussion about *The Pink Panther Strikes Again*:
'We've all made a lot of money, and it looks as if we shall all make
even more on this one. Money makes you watertight; as Kubrick
used to say, "Get some FUCK YOU money in the bank, then you
can afford to mess about." He's proved that. Having earned my
FUCK YOU money, has it made much difference? You see, I've
never got hung up on money, I think that's the secret. I've never
been a manipulator of money. Okay, fine, a couple of people
around me have done wonderful things for me [accountants,
lawyers and such] – made sure I haven't acted foolishly and so
on. But I've never coveted money, like some people do. I've
never hoarded the stuff. I've always thought, great, it's good to have
a few bob because you can go out and get the goods. Buy yourself a
nice home ... I always knew I could take care of myself [but]
I never knew I would get into this sort of league. But listen, what
can you buy? I know the old saying about all the things that money
cannot buy. There is a lot of truth in that ... I'll tell you what, it
gives me a certain amount of confidence. People somehow treat
you differently. It's strange how in awe some people are of
money. . . .'

---

* The inestimable Hugh Kenner's discovery, in *A Colder Eye: The Modern Irish
  Writers* (New York, 1983), page 212.

Miranda wasn't in awe of money, nor was she extravagant; she simply expected there to be plenty of it in the background or as part of the air she breathed. It was what facilitated leisure – which to Sellers looked from a distance like happiness. Sellers had met her at the London to Melbourne car rally at Crystal Palace in 1969. He fed her with marijuana-spiked honey and later, or on another occasion, he tried to be impressive by consuming sugar lumps soaked with LSD, which made him sick. He was a middle-aged man in the Age of Aquarius, an era of Krays and Carnaby Street, sex and drugs. The mockery of, and underlying affection for, the Union Jack and the national anthem, the loony patriotism of the 'I'm Backing Britain' (over a cliff – as Milligan would add) campaign, all goes back to *The Goon Show*; and whatever else it demonstrates of Sellers' caprices, *Casino Royale* is a window on the fashions of the time: yellowish gold armour-plate mini-skirts, feathery head-dresses, Victoriana crossed with the mystic East, and so on, created by Guy Laroche, Paco Rabanne and Julie Harris.

Dressed in loosely-knotted scarves and snakeskin jerkins, Sellers and his very youthful moll were familiar features on the Swinging London scene: the Trattoria Terrazza, Soho, San Lorenzo's, Beau-champ Place, Annabel's, Berkeley Square (named for the Marquess of Londonderry's sister) and Tramps, Jermyn Street – where Sellers and Miranda held their wedding reception. If peers and prosperous paupers met and mingled, our man was there, spreading the gospel of self-indulgence; he was frantic to be part of the frivolity. On January 16th 1969 he told a crowd of four hundred and fifty students: 'I've used marijuana with groups of friends and there's no harm in it . . . I mean, it's better than drink. . . . Some of the hard drugs are bad – LSD is a frightening thing. But marijuana is all right, and court sentences for using it are ridiculous. It heightens the senses and one of the best ways of using it is when listening to music. You can hear music as you've never heard it before.'

One of the people influenced by these words and who tried to follow his example was his own son, who was suspended from school, King Alfred's, North London, for three weeks and threatened with expulsion. As Michael told me: 'He came up to the school where I'd been caught smoking pot and gave me this whole lecture in front of the headmistress: "You can't do that, it's setting a bad example . . . it's against the law . . . it's not right . . . blah blah blah. . . ." Next day he's at the London School of Economics. They ask him if he smokes cannabis. "Yeah, it's great. . ." Didn't do my case any good! He couldn't handle drink and drugs at all. It took him too far over the edge. It made him more of what he was – he got reflective and introverted, and this induced his paranoia. Drugs wound him up, and he began to have doubts about himself and whether he could act. I've seen him take cocaine – especially when he was on the fringes of the pop industry. He had the same manager as George Harrison and he was introduced to people like Keith Moon – became friendly with him shortly before he died. Cocaine was free and running at those parties. It didn't do him any good. He was tempting fate. He didn't care. He was more interested in getting stoned and enjoying himself.'

☆　★　☆

Here is a curiosity, and a post-scriptum to the above. God knows how it came into being or why it was smuggled out, but a bootleg tape-recording is in my possession of Sellers having a seriously relaxed chat about hallucinogens with the Beatles, during an off-duty encounter at the Apple HQ. As a testament to Sellers' rapport with John Lennon – and as a souvenir of a meeting between great men of the Me Decade – it has minor historical significance. This is my transcription. It has an inconsequential surreal rapture.

LENNON:	Now, what do you think about Mock-Tudor Shithouses in Weybridge and places like that?
RINGO:	I don't mind them being in Weybridge – it's just when they try and put them in London, they get in the way of the traffic.
LENNON:	As you said yesterday, neither your arse nor your elbow.
RINGO:	I said that?
LENNON:	I'll never forget it . . . Pull up a star's seat. We've

been lucky enough this evening to secure the
talents of Mr Peter Sellers here – who is going to
give us Number Three.

SELLERS: Number Three, folks, Number Three.

LENNON: How about that, folks? That was Number Three
from Peter Sellers. Now on to the next round.

SELLERS: And there's more where that came from.

LENNON: If we ask him really nicely he'll probably do
Number Five.

SELLERS: Yes I might.

LENNON: Over to you Peter.

RINGO: He *is* doing Number Five.

SELLERS: I can't count that far these days – I used to be
able to.

[*Soft laid-back giggles from everybody*]

LENNON: Do you remember when I gave you that grass in
Piccadilly?

SELLERS: Really stoned me out of my mind, really. Acapulco gold, wasn't it? Fantastic.

LENNON: Exactly.

SELLERS: Sorry I'm not holding any right now.

LENNON: We can't get it.

SELLERS: Oh yeah?

LENNON: I've given up, you know – as stated by 'Unter
Damn' Yer [Hunter Davies] in *The Beatles'
Actual Life Story*.

SELLERS: Well, I'm sorry about that, fellas, but I, you
know, if I'd known I was going to see you, of
course, I would have had some on me. Because I
know how you love it and dig chewing that
thing.

McCARTNEY:* Got you, Pete. You got it? Can you dig it?

SELLERS: *Ohh* yes, God I can dig it.

---

* Paul McCartney wrote and performed the soundtrack for *The Magic Christian* –
the lyrics are grab, grab, grab;
   'If you want it, here it is, come and get it,
   But you'd better hurry 'cause it's going fast.'

LENNON:	Do you want to make the scene in the Gents lavatory?
SELLERS:	That's a groove.
LENNON:	Way out.
SELLERS:	[*puzzled*] Exit?
LENNON:	Just don't leave the needles lying around, you know. We've got a bad reputation.

☆ ★ ☆

The Sixties' combination of bliss and depression, insouciance and willed chaos, mock innocence and authentic brutishness could have been an emanation of Sellers' mood and toy-life. The relationship with Miranda was up and down, on and off. He was always arguing with her. He deliberately crashed his Rolls because of something she'd said – he didn't like women to have minds of their own. (She wouldn't retract, so he sent the car into reverse and rammed the vehicle behind as well.) He took her on his yacht ('I don't use it very much now,' he sighed, affecting aristocratic disdain. 'I charter it mainly. . . Actually I think material possessions are a bit of a bind really. Oh, you imagine it would be nice to have a boat, then you take on all the problems of owning a boat and there are many, so it becomes something of a problem') and he introduced her to Leslie Bricusse, Tony Newley, David Niven and Roger Moore. He courted her for two years, spoiling her rotten with frocks from Zandra Rhodes and Yves St Laurent – whilst simultaneously, though of course also separately, he romanced Francesca Hilton (Zsa Zsa Gabor's daughter) and Titi Wachtmeister (former girlfriend of Britt's younger brother), whom he thought seriously of marrying because the photographs he'd taken of her in the shower were 'beautiful'.

He cavorted like his James Bond character from *Casino Royale*: 'a bounder and a vulgarian, a joke shop spy, a sexual acrobat who leaves a trail of beautiful dead women behind him like blown roses' – and it was Miranda whom he selected for capture on August 24th 1970. She was so surprised that she was going to be a bride, she didn't buy a special kaftan until the morning of the ceremony, which was held at the Caxton Hall (where Sellers had married Anne nineteen years previously). The bridesmaids were Tabitha and Thomasina, Miranda's dogs. The Best Man was Bert Mortimer, ever faithful, ever true. (Was it Sixties hypergamy in action?) He married her to spite her – to spite everybody. He phoned Anne and Britt moments before the service began to remonstrate with them. 'Look what you made me do! I'm having to marry a third time because my marriages to you didn't work.' They had divorced him; by his crazy reasoning, he could therefore put the blame for a doomed-from-the-start relationship squarely on the shoulders of Miranda's predecessors. His conception of cause and effect was the wayward child's – shifting responsibility on to its elders for its own malice and misdemeanours.

For the first year the couple lived in Cheyne Gardens, near the Albert Bridge. Sellers told visitors, 'This isn't my world actually. It belongs to an estate agent. It's a rented world. Rentaworld!' The unrealities intensified. The Irish government had declared the republic a tax haven for writers and artists. It was hoped that the members of High Bohemia would acquire the crumbling Georgian mansions and unwanted neo-gothick castles, which came with stabling for a thousand stallions, mead vats, pit bull kennels and village idiot servantry running the laundry through a gin still. After a party at San Lorenzo's on March 25th 1971 – the entire place bedecked with emerald green balloons and streamers in his honour, and with a guest list that included Ma'am Darling and Snowdon, Joan Collins, Warren Beatty and Shirley MacLaine – Sellers duly moved to a palatial residence, beyond the reach of the Inland Revenue, in the village of Maynooth, a few miles outside Dublin. Here, surrounded by a five mile stone wall, with five entrance lodges, was an estate fit for Rex Finchley and his queen. Carton House, Co. Kildare, was formerly the seat of the Dukes of Leinster. It abounds with colonnades, baroque plasterwork, Chinese Chippendale giltwood overmantels and barrel-vaulted ceilings covered in interlocking circles of oak and vine leaves. There are over a thousand acres of private park, containing cows, two and a half thousand pheasants and five hundred duck 'reared to enhance the wild population'.

Miranda, he said, 'is rather a special type of girl in so much that she is concerned with making a home'. Her concept of domesticity, however, wasn't what he'd led himself to expect. It wasn't connected to any innate motherliness. She designed water gardens and her taste for interior decoration tended towards psychedelic purple murals and ultra-violet lamps – which was all very hip and groovy. But what about washing up the saucepans? Where was her devotion? Where was Peg?

'Miranda we didn't really get on with,' Sarah Sellers told me, speaking on behalf of the whole family. 'She wasn't too crazy about us, either; but it wasn't malicious or intentional. She just had her life and ideas about how children should behave, and we didn't fit in very well . . .'

Neither did Sellers. His wife was alien to him. In London, there had been the clubs and discos to hide in; life had been given the illusion of liveliness. Exiled in Ireland, away from excitement, he and Miranda were on their own as a couple for the first time and Sellers felt a sterility round him. Like many in her class, raised to be seen and not heard, shoved off to boarding school and drilled in etiquette and good form, Miranda was courteous and cold. Her emotional relationships, like those of Lord Greystoke (apes), Princess Anne (horses) or John Aspinall (apes again), were with animals.* She filled Carton House with yapping dogs, cats and parrots; they were called her 'babies' and named for the anthropomorphised fauna in Beatrix Potter. Whilst she believed in governesses and draughty attic nurseries for human children, the fur and feather brigade were almost encouraged to befoul the floors and furniture. They were fed on fillet steaks and roast chicken; and when Michael, Sarah and Victoria came to stay, all Sellers' own real infants got to eat were Heinz baked beans.

---

* Also see the complete works of Jilly Cooper – where you have to keep alert to tell when she is describing men and when she is referring to handsome golden retrievers.

If Sellers had hoped that his wife's affection for her pets would be superceded by a new slavishness towards him, he'd misread her strength of character. She was not malleable. The serenity and invulnerability which she represented (and embodied), and which he had wanted to procure, defeated him. Miranda (in his view) was destroying him. She failed to notice him. Instead of being replenished, he felt belittled, subsidiary. The Anglo-Irish gentry, whom she seemed to know already, the Hely-Hutchinsons, the Knatchbull Huggessons, he spurned as stiff and stupid; they (he guessed) considered him ridiculous and impudent. Sellers hardened. 'I'm pissed off with the pleasures of society and Miranda's pissed off with me. That's what you get for being such a bloody snob [meaning himself?] I think that all Miranda ever really wanted was a bit of rough, a stroll across the tracks'. How could he assert himself? He crept downstairs one night and strangled a cockatoo. He threw a puppy in a swimming pool (whence it was rescued by Michael). He tore up the album of wedding photographs and confiscated Miranda's jewellery. He then decided to commit suicide.

☆ ★ ☆

It all sounds horrible from beginning to end. There was never an atmosphere of trust and easiness, and Miranda – now Miranda, Lady Nuttall and a friend of the Earl of Stockton – told me that 'my marriage to Peter was a difficult and ultimately painful time in my life'. When he'd realised she wasn't under his influence, Sellers had done his best to tear her nerves. As the falsely accused Hermione says to Leontes, so Sellers' wives could have said to him: *My life stands in the level of your dreams*. The paranoia which gathered momentum and destroyed the marriage to Anne, which had wrecked the marriage to Britt, and which would poison his relationship with Lynne, put paid to this alliance, too. Sellers was dejected to find out that he wasn't the person he wanted to be – and so he reasoned that the people he was with weren't what he thought they'd be, either. The worse his behaviour, the more Miranda had sought refuge with her menagerie; and at one point she fell ill with a rare strain of meningitis and was sent to a hospital in Oxford for specialist treatment. Sellers started to eavesdrop on her phone calls and brought his usual gamut of groundless suspicions into play: who had she been seeing? Was she having an affair? 'I want proof of your innocence.'

It looked like he was going to start getting violent. Instead, he was gripped with an ennui so stultifying, he thought he was dying. Was it, he wondered, his heart which was murmuring to him? 'I keep getting these moments of blackness,' he said. 'If you have thirteen [*sic*] heart attacks in a row, and the supply of blood is stopped for two minutes – I think something must happen. They did tell me I'd suffered no brain damage at all. I'm pretty sure deep down, and this is something only I know, that I come across these periods of blankness, loss of memory.' It was the nearest he came to confessing he was mad, that he needed psychiatric help. (He'd return to the idea prior to *Being There*: 'They . . . told me that I did not suffer any brain damage, but I have reason to believe that I did. My mind has deteriorated since then. I think I'm probably going a little soft in the head, which is why I have something in common with Chance.')

Sellers took to his bed for days on end – the gentleman of leisure turned into a shuffling recluse, who made a dash for the refrigerator at midnight when the rest of the household was asleep. He refused to speak to anybody, except Peg (through a ouija board). He played his private archive of radio tapes – *Variety Bandbox, Ray's a Laugh*, and especially *The Goon Show*. We can see, from what he'd told Barry Took at the mansion in October 1971, just where his mind was wandering – into the past. 'As a matter of fact, I have all my early recordings. I've got my very first broadcast . . . *Henry Hall's Guest Night, Variety Bandbox* . . . I could always get a *Workers' Playtime*. I remember Bill Gates, who was a very kind chap, who used to get me on when they were appearing at the corset factory. I remember taking these corsets home to my mother: [factory girl voice] "What size would your mother like? Here's our medium." I did ten minute things – those ten minute spots if you got ten minutes. It was such a struggle to get on them . . . I've never thought of anything other than I miss doing *The Goon Shows* on Sundays. The big thing in my life. If anyone said to me: "When did you have the most fun? What were your happiest days? Well, they were the Sundays ... what I did then, what I was part of, the Goons. . .'

Out of this longing came *The Last Goon Show of All*, recorded in London on April 30th 1972, with the royal family, Anne, the children, and Britt, in the audience. Sellers, who had scaled every height and removed every human obstacle without compunction, in order to get himself off radio and into films – because 'I always had an ambition to work in films as an art form' – looked to Goonery as a world without restrictions. Cocksure, standing behind the microphone, he had been fulfilled. *The Goon Show* was the one great good place where his raging and destructive fantasies could be converted into comedy. Alone in Ireland (Took says he was 'separated from his then wife, Miranda'), he was eager for yesteryear, and if time-machines existed to get him back where he could start over, he'd have been the first to buy the biggest and the best. Because he was a sentimentalist, he was quite able to overlook the fact that he'd always been unsatisfied and fretful; he was quite able to forget how he'd rejected Milligan. Nothing mattered except that he was absorbed and never gave way.

But still the bitterness persisted. Finally, he opened a drawer and took out the kitchen scissors. He went back to his room and toyed with the blades. In a frenzied rage, he gave his arteries a miss and chopped off all his hair. 'He looked ghastly,' said Bert Mortimer. 'I said, "God, what have you done?" Slowly he replied, "I think I'll become a monk – I'm going to join a monastery."'

It was this peculiar penitent who made *A Day at the Beach, Where Does It Hurt?, Alice's Adventures in Wonderland, The Block-house, The Optimists of Nine Elms, Soft Beds, Hard Battles*, and *Ghost in the Noonday Sun*. If Miranda was the wife people beneath the rank of baronet never knew ('She's not in this industry to begin with,' said Sellers, listing her virtues, 'I think it's a mistake to marry into this industry'), then these are the films hardly anybody saw.

Despite this, the Aer Lingus shuttle between Heathrow and Dublin was laden with producers and directors bearing projects to Maynooth. 'I went to Ireland to show him the script of *The Blockhouse*,' says Clive Rees. 'Bert Mortimer said he was out shooting coot with an air pistol. We had lunch with him and he said, "Yes". We came back to England and his agent said, "The answer is definitely NO." We said, "Can we get in touch with him?" Dennis Selinger didn't want us to. But Anthony Rufus-Isaacs rang him up direct and Peter said, "I'm going to do it. Don't worry."'

Leslie Linder wasn't so fortunate with the Hitler fantasy, *The Phantom v. The Fourth Reich*; neither, for a while, were the Boultings, with their Nazi occupied brothel comedy, originally entitled *The Saga of the Six Black Virgins*. Roy went across the Irish Sea and was able to claim, 'Peter's with us. The contract will be drawn up right away.' He returned to London, and the inevitable communiqué from Selinger: 'Roy, I don't quite know how to tell you this. Peter has gone cold on the subject. He's not going to do it.' Much to the Boulting twins' surprise, some months later Denis O'Brien telephoned: 'I've been talking with Peter. He thinks he made a mistake. Now he wants to do *Soft Beds, Hard Battles*. What are the chances?'

☆ ★ ☆

Can a thread be traced through his Irish phase films, so to dub them? *Alice's Adventures in Wonderland* was Sellers' second outing with Lewis Carroll. His first, Jonathan Miller's television film of 1966, is one of the best literary adaptations that I know. (It is perfection.) Talk about 'Off with their heads', the characters here are off their heads. It is a crazy, beautiful interpretation of the Victorian mind, and it seems to be set in the park of a neo-gothick haunted house that is actually an asylum. (A prediction of Sellers' court at Maynooth?) There are wonderful images: a broken rocking-horse in the long grass and nettles; a wrought iron cage containing pure white greyhounds – they are like heavenly hounds. The soundtrack is a complicated mix of hymns, music box tinkles, bird shrieks, whirring insects, and oriental plonks and strummings by Leon Goossens (oboe) and Ravi Shankar (sitar). Added to that medley are human cries and whispers. The mood manages to be both languor-ous and feverish – i.e. manic-depressive – and Alice's pre-adol-escent obsession with identity ('Who am I? That's the great puzzle') leads to the overwhelming answer: Nobody ever knows.

In this film, people's extraordinary gibberings, their energies and lassitude, are all seen as a means of avoiding stark reality and dread. Rules, regulations, laws (social and moral); religion and patriotism: they are structures created to give an illusion of order and purpose. Wilfrid Brambell, as the White Rabbit, is mad about time's passage and terrified he'll be late; the Hatter, March Hare and Dormouse, by contrast, have beaten time. They are stuck in a permanent six o'clock timewarp, their tea-table cobwebby and buzzed by wasps and the dronings of bugs and flies. (Peter Cook, Michael Gough, and Wilfrid Lawson form a gaunt, funereal trio.) Alan Bennett and Finlay Currie play a pair of Oxford dons, endlessly and meaning-lessly disputing points of medieval history – pedantry is another way of keeping back encroaching chaos. Their audience (other aca-demics? Undergraduates?) mutter and nod enthusiastically, and break into a jerky, zomboid race around the interior of a deserted chapel. Happily, there are prizes for each contestant. Everybody wins; everybody loses. It is the same difference.

If Carroll's fable has a message, in amongst its satire on Senior Common Room conversation, Christ Church mathematics lectur-ing and high-table rituals, it is that adulthood and/or maturity are not worth attaining. What awaits the keen and expectant child is disappointment, exasperation, despair. (Like *Peter Pan*, it is an in-dictment of adulthood.) Can anything have been more up Sellers' street? (Miller seems to be giving us a picture of the inside of Sellers' head.) 'I'm afraid I don't know just at the moment', says Alice, as the paranoia-inducing question *Who are you? Who are you?* gathers in intensity. 'I know who I was when I got up this morning, but I've changed several times since then . . . I'm afraid I can't explain myself. I'm not myself, you see.' ('No, I *don't* see!' snaps Michael Redgrave, as a dominie in a smoking cap, the cater-pillar.)

Sellers himself plays the King of Hearts. Along with university professors, churchmen and aesthetes (Malcolm Muggeridge and John Gielgud as the Gryphon and the Mock Turtle capering on the sea shore), the other illustrious public rôle-players and inmates of the bobby-hatch are royalty. Much of the hymn singing and band music that fills the film flows from the King and Queen's processions. They are always having processions. (Pageantry joins pedantry as a way of using up time.) Dwarves out of Velázquez paintings, roundheads and cavaliers, bishops, bewigged judges, the footmen from Versailles, minstrels strumming mandolins: these cavalcades mix Oxford's Encaenia, the fancy dress of the House of Lords, and the carryings-on of a military march-past. The institutions of power are in endless, flagging movement. Sellers, in an elaborate Austro-Hungarian tunic, totters and stoops in the rear column, his voice Henry Crun's. Confronted with the imbecility of the Knave of Hearts, he says, 'But at least he's tall – very tall.' If everybody else in wonderland is strident, sure of themselves as madmen are, Sellers' King is dotty and bewildered. He's aware that he could be dreaming.

He's next seen at the trial – England's legal system, its arcana and pettifoggery being Carroll's final target. Sellers, in an outsize judge's wig and wielding an ear trumpet, presides. (As when he's Queen Victoria at Balmoral, he's in his element.) The courtroom is a dark theatre. In the galleries and boxes, people are taking baths, shaving, cooking – they live there. The King tries to keep order – 'I'll have you executed. I can have *anybody* executed. Power – the power, you know' – but he is ignored. When the Cook refuses to give evidence ('Shan't!'), Sellers times his response impeccably. 'Well,' he says, 'That's the end of that then.' He falls off his throne; he does bits of business with the wig and ear-trumpet. 'Let's not have another witness – let's have a song,' he says, and a gloriously discordant chorus of the 'Eton Boating Song' ensues, complete with poultry accompaniment and noises out of *The Goon Show*. 'Ah,' he says. 'They don't reach verdicts like that any more.' He then sleeps, snores, makes animal noises, and collapses with a heart attack. It is funny, inventive, indulgent.

The feature directed by William Sterling seven years later returns to Carroll's text – from which Miller's film had taken wing – and quite misses its higgledy-piggledy spirit – which Miller had indisputably captured. It is leaden, as Sellers warned when he was interviewed on the set at Shepperton: 'I think they stuck very, very closely to the Lewis Carroll original. Will Sterling, the director, also wrote the screenplay. There was certainly no improvised dialogue at all. The script was very straight' – and boring, he might have added. (There are hopeless songs, with a chug-chug beat and an insidious chink-chink harpsichord, perpetrated by John Barry and Don Black, to further drag us down.) 'I've been trying to remember how old I was when I first read *Alice*. I think about fourteen. I re-read the book when I did Jonathan Miller's television version a few years ago. I wanted to see the difference between his interpretation and the original one. . . .'

There is much in Carroll to appeal to Sellers – in addition to the identity crisis already mentioned. The whacky logic, the mathematics and conundrums, suggest *The Goon Show*, as does the baby transmogrifying into a pig or Alice's alarming growth and shrinkage. The Duchess and the Cook, smashing plates and chucking pepper about, are a music hall duo – and many of the merry andrews Alice meets are vaudeville or pantomime grotesques. There are sexual themes, too, in the story. Alice Liddell is Lolita, and Sellers' eye appraised Fiona Fullerton, who was golden-haired and budding: 'I think Fiona Fullerton, who plays Alice, will be marvellous. She's fifteen, and seems to be very confident of herself. When I joined the film, they had already been shooting for some time, and she seemed to be perfectly at ease.'

The film is at least a triumph of casting direction: Ralph Richardson as a bad tempered caterpillar, puffing on his hookah (he is more distrait than Michael Redgrave); Flora Robson's fierce features were made for the psychotic Queen; and Peter Bull's fat-faced glare is so like Tenniel's Duchess, it makes you believe in reincarnation. Other make-ups and costume designs, however, eclipse the actor: the Mock Turtle (Michael Hordern), the White Rabbit

(Michael Crawford) or Milligan's brilliant green Gryphon – it could be anyone in there. (Milligan is recognisable only by his voice, which is pitched halfway between Moriarty and Minnie Bannister.) My personal favourite is Sir Robert Helpmann as the Mad Hatter. He plays the rôle like a zany ballet Hamlet.

But it is only really worth sitting through for Sellers, who transcends the puppet-theatre monotony: 'I was originally asked to play several rôles, but there just wasn't time . . . so I chose the March Hare character . . . I've studied the wild antics of live hares in the countryside round my home in Ireland. They do actually seem to go mad. It's part of the mating season during March. That's what Lewis Carroll meant in his book. They really do go ape. They come up and look at you, then tear about all over the place at a most alarming rate.'

Did he recognise a kinship, I wonder? The alternating mania and numbness? 'This rôle was a complete departure for me. I've never been asked to portray an animal before, but I must say it was really fun to do. I had a lengthy make-up session early every morning to turn me into the March Hare . . . I play the March Hare as a vocal characterisation. I speak through a false set of buck teeth, which gives a sort of lisp, and I invented a voice for it.'

Sellers came out with a deep, gurgling, twitchy tone – the exact opposite to Michael Gough, in the Miller film, who stammers and rocks back and forth, catatonically clenching his fists and jaw. Gough's Hare was clinically, authentically mad; Sellers' is gloriously eccentric. His costume, an olive jacket, primrose tie, billowing handkerchief and spats, makes him a dandy. He is wonderfully jumpy. His legs stretch and bend in different ways at once. His ears, which have grass and straw wreathed about them, flop and twitch like radar. His eyes, too, rotate, cross and wriggle alertly. (The whites of Sellers' eyes are so pure, they are the brightest things on the screen: they seem to give off light.) There is a moment in the trial scene, when he is sitting in the well of the court, and not particularly the centre of attention, which is simple and awesome: Sellers lets a quiver or shudder run along his spine that is exactly like a rabbit or hare. The detail is over in a flash, but I'll never forget it. Watching the wild things in the green fields of Maynooth paid off. Sellers is jiving, electric.

He has our sympathy for hating the dud picture that encased such a jewel of a performance. The evening of the première a few weeks before Christmas, 1972, was also the last time he saw Angela Morley, who at that time may still have been Wally Stott. 'I was at the Trattoo restaurant. Spike and Peter had been to the opening of *Alice's Adventures in Wonderland* and they came in looking for a drink. They weren't too happy about how it had gone and what they thought of it. They came and sat near Alan Clare, who was playing the piano in the bar, and Peter started to make up Russian songs – the kind which start very slowly and tragically and gradually get faster and faster.' Miss Morley didn't tell me whether she spoke to Sellers, or if she was acknowledged. If the star had pumped the paw of the conductor of *The Goon Show* orchestra, then what? Sellers always stalled when he met the living witnesses of his past. 'He'd telephone me from the pool-side in California, or from some location,' says Herbert Kretzmer. 'Always difficult conversations. After he'd told a few of the latest jokes, he'd have nothing more to say.' The forlornest example of this blankness is contributed by Michael Gough, who was Tamise, you'll recall, in *Mister Topaze*: 'Peter and I were in a hotel in Tours, the unit were some miles away. We ate and drank the most expensive things on the menu – I remonstrated – the company will never stand for this. . . . When I left I discovered he'd paid my bill. . . . Much later I was on the set of [Miller's] *Alice in Wonderland*, and there was a shout of "Micky Gough!" and we embraced and he had nothing to say. It was almost as though he was playing the part of an "Old Friend". Sad, because nearly always actors pick up old relationships just where we put them down.'

☆　★　☆

In both of his *Alice* efforts, Sellers is clownish, out of vaudeville. It constantly haunted him, the side shows, the rough magic, and we can see how his memory worked. *The Optimists of Nine Elms* and

Soft Beds, Hard Battles, with its multiple-rôle quick-change artistry, also see him seeking sanctuary in frowzy music hall. (After dinner in Maynooth he used to enjoy singing himself to sleep with the ukelele.) Though he'd gathered strength from it – and had surpassed it – he could not escape. It contributed to his feeling that he was going bad inside. Thus, his attraction to the umbrageousness of *A Day at the Beach* and *The Blockhouse*; their dreariness conveys the bottomless pit into which Sellers had fallen – and by *Ghost in the Noonday Sun*, his mind was crumbling into so many pieces, he was swirling like dust.

It was that film, nevertheless, which coincidentally, fortuitously, what you will, restored him to popularity. He turned up at Kyrenia harbour during a night shoot and said he was going to make a commercial for Benson and Hedges cigarettes, to be produced by Anthony Rufus-Isaacs' company. He wanted Peter Medak to direct it.

'Peter, I can't get you to shoot this film, let alone a commercial,' said Medak – who told me, 'Needless to say I ended up doing it in Cyprus on our only day off. It won several awards. Sellers and Milligan are breaking into a customs warehouse where all this gold is kept; they stack the gold into Spike's pockets – all done to a stopwatch, like a time and motion study. They march out. Sellers orders Spike into the boat and he crashes through the bottom of it and it starts to sink . . . Peter decided to play it as Clouseau, and we had more fun with this commercial than on the whole movie. This is when Peter had the idea to revive Clouseau – originally for television, backed by Lew Grade. Within six months he was making *The Return of the Pink Panther*.

'Anyway, we get to the all-important pack-shot, and there was trouble. They were meant to come out of the warehouse with the gold and Peter was to take out the Benson and Hedges packet and let it flash in the sunlight. "Oh, not me, daddy," he said. "I'm not allowed to touch cigarettes any more." Spike said he was chairman of the anti-smoking league. James Villiers was in it. He said, "Sure, lovey, any time," and Jimmy was only getting two thousand pounds for this job. Spike got twenty thousand which he donated to charity. Sellers got a new Mercedes as his fee, and poor old Jim did all the work. The entire thing done in five hours.'

Whenever he didn't fancy putting himself out, which was often, there was his heart. 'On the first day of shooting,' says Medak, reverting to *Ghost in the Noonday Sun*, 'the first scene was a long tracking shot – the scene in the black and white sequence where Peter Boyle leads the slaves tethered by a rope, and Sellers is at the end of the rope with his cooking cans. We were in the sand dunes, very isolated. After the second take, Peter, who was half a mile away, clutched his chest, and on the walkie-talkie he sent a message back that he had cardiac pains. Everybody panicked – everybody thought he was getting another heart attack. "I can't do this, baby," he said, and he was whisked away. So we then stopped shooting. The next morning I had the same tracking shot. He went insane. "How do you expect me to do this? I couldn't do this yesterday?" – "Well, maybe you don't have a chest pain now – it is flat where you are – you just have to walk."'

It was nostalgia for his heart attack which drew him to the hospital comedy, *Where Does It Hurt?*, made in Los Angeles the previous year, 1972. The critics have buried it. 'It ranks as the most technically atrocious fiasco ever associated with Sellers' film career' (Michael Starr); 'colourless, tasteless and, with its crude gags on malpractice and appendectomies, decidedly malodorous' (Derek Sylvester); 'At the end of a dismal comedy called *Where Does It Hurt?* he took to his bed for weeks. He had lost so much weight from not eating, he quickly developed bed sores' (Evans); 'Neither *Where Does It Hurt?*, nor *Alice's Adventures in Wonderland* ... brought him any substantial benefit' (Walker). In fact, though we keep seeing the tops of sets and the obtruding boom microphone, it isn't so awful. My complaint would be that it is not tasteless *enough*.

'It was an offer of work,' says son Michael. 'He spent a lot of time with the script trying out various American voices and walks. "What do you think of this interpretation? ... This? ... Do you think he'd sound like this?" Different inflexions, breaking down the sentences into different phrases, to see how they'd come out.'

Sellers is Mr Hoffnagel, the corrupt administrator of Vista Vue Hospital. After so many suave rôles, it is good to have him back where he belongs, playing a twinkling shit. The voice he settled on was Nixon's;* the walk, a lop-sided glide, is that of a shyster thrown off-balance by his own crooked schemes. Hoffnagel runs the hospital as a big business (or as Nixon ran the country); and illness isn't something to be cured, and the patient sent on his way. Illness is there to be cosseted, coaxed, invested in. ('If you were legitimate, you could be president,' Hoffnagel is told. 'I could never work on a straight salary,' he laments. 'They'd have to give me five per cent of the country. That's two and a half states. They'd never go for that.')

It is one thing to bleed patients from the wallet once they have discovered their growths and ailments. At Vista Vue they have invented the concept of 'creative medicine' which ensnares the healthy, too. 'It is infinitely wiser to treat diseases before they begin', Hoffnagel purrs. 'Can the average prostate ever be completely trusted never, *never*, to flare up?' He sweet-talks the patients and they beg for the knife. 'You elect to operate . . . before the need arises.' He is every over-the-top insurance salesman and fraudulent television evangelist you pray you'll never meet. Instead of transferring them to the morgue, he charges full-rates for corpses staying on in a room. He insists on plenty of salt in the food to make people thirsty – they buy cans of Pepsi from a vending machine and the coins tinkle down a chute into his office through a hole in the wall. He fiddles with the accounts from the maternity ward – he pretends a baby had inherited mild gonorrhoea from the father, and he adds the price of penicillin shots to the invoice. 'It was a serious infection – thank God we saved that baby,' he murmurs – and the sinister

---

* Sellers repeated it in 1974 on the LP, *He's Innocent of Watergate, or Dick's Last Stand*, being 'fragments of fifteen tapes recently found secreted in the false bottom of a flowerbed in the White House Gardens'. The script was by Milligan, Alan Coren, N.F. Simpson, John Bird, Barry Took, Richard Ingrams, and Barry Fantoni. In addition to Nixon – who grows more Hitlerian and ends his days not in the bunker but as a busker – Sellers was also President Amin of Uganda and the British ambassador.

thing is, he believes it as he writes it. He is a wise guy so deep into con tricks he can take himself in.

Money and medicine are a fertile theme – a computer print-out at the bottom of the screen keeps the running total of a poor sap's full check-up (urinalysis, proctological examinations, a barium enema); and one lady, in for a hysterectomy, tries to settle her account with Green Shield stamps. Hoffnagel counts her spools and spools of stickers and informs her she's short. 'Shove your hysto,' she snaps, 'I'll get me a colour TV.' She is one of Vista Vue's few failures. The wards are full of fools being parted from their assets. The doctors keep performing exploratory surgery until the patients reach bankruptcy. There is a psychological need to be ill. 'If you show me a patient without a scar, you'll show me a patient ashamed to face family and employer.'

For all this, the hospital is gloriously inefficient. The wrong doctors administer the wrong injections to the wrong patients. The consultants, who are busy cheating on each other's wives, rely on Hoffnagel to field malpractice suits. Mr Nishimoto, the laboratory assistant, regularly confuses the blood and urine samples (his moment of glory was testing John Wayne's pee); and a nurse, coming across a dead body, chastises herself: 'Oh Christ, if I don't write things down it's forgetsville.'

Where Does It Hurt? is a television episode of *MASH* without the integrity; if Mel Brooks decided to spoof hospital sitcoms, it would be up to this standard. Like *Blazing Saddles*, which ends with a free-for-all, somehow the hospital is turned into a whore house ('Big, beautiful tits' lusts Hoffnagel), complete with a Mexican band, balloons and streamers. Alarm bells and phones ring unheeded. The drunken doctors perform a circumcision on a young man ('Some day he might want to marry Barbra Streisand') and disinfect the snip with a splash of Bushmills. Hoffnagel sets up a secret camera to film the illicit fornications and general medical incompetence (blackmail material for later) and he has sex with a nurse in a linen cupboard. . .

Yes, it is crummy beyond, really. Slapdash in a way that isn't energetic. But Sellers breaks free, and his character is at a remove in any event. Clad in an immaculate brown suit and with brown lenses in his spectacles – he's a streak of brown lightning – he appears happy and comprehensively spurious as a minor Richard III, bribing and threatening. ('You are about to join the ranks of the unemployed,' he says to any member of staff which crosses him.) He dodges and swerves through the building, checking his watch, disappearing behind secret doors and spying through two-way mirrors – he shimmers and hovers like a hobgoblin. 'Even as a child I was not well-liked,' the arch-grifter says, shedding crocodile tears. 'My mother paid other kids to play with me. . . It is simply that I am cursed with a shitty personality.'

He claims to be cursed; like Richard, descanting on his own deformity, he knows he is blessed. Hoffnagel is consummate. He loves himself. He loves totting up inflated bills and dreaming up forbidden activities. The last plot is seriously sicko – even without its connections to, and echoes of, Sellers' own sessions on a hospital slab. He decides he wants to be operated on. He'll then sue for malpractice, make a mint, and split the insurance pay out with the quacks. The sight of Hoffnagel – or Sellers – bandaged for surgery, lying there in state, is disconcerting, to pitch it no higher. He is meditating – and when a slight smile plays across his face, Sellers is definitely no longer in character. He is inscrutable – an anticipation of Chance, on the consulting-room bed at the Rand mansion, repeating the scene that was in the contentious out-take compilation (so admired by John Updike); and he is also in position to be the mummified Fu. Hoffnagel disappears to be replaced by the Sellers who believed that death wasn't an opposite to life, but a status that shared the winter with birth.

☆ ★ ☆

Is that what Sellers was, in the final analysis (not to say urinalysis): a shitty personality? A man who always had to have his own way? Who was averse to behaving naturally? The connoisseur of shits and shittiness in the present century is Kingsley Amis. In his novel *I Want It Now*, the hero, Ronnie Appleyard, 'a hypocritical affected vain little shit', is a Sellers-like media star on the alert for fame, money and a giant's helping of sex. He befriends only those who can advance his career or whom he can get something out of: 'he had been a bastard to plenty of people in the past and doubtless would be again any day. . .' After a visit to America, however, he realises he hasn't got what it takes: 'I've had to give up trying to be a dedicated, full-time shit. I couldn't make it, hadn't the strength of character. Which is a pity in a way, because when you fall back into the ranks of the failed shits or amateur shits or incidental shits you start taking on responsibility for other people.'

There was no equivalent moral awakening with Sellers. In a novel you can improve him, begin with his ambitiousness and gradually have him perceive just how degrading the pursuit of almightiness gets to be; in fiction, characters can mend their ways. What shall it profit a man, if he shall gain the whole world, and lose his own soul? runs the rubric in the great tradition – i.e. in the books of Jane Austen, George Eliot, Henry James, Joseph Conrad, and D.H. Lawrence. On the other hand, the conscience-free fellow can have an awful lot of fun. Ronnie Appleyard may reform, because he discovered he has a sense of duty, but no such qualms spoil Roger Micheldene's pleasure-seeking, in *One Fat Englishman*: 'the only thing to do is do what you want. Any means are justifiable for getting what you want, up to and including murder.'

If Appleyard might allude to the youngish Sellers on the make, Micheldene to the burly Sellers *passim*, Sir Roy Vandervane, in *Girl, Twenty*, is the celebrated Sellers of the Sixties. There do seem to be a number of marked resemblances. Vandervane lives on the expensive fringe of Hertfordshire, where the barns of his mansion have been converted into studios; he is a satyromaniac who chases starlets and neglects his wife – very young girls tone him up. He is always 'thinking up new ways of being a shit that you can't help taking your hat off to him for'. He argues in favour of legalised pot and frequents night-clubs with their loud pop noises. He berates policemen, traffic wardens and petty officials, calling them bastards and fascists (though 'fascists and bastards were interchangeable');

and he is always coming out with vocal impersonations and mimicries.

Like Sellers, Vandervane (a distinguished orchestra conductor) is a middle-aged delinquent. He feels compromised by the rôle of beloved husband and father – he bridles at the idea of limitations and accountability and he refuses to be told to do anything by anybody. To keep basic decency at bay, he devises self-protective strategies, 'hostile, wounding, designed to humiliate' the opposition. With all this he has considerable charm, and far from being repulsed, people find him attractive, compelling: 'the tonic effect of going to see Roy uplifts the spirits'. In this way he is related to Alun Weaver in *The Old Devils*, a professional media Welshman with a CBE. Weaver (a corrupt elder version of Lewis from *That Uncertain Feeling* a.k.a. *Only Two Can Play*) is an adulterer and deceiver, a chancer who desperately needs the publicity and attention he pretends to despise, and yet 'it may go against the grain to admit it, but one's spirits do tend to lift a degree or so at the sight of him'. As with Vandervane, we have to decide whether 'a fraud who's come out is more believable than a closet fraud'. He makes a big show of hating Americans ('They do say fuck off in America, don't they?') and of being rude to waiters and underlings. Linked with this bullying is his self-pitying sentimentality – he wants to tour the old sights and haunts with his former chums. If it isn't possible to put the clocks back, he can at least measure for himself how far he has risen, how far away he got in terms of success.

To be a shit you have to be anxious to seize the initiative; you have to crow; you are calculating: as Helene says to Micheldene, in respect of his attitude toward intercourse, but not only that:

> It's all for you, all that, isn't it? You think of it and you do it. Like a lot of men. You know, the first few years I slept with people I thought it was all a thing they did to you. If you happened to enjoy it and you showed it that was all right, that was fine because it told them how good they were, but you didn't have to enjoy it too much because you weren't there for that. . .

(This speech is repeated in modified form in *The Old Devils*: 'It was all over in seconds but she got quite a lot in. Bloody this and fucking that, what would you, and selfish monster and windbag and hypocrite and broken down Don Juan and phony Welshman'. In the television adaptation, Weaver [John Stride] is also called 'the thinking woman's Harry Secombe'.)

☆ ★ ☆

If I sound in danger of making the claim that Sir Kingsley's great subject has been variations on a theme of Sellers, this is not only the besotted biographer speaking. When I began assembling material for this book, in July 1989, I wrote to ask him if he had any comments to make about *Only Two Can Play*: 'Did you meet Sellers, and how did he strike you? Etc. Usual biographer's catechism.' I received the following by return of post.

[London]

Dear Mr Lewis,
It so happens that I have a few thoughts to offer about Peter Sellers, whom I met on several occasions when he came down to Swansea to film *Only Two Can Play*.

Most of the cast were installed at the Grand Hotel, Swansea, which in those days was a slightly above average ordinary Station hotel such as you might expect to find in the West of England – certainly clean and cheerful. Mai Zetterling, then an international star, took a look round the bedroom she was offered and gracefully said it would do very well. Sellers walked out, not very politely, and installed himself at Porthcawl, some miles down the coast, in a hotel which we all delightedly learned was far inferior to the Grand. Here Kenneth Griffith taught him the Swansea accent, but so brilliantly that 'John Lewis' sounded *exactly* like the kind of educated upper-working-class valleys Welshman I had had in mind.*

At a very meagre lunch he threw me in Swansea, he informed me that he and Spike Milligan had between them invented the

---

* For Griffith's version of this story, see pages 489–900.

whole of post-war British humour, principally via the Goon Show. Over all, he impressed me as one of the most self-satisfied shits I have ever met. He did, however, impart one interesting item of information, that a stuntman he once talked to had told him that what he most enjoyed was going through a plate glass window.

. . .

Yours,
Kingsley Amis

In further letters to me, after I'd told him about my meeting with Kenneth Griffith, amongst other items of gossip, Sir Kingsley vouchsafed that 'I have not myself found Kenneth Griffith quite the charming chap you see him as. Dotty, certainly, and a bit of a shit with it. Sellers was of course a larger shit and the less said about him the better. A good actor, though.' (These opinions were broadcast publicly in his *Memoirs*, published in 1991: Sellers gets to be called a 'comedian in several senses' and Griffith is a 'fine actor and nasty little subversive creep' – which seems rather to confuse him with his part in the film, Euan Jenkins.)

☆ ★ ☆

In fact, to call Sellers a shit demeans him; his faults and cunning are in a different league. To call him mad, as I have often done throughout this book, excuses him ('Peter was psychiatrically cruel,' Milligan told me. 'His judgement was not that of a normal person'). What I think we need to do is revert to more ancient terminology, when summing him up. He had an evil streak in him. Sellers was evil. At the end of the last chapter, when I was in the graveyard, I promised you a further concluding point, and this is it. He was a destroyer. He was pandemonium.

I don't mean that he was a black and white horror movie ghoul liable to jump out from the shadows at any moment; neither was he involved with devil-worship cults, or similar supernatural lunacies, or at least not all the time. The meaning of Sellers came to me only recently, when I was reading about Henry James' remarkable family. His father, William, once had a famous apprehension of evil: 'To all appearances it was a perfectly insane and abject terror, without ostensible cause, and only to be accounted for, to my perplexed imagination, by some damned shape squatting invisible to me within the precincts of the room, and raying out from his fetid personality influences fatal to life.' Henry James himself sensed this morbidity during a period of illness, 'a black bad time . . . of horrible nervous . . . melancholia'; and his sister Alice once said 'physical pain, however great, ends in itself and falls away, whilst moral discords and nervous horrors sear the soul'.

The James' acknowledged evil ('Portentous evil . . . the hot breath of the pit') and wrote about it; Sellers yielded to it, he embodied it. There was a darkness wheeling about him. This is the strong impression I am left with after spending twenty-five thousand hours in his company; and I don't believe my intuitions can totally be discounted as those of an author who, approaching the end of a long and difficult task, starts to resent his subject for consuming so much of his life, though there must be a bit of that abroad, too. Sellers was petulant, ecstatic; he was brutal and intense. To follow up this grand opera generalisation with the 'brief illustration, the offered example, . . . the limited deplorable presentable instance', as James acknowledged when crafting *The Turn of the Screw*, is rather to shrink and render cursory with 'weak specifications' that which needs to be left to the imagination.

However, let us start with his insidious behaviour towards his children. The underlinings in my copy of *P.S. I Love You* are like a condensed version of my own text: *Whims and insanities . . . he could snarl like a tortured animal . . . insanely jealous . . . my father's temper, once lost, being utterly uncontrollable . . . He threw a tantrum . . . near schizophrenic effect on his own character . . . his demented mind . . . a myriad of ideas, both creative and conspiratorial . . . 'You're going back to your mother's and I never want to see you again' . . . a bitter row broke out . . . He kept a 'shit-list' of producers, directors, newspaper columnists and critics aligned against him . . . storms gathered . . . he once again became over-possessive . . . the Polo Lounge ground to a halt as his temper gathered fury . . . One of his familiar black moods descended . . . He threatened to kill Lynne's dog . . . 'I've set you up for life and you're ungrateful . . . What kind of son are you?' . . . 'Good luck with your career, if you ever choose one' . . . He had lost interest in the world . . . Dad was alone and suspicious of everyone . . . 'Dear Sarah . . . I shall be happy if I never hear from you again . . . I won't tell you what I think of you' . . . A frail, ailing figure . . . Lynne married David Frost. It was six months to the very day that Dad died. . .*

It is possible to explain away his iniquities by saying, well, Sellers was a basic, crude performing mechanism. He simply played certain rôles. The client going to see the lawyer; the famous face in the restaurant; the fêted actor on the sound stage; the millionaire behind the wheel of a Rolls Royce. He had no idea of what a father was meant to do. What did it mean to be 'Peter Sellers' children'? He had no conception of domestic life – they don't show ordinary domestic life in the movies. He was no sort of father to Michael, Sarah, or Victoria because the part did not inspire him. They must have wondered who this person was, permissive and suddenly harsh, flying in and out of their lives for a few days at a time, wanting everything to operate in his favour.

Though there is much to recommend a mask-behind-the-mask-interpretation – Sellers, the compulsive mimic, who had no mind or philosophy getting in the way – it is too exculpatory and limited for my taste. He was ignorant, but he wasn't stupid. He never had any desire to put the effort into learning anything; he was an uneducated man who couldn't hold an intellectual conversation, but he knew what he was doing. He was no fool; he was egotistically sublime. He rejected his children because, by virtue of their very existence, they made him belong to material reality; they compromised, or revoked, his fantasy lives. They gave him a cold feeling – like a memento mori. They were also a boring responsibility, a bondage, and he wasn't going to accept that. There was nothing he could get out of them – no advantage. Any school achievements or gifts they might have made he mocked and threw out.* He had no use for his children, and his lack of consideration was completely consistent. (That they were left high and dry in his will quite fits the pattern.)

Victoria got the worst of it. Sellers didn't want her to be born. 'I've got Michael, I've got Sarah. I don't want any more children.' Only the intercession of Bryan Forbes and Nanette Newman prevented Sellers from ordering Britt to have an abortion. He was making *What's New, Pussycat?* when the baby appeared, on January 20th 1965. He was so pre-occupied with the re-starting of his career – his performance as Fritz Fassbender being his first major post-coronary rôle – he dumped his wife on the pavement outside the Welbeck Street Clinic, without so much as carrying her suitcase in through the door. (Not for him any father-in-attendance rubbish.) Congratulatory telegrams arrived by the thousand, but Peg was not impressed. She only ever referred to Victoria as 'it'; Sellers seems to have followed this example. He never allowed his young daughter a separate existence. She was simply handy as a way of imperilling Britt. 'Don't listen to what your mother says,' he commanded, 'only listen to me.' (Britt had seen Sellers through his convalescence; she had administered his complex and heavy medication. This is how he treated her, like dirt.)

The baby was raised by nurses and strings of nannies, and Britt had to ensure that Victoria was hidden out of sight and earshot by the time the master returned from the studios. He was so competitive, he was jealous if he sensed his wife used her energies up being a mother. She had to be all for him. Here's how, in 1966, she felt obliged to set her routine: '. . . while I am young and fairly newly-married I feel it's important I spend as much time as I can with my husband. Obviously, when Victoria gets a bit older I would

---

* E.g. table mats, pen holders, poster paint pictures – all the stuff children cart home from school. Sellers' reaction was to write this sort of thank-you letter: 'Dear Sarah, I have just been given what I believe to be your Christmas presents . . . I know it is the thought that counts and not the money. But what a thought. Yours, Dad.'

want to spend more time with her – when she can actually talk and I can teach her things. I don't say I can't talk to her now because I can but I don't think she understands me! And so much of the time it makes little difference whether I am there or nanny is there . . . In six months or a year's time she will want more from her mother and I will have to give her more. That does not mean I will have to give my husband *less* time but that I may have to take more time off from my own career.'

Britt's dilemma – trying to be a good mother whilst also supplying Sellers' extensive demands for subservience – tied her in knots: '. . . look at mothers who spend whole days with their children. I'm sure you don't think they sit on the floor playing with them for eight hours a day. They take them shopping in the pram, leave them outside the shop, load the pram full of parcels. They run home, cook the lunch, give the child lunch, then put it [*sic*] to bed. They clean the home. When the child wakes they put them in a playroom or in the kitchen while they get on with the washing or evening cooking. So, you see, an ordinary child [ie. a child not delivered into the care of a full domestic staff; a child whose impetuous papa has not moved everybody into the Dorchester] might *see* more of its mother but might not *feel* more if you understand me. She might not necessarily *feel* more love and affection.'

No matter how conscientious or compliant Britt was, Sellers would have been dissatisfied. It had appealed to his vanity to woo and win a beautiful woman; but having made the conquest he was bored with her and wanted to kill her. Indeed, he despised her for trying to love him – he was both smart and twisted enough to see that as a flaw in her nature. (Also, young and gorgeous, she reminded him he was growing old.) Many of the quarrels and fights, already discussed, which took place during the making of *After the Fox* or *The Bobo*, unfolded with Victoria present. As Hattie Stevenson recalls: 'We spent a lot of time in Naples and Rome. He had really pushed to have Britt in those films, and after the first day of shooting he was distraught: "Oh God, she's useless. Why did I think she could act? Why did I want her cast?" Bert and I had to fly to Sweden. They'd had a row and we had to take Victoria, who was then a baby, to Stockholm – where Britt had already gone. We had to take the baby back to her. We had to fly to Sweden and then return to Italy immediately. Britt tried very hard – within a few months she knew she'd never be happy with him, but she still tried with him; she still worked at it. He became terribly possessive of her. She couldn't go anywhere in the end.'

The innocent child in their midst was the battle ground (or battle trophy?). Victoria was to be victimised – as anybody could tell from the statement read out in the London Divorce Court on December 18th 1968. Mr Joseph Jackson QC, appearing for Sellers, said: 'They know that even if they have failed with their marriage they must not fail over Victoria. They are both devoted to her. They have her interests vitally at heart.' The judge gave Sellers and Britt joint custody of the girl, who was not quite four, which meant there was going to have to be collaboration and agreement over major matters such as schools; but daily 'care and control' did go to the mother. Britt was granted a decree nisi on the grounds of her husband's cruelty – and Sellers, who was not in court, did not instruct his lawyers to deny that cruelty. Mr Jackson said: 'My client very much regrets that his marriage has broken down and, in so far as it is appropriate to do so, he wishes his wife well. He has made proper provision for his wife and daughter, as befits a man in his profession. [What is that meant to mean?] He is entirely satisfied that his wife will behave responsibly towards Victoria. I think that both of them have been very sensible over what I could call their "common asset".'

If only Sellers' learned friend had realised the implications of his little legal quip! Sellers felt he was being officially sanctioned to treat Victoria as a bit of impassive property. Famously crude and abandoned over goods and chattels, he consigned his flesh and blood to the ranks of cameras and cars (and dolly birds) – an object he could pretend to be occupied with and then neglect. As part of his courting of the royal family, for example, he gave Viscount Linley and Sarah Armstrong Jones a palomino pony, Buttercup –

Victoria's. Sellers' daughter went in the paddock one day and the animal was gone. Cruel? Thoughtless? Spiteful? It mattered nothing to him that his daughter might have feelings that could be hurt. In recent years, Victoria has tried to be understanding: 'I really missed that pony. But you just had to accept that that was the way Dad was'. She then added a gloss to the resigned remark which, subsconsciously I am sure, goes right to the heart of her father's evil nature. 'It was an object to him, and he never got fond of objects. Once they'd stopped being new toys to him, he'd give them away or sell them.'

What went for Buttercup went for people; and as if the royal family was short of nags! But he wasn't giving the Snowdon babes a present so much as hoping he could bustle closer to the throne. The custom-built silver blue Aston Martin which he sold to Lord Snowdon for £3,000 was also part of this crackpot campaign. (As Britt has said, 'for all the money that exchanged hands he might just as well have given it to Tony.') He was only generous if there was an end in view, or to get allies, or to get a reaction. Indeed, generosity was a perverted concept where Sellers was concerned – he felt momentarily better for the attention/gratitude he inspired; he liked having the power to spend and surprise; he was bragging (it was self-glory) and he didn't give a tuppenny fuck for the actual recipients. He didn't care about the effects on other people of his generosity or non-generosity. He'd often tell his children he was hard up – and then they'd discover that (say) Miranda's relatives had been given saloon cars or thousands of pounds worth of photographic equipment.

He resented spending money on his children, but he didn't stint on wasting fortunes, over the years, surging after Britt with solicitor's letters. He opposed all her ideas about education on principle, with the upshot that Victoria was frequently uprooted and made to traipse Sweden, England and America in search of a suitable lycée. He called Britt filthy names in front of the child, to make her tearful, and he expected to get from her what Britt said about him – all the while scaring her 'by threatening to have Britt arrested and thrown into jail, and that he would seek custody of her; then she would live with him permanently because her mother was a bad influence. . .'

You'd have thought a speech of that kidney had gone out with Charles Dickens' personages, Ralph Nickleby or Edward Murdstone, but no; and far from his being interested in keeping Victoria, protecting her or contemplating her welfare – she didn't exist – it was the act of throwing her back and snatching her away which provided Sellers with amusement.* 'After another row with Britt [Dad] took his revenge by refusing to invite Victoria to stay,' Michael has said. On another occasion, Victoria was on her way to the airport, with the flight tickets in her pocket, when Sellers cancelled a long-promised holiday.

They did, however, eventually reach a beach. 'The only time I really saw him militant,' Herbert Lom says, and he must have acquired a strong basis for comparison, 'was when he was fighting Britt for custody of Victoria. He was happy at the prospect of taking Victoria on holiday – a grand beach house was procured for three weeks. After three days he was back. "We grew bored with each other." Tragic. As a father I'm sure he was a monster.'

☆ ★ ☆

And as an ex-husband. He commissioned a private dick to shadow Britt *after* the divorce. He intimated that he would apply to have Victoria made a ward of court if her mother took a boyfriend. Meantime, of course, Sellers was tom-catting like billy-o and telephoning his ex-wife to boast of his conquests. Mia Farrow, soon to be a famous Earth Mother, was in his harem. ('EXIT BRITT, ENTER MIA' blazed the tabloids.) They dressed in kaftans and beads, lit joss sticks, and watched the sky for UFOs. (On one trip into the desert to have a mystical experience, they were secretly followed by Roman Polanski, who threw rocks and made funny

---

* Do I need to spell out that we have toppled headlong into *What Maisie Knew?* Go and see for yourself: *The Complete Notebooks of Henry James*, edited by Leon Edel and Lyall H. Powers, (New York, 1987), pages 147–51 and 161–7.

noises. 'Did you hear that?' whispered Sellers. 'What was it?' hissed Mia. 'I don't know, but it was fantastic. *Fantastic!*')

Sellers was fascinated by the flower-power paraphernalia of the Sixties. (He could hide his evil behind it.) He burned incense and chanted sanskrit before a statue of Buddha; he acquired an altar, complete with a porcelain three-headed elephant and velvet prayer cushions. He was a proselytiser for Ravi Shankar. The film which exhibited much of the cock and bull – the pretences – was *I Love You, Alice B. Toklas*, in which the Jewish lawyer dropped out to become a hippy. 'It is really a full-blown story of a man and the metamorphosis that comes about when he is exposed to pot . . . Alice B. Toklas' chocolate brownies with hashish in them [are] the springboard for a change in the man,' explained Hy Averback, the director. The picture is awash with paisley swirls, beads, shawls, oriental rugs and copies of Mao's little red book. Grass, dope, and weeds of every description are rolled and smoked. There is a scene set in the casbah on Venice beach – where hippies were invented? – and a great deal of astrological claptrap gets spoken: 'Flower in the crannied wall, if I could but understand what you are, root and all, and all-in-all, I should know what God and man is . . .' intones a big hairy earnest silly sod.

'Our writers [Paul Mazursky and Larry Tucker] did tremendous research on hippies,' said Averback. 'We have also employed real hippies on the film. We find we get an honesty out of their performances, whereas to have actors assume these things . . . One of the gentlemen we are using actually has a hippy commune in Northern California. He plays our guru; and we have Lou Gottlieb, and he's absolutely brilliant. Lou was formerly in show business . . . Lou has fallen out [*sic*] . . . and he is an extremely brilliant man, who has turned out to be a brilliant performer for our film. . . .'

As it is possible to detect from this effusion, *I Love You, Alice B. Toklas* contained elements of documentary. 'I'll tell you a strange thing,' said Sellers a decade afterwards. 'During the making of [it] in 1968, there were two cuts, ours and the studios. I wish you'd seen the original with the interviews with Allen Ginsberg and Timothy

Leary. Paul Mazursky and Larry Tucker and myself, we even got in the lab at night and *we* cut the film. Can you believe it. We bribed the guard, we spent all night with an editor, and when the schmucks came in the following day, we were there bright and early as though we'd just arrived, and we said, "Listen, we don't like the finished film. We think you should see our attempts." So they see it, and they say: "Too weird. Who the *fuck* is Ginsberg? Who the *fuck* is Leary? People are gonna know about Ginsberg and Leary in Orange County? O man dat's ridiculous." I said, "They're not for Orange County, they're for the *World*."'

With its *Reds* or *Zelig*-style talking heads lopped off, *I Love You, Alice B. Toklas* still retains a documentary value. It is Sellers' life and times which are on show. The guru's questioning, 'Who are you? Do you know who you are?' fits with Sellers' own endless ego trip; and Harold Fine, anxious, angry, Jewish, mother-dominated, is simply saturnine Sellers with a Californian accent. The satirical barb, too, hits him palpably: the successful man agitated because he thinks he is missing out. Harold grows his hair and walks barefoot, but he hasn't really altered his personality (only his wardrobe) – he is still possessive of Nancy, the girl he meets who munches oranges complete with peel – and who, as played by Leigh Taylor-Young, is a dead-ringer for Britt. He doesn't quite appreciate the grotesques who have taken up residence in his apartment, daubing horoscopes on the walls, lying unconscious in the bath tub, leaving their syringes about. (It has the squalor of a squat.) When Nancy is seen painting psychedelic mauve squiggles on another guy's body, he explodes. 'I like him,' the Lolita says ingenuously. 'Is there anyone you don't like?' snarls her Humbert Humbert. She accuses him of being unhip. Sellers then riffs: 'I'm probably the hippest guy around here. I got pot, I got acid, I got LSD cubes. I got this thing here [his medallion]. I am so hip it hurts. That's how hip I am. Don't tell me about hip.' – 'It's very unhip to say you're hip, Harold,' responds the waif. 'And it's very unhip of you to tell me I am unhip,' he says, having the last word.

For Harold, the hippy-business is street theatre, a dodge; the drug culture enables him to block out his family problems – he can't confront them, he still can't cope. Intoxicated by marijuana, he says he doesn't have 'hatred and violence' in his soul any more – but he does, and Sellers himself did. The hippy antics were completely bogus, the latest posture among many, as witness his anti-nirvana-like behaviour whilst making the film. He wanted the crew changed because he said they didn't like him and were leaking stories to the press.* He was often late and he held up the production for footling reasons. Jo Van Fleet (who played Harold's mother) reprimanded him for leaving the company standing around. Sellers flew at her. How dare she call him unprofessional! She was the unprofessional one, for calling *him* unprofessional! 'How dare you say this to *me*! Not only are *you* unprofessional, nobody *likes* you!', he screamed.

The cadences of the hip-unhip dialogue can be heard in that; and staying in a shitty vein, he had the script girl sacked because she was wearing a purple dress – the colour was giving off bad vibes, he argued. Bad vibes seemed to reach Sellers like a dog whistle. The air was full of pulses and wing beats, as Roman Polanski discovered: 'Peter's idiosyncrasies could be a drag . . . I grew to dread the moment when, after ordering [in a restaurant], Peter would whisper: "Ro, I can't stand it. Bad vibes in here. . . Let's go somewhere else."'

☆ ★ ☆

To continue with sartorial matters – *I Love You, Alice B. Toklas* was the closest destiny ever took Sellers to being the dashing swashbuckler. I wonder if he knew? The costumes for the film, the hippy robes and rags, were reconstituted from colourful fabrics found in the Warner warehouse. Sellers' fur-trimmed jerkin was made from

---

* It was reported in the *Los Angeles Times*, on January 8th 1968, that 'Peter Sellers is behaving like a brat. He has threatened to walk off his new movie *I Love You, Alice B. Toklas*. . . He contends there is a spy on the set. . . Sellers' temper is hardly a secret deserving of espionage. It may now be time for Peter Sellers, one of our great comedy actors, to return to acting in earnest. . .'

an Errol Flynn cloak of the Thirties. 'I had to poke around in the stockroom to find it,' said the dress designer, Theda Van Runkle. 'It was much more meaningful than just finding a piece of cloth in a sale and trying to force something. I just let it happen . . . we just had fun. Just like a party.'

What for Harold was a masked ball and an affectation, however, with Sellers with hypocrisy. The yogic dumb-shows in the film are there to be laughed at; the standing-on-his-head and lotus position meditations, which Sellers went in for, were party tricks, too, but what bestowed a particular perfidiousness upon them was the way he pretended to have achieved the calm-dignity-grace of Buddhist ethics. (Sellers was a mock priest.) 'What I am aware of', he stated as late as December 1976, 'is that I'm never one for feelings of revenge. It's anti my beliefs in yoga . . . I've got nothing to come out now. Nothing up my sleeve. I'm clean, bare, naked. That's fine. . .'

It was fine, too, to bring Victoria to Ireland and banish her to remote icy bed chambers; it was fine, if Britt remonstrated with him over the maintenance arrears, to send the child a letter saying she should no longer regard him as her father; it was fine, if she did come and stay, to 'let me do anything I wanted because that was his way of getting back at Mum . . . Then he could be completely cold and distant as though I wasn't even in the room.' Any discipline or routine Britt may have established Sellers delighted in wrecking – and he would have condoned his daughter's career as a nude model, we can be certain of that. 'Mum might freak out, so I'm avoiding her,' said Victoria, when her acceptance of a *Playboy* assignment was announced. 'But I don't think Dad would have been all that negative.'

The feature spread, with photographs by Richard Fegley, was published in the issue of April 1986, when Victoria was twenty. Had Sellers lived to see her thus exposed, I'd be afraid for her. ('We used to have our own names for one another. I was Toria to him, or sometimes Torikins, and I'd call him Daddles. And we had a silly game we'd play. He'd creep up on me and then make a weird noise and jump out at me and grab my bum. . . Then he'd walk away, and I'd sneak up on him – and we'd end up chasing each other all over the place.') The excuse for Victoria's strip-tease was Sellers' own *Playboy* pictorial of April 1964, called 'Sellers Mimes the Movie Lovers'. In that he (rather brilliantly) impersonated José Ferrer in *Moulin Rouge*, Rudolf Valentino in *The Sheik*, Francis X. Bushman in *Ben Hur*, Bela Lugosi in *Dracula*, James Stewart in *Destry Rides Again*, Cary Grant in *Notorious*, Groucho in *A Night at the Opera* – and then he was himself (as it were) in *The World of Henry Orient*. Needless to say, Sellers is completely clad in the various costumes (wild west gunslinger, Roman centurion gear, etc.); he stares at the camera in mute appeal whilst the playmates, with a hint of nipple, try to paw and fondle him. Sellers' 'near-miraculous metamorphoses to the celluloid amorists of yesteryear . . . is very much Peter's own [idea] . . . The enjoyment of Peter's antic updating of famous love scenes from film classics . . . is quite universal and devastatingly comedic . . .' we were told, a little bewilderingly.

Two decades on, the feature 'Best Sellers: Peter's Daughter Victoria Joins the Family Business', is not only complementary; it is like delayed action incest. Sellers version of Cary Grant, Valentino, Groucho and Lugosi are reprised and inset, to look down upon Victoria – leggy and pawky – as Ingrid Bergman in *Casablanca*, Elizabeth Taylor in *Cleopatra*, Jane Russell in *The Outlaw*, Raquel Welch in *One Million Years B.C.*, Sophia Loren (*Sophia Loren?*) in *Yesterday, Today and Tomorrow*, Brooke Shields in *The Blue Lagoon*, Maria Schneider in *Last Tango in Paris*, Brigitte Bardot in *And God Created Woman* and Kathleen Turner in *Body Heat*.

Sellers, in his assignment, had managed to spoof the notion of practised lechery. We admire his facial expressions first and only then hunt for the tastefully posed – scarcely exposed – knockers. With Victoria, breasts, bottom and beaver push towards the lens, like plastic flowers seeking the sun. The emphasis on body parts is almost pornographic, or shall I say fatuous? Victoria doesn't adapt her expression to the sirens she is ostensibly imitating. She does not resemble the screen vamps, nor can she get into the spirit of them. She seems to have nothing to bring out. Despite the elaborate sets, make-up and general scene-setting, she isn't an actress, as such. She's trying hard and, as I look at these photos, she does seem very young and vulnerable. What I see, behind her eyes and embarrassment, is her father and a process of dehumanisation.

So much for sex; now it is the turn of drugs. Narcotics gripped and blighted her life after Sellers' death. Following the funeral, when she had been screamed at unnecessarily by Lynne, Victoria went through a long period of uglifying herself as a punk rocker. In May 1986, she pleaded guilty to knowing about an international cocaine ring run by her violent boyfriend, Reed Wallace. The Assistant United States Attorney, Judy Russell, in consultation with the Drug Enforcement Administration, agreed to a light sentence on conspiracy charges after Victoria had promised to be a prosecution witness against the gang. In Newark, New Jersey, she was given a suspended jail sentence and ordered to do six hundred hours of community service; the sentencing judge had every right to have put her behind bars for twenty years and to have fined her a quarter of a million dollars.

That the girl turned out this way can be no surprise.* Her ideas

---

* As we go to press, news is reaching me of Victoria's prostitution and her association with an alleged Hollywood bawd, Heidi Fleiss, who is currently (August 1993) facing pimping, pandering and sale of narcotics charges – but who, more to the point, had a celebrity clientele which would fork out over a thousand bucks a throw. According to reports, Fleiss was once a familiar sight at 'On the Rox', a night-club where Victoria worked as a hostess. 'Heidi would be with a group of girls in the corner,' explains *Time*. 'You'd see her get up and talk to a guy by the bar, then she'd go back and get a girl, and then the girl would go over and sit on the guy's lap while he ran his hand under her clothes.'

It would seem that Fleiss used Victoria's surname and connections to give her parties a showbiz glimmer. Victoria, in her turn, enjoyed Heidi's high life and gaiety – and they ended up sharing a house together. 'It is not thought', warns Sharon Churcher in the *Mail on Sunday*, 'that Victoria knew anything about Fleiss' activities . . . But the irony is that Victoria Sellers believes that by standing by her friend, she will somehow benefit from it . . . The truth is that Hollywood society, which is closing ranks against Fleiss, will shun anyone who publicly defends her – that will include Victoria Sellers.'

The truth is less innocent and more murky. Whilst we can admire Victoria's of right and wrong, good and bad, had been formed by a father who not only refused to take her calls if she'd worn a frock he didn't like the colour of – he'd rant: 'As far as I'm concerned you can get the next plane and go home. I never want to see you again. Your behaviour is disgusting. . .' Etc. Etc. Be on the receiving end of a repudiation like that, because there's a hint of purple in your warp and woof, and what's the worry with real vices? Sellers had seen to it that his daughter was lurid and apathetic. He inspired a malaise. As Victoria's probation officer, James Brouchard, said, 'Our concern is not that she is not sincere in wishing to kick drugs, but that she is incapable.'

She has, in fairness, been rehabilitated somewhat, and in October 1992 she said: 'Drugs are behind me. They nearly ruined my life. . . It's humiliating to have to keep taking drug tests but it's a small price to pay rather than going to jail.' Michael and Sarah were not corrupted by their father, but they were no less affected and shell-shocked: 'Having been brought up like that,' Michael said to me, 'unable to relax when he was around, the mechanism for dealing with it all is alive and well in me – but it has no place. People say I'm aloof and offish. It's not that – it is an inbuilt mechanism that prevents me from being totally open, because I was emotionally trampled on when younger; I've been taken advantage of, and the result is I have few friends. I have no old school friends, because of the way he moved me around. I find it difficult to trust people and to make new friends. . .'

The evil that men do lives after them (the good is oft interred with their bones – though I'm not convinced of that, either).

---

loyal stand – which is not something her father would have bothered to take up on anybody's behalf – this little episode would all seem to comply with my belief that, such was the climate of her childhood, Victoria's adult conception of right and wrong is going to be fitful. Her father's dead hand continues to reach out – and, indeed, now that it is common knowledge that Victoria has worked as a high-class hooker ('The guy wasn't repulsive and it was straight sex – which was over in three minutes. I remember taking a huge sigh of relief. I knew then I could do it. It was easy money'), my only concern is that posterity will acknowledge Sellers purely because he was the papa of little Vicki.

After he'd made *The Magic Christian*, and had given lots of press interviews to peddle the money-can't-buy-happiness/everybody-has-their-price theme, Sellers, steeped in decay and gloat, evangelised as follows: 'Love, in the fullest sense of the word, contributes to my search for happiness. Not just physical, sexual love – I mean just love for people, from one person to another. *That*. Getting to that – getting yourself together to get into that position – trying not to be uptight about people. You know when somebody says something that makes you rile a bit – trying to kill that if you can. I've been unsuccessful at this, but that would be my aim.'

Would be his aim, except . . .: note that use of the conditional tense. In fact, Sellers had long before renounced love in order to gain power. That, I now see, has been the theme of my book; it is what gives Sellers' story a moral dimension. Even his money – like the gold at the bottom of the Rhine in the mythology of gods and dragons – has been cursed. In the thirteen years since Sellers' death, his widow and the beneficiary of his estate has continued to live very much in his shadow. The money has done nothing for her. Lynne is shut off from the rest of the world, save for her mother and grandmother. A friend who has observed her plight told me: 'Mrs Sellers, now Mrs Unger, never really did recover from the death of Peter Sellers . . . In as much as you are interested in the psychopathology of artists, you might also cast an eye at their spouses. Hers is a tragedy, being swept off her feet at a very early age by someone who was both used to getting his way in everything and very aware of his mortality and fragility. She has had a rotten time of it for the past ten years and all that wealth has given her no satisfaction . . . Her health is poor and her spirits are low, but I have intimations that she is beginning at last to take charge of her life – at least I hope so . . . I think that one of the qualifications of artists should be a vow of celibacy. They should be confined to ruining only their own lives.'

☆　★　☆

There was a devil in Peter, which is rather terrifyingly on view in

Tessa Dahl's novel *Working for Love* – though perhaps novel is not the most accurate term I could deploy. To tell her tale about a girl called Molly breaking away and growing up, Miss Dahl's cast includes a brain-damaged elder brother, an elder sister who dies of measles, an Iowa-born famous actress mother struck down by strokes, and an irascible artist father nearly seven feet tall. They live in a gypsy-style house packed with Francis Bacons and fine furniture . . . Anybody who knows just a little of Roald Dahl's marriage to Patricia Neal, and of the misfortune after misfortune which beset them, will see at once that this is fiction heavily reliant upon fact. Autobiography provides a frame for what reads like an impassioned, accusatory letter home. What is the point of all this for Sellers? Tessa Dahl had an affair with him when she was in her late teens. As Michael says in *P.S. I Love You*: 'Tessa was flattered and gave the impression that she was going to organise Dad's life for him. She established herself in the apartment at Roebuck House answering telephone calls and the doorbell with great self-assurance. But this time, thankfully, Dad recognised the danger signs and asked Tessa to leave . . . He didn't show much consideration when it came to giving the marching orders . . . He just told Tessa to go. And closed the door.'

Molly, at a similar stage in her development (aged eighteen) as her creator was when she knew Sellers, has a relationship with a film-world fellow – who is called Peter. This is presumptive evidence, I know; but even if the Peter in *Working for Love* is complete invention, the character remains a plausible portrait of Sellers-like evil. Sellers' behaviour with young women is here; and, by the by, a picture of what it must be like to be a child of a very famous man is here, too: 'This glorious man, my life and love who was never quite within my reach. Whom I could never quite fascinate or please. . .'

Molly's battle is to try and force her individual personality on the world when she is hemmed in by various demanding egomaniacs. She, as a child, tries to keep the peace; she cooks and she cleans. As a result, she is looked down on as a home-maker and a go-between. Love, she discovered, means protection – but it can also mean possession and control; and it can easily switch to rejection and contempt. The chief villain is her father – and she is aware that her great self-destructive fault is to look for father-figures in the men she falls for – men who try to dominate her emotionally. It is a dilemma, and it is level-headedly, sparely put: if Molly tries to express her rage for independence, that is wrong; if she cowers and takes the humiliations, that is used against her, also. Bitterness and jealousy, not acceptance and delight, are the sensations which shoot back and forth between people who are close, whether by blood or by marriage.

I was amazed when I came across one of Molly's speeches. Her eloquence is applicable to any of the women – but not only the women – who entered Sellers' force-field: 'I began to realise that I couldn't go on allowing you to control me through your manipulation and constant put-downs . . . [Molly says to her ex-husband, Jack, who could be named for the Ripper]. I don't need you. I don't need your constant tyranny. All we have is money, nothing else. No partnership, no caring, no sharing. I've done everything to be what you want me to be . . . I've grovelled, I've begged, I've been reduced to a pulp. For what? To make you feel important . . . The only way you can retain your position of power is to keep pushing me down. The game is to keep me down. Criticise and control, as long as I'm kept lower than you I will never rise to be your equal. Your greatest fear is that maybe I'll realise that I am stronger than you, more powerful than you and could, maybe, be as successful. You cannot operate without a dependent partner. You resent me, Jack, and you are dead scared of losing me.'

If the love = pain idiom is soap opera, the emotional temperature tends more towards Verdi and Donizetti than afternoon television shows (translate Molly's words into Italian and we have an aria for Dame Joan Sutherland); and when the Peter character makes his entrance, in a puff of smoke, the torpidity and suffering take on a new intensity and belong on the stage of La Scala, Milan, not 'in a block of mansion flats'. Peter is a friend of Molly's mother (as Sellers was of Patricia Neal). He quickly seduces the girl ('Peter . . . could show me, teach me, mould me') and after she's had an argument with her parents, she turns up on his doorstep. 'Well, well, what have we here?' – 'Please can I come and stay with you Peter?' – 'My poor darling, my poor little girl. Well, don't worry, I'm here now. I'll look after you.'

He quickly bores of her prattle and presence. 'Peter was a very bitter man. He was racked with jealousy and envy ... his eyes would start to narrow and the taunting would begin ... His lips would start to sneer, his voice would develop a sing-song quality and venom would pour out. Accusations, twisted statements, vehement insisting that I had committed some wrong. I would argue, I would plead my innocence.'

To no avail, of course. Peter enjoys talking himself into a paranoid rage so that he can justify his resorting to violence. Molly's skull is cracked repeatedly against a wall; she is slammed in the kidneys. She flees back to her father and mother, but they don't want her particularly. She returns to London and is nearly battered to death. 'You fucking bitch, you lousy fucking bitch. You disobeyed me, you ran to Daddy. Well, I was right, wasn't I? He should have done this to you years ago, then perhaps I wouldn't have to be doing it.' After a few hours of administering kicks, slaps, punches and gougings, Peter telephones Molly's old man: 'You did it mentally old boy, so I've finished the job. Listen, yes, that's right old boy, that's her you can hear. Well, I don't want her any more. You can have her. . .'

The mother comes and collects the limp girl. Nobody thinks of reproaching Peter, or of punishing him. (There'd be no point. It is in Lucifer's nature to try and exterminate angels.) He'd no doubt get away with murder, as Sellers always did. He calmly brushes his teeth and goes to bed.

☆ ★ ☆

Fearless vampire killer that I am, I think I have got the hang of detecting his permeations by now. If Tessa Dahl's novel – a reworking of beauty-and-the-beast where brackish beastliness wins – is not about Sellers actually, it can, in my judgement, be about Sellers allegorically. (*Hoffman* is the dark side of *There's a Girl in My*

Soup and *Working for Love* might contain perverse and poisoned elements of both of those.) So much suits him: his smotherings; his refusal to treat people as equals, only as competitors and cast-offs; his complete freedom and loathings; his subjections. It is irrelevant whether Sellers physically did to Tessa Dahl what Peter does to Molly (I very much hope he did not);* the psychological truth of her book transcends the limitations of experience or verifiable history. *Working for Love* describes possession by demons; it is an example of Sellers' afterlife in imaginative literature.

There are demons in Roald Dahl's books, too. (They are called children.) Sellers wanted to make a film of *Charlie and the Chocolate Factory*, and he would have been brilliant as the eccentric confectioner, who is half traditional twinkling mad inventor and half psychopath. 'I did not know Peter Sellers at all well,' Dahl wrote to me, 'but it is true that he wanted very much the part of Willy Wonka and I wanted him to have it. The Hollywood director would not accept him because by then in the director's words, "he had become unreliable and might not necessarily turn up on time".' Instead, in *Willy Wonka and the Chocolate Factory*, made in 1971, there is Gene Wilder, whom Sellers had so admired in *The Producers*.† Wilder gives Wonka a hysteric, cruel edge, but there is no mystique or flamboyance. I'd have laid out a lot to see Sellers' face

---

* Some considerable time *before* I'd read her novel, and following a letter from her father in which he'd told me 'My daughter, Tessa, knew Sellers a bit', she'd turned down my request for an interview. 'Peter should be allowed to rest in peace,' she informed me. I am ashamed of my response. I scrawled HOLY CHRIST WHAT SANCTIMONIOUS BALLS on her envelope and mailed it back. I at least demonstrated, through my callous stupidity, that behaving badly and ungraciously was not a Sellers monopoly. I unreservedly apologise. However if we leave perturbed spirits to try and R.I.P., what does that mean for the art of biography?

† Sellers once had a thought running through his head to return to the stage in an adaptation of the Mel Brooks film. 'I had never met Mel before, and we just went walking around New York together, having a good time, going to the Russian Tea Room, talking, talking, talking.' Sellers would have been Max Bialystock, the Zero Mostel part; Kenneth Griffith was to be Bloom. In the end, Sellers had to content himself with going on chat shows, Milligan's *This Is Your Life*, etc.,

when the children are tortured and disappear – Augustus Gloop getting sucked up the waste pipe of the chocolate vat and Violet turning into a giant blueberry, to name only a pair of delights.

He was always massacring innocents, so to speak. After the turning-point in the early Sixties, when he zoomed from star to superstar status, his refractoriness intensified; and the destructive forces which made a hell of his private life created such despondency on his film sets, clearly the man and the artist were one. Roy Boulting has said that his relationship with Sellers during the making of *There's a Girl in My Soup* 'had been a very abrasive one. I emerged from it worn, shaken and swearing that I would never endure such an experience again. What I did not know until later was that Peter himself was suffering domestic traumas at the time that left him nervy, irritable and deeply unhappy.' Yet he always had domestic traumas on the go. He inculcated them; they were one of his diversions, thinking up new ways of being repulsive. If he played up at work, therefore, because of discord at home, this wasn't a case of straightforward coincidence or correlation. It was his nature.

Fame facilitated the release of all the unpleasantness in him. His faculties, too, altered. He went from being the sort of actor who entered into his characters and revealed their oddities and quirks and became – or tried to become – the kind of performer who insisted on his own ego and vision. The earlier Sellers, as it were, was like Coleridge's idea about Shakespeare, 'darting himself forth and passing into all the forms of human character and passion'; whilst the later Sellers was more Miltonic, intent 'on attracting all forms and things to himself, into the unity of his own grand Ideal' – which in Sellers' case meant being able to indulge his selfishness and riot. This is why, after *Doctor Strangelove*, characters come to resemble one another: Evelyn Tremble, in *Casino Royale*, is an Anglicised Harold Fine, from *I Love You, Alice B. Toklas*; Benjamin Hoffman and Robert Danvers are shadowy and sunny twins; Chance and Fu

---

dressed up as Kenneth Mars' Nazi playwright, author of the surprise hit musical *Springtime for Hitler*.

Manchu are serene and godlike, and Nayland Smith and Fu recognise a kinship. Then there's *The Prisoner of Zenda*, which is about a pair of brothers ... Sellers was a one-man family, and he felt ranged against the world.

Once awakened, his evil nature created the problems he could then complain about. As Wolf Mankowitz says: 'Sellers' poor standards of behaviour would create the most unbelievable mess – because by *Casino Royale*, say, he was pretty well round the bend and couldn't function properly. He'd change the order of shooting on what might be very complicated films. He'd be "unavailable" or he'd constantly change his timing, making it difficult to splice material together. Charlie Feldman expected a four-and-a-half million budget. It ran away to the tune of twenty-eight million. The eventual film doesn't make sense. Nothing connects. I wrote it as a quartet of Bonds. Who is James Bond? Is he this? Is he that? Is he really 007? Is he really ... Just a joke. Because of Sellers it was cut, re-cut, screwed around with a thousand different ways. There were different directors; different writers were working on scripts for different actors.* Joe McGrath, Sellers and Terry Southern came up with their own versions of the script, full of dream sequences. Charlie agreed to anything to keep Sellers happy. He gave him a white Rolls Royce on the first day of shooting, just as a come-on.'

If he had intended to bribe Sellers into being complaisant, Feldman found the opposite was happening. 'Feldman was glad to get Sellers at any price,' says Joe McGrath. 'He'd put up the money for

---

* For example:

February 13th 1991

Dear Roger Lewis,

 ... Worked two weeks and wrote scenes nobody ever used. Was told there was no script at all for the movie when shooting began, and that on some days Sellers flatly refused to 'go' ... Good luck with the project. Sellers was a favourite of everyone's ...

Cordially,
Joseph Heller.

Sellers' personal insurance on *What's New, Pussycat?* – after his heart attack, nobody would cover him – but Sellers wouldn't be beguiled. "Even at that time Feldman was devious," Sellers told me. "At the end there's a go-cart sequence. The idea had come up and they'd shot it without my permission." There was a great row with Charlie. Sellers eventually agreed to go back and do some close-ups, driving a go-cart, and allowed the scene to be shown. He said to me, "I should have been aware of that – that's what he'll do on *Casino Royale*."'

Sellers imputed underhand tactics to the producer, and his mistrust spread across the film like a cancer. 'I walked off the film after six or seven weeks' shooting,' says McGrath. 'I told Feldman, "It's pointless going on. There's no control. Nobody has any overall feeling for the film and what's happening". Sellers phoned me and said, "Come back. He's going to give you a Rolls Royce." I said, "I don't want a Rolls Royce". Two years later I was in Beverly Hills and a guy named Jerry Bressler, who ended up having a credit as Executive Producer, pulled up in a white Corniche and said, "Are you Joe McGrath? I'm driving your Rolls Royce." He gave it to Jerry Bressler.'

McGrath was responsible for the seduction scene, in which Tremble dressed up as Hitler and Napoleon to try and impress Ursula Andress. 'A typical Sellers scene,' says McGrath. 'He wrote to me later: "Looking back on it, I realise I should have stuck with you. I should have stuck with that, because that scene had the strange Goonish vision you and I know about, so please let's work together again." Hence *The Magic Christian* and *The Great McGonagall*. Milligan phoned him up, over *Casino Royale*, and said that the disguise sequence, where Ursula is photographing him, was wonderful. "Peter, what went wrong with the rest of the movie?" Our script [the Sellers-Southern-McGrath version] would then have had Peter playing a lot of other parts – disguises. That was the whole point of the scene: "I'll show you what I can do, who I can turn into." Tremble as Hitler, Tremble as Napoleon. I was meeting with Sellers and writing it at the Dorchester, and then shooting it.'

Or not shooting it, because his nibs had his little tantrum about Welles. Whatever it was that emanated from the hotel suite, it was nevertheless Mankowitz's job to try and co-ordinate it with his own proliferating draft screenplays. By June 9th 1966, *he'd* had enough, and he instructed his agent, John Heyman, to send Feldman the following letter:

[...]

Wolf feels that there really is very little more he can contribute to CASINO ROYALE. He also points out that in the past two weeks he has done –
1) rewrites for the last sequence [the gunfight at the casino].*
2) rewrites and cuts for the Tremble sequence which was in total chaos and is now ordered and effective.
3) new link scenes for Niven [in an office talking on the phone].
4) additional material for Cooper – which, even if it doesn't

---

*   MEMORANDUM

TO: C. K. Feldman
FROM: Wolf Mankowitz

re *Casino Royale sequence*

Herewith a suggested fight and chase development which follows the end of the game between Sellers and Welles.

Instead of Welles doing his disappearing trick in the wheel-chair as at present suggested, he makes a signal – perhaps coloured rockets going up from rocket emplacements in his chair.

On getting the signal, a number of Casino servants, who were all assumed to be men before, pull down zippers and reveal themselves to be wearing basic killer-girl costumes. They back up Le Chiffre and advance upon Sellers, Vesper, Mathis and his plain-clothes men.

There follows a Western-style fight between the killer-girls (being directed by Le Chiffre from his wheel-chair), and the Sellers group, resulting in the total destruction of the Casino salon, Wild West Style, breaking up of furniture, mirrors, etc.. At end of fight actual cowboys on horses materialise and gallop through, or the Texas cavalry. Obviously this can go as mad as the game between Sellers and Welles.

Welles makes his get-away in the wheel chair and we go into the chase sequence which, to my knowledge, has not yet been rediscussed in detail.

996

satisfy you, is the best he has been able to come up with.
5) some cuts on Mata Bond and story discussion with Karel
Reisz [for scenes directed by Ken Hughes].

. . .

The problems alluded to in point (2) gave rise to all the other
predicaments. Point (4), by the way, connects with a long memorandum, previously delivered to Feldman, in which Mankowitz
outlined how a burly middle-aged nondescript played by Terence
Cooper could be incorporated into the story to fill the gap left by
the errant Sellers: 'Introduce Cooper as black sheep nephew of Sir
James Bond who has been under contract to the Secret Service and
is a completely useless cocksman. His deal with the Secret Service is
the result of James Bond's retirement arrangements. [Later he
is shot] but the effects are not fatal. Still wounded, Cooper fights
his way right through [the rest of the film] taking over all the
action material at present carried by Sellers and Andress who we
write out . . . entirely.' At the end, Sir James was to go back into
retirement and Cooper was to take over as head of the Secret
Service.

If you watch the picture, therefore, and wonder who this big boring lump is and what he is doing, he is standing in for Sellers.
(Another idea was to have replaced Sellers with Danny La Rue, 'the
best drag-artist in the world'. La Rue would have been Mata Bond,
'with the awful revelation to Bond at the end that his illegitimate
child is a pouf. . . . This gives us [a] vaudeville reference and I think
the idea of someone as distinguished as Sir James Bond having a
low burlesque comic for a son is quite funny,' Mankowitz wrote un-
convincingly to Feldman.) It is also clear, from my examination of
the material edited and presented under point (2) that Sellers didn't
execute the photography sequence with that much dedication.
Tremble has been invited to Vesper Lynd's pad, a Sixties dream-
scape of round beds, sunken floors, mirrors, fish tanks, Tiffany
lamps and Klimt posters. He dresses up as Hitler, Napoleon, and
Toulouse Lautrec – and that's it. They are meant to be discussing

baccarat and working up to making love, but Sellers is glassy. He doesn't bother to speak in Germanic, French, or Groucho Marx voices, as indicated by the script. Nor did he pursue his original idea to make Tremble a boy from Birmingham: 'It's the most unattractive, the least sexy accent in Britain,' he'd told Joe McGrath. 'James Bond parodied as Black Country. The epitome of the Secret Service with a horrible whine – there are possibilities . . .'

'We could have done a whole sequence of him starting off with the Birmingham accent and then losing it,' says McGrath. 'When he's taken down to the basement of Harrods and they fix him up with the clothes and gadgets, they could have given him elocution lessons.'

Clearly, Sellers was more interested in making trouble than making a film – here's how the genesis of *Hoffman* was described to me: 'Between the time when I had been advanced money and supported by the London head of Columbia, and the time when the script was finished and I'd acquired the interest of Peter, the hierarchy of Columbia in London had changed,' explained Ben Arbeid. 'A different man altogether, called John Van Eyssen, an ex-actor, had become Head of Production. As was my obligation, when the script was finished and the project was put together, it was submitted to Columbia for first refusal. Van Eyssen rejected it, criticising the script. He said it needed fixing, and he waved his arms about. When Alvin Rakoff asked for some suggestions, he said, "I'm not going to be the buyer and the seller." By the end of the week, a new deal was signed with Bryan Forbes and EMI. I then had the job of informing Columbia formally that I was withdrawing the film, in view of their attitude, and that any money advanced would be returned etc. etc. I felt I had to inform Peter, because he was still expecting to work for Columbia, about Van Eyssen's coolness. "I understand," he said. "Don't worry – I think I know why. . . You know he was an actor, a lousy actor? Well, it was only a year or so ago that Miranda and I were guests on Sam Spiegel's yacht at Cannes. So was John Van Eyssen, whom I found myself sitting next to at dinner. I can't deny that I was a little high on marijuana. I said, 'How you doing John?' – 'Oh, fine.' – 'What are you doing, John?' – 'I'm now the Head of Production at Columbia Pictures.' At which point I fell off my chair in hysteria, and pointed at him and said: 'You, you cunt, you couldn't even act the part.' You can get an idea why he didn't want to do *Hoffman* with me in it."'

☆ ★ ☆

Once established at EMI, Elstree, Sellers decided to turn the director's bowels to water. 'To get to know Peter, I'd accompanied him to a veteran car sale at Olympia. He was already showing signs of anxiety about various things – "The part's unplayable" – and I tried to reassure him saying we'd rehearse for a few days, we'll ease into it, settle things – a quiet rehearsal, without anybody else present who'd distract him. "We'll decide later who we get rid of and who we don't." He said this very pointedly, and I thought, well, he means me. His conversation began to have a manic feel about it. I was called to this meeting, where Ernie Gebler had got hold of a print of the television play, *Call Me Daddy* – Donald Pleasence and Judy Cornwell doing the original of *Hoffman* in 1967, when it had won an EMMY for ABC. It was run. The quality of the recording was appalling, but there was enough there to see how it was done. When it had finished, Peter said, "Well, *he* didn't know how to play the part either. That's what I mean." I decided not to defend the production, though I was a bit surprised he'd decided to attack a fellow actor – so I talked about what could be done. We'd have more time before we started to rehearse and get it right, I argued. We talked and talked, and finally Peter said, "I don't think you and I will ever get on anyway, Alvin." I was absolutely taken aback and upset. I left the meeting. Ben Arbeid followed me to the door and I said to him, "There are certain things that ought to be said that I'm not saying." – "Come back and say them." – "No, no." Ben insisted that I went back. I went back into the room, and Peter was sitting with Bert Mortimer. I said, "I understand Peter's anxiety – he was an actor who didn't know how to play a part; but what wasn't right, what I didn't appreciate, was the fact that I'd taken this very short idea from Ernie Gebler, made it into this television script by the actors' contribution – Donald and Judy coming up with ideas – but,

999

without bragging too much, primarily me coming up with ideas –
and we'd extended the story. It is a great basic premise: a man
wants to get a girl into his flat to show how much he loves her. He's
had all kinds of sexual fantasies, which he can't perform . . . From
that television play, Ernie had written a book and a screenplay. My
thanks for doing all this on the author's behalf was to be dismissed."
I remember going down the stairs and reminding myself to tell Ben
that I do have a contract – so I can be dismissed from the meeting,
but not the picture. But I didn't point this out. The next day Dennis
Selinger rang and said, "Bert says how brave you'd been confronting Sellers and walking out of the picture." – "Just a second
Dennis," I said, "I didn't walk out of the picture, and I've got a
contract." I rang Ben; he said, "It is debatable as to whether you
walked out of the picture or the meeting." Ben agreed with me, "I
hired you. Peter can't fire you – only I can fire you." Then began
horrendous days of waiting to see what would happen. Behind the
scenes machinations were going on – Peter trying to get Bryan
Forbes to direct it; Ernie wanting to direct it. Ernie thought he and
Peter could direct it between them. Eventually, a phone call came
from Peter, much to my relief, "Let's see if we can get together."

'We were supposed to rehearse for two weeks – Peter couldn't
stand rehearsing, as is well known. He keep saying filming and film
making is not rehearsing; I pointed out that Rod Steiger is always
desperate to rehearse. You can sort your problems out and you
haven't got a hundred crew members staring at you, and you aren't
worried about the time ticking away . . . You are doing it quietly in
a rehearsal room. Peter didn't see this. Ben had made it a condition
that the author not be present – knowing that Peter and Ernie had
defended each other – but I felt this was a mistake: I thought it
would be easier to have Ernie in front of me, so that any conversations would be more out in the open. As I'd tried to say to Peter,
that day at the car auction, the author must realise you'll change the
words – you've got to make adjustments.

'Peter did enjoy the novelty of moving around the markers we'd
laid out for the set, but by the third day he was suddenly in one of
his other moods:

'"We should be on the proper set. I can't pretend. I can't see the fucking wall that's meant to be here."

'"Do you want to abandon rehearsal?"

'"I've done enough. There's nothing to do here. I'm prepared to shoot."

'We did a night shoot. He and Sinead coming back from the restaurant. Two takes. The relationship between he and I was getting better – by the time we got into the studio, we were virtually friends. He came back here in the evening – he said he loved my wife's curtains, which are still up. He loved this Bedford Park house. I'd moved here in 1968. He arranged for the installation of the hi-fi equipment – all that bank of stuff, speakers all over the house, wires under the floors. "Oh, I can do that!" he exclaimed when I said I wanted a hi-fi set. "How much can I spend?" I'd thought about forty pounds – this was a quarter of a century ago. Knowing it was Peter, I said: "Two hundred pounds." The bill was a *thousand* pounds. "Peter, what have you done to me?" He came here with Sinead. Bert was shadowing him. He was just getting rid of Miranda, wasn't he? Miranda said to me, during the shooting – she came on the set – not knowing he was seeing Sinead, "He loves being in this picture now." He had several rows with Sinead, whom he called Cyanide or Senapod. Peter bought her a solid gold nugget cigarette lighter. She got into a row with him, and she was driving past Regent's Park canal, and with her Irish temper, she made the cab stop, and she hurled this ingot into the water. "Tell us where it is, we'll send divers down!" we all said.

'The last day of shooting, a van appeared with gifts for everybody – Leica cameras, television sets. He put his arms around Ben and I and said, "I can't give you two guys enough – so what I want you to do is to take your wives and go away for a week's holiday – to anywhere you like in the world – and send me the bill." I said thank you very much. Ben was thrilled by this. When Peter was out of earshot I said, "I would've settled for a Leica quite happily." – "Why?" – "We can't do it can we? Can't go away for a week and send him the bill?" Ben eventually went on a trip and he did send

Peter the bill – as a joke. Sellers did forget about his promise, of course he did.

'The last time I saw Peter, I was waiting for him to come up to Elstree to do some post syncing, and he was in a car he'd just acquired, a Ferrari, accompanied by the legendary Bert – and Peter was driving and he lost control of it coming up the Finchley Road. He got out of the car, hailed a taxi, and never went near the Ferrari again. He just abandoned it. A jinxed car. He was always talking about things emanating bad vibes. So he was in a *terribly* bad mood, and a bit frightened. To me, the picture generally suffered because of his moodiness. You can't have the director virtually fired and then re-hired – if you go through any chicanery, rockiness, with a director, it's there all the time. My relationship with Peter went from a disaster, to warmth, to oblivion, which is true of most of his relationships, I believe.'

☆ ★ ☆

On November 24th 1969, Sellers bought a page in the trade paper, *Today's Cinema*, and informed its readers: '*Hoffman* was not only a motion picture – it was an experience I will always remember' – with dread. 'He hated the film after it was finished,' says Arbeid. 'He wanted it burnt.' This was a frequent invocation, which had nothing to do with his retroactive wish that he'd done better. (A consistently crappy Sellers thing was his allegation that he was a perfectionist.) Sellers wanted to destroy his films because he saw, with considerable mortification, that they were self-revelations. As he put it, 'I'm too close to all of them to be objective. I couldn't stand outside any of those characters – I've got to *be* them. So I could never be "critical". . .'

To the present purpose, therefore, comes Lionel Meadows, from *Never Let Go*; the energy Sellers found for the character suggests a fascination with evil. (Pasolini, the director of evil, would have relished Sellers, I think.) But after that film, he played it safe. He became more of a cartoon actor, throughout the Sixties, and refused to allow the public to appreciate his capabilities – instead, his

lechery was caricatured (*What's New, Pussycat?*), his vanity was
mocked (*The World of Henry Orient*), his explosive temper was
Latinised (*After the Fox*), his solitariness was made clumsy (Clouseau's appearances) etc. His propensity to go over the top for its
own sake was often unrestrained, rather than inventive (Evelyn
Tremble, in a related though opposite way, is so muted, he's bland
– which is not the same thing as his being understated); or perhaps
it was simply that, after his heart attack, he had to show off and
convince us of his irrepressibility? And is that why, in contrast to
the black and white movies of the Fifties and early Sixties, he's
often less than recognisably human?

Whatever, he was still egotistical beyond, and if his film rôles
made comic capital out of the seven deadly sins – pride (Robert
Danvers), anger (Aldo Vanucci), envy (Harold Fine), lust (Fritz
Fassbender), gluttony (Danvers again, also Hoffman's food/sex
imagery), avarice (Mr Hoffnagel) and sloth (Dr Pratt) – in real life
he was increasingly disabled by his appetites. His versatility was
compromised by pettiness and spite; his determination and ambition became a coarse kind of stubbornness; and his mercurialism
and affectations, out of which he had once made art, left him dissipated. If, on the screen, his performances came to be
self-indulgent turns, hollow at the core, that is because his juice was
being deployed to spoil the films he was in, as he was making them
– not only before or after the shoot, like *Hoffman*; not merely with
stops and starts and delays, like *Casino Royale*, but as the cameras
turned.

'The one thing he enjoyed was manoeuvring and manipulating,'
says Peter Medak. 'He'd do a deal with a producer, and then decide
he deserved more money. For *Ghost in the Noonday Sun*, he
doubled his money, and the producers had to cave in or the picture
wouldn't have gone ahead and they'd already built this pirate ship
in Athens. To save money, to pay Peter, they'd fitted it with two re-
holed engines. Every day the engines broke down. Other boats
would come and rescue us and supply us with food. I was told that a
week after we left, one of the skippers of the catering ships, called

Kostas, claimed salvage in the courts and got the boat – he said he'd rescued it. It was then sunk in the harbour at Kyrenia when the Turks invaded.

'To this day, the producers think I was a party to the games, which I wasn't. I tried to reason with Peter, but he wouldn't listen – and it suited his purpose – whatever that was – to create a situation between me and the producers. Gareth Wigan came out to Cyprus to supervise. His whole job was to organise the schedule so that we kept shooting, and that basically every scene in the script was legally shot – so long as it was shot, Columbia couldn't object to paying for the film. We'd have made the film we were contracted to make. So it was like running a factory – an endurance test. All because of Peter – his contumeliousness. Sometimes he got carried away and started acting – sometimes, you can see it in the film, he'd switch off right in the middle of a scene – comes right out of character and stops acting. We'd created this Irish character who was so stupid he had no forehead. As the picture progressed, the forehead got higher and higher because he couldn't be bothered to put any make-up on. He had lots of problems – he'd just broken up with Liza Minnelli, whom he was infatuated by. He was on drugs – marijuana, I don't know what else. He created terrible problems with himself and Tony Franciosa. He alienated everybody.'

☆ ★ ☆

The Minnelli episode, which wrecked the production schedule of *Soft Beds, Hard Battles* such that the Boultings were nearly bankrupted, in addition to imperilling *Ghost in the Noonday Sun*, and the future career of its helmsmen, was a fast-motion version of all his other love-affairs – a world which turned from glee to wearisomeness. (He was still married to Miranda, but no matter.) He was glad to be with a show business creature again, after the blue-blood experiment and the Irish exiles; and Liza,[*] who always has about

---

[*] My publisher's legal advisers have requested that I make it clear that this whole paragraph refers only to Liza Minnelli's characters. I am happy to assert this fact and to concur that my descriptions would be impertinent and misleading if applied to a real human being.

her the flooziness of Sally Bowles, reminded him of a successful version of his mother – Peg, the cabaret performer, eager to perform, to give out . . . Liza, too, was a bird-woman – her eyelashes are like the wings of an injured crow; and is Loren there, also, in those dark and lumpy features? In that automatic flirtatiousness? Yet where Loren plays duchesses, countesses from Hong Kong – millionairesses – Liza's public persona is vampish, a bit sleazy; she is ripe and erotic, very much the daughter of the fag-hag of fag-hags, Judy Garland.

Sellers was impassioned by these connections and reverberations. Liza had opened at the Palladium on May 11th 1973, for three nights. Sellers was so excited, he stood up at the première and began taking photographs, no doubt infringing any amount of copyright laws. He came back for the second and third performances, and similarly bounded about popping flash bulbs. Liza's reaction was magnificent. Since Sellers was so keen, she invited herself and full company back to his bijou house, at 11 Eaton Mews North, and did a selection of her numbers specially for him in the lounge-room. 'Peter was overwhelmed,' Bert Mortimer, who was also squeezed on to the premises, commented. (I'm imagining something like the stateroom scene in *A Night at the Opera*.) 'It was Liza's zany zing that really got to him.'

Perhaps because of her energy, perhaps because she was always aware of the omnipresent camera, Sellers called her 'Flash'. He had this sobriquet inscribed on a miniature tape recorder, which was one of his first presents. They attended Noël Coward's Memorial Service together; they decided they were in love. 'I fell in love with this man, and I am pleased to say he fell in love with me,' Liza told the press. 'I have always been an admirer of his wonderful talent and we both believe in humour and in having good times.' Sellers drove his fan up to Hampstead to show her off to Anne.

'It was a bit odd coming to my house anyway,' she recalls, of this curious visit. Was Sellers wanting his former wife's approval? Or was he gloating? Both, probably. Sellers was now talking of marriage – and a formal engagement had been announced on May

22nd. Liza, however, took Anne's chum, Loretta Feldman, aside and said: 'How the hell did he ever let her go? He's got to be out of his mind!' (Well, yes.)

Liza had to return to America, for a professional engagement in Chicago. She came back to London on June 4th, with the intention of staying at the Savoy. Sellers had other plans. He met her at Heathrow and she stayed for over two weeks at Eaton Mews North. So that she could continue to rehearse her songs, he'd sent a removal lorry to Hampstead to confiscate Sarah's Knight's piano. 'During their hot passionate . . . relationship,' Bert Mortimer said, 'they spent virtually every night together' – not only in the obvious place, but at clubs and discos. As a result, Sellers, who had six a.m. calls for the Boulting film, would slump, snort and snore in the make-up chair. Liza accompanied him to Shepperton and made breakfasts of spaghetti. She then applauded his transformations into Nazis, Japanese generals, and French persons. 'It is terrific', she said, 'to find yourself in love with a genius'.

The production shut down so that the genius could recuperate, and grow bored with his new conquest. It was obvious to anybody that Liza's need for excitement upon excitement would pall on him. So it proved. He began to complain of her high definition personality to Bert Mortimer: 'I just can't keep up the pace with her!' he lamented (multiple orgasms or dancing at Tramps?) To Michael he moaned about her entourage of secretaries and executive assistants – he didn't like his queen to come with a court of her own. Liza wouldn't budge. 'These are my friends, Peter. They're always going to be my friends.'

The whole romance was followed by the press – which could see it was a joke from first to last. The couple were accompanied by journalists when they decided to double-check with a clairvoyant and see if they had a future. Frederick Davies, Liza's choice of soothsayer, read the Tarot pack and informed his clients that the prognosis did not look good. ('Why didn't she go to my fucking clairvoyant?' demanded Sellers with memorable semi-conscious irony.) By June 20th, the two stars had collided and left each other's orbit.

'It's over, but Peter is marvellous and we had a lovely, lovely time,' pronounced Liza. 'Regrets? No, I have none.'

The relationship finished as it had begun – five weeks previously – with a crowd of people present. 'When he parted from Liza Minnelli they had a rave-up at the Trattoo which went on for four solid days', says Alan Clare, who played the piano for those ninety-six hours. 'The entire love-affair was like a publicity stunt.'

☆ ★ ☆

Sellers had enjoyed and encouraged the press attention – 'Liza Minnelli and Peter Sellers at Shepperton film studios yesterday . . . Miss Minnelli held a press conference to announce that the engagement to Desi Arnaz Jr was off and that she is in love with Sellers' (*Guardian*); 'On the film set Liza lovingly sees through one of Peter's disguises' (*Sunday Mirror*); etc. etc. If he read about himself in the public prints, it had to be true. But Liza wrong-footed him when it came to announcing their dissolution. He hated it that the public were being told that *she* was leaving *him*. 'It's true, but it was for Liza to say so,' he pseudo-gallantly said when asked to confirm the news. 'We are finished, but it was not my wish.'

It was with an affectedly broken-hearted Sellers that Medak had to contend during pre-production. ('I wasn't sure he'd ever read the script' the director told me); but by the autumn of 1973, when they were in Cyprus, Minnelli's effects were wearing off. He gave himself booster shots of amorous wrangling by squiring Titi Wachtmeister, another Britt lookalike, but fresh sport was required. Sellers had to devise a new torture. Hence, his decision to harass Tony Franciosa. 'He mocked Franciosa without mercy,' says Medak. 'He walked down the street shouting, "You fucking western cowboy." On the set he yelled, "Come on you American cowboy, you can act better than that." I did a take. We cut. The boat had to be turned around in a big circle to get the sun in the right place for another take. Peter took his wig off and was leaning over the poop deck. Franciosa came over to me and said, "I'm going to fucking kill that son of a bitch – if he says one more word, and provokes me once more, I'll knock him out and not be responsible. . ." He was getting worked up talking to me. He picked his heavy sword up and I thought he was going to cut Sellers' head into two halves. He stopped an inch above Sellers' head – Peter was turned away, and didn't see. But Bert Mortimer saw this. I pulled Tony away. Five minutes later, Bert was with the make-up men, the Framptons, whispering to Peter. Two seconds later, Peter throws his wig and boots into the sea and jumps into a speedboat. I got in after him. "That fucking man tried to kill me," he screamed. "Who the fuck does he think he is? I refuse to be in the same frame as him!" I reported that to Gareth Wigan, who said, "You'll just have to do it in separate frames, then, won't you?" There was meant to be a whole confrontation scene between the two characters at the end. How could we do it?'

It was a repeat of Sellers' Welles aversion. The duel, instead of being on screen, was between the actors on the set – or simply deep in Sellers' mind. I asked Franciosa for his recollections and the first thing he said to me was: 'Why wouldn't Sellers see a psychiatrist?' Then he went on: 'I was a great Sellers admirer. I was a fan. Then I was to work with him. He seemed to have a lot of problems, though nobody knew their source. He was unhappy with Medak, I couldn't see why. I don't think Sellers had reasons for behaving as he did, certainly none that I could see. He just seemed to want to sabotage the production. Medak was shooting correctly. Everybody was doing their best, under trying conditions on the ship. Sellers wouldn't cooperate. We did have a few harsh words – which made me unhappy, as I'd had such a respect for his talent. He didn't speak to me after a while, and I was very sad that he felt this way. From my personal point of view, I spent a glorious two months on Cyprus with my wife and children – and I do believe that Sellers took against me even for this.'

I should think that Franciosa's ability to return to, and seek sanctuary amongst, a happy family atmosphere would have rattled Sellers no end. He'd have been convulsed with jealousy – and resentment that his attempts to undermine his co-star were not working. Franciosa had also refused to vote with him for the sacking of the director, and as he told me: 'Sellers was adversarial. He was paranoid about people around him. If you disagreed with him at all, as I did over his desire to sack Medak, you were confronting his paranoia. He had profound problems!'

His immediate one was how to wreck the film if the director was staying put, his co-star remained relatively unflurried, and Gareth Wigan was keeping a cautious eye on all and sundry. Of course! Why hadn't he thought of this one before? Brilliant! If there is one thing you need as a basic skill when making films it is a chap to focus the camera. So Sellers sacked the cinematographer, Larry Pizer.

This was a particularly injurious and shitty deed, because Pizer had shot *The Optimists of Nine Elms* and Sellers therefore knew that he was trifling with a totally competent and distinguished technician. They'd parted from the earlier film on good terms and Sellers had said, 'I look forward to seeing you on the next one, Larry!' Pizer had scouted for locations and had viewed the boat at Pireus. He helped the art director to design the bridge and the entrances to the cabins, so that the vessel would adapt itself to the shooting. Work began and (as he told me) 'one became aware of a lot of tension on the set and a feeling of people being careful of what they said, and looking at their watches – and suddenly I was asked to leave. I'd been working fourteen hour days in the heat and the dust. I remember a party with Peter – he was singing all his Old Sam the busker songs, and his daughter, Victoria, who was about eight, was on my lap, joining in. A happy evening – Peter was singing – but why was I suddenly invited out of the blue at a moment's notice to go and join him? The following morning I was told to leave the picture. What was especially upsetting, and what I found strange, was that I was told to leave that very day – I was handed a plane ticket for a flight leaving at midnight. They wanted me out of the place like I had some terrible contagious disease, and I had to be wiped out. Very odd. I flatly refused to leave so quickly – an impossible demand, quite apart from the fact I was exhausted. I think I upset Sellers by hanging around until the next day. I did see, in the hotel, members of the cast and crew – and of course there was this fear that I'd do something detrimental to the morale of the unit. But Sellers had wanted the director of photography to disappear off the face of the earth overnight. Cast and crew were indeed bewildered by the event; they clubbed together and bought me a brass ship's lamp.

'Peter had asked me to his party, for his sake or my sake? I'll never know. He didn't say a word or indicate anything about what was going to happen. He clearly knew. His decision, the director of photography's going. That last supper . . . Peter Medak was very upset, but he was in no position to help me, or to offer any explanations. Oh, no, they all said, it had nothing to do with my work. They were thrilled with what I'd shot . . . I'd given my total dedication to the man in charge of the picture, that's the person I'm responsible to, the director, and this I did on *Ghost in the Noonday Sun*. I was busy making the picture look good – did my departure improve it? I wasn't there! But I left a whole camera crew there . . . .'*

It was precisely because Pizer was making the picture look good, and heeding Medak's instructions, that Sellers had to have him exterminated – he was the strong link in the chain. That was devious enough. What was shabby to the point of criminality was the note, signed with his Shanti Om mystic monogram, which he sent to Pizer's home at Harrow Weald, Middlesex, to greet the chastened cinematographer on his return:

Kyrenia
Sunday 30th [October 1973]

My dear friend Larry,

There is no *clear* answer to the reason for your going except that Medak was thought to need an iron willed cameraman because he is unable to make his mind up. Chaos is supreme here and I

---

* Larry Pizer's position was taken over by Michael Reed, whose credits included *Dracula Prince of Darkness* and *On Her Majesty's Secret Service*.

await Milligan (if he decides to come) with eagerness, as if all is not clear *then* – thank God we will all go home.

It's easy to say but don't be unhappy, it has NOTHING to do with you.

Your true friend . . .

Sellers refused to view himself as a participant in the dramas and upheavals he'd set going; yet he was at least in the right of it when he emphasised Pizer's innocence. Was he subconsciously admitting that it had EVERYTHING to do with himself? But it is shameful behaviour, unameliorated, as it turned out, by Milligan's arrival. ('Once Spike arrived he eased up a little bit,' says Medak, 'but then he got bored with that as well.')

'Nobody on the film was funny,' Milligan told me. 'Not the director, not Tony Franciosa, not Peter, not anybody. Medak is a very lovely man, but because Peter kept leaving Cyprus to go back to England, the film was dead from the start . . . What I did was I decided to make the gang of pirates idiots and failures – you saw them singing for alms in the streets of Tangiers. They sight a duck at sea and go after it in a long boat with a cannon and blow it out of the water. A lot of that went on. They are total failures as pirates. They can't get it together. They try to get to a Greek island and land in Co. Cork. That's what I tried to do to it. But every day was a miserable episode. Tony Franciosa claimed that I was baby-sitting for Peter Sellers,* which was a bloody insult. He threatened he was going to kill us. So I went up to him and said, "What's all this?" He said, "You came on the film to babysit for Sellers." – "If that's

---

* In that Milligan joined the film in mid-production, to re-write the script and incorporate a major character for himself, called Billy Bombay, and that all this was done at Sellers' initial request and insistence; and given that, as ever, the film company was trying desperately to appease Sellers, you can see how Franciosa came to use this – albeit pejorative – term. The subsequent surfacing of Sellers/Milligan rivalries on the film I have discussed elsewhere.

what you think, I'm leaving tomorrow." And I did. I got on a plane the next morning and that was it.'

☆　★　☆

As we can see, Sellers was not lackadaisical or an eccentric; he was not careless, lazy, or simply childish. He was systematically destructive, putting a great deal of effort into his backstairs plotting. (It's where his audacity went.) He was amazingly inconsiderate – people would write scripts, build sets, prepare shots, and he'd disappear. That (as it might be) ninety crew members were sweltering on a galleon, getting it ready for his big scene, only encouraged him to whizz away from them in his luxury yacht. 'He did this because he enjoyed it,' a veteran Key-Grip told me. 'On one occasion I had to build a long track for the camera crane. It took me four hours to carry the equipment across the dunes to the location. A big set-up rig. Just as I'd finished, a message came over the short-wave radio: "Wrap it. Sellers won't come and do the scene." This happened all the time. A nasty man. Even now I can never come to terms with how brilliant people say he was . . .'

After *Doctor Strangelove*, nobody, from the director down to the caterers' runners, was immune to his chicanery. You never knew when he'd become crackbrain. Clive Rees told me that, throughout the making of *The Blockhouse*, he was 'fully expecting typical Sellers bad behaviour at any moment – and this was a great strain. One had to be very sensitive with him. No point in being either histrionic or acquiescent; you couldn't bawl or crawl. At last it came – Sellers turned up in a kaftan and a long wig. He was also stoned. I decided to ignore him and eventually he fell asleep in a corner. He phoned me up at three o'clock in the morning: "You didn't like my poncho?" – "I think Clint Eastwood has given them new meaning." – "My wig?" – "I hated it."'

Anthony Simmons had to endure a similar bout of unbidden inspiration. 'There was to be a busking sequence outside the Prince of Wales and the Windmill Theatre. An expensive day for us, on our tiny budget, because of the extras, and it was a Sunday – overtime for the crew. I got a call at three a.m. Peter suddenly had all these marvellous ideas about what he was going to do. He was going to have Old Sam strip naked and arrive on a white horse – and he was going to do all his music hall act on this white horse outside the Windmill. "Fine, Peter. See you tomorrow morning." In the morning he'd totally forgotten all about it. We didn't have any white horse, but I fear if we'd been a big studio with lots of money, that's what he'd have insisted on – white horses. People gave in to his crazy whims.'

They did, always. If he had accomplished good work, he still liked to retain the right to go back and spoil it. He couldn't set fire to *Hoffman*, but he made sure he pooh-poohed it in the press. Likewise he decried *The Prisoner of Zenda* ('I advise people not to go to see it'), *Murder by Death* ('the epitome of eight millimetre home-movie making'), and just about everything else, including his own life, or Life. I'm referring to his behaviour towards Peter Evans and the composition of *The Mask Behind the Mask*, which was first published in 1968. 'I had nothing to do with the book at all,' Sellers claimed. 'It was Peter Evans' own brain child. He knows that. I couldn't stop him from going to see the people who talk about me. I knew about the book being done and I expressed my displeasure at his doing it. I asked him to wait until much later in my career, and then to do one from the masses of notes on the things I've done and the people I've met and the incredible situations I've been in. At some time in my life I mean to make them into book form. The true story! But I didn't want it then. The book wasn't done with my approval.'

No more was ever heard of 'The Sellers Papers', if such an archive, or *nachlass*, existed, which I doubt. Nor was Sellers being fair to Evans' book, which is indeed a true story, in so far as it went. Where his comments verge on the definitely false, however, is the impression he gave of being completely asunder from the project. In fact, it was practically an authorised biography. As Evans explained to me: 'He was very excited and pleased that, by leaving my job at the *Express*, I'd have more time to work on his Life – I had all the speeches about how thrilled and honoured he was, and yet he knew it was a gamble, my leaving a salaried job in Fleet Street. Just before I started writing the book, having interviewed him extensively, I went on holiday to Malta. My secretary phoned me and read out this letter:'

> 37 Panton Street,
> Haymarket,
> London, SW1
> September 12th 1966

Dear Peter,

I have given a very great deal of thought to our proposed project on my life story, including dying and everything, and I have a strong feeling that this is not the time to do it, even though I think your idea for the general layout is the best yet. I won't bore you with the whys and wherefores; enough that you know, in the words of Fred Kite, that: 'I have withdrawn, meditated, consulted, convened and my decision has been democratically arrived at.'

I think later on, much later on, would be better for me – perhaps in about eight or nine years. Of course it may be that nobody will be interested by then, but the reverse also applies, and I know I am just coming into my most productive period right now.

I wish that you will understand my feelings, Peter, and not be disappointed.

. . .

> All good wishes,
> As ever,
> *Peter Sellers*

'Just like that! He'd known I'd given up my job. He'd decided the time wasn't right! I was pretty angry – my first reaction – and apprehensive about my future. He was in Rome making *After the Fox*. I immediately flew from Malta to see him. He was living on the Appian Way, a beautiful big film-star house, built by Mussolini.

I turned up there unannounced at ten o'clock at night, and Sellers was sitting down with Britt in a huge fascistic-brutalist chamber lit by candles – all slanting shadows and pillars. She was at one end of this long table, he was at the other. "Hello, love," he said. "Fantastic to see you . . . ." He didn't ask me why I'd turned up, and didn't mention the letter. He instantly wanted to open the Dom Perignon – he was living on this scale by now, and playing the rôle of International Movie Star. This I found bizarre – I was used to seeing him out at Whetstone; and from Whetstone, suddenly to be in these vast mansions . . . I can almost picture him in a monogrammed velvet robe. . . . Finally, I said how upset I was by the letter. "What letter? Oh, that letter. Well – you understand. . ." – "No, I don't understand. We had an arrangement. We have been working together on this project for nearly a year. I gave up my job, having discussed this with you; I must tell you, whether you continue to work with me or not, I'm going to write a book about you. I have a contractual commitment. . ."

'It ended with his saying: "Great, I'm all excited again. It's a wonderful idea – let's go forward together."

'Until then I'd not personally experienced his betrayals and changes of heart. I came back to London; I went back to Italy and saw him on a ten week picture at Cinecitta, *The Bobo*. He welcomed me, though I could see the picture was in a lot of trouble, and this was affecting him. Enormously. Problems with himself, and movie making, and with the responsibilities of being a star. The whole production revolved around him. Already he was having trouble with Britt. I could see that this was going to be a difficult book to write with him – and he announced for a second time that he wouldn't co-operate with me, with the consequence that I informed him it would in any event be a better book without him in many ways. I wasn't too worried by this stage – because he was never threatening to injunct the book itself. He just didn't want to be part of it any more.'

He'd lost interest in his Life, or anyway in Evans' version of it – and if Evans' synopsis, which sketched him as a Sixties show-biz personality, was 'the best yet', was he inviting tenders? (Walker, in the preface to his Authorised Biography – which makes no reference to the existence of Evans' opus, an omission which I find extraordinary – lets us know that Sellers 'several times ... encouraged me to consider writing this book ... I cried off, protesting that it was too soon'.) I suspect that Sellers had a fear of too many facts. A biography is an extended obituary – there you are, mapped out. His changeling fantasies; his sentimental revisions of the past: how could they stand up to scrutiny? Biographers have a habit of bringing their subjects down to earth, to make them a bundle of foibles, a string of causes and effects – just like you and me, with a bit of Freud thrown in the stew to explain away creativity. How could Sellers countenance any of that? How could he bear to have a stranger, assuming the vantage point of God, look down upon his life from above and confront him with his misdeeds? How could he dare be made explicable – levelled – by tabloid journalists?* In

---

* '... biography has often been allotted to writers who seem very little acquainted with the nature of their task, or very negligent about the performance. They rarely afford any other account than might be collected from public papers, but imagine themselves writing a life, when they exhibit a chronological series of actions or preferments; and have so little regard to the manners of behaviour of their heroes, that more knowledge may be gained of a man's real character by a short conversation with one of his servants than from a formal and studied narrative, begun with his pedigree, and ended with his funeral.

'There are indeed, some natural reasons why these narratives are often written by such as were not likely to give much instruction or delight, and why most accounts of particular persons are barren and useless. If a life be delayed till interest and envy are at an end, we may hope for impartiality, but must expect little intelligence; for the incidents which give excellence to biography are of a volatile and evanescent kind, such as soon escape the memory, and are rarely transmitted by tradition. We know how few can portray a living acquaintance, except by his most prominent and observable particularities, and the grosser features of his mind; and it may be easily imagined how much of this little knowledge may be lost in imparting it, and how soon a succession of copies will lose all resemblance of the original.'

Samuel Johnson, *Rambler*, No. 60. Quoted by Boswell in his Introductory section to the *Life*.

The Evil That Men Do

Tony Palmer's documentary, *Will the Real Peter Sellers (Stand Up)?*,[*] Milligan, who is providing the commentary, suddenly rounds on the camera crew and says: 'How can you encompass a lifetime? Do you think that by showing his agony to other people you will in any way help him? In Peter's case this is crucial, because he's so emotionally defenceless. . .'

I am not so sure about the defencelessness – that's where the tantrums and shrewd bullyings came in handy. Sadism was his shield. But Milligan has a point about the biographical pursuit and intervention – the chase, the quest. For how *do* you tell the story of another man's life? Proust took a thousand pages to describe a chap turning over in bed; Joyce wrote a long novel about a fellow's day out in Dublin. As these examples from pure fiction suggest, the *last* thing a biography should try and be is objective. (I am not a camera.) If you want to know a man's heart, you have to find a structure and form that suits each individual subject – and out of this can come a dialogue (so to speak) between the author of a book

---

[*] Q: Did you recognise yourself at all in that portrait?

A: No, not at all, no. No.

Sellers also said, in 1971: 'The film? Well, that wasn't me at all. I absolutely refute it completely. It made me out to be some sort of strange, hermit-like recluse. I'm not! It had nothing to do with me . . . I didn't like it. . .' Made in 1969, the documentary was shelved by the BBC and only shown for the first time complete at the British Film Institute/National Film Theatre on June 28th 1989.

It is a fantastic film – as intricate and chaotic as a modern painting – lots of slewed juxtapositions, parallels, allusions, overlaps of ideas and references, seemingly edited by an extremely gifted maniac. On top of that there is a cacophonous sound-track, with everything from Peruvian flutes to sci-fi hums and drones. Every so often there are images of death, blood, explosiveness: dying bulls at a corrida (with Sellers in the audience filming it for his home-movie collection); Sellers speeding along in his cars – and shots of cars in flames; Sellers on his yacht, with Sibelius booming across the water . . . I was knocked out by it – Tony Palmer ran the complete print for me. I wrote him a fan letter afterwards. 'The source of Sellers' comedy was sorrow, and this you showed,' was one of my less gushing remarks. Mr Palmer replied: 'I don't agree with a word you say about the film but I am glad you liked it.'

and the person he is writing it about. That, anyway, has been my own intention. Unlike Evans, Walker, Stark et al, I never knew Sellers personally. Now I know him intimately; he haunts me; he is always just around the corner, as a sly ghost. I have stood outside his houses and on the pier at Ilfracombe. I have visited his birthplace – at the junction of Southsea Terrace and Castle Road, Southsea; and I have seen the woebegone plastic plaque nailed under the eaves of what is now a Chinese Take Away:

PETER SELLERS
Film Actor and Comedian
Was born in the flat
Above these premises
On 8th September 1925

Presented by the Post Office
1985

– I have tried on his old costumes. . . And all for what? To be as he was?

☆ ★ ☆

He forswore Evans and Palmer; he relinquished his children and his films (his brainchildren); he wanted to be strangely vanished. One piece of labour he did get his hands on was the album *He's Innocent of Watergate*, produced by the former ring-master of *The Goon Show*, Peter Eton. 'We did a thing on Nixon,' says John Bluthal. 'Six months later I'm in Australia and I see it in a record shop. I buy it. I listen to it. I had about two lines left. I came back to England. I see Spike. "Spike, what's this? This isn't what we did." – "Oh yeah. Bloody Peter. He got a new cast a week later and re-did the whole album."'

That was unforgivable. Milligan had been part of the development side of the project, and Sellers overrode him. (He overrode Eton, too, who was so embarrassed by the tinkerings he removed his name from the sleeve. Now the disc is credited to Pismo Clam – an old W. C. Fields pseudonym.) Why did he re-record the Watergate spoof? Like the re-takes of the Cleese scenes in *The Magic*

Christian – because Bluthal and Milligan were *too good*. Two tracks
were deleted in their entirety: a visit to the Church of St Anthony,
patron saint of the CIA: Nixon goes to confession at three a.m. (evidently Sellers' witching hour), because that is the only hour his
bodyguard goes to sleep. Father O'Brien, played by Milligan, hears
the confession: Nixon is really two personalities the President, *and*
Mr Nixon. Father O'Brien is confused: 'I can't take two at a time.'
On the other track, Nixon is at large in Forty-Second Street. 'Take
me to the White House,' he tells a cab driver. The conversation in
the taxi (the driver being Bluthal), is apparently recorded by a dwarf
secreted under the seat.

I'm not suggesting that masterpieces in the History of Western
Comedy have been lost;* I am suggesting that there was a barely
hidden fury in Sellers, and you could never be certain when it
would surface, or to what extent, or why he was getting into conflicts at all. Often, people didn't know that they were going to be his
victims – or that he'd be having this sort of duplicitous exchange
with Joe McGrath. It is three in the morning. The phone rings.

'Will you take over the movie?'

'No. Peter.'

'What you are saying is you're *refusing* to take this movie over?'

'Yes.'

'Why?'

'First of all, you didn't ask me to direct it or be involved
originally; second, I haven't seen the script; third, I don't like taking
over from other directors. You've got to have some sort of loyalty to
your craft. People don't end up being directors as an accident,
Peter. It takes time. If [insert name] has got a director's ticket, it
means something.'

---

* *He's Innocent of Watergate* comes under the heading of 'minute particulars': '[it is
not always in] the most distinguished achievements that men's virtues or vices
may be best discerned; but very often an action of small note, a short saying, or a
jest, shall distinguish a person's real character more than the greatest sieges, or
the most important battles'.

Plutarch's *Life of Alexander*. (Langhorne's translation.)

'The bloody old thing wants us to rehearse.'

'I don't even want to get into it, Peter.'

'You are turning me down.'

'Yes.'

'Right, I'm off.'

McGrath might not hear from Sellers for six or seven weeks. Then would come another inconvenient phone call from the hotel on location.

'Will you come over and take over the direction?'

'Look, I didn't want to even before you started shooting.'

'Well, it's just a disaster. I've got no confidence in . . .'

'Peter, you haven't got confidence in *anybody*.'

'Why don't you come and take over?'

'It's too late – it's silly.'

Et and no doubt cetera. 'He had no conception of allegiance,' McGrath told me. 'He'd only have lost confidence in me as well, as on *Casino Royale*. "This isn't working out. I don't have any confidence in you." Totally self-centred. He'd get in a state if he couldn't control things, yet he'd have a big enough problem with his own part, let alone trying to control an entire production. . .'

It was megalomania. He disposed of people who displeased him. He trusted no one. Dr Thomas Stuttaford, in his column 'Medical Briefing' in *The Times*, on February 7th 1991, would seem to be trying to define a Sellers-type:

> They disregard the usual rules of society as they seek to achieve their own ends. They are impulsive and demand immediate self-gratification; if frustrated in their objectives, they will not respond to reason but are likely to become increasingly violent and aggressive; rather than capitulate they would prefer to sacrifice their own life . . . or that of others . . . [They] are sexually irresponsible, albeit successful, for provided that life is going their way they are often charming and plausible. These same characteristics can be used to manipulate the gullible, hence perhaps Hitler's love of the uncritical, whether unsophisticated children, impressionable women or fawning dogs.

Dr Stuttaford was attempting to describe the personality of a psychopath, with particular reference to Saddam Hussein ('Many leaders have some psychopathic tendencies and ... learn to manipulate society, some with charm, while others rely on fear'). If this seems laughably hyperbolic in relation to a nutty actor with a weak heart who cooled thirteen years ago, this is what Milligan said in 1969: 'First there was Hitler, who loved Wagner, children, flowers and sunset, and then he goes and murders six million Jews. Peter can't work off his madness – it's all bottled up in him. Peter's biggest rage is that he can't be violent like Hitler. Don't mistake him. He's full of rage – the rage of a murderer.'

We must be grateful, in that case, that he was *only* an actor (if, that is, you accept Kingsley Amis' definition of actors as 'stupid, ignorant and eaten up with themselves'. I don't myself). What Sellers represented was an attitude of mind. He seemed to want to pay people back, get one over on them. It was fatal to try and be friendly. (He behaved especially badly to those who did the most for him – by being sympathetic, or in taking him at his word, they gave credibility to and confirmed his fantasies, depressions and fears.) His ambitiousness, which had made him, proceeded to un-make him – his destructiveness was the other panel in the diptych. His rage found its first pure expression in *The Goon Show*, and Milligan was right to say 'from it has sprung everything': the Fifties fustian, the cackling demons, the Hitler jokes, the cockiness, the misanthropy, the irresponsibility. ... That is what Sellers took away from his radio days, and it was made to conform with what I have chosen to call his evil dimension – his psychopathy – which gripped him after his first marriage, his first divorce, his first heart attack, his ending of the world in *Doctor Strangelove* – that period in and around 1963, which forms the bend in the river.

☆ ★ ☆

Epilogue
Who's the Man?

> I know him very well indeed. Sometimes he bores me, sometimes he frightens me. Frequently he bewilders me. Occasionally he astonishes me, and sometimes I think he's mad. *Sellers describing Sellers.*

He had the lot – beautiful women (and he was either fat and plug-ugly or thin and goofy); great riches (think how he started, on the road with the saltimbanques); there was an element of fairy story in his rise (let alone the mythic themes of doubles and duality); he was world famous. Insanity was the last luxury left, the only blockhouse he could hide in.

What with the ferment going on inside him already, trying to cope with the flow of external phenomena, on top, was beyond him. He wanted to still it, as with a camera. He abused kindnesses, to see how far he could push people – like his wives or Janette Scott: they were subjected to crazy tests or psychological siege. He played practical jokes on those who might otherwise have been his chums, to show them who was boss. Here is a late entry, c/o an anonymous source: 'There was a young unmarried man who believed Peter was fond of him, called Anthony. He called Peter "Pete", which he hated, so Anthony was called Ant, an insect name, right? One way he had of cheering himself up was to telephone Ant and play a joke on him. He'd suggest that Ant came over to Roebuck House, in Victoria, for yoga and a curry – and Peter would instruct his wife to lace Ant's portion with extra chilli and spices. Ant would get very red in the face – he'd flush easily anyway, there must have been something wrong with him. He'd get redder and redder, like a cartoon, and Peter would have a great time! Ant hadn't got the guts to say anything. Peter would say, "Great curry, this. Isn't it a good curry, Ant? Lynne, you can make a great curry." Ant would be going crimson-to-black, not wanting to admit he was nearly burning to death.'

This is funny only so long as you don't happen to be the Ant in question, and even then, after a moment's reflection, it is possible to see it as one of the spiteful little bits of shit Sellers did on people. The well-being of others did not concern him. Only a constant succession of toys – or the turning of individuals into automata, as above – kept him happy. Hence the hi-fi, cameras and cars ('I could spend hours wondering whether to buy myself an East German 1,000 De Luxe Wartburg saloon, gearbox ratios I 3.273, II 2.133, III 1.368, IV 0.956, rev. 4.440; or, alternatively, a People's Chinese Dong Feng'). The inhumanity of machines, and the sets of data which he could reel off about them, gave him the illusion of being scrupulous and rational – a clear-headed scientist. What he liked about his yacht – after the money it cost and the prestige it bought – were the specifications. 'This boat has two General Motor diesels, each 600-horsepower. It is the only boat in the world with these engines. An engineer flew from Detroit to Monte Carlo to install them. We cruise at twenty-three knots! Top speed twenty-seven. . .' The boat, eighteen metres long and fifty tons in weight, had a rotation radar dish, echo-sounding apparatus, automatic pilot, a radio telephone system, full air-conditioning, automatic anchor winches – all in addition to the engines. 'They have turbo blowers, principally because my kids get bored at sea, so when we go somewhere, we have to get there fast.' There was also a bicycle on board, so that the fed-up passengers could whizz away inland.

Of course, the speed boat/fear of boredom business was a personal anxiety of the master's. Sellers' children didn't have disaffections of their own, not so far as he was concerned. That is why he so often trained cameras on them. To have, later, his children playing over his walls as home-movies was preferable to having them in the home, as real people. Home-movies kept them at a distance – he could turn their caperings into a story, and give random life a form, a narrative. I am not being fanciful. In July 1970 he contributed his advice on home-movie making to some magazine or other and he stressed the importance of devising 'a theme and movement, and everything else fits in'. Whilst magic lantern images danced on a sheet – Victoria as a baby on a beach, Michael rowing a black rubber dinghy, with cutaway shots to cypress trees, terracotta roof-scapes, and patches of deep blue water – Sellers said: 'I think the main reason for this great nostalgia and excitement in home-movies, and why they have become so popular, is that you can watch your children growing. They themselves don't particularly enjoy the films now, but I wonder how they'll feel in years to come. It's like a short piece of cine-film I saw of my father the other day, from some time in the Twenties. Before that I'd only seen old faded shots of him. Then, there he was on the film, a young man, larking about, alive and moving.'

Where is that fragment of Bill now? What happened to Sellers' own trove, which was apparently destined for Michael, Sarah and Victoria when they grew up? Destroyed in one of his fits of pique? Thrown out by his widow's assigns, who can have had no interest in forgotten foreign holidays or baby-on-the-lawn stuff? (Who can deny Michael's words: 'When he was alive you'd think, God, when you're gone it will be different. That shadow won't be over me any more. But even in his death he's denied me my right – not the money; but I should have been allowed to go to Switzerland and sift through everything that was his. Because he was my father. I should have been allowed to find out about things.')

Sellers had adored photography because it brought back a remembrance of things past; in his last months he hated it for the same reason. (Hence the bonfires at La Haute Grange.) Pictures were evidence of time's passage – no mystery there – but they also reminded him that his happy days were now very far off. During one of his final trips to London, he bade his chauffeur, Peter Greenwood, take him on a tour of his favourite shutterbug shops. The car was piled high with new cameras and cine equipment, thousands of pounds' worth. Just as he was being returned to the Dorchester, Sellers turned to his driver and said: 'You have it. Photograph your baby growing up.'

It was a generous gesture, yet there was weariness and bitterness in Sellers' tone. He was in a leave-taking mood. He wanted to be rid of things. His preferred occupation was to sit alone in the dark. 'I don't mind being alone,' he claimed. 'I really don't mind. I'm quite happy to sit here and look out of the window.' Was the view, through a charmed magic casement opening on to faery-lands forlorn, similar to staring desultorily at an uneditable jumble on a home-movie screen? (Sellers' recommendation: a forty square inch Luxor Screen, £8.10s from Johnsons of Hendon.) He was always self-isolating. As Janette Scott testified, he would lock himself in bathrooms – and he had a fondness of rooms entirely made of mirrors, where his image could repeat itself and stretch away to the vanishing point forever. His Clarges Street apartment had curved, cracked and mottled mirrors. With the curtains drawn and Sellers in dark glasses it resembled a crypt – 'a general air of gloom used to hang over the meetings,' recalls Jocelyn Rickards, who met him there when she was to have designed the costumes for *The Magic Christian*.

Dressing-rooms have a triptych of mirrors, and Sellers liked to watch himself take shape as somebody new. 'I walk around, trying different accents, feeling my way to the character. I do this every time,' he once said of his methodology. 'I stare at my own image in the mirror every morning, waiting for the other fellow – the man I'm going to play to emerge, and stare back at me. I am waiting for this stranger to come into my life. When it happens, I have this flush of happiness.' He waited for a double – a lost twin, or brother? The process certainly sounds supernatural. In a way, he was *never* alone, if these alien voices and detachable identities could pour forth at will.

He could fill an empty space with echoes and shadow play – which is why, to other members of the human race who visited him, his residences were eerie and vacant. 'I never remember him living in a place that seemed lived-in,' says Joe McGrath. 'It was always as if he'd moved into a hotel room. He was never at home anywhere. When he'd moved into the Hampstead penthouse, before he got rid of Anne, he asked me, because of my background at the Royal College of Art, to go up Bond Street with him. He wanted to buy some paintings. We went around the galleries, and he had a lot of money to spend. In those days you could buy Bonnards or Raoul Dufys for less than three thousand pounds. "If I could afford it, I'd buy these Impressionists, Peter." He ended up buying some cheap prints. Years later, when they'd soared in price, he said he wished he'd bought those Impressionists – yet he'd never quibbled about spending forty thousand on a Rolls Royce. . . .'

There was something about him that didn't like old things. Always it had to be the most up-to-date cameras, cars and gadgets. Was he fearful of the intellectual/cultural aspects of art works? Or was it their rootedness – their antiquity – which unsettled him? Also, if you are only happy in a hotel, or somewhere that resembles a hotel, that says a great deal about your own impermanence. It is as if everywhere he stayed was a preliminary to that final scene in the Dorchester, enacted in the suite that is not there now, when he went blue and was stretchered to Intensive Care.

Somebody who saw him as very much the morose magus in his tower was Kenneth Griffith: 'Bernard Miles was always asking me to act at the Mermaid, in *Don't Let Summer Come*. I loved Bernard Miles, and Donald Wolfit, the real old rogues of the theatre. So Bernard said, "Kenny, you've got to do it." I said, "Bernard, I can't afford to do it. Oh, all right, for fifty quid a week." – "Fifty pounds a week!" – "All right, forty-five pounds, and Bernard, a bottle of Guinness for every performance." And he wheeled in crates and crates of Guinness. Beer reached the ceiling. And I get a call from Peter, just at this time, the early Sixties. He is living in a penthouse suite at the Dorchester.

'"Kenny, I've got to talk to you."

'"Well, you know. . ."

'"Soon, it's a bit urgent."

'"Peter, I'm doing this show. . ." Ten times a week! Shit! Anyway, my doctor intervened, and I was really knocked out. They cut out a few matinées.

'". . . We don't come down until ten forty-five."

'"That's fine, Kenny. Come on afterwards, and we'll have a real good meal."

'Now, he's in the penthouse of the Dorchester – I got on the Underground at Blackfriars, went to Hyde Park Corner. I was unshaven, and I sloped up to the Dorchester. It was eleven fifteen – and they were all waiting. "Mr Griffith, ah, Mr Griffith. . ." The manager, etc. "Mr Sellers has asked us to look after you." I was put in the special express lift and taken up. It was a vast place, Sellers' suite, with a roaring log fire. A real log fire at the top of the Dorchester.

'"How are you, Kenny?"

'It always lifted me up to see him. I always felt lifted up by his company.

'"I'm feeling fine."

'"We'll have the grub brought up here."

'It was wheeled in. Caviar, champagne, turkey. Everything was so opulent.

'"Something worrying you, Kenny?"

'"I'm a bit battered, doing this play which I shouldn't have done."

'"There's something else worrying you, isn't there? You've got to tell me. If anything is worrying you, *you've got to tell me* . . ."

'"Well I've had a hell of a two years actually. I bought a house in Islington on a short mortgage, which I agreed to repay in three years, and it has been a struggle, a *real slog*, and it has taken it out of me; but I've beaten it now, because I've paid it off."

'"You've really paid it all off?"

'"Virtually. There's under two thousand pounds left."

'So I was eating away by this great roaring fire, and he got up and went to a grand piano, and I saw him scribbling something – and he gave me a cheque for two thousand pounds.

'"Don't tear it up, I beg you," he said. "Look, I'll be on to Bill in the morning" – that was his accountant who went to Switzerland with some of the loot – "and I'll tell him to 'lose' it." I'd not heard the expression before. "Kenny, I won't even *know*. I won't know it's gone."

'I tore it up. I said, "Peter, I promise you – if ever I feel I'm beaten, I'll let you know."

'He was begging me. Years and years later, I retold this story to him, on the last time I saw him, with Lynne Frederick, at their apartment down in Victoria – at the top of another big building. He was always asking me to go and have a chat. Always asking me to act with him. And she came in from some modelling assignment in France. So what I did was, I said, "You know how one's imagination plays tricks on the memory? Things you believe happened and you can't believe they happened?" She was sitting there. His eyes were fixed on me. Lynne and Peter's eyes were riveted on me, as I went over this story. Something disturbed him about this, and right at the end I said, "You gave me this cheque. . ." And he said, "Yes, and you tore it up, didn't you, you bugger?"'

☆ ★ ☆

Was he trying to buy somebody off? Grope for friendship? Connect somebody to him? Ensure gratitude? Express his lordliness? It is his loneliness which comes through in the story; his misjudgement. Griffith, in conjuring up this account of Sellers in his nocturnal world, could be describing an encounter with a gangster – Don Vito Corleone, perhaps. It was Sellers, incidentally, whom Coppola wanted for the rôle of the devious Hyman Roth in *The Godfather Part Two*. Lee Strasberg, who did take the part, is just about unimprovable on, but I'd like to have seen Sellers in that murky and primitive society of loyalty and betrayal, ritual and murder. (Where Brando was bull-like, minotaur-like, Hyman Roth, in the second film, is all Jewish patter and frail health: his power and fury simmer behind his eyes, and his cracked smile and patronage are terrifying.)

If Sellers inhabited castles in the air, his characters, too, were provided with mysterious retreats. Old Sam has his eyrie, papered with music hall posters, which is reached by a vertiginous rusty outside staircase. 'Peter came up with a sight gag,' says Larry Pizer, 'when the character arrived home drunk and distressed after the death of his dog. He tries to walk up the iron steps. He staggers towards the steps, and makes it up three or four, and staggers back, his impetus unable to take him further. Wearing a huge coat with huge pockets and, like ballast, he occasionally reveals empty bottles and throws them away. With the reduction in weight, he makes it up some more steps, falls back again, and throws more ballast out from his pockets – eventually, having dispensed enough, he has a run, and makes it right to the top of the stairs. This shot went on forever! Wonderful to see – he suddenly just did it! We kept turning, turning, turning to take it all in.'

It is not retained in the finished film, alas. 'It was obvious from the moment we arrived on the set that we were going to have to cut the scene,' Anthony Simmons has told me. 'It was a classic example of what happened on the "Pink Panther" sets, i.e. Peter playing for the crew, to amuse them. . . Peter said, "OK, Tone, you set up the camera and let me show you how . . ." It *was* funny – for the crew. But grossly over-the-top and too long for the film.'

There was no need for solicitude in *What's New, Pussycat?*, another film where a Sellers character has a particular relationship with his surroundings. Dr Fassbender lives in an Art Nouveau funhouse – a folly of windows and mazy passageways. The film begins with the psychiatrist being chased around the balconies and turrets by his Brünnhilde of a bride. She is accusing him of having a mistress, and demands to know how pretty she is by comparison. 'Prettier than you?' screeches Fassbender. '*I* am prettier than you!' He also insists she shut up: 'Silence, when you are shouting at me!' (Sellers, ad-libbing, purloins the Lionel Jeffries line from *Two Way Stretch*.) The camera remains outside the building. We never know where the two warring figures will pop up next. (They are like puppets, Punch and Judy.) What we are certain of, however, is that the teetering, rambling edifice, all curlicues and battlements, is an image of the insides of Fassbender's head – Sellers', too, with the bric-à-brac, shadowy corners, flights of fancy; it is half-ruin, half-Xanadu. (Clare Quilty may have been a riotous resident at one time.).

Dr Strangelove and Rouquet have their bunkers; Dodger Lane his gaol cell; John Lewis his library; Dr Pratt his cat-infested consulting room; and Clouseau his Cato-booby-trapped flat-cum-gymnasium. *The Party* might be said to be about Hrundi's dangerous liaison with a Hollywood mansion, its gadgetry and sliding walls; and *Hoffman* and *There's a Girl in My Soup* are about Wendy Houses and bachelor pads – habitats which are so important to, and revealing of, their owners. *Being There*, I think, would be much less of a film, atmospherically, without that cathedral-sized ice palace of Biltmore; and *The Prisoner of Zenda*, *Murder by Death*, and *The Fiendish Plot of Dr Fu Manchu* unfold in ornate, encrusted, Ruritanian lodges, towers or hideaways, which are all the more apt and beautiful, perhaps, because, like Mrs Wilberforce's villa in *The Ladykillers*, they are mere movie sets, built not to last.

Then there are the islands: Gaillardia and Huwyat, for example. Aldo Vanucci turns Ischia into a film set in *After the Fox* (he pretends to take a call from Sophia Loren: 'I'm sorry. There's no part for you in this picture ... She'll kill me, it'll be in all the Italian newspapers'); and then there is the Cyprus carry-on of *Ghost in the Noonday Sun*, which provides my favourite expanding and contracting perspective on Sellers the hopping hobgoblin: 'One day I was shooting with a helicopter,' says Medak. 'Peter had to be way below on this boat. I was giving him my direction by radio. This argument started between me and Peter, because I wanted him to go near Franciosa, and he didn't want to go near him. He refused to share a shot with him, and wasted half a day's work. He wouldn't do what I wanted, and I'm two thousand feet up, and conditions are right for the camera to swoop down over him, and he wouldn't do it. I got so angry I said for the pilot to take us ten thousand feet up. We are sitting up there having a beer and I see warships over there, warships over there. I look up. Russian and American jets are screaming across the sky. It was just before the Arab-Israeli War broke out. So war is about to break out up here, and there's that lunatic on a pirate ship below. . .'

☆　☆　☆

It had always been his ambition, when he had the lolly, to purchase his own desert island and live like Robinson Crusoe, all-powerful in his own little world. As early as 1954, he had said he was labouring towards and searching for an island – to get right away and live in a state of idyllic happiness, like a noble savage. He never did get his island, but he did buy that boat, *The Bobo*, later re-named *The Victoria Maria* ('which may have been the only public compliment he ever paid to one of us,' says Michael).

'My real home is on the boat,' he said, 'got all my bits in there. I know the crew. They know me. They don't bother me. They keep out of my way. I can run the boat myself. You're not stuck in one place. You get out to sea – and there's nobody there. Just nobody there. Vast expanses of blue. When it's lovely weather, I know nothing nicer than being at sea on a yacht, putting into ports when you want to put in, getting off when you want to get off, eating on board, swimming – it's the ultimate luxury. If you said to me, what is the most material super-luxury you have in your life, I'd say my boat. . .'

Of course, yellow sands and wild waves soon lost their appeal. Though he kept saying, 'It's the only place where I can relax. There is no one there but the water' – the sea and being adrift – the dead calm – like the peace and the snows of his Alpine fastness, made him moody and reflective, his mind dwelling on imagined hurts and insults. He once went stir-crazy in the Adriatic and the gleaming white motor yacht, flying the Panamanian flag, had to return to Venice. They dropped anchor off the Piazza San Marco, and Sellers thought it a huge laugh to rant and rave on the poop deck, pretending to be Hitler addressing a rally. Later, he changed voices and used a megaphone to give the vote-garnering speech of a

British Conservative candidate: 'Let me, as a good politician, make my position quite clear. . .' Didn't anybody *ever* think to knock the mad bastard off?

Hattie Stevenson, who had the unenviable task of keeping abreast of her master's non-stop global criss-crossings, says that 'his answer to everything was hiring speedboats or yachts. Nuts about that. All through their lives, the main meeting point for his children was to get them on a boat. I don't know why, but I remember this.' I should think it would have registered with anybody who knew Sellers that boats and oceans were his symbol of escape – to vanish into the wilderness. As Louis MacNeice might have said, or Ralph Reader, when you are riding along on the crest of a wave, time is away and somewhere else. But Sellers was often somewhere else, too: his notorious non-appearance after he had invited Nanette Newman and Bryan Forbes; the occasions when his children arrived on board to find their father packing up and leaving. If ever he invited one of his wives on a cruise, she was soon his ex-wife. The engine's throb and the vastness of the dark green oceans filled him with nausea. Alan Clare's wife, Bloom, recalls receiving an urgent ship-to-shore telephone call from the Aegean: 'I am sailing around the Greek islands,' explained Sellers, 'and I'm bored to death.'

The beauty of natural scenery, the majesty of the Greek civilisation's sticks and stones, etc., reminded him of his own irrelevance; his puniness in the scheme of things.* As Milligan said: 'When the boat was finished, he thought, "Well, there's the blue moon; there's the stars . . . So what happens now? I've seen the stars before; I've seen the ocean; I've heard the music; I know the tune – what else is there? Nothing else? Let's all go back to London." Like everything else in his life, faced with the reality,

---

* The watch upon my wrist
  Would soon forget that I exist,
  If I were not reminded
  By days when I forget to wind it.
  W.H. Auden.

he had no choice but to run away. The yacht: his home: all a dream.'

Sellers didn't need semaphores to see the comparison between aimlessly voyaging aboard his boats and pleasure steamers and wandering London with Peg or touring the rackety music halls as a child. He was richer, but no happier. Within the adult Sellers, searching for distractions, was still the St Aloysius' Jew who had to keep on the move. Feeling a sense of entrapment, separated, he identified with the nothingness and mindlessness of his surroundings, which were closing in. Air, earth, fire, water. The monotony, too, the vibration of the waves and sea-swell, was rhythmic, like a drumming – a heart-beat, familiar and lulling. Sellers, in his entrails, knew that there was something about sailing ships and the sea which would explain him. The sea, Elias Canetti once said, is like a powerful crowd; a mob: it 'is multiple, it moves, and it is dense. Its multiplicity lies in its waves . . . it can soothe or threaten or break out in storms. Its sublimity is enhanced by the thought of what it contains, the multitudes of plants and animals hidden within it; it is an image of stilled humanity; all life flows into it and it contains all life.' Gazing for hours out at the sea's flashing surface, freely floating, Sellers was seeing himself as a desert island,* a desolate atoll. To try and know him, Milligan has said, was 'like going to a desert island. In the middle is a lake, and in the middle of

---

* Here, by the way, are Sellers' *Desert Island Discs* (February 4th 1957):

'I Want a Big Butter and Egg Man,' performed by Bobby Hackett and his Jazz Band.

Rodgers/Hammerstein, 'I Have Dreamed' (*The King and I*), sung by Rita Moreno and Carlos Rivas.

Delius, 'On Hearing the First Cuckoo in Spring', played by the London Symphony Orchestra, conducted by Anthony Collins.

Berlin, 'Cheek to Cheek', sung by Ella Fitzgerald and Louis Armstrong.

Debussy, 'Prelude No. 8', played by Hans Henkemans.

Victor Young, 'White' (*Tone Poems of Colour*), orchestra conducted by Frank Sinatra.

Raksin/Mercer, 'Laura', sung by Erroll Garner.

Rodgers/Hart, 'I Like to Recognise the Tune', sung by Mel Tormé.

that, another deserted island. He's that lonely. He's desperate to be happy, successful, wanted, happily married. He's desperate not to destroy his past. It's all desperation. He *is* desperation.'

☆　☆　☆

I can't leave him there, can I, spinning and twirling through space – like Milton's Satan ('Me miserable! Which way I fly is hell; myself am hell . . .'); like the Peter Pan of Peter Pans, playing on and on until we wake up? I will order the curtain down with the following letter. Perhaps, because it doesn't strive for effect, I find it almost intolerably moving. Here's the Sellers it is possible to have a salmon leap of sympathy for; also Sellers the unfaithful rascal and egotist, who wanted everything out of life and ended up with less than nothing of any consequence – and who was content, fleetingly, only up above the world so high, amongst the cumulus, travelling nowhere in particular or freely falling:

> Los Angeles,
> CA 90045
> April 2, 1991

Dear Mr Lewis,

Sorry to have taken so long getting around to writing this. Time just disappears. It's hard to believe that I dated Peter twenty years ago. (I am now forty-eight.)

I first met him on a Pan Am flight from Los Angeles to London. I ran into him again at Sharon Tate's wedding * at the London Playboy Club where several crew members had been invited by Sammy Davis. In those days, 1970 or so, on the 707

---

* The Tate-Polanski nuptial was on January 20th 1968 at the Chelsea Registry Office in the King's Road. The party at the Playboy Club afterwards 'was attended by what seemed like the whole of London and half of Hollywood,' according to the groom. The Manson Family's murder of Sharon and some of her friends took place in Los Angeles, at Cielo Drive, on August 9th 1969. Sellers offered a reward for any information which might lead to the capture of the killers.

we carried a lot of entertainers and they were always inviting crew members to different events.

Peter drove me back to the hotel after the wedding reception and I started dating him at that time. I enjoyed Peter's company and saw him whenever I was in London. I saw him a few times in Los Angeles also.

I felt that Peter was always searching for the normal life he thought he wanted but if he ever found it I think it would have bored him to death. He did say that all he ever wanted was a wife to come home to and a normal family life, but look who he married.

He did ask me to marry him, but I knew I couldn't live his life-style, any more than he could live mine. I think he was attracted to me because I did represent that 'normal' life. He was also looking for some answers through religion. He asked a lot of questions about Catholicism, my faith.

I found him to be very generous, but since I am not very materialistic, that didn't impress me. If I mentioned I'd been looking for a new radio or that I liked a certain thing, the next thing I knew, he'd buy it for me. I soon learned not to mention wanting anything.

Peter also told me that Britt told him he was 'unlivable with'. I never had a major disagreement with Peter, but I could tell by the way he would change personalities that it would be like living with a different person every few days. We would walk into an Indian restaurant and he would become Indian. He would walk past a globe and he was Inspector Clouseau.

During the time I was dating him he was making the movie 'Hoffman'. I went to visit him on the set and found a person I did not know at all. He had become the person he was playing in that movie. (I never did get to see that movie.) I asked him how long he would be like that and he said until he finished the movie. I told him to call me when the movie was finished and left. He called.

We would occasionally go to restaurants, but spent a lot of time at his flat in Mayfair, was it the Samuel Pepys building? I can remember his quite ineptly trying to clean the oven because 'help was hard to find'. We would do simple and silly things like listen to Tiny Tim singing 'Tip Toe through the Tulips' or watch 'The Producers' one of his favourite movies at the time. He didn't have a projection room in the flat, just a projector and movie screen in the living room. He loved electronic gadgets. (I am sort of rambling, because I don't know what will be of interest to you.) I also felt Peter was at times very shy and trying to impress me. I remember he was telling a joke one day and messed it up. He seemed embarrassed and said, 'Imagine me messing up a joke.'

It was more enjoyable to spend time alone with Peter because he often became another person when a third person entered the room. Unfortunately I'm not good with dates, but I remember one flight he was on when I was a working flight attendant. Robert Goulet, the singer, was also in First Class, with four other passengers. When we arrived in Los Angeles, Peter was the first to disembark. He kissed me on the cheek as he got off the plane. Robert Goulet was the next one to exit and in true show business fashion also kissed me on the cheek. At this time another male passenger exited and figuring this was the way it was done also kissed me on the cheek. At this point the ground agent looked at me and said: 'Wow, that must have been some flight!'

I dated Peter about two years, but of course didn't see him all that often since he was in London and I was in Los Angeles. I'd be in London on my Pan Am trips two or three times a month and usually would see him then.

As I said, I'm not good at dates, but know it was just after he'd been going with Liza Minnelli and before he married Miranda. I kept in touch with him a few years after he married Miranda, but then lost contact with him before he died.

I also remember he was a little superstitious. He was supposed to visit me in Los Angeles, but that was the time a plane crashed off the coast of Los Angeles, on the landing approach, and he decided that was a sign and he shouldn't come to L.A. A week before Peter married Miranda I visited him while I was in London. He told me he was through with her, she was out of his life and he felt great. A week later I read he'd married her. I sent him a message that simply said 'WHY?' His reply was 'It seemed like a good idea at the time.'

I feel that sentence summed up his philosophy of life. He seemed to always be starting over, to be reinventing his life: 'today is the first day of the rest of your life' philosophy. I feel that was the reason he left so little money to his children. I can just see him getting up one day and saying, 'Wouldn't it be great if the kids could make it on their own?' I really don't know if he was always changing his Will, but I would think it would be in character.

I just found a date, 12/1/69. I had purchased a copy of *Peter Sellers: The Mask Behind the Mask*. I asked him to autograph it and he wrote: 'For Alice, This book supposedly about me was written entirely without my permission. However, now that you have a copy you'll know that inside these pages there is no Peter Sellers only photographs. Love and good luck always, Peter 12/1/69'.

By the way, Goldie Hawn was on a flight of mine shortly after Peter died. She told me she'd had a 'psychic experience' and Peter had told her he was finally happy and at peace. She also said that when he was at her place he walked around the house saying this was all he ever wanted, a home and family.

Can't think of too much else. Hope some of it will be useful. I now work for United Airlines, having left Pan Am when they sold the Pacific routes to UAL. I'm still living in LA, near the airport, with ten cats. I'm still single . . . maybe after saying I have ten cats already made that evident . . . and work as a substitute teacher in the elementary grades on my days off.

Let me know if I can be of any other help. Also, how are

Michael and Sarah doing? I think they got a bad deal. From
Peter and his widow.[*]

I've enjoyed doing this. It's brought back some very pleasant
memories of days gone by. 'Those Were the Days my Friends',
another song Peter and I listened to a lot.

Alice Joyce

---

[*] When asked if she would consider settling some of Sellers' money on his children, Lynne told the press: 'A Will surely reflects the attitudes and feelings of
the man who made it. And the fact is that between Peter and his children there
was not too great an understanding.' *Daily Mail*, November 24th 1980.

Appendix
A Day at the Beach

There was one Sellers film I never found, the above-named *A Day at the Beach*. The screenplay was written by Roman Polanski in 1968 – after his marriage to Sharon Tate and before her murder. It was based on a short-story by a Dutch writer, Heere Heresma, and it was made as a low-budget operation under the aegis of Cadre Films, the company which had produced *Rosemary's Baby*. Polanski explains that 'it concerned an alcoholic who takes his small daughter on a day-trip to a seaside town – an outing that ends in a prolonged binge and, ultimately, in disaster. This was to be Simon Hessera's first directorial attempt and Paramount were dragging their feet over financing it. Charlie Bluhdorn and Bob Evans were in London on business, so Gene Gutowski decided to make a final pitch. I flew over for a working lunch with them at Gene's apartment. Peter Sellers, who had agreed to play an unpaid cameo part, was also invited, as, of course, was Simon. Between them, Peter and Simon so mesmerised Bluhdorn with their clowning that he'd have signed anything. Paramount had some funds in Denmark it wanted to invest, so Simon flew to Copenhagen to line things up for shooting there.'

The story is continued by Graham Stark, in his *Remembering Peter Sellers*. He received a phone call, purportedly from Gutowski, but he was convinced it was Sellers playing a prank: 'Pliz, to Graham Stark I would like to speak . . . No Pleez. Am Gene Gutowski, prodoocer for Roman Polanski. Am not Peeter Sellers, but am calling *about* Peeter Sellers . . . Peeter is not charging for being in feelm. Peter is doing feelm for free . . . However, Peeter only play part in feelm if you play other part . . . You like play old queen?'

Enough of this speech-spelling. The upshot was that Stark and Sellers were to appear as a pair of ageing homosexual knick-knack shop proprietors. Sellers was dressed up in a pale-blue pullover and a chiffon scarf; Stark had gold teeth fitted, and he was made to wear rings and medallions. All looked set for an amusing scene when Sellers decided to sulk. Hessera wanted Sellers and Stark to improvise some comedy – but 'Peter's chin went up, the eyes narrowed, and he said, "If you wanted Laurel and Hardy why didn't you book them?"' Sellers refused to perform at all until Stark, much to his embarrassment, took over the direction of the brief sequence. '"Well," I said tentatively, "Peter could start over here and I can come through the beaded curtain . . ."'

A little of the Copenhagen episode is preserved in Tony Palmer's documentary, *Will the Real Peter Sellers (Stand Up)?* Sellers and Stark are seen posing beside the Little Mermaid statue, for a press call. Sellers decides to look 'for the real Peter Sellers' and hunts under stones and behind trees, whilst Stark laughs loudly (it is actually more of a strange jaw-dropped hiss). We later see Sellers improvising in a bar at the beach. He is in character now, and transformed. His hair seems fluffier, his mannerisms are mincing. His voice has the affected bored drawl of the bitter middle-aged homosexual. 'This young man wants three bottles and an opener,' he says with incredible languor. 'He doesn't open them with his teeth like you do.' He has fun with 'opener', which comes out as 'ope-nahh'. Sellers then says, on the commentary soundtrack, referring to his camp delivery, but not only to that voice: 'I talk it all the time, on and off the set – rather disturbing for friends, who think you've gone mad.'

The uneasiness which prevailed during Sellers' scene seemed to beleaguer the whole production. 'I saw the rushes almost daily, and the male lead, Mark Burns, simply wasn't right for the part,' Polanski has written. 'By now, however, it was too late to

change.' The completed film was screened once for Paramount
executives in Paris in 1970. The negative was shipped to the company's vaults in London – and apparently lost. The company had
decided that the film was not commercially viable and should not
be distributed. 'It is absolutely enervating – unwatchable' was the
evaluation.

I felt I had to see it. I first wrote to Paramount on November 7th
1989 ('Any help you can give me will be most useful', etc.). No reply. I wrote again, photocopying and enclosing my original note.
No reply. I telephoned the company's head office, in central
London, and was re-routed to UIP House, 45 Beadon Road, Hammersmith. Over the following months I spoke to any number of
people, on any number of different extensions. On July 17th 1990,
my phone bill and frustration ever-increasing, I sent a fax to a new
name I'd been given, Sue Wright:

> I have been searching for a print of A DAY AT THE BEACH . . .
> So far I've been passed, after many a fruitless phone call and un-
> answered letter, from Ian Scorer to Michael O'Sullivan (I called and
> wrote on March 30th, and he said 'leave it with me') to you (via
> various anons.) SURELY A FILM CAN'T DISAPPEAR WITH-
> OUT TRACE?

Again, I received no reply of any kind. In October 1990, I got
hold of Mr Les Beard, who said he was the Paramount archivist. At
last, here was a bit of news. He confirmed that he had taken
possession of the (only) print on August 11th 1969. The negative
and another 'work print' were sent to America; a 'television' copy of
the negative was also made, though it was not possible to sell it to
any network. Because of the decision not to release the film to the
public – with all the concomitant legal and fiscal ramifications – the
only print (left in England) was cut up for library footage – doors
shutting; seascapes; street scenes: any shot that did not contain an
artiste was preserved. Two hundred cans of 'pos. trims' i.e.
everything else that was left over pertaining to the production,
were destroyed. There were no 'dupe prints' made; all that was
now known to exist was the 'fine grain negative,' ostensibly in

America. If I wanted to see A Day at the Beach I was going to have to write to a Mr Ted Gagliano, at Paramount Pictures Corp., 5555 Melrose Avenue, Hollywood, CA 90038, and see if there was any viewable material there, amidst the 'shit and oranges' (Sellers' description of California). I duly sent an account of the quest off by Air Mail on November, 19th 1990. ('I am very grateful for your help and look forward to hearing from you . . .'). No reply.

Meantime, back in March, Simon Williams had put me in touch with Mark Burns. As I had not seen the film in which he had appeared, I did not feel I could interview him properly. But in a brief telephone chat he did reveal one extraordinarily interesting fact: that Sellers had wanted to play the rôle he, Burns, had taken. This altered the nature of my fascination in *A Day at the Beach* considerably. From not wanting to give up the chase simply because (i) I do not like to be defeated when it comes to research; (ii) I was trying to be complete (and conscientious) – now here was a real reason to find the film. One of the questions I have addressed in this book was what precisely attracted Sellers to certain rôles? His affinity with certain sorts (Chance, Lionel Meadows, Topaze, etc.) is revealing. In *A Day at the Beach*, the central character is not in control of himself – and *this* is what Sellers responded to. Bernie is not only irresponsible; he's beyond redemption. The film is about an indignant man's mental and moral collapse. (Can Polanski possibly have had Sellers in mind? As we know they were friends.)

The same week as I spoke to Mr Burns, the curator of De Danske Filmmuseum had written to me (I should add that virtually every public film collection, archive, storehouse, and university department of cinema studies in the world had heard from me, re. Sellers, over the years):

[Medlem af Fédération
Internationale des

A Day at the Beach

Archives du Film,]
St. Søndervoldstraede 4,
DK-1419 København K.
March 8th 1990

Dear Sir,

Thank you for your letter of February 28th concerning A DAY
AT THE BEACH. The film had its Danish première on April
17th 1972 and was distributed by Cinema International
Corporation, from which we did not receive prints at that time.
Therefore we do not have a print in our collection and no prints
are in existence in Denmark.

We have however stills and a file with documentation on the
films (articles, reviews etc.). All this material is in Danish. The
only material in English is the material of which I enclose
photocopies for you.

. . .

So: the film *was* shown to a non-Paramount audience of some
description; and, also, Mr Burns had told me, 'the film ran for years
in Paris – it had a cult appeal. Simon Hessera lives in Paris.' This
sounds like the apocryphal fate of *The Blockhouse* – its having a cult
following in Lisbon. . .

The Danes sent me two documents. The first is a typed 'Unit
List' – the whereabouts of the crew, their telephone numbers and
hotel rooms. Of note here is the news that the director of photography was Otto Heller, the cinematographer on *The Ladykillers*;
and for the record, the picture was shot at the ASA Film Studios,
Asavaenget, Lyngby, outside the capital. But much more important
was the other bundle of papers – a long synopsis of the movie,
which, with grateful acknowledgements to the Danish Film
Museum, I hereby append. (I have done my best to correct spelling,
grammar and punctuation flaws – I doubt if its author knew English

1043

as a first language.) When you read it, I want you to ask yourself what was pulling Sellers towards the story of a man having a drunken and bad day at the beach. Bernie rebuffs offers of friendship; he is provocative, overbearing, ugly, maudlin. (This is the Polanski of *Repulsion*.) He evinces Sellers' own isolating behaviour – that, for all the sentimental weeping and wailing, he needs to be alone (neurosis suits him). This synopsis* suggests a film that is an allegory of Sellers' emotional destructiveness; and the seaside setting – why, it's the Ilfracombe world of Sellers' childhood; and more harrowingly, this is how he treated his own children, too. (Hessera has said 'This problem of child abuse and abandonment ... it is so contemporary'). To read the synopsis is to picture Sellers

---

* I have a post scriptum to my (failed) quest. It would seem that my search was duplicated by the director – who was, however, more successful. Whether it was my own badgerings which stirred Paramount up in the first instance, we'll never know – I drew so many blanks with them. But in the *Los Angeles Times* (Calendar Section), on February 14th 1993, there was an article called 'You Never Knew Peter Sellers Spent "A Day at the Beach"?' by Jane Galbraith:

> Using the *nom de cinema* A. Queen, Sellers played a homosexual shopkeeper in *A Day at the Beach*, a Paramount picture that only recently was uncovered in the studio's London vaults, where it had been lost for 23 years ...

> Sellers – who died in 1980 – appears in the film for only five minutes, yet as director Simon Hessera admits, the actor's presence may help the film's chances of getting a theatrical launch. He has just bought the rights from the studio and has had the negative restored.

> 'My God! It's a beautiful film. I did a wonderful job, the actors did a wonderful job. Why shouldn't it come out?' the French-born film maker said.
> . . .

> Even though the first-time film maker had the good fortune of working with Polanski and Paramount, his misfortunes started to pile up once the movie was in the can ... [Following the decision not to release it] it was reported lost due to a mix-up in paperwork. Having no cachet, Hessera hoped that Polanski, a close friend of then-Paramount production chief Bob Evans, would be able to spur a search for lost film cans. But, as Hessera remembers the time, Polanski was 'incapable' of much of anything – the Polish-born director was still consumed with the traumatic emotional aftershocks of wife Sharon Tate's brutal murder ...

and Victoria, say – except in place of drink, Sellers had his dimension of natural evil.

☆ ★ ☆

'A Day at the Beach'
Synopsis

Bernie (MARK BURNS), an unkempt work-shy alcoholic, is walking through the rain in the early morning. The streets are deserted except for a milkman. Bernie is on his way to take his polio-stricken six year-old daughter, Winnie, (BEATRICE EDNEY) out to the beach for the day. After Winnie was born, her mother, Melissa (FIONA LEWIS) married the neat, industrious Carl (JORGEN KIIL) as a refuge from her impossible relationship with Bernie. It is still too early for Bernie to collect Winnie so he enters a block of offices and persuades the Caretaker to let him shelter from the rain until it is time for him to station himself outside the block of flats where Melissa and Carl live.

As Carl is about to get into his car to go to work, Bernie approaches him. The two men despise each other, but Bernie has no compunction in borrowing some money from Carl. When Carl has driven away, Bernie, going up in the lift, is surprised to find that Carl had handed him a ten pound note. Still contemptuous, he tucks it into his sock. Melissa receives him without enthusiasm, suspecting that he might be drunk; and while she is getting dressed, Bernie helps himself to food and a couple of magazines. Melissa taunts him with his fecklessness and praises Carl for his consideration. Bernie retaliates by outlining her reasons for marrying Carl after Winnie was born and Melissa bursts into tears. He caresses her a little, and then breaks away. While Melissa is getting Winnie ready to go out, Bernie gulps down a couple of large vodkas.

Hand in hand, Winnie and her father set out. She is delighted when he is rude to a pompously condescending Lady (RANDI MIEHELSEN) as they emerge from the foyer. She does not know their true relationship and calls him 'Uncle Bernard'. He is concerned because she limps and has to wear a leg iron, but Winnie seems not to notice her affliction and scampers on ahead of him. At the station, Bernie is accosted by Louis (BERTIL LAURING) to whom he owes money. Pleading that he has nothing but small change, Bernie thrusts a handful of coins into Louis's hand and then begs back half-a-crown for the train fare. Furious, Louis strikes Bernie and walks away muttering threats. Winnie shouts after him in anger and sets about comforting Uncle Bernard. On the train, Bernie refuses to recognise the Conductor (OLE MONTY) as a former drinking companion and brusquely dismisses him. When they arrive at the seaside, Bernie offers Winnie something to eat. She wants chips 'though Daddy doesn't like me to,' which sets Bernie off on such a tirade against Carl that Winnie becomes frightened and, to mollify her, Bernie quickly takes her into a snack bar.

After eating, they enter a souvenir shop on the promenade where Bernie buys Winnie a seashell and shows her how to listen to it. They walk on and Bernie talks to a Fisherman (JORGEN LANG-BAEK). For once, because fishing is his sport, Bernie is pleasant and is in a good mood when he joins Winnie in an empty beach café where she is sheltering from the rain. Happy, Winnie goes inside to fetch the waitress, (SISSE REINGARD) whom Bernie immediately attacks because she is wearing slacks and a sweater. She explains that she is the daughter of the Proprietress (EVA DAHLBECK), but Bernie tells her to go away and fetch her mother. When the owner of the café appears, she has such a friendly air that Bernie invites her and her daughter to join him. They decide on coffee, Winnie wants lemonade, and Bernie orders beer in a carefully off-hand way. When the Proprietress makes a veiled reference to Winnie's deformity, Bernie's mood changes and he becomes truculent again; he takes a familiar attitude with the daughter and orders more beer. After a few sharp exchanges between Bernie and the Proprietress, Winnie becomes impatient and asks to go and play. Once she has gone the atmosphere in the café deteriorates still further. Bernie is deliberately rude and provoking and leaves after refusing to pay the bill in full.

As they hurry away in the rain, Winnie realises that she has left her shell in the café. She wants to go back for it and cannot understand why Uncle Bernard refuses. Tearful, dismayed, and drenched to the skin, Winnie is inconsolable until Bernie tells her to run ahead to look at the shops where they may find another shell. When she has gone, Bernie carefully separates a couple of notes from his

money and puts them in his sock. Winnie, investigating some nets
drying further along the beach, knocks over one of the supporting
poles and is trapped underneath. Terrified, she begins to scream,
but Bernie does not hear her; he is busy buying some cigarettes and
inspecting a large shell which is for sale in the shop. The Salesman
(A. QUEEN [SELLERS]) invites him in to look round, and Bernie
encounters Pipi (STARK), a vulgar gaudily-dressed obese man who,
because he has money invested in the shop, is able to prevent the
Salesman from forming new friendships. Bernie, sensing that Pipi is
interested in him, suggests that he should bring some beer. Pipi is
elated and goes to bring three bottles which Bernie pockets without
attempting to pay. In his usual fashion, Bernie is rude to Pipi –
much to the satisfaction of the Salesman.

When he emerges from the shop he cannot see Winnie anywhere. Bernie trudges along in the rain calling her name. When he
nears the pier, Winnie gets up from a basket chair, sobbing
piteously. She is quite beside herself but Bernie sits with her in a
chair and gives her the big shell he has bought. Winnie is completely happy again and Bernie celebrates with a bottle of beer.
Winnie puts the shell to her ear and tells Bernie it says he is the
sweetest uncle in the world. She kisses him shyly but Bernie is upset
by her affection and warns her not to become too fond of him. The
beer begins to take its effect and he staggers down to the edge of the
sea and rages about the decadent state of the world. He falls on to
his knees and throws handfuls of sand into the air in helpless anger.
Winnie shrieks with laughter and begs him to do it again, but first
Bernie must drink more beer and he sits down once more in the basket chair. Along comes the Collector (JACK MACGOWRAN) and
demands his fee, but Bernie is rude and overbearing and continues
to drink. Winnie is frightened by Bernie's attitude, and Bernie re-
lents and pays twice as much as he need, then kneels before the old
man in mock submission, and forces the Collector to place his boot
on his neck. Winnie thinks this is great fun and demands that Bernie place his boot on her neck, but Bernie dismisses this notion as
crazy and stalks off under the pier.

By now they are soaked to the skin and Bernie had drunk the last
of his beer. They go into a warm café where Winnie has a meal of
pancakes. Bernie manages to leave without paying in spite of the

kindness of the Cook (ARNE SELDORF), who has dried their coats on the stove. The rain has stopped and they go off for a ride on the dodgem cars, but Bernie is becoming bored and is seeking an opportunity to find another drink. He is saved when a poet friend, Michael (MAURICE ROEVES), arrives in a bubble car with his wife Tonie (JOANNA DUNHAM) and their four-year-old son. Bernie senses a drinking companion and starts to flatter Michael about his poetry. Pleading that Winnie has been out in the wet all day, Bernie drives off with her and Michael, leaving a disgruntled Tonie behind on the promenade with her son. Bernie takes Michael to a disreputable bar, pleading that it is just the place for a couple of outcasts. Soon Michael becomes uneasy and wants to return for Tonie and the boy. Bernie, afraid that he is going to be left alone with Winnie and so not able to drink, snatches Michael's wristwatch and gives it to the Barkeeper (MICHAEL HILDENSHEIM) as a security for his return. When Michael has gone, Bernie suddenly remembers Winnie and rushes outside, only to find that she is no longer there. He hopefully assumes that Michael has taken her and goes back to his drinking.

Soon Michael and Tonie return, leaving the children in the car. Bernie can now get down to some serious drinking with an easy conscience. They switch to gin, and Michael, unused to drinking, quickly gets drunk, which gives Bernie an opportunity to squeeze Tonie's knee and kiss her. Michael, spouting poetry and beginning to feel ill, hardly notices what is happening; and Tonie, although she spurns Bernie's advances at first, soon becomes excited and arranges to see him again. Bernie reacts to Michael's condition only by insisting that he should drink more.

Outside it is now dusk. Bernie finds Winnie still in the bubble car with the little boy asleep on her shoulder. She is glad to be released. Tonie appears, remorseful that she has neglected her son and warns Bernie that Michael is coming out to pick a fight.

Winnie is tired and wants to go home. Bernie walks steadily – with the concentration of the experienced drunk. He addresses a passing Girl (GRIT FJELDMOSE) assuring her totally unnecessarily that he is not intoxicated. Shortly, he stops in a cemetery and leans against the railings in the rain. Winnie tells him again that she wants to go home, but Bernie has to have another drink; and, on the pretext of phoning her mother, he hurries across the street to a bar. He coaxes Winnie to stay in the street by asking her to start counting, and to see how long it takes to make the call. Trusting him, she begins to count.

Inside the bar Bernie meets the Man From Ghana (TOM HEATHCOTE) – a phlegmatic customer, a man who has drunk his whisky in bars all over the world, and who is surprised by nothing. Bernie does his best to impress him, but the Man From Ghana fails to react. Even when Bernie is rude to the Barmaid (LILLY BROBERG) he remains unmoved. Bernie makes a last effort and refuses to pay for his drink, but neither the Man From Ghana nor the Barmaid take the slightest notice. Bernie is defeated and leaves when a Workman (HOLGER PERFORT) rushes in demanding to know who is supposed to be in charge of the child standing outside.

It is now completely dark in the street. Half a dozen passers-by have formed a circle round Winnie who is sobbing uncontrollably. When she sees Bernie she rushes up to him and flings her arms tightly round his neck, demanding to know where he has been. Chastened by the scandalised remarks of a couple of women, Bernie consoles Winnie and promises to find a taxi to take her home. He picks her up in his arms and walks away, but as soon as he is out of sight of the shocked group of people, he carries Winnie into a sandwich bar and orders some black coffee for himself and some hot soup for the little girl. The coffee sobers him to the point where he needs another drink. He tells Winnie that it really won't be long now and rings the bell of a wine and spirit shop which has already closed for the night. Pleading that a sick friend needs a bottle of gin to ease his suffering, Bernie forces his way into the shop. The Shopkeeper (JOHN FRANKLYN) wraps up the gin and Bernie asks him to bring some beer and some lemonade for Winnie. While the Shopkeeper is fetching the beer, Bernie steals a flask of brandy from a shelf and puts it into his pocket. Bernie is now very drunk – his vision blurred, his speech thick – but the Shopkeeper is a friendly man and continues to drink with him. Finally Bernie says he needs a sandwich and staggers out of the shop dragging the sleepy Winnie with him. He has reached the final stages of perfect drunkenness. He stumbles on, his daughter trying to keep up.

'This is my hour, Winnie. Glorious, glorious . . .'

Later that night, Bernie is lying in a hole in the beach without his jacket. As he tries to get up, he feels the brandy flask between his legs and he takes a careful drink. It is too much for him. His stomach turns over and the brandy spills down his chest. Utterly revolted with himself, he starts to scream and flings himself, in desperation, face down in the sand. Suddenly he remembers Winnie. Frantically he calls for her . . . but there is no reply. He tries to get up, but falls time after time. In his anxiety he begins shouting and knocking over chairs. The beach stretches deserted before him. He begins to run wildly . . . zigzagging . . . stumbling again and again.

Winnie is asleep in a basket chair wrapped in Bernie's coat. Wakened by Bernie's far-off cries, she sits up shivering. Bernie comes running past, trips, and hits his head on the side of the chair. Raising himself up he grasps Winnie's legs and bursts into sobs. It is now Winnie's turn to comfort him.

'Don't cry Uncle Bernard. Please don't cry.'

She wipes his tears with her scarf.

'Everything will be all right. You'll see, you'll feel better.'

She takes his jacket and puts it round his shoulders. Bernie buries his head in his hands and turns to whimpering. Winnie takes command and tells him that she will find a taxi and take him home.

Winnie carefully leads Bernie along as if he were blind. His state worsens with every step. Finally he stumbles, crashes head first into the cobbles and lies still. Winnie speaks to him but he lies senseless, spread-eagled on the wet stones, a bubble of saliva dribbling from his mouth. She calls to him, but Bernie does not hear. She looks round helplessly and starts to cry. As she realises the hopelessness of the situation the cry becomes a desperate, lonely wail. The vast square is deserted. Only two solitary figures remain. A little girl in a leg iron whose wail has now become a ceaseless whimper . . . and a shapeless man lying in a puddle.

Afterword

'Happy endings are only possible if you don't tell the rest of the story.'

Orson Welles

Did this book – i.e. did I – kill Lynne Frederick? She turned up her toes on April 27th 1994, the eve of my hardback publication day, and that's a very eerie coincidence. For some weeks previously the newspapers had been previewing my material – and given that she professed to idolise Sellers ('I am still in love with Peter, I hold his memory very dear,' she'd said after her divorce from Dr Barry Unger in 1991), how was she going to react to my portrait of her fatal marriage? To my account of Sellers as a sort of evil father-figure? He was evil, and this book details what Charles Laughton called the *strain* of being evil, so it was quite likely that Lynne would object, yammer about 'an insult to his memory' and so on. She'd go into screaming orbit, unleash the dogs of war (i.e. expensive lawyers). Instead of which she choked on spaghetti and meatballs and ended up as cadaver no. 94-3840 in the Beverly Hills police department morgue.

In fact, if I (fancifully) contributed to her exit it was only because I'd written what she knew to be the truth; and how could she bear the truth? She'd married Sellers virtually in good faith – believing, like Dorothea of Casaubon in *Middlemarch*, that his 'odd habits would be a glorious piety to endure' – and yet he systematically destroyed her, preying upon her weakness and devotion. 'She'd hang on to his words,' Sarah Sellers told the *Daily Express* on May 4th. 'If

Dad said something unpleasant about someone in passing, she'd echo it six times more.' Lynne, to appease him, grew to be like him. She became, a film executive told me, 'Iago whispering into Othello's ear' – compounding Sellers' megalomania and causing directors and crew to be sacked. Determined not to let him down, she was pulled towards the abyss at Sellers' core; and, unable to reconcile his genius as a performer with the intensities of his madness as a man – his shiftiness, his fluidity – she embarked upon what the Los Angeles coroner called 'a history of alcohol and seizures' and the route towards her under-attended funeral at the Little Chapel of the Dawn in Santa Monica at the age of thirty-nine.

She'd wanted a consuming passion, and (as Wilde said of Salome) she was consumed by it. About this she never had illusions: 'I learned what it really meant to love another person. A total all-consuming love. It consumed every minute of my life,' she claimed with an irony that emerges only now. But was it love? Wasn't it, in its self-destructiveness and its total absence of happy memories, more akin to hate? She was immersed in Sellers; he held her attention for so long, her view of him was a delusion (as Sellers' was for Peg, whom he could find no fault with once she was dead). She forgot – and spent the fourteen years of her widowhood sinking deeper down a drain of vodka and pills in order to forget – the reality, the bitterness, the threats and counter-threats and legal communiqués. Sellers, indeed, was set to divorce her – his lawyer was to return to the Dorchester on the afternoon of July 22nd 1980 with the papers for his signature. As we know, Sellers croaked into his Dover sole. He was, as it happens, seriously deceased – brain dead – long before he reached the Middlesex Hospital, attached to wires and tubes. That was all a grisly farce for Lynne's benefit. She had to fly from America and insisted on giving that weepin' an' wailin' act for the photographers; and if you've watched her in *Vampire Circus* or *Voyage of the Damned*, you'll agree it was her best performance – one which sickened Sellers' real family and friends. Even before the funeral she was giving press interviews in the hotel suite; she went over the will avidly with a solicitor; she began speaking on the phone to David Frost – whom she was to marry a few months later. It was her finest hour.

I have yet to find anyone with a good word to say about Lynne: a hypocrite, a nymphomaniac, a hysteric; she was impossible to do business with; she was prone to screaming and crying. (To me, in a transcontinental phone call that went on and on, she played the part of a coquettish little girl.) She was self-destructing. Her lawyer told me back in 1989, 'She is not going to live very long. You just get that feeling about her.' She carried with her a sense of morbidity, of shadows and unrest. She'd failed to evolve. Despite two intervening marriages she was still Mrs Peter Sellers on her credit cards; she still wore Peg's wedding ring. 'Lynne talked about Peter constantly. You know . . . what might have been,' the few people who met her reported. She lived in the past and denied herself a future (she retained no agent or publicist; she did not open her mail); but it was an invented past, as she secretly knew. Nobody was allowed to mention the Dorchester heart attack; she was suspicious and jealous of people who'd known Sellers before she'd come along – the worthy Milligan was sent packing, for example, when he asked for the return of some comedy material; Sellers' children were refused access to photos their father had taken of them.

It was the actual past, the past detailed in this book, which ate her mind away. As Michael Sellers remarked with grim satisfaction: 'As we understand it, she's not a very happy person. A bloated alcoholic drug addict.' Another enemy crowed, 'She was haunted by guilt which finally destroyed her.' It wasn't guilt – it was a sense of waste. You don't only have to be partial to wrecks, ruins and witches (from Lucia di Lammermoor to Norma Desmond) to appreciate her tragedy that, not allowing Sellers' life to end, Lynne's never began. She was virtually his last victim. She'd get up late and start boozing on her own; she squandered her inheritance, £2,500 a week going on nose candy. (Sellers did nothing good with his money when he lived, and nothing good was done with it when he died.) Her slender figure ballooned to fourteen stone. She pined and raged, and perhaps in her rise and fall, her thinness and fatness, and the way that she was melancholy and craven ('We can never forget how callous she was after our father died,' says Michael), we have an encapsulation of Sellers' own personality. Lynne was, in a way, his supernatural double or fellow lost soul; except that she acquired his insanities without the compensations of his genius.

☆ ★ ☆

Currently there is a wrangle about the destination of Lynne's ashes. She'd wanted to be sprinkled under Sellers' rose bush at Golders Green – though might not that create an atomic explosion like the quicklime put down to rid Trafalgar Square of squawking birds in 'The Starlings' episode of *The Goon Show*? The scheme is certainly repugnant to Sellers' children, and the events of the past six months have made me wonder if my Sellers file can ever be closed. I'm still being sent clippings; the *Newsletter* of the Goon Show Preservation Society continues to compile its notes and queries with the diligence of *Der Shakespeare Jahrbuch*; the man who pinched Sophia Loren's jewels when she was making *The Millionairess* was only arrested in March 1994 – thirty-four years after the theft ('We hired a Rolls Royce to blend in because it was a very rich area,' bragged Ray 'The Cat' Jones); and Peter Ackroyd has published a novel about Dan Leno, whom Sellers believed himself to be the reincarnation of . . .

This is a long book – it could easily be longer, a *gesamtkunstwerk*, to use a word that once wafted around Wahnfried. Biography is an ever-widening sea: new facts, new names, the criss-cross of relationships; there is always more to add – and add to *that* the biographer's endless reconsiderations . . . What is the truth? What is the answer? It was my intention, by devising a non-circumspect all-inclusive style, consisting of interconnecting monologues and digressions, to get just this flux and reflux on to my pages – so that here we have a meditation on Sellers which is also, perhaps primarily, a book about somebody finding out about Sellers. For as in that old joke about the Grail Knights – What would they do with it if they found it? – it is the quest which counts; what happens on the journey, as I wrestle with and try to understand what Nabokov would call Sellers' 'inner attitude in regard to the outer world'.

Afterword

To explore the issues involved when imposing order and finding patterns and directions in another person's life, I have put a fallible sleuth* actually in the text, groping and swerving, following clues, meeting people, making mistakes, coming to conclusions (some of which were unpalatable to fans and reviewers) – and perhaps, in the process of re-living a life that is not his own, he loses his identity and takes on Sellers'? Though I remain fascinated with the relationship of the biographer to his work, thankfully this book can be read without ever dealing with that level if you don't want to; and though many critics have called this book *definitive*, it is not.†

First, anecdotes previously unknown to me have come to light: Sellers taking a goat into the Dorchester lift, announcing that he was going to kill it and barbecue it in the bathroom (his protest against Arabs residing in his favourite hotel); Sellers, in late 1950, appearing at the Grimsby Fish Merchants' Annual Dinner Dance, at the Winter Gardens, Cleethorpes ('a little bit of last night's supper left in the teeth is very tasty on a cold morning'); Sellers participating in The Who's *Tommy* at the Royal Albert Hall in December 1972, playing (as a Nazi stormtrooper) the role of the Doctor: 'He seems to be completely unreceptive/The tests I gave him show no sense at all/He hears but cannot answer to your call'; Sellers in a daze because he'd been thwacked over the noggin, so that a picture frame was round his neck and glass covered his face:

---

* 'certifiably egomaniacal' (*London Review of Books*); 'wilfully swinish' (*Independent*); 'mad' (*Sunday Times*); 'has a screw loose' (*Spectator*); 'he chooses to litter his text with wholly unnecessary four-letter words' (*Sunday Telegraph*); 'the Welsh Bitch' (*New Statesman*); 'He has escaped from all constraint. He is mad, unhinged, certifiable: all the things he imputes to Peter Sellers' (Alexander Walker in the *Evening Standard*); 'He is as mean-minded as they come . . . a monstrously vain ego – not Peter Sellers' – intrudes' (*Irish Sunday Independent*); etc., etc.

† If, as Michael Kinsley has said, on American television the word 'talent' is an insult, so too, I can report, are 'definitive' and 'dedicated' perjorative terms when used by harsh and hasty British reviewers: 'The facts of Sellers' work and life are certainly there – in train-spotting detail,' mocked a woman of no importance in *The Times*.

'She hit me with me mum!' he whimpered, which was indeed the truth, as Britt Ekland had brandished a cherished photograph of that appalling pterodactyl Peg in self-defence . . .

Then there are the people I failed to find and interview – for example, Mr Walter Jokel, who knew Sellers from 1948 and attended the private funeral service and subsequent reception at the Dorchester. Jokel was Sellers' and Milligan's personal manager in the early days, and introduced him to Bill Wills (who *is* dead), his secretary, Sue Evans, and Patricia Hammond (a name which is new to me), who took over when Miss Evans had a leave of absence. 'Even Britt Ekland in her book *True Britt* writes about me,' chides Mr Jokel in a recent letter.

No joke at all was the fate of a lady, who wrote to me last May:

> At the time that Ted Levy, architect, met Anne and Peter Sellers, I was his wife. We were living together in a house we had recently bought in New End, Hampstead. We had a son who was five. I cannot speak of the accuracy of the information given to you by Anne Sellers-Levy nor Michael Sellers in general. However, I can tell you [that] I was in my mid-twenties when my marriage broke up . . . Michael Sellers was old enough to remember coming to my son's fifth birthday party, yet he states [in *P.S. I Love You*] that when his mother met Ted, Ted was separated from his wife. Further on he states that Ted and myself were separated on the recommendation of a psychiatrist. Fact! I was pregnant when Ted left. He made me have an abortion. In those days a psychiatrist had to sanction it . . . Also, for the record, on the night when Peter Sellers and I went to look for Ted and Anne at Golden Yard, it was Anne who was screaming, not me. I was quiet, overwhelmed by the screaming and theatricals I was witnessing. It was Anne who ran into the kitchen and came out with a bread knife, aiming it at Peter [who was] morose, hideously self-centred and nasty.

Well, it was a long time ago. But my point is that as Sellers had made life absolute hell for Anne, his first wife, and their children, he'd therefore prepared the ground for her to seek the sanctuary of somebody else. That somebody else was unfortunately my correspondent's first husband – and the knock-on effects were additionally destructive and painful, evidently, to Ted's family. Adam, the five year old, grew up to be severely mentally disturbed; he lived in terrible hostels for the homeless and when Levy died (I was told):

> Anne turned her back on us and swooped her family into the service. The rabbi who officiated shook hands with Anne, Michael, Sarah and Katie and Loretta Feldman. Adam was completely ignored. He looked awful, hunched and cold. I took him to the rabbi and said he was Ted's only son . . .

Nobody wants to be reminded of ancient injustice, old wives, cast-off families – that pile of debris, the past. Yet is there any link between this lad's psychiatric distress and the 'loss' of his father in the divorce? ('Yes, I do think that Ted's absence had a profound effect on Adam's mental state.') How much blame for this can be assigned to Sellers – for was he not the first to disrupt people's harmony, like Alberich, whose cavortings on the bank of the Rhine bring about, several music dramas later, the end of the world? (Sellers embodied Original Sin.) If he was the initiator, years ago, if my correspondent and her son were innocents dragged into his orbit, where and when can his actions and decisions be said to start ceasing to matter?

☆ ★ ☆

Which brings us to Victoria, who told the *Daily Mail* in July 1994 that 'my dad was really nice and normal'. She's been in and out of the slammer so often I've given up keeping track. The latest news, which will be way out of date by the time you read this, is that she faces a possible two-year sentence on a charge of receiving stolen goods. Her lover, Oscar Lopez, and his friend, Anthony Zapata, have been arrested at her house and accused of murder and armed robberies – all this in addition to the Heidi Fleiss shenanigans, which are the subject of a footnote on pages 986–7.

Victoria once said, 'I want to be a comedy actress, a kind of female Peter Sellers,' and she is indeed a comedian in a certain sense. She is not only daughter to Sellers' blood – but to his manners. Victoria has come in for his sultry, long, thin face – the Portuguese Jewish coloration – and his fecklessness and amorality.

Her alleged contempt for proprieties, for law, order and the feelings of others, is a dreadful resurfacing of her father's mentality – of his way of looking dead behind the eyes. To try and expel him from her system she is undergoing $10,000 worth of plastic surgery: 'Miss Sellers said she wanted to be rid of creases around her mouth which make her look like her late father,' readers of the *Evening Standard* were told on September 27th 1994. Apparently she wants to start looking like Audrey Hepburn instead.

So much is easily said: that the innocent and cunning Victoria is the spawn of a shameful human being who, through his films and other repercussions, is still laughingly alive. Sellers had never allowed her mother to be maternal. The way he reasoned it, attention spent on the baby meant less time spent on him. A good mother was a disloyal wife. Victoria was raised in hotel suites by nannies, and Britt – in despair – claimed that not only did she never change any nappies, but also, 'I could dispense with the necessity of breast feeding, the thought of which was alien to my nature.' Victoria was never to be read bedtime stories, nor did anyone sit 'at a kitchen table with a tube of glue and make animal cardboard cutouts . . .' She was purposefully neglected and being outrageous became her way of registering that she existed. She has had involvements with cocaine trafficking gangs, and after the modelling and hostessing at night-clubs it was inevitable that she would think that being a hooker was an up-market career path. (Her sole consolation is to gloat on Lynne's worse fate: 'The fact that she blew up as a big fat giant and was drinking vodka all day long, taking pills and doing coke – I don't know but that makes me feel better.')

Britt, who must loathe and fear the side of Victoria that resembles Sellers, optimistically stated in 1992 that 'all Victoria's problems are in the past'. She meant over and done with. The real meaning is that it is in the dark intricacies of her past that Victoria's present problems have their roots. She has no conception of right and wrong; she is a naughty, naughty girl – and she appears to enjoy every minute of it.

R. L., Manitoba, January 1995

Sources and Acknowledgements

> Not that I quite know indeed what situations the seeking fabulist
> does 'find'; he seeks them enough assuredly, but his discoveries are,
> like those of the navigator, the chemist, the biologist, scarce more
> than alert recognitions. He comes upon the interesting thing as
> Columbus came upon the isle of San Salvador, because he had
> moved in the right direction for it . . .'
>
> Preface to *The Aspern Papers*, by Henry James

I was Professor Humbert Humbert pursuing Quilty – or perhaps
Clouseau chasing Sir Charles Phantom, the famous Litton (as he
puts it). As long ago as August 1989 there was a reporter from the
Sunday Mirror on my doorstep, wanting to know my intentions.
GOON FURY AT A 'SLUR' ON SELLERS ran the subsequent
headline. 'The author would only have been eighteen when Peter
died and could not have even met him,' Michael Bentine was
quoted as saying. 'The two other books written about Peter are both
rubbish – and this sounds exactly the same.' As I'd not yet written a
word, this seemed a bit scathing – and, in fairness, when he discovered my work was still in progress, Mr Bentine did apologise to
me and was amiableness itself. But word was out and the following
year the tabloids had another go at scuppering the project. IN-
SPECTOR CLOUSEAU'S SNORTIN' SEX SECRETS, bellowed
the *Sunday Sport*, on July 22nd 1990. 'Sex-crazed ex-Goon Peter
Sellers died a gibbering LOONY after DESTROYING himself
with mind-blowing BONKING drugs, we can reveal today . . . The
zany star MASHED his brains in a bizarre bid to get a better

STIFFY and in an EXPLOSIVE new book it is claimed the man who made millions laugh had a long history of mental problems . . .'

Again, I'd not yet started to scribble – but as an example of long-distance mind-reading it is pretty impressive. Not funny at all was the punishment I received over a two-year period from an eminent firm of British libel lawyers on behalf of a client who was once – hilariously but quite misleadingly – described by John Le Mesurier as 'the only man in London with a flat up Peter Sellers' arse'. People were starting to get jittery – fearful of my investigations. On April 18th 1991, my solicitor, Richard Sykes, received a summons for 'Notes and Transcripts of Mr Lewis' interviews with those that he saw in connection with his proposed book . . . and Correspondence between Mr Lewis and others concerning his proposed book – relevant to malice'. I instructed my lawyer to issue a Grade A Fuck Off (to use a legal term). He did so – but it took a Queen's Counsel and getting on for a six figure sum to despatch the opposition. It was all too complicated and Kafka-esque and an eye-opening glimpse into the British concept of justice – its priggishness and its relish for vague concepts ('reputation' for one) which, as David Hare says in *Murmuring Judges*, cannot be proved. One thing was clear, however. The Velociraptors in *Jurassic Park*, all agile fangs and claws, never became extinct. They'd evolved into devotees of Peter Carter-Ruck's tip-top text books on defamation and slander.

As a result of the legal hair-pulling, I became the more resolved to carry on and root out the truth. Eventually I had accumulated a wide Sargasso Sea of documents and letters, statements from Sellers' acquaintances, papers, fragments, diary jottings, tape recordings and pictures. Like Boswell, I know exactly how it feels to have 'spared no pains in obtaining materials concerning [my subject], from every quarter where I could discover that they were to be found, and have been favoured with the most liberal communications.' It therefore gives me much pleasure to acknowledge my indebtedness to the following authors, publishers, institutions and individuals out of whose words and works the present book has been created:

Sources and Acknowledgements

(a) *Principal printed material cited and quoted*

i. Books

ALLEN, Steve. *Funny People* (New York, 1981).

AMIS, [Sir] Kingsley. *That Uncertain Feeling* (London, 1955).
   I Want It Now (London, 1968).
   Girl, Twenty (London, 1971).
   The Old Devils (London, 1986).
   The Amis Collection (London, 1990).
   Memoirs (London, 1991).

ANON. *A Pictorial and Descriptive Guide to Ilfracombe*, Tenth Edition [no date – c. 1930s].

BACH, Steven. *Final Cut* (London, 1985).

BALCON, [Sir] Michael. *Michael Balcon Presents a Lifetime of Films* (London, 1969).

BARTHES, Roland. *Camera Lucida* (New York, 1981).

BEHAN, Dominic. *Milligan* (London, 1988).

BELL, Simon, et al. *Who's Had Who* (London, 1987).

BENDAZZI, G. *The Films of Woody Allen* (Milan, 1984).

BENTINE, Michael. *The Long Banana Skin* (London, 1975).
   The Best of Bentine (St Albans, 1983).
   The Reluctant Jester (London, 1992).

BERGAN, Ronald. *Beyond the Fringe . . . And Beyond* (London, 1989).

BIRKIN, Andrew. *J. M. Barrie and the Lost Boys* (London, 1979).

BRODE, Douglas. *Woody Allen: His Films and Career* (New York, 1985).

BULL, Peter. *I Say, Look Here* (London, 1965).
   Life is a Cucumber (London, 1973).

BYGRAVES, Max. *I Wanna Tell You a Story* (London, 1976).
   Afterthoughts (London, 1988).

CHAPLIN, Charles. *My Autobiography* (London, 1964).

CHAPMAN, Graham. *A Liar's Autobiography* (London, 1980).

CIMENT, Michel. *Kubrick* (New York, 1982).

COLLINS, Doris. *Woman of Spirit* (London, 1983).

CREWE, Quentin. *Well, I Forget the Rest* (London, 1991).

DAHL, Tessa. *Working For Love* (London, 1988).

DAVIDSON, Gerald and John M. Neale. *Abnormal Psychology: An Experimental Clinical Approach* (Toronto, 1978).

DRAPER, Alfred. *The Story of the Goons* (London, 1976).

DUNN, Clive. *Permission to Speak* (London, 1986).

EKLAND, Britt. *True Britt* (London, 1980).

   Sensual Beauty – and How to Achieve It (London, 1984).

EMETT, Rowland. *From Punch to Chitty Chitty Bang Bang . . . and Beyond* [sale exhibition catalogue, Chris Beetles Ltd.] (London, 1988).

EVANS, Peter. *The Mask Behind the Mask* (London, 1968; updated edition, 1980).

   Soft Beds, Hard Battles (London, 1974).

FIELD, Andrew. *The Life and Art of Vladimir Nabokov* (London, 1986).

FLASHNER, Graham. *Fun with Woody* (New York, 1987).

FLEISCHMAN, Sid. *The Ghost in the Noonday Sun* (Boston, 1965).

FORBES, Bryan. *Notes for a Life* (London, 1974).

FRANCIS, Anne. *Julian Wintle: A Memoir* (Brighton, 1984).

FRAYN, Michael. *The Book of Fub* (London, 1963).

FREEDLAND, Michael. *Liza With a Z* (London, 1988).

FUSSELL, Paul. *Wartime: Understanding and Behaviour in the Second World War* (New York, 1989).

GEBLER, Ernest. *Hoffman* (London, 1969).

GELDRAY, Max. *Goon with the Wind* (London, 1989).

GELMIS, Joseph. *The Film Director as Superstar* (New York, 1970).

GILLIAT, Penelope. *To Wit: In Celebration of Comedy* (London, 1990).

GIFFORD, Denis. *The Armchair Odeon* (n.p., n.d.).

GRADE, Lew. *Still Dancing* (London, 1987).

GRAHAM, Sheilah. 'Caesar Sellers', in *Scratch an Actor* (London, 1969).

GROBEL, Lawrence. *The Hustons* (London, 1990).

GUINNESS, [Sir] Alec. *Blessings in Disguise* (London, 1985).

GUNDEN, Kenneth Von. *Alec Guinness: The Films* (North Carolina, 1987).

Sources and Acknowledgements

HACKNEY, Alan. *I'm All Right, Jack* (London, 1958).

HAILL, Catherine. *Dear Peter Pan* [Foreword by Nanette Newman], (London, 1983).

HARWOOD, Ronald, ed. *Dear Alec: Guinness at Seventy-Five* (London, 1989).

HILL, Leonard. *Saucy Boy: The Life Story of Benny Hill* (London, 1990).

JULIAN, Desmond G. *Cardiology*, Fifth Edition (London, 1988).

KEMP, Philip. *Lethal Innocence: The Cinema of Alexander Mackendrick* (London, 1991).

KENNER, Hugh. *Paradox in Chesterton* (London, 1948).

KOSINSKI, Jerzy. *Being There* (New York, 1970).

KOTSILIBAS-DAVIS, James. *Myrna Loy: Being and Becoming* (London, 1987).

LAX, Eric. *Woody Allen: A Biography* (London, 1991).

LEAMING, Barbara. *Orson Welles* (London, 1985).

LEHMAN, Peter and William Luhr, *Blake Edwards* (Ohio, 1981).

LE MESURIER, Joan. *Lady Don't Fall Backwards* (London, 1988).

LEWIS, Roger. *Stage People* (London, 1989).

ed. *Confessions of a Justified Sinner* (London, 1992).

LODGE, David. *Up the Ladder to Obscurity* (Bognor Regis, 1986).

MacLAINE, Shirley. *Out On a Limb* (London, 1983).

McKERN, Leo. *Just Resting* (London, 1983).

MAGRIEL, Paul, ed. *Memoirs of the Life of Daniel Mendoza* (London, 1951).

MARTIN, George. *All You Need Is Ears* (London, 1979).

MASON, James. *Before I Forget* (London, 1981).

MILLIGAN, Spike. *The Goon Show Scripts* (London, 1972).

More Goon Show Scripts (London, 1973).

The Book of the Goons (London, 1974).

The Great McGonagall Scrapbook (London, 1975).

William McGonagall: The Truth at Last [illustrated by Sellers], (London, 1976).

The Spike Milligan Letters (London, 1977).

Indefinite Articles & Scunthorpe (London, 1981).

More Spike Milligan Letters (London, 1984).

Where Have All the Bullets Gone? (London, 1985).

Goodbye Soldier (London, 1986).

The Lost Goon Shows (London, 1987).

Scunthorpe Revisted (London, 1989).

MINNEY, R.J. *Puffin Asquith* (London, 1973).

MORTIMER, John. *Clinging to the Wreckage* (London, 1982).

NABOKOV, Vladimir. *Lolita* (London, 1959).

Lolita: A Screenplay (New York, 1974).

Selected Letters: 1940–1977 (London, 1990).

NATHAN, David. *The Laughtermakers* (London, 1971).

OAKES, Philip. *Tony Hancock* (London, 1975).

OWEN, Maureen. *The Crazy Gang* (London, 1986).

PARRISH, Robert. *Hollywood Doesn't Live Here Anymore* (Boston, 1988).

PERRY, George. *Forever Ealing* (London, 1981).

PETRUCELLI, Alan W. *Liza! Liza!* (Bromley, 1983).

PLOMLEY, Roy. *Plomley's Pick* (London, 1982).

POLANSKI, Roman. *Roman* (London, 1984).

POWELL, Michael. *Million Dollar Movie* (London, 1992).

RANDALL, Alan and Ray Seaton. *George Formby* (London, 1974).

RAPHAEL, Frederic. *Think of England* (London, 1986).

RAY, Satyajit. *The Chess Players* [includes *The Alien*] (London, 1989).

RAY, Ted. *Raising the Laughs* (London, 1952).

My Turn Next (London, 1963).

READER, Ralph. *It's Been Terriffic* (London, 1953).

Ralph Reader Remembers (London, 1974).

RICKARDS, Jocelyn. *The Painted Banquet* (London, 1987).

ROSS, Lilian and Helen. *The Player: A Profile of an Art* (New York, 1962).

ROSSO de, Diana. *James Mason: A Personal Biography* (London, 1989).

RUTHERFORD, Margaret. *An Autobiography* (London, 1972).

SCUDAMORE, Pauline. *Spike Milligan: A Biography* (London, 1985).

ed. *Dear Robert, Dear Spike: The Graves–Milligan Correspondence* (Stroud, 1991).

SECOMBE, Sir Harry. *Arias and Raspberries* (London, 1989).

SELLERS, Michael. *P.S., I Love You* (London, 1981).

SHERRIN, Ned. *A Small Thing – Like an Earthquake* (London, 1983).

SHILLINGFORD, J. P. *Coronary Heart Disease* (London, 1981).

SIMMONS, Anthony. *The Optimists of Nine Elms* (London, 1964); [a 1974 edition contains stills from the film].

SINCLAIR, David. *Snowdon: A Man for Our Times* (London, 1982).

SONTAG, Susan. *On Photography* (New York, 1977).

STARK, Graham. *Remembering Peter Sellers* (London, 1990).

STARR, Michael. *Peter Sellers: A Film History* (London, 1992).

SYLVESTER, Derek. *Peter Sellers* (New York, 1981).

TAYLOR, John. *Love, Cricket, Peter Sellers* (Birmingham, 1988).

TAYLOR, John Russell. *Alec Guinness: A Celebration* (London, 1984).

TERRY-THOMAS. *Terry-Thomas Tells Tales* (London, 1990).

THURBER, James. 'The Catbird Seat', in *The Thurber Carnival* (London, 1945).

TODD, Richard. *In Camera* (London, 1989).

TOMLINSON, David. *Luckier than Most* (London, 1990).

TOOK, Barry. *Comedy Greats* (Northamptonshire, 1979).
Laughter in the Air (London, 1976).
A Point of View (London, 1990).

WALKER, Alexander. *Stanley Kubrick Directs* (New York, 1971).
Peter Sellers: The Authorized Biography (London, 1981; reprinted with an Afterword, 1990).

WHICKER, Alan. *Within Whicker's World* (London, 1982).

WILMUT, Roger. *The Goon Show Companion* (London, 1976).
Kindly Leave the Stage (London, 1985).

WINTERS, Shelley. *Best of Times, Worst of Times* (New York, 1990).

ZEC, Donald. *Sophia Loren* (London, 1975).

ZETTERLING, Mai. *All Those Tomorrows* (London, 1985).

ZOLOTOW, Maurice. *Billy Wilder in Hollywood* (London, 1977).

ii. Periodicals and Newspapers

ANON. 'Being There'. *Listener*, July 31st 1980.

'The Changing Face of Sellers', *Film Show Annual*, 1962.

'Dan Mendoza', *Egan's Boxiana*, Vols I and III, 1818.

'The Day Peter Sellers Died', *Headlines*, Number 53.

'For TV Humour, A Goon Twist', *TV Mirror*, March 31st 1956.

'Friends Mourn Sellers', *Sunday Telegraph*, July 27th 1980.

'How to Get into Films', *Films and Filming*, May 1961.

'It's Sellers for President', *Evening News*, April 3rd 1979.

'Life Lines of Peter Sellers', *Musical Express*, December 9th 1960.

'Memoirs of Dan Mendoza', *The Fancy*, Vol. II, 1826.

Miscellanies of the Jewish Historical Society of England, Vol. V.

'Peter Sellers' [obituary], *The Stage and Television Today*, July 31st 1980.

'The Sellers Marriage Go Round', *TV Times*, March 15th 1986.

Profile of Dennis Main Wilson, *Observer*, June 26th 1988.

'Seven Characters in search of one voice – and the object is PETER SELLERS', *Sound and Vision*, October 1950.

'Should Sellers Have Said It?' *Sun*, January 16th 1969.

'Spiked', *Listener*, September 30th 1982.

St Aloysius' College: 1879–1979 [Centenary brochure].

'String and Teeth: The Property of Spike Milligan, Esq.' [Lot 215 in a Christie's auction catalogue, c. April 1981.]

'Years of Fun with Peter Sellers', *Sun*, April 15th 1980.

AYRE, Leslie. 'Who Would Be a BBC Announcer?' *Radio Times*, March 21st 1958.

BARBER, Lynn. 'The Unforgiving Goon', *Independent on Sunday*, September 9th 1990.

BALL, Ian. 'Plea Deal for Miss [Victoria] Sellers', *Daily Telegraph*, May 25th 1986.

BAUER, Ed. 'Our Marriage Won't Last [says Lynne]', *Titbits*, March 15th 1980.

BERMAN, Charles. 'No Lynne, No Me, Angry Peter Told the Palace', *Daily Mirror*, June 28th 1983.

BILLINGTON, Michael. 'Hancock's Laugh Hour', *Radio Times*, April 20th 1985.

BOULTING, Roy and John. 'Sellers Market', *New Standard*, September 29th 1981.

'Notes from a director's thought-book', *Films and Filming*, February and March 1974.

CALLAN, Paul. 'Talks to Lynne Frederick', *Daily Mirror*, October 6th 1981.

'Turmoil of the star's daughter on drug charges', *Daily Mirror*, March 14th 1986.

CASTELL, David. 'Best Sellers', *Films Illustrated*, February 1976.

CHAMBERS, Peter. 'Sellers Buys His Second Cadillac', [source untraced].

CLAYTON, Freddy. 'Meet Peter Sellers', *The Musician* [c. 1970.] 'Spike, Peter and Harry Who?' *Punch* [c. 1976.]

COWLEY, Elizabeth. 'The Best Sellers Buys', *Radio Times* [date untraced].

CRAWLEY, Tony. 'Kosinski, body and soul', *Films Illustrated*, September 1980.

DANGAARD, Colin. 'Loving – one day at a time', *Daily Express*, July 14th 1978.

DAVIES, Shan. 'Bert Mortimer: the Man Who Knew Sellers Best', *Sunday People*, August 3rd 1980.

DAVIS, Victor. 'Sellers, the mad genius, by Pink Panther Blake', *Daily Express*, December 14th 1982.

DONNELLY, Paul. 'Behind the Mask: The Secret World of Peter Sellers', *Idols*, No. 15, May 1989.

DUNCAN, Andrew. 'A Most Successful Ongoing Failure', *Radio Times* [c. July 1987].

EDWARDS, Blake and Julie Andrews. 'Interview', *Playboy*, December 1982.

EDWARDS, Lewis. 'Daniel Mendoza', *Transactions of the Jewish Historical Society of England*, Vol. XV, 1938.

FAWCETT, Ian. 'I Want to Start Living Again', *Photoplay*, April 1965.

FERGUSSON, Ken. 'Sellers', *Photoplay Film Monthly*, June 1971.

FORBES, Bryan. 'On the dark side of the Goon', *Independent*, July 21st 1990.

FOSTER, Edwin. 'Guess Who Is Playing Sellers' Sister – It's Britt!', *Showtime*, November 1966.

FRANKLIN, Olga. 'In Search of Sellers', *Daily Mail*, June 21st, 22nd and 23rd 1960.

FRATER, Alexander. 'Status Symbols Are a Lot of Bananas!', *Sunday Telegraph Magazine* [c. 1968].

FROST, Tony, 'Sellers' Last Pledge', *Sunday Mirror*, July 27th 1980.

GRAHAM, Keith. 'Send for Sellers', *TV Mirror*, October 30th 1954.

GRANT, Steve. 'The Laugh Donor', *Time Out*, February 20th 1986.

GLAZER, Mitchell. 'The Strange World of Peter Sellers', *Rolling Stone*, April 17th 1980.

GRETTON, Charles. 'The Tragic Secret of Spike Milligan', *TV Mirror* February 1st 1958.

GRIFFITH, Kenneth. 'Looking for the best of Sellers', *The Times*, October 8th 1981.

HAIGH, Peter S. 'Peter Sellers: Star Interview', [source untraced, c. 1960].

HALL, Judith. 'Why Victoria Sellers' heart will always belong to Daddy', [source untraced, c. 1981].

HART, Melanie. 'Victoria Sellers', *Hello*, [late 1992].

HILL, Derek, 'Camera Magic', *Amateur Cine World*, February 1959.

HUTCHINS, Chris. 'Why I Worried about Lynne's Marriage – interview with Iris Frederick' [source untraced, c. 1978].

HUTCHINSON, Tom. 'Look Out – Here They Are', *Picturegoer*, November 26th 1955.

'The Naked Truth', *Picturegoer*, July 20th 1957.

'The Search for Peter Sellers', *Picturegoer*, December 19th 1959.

'Sellers Outgrows the Goons', *Picturegoer*, [c. 1960].

JOSEPH, Joe. 'What's it all about, Michael [Caine]?' *The Times*, August 26th 1992.

KOFF, Sidney. 'I think I'm having a heart attack', *Modern Screen*, July 1964.

KRETZMER, Herbert. 'Goon in a Nightmare', *Daily Sketch*, February 28th 1958.

'Sellers: Now I Will Tear My Palace to Bits', *Daily Sketch*, March 9th 1963

'A Wizard Running the Peter Sellers Empire', *Daily Sketch*, June 15th 1963.

LAWRENCE, Hamilton. 'Should You Tip Your Pilot?' *Mensan* (San Diego), February 1984.

LEACH, Robin. 'Death is not far away, said Peter', *News of the World*, July 27th 1980.

LEE, Carol. 'Lynne Makes a New Date with Sellers [via a spirit medium]', *News of the World*, August 10th 1980.

LEE-POTTER, Lynda. 'Yes, Dad was an idiot [says Michael]', *Daily Mail*, September 29th 1981.

LEWIN, David. 'Peter the Great', *Sunday Mirror*, August 3rd, 10th and 17th 1980.

'Exclusive! Lynne Frederick Sellers', *Woman's Own* [late 1980].

LINDEN, Livia. 'The Way They Were: Peter Sellers', *Rona Barrett's Hollywood*, July 1980.

MANN, Roderick. 'If he is happier without me, says Mrs Sellers', [Lynne responds to Sellers' desire for a divorce] *Sunday Express*, May 20th 1979.

MARLBOROUGH, Douglas. 'Sophia scares so-shy Sellers', *Daily Mail*, May 19th 1960.

McASH, Ian F. 'Said the March Hare', *Film Review*, (1972).

'The Changing Face of Peter Sellers', *Films Illustrated*, May 1974.

MIDWINTER, Janet. 'Sellers Dies', *Sun*, July 24th 1980.

MORRIS, Ronald. 'By Gad, Sir,' *Picturegoer*, September 20th 1958.

MORTIMER, John. 'Second Opinion', *Films and Filming*, May 1963.

'Creative Force of a Meticulous Clown', *Sunday Times*, July 27th 1980.

O'DOWD, Brian. 'My Friend Peter Sellers', *Hollywood Studio Magazine* [c. 1980].

OUGHTON, Frederick. 'The Secret Life of Peter Sellers', *Picturegoer Film Annual*, 1959–60.

OWEN, Jane. 'Britt – the Unwanted Mourner', *Sunday People*, July 27th 1980.

PACTER, Trudi. 'Tears and Tantrums Finished Us', *Sunday Mirror* [c. August 1980].

'Secrets of the Superset', *Sunday Mirror*, November 11th 1980.

PEDRICK, Gale. 'Finkel's Café', *Radio Times*, June 29th 1956.

PETERSEN, Eric. 'Victoria Sellers', *Hello*, October 13th 1990.

POWELL, Dilys. 'Peter Sellers: A Recorded Dialogue', *Sunday Times*, January 14th and 21st 1962.

'The delicate balance of Peter Sellers', *Sunday Times*, July 27th 1980.

PURSER, Philip. 'Beyond Experience', *Sunday Telegraph Magazine* [c. November 1972].

READ, Piers Paul. 'Small Expectations: profile of Alec Guinness', *Independent Magazine*, October 1st 1988.

ROCHE, Ken. 'On the Trail of the Real Peter Sellers', *TV Times*, Christmas issue, 1983.

RUSSELL, Sue. 'Meet Mademoiselle Clouseau [i.e. Victoria],' *You Magazine*, November 15th 1992.

SALE, Jonathan. 'The Men in the Goons', *Punch*, September 26th 1979.

SALEWICZ, Chris. 'Comic View: Milligan on Sellers', *Sunday Times*, [c. 1980].

SAVAGE, Paul. 'Peter Sellers is a keen home movie maker', *Sunday Telegraph Magazine*, July 3rd 1970.

SAXTY, Dick. 'Was Sophia the big love of Sellers?' [source untraced].

SCHICKEL, Richard. 'Sellers Strikes Again', *Time Magazine*, March 3rd 1980.

SEDWARDS, Lisa. 'Victoria's Victory', *Daily Express*, October 1st 1992.

SELLERS, Peter. 'You Tell Me', *Picturegoer*, February 19th 1955.
'Star Turn Table', *TV Times*, July 20th 1956.
'A Serious Look at Laughter', *Films and Filming*, March 1960.
[Entry] *Current Biography 1960* (New York).
'Candid Conversation', *Playboy*, October 1962.
'Sellers Mimes the Movie Lovers', *Playboy*, April 1964.
'New Books about Cars', *Sunday Times*, October 24th 1965.
'My First Encounter with an Impressario', in *The Vogue Bedside Book*, ed. Josephine Ross (London, 1984).

SELLERS, Victoria. 'Best Sellers', *Playboy*, April 1986.

SHERIFF, Paul. 'Designing for an Heiress', *Films and Filming*, November 1960.

SIMONS, Judith, 'Inspired – by the NAAFI canteen', *Daily Express* [c. 1979].

SINEUX, Michel. 'Bye Bye Birdie-Num-Num', *Positif* (Paris), February 1981.

SMITH, Marjorie. 'He Was Just One of the Boys', *My Weekly*, June 7th 1980.

SPEED, F. Maurice. 'The Sellers Story', *Film Review* (1964).

STAMP, Gavin. 'Dreams and Nightmares of a Changing City', *Times*, November 3rd 1990.

STARK, Graham. 'The Peter Sellers Only I Knew', *Woman's Realm*, July 3rd, 1983.

STOPPARD, Tom. 'The Constance Cummings Story', *Bristol Evening World*, May 12th 1960.

STUTTAFORD, Thomas. 'Portrait of a President', *Times*, February 7th 1991.

TAYLOR, Norman. 'Best Sellers', *Film Review*, March 1959.

THIRKELL, Arthur. 'Who Is This Man?' [source untraced, c. 1961].

TOMKIES, Mike. 'My Man Peter', *Photoplay*, September 1966.

WAGGONER, Walter. 'Arrival of Sellers', *New York Times Magazine*, March 27th 1960.

WALKER, Alexander. 'Alas, Some of them Die', *Evening Standard*, July 24th 1980.

'My Life with Peter Sellers [i.e. Lynne's]', *Evening Standard*, August 14th 1981.

WALKER, Derek. 'He Doesn't Want to be Funny', *Picturegoer*, July 21st 1956.

WALKER, John. 'A Role that Mirrors the Real Sellers?', *Now*, June 6th 1980.

WARGA, Wayne. 'Not Exactly Being There', *Los Angeles Times*, March 30th 1980.

WAUGH, Auberon. 'The Last Thoughts of Peter Sellers', *Sunday Telegraph*, July 27th 1980.

WELLS, Tony. 'The Waltz of the Corridors', *Today*, January 19th 1963.

WIGG, David. 'My Beloved Peter', *Daily Express*, July 31st 1981.

'Ohh, Dick [Emery] You Were Wonderful', *Daily Express*, January 3rd 1983.

WILSON, Cecil. 'Mr Sellers Buys Car No. 53', *Daily Mail*, May 6th 1960.

ZASLOW, Esther. 'Why Peter Sellers is so afraid of real women', *Hollywood Screen Parade*, June 1969.

ZEC, Donald. 'Wham! 24 Hours from Meeting to Mating [with Liza Minnelli]', *Daily Mirror*, September 26th 1977.

(b) *Institutions*

I am grateful to the following curators, archivists and reference librarians, administrators, managers and editors: Bantam Press (Nina Martyn); BBC Enterprises Ltd.; BBC Written Archives Centre, Caversham Park (Jacqueline Kavanagh); Bloomsbury and Islington Health Authority; Bradford Cathedral (Barbara L. Craven); Brothers of Our Lady of Mercy (Bro. F. Kean); Bodleian Library, Oxford (Miss M. Sheldon-Williams); Boston University, Special Collections (Mugar Memorial Library – curator: Howard B. Gotlieb); Chichester Festival Theatre (Paul Rogerson); EMI Music

Archives (Sarah Hobbs); Entertainment Artistes' Benevolent Fund (Peter Elliott); Evergreen Communications Ltd. (Peter Morley); The Goon Show Preservation Society (Mark Cousins, Mike Coveney, Bill Nunn, Tony Reynolds and Keith Vincent); Hampshire County Council (J. Thorn, Divisional Librarian); Ilfracombe Museum (Joy Slocombe, Hon. Curator and Secretary); The Jewish Historical Society (Charles Tucker); Library and Museum of the United Grand Lodge of England, Freemasons' Hall (K. A. McQuillan); Library of Congress, Motion Picture, Broadcasting and Recorded Sound Division (Madeline F. Matz); the Library of St John's College, Oxford; the Library of Wolfson College, Oxford; the *Los Angeles Times*; the Middlesex Hospital (Jim Stapleton, Medical Records Manager); *The Nation* (Nicholas W. P. Clegg); National Film Archive / British Film Institute; National Film Information Service, Academy Foundation (Kristine Krueger); Omega Lighting (Keith Applin); Pan American Airways (Barbara Yager, Flight Services Headquarters); Parkfield Entertainment (Ken Hill); The Raymond Mander and Joe Mitchenson Theatre Collection; Robson Books (Cheryll Roberts); Southbrook Group Ltd. (Sue J. Coombes); The Spanish and Portuguese Jews' Congregation (Miss Miriam Rodrigues-Pereira); Spike Milligan Productions Ltd. (Norma Farnes); St Aloysius' College (J. A. Mackersie, Headmaster); Stoll Moss Archives, Theatre Royal, Drury Lane (George Hoare); Strategic Marketing (EMI Records UK – David Hughes, and J. Nagle, Publicity Department); the *Sunday Times Magazine* (Susan Raven); Telstar Video Entertainment; Tessa Le Bars Management; Thames Television (Joanna Wood); Twentieth Century Fox (Paul Higginson); University of California, Los Angeles, Film and Television Archive (Charles Hopkins).

(c) *Individuals*

I wish to thank the following people, whom I had the joy of interviewing and/or corresponding with expressly for this book: Dave Allen; Sir Kingsley Amis; John Antrobus; the late Ben Arbeid;

Steven Bach; the late Terence Baker; Ken Barnes; Michael Bentine; Dick Bentley; the late Peta Bentley; John Bird; Ron Bishop (son of Waldini); John Bluthal; Roy Boulting; Peter Boyle; Ronnie Bridges; Tony Britton; Mark Burns; Max Bygraves; Dave Callaghan; Ian Carmichael; the late Alan Clare; Bloom Clare; Doris Collins; Bryan Connon; Alan Cooper; the late Theo Cowan; Gerry Crampton; Quentin Crewe; Bernard Cribbins; Charles Critchton; Constance Cummings; Sinead Cusack; the late Roald Dahl; Monja Danischewsky; Clive Donner; Alfred Draper; Joe Dunne; Mathew Dunne; Shirley Eaton; Martin Esslin; Peter Evans; Bryan Forbes; Anthony Franciosa; Michael Frayn; Dennis Frazer; Liz Frazer; Iris Frederick; the late Lynne Frederick (Mrs Barry Unger); Ray Galton; Kathy Ganis Gardner; Lord Grade of Elstree; Mike Grady; Kenneth Griffith; the late Dimitri de Grunwald; Michael Gough; Val Guest; Sir Alec Guinness; Piers Haggard; John Hamilton; Hermione Harvey; Mary Harvey; Joseph Heller; John Heyman; the late Benny Hill; Al Hix; the late Jack Hobbs; Mr Justice Hobhouse; Ken Hughes; the late Raymond Huntley; David Jacobs; Michael Jeffery; Dr A. P. Joseph; Alice Joyce; Miriam Karlin; Elliot Kastner; Jeremy Kemp; Philip Kemp; Deborah Kerr; Dennis King; the late Jerzy Kosinski; Herbert Kretzmer; Bert Kwouk; Col. Hamilton Lawrence; Rosemary Leach; Peter Lepino; Dick Lester; Anne Levy; Leslie Linder; Russell Lloyd; David Lodge; Herbert Lom; Shirley MacLaine; Wolf Mankowitz; Vera Marks; Joe McGrath; Peter Medak; Murray Melvin; Gerald Mendoza; Beatrix Miller; Jonathan Miller; Spike Milligan; Charlotte Mitchell; the late Joe Mitchenson; Angela Morley (Wally Stott); Sheridan Morley; Peggy Mount; Frank Muir; the late Stanley Myers; Margaretta Neilly (Paddy Black); Anthony Newley; Peter Noble; Tony Palmer (and his staff at Isolde Films); Michael Parkinson; Elaine Parsons; John Penrose; Tom Pevsner; Larry Pizer; Miranda Quarry; Alvin Rakoff; Frederic Raphael; Robin Ray; the late Satyajit Ray; the Marquess of Reading; Clive Rees; Elwood Rickless; the late Cardew Robinson; Norman Rossington; Colin Ross-Munro Q.C.; Sir Evelyn de Rothschild; Pierre Rouve; Lord Anthony Rufus-Isaacs; Jack Salt; Prunella

Scales; Danny Schelmerdine; Victor Schlienger; Janette Scott; Anne Scott-James (Lady Lancaster); Ronald Searle; Michael Sellers; Sarah Sellers; Michael Selsman; John Sessions; Bryn Siddall; Anthony Simmons; Alan Simpson; Hattie Stevenson; J.E. Sumpton; John Taylor; Lady (Peggy) Tedder; the late Andrew Timothy; Richard Todd; David Tomlinson; Barry Took; Peter Vaughan; Hugo Vickers; Darren Vidler; Dick Vosburgh; Alexander Walker; Ray Walston; Auberon Waugh; John Wells; Gareth Wigan; Frank Wildish; Simon Williams; and Donald Zec.

(d) *Photograph acknowledgements*

The plates in this book emanate from the following sources, to whom the publishers gratefully offer acknowledgement: Author Collection (nos. 6, 7, 16 [National Screen Service Ltd.], 18 [photograph by Ricki Howell, © Allen Hutton Gallery, Whetstone], 29 [Warner-Pathe Distributors Ltd.], 31, 34, 40, 41 [Universal City Studios Inc.], 43, 46); George Brown Collection (2 [Adelphi Films Ltd.], 3, 4, 5 [Group 3 Ltd.], 8 [Columbia Pictures Corp. Ltd.], 9, 11 [photograph by Harry Gillard], 12, 13, 19, 27, 30, 35 [Hemdale International Films], 44); Peter Evans and Bryan Connon (1); Michael Jeffery (42, 47); Peter Medak (37, 38); Satyajit Ray (28); Michael Sellers Collection (10, 14 [photograph by Norman Hargood], 15 [photograph by George Ward: Rank Productions Ltd.], 17, 20, 22 [photograph by Norman Hargood], 23, 26, 32, 33, 36 [Scotia-Barber Distributors], 9, 45; Hattie Stevenson (21, 24, 25). *n.b.* Dates in the captions refer to the year photographs were taken – which may not necessarily be the same as the year films were released.

(e) *Special acknowledgements*

To assemble my own archive of Sellers material, I acquired the collections of clippings and memorabilia which were formerly in the possession of Larry Turnbull, of Cardiff; J. Skinner gave me all the Sellers material which was on file at his Celebrity Information

Bureau; and I am grateful to Tony Broughton, of West Sussex, for lending me dozens of videotapes of Sellers' out-of-the-way films. I have also made full use of the articles and reminiscences published over the years in the quarterly *Newsletter* of the Goon Show Preservation Society. The full set of the (defunct) *Goonews*, given to me by Bill Nunn, was also of much interest. Dr Bernard Richards, of Brasenose College, Oxford, and Francis Wheen, of *Private Eye*, sent me useful articles and provided general enlightenment, as did (as ever) Mark Rylance, John Bayley and Iris Murdoch. George Brown was virtually my acting (unpaid) research assistant. Hardly a fortnight went by without his sending letters and nuggets; this book would be much impoverished without his discoveries. Al Hix performed a similar function for me from America. I am much indebted to such selfless vigilance.

Of the other people who helped me, it would be invidious to start singling them out and ranking them – but I want it to be recorded that Roy Boulting opened his address book and introduced me to, amongst others, the members of Sellers' family. Michael Sellers, his mother, Anne Levy, and his sister, Sarah Sellers, endured months of my cross-examinations. Peter Evans, who had mapped out Sellers *with* Sellers, also gave me hours of his time – as well as copies of letters and interview transcripts he had not, owing to the pressure of space, been able to include in his own book. Wolf Mankowitz let me loose in his extensive archives; Peter Medak succumbed to a long interview and loaned me the original battle-scarred copy of the *Ghost in the Noonday Sun* script, plus some marvellous photographs; Spike Milligan rose from his sickbed to give me a candid interview at this house near Rye; and Clive Rees screened *The Blockhouse*.

On a personal level, David Huw Harries, my old school pal, will be amused to see the results of my teenage Sellers fad. He'd always said that his auntie, Elaine Parsons, had taught Sellers to play the drums, and frankly I'd never believed him. But Sellers' origins – his end-of-the-pier beginnings which haunted him and were part of the sadness which followed him, were right there in Wales, where I grew up. Through Elaine Parsons I met other survivors of that music hall era, and I was off.

Leslie Gardner, my agent, and Mark Booth, my editor, have been models of patience and wise counsel – which I frequently and no doubt infuriatingly disregarded. This is, after all, my book – and all the research, classified above, was only a preliminary. Sellers still had to be conjured up in the writing – all by hand, non-stop over eleven months with a Waterman fountain pen – and for this reason I must emphasise that this is *my* version of Sellers, a Sellers ordered and shaped by *my* own imagination and judgements. I make no claims for objectivity or comprehensiveness. (Why ever should I? The concept of a definitive biography is a nonsense. The best you can hope for is a spirited and unsettling personal essay – and this [Poop! Poop!] is what you are now holding in your hands). The typing was done in a matter of weeks by Suzanne Anderson and Lesley Caldwell. My conscientious copy-editor and proof-reader was Kate Pleydell-Bouverie – a name the Goons would have savoured.

My flesh and blood – that's Anna, Tristan, Oscar and Sébastien – won't believe that this book is finished, and I can never adequately thank them for enduring the hardships and deprivations which its long genesis and frenzied composition imposed upon them. If it wasn't for the very practical assistance and alms yielded by my parents-in-law and my brother-in-law, the last chapters wouldn't have been written in France – they'd have been collected from the Marshalsea, whither we'd have had to go, like the Dorrits.

For mid-way through my research I decided I could no longer bear to remain in Oxford as a classroom technician (to use Gore Vidal's apt and contemptuous phrase). I moved the family to Normandy and metamorphosed from a quicksilvery don to a morose writer-in-exile – a non-smoking Anthony Burgess. This book, then, changed my life. Children of mine, not born when I began it, were able to tell their teacher, Mme. Claudine Chastang, that papa was not, like everybody else in the bocage, a peasant farmer, a wood-cutter or an iron foundryman. His metier was 'Piter Séleux et tout le bataclan du tralala'.* I couldn't put it better myself.

Roger Lewis
Oxford, July 11th 1989
France, July 11th 1993.

---

* *Peter Sellers and all the rest of that general rubbish.*

Index

Index

Index

ALSO AVAILABLE IN ARROW

Something Like Fire:
Peter Cook Remembered

Lin Cook ed.

An intimate and entertaining portrait of one of comedy's greatest geniuses b
those who knew Peter Cook best and can write about his rare talent. The cor
tributors include Clive Anderson, Alan Bennett, John Cleese, Stephen Fry, Willian
Goldman, Barry Humphries, Eric Idle, Dudley Moore and Michael Palin.

'Read it for yourself. No other biography will ever better tell the truth'
The Times

'One thing nearly all of the friends invited to contribute to this book have in
common: by God they can write . . . The authors are a ministry of all the
talents; the book is most enjoyable'
Spectator

'This book contains excellent contributions by comic writers. The gems are
Peter Cook's'
Sunday Times

arrow books